Office of Government Commerce

Service Design

London: TSO

TSO

Published by TSO (The Stationery Office) and available from:

Online
www.tsoshop.co.uk

Mail, Telephone, Fax & E-mail
TSO
PO Box 29, Norwich, NR3 1GN
Telephone orders/General enquiries: 0870 600 5522
Fax orders: 0870 600 5533
E-mail: customer.services@tso.co.uk
Textphone 0870 240 3701

TSO Shops
123 Kingsway, London, WC2B 6PQ
020 7242 6393 Fax 020 7242 6394
16 Arthur Street, Belfast BT1 4GD
028 9023 8451 Fax 028 9023 5401
71 Lothian Road, Edinburgh EH3 9AZ
0870 606 5566 Fax 0870 606 5588

TSO@Blackwell and other Accredited Agents

First published 2007

ISBN 978 0 11 331047 0

Printed in the United Kingdom for The Stationery Office

Contents

List of figures

All diagrams in this publication are intended to provide an illustration of ITIL Service Management Practice concepts and guidance. They have been artistically rendered to visually reinforce key concepts and are not intended to meet a formal method or standard of technical drawing. The ITIL Service Management Practices Integrated Service Model conforms to technical drawing standards and should be referred to for complete details. Please see www.best-management-practice.com/itil for details.

List of tables

OGC's foreword

Since its creation, ITIL has grown to become the most widely accepted approach to IT Service Management in the world. However, along with this success comes the responsibility to ensure that the guidance keeps pace with a changing global business environment. Service Management requirements are inevitably shaped by the development of technology, revised business models and increasing customer expectations. Our latest version of ITIL has been created in response to these developments.

This is one of five core publications describing the IT Service Management practices that make up ITIL. They are the result of a two-year project to review and update the guidance. The number of Service Management professionals around the world who have helped to develop the content of these publications is impressive. Their experience and knowledge have contributed to the content to bring you a consistent set of high-quality guidance. This is supported by the ongoing development of a comprehensive qualifications scheme, along with accredited training and consultancy.

Whether you are part of a global company, a government department or a small business, ITIL gives you access to world-class Service Management expertise. Essentially, it puts IT services where they belong – at the heart of successful business operations.

Peter Fanning

Acting Chief Executive

Office of Government Commerce

Chief Architect's foreword

Great services do not exist by accident. They have to be carefully planned and designed. Service Design is the means to achieve this. The best Service Strategy cannot be realized without well-designed services. Effective Service Design can lead organizations to greater gains in quality and cost-effectiveness. It reduces the risk of costly compensating for design flaws in the operational environment and ensures that services will perform as they are intended and bring measurable value to the business objectives.

In the past, the IT world has been viewed in two parts – the development world and the operational world. A lack of synergy between these worlds often produces a serious side effect – the business objectives are not met.

A main objective of Service Design is to eliminate this old-world view and bring IT service into a single, consolidated view of designing services within the realities, constraints and opportunities of live operation.

The opportunity to take advantage of new technologies, maximize the use of existing infrastructure, applications, data and knowledge comes to life within the pages of this publication.

Service Design broadens our horizons and helps us to see a larger, more cohesive view of IT Service Management.

Any IT organization that wants to maximize its potential to meet business objectives and business value needs this publication in its arsenal of capabilities.

Service Design is powerful guidance and a cornerstone of practical skills, tools and methods for achieving service excellence.

Sharon Taylor

Chief Architect, ITIL Service Management Practices

Preface

'Quality in a product or service is not what the supplier puts in. It is what the customer gets out and is willing to pay for.'

Peter Drucker, American management guru.

The ITIL Service Management practices are based on this idea. Services are assets from which the customer gains value. How well services are designed with the customers' needs in mind will predict the value that can be derived from them. In the absence of Service Design, service will evolve informally, often without taking advantage of the broader perspective – the business view.

The Service Design phase of the ITIL Service Lifecycle takes business requirements and, using five aspects for Service Design, creates services and their supporting practices that meet business demands for quality, reliability and flexibility. Service Design is iterative throughout the Service Lifecycle, and begins with a solid blueprint that enables the build, test and release stages of Service Transition through the Service Design Package.

Readers will learn about design principles for application, infrastructure, processes and resources, as well as sourcing models. Service Managers will also find guidance on the engineering of sound requirements, Supplier Management and key design considerations for service outsourcing.

Whether you are an internal or external service provider, you are part of a value network and fill a critical role in the Service Lifecycle, by integrating the best practices for Service Design and the ITIL Service Lifecycle into innovative products for the business customer. The Service Design publication provides the knowledge and skills required to assemble the best combination of service assets to produce measurable, scalable and innovative services, along the path to service excellence.

Any IT service provider who is expected to deliver quality to the business customer must have the capability to design services that meet expectations, then go on to exceed those expectations.

The guidance in this publication will help achieve this.

Contact information

Full details of the range of material published under the ITIL banner can be found at www.best-management-practice.com/itil

For further information on qualifications and training accreditation, please visit www.itil-officialsite.com. Alternatively, please contact:

APMG Service Desk
Sword House
Totteridge Road
High Wycombe
Buckinghamshire
HP13 6DG

Tel: +44 (0) 1494 452450
E-mail: servicedesk@apmg.co.uk

Acknowledgements

Chief Architect and authors

Sharon Taylor (Aspect Group Inc)   Chief Architect

Vernon Lloyd (Fox IT)   Author

Colin Rudd (IT Enterprise
Management Services Ltd – ITEMS)   Author

ITIL authoring team

The ITIL authoring team contributed to this guide through commenting on content and alignment across the set. So thanks are also due to the other ITIL authors, specifically Jeroen Bronkhorst (HP), David Cannon (HP), Gary Case (Pink Elephant), Ashley Hannah (HP), Majid Iqbal (Carnegie Mellon University), Shirley Lacy (ConnectSphere), Ivor Macfarlane (Guillemot Rock), Michael Nieves (Accenture), Stuart Rance (HP), George Spalding (Pink Elephant) and David Wheeldon (HP).

Mentors

Tony Jenkins
Sergio Rubinato Filho

Further contributions

A number of people generously contributed their time and expertise to this Service Design publication. Jim Clinch, as OGC Project Manager, is grateful to the support provided by Jenny Dugmore, Convenor of Working Group ISO/IEC 20000, Janine Eves, Carol Hulm, Aidan Lawes and Michiel van der Voort.

The authors would also like to thank Tony Jenkins, DOMAINetc and Steve Rudd IT Enterprise Management Service Limited (ITEMS).

In order to develop ITIL v3 to reflect current best practice and produce publications of lasting value, OGC consulted widely with different stakeholders throughout the world at every stage in the process. OGC would also like to thank the following individuals and their organisations for their contributions to refreshing the ITIL guidance:

The ITIL Advisory Group

Pippa Bass, OGC; Tony Betts, Independent; Megan Byrd, Bank of America; Alison Cartlidge, Xansa; Diane Colbeck, DIYmonde Solutions Inc; Ivor Evans, DIYmonde Solutions Inc; Karen Ferris, ProActive; Malcolm Fry, FRY-Consultants; John Gibert, Independent; Colin Hamilton, RENARD Consulting Ltd; Lex Hendriks, EXIN; Signe Marie Hernes, Det Norske Veritas; Carol Hulm, British Computer Society-ISEB; Tony Jenkins, DOMAINetc; Phil Montanaro, EDS; Alan Nance, ITPreneurs; Christian Nissen, Itilligence; Don Page, Marval Group; Bill Powell, IBM; Sergio Rubinato Filho, CA; James Siminoski, SOScorp; Robert E. Stroud, CA; Jan van Bon, Inform-IT; Ken Wendle, HP; Paul Wilkinson, Getronics PinkRoccade; Takashi Yagi, Hitachi

Reviewers

Kamal Kishore Arora, Infosys Technologies; Martin Andenmatten, Independent; Pierre Bernard, Pink Elephant; Wills Damasio, Quint Wellington Redwood; Catalin Danila, GlaxoSmithKline, SRL Romania; Juergen Dierlamm, Rechtsanwaltkanzlei Dierlamm; Thomas Dressler, EDV-Beratung; Fouad El Sioufy, TUV Rheinland Secure iT GmbH; Jaime Eduardo Facioli, Kalendae IT service Management; Juergen Feldges, DNV; Prasad Gadgil, Satyam Computer Services Ltd; Kingshuk Ghosh, HP; Sandeep Gondhalekar, Quint Wellington Redwood; John Graham, Educad; Juergen Gross, Independent; Tsuyoshi Hamada, HP; Colin Hamilton, RENARD Consulting Ltd; Christoph Herwig, Accenture; Thomas Hess, Pluralis AG; Chris Jones, Ariston Strategic Consulting; Daniel Keller, Swiss SUIT; Hendrikje Kuhne, Ktp-organisationsterberatung; Jane Link, Acerit Limited; Paul Martini, HP; Raimund Martl, HP; Alan Nance, Itpreneurs; Christian Nissen, Itilligence; Glen Notman, Pink Elephant; Tuomas Nurmela, TietoEnator Processing & Network Oy; Benjamin Orazem, SRC.SI; Gerard Persoon, E.Novation; Neil Pinkerton, Laughingtree; Christian Probst, Quint Wellington Redwood; Rajesh Radhakrishnan, IBM; Brian Rowlatt, LogicaCMG; Sutirtha Roy Chowdhury, Sierra Systems; Alexander Sapronov, HP; Frances Scarff, OGC; Alan Shepherd, Deutsche Bank AG; Rob Stroud, CA; Michael Tomkinson, BT; Ken Turbitt, BMC Software; Wiley Vasquez, BMC Software; Ettiene Vermeulen, Datacentrix; Joachim von Caron, Lufthansa Systems; Andreas Weinberger, DekaBank; Sven Werner, Unilog Avinci GmbH; Theresa Wright, Computacenter Services; Geoffrey Wyeth, Independent; Rob Young, Fox IT

Introduction

1

1 Introduction

The primary objective of Service Management is to ensure that the IT services are aligned to the business needs and actively support them. It is imperative that the IT services underpin the business processes, but it is also increasingly important that IT acts as an agent for change to facilitate business transformation.

All organizations that use IT will depend on IT to be successful. If IT processes and IT services are implemented, managed and supported in the appropriate way, the business will be more successful, suffer less disruption and loss of productive hours, reduce costs, increase revenue, improve public relations and achieve its business objectives.

Most authorities now identify four types of IT assets that need to be acquired and managed in order to contribute to effective IT service provision. These are IT infrastructure, applications, information and people. Specifically there is a strong emphasis on the acquisition, management and integration of these assets throughout their 'birth to retirement' lifecycle. The delivery of quality IT services depends on the effective and efficient management of these assets.

These assets on their own, however, are not enough to meet the Service Management needs of the business. ITIL Service Management practices use these four asset types as part of a set of capabilities and resources called 'service assets'.

An IT service, used in support of business processes, is constructed from a combination of IT assets and externally provided 'underpinning' services. Once in place, an IT service must be supported throughout its 'life', during which time it may be modified many times, either through technological innovation, changing business environment, changing usage of the service, changing its service quality parameters, or changing its supporting IT assets or capabilities (e.g. a change in an application software component to provide additional functionality). Eventually the IT service is retired, when business processes no longer have a use for it or it is no longer cost-effective to run. Service Transition is involved in the build and deployment of the service and day-to-day support, and delivery of the service is the role of Service Operation, while Continual Service Improvement implements best practice in the optimize and retire stages.

From this perspective, Service Design can be seen as gathering service needs and mapping them to requirements for integrated services, and creating the design specifications for the service assets needed to provide services. A particular feature of this approach is a strong emphasis on re-use during design.

The main aim of Service Design is to design IT services, together with the governing IT practices, processes and policies, to realize the strategy and to facilitate the introduction of these services into the live environment ensuring quality service delivery, customer satisfaction and cost-effective service provision. Service Design should also design the IT services effectively so that they don't need a great deal of improvement during their lifecycle. However, continual improvement should be embedded in all Service

	Capabilities			Resources	
A1	Management			Financial capital	A9
A2	Organization			Infrastructure	A8
A3	Processes			Applications	A7
A4	Knowledge			Information	A6
	People	A5		People	

Figure 1.1 Resources and capabilities are the basis for value creation

Design activities to ensure that the solutions and designs become even more effective over time and to identify changing trends in the business that may offer improvement opportunities. Service Design activities can be periodic or exception-based when they may be triggered by a specific business need or event.

If services or processes are not designed they will evolve organically. If they evolve without proper controls, the tendency is simply to react to environmental conditions that have occurred rather than to understand clearly the overall vision and overall needs of the business. Designing to match the anticipated environment is much more effective and efficient, but often impossible – hence the need to consider iterative and incremental approaches to Service Design. Iterative and incremental approaches are essential to ensure that services introduced to the live environment adapt and continue to remain in line with evolving business needs. In the absence of formalized Service Design, services will often be unduly expensive to run, prone to failure, resources will be wasted and services will not be fully aligned to business needs. It is unlikely that any improvement programme will ever be able to achieve what proper design would achieve in the first place. Without Service Design, cost-effective service is not possible. The human aspects of Service Design are also of the utmost importance, and these will be explored in detail later in this publication.

1.1 OVERVIEW

This publication forms part of the overall ITIL Service Management practices and covers the design of appropriate and innovative IT services to meet current and future agreed business requirements. It describes the principles of Service Design and looks at identifying, defining and aligning the IT solution with the business requirements. It also introduces the concept of the Service Design Package and looks at selecting the appropriate Service Design model. The publication also discusses the fundamentals of the design processes and the five aspects of the design:

- Services
- Design of Service Management systems and tools, especially the Service Portfolio
- Technology architectures and management systems
- Processes
- Measurement methods and metrics.

The publication covers the methods, practices and tools to achieve excellence in Service Design. It enforces the principle that the initial Service Design should be driven by a number of factors, including the functional requirements, the requirements within the Service Level Agreements (SLAs), the business benefits and the overall design constraints.

Chapter 4 explains the end-to-end process of the areas key to successful Service Design. These processes are utilized by all other stages of the Service Lifecycle, and other processes are taken into account by Service Design. However, it is here that Service Catalogue Management, Service Level Management, Capacity Management, Availability Management, IT Service Continuity Management, Information Security Management and Supplier Management are covered in detail.

The appendices to this publication give examples of the Service Design Package, Service Acceptance Criteria, process documentation templates, design and planning documents, environmental architectures and standards, sample SLAs, OLAs and Service Catalogue and the Service Management process maturity framework.

1.2 CONTEXT

1.2.1 Service Management

Information technology (IT) is a commonly used term that changes meaning with context. From the first perspective, IT systems, applications, and infrastructure are components or sub-assemblies of a larger product. They enable or are embedded in processes and services. From the second perspective, IT is an organization with its own set of capabilities and resources. IT organizations can be of various types, such as business functions, shared services units, and enterprise-level core units.

From the third perspective, IT is a category of services utilized by business. They are typically IT applications and infrastructure that are packaged and offered as services by internal IT organizations or external service providers. IT costs are treated as business expenses. From the fourth perspective, IT is a category of business assets that provide a stream of benefits for their owners, including but not limited to revenue, income and profit. IT costs are treated as investments.

1.2.2 Good practice in the public domain

Organizations operate in dynamic environments with the need to learn and adapt. There is a need to improve performance while managing trade-offs. Under similar pressure, customers seek advantage from service providers. They pursue sourcing strategies that best serve their own business interests. In many countries, government agencies and non-profits have a similar tendency to outsource for the sake of operational effectiveness. This puts additional pressure on service providers to maintain a competitive advantage with respect to the alternatives that customers may have. The increase in outsourcing has particularly exposed internal service providers to unusual competition.

To cope with the pressure, organizations benchmark themselves against peers and seek to close gaps in capabilities. One way to close such gaps is the adoption of good practices in wide industry use. There are several sources for good practices, including public frameworks, standards, and the proprietary knowledge of organizations and individuals (Figure 1.2).

Public frameworks and standards are attractive when compared with proprietary knowledge:

■ Proprietary knowledge is deeply embedded in organizations and therefore difficult to adopt, replicate or transfer, even with the cooperation of the owners. Such knowledge is often in the form of tacit knowledge that is inextricable and poorly documented.

■ Proprietary knowledge is customized for the local context and specific business needs to the point of being idiosyncratic. Unless the recipients of such knowledge have matching circumstances, the knowledge may not be as effective in use.

■ Owners of proprietary knowledge expect to be rewarded for their long-term investments. They may make such knowledge available only under commercial terms through purchases and licensing agreements.

■ Publicly available frameworks and standards such as ITIL, COBIT, CMMI, eSCM-SP, PRINCE2, ISO 9000, ISO/IEC 20000, and ISO/IEC 27001 are validated across a diverse set of environments and situations rather than the limited experience of a single organization. They are subject to broad review across multiple organizations and disciplines. They are vetted by diverse sets of partners, suppliers and competitors.

■ The knowledge of public frameworks is more likely to be widely distributed among a large community of professionals through publicly available training and certification. It is easier for organizations to acquire such knowledge through the labour market.

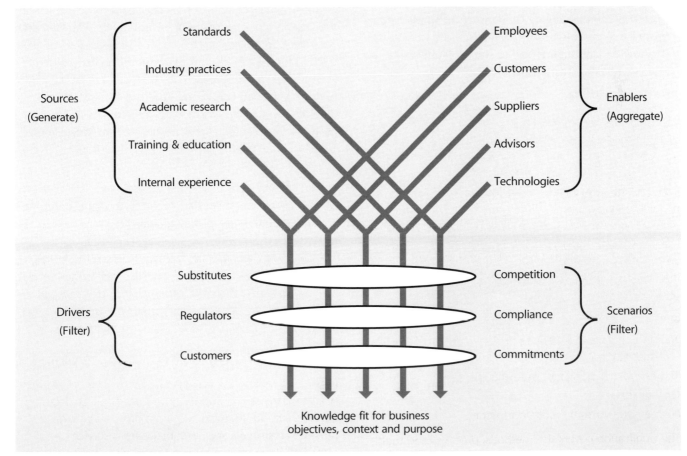

Figure 1.2 Sourcing of Service Management practice

Ignoring public frameworks and standards can needlessly place an organization at a disadvantage. Organizations should cultivate their own proprietary knowledge on top of a body of knowledge based on public frameworks and standards. Collaboration and coordination across organizations are easier on the basis of shared practices and standards.

1.2.3 ITIL and good practice in Service Management

The context of this publication is the ITIL Framework as a source of good practice in Service Management. ITIL is used by organizations worldwide to establish and improve capabilities in Service Management. ISO/IEC 20000 provides a formal and universal standard for organizations seeking to have their Service Management capabilities audited and certified. While ISO/IEC 20000 is a standard to be achieved and maintained, ITIL offers a body of knowledge useful for achieving the standard.

The ITIL Library has the following components:

- The ITIL Core – best practice guidance applicable to all types of organizations who provide services to a business
- The ITIL Complementary Guidance – a complementary set of publications with guidance specific to industry sectors, organization types, operating models and technology architectures.

The ITIL Core consists of five publications (Figure 1.3). Each provides the guidance necessary for an integrated approach, as required by the ISO/IEC 20000 standard specification:

- Service Strategy
- Service Design
- Service Transition
- Service Operation
- Continual Service Improvement.

Each publication addresses capabilities having direct impact on a service provider's performance. The structure of the Core is in the form of a lifecycle. It is iterative and multidimensional. It ensures organizations are set up to leverage capabilities in one area for learning and improvements in others. The Core is expected to provide structure, stability and strength to Service Management capabilities with durable principles, methods and tools. This serves to protect investments and provide the necessary basis for measurement, learning and improvement.

The guidance in ITIL can be adapted for use in various business environments and organizational strategies. The Complementary Guidance provides flexibility to implement the Core in a diverse range of environments. Practitioners can select Complementary Guidance as needed to provide traction for the Core in a given business context, much like tyres are selected based on the type of vehicle, purpose and road conditions. This is to increase the durability and portability of knowledge assets and to protect investments in Service Management capabilities.

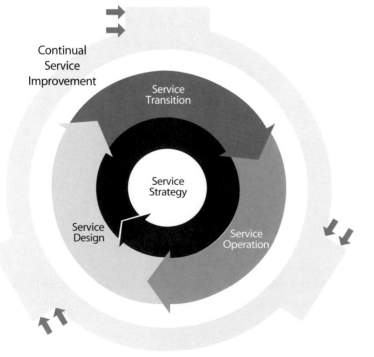

Figure 1.3 ITIL Core

1.2.3.1 Service Strategy

The Service Strategy publication provides guidance on how to design, develop and implement Service Management, not only as an organizational capability but also as a **strategic asset**. Guidance is provided on the principles underpinning the practice of Service Management, which are useful for developing Service Management policies, guidelines and processes across the ITIL Service Lifecycle. Service Strategy guidance is useful in the context of Service Design, Service Transition, Service Operation, and Continual Service Improvement. Topics covered in Service Strategy include the development of markets – internal and external, service assets, service catalogue, and implementation of strategy through the Service Lifecycle. Financial Management, Service Portfolio Management, Organizational Development and Strategic Risks are among other major topics.

Organizations use the guidance to set objectives and expectations of performance towards serving customers and market spaces, and to identify, select and prioritize opportunities. Service Strategy is about ensuring that organizations are in a position to handle the costs and risks associated with their Service Portfolios, and are set up not just for operational effectiveness but also for distinctive performance. Decisions made with respect to Service Strategy have far-reaching consequences, including those with delayed effect.

Organizations already practising ITIL use this publication to guide a strategic review of their ITIL-based Service Management capabilities and to improve the alignment between those capabilities and their business strategies. This publication of ITIL encourages readers to stop and think about why something is to be done before thinking of how. Answers to the first type of questions are closer to the customer's business. Service Strategy expands the scope of the ITIL Framework beyond the traditional audience of IT Service Management professionals.

1.2.3.2 Service Design

The Service Design publication provides guidance for the design and development of services and Service Management processes. It covers design principles and methods for converting strategic objectives into portfolios of services and service assets. The scope of Service Design is not limited to new services. It includes the changes and improvements necessary to increase or maintain value to customers over the lifecycle of services, the continuity of services, achievement of service levels and conformance to standards and regulations. It guides organizations on how to develop design capabilities for Service Management.

1.2.3.3 Service Transition

The Service Transition publication provides guidance for the development and improvement of capabilities for transitioning new and changed services into operations. This publication provides guidance on how the requirements of Service Strategy encoded in Service Design are effectively realized in service operations while controlling the risks of failure and disruption. The publication combines practices in Release Management, Programme Management and risk management, and places them in the practical context of Service Management. It provides guidance on managing the complexity related to changes to services and Service Management processes – preventing undesired consequences while allowing for innovation. Guidance is provided on transferring the control of services between customers and service providers.

1.2.3.4 Service Operation

This publication embodies practices in the management of service operations. It includes guidance on achieving effectiveness and efficiency in the delivery and support of services so as to ensure value for the customer and the service provider. Strategic objectives are ultimately realized through service operations, therefore making it a critical capability. Guidance is provided on how to maintain stability in service operations, allowing for changes in design, scale, scope and service levels. Organizations are provided with detailed process guidelines, methods and tools for use in two major control perspectives: reactive and proactive. Managers and practitioners are provided with knowledge allowing them to make better decisions in areas such as managing the availability of services, controlling demand, optimizing capacity utilization, scheduling operations and fixing problems. Guidance is provided on supporting operations through new models and architectures such as shared services, utility computing, internet services and mobile commerce.

1.2.3.5 Continual Service Improvement

This publication provides instrumental guidance in creating and maintaining value for customers through better design, transition and operation of services. It combines principles, practices and methods from quality management, Change Management and capability improvement. Organizations learn to realize incremental and large-scale improvements in service quality, operational efficiency and business continuity. Guidance is provided for linking improvement efforts and outcomes with service strategy, design, transition and operation. A closed-loop feedback system, based on the

Plan–Do–Check–Act (PDCA) model specified in ISO/IEC 20000, is established and capable of receiving inputs for change from any planning perspective.

1.3 PURPOSE

The aim of this publication is to give the reader guidance on using recommended practices when designing IT services and IT Service Management processes.

This publication follows on from the Service Strategy publication, which provides guidance on alignment and integration of the business needs to IT. It enables the reader to assess the requirements when designing a service, and documents industry best practice for the design of IT services and processes.

Although this publication can be read in isolation, it is recommended that it be used in conjunction with the other ITIL publications. The guidance in the ITIL publications is applicable generically. It is neither bureaucratic nor unwieldy if utilized sensibly and in full recognition of the business needs of the organization. Service Design is important for setting the stage to deliver services effectively to the business and meet the demand for growth and change. Enhancement is typically greater in cost and resource than development. Significant consideration should therefore be given to designing for the ease and economy of support over the whole lifecycle, but more importantly it is not possible to completely re-engineer a service once in production. It may be possible to get close, but it will be impossible to get back to a design once something is running. Retrofitting the design is difficult and costly and never achieves what could have been achieved if designed properly in the first place.

1.4 USAGE

This publication is relevant to anyone involved in the design, delivery or support of IT services. It will have relevance to the IT Architect, IT managers and practitioners at all levels. All the publications in the ITIL Service Management Core Library need to be read to fully appreciate and understand the overall lifecycle of services and of IT Service Management.

There are several ways of delivering an IT service, such as in-house, outsourced and partnership. This publication is generally relevant to all methods of service provision. So those involved in delivering IT services – within their own organization, in outsourced service provision or working in partnerships – will find that this publication is applicable to them. Business managers may find the publication helpful in understanding and establishing best practice IT services and support. Managers from supplier organizations will also find this publication relevant when setting up agreements for the delivery and support of services.

Service Management as a practice

2

2   Service Management as a practice

2.1   WHAT IS SERVICE MANAGEMENT?

Service Management is a set of specialized organizational capabilities for providing value to customers in the form of services. The capabilities take the form of functions and processes for managing services over a lifecycle, with specializations in strategy, design, transition, operation and continual improvement. The capabilities represent a service organization's capacity, competency and confidence for action. The act of transforming resources into valuable services is at the core of Service Management. Without these capabilities, a service organization is merely a bundle of resources that by itself has relatively low intrinsic value for customers.

> Service Management is a set of specialized organizational capabilities for providing value to customers in the form of services.

Organizational capabilities are shaped by the challenges they are expected to overcome. Service Management capabilities are similarly influenced by the following challenges that distinguish services from other systems of value creation such as manufacturing, mining and agriculture:

- Intangible nature of the output and intermediate products of service processes: difficult to measure, control and validate (or prove)
- Demand is tightly coupled with customer's assets: users and other customer assets such as processes, applications, documents and transactions arrive with demand and stimulate service production
- High level of contact for producers and consumers of services: little or no buffer between the customer, the front-office and back-office
- The perishable nature of service output and service capacity: there is value for the customer from assurance on the continued supply of consistent quality. Providers need to secure a steady supply of demand from customers.

Service Management, however, is more than just a set of capabilities. It is also a professional practice supported by an extensive body of knowledge, experience and skills. A global community of individuals and organizations in the public and private sectors fosters its growth and maturity. Formal schemes exist for the education, training and certification of practising organizations, and individuals influence its quality. Industry best practices, academic research and formal standards contribute to its intellectual capital and draw from it.

The origins of Service Management are in traditional service businesses such as airlines, banks, hotels and phone companies. Its practice has grown with the adoption by IT organizations of a service-oriented approach to managing IT applications, infrastructure and processes. Solutions to business problems and support for business models, strategies and operations are increasingly in the form of services. The popularity of shared services and outsourcing has contributed to the increase in the number of organizations who are service providers, including internal organizational units. This, in turn, has strengthened the practice of Service Management, at the same time imposing greater challenges on it.

2.2   WHAT ARE SERVICES?

2.2.1   The value proposition

> A service is a means of delivering value to customers by facilitating outcomes customers want to achieve without the ownership of specific costs and risks.

Services are a means of delivering value to customers by facilitating outcomes customers want to achieve without the ownership of specific costs and risks. Services facilitate outcomes by enhancing the performance of associated tasks and reducing the effect of constraints. The result is an increase in the probability of desired outcomes.

Over the years, organizations have debated the definition of a 'service'. The illustration in Figure 2.1 is an example of the realization that service is really about delivering value to customers.

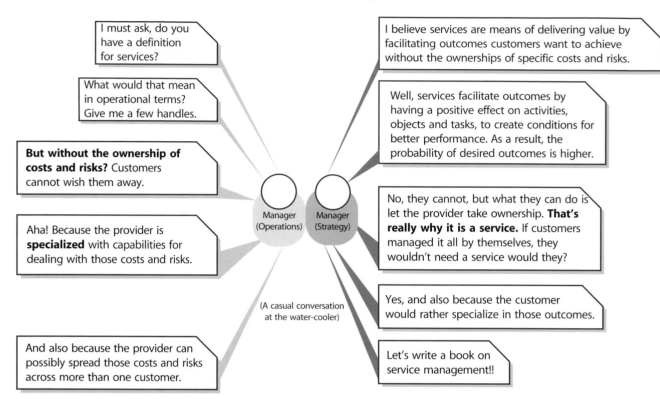

Figure 2.1 A conversation about the definition and meaning of services

2.3 FUNCTIONS AND PROCESSES ACROSS LIFECYCLE

2.3.1 Functions

Functions are units of organizations specialized to perform certain types of work and responsible for specific outcomes. They are self-contained, with capabilities and resources necessary for their performance and outcomes. Capabilities include work methods internal to the functions. Functions have their own body of knowledge, which accumulates from experience. They provide structure and stability to organizations.

Functions are means to structure organizations to implement the specialization principle. Functions typically define roles and the associated authority and responsibility for a specific performance and outcomes. Coordination between functions through shared processes is a common pattern in organization design. Functions tend to optimize their work methods locally to focus on assigned outcomes. Poor coordination between functions, combined with an inward focus, leads to functional silos that hinder the alignment and feedback that are critical to the success of the organization as a whole. Process models

help avoid this problem with functional hierarchies by improving cross-functional coordination and control. Well-defined processes can improve productivity within and across functions.

2.3.2 Processes

Processes are examples of closed-loop systems because they provide change and transformation towards a goal, and utilize feedback for self-reinforcing and self-corrective action (Figure 2.2). It is important to consider the entire process or how one process fits into another.

Process definitions describe actions, dependencies and sequence. Processes have the following characteristics:

■ **Measurable** – we are able to measure the process in a relevant manner. It is performance driven. Managers want to measure cost, quality and other variables while practitioners are concerned with duration and productivity.

■ **Specific results** – the reason a process exists is to deliver a specific result. This result must be individually identifiable and countable. While we can count changes, it is impossible to count how many Service Desks were completed.

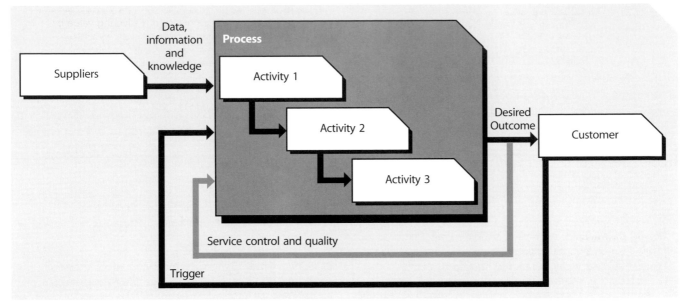

Figure 2.2 A basic process

- **Customers** – every process delivers its primary results to a customer or stakeholder. Customers may be internal or external to the organization, but the process must meet their expectations.
- **Responds to a specific event** – while a process may be ongoing or iterative, it should be traceable to a specific trigger.

There is often confusion around functions, processes, roles and activities. Functions are often mistaken for processes, and processes mistaken for functions. Service Design, as well as being a stage in the lifecycle of a service, can itself be seen by some organizations as a function, by others as a role or a set of processes or as an activity. Whether or not it is a function, role, activity or set of processes depends entirely on the size, structure and culture of an organization. It is important that however it is defined and implemented within an organisation, the success of the function, process, role or activity is measured and continually improved.

2.3.3 Specialization and coordination across the lifecycle

Specialization and coordination are necessary in the lifecycle approach. Feedback and control between the functions and processes within and across the elements of the lifecycle make this possible. The dominant pattern in the lifecycle is the sequential progress starting from SS

through SD–ST–SO and back to SS through CSI. That, however, is not the only pattern of action. Every element of the lifecycle provides points for feedback and control.

The combination of multiple perspectives allows greater flexibility and control across environments and situations. The lifecycle approach mimics the reality of most organizations, where effective management requires the use of multiple control perspectives. Those responsible for the design, development and improvement of processes for Service Management can adopt a process-based control perspective. For those responsible for managing agreements, contracts and services may be better served by a lifecycle-based control perspective with distinct phases. Both these control perspectives benefit from systems thinking. Each control perspective can reveal patterns that may not be apparent from the other.

2.4 SERVICE DESIGN FUNDAMENTALS

2.4.1 Purpose/goal/objective

The main purpose of the Service Design stage of the lifecycle is the design of new or changed services for introduction into the live environment. It is important that a holistic approach to all aspects of design is adopted, and that when changing or amending any of the individual elements of design all other aspects are considered. Thus when designing and developing a new application, this shouldn't be done in isolation, but should also consider the impact on the overall service, the management systems and tools (e.g. Service Portfolio and Service Catalogue), the architectures, the technology, the Service Management processes and the necessary measurements and metrics. This will ensure not only that the functional elements are addressed by the design, but also that all of the management and operational requirements are addressed as a fundamental part of the design and are not added as an afterthought.

> **Key message**
>
> A holistic approach should be adopted for all Service Design aspects and areas to ensure consistency and integration within all activities and processes across the entire IT technology, providing end-to-end business-related functionality and quality.

Not every change within an IT service will require the instigation of Service Design activity. It will only be required where there is 'significant' change. Every organization must define what constitutes 'significant' so that everyone within the organization is clear as to when Service Design activity is instigated. Therefore all changes should be assessed for their impact on Service Design activities to determine whether they are significant in terms of requiring Service Design activity. This should be part of the Change Management process impact assessment within the Service Transition publication of ITIL.

2.4.2 Scope

There are five individual aspects of Service Design considered within this publication. These are the design of:

- New or changed services
- Service Management systems and tools, especially the Service Portfolio, including the Service Catalogue
- Technology architecture and management systems
- The processes required
- Measurement methods and metrics.

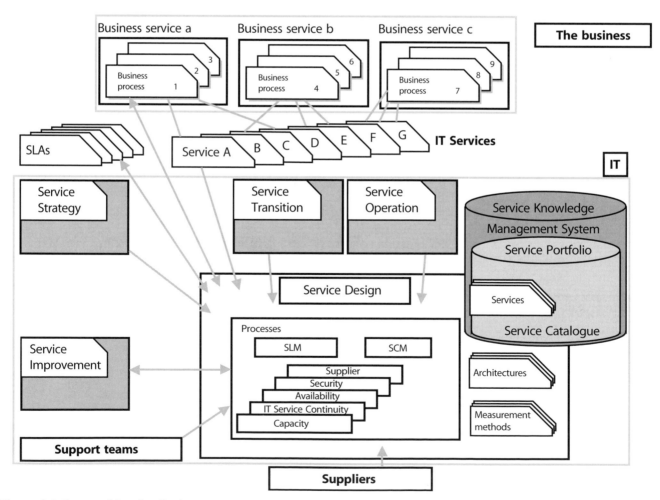

Figure 2.3 Scope of Service Design

The Service Design stage of the lifecycle starts with a set of new or changed business requirements and ends with the development of a service solution designed to meet the documented needs of the business. This developed solution, together with its Service Design Package (SDP – see Appendix A), is then passed to Service Transition to evaluate, build, test and deploy the new or changed service. On completion of these transition activities, control is transferred to the Service Operation stage of the Service Lifecycle. The activities involved in these stages are outlined in section 3. The overall scope of Service Design and the five aspects of design and how they interact are illustrated in Figure 2.3.

The main aim of Service Design is the design of new or changed services. The requirements for these new services are extracted from the Service Portfolio. Each requirement is analysed, documented and agreed, and a solution design is produced that is then compared with the strategies and constraints from Service Strategy to ensure that it conforms to corporate and IT policies. Each individual Service Design is also considered in conjunction with each of the other aspects of Service Design:

■ **The Service Management systems and tools, especially the Service Portfolio**: to ensure that this new or changed service is consistent with all other services, and that all other services that interface, support or depend on the new or changed services are consistent with the new service. If not, either the design of the new service or the other existing services will need to be adapted. Also the Service Management systems and tools should be reviewed to ensure they are capable of supporting the new or changed service.

■ **The technology architectures and management systems**: to ensure that all the technology architectures and management systems are consistent with the new or changed service and have the capability to operate and maintain the new service. If not, then either the architectures or management systems will need to be amended or the design of the new service will need to be revised.

■ **The processes**: to ensure that the processes, roles, responsibilities and skills have the capability to operate, support and maintain the new or changed service. If not, the design of the new service will need to be revised or the existing process capabilities will need to be enhanced. This includes all IT and Service Management processes, not just the key Service Design processes.

■ **The measurement methods and metrics**: to ensure that the existing measurement methods can provide the required metrics on the new or changed service. If not, then the measurement methods will need to be enhanced or the service metrics will need to be revised.

If all the above activities are completed during the Service Design stage, this will ensure that there will be minimal issues arising during the subsequent stages of the Service Lifecycle. Therefore Service Design must consolidate the key design issues and activities of all IT and Service Management processes within its own design activities, to ensure that all aspects are considered and included within all designs for new or changed services as part of everyday process operation.

The ability to measure and demonstrate value to the business requires the capability to link business outcomes, objectives and their underpinning processes and functions to the IT services and their underpinning assets, processes and functions. This value should be articulated by:

■ Agreeing service levels, SLAs and targets across the whole enterprise, ensuring critical business processes receive most attention

■ Measuring IT quality in business/user terms, reporting what is relevant to users (e.g. customer satisfaction, business value)

■ Mapping business processes to IT infrastructure, since new components are added continuously, increasing the possibility of disruptions caused by IT and loss of focus on business services and processes

■ Mapping business processes to business and service measurements, making services focus on IT measurements related to key aspects of business performance

■ Mapping infrastructure resources to services in order to take full advantage of critical IT components within the Configuration Management System (CMS), which are linked to critical business processes. This may also use information within the complete Service Knowledge Management System (SKMS). More information can be found on the CMS within the Service Transition publication

■ Providing end-to-end performance monitoring and measurement of online business processes, periodically reported against SLA targets.

Often the design of a major new or changed service will require that design changes are considered, and often affect or are affected by all of the other four phases of the Service Lifecycle. It is essential, therefore, that IT systems and services are designed, planned, implemented and managed appropriately for the business as a whole. The requirement then is to provide IT services that:

■ Are business- and customer-oriented, focused and driven

■ Are cost-effective and secure

■ Are flexible and adaptable, yet fit for purpose at the point of delivery

■ Can absorb an ever-increasing demand in the volume and speed of change

■ Meet increasing business demands for continuous operation

■ Are managed and operated to an acceptable level of risk

■ Are responsive, with appropriate availability matched to business needs.

With all these pressures on both IT and the business, the temptation – and unfortunately the reality in some cases – is to 'cut corners' on the design and planning processes or to ignore them completely. However, in these situations the design and planning activities are even more essential to the overall delivery of quality services. Therefore, more time rather than less should be devoted to the design processes and their implementation.

In order that effective, quality design can be achieved, even when timescales are short and pressure to deliver services is high, organizations should ensure that the importance of the Service Design function is fully understood and that support is provided to maintain and mature Service Design as a fundamental element of Service Management. Organizations should strive continually to review and improve their Service Design capability, in order that Service Design can become a consistent and repeatable practice, enabling organizations to deliver quality services against challenging timescales. Having a mature Service Design practice will also enable organizations to reduce risk in the transition and operational stages of service.

In general, the key to the successful provision of IT services is an appropriate level of design and planning to determine which projects, processes and services will have the greatest impact or benefit to the business. With the appropriate level of thought, design, preparation and planning, effort can be targeted at those areas that will yield the greatest return. Risk assessment and management are key requirements within all design activities. Therefore all five aspects of Service Design must include risk assessment and management as an integrated, inherent part of everything they do. This will ensure that the risks involved in the provision of services and the operation of processes, technology and measurement methods are aligned with business risk and impact, because risk assessment and management are embedded within all design processes and activities.

Many designs, plans and projects fail through a lack of preparation and management. The implementation of ITIL Service Management as a practice is about preparing and planning the effective and efficient use of the four Ps: the People, the Processes, the Products (services, technology and tools) and the Partners (suppliers, manufacturers and vendors), as illustrated in Figure 2.4.

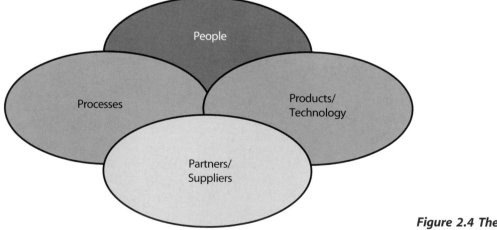

Figure 2.4 The Four Ps

However, there is no benefit in producing designs, plans, architectures and policies and keeping them to yourself. They must be published, agreed, circulated and actively used.

In order to ensure that business and IT services remain synchronized, many organizations form committees of senior management from the business and IT organizations. The committee carries the overall accountability for setting governance, direction, policy and strategy for IT services. Many organizations refer to this group as the IT Strategy or Steering Group. (ISG). The function of an ISG is to act as a partnership between IT and the business. It should meet regularly and review the business and IT strategies, designs, plans, service portfolio, architectures and policies to ensure that they are closely aligned with each other. It should provide the vision, set direction and determine priorities of individual programmes and projects to ensure that IT is aligned and focused on business targets and drivers. The group should also ensure that unrealistic timescales, which could jeopardize quality or disrupt normal operational requirements, are not imposed or attempted by either the business or IT. See Figure 2.5.

The ISG will include discussions on all aspects of the business that involve IT service, as well as proposed or possible change at a strategic level. Subjects for the ISG to discuss may include:

- **Reviewing business and IT plans**: to identify any changes in either area that would trigger the need to create, enhance or improve services
- **Demand planning**: to identify any changes in demand for both short- and long-term planning horizons; such changes may be increases or decreases in demand, and concern both business-as-usual and projects
- **Project authorization and prioritization**: to ensure that projects are authorized and prioritized to the mutual satisfaction of both the business and IT
- **Review of projects**: to ensure that the expected business benefits are being realized in accordance with project business cases, and to identify whether the projects are on schedule
- **Potential outsourcing**: to identify the need and content of sourcing strategies for the IT service provision

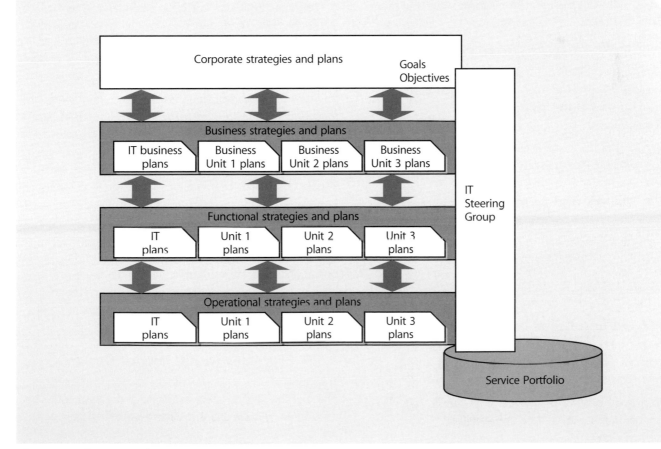

Figure 2.5 The IT Steering/Strategy Group

- **Business/IT strategy review**: to discuss major changes to business strategy and major proposed changes to IT strategy and technology, to ensure continued alignment
- **Business Continuity and IT Service Continuity**: the group, or a working party from the group, is responsible for aligning Business Continuity and IT Service Continuity strategies
- **Policies and standards**: the ISG is responsible for ensuring that IT policies and standards, particularly in relation to financial strategy and performance management, are in place and aligned with the overall corporate vision and objectives.

The IT Steering Group sets the direction for policies and plans from corporate to operational levels of IT organization and ensures that they are consistent with corporate level strategies. See Figure 2.5.

The ISG has an important role to play in the alignment of business and IT strategies and plans as illustrated in Figure 2.5. As can be seen, the Service Portfolio is a key source of input to the ISG in its decision-making role, which enables the ISG to:

- Direct and steer the selection of investment in those areas that yield the greatest business value and return on investment

- Perform effective programme and project selection, prioritization and planning

- Exercise effective ongoing governance and active management of the 'pipeline' of business requirements

- Ensure that the projected business benefits of programmes and projects are realized.

2.4.3 Value to business

With good Service Design, it is possible to deliver quality, cost-effective services and to ensure that the business requirements are being met.

The following benefits result from good Service Design practice:

- **Reduced Total Cost of Ownership (TCO)**: cost of ownership can only be minimized if all aspects of services, processes and technology are designed properly and implemented against the design

- **Improved quality of service**: both service and operational quality will be enhanced

- **Improved consistency of service**: as services are designed within the corporate strategy, architectures and constraints

- **Easier implementation of new or changed services**: as there is integrated and full Service Design and the production of comprehensive SDPs

- **Improved service alignment**: involvement from the conception of the service, ensuring that new or changed services match business needs, with services designed to meet Service Level Requirements

- **More effective service performance**: with incorporation and recognition of Capacity, Financial Availability and IT Service Continuity Plans

- **Improved IT governance**: assist with the implementation and communication of a set of controls for effective governance of IT

- **More effective Service Management and IT processes**: processes will be designed with optimal quality and cost-effectiveness

- **Improved information and decision-making**: more comprehensive and effective measurements and metrics will enable better decision-making and continual improvement of Service Management practices in the design stage of the Service Lifecycle.

2.4.4 Optimizing design performance

The optimizing of design activities requires the implementation of documented processes, together with an overriding quality management system (such as ISO 9001) for their continual measurement and improvement. It is important that when considering the improvement and optimization of the Service Design activities, the impact of the activities on all stages of the lifecycle should be measured and not just the impact on the design stage. Therefore Service Design measurements and metrics should look at the amount of rework activity and improvement activity that is needed on transition, operation and improvement activities as a result of inadequacies within the design of new and changed service solutions. More information on measurement of Service Design can be found in section 8.5.

2.4.5 Processes within Service Design

This publication details processes required in the design phase of the Service Lifecycle. These processes cannot be considered in isolation, as their true value will only be realized when interfaces between the processes are identified and actioned. The following processes are detailed in this publication:

- **Service Catalogue Management**: to ensure that a Service Catalogue is produced and maintained, containing accurate information on all operational services and those being prepared to be run operationally

- **Service Level Management**: negotiates, agrees and documents appropriate IT service targets with representatives of the business, and then monitors and produces reports on the service provider's ability to deliver the agreed level of service

- **Capacity Management**: to ensure that cost-justifiable IT capacity in all areas of IT always exists and is matched to the current and future agreed needs of the business, in a timely manner

- **Availability Management**: to ensure that the level of service availability delivered in all services is matched to, or exceeds, the current and future agreed needs of the business, in a cost-effective manner

- **IT Service Continuity Management**: to ensure that the required IT technical and service facilities (including computer systems, networks, applications, data repositories, telecommunications, environment, technical support and Service Desk) can be resumed within required, and agreed, business timescales

- **Information Security Management**: to align IT security with business security, and ensure that information security is effectively managed in all service and Service Management activities

- **Supplier Management**: to manage suppliers and the services they supply, to provide seamless quality of IT service to the business, ensuring value for money is obtained.

These are only some of the processes described in the ITIL Service Management practice guidance. All processes within the Service Management Lifecycle must be linked closely together for managing, designing, supporting and maintaining the services, IT infrastructure, environment, applications and data. Other processes are described in detail in other publications within the ITIL Service Management Practices core library. The interfaces between every process and every other process need to be clearly defined when designing a service or improving or implementing a process. These interfaces are described in detail in section 4 and include not only the interfaces to each of the Service Design processes, but also interfaces to processes within other stages of the lifecycle.

When designing a service or a process, it is imperative that all the roles are clearly defined. A trademark of high performing organizations is the ability to make the right decisions quickly and execute them quickly. Whether the decision involves a strategic choice or a critical operation, being clear on who has input, who decides and who takes action will enable the organization to move forward quickly.

Service Design principles

3

3 Service Design principles

IT Service Design is a part of the overall business change
process. This business change process and the role of IT
are illustrated in Figure 3.1.

Once accurate information has been obtained on what is
required and signed off, with regard to the changed needs
of the business, the plan for the delivery of a service to
meet the agreed need can be developed.

The role of the Service Design stage within this overall
business change process can be defined as:

> 'The design of appropriate and innovative IT services,
> including their architectures, processes, policies and
> documentation, to meet current and future agreed
> business requirements.'

It is important that the right interfaces and links to the
design activities exist. When designing new or changed
services, it is vital that the entire Service Lifecycle and ITSM
processes are involved from the outset. Often difficulties
occur in operations when a newly designed service is
handed over for live running at the last minute. The
following are actions that need to be undertaken from the
outset of a Service Design to ensure that the solution
meets the requirements of the business:

- The new service solution should be added to the
  overall Service Portfolio from the concept phase, and
  the Service Portfolio should be updated to reflect the
  current status through any incremental or iterative
  development. This will be beneficial not only from the
  financial perspective, but also from all other areas
  during design.

- As part of the initial service/system analysis, there
  will be a need to understand the Service Level
  Requirements (SLRs) for the service when it goes live.

- From the SLRs, the Capacity Management team can
  model this within the current infrastructure to
  ascertain if this will be able to support the new
  service. If time allows, the results from the modelling
  activities can be built into the Capacity Plan.

- If new infrastructure is required for the new service, or
  extended support, Financial Management will need to
  be involved to set the budget.

- An initial Business Impact Analysis and risk assessment
  should be conducted on services well before
  implementation as invaluable input into IT Service
  Continuity Strategy, Availability Design and Capacity
  Planning.

- The Service Desk will need to made aware of new
  services well in advance of live operation to prepare
  and train Service Desk staff and potentially IT
  customer staff.

- Service Transition can start planning the
  implementation and build into the change schedule.

- Supplier Management will need to be involved if
  procurement is required for the new service.

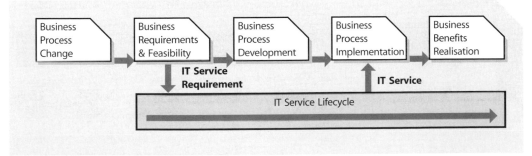

Figure 3.1 The business change process

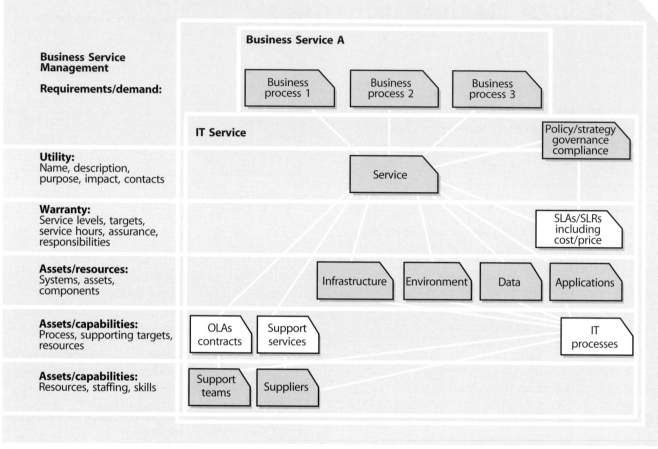

Figure 3.2 Service composition

The composition of a service and its constituent parts is illustrated in Figure 3.2.

Service Design must consider all these aspects when designing service solutions to meet new and evolving business needs:

■ **Business process**: to define the functional needs of the service being provided, e.g. telesales, invoicing, orders, credit checking

■ **Service**: the service itself that is being delivered to the customers and business by the service provider, e.g. e-mail, billing

■ **SLAs/SLRs**: the documents agreed with the customers that specify the level, scope and quality of service to be provided

■ **Infrastructure**: all of the IT equipment necessary to delivery the service to the customers and users, including servers, network circuits, switches, PCs, telephones

■ **Environment**: the environment required to secure and operate the infrastructure, e.g. data centres, power, air conditioning

■ **Data**: the data necessary to support the service and provide the information required by the business processes, e.g. customer records, accounts ledger

■ **Applications**: all of the software applications required to manipulate the data and provide the functional requirements of the business processes, e.g. ERM, Financial, CRM

■ **Support Services**: any services that are necessary to support the operation of the delivered service, e.g. a shared service, a managed network service

■ **Operational Level Agreements (OLAs) and contracts**: any underpinning agreements necessary to deliver the quality of service agreed within the SLA

■ **Support Teams**: any internal support teams providing second- and third-line support for any of the components required to provide the service, e.g. Unix, mainframe, networks

■ **Suppliers**: any external third parties necessary to provide third- and fourth- line support for any of the components required to provide the service, e.g. networks, hardware, software.

The design activities must not just consider each of the components above in isolation, but must also consider the relationships between each of the components and their interactions and dependencies on any other components and services, in order to provide an effective and comprehensive solution that meets the business needs.

3.1 GOALS

The main goals and objectives of Service Design are to:

■ Design services to satisfy business objectives, based on the quality, compliance, risk and security requirements, delivering more effective and efficient IT and business solutions and services aligned to business needs by coordinating all design activities for IT services to ensure consistency and business focus

■ Design services that can be easily and efficiently developed and enhanced within appropriate timescales and costs and, wherever possible, reduce, minimize or constrain the long-term costs of service provision

■ Design efficient and effective processes for the design, transition, operation and improvement of high-quality IT services, together with the supporting tools, systems and information, especially the Service Portfolio, to manage services through their lifecycle

■ Identify and manage risks so that they can be removed or mitigated before services go live

■ Design secure and resilient IT infrastructures, environments, applications and data/information resources and capability that meet the current and future needs of the business and customers

■ Design measurement methods and metrics for assessing the effectiveness and efficiency of the design processes and their deliverables

■ Produce and maintain IT plans, processes, policies, architectures, frameworks and documents for the design of quality IT solutions, to meet current and future agreed business needs

■ Assist in the development of policies and standards in all areas of design and planning of IT services and processes, receiving and acting on feedback on design processes from all other areas and incorporating the actions into a continual process of improvement

■ Develop the skills and capability within IT by moving strategy and design activities into operational tasks, making effective and efficient use of all IT service resources

■ Contribute to the improvement of the overall quality of IT service within the imposed design constraints, especially by reducing the need for reworking and enhancing services once they have been implemented in the live environment.

3.2 BALANCED DESIGN

For any new business requirements, the design of services is a delicate balancing act, ensuring that not only the functional requirements but also the performance targets are met. All of this needs to be balanced with regard to the resources available within the required timescale and the costs for the new services. Jim McCarthy, author of *Dynamics of Software Development*, states: 'As a development manager, you are working with only three things':

■ **Functionality**: the service or product and its facilities, functionality and quality, including all of the management and operational functionality required

■ **Resources**: the people, technology and money available

■ **Schedule**: the timescales.

These are shown in Figure 3.3.

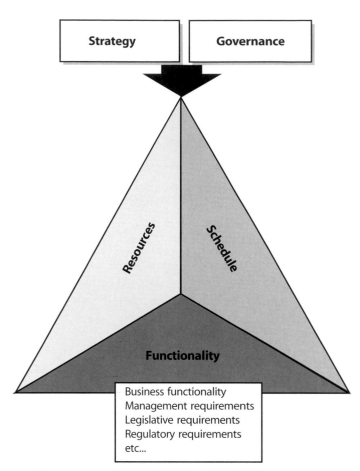

Business functionality
Management requirements
Legislative requirements
Regulatory requirements
etc...

Figure 3.3 Project elements in a triangulated relationship

This concept is extremely important to Service Design activities and to the balance between the effort that is spent in the design, development and delivery of services in response to business requirements. Service Design is a delicate balancing act of all three elements and the constant dynamic adjustment of all three to meet changing business needs. Changing one side of the triangle invariably has an impact on at least one of the other sides if not both of them. It is vital therefore that the business drivers and needs are fully understood in order that the most effective business solutions are designed and delivered, using the most appropriate balance of these three elements. It is likely that business drivers and needs will change during design and delivery, due to market pressures. The functionality and resources should be considered for all stages of the Service Lifecycle, so that services are not only designed and developed effectively and efficiently, but that the effectiveness and efficiency of the service is maintained throughout all stages of its lifecycle.

Due consideration should be given within Service Design to all subsequent stages within the Service Lifecycle. Often designers and architects only consider the development of a new service up to the time of implementation of the service into the live environment. A holistic approach to

the design of IT services should be adopted to ensure that a fully comprehensive and integrated solution is designed to meet the agreed requirements of the business. This approach should also ensure that all of the necessary mechanisms and functionality are implemented within the new service so that it can be effectively managed and improved throughout its operational life to achieve all of its agreed service targets. A formal, structured approach should be adopted to ensure that all aspects of the service are addressed and ensure its smooth introduction and operation within the live environment.

The most effective IT service providers integrate all five aspects of design rather than design them in isolation. This ensures that an integrated Enterprise Architecture is produced, consisting of a set of standards, designs and architectures that satisfy all of the management and operational requirements of services as well as the functionality required by the business. This integrated design ensures that when a new or changed service is implemented, it not only provides the functionality required by the business, but also meets and continues to meet all its service levels and targets in all areas. This ensures that no (or absolute minimum) weaknesses will need to be addressed retrospectively.

In order to achieve this, the overall management of these design activities needs to ensure:

■ Good communication between the various design activities and all other parties, including the business and IT planners and strategists

■ The latest versions of all appropriate business and IT plans and strategies are available to all designers

■ All of the architectural documents and design documents are consistent with all business and IT policies and plans

■ The architectures and designs:

● Are flexible and enable IT to respond quickly to new business needs

● Integrate with all strategies and policies

● Support the needs of other stages of the Service Lifecycle

● Facilitate new or changed quality services and solutions, aligned to the needs and timescales of the business.

3.3 IDENTIFYING SERVICE REQUIREMENTS

Service Design must consider all elements of the service by taking a holistic approach to the design of a new service. This approach should consider the service and its constituent components and their inter-relationships, ensuring that the services delivered meet the functionality and quality of service expected by the business in all areas:

■ The scalability of the service to meet future requirements, in support of the long-term business objectives

■ The business processes and business units supported by the service

■ The IT service and the agreed business functionality and requirements

■ The service itself and its Service Level Requirement (SLR) or Service Level Agreement (SLA)

■ The technology components used to deploy and deliver the service, including the infrastructure, the environment, the data and the applications

■ The internally supported services and components and their associated Operational Level Agreements (OLAs)

■ The externally supported services and components and their associated underpinning contracts, which will often have their own related agreements and/or schedules

■ The performance measurements and metrics required

■ The legislated or required security levels.

The relationships and dependencies between these elements are illustrated in Figure 3.4.

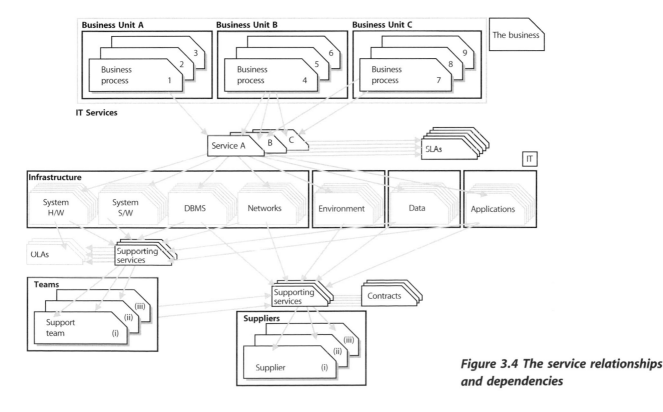

Figure 3.4 The service relationships and dependencies

No service can be designed, transitioned and operated in isolation. The relationship of each service to its supporting components and services must be clearly understood and recognized by all people within the service provider organization. It is also essential that all targets contained within supporting agreements, such as OLAs and contracts, underpin those agreed between the service provider and its customers. Some of these concepts are discussed in more detail in later sections of the publication, with respect to the individual aspects of Service Design. However, when an individual aspect of a service is changed, all other areas of the service should also be considered to ensure that any amendments necessary to support the change are included in the overall design. Increasingly, services are complex and are delivered by a number of partner or supplier organizations. Where multiple service providers are involved in delivery of a service, it is vital that a central Service Design authority is established, to ensure services and processes are fully integrated across all parties.

Within the specific area of technology there are four separate technology domains that will need to be addressed, as they are the supporting components of every service and contribute to its overall performance:

- **Infrastructure**: the management and control of all infrastructure elements, including mainframes, servers, network equipment, database systems, storage area networks (SANs), network-attached storage (NAS), systems software, utilities, backup systems, firewalls, development and test environments, management tools, etc.
- **Environmental**: the management and control of all environmental aspects of all major equipment rooms, including the physical space and layout, power, air conditioning, cabling, physical security, etc.
- **Data**: the management and control of all data and information and its associated access, including test data where applicable
- **Applications**: the management and control of all applications software, including both bought-in applications and in-house developed applications software.

3.4 IDENTIFYING AND DOCUMENTING BUSINESS REQUIREMENTS AND DRIVERS

IT must retain accurate information on business requirements and drivers if it is to provide the most appropriate catalogue of services with an acceptable level of service quality that is aligned to business needs. Business drivers are the people, information and tasks that

support the fulfilment of business objectives. This requires that IT develops and maintains close, regular and appropriate relationships and exchange of information in order to understand the operational, tactical and strategic requirements of the business. This information needs to be obtained and agreed in two main areas to maintain service alignment:

- **Information on the requirements of existing services** – what changes will be required to existing services with regard to:
  - New facilities and functionality requirements
  - Changes in business processes, dependencies, priorities, criticality and impact
  - Changes in volumes of service transactions
  - Increased service levels and service level targets due to new business driver, or reduced for old services, lowering priority for those due for replacement
  - Additional needs for Service Management information.
- **Information on the requirements of new services**:
  - Facilities and functionality required
  - Management information required and management needs
  - Business processes supported, dependencies, priorities, criticality and impact
  - Business cycles and seasonal variations
  - Service level requirements and service level targets
  - Business transaction levels, service transaction levels, numbers and types of users and anticipated future growth
  - Business justification, including the financial and strategic aspects
  - Predicted level of change, e.g. known future business requirements or enhancement
  - Level of business capability or support to be provided, e.g. local business-based support.

This collection of information is the first and most important stage for designing and delivering new services or major changes to existing services. The need for accurate and representative information from the business is paramount. This must be agreed and signed off with senior representatives within the business. If incorrect or misleading information is obtained and used at this stage, then all subsequent stages will be delivering services that do not match the needs of the business. Also, there must be some formal process for the agreement and acceptance of changes to the business requirements, as these will often change and evolve during the Service

Lifecycle. The requirements and the design must evolve with the changing business environment to ensure that the business expectations are met. However, this must be a carefully managed process to ensure that the rate of change is kept at an agreed and manageable level, and does not 'swamp' and excessively delay the project or its implementation.

In order to design and deliver IT services that meet the needs of the customers and the business, clear, concise, unambiguous specifications of the requirements must be documented and agreed. Time spent in these activities will prevent issues and discussion from arising later with regard to variances from customer and business expectation. This business requirements stage should consist of:

■ Appointment of a project manager, the creation of a project team and the agreement of project governance by the application of a formal, structured project methodology

■ Identification of all stakeholders, including the documentation of all requirements from all stakeholders and stakeholder benefits they will obtain from the implementation

■ Requirements analysis, prioritization, agreement and documentation

■ Determination and agreement of outline budgets and business benefits. The budget must be committed by management, because it is normal practice to decide next year's budget in the last quarter of the previous year, so any plans must be submitted within this cycle

■ Resolution of the potential conflict between business units and agreement on corporate requirements

■ Sign-off processes for the agreed requirements and a method for agreeing and accepting changes to the agreed requirements. Often the process of developing requirements is an iterative or incremental approach that needs to be carefully controlled to manage 'scope creep'

■ Development of a customer engagement plan, outlining the main relationships between IT and the business and how these relationships and necessary communication to wider stakeholders will be managed.

Where service requirements are concerned, they sometimes come with a price tag (which might not be entirely known at this stage), so there always needs to be a balance between the service achievable and the cost. This may mean that some requirements may be too costly to include and may have to be dropped during the financial assessment involved within the design process.

If this is necessary, all decisions to omit any service requirements from the design of the service must be documented and agreed with the representatives of the business. There is often a difficulty when what the business wants and the budget allocated for the solution do not take into account the full service costs, including the ongoing costs.

3.5 DESIGN ACTIVITIES

All design activities are triggered by changes in business needs or service improvements. A structured and holistic approach to the design activities should be adopted, so that all available information is considered to ensure consistency and integration is achieved throughout the IT service provider organization, within all design activities.

> **Key message**
> Architectures and designs should be kept, clear, concise, simple and relevant. All too often, designs and architectures are complex and theoretical and do not relate to the 'real world'.

The main problem today is that organizations often only focus on the functional requirements. A design or architecture by definition needs to consider all design aspects. It is not a smaller organization that combines these aspects, it is a sensible one.

The design processes activities are:

■ Requirements collection, analysis and engineering to ensure that business requirements are clearly documented and agreed

■ Design of appropriate services, technology, processes, information and process measurements to meet business requirements

■ Review and revision of all processes and documents involved in Service Design, including designs, plans, architectures and policies

■ Liaison with all other design and planning activities and roles, e.g. solution design

■ Production and maintenance of IT policies and design documents, including designs, plans, architectures and policies

■ Revision of all design documents, and planning for the deployment and implementation of IT strategies using 'roadmaps', programmes and project plans

■ Risk assessment and management of all design processes and deliverables

■ Ensuring alignment with all corporate and IT strategies and policies.

The inputs to the various design activities are:

- Corporate visions, strategies, objectives, policies and plans, business visions, strategies, objectives and plans, including Business Continuity Plans (BCPs)
- Constraints and requirements for compliance with legislated standards and regulations
- IT strategies and strategic documents (from Service Strategy):
  - All IT strategies, policies and strategic plans
  - Details of business requirements
  - All constraints, financial budgets and plans
  - The Service Portfolio
  - Service Management visions, strategies, policies, objectives and plans
  - IT and Service Management processes, risks and issues registers
  - Service Transition plans (Change, Configuration and Release and Deployment Management Plans)
  - Security policies, handbooks and plans
  - The procurement and contract policy, supplier strategy and Supplier Management processes
  - The current staff knowledge, skills and capability
  - IT business plans, Business and IT Quality Plans and policies
  - Service Management plans, including Service Level Management Plans, SLAs and SLRs, Service Improvement Plan (SIP), Capacity Plans, Availability Plans, IT Service Continuity Plans
- Measurement tools and techniques.

The deliverables from the design activities are:

- Suggested revisions to IT strategies and policies
- Revised designs, plans and technology and management architectures, including:
  - The IT infrastructure and infrastructure management and environmental strategy, designs, plans, architectures and policies
  - The applications and data strategies, designs, plans, architectures and policies
- Designs for new or changed services, processes and technologies
- Process review and analysis reports, with revised and improved processes and procedures
- Revised measurement methods and processes
- Managed levels of risk, and risk assessment and management reports

- Business cases and feasibility studies, together with Statements of Requirements (SORs) and Invitations to Tender (ITTs)
- Comments and feedback on all other plans
- Business benefit and realization reviews and reports.

3.6 DESIGN ASPECTS

An overall, integrated approach should be adopted for the design activities documented in the previous section and should cover the design of:

- Service solutions, including all of the functional requirements, resources and capabilities needed and agreed
- Service Management systems and tools, especially the Service Portfolio for the management and control of services through their lifecycle
- Technology architectures and management architectures and tools required to provide the services
- Processes needed to design, transition, operate and improve the services
- Measurement systems, methods and metrics for the services, the architectures and their constituent components and the processes.

The key aspect is the design of new or changed service solutions to meet changing business needs. Every time a new service solution is produced, it needs to be checked against each of the other aspects to ensure that it will integrate and interface with all of the other services already in existence. These five aspects of Service Design are covered in more detail in the following sections. The plans produced by Service Design for the design, transition and subsequent operation of these five different aspects should include:

- The approach taken and the associated timescales
- The organizational impact of the new or changed solution on both the business and IT
- The commercial impact of the solution on the organization, including the funding, costs and budgets required
- The technical impact of the solution and the staff and their roles, responsibilities, skills, knowledge, training and competences required to deploy, operate, maintain and optimize the new solution to the business
- The commercial justification assessment of the impact of the solution on existing business – this impact must be assessed from the point of view of IT and Service Management processes, including both their capacity and performance

- The assessment and mitigation of risks to services, processes and Service Management activities

- Communication planning and all aspects of communication with all interested parties

- The impact of the solution on new or existing contracts or agreements

- The expected outcomes from the operation of the new or changed service in measurable terms, generally expressed within new or existing Service Level Agreements (SLAs), service levels and customer satisfaction

- The production of a Service Design Package (see Appendix A) containing everything necessary for the subsequent testing, introduction and operation of the solution or service

- The production of a set of Service Acceptance Criteria (SAC) (see Appendix B) that will be used to ensure that the service provider is ready to deliver and support the new or changed service in the live environment.

3.6.1 Designing service solutions

There are many activities that have to be completed within the Service Design stage for a new or changed service. A formal and structured approach is required to produce the new service at the right cost, functionality, quality and within the right time frame. This process and its constituent stages are illustrated in Figure 3.5, together with the other major areas that will need to be involved within the process. This process must be iterative/incremental to ensure that the service delivered meets the evolving and changing needs of the business during the business process development and the IT Service Lifecycle. Additional project managers and project teams may need to be allocated to manage the stages within the lifecycle for the deployment of the new service.

The role of the project team within this activity of delivering new and changing IT services to the business and its relationship to design activities is illustrated in Figure 3.5.

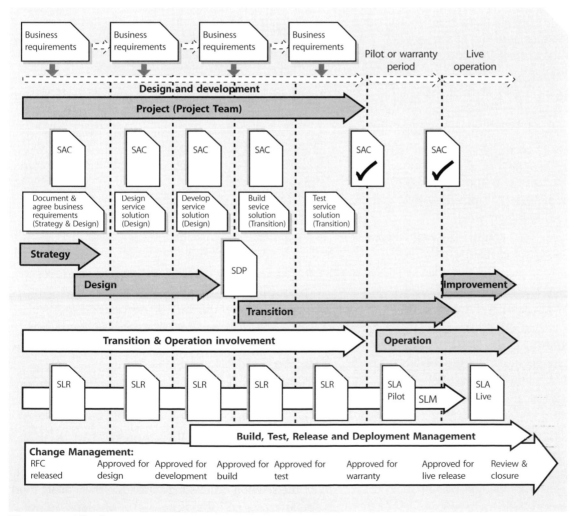

Figure 3.5 Aligning new services to business requirements

Figure 3.5 shows the lifecycle of a service from the initial or changed business requirement through the design, transition and operation stages of the lifecycle. It is important that there is effective transfer of knowledge at all stages between the operational staff and the project staff to ensure smooth progression through each of the stages illustrated.

The areas that need to be considered within the design of the service solution should include:

- Analyse the agreed business requirements
- Review the existing IT services and infrastructure and produce alternative service solutions, with a view to re-using or exploiting existing components and services wherever possible
- Design the service solutions to the new requirements, including their constituent components, in terms of the following, and document this design:
  - The facilities and functionality required, and information required for the monitoring of the performance of the service or process
  - The business processes supported, dependencies, priorities, criticality and impact of the service, together with the business benefits that will be delivered by the service
  - Business cycles and seasonal variations, and the related business transaction levels, service transaction levels, the numbers and types of users and anticipated future growth, and the business continuity requirements
  - Service Level Requirements and service level targets and the necessary service measuring, reporting and reviewing activities
  - The timescales involved and the planned outcomes from the new service and the impact on any existing services
  - The requirements for testing, including any User Acceptance Testing (UAT) and responsibilities for managing the test results
- Ensure that the contents of the Service Acceptance Criteria (SAC) are incorporated and the required achievements planned into the initial design
- Evaluate and cost alternative designs, highlighting advantages as well as disadvantages of the alternatives
- Agree the expenditure and budgets
- Re-evaluate and confirm the business benefits, including the Return on Investment (RoI) from the service, including identification and quantification of all service costs and all business benefits and increased revenues. The costs should cover the Total Cost of Ownership (TCO) of the service and include

start-up costs such as design costs, transition costs, project budget, and all ongoing operational costs, including management, support and maintenance

- Agree the preferred solution and its planned outcomes and targets (Service Level Requirement (SLR))
- Check the solution is in balance with all corporate and IT strategies, policies, plans and architectural documents. If not, revise either the solution or the strategic documentation (taking into account the effect on other strategic documents, services and components) wherever possible re-using or exploiting existing components (e.g. software objects, 'corporate' data, hardware), unless the strategy dictates otherwise. The changing of strategy will involve a significant amount of work and would be done in conjunction with Service Strategy
- Ensure that all of the appropriate corporate and IT governance and security controls are included with the solution
- Complete an IT 'organizational readiness assessment' to ensure that the service can be effectively operated to meet its agreed targets and that the organization has the appropriate capability to deliver to the agreed level. This will include:
  - The commercial impact on the organization from both a business and IT perspective, including all of the business benefits and all of the costs (both one-off project costs and the ongoing annual operation costs) involved in the design, development and ongoing operation and support of the service
  - Assessment and mitigation of the risks associated with the new or changed service, particularly with regard to the operation, security, availability and continuity of the service
  - The business capability and maturity. This activity should be performed by the business itself to ensure that all of the right processes, structure, people, roles, responsibilities and facilities are in place to operate the new service
  - The IT capability and maturity:
    - The environment and all areas of technology, having considered the impact on existing components of the infrastructure and existing services
    - The IT organizational structure and the roles and responsibilities
    - The IT processes and their documentation
    - The skills, knowledge and competence of the staff

- The IT management processes and supporting tools
- The supplier and supporting agreements necessary to maintain and deliver the service
- The assembly of a Service Design Package (SDP) for the subsequent transition, operation and improvement of the new or changed service solution.

3.6.2 Designing supporting systems, especially the Service Portfolio

The most effective way of managing all aspects of services through their lifecycle is by using appropriate management systems and tools to support and automate efficient processes. The Service Portfolio is the most critical management system used to support all processes and describes a provider's services in terms of business value. It articulates business needs and the provider's response to those needs. By definition, business value terms correspond to market terms, providing a means for comparing service competitiveness across alternative providers. By acting as the basis of a decision framework, a service portfolio either clarifies or helps to clarify the following strategic questions:

- Why should a customer buy these services?
- Why should they buy these services from you?
- What are the pricing or chargeback models?
- What are my strengths and weaknesses, priorities and risk?
- How should my resources and capabilities be allocated?

See Figure 3.6. Ideally the Service Portfolio should form part of a comprehensive Service Knowledge Management System (SKMS) and registered as a document in the Configuration Management System (CMS). Further information is provided on both the CMS and the SKMS within the Service Transition publication.

Figure 3.6 is a depiction of the relationship of the Service Portfolio with the SKMS.

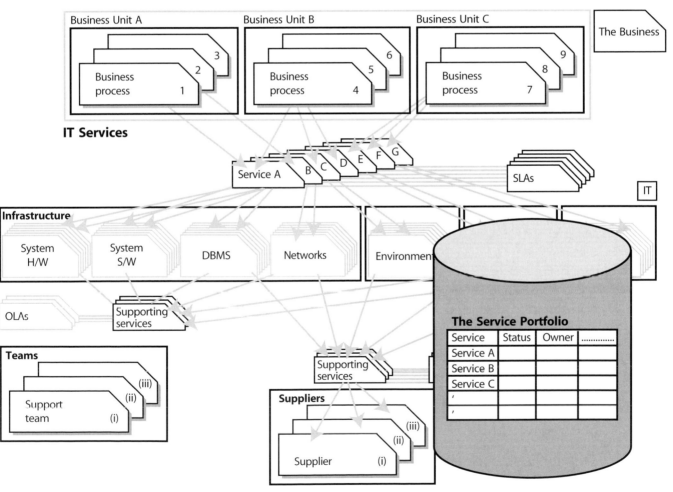

Figure 3.6 The Service Portfolio – a central repository

Once a strategic decision to charter a service is made, this is the stage in the Service Lifecycle when Service Design begins architecting the service, which will eventually become part of the Service Catalogue. The Service Portfolio should contain information relating to every service and its current status within the organization. The options of status within the Service Portfolio should include:

■ **Requirements**: a set of outline requirements have been received from the business or IT for a new or changed service

■ **Defined**: the set of requirements for the new service are being assessed, defined and documented and the SLR is being produced

■ **Analysed**: the set of requirements for the new service are being analysed and prioritized

■ **Approved**: the set of requirements for the new service have been finalized and authorized

■ **Chartered**: the new service requirements are being communicated and resources and budgets allocated

■ **Designed**: the new service and its constituent components are being designed – and procured, if required

■ **Developed**: the service and its constituent components are being developed or harvested, if applicable

■ **Built**: the service and its constituent components are being built

■ **Test**: the service and its constituent components are being tested

■ **Released**: the service and its constituent components are being released

■ **Operational**: the service and its constituent components are operational within the live environment

■ **Retired**: the service and its constituent components have been retired.

The Service Portfolio would therefore contain details of all services and their status with respect to the current stage within the Service Lifecycle, as illustrated in Figure 3.7.

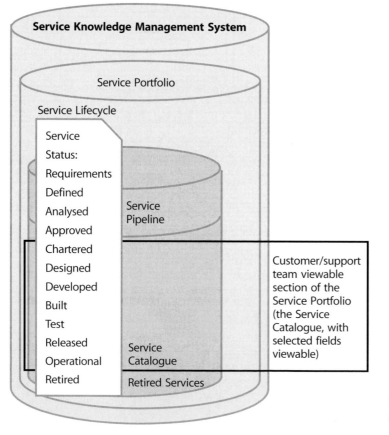

Figure 3.7 The Service Portfolio and its contents

Customers and users would only be allowed access to those services within the Service Portfolio that were of a status between 'chartered' and 'operational', as illustrated by the box in Figure 3.7, i.e. those services contained within the Service Catalogue. Service Strategy and Service Design personnel would need access to all records within the Service Portfolio, as well as other important areas such as Change Management. Other members of the service provider organization would have access to a permitted subset of the records within the Service Portfolio. Although the Service Portfolio is designed by Service Design, it is owned and managed by Service Strategy within the Service Portfolio Management process. Full details on Service Portfolio Management are discussed in the Service Strategy publication.

The Service Pipeline is a subset of the overall Service Portfolio and contains details of all of the business requirements that have not yet become services released to the live environment. It is used as a basis for the definition, analysis, prioritization and approval, by the ISG and Service Strategy, of all requests for new or changed services, to ensure that new and changed services are aligned to business requirements. It will principally be used as input to the activities of the Service Strategy and Service Design stages of the Service Lifecycle. It also provides valuable input to the activities of the Service Transition stage of the lifecycle in determining the services to be released. The Service Catalogue Management process must ensure that all of the details within the Service Portfolio are accurate and up-to-date as the requirement and its new or changed service is migrated into the live environment. This will involve close liaison with all Service Transition activities.

Various elements of the same service can have different statuses at the same time. Otherwise the Service Portfolio would be unable to support 'incremental and iterative' development. Each organization should carefully design its Service Portfolio, the content and the access allowed to the content. The content should include:

■ Service name
■ Service description
■ Service status
■ Service classification and criticality
■ Applications used
■ Data and/or data schema used
■ Business processes supported
■ Business owners
■ Business users
■ IT owners

■ Service warranty level, SLA and SLR references
■ Supporting services
■ Supporting resources
■ Dependent services
■ Supporting OLAs, contracts and agreements
■ Service costs
■ Service charges (if applicable)
■ Service revenue (if applicable)
■ Service metrics.

The Service Portfolio is the main source of information on the requirements and services and needs to be very carefully designed to meet all the needs of all its users. The design of the Service Portfolio needs to be considered in the same way as the design of any other IT service to ensure that it meets all of these needs. This approach should also be used for all of the other Service Management information systems, including the:

■ Service Knowledge Management System (SKMS)
■ Configuration Management System (CMS)
■ Service Desk system
■ Capacity Management Information System (CMIS)
■ Availability Management Information System (AMIS)
■ Security Management Information System (SMIS)
■ Supplier and Contracts Database (SCD).

3.6.3 Designing technology architectures

The architectural design activities within an IT organization are concerned with providing the overall strategic 'blueprints' for the development and deployment of an IT infrastructure – a set of applications and data that satisfy the current and future needs of the business. Although these aspects underpin the delivery of quality IT services, they alone cannot deliver quality IT services, and it is essential that the people, process and partner/supplier aspects surrounding these technological components (products) are also considered.

'Architecture' is a term used in many different contexts. In this context it is defined as:

> The fundamental organization of a system, embodied in its components, their relationships to each other and to the environment, and the principles guiding its design and evolution.

'System' in this definition is used in the most general, not necessarily IT, sense:

> 'a collection of components organized to accomplish a specific function or set of functions'.

So the system could be, for example, a whole organization, a business function, a product line or an information system. Each of these systems will have an 'architecture' as defined earlier, made up of the components of the system, the relationships between them (such as control interfaces and data exchanges), the relationships between the system and its environment (political, organizational, technological, etc.) and the design principles that inform, guide and constrain its structure and operation, as well as its future development.

In essence, architectural design can be defined as:

> 'The development and maintenance of IT policies, strategies, architectures, designs, documents, plans and processes for the deployment and subsequent operation and improvement of appropriate IT services and solutions throughout an organization.'

The work of architectural design needs to assess and reconcile many types of needs, some of which may be in conflict with one another. The work should ensure that:

■ The IT infrastructures, environments, data, applications and external services serve the needs of the business, its products and services. This activity not only includes the technology components but also the management of them

■ The right balance is struck between innovation, risk and cost whilst seeking a competitive edge, where desired by the business

■ There is compliance with relevant architectural frameworks, strategies, policies, regulations and standards

■ A coordinated interface is provided between IT designers and planners, strategists, business designers and planners.

The architectural design activities should use input from the business, Service Strategy, its plans, designers and planners to develop appropriate designs, plans, architectures and policies for all areas of IT. These designs, plans, architectures and policies should cover all aspects of IT, including roles and responsibilities, services, technology, architecture and frameworks, processes and procedures, partners and suppliers and management methods. The architectural design process must also cover all areas of technology, including the infrastructure, environment, applications and data and be closely linked to the overall business planning and design processes.

Any enterprise is a complex system, with many types of components including its staff, business functions and processes, organizational structure and physical distribution, information resources and information systems, financial and other resources including technology, and the strategies, plans, management, policies and governance structures that drive the enterprise. An Enterprise Architecture should show how all these components (and others) are integrated in order to achieve the business objectives, both now and in the future.

The complete Enterprise Architecture can be large and complex. Here we are interested in those architectures concerned with the business of the organization and the information systems that support it. Each of these architectures calls on distinct architectural disciplines and areas of expertise, as illustrated in Figure 3.8.

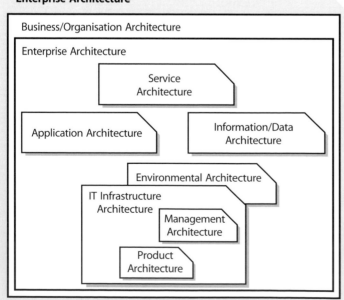

Figure 3.8 Enterprise Architecture

Enterprise Architecture is defined by Gartner as:

> 'the process of translating business vision and strategy into effective enterprise change, by creating, communicating and improving key principles and models that describe the enterprise's future states and enable its evolution'.

There are many proprietary and non-proprietary frameworks for the development of an Enterprise Architecture, as illustrated in Table 3.1.

These frameworks include descriptions of the organizational structure, business processes, planning and control systems, management and governance mechanisms, policies and procedures of the enterprise. They show how these components interoperate and contribute to the achievement of business goals and objectives, and provide the basis for identifying the requirements for information systems that support these business processes.

Table 3.1   Enterprise Architecture frameworks

Full framework name	Framework acronym
Architecture of Integrated Information Systems Framework	ARIS
Bredemeyer Framework	Bredemeyer
Business Transformation Enablement Programme Transformation Framework	BTEP
Command, Control, Communications, Computers Intelligences Surveillance and Reconnaissance	C4ISR
CSC Catalyst	Catalyst
Computer Integrated Manufacturing Open Systems Architecture	CIMOSA
Enterprise Architecture Framework	Gartner
Enterprise Architecture Planning	EAP
Extended Enterprise Architecture Framework	E2AF
FEA Reference Models	FEA
Generalized Enterprise Reference Architecture and Methodology	GERAM
Integrated Architecture Framework	IAF
Pillars of EA	Forrester
Reference Model for Open Distributed Processing	RM-ODP
Technical Architectural Framework Information Management	TAFIM
Treasury Enterprise Architecture Framework	TFAF
TOGAF Technical Reference Model	TOGAF
Zachman Framework	Zachman

The Enterprise Architecture should be an integrated element of the Business Architecture and should include the following major areas:

- **Service Architecture**, which translates applications, infrastructure, organization and support activities into a set of services. The Service Architecture provides the independent, business integrated approach to delivering services to the business. It provides the model for making a distinction between the Service Architecture, the Application Architecture, the Data Architecture and the Infrastructure Architecture. It also provides fault tolerance, future proofing and security controls. This means that, potentially, changes occurring within any technology architectures will be transparent to the users of the service – for example, web-based self-service delivery mechanisms. It should include not just the services themselves and their overall integration, but also the management of those services.

- **Application Architecture**, which provides a blueprint for the development and deployment of individual applications, maps business and functional requirements on to applications, and shows the inter-relationships between applications. Emerging Application Architectures are likely to be component-based. Such an approach maximizes re-use and helps to maintain flexibility in accommodating changes in sourcing policy.

- **Data/Information Architecture**, which describes the logical and physical data assets of the enterprise and the data management resources. It shows how the information resources are managed and shared for the benefit of the enterprise. A strategy on centralized versus distributed data will almost certainly have been devised as part of such an architecture. The Data/Information Architecture will include consideration of data warehousing technologies that facilitate the exploitation of corporate information assets. It will increasingly cover content management and the facilities for delivery of information over multiple channels.

- **IT Infrastructure Architecture**, which describes the structure, functionality and geographical distribution of the hardware, software and communications components that underpin and support the overall architecture, together with the technical standards applying to them. This should also include a 'Product Architecture' that describes the particular proprietary products and industry standards that the enterprise uses to implement the infrastructure in conformance with the IT Infrastructure Architecture principles

- **Environmental Architecture**, which describes all aspects, types and levels of environment controls and their management. An illustration of the type of environmental information required is included in Appendix E.

The relationships between these architectural perspectives can be seen in Figure 3.9. The development, documentation and maintenance of business and IT architectures will typically form part of the processes of strategic thinking and strategy development in the organization.

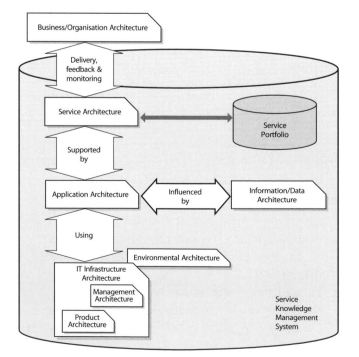

Figure 3.9 Architectural relationships

Within the framework described earlier, it is possible to identify (at least) three architectural roles. These could all report to a senior 'Enterprise Architect' in the organization:

- **Business/Organizational Architect**: concerned with business models, business processes and organizational design – the structural and functional components of the organization and their relationship, and how the business functions and activities of the organization are distributed among them; also the governance of the organization and the roles and responsibilities required
- **Service Architect** (often separate roles of Applications Architect and Information/Data Architect): concerned with the Service, Data and Application Architectures – the logical architectures supporting the business and the relationships between them
- **IT Infrastructure Architect**: concerned with the physical technology model, the infrastructure components and their relationships, including choices of technologies, interfaces and protocols, and the selection of products to implement the infrastructure.

In some organizations, the roles of Business/Organizational Architect, Information Systems Architect (or possibly separate roles of Applications Architect and Data Architect) and IT Infrastructure Architect will be separate functions. In others, some or all of the roles may be combined. The roles may reside in separate parts of the organization or even outside it. For example:

- The Business/Organizational Architect role may reside within the Business Strategy and Planning function in the corporate HQ
- The Service Architect role may form part of an internal function with responsibility for handling relationships between the business, external suppliers and IT partners relating to Service issues. A key responsibility of such a function is the maintenance of the Service Architecture. This function may be within an IT function or within the business side of an organization
- The IT Infrastructure Architect role may reside with the service provider/partner who is responsible for producing the IT Infrastructure Architecture used for the delivery of IT services to the organization.

If the necessary architectures are in place, then the role of Service Design is affected in the following ways:

- Must work within the agreed architectural framework and standards
- Will be able to re-use many of the assets created as part of the architecture
- Should work closely with all three architectural roles to

ensure maximum benefit from the work done in creating the architecture.

If architecture design is to be accomplished effectively and economically, the documents, processes and activities of the business and architectural design should be closely coordinated and synchronized. A list of these design documents and their content is contained in Appendices C and D. The individual details of technology included within architectural design are considered in the following sections.

> Key message:
>
> The real benefit and RoI of the Enterprise Architecture comes not from the architecture itself, but from the ability of an organization to design and implement projects and solutions in a rapid and consistent manner.

3.6.3.1 Technology Management

A strategic approach should be adopted with regard to the planning of an information technology and its management. This implies creating 'architectures' or 'blueprints' for the long-term framework of the technology used and planned. IT planners, designers and architects need to understand the business, the requirements and the current technology in order to develop appropriate IT architectures for the short, medium and long term. Technology design also needs to take account of the likely IT services that it will underpin, or at least the types of service from an understanding of the business and its future direction, because the business will demand IT services, and they will need an appropriate technology to provide and deliver those services. If it is possible to provide a longer-term technology, which can underpin a number of IT services, then taking a strategic approach will provide benefit in the longer term.

Architectures need to be developed within the major areas of technology.

Technology architectures

Architectures are needed in all areas of IT infrastructure. Where relevant they need to be developed in the following areas:

- Applications and systems software
- Information, data and data base including information security and confidentiality, data warehousing and data mining
- Infrastructure design and architecture:
    - Central server, mainframe architectures, distributed regional servers, including local file and print servers

- Data networks (LANs, MANs, WANs, protocols, etc.), internet, intranet and extranet systems
- Converged network technologies, including voice networks (PABXs, Centrex, handsets, mobiles, faxes, etc.)
- Client systems (desktop PCs, laptop PCs, mobile access devices (hand-held devices, mobile phones, palmtops, PDAs, scanners, etc.)
- Storage devices, Storage Area Networks (SANs), Network Attached Storage (NAS) including backup and recovery systems and services (servers, robots, etc.)
- Document storage, handling and management
- Specialist areas of technology such as EPOS, ATMs, scanning devices, GPS systems, etc.
- Environmental systems and equipment, including their monitoring and management.

This will result in a hierarchy of architectures, which will need to be dovetailed to construct an integrated set of technology architectures for the organization. The Infrastructure Architecture should aim to provide relatively few standardized platforms for hosting applications. It must also lay down standards for application architectures that are to be hosted in controlled data centres so that these fit in with the standardized operating, monitoring and security requirements.

Management architectures

IT must manage costs, deliver the right services at the right time, secure information assets, provide dependable service and lead the business in leveraging technologies. This requires automated procedures and management tools in order to achieve this effectively and efficiently. The selection of an appropriate management architecture is key to establishing the required level of control and automation. There are two separate approaches to developing a management architecture:

- **Selecting a proprietary management architecture**: this is based on selecting a single set of management products and tools from a single proprietary management solutions supplier. This approach will normally require less effort, will support and integrate within an overall tool architecture, but will often mean that compromises will have to be made with management functionality and facilities, which may result in gaps.
- **Selecting a 'best of breed' architecture**: this approach involves the selection of a set of 'best of breed' management tools and products from a number of management solutions suppliers and then integrating them to provide a comprehensive

management solution. This will generally require more effort in the integration of the tools into a single comprehensive management solution but will often provide greater management functionality and facilities leading to long-term cost savings.

The challenges for IT management are to coordinate and work in partnership with the business in the building of these management solutions, supporting the appropriate processes and providing the required measurements and metrics. This has to be achieved while reducing or optimizing the costs involved, particularly the annual, ongoing costs. The best way of minimizing costs is to design cleverly and carefully – for example, making best use of capacity so that additional capacity is not unnecessarily bought (with its associated ongoing costs), or designing a backup/recovery solution that doesn't require a complete additional set of infrastructure. Considerable costs can be saved by intelligent and careful design, using technology that is supportable and causes few problems in the operational environment.

The main method of realizing these goals is to design solutions that give a reduction in the overall network management and support costs, while maintaining or even improving the quality of service delivered to the business.

To gain the greatest benefit from the use of the Four Ps, organizations should determine the roles of processes and people, and then implement the tools to automate the processes, facilitating people's roles and tasks. The best way of achieving this is to develop a model or architecture based on these principles. This architecture should facilitate the implementation of a set of integrated tools and processes that support 'end-to-end' management of all areas of the technology used, ensuring that there are no gaps and no 'technical silos'.

However, IT faces a big challenge in developing and maintaining the soft skills required to perform these management roles and processes effectively. In the truly efficient organizations, these roles and processes are aligned to those of the business. This ensures that the business and IT Management processes and information have similar targets and goals. However, all too often, organizations devote insufficient time and effort to the development of the soft skills (for example, interpersonal skills, communication skills, meeting skills) necessary for the processes and the business alignment to be effectively achieved.

There are five areas that need to be considered with regard to the design of a management architecture, as illustrated in Figure 3.10.

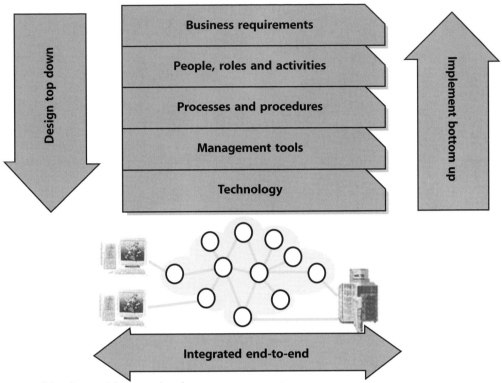

Figure 3.10 Integrated business-driven technology management

The relationships between these architectural perspectives can be seen in the diagram above. The development, documentation and maintenance of business and IT architectures will typically form part of the processes of strategic thinking and strategy development in the organization.

These five management areas to be considered can be briefly defined as:

- **Business**: the needs, requirements, processes, objectives and goals of the business units and managers within the organization
- **People**: the scope, tasks and activities of the managers and staff involved in the management of the provision of IT services
- **Processes**: the processes and procedures used to manage IT services to the business and its customers
- **Tools**: the management and support tools required to effectively manage the IT infrastructure
- **Technology**: the IT products and technology used to deliver the service and information to the right person, in the right place at the right time.

Such an architecture can be used to design and implement efficient, effective and integrated management solutions that are aligned to the business requirements of the organization and its Business Managers. This management architecture can be applied within an organization to:

- **Design from the top down**, ensuring that the Service Management and technology management processes, tools and information are aligned with the business needs and goals
- **Implement from the bottom up**, ensuring that efficient and effective Service Management and technology management processes are fully integrated with the tools and technology in use within the organization
- **Integrate processes and tools**, ensuring greater exploitation of tools in the management and support of technology and end-to-end processes.

These bullet points are also illustrated in Figure 3.10.

The key to the development of a management architecture is to ensure that it is driven by business needs and not developed for IT needs in isolation:

> Management architectures need to be:
> '... business aligned, NOT technology driven'.

Within this overall structure, a management architecture is needed that can be applied to all areas of IT Management and not just to individual isolated areas. This can then be implemented in a coordinated programme of inter-working, to provide overall end-to-end Enterprise Management so essential to the effective management of today's IT infrastructure. If only individual areas buy into the architecture, then individual 'islands of excellence' will develop and it will be impossible to provide the complete end-to-end solutions required to support today's e-business solutions.

As well as ensuring that all areas of the IT are integrated, it is vital that the management architecture is developed from the business and service perspective (i.e. 'top down'). Therefore, the key elements to agree and define before developing the management architecture are:

■ Management of the business processes: What are the business processes and how do they relate to network and IT services and components?

■ Management of service quality: What is service quality? How and where will it be measured?

These are the key elements that need to be determined by SLM and IT Management. They provide crucial input to the development of business-focused management architectures. All too often management tools and processes have been focused on components and component management rather than services and business processes. This needs to be changed, with emphasis clearly on the design of management systems, processes and tools that are driven by business needs and are focused on the management of business processes and IT services. If the appropriate management architecture is designed and implemented, this will allow Service Management processes to focus on managing services and service quality and operate from end-to-end across the entire IT enterprise, providing true Enterprise Service Management. This will truly facilitate the management of services to ensure that services and service quality are closely aligned to the needs of the business.

The architectures described suggest that the future of network and systems management will be less focused on the technology and become more integrated with the overall requirements of the business and IT Management. These new systems and processes are already starting to evolve as the management standards for the exchange of management information between tools become more

fully defined, by organizations such as the Distributed Management Task Force (DMTF). In essence, management systems will become:

■ More focused on business needs

■ More closely aligned to business processes

■ Less dependent on specific technology and more 'service-centric'

■ More integrated with other management tools and processes as the management standards evolve. This will involve the integration of systems management, operational management and Service Management tools and processes, with fewer 'technology silos' and 'islands of excellence'

■ Part of end-to-end management systems and processes, more focused on provision of quality and customer services

■ More flexible. There will be a move away from some of the more rigid, single supplier frameworks to a more open 'best-of-breed' approach.

3.6.4 Designing processes

This section provides a general introduction to process theory and practice, which is the basis for the design of ITIL processes that are used in the Service Lifecycle. A process model enables understanding and helps to articulate the distinctive features of a process.

A process is a structured set of activities designed to accomplish a specific objective. A process takes one or more inputs and turns them into defined outputs. A process includes all of the roles, responsibilities, tools and management controls required to reliably deliver the outputs. A process may also define or revise policies, standards, guidelines, activities, processes, procedures and work instructions if they are needed.

Process control can be defined as:

> The activity of planning and regulating a process, with the objective of performing a process in an effective, efficient and consistent manner.

Processes, once defined, should be documented and controlled. Once under control, they can be repeated and become manageable. Degrees of control over processes can be defined, and then process measurement and metrics can be built in to the process to control and improve the process, as illustrated in Figure 3.11.

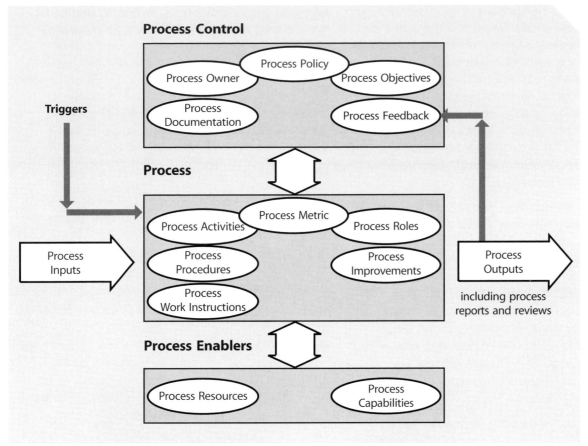

Figure 3.11 The generic process elements

The generic process elements show data enters the process, is processed, is output and the outcome is measured and reviewed. This very basic description underpins any process description. A process is always organized around a set of objectives. The main outputs from the process should be driven by the objectives and should always include process measurements (metrics), reports and process improvement.

Each process should be owned by a process owner, who should be responsible for the process and its improvement and for ensuring that a process meets its objectives. The objectives of any IT process should be defined in measurable terms and should be expressed in terms of business benefits and underpinning business strategy and goals. Service Design should assist each process owner with the design of processes, in order to ensure that all processes use standard terms and templates, are consistent and integrate with each other to provide end-to-end integration across all areas.

The output produced by a process has to conform to operational norms that are derived from business objectives. If products conform to the set norm, the process can be considered effective (because it can be repeated, measured and managed). If the activities are

carried out with a minimum use of resources, the process can also be considered efficient. Process analysis, results and metrics should be incorporated in regular management reports and process improvements.

All these areas should be included within the design of any process. These new ITIL publications have been written around 'sets of processes' that reflect the stages in the lifecycle of a service. The Service Design set of processes detailed in this publication covers the processes principally related to all aspects of design.

Working with defined processes has been the foundation of ITIL from its beginning. By defining what the organization's activities are, which inputs are necessary and which outputs will result from the process, it is possible to work in a more efficient and effective manner. Measuring and steering the activities increases this effectiveness. Finally, by adding norms to the process, it is possible to add quality measures to the output.

This approach underpins the Plan–Do–Check–Act cycle of continual improvement for any quality-management system. Plan the purpose of the process in such a way that process actions can be reviewed, assessed or audited for successful achievement and improved.

Norms define certain conditions that the results should meet. Defining norms introduces quality aspects to the process. Even before starting, it is important to think about what the process outcomes should look like. To discover whether or not process activities are contributing optimally to the business goal and the objectives of the process, aligned to business goals, the effectiveness should be measured on a regular basis. Measuring allows comparison of what has actually been done with what the organization set out to do, and to identify and implement improvements within the process.

Each organization should adopt a formalized approach to the design and implementation of Service Management processes. The objective should not be to design 'perfect processes', but to design practical and appropriate processes with 'in-built' improvement mechanisms, so that the effectiveness and efficiency of the processes are improved in the most suitable manner for the organization. Documentation standards, processes and templates should be used to ensure that the processes are easily adopted throughout the organization. Some example process documentation templates are included in Appendix C.

The goal for now and in the future is to design processes and support these with tools that can provide integration between organizations. This has now become possible because management tools are providing support of open standards, such as the Distributed Management Task Force (DMTF), that support the exchange of information based on ITIL concepts, such as incidents, problems and changes with standard formats and contents. This allows service providers to support efficient and effective process interfaces with their main suppliers with automated exchange of key operational information in real time.

3.6.5 Design of measurement systems and metrics

'If you can't measure it then you can't manage it.'

In order to manage and control the design processes, they have to be monitored and measured. This is true for all aspects of the design processes. Measurements and metrics are covered in detail in the Continual Service Improvement publication. This section covers those aspects that are particularly relevant and appropriate to measuring the quality of the design processes and their deliverables.

Care should be exercised when selecting measurements and metrics and the methods used to produce them. This is because the metrics and measurements chosen will actually affect and change the behaviour of people working within the activities and processes being measured, particularly where this relates to objectives, personal and team performance and performance-related pay schemes. Therefore only measurements that encourage progression towards meeting business objectives or desired behavioural change should be selected.

In all the design activities the requirement should be to:

- Design solutions that are 'fit for purpose'
- Design for the appropriate level of quality – not over-engineered or under-engineered
- Design solutions that are 'right first time' and meet their expected targets
- Design solutions that minimize the amount of 'rework' or 'add-ons' that have to be rapidly developed after solutions have been deployed
- Design solutions that are effective and efficient from the perspective of the business and the customers. The emphasis should be on the solutions that are effective above all and that are efficient within the constraint of remaining effective.

Measurement methods and metrics should reflect these requirements and be designed to measure the ability of design processes to match these requirements. All of the measurements and metrics used should reflect the quality and success of the design processes from the perspective of the business, customers and users. They need to reflect the ability of the delivered solutions to meet the identified and agreed requirements of the business.

The process measurements selected need to be appropriate for the capability and maturity of the processes being measured. Immature processes are not capable of supporting sophisticated measurements, metrics and measurement methods. There are four types of metrics that can be used to measure the capability and performance of processes:

- **Progress**: milestones and deliverables in the capability of the process
- **Compliance**: compliance of the process to governance requirements, regulatory requirements and compliance of people to the use of the process.
- **Effectiveness**: the accuracy and correctness of the process and its ability to deliver the 'right result'
- **Efficiency**: the productivity of the process, its speed, throughput and resource utilization.

Measurements and metrics should develop and change as the maturity and capability of a process develops. Initially, with immature processes the first two levels of metrics should be used to measure the progress and compliance of the process as it develops in maturity. As the process maturity develops, greater use should be made of effectiveness and efficiency metrics, but not to the detriment of compromising the progress or compliance of the process.

The selection of the metrics, the point of measurement and the methods of measuring, calculating and reporting on the metrics must be carefully designed and planned. The primary metrics should always focus on determining the effectiveness and the quality of the solutions provided. Secondary metrics can then measure the efficiency of the processes used to produce and manage the solution. The priority should always be to ensure that the processes provide the correct results for the business. Therefore the measurement methods and metrics should always provide this business-focused measurement above all.

The most effective method of measurement is to establish a 'Metrics Tree' or 'KPI tree'. Too many organizations collect measurement in individual areas, but fail to aggregate them together and gain the full benefit of the measurements, and therefore suffer because:

■ Measurements are not aligned with business objectives and needs

■ There is no overall visibility of the 'top-level' picture

■ There are gaps in areas where measurements are not recorded

■ Individual areas are well measured and others are poorly measured or are not measured

■ There is no consistency in the method, presentation and calculation of the measurements

■ Decisions and improvement actions are based on incomplete or inaccurate information.

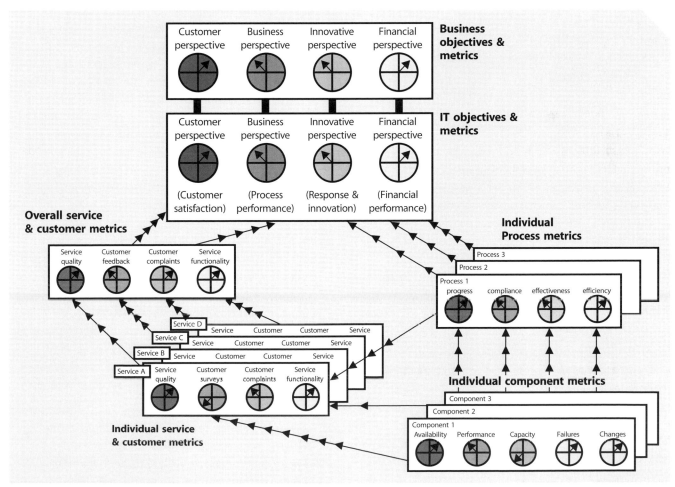

Figure 3.12 The Metrics Tree

Therefore organizations should attempt to develop automated measurement systems based on a form of 'Metrics Tree' such as that illustrated in Figure 3.12.

The tree in Figure 3.12 is illustrative of an example of a Metrics Tree based on a typical Balanced Scorecard. Balanced Scorecards represent a management system that enables increasing numbers of organizations to clarify their vision and strategy into action. They provide feedback regarding the internal business processes and external outcomes in order continually to improve strategic performance and results. This enables everybody within the organization to get a picture of the performance of the organization at the appropriate level:

■ Business managers and customers can get a 'top-level' business 'dashboard', aligned with business needs and processes
■ Senior IT managers and customers can focus on the top-level IT management dashboard
■ Service managers and customers can focus on the performance of particular services
■ Process owners and managers can view the performance of their processes
■ Technical specialists can look at the performance of individual components
■ The dashboard also presents an opportunity to view trends over time, rather than static data, so that potential performance degradation can be identified and rectified at an early stage.

This means that within a hierarchical metrics system, each person in the organization can get access to an appropriate level of information and measurement that suits their particular need. It gives senior management the opportunity to monitor a top-level dashboard to ensure that services continue to be delivered to their agreed levels, and it also provides the capability for technical specialists and processes owners to drill down to the detail to analyse variance from agreed service, component or process performance.

Obviously the collection, analysis and presentation of this data can be a very labour-intensive activity and therefore should be automated wherever possible. This can be achieved using analysis tools based on macros, scripts, spreadsheets, or preferably on specific web-based solutions. The measurements at each of the levels should be specifically defined to meet the needs of the business, customers and users of the information.

More detailed information on measurements, metrics and measurement methods are contained in the Continual Service Improvement publication.

3.7 THE SUBSEQUENT DESIGN ACTIVITIES

Once the desired service solution has been designed, then the subsequent activities must also be completed with the Service Design stage before the solution passes into the Service Transition stage.

3.7.1 Evaluation of alternative solutions

An additional evaluation stage may be necessary if external supplier services and solutions are involved. This consists of the following:

■ Selecting a set of suppliers and completing a tendering process. This will require the production and completion of:
  ● Documentation of the scope of the service and production of a Statement of Requirement (SoR) and/or a Terms of Reference (ToR) document
  ● Request For Information (RFI), Request For Proposal (RFP), Request For Quotation (RFQ) and Invitation To Tender (ITT) documents
  ● Producing and agreeing a set of solution and supplier evaluation criteria and a scoring process.
■ Evaluation and review of supplier responses and selection of the preferred supplier(s) and their proposed solution(s). This may also involve running trials or even prototyping or proof of concept activities if significant new concepts or technology are involved in the new service in order to ensure that new components meet their expectations.
■ Evaluation and costing of the alternative designs, possibly including identification of potential suppliers and evaluation of their alternative proposals, technologies, solutions and contracts. There is a need to ensure that costing covers one-off costs and ongoing costs of operation and ownership, including support and maintenance.

3.7.2 Procurement of the preferred solution

It is possible that no external elements will be required for the solution. However, this is unusual as suppliers of software at least are highly likely to be involved. Where external suppliers are involved in the preferred solution, the stages consist of:

■ Completing all necessary checks on the preferred supplier
■ Finalizing the terms and conditions of any new contracts, ensuring that all corporate policies are enforced
■ The procurement of the selected solution.

3.7.3 Develop the service solution

The development stage consists of translating the Service Design into a plan for the development, re-use or redevelopment of the components required to deliver the service and the subsequent implementation of the developed service. It may need to be developed into a programme of plans, if this is a major service change. Each plan or project within the programme will be responsible for delivering one or more components of the service and will include:

- The needs of the business
- The strategy to be adopted for the development and or purchase of the solution
- The timescales involved
- The resources required, taking into consideration facilities, IT infrastructure and the right personnel skills in order to ensure the delivery service meets the customer's needs
- The development of the service and its constituent components, including the management and other operational mechanisms, such as measurement, monitoring and reporting
- Service and component test plans.

Careful project management will need to be used to ensure that conflict is avoided and that the compatible components are developed from the various different development activities

3.8 DESIGN CONSTRAINTS

All design activities operate within many constraints. These constraints come from the business and Service Strategy and cover many different areas, as illustrated in Figure 3.13.

This means that designers are not always 'free' to design the most appropriate solution for the business, because it does not fall within the imposed constraints, as illustrated in Figure 3.13. The most obvious constraint is the financial one. There may be insufficient budget available for the most appropriate solution, therefore a cheaper alternative service would have to be identified and agreed with the business. The designer can only provide the solution that fits within all of the currently known constraints, or else try lifting or renegotiating some of the constraints – for instance, by obtaining a bigger budget. In Figure 3.13, not only will more budget need to be obtained to implement the desired solution, but it would also be non-compliant with some of the relevant standards and regulations. So in this case an alternative, cheaper compliant solution would be probably be required.

So the Service Design processes must recognize the fact that they are free to design solutions, but they are working in an environment where many external factors can influence the design.

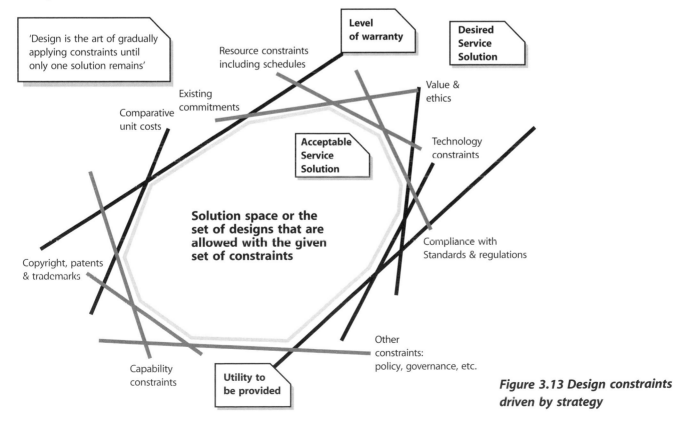

Figure 3.13 Design constraints driven by strategy

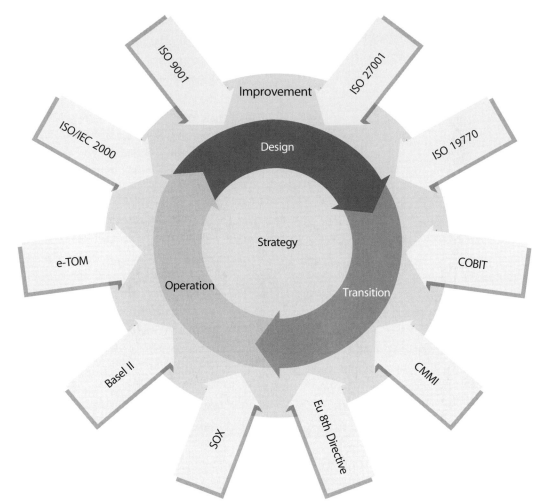

Figure 3.14 External influences on solution design

Many of these external influences are from the need for good corporate and IT governance, and others are from the requirement for compliance with regulations, legislation and international standards, as illustrated in Figure 3.14. It is essential, therefore, that all designers recognize these and ensure that the designs and solutions they produce have all of the necessary controls and capability within them.

3.9   SERVICE ORIENTED ARCHITECTURE

Business process and solutions should be designed and developed using a Service Oriented Architecture (SOA) approach. The SOA approach is considered best practice and is used by many organizations to improve their effectiveness and efficiency in the provision of IT services.

SOA is defined by OASIS (www.oasis-open.org) as:

> 'A paradigm for organizing and utilizing distributed capabilities that may be under the control of different ownership domains. It provides a uniform means to offer, discover, interact with and use capabilities to produce desired effects consistent with measurable preconditions and expectations.'

OASIS (Organization for the Advancement of Structured Information Standards) is a not-for-profit, international consortium that drives the development, convergence and adoption of e-business standards. SOA brings value and agility to an organization by encouraging the development of 'self-contained' services that are re-usable. This, in turn, promotes a flexible and modular approach to the development of 'shared services' that can be used in many different areas of the business. More and more organizations are converting business processes to common 'packaged services' that can be used and shared by many areas of the business.

Wherever possible, IT service provider organizations should use the SOA and principles to develop flexible, re-usable IT services that are common and can be shared and exploited across many different areas of the business. When this approach is used, it is essential that IT:

■ Defines and determines what a service is

■ Understands and clearly identifies interfaces and dependencies between services

■ Utilizes standards for the development and definition of services

■ Uses common technology and tool-sets

■ Investigates and understands the impact of changes to 'shared services'

■ Ensures that SOA-related training has been planned and achieved for the IT people in order to establish a common language and improve the implementation and support of the new or changed services.

When SOA principles are used by the IT service provider organization, it is critical that an accurate Service Catalogue is maintained as part of an overall Service Portfolio and Configuration Management System (CMS). Adopting this approach can significantly reduce the time taken to deliver new solutions to the business and to move towards a Business Service Management (BSM) capability. The Service Catalogue will also show the relationship between services and applications. A single application could be part of more than one service, and a single service could utilize more than one application.

3.10 BUSINESS SERVICE MANAGEMENT

Business Service Management (BSM) is a strategy and an approach to enable IT components to be linked to the goals of the business. This way the impact of technology on the business and how business change may impact technology can both be predicted. The creation of a totally integrated Service Catalogue – including business units, processes and services, and their relationships and dependencies on IT services, technology and components – is crucial to increasing the IT service provider's capability to deliver BSM. All aspects of Service Design are vital elements in supporting and enhancing the Business Service Management capability of the IT service provider, particularly the design of the Service Portfolio, the Service Catalogue and the individual IT services. All of these activities will also improve the alignment of IT service provision with business and its evolving needs. See Figure 3.15.

BSM enables an IT service provider organization to:

■ Align IT service provision with business goals and objectives

■ Prioritize all IT activities on business impact and urgency, ensuring critical business processes and services receive the most attention

■ Increase business productivity and profitability through the increased efficiency and effectiveness of IT processes

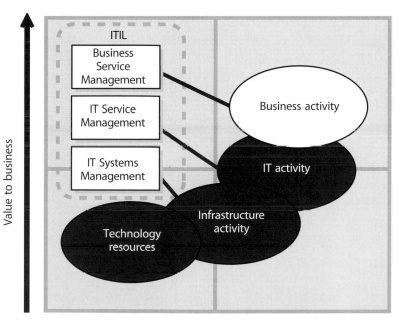

Figure 3.15 The IT management continuum

■ Support the requirements for corporate governance with appropriate IT governance and controls

■ Create competitive advantage through the exploitation and innovation of IT infrastructure as a whole

■ Improve service quality, customer satisfaction and user perception

■ Ensure regulatory and legislative compliance

■ Ensure appropriate levels of protection on all IT and information assets

■ Ensure that IT services are aligned and continue to be aligned with changing business needs.

Figure 3.15 illustrates the relationship of service activities and Service Management, and the reach and range they offer in value to the business and IT.

3.11 SERVICE DESIGN MODELS

The model selected for the design of IT services will depend mainly on the model selected for the delivery of IT services. Before adopting a design model for a major new service, a review of the current capability and provisions with respect to all aspects of the delivery of IT services should be conducted. This review should consider all aspects of the new service, including the:

■ Business drivers and requirements

■ Scope and capability of the existing service provider unit

■ Demands, targets and requirements of the new service

■ Scope and capability of external suppliers

■ Maturity of the organizations currently involved and their processes

■ Culture of the organizations involved

■ IT infrastructure, applications, data, services and other components involved

■ Degree of corporate and IT governance and the level of ownership and control required

■ Budgets and resources available

■ Staff levels and skills.

This review/assessment provides a structured mechanism for determining an organization's capabilities and state of readiness for delivering new or revised services in support of defined business drivers and requirements. The information obtained from such an assessment can be used in determining the delivery strategy for a particular IT service or IT system. The delivery strategy is the approach taken to move an organization from a known state, based on the readiness assessment, to a desired state, determined by the business drivers and needs. There are many ways to prepare an organization for deploying a

new service. The method and strategy selected should be based on the solution the organization chooses for fulfilling its key business drivers, as well as the capabilities of the IT organization and its partners. The scale of options available is quite large, and not every option needs be considered in every case. However, keeping all the options available for consideration is key for designing and operating innovative solutions to the most difficult business challenges. In the end, this may be the difference between a failed project – or even a failed company – and a successful one.

These two models, for the design and delivery of IT services, are closely related and are considered in the following two sections.

3.11.1 Delivery model options

Although the readiness assessment determines the gap between the current and desired capabilities, an IT organization should not necessarily try to bridge that gap by itself. There are many different delivery strategies that can be used. Each one has its own set of advantages and disadvantages, but all require some level of adaptation and customization for the situation at hand. Table 3.2 lists the main categories of sourcing strategies with a short abstract for each. Delivery practices tend to fall into one of these categories or some variant of them.

Table 3.2 highlights a key point: the set of delivery strategies varies widely and ranges from a relatively straightforward situation, solely managed within the boundaries of a company, all the way to a full KPO situation. This broad range of alternatives provides significant flexibility, but often with added complexity, and in some cases additional risk. The advantages and disadvantages of each type of delivery strategy are discussed in Table 3.3 below.

All of the above arrangements can be provided in both an off-shore or on-shore situation. In the on-shore case, both organizations are based within the same country/continent, whereas in the off-shore situation the organizations are in different countries/continents. Very complex sourcing arrangements exist within the IT industry and it is impossible to cover all combinations and their implications here. ITIL Service Management Practice Complementary Series will provide additional guidance on sourcing strategies.

Mergers and acquisitions can also complicate the issues. These situations occur when one company acquires or merges with another company for cash and/or equity swaps of the company's stock. Again, this occurs generally in response to industry consolidations, market expansion,

Table 3.2 Main service delivery strategies

Delivery strategy	Description
Insourcing	This approach relies on utilizing internal organizational resources in the design, development, transition, maintenance, operation and/or support of new, changed or revised services or data centre operations
Outsourcing	This approach utilizes the resources of an external organization or organizations in a formal arrangement to provide a well-defined portion of a service's design, development, maintenance, operations and/or support. This includes the consumption of services from Application Service Providers (ASPs) described below
Co-sourcing	Often a combination of insourcing and outsourcing, using a number of outsourcing organizations working together to co-source key elements within the lifecycle. This generally involves using a number of external organizations working together to design, develop, transition, maintain, operate and/or support a portion of a service
Partnership or multi-sourcing	Formal arrangements between two or more organizations to work together to design, develop, transition, maintain, operate and/or support IT service(s). The focus here tends to be on strategic partnerships that leverage critical expertise or market opportunities.
Business Process Outsourcing (BPO)	The increasing trend of relocating entire business functions using formal arrangements between organizations where one organization provides and manages the other organization's entire business process(es) or functions(s) in a low-cost location. Common examples are accounting, payroll and call centre operations
Application Service Provision	Involves formal arrangements with an Application Service Provider (ASP) organization that will provide shared computer-based services to customer organizations over a network. Applications offered in this way are also sometimes referred to as on-demand software/applications. Through ASPs, the complexities and costs of such shared software can be reduced and provided to organizations that could otherwise not justify the investment
Knowledge Process Outsourcing (KPO)	The newest form of outsourcing, KPO is a step ahead of BPO in one respect. KPO organizations provide domain-based processes and business expertise rather than just process expertise, and require advanced analytical and specialized skills from the outsourcing organization

or in direct response to competitive pressures. If companies that have different service delivery strategies are acquired or merge, a period of review and consolidation is often required to determine the most appropriate sourcing strategy for the newly merged organization. However, mergers and acquisitions can often provide organizations with the opportunity to consolidate the best practice from each organization, thereby improving the overall service capability and achieving synergies across the organization. Opportunities will also exist to provide improved career development options to Service Management personnel and to consolidate supplier contract for services.

3.11.2 Design and development options

The delivery strategies are relevant to both the design and transition stages of the Service Lifecycle as well as the operation stage. Extreme care must be taken when selecting different strategies for different stages of the lifecycle to ensure that all organizations involved clearly understand their individual roles and responsibilities, and also every other organization's role and responsibility to ensure acceptance and handover processes are clearly defined, agreed and accepted.

Table 3.3 Advantages and disadvantages of service delivery strategies

Delivery strategy	Advantages	Disadvantages
Insourcing	Direct control Freedom of choice Rapid prototyping of leading-edge services Familiar policies and processes Company-specific knowledge	Scale limitations Cost and time to market for services readily available outside Dependent on internal resources and their skills and competencies
Outsourcing	Economies of scale Purchased expertise Supports focus on company core competencies Support for transient needs Test drive/trial of new services	Less direct control Exit barriers Solvency risk of suppliers Unknown supplier skills and competencies More challenging business process integration Increased governance and verification
Co-sourcing	Time to market Leveraged expertise Control Use of specialized providers	Project complexity Intellectual property and copyright protection Culture clash between companies
Partnership or multi-sourcing	Time to market Market expansion/entrance Competitive response Leveraged expertise Trust, alignment and mutual benefit 'Risk and reward' agreements	Project complexity Intellectual property and copyright protection Culture clash between companies
Business Process Outsourcing (BPO)	Single point of responsibility 'One-stop shop' Access to specialist skills Risk transferred to the outsource Low-cost location	Culture clash between companies Loss of business knowledge Loss of relationship with the business
Application Service Provision	Access to expensive and complex solutions Low-cost location Support and upgrades included Security and ITSCM options included	Culture clash between companies Access to facilities only, not knowledge Often usage-based charging models
Knowledge Process Outsourcing (KPO)	Access to specialist skills, knowledge and expertise Low-cost location Significant cost savings	Culture clash between companies Loss of internal expertise Loss of relationship with the business

Service Design processes

4

4 Service Design processes

This chapter describes and explains the fundamentals of the key supporting Service Design processes. These processes are principally responsible for providing key information to the design of new or changed service solutions. There are five aspects of design that need to be considered:

- The design of the services, including all of the functional requirements, resources and capabilities needed and agreed
- The design of Service Management systems and tools, especially the Service Portfolio, for the management and control of services through their lifecycle
- The design of the technology architectures and management systems required to provide the services
- The design of the processes needed to design, transition, operate and improve the services, the architectures and the processes themselves
- The design of the measurement methods and metrics of the services, the architectures and their constituent components and the processes.

A results-driven approach should be adopted for each of the above five aspects. In each, the desired business outcomes and planned results should be defined so that what is delivered meets the expectations of the customers and users. Thus this structured approach should be adopted within each of the five aspects to deliver quality, repeatable consistency and continual improvement throughout the organization. There are no situations within IT service provision with either internal or external service providers where there are no processes in the Service Design area. All IT service provider organizations already have some elements of their approach to these five aspects in place, no matter how basic. Before starting on the implementation of the improvement of activities and processes, a review should be conducted of what elements are in place and working successfully. Many service provider organizations already have mature processes in place for designing IT services and solutions.

All designs and design activities need to be driven principally by the business needs and requirements of the organization. Within this context they must also reflect the needs of the strategies, plans and policies produced by Service Strategy processes, as illustrated in Figure 4.1.

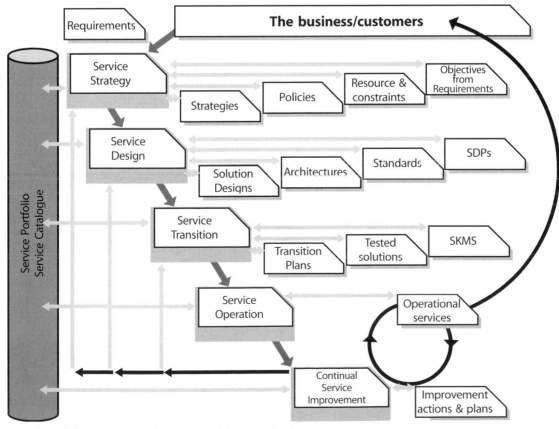

Figure 4.1 The key links, inputs and outputs of Service Design

Figure 4.1 gives a good overview of the links, inputs and outputs involved at each stage of the Service Lifecycle. It illustrates the key outputs produced by each stage, which are used as inputs by the subsequent stages. The Service Portfolio acts as 'the spine' of the Service Lifecycle. It is the single integrated source of information on the status of each service, together with other service details and the interfaces and dependencies between services. The information within the Service Portfolio is used by the activities within each stage of the Service Lifecycle.

The key output of the Service Design stage is the design of service solutions to meet the changing requirements of the business. However, when designing these solutions, input from many different areas needs to be considered within the various activities involved in designing the service solution, from identifying and analysing requirements, through to building a solution and SDP to hand over to Service Transition.

In order to develop effective and efficient service solutions that meet and continue to meet the requirements of the business and the needs of IT, it is essential that all the inputs and needs of all other areas and processes are

reconsidered within each of the Service Design activities, as illustrated in Figure 4.2. This will ensure that all service solutions are consistent and compatible with existing solutions and will meet the expectations of the customers and users. This will most effectively be achieved by consolidating these facets of the key processes into all of these Service Design activities, so that all inputs are automatically referenced every time a new or changed service solution is produced.

4.1 SERVICE CATALOGUE MANAGEMENT

4.1.1 Purpose/goal/objective

The purpose of Service Catalogue Management is to provide a single source of consistent information on all of the agreed services, and ensure that it is widely available to those who are approved to access it.

The goal of the Service Catalogue Management process is to ensure that a Service Catalogue is produced and maintained, containing accurate information on all operational services and those being prepared to be run operationally.

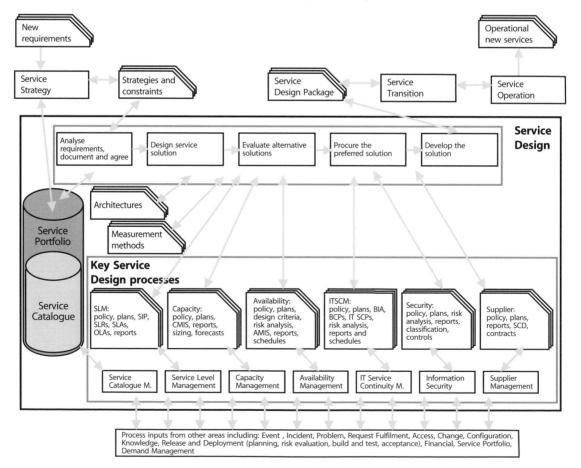

Figure 4.2 Service Design – the big picture

The objective of Service Catalogue Management is to manage the information contained within the Service Catalogue, and to ensure that it is accurate and reflects the current details, status, interfaces and dependencies of all services that are being run, or being prepared to run, in the live environment.

4.1.2 Scope

The scope of the Service Catalogue Management process is to provide and maintain accurate information on all services that are being transitioned or have been transitioned to the live environment.

The Service Catalogue Management activities should include:

- Definition of the service
- Production and maintenance of an accurate Service Catalogue
- Interfaces, dependencies and consistency between the Service Catalogue and Service Portfolio
- Interfaces and dependencies between all services and supporting services within the Service Catalogue and the CMS
- Interfaces and dependencies between all services, and supporting components and Configuration Items (CIs) within the Service Catalogue and the CMS.

4.1.3 Value to the business

The Service Catalogue provides a central source of information on the IT services delivered by the service provider organization. This ensures that all areas of the business can view an accurate, consistent picture of the IT services, their details and their status. It contains a customer-facing view of the IT services in use, how they are intended to be used, the business processes they enable, and the levels and quality of service the customer can expect for each service.

4.1.4 Policies, principles and basic concepts

Over the years, organizations' IT infrastructures have grown and developed, and there may not be a clear picture of all the services currently being provided and the customers of each service. In order to establish an accurate picture, it is recommended that an IT Service Portfolio containing a Service Catalogue is produced and maintained to provide a central, accurate set of information on all services and to develop a service-focused culture.

The Service Portfolio should contain all the future requirements for services and the Service Catalogue should contain details of all services currently being provided or those being prepared for transition to the live environment, a summary of their characteristics, and details of the customers and maintainers of each. A degree of 'detective work' may be needed to compile this list and agree it with the customers (sifting through old documentation, searching program libraries, talking with IT staff and customers, looking at procurement records and talking with suppliers and contractors etc.). If a CMS or any sort of asset database exists, these may provide valuable sources of information, although they should be verified before inclusion within either the Service Portfolio or Service Catalogue. The Service Portfolio is produced as part of Service Strategy and should include participation by those involved in Service Design, Transition, Operation and Improvement. Once a service is 'chartered' (being developed for use by customers, Service Design produces the specifications for the service and it is at this point that the service should be added to the Service Catalogue.

Each organization should develop and maintain a policy with regard to both the Portfolio and the Catalogue, relating to the services recorded within them, what details are recorded and what statuses are recorded for each of the services. The policy should also contain details of responsibilities for each section of the overall Service Portfolio and the scope of each of the constituent sections.

The Service Catalogue Management process produces and maintains the Service Catalogue, ensuring that a central, accurate and consistent source of data is provided, recording the status of all operational services or services being transitioned to the live environment, together with appropriate details of each service.

What is a service? This question is not as easy to answer as it may first appear, and many organizations have failed to come up with a clear definition in an IT context. IT staff often confuse a 'service' as perceived by the customer with an IT system. In many cases one 'service' can be made up of other 'services' (and so on), which are themselves made up of one or more IT systems within an overall infrastructure including hardware, software, networks, together with environments, data and applications. A good starting point is often to ask customers which IT services they use and how those services map onto and support their business processes. Customers often have a greater clarity of what they believe a service to be. Each organization needs to develop a policy of what is a service and how it is defined and agreed within their own organization.

To avoid confusion, it may be a good idea to define a hierarchy of services within the Service Catalogue, by qualifying exactly what type of service is recorded, e.g. business service (that which is seen by the customer). Alternatively, supporting services, such as infrastructure services, network services, application services (all invisible to the customer, but essential to the delivery of IT services) will also need to be recorded. This often gives rise to a hierarchy of services incorporating customer services and other related services, including supporting services, shared services and commodity services, each with defined and agreed service levels.

When initially completed, the Service Catalogue may consist of a matrix, table or spreadsheet. Many organizations integrate and maintain their Service Portfolio and Service Catalogue as part of their CMS. By defining each service as a Configuration Item (CI) and, where appropriate, relating these to form a service hierarchy, the organization is able to relate events such as incidents and RFCs to the services affected, thus providing the basis for service monitoring and reporting using an integrated tool (e.g. 'list or give the number of incidents affecting this particular service'). It is therefore essential that changes within the Service Portfolio and Service Catalogue are subject to the Change Management process.

The Service Catalogue can also be used for other Service Management purposes (e.g. for performing a Business Impact Analysis (BIA) as part of IT Service Continuity Planning, or as a starting place for re-distributing workloads, as part of Capacity Management). The cost and effort of producing and maintaining the catalogue, with its relationships to the underpinning technology components, is therefore easily justifiable. If done in conjunction with prioritization of the BIA, then it is possible to ensure that the most important services are covered first. An example of a simple Service Catalogue that can be used as a starting point is given in Appendix G.

The Service Catalogue has two aspects:

■ **The Business Service Catalogue:** containing details of all the IT services delivered to the customer, together with relationships to the business units and the business process that rely on the IT services. This is the customer view of the Service Catalogue.

■ **The Technical Service Catalogue:** containing details of all the IT services delivered to the customer, together with relationships to the supporting services, shared services, components and CIs necessary to support the provision of the service to the business. This should underpin the Business Service Catalogue and not form part of the customer view.

The relationship between these two aspects is illustrated in Figure 4.3.

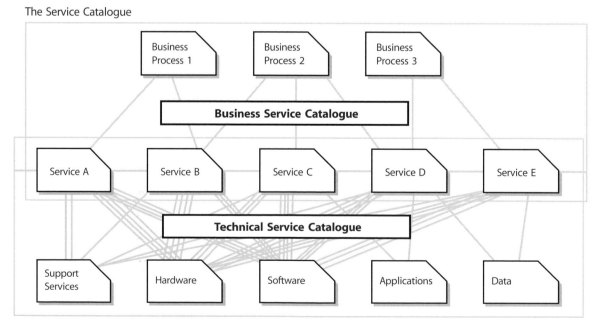

Figure 4.3 The Business Service Catalogue and the Technical Service Catalogue

Some organizations only maintain either a Business Service Catalogue or a Technical Service Catalogue. The preferred situation adopted by the more mature organizations maintains both aspects within a single Service Catalogue, which is part of a totally integrated Service Management activity and Service Portfolio. More information on the design and contents of a Service Catalogue is contained in Appendix G. The Business Service Catalogue facilitates the development of a much more proactive or even pre-emptive SLM process, allowing it to develop more into the field of Business Service Management. The Technical Service Catalogue is extremely beneficial when constructing the relationship between services, SLAs, OLAs and other underpinning agreements and components, as it will identify the technology required to support a service and the support group(s) that support the components. The combination of a Business Service Catalogue and a Technical Service Catalogue is invaluable for quickly assessing the impact of incidents and changes on the business. An example of relationships between the Business and Technical portions of a Service Catalogue is shown in Figure 4.4.

4.1.5 Process activities, methods and techniques

The key activities within the Service Catalogue Management process should include:

- Agreeing and documenting a service definition with all relevant parties
- Interfacing with Service Portfolio Management to agree the contents of the Service Portfolio and Service Catalogue
- Producing and maintaining a Service Catalogue and its contents, in conjunction with the Service Portfolio
- Interfacing with the business and IT Service Continuity Management on the dependencies of business units and their business processes with the supporting IT services, contained within the Business Service Catalogue
- Interfacing with support teams, suppliers and Configuration Management on interfaces and dependencies between IT services and the supporting services, components and CIs contained within the Technical Service Catalogue

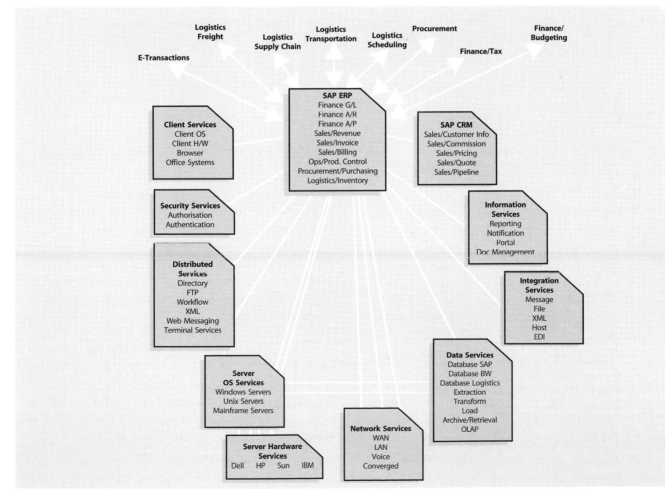

Figure 4.4 Example Service Catalogue

■ Interfacing with Business Relationship Management and Service Level Management to ensure that the information is aligned to the business and business process.

4.1.6 Triggers, inputs, outputs and interfaces

There are a number of sources of information that are relevant to the Service Catalogue Management process. These should include:

■ Business information from the organization's business and IT strategy, plans and financial plans, and information on their current and future requirements from the Service Portfolio

■ Business Impact Analysis, providing information on the impact, priority and risk associated with each service or changes to service requirements

■ Business requirements: details of any agreed, new or changed business requirements from the Service Portfolio

■ The Service Portfolio

■ The CMS

■ Feedback from all other processes.

The triggers for the Service Catalogue Management process are changes in the business requirements and services, and therefore one of the main triggers is Request For Changes (RFCs) and the Change Management process. This will include new services, changes to existing services or services being retired.

The process outputs of SCM are:

■ The documentation and agreement of a 'definition of the service'

■ Updates to the Service Portfolio: should contain the current status of all services and requirements for services

■ The Service Catalogue: should contain the details and the current status of every live service provided by the service provider or service being transitioned into the live environment, together with the interfaces and dependencies. An example of a Service Catalogue is contained in Appendix G.

4.1.7 Information management

The key information within the Service Catalogue Management process is that contained within the Service Catalogue. The main input for this information comes from the Service Portfolio and the business via either the Business Relationship Management (BRM) or Service Level Management (SLM) processes. This information needs to be verified for accuracy before being recorded within the Service Catalogue. The information and the Service Catalogue itself need to be maintained using the Change Management process.

4.1.8 Key Performance Indicators

The two main Key Performance Indicators (KPIs) associated with the Service Catalogue and its management are:

■ The number of services recorded and managed within the Service Catalogue as a percentage of those being delivered and transitioned in the live environment

■ The number of variances detected between the information contained within the Service Catalogue and the 'real-world' situation.

Other measurements and KPIs that could be used are:

■ Business users' awareness of the services being provided, i.e. percentage increase in completeness of the Business Service Catalogue against operational services

■ IT staff awareness of the technology supporting the services:
  ● Percentage increase in completeness of the Technical Service Catalogue against IT components that support the services
  ● Service Desk having access to information to support all live services, measured by the percentage of incidents without the appropriate service-related information.

4.1.9 Challenges, Critical Success Factors and risks

The major challenge facing the Service Catalogue Management process is that of maintaining an accurate Service Catalogue as part of a Service Portfolio, incorporating both the Business Service Catalogue and the Technical Service Catalogue as part of an overall CMS and SKMS. This is best approached by developing stand-alone spreadsheets or databases before trying to integrate the Service Catalogue and Service Portfolio within the CMS or SKMS. In order to achieve this, the culture of the organization needs to accept that the Catalogue and Portfolio are essential sources of information that everyone within the IT organization needs to use and help maintain. This will often assist in the standardization of the Service Catalogue and the Service Portfolio and enable increase in cost performance through economies of scale.

The main Critical Success Factors for the Service Catalogue Management process are:

- An accurate Service Catalogue
- Business users' awareness of the services being provided
- IT staff awareness of the technology supporting the services.

The risks associated with the provision of an accurate Service Catalogue are:

- Inaccuracy of the data in the catalogue and it not being under rigorous Change control
- Poor acceptance of the Service Catalogue and its usage in all operational processes. The more active the catalogue is, the more likely it is to be accurate in its content
- Inaccuracy of information received from the business, IT and the Service Portfolio, with regard to service information
- The tools and resources required to maintain the information
- Poor access to accurate Change Management information and processes
- Poor access to and support of appropriate and up-to-date CMS and SKMS
- Circumvention of the use of the Service Portfolio and Service Catalogue
- The information is either too detailed to maintain accurately or at too high a level to be of any value. It should be consistent with the level of detail within the CMS and the SKMS.

4.2 SERVICE LEVEL MANAGEMENT

Service Level Management (SLM) negotiates, agrees and documents appropriate IT service targets with representatives of the business, and then monitors and produces reports on the service provider's ability to deliver the agreed level of service. SLM is a vital process for every IT service provider organization in that it is responsible for agreeing and documenting service level targets and responsibilities within SLAs and SLRs, for every activity within IT. If these targets are appropriate and accurately reflect the requirements of the business, then the service delivered by the service providers will align with business requirements and meet the expectations of the customers and users in terms of service quality. If the targets are not aligned with business needs, then service provider activities and service levels will not be aligned with business expectations and problems will develop. The SLA is effectively a level of assurance or warranty with regard to the level of service quality delivered by the service provider for each of the services delivered to the business.

The success of SLM is very dependent on the quality of the Service Portfolio and the Service Catalogue and their contents, because they provide the necessary information on the services to be managed within the SLM process.

4.2.1 Purpose/goal/objective

The goal of the Service Level Management process is to ensure that an agreed level of IT service is provided for all current IT services, and that future services are delivered to agreed achievable targets. Proactive measures are also taken to seek and implement improvements to the level of service delivered.

The purpose of the SLM process is to ensure that all operational services and their performance are measured in a consistent, professional manner throughout the IT organization, and that the services and the reports produced meet the needs of the business and customers.

The objectives of SLM are to:

- Define, document, agree, monitor, measure, report and review the level of IT services provided
- Provide and improve the relationship and communication with the business and customers
- Ensure that specific and measurable targets are developed for all IT services
- Monitor and improve customer satisfaction with the quality of service delivered
- Ensure that IT and the customers have a clear and unambiguous expectation of the level of service to be delivered
- Ensure that proactive measures to improve the levels of service delivered are implemented wherever it is cost-justifiable to do so.

4.2.2 Scope

SLM should provide a point of regular contact and communication to the customers and business managers of an organization. It should represent the IT service provider to the business, and the business to the IT service provider. This activity should encompass both the use of existing services and the potential future requirements for new or changed services. SLM needs to manage the expectation and perception of the business, customers and users and ensure that the quality of service delivered by the service provider is matched to those expectations and needs. In order to do this effectively, SLM should establish and maintain SLAs for all current live services and manage the level of service provided to meet the targets and quality measurements contained within the SLAs. SLM should also produce and agree SLRs for all planned new or changed services.

This will enable SLM to ensure that all the services and components are designed and delivered to meet their targets in terms of business needs. The SLM processes should include the:

- Development of relationships with the business
- Negotiation and agreement of current requirements and targets, and the documentation and management of SLAs for all operational services
- Negotiation and agreement of future requirements and targets, and the documentation and management of SLRs for all proposed new or changed services
- Development and management of appropriate Operational Level Agreements (OLAs) to ensure that targets are aligned with SLA targets
- Review of all underpinning supplier contracts and agreements with Supplier Management to ensure that targets are aligned with SLA targets
- Proactive prevention of service failures, reduction of service risks and improvement in the quality of service, in conjunction with all other processes
- Reporting and management of all services and review of all SLA breaches and weaknesses
- Instigation and coordination of a Service Improvement Plan (SIP) for the management, planning and implementation of all service and process improvements.

4.2.3 Value to the business

SLM provides a consistent interface to the business for all service-related issues. It provides the business with the agreed service targets and the required management information to ensure that those targets have been met. Where targets are breached, SLM should provide feedback on the cause of the breach and details of the actions taken to prevent the breach from recurring. Thus SLM provides a reliable communication channel and a trusted relationship with the appropriate customers and business representatives.

4.2.4 Policies/principles/basic concepts

SLM is the name given to the processes of planning, coordinating, drafting, agreeing, monitoring and reporting of SLAs, and the ongoing review of service achievements to ensure that the required and cost-justifiable service quality is maintained and gradually improved. However, SLM is not only concerned with ensuring that current services and SLAs are managed, but it is also involved in ensuring that new requirements are captured and that new or changed services and SLAs are developed to match the business needs and expectations. SLAs provide the

basis for managing the relationship between the service provider and the customer, and SLM provides that central point of focus for a group of customers, business units or lines of business.

An SLA is a written agreement between an IT service provider and the IT customer(s), defining the key service targets and responsibilities of both parties. The emphasis must be on agreement, and SLAs should not be used as a way of holding one side or the other to ransom. A true partnership should be developed between the IT service provider and the customer, so that a mutually beneficial agreement is reached – otherwise the SLA could quickly fall into disrepute and a 'blame culture' could develop that would prevent any true service quality improvements from taking place.

SLM is also responsible for ensuring that all targets and measures agreed in SLAs with the business are supported by appropriate underpinning OLAs or contracts, with internal support units and external partners and suppliers. This is illustrated in Figure 4.5.

Figure 4.5 shows the relationship between the business and its processes and the services, and the associated technology, supporting services, teams and suppliers required to meet their needs. It demonstrates how important the SLAs, OLAs and contracts are in defining and achieving the level of service required by the business.

An OLA is an agreement between an IT service provider and another part of the same organization that assists with the provision of services – for instance, a facilities department that maintains the air conditioning, or network support team that supports the network service. An OLA should contain targets that underpin those within an SLA to ensure that targets will not be breached by failure of the supporting activity.

4.2.5 Process activities, methods and techniques

The key activities within the SLM process should include:

- Determine, negotiate, document and agree requirements for new or changed services in SLRs, and manage and review them through the Service Lifecycle into SLAs for operational services
- Monitor and measure service performance achievements of all operational services against targets within SLAs
- Collate, measure and improve customer satisfaction
- Produce service reports

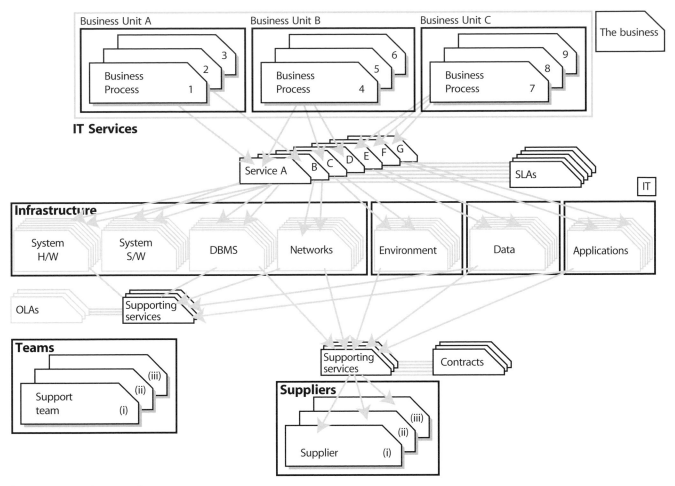

Figure 4.5 Service Level Management

- Conduct service review and instigate improvements within an overall Service Improvement Plan (SIP)
- Review and revise SLAs, service scope OLAs, contracts, and any other underpinning agreements
- Develop and document contacts and relationships with the business, customers and stakeholders
- Develop, maintain and operate procedures for logging, actioning and resolving all complaints, and for logging and distributing compliments
- Log and manage all complaints and compliments
- Provide the appropriate management information to aid performance management and demonstrate service achievement
- Make available and maintain up-to-date SLM document templates and standards.

The interfaces between the main activities are illustrated in Figure 4.6.

Although Figure 4.6 illustrates all the main activities of SLM as separate activities, they should be implemented as one integrated SLM process that can be consistently applied to all areas of the businesses and to all customers. These activities are described in the following sections.

4.2.5.1 Designing SLA frameworks

Using the Service Catalogue as an aid, SLM must design the most appropriate SLA structure to ensure that all services and all customers are covered in a manner best suited to the organization's needs. There are a number of potential options, including the following.

Service-based SLA

This is where an SLA covers one service, for all the customers of that service – for example, an SLA may be established for an organization's e-mail service – covering all the customers of that service. This may appear fairly straightforward. However, difficulties may arise if the specific requirements of different customers vary for the same service, or if characteristics of the infrastructure mean that different service levels are inevitable (e.g. head office staff may be connected via a high-speed LAN, while local offices may have to use a lower-speed WAN line). In such cases, separate targets may be needed within the

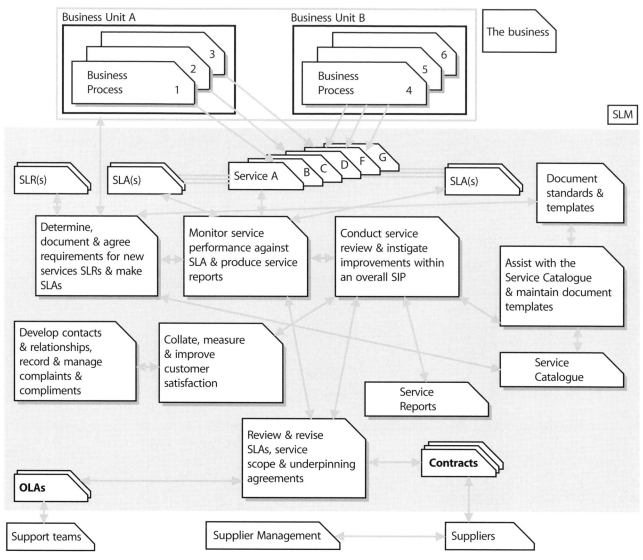

Figure 4.6 The Service Level Management process

one agreement. Difficulties may also arise in determining who should be the signatories to such an agreement. However, where common levels of service are provided across all areas of the business, e.g. e-mail or telephony, the service-based SLA can be an efficient approach to use. Multiple classes of service, e.g. gold, silver and bronze, can also be used to increase the effectiveness of service-based SLAs.

Customer-based SLA

This is an agreement with an individual customer group, covering all the services they use. For example, agreements may be reached with an organization's finance department covering, say, the finance system, the accounting system, the payroll system, the billing system, the procurement system, and any other IT systems that they use. Customers often prefer such an agreement, as all of their requirements are covered in a single document.

Only one signatory is normally required, which simplifies this issue.

> **Hints and tips**
>
> A combination of either of these structures might be appropriate, providing all services and customers are covered, with no overlap or duplication.

Multi-level SLAs

Some organizations have chosen to adopt a multi-level SLA structure. For example, a three-layer structure as follows:

- **Corporate level:** covering all the generic SLM issues appropriate to every customer throughout the organization. These issues are likely to be less volatile, so updates are less frequently required

■ **Customer level:** covering all SLM issues relevant to the particular customer group or business unit, regardless of the service being used

■ **Service level:** covering all SLM issues relevant to the specific service, in relation to a specific customer group (one for each service covered by the SLA).

As shown in Figure 4.7, such a structure allows SLAs to be kept to a manageable size, avoids unnecessary duplication, and reduces the need for frequent updates. However, it does mean that extra effort is required to maintain the necessary relationships and links within the Service Catalogue and the CMS.

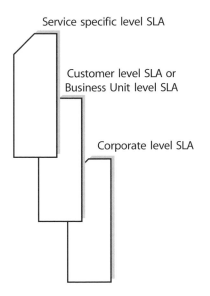

Service specific level SLA

Customer level SLA or Business Unit level SLA

Corporate level SLA

Figure 4.7 Multi-level SLAs

Many organizations have found it valuable to produce standards and a set of proformas or templates that can be used as a starting point for all SLAs, SLRs and OLAs. The proforma can often be developed alongside the draft SLA. Guidance on the items to be included in an SLA is given in Appendix F. Developing standards and templates will ensure that all agreements are developed in a consistent manner, and this will ease their subsequent use, operation and management.

Hints and tips

Make roles and responsibilities a part of the SLA. Consider three perspectives – the IT provider, the IT customer and the actual users.

The wording of SLAs should be clear and concise and leave no room for ambiguity. There is normally no need for agreements to be written in legal terminology, and plain language aids a common understanding. It is often helpful to have an independent person, who has not been involved with the drafting, to do a final read-through. This often throws up potential ambiguities and difficulties that can then be addressed and clarified. For this reason alone, it is recommended that all SLAs contain a glossary, defining any terms and providing clarity for any areas of ambiguity.

It is also worth remembering that SLAs may have to cover services offered internationally. In such cases the SLA may have to be translated into several languages. Remember also that an SLA drafted in a single language may have to be reviewed for suitability in several different parts of the world (i.e. a version drafted in Australia may have to be reviewed for suitability in the USA or the UK – and differences in terminology, style and culture must be taken into account).

Where the IT services are provided to another organization by an external service provider, sometimes the service targets are contained within a contract and at other times they are contained within an SLA or schedule attached to the contract. Whatever document is used, it is essential that the targets documented and agreed are clear, specific and unambiguous, as they will provide the basis of the relationship and the quality of service delivered.

4.2.5.2 Determine, document and agree requirements for new services and produce SLRs

This is one of the earliest activities within the Service Design stage of the Service Lifecycle. Once the Service Catalogue has been produced and the SLA structure has been agreed, a first SLR must be drafted. It is advisable to involve customers from the outset, but rather than going along with a blank sheet to start with, it may be better to produce a first outline draft of the performance targets and the management and operational requirements, as a starting point for more detailed and in-depth discussion. Be careful, though, not to go too far and appear to be presenting the customer with a 'fait accompli'.

It cannot be over-stressed how difficult this activity of determining the initial targets for inclusion with an SLR or SLA is. All of the other processes need to be consulted for their opinion on what are realistic targets that can be achieved, such as Incident Management on incident targets. The Capacity and Availability Management processes will be of particular value in determining appropriate service availability and performance targets. If there is any doubt, provisional targets should be included within a pilot SLA that is monitored and adjusted through a service warranty period, as illustrated in Figure 3.5.

While many organizations have to give initial priority to introducing SLAs for existing services, it is also important to establish procedures for agreeing Service Level Requirements (SLRs) for new services being developed or procured.

The SLRs should be an integral part of the Service Design criteria, of which the functional specification is a part. They should, from the very start, form part of the testing/trialling criteria as the service progresses through the stages of design and development or procurement. This SLR will gradually be refined as the service progresses through the stages of its lifecycle, until it eventually becomes a pilot SLA during the early life support period. This pilot or draft SLA should be developed alongside the service itself, and should be signed and formalized before the service is introduced into live use.

It can be difficult to draw out requirements, as the business may not know what they want – especially if not asked previously – and they may need help in understanding and defining their needs, particularly in terms of capacity, security, availability and IT service continuity. Be aware that the requirements initially expressed may not be those ultimately agreed. Several iterations of negotiations may be required before an affordable balance is struck between what is sought and what is achievable and affordable. This process may involve a redesign of the service solution each time.

If new services are to be introduced in a seamless way into the live environment, another area that requires attention is the planning and formalization of the support arrangements for the service and its components. Advice should be sought from Change Management and Configuration Management to ensure the planning is comprehensive and covers the implementation, deployment and support of the service and its components. Specific responsibilities need to be defined and added to existing contracts/OLAs, or new ones need to be agreed. The support arrangements and all escalation routes also need adding to the CMS, including the Service Catalogue where appropriate, so that the Service Desk and other support staff are aware of them. Where appropriate, initial training and familiarization for the Service Desk and other support groups and knowledge transfer should be completed before live support is needed.

It should be noted that additional support resources (i.e. more staff) may be needed to support new services. There is often an expectation that an already overworked support group can magically cope with the additional effort imposed by a new service.

Using the draft agreement as a basis, negotiations must be held with the customer(s), or customer representatives to finalize the contents of the SLA and the initial service level

targets, and with the service providers to ensure that these are achievable.

4.2.5.3 Monitor service performance against SLA

Nothing should be included in an SLA unless it can be effectively monitored and measured at a commonly agreed point. The importance of this cannot be overstressed, as inclusion of items that cannot be effectively monitored almost always results in disputes and eventual loss of faith in the SLM process. A lot of organizations have discovered this the hard way and as a result have absorbed heavy costs, both in a financial sense as well as in terms of negative impacts on their credibility.

> **Anecdote**
>
> A global network provider agreed availability targets for the provision of a managed network service. These availability targets were agreed at the point where the service entered the customer's premises. However, the global network provider could only monitor and measure availability at the point the connection left its premises. The network links were provided by a number of different national telecommunications service providers, with widely varying availability levels. The result was a complete mismatch between the availability figures produced by the network provider and the customer, with correspondingly prolonged and heated debate and argument.

Existing monitoring capabilities should be reviewed and upgraded as necessary. Ideally this should be done ahead of, or in parallel with, the drafting of SLAs, so that monitoring can be in place to assist with the validation of proposed targets.

It is essential that monitoring matches the customer's true perception of the service. Unfortunately this is often very difficult to achieve. For example, monitoring of individual components, such as the network or server, does not guarantee that the service will be available so far as the customer is concerned. Customer perception is often that although a failure might affect more than one service, all they are bothered about is the service they cannot access at the time of the reported incident – though this is not always true, so caution is needed. Without monitoring all components in the end-to-end service (which may be very difficult and costly to achieve) a true picture cannot be gained. Similarly, users must be aware that they should report incidents immediately to aid diagnostics, especially if they are performance-related, so that the service provider is aware that service targets are being breached.

A considerable number of organizations use their Service Desk, linked to a comprehensive CMS, to monitor the customer's perception of availability. This may involve making specific changes to incident/problem logging screens and may require stringent compliance with incident logging procedures. All of this needs discussion and agreement with the Availability Management process.

The Service Desk is also used to monitor incident response times and resolution times, but once again the logging screen may need amendment to accommodate data capture, and call-logging procedures may need tightening and must be strictly followed. If support is being provided by a third party, this monitoring may also underpin Supplier Management.

It is essential to ensure that any incident/problem-handling targets included in SLAs are the same as those included in Service Desk tools and used for escalation and monitoring purposes. Where organizations have failed to recognize this, and perhaps used defaults provided by the tool supplier, they have ended up in a situation where they are monitoring something different from that which has been agreed in the SLAs, and are therefore unable to say whether SLA targets have been met, without considerable effort to manipulate the data. Some amendments may be needed to support tools, to include the necessary fields so that relevant data can be captured.

Another notoriously difficult area to monitor is transaction response times (the time between sending a screen and receiving a response). Often end-to-end response times are technically very difficult to monitor. In such cases it may be appropriate to deal with this as follows:

- Include a statement in the SLA along the following lines: 'The services covered by the SLA are designed for high-speed response and no significant delays should be encountered. If a response time delay of more than x seconds is experienced for more than y minutes, this should be reported immediately to the Service Desk'.
- Agree and include in the SLA an acceptable target for the number of such incidents that can be tolerated in the reporting period.
- Create an incident category of 'poor response' (or similar) and ensure that any such incidents are logged accurately and that they are related to the appropriate service.
- Produce regular reports of occasions where SLA transaction response time targets have been breached, and instigate investigations via Problem Management to correct the situation.

This approach not only overcomes the technical difficulties of monitoring, but also ensures that incidents of poor response are reported at the time they occur. This is very important, as poor response is often caused by a number of transient interacting events that can only be detected if they are investigated immediately.

The preferred method, however, is to implement some form of automated client/server response time monitoring in close consultation with the Service Operation. Wherever possible, implement sampling or 'robot' tools and techniques to give indications of slow or poor performance. These tools provide the ability to measure or sample actual or very similar response times to those being experienced by a variety of users, and are becoming increasingly available and increasingly more cost-effective to use.

> **Hints and tips**
>
> Some organizations have found that, in reality, 'poor response' is sometimes a problem of user perception. The user, having become used to a particular level of response over a period of time, starts complaining as soon as this is slower. Take the view that 'if the user thinks the service is slow, then it is'.

If the SLA includes targets for assessing and implementing Requests for Change (RFCs), the monitoring of targets relating to Change Management should ideally be carried out using whatever Change Management tool is in use (preferably part of an integrated Service Management support tool) and change logging screens and escalation processes should support this.

4.2.5.4 Collate, measure and improve customer satisfaction

There are a number of important 'soft' issues that cannot be monitored by mechanistic or procedural means, such as customers' overall feelings (these need not necessarily match the 'hard' monitoring). For example, even when there have been a number of reported service failures, the customers may still feel positive about things, because they may feel satisfied that appropriate actions are being taken to improve things. Of course, the opposite may apply, and customers may feel dissatisfied with some issues (e.g. the manner of some staff on the Service Desk) when few or no SLA targets have been broken.

From the outset, it is wise to try and manage customers' expectations. This means setting proper expectations and appropriate targets in the first place, and putting a systematic process in place to manage expectations going forward, as satisfaction = perception – expectation (where a zero or positive score indicates a satisfied customer).

SLAs are just documents, and in themselves do not materially alter the quality of service being provided (though they may affect behaviour and help engender an appropriate service culture, which can have an immediate beneficial effect, and make longer-term improvements possible). A degree of patience is therefore needed and should be built into expectations.

Where charges are being made for the services provided, this should modify customer demands. (Customers can have whatever they can cost-justify – providing it fits within agreed corporate strategy – and have authorized budget for, but no more.) Where direct charges are not made, the support of senior business managers should be enlisted to ensure that excessive or unrealistic demands are not placed on the IT provider by any individual customer group.

It is therefore recommended that attempts be made to monitor customer perception on these soft issues. Methods of doing this include:

- Periodic questionnaires and customer surveys
- Customer feedback from service review meetings
- Feedback from Post Implementation Reviews (PIRs) conducted as part of the Change Management process on major changes, releases, new or changed services, etc.
- Telephone perception surveys (perhaps at random on the Service Desk, or using regular customer liaison representatives)
- Satisfaction survey handouts (left with customers following installations, service visits, etc.)
- User group or forum meetings
- Analysis of complaints and compliments.

Where possible, targets should be set for these and monitored as part of the SLA (e.g. an average score of 3.5 should be achieved by the service provider on results given, based on a scoring system of 1 to 5, where 1 is poor performance and 5 is excellent). Ensure that if users provide feedback they receive some return, and demonstrate to them that their comments have been incorporated in an action plan, perhaps a SIP. All customer satisfaction measurements should be reviewed, and where variations are identified, they should be analysed with action taken to rectify the variation.

4.2.5.5 Review and revise underpinning agreements and service scope

IT service providers are dependent to some extent on their own internal technical support teams or on external partners or suppliers. They cannot commit to meeting SLA targets unless their own support team's and suppliers' performances underpin these targets. Contracts with external suppliers are mandatory, but many organizations have also identified the benefits of having simple agreements with internal support groups, usually referred to as OLAs. 'Underpinning agreements' is a term used to refer to all underpinning OLAs, SLAs and contracts.

Often these agreements are referred to as 'back-to-back' agreements. This is to reflect the need to ensure that all targets within underpinning or 'back-to-back' agreements are aligned with, and support, targets agreed with the business in SLAs or OLAs. There may be several layers of these underpinning or 'back-to-back' agreements with aligned targets. It is essential that the targets at each layer are aligned with, and support, the targets contained within the higher levels (i.e. those closest to the business targets).

OLAs need not be very complicated, but should set out specific back-to-back targets for support groups that underpin the targets included in SLAs. For example, if the SLA includes overall time to respond and fix targets for incidents (varying on the priority levels), then the OLAs should include targets for each of the elements in the support chain. It must be understood, however, that the incident resolution targets included in SLAs should not normally match the same targets included in contracts or OLAs with suppliers. This is because the SLA targets must include an element for all stages in the support cycle (e.g. detection time, Service Desk logging time, escalation time, referral time between groups etc, Service Desk review and closure time – as well as the actual time fixing the failure).

The SLA target should cover the time taken to answer calls, escalate incidents to technical support staff, and the time taken to start to investigate and to resolve incidents assigned to them. In addition, overall support hours should be stipulated for all groups that underpin the required service availability times in the SLA. If special procedures exist for contacted staff (e.g. out-of-hours telephone support) these must also be documented.

OLAs should be monitored against OLA and SLA targets, and reports on achievements provided as feedback to the appropriate managers of each support team. This highlights potential problem areas, which may need to be addressed internally or by a further review of the SLA or OLA. Serious consideration should be given to introducing formal OLAs for all internal support teams, which contribute to the support of operational services.

Before committing to new or revised SLAs, it is therefore important that existing contractual arrangements are investigated and, where necessary, upgraded. This is likely to incur additional costs, which must either be absorbed by IT or passed on to the customer. In the latter case, the customer must agree to this, or the more relaxed targets in existing contracts should be agreed for inclusion in SLAs. This activity needs to be completed in close consultation with the Supplier Management process, to ensure not only that SLM requirements are met, but also that all other process requirements are considered, particularly supplier and contractual policies and standards.

4.2.5.6 Produce service reports

Immediately after the SLA is agreed and accepted, monitoring must be instigated, and service achievement reports must be produced. Operational reports must be produced frequently (weekly – perhaps even more frequently) and, where possible, exception reports should be produced whenever an SLA has been broken (or threatened, if appropriate thresholds have been set to give an 'early warning'). Sometimes difficulties are encountered in meeting the targets of new services during the early life support period because of the high volume of RFCs. Limiting the number of RFCs processed during the early life support period can limit the impact of changes.

The SLA reporting mechanisms, intervals and report formats must be defined and agreed with the customers. The frequency and format of Service Review Meetings must also be agreed with the customers. Regular intervals are recommended, with periodic reports synchronized with the reviewing cycle.

Periodic reports must be produced and circulated to customers (or their representatives) and appropriate IT managers a few days in advance of service level reviews, so that any queries or disagreements can be resolved ahead of the review meeting. The meeting is not then diverted by such issues.

The periodic reports should incorporate details of performance against all SLA targets, together with details of any trends or specific actions being undertaken to improve service quality. A useful technique is to include a SLA Monitoring (SLAM) chart at the front of a service report to give an 'at-a-glance' overview of how achievements have measured up against targets. These are most effective if colour coded (Red, Amber, Green, and sometimes referred to as RAG charts as a result). Other interim reports may be required by IT management for OLA or internal performance reviews and/or supplier or contract management. This is likely to be an evolving process – a first effort is unlikely to be the final outcome.

The resources required to produce and verify reports should not be underestimated. It can be extremely time-consuming, and if reports do not reflect the customer's own perception of service quality accurately, they can make the situation worse. It is essential that accurate information from all areas and all processes (e.g. Incident Management, Problem Management, Availability Management, Capacity Management, Change and Configuration Management) is analysed and collated into a concise and comprehensive report on service performance, as measured against agreed business targets.

SLM should identify the specific reporting needs and automate production of these reports, as far as possible. The extent, accuracy and ease with which automated reports can be produced should form part of the selection criteria for integrated support tools. These service reports should not only include details of current performance against targets, but should also provide historic information on past performance and trends, so that the impact of improvement actions can be measured and predicted.

4.2.5.7 Conduct service reviews and instigate improvements within an overall SIP

Periodic review meetings must be held on a regular basis with customers (or their representatives) to review the service achievement in the last period and to preview any issues for the coming period. It is normal to hold such meetings monthly or, as a minimum, quarterly.

Actions must be placed on the customer and provider as appropriate to improve weak areas where targets are not being met. All actions must be minuted, and progress should be reviewed at the next meeting to ensure that action items are being followed up and properly implemented.

Particular attention should be focused on each breach of service level to determine exactly what caused the loss of service and what can be done to prevent any recurrence. If it is decided that the service level was, or has become, unachievable, it may be necessary to review, renegotiate, review-agree different service targets. If the service break has been caused by a failure of a third-party or internal support group, it may also be necessary to review the underpinning agreement or OLA. Analysis of the cost and impact of service breaches provides valuable input and justification of SIP activities and actions. The constant need for improvement needs to be balanced and focused on those areas most likely to give the greatest business benefit.

Reports should also be produced on the progress and success of the SIP, such as the number of SIP actions that were completed and the number of actions that delivered their expected benefit.

4.2.5.8 Review and revise SLAs, service scope and underpinning agreements

All agreements and underpinning agreements, including SLAs, underpinning contracts and OLAs, must be kept up-to-date. They should be brought under Change and Configuration Management control and reviewed periodically, at least annually, to ensure that they are still current and comprehensive, and are still aligned to business needs and strategy.

These reviews should ensure that the services covered and the targets for each are still relevant – and that nothing significant has changed that invalidates the agreement in any way (this should include infrastructure changes, business changes, supplier changes, etc.). Where changes are made, the agreements must be updated under Change Management control to reflect the new situation. If all agreements are recorded as CIs within the CMS, it is easier to assess the impact and implement the changes in a controlled manner.

These reviews should also include the overall strategy documents, to ensure that all services and service agreements are kept in line with business and IT strategies and policies.

4.2.5.9 Develop contacts and relationships

It is very important that SLM develops trust and respect with the business, especially with the key business contacts. Using the Service Catalogue, especially the Business Service Catalogue element of it, enables SLM to be much more proactive. The Service Catalogue provides the information that enables SLM to understand the relationships between the services and the business units and business process that depend on those services. It should also provide the information on all the key

business and IT contacts relating to the services, their use and their importance. In order to ensure that this is done in a consistent manner, SLM should perform the following activities:

- Confirm stakeholders, customers and key business managers and service users.
- Assist with maintaining accurate information within the Service Portfolio and Service Catalogue.
- Be flexible and responsive to the needs of the business, customers and users, and understand current and planned new business processes and their requirements for new or changed services, documenting and communicating these requirements to all other processes as well as facilitating and innovating change wherever there is business benefit.
- Develop a full understanding of business, customer and user strategies, plans, business needs and objectives, ensuring that IT are working in partnership with the business, customers and users, developing long-term relationships.
- Regularly take the customer journey and sample the customer experience, providing feedback on customer issues to IT. (This applies to both IT customers and also the external business customers in their use of IT services).
- Ensure that the correct relationship processes are in place to achieve objectives and that they are subjected to continuous improvement.
- Conduct and complete customer surveys, assist with the analysis of the completed surveys and ensure that actions are taken on the results.
- Act as an IT representative on organizing and attending user groups.
- Proactively market and exploit the Service Portfolio and Service Catalogue and the use of the services within all areas of the business.
- Work with the business, customers and users to ensure that IT provides the most appropriate levels of service to meet business needs currently and in the future.
- Promote service awareness and understanding.
- Raise the awareness of the business benefits to be gained from the exploitation of new technology.
- Facilitate the development and negotiation of appropriate, achievable and realistic SLRs and SLAs between the business and IT.
- Ensure the business, customers and users understand their responsibilities/commitments to IT (i.e. IT dependencies).
- Assist with the maintenance of a register of all outstanding improvements and enhancements.

4.2.5.10 Complaints and compliments

The SLM process should also include activities and procedures for the logging and management of all complaints and compliments. The logging procedures are often performed by the Service Desk as they are similar to those of Incident Management and Request Fulfilment. The definition of a complaint and compliment should be agreed with the customers, together with agreed contact points and procedures for their management and analysis. All complaints and compliments should be recorded and communicated to the relevant parties. All complaints should also be actioned and resolved to the satisfaction of the originator. If not, there should be an escalation contact and procedure for all complaints that are not actioned and resolved within an appropriate timescale. All outstanding complaints should be reviewed and escalated to senior management where appropriate. Reports should also be produced on the numbers and types of complaints, the trends identified and actions taken to reduce the numbers received. Similar reports should also be produced for compliments.

4.2.6 Triggers, inputs, outputs and interfaces

There are many triggers that instigate SLM activity. These include:

- Changes in the Service Portfolio, such as new or changed business requirements or new or changed services
- New or changed agreements, SLRs, SLAs, OLAs or contracts
- Service review meetings and actions
- Service breaches or threatened breaches
- Compliments and complaints
- Periodic activities such as reviewing, reporting and customer satisfaction surveys
- Changes in strategy or policy.

4.2.6.1 SLM process inputs

There are a number of sources of information that are relevant to the Service Level Management process. These should include:

- Business information: from the organization's business strategy, plans, and financial plans and information on their current and future requirements
- Business Impact Analysis: providing information on the impact, priority, risk and number of users associated with each service
- Business requirements: details of any agreed, new or changed business requirements
- The strategies, policies and constraints from Service Strategy
- The Service Portfolio and Service Catalogue
- Change information: from the Change Management process with a forward schedule of changes and a need to assess all changes for their impact on all services
- CMS: containing information on the relationships between the business services, the supporting services and the technology
- Customer and user feedback, complaints and compliments
- Other inputs: including advice, information and input from any of the other processes (e.g. Incident Management, Capacity Management and Availability Management), together with the existing SLAs, SLRs, and OLAs and past service reports on the quality of service delivered.

4.2.6.2 SLM process outputs

The outputs of Service Level Management should include:

- Service reports: providing details of the service levels achieved in relation to the targets contained within SLAs. These reports should contain details of all aspects of the service and its delivery, including current and historical performance, breaches and weaknesses, major events, changes planned, current and predicted workloads, customer feedback, and improvement plans and activities
- Service Improvement Plan (SIP): an overall programme or plan of prioritized improvement actions, encompassing all services and all processes, together with associated impacts and risks
- The Service Quality Plan: documenting and planning the overall improvement of service quality
- Document templates: standard document templates, format and content for SLAs, SLRs and OLAs, aligned with corporate standards
- Service Level Agreements (SLAs): a set of targets and responsibilities should be documented and agreed within an SLA for each operational service
- Service Level Requirements (SLRs): a set of targets and responsibilities should be documented and agreed within an SLR for each proposed new or changed service
- Operational Level Agreements (OLAs): a set of targets and responsibilities should be documented and agreed within an OLA for each internal support team
- Reports on OLAs and underpinning contracts

- Service review meeting minutes and actions: all meetings should be scheduled on a regular basis, with planned agendas and their discussions and actions recorded and progressed
- SLA review and service scope review meeting minutes: summarizing agreed actions and revisions to SLAs and service scope
- Revised contracts: changes to SLAs or new SLRs may require existing underpinning contracts to be changed, or new contracts to be negotiated and agreed.

4.2.7 Key Performance Indicators

Key Performance Indicators (KPIs) and metrics can be used to judge the efficiency and effectiveness of the SLM activities and the progress of the SIP. These metrics should be developed from the service, customer and business perspective and should cover both subjective and objective measurements such as the following.

Objective:

- Number or percentage of service targets being met
- Number and severity of service breaches
- Number of services with up-to-date SLAs
- Number of services with timely reports and active service reviews.

Subjective:

- Improvements in customer satisfaction.

More information on KPIs, measurements and improvements can be found in the following section and in the Continuous Service Improvement publication.

> **Hints and tips**
>
> Don't fall into the trap of using percentages as the only metric. It is easy to get caught out when there is a small system with limited measurement points (i.e. a single failure in a population of 100 is only 1%; a single failure in a population of 50 is 2% – if the target is 98.5%, then the SLA is already breached). Always go for number of incidents rather than a percentage on populations of less than 100, and be careful when targets are accepted. This is something organizations have learned the hard way.

The SLM process often generates a good starting point for a SIP – and the service review process may drive this, but all processes and all areas of the service provider organization should be involved in the SIP.

Where an underlying difficulty has been identified that is adversely impacting on service quality, SLM must, in conjunction with Problem Management and Availability Management, instigate a SIP to identify and implement whatever actions are necessary to overcome the difficulties and restore service quality. SIP initiatives may also focus on such issues as user training, service and system testing and documentation. In these cases, the relevant people need to be involved and adequate feedback given to make improvements for the future. At any time, a number of separate initiatives that form part of the SIP may be running in parallel to address difficulties with a number of services.

Some organizations have established an up-front annual budget held by SLM from which SIP initiatives can be funded. This means that action can be undertaken quickly and that SLM is demonstrably effective. This practice should be encouraged and expanded to enable SLM to become increasingly proactive and predictive. The SIP needs to be owned and managed, with all improvement actions being assessed for risk and impact on services, customers and the business, and then prioritized, scheduled and implemented.

If an organization is outsourcing its Service Delivery to a third party, the issue of service improvement should be discussed at the outset and covered (and budgeted for) in the contract, otherwise there is no incentive during the lifetime of the contract for the supplier to improve service targets if they are already meeting contractual obligations and additional expenditure is needed to make the improvements.

4.2.7.1 KPIs

Manage the overall quality of IT service needed, both in the number and level of services provided and managed:

- Percentage reduction in SLA targets missed
- Percentage reduction in SLA targets threatened
- Percentage increase in customer perception and satisfaction of SLA achievements, via service reviews and Customer Satisfaction Survey responses
- Percentage reduction in SLA breaches caused because of third-party support contracts (underpinning contracts)
- Percentage reduction in SLA breaches caused because of internal Operational Level Agreements (OLAs).

Deliver service as previously agreed at affordable costs:

- Total number and percentage increase in fully documented SLAs in place
- Percentage increase in SLAs agreed against operational services being run
- Percentage reduction in the costs associated with service provision

- Percentage reduction in the cost of monitoring and reporting of SLAs
- Percentage increase in the speed and of developing and agreeing appropriate SLAs
- Frequency of service review meetings.

Manage business interface:

- Increased percentage of services covered by SLAs
- Documented and agreed SLM processes and procedures are in place
- Reduction in the time taken to respond to and implement SLA requests
- Increased percentage of SLA reviews completed on time
- Reduction in the percentage of outstanding SLAs for annual renegotiation
- Reduction in the percentage of SLAs requiring corrective changes (for example, targets not attainable; changes in usage levels). Care needs to be taken when using this KPI
- Percentage increase in the coverage of OLAs and third-party contracts in place, whilst possibly reducing the actual number of agreements (consolidation and centralization)
- Documentary evidence that issues raised at service and SLA reviews are being followed up and resolved
- Reduction in the number and severity of SLA breaches
- Effective review and follow-up of all SLA, OLA and underpinning contract breaches.

4.2.8 Information Management

SLM provides key information on all operational services, their expected targets and the service achievements and breaches for all operational services. It assists Service Catalogue Management with the management of the Service Catalogue and also provides the information and trends on customer satisfaction, including complaints and compliments.

SLM is crucial in providing information on the quality of IT service provided to the customer, and information on the customer's expectation and perception of that quality of service. This information should be widely available to all areas of the service provider organization.

4.2.9 Challenges, Critical Success Factors and risks

One challenge faced by SLM is that of identifying suitable customer representatives with whom to negotiate. Who 'owns' the service? In some cases, this may be obvious, and a single customer manager is willing to act as the

signatory to the agreement. In other cases, it may take quite a bit of negotiating or cajoling to find a representative 'volunteer' (beware that volunteers often want to express their own personal view rather than represent a general consensus), or it may be necessary to get all customers to sign.

If customer representatives exist who are able genuinely to represent the views of the customer community, because they frequently meet with a wide selection of customers, this is ideal. Unfortunately, all too often representatives are head-office based and seldom come into contact with genuine service customers. In the worst case, SLM may have to perform his/her own programme of discussions and meetings with customers to ensure true requirements are identified.

Anecdote

On negotiating the current and support hours for a large service, an organization found a discrepancy in the required time of usage between Head Office and the field office's customers. Head Office (with a limited user population) wanted service hours covering 8.00 to 18.00, whereas the field office (with at least 20 times the user population) stated that starting an hour earlier would be better – but all offices closed to the public by 16.00 at the latest, and so wouldn't require a service much beyond this. Head Office won the 'political' argument, and so the 8.00 to 18.00 band was set. When the service came to be used (and hence monitored) it was found that service extensions were usually asked for by the field office to cover the extra hour in the morning, and actual usage figures showed that the service had not been accessed after 17.00, except on very rare occasions. The Service Level Manager was blamed by the IT staff for having to cover a late shift, and by the customer representative for charging for a service that was not used (i.e. staff and running costs).

Hints and tips

Care should be taken when opening discussions on service levels for the first time, as it is likely that 'current issues' (the failure that occurred yesterday) or long-standing grievances (that old printer that we have been trying to get replaced for ages) are likely to be aired at the outset. Important though these may be, they must not be allowed to get in the way of establishing the longer-term requirements. Be aware, however, that it may be necessary to address any issues raised at the outset before gaining any credibility to progress further.

If there has been no previous experience of SLM, then it is advisable to start with a draft SLA. A decision should be made on which service or customers are to be used for the draft. It is helpful if the selected customer is enthusiastic and wishes to participate – perhaps because they are anxious to see improvements in service quality. The results of an initial customer perception survey may give pointers to a suitable initial draft SLA.

Hints and tips

Don't pick an area where large problems exist as the first SLA. Try to pick an area that is likely to show some quick benefits and develop the SLM process. Nothing encourages acceptance of a new idea quicker than success.

One difficulty sometimes encountered is that staff at different levels within the customer community may have different objectives and perceptions. For example, a senior manager may rarely use a service and may be more interested in issues such as value for money and output, whereas a junior member of staff may use the service throughout the day, and may be more interested in issues such as responsiveness, usability and reliability. It is important that all of the appropriate and relevant customer requirements, at all levels, are identified and incorporated in SLAs.

Some organizations have formed focus groups from different levels from within the customer community to help ensure that all issues have been correctly addressed. This takes additional resources, but can be well worth the effort.

The other group of people that has to be consulted during the whole of this process is the appropriate representatives from within the IT provider side (whether internal or from an external supplier or partner). They need to agree that targets are realistic, achievable and affordable. If they are not, further negotiations are needed until a compromise acceptable to all parties is agreed. The views of suppliers should also be sought, and any contractual implications should be taken into account during the negotiation stages.

Where no past monitored data is available, it is advisable to leave the agreement in draft format for an initial period, until monitoring can confirm that initial targets are achievable. Targets may have to be re-negotiated in some cases. Many organizations negotiate an agreed timeframe for IT to negotiate and create a baseline for establishing realistic service targets. When targets and timeframes have been confirmed, the SLAs must be signed.

Once the initial SLA has been completed, and any early difficulties overcome, then move on and gradually introduce SLAs for other services/customers. If it is decided from the outset to go for a multi-level structure, it is likely that the corporate-level issues have to be covered for all customers at the time of the initial SLA. It is also worth trialling the corporate issues during this initial phase.

Hints and tips

Don't go for easy targets at the corporate level. They may be easy to achieve, but have no value in improving service quality or credibility. Also, if the targets are set at a sufficiently high level, the corporate SLA can be used as the standard that all new services should reach.

One point to ensure is that at the end of the drafting and negotiating process, the SLA is actually signed by the appropriate managers on the customer and IT service provider sides to the agreement. This gives a firm commitment by both parties that every attempt will be made to meet the agreement. Generally speaking, the more senior the signatories are within their respective organizations, the stronger the message of commitment. Once an SLA is agreed, wide publicity needs to be used to ensure that customers, users and IT staff alike are aware of its existence and of the key targets.

Steps must be taken to advertise the existence of the new SLAs and OLAs amongst the Service Desk and other support groups, with details of when they become operational. It may be helpful to extract key targets from these agreements into tables that can be on display in support areas, so that staff are always aware of the targets to which they are working. If support tools allow, these targets should be recorded within the tools, such as within a Service Catalogue or CMS, so that their content can be made widely available to all personnel. They should also be included as thresholds, and automatically alerted against when a target is threatened or actually breached. SLAs, OLAs and the targets they contain must also be publicized amongst the user community, so that users are aware of what they can expect from the services they use, and know at what point to start expressing dissatisfaction.

It is important that the Service Desk staff are committed to the SLM process, and become proactive ambassadors for SLAs, embracing the necessary service culture, as they are the first contact point for customers' incidents, complaints and queries. If the Service Desk staff are not fully aware of SLAs in place, and do not act on their contents, customers very quickly lose faith in SLAs.

4.2.9.1 *Critical Success Factors*

The main Critical Success Factors for the Service Catalogue Management process are:

- Manage the overall quality of IT services required
- Deliver the service as previously agreed at affordable costs
- Manage the interface with the business and users.

The risks associated with regard to the provision of an accurate Service Catalogue are:

- A lack of accurate input, involvement and commitment from the business and customers
- The tools and resources required to agree, document, monitor, report and review agreements and service levels
- The process becomes a bureaucratic, administrative process rather than an active and proactive process delivering measurable benefit to the business
- Access to and support of appropriate and up-to-date CMS and SKMS
- Bypassing the use of the SLM processes
- Business and customer measurements are too difficult to measure and improve, so are not recorded
- Inappropriate business and customer contacts and relationships are developed
- High customer expectations and low perception
- Poor and inappropriate communication is achieved with the business and customers.

4.3 CAPACITY MANAGEMENT

Capacity Management is a process that extends across the Service Lifecycle. A key success factor in managing capacity is ensuring it is considered during the design stage. It is for this reason that the Capacity Management process is included in this publication. Capacity Management is supported initially in Service Strategy where the decisions and analysis of business requirements and customer outcomes influence the development of patterns of business activity (PBA), levels of service (LOS) and service level packages (SLPs). This provides the predictive and ongoing capacity indicators needed to align capacity to demand.

4.3.1 Purpose/goal/objective

'The goal of the Capacity Management process is to ensure that cost-justifiable IT capacity in all areas of IT always exists and is matched to the current and future agreed needs of the business, in a timely manner'.

The purpose of Capacity Management is to provide a point of focus and management for all capacity- and performance-related issues, relating to both services and resources.

The objectives of Capacity Management are to:

- Produce and maintain an appropriate and up-to-date Capacity Plan, which reflects the current and future needs of the business
- Provide advice and guidance to all other areas of the business and IT on all capacity- and performance-related issues
- Ensure that service performance achievements meet or exceed all of their agreed performance targets, by managing the performance and capacity of both services and resources
- Assist with the diagnosis and resolution of performance- and capacity-related incidents and problems
- Assess the impact of all changes on the Capacity Plan, and the performance and capacity of all services and resources
- Ensure that proactive measures to improve the performance of services are implemented wherever it is cost-justifiable to do so.

4.3.2 Scope

The Capacity Management process should be the focal point for all IT performance and capacity issues. Technology management functions such as Network Support, Server Support or Operation Management may carry out the bulk of the day-to-day operational duties, but will provide performance information to the Capacity Management process. The process should encompass all areas of technology, both hardware and software, for all IT technology components and environments. Capacity Management should also consider space planning and environmental systems capacity as well as certain aspects of human resources, but only where a lack of human resources could result in a breach of SLA or OLA targets, a delay in the end-to-end performance or service response time, or an inability to meet future commitments and plans (e.g. overnight data backups not completed in time because no operators were present to load tapes).

In general, human resource management is a line management responsibility, though the staffing of a Service Desk should use identical Capacity Management techniques. The scheduling of human resources, staffing levels, skill levels and capability levels should therefore be included within the scope of Capacity Management. The driving force for Capacity Management should be the business requirements of the organization and to plan the resources needed to provide service levels in line with SLAs and OLAs. Capacity Management needs to understand the total IT and business environments, including:

■ The current business operation and its requirements, through the patterns of business activity

■ The future business plans and requirements via the Service Portfolio

■ The service targets and the current IT service operation though SLAs and Standard Operating Procedures

■ All areas of IT technology and its capacity and performance, including infrastructure, data, environment and applications.

Understanding all of this will enable Capacity Management to ensure that all the current and future capacity and performance aspects of services are provided cost-effectively.

Capacity Management is also about understanding the potential for the delivery of new services. New technology needs to be understood and, if appropriate, used to innovate and deliver the services required by the customer. Capacity Management needs to recognize that the rate of technological change will probably increase and that new technology should be harnessed to ensure that the IT services continue to satisfy changing business expectations. A direct link to the Service Strategy and Service Portfolio is needed to ensure that emerging technologies are considered in future service planning.

The Capacity Management process should include:

■ Monitoring patterns of business activity and service-level plans through performance, utilization and throughput of IT services and the supporting infrastructure, environmental, data and applications components and the production of regular and ad hoc reports on service and component capacity and performance

■ Undertaking tuning activities to make the most efficient use of existing IT resources

■ Understanding the agreed current and future demands being made by the customer for IT resources, and producing forecasts for future requirements

■ Influencing demand management, perhaps in conjunction with Financial Management

■ Producing a Capacity Plan that enables the service provider to continue to provide services of the quality defined in SLAs and that covers a sufficient planning timeframe to meet future service levels required as defined in the Service Portfolio and SLRs

■ Assistance with the identification and resolution of any incidents and problems associated with service or component performance

■ The proactive improvement of service or component performance wherever it is cost-justifiable and meets the needs of the business.

Managing the capacity of large distributed IT infrastructures is a complex and demanding task, especially when the IT capacity and the financial investment required is ever-increasing. Therefore it makes even more sense to plan for growth. While the cost of the upgrade to an individual component in a distributed environment is usually less than the upgrade to a component in a mainframe environment, there are often many more components in the distributed environment that need to be upgraded. Also there could now be economies of scale, because the cost per individual component could be reduced when many components need to be purchased. Capacity Management should have input to the Service Portfolio and procurement process to ensure that the best deals with suppliers are negotiated.

Capacity Management provides the necessary information on current and planned resource utilization of individual components to enable organizations to decide, with confidence:

■ Which components to upgrade (i.e. more memory, faster storage devices, faster processors, greater bandwidth)

■ When to upgrade – ideally this is not too early, resulting in expensive over-capacity, nor too late, failing to take advantage of advances in new technology, resulting in bottle-necks, inconsistent performance and, ultimately, customer dissatisfaction and lost business opportunities

■ How much the upgrade will cost – the forecasting and planning elements of Capacity Management feed into budgetary lifecycles, ensuring planned investment.

Many of the other processes are less effective if there is no input to them from the Capacity Management process. For example:

■ Can the Change Management process properly assess the effect of any change on the available capacity?

■ When a new service is implemented, can the SLM process be assured that the SLRs of the new service are achievable, and that the SLAs of existing services will not be affected?

■ Can the Problem Management process properly diagnose the underlying cause of incidents caused by poor performance?

■ Can the IT Service Continuity process accurately determine the capacity requirements of the key business processes?

Capacity Management is one of the forward-looking processes that, when properly carried out, can forecast business events and impacts often before they happen. Good Capacity Management ensures that there are no surprises with regard to service and component design and performance.

Capacity Management has a close, two-way relationship with the Service Strategy and planning processes within an organization. On a regular basis, the long-term strategy of an organization is encapsulated in an update of the business plans. The Service Strategy will reflect the business plans and strategy, which are developed from the organization's understanding of the external factors such as the competitive marketplace, economic outlook and legislation, and its internal capability in terms of manpower, delivery capability, etc. Often a shorter-term tactical plan, or business change plan is developed to implement the changes necessary in the short to medium term to progress the overall business plan and Service Strategy. Capacity Management needs to understand the short-, medium- and long-term plans of the business while providing information on the latest ideas, trends and technologies being developed by the suppliers of computing hardware and software.

The organization's business plans drive the specific IT Service Strategy, the contents of which Capacity Management needs to be familiar with, and to which Capacity Management needs to have had significant and ongoing input. The right level of capacity at the right time is critical. Service Strategy plans will be helpful to capacity planning by identifying the timing for acquiring and implementing new technologies, hardware and software.

4.3.3 Value to the business

Capacity Management is responsible for ensuring that IT resources are planned and scheduled to provide a consistent level of service that is matched to the current and future needs of the business, as agreed and documented within SLAs and OLAs. In conjunction with the business and their plans, Capacity Management provides a Capacity Plan that outlines the IT resources and funding needed to support the business plan, together with a cost justification of that expenditure.

4.3.4 Policies/principles/basic concepts

Capacity Management ensures that the capacity and performance of the IT services and systems matches the evolving agreed demands of the business in the most cost-effective and timely manner. Capacity Management is essentially a balancing act:

■ **Balancing costs against resources needed:** the need to ensure that processing capacity that is purchased is cost-justifiable in terms of business need, and the need to make the most efficient use of those resources.

■ **Balancing supply against demand:** the need to ensure that the available supply of IT processing power matches the demands made on it by the business, both now and in the future. It may also be necessary to manage or influence the demand for a particular resource.

Capacity Management processes and planning must be involved in all stages of the Service Lifecycle from Strategy and Design, through Transition and Operation to Improvement. From a strategic perspective, the Service Portfolio contains the IT resources and capabilities. The advent of Service Oriented Architecture, virtualization and the use of value networks in IT service provision are important factors in the management of capacity. The appropriate capacity and performance should be designed into services and components from the initial design stages. This will ensure not only that the performance of any new or changed service meets its expected targets, but also that all existing services continue to meet all of their targets. This is the basis of stable service provision.

The overall Capacity Management process is continually trying cost-effectively to match IT resources and capacity to the ever-changing needs and requirements of the business. This requires the tuning and optimization of the current resources and the effective estimation and planning of the future resources, as illustrated in Figure 4.8.

Capacity Management is an extremely technical, complex and demanding process, and in order to achieve results, it requires three supporting sub-processes.

One of the key activities of Capacity Management is to produce a plan that documents the current levels of resource utilization and service performance and, after consideration of the Service Strategy and plans, forecasts the future requirements for new IT resources to support the IT services that underpin the business activities. The plan should indicate clearly any assumptions made. It should also include any recommendations quantified in terms of resource required, cost, benefits, impact, etc.

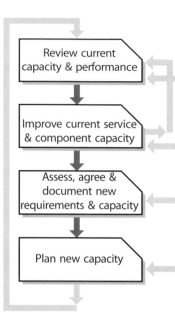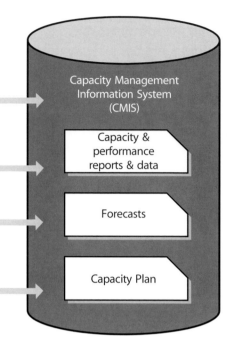

Figure 4.8 The Capacity Management process

The production and maintenance of a Capacity Plan should occur at pre-defined intervals. It is, essentially, an investment plan and should therefore be published annually, in line with the business or budget lifecycle, and completed before the start of negotiations on future budgets. A quarterly re-issue of the updated plan may be necessary to take into account changes in service plans, to report on the accuracy of forecasts and to make or refine recommendations. This takes extra effort but, if it is regularly updated, the Capacity Plan is more likely to be accurate and to reflect the changing business need.

The typical contents of a Capacity Plan are described in Appendix J.

4.3.4.1 Business Capacity Management

This sub-process translates business needs and plans into requirements for service and IT infrastructure, ensuring that the future business requirements for IT services are quantified, designed, planned and implemented in a timely fashion. This can be achieved by using the existing data on the current resource utilization by the various services and resources to trend, forecast, model or predict future requirements. These future requirements come from the Service Strategy and Service Portfolio detailing new processes and service requirements, changes, improvements, and also the growth in the existing services.

4.3.4.2 Service Capacity Management

The focus of this sub-process is the management, control and prediction of the end-to-end performance and capacity of the live, operational IT services usage and workloads. It ensures that the performance of all services, as detailed in service targets within SLAs and SLRs, is monitored and measured, and that the collected data is recorded, analysed and reported. Wherever necessary, proactive and reactive action should be instigated, to ensure that the performance of all services meets their agreed business targets. This is performed by staff with knowledge of all the areas of technology used in the delivery of end-to-end service, and often involves seeking advice from the specialists involved in Component Capacity Management. Wherever possible, automated thresholds should be used to manage all operational services, to ensure that situations where service targets are breached or threatened are rapidly identified and cost-effective actions to reduce or avoid their potential impact implemented.

4.3.4.3 Component Capacity Management

The focus in this sub-process is the management, control and prediction of the performance, utilization and capacity of individual IT technology components. It ensures that all components within the IT infrastructure that have finite resource are monitored and measured, and that the collected data is recorded, analysed and reported. Again, wherever possible, automated thresholds should be implemented to manage all components, to ensure that situations where service targets are breached or threatened by component usage or performance are rapidly identified, and cost-effective actions to reduce or avoid their potential impact are implemented.

There are many similar activities that are performed by each of the above sub-processes, but each sub-process has a very different focus. Business Capacity Management is focused on the current and future business requirements, while Service Capacity Management is focused on the delivery of the existing services that support the business, and Component Capacity Management is focused on the IT infrastructure that underpins service provision. The role that each of these sub-processes plays in the overall process and the use of management tools is illustrated in Figure 4.9.

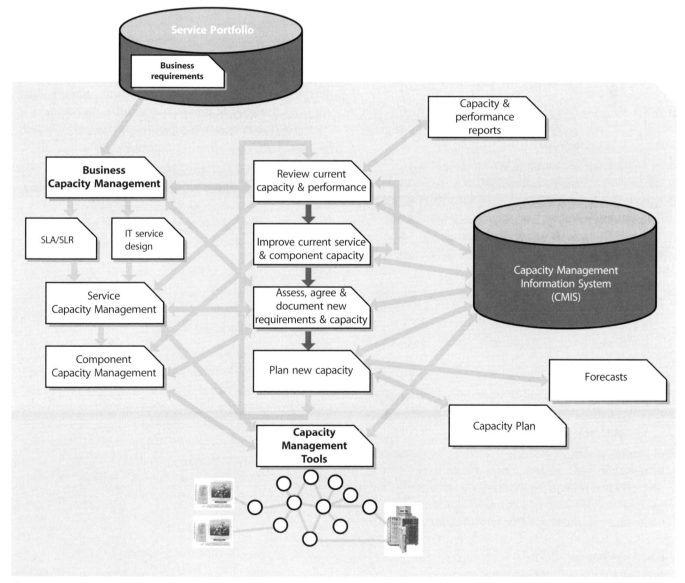

Figure 4.9 Capacity Management sub-processes

The tools used by Capacity Management need to conform to the organization's management architecture and integrate with other tools used for the management of IT systems and automating IT processes. The monitoring and control activities within Service Operation will provide a good basis for the tools to support and analyse information for Capacity Management.

4.3.5 Process activities, methods and techniques

Some activities in the Capacity Management process are reactive, while others are proactive. The proactive activities of Capacity Management should include:

■ Pre-empting performance issues by taking the necessary actions before they occur

■ Producing trends of the current component utilization and estimating the future requirements, using trends and thresholds for planning upgrades and enhancements

■ Modelling and trending the predicted changes in IT services, and identifying the changes that need to be made to services and components of the IT infrastructure and applications to ensure that appropriate resource is available

■ Ensuring that upgrades are budgeted, planned and implemented before SLAs and service targets are breached or performance issues occur

■ Actively seeking to improve service performance wherever it is cost-justifiable

■ Tuning and optimizing the performance of services and components.

The reactive activities of Capacity Management should include:

■ Monitoring, measuring, reporting and reviewing the current performance of both services and components

■ Responding to all capacity-related 'threshold' events and instigating corrective action

■ Reacting to and assisting with specific performance issues. For example, the Service Desk may refer incidents of poor performance to Technology Management, which will employ Capacity Management techniques to resolve them.

Key message

The more successful the proactive and predictive activities of Capacity Management, the less need there will be for the reactive activities of Capacity Management.

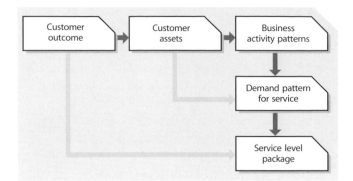

Figure 4.10 Capacity must support business requirements

4.3.5.1 Business Capacity Management

The main objective of the Business Capacity Management sub-process is to ensure that the future business requirements (customer outcomes) for IT services are considered and understood, and that sufficient IT capacity to support any new or changed services is planned and implemented within an appropriate timescale. Figure 4.10 illustrates that BCM is influenced by the business patterns of activity and how services are used.

The Capacity Management process must be responsive to changing requirements for capacity demand. New services or changed services will be required to underpin the changing business. Existing services will require modification to provide extra functionality. Old services will become obsolete, freeing up spare capacity. As a result, the ability to satisfy the customers' SLRs and SLAs will be affected. It is the responsibility of Capacity Management to predict the demand for capacity for such changes and manage the demand.

These new requirements may come to the attention of Capacity Management from many different sources and for many different reasons, but the principal sources of supply should be the Pattern of Business Activity from Demand Management and the Service Level Packages produced for the Service Portfolio. These indicate a window of future predictors for capacity. Such examples could be a recommendation to upgrade to take advantage of new technology, or the implementation of a tuning activity to resolve a performance problem. Figure 4.11 shows the cycle of demand management.

Capacity Management needs to be included in all strategic, planning and design activities, being involved as early as possible within each process, such as:

■ Assisting and supporting the development of Service Strategy

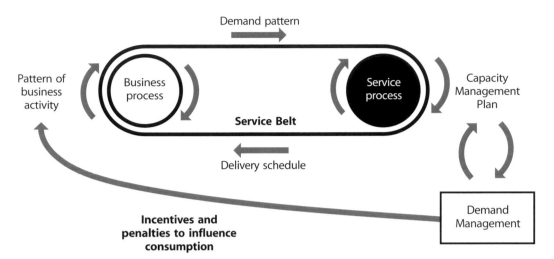

Figure 4.11 Capacity Management takes particular note of demand pattern

■ Involvement in the review and improvement of IT strategies and policies

■ Involvement in the review and improvement of technology architectures.

> **Key message**
> Capacity Management should not be a last-minute 'tick in the box' just prior to customer acceptance and operational acceptance.

If early involvement can be achieved from Capacity Management within these processes, then the planning and design of IT capacity can be closely aligned with business requirements and can ensure that service targets can be achieved and maintained.

Assist with agreeing Service Level Requirements

Capacity Management should assist SLM in understanding the customers' capacity and performance requirements, in terms of required service/system response times, expected throughput, patterns of usage and volume of users. Capacity Management should help in the negotiation process by providing possible solutions to a number of scenarios. For example, if the volume of users is less than 2,000, then response times can be guaranteed to be less than two seconds. If more than 2,000 users connect concurrently, then extra network bandwidth is needed to guarantee the required response time, or a slower response time will have to be accepted. Modelling, trending or application sizing techniques are often employed here to ensure that predictions accurately reflect the real situation.

Design, procure or amend service configuration

Capacity Management should be involved in the design of new or changing services and make recommendations for the procurement of hardware and software, where performance and/or capacity are factors. In some instances Capacity Management instigates the implementation of the new requirement through Change Management, where it is also involved as a member of the Change Advisory Board. In the interest of balancing cost and capacity, the Capacity Management process obtains the costs of alternative proposed solutions and recommends the most appropriate cost-effective solution.

Verify SLA

The SLA should include details of the anticipated service throughputs and the performance requirements. Capacity Management advises SLM on achievable targets that can be monitored and on which the Service Design has been based. Confidence that the Service Design will meet the SLRs and provide the ability for future growth can be gained by using modelling, trending or sizing techniques.

Support SLA negotiation

The results of the predictive techniques provide the verification of service performance capabilities. There may be a need for SLM to renegotiate SLAs based on these findings. Capacity Management provides support to SLM should renegotiations be necessary, by recommending potential solutions and associated cost information. Once assured that the requirements are achievable, it is the responsibility of SLM to agree the service levels and sign the SLA.

Control and implementation

All changes to service and resource capacity must follow all IT processes such as Change, Release, Configuration and Project Management to ensure that the right degree of control and coordination is in place on all changes and that any new or change components are recorded and tracked through their lifecycle.

4.3.5.2 Service Capacity Management

The main objective of the Service Capacity Management sub-process is to identify and understand the IT services, their use of resource, working patterns, peaks and troughs, and to ensure that the services meet their SLA targets, i.e. to ensure that the IT services perform as required. In this sub-process, the focus is on managing service performance, as determined by the targets contained in the agreed SLAs or SLRs.

The Service Capacity Management sub-process ensures that the services meet the agreed capacity service targets. The monitored service provides data that can identify trends from which normal service levels can be established. By regular monitoring and comparison with these levels, exception conditions can be defined, identified and reported on. Therefore Capacity Management informs SLM of any service breaches or near misses.

There will be occasions when incidents and problems are referred to Capacity Management from other processes, or it is identified that a service could fail to meet its SLA targets. On some of these occasions, the cause of the potential failure may not be resolved by Component Capacity Management. For example, when the failure is analysed it may be found that there is no lack of capacity, or no individual component is over-utilized. However, if the design or coding of an application is inefficient, then the service performance may need to be managed, as well as individual hardware or software resources. Service Capacity Management should also be monitoring service workloads and transactions to ensure that they remain within agreed limitations and thresholds.

The key to successful Service Capacity Management is to forecast issues, wherever possible, by monitoring changes in performance and monitoring the impact of changes. So this is another sub-process that has to be proactive and predictive, even pre-emptive, rather than reactive. However, there are times when it has to react to specific performance problems. From a knowledge and understanding of the performance requirements of each of the services being used, the effects of changes in the use of services can be estimated, and actions taken to ensure that the required service performance can be achieved.

4.3.5.3 Component Capacity Management

The main objective of Component Capacity Management (CCM) is to identify and understand the performance, capacity and utilization of each of the individual components within the technology used to support the IT

services, including the infrastructure, environment, data and applications. This ensures the optimum use of the current hardware and software resources in order to achieve and maintain the agreed service levels. All hardware components and many software components in the IT infrastructure have a finite capacity that, when approached or exceeded, has the potential to cause performance problems.

This sub-process is concerned with components such as processors, memory, disks, network bandwidth, network connections etc. So information on resource utilization needs to be collected on a continuous basis. Monitors should be installed on the individual hardware and software components, and then configured to collect the necessary data, which is accumulated and stored over a period of time. This is an activity generally carried out through monitoring and control within Service Operation. A direct feedback to CCM should be applied within this sub-process.

As in Service Capacity Management, the key to successful CCM is to forecast issues, wherever possible, and it therefore has to be proactive and predictive as well. However, there are times when CCM has to react to specific problems that are caused by a lack of capacity, or the inefficient use of the component. From a knowledge and understanding of the use of resource by each of the services being run, the effects of changes in the use of services can be estimated and hardware or software upgrades can be budgeted and planned. Alternatively, services can be balanced across the existing resources to make most effective use of the current resources.

4.3.5.4 The underpinning activities of Capacity Management

The activities described in this section are necessary to support the sub-processes of Capacity Management, and these activities can be done both reactively or proactively, or even pre-emptively.

The major difference between the sub-processes is in the data that is being monitored and collected, and the perspective from which it is analysed. For example, the level of utilization of individual components in the infrastructure – such as processors, disks, and network links – is of interest in Component Capacity Management, while the transaction throughput rates and response times are of interest in Service Capacity Management. For Business Capacity Management, the transaction

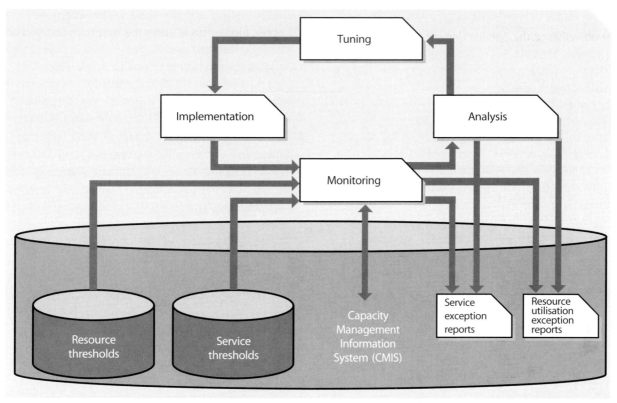

Figure 4.12 Iterative ongoing activities of Capacity Management

throughput rates for the online service need to be translated into business volumes – for example, in terms of sales invoices raised or orders taken. The biggest challenge facing Capacity Management is to understand the relationship between the demands and requirements of the business and the business workload, and to be able to translate these in terms of the impact and effect of these on the service and resource workloads and utilizations, so that appropriate thresholds can be set at each level.

Tuning and optimization activities

A number of the activities need to be carried out iteratively and form a natural cycle, as illustrated in Figure 4.12.

These activities provide the basic historical information and triggers necessary for all of the other activities and processes within Capacity Management. Monitors should be established on all the components and for each of the services. The data should be analysed using, wherever possible, expert systems to compare usage levels against thresholds. The results of the analysis should be included in reports, and recommendations made as appropriate. Some form of control mechanism may then be put in place to act on the recommendations. This may take the

form of balancing services, balancing workloads, changing concurrency levels and adding or removing resources. All of the information accumulated during these activities should be stored in the Capacity Management Information System (CMIS) and the cycle then begins again, monitoring any changes made to ensure they have had a beneficial effect and collecting more data for future actions.

Utilization monitoring

The monitors should be specific to particular operating systems, hardware configurations, applications, etc. It is important that the monitors can collect all the data required by the Capacity Management process, for a specific component or service. Typical monitored data includes:

- Processor utilization
- Memory utilization
- Per cent processor per transaction type
- IO rates (physical and buffer) and device utilization
- Queue lengths
- Disk utilization
- Transaction rates
- Response times

- Batch duration
- Database usage
- Index usage
- Hit rates
- Concurrent user numbers
- Network traffic rates.

In considering the data that needs to be included, a distinction needs to be drawn between the data collected to monitor capacity (e.g. throughput) and the data to monitor performance (e.g. response times). Data of both types is required by the Service and Component Capacity Management sub-processes. This monitoring and collection needs to incorporate all components in the service, thus monitoring the 'end-to-end' customer experience. The data should be gathered at total resource utilization level and at a more detailed profile for the load that each service places on each particular component. This needs to be carried out across the whole technology, host or server, the network, local server and client or workstation. Similarly the data needs to be collected for each service.

Part of the monitoring activity should be of thresholds and baselines or profiles of the normal operating levels. If these are exceeded, alarms should be raised and exception reports produced. These thresholds and baselines should have been determined from the analysis of previously recorded data, and can be set at both the component and service level. All thresholds should be set below the level at which the component or service is over-utilized, or below the targets in the SLAs. When the threshold is reached or threatened, there is still an opportunity to take corrective action before the SLA has been breached, or the resource has become over-utilised and there has been a period of poor performance. The monitoring and management of these events, thresholds and alarms is covered in detail in the Service Operation publication.

Often it is more difficult to get the data on the current business volumes as required by the Business Capacity Management sub-process. These statistics may need to be derived from the data available to the Service and Component Capacity Management sub-processes.

Response time monitoring

Many SLAs have user response times as one of the targets to be measured, but equally many organizations have great difficulty in supporting this requirement. User response times of IT and network services can be monitored and measured by the following:

- **Incorporating specific code within client and server applications software.** This can be used to provide complete 'end-to-end' service response times or intermediate timing points to break down the overall response into its constituent components. The figures obtained from these tools give the actual response times as perceived by the users of a service.

- **Using 'robotic scripted systems' with terminal emulation software.** These systems consist of client systems with terminal emulation software (e.g. browser or Telnet systems) and specialized scripted software for generating and measuring transactions and responses. These systems generally provide sample 'end-to-end' service response times and are useful for providing representative response times, particularly for multi-phase transactions or complex interactions. These only give sample response times, not the actual response times as perceived by the real users of the service.

- **Using distributed agent monitoring software.** Useful information on service response times can be obtained by distributing agent systems with monitoring software at different points of a network (e.g. within different countries on the internet). These systems can then be used to generate transactions from a number of locations and give periodic measurements of an internet site as perceived by international users of an internet website. However, again the times received are only indications of the response times and are not the real user response times.

- **Using specific passive monitoring systems.** Tracking a representative sample number of client systems. This method relies on the connection of specific network monitoring systems, often referred to as 'sniffers' being inserted at appropriate points within the network. These can then monitor, record and time all traffic passing a particular point within the network. Once recorded, this traffic can then be analysed to give detailed information on the service response times. Once again, however, these can only be used to give an approximation to the actual user response times, although these are often very close to the real-world situation, but this depends on the position of the monitor itself within the IT infrastructure.

In some cases, a combination of a number of systems may be used. The monitoring of response times is a complex process even if it is an in-house service running on a private network. If this is an external internet service, the process is much more complex because of the sheer number of different organizations and technologies involved.

> **Anecdote**
>
> A private company with a major website implemented a website monitoring service from an external supplier that would provide automatic alarms on the availability and responsiveness of their website. The availability and speed of the monitoring points were lower than those of the website being monitored. Therefore the figures produced by the service were of the availability and responsiveness of the monitoring service itself, rather than those of the monitored website.

> **Hints and tips**
>
> When implementing external monitoring services, ensure that the service levels and performance commitments of the monitoring service are in excess of those of the service(s) being monitored.

Analysis

The data collected from the monitoring should be analysed to identify trends from which the normal utilization and service levels, or baselines, can be established. By regular monitoring and comparison with this baseline, exception conditions in the utilization of individual components or service thresholds can be defined, and breaches or near misses in the SLAs can be reported and actioned. Also the data can be used to predict future resource usage, or to monitor actual business growth against predicted growth.

Analysis of the data may identify issues such as:

- 'Bottlenecks' or 'hot spots' within the infrastructure
- Inappropriate distribution of workload across available resources
- Inappropriate database indexing
- Inefficiencies in the application design
- Unexpected increase in workloads or transaction rates
- Inefficient scheduling or memory usage.

The use of each component and service needs to be considered over the short, medium and long term, and the minimum, maximum and average utilization for these periods recorded. Typically, the short-term pattern covers the utilization over a 24-hour period, while the medium term may cover a one- to four-week period, and the long term a year-long period. Over time, the trend in the use of the resource by the various IT services will become apparent. The usefulness of this information is further enhanced by recording any observed contributing factors to peaks or valleys in utilization – for example, if a change of business process or staffing coincides with any deviations from the normal utilization.

It is important to understand the utilization in each of these periods, so that changes in the use of any service can be related to predicted changes in the level of utilization of individual components. The ability to identify the specific hardware or software components on which a particular IT service depends is improved greatly by an accurate, up-to-date and comprehensive CMS.

When the utilization of a particular resource is considered, it is important to understand both the total level of utilization and the utilization by individual services of the resource.

> **Example**
>
> If a processor that is 75% loaded during the peak hour is being used by two different services, A and B, it is important to know how much of the total 75% is being used by each service. Assuming the system overhead on the processor is 5%, the remaining 70% load could be split evenly between the two services. If a change in either Service A or Service B is estimated to double its loading on the processor, then the processor would be overloaded.
>
> However, if service A uses 60% and Service B uses 10% of the processor, then the processor would be overloaded if service A doubled its loading on the processor. But if service B doubled its loading on the processor, then the processor would not necessarily be overloaded.

Tuning

The analysis of the monitored data may identify areas of the configuration that could be tuned to better utilize the service, system and component resources or improve the performance of the particular service.

Tuning techniques that are of assistance include:

- Balancing workloads and traffic – transactions may arrive at the host or server at a particular gateway, depending on where the transaction was initiated; balancing the ratio of initiation points to gateways can provide tuning benefits
- Balancing disk traffic – storing data on disk efficiently and strategically, e.g. striping data across many spindles may reduce data contention
- Definition of an accepted locking strategy that specifies when locks are necessary and the appropriate level, e.g. database, page, file, record and row – delaying the lock until an update is necessary may provide benefits
- Efficient use of memory – may include looking to utilize more or less memory, depending on the circumstances.

Before implementing any of the recommendations arising from the tuning techniques, it may be appropriate to consider testing the validity of the recommendation. For example, 'Can Demand Management be used to avoid the need to carry out any tuning?' or 'Can the proposed change be modelled to show its effectiveness before it is implemented?'

Implementation

The objective of this activity is to introduce to the live operation services any changes that have been identified by the monitoring, analysis and tuning activities. The implementation of any changes arising from these activities must be undertaken through a strict, formal Change Management process. The impact of system tuning changes can have major implications on the customers of the service. The impact and risk associated with these types of changes are likely to be greater than that of other different type of changes.

It is important that further monitoring takes place, so that the effects of the change can be assessed. It may be necessary to make further changes or to regress some of the original changes.

Exploitation of new technology

This involves understanding new techniques and new technology and how they can be used to support the business and innovate improvements. It may be appropriate to introduce new technology to improve the provision and support of the IT services on which the organization is dependent. This information can be gathered by studying professional literature (magazine and press articles) and by attending:

- Promotional seminars by hardware and software suppliers
- User group meetings of suppliers of potential hardware and software
- User group meetings for other IT professionals involved in Capacity Management.

Each of these provides sources of information relating to potential techniques, technology, hardware and software, which might be advantageous for IT to implement to realize business benefits. However, at all times Capacity Management should recognize that the introduction and use of this new technology must be cost-justified and deliver real benefit to the business. It is not just the new technology itself that is important, but Capacity Management should also keep aware of the advantages to be obtained from the use of new technologies, using techniques such as 'grid computing', 'virtualization' and 'on-demand computing'.

Designing resilience

Capacity Management assists with the identification and improvement of the resilience within the IT infrastructure or any subset of it, wherever it is cost-justified. In conjunction with Availability Management, Capacity Management should use techniques such as Component Failure Impact Analysis (CFIA, as described in section 4.4 on Availability Management) to identify how susceptible the current configuration is to the failure or overload of individual components and make recommendations on any cost-effective solutions.

Capacity Management should be able to identify the impact on the available resources of particular failures, and the potential for running the most important services on the remaining resources. So the provision of spare capacity can act as resilience or fail-over in failure situations.

The requirements for resilience in the IT infrastructure should always be considered at the time of the service or system design. However, for many services, the resilience of the service is only considered after it is in live operational use. Incorporating resilience into Service Design is much more effective and efficient than trying to add it at a later date, once a service has become operational.

4.3.5.5 Threshold management and control

The technical limits and constraints on the individual services and components can be used by the monitoring activities to set the thresholds at which warnings and alarms are raised and exception reports are produced. However, care must be exercised when setting thresholds, because many thresholds are dependent on the work being run on the particular component.

The management and control of service and component thresholds is fundamental to the effective delivery of services to meet their agreed service levels. It ensures that all service and component thresholds are maintained at the appropriate levels and are continuously, automatically monitored, and alerts and warnings generated when breaches occur. Whenever monitored thresholds are breached or threatened, then alarms are raised and breaches, warnings and exception reports are produced. Analysis of the situation should then be completed and remedial action taken whenever justified, ensuring that the situation does not recur. The same data items can be used to identify when SLAs are breached or likely to be breached or when component performance degrades or is likely to be degraded. By setting thresholds below or above the actual targets, action can be taken and a breach of the SLA targets avoided. Threshold monitoring should not only alarm on exceeding a threshold, but should also monitor the rate of change and predict when the threshold will be reached. For example, a disk-space monitor should monitor the rate of growth and raise an alarm when the current rate will cause the disk to be full within the next N days. If a 1GB disk has reached 90% capacity, and is growing at 100KB per day, it will be 1,000 days before it is full. If it is growing at 10MB per day, it will only be 10 days before it is full. The monitoring and management of these events and alarms is covered in detail in the Service Operations publication.

There may be occasions when optimization of infrastructure components and resources is needed to maintain or improve performance or throughput. This can often be done through Workload Management, which is a generic term to cover such actions as:

- Rescheduling a particular service or workload to run at a different time of day or day of the week, etc. (usually away from peak times to off-peak windows) – which will often mean having to make adjustments to job-scheduling software
- Moving a service or workload from one location or set of CIs to another – often to balance utilization or traffic
- Technical 'virtualization': setting up and using virtualization techniques and systems to allow the movement of processing around the infrastructure to give better performance/resilience in a dynamic fashion

- Limiting or moving demand for components or resources through Demand Management techniques, in conjunction with Financial Management (see section 4.3.5.6).

It will only be possible to manage workloads effectively if a good understanding exists of which workloads will run at what time and how much resource utilization each workload places on the IT infrastructure. Diligent monitoring and analysis of workloads, together with a comprehensive CMIS, are therefore needed on an ongoing operational basis.

4.3.5.6 Demand Management

The prime objective of Demand Management is to influence user and customer demand for IT services and manage the impact on IT resources.

This activity can be carried out as a short-term requirement because there is insufficient current capacity to support the work being run, or, as a deliberate policy of IT management, to limit the required capacity in the long term.

Short-term Demand Management may occur when there has been a partial failure of a critical resource in the IT infrastructure. For example, if there has been a failure of a processor within a multi-processor server, it may not be possible to run the full range of services. However, a limited subset of the services could be run. Capacity Management should be aware of the business priority of each of the services, know the resource requirements of each service (in this case, the amount of processor power required to run the service) and then be able to identify which services can be run while there is a limited amount of processor power available.

Long-term Demand Management may be required when it is difficult to cost-justify an expensive upgrade. For example, many processors are heavily utilized for only a few hours each day, typically 10.00-12.00 and 14.00-16.00. Within these periods, the processor may be overloaded for only one or two hours. For the hours between 18.00-08.00, these processors are only very lightly loaded and the components are under-utilized. Is it possible to justify the cost of an upgrade to provide additional capacity for only a few hours in 24 hours? Or is it possible to influence the demand and spread the requirement for resource across 24 hours, thereby delaying or avoiding altogether the need for a costly upgrade?

Demand Management needs to understand which services are utilizing the resource and to what level, and the schedule of when they must be run. Then a decision can be made on whether it will be possible to influence the use of resource and, if so, which option is appropriate.

The influence on the services that are running could be exercised by:

- **Physical constraints:** for example, it may be possible to stop some services from being available at certain times, or to limit the number of customers who can use a particular service – for example, by limiting the number of concurrent users; the constraint could be implemented on a specific resource or component – for example, by limiting the number of physical connections to a network router or switch
- **Financial constraints:** if charging for IT services is in place, reduced rates could be offered for running work at times of the day when there is currently less demand for the resource. This is known as differential charging.

4.3.5.7 Modelling and trending

A prime objective of Capacity Management is to predict the behaviour of IT services under a given volume and variety of work. Modelling is an activity that can be used to beneficial effect in any of the sub-processes of Capacity Management.

The different types of modelling range from making estimates based on experience and current resource utilization information, to pilot studies, prototypes and full-scale benchmarks. The former is a cheap and reasonable approach for day-to-day small decisions, while the latter is expensive, but may be advisable when implementing a large new project or service. With all types of modelling, similar levels of accuracy can be obtained, but all are totally dependent on the skill of the person constructing the model and the information used to create it.

Baselining

The first stage in modelling is to create a baseline model that reflects accurately the performance that is being achieved. When this baseline model has been created, predictive modelling can be done, i.e. ask the 'What if?' questions that reflect failures, planned changes to the hardware and/or the volume/variety of workloads. If the baseline model is accurate, then the accuracy of the result of the potential failures and changes can be trusted.

Effective Capacity Management, together with modelling techniques, enables Capacity Management to answer the 'What if?' questions. What if the throughput of Service A doubles? What if Service B is moved from the current server onto a new server – what will be the effect on the response times of the two services?

Trend analysis

Trend analysis can be done on the resource utilization and service performance information that has been collected by the Capacity Management process. The data can be analysed in a spreadsheet, and the graphical and trending and forecasting facilities used to show the utilization of a particular resource over a previous period of time, and how it can be expected to change in the future.

Typically, trend analysis only provides estimates of future resource utilization information. Trend analysis is less effective in producing an accurate estimate of response times, in which case either analytical or simulation modelling should be used. Trend analysis is most effective when there is a linear relationship between a small number of variables, and less effective when there are non-linear relationships between variables or when there are many variables.

Analytical modelling

Analytical models are representations of the behaviour of computer systems using mathematical techniques, e.g. multi-class network queuing theory. Typically, a model is built using a software package on a PC, by specifying within the package the components and structure of the configuration that needs to be modelled, and the utilization of the components, e.g. processor, memory and disks, by the various workloads or applications. When the model is run, the queuing theory is used to calculate the response times in the computer system. If the response times predicted by the model are sufficiently close to the response times recorded in real life, the model can be regarded as an accurate representation of the computer system.

The technique of analytical modelling requires less time and effort than simulation modelling, but typically it gives less accurate results. Also, the model must be kept up-to-date. However, if the results are within 5% accuracy for utilization, and 15–20% for online application response times, the results are usually satisfactory.

Simulation modelling

Simulation involves the modelling of discrete events, e.g. transaction arrival rates, against a given hardware configuration. This type of modelling can be very accurate in sizing new applications or predicting the effects of changes on existing applications, but can also be very time-consuming and therefore costly.

When simulating transaction arrival rates, have a number of staff enter a series of transactions from prepared scripts, or use software to input the same scripted transactions with a random arrival rate. Either of these approaches takes time and effort to prepare and run. However, it can be cost-justified for organizations with very large services and systems where the major cost and the associated performance implications assume great importance.

4.3.5.8 Application sizing

Application sizing has a finite lifespan. It is initiated at the design stage for a new service, or when there is a major change to an existing service, and is completed when the application is accepted into the live operational environment. Sizing activities should include all areas of technology related to the applications, and not just the applications themselves. This should include the infrastructure, environment and data, and will often use modelling and trending techniques.

The primary objective of application sizing is to estimate the resource requirements to support a proposed change to an existing service or the implementation of a new service, to ensure that it meets its required service levels. To achieve this, application sizing has to be an integral part of the Service Lifecycle.

During the initial requirements and design, the required service levels must be specified in an SLR. This enables the Service Design and development to employ the pertinent technologies and products to achieve a design that meets the desired levels of service. It is much easier and less expensive to achieve the required service levels if Service Design considers the required service levels at the very beginning of the Service Lifecycle, rather than at some later stage.

Other considerations in application sizing are the resilience aspects that it may be necessary to build into the design of new services. Capacity Management is able to provide advice and guidance to the Availability Management process on the resources required to provide the required level of performance and resilience.

The sizing of the application should be refined as the design and development process progresses. The use of modelling can be used within the application sizing process.

The SLRs of the planned application developments should not be considered in isolation. The resources to be utilized by the application are likely to be shared with other services, and potential threats to existing SLA targets must be recognized and managed.

When purchasing software packages from external suppliers, it is just as important to understand the resource requirements needed to support the service. Often it can be difficult to obtain this information from the suppliers

and it may vary, depending on throughput. Therefore, it is beneficial to identify similar customers of the product and to gain an understanding of the resource implications from them. It may be pertinent to benchmark, evaluate or trial the product prior to purchase.

> **Key message**
> Quality must be built in.

Some aspects of service quality can be improved after implementation (additional hardware can be added to improve performance, for example). Others – particularly aspects such as reliability and maintainability of applications software – rely on quality being 'built in', since to attempt to add it at a later stage is, in effect, redesign and redevelopment, normally at a much higher cost than the original development. Even in the hardware example quoted above, it is likely to cost more to add additional capacity after service implementation rather than as part of the original project.

4.3.6 Triggers, inputs, outputs and interfaces

There are many triggers that will initiate Capacity Management activities. These include:

- Service breaches, capacity or performance events and alerts, including threshold events
- Exception reports
- Periodic revision of current capacity and performance and the review of forecasts, reports and plans
- New and changed services requiring additional capacity
- Periodic trending and modelling
- Review and revision of business and IT plans and strategies
- Review and revision of designs and strategies
- Review and revision of SLAs, OLAs, contracts or any other agreements.

There are a number of sources of information that are relevant to the Capacity Management process. Some of these are as follows.

4.3.6.1 Inputs

- **Business information:** from the organization's business strategy, plans and financial plans, and information on their current and future requirements.
- **Service and IT information:** from Service Strategy, the IT strategy and plans and current budgets, covering all areas of technology and technology plans,

including the infrastructure, environment, data and applications, and the way in which they relate to business strategy and plans.

■ **Component performance and capacity information:** of both existing and new technology, from manufacturers and suppliers.

■ **Service performance issues:** the Incident and Problem Management processes, with incidents and problems relating to poor performance.

■ **Service information:** from the SLM process, with details of the services from the Service Portfolio and the Service Catalogue and service level targets within SLAs and SLRs, and possibly from the monitoring of SLAs, service reviews and breaches of the SLAs.

■ **Financial information:** from Financial Management, the cost of service provision, the cost of resources, components and upgrades, the resultant business benefit and the financial plans and budgets, together with the costs associated with service and component failure. Some of the costs of components and upgrades to components will be obtained from procurement, suppliers and manufacturers.

■ **Change information:** from the Change Management process, with a Change Schedule and a need to assess all changes for their impact on the capacity of the technology.

■ **Performance information:** from the Capacity Management Information System (CMIS) on the current performance of both all existing services and IT infrastructure components.

■ **CMS:** containing information on the relationships between the business, the services, the supporting services and the technology.

■ **Workload information:** from the IT Operations team, with schedules of all the work that needs to be run, and information on the dependencies between different services and information, and the interdependencies within a service.

4.3.6.2 Outputs

The outputs of Capacity Management are used within all other parts of the process, by many other processes and by other parts of the organization. Often this information is supplied as electronic reports or displays on shared areas, or as pages on intranet servers, to ensure the most up-to-date information is always used. The information provided is as follows:

■ **The Capacity Management Information System (CMIS):** holds the information needed by all sub-processes within Capacity Management. For example,

the data monitored and collected as part of Component and Service Capacity Management is used in Business Capacity Management to determine what infrastructure components or upgrades to components are needed, and when.

■ **The Capacity Plan:** used by all areas of the business and IT management. and is acted on by the IT service provider and senior management of the organization to plan the capacity of the IT infrastructure. It also provides planning input to many other areas of IT and the business. It contains information on the current usage of service and components, and plans for the development of IT capacity to meet the needs in the growth of both existing service and any agreed new services. The Capacity Plan should be actively used as a basis for decision-making. Too often, Capacity Plans are created and never referred to or used.

■ **Service performance information and reports:** used by many other processes. For example, the Capacity Management process assists Service Level Management with the reporting and reviewing of service performance and the development of new SLRs or changes to existing SLAs. It also assists the Financial Management process by identifying when money needs to be budgeted for IT infrastructure upgrades, or the purchase of new components.

■ **Workload analysis and reports:** used by IT Operations to assess and implement changes in conjunction with Capacity Management to schedule or reschedule when services or workloads are run, to ensure that the most effective and efficient use is made of the available resources.

■ **Ad hoc capacity and performance reports:** used by all areas of Capacity Management, IT and the business to analyse and resolve service and performance issues.

■ **Forecasts and predictive reports:** used by all areas to analyse, predict and forecast particular business and IT scenarios and their potential solutions.

■ **Thresholds, alerts and events.**

4.3.7 Key Performance Indicators

Some of the KPIs and metrics that can be used to judge the efficiency and effectiveness of the Capacity Management activities should include:

■ Accurate business forecasts:
  ● Production of workload forecasts on time
  ● Percentage accuracy of forecasts of business trends
  ● Timely incorporation of business plans into the Capacity Plan

- Reduction in the number of variances from the business plans and Capacity Plans.

- Knowledge of current and future technologies:
    - Increased ability to monitor performance and throughput of all services and components
    - Timely justification and implementation of new technology in line with business requirements (time, cost and functionality)
    - Reduction in the use of old technology, causing breached SLAs due to problems with support or performance.

- Ability to demonstrate cost-effectiveness:
    - Reduction in last-minute buying to address urgent performance issues
    - Reduction in the over-capacity of IT
    - Accurate forecasts of planned expenditure
    - Reduction in the business disruption caused by a lack of adequate IT capacity
    - Relative reduction in the cost of production of the Capacity Plan.

- Ability to plan and implement the appropriate IT capacity to match business needs:
    - Percentage reduction in the number of incidents due to poor performance
    - Percentage reduction in lost business due to inadequate capacity
    - All new services implemented match Service Level Requirements (SLRs)
    - Increased percentage of recommendations made by Capacity Management are acted on
    - Reduction in the number of SLA breaches due to either poor service performance or poor component performance.

4.3.8 Information Management

The aim of the CMIS is to provide the relevant capacity and performance information to produce reports and support the Capacity Management process. These reports provide valuable information to many IT and Service Management processes. These reports should include the following.

Component-based reports

For each component there should be a team of technical staff responsible for its control and management. Reports must be produced to illustrate how components are performing and how much of their maximum capacity is being used.

Service-based reports

Reports and information must also be produced to illustrate how the service and its constituent components are performing with respect to their overall service targets and constraints. These reports will provide the basis of SLM and customer service reports.

Exception reports

Reports that show management and technical staff when the capacity and performance of a particular component or service becomes unacceptable are also a required from analysis of capacity data. Thresholds can be set for any component, service or measurement within the CMIS. An example threshold may be that processor percentage utilization for a particular server has breached 70% for three consecutive hours, or that the concurrent number of logged-in users exceeds the agreed limit.

In particular, exception reports are of interest to the SLM process in determining whether the targets in SLAs have been breached. Also the Incident and Problem Management processes may be able to use the exception reports in the resolution of incidents and problems.

Predictive and forecast reports

To ensure the IT service provider continues to provide the required service levels, the Capacity Management process must predict future workloads and growth. To do this, future component and service capacity and performance must be forecast. This can be done in a variety of ways, depending on the techniques and the technology used. Changes to workloads by the development and implementation of new functionality and services must be considered alongside growth in the current functionality and services driven by business growth. A simple example of a capacity forecast is a correlation between a business driver and a component utilization, e.g. processor utilization against the number of customer accounts. This data can be correlated to find the effect that an increase in the number of customer accounts will have on the processor utilization. If the forecasts on future capacity requirements identify a requirement for increased resource, this requirement needs to be input into the Capacity Plan and included within the IT budget cycle.

Often capacity reports are consolidated together and stored on an intranet site so that anyone can access and refer to them.

4.3.8.1 Capacity Management Information System

Often capacity data is stored in technology-specific tools and databases, and full value of the data, the information and its analysis is not obtained. The true value of the data can only be obtained when the data is combined into a single set of integrated, information repositories or set of databases.

The Capacity Management Information System (CMIS) is the cornerstone of a successful Capacity Management process. Information contained within the CMIS is stored and analysed by all the sub-processes of Capacity Management because it is a repository that holds a number of different types of data, including business, service, resource or utilization and financial data, from all areas of technology.

However, the CMIS is unlikely to be a single database, and probably exists in several physical locations. Data from all areas of technology, and all components that make up the IT services, can then be combined for analysis and provision of technical and management reporting. Only when all of the information is integrated can 'end-to-end' service reports be produced. The integrity and accuracy of the data within the CMIS needs to be carefully managed. If the CMIS is not part of an overall CMS or SKMS, then links between these systems need to be implemented to ensure consistency and accuracy of the information recorded within them.

The information in the CMIS is used to form the basis of performance and Capacity Management reports and views that are to be delivered to customers, IT management and technical personnel. Also, the data is utilized to generate future capacity forecasts and allow Capacity Management to plan for future capacity requirements. Often a web interface is provided to the CMIS to provide the different access and views required outside of the Capacity Management process itself.

The full range of data types stored within the CMIS is as follows.

Business data

It is essential to have quality information on the current and future needs of the business. The future business plans of the organization need to be considered and the effects on the IT services understood. The business data is used to forecast and validate how changes in business drivers affect the capacity and performance of the IT infrastructure. Business data should include business

transactions or measurements such as the number of accounts, the number of invoices generated, the number of product lines.

Service data

To achieve a service-orientated approach to Capacity Management, service data should be stored within the CMIS. Typical service data are transaction response times, transaction rates, workload volumes, etc. In general, the SLAs and SLRs provide the service targets for which the Capacity Management process needs to record and monitor data. To ensure that the targets in the SLAs are achieved, SLM thresholds should be included, so that the monitoring activity can measure against these service thresholds and raise exception warnings and reports before service targets are breached.

Component utilization data

The CMIS also needs to record resource data consisting of utilization, threshold and limit information on all of the technological components supporting the services. Most of the IT components have limitations on the level to which they should be utilized. Beyond this level of utilization, the resource will be over-utilized and the performance of the services using the resource will be impaired. For example, the maximum recommended level of utilization on a processor could be 80%, or the utilization of a shared Ethernet LAN segment should not exceed 40%.

Also, components have various physical limitations beyond which greater connectivity or use is impossible. For example, the maximum number of connections through an application or a network gateway is 100, or a particular type of disk has a physical capacity of 15Gb. The CMIS should therefore contain, for each component and the maximum performance and capacity limits, current and past utilization rates and the associated component thresholds. Over time this can require vast amounts of data to be accumulated, so there need to be good techniques for analysing, aggregating and archiving this data.

Financial data

The Capacity Management process requires financial data. For evaluating alternative upgrade options, when proposing various scenarios in the Capacity Plan, the financial cost of the upgrades to the components of the IT infrastructure, together with information about the current IT hardware budget, must be known and included in the considerations. Most of this data may be available from the Financial Management for IT services process, but

Capacity Management needs to consider this information when managing the future business requirements.

4.3.9 Challenges, Critical Success Factors and risks

One of the major challenges facing Capacity Management is persuading the business to provide information on its strategic business plans, to enable the IT service provider organization to provide effective Business Continuity Management (BCM). This is particularly true in outsourced situations where there may be commercial or confidential reasons why this data cannot be shared. Even if the data on the strategic business plan is available, there may be issues with regard to the quality or accuracy of the data contained within the business plans with regard to BCM.

Another challenge is the combination of all of the CCM data into an integrated set of information that can be analysed in a consistent manner to provide details of the usage of all components of the services. This is particularly challenging when the information from the different technologies is provided by different tools in differing formats. Often the quality of component information on the performance of the technology is variable in both its quality and accuracy.

The amounts of information produced by BCM, and especially SCM and CCM, are huge and the analysis of this information is difficult to achieve. The people and the processes need to focus on the key resources and their usage, whilst not ignoring other areas. In order to do this, appropriate thresholds must be used, and reliance placed on the tools and technology to automatically manage the technology and provide warnings and alerts when things deviate significantly from the 'norm'.

The main CSFs for the Capacity Management process are:

- Accurate business forecasts
- Knowledge of current and future technologies
- Ability to demonstrate cost-effectiveness
- Ability to plan and implement the appropriate IT capacity to match business need.

Some of the major risks associated with Capacity Management include:

- A lack of commitment from the business to the Capacity Management process
- A lack of appropriate information from the business on future plans and strategies

- A lack of senior management commitment or a lack of resources and/or budget for the Capacity Management process
- SCM and CCM performed in isolation because BCM is difficult, or there is a lack of appropriate and accurate business information
- The processes become too bureaucratic or manually intensive
- The processes focus too much on the technology (CCM) and not enough on the services (SCM) and the business (BCM)
- The reports and information provided are too bulky or too technical and do not give the information required or appropriate to the customers and the business.

4.4 AVAILABILITY MANAGEMENT

4.4.1 Purpose/goal/objective

The goal of the Availability Management process is to ensure that the level of service availability delivered in all services is matched to or exceeds the current and future agreed needs of the business, in a cost-effective manner.

The purpose of Availability Management is to provide a point of focus and management for all availability-related issues, relating to both services and resources, ensuring that availability targets in all areas are measured and achieved.

The objectives of Availability Management are to:

- Produce and maintain an appropriate and up-to-date Availability Plan that reflects the current and future needs of the business
- Provide advice and guidance to all other areas of the business and IT on all availability-related issues
- Ensure that service availability achievements meet or exceed all their agreed targets, by managing services and resources-related availability performance
- Assist with the diagnosis and resolution of availability-related incidents and problems
- Assess the impact of all changes on the Availability Plan and the performance and capacity of all services and resources
- Ensure that proactive measures to improve the availability of services are implemented wherever it is cost-justifiable to do so.

Availability Management should ensure the agreed level of availability is provided. The measurement and monitoring of IT availability is a key activity to ensure availability levels are being met consistently. Availability Management should look to continually optimize and proactively improve the availability of the IT infrastructure, the services and the supporting organization, in order to provide cost-effective availability improvements that can deliver business and customer benefits.

4.4.2 Scope

The scope of the Availability Management process covers the design, implementation, measurement, management and improvement of IT service and component availability. Availability Management needs to understand the service and component availability requirements from the business perspective in terms of the:

- Current business processes, their operation and requirements
- Future business plans and requirements
- Service targets and the current IT service operation and delivery
- IT infrastructure, data, applications and environment and their performance
- Business impacts and priorities in relation to the services and their usage.

Understanding all of this will enable Availability Management to ensure that all the services and components are designed and delivered to meet their targets in terms of agreed business needs. The Availability Management process:

- Should be applied to all operational services and technology, particularly those covered by SLAs. It can also be applied to those IT services deemed to be business critical regardless of whether formal SLAs exist
- Should be applied to all new IT services and for existing services where Service Level Requirements (SLRs) or Service Level Agreements (SLAs) have been established
- Should be applied to all supporting services and the partners and suppliers (both internal and external) that form the IT support organization as a precursor to the creation of formal agreements
- Considers all aspects of the IT services and components and supporting organizations that may impact availability, including training, skills, process effectiveness, procedures and tools.

The Availability Management process does not include Business Continuity Management and the resumption of business processing after a major disaster. The support of BCM is included within IT Service Continuity Management (ITSCM). However, Availability Management does provide key inputs to ITSCM, and the two processes have a close relationship, particularly in the assessment and management of risks and in the implementation of risk reduction and resilience measures.

The Availability Management process should include:

- Monitoring of all aspects of availability, reliability and maintainability of IT services and the supporting components, with appropriate events, alarms and escalation, with automated scripts for recovery
- Maintenance of a set of methods, techniques and calculations for all availability measurements, metrics and reporting
- Assistance with risk assessment and management activities
- Collection of measurements, analysis and production of regular and ad hoc reports on service and component availability
- Understanding the agreed current and future demands of the business for IT services and their availability
- Influencing the design of services and components to align with business needs
- Producing an Availability Plan that enables the service provider to continue to provide and improve services in line with availability targets defined in Service Level Agreements (SLAs), and to plan and forecast future availability levels required, as defined in Service Level Requirements (SLRs)
- Maintaining a schedule of tests for all resilient and fail-over components and mechanisms
- Assistance with the identification and resolution of any incidents and problems associated with service or component unavailability
- Proactive improvement of service or component availability wherever it is cost-justifiable and meets the needs of the business.

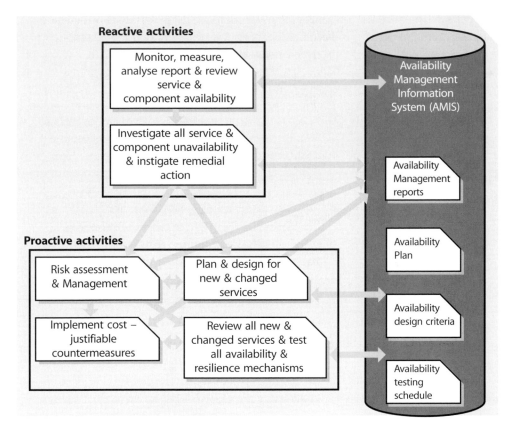

Figure 4.13 The Availability Management process

4.4.3 Value to the business

The Availability Management process ensures that the availability of systems and services matches the evolving agreed needs of the business. The role of IT within the business is now pivotal. The availability and reliability of IT services can directly influence customer satisfaction and the reputation of the business. This is why Availability Management is essential in ensuring IT delivers the right levels of service availability required by the business to satisfy its business objectives and deliver the quality of service demanded by its customers. In today's competitive marketplace, customer satisfaction with service(s) provided is paramount. Customer loyalty can no longer be relied on, and dissatisfaction with the availability and reliability of IT service can be a key factor in customers taking their business to a competitor.

The Availability Management process and planning, just like Capacity Management, must be involved in all stages of the Service Lifecycle, from Strategy and Design, through Transition and Operation to Improvement. The appropriate availability and resilience should be designed into services and components from the initial design stages. This will ensure not only that the availability of any new or changed service meets its expected targets, but also that

all existing services and components continue to meet all of their targets. This is the basis of stable service provision.

4.4.4 Policies/principles/basic concepts

The Availability Management process is continually trying to ensure that all operational services meet their agreed availability targets, and that new or changed services are designed appropriately to meet their intended targets, without compromising the performance of existing services. In order to achieve this, Availability Management should perform the reactive and proactive activities illustrated in Figure 4.13.

The reactive activities of Availability Management consist of monitoring, measuring, analysing, reporting and reviewing all aspects of component and service availability. This is to ensure that all agreed service targets are measured and achieved. Wherever deviations or breaches are detected, these are investigated and remedial action instigated. Most of these activities are conducted within the Operations stage of the lifecycle and are linked into the monitoring and control activities, Event and Incident Management processes. (See the Service Operation publication.)

The proactive activities consist of producing recommendations, plans and documents on design guidelines and criteria for new and changed services, and the continual improvement of service and reduction of risk in existing services wherever it can be cost-justified. These are key aspects to be considered within Service Design activities.

An effective Availability Management process, consisting of both the reactive and proactive activities, can 'make a big difference' and will be recognized as such by the business, if the deployment of Availability Management within an IT organization has a strong emphasis on the needs of the business and customers. To reinforce this emphasis, there are several guiding principles that should underpin the Availability Management process and its focus:

- Service availability is at the core of customer satisfaction and business success: there is a direct correlation in most organizations between the service availability and customer and user satisfaction, where poor service performance is defined as being unavailable.
- Recognizing that when services fail, it is still possible to achieve business, customer and user satisfaction and recognition: the way a service provider reacts in a failure situation has a major influence on customer and user perception and expectation.
- Improving availability can only begin after understanding how the IT services support the operation of the business.
- Service availability is only as good as the weakest link on the chain: it can be greatly increased by the elimination of Single Points of Failure (SPoFs) or an unreliable or weak component.
- Availability is not just a reactive process. The more proactive the process, the better service availability will be. Availability should not purely react to service and component failure. The more events and failures are predicted, pre-empted and prevented, the higher the level of service availability.
- It is cheaper to design the right level of service availability into a service from the start rather than try and 'bolt it on' subsequently. Adding resilience into a service or component is invariably more expensive than designing it in from the start. Also, once a service gets a bad name for unreliability, it becomes very difficult to change the image. Resilience is also a key consideration of ITSCM, and this should be considered at the same time.

The scope of Availability Management covers the design, implementation, measurement and management of IT service and infrastructure availability. This is reflected in the process description shown in Figure 4.13 and described in the following paragraphs.

The Availability Management process has two key elements:

- Reactive activities: the reactive aspect of Availability Management involves the monitoring, measuring, analysis and management of all events, incidents and problems involving unavailability. These activities are principally involved within operational roles.
- Proactive activities: the proactive activities of Availability Management involve the proactive planning, design and improvement of availability. These activities are principally involved within design and planning roles.

Availability Management is completed at two inter-connected levels:

- **Service availability:** involves all aspects of service availability and unavailability and the impact of component availability, or the potential impact of component unavailability on service availability
- **Component availability:** involves all aspects of component availability and unavailability.

Availability Management relies on the monitoring, measurement, analysis and reporting of the following aspects:

Availability: the ability of a service, component or CI to perform its agreed function when required. It is often measured and reported as a percentage:

$$\text{Availability (\%)} = \frac{\text{(Agreed Service Time (AST) – downtime)}}{\text{Agreed Service Time (AST)}} \times 100\,\%$$

Note: Downtime should only be included in the above calculation when it occurs within the Agreed Service Time (AST). However, total downtime should also be recorded and reported.

Reliability: a measure of how long a service, component or CI can perform its agreed function without interruption. The reliability of the service can be improved by increasing the reliability of individual components or by increasing the resilience of the service to individual component failure (i.e. increasing the component redundancy, e.g. by using load-balancing techniques). It is often measured and reported as Mean Time Between Service Incidents (MTBSI) or Mean Time Between Failures (MTBF):

$$\text{Reliability (MTBSI in hours)} = \frac{\textbf{Available time in hours}}{\textbf{Number of breaks}}$$

$$\text{Reliability (MTBF in hours)} = \frac{\textbf{Available time in hours} - \textbf{Total downtime in hours}}{\textbf{Number of breaks}}$$

Maintainability: a measure of how quickly and effectively a service, component or CI can be restored to normal working after a failure. It is measured and reported as Mean Time to Restore Service (MTRS) and should be calculated using the following formula:

$$\text{Maintainability (MTRS in hours)} = \frac{\textbf{Total downtime in hours}}{\textbf{Number of service breaks}}$$

MTRS should be used to avoid the ambiguity of the more common industry term Mean Time To Repair (MTTR), which in some definitions includes only repair time, but in others includes recovery time. The downtime in MTRS covers all the contributory factors that make the service, component or CI unavailable:

- Time to record
- Time to respond
- Time to resolve
- Time to physically repair or replace
- Time to recover.

Example: A situation where a 24 x 7 service has been running for a period of 5,020 hours with only two breaks, one of six hours and one of 14 hours, would give the following figures:

Availability = (5,020-(6+14)) / 5,020 x 100 = 99.60%

Reliability (MTBSI) = 5,020 / 2 = 2,510 hours

Reliability (MTBF) = 5,020-(6+14) / 2 = 2,500 hours

Maintainability (MTRS) = (6+14) / 2 = 10 hours

Serviceability: the ability of a third-party supplier to meet the terms of their contract. Often this contract will include agreed levels of availability, reliability and/or maintainability for a supporting service or component.

These aspects and their inter-relationships are illustrated in Figure 4.14.

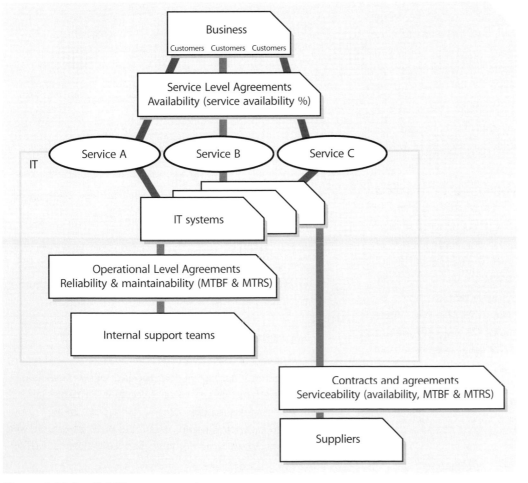

Figure 4.14 Availability terms and measurements

Although the principal service target contained within SLAs for the customers and business is availability, as illustrated in Figure 4.14, some customers also require reliability and maintainability targets to be included as well. Where these are included they should relate to service reliability and maintainability targets, whereas the reliability and maintainability targets contained in OLAs and contracts relate to component and supporting service targets and can often include availability targets relating to the relevant components or supporting services.

The term Vital Business Function (VBF) is used to reflect the business critical elements of the business process supported by an IT service. An IT service may support a number of business functions that are less critical. For example, an automated teller machine (ATM) or cash dispenser service VBF would be the dispensing of cash. However, the ability to obtain a statement from an ATM may not be considered as vital. This distinction is important and should influence availability design and associated costs. The more vital the business function generally, the greater the level of resilience and availability that needs to be incorporated into the design required in the supporting IT services. For all services, whether VBFs or not, the availability requirements should be determined by the business and not by IT. The initial availability targets are often set at too high a level, and this leads to either over-priced services or an iterative discussion between the service provider and the business to agree an appropriate compromise between the service availability and the cost of the service and its supporting technology.

Certain VBFs may need special designs, which are now being used as a matter of course within Service Design plans, incorporating:

- **High availability:** a characteristic of the IT service that minimizes or masks the effects of IT component failure to the users of a service.
- **Fault tolerance:** the ability of an IT service, component or CI to continue to operate correctly after failure of a component part.
- **Continuous operation:** an approach or design to eliminate planned downtime of an IT service. Note that individual components or CIs may be down even though the IT service remains available.
- **Continuous availability:** an approach or design to achieve 100% availability. A continuously Available IT service has no planned or unplanned downtime.

Industry view

Many suppliers commit to high availability or continuous availability solutions only if stringent environmental standards and resilient processes are used. They often agree to such contracts only after a site survey has been completed and additional, sometimes costly, improvements have been made.

Availability Management commences as soon as the availability requirements for an IT service are clear enough to be articulated. It is an ongoing process, finishing only when the IT service is decommissioned or retired. The key activities of the Availability Management process are:

- Determining the availability requirements from the business for a new or enhanced IT service and formulating the availability and recovery design criteria for the supporting IT components
- Determining the VBFs, in conjunction with the business and ITSCM
- Determining the impact arising from IT service and component failure in conjunction with ITSCM and, where appropriate, reviewing the availability design criteria to provide additional resilience to prevent or minimize impact to the business
- Defining the targets for availability, reliability and maintainability for the IT infrastructure components that underpin the IT service to enable these to be documented and agreed within SLAs, OLAs and contracts
- Establishing measures and reporting of availability, reliability and maintainability that reflect the business, user and IT support organization perspectives
- Monitoring and trend analysis of the availability, reliability and maintainability of IT components
- Reviewing IT service and component availability and identifying unacceptable levels
- Investigating the underlying reasons for unacceptable availability
- Producing and maintaining an Availability Plan that prioritizes and plans IT availability improvements.

4.4.5 Process activities, methods and techniques

The Availability Management process depends heavily on the measurement of service and component achievements with regard to availability.

'What to measure and how to report it' inevitably depends on which activity is being supported, who the recipients are and how the information is to be utilized. It is important to recognize the differing perspectives of availability to ensure measurement and reporting satisfies these varied needs:

■ The business perspective considers IT service availability in terms of its contribution or impact on the VBFs that drive the business operation.

■ The user perspective considers IT service availability as a combination of three factors, namely the frequency, the duration and the scope of impact, i.e. all users, some users, all business functions or certain business functions – the user also considers IT service availability in terms of response times. For many performance-centric applications, poor response times are considered equal in impact to failures of technology.

■ The IT service provider perspective considers IT service and component availability with regard to availability, reliability and maintainability.

In order to satisfy the differing perspectives of availability, Availability Management needs to consider the spectrum of measures needed to report the 'same' level of availability in different ways. Measurements need to be meaningful and add value if availability measurement and reporting are ultimately to deliver benefit to the IT and business organizations. This is influenced strongly by the combination of 'what you measure' and 'how you report it'.

4.4.5.1 The reactive activities of Availability Management

Monitor, measure, analyse and report service and component availability

A key output from the Availability Management process is the measurement and reporting of IT availability. Availability measures should be incorporated into SLAs, OLAs and any underpinning contracts. These should be reviewed regularly at Service Level review meetings. Measurement and reporting provide the basis for:

■ Monitoring the actual availability delivered versus agreed targets

■ Establishing measures of availability and agreeing availability targets with the business

■ Identifying unacceptable levels of availability that impact the business and users

■ Reviewing availability with the IT support organization

■ Continual improvement activities to optimize availability.

The IT service provider organizations have, for many years, measured and reported on their perspective of availability. Traditionally these measures have concentrated on component availability and have been somewhat divorced from the business and user views. Typically these traditional measures are based on a combination of an availability percentage (%), time lost and the frequency of failure. Some examples of these traditional measures are as follows:

■ **Per cent available** – the truly 'traditional' measure that represents availability as a percentage and, as such, much more useful as a component availability measure than a service availability measure. It is typically used to track and report achievement against a service level target. It tends to emphasize the 'big number' such that if the service level target was 98.5% and the achievement was 98.3%, then it does not seem that bad. This can encourage a complacent behaviour within the IT support organization.

■ **Per cent unavailable** – the inverse of the above. This representation, however, has the benefit of focusing on non-availability. Based on the above example, if the target for non-availability is 1.5% and the achievement was 1.7%, then this is a much larger relative difference. This method of reporting is more likely to create awareness of the shortfall in delivering the level of availability required.

■ **Duration** – achieved by converting the percentage unavailable into hours and minutes. This provides a more 'human' measure that people can relate to. If the weekly downtime target is two hours, but one week the actual downtime was four hours; this would represent a trend leading to an additional four days of non-availability to the business over a full year. This type of measure and reporting is more likely to encourage focus on service improvement.

■ **Frequency of failure** – used to record the number of interruptions to the IT service. It helps provide a good indication of reliability from a user perspective. It is best used in combination with 'duration' to take a balanced view of the level of service interruptions and the duration of time lost to the business.

■ **Impact of failure** – this is the true measure of service unavailability. It depends on mature incident recording where the inability of users to perform their business tasks is the most important piece of information captured. All other measures suffer from a potential to mask the real effects of service failure and are often converted to a financial impact.

The business may have, for many years, accepted that the IT availability that they experience is represented in terms of component availability rather than overall service or business availability. However, this is no longer being viewed as acceptable and the business is keen to better represent availability in measure(s) that demonstrate the positive and negative consequences of IT availability on their business and users.

Key messages

The most important availability measurements are those that reflect and measure availability from the business and user perspective.

Availability Management needs to consider availability from both a business/IT service provider perspective and from an IT component perspective. These are entirely different aspects, and while the underlying concept is similar, the measurement, focus and impact are entirely different.

The sole purpose of producing these availability measurements and reports, including those from the business perspective, is to improve the quality and availability of IT service provided to the business and users. All measures, reports and activities should reflect this purpose.

Availability, when measured and reported to reflect the experience of the user, provides a more representative view on overall IT service quality. The user view of availability is influenced by three factors:

- Frequency of downtime
- Duration of downtime
- Scope of impact.

Measurements and reporting of user availability should therefore embrace these factors. The methodology employed to reflect user availability could consider two approaches:

- **Impact by user minutes lost:** this is to base calculations on the duration of downtime multiplied by the number of users impacted. This can be the basis to report availability as lost user productivity, or to calculate the availability percentage from a user perspective, and can also include the costs of recovery for lost productivity (e.g. increased overtime payments).

- **Impact by business transaction:** this is to base calculations on the number of business transactions that could not be processed during the period of downtime. This provides a better indication of business impact reflecting differing transaction processing profiles across the time of day, week etc. In many instances it may be the case that the user impact correlates to a VBF, e.g. if the user takes customer purchase orders and a VBF is customer sales. This single measure is the basis to reflect impact to the business operation and user.

The method employed should be influenced by the nature of the business operation. A business operation supporting data entry activity is well suited to reporting that reflects user productivity loss. Business operations that are more customer-facing, e.g. ATM services, benefit from reporting transaction impact. It should also be noted that not all business impact is user-related. With increasing automation and electronic processing, the ability to process automated transactions or meet market cut-off times can also have a large financial impact that may be greater than the ability of users to work.

The IT support organization needs to have a keen awareness of the user experience of availability. However, the real benefits come from aggregating the user view into the overall business view. A guiding principle of the Availability Management process is that **'Improving availability can only begin when the way technology supports the business is understood'.** Therefore Availability Management isn't just about understanding the availability of each IT component, but is all about understanding the impact of component failure on service and user availability. From the business perspective, an IT service can only be considered available when the business is able to perform all vital business functions required to drive the business operation. For the IT service to be available, it therefore relies on all components on which the service depends being available, i.e. systems, key components, network, data and applications.

The traditional IT approach would be to measure individually the availability of each of these components. However, the true measure of availability has to be based on the positive and negative impacts on the VBFs on which the business operation is dependent. This approach ensures that SLAs and IT availability reporting are based on measures that are understood by both the business and IT. By measuring the VBFs that rely on IT services, measurement and reporting becomes business-driven, with the impact of failure reflecting the consequences to the business. It is also important that the availability of the services is defined and agreed with the business and reflected within SLAs. This definition of availability should include:

- What is the minimum available level of functionality of the service?
- At what level of service response is the service considered unavailable?
- Where will this level of functionality and response be measured?
- What are the relative weightings for partial service unavailability?
- If one location or office is impacted, is the whole service considered unavailable, or is this considered to be 'partial unavailability'? This needs to be agreed with the customers.

Reporting and analysis tools are required for the manipulation of data stored in the various databases utilized by Availability Management. These tools can either be platform- or PC-based and are often a combination of the two. This will be influenced by the database repository technologies selected and the complexity of data processing and reporting required. Availability Management, once implemented and deployed, will be required to produce regular reports on an agreed basis, e.g. monthly availability reports, Availability Plan, Service Failure Analysis (SFA) status reports, etc. The activities involved within these reporting activities can require much manual effort and the only solution is to automate as much of the report generation activity as possible. For reporting purposes, organizational reporting standards should be used wherever possible. If these don't exist, IT standards should be developed so that IT reports can be developed using standard tools and techniques. This means that the integration and consolidation of reports will subsequently be much easier to achieve.

Unavailability analysis

All events and incidents causing unavailability of services and components should be investigated, with remedial actions being implemented within either the Availability Plan or the overall SIP. Trends should be produced from this analysis to direct and focus activities such as Service Failure Analysis (SFA) to those areas causing the most impact or disruption to the business and the users.

The overall costs of an IT service are influenced by the levels of availability required and the investments required in technology and services provided by the IT support organization to meet this requirement. Availability certainly does not come for free. However, it is important to reflect that the unavailability of IT also has a cost, therefore

unavailability isn't free either. For highly critical business processes and VBFs, it is necessary to consider not only the cost of providing the service, but also the costs that are incurred from failure. The optimum balance to strike is the cost of the availability solution weighed against the costs of unavailability.

Before any SLR is accepted, and ultimately the SLR or SLA is negotiated and agreed between the business and the IT organization, it is essential that the availability requirements of the business are analysed to assess if/how the IT service can deliver the required levels of availability. This applies not only to new IT services that are being introduced, but also to any requested changes to the availability requirements of existing IT services.

The cost of an IT failure could simply be expressed as the number of business or IT transactions impacted, either as an actual figure (derived from instrumentation) or based on an estimation. When measured against the VBFs that support the business operation, this can provide an obvious indication of the consequence of failure. The advantage of this approach is the relative ease of obtaining the impact data and the lack of any complex calculations. It also becomes a 'value' that is understood by both the business and IT organization. This can be the stimulus for identifying improvement opportunities and can become a key metric in monitoring the availability of IT services.

The major disadvantage of this approach is that it offers no obvious monetary value that would be needed to justify any significant financial investment decisions for improving availability. Where significant financial investment decisions are required, it is better to express the cost of failure arising from service, system, application or function loss to the business as a monetary 'value'.

The monetary value can be calculated as a combination of the tangible costs associated with failure, but can also include a number of intangible costs. The monetary value should also reflect the cost impact to the whole organization, i.e. the business and IT organization.

Tangible costs can include:

- Lost user productivity
- Lost IT staff productivity
- Lost revenue
- Overtime payments
- Wasted goods and material
- Imposed fines or penalty payments.

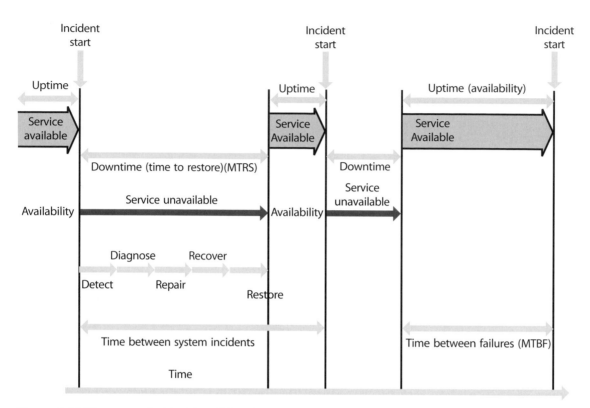

Figure 4.15 The expanded incident lifecycle

These costs are often well understood by the finance area of the business and IT organization, and in relative terms are easier to obtain and aggregate than the intangible costs associated with an IT failure.

Intangible costs can include:

- Loss of customers
- Loss of customer goodwill (customer dissatisfaction)
- Loss of business opportunity (to sell, gain new customers or revenue, etc.)
- Damage to business reputation
- Loss of confidence in IT service provider
- Damage to staff morale.

It is important not simply to dismiss the intangible costs (and the potential consequences) on the grounds that they may be difficult to measure. The overall unavailability of service, the total tangible cost and the total intangible costs arising from service unavailability are all key metrics in the measurement of the effectiveness of the Availability Management process.

The expanded incident lifecycle

A guiding principle of Availability Management is to recognize that it is still possible to gain customer satisfaction even when things go wrong. One approach to help achieve this requires Availability Management to ensure that the duration of any incident is minimized to

enable normal business operations to resume as quickly as possible. An aim of Availability Management is to ensure the duration and impact from incidents impacting IT services are minimized, to enable business operations to resume as quickly as is possible. The analysis of the 'expanded incident lifecycle' enables the total IT service downtime for any given incident to be broken down and mapped against the major stages through which all incidents progress (the lifecycle). Availability Management should work closely with Incident Management and Problem Management in the analysis of all incidents causing unavailability.

A good technique to help with the technical analysis of incidents affecting the availability of components and IT services is to take an incident 'lifecycle' view. Every incident passes through several major stages. The time elapsed in these stages may vary considerably. For Availability Management purposes, the standard incident 'lifecycle', as described within Incident Management, has been expanded to provide additional help and guidance particularly in the area of 'designing for recovery'. Figure 4.15 illustrates the expanded incident lifecycle.

From the above it can be seen that an incident can be broken down into individual stages within a lifecycle that can be timed and measured. This lifecycle view provides an important framework in determining, amongst others, systems management requirements for event and incident detection, diagnostic data capture requirements and tools for diagnosis, recovery plans to aid speedy recovery and how to verify that IT service has been restored. The individual stages of the lifecycle are considered in more detail as follows.

- **Incident detection:** the time at which the IT service provider organization is made aware of an incident. Systems management tools positively influence the ability to detect events and incidents and therefore to improve levels of availability that can be delivered. Implementation and exploitation should have a strong focus on achieving high availability and enhanced recovery objectives. In the context of recovery, such tools should be exploited to provide automated failure detection, assist failure diagnosis and support automated error recovery, with scripted responses. Tools are very important in reducing all stages of the incident lifecycle, but principally the detection of events and incidents. Ideally the event is automatically detected and resolved, before the users have noticed it or have been impacted in any way.

- **Incident diagnosis:** the time at which diagnosis to determine the underlying cause has been completed. When IT components fail, it is important that the required level of diagnostics is captured, to enable problem determination to identify the root cause and resolve the issue. The use and capability of diagnostic tools and skills is critical to the speedy resolution of service issues. For certain failures, the capture of diagnostics may extend service downtime. However, the non-capture of the appropriate diagnostics creates and exposes the service to repeat failures. Where the time required to take diagnostics is considered excessive, or varies from the target, a review should be instigated to identify if techniques and/or procedures can be streamlined to reduce the time required. Equally the scope of the diagnostic data available for capture can be assessed to ensure only the diagnostic data considered essential is taken. The additional downtime required to capture diagnostics should be included in the recovery metrics documented for each IT component.

- **Incident repair:** the time at which the failure has been repaired/fixed. Repair times for incidents should be continuously monitored and compared against the targets agreed within OLAs, underpinning contracts and other agreements. This is particularly important with respect to externally provided services and supplier performance. Wherever breaches are observed,

techniques should be used to reduce or remove the breaches from similar incidents in the future.

- **Incident recovery:** the time at which component recovery has been completed. The backup and recovery requirements for the components underpinning a new IT service should be identified as early as possible within the design cycle. These requirements should cover hardware, software and data and recovery targets. The outcome from this activity should be a documented set of recovery requirements that enables the development of appropriate recovery plans. To anticipate and prepare for performing recovery such that reinstatement of service is effective and efficient requires the development and testing of appropriate recovery plans based on the documented recovery requirements. Wherever possible, the operational activities within the recovery plan should be automated. The testing of the recovery plans also delivers approximate timings for recovery. These recovery metrics can be used to support the communication of estimated recovery of service and validate or enhance the Component Failure Impact Analysis documentation. Availability Management must continuously seek and promote faster methods of recovery for all potential Incidents. This can be achieved via a range of methods, including automated failure detection, automated recovery, more stringent escalation procedures, exploitation of new and faster recovery tools and techniques. Availability requirements should also contribute to determining what spare parts are kept within the Definitive Spares to facilitate quick and effective repairs, as described within the Service Transition publication.

- **Incident restoration:** the time at which normal business service is resumed. An incident can only be considered 'closed' once service has been restored and normal business operation has resumed. It is important that the restored IT service is verified as working correctly as soon as service restoration is completed and before any technical staff involved in the incident are stood down. In the majority of cases, this is simply a case of getting confirmation from the affected users. However, the users for some services may be customers of the business, i.e. ATM services, internet-based services. For these types of services, it is recommended that IT service verification procedures are developed to enable the IT service provider organization to verify that a restored IT service is now working as expected. These could simply be visual checks of transaction throughput or user simulation scripts that validate the end-to-end service.

Each stage, and the associated time taken, influences the total downtime perceived by the user. By taking this approach it is possible to see where time is being 'lost' for the duration of an incident. For example, the service was unavailable to the business for 60 minutes, yet it only took five minutes to apply a fix – where did the other 55 minutes go?

Using this approach identifies possible areas of inefficiency that combine to make the loss of service experienced by the business greater than it need be. These could cover areas such as poor automation (alerts, automated recovery etc.), poor diagnostic tools and scripts, unclear escalation procedures (which delay the escalation to the appropriate technical support group or supplier), or lack of comprehensive operational documentation. Availability Management needs to work in close association with Incident and Problem Management to ensure repeat occurrences are eliminated. It is recommended that these measures are established and captured for all availability incidents. This provides Availability Management with metrics for both specific incidents and trending information. This information can be used as input to SFA assignments, SIP activities and regular Availability Management reporting and to provide an impetus for continual improvement activity to pursue cost-effective improvements. It can also enable targets to be set for specific stages of the incident lifecycle. While accepting that each incident may have a wide range of technical complexity, the targets can be used to reflect the consistency of how the IT service provider organization responds to incidents.

An output from the Availability Management process is the real-time monitoring requirements for IT services and components. To achieve the levels of availability required and/or ensure the rapid restoration of service following an IT failure requires investment and exploitation of a systems management toolset. Systems management tools are an essential building block for IT services that require a high level of availability and can provide an invaluable role in reducing the amount of downtime incurred. Availability Management requirements cover the detection and alerting of IT service and component exceptions, automated escalation and notification of IT failures and the automated recovery and restoration of components from known IT failure situations. This makes it possible to identify where 'time is being lost' and provides the basis for the identification of factors that can improve recovery and restoration times. These activities are performed on a regular basis within Service Operation.

Service Failure Analysis

Service Failure Analysis (SFA) is a technique designed to provide a structured approach to identifying the underlying causes of service interruptions to the user. SFA utilizes a range of data sources to assess where and why shortfalls in availability are occurring. SFA enables a holistic view to be taken to drive not just technology improvements, but also improvements to the IT support organization, processes, procedures and tools. SFA is run as an assignment or project, and may utilize other Availability Management methods and techniques to formulate the recommendations for improvement. The detailed analysis of service interruptions can identify opportunities to enhance levels of availability. SFA is a structured technique to identify improvement opportunities in end-to-end service availability that can deliver benefits to the user. Many of the activities involved in SFA are closely aligned with those of Problem Management, and in a number of organizations these activities are performed jointly by Problem and Availability Management.

The high-level objectives of SFA are:

- To improve the overall availability of IT services by producing a set of improvements for implementation or input to the Availability Plan
- To identify the underlying causes of service interruption to users
- To assess the effectiveness of the IT support organization and key processes
- To produce reports detailing the major findings and recommendations
- That availability improvements derived from SFA-driven activities are measured.

SFA initiatives should use input from all areas and all processes including, most importantly, the business and users. Each SFA assignment should have a recognized sponsor(s) (ideally, joint sponsorship from the IT and business) and involve resources from many technical and process areas. The use of the SFA approach:

- Provides the ability to deliver enhanced levels of availability without major cost
- Provides the business with visible commitment from the IT support organization
- Develops in-house skills and competencies to avoid expensive consultancy assignments related to availability improvement
- Encourages cross-functional team working and breaks barriers between teams, and is an enabler to lateral

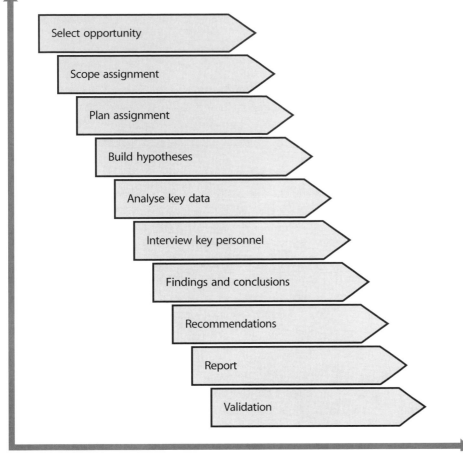

Figure 4.16 The structured approach to Service Failure Analysis (SFA)

thinking, challenging traditional thoughts and providing innovative, and often inexpensive, solutions

■ Provides a programme of improvement opportunities that can make a real difference to service quality and user perception

■ Provides opportunities that are focused on delivering benefit to the user

■ Provides an independent 'health check' of IT Service Management processes and is the stimulus for process improvements.

To maximize both the time of individuals allocated to the SFA assignment and the quality of the delivered report, a structured approach is required. This structure is illustrated in Figure 4.16. This approach is similar to many consultancy models utilized within the industry, and in many ways Availability Management can be considered as providing via SFA a form of internal consultancy.

The above high-level structure is described briefly as follows.

■ **Select opportunity:** prior to scheduling an SFA assignment, there needs to be agreement as to which IT service or technology is to be selected. It is

recommended that an agreed number of assignments are scheduled per year within the Availability Plan and, if possible, the IT services are selected in advance as part of the proactive approach to Availability Management. Before commencing with the SFA, it is important that the assignment has a recognized sponsor from within the IT organization and/or the business and that they are involved and regularly updated with progress of the SFA activity. This ensures organizational visibility to the SFA and ensures recommendations are endorsed at a senior level within the organization.

■ **Scope assignment:** this is to state explicitly what areas are and are not covered within the assignment. This is normally documented in Terms of Reference issued prior to the assignment.

■ **Plan assignment:** the SFA assignment needs to be planned a number of weeks in advance of the assignment commencing, with an agreed project plan and a committed set of resources. The project should look at identifying improvement opportunities that benefit the user. It is therefore important that an end-to-end view of the data and Management Information

System (MIS) requirements is taken. The data and documentation should be collected from all areas and analysed from the user and business perspective. A 'virtual' SFA team should be formed from all relevant areas to ensure that all aspects and perspectives are considered. The size of the team should reflect the scope and complexity of the SFA assignment.

■ **Build hypothesis:** this is a useful method of building likely scenarios, which can help the study team draw early conclusions within the analysis period. These scenarios can be built from discussing the forthcoming assignment with key roles, e.g. senior management and users, or by using the planning session to brainstorm the list from the assembled team. The completed hypotheses list should be documented and input to the analysis period to provide some early focus on the data and Management Information System (MIS) that match the individual scenarios. It should be noted that this approach also eliminates perceived issues, i.e. no data or MIS substantiates what is perceived to be a service issue.

■ **Analyse data:** the number of individuals that form the SFA team dictates how to allocate specific analysis responsibilities. During this analysis period the hypotheses list should be used to help draw some early conclusions.

■ **Interview key personnel:** it is essential that key business representatives and users are interviewed to ensure the business and user perspectives are captured. It is surprising how this dialogue can identify quick win opportunities, as often what the business views as a big issue can be addressed by a simple IT solution. Therefore these interviews should be initiated as soon as possible within the SFA assignment. The study team should also seek input from key individuals within the IT service provider organization to identify additional problem areas and possible solutions that can be fed back to the study team. The dialogue also helps capture those issues that are not easily visible from the assembled data and MIS reports.

■ **Findings and conclusions:** after analysis of the data and MIS provided, interviews and continual revision of the hypothesis list, the study team should be in a position to start documenting initial findings and conclusions. It is recommended that the team meet immediately after the analysis period to share their individual findings and then take an aggregate view to form the draft findings and conclusions. It is important

that all findings can be evidenced by facts gathered during the analysis. During this phase of the assignment, it may be necessary to validate finding(s) by additional analysis to ensure the SFA team can back up all findings with clear documented evidence.

■ **Recommendations:** after all findings and conclusions have been validated, the SFA team should be in a position to formulate recommendations. In many cases, the recommendations to support a particular finding are straightforward and obvious. However, the benefit of bringing a cross-functional team together for the SFA assignment is to create an environment for innovative lateral-thinking approaches. The SFA assignment leader should facilitate this session with the aim of identifying recommendations that are practical and sustainable once implemented.

■ **Report:** the final report should be issued to the sponsor with a management summary. Reporting styles are normally determined by the individual organizations. It is important that the report clearly shows where loss of availability is being incurred and how the recommendations address this. If the report contains many recommendations, an attempt should be made to quantify the availability benefit of each recommendation, together with the estimated effort to implement. This enables informed choices to be made on how to take the recommendations forward and how these should be prioritized and resourced.

■ **Validation:** it is recommended that for each SFA, key measures that reflect the business and user perspectives prior to the assignment are captured and recorded as the 'before' view. As SFA recommendations are progressed, the positive impacts on availability should be captured to provide the 'after' view for comparative purposes. Where anticipated benefits have not been delivered, this should be investigated and remedial action taken. Having invested time and effort in completing the SFA assignment, it is important that the recommendations, once agreed by the sponsor, are then taken forward for implementation. The best mechanism for achieving this is by incorporating the recommendations as activities to be completed within the Availability Plan or the overall SIP. The success of the SFA assignment as a whole should be monitored and measured to ensure its continued effectiveness.

Hints and tips

Consider categorizing the recommendations under the following headings:
DETECTION: Recommendations that, if implemented, will provide enhanced reporting of key indicators to ensure underlying IT service issues are detected early to enable a proactive response.
REDUCTION: Recommendations that, if implemented, will reduce or minimize the user impact from IT service interruption, e.g. recovery and/or restoration can be enhanced to reduce impact duration.
AVOIDANCE: Recommendations that, if implemented, will eliminate this particular cause of IT service interruption.

4.4.5.2 The proactive activities of Availability Management

The capability of the Availability Management process is positively influenced by the range and quality of proactive methods and techniques utilized by the process. The following activities are the proactive techniques and activities of the Availability Management process.

Identifying Vital Business Functions (VBFs)

The term Vital Business Function (VBF) is used to reflect the business critical elements of the business process supported by an IT service. The service may also support less critical business functions and processes, and it is important that the VBFs are recognized and documented to provide the appropriate business alignment and focus.

Designing for availability

The level of availability required by the business influences the overall cost of the IT service provided. In general, the higher the level of availability required by the business, the higher the cost. These costs are not just the procurement of the base IT technology and services required to underpin the IT infrastructure. Additional costs are incurred in providing the appropriate Service Management processes, systems management tools and high-availability solutions required to meet the more stringent availability requirements. The greatest level of availability should be included in the design of those services supporting the most critical of the VBFs.

When considering how the availability requirements of the business are to be met, it is important to ensure that the level of availability to be provided for an IT service is at the level actually required, and is affordable and cost-justifiable to the business. Figure 4.17 indicates the products and processes required to provide varying levels of availability and the cost implications.

Base product and components

The procurement or development of the base products, technology and components should be based on their capability to meet stringent availability and reliability requirements. These should be considered as the cornerstone of the availability design. The additional investment required to achieve even higher levels of availability will be wasted and availability levels not met if these base products and components are unreliable and prone to failure.

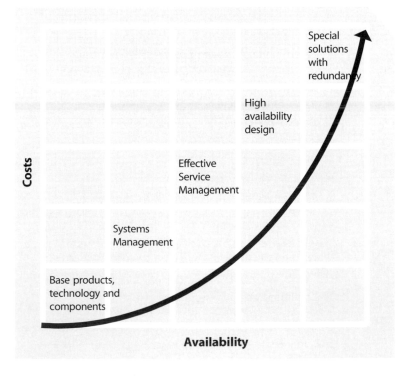

Figure 4.17 Relationship between levels of availability and overall costs

Systems management

Systems management should provide the monitoring, diagnostic and automated error recovery to enable fast detection and speedy resolution of potential and actual IT failure.

Service Management processes

Effective Service Management processes contribute to higher levels of availability. Processes such as Availability Management, Incident Management, Problem Management, Change Management, Configuration Management, etc. play a crucial role in the overall management of the IT service.

High-availability design

The design for high availability needs to consider the elimination of SPoFs and/or the provision of alternative components to provide minimal disruption to the business operation should an IT component failure occur. The design also needs to eliminate or minimize the effects of planned downtime to the business operation normally required to accommodate maintenance activity, the implementation of changes to the IT infrastructure or business application. Recovery criteria should define rapid recovery and IT service reinstatement as a key objective within the designing for recovery phase of design.

Special solutions with full redundancy

To approach continuous availability in the range of 100% requires expensive solutions that incorporate full mirroring or redundancy. Redundancy is the technique of improving availability by using duplicate components. For stringent availability requirements to be met, these need to be working autonomously in parallel. These solutions are not just restricted to the IT components, but also to the IT environments, i.e. data centres, power supplies, air conditioning and telecommunications.

Where new IT services are being developed, it is essential that Availability Management takes an early and participating design role in determining the availability requirements. This enables Availability Management to influence positively the IT infrastructure design to ensure that it can deliver the level of availability required. The importance of this participation early in the design of the IT infrastructure cannot be underestimated. There needs to be a dialogue between IT and the business to determine the balance between the business perception of the cost of unavailability and the exponential cost of delivering higher levels of availability.

As illustrated in Figure 4.17, there is a significant increase in costs when the business requirement is higher than the optimum level of availability that the IT infrastructure can deliver. These increased costs are driven by major redesign of the technology and the changing of requirements for the IT support organization.

It is important that the level of availability designed into the service is appropriate to the business needs, the criticality of the business processes being supported and the available budget. The business should be consulted early in the Service Design lifecycle so that the business availability needs of a new or enhanced IT service can be costed and agreed. This is particularly important where stringent availability requirements may require additional investment in Service Management processes, IT service and System Management tools, high-availability design and special solutions with full redundancy.

It is likely that the business need for IT availability cannot be expressed in technical terms. Availability Management therefore provides an important role in being able to translate the business and user requirements into quantifiable availability targets and conditions. This is an important input into the IT Service Design and provides the basis for assessing the capability of the IT design and IT support organization in meeting the availability requirements of the business.

The business requirements for IT availability should contain at least:

- A definition of the VBFs supported by the IT service
- A definition of IT service downtime, i.e. the conditions under which the business considers the IT service to be unavailable
- The business impact caused by loss of service, together with the associated risk
- Quantitative availability requirements, i.e. the extent to which the business tolerates IT service downtime or degraded service
- The required service hours, i.e. when the service is to be provided
- An assessment of the relative importance of different working periods
- Specific security requirements
- The service backup and recovery capability.

Once the IT technology design and IT support organization are determined, the service provider organization is then in a position to confirm if the availability requirements can be met. Where shortfalls are identified, dialogue with the business is required to present the cost options that exist to enhance the proposed design to meet the availability requirements. This enables the business to reassess if lower or higher levels of availability are required, and to understand the appropriate impact and costs associated with their decision.

Determining the availability requirements is likely to be an iterative process, particularly where there is a need to balance the business availability requirement against the associated costs. The necessary steps are:

■ Determine the business impact caused by loss of service

■ From the business requirements, specify the availability, reliability and maintainability requirements for the IT service and components supported by the IT support organization

■ For IT services and components provided externally, identify the serviceability requirements

■ Estimate the costs involved in meeting the availability, reliability, maintainability and serviceability requirements

■ Determine, with the business, if the costs identified in meeting the availability requirements are justified

■ Determine, from the business, the costs likely to be incurred from loss or degradation of service

■ Where these are seen as cost-justified, define the availability, reliability, maintainability and serviceability requirements in agreements and negotiate into contracts.

Hints and tips

If costs are seen as prohibitive, either:

■ Reassess the IT infrastructure design and provide options for reducing costs and assess the consequences on availability; or

■ Reassess the business use and reliance on the IT service and renegotiate the availability targets within the SLA.

The SLM process is normally responsible for communicating with the business on how its availability requirements for IT services are to be met and negotiating the SLR/SLA for the IT Service Design process. Availability Management therefore provides important support and input to the both SLM and design processes during this period. While higher levels of availability can often be provided by investment in tools and technology, there is no justification for providing a higher level of availability than that needed and afforded by the business. The reality is that satisfying availability requirements is always a balance between cost and quality. This is where Availability Management can play a key role in optimizing

availability of the IT Service Design to meet increasing availability demands while deferring an increase in costs.

Designing service for availability is a key activity driven by Availability Management. This ensures that the required level of availability for an IT service can be met. Availability Management needs to ensure that the design activity for availability looks at the task from two related, but distinct, perspectives:

■ **Designing for availability:** this activity relates to the technical design of the IT service and the alignment of the internal and external suppliers required to meet the availability requirements of the business. It needs to cover all aspects of technology, including infrastructure, environment, data and applications.

■ **Designing for recovery:** this activity relates to the design points required to ensure that in the event of an IT service failure, the service and its supporting components can be reinstated to enable normal business operations to resume as quickly as is possible. This again needs to cover all aspects of technology.

Additionally, the ability to recover quickly may be a crucial factor. In simple terms, it may not be possible or cost-justified to build a design that is highly resilient to failure(s). The ability to meet the availability requirements within the cost parameters may rely on the ability consistently to recover in a timely and effective manner. All aspects of availability should be considered in the Service Design process and should consider all stages within the Service Lifecycle.

The contribution of Availability Management within the design activities is to provide:

■ The specification of the availability requirements for all components of the service

■ The requirements for availability measurement points (instrumentation)

■ The requirements for new/enhanced systems and Service Management

■ Assistance with the IT infrastructure design

■ The specification of the reliability, maintainability and serviceability requirements for components supplied by internal and external suppliers

■ Validation of the final design to meet the minimum levels of availability required by the business for the IT service.

If the availability requirements cannot be met, the next task is to re-evaluate the Service Design and identify cost-justified design changes. Improvements in design to meet the availability requirements can be achieved by reviewing the capability of the technology to be deployed in the proposed IT design. For example:

- The exploitation of fault-tolerant technology to mask the impact of planned or unplanned component downtime
- Duplexing, or the provision of alternative IT infrastructure components to allow one component to take over the work of another component
- Improving component reliability by enhancing testing regimes
- Improved software design and development
- Improved processes and procedures
- Systems management enhancements/exploitation
- Improved externally supplied services, contracts or agreements
- Developing the capability of the people with more training.

Hints and tips

Consider documenting the availability design requirements and considerations for new IT services and making them available to the design and implementation functions. Longer term seek to mandate these requirements and integrate within the appropriate governance mechanisms that cover the introduction of new IT services.

Part of the activity of designing for availability must ensure that all business, data and information security requirements are incorporated within the Service Design. The overall aim of IT security is 'balanced security in depth', with justifiable controls implemented to ensure that the Information Security Policy is enforced and that continued IT services within secure parameters (i.e. confidentiality, integrity and availability) continue to operate. During the gathering of availability requirements for new IT services, it is important that requirements that cover IT security are defined. These requirements need to be applied within the design phase for the supporting technology. For many organizations, the approach taken to IT security is covered by an Information Security Policy owned and maintained by Information Security Management. In the execution of the security policy, Availability Management plays an important role in its operation for new IT services.

Where the business operation has a high dependency on IT service availability, and the cost of failure or loss of business reputation is considered not acceptable, the business may define stringent availability requirements. These factors may be sufficient for the business to justify the additional costs required to meet these more demanding levels of availability. Achieving agreed levels of availability begins with the design, procurement and/or development of good-quality products and components. However, these in isolation are unlikely to deliver the sustained levels of availability required. To achieve a consistent and sustained level of availability requires investment in and deployment of effective Service Management processes, systems management tools, high-availability design and ultimately special solutions with full mirroring or redundancy.

Designing for availability is a key activity, driven by Availability Management, which ensures that the stated availability requirements for an IT service can be met. However, Availability Management should also ensure that within this design activity there is focus on the design elements required to ensure that when IT services fail, the service can be reinstated to enable normal business operations to resume as quickly as is possible. 'Designing for recovery' may at first sound negative. Clearly good availability design is about avoiding failures and delivering, where possible, a fault-tolerant IT infrastructure. However, with this focus is too much reliance placed on technology, and has as much emphasis been placed on the fault tolerance aspects of the IT infrastructure? The reality is that failures will occur. The way the IT organization manages failure situations can have a positive effect on the perception of the business, customers and users of the IT services.

Key message

Every failure is an important 'moment of truth' – an opportunity to make or break your reputation with the business.

By providing focus on the 'designing for recovery' aspects of the overall availability, design can ensure that every failure is an opportunity to maintain and even enhance business and user satisfaction. To provide an effective 'design for recovery', it is important to recognize that both the business and the IT organization have needs that must be satisfied to enable an effective recovery from IT failure.

These are informational needs that the business requires to help them manage the impact of failure on their business and set expectation within the business, user community and their business customers. These are the skills, knowledge, processes, procedures and tools required to enable the technical recovery to be completed in an optimal time.

> **Hints and tips**
>
> Consider documenting the recovery design requirements and considerations for new IT services and make them available to the areas responsible for design and implementation. In the longer term, seek to mandate these requirements and integrate them within the appropriate governance mechanisms that cover the introduction of new IT services.

A key aim is to prevent minor incidents from becoming major incidents by ensuring the right people are involved early enough to avoid mistakes being made and to ensure the appropriate business and technical recovery procedures are invoked at the earliest opportunity. The instigation of these activities is the responsibility of the Incident Management process and a role of the Service Desk. To ensure business needs are met during major IT service failures, and to ensure the most optimal recovery, the Incident Management process and Service Desk need to have defined and to execute effective procedures for assessing and managing all incidents.

> **Key message**
>
> The above are not the responsibilities of Availability Management. However, the effectiveness of the Incident Management process and Service Desk can strongly influence the overall recovery period. The use of Availability Management methods and techniques to further optimize IT recovery may be the stimulus for subsequent continual improvement activities to the Incident Management process and the Service Desk.

In order to remain effective, the maintainability of IT services and components should be monitored, and their impact on the 'expanded incident lifecycle' understood, managed and improved.

Component Failure Impact Analysis

Component Failure Impact Analysis (CFIA) can be used to predict and evaluate the impact on IT service arising from component failures within the technology. The output from a CFIA can be used to identify where additional resilience should be considered to prevent or minimize the impact of component failure to the business operation and users. This is particularly important during the Service Design stage, where it is necessary to predict and evaluate the impact on IT service availability arising from component failures within the proposed IT Service Design. However, the technique can also be applied to existing services and infrastructure.

CFIA is a relatively simple technique that can be used to provide this information. IBM devised CFIA in the early 1970s, with its origins based on hardware design and configuration. However, it is recommended that CFIA be used in a much wider context to reflect the full scope of the IT infrastructure, i.e. hardware, network, software, applications, data centres and support staff. Additionally the technique can also be applied to identify impact and dependencies on IT support organization skills and competencies amongst staff supporting the new IT service. This activity is often completed in conjunction with ITSCM and possibly Capacity Management.

The output from a CFIA provides vital information to ensure that the availability and recovery design criteria for the new IT service is influenced to prevent or minimize the impact of failure to the business operation and users. CFIA achieves this by providing and indicating:

- SPoFs that can impact availability
- The impact of component failure on the business operation and users
- Component and people dependencies
- Component recovery timings
- The need to identify and document recovery options
- The need to identify and implement risk reduction measures.

The above can also provide the stimulus for input to ITSCM to consider the balance between recovery options and risk reduction measures, i.e. where the potential business impact is high there is a need to concentrate on high-availability risk reduction measures, i.e. increased resilience or standby systems.

Having determined the IT infrastructure configuration to be assessed, the first step is to create a grid with CIs on one axis and the IT services that have a dependency on the CI on the other, as illustrated in Figure 4.18. This information should be available from the CMS, or alternatively it can be built using documented configuration charts and SLAs.

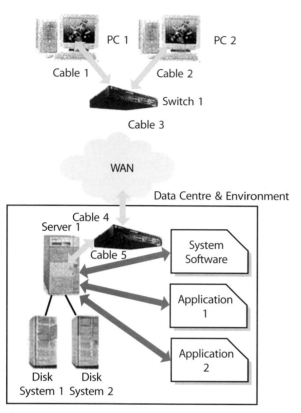

CI	Service 1	Service 2
PC1	M	M
PC2	M	M
Cable 1	M	M
Cable 2	M	M
Switch 1	X	X
Cable 3	X	X
WAN	X	X
Cable 4	X	X
Switch 2	X	X
Cable 5	X	X
Data Centre	X	X
Server 1	X	X
Disk 1	A	A
Disk 2	A	A
System S/W	X	X
Application 1	X	
Application 2		X

Figure 4.18 Component Failure Impact Analysis

The next step is to perform the CFIA and populate the grid as follows:

■ Leave a blank when a failure of the CI does not impact the service in any way
■ Insert an 'X' when the failure of the CI causes the IT service to be inoperative
■ Insert an 'A' when there is an alternative CI to provide the service
■ Insert an 'M' when there is an alternative CI, but the service requires manual intervention to be recovered.

Having built the grid, CIs that have a large number of Xs are critical to many services and can result in high impact should the CI fail. Equally, IT services having high counts of Xs are complex and are vulnerable to failure. This basic approach to CFIA can provide valuable information in quickly identifying SPoFs, IT services at risk from CI failure and what alternatives are available should CIs fail. It should also be used to assess the existence and validity of recovery procedures for the selected CIs. The above example assumes common infrastructure supporting multiple IT services. The same approach can be used for a single IT service by mapping the component CIs against the VBFs and users supported by each component, thus understanding the impact of a component failure on the business and user. The approach can also be further

refined and developed to include and develop 'component availability weighting' factors that can be used to assess and calculate the overall effect of the component failure on the total service availability.

To undertake an advanced CFIA requires the CFIA matrix to be expanded to provide additional fields required for the more detailed analysis. This could include fields such as:

■ **Component availability weighting:** a weighting factor appropriate to the impact of failure of the component on the total service availability. For example, if the failure of a switch can cause 2,000 users to lose service out of a total service user base of 10,000, then the weighting factor should be 0.2, or 20%
■ **Probability of failure:** this can be based on the reliability of the component as measured by the Mean Time Between Failures (MTBF) information if available or on the current trends. This can be expressed as a low/medium/high indicator or as a numeric representation
■ **Recovery time:** this is the estimated recovery time to recover the CI. This can be based on recent recovery timings, recovery information from disaster recovery testing or a scheduled test recovery

- **Recovery procedures:** this is to verify that up-to-date recovery procedures are available for the CI
- **Device independence:** where software CIs have duplex files to provide resilience, this is to ensure that file placements have been verified as being on separate hardware disk configurations. This also applies to power supplies – it should be verified that alternate power supplies are connected correctly
- **Dependency:** this is to show any dependencies between CIs. If one CI failed, there could be an impact on other CIs – for example, if the security CI failed, the operating system might prevent tape processing.

Single Point of Failure analysis

A Single Point of Failure (SPoF) is any component within the IT infrastructure that has no backup or fail-over capability, and has the potential to cause disruption to the business, customers or users when it fails. It is important that no unrecognized SPoFs exist within the IT infrastructure design or the actual technology, and that they are avoided wherever possible.

The use of SPoF analysis or CFIA as techniques to identify SPoFs is recommended. SPoF and CFIA analysis exercises should be conducted on a regular basis, and wherever SPoFs are identified, CFIA can be used to identify the potential business, customer or user impact and help determine what alternatives can or should be considered to cater for this weakness in the design or the actual infrastructure. Countermeasures should then be implemented wherever they are cost-justifiable. The impact and disruption caused by the potential failure of the SPoF should be used to cost-justify its implementation.

Fault Tree Analysis

Fault Tree Analysis (FTA) is a technique that can be used to determine the chain of events that causes a disruption to IT services. FTA, in conjunction with calculation methods, can offer detailed models of availability. This can be used to assess the availability improvement that can be achieved by individual technology component design options. Using FTA:

- Information can be provided that can be used for availability calculations
- Operations can be performed on the resulting fault tree; these operations correspond with design options
- The desired level of detail in the analysis can be chosen.

FTA makes a representation of a chain of events using Boolean notation. Figure 4.19 gives an example of a fault tree.

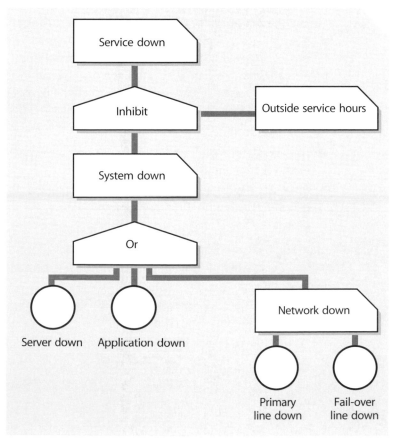

Figure 4.19 Example Fault Tree Analysis

Essentially FTA distinguishes the following events:

■ **Basic events** – terminal points for the fault tree, e.g. power failure, operator error. Basic events are not investigated in great depth. If basic events are investigated in further depth, they automatically become resulting events.

■ **Resulting events** – intermediate nodes in the fault tree, resulting from a combination of events. The highest point in the fault tree is usually a failure of the IT service.

■ **Conditional events** – events that only occur under certain conditions, e.g. failure of the air-conditioning equipment only affects the IT service if equipment temperature exceeds the serviceable values.

■ **Trigger events** – events that trigger other events, e.g. power failure detection equipment can trigger automatic shutdown of IT services.

These events can be combined using logic operators, i.e.:

■ **AND-gate** – the resulting event only occurs when all input events occur simultaneously

■ **OR-gate** – the resulting event occurs when one or more of the input events occurs

■ **Exclusive OR-gate** – the resulting event occurs when one and only one of the input events occurs

■ **Inhibit gate** – the resulting event only occurs when the input condition is not met.

This is the basic FTA technique. This technique can also be refined, but complex FTA and the mathematical evaluation of fault trees are beyond the scope of this publication.

Modelling

To assess if new components within a design can match the stated requirements, it is important that the testing regime instigated ensures that the availability expected can be delivered. Simulation, modelling or load testing tools to generate the expected user demand for the new IT service should be seriously considered to ensure components continue to operate under anticipated volume and stress conditions.

Modelling tools are also required to forecast availability and to assess the impact of changes to the IT infrastructure. Inputs to the modelling process include descriptive data of the component reliability, maintainability and serviceability. A spreadsheet package to perform calculations is usually sufficient. If more detailed and accurate data is required, a more complex modelling tool may need to be developed or acquired. The lack of readily available availability modelling tools in the marketplace may require such a tool to be developed and maintained 'in-house', but this is a very expensive and time-consuming activity that should only be considered where the investment can be justified. Unless there is a clearly perceived benefit from such a development and the ongoing maintenance costs, the use of existing tools and spreadsheets should be sufficient. However, some System Management tools do provide modelling capability and can provide useful information on trending and forecasting availability needs.

Risk Analysis and Management

To assess the vulnerability of failure within the configuration and capability of the IT service and support organization it is recommended that existing or proposed IT infrastructure, service configurations, Service Design and supporting organization (internal and external suppliers) are subject to formal Risk Analysis and Management exercises. Risk Analysis and Management is a technique that can be used to identify and quantify risks and justifiable countermeasures that can be implemented to protect the availability of IT systems. The identification of risks and the provision of justified countermeasures to reduce or eliminate the threats posed by such risks can play an important role in achieving the required levels of availability for a new or enhanced IT service. Risk Analysis should be undertaken during the design phase for the IT technology and service to identify:

■ Risks that may incur unavailability for IT components within the technology and Service Design

■ Risks that may incur confidentiality and/or integrity exposures within the IT technology and Service Design.

Most risk assessment and management methodologies involve the use of a formal approach to the assessment of risk and the subsequent mitigation of risk with the implementation of subsequent cost-justifiable counter-measures, as illustrated in Figure 4.20.

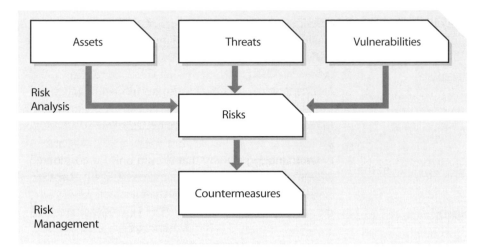

Figure 4.20 Risk Analysis and Management

Risk Analysis involves the identification and assessment of the level (measure) of the risks calculated from the assessed values of assets and the assessed levels of threats to, and vulnerabilities of, those assets. Risk is also determined to a certain extent by its acceptance. Some organizations and businesses may be more willing to accept risk whereas others cannot.

Risk management involves the identification, selection and adoption of countermeasures justified by the identified risks to assets in terms of their potential impact on services if failure occurs, and the reduction of those risks to an acceptable level. Risk management is an activity that is associated with many other activities, especially ITSCM, Security Management and Service Transition. All of these risk assessment exercises should be coordinated rather than being separate activities.

This approach, when applied via a formal method, ensures coverage is complete, together with sufficient confidence that:

- All possible risks and countermeasures have been identified
- All vulnerabilities have been identified and their levels accurately assessed
- All threats have been identified and their levels accurately assessed
- All results are consistent across the broad spectrum of the technology reviewed
- All expenditure on selected countermeasures can be justified.

Formal Risk Analysis and Management methods are now an important element in the overall design and provision of IT services. The assessment of risk is often based on the probability and potential impact of an event occurring. Counter-measures are implemented wherever they are cost-justifiable, to reduce the impact of an event, or the probability of an event occurring, or both.

Management of Risk (M_o_R) provides an alternative generic framework for the management of risk across all parts of an organization – strategic, programme, project and operational. It incorporates all the activities required to identify and control the exposure to any type of risk, positive or negative, that may have an impact on the achievement of your organization's business objectives.

M_o_R provides a framework that is tried, tested and effective to help you eliminate – or manage – the risks involved in reaching your goals. M_o_R adopts a systematic application of principles, approach and processes to the task of identifying, assessing and then planning and implementing risk responses. Guidance stresses a collaborative approach and focuses on the following key elements:

- Developing a framework that is transparent, repeatable and adaptable
- Clearly communicating the policy and its benefits to all staff
- Nominating key individuals in senior management to 'own' risk management initiatives and ensure they move forwards
- Ensuring the culture engages with and supports properly considered risk, including innovation
- Embedding risk management systems in management and applying them consistently
- Ensuring that risk management supports objectives – rather than vice versa
- Explicitly assessing the risks involved in working with other organizations
- Adopting a no-blame approach to monitoring and reviewing risk assessment activity.

Availability testing schedule

A key deliverable from the Availability Management process is the 'availability testing schedule'. This is a schedule for the regular testing of all availability mechanisms. Some availability mechanisms, such as 'load balancing', 'mirroring' and 'grid computing', are used in the provision of normal service on a day-by-day basis; others are used on a fail-over or manual reconfiguration basis. It is essential, therefore, that all availability mechanisms are tested in a regular and scheduled manner to ensure that when they are actually needed for real they work. This schedule needs to be maintained and widely circulated so that all areas are aware of its content and so that all other proposed activities can be synchronized with its content, such as:

■ The change schedule
■ Release plans and the release schedule
■ All transition plans, projects and programmes
■ Planned and preventative maintenance schedules
■ The schedule for testing IT service continuity and recovery plans
■ Business plans and schedules.

Planned and preventative maintenance

All IT components should be subject to a planned maintenance strategy. The frequency and levels of maintenance required varies from component to component, taking into account the technologies involved, criticality and the potential business benefits that may be introduced. Planned maintenance activities enable the IT support organization to provide:

■ Preventative maintenance to avoid failures
■ Planned software or hardware upgrades to provide new functionality or additional capacity
■ Business requested changes to the business applications
■ Implementation of new technology and functionality for exploitation by the business.

The requirement for planned downtime clearly influences the level of availability that can be delivered for an IT service, particularly those that have stringent availability requirements. In determining the availability requirements for a new or enhanced IT service, the amount of downtime and the resultant loss of income required for planned maintenance may not be acceptable to the business. This is becoming a growing issue in the area of 24 x 7 service operation. In these instances, it is essential that continuous operation is a core design feature to enable maintenance activity to be performed without impacting the availability of IT services.

Where the required service hours for IT services are less than 24 hours per day and/or seven days per week, it is likely that the majority of planned maintenance can be accommodated without impacting IT service availability. However, where the business needs IT services available on a 24-hour and seven-day basis, Availability Management needs to determine the most effective approach in balancing the requirements for planned maintenance against the loss of service to the business. Unless mechanisms exist to allow continuous operation, scheduled downtime for planned maintenance is essential if high levels of availability are to be achieved and sustained. For all IT services, there should logically be a 'low-impact' period for the implementation of maintenance. Once the requirements for managing scheduled maintenance have been defined and agreed, these should be documented as a minimum in:

■ SLAs
■ OLAs
■ Underpinning contracts
■ Change Management schedules
■ Release and Deployment Management schedules.

> **Hints and tips**
>
> Availability Management should ensure that building in preventative maintenance is one of the prime design considerations for a '24 x 7' IT service.

The most appropriate time to schedule planned downtime is clearly when the impact on the business and its customers is least. This information should be provided initially by the business when determining the availability requirements. For an existing IT service, or once the new service has been established, monitoring of business and customer transactions helps establish the hours when IT service usage is at its lowest. This should determine the most appropriate time for the component(s) to be removed for planned maintenance activity.

To accommodate the individual component requirements for planned downtime while balancing the IT service availability requirements of the business provides an opportunity to consider scheduling planned maintenance to multiple components concurrently. The benefit of this approach is that the number of service disruptions required to meet the maintenance requirements is reduced. While this approach has benefits, there are potential risks that need to be assessed. For example:

■ The capability of the IT support organization to coordinate the concurrent implementation of a high number of changes

- The ability to perform effective problem determination where the IT service is impacted after the completion of multiple changes
- The impact of change dependency across multiple components where back-out of a failed change requires multiple changes to be removed.

The effective management of planned downtime is an important contribution in meeting the required levels of availability for an IT service. Where planned downtime is required on a cyclic basis to an IT component(s), the time that the component is unavailable to enable the planned maintenance activity to be undertaken should be defined and agreed with the internal or external supplier. This becomes a stated objective that can be formalized, measured and reported. All planned maintenance should be scheduled, managed and controlled to ensure that the individual objectives and time slots are not exceeded and to ensure that activities are coordinated with all other schedules of activity to minimize clashes and conflict (e.g. change and release schedules, testing schedules.) In addition they provide an early warning during the maintenance activity of the time allocated to the planned outage duration being breached. This can enable an early decision to be made on whether the activity is allowed to complete with the potential to further impact service or to abort the activity and instigate the back-out plan. Planned downtime and performance against the stated objectives for each component should be recorded and used in service reporting.

Production of the Projected Service Outage (PSO) document

Availability Management should produce and maintain the PSO document. This document consists of any variations from the service availability agreed within SLAs. This should be produced based on input from:

- The change schedule
- The release schedules
- Planned and preventative maintenance schedules
- Availability testing schedules
- ITSCM and Business Continuity Management testing schedules.

The PSO contains details of all scheduled and planned service downtime within the agreed service hours for all services. These documents should be agreed with all the appropriate areas and representatives of both the business and IT. Once the PSO has been agreed, the Service Desk should ensure that it is communicated to all relevant parties so that everyone is made aware of any additional, planned service downtime.

Continual review and improvement

Changing business needs and customer demand may require the levels of availability provided for an IT service to be reviewed. Such reviews should form part of the regular service reviews with the business undertaken by SLM. Other input should also be considered on a regular basis from ITSCM, particularly from the updated Business Impact Analysis and Risk Analysis exercises. The criticality of services will often change and it is important that the design and the technology supporting such services is regularly reviewed and improved by Availability Management to ensure that the change of importance in the service is reflected within a revised design and supporting technology. Where the required levels of availability are already being delivered, it may take considerable effort and incur significant cost to achieve a small incremental improvement within the level of availability.

A key activity for Availability Management is continually to look at opportunities to optimize the availability of the IT infrastructure in conjunction with Continual Service Improvement activities. The benefits of this regular review approach are that, sometimes, enhanced levels of availability may be achievable, but with much lower costs. The optimization approach is a sensible first step to delivering better value for money. A number of Availability Management techniques can be applied to identify optimization opportunities. It is recommended that the scope should not be restricted to the technology, but also include a review of both the business process and other end-to-end business-owned responsibilities. To help achieve these aims, Availability Management needs to be recognized as a leading influence over the IT service provider organization to ensure continued focus on availability and stability of the technology.

Availability Management can provide the IT support organization with a real business and user perspective on how deficiencies within the technology and the underpinning process and procedure impact on the business operation and ultimately their customers. The use of business-driven metrics can demonstrate this impact in real terms and, importantly, also help quantify the benefits of improvement opportunities. Availability Management can play an important role in helping the IT service provider organization recognize where it can add value by exploiting its technical skills and competencies in an availability context. The continual improvement technique can be used by Availability Management to harness this technical capability. This can be used with either small groups of technical staff or a wider group within a workshop or SFA environment.

The impetus to improve availability comes from one or more of the following:

- The inability for existing or new IT services to meet SLA targets on a consistent basis
- Period(s) of IT service instability resulting in unacceptable levels of availability
- Availability measurement trends indicating a gradual deterioration in availability
- Unacceptable IT service recovery and restoration times
- Requests from the business to increase the level of availability provided
- Increasing impact on the business and its customers of IT service failures as a result of growth and/or increased business priorities or functionality
- A request from SLM to improve availability as part of an overall SIP
- Availability Management monitoring and trend analysis.

Availability Management should take a proactive role in identifying and progressing cost-justified availability improvement opportunities within the Availability Plan. The ability to do this places reliance on having appropriate and meaningful availability measurement and reporting. To ensure availability improvements deliver benefits to the business and users, it is important that measurement and reporting reflects not just IT component availability but also availability from a business operation and user perspective.

Where the business has a requirement to improve availability, the process and techniques to reassess the technology and IT service provider organization capability to meet these enhanced requirements should be followed. An output of this activity is enhanced availability and recovery design criteria. To satisfy the business requirement for increased levels of availability may require additional financial investment to enhance the underpinning technology and/or extend the services provided by the IT service provider organization. It is important that any additional investment to improve the levels of availability delivered can be cost-justified. Determining the cost of unavailability as a result of IT failure(s) can help support any financial investment decision in improving availability.

4.4.6 Triggers, inputs, outputs and interfaces

Many events may trigger Availability Management activity. These include:

- New or changed business needs or new or changed services

- New or changed targets within agreements, such as SLRs, SLAs, OLAs or contracts
- Service or component breaches, availability events and alerts, including threshold events, exception reports
- Periodic activities such as reviewing, revising or reporting
- Review of Availability Management forecasts, reports and plans
- Review and revision of business and IT plans and strategies
- Review and revision of designs and strategies
- Recognition or notification of a change of risk or impact of a business process or VBF, an IT service or component
- Request from SLM for assistance with availability targets and explanation of achievements.

The key interfaces that Availability Management has with other processes are:

- **Incident and Problem Management:** in providing assistance with the resolution and subsequent justification and correction of availability incidents and problems
- **Capacity Management:** with the provision of resilience and spare capacity
- **IT Service Continuity Management:** with the assessment of business impact and risk and the provision of resilience, fail-over and recovery mechanisms
- **Service Level Management:** assistance with the determining of availability targets and the investigation and resolution of service and component breaches.

4.4.6.1 Inputs

A number of sources of information are relevant to the Availability Management process. Some of these are as follows:

- **Business information:** from the organization's business strategy, plans and financial plans, and information on their current and future requirements, including the availability requirements for new or enhanced IT services
- **Business impact information:** from BIAs and assessment of VBFs underpinned by IT services
- **Previous Risk Analysis** and Assessment reports and a risk register
- **Service information:** from the Service Portfolio and the Service Catalogue,
- **Service information:** from the SLM process, with

details of the services from the Service Portfolio and the Service Catalogue, service level targets within SLAs and SLRs, and possibly from the monitoring of SLAs, service reviews and breaches of the SLAs

■ **Financial information:** from Financial Management, the cost of service provision, the cost of resources and components

■ **Change and release information:** from the Change Management process with a Change Schedule, the Release Schedule from Release Management and a need to assess all changes for their impact on service availability

■ **Configuration Management:** containing information on the relationships between the business, the services, the supporting services and the technology

■ **Service targets:** from SLAs, SLRs, OLAs and contracts

■ **Component information:** on the availability, reliability and maintainability requirements for the technology components that underpin IT service(s)

■ **Technology information:** from the CMS on the topology and the relationships between the components and the assessment of the capabilities of new technology

■ **Past performance:** from previous measurements, achievements and reports and the Availability Management Information System (AMIS)

■ **Unavailability and failure information:** from incidents and problems.

4.4.6.2 Outputs

The outputs produced by Availability Management should include:

■ The Availability Management Information System (AMIS)

■ The Availability Plan for the proactive improvement of IT services and technology

■ Availability and recovery design criteria and proposed service targets for new or changed services

■ Service availability, reliability and maintainability reports of achievements against targets, including input for all service reports

■ Component availability, reliability and maintainability reports of achievements against targets

■ Revised risk analysis reviews and reports and an updated risk register

■ Monitoring, management and reporting requirements for IT services and components to ensure that deviations in availability, reliability and maintainability are detected, actioned, recorded and reported

■ An Availability Management test schedule for testing all availability, resilience and recovery mechanisms

■ The planned and preventative maintenance schedules

■ The Projected Service Outage (PSO) in conjunction with Change and Release Management

■ Details of the proactive availability techniques and measures that will be deployed to provide additional resilience to prevent or minimize the impact of component failures on the IT service availability

■ Improvement actions for inclusion within the SIP.

4.4.7 Key Performance Indicators

Many KPIs can be used to measure the effectiveness and efficiency of Availability Management, including the following examples:

Manage availability and reliability of IT service:

■ Percentage reduction in the unavailability of services and components

■ Percentage increase in the reliability of services and components

■ Effective review and follow-up of all SLA, OLA and underpinning contract breaches

■ Percentage improvement in overall end-to-end availability of service

■ Percentage reduction in the number and impact of service breaks

■ Improvement in the MTBF (Mean Time Between Failures)

■ Improvement in the MTBSI (Mean Time Between Systems Incidents)

■ Reduction in the MTRS (Mean Time to Restore Service).

Satisfy business needs for access to IT services:

■ Percentage reduction in the unavailability of services

■ Percentage reduction of the cost of business overtime due to unavailable IT

■ Percentage reduction in critical time failures, e.g. specific business peak and priority availability needs are planned for

■ Percentage improvement in business and users satisfied with service (by CSS results).

Availability of IT infrastructure achieved at optimum costs:

■ Percentage reduction in the cost of unavailability

■ Percentage improvement in the Service Delivery costs

■ Timely completion of regular Risk Analysis and system review

■ Timely completion of regular cost-benefit analysis

established for infrastructure Component Failure Impact Analysis (CFIA)

- Percentage reduction in failures of third-party performance on MTRS/MTBF against contract targets
- Reduced time taken to complete (or update) a Risk Analysis
- Reduced time taken to review system resilience
- Reduced time taken to complete an Availability Plan
- Timely production of management reports
- Percentage reduction in the incidence of operational reviews uncovering security and reliability exposures in application designs.

4.4.8 Information Management

The Availability Management process should maintain an AMIS that contains all of the measurements and information required to complete the Availability Management process and provide the appropriate information to the business on the level of IT service provided. This information, covering services, components and supporting services, provides the basis for regular, ad hoc and exception availability reporting and the identification of trends within the data for the instigation of improvement activities. These activities and the information contained within the AMIS provide the basis for developing the content of the Availability Plan.

In order to provide structure and focus to a wide range of initiatives that may need to be undertaken to improve availability, an Availability Plan should be formulated and maintained. The Availability Plan should have aims, objectives and deliverables and should consider the wider issues of people, processes, tools and techniques as well as having a technology focus. In the initial stages it may be aligned with an implementation plan for Availability Management, but the two are different and should not be confused. As the Availability Management process matures, the plan should evolve to cover the following:

- Actual levels of availability versus agreed levels of availability for key IT services. Availability measurements should always be business- and customer-focused and report availability as experienced by the business and users.
- Activities being progressed to address shortfalls in availability for existing IT services. Where investment decisions are required, options with associated costs and benefits should be included.
- Details of changing availability requirements for existing IT services. The plan should document the options available to meet these changed requirements.

Where investment decisions are required, the associated costs of each option should be included.

- Details of the availability requirements for forthcoming new IT services. The plan should document the options available to meet these new requirements. Where investment decisions are required, the associated costs of each option should be included.
- A forward-looking schedule for the planned SFA assignments.
- Regular reviews of SFA assignments should be completed to ensure that the availability of technology is being proactively improved in conjunction with the SIP.
- A technology futures section to provide an indication of the potential benefits and exploitation opportunities that exist for planned technology upgrades. Anticipated availability benefits should be detailed, where possible based on business-focused measures, in conjunction with Capacity Management. The effort required to realize these benefits where possible should also be quantified.

During the production of the Availability Plan, it is recommended that liaison with all functional, technical and process areas is undertaken. The Availability Plan should cover a period of one to two years, with a more detailed view and information for the first six months. The plan should be reviewed regularly, with minor revisions every quarter and major revisions every half year. Where the technology is only subject to a low level of change, this may be extended as appropriate.

It is recommended that the Availability Plan is considered complementary to the Capacity Plan and Financial Plan, and that publication is aligned with the capacity and business budgeting cycle. If a demand is foreseen for high levels of availability that cannot be met due to the constraints of the existing IT infrastructure or budget, then exception reports may be required for the attention of both senior IT and business management.

In order to facilitate the production of the Availability Plan, Availability Management may wish to consider having its own database repository. The AMIS can be utilized to record and store selected data and information required to support key activities such as report generation, statistical analysis and availability forecasting and planning. The AMIS should be the main repository for the recording of IT availability metrics, measurements, targets and documents, including the Availability Plan, availability measurements, achievement reports, SFA assignment reports, design criteria, action plans and testing schedules.

> **Hints and tips**
>
> Be pragmatic, define the initial tool requirements and identify what is already deployed that can be used and shared to get started as quickly as possible. Where basic tools are not already available, work with the other IT service and systems management processes to identify common requirements with the aim of selecting shared tools and minimizing costs. The AMIS should address the specific reporting needs of Availability Management not currently provided by existing repositories and integrate with them and their contents.

4.4.9 Challenges, Critical Success Factors and risks

Availability Management faces many challenges, but probably the main challenge is to actually meet the expectations of the customers, the business and senior management. These expectations are that services will always be available not just during their agreed service hours, but that all services will be available on a 24-hour, 365-day basis. When they aren't, it is assumed that they will be recovered within minutes. This is only the case when the appropriate level of investment and design has been applied to the service, and this should only be made where the business impact justifies that level of investment. However, the message needs to be publicized to all customers and areas of the business, so that when services do fail they have the right level of expectation on their recovery. It also means that Availability Management must have access to the right level of quality information on the current business need for IT services and its plans for the future. This is another challenge faced by many Availability Management processes.

Another challenge facing Availability Management is the integration of all of the availability data into an integrated set of information (AMIS) that can be analysed in a consistent manner to provide details on the availability of all services and components. This is particularly challenging when the information from the different technologies is often provided by different tools in differing formats.

Yet another challenge facing Availability Management is convincing the business and senior management of the investment needed in proactive availability measures. Investment is always recognized once failures have occurred, but by then it is really too late. Persuading

businesses and customers to invest in resilience to avoid the possibility of failures that may happen is a difficult challenge. Availability Management should work closely with Service Continuity Management, Security Management and Capacity Management in producing the justifications necessary to secure the appropriate investment.

The main CSFs for the Availability Management process are:

■ Manage availability and reliability of IT service
■ Satisfy business needs for access to IT services
■ Availability of IT infrastructure, as documented in SLAs, provided at optimum costs.

Some of the major risks associated with Availability Management include:

■ A lack of commitment from the business to the Availability Management process
■ A lack of commitment from the business and a lack of appropriate information on future plans and strategies
■ A lack of senior management commitment or a lack of resources and/or budget to the Availability Management process
■ The reporting processes become very labour-intensive
■ The processes focus too much on the technology and not enough on the services and the needs of the business
■ The Availability Management information (AMIS) is maintained in isolation and is not shared or consistent with other process areas, especially ITSCM, Security Management and Capacity Management. This investment is particularly important when considering the necessary service and component backup and recovery tools, technology and processes to meet the agreed needs.

4.5 IT SERVICE CONTINUITY MANAGEMENT

4.5.1 Purpose/goal/objective

> 'The goal of ITSCM is to support the overall Business Continuity Management process by ensuring that the required IT technical and service facilities (including computer systems, networks, applications, data repositories, telecommunications, environment, technical support and Service Desk) can be resumed within required, and agreed, business timescales.'

As technology is a core component of most business processes, continued or high availability of IT is critical to the survival of the business as a whole. This is achieved by introducing risk reduction measures and recovery options. Like all elements of ITSM, successful implementation of ITSCM can only be achieved with senior management commitment and the support of all members of the organization. Ongoing maintenance of the recovery capability is essential if it is to remain effective. The purpose of ITSCM is to maintain the necessary ongoing recovery capability within the IT services and their supporting components.

The objectives of ITSCM are to:

- Maintain a set of IT Service Continuity Plans and IT recovery plans that support the overall Business Continuity Plans (BCPs) of the organization
- Complete regular Business Impact Analysis (BIA) exercises to ensure that all continuity plans are maintained in line with changing business impacts and requirements
- Conduct regular Risk Analysis and Management exercises, particularly in conjunction with the business and the Availability Management and Security Management processes, that manage IT services within an agreed level of business risk
- Provide advice and guidance to all other areas of the business and IT on all continuity- and recovery-related issues
- Ensure that appropriate continuity and recovery mechanisms are put in place to meet or exceed the agreed business continuity targets
- Assess the impact of all changes on the IT Service Continuity Plans and IT recovery plans
- Ensure that proactive measures to improve the availability of services are implemented wherever it is cost-justifiable to do so
- Negotiate and agree the necessary contracts with suppliers for the provision of the necessary recovery capability to support all continuity plans in conjunction with the Supplier Management process.

4.5.2 Scope

ITSCM focuses on those events that the business considers significant enough to be considered a disaster. Less significant events will be dealt with as part of the Incident Management process. What constitutes a disaster will vary from organization to organization. The impact of a loss of a business process, such as financial loss, damage to reputation or regulatory breach, is measured through a BIA exercise, which determines the minimum critical requirements. The specific IT technical and service requirements are supported by ITSCM. The scope of ITSCM within an organization is determined by the organizational structure, culture and strategic direction (both business and technology) in terms of the services provided and how these develop and change over time.

ITSCM primarily considers the IT assets and configurations that support the business processes. If (following a disaster) it is necessary to relocate to an alternative working location, provision will also be required for items such as office and personnel accommodation, copies of critical paper records, courier services and telephone facilities to communicate with customers and third parties.

The scope will need to take into account the number and location of the organization's offices and the services performed in each.

ITSCM does not usually directly cover longer-term risks such as those from changes in business direction, diversification, restructuring, major competitor failure, and so on. While these risks can have a significant impact on IT service elements and their continuity mechanisms, there is usually time to identify and evaluate the risk and include risk mitigation through changes or shifts in business and IT strategies, thereby becoming part of the overall business and IT Change Management programme.

Similarly, ITSCM does not usually cover minor technical faults (for example, non critical disk failure), unless there is a possibility that the impact could have a major impact on the business. These risks would be expected to be covered mainly through the Service Desk and the Incident Management process, or resolved through the planning associated with the processes of Availability Management, Problem Management, Change Management, Configuration Management and 'business as usual' operational management.

The ITSCM process includes:

- The agreement of the scope of the ITSCM process and the policies adopted.
- Business Impact Analysis (BIA) to quantify the impact loss of IT service would have on the business.
- Risk Analysis (RA) – the risk identification and risk assessment to identify potential threats to continuity and the likelihood of the threats becoming reality. This also includes taking measures to manage the identified threats where this can be cost-justified.
- Production of an overall ITSCM strategy that must be integrated into the BCM strategy. This can be produced following the two steps identified above, and is likely to include elements of risk reduction as well as selection of appropriate and comprehensive recovery options.

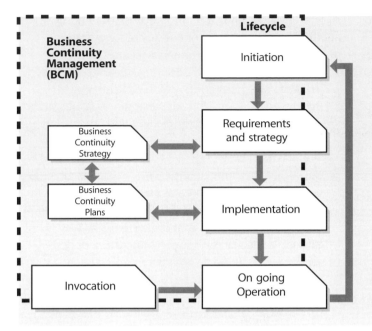

Figure 4.21
Lifecycle of
Service
Continuity
Management

- Production of an ITSCM plan, which again must be integrated with the overall BCM plans.
- Testing of the plans.
- Ongoing operation and maintenance of the plans.

4.5.3 Value to the business

ITSCM provides an invaluable role in supporting the Business Continuity Planning process. In many organizations, ITSCM is used to raise awareness of continuity and recovery requirements and is often used to justify and implement a Business Continuity Planning process and Business Continuity Plans. The ITSCM should be driven by business risk as identified by Business Continuity Planning, and ensures that the recovery arrangements for IT services are aligned to identified business impacts, risks and needs.

4.5.4 Policies/principles/basic concepts

A lifecycle approach should be adopted to the setting up and operation of an ITSCM process. Figure 4.21 shows the lifecycle of ITSCM, from initiation through to continual assurance that the protection provided by the plan is current and reflects all changes to services and service levels. ITSCM is a cyclic process through the lifecycle to ensure that once service continuity and recovery plans have been developed they are kept aligned with Business Continuity Plans (BCPs) and business priorities. Figure 4.21 also shows the role played within the ITSCM process of BCM.

Initiation and requirements stages are principally BCM activities. ITSCM should only be involved in these stages to support the BCM activities and to understand the

relationship between the business processes and the impacts caused on them by loss of IT service. As a result of these initial BIA and Risk Analysis activities, BCM should produce a Business Continuity Strategy, and the first real ITSCM task is to produce an ITSCM strategy that underpins the BCM strategy and its needs.

The Business Continuity Strategy should principally focus on business processes and associated issues (e.g. business process continuity, staff continuity, buildings continuity). Once the Business Continuity Strategy has been produced, and the role that IT services has to provide within the strategy has been determined, an ITSCM strategy can be produced that supports and enables the Business Continuity Strategy. This ensures that cost-effective decisions can be made, considering all the 'resources' to deliver a business process. Failure to do this tends to encourage ITSCM options that are faster, more elaborate and expensive than are actually needed.

The activities to be considered during initiation depend on the extent to which continuity facilities have been applied within the organization. Some parts of the business may have established individual Business Continuity Plans based around manual work-arounds, and IT may have developed continuity plans for systems perceived to be critical. This is good input to the process. However, effective ITSCM depends on supporting critical business functions. The only way of implementing effective ITSCM is through the identification of critical business processes and the analysis and coordination of the required technology and supporting IT services.

This situation may be even more complicated in outsourcing situations where an ITSCM process within an external service provider or outsourcer organization has to meet the needs not only of the customer BCM process and strategy, but also of the outsourcer's own BCM process and strategy. These needs may be in conflict with one another, or may conflict with the BCM needs of one of the other outsourcing organization's customers.

However, in many organizations BCM is absent or has very little focus, and often ITSCM is required to fulfil many of the requirements and activities of BCM. The rest of this section has assumed that ITSCM has had to perform many of the activities required by BCM. Where a BCM process is established with Business Continuity Strategies and Plans in place, these documents should provide the focus and drive for establishing ITSCM.

4.5.5 Process activities, methods and techniques

The following sections contain details of each of the stages within the ITSCM lifecycle.

4.5.5.1 Stage 1 – Initiation

The initiation process covers the whole of the organization and consists of the following activities:

- **Policy setting** – this should be established and communicated as soon as possible so that all members of the organization involved in, or affected by, Business Continuity issues are aware of their responsibilities to comply with and support ITSCM. As a minimum, the policy should set out management intention and objectives.
- **Specify terms of reference and scope** – this includes defining the scope and responsibilities of all staff in the organization. It covers such tasks as undertaking a Risk Analysis and Business Impact Analysis and determination of the command and control structure required to support a business interruption. There is also a need to take into account such issues as outstanding audit points, regulatory or client requirements and insurance organization stipulations, and compliance with standards such as ISO 27001, the Standard on Information Security Management, which also addresses Service Continuity requirements.
- **Allocate resources** – the establishment of an effective Business Continuity environment requires considerable resource in terms of both money and manpower. Depending on the maturity of the organization, with respect to ITSCM, there may be a requirement to familiarize and/or train staff to accomplish the Stage 2 tasks. Alternatively, the use of experienced external consultants may assist in completing the analysis more quickly. However, it is important that the organization

can then maintain the process going forward without the need to rely totally on external support.

- **Define the project organization and control structure** – ITSCM and BCM projects are potentially complex and need to be well organized and controlled. It is strongly advisable to use a recognized standard project planning methodology such as Projects IN a Controlled Environment (PRINCE2®) or Project Management Body Of Knowledge (PMBOK®).
- **Agree project and quality plans** – plans enable the project to be controlled and variances addressed. Quality plans ensure that the deliverables are achieved and to an acceptable level of quality. They also provide a mechanism for communicating project resource requirements and deliverables, thereby obtaining 'buy-in' from all necessary parties.

4.5.5.2 Stage 2 – Requirements and strategy

Ascertaining the business requirements for IT service continuity is a critical component in order to determine how well an organization will survive a business interruption or disaster and the costs that will be incurred. If the requirements analysis is incorrect, or key information has been missed, this could have serious consequences on the effectiveness of ITSCM mechanisms.

This stage can effectively be split into two sections:

- **Requirements** – perform Business Impact Analysis and risk assessment
- **Strategy** – following the requirements analysis, the strategy should document the required risk reduction measures and recovery options to support the business.

Requirements – Business Impact Analysis

The purpose of a Business Impact Analysis (BIA) is to quantify the impact to the business that loss of service would have. This impact could be a 'hard' impact that can be precisely identified – such as financial loss – or 'soft' impact – such as public relations, morale, health and safety or loss of competitive advantage. The BIA will identify the most important services to the organization and will therefore be a key input to the strategy.

The BIA identifies:

- The form that the damage or loss may take – for example:
  - Lost income
  - Additional costs
  - Damaged reputation
  - Loss of goodwill
  - Loss of competitive advantage
  - Breach of law, health and safety

- Risk to personal safety
- Immediate and long-term loss of market share
- Political, corporate or personal embarrassment
- Loss of operational capability – for example, in a command and control environment

■ How the degree of damage or loss is likely to escalate after a service disruption, and the times of the day, week, month or year when disruption will be most severe

■ The staffing, skills, facilities and services (including the IT services) necessary to enable critical and essential business processes to continue operating at a minimum acceptable level

■ The time within which minimum levels of staffing, facilities and services should be recovered

■ The time within which all required business processes and supporting staff, facilities and services should be fully recovered

■ The relative business recovery priority for each of the IT services.

One of the key outputs from a BIA exercise is a graph of the anticipated business impact caused by the loss of a business process or the loss of an IT service over time, as illustrated in Figure 4.22.

This graph can then be used to drive the business and IT continuity strategies and plans. More preventative measures need to be adopted with regard to those processes and services with earlier and higher impacts,

whereas greater emphasis should be placed on continuity and recovery measures for those where the impact is lower and takes longer to develop. A balanced approach of both measures should be adopted to those in between.

These items provide the drivers for the level of ITSCM mechanisms that need to be considered or deployed. Once presented with these options, the business may decide that lower levels of service or increased delays are more acceptable, based on a cost-benefit analysis, or it maybe that comprehensive disaster prevention measures will need to be implemented.

These assessments enable the mapping of critical service, application and technology components to critical business processes, thus helping to identify the ITSCM elements that need to be provided. The business requirements are ranked and the associated ITSCM elements confirmed and prioritized in terms of risk reduction and recovery planning. The results of the BIA, discussed earlier, are invaluable input to several areas of process design including Service Level Management to understand the required service levels.

Impacts should be measured against particular scenarios for each business process, such as an inability to settle trades in a money market dealing process, or an inability to invoice for a period of days. An example is a money market dealing environment where loss of market data information could mean that the organization starts to lose money immediately as trading cannot continue. In

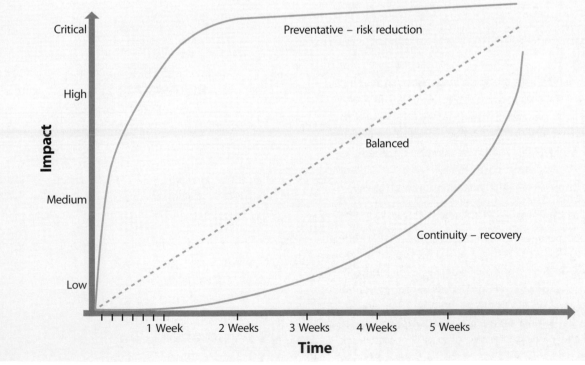

Figure 4.22 Graphical representation of business impacts

addition, customers may go to another organization, which would mean potential loss of core business. Loss of the settlement system does not prevent trading from taking place, but if trades already conducted cannot be settled within a specified period of time, the organization may be in breach of regulatory rules or settlement periods and suffer fines and damaged reputation. This may actually be a more significant impact than the inability to trade because of an inability to satisfy customer expectations.

It is also important to understand how impacts may change over time. For instance, it may be possible for a business to function without a particular process for a short period of time. In a balanced scenario, impacts to the business will occur and become greater over time. However, not all organizations are affected in this way. In some organizations, impacts are not apparent immediately. At some point, however, for any organization, the impacts will accrue to such a level that the business can no longer operate. ITSCM ensures that contingency options are identified so that the appropriate measure can be applied at the appropriate time to keep business impacts from service disruption to a minimum level.

When conducting a BIA, it is important that senior business area representatives' views are sought on the impact following loss of service. It is also equally important that the views of supervisory staff and more junior staff are sought to ensure all aspects of the impact following loss of service are ascertained. Often different levels of staff will have different views on the impact, and all will have to be taken into account when producing the overall strategy.

In many organizations it will be impossible, or it will not be cost-justifiable, to recover the total service in a very short timescale. In many cases, business processes can be re-established without a full complement of staff, systems and other facilities, and still maintain an acceptable level of service to clients and customers. The business recovery objectives should therefore be stated in terms of:

■ The time within which a pre-defined team of core staff and stated minimum facilities must be recovered
■ The timetable for recovery of remaining staff and facilities.

It may not always be possible to provide the recovery requirements to a detailed level. There is a need to balance the potential impact against the cost of recovery

to ensure that the costs are acceptable. The recovery objectives do, however, provide a starting point from which different business recovery and ITSCM options can be evaluated.

Requirements – Risk Analysis

The second driver in determining ITSCM requirements is the likelihood that a disaster or other serious service disruption will actually occur. This is an assessment of the level of threat and the extent to which an organization is vulnerable to that threat. Risk Analysis can also be used in assessing and reducing the chance of normal operational incidents and is a technique used by Availability Management to ensure the required availability and reliability levels can be maintained. Risk Analysis is also a key aspect of Information Security Management. A diagram on Risk Analysis and Management (Figure 4.20) is contained within the Availability Management process in section 4.4.

A number of Risk Analysis and Management methods are available for both the commercial and government sectors. Risk Analysis is the assessment of the risks that may give rise to service disruption or security violation. Risk management is concerned with identifying appropriate risk responses or cost-justifiable counter-measures to combat those risks.

A standard methodology, such as the Management of Risk (M_o_R), should be used to assess and manage risks within an organization. The M_o_R framework is illustrated in Figure 4.23.

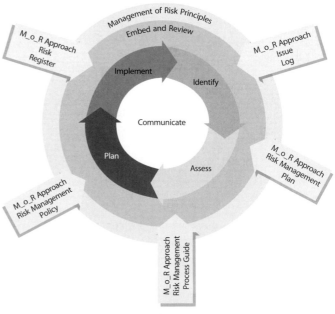

Figure 4.23 Management of Risk

The M_o_R approach is based around the above framework, which consists of the following:

- **M_o_R principles:** these principles are essential for the development of good risk management practice and are derived from corporate governance principles.
- **M_o_R approach:** an organization's approach to these principles needs to be agreed and defined within the following living documents:
  - Risk Management Policy
  - Process Guide
  - Plans
  - risk registers
  - Issue Logs.
- **M_o_R Processes:** the following four main steps describe the inputs, outputs and activities that ensure that risks are controlled:
  - **Identify:** the threats and opportunities within an activity that could impact the ability to reach its objective
  - **Assess:** the understanding of the net effect of the identified threats and opportunities associated with an activity when aggregated together
  - **Plan:** to prepare a specific management response that will reduce the threats and maximize the opportunities
  - **Implement:** the planned risk management actions, monitor their effectiveness and take corrective action where responses do not match expectations.
- **Embedding and reviewing M_o_R:** having put the principles, approach and processes in place, they need to be continually reviewed and improved to ensure they remain effective.
- **Communication:** having the appropriate communication activities in place to ensure that everyone is kept up-to-date with changes in threats, opportunities and any other aspects of risk management.

This M_o_R method requires the evaluation of risks and the development of a risk profile, such as the example in Figure 4.24.

Figure 4.24 shows an example risk profile, containing many risks that are outside the defined level of 'acceptable risk'. Following the Risk Analysis it is possible to determine appropriate risk responses or risk reduction measures (ITSCM mechanisms) to manage the risks, i.e. reduce the risk to an acceptable level or mitigate the risk. Wherever possible, appropriate risk responses should be implemented to reduce either the impact or the

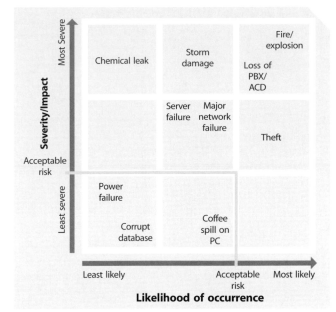

Figure 4.24 Example summary risk profile

likelihood, or both, of these risks from manifesting themselves.

In the context of ITSCM, there are a number of risks that need to be taken into consideration. The following is not a comprehensive list but does give some examples of risks and threats that need to be addressed by the ITSCM process.

IT Service Continuity Strategy

The results of the Business Impact Analysis and the Risk Analysis will enable appropriate Business and IT Service Continuity strategies to be produced in line with the business needs. The strategy will be an optimum balance of risk reduction and recovery or continuity options. This includes consideration of the relative service recovery priorities and the changes in relative service priority for the time of day, day of the week, and monthly and annual variations. Those services that have been identified as high impacts in the short term within the BIA will want to concentrate efforts on preventative risk reduction methods – for example, through full resilience and fault tolerance – while an organization that has low short-term impacts would be better suited to comprehensive recovery options, as described in the following sections. Similar advice and guidance can be found in the Business Continuity Institute's BCI Good Practice Guidelines.

Risk response measures

Most organizations will have to adopt a balanced approach where risk reduction and recovery are complementary and both are required. This entails reducing, as far as possible, the risks to the continued

Table 4.1 Examples of risks and threats

Risk	Threat
Loss of internal IT systems/networks, PABXs, ACDs, etc.	Fire Power failure Arson and vandalism Flood Aircraft impact Weather damage, e.g. hurricane Environmental disaster Terrorist attack Sabotage Catastrophic failure Electrical damage, e.g. lightning Accidental damage Poor-quality software
Loss of external IT systems/networks, e.g. e-commerce servers, cryptographic systems	All of the above Excessive demand for services Denial of service attack, e.g. against an internet firewall Technology failure, e.g. cryptographic system
Loss of data	Technology failure Human error Viruses, malicious software, e.g. attack applets
Loss of network services	Damage or denial of access to network service provider's premises Loss of service provider's IT systems/networks Loss of service provider's data Failure of the service provider
Unavailability of key technical and support staff	Industrial action Denial of access to premises Resignation Sickness/injury Transport difficulties
Failure of service providers, e.g. outsourced IT	Commercial failure, e.g. insolvency Denial of access to premises Unavailability of service provider's staff Failure to meet contractual service levels

provision of the IT service and is usually achieved through Availability Management. However well planned, it is impossible to completely eliminate all risks – for example, a fire in a nearby building will probably result in damage, or at least denial of access, as a result of the implementation of a cordon. As a general rule, the invocation of a recovery capability should only be taken as a last resort. Ideally, an organization should assess all of the risks to reduce the potential requirement to recover the business, which is likely to include the IT services.

The risk reduction measures need to be implemented and should be instigated in conjunction with Availability Management, as many of these reduce the probability of failure affecting the availability of service. Typical risk reduction measures include:

- Installation of UPS and backup power to the computer
- Fault-tolerant systems for critical applications where even minimal downtime is unacceptable – for example, a banking system
- RAID arrays and disk mirroring for LAN servers to prevent against data loss and to ensure continued availability of data
- Spare equipment/components to be used in the event of equipment or component failure – for example, a spare LAN server already configured with the standard configuration and available to replace a faulty server with minimum build and configuration time

- The elimination of SpoFs, such as single access network points or single power supply into a building
- Resilient IT systems and networks
- Outsourcing services to more than one provider
- Greater physical and IT-based security controls
- Better controls to detect service disruptions, such as fire detection systems, coupled with suppression systems
- A comprehensive backup and recovery strategy, including off-site storage.

The above measures will not necessarily solve an ITSCM issue and remove the risk totally, but all or a combination of them may significantly reduce the risks associated with the way in which services are provided to the business.

Off-site storage

One risk response method is to ensure all vital data is backed up and stored off-site. Once the recovery strategy has been defined, an appropriate backup strategy should be adopted and implemented to support it. The backup strategy must include regular (probably daily) removal of data (including the CMS to ease recovery) from the main data centres to a suitable off-site storage location. This will ensure retrieval of data following relatively minor operational failure as well as total and complete disasters. As well as the electronic data, all other important information and documents should be stored off-site, with the main example being the ITSCM plans.

ITSCM recovery options

An organization's ITSCM strategy is a balance between the cost of risk reduction measures and recovery options to support the recovery of critical business processes within agreed timescales. The following is a list of the potential IT recovery options that need to be considered when developing the strategy.

Manual work-arounds

For certain types of services, manual work-arounds can be an effective interim measure for a limited timeframe until the IT service is resumed. For instance, a Service Desk call-logging service could survive for a limited time using paper forms linked to a laptop computer with a spreadsheet.

Reciprocal arrangements

In the past, reciprocal arrangements were typical contingency measures where agreements were put in place with another organization using similar technology. This is no longer effective or possible for most types of IT systems, but can still be used in specific cases – for example, setting up an agreement to share high-speed printing facilities. Reciprocal arrangements can also be used for the off-site storage of backups and other critical information.

Gradual recovery

This option (sometimes referred to as 'cold standby') includes the provision of empty accommodation, fully equipped with power, environmental controls and local network cabling infrastructure, telecommunications connections, and available in a disaster situation for an organization to install its own computer equipment. It does not include the actual computing equipment, so is not applicable for services requiring speedy recovery, as set-up time is required before recovery of services can begin. This recovery option is only recommended for services that can bear a delay of recovery time in days or weeks, not hours. Any non-critical service that can bear this type of delay should take into account the cost of this option versus the benefit to the business before determining if a gradual recovery option should be included in the ITSCM options for the organization.

The accommodation may be provided commercially by a third party, for a fee, or may be private, (established by the organization itself) and provided as either a fixed or portable service.

A portable facility is typically a prefabricated building provided by a third party and located, when needed, at a predetermined site agreed with the organization. This may be in another location some distance from the home site, perhaps another owned building. The replacement computer equipment will need to be planned, but suppliers of computing equipment do not always guarantee replacement equipment within a fixed deadline, though they would normally do so under their best efforts.

Intermediate recovery

This option (sometimes referred to as 'warm standby') is selected by organizations that need to recover IT facilities within a predetermined time to prevent impacts to the business process. The predetermined time will have been agreed with the business during the BIA.

Most common is the use of commercial facilities, which are offered by third-party recovery organizations to a number of subscribers, spreading the cost across those subscribers. Commercial facilities often include operation, system management and technical support. The cost varies depending on the facilities requested, such as processors, peripherals, communications, and how quickly the services must be restored.

The advantage of this service is that the customer can have virtually instantaneous access to a site, housed in a secure building, in the event of a disaster. It must be understood, however, that the restoration of services at the site may take some time, as delays may be encountered while the site is re-configured for the organization that invokes the service, and the organization's applications and data will need to be restored from backups.

One potentially major disadvantage is the security implications of running IT services at a third party's data centre. This must be taken into account when planning to use this type of facility. For some organizations, the external intermediate recovery option may not be appropriate for this reason.

If the site is invoked, there is often a daily fee for use of the service in an emergency, although this may be offset against additional cost of working insurance.

Commercial recovery services can be provided in self-contained, portable or mobile form where an agreed system is delivered to a customer's site, within an agreed time.

Fast recovery
This option (sometimes referred to as 'hot standby') provides for fast recovery and restoration of services and is sometimes provided as an extension to the intermediate recovery provided by a third-party recovery provider. Some organizations will provide their own facilities within the organization, but not on an alternative site to the one used for the normal operations. Others implement their own internal second locations on an alternative site to provide more resilient recovery.

Where there is a need for a fast restoration of a service, it is possible to 'rent' floor space at the recovery site and install servers or systems with application systems and

communications already available, and data mirrored from the operational servers. In the event of a system failure, the customers can then recover and switch over to the backup facility with little loss of service. This typically involves the re-establishment of the critical systems and services within a 24-hour period.

Immediate recovery
This option (also often referred to as 'hot standby', 'mirroring', 'load balancing' or 'split site') provides for immediate restoration of services, with no loss of service. For business critical services, organizations requiring continuous operation will provide their own facilities within the organization, but not on the same site as the normal operations. Sufficient IT equipment will be 'dual located 'in either an owned or hosted location to run the compete service from either location in the event of loss of one facility, with no loss of service to the customer. The second site can then be recovered whilst the service is provided from the single operable location. This is an expensive option, but may be justified for critical business processes or VBFs where non-availability for a short period could result in a significant impact, or where it would not be appropriate to be running IT services on a third party's premises for security or other reasons. The facility needs to be located separately and far enough away from the home site that it will not be affected by a disaster affecting that location. However, these mirrored servers and sites options should be implemented in close liaison with Availability Management as they support services with high levels of availability.

The strategy is likely to include a combination of risk response measures and a combination of the above recovery options, as illustrated in Figure 4.25.

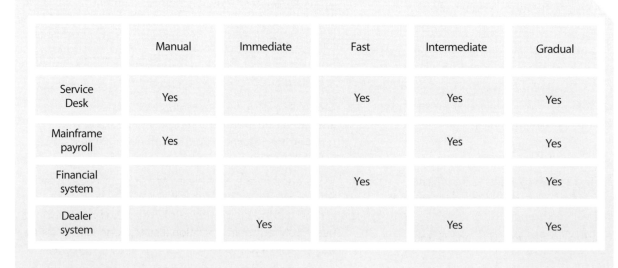

	Manual	Immediate	Fast	Intermediate	Gradual
Service Desk	Yes		Yes	Yes	Yes
Mainframe payroll	Yes			Yes	Yes
Financial system			Yes		Yes
Dealer system		Yes		Yes	Yes

Figure 4.25 Example set of recovery options

Figure 4.25 shows that a number of options may be used to provide continuity of service. An example from Figure 4.25 shows that, initially, continuity of the Service Desk is provided using manual processes such as a set of forms, and maybe a spreadsheet operating from a laptop computer, whilst recovery plans for the service are completed on an alternative 'fast recovery' site. Once the alternative site has become operational, the Service Desk can switch back to using the IT service. However, use of the external 'fast recovery' alternative site is probably limited in duration, so while running temporarily from this site, the 'intermediate site' can be made operational and long-term operations can be transferred there.

Different services within an organization require different in-built resilience and different recovery options. Whatever option is chosen, the solution will need to be cost-justified. As a general rule, the longer the business can survive without a service, the cheaper the solution will be. For example, a critical healthcare system that requires continuous operation will be very costly, as potential loss of service will need to be eliminated by the use of immediate recovery, whereas a service the absence of which does not severely affect the business for a week or so could be supported by a much cheaper solution, such as intermediate recovery.

As well as the recovery of the computing equipment, planning needs to include the recovery of accommodation and infrastructure for both IT and user staff. Other areas to be taken into account include critical services such as power, telecommunications, water, couriers, post, paper records and reference material.

It is important to remember that the recovery is based around a series of stand-by arrangements including accommodation, procedures and people, as well as systems and telecommunications. Certain actions are necessary to implement the stand-by arrangements. For example:

- Negotiating for third-party recovery facilities and entering into a contractual arrangement
- Preparing and equipping the stand-by accommodation
- Purchasing and installing stand-by computer systems.

4.5.5.3 Stage 3 – Implementation

Once the strategy has been approved, the IT Service Continuity Plans need to be produced in line with the Business Continuity Plans.

ITSCM plans need to be developed to enable the necessary information for critical systems, services and facilities to either continue to be provided or to be reinstated within an acceptable period to the business. An example ITSCM recovery plan is contained in Appendix K. Generally the Business Continuity Plans rely on the availability of IT services, facilities and resources. As a consequence of this, ITSCM plans need to address all activities to ensure that the required services, facilities and resources are delivered in an acceptable operational state and are 'fit for purpose' when accepted by the business. This entails not only the restoration of services and facilities, but also the understanding of dependencies between them, the testing required prior to delivery (performance, functional, operational and acceptance testing) and the validation of data integrity and consistency.

It should be noted that the continuity plans are more than just recovery plans, and should include documentation of the resilience measures and the measures that have been put into place to enable recovery, together with explanations of why a particular approach has been taken (this facilitates decisions should invocation determine that the particular situation requires a modification to the plan). However, the format of the plan should enable rapid access to the recovery information itself, perhaps as an appendix that can be accessed directly. All key staff should have access to copies of all the necessary recovery documentation.

Management of the distribution of the plans is important to ensure that copies are available to key staff at all times. The plans should be controlled documents (with formalized documents maintained under Change Management and Configuration Management control) to ensure that only the latest versions are in circulation and each recipient should ensure that a personal copy is maintained off-site.

The plan should ensure that all details regarding recovery of the IT services following a disaster are fully documented. It should have sufficient details to enable a technical person unfamiliar with the systems to be able to follow the procedures. The recovery plans include key details such as the data recovery point, a list of dependent systems, the nature of the dependency and their data recovery points, system hardware and software requirements, configuration details and references to other relevant or essential information about the service and systems.

It is a good idea to include a checklist that covers specific actions required during all stages of recovery for the service and system. For example, after the system has been restored to an operational state, connectivity checks, functionality checks or data consistency and integrity checks should be carried out prior to handing the service over to the business.

There are a number of technical plans that may already exist within an organization, documenting recovery procedures from a normal operational failure. The development and maintenance of these plans will be the responsibility of the specialist teams, but will be coordinated by the Business Continuity Management team. These will be useful additions or appendices to the main plan. Additionally, plans that will need to be integrated with the main BCP are:

- **Emergency Response Plan:** to interface to all emergency services and activities
- **Damage Assessment Plan:** containing details of damage assessment contacts, processes and plans
- **Salvage Plan:** containing information on salvage contacts, activities and processes
- **Vital Records Plan:** details of all vital records and information, together with their location, that are critical to the continued operation of the business
- **Crisis Management and Public Relations Plan:** the plans on the command and control of different crisis situations and management of the media and public relations
- **Accommodation and Services Plan:** detailing the management of accommodation, facilities and the services necessary for their continued operation
- **Security Plan:** showing how all aspects of security will be managed on all home sites and recovery sites
- **Personnel Plan:** containing details of how all personnel issues will be managed during a major incident
- **Communication Plan:** showing how all aspects of communication will be handled and managed with all relevant areas and parties involved during a major incident
- **Finance and Administration Plan:** containing details of alternative methods and processes for obtaining possible emergency authorization and access to essential funds during a major incident.

Finally, each critical business area is responsible for the development of a plan detailing the individuals who will be in the recovery teams and the tasks to be undertaken on invocation of recovery arrangements.

The ITSCM Plan must contain all the information needed to recover the IT systems, networks and telecommunications in a disaster situation once a decision to invoke has been made, and then to manage the business return to normal operation once the service disruption has been resolved. One of the most important inputs into the plan development is the results of the Business Impact Analysis. Additionally other areas will

need to be analysed, such as Service Level Agreements (SLA), security requirements, operating instructions and procedures and external contracts. It is likely that a separate SLA with alternative targets will have been agreed if running at a recovery site following a disaster.

Other areas that will need to be implemented following the approval of the strategy are:

Organization planning

During the disaster recovery process, the organizational structure will inevitably be different from normal operation and is based around:

- Executive – including senior management/executive board, with overall authority and control within the organization and responsible for crisis management and liaison with other departments, divisions, organizations, the media, regulators, emergency services etc.
- Coordination – typically one level below the executive group and responsible for coordinating the overall recovery effort within the organization
- Recovery – a series of business and service recovery teams, representing the critical business functions and the services that need to be established to support these functions. Each team is responsible for executing the plans within their own areas and for liaison with staff, customers and third parties. Within IT the recovery teams should be grouped by IT service and application. For example, the infrastructure team may have one or more people responsible for recovering external connections, voice services, local area networks, etc. and the support teams may be split by platform, operating system or application. In addition, the recovery priorities for the service, application or its components identified during the Business Impact Analysis should be documented within the recovery plans and applied during their execution.

Testing

Experience has shown that recovery plans that have not been fully tested do not work as intended, if at all. Testing is therefore a critical part of the overall ITSCM process and the only way of ensuring that the selected strategy, standby arrangements, logistics, business recovery plans and procedures will actually work in practice.

The IT service provider is responsible for ensuring that the IT services can be recovered in the required timescales with the required functionality and the required performance following a disaster.

There are four basic types of tests that can be undertaken:

- **Walk-through tests** can be conducted when the plan has been produced simply by getting the relevant people together to see if the plan(s) at least work in a simulated way.
- **Full tests** should be conducted as soon as possible after the plan production and at regular intervals of at least annually thereafter. They should involve the business units to assist in proving the capability to recover the services appropriately. They should, as far as possible, replicate an actual invocation of all stand-by arrangements and should involve external parties if they are planned to be involved in an actual invocation. The tests must not only prove recovery of the IT services but also the recovery of the business processes. It is recommended that an independent observer records all the activities of the tests and the timings of the service recovery. The observer's documentation of the tests will be vital input into the subsequent post mortem review. The full tests may be announced or unannounced. The first test of the plan is likely to be announced and carefully planned, but subsequent tests may be 'sprung' on key players without warning. It is also essential that many different people get involved, including those not very familiar with the IT service and systems, as the people with the most knowledge may not be available when a disaster actually occurs.
- **Partial tests** can also be undertaken where recovery of certain elements of the overall plan is tested, such as single services or servers. These types of tests should be in addition to the full test not instead of the full test. The full test is the best way of testing that all services can be recovered in required timescales and can run together on the recovery systems.
- **Scenario tests** can be used to test reactions and plans to specific conditions, events and scenarios. They can include testing that BCPs and IT Service Continuity Plans interface with each other, as well as interfacing with all other plans involved in the handling and management of a major incident.

All tests need to be undertaken against defined test scenarios, which are described as realistically as possible. It should be noted, however, that even the most comprehensive test does not cover everything. For example, in a service disruption where there has been injury or even death to colleagues, the reaction of staff to a crisis cannot be tested and the plans need to make allowance for this. In addition, tests must have clearly defined objectives and Critical Success Factors, which will be used to determine the success or otherwise of the exercise.

4.5.5.4 Stage 4 – Ongoing operation

This stage consists of the following:

- **Education, awareness and training** – this should cover the organization and, in particular, the IT organization, for service continuity-specific items. This ensures that all staff are aware of the implications of business continuity and of service continuity and consider these as part of their normal working, and that everyone involved in the plan has been trained in how to implement their actions.
- **Review** – regular review of all of the deliverables from the ITSCM process needs to be undertaken to ensure that they remain current.
- **Testing** – following the initial testing, it is necessary to establish a programme of regular testing to ensure that the critical components of the strategy are tested, preferably at least annually, although testing of IT Service Continuity Plans should be arranged in line with business needs and the needs of the BCPs. All plans should also be tested after every major business change. It is important that any changes to the IT technology are also included in the strategy, implemented in an appropriate fashion and tested to ensure that they function correctly within the overall provision of IT following a disaster. The backup and recovery of IT service should also be monitored and tested to ensure that when they are needed during a major incident, they will operate as needed. This aspect is covered more fully in the Service Operation publication
- **Change Management** – the Change Management process should ensure that all changes are assessed for their potential impact on the ITSCM plans. If the planned change will invalidate the plans, then the plan must be updated before the change is implemented, and it should be tested as part of the change testing. The plans themselves must be under very strict Change Management and Configuration Management control. Inaccurate plans and inadequate recovery capabilities may result in the failure of BCPs. Also, on an ongoing basis, whenever there are new services or where services have major changes, it is essential that a BIA and risk assessment is conducted on the new or changed service and the strategy and plans updated accordingly.

Invocation

Invocation is the ultimate test of the Business Continuity and ITSCM Plans. If all the preparatory work has been successfully completed, and plans developed and tested, then an invocation of the Business Continuity Plans should be a straightforward process, but if the plans have not been tested, failures can be expected. It is important that due consideration is given to the design of all invocation processes, to ensure that they are fit for purpose and interface to all other relevant invocation processes.

Invocation is a key component of the plans, which must include the invocation process and guidance. It should be remembered that the decision to invoke, especially if a third-party recovery facility is to be used, should not be taken lightly. Costs will be involved and the process will involve disruption to the business. This decision is typically made by a 'crisis management' team, comprising senior managers from the business and support departments (including IT), using information gathered through damage assessment and other sources.

A disruption could occur at any time of the day or night, so it is essential that guidance on the invocation process is readily available. Plans must be available to key staff in the office and away from the office.

The decision to invoke must be made quickly, as there may be a lead-time involved in establishing facilities at a recovery site. In the case of a serious building fire, the decision may be fairly easy to make. However, in the case of power failure or hardware fault, where a resolution is expected within a short period, a deadline should be set by which time if the incident has not been resolved, invocation will take place. If using external services providers, they should be warned immediately if there is a chance that invocation might take place.

The decision to invoke needs to take into account the:

■ Extent of the damage and scope of the potential invocation
■ Likely length of the disruption and unavailability of premises and/or services
■ Time of day/month/year and the potential business impact. At year-end, the need to invoke may be more pressing, to ensure that year-end processing is completed on time.

Therefore the design of the invocation process must provide guidance on how all of these areas and circumstances should be assessed to assist the person invoking the continuity plan.

The ITSCM Plan should include details of activities that need to be undertaken, including:

■ Retrieval of backup tapes or use of data vaulting to retrieve data
■ Retrieval of essential documentation, procedures, workstation images, etc. stored off-site
■ Mobilization of the appropriate technical personnel to go to the recovery site to commence the recovery of required systems and services
■ Contacting and putting on alert telecommunications suppliers, support services, application vendors, etc. who may be required to undertake actions or provide assistance in the recovery process.

The invocation and initial recovery is likely to be a time of high activity, involving long hours for many individuals. This must be recognized and managed by the recovery team leaders to ensure that breaks are provided and prevent 'burn-out'. Planning for shifts and handovers must be undertaken to ensure that the best use is made of the facilities available. It is also vitally important to ensure that the usual business and technology controls remain in place during invocation, recovery and return to normal to ensure that information security is maintained at the correct level and that data protection is preserved.

Once the recovery has been completed, the business should be able to operate from the recovery site at the level determined and agreed in the strategy and relevant SLA. The objective, however, will be to build up the business to normal levels, maintain operation from the recovery site in the short term and vacate the recovery site in the shortest possible time. Details of all these activities need to be contained within the plans. If using external services, there will be a finite contractual period for using the facility. Whatever the period, a return to normal must be carefully planned and undertaken in a controlled fashion. Typically this will be over a weekend and may include some necessary downtime in business hours. It is important that this is managed well and that all personnel involved are aware of their responsibilities to ensure a smooth transition.

4.5.6 Triggers, inputs, outputs and interfaces

Many events may trigger ITSCM activity. These include:

■ New or changed business needs, or new or changed services
■ New or changed targets within agreements, such as SLRs, SLAs, OLAs or contracts
■ The occurrence of a major incident that requires assessment for potential invocation of either Business or IT Continuity Plans

■ Periodic activities such as the BIA or Risk Analysis activities, maintenance of Continuity Plans or other reviewing, revising or reporting activities

■ Assessment of changes and attendance at Change Advisory Board meetings

■ Review and revision of business and IT plans and strategies

■ Review and revision of designs and strategies

■ Recognition or notification of a change of risk or impact of a business process or VBF, an IT service or component

■ Initiation of tests of continuity and recovery plans.

Integration and interfaces exist from ITSCM to all other processes. Important examples are as follows:

■ **Change Management** – all changes need to be considered for their impact on the continuity plans, and if amendments are required to the plan, updates to the plan need to be part of the change. The plan itself must be under Change Management control.

■ **Incident and Problem Management** – incidents can easily evolve into major incidents or disasters. Clear criteria need to be agreed and documented on for the invocation of the ITSCM plans.

■ **Availability Management** – undertaking Risk Analysis and implementing risk responses should be closely coordinated with the availability process to optimize risk mitigation.

■ **Service Level Management** – recovery requirements will be agreed and documented in the SLAs. Different service levels could be agreed and documented that could be acceptable in a disaster situation.

■ **Capacity Management** – ensuring that there are sufficient resources to enable recovery onto replacement computers following a disaster.

■ **Configuration Management** – the CMS documents the components that make up the infrastructure and the relationship between the components. This information is invaluable for all the stages of the ITSCM lifecycle, the maintenance of plans and recovery facilities.

■ **Information Security Management** – a very close relationship exists between ITSCM and Information Security Management. A major security breach could be considered a disaster, so when conducting BIA and Risk Analysis, security will be a very important consideration.

4.5.6.1 Inputs

There are many sources of input required by the ITSCM process:

■ Business information: from the organization's business strategy, plans and financial plans, and information on their current and future requirements

■ IT information: from the IT strategy and plans and current budgets

■ A Business Continuity Strategy and a set of Business Continuity Plans: from all areas of the business

■ Service information: from the SLM process, with details of the services from the Service Portfolio and the Service Catalogue and service level targets within SLAs and SLRs

■ Financial information: from Financial Management, the cost of service provision, the cost of resources and components

■ Change information: from the Change Management process, with a Change Schedule and a need to assess all changes for their impact on all ITSCM plans

■ CMS: containing information on the relationships between the business, the services, the supporting services and the technology

■ Business Continuity Management and Availability Management testing schedules

■ IT Service Continuity Plans and test reports from supplier and partners, where appropriate.

4.5.6.2 Outputs

The outputs from the ITSCM process include:

■ A revised ITSCM policy and strategy

■ A set of ITSCM plans, including all Crisis Management, Emergency Response Plans and Disaster Recovery Plans, together with a set of supporting plans and contracts with recovery service providers

■ Business Impact Analysis exercises and reports, in conjunction with BCM and the business

■ Risk Analysis and Management reviews and reports, in conjunction with the business, Availability Management and Security Management

■ An ITSCM testing schedule

■ ITSCM test scenarios

■ ITSCM test reports and reviews.

Forecasts and predictive reports are used by all areas to analyse, predict and forecast particular business and IT scenarios and their potential solutions.

4.5.7 Key Performance Indicators

IT services are delivered and can be recovered to meet business objectives:

■ Regular audits of the ITSCM Plans to ensure that, at all times, the agreed recovery requirements of the business can be achieved

- All service recovery targets are agreed and documented in SLAs and are achievable within the ITSCM Plans
- Regular and comprehensive testing of ITSCM Plans
- Regular reviews are undertaken, at least annually, of the business and IT continuity plans with the business areas
- Negotiate and manage all necessary ITSCM contracts with third party
- Overall reduction in the risk and impact of possible failure of IT services.

Awareness throughout the organizations of the plans:

- Ensure awareness of business impact, needs and requirements throughout IT
- Ensure that all IT service areas and staff are prepared and able to respond to an invocation of the ITSCM Plans
- Regular communication of the ITSCM objectives and responsibilities within the appropriate business and IT service areas.

4.5.8 Information Management

ITSCM needs to record all of the information necessary to maintain a comprehensive set of ITSCM plans. This information base should include:

- Information from the latest version of the BIA
- Comprehensive information on risk within a Risk Register, including risk assessment and risk responses
- The latest version of the BCM strategy and BCPs
- Details relating to all completed tests and a schedule of all planned tests
- Details of all ITSCM Plans and their contents
- Details of all other plans associated with ITSCM Plans
- Details of all existing recovery facilities, recovery suppliers and partners, recovery agreements and contracts, spare and alternative equipment
- Details of all backup and recovery processes, schedules, systems and media and their respective locations.

All the above information needs to be integrated and aligned with all BCM information and all the other information required by ITSCM. Interfaces to many other processes are required to ensure that this alignment is maintained.

4.5.9 Challenges, Critical Success Factors and risks

One of the major challenges facing ITSCM is to provide appropriate plans when there is no BCM process. If there is no BCM process, then IT is likely to make incorrect assumptions about business criticality of business processes and therefore adopt the wrong continuity strategies and options. Without BCM, expensive ITSCM solutions and plans will be rendered useless by the absence of corresponding plans and arrangements within the business. Also, if BCM is absent, then the business may fail to identify inexpensive non-IT solutions and waste money on ineffective, expensive IT solutions.

In some organizations, the business perception is that continuity is an IT responsibility, and therefore the business assumes that IT will be responsible for disaster recovery and that IT services will continue to run under any circumstances. This is especially true in some outsourced situations where the business may be reluctant to share its BCM information with an external service provider.

If there is a BCM process established, then the challenge becomes one of alignment and integration. ITSCM must ensure that accurate information is obtained from the BCM process on the needs, impact and priorities of the business, and that the ITSCM information and plans are aligned and integrated with those of the business. Having achieved that alignment, the challenge becomes one of keeping them aligned by management and control of business and IT change. It is essential, therefore, that all documents and plans are maintained under strict Change Management and Configuration Management control.

The main CSFs for the ITSCM process are:

- IT services are delivered and can be recovered to meet business objectives
- Awareness throughout the organization of the business and IT Service Continuity Plans.

Some of the major risks associated with ITSCM include:

- Lack of commitment from the business to the ITSCM processes and procedures
- Lack of commitment from the business and a lack of appropriate information on future plans and strategies
- Lack of senior management commitment or a lack of resources and/or budget for the ITSCM process
- The processes focus too much on the technology issues and not enough on the IT services and the needs and priorities of the business

■ Risk Analysis and Management are conducted in isolation and not in conjunction with Availability Management and Security Management

■ ITSCM plans and information become out-of-date and lose alignment with the information and plans of the business and BCM.

4.6 INFORMATION SECURITY MANAGEMENT

4.6.1 Purpose/goal/objective

'The goal of the ISM process is to align IT security with business security and ensure that information security is effectively managed in all service and Service Management activities'.

ISM needs to be considered within the overall corporate governance framework. Corporate governance is the set of responsibilities and practices exercised by the board and executive management with the goal of providing strategic direction, ensuring the objectives are achieved, ascertaining the risks are being managed appropriately and verifying that the enterprise's resources are used effectively.

Information security is a management activity within the corporate governance framework, which provides the strategic direction for security activities and ensures objectives are achieved. It further ensures that the information security risks are appropriately managed and that enterprise information resources are used responsibly. The purpose of ISM is to provide a focus for all aspects of IT security and manage all IT security activities.

The term 'information' is used as a general term and includes data stores, databases and metadata. The objective of information security is to protect the interests of those relying on information, and the systems and communications that deliver the information, from harm resulting from failures of availability, confidentiality and integrity.

For most organizations, the security objective is met when:

■ Information is available and usable when required, and the systems that provide it can appropriately resist attacks and recover from or prevent failures (availability)

■ Information is observed by or disclosed to only those who have a right to know (confidentiality)

■ Information is complete, accurate and protected against unauthorized modification (integrity)

■ Business transactions, as well as information exchanges between enterprises, or with partners, can be trusted (authenticity and non-repudiation).

Prioritization of confidentiality, integrity and availability must be considered in the context of business and business processes. The primary guide to defining what must be protected and the level of protection has to come from the business. To be effective, security must address entire business processes from end to end and cover the physical and technical aspects. Only within the context of business needs and risks can management define security.

4.6.2 Scope

The ISM process should be the focal point for all IT security issues, and must ensure that an Information Security Policy is produced, maintained and enforced that covers the use and misuse of all IT systems and services. ISM needs to understand the total IT and business security environment, including the:

■ Business Security Policy and plans

■ Current business operation and its security requirements

■ Future business plans and requirements

■ Legislative requirements

■ Obligations and responsibilities with regard to security contained within SLAs

■ The business and IT risks and their management.

Understanding all of this will enable ISM to ensure that all the current and future security aspects and risks of the business are cost-effectively managed.

The ISM process should include:

■ The production, maintenance, distribution and enforcement of an Information Security Policy and supporting security policies

■ Understanding the agreed current and future security requirements of the business and the existing Business Security Policy and plans

■ Implementation of a set of security controls that support the Information Security Policy and manage risks associated with access to services, information and systems

■ Documentation of all security controls, together with the operation and maintenance of the controls and their associated risks

■ Management of suppliers and contracts regarding access to systems and services, in conjunction with Supplier Management

■ Management of all security breaches and incidents associated with all systems and services

■ The proactive improvement of security controls, and security risk management and the reduction of security risks

- Integration of security aspects within all other IT SM processes.

To achieve effective information security governance, management must establish and maintain an Information Security Management System (ISMS) to guide the development and management of a comprehensive information security programme that supports the business objectives.

4.6.3 Value to the business

ISM ensures that an Information Security Policy is maintained and enforced that fulfils the needs of the Business Security Policy and the requirements of corporate governance. ISM raises awareness of the need for security within all IT services and assets throughout the organization, ensuring that the policy is appropriate for the needs of the organization. ISM manages all aspects of IT and information security within all areas of IT and Service Management activity.

ISM provides assurance of business processes by enforcing appropriate security controls in all areas of IT and by managing IT risk in line with business and corporate risk management processes and guidelines.

4.6.4 Policies/principles/basic concepts

Prudent business practices require that IT processes and initiatives align with business processes and objectives. This is critical when it comes to information security, which must be closely aligned with business security and business needs. Additionally all processes within the IT organization must include security considerations.

Executive management is ultimately responsible for the organization's information and is tasked with responding to issues that affect its protection. In addition, boards of directors are expected to make information security an integral part of corporate governance. All IT service provider organizations must therefore ensure that they have a comprehensive ISM policy(s) and the necessary security controls in place to monitor and enforce the policies.

4.6.4.1 Security framework

The Information Security Management process and framework will generally consist of:

- An Information Security Policy and specific security policies that address each aspect of strategy, controls and regulation
- An Information Security Management System (ISMS), containing the standards, management

procedures and guidelines supporting the information security policies

- A comprehensive security strategy, closely linked to the business objectives, strategies and plans
- An effective security organizational structure
- A set of security controls to support the policy
- The management of security risks
- Monitoring processes to ensure compliance and provide feedback on effectiveness
- Communications strategy and plan for security
- Training and awareness strategy and plan.

4.6.4.2 The Information Security Policy

Information Security Management activities should be focused on and driven by an overall Information Security Policy and a set of underpinning specific security policies. The ITP should have the full support of top executive IT management and ideally the support and commitment of top executive business management. The policy should cover all areas of security, be appropriate, meet the needs of the business and should include:

- An overall Information Security Policy
- Use and misuse of IT assets policy
- An access control policy
- A password control policy
- An e-mail policy
- An internet policy
- An anti-virus policy
- An information classification policy
- A document classification policy
- A remote access policy
- A policy with regard to supplier access of IT service, information and components
- An asset disposal policy.

These policies should be widely available to all customers and users, and their compliance should be referred to in all SLRs, SLAs, contracts and agreements. The policies should be authorized by top executive management within the business and IT, and compliance to them should be endorsed on a regular basis. All security policies should be reviewed – and, where necessary, revised – on at least an annual basis.

4.6.4.3 The Information Security Management System (ISMS)

The framework or the ISMS in turn provides a basis for the development of a cost-effective information security programme that supports the business objectives. It will involve the Four Ps of People, Process, Products and

Customers – Requirements – Business Needs

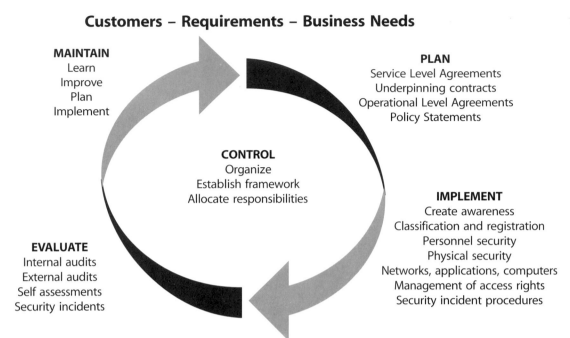

Figure 4.26 Framework for managing IT security

technology as well as Partners and suppliers to ensure high levels of security are in place.

ISO 27001 is the formal standard against which organizations may seek independent certification of their ISMS (meaning their frameworks to design, implement, manage, maintain and enforce information security processes and controls systematically and consistently throughout the organizations). The ISMS shown in Figure 4.26 shows an approach that is widely used and is based on the advice and guidance described in many sources, including ISO 27001.

The five elements within this framework are as follows:

Control

The objectives of the control element of the ISMS are to:

■ Establish a management framework to initiate and manage information security in the organization
■ Establish an organization structure to prepare, approve and implement the Information Security Policy
■ Allocate responsibilities
■ Establish and control documentation.

Plan

The objective of the plan element of the ISMS is to devise and recommend the appropriate security measures, based on an understanding of the requirements of the organization.

The requirements will be gathered from such sources as business and service risk, plans and strategies, SLAs

and OLAs and the legal, moral and ethical responsibilities for information security. Other factors, such as the amount of funding available and the prevailing organization culture and attitudes to security, must be considered.

The Information Security Policy defines the organization's attitude and stance on security matters. This should be an organization-wide document, not just applicable to the IT service provider. Responsibility for the upkeep of the document rests with the Information Security Manager.

Implement

The objective of the implementation of the ISMS is to ensure that appropriate procedures, tools and controls are in place to underpin the Information Security Policy.

Amongst the measures are:

■ **Accountability for assets** – Configuration Management and the CMS are invaluable here
■ **Information classification** – information and repositories should be classified according to the sensitivity and the impact of disclosure.

The successful implementation of the security controls and measures is dependent on a number of factors:

■ The determination of a clear and agreed policy, integrated with the needs of the business
■ Security procedures that are justified, appropriate and supported by senior management
■ Effective marketing and education in security requirements
■ A mechanism for improvement.

Evaluation

The objectives of the evaluation element of the ISMS are to:

■ Supervise and check compliance with the security policy and security requirements in SLAs and OLAs

■ Carry out regular audits of the technical security of IT systems

■ Provide information to external auditors and regulators, if required.

Maintain

The objectives of this maintain element of the ISMS are to:

■ Improve security agreements as specified in, for example, SLAs and OLAs

■ Improve the implementation of security measures and controls.

This should be achieved using a PDCA (Plan–Do–Check–Act) cycle, which is a formal approach suggested by ISO 27001 for the establishment of the Information Security Management System (ISMS) or framework. This cycle is described in more detail in the Continual Service Improvement publication.

Security governance

Information security governance, when properly implemented, should provide six basic outcomes:

■ Strategic alignment:
  ● Security requirements should be driven by enterprise requirements
  ● Security solutions need to fit enterprise processes
  ● Investment in information security should be aligned with the enterprise strategy and agreed-on risk profile.
■ Value delivery:
  ● A standard set of security practices, i.e. baseline security requirements following best practices
  ● Properly prioritized and distributed effort to areas with greatest impact and business benefit
  ● Institutionalized and commoditized solutions
  ● Complete solutions, covering organization and process as well as technology
  ● A culture of continual improvement.
■ Risk management:
  ● Agreed-on risk profile
  ● Understanding of risk exposure
  ● Awareness of risk management priorities
  ● Risk mitigation
  ● Risk acceptance/deference.

■ Performance Management:
  ● Defined, agreed and meaningful set of metrics
  ● Measurement process that will help identify shortcomings and provide feedback on progress made resolving issues
  ● Independent assurance.
■ Resource management:
  ● Knowledge is captured and available
  ● Documented security processes and practices
  ● Developed security architecture(s) to efficiently utilize infrastructure resources.
■ Business process assurance.

4.6.5 Process activities, methods and techniques

The purpose of the ISM process is to ensure that the security aspects with regard to services and all Service Management activities are appropriately managed and controlled in line with business needs and risks:

The key activities within the ISM process are:

■ Production, review and revision of an overall Information Security Policy and a set of supporting specific policies

■ Communication, implementation and enforcement of the security policies

■ Assessment and classification of all information assets and documentation

■ Implementation, review, revision and improvement of a set of security controls and risk assessment and responses

■ Monitoring and management of all security breaches and major security incidents

■ Analysis, reporting and reduction of the volumes and impact of security breaches and incidents

■ Schedule and completion of security reviews, audits and penetration tests.

The interactions between these key activities are illustrated in Figure 4.27.

The developed Information Security Management processes, together with the methods, tools and techniques, constitute the security strategy. The security manager should ensure that technologies, products and services are in place and that the overall policy is developed and well published. The security manager is also responsible for security architecture, authentication, authorization, administration and recovery.

The security strategy also needs to consider how it will embed good security practices into every area of the business. Training and awareness are vital in the overall

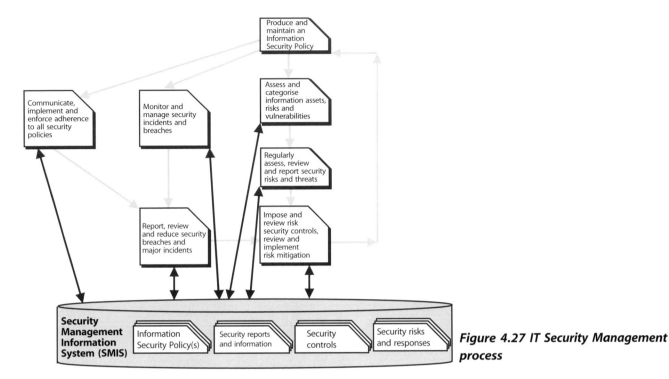

Figure 4.27 IT Security Management process

strategy, as security is often weakest at the end-user stage. It is here, as well, that there is a need to develop methods and processes that enable the policies and standards to be more easily followed and implemented.

Resources need to be assigned to track developments in these enabling technologies and the products they support. For example, privacy continues to be important and, increasingly, the focus of government regulation, making privacy compliance technologies an important enabling technology.

4.6.5.1 Security controls

The Information Security Manager must understand that security is not a step in the lifecycle of services and systems and that security cannot be solved through technology. Rather, information security must be an integral part of all services and systems and is an ongoing process that needs to be continuously managed using a set of security controls, as shown in Figure 4.28.

The set of security controls should be designed to support and enforce the Information Security Policy and to minimize all recognized and identified threats. The controls will be considerably more cost-effective if included within the design of all services. This will ensure the continued protection of all existing services and that new services and access to them are in line with the policy.

Security measures can be used at a specific stage in the prevention and handling of security incidents, as illustrated in Figure 4.28. Security incidents are not solely caused by technical threats – statistics show that, for example, the large majority stem from human errors (intended or not) or procedural errors, and often have implications in other fields such as safety, legal or health.

The following stages can be identified. At the start there is a risk that a threat will materialize. A threat can be anything that disrupts the business process or has negative impact on the business. When a threat

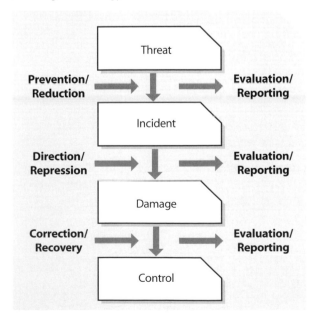

Figure 4.28 Security controls for threats and incidents

materializes, we speak of a security incident. This security incident may result in damage (to information or to assets) that has to be repaired or otherwise corrected. Suitable measures can be selected for each of these stages. The choice of measures will depend on the importance attached to the information.

■ **Preventive:** security measures are used to prevent a security incident from occurring. The best-known example of preventive measures is the allocation of access rights to a limited group of authorized people. The further requirements associated with this measure include the control of access rights (granting, maintenance and withdrawal of rights), authorization (identifying who is allowed access to which information and using which tools), identification and authentication (confirming who is seeking access) and access control (ensuring that only authorized personnel can gain access).

■ **Reductive:** further measures can be taken in advance to minimize any possible damage that may occur. These are 'reductive' measures. Familiar examples of reduction measures are making regular backups and the development, testing and maintenance of contingency plans.

■ **Detective:** if a security incident occurs, it is important to discover it as soon as possible – detection. A familiar example of this is monitoring, linked to an alert procedure. Another example is virus-checking software.

■ **Repressive:** measures are then used to counteract any continuation or repetition of the security incident. For example, an account or network address is temporarily blocked after numerous failed attempts to log on or the retention of a card when multiple attempts are made with a wrong PIN number.

■ **Corrective:** The damage is repaired as far as possible using corrective measures. For example, corrective measures include restoring the backup, or returning to a previous stable situation (roll-back, back-out). Fallback can also been seen as a corrective measure.

The documentation of all controls should be maintained to reflect accurately their operation, maintenance and their method of operation.

4.6.5.2 Management of security breaches and incidents

In the case of serious security breaches or incidents, an evaluation is necessary in due course, to determine what went wrong, what caused it and how it can be prevented in the future. However, this process should not be limited to serious security incidents. All breaches of security and security incidents need to be studied in order to gain a full picture of the effectiveness of the security measures as a whole. A reporting procedure for security incidents is required to be able to evaluate the effectiveness and efficiency of the present security measures based on an insight into all security incidents. This is facilitated by the maintenance of log files and audit files and, of course, the incident records of the Service Desk function. The analysis of these statistics on security issues should lead to improvement actions focused on the reduction of the impact and volume of all security breaches and incidents, in conjunction with Problem Management.

4.6.6 Triggers, inputs, outputs and interfaces

ISM activity can be triggered by many events. These include:

■ New or changed corporate governance guidelines

■ New or changed Business Security Policy

■ New or changed corporate risk management processes and guidelines

■ New or changed business needs or new or changed services

■ New or changed requirements within agreements, such as SLRs, SLAs, OLAs or contracts

■ Review and revision of business and IT plans and strategies

■ Review and revision of designs and strategies

■ Service or component security breaches or warnings, events and alerts, including threshold events, exception reports

■ Periodic activities, such as reviewing, revising or reporting, including review and revision of ISM policies, reports and plans

■ Recognition or notification of a change of risk or impact of a business process or VBF, an IT service or component

■ Requests from other areas, particularly SLM for assistance with security issues.

The effective and efficient implementation of an Information Security Policy within an organization will, to a large extent, be dependent on good Service Management processes. Indeed, the effective implementation of some processes can be seen as a pre-requisite for effective security control. The key interfaces that ISM has with other processes are as follows:

■ Incident and Problem Management: in providing assistance with the resolution and subsequent justification and correction of security incidents and problems. The Incident Management process must include the ability to identify and deal with security incidents. Service Desk and Service Operations staff must 'recognize' a security incident.

- ITSCM: with the assessment of business impact and risk, and the provision of resilience, fail-over and recovery mechanisms. Security is a major issue when continuity plans are tested or invoked. A working ITSCM plan is a mandatory requirement for ISO 27001.
- SLM: assistance with the determining of security requirements and responsibilities and their inclusion within SLRs and SLAs, together with the investigation and resolution of service and component security breaches.
- Change Management: ISM should assist with the assessment of every change for impact on security and security controls. Also ISM can provide information on unauthorized changes.
- Legal and HR issues must be considered when investigating security issues.
- Configuration Management will give the ability to provide accurate asset information to assist with security classifications. Having an accurate CMS is therefore an extremely useful ISM input.
- Security is often seen as an element of Availability Management, with Confidentiality Integrity and Availability (CIA) being the essence of Availability and ISM. Also, ISM should work with both Availability Management and ITSCM to conduct integrated Risk Analysis and Management exercises.
- Capacity Management must consider security implications when selecting and introducing new technology. Security is an important consideration when procuring any new technology or software.
- Financial Management should provide adequate funds to finance security requirements.
- Supplier Management should assist with the joint management of suppliers and their access to services and systems, and the terms and conditions to be included within contracts concerning supplier responsibilities.

4.6.6.1 Inputs

Information Security Management will need to obtain input from many areas, including:

- Business information: from the organization's business strategy, plans and financial plans, and information on their current and future requirements.

- Corporate governance and business security policies and guidelines, security plans, Risk Analysis and responses
- IT information: from the IT strategy and plans and current budgets
- Service information: from the SLM process with details of the services from the Service Portfolio and the Service Catalogue and service level targets within SLAs and SLRs, and possibly from the monitoring of SLAs, service reviews and breaches of the SLAs
- Risk Analysis processes and reports: from ISM, Availability Management and ITSCM
- Details of all security events and breaches: from all areas of IT and SM, especially Incident Management and Problem Management
- Change information: from the Change Management process with a Change Schedule and a need to assess all changes for their impact on all security policies, plans and controls
- CMS: containing information on the relationships between the business, the services, supporting services and the technology
- Details of partner and supplier access: from Supplier Management and Availability Management on external access to services and systems.

4.6.6.2 Outputs

The outputs produced by the Information Security Management process are used in all areas and should include:

- An overall Information Security Management Policy, together with a set of specific security policies
- A Security Management Information System (SMIS), containing all the information relating to ISM
- Revised security risk assessment processes and reports
- A set of security controls, together with details of the operation and maintenance and their associated risks
- Security audits and audit reports
- Security test schedules and plans, including security penetration tests and other security tests and reports
- A set of security classifications and a set of classified information assets
- Reviews and reports of security breaches and major incidents
- Policies, processes and procedures for managing partners and suppliers and their access to services and information.

4.6.7 Key Performance Indicators

Many KPIs and metrics can be used to assess the effectiveness and efficiency of the ISM process and activities. These metrics need to be developed from the service, customer and business perspective such as:

- Business protected against security violations:
  - Percentage decrease in security breaches reported to the Service Desk
  - Percentage decrease in the impact of security breaches and incidents
  - Percentage increase in SLA conformance to security clauses.

- The determination of a clear and agreed policy, integrated with the needs of the business: decrease in the number of non-conformances of the ISM process with the business security policy and process.

- Security procedures that are justified, appropriate and supported by senior management:
  - Increase in the acceptance and conformance of security procedures
  - Increased support and commitment of senior management.

- A mechanism for improvement:
  - The number of suggested improvements to security procedures and controls
  - Decrease in the number of security non-conformance detected during audits and security testing.

- Information security is an integral part of all IT services and all ITSM processes: increase in the number of services and processes conformant with security procedures and controls.

- Effective marketing and education in security requirements, IT staff awareness of the technology supporting the services:
  - Increased awareness of the security policy and its contents, throughout the organization
  - Percentage increase in completeness of the technical Service Catalogue against IT components supporting the services
  - Service Desk supporting all services.

4.6.8 Information Management

All the information required by ISM should be contained within the SMIS. This should include all security controls, risks, breaches, processes and reports necessary to support and maintain the Information Security Policy and the ISMS. This information should cover all IT services and components and needs to be integrated and maintained in alignment with all other IT information management systems, particularly the Service Portfolio and the CMS. The SMIS will also provide the input to security audits and reviews and to the continual improvement activities so important to all ISMSs. The SMIS will also provide invaluable input to the design of new systems and services.

4.6.9 Challenges, Critical Success Factors and risks

ISM faces many challenges in establishing an appropriate Information Security Policy with an effective supporting process and controls. One of the biggest challenges is to ensure that there is adequate support from the business, business security and senior management. If these are not available, it will be impossible to establish an effective ISM process. If there is senior IT management support, but there is no support from the business, IT security controls and risk assessment will be severely limited in what they can achieve because of this lack of support from the business. It is pointless implementing security policies, procedures and controls in IT if these cannot be enforced throughout the business. The major use of IT services and assets is outside of IT, and so are the majority of security threats and risks.

In some organizations the business perception is that security is an IT responsibility, and therefore the business assumes that IT will be responsible for all aspects of IT security and that IT services will be adequately protected. However, without the commitment and support of the business and business personnel, money invested in expensive security controls and procedures will be largely wasted and they will mostly be ineffective.

If there is a business security process established, then the challenge becomes one of alignment and integration. ISM must ensure that accurate information is obtained from the business security process on the needs, risks, impact and priorities of the business and that the ISM policies, information and plans are aligned and integrated with those of the business. Having achieved that alignment, the challenge becomes one of keeping them aligned by management and control of business and IT change using strict Change Management and Configuration Management control. Again, this requires support and commitment from the business and senior management.

The main CSFs for the ISM process are:

- Business protected against security violations
- The determination of a clear and agreed policy, integrated with the needs of the business

- Security procedures that are justified, appropriate and supported by senior management
- Effective marketing and education in security requirements
- A mechanism for improvement
- Information security is an integral part of all IT services and all ITSM processes
- The availability of services is not compromised by security incidents
- Clear ownership and awareness of the security policies amongst the customer community.

Information systems can generate many direct and indirect benefits, and as many direct and indirect risks. These risks have led to a gap between the need to protect systems and services and the degree of protection applied. The gap is caused by internal and external factors, including the widespread use of technology, increasing dependence of the business on IT, increasing complexity and interconnectivity of systems, disappearance of the traditional organizational boundaries and increasingly onerous regulatory requirements.

This means that there are new risk areas that could have a significant impact on critical business operations, such as:

- Increasing requirements for availability and robustness
- Growing potential for misuse and abuse of information systems affecting privacy and ethical values
- External dangers from hackers, leading to denial-of-service and virus attacks, extortion, industrial espionage and leakage of organizational information or private data.

Because new technology provides the potential for dramatically enhanced business performance, improved and demonstrated information security can add real value to the organization by contributing to interaction with trading partners, closer customer relationships, improved competitive advantage and protected reputation. It can also enable new and easier ways to process electronic transactions and generate trust. In today's competitive global economy, if an organization wants to do business, it may well be asked to present details of its security posture and results of its past performance in terms of tests conducted to ensure security of its information resources.

Other areas of major risks associated with ISM include:

- A lack of commitment from the business to the ISM processes and procedures
- Lack of commitment from the business and a lack of appropriate information on future plans and strategies

- A lack of senior management commitment or a lack of resources and/or budget for the ISM process
- The processes focus too much on the technology issues and not enough on the IT services and the needs and priorities of the business
- Risk assessment and management is conducted in isolation and not in conjunction with Availability Management and ITSCM
- ISM policies, plans, risks and information become out-of-date and lose alignment with the corresponding relevant information and plans of the business and business security.

4.7 SUPPLIER MANAGEMENT

4.7.1 Purpose/goal/objective

'The goal of the Supplier Management process is to manage suppliers and the services they supply, to provide seamless quality of IT service to the business, ensuring value for money is obtained.'

The Supplier Management process ensures that suppliers and the services they provide are managed to support IT service targets and business expectations. The aim of this section is to raise awareness of the business context of working with partners and suppliers, and how this work can best be directed toward realising business benefit for the organization.

It is essential that Supplier Management processes and planning are involved in all stages of the Service Lifecycle, from strategy and design, through transition and operation, to improvement. The complex business demands require the complete breadth of skills and capability to support provision of a comprehensive set of IT services to a business, therefore the use of value networks and the suppliers and the services they provide are an integral part of any end-to-end solution. Suppliers and the management of suppliers and partners are essential to the provision of quality IT services.

The purpose of the Supplier Management process is to obtain value for money from suppliers and to ensure that suppliers perform to the targets contained within their contracts and agreements, while conforming to all of the terms and conditions.

The main objectives of the Supplier Management process are to:

- Obtain value for money from supplier and contracts
- Ensure that underpinning contracts and agreements with suppliers are aligned to business needs, and

support and align with agreed targets in SLRs and SLAs, in conjunction with SLM

- Manage relationships with suppliers
- Manage supplier performance
- Negotiate and agree contracts with suppliers and manage them through their lifecycle
- Maintain a supplier policy and a supporting Supplier and Contract Database (SCD).

4.7.2 Scope

The Supplier Management process should include the management of all suppliers and contracts needed to support the provision of IT services to the business. Each service provider should have formal processes for the management of all suppliers and contracts. However, the processes should adapt to cater for the importance of the supplier and/or the contract and the potential business impact on the provision of services. Many suppliers provide support services and products that independently have a relatively minor, and fairly indirect, role in value generation, but collectively make a direct and important contribution to value generation and the implementation of the overall business strategy. The greater the contribution the supplier makes to business value, the more effort the service provider should put into the

management of the supplier and the more that supplier should be involved in the development and realization of the business strategy. The smaller the supplier's value contribution, the more likely it is that the relationship will be managed mainly at an operational level, with limited interaction with the business. It may be appropriate in some organizations, particularly large ones, to manage internal teams and suppliers, where different business units may provide support of key elements.

The Supplier Management process should include:

- Implementation and enforcement of the supplier policy
- Maintenance of a Supplier and Contract Database (SCD)
- Supplier and contract categorization and risk assessment
- Supplier and contract evaluation and selection
- Development, negotiation and agreement of contracts
- Contract review, renewal and termination
- Management of suppliers and supplier performance
- Agreement and implementation of service and supplier improvement plans
- Maintenance of standard contracts, terms and conditions

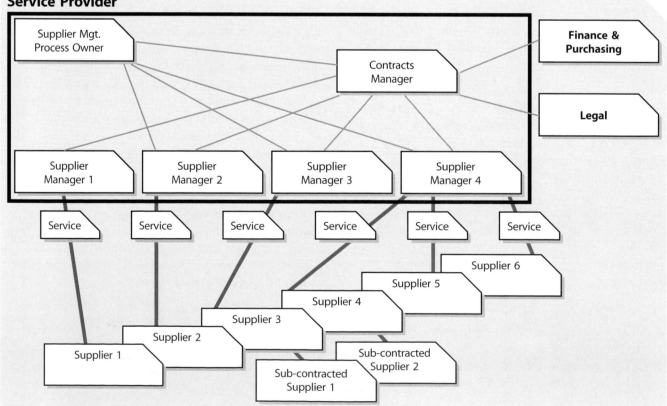

Figure 4.29 Supplier Management – roles and interfaces

- Management of contractual dispute resolution
- Management of sub-contracted suppliers.

IT Supplier Management often has to comply with organizational or corporate standards, guidelines and requirements, particularly those of corporate legal, finance and purchasing, as illustrated in Figure 4.29.

In order to ensure that suppliers provide value for money and meet their service targets, the relationship between each supplier should be owned by an individual within the service provider organization. However, a single individual may own the relationship for one or many suppliers, as illustrated in Figure 4.29. To ensure that relationships are developed in a consistent manner and that suppliers' performance is appropriately reviewed and managed, roles need to be established for a Supplier Management process owner and a Contracts Manager. In smaller organizations, these separate roles may be combined into a single responsibility.

4.7.3 Value to the business

The main objectives of the Supplier Management process are to provide value for money from suppliers and contracts and to ensure that all targets in underpinning supplier contracts and agreements are aligned to business needs and agreed targets within SLAs. This is to ensure the delivery to the business of end-to-end, seamless, quality IT services that are aligned to the business's expectation. The Supplier Management process should align with all

corporate requirements and the requirements of all other IT and SM processes, particularly ISM and ITSCM. This ensures that the business obtains value from supporting supplier services and that they are aligned with business needs.

4.7.4 Policies/principles/basic concepts

The Supplier Management process attempts to ensure that suppliers meet the terms, conditions and targets of their contracts and agreements, whilst trying to increase the value for money obtained from suppliers and the services they provide. All Supplier Management process activity should be driven by a supplier strategy and policy from Service Strategy. In order to achieve consistency and effectiveness in the implementation of the policy, a Supplier and Contracts Database (SCD) should be established, as illustrated in Figure 4.30, together with clearly defined roles and responsibilities.

Ideally the SCD should form an integrated element of a comprehensive CMS or SKMS, recording all supplier and contract details, together with details of the type of service(s) or product(s) provided by each supplier, and all other information and relationships with other associated CIs. The services provided by suppliers will also form a key part of the Service Portfolio and the Service Catalogue. The relationship between the supporting services and the IT and business services they support are key to providing quality IT services.

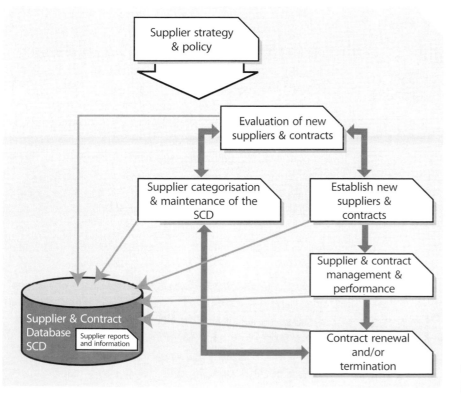

Figure 4.30 Supplier Management process

This information within the SCD will provide a complete set of reference information for all Supplier Management procedures and activities:

- Supplier categorization and maintenance of the Supplier and Contracts Database (SCD)
- Evaluation and set-up of new suppliers and contracts
- Establishing new suppliers
- Supplier and Contract Management and performance
- Contract renewal and termination.

The first two elements within the above list are covered within the Service Design stage. The third element is part of Service Transition, and the last two are part of the Service Operation stage and are covered in more detail in those publications.

4.7.5 Process activities, methods and techniques

This section provides more detail on the Supplier Management process, its sub-processes and activities, and the management of the contract lifecycle.

When dealing with external suppliers, it is strongly recommended that a formal contract with clearly defined, agreed and documented responsibilities and targets is established and managed through the stages of its lifecycle, from the identification of the business need to the operation and cessation of the contract:

- Identification of business need and preparation of the business case:
  - Produce a Statement of Requirement (SOR) and/or Invitation To Tender (ITT)
  - Ensure conformance to strategy/policy
  - Prepare the initial business case, including options (internal and external), costs, timescales, targets, benefits, risk assessment.
- Evaluation and procurement of new contracts and suppliers:
  - Identify method of purchase or procurement
  - Establish evaluation criteria – for example, services, capability (both personnel and organization), quality and cost
  - Evaluate alternative options
  - Select
  - Negotiate contracts, targets and the terms and conditions, including responsibilities, closure, renewal, extension, dispute, transfer
  - Agree and award the contract.

- Establish new suppliers and contracts:
  - Set up the supplier service and contract, within the SCD and any other associated corporate systems
  - Transition of service
  - Establish contacts and relationships.
- Supplier and contract categorization:
  - Assessment or reassessment of the supplier and contract
  - Ensure changes progressed through Service Transition
  - Categorization of the supplier
  - Update of SCD
  - Ongoing maintenance of the SCD.
- Manage the supplier and contract performance:
  - Management and control of the operation and delivery of service/products
  - Monitor and report (service, quality and costs)
  - Review and improve (service, quality and costs)
  - Management of the supplier and the relationship (communication, risks, changes, failures, improvements, contacts, interfaces)
  - Review, at least annually, service scope against business need, targets and agreements
  - Plan for possible closure/renewal/extension.
- End of term:
  - Review (determine benefits delivered, ongoing requirement)
  - Renegotiate and renew or terminate and/or transfer.

The business, IT, finance, purchasing and procurement need to work together to ensure that all stages of the contract lifecycle are managed effectively. All areas need to be jointly involved in selecting the solution and managing the ongoing performance of the supplier, with each area taking responsibility for the interests of their own area, whilst being aware of the implications on the organization as a whole. The processes involved in the stages of the contract lifecycle are explained in detail in the following sections.

4.7.5.1 Evaluation of new suppliers and contracts

The activities associated with the identification of business needs and the subsequent evaluation of new suppliers and contracts are part of the Service Design process. The outputs from this area provide the inputs to all other stages of the contract lifecycle. IT is vital to the ongoing success of the contract and the relationship that the business is closely involved in all aspects of these activities. Every organization should have templates and a formal method for the production of business cases and their approval and sign-off. The detailing of the business needs and the content of the business case should be agreed, approved and signed off by both the business and IT.

When selecting a new supplier or contract, a number of factors need to be taken into consideration, including track record, capability, references, credit rating and size relative to the business being placed. In addition, depending on the type of supplier relationship, there may be personnel issues that need to be considered. Each organization should have processes and procedures for establishing new suppliers and contracts.

While it is recognized that factors may exist that influence the decision on type of relationship or choice of supplier (e.g. politics within the organization, existing relationships), it is essential that in such cases the reasoning is identified and the impact fully assessed to ensure costly mistakes are avoided.

Services may be sourced from a single supplier or multi-sourced. Services are most likely to be sourced from two or more competing suppliers where the requirement is for standard services or products that are readily available 'off-the-shelf'. Multi-sourcing is most likely to be used where cost is the prime determinant, and requirements for developing variants of the services are low, but may also be undertaken to spread risk. Suppliers on a multi-source list may be designated with 'Preferred Supplier' status within the organization, limiting or removing scope for use of other suppliers.

Partnering relationships are established at an executive level and are dependent on a willingness to exchange strategic information to align business strategies. Many strategically important supplier relationships are now positioned as partnering relationships. This reflects a move away from traditionally hierarchical relationships, where the supplier acts subordinately to the customer organization, to one characterized by:

- **Strategic alignment:** good alignment of culture, values and objectives, leading to an alignment of business strategies
- **Integration:** a close integration of the processes of the two organizations
- **Information flow:** good communication and information exchange at all levels, especially at the strategic level, leading to close understanding
- **Mutual trust:** a relationship built on mutual trust between the organizations and their individuals

- **Openness:** when reporting on service performance, costs and Risk Analysis
- **Collective responsibility:** joint partnership teams taking collective responsibility for current performance and future development of the relationship
- **Shared risk and reward:** e.g. agreeing how investment costs and resultant efficiency benefits are shared, or how risks and rewards from fluctuations in material costs are shared.

Both parties derive benefits from partnering. An organization derives progressively more value from a supplier relationship as the supplier's understanding of the organization as a whole increases, from its IT inventory architectures through to its corporate culture, values and business objectives. With time, the supplier is able to respond more quickly and more appropriately to the organization's needs. The supplier benefits from a longer-term commitment from the organization, providing it with greater financial stability, and enabling it to finance longer-term investments, which benefit its customers.

A partnership makes it possible for the parties to align their IT infrastructures. Joint architecture and risk control agreements allow the partners to implement a range of compatible solutions from security, networking, data/information interchange, to workflow and application processing systems. This integration can provide service improvements and lowered costs. Such moves also reduce risks and costs associated with one-off tactical solutions, put in place to bridge a supplier's IT with that of the organization.

The key to a successful partnering relationship is being absolutely clear about the benefits and costs such a relationship will deliver before entering into it. Both parties then know what is expected of them at the outset. The success of the partnership may involve agreeing the transfer of staff to the partner or outsourcing organization as part of the agreement and relationship.

Service provider organizations should have documented and formal processes for evaluating and selecting suppliers based on:

- Importance and impact: the importance of the service to the business, provided by the supplier
- Risk: the risks associated with using the service
- Costs: the cost of the service and its provision.

Often other areas of the service provider organization, such as Legal, Finance and Purchasing, will get involved with this aspect of the process. Service provider organizations should have processes covering:

- Production of business case documents
- Production of SoR and Invitations to Tender or proposal documents
- Formal evaluation and selection of suppliers and contracts
- The inclusion of standard clauses, terms and conditions within contracts, including early termination, benchmarking, exit or transfer of contracts, dispute resolution, management of sub-contracted suppliers and normal termination
- Transitioning of new contracts and suppliers.

These processes may, and should be, different, based on the type, size and category of the supplier and the contract.

The nature and extent of an agreement depends on the relationship type and an assessment of the risks involved. A pre-agreement Risk Analysis is a vital stage in establishing any external supplier agreement. For each party, it exposes the risks that need to be addressed and needs to be as comprehensive as practical, covering a wide variety of risks, including financial, business reputation, operational, regulatory and legal.

A comprehensive agreement minimizes the risk of disputes arising from a difference of expectations. A flexible agreement, which adequately caters for its adaptation across the term of the agreement, is maintainable and supports change with a minimum amount of renegotiation.

The contents of a basic underpinning contract or service agreement are as follows:

- **Basic terms and conditions:** the term (duration) of the contract, the parties, locations, scope, definitions and commercial basis.
- **Service description and scope:** the functionality of the services being provided and its extent, along with constraints on the service delivery, such as performance, availability, capacity, technical interface and security. Service functionality may be explicitly defined, or in the case of well-established services, included by reference to other established documents, such as the Service Portfolio and the Service Catalogue.
- **Service standards:** the service measures and the minimum levels that constitute acceptable performance and quality, e.g. IT may have a performance requirement to respond to a request for a new desktop system in 24 hours, with acceptable service deemed to have occurred where this performance requirement is met in 95% of cases.

Service levels must be realistic, measurable and aligned to the organization's business priorities and underpin the agreed targets within SLRs and SLAs.

- **Workload ranges:** the volume ranges within which service standards apply, or for which particular pricing regimes apply.
- **Management Information (MI):** the data that must be reported by the supplier on operational performance – take care to ensure that MI is focused on the most important or headline reporting measures on which the relationship will be assessed. Key Performance Indicators (KPIs) and Balanced Scorecards (BSCs) may form the core of reported performance data.
- **Responsibilities and dependencies:** description of the obligations of the organization (in supporting the supplier in the service delivery efforts) and of the supplier (in its provision of the service), including communication, contacts and escalation.

An extended service agreement may also contain:

- Service debit and credit regime (incentives and penalties)
- Additional performance criteria.

The following gives a limited sample of the legal and commercial topics typically covered by a service or contractual agreement:

- Scope of services to be provided
- Service performance requirements
- Division and agreement of responsibilities
- Contact points, communication and reporting frequency and content
- Contract review and dispute resolution processes
- Price structure
- Payment terms
- Commitments to change and investment
- Agreement change process
- Confidentiality and announcements
- Intellectual property rights and copyright
- Liability limitations
- Termination rights of each party
- Obligations at termination and beyond.

The final form of an agreement, and some of the terminology, may be dictated by the views and preferences of the procurement and legal departments, or by specialist legal firms.

Tip

Seek legal advice when formalizing external supply agreements.

Formal contracts

Formal contracts are appropriate for external supply arrangements that make a significant contribution to the delivery and development of the business. Contracts provide for binding legal commitments between customer and supplier, and cover the obligations each organization has to the other from the first day of the contract, often extending beyond its termination. A contract is used as the basis for external supplier agreements where an enforceable commitment is required. High-value and/or strategic relationships are underpinned by a formal contract. The formality and binding nature of a contract are not at odds with the culture of a partnering agreement, but rather form the basis on which trust in the relationship may be founded.

A contract is likely to be structured with a main body containing the commercial and legal clauses, and with the elements of a service agreement, as described earlier, attached as schedules. Contracts may also include a number of other related documents as schedules, for example:

- Security requirements
- Business continuity requirements
- Mandated technical standards
- Migration plans (agreed pre-scheduled change)
- Disclosure agreements.

Most large organizations have procurement and legal departments specializing in sourcing contracts. Specialist legal firms may be employed to support the internal procurement and legal function when establishing significant formal contracts.

Underpinning agreements

In ITIL an SLA is defined as a 'written agreement between a service provider and the customer(s) that documents agreed service levels for a service'. Service providers should be aware that SLAs are widely used to formalize service-based relationships, both internally and externally, and that while conforming to the definition above, these agreements vary considerably in the detail covered.

Key message

The views of some organizations, such as the Chartered Institute of Purchase and Supply (CIPS) and various specialist lawyers, are that SLAs ought not to be used to manage external relationships unless they form part of an underlying contract. The Complete Guide to Preparing and Implementing Service Level Agreements (2001) emphasizes that a stand-alone SLA may not be legally enforceable but instead 'represents the goodwill and faith of the parties signing it'. Therefore it is in service providers' and suppliers' interests to ensure that SLAs are incorporated into an appropriate contractual framework that meets the ITIL objective that SLAs are binding agreements.

SLAs, underpinning agreements and contracts should be reviewed on a regular basis to ensure performance conforms to the service levels that have been agreed.

The organization is likely to be dependent on its own internal support groups to some extent. To be able to achieve SLA targets, it is advisable to have formal arrangements in place with these groups. Operational Level Agreements (OLAs) ensure that underpinning services support the business/IT SLA targets. OLAs focus on the operational requirements that the services need to meet. This is a non-contractual, service-oriented document describing services and service standards, with responsibilities and obligations where appropriate.

Just as with SLAs, it is important that OLAs are monitored to highlight potential problems. The Service Level Manager has the overall responsibility to review performance against targets so that action can be taken to remedy, and prevent future recurrence of, any OLA breaches. Depending on the size of the organization and variety of services, e.g. SLAs and OLAs, a Service Level Manager should take responsibility for their service or set of services.

4.7.5.2 Supplier categorization and maintenance of the Supplier and Contracts Database (SCD)

The Supplier Management process should be adaptive and spend more time and effort managing key suppliers than less important suppliers. This means that some form of categorization process should exist within the Supplier Management process to categorize the supplier and their importance to the service provider and the services provided to the business. Suppliers can be categorized in many ways, but one of the best methods for categorizing

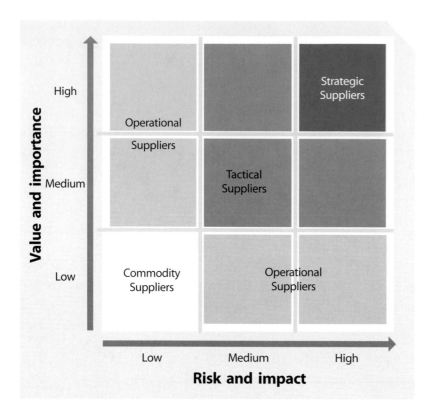

Figure 4.31 Supplier categorization

suppliers is based on assessing the risk and impact associated with using the supplier, and the value and importance of the supplier and their services to the business, as illustrated in Figure 4.31.

The amount of time and effort spent managing the supplier and the relationship can then be appropriate to its categorization:

■ **Strategic:** for significant 'partnering' relationships that involve senior managers sharing confidential strategic information to facilitate long-term plans. These relationships would normally be managed and owned at a senior management level within the service provider organization, and would involve regular and frequent contact and performance reviews. These relationships would probably require involvement of Service Strategy and Service Design resources, and would include ongoing specific improvement programmes (e.g. a network service provider, supplying worldwide networks service and their support).

■ **Tactical:** for relationships involving significant commercial activity and business interaction. These relationships would normally be managed by middle management and would involve regular contact and performance reviews, often including ongoing improvement programmes (e.g. a hardware maintenance organization providing resolution of server hardware failures).

■ **Operational:** for suppliers of operational products or services. These relationships would normally be managed by junior operational management and would involve infrequent but regular contact and performance reviews (e.g. an internet hosting service provider, supplying hosting space for a low-usage, low-impact website or internally used IT service).

■ **Commodity:** for suppliers that provide low-value and/or readily available products and services, which could be alternatively sourced relatively easily (e.g. paper or printer cartridge suppliers).

Strategically important supplier relationships are given the greatest focus. It is in these cases that Supplier Managers have to ensure that the culture of the service provider organization is extended into the supplier domain so that the relationship works beyond the initial contract. The rise in popularity of external sourcing, and the increase in the scope and complexity of some sourcing arrangements, has resulted in a diversification of types of supplier relationship. At a strategic level, it is important to understand the options that are available so that the most suitable type of supplier relationship can be established to gain maximum business benefit and evolves in line with business needs.

A number of factors, from the nature of the service to the overall cost, determine the importance of a supplier from a business perspective. As shown later, the greater the business significance of a supplier relationship, the more the business needs to be involved in the management and development of a relationship. A formal categorization approach can help to establish this importance.

The business value, measured as the contribution made to the business value chain, provides a more business-aligned assessment than pure contract price. Also, the more standard the services being procured, the lower the dependence the organization has on the supplier, and the more readily the supplier could be replaced (if necessary). Standardized services support the business through minimal time to market when deploying new or changed business services, and in pursuing cost-reduction strategies. More information on this subject can be found in the Service Strategy publication.

The more customized those services are, the greater the difficulty in moving to an alternative supplier. Customization may benefit the business, contributing to competitive advantage through differentiated service, or may be the result of operational evolution.

Tailored services increase the dependence on the supplier, increase risk and can result in increased cost. From a supplier perspective, tailored services may decrease their ability to achieve economies of scale through common operations, resulting in narrowed margins, and reduced capital available for future investment.

Standard products and services are the preferred approach unless a clear business advantage exists, in which case a strategic supplier delivers the tailored service.

Having established the type of supplier, the relationship then needs to be formalized. In the discussion below, the term 'agreement' is used generically to refer to any formalization of a relationship between customer and supplier organizations, and may range from the informal to comprehensive legally binding contracts. Simple, low-value relationships may be covered by a supplier's standard terms and conditions, and be managed wholly by IT. A relationship of strategic importance to the business, on the other hand, requires a comprehensive contract that ensures that the supplier supports evolving business needs throughout the life of the contract. A contract needs to be managed and developed in conjunction with procurement and legal departments and business stakeholders.

A business service may depend on a number of internal and/or external suppliers for its delivery. These may include a mixture of strategic suppliers and commodity suppliers. Some suppliers supply directly to the organization; others are indirect or sub-contracted suppliers working via another supplier. Direct suppliers are directly managed by the service provider; indirect or sub-contracted suppliers are managed by the leading supplier. Any one supplier may provide products or services used to support a number of different business services.

Supply chain analysis shows the mapping between business services and supplier services. Analysis of business processes will reveal the suppliers involved in each process and the points of hand-off between them. Management of the supply chain ensures that functional boundaries and performance requirements are clearly established for each supplier to ensure that overall business service levels are achieved. Business services are most likely to meet their targets consistently where there are a small number of suppliers in the supply chain, and where the interfaces between the suppliers in the chain are limited, simple and well-defined.

Reducing the number of direct suppliers reduces the number of relationships that need to be managed, the number of peer-to-peer supplier issues that need to be resolved, and reduces the complexity of the Supplier Management activities. Some organizations may successfully reduce or collapse the whole supply chain around a single service provider, often referred to as a 'prime' supplier. Facilities management is often outsourced to a single specialist partner or supplier, who may in turn subcontract restaurant services, vending machine maintenance and cleaning.

Outsourcing entire business services to a single 'prime supplier' may run additional risks. For these reasons, organizations need to consider carefully their supply chain strategies ahead of major outsourcing activity. The scope of outsourced services needs to be considered to reduce the number of suppliers, whilst ensuring that risk is managed and it fits with typical competencies in the supply market.

The SCD is a database containing details of the organization's suppliers, together with details of the products and services that they provide to the business (e.g. e-mail service, PC supply and installation, Service Desk), together with details of the contracts. The SCD contains supplier details, a summary of each product/service (including support arrangements), information on the ordering process and, where applicable, contract details. Ideally the SCD should be contained within the overall CMS.

SCDs are beneficial because they can be used to promote preferred suppliers and to prevent purchasing of unapproved or incompatible items. By coordinating and controlling the buying activity, the organization is more likely to be able to negotiate preferential rates.

4.7.5.3 Establishing new suppliers and contracts

Adding new suppliers or contracts to the SCD needs to be handled via the Change Management process, to ensure that any impact is assessed and understood. In most organizations, the SCD is owned by the Supplier Management process or the procurement or purchasing department. The SCD provides a single, central focal set of information for the management of all suppliers and contracts.

Risk management, working with suppliers, centres on assessing vulnerabilities in each supplier arrangement or contract that pose threats to any aspect of the business, including business impact, probability, customer satisfaction, brand image, market share, profitability, share price or regulatory impacts or penalties (in some industries).

The nature of the relationship affects the degree of risk to the business. Risks associated with an outsourced or

strategic supplier are likely to be greater in number, and more complex to manage, than with internal supply. It is rarely possible to 'outsource' risk, although sometimes some of the risk may be transferred to the outsourcing organization. Blaming a supplier does not impress customers or internal users affected by a security incident or a lengthy system failure. New risks arising from the relationship need to be identified and managed, with communication and escalation as appropriate.

A substantial risk assessment should have been undertaken pre-contract, but this needs to be maintained in the light of changing business needs, changes to the contract scope, or changes in the operational environment.

The service provider organization and the supplier must consider the threats posed by the relationship to their own assets, and have their own risk profile. Each must identify their respective risk owners. In a well-functioning relationship, it is possible for much or all of the assessment to be openly shared with the other party. By involving supplier experts in risk assessments, especially in Operational Risk Assessments (ORAs), the organization may gain valuable insights into how best to mitigate risks, as well as improving the coverage of the assessment.

When evaluating risks of disruption to business services or functions, the business may have different priorities for service/function restoration. Business Impact Analysis (BIA) is a method used to assess the impacts on different areas of the business, resulting from a loss of service. Risk assessment and BIA activities relating to suppliers and contracts should be performed in close conjunction with Service Continuity Management, Availability Management and Information Security Management, with a view to reducing the impact and probability of service failure as a result of supplier or supplier service failure.

Once these activities have been completed and the supplier and contract information has been input into the SCD, including the nominated individuals responsible for managing the new supplier and/or contracts, frequency of service/supplier review meetings and contractual review meetings needs to be established, with appropriate break points, automated thresholds and warnings in place. The introduction of new suppliers and contracts should be handled as major changes through transition and into operation. This will ensure that appropriate contacts and communication points are established.

4.7.5.4 Supplier and Contract Management and performance

At an operational level, integrated processes need to be in place between an organization and its suppliers to ensure efficient day-to-day working practices. For example:

- Is the supplier expected to conform to the organization's Change Management process or any other processes?
- How does the Service Desk notify the supplier of incidents?
- How is CMS information updated when CIs change as a result of supplier actions? Who is responsible?

There may be a conflict of interest between the service provider organization and their supplier, especially with regard to the Change Management, Incident Management, Problem Management and Configuration Management processes. The supplier may want to use their processes and systems, whereas the service provider organization will want to use their own processes and systems. If this is the case, clear responsibilities and interfaces will need to be defined and agreed.

These and many other areas need to be addressed to ensure smooth and effective working at an operational level. To do so, all touch points and contacts need to be identified and procedures put in place so that everyone understands their roles and responsibilities. This should include identification of the single, nominated individual responsible for ownership of each supplier and contract. However, an organization should take care not to automatically impose its own processes, but to take the opportunity to learn from its suppliers.

> **Example**
>
> A contract had been awarded for a customized Stores Control System for which the organization's IT department had developed processes to support the live service once it was installed. This included procedures for recording and documenting work done on the service by field engineers (e.g. changes, repairs, enhancement and reconfigurations). At a project progress meeting, the supplier confirmed that they had looked at the procedures and could follow them if required. However, having been in this situation many times before, they had already developed a set of procedures to deal with such events. These procedures were considerably more elegant, effective and easier to follow than those developed and proposed by the organization.

In addition to process interfaces, it is essential to identify how issues are handled at an operational level. By having clearly defined and communicated escalation routes, issues are likely to be identified and resolved earlier, minimizing the impact. Both the organization and the supplier benefit from the early capture and resolution of issues.

Both sides should strive to establish good communication links. The supplier learns more about the organization's business, its requirements and its plans, helping the supplier to understand and meet the organization's needs. In turn, the organization benefits from a more responsive supplier who is aware of the business drivers and any issues, and is therefore more able to provide appropriate solutions. Close day-to-day links can help each party to be aware of the other's culture and ways of working, resulting in fewer misunderstandings and leading to a more successful and long-lasting relationship.

Two levels of formal review need to take place throughout the contract lifecycle to minimize risk and ensure the business realizes maximum benefit from the contract:

- **Service/supplier performance reviews:** reports on performance should be produced on a regular basis, based on the category of supplier, and should form the basis of service review meetings. The more important the supplier, the more frequent and extensive the reports and reviews should be
- **Service, service scope and contract reviews:** these should also be conducted on a regular basis, at least annually for all major suppliers. The objective of these should be to review the service, overall performance, service scope and targets and the contract, together with any associated agreements. This should be compared with the original business needs and the current business needs to ensure that supplier and contracts remain aligned to business needs and continue to deliver value for money.

Formal performance review meetings must be held on a regular basis to review the supplier's performance against service levels, at a detailed operational level. These meetings provide an opportunity to check that the ongoing service performance management remains focused on supporting business needs. Typical topics include:

- Service performance against targets
- Incident and problem reviews, including any escalated issues
- Business and customer feedback

- Expected major changes that will (or may) affect service during the next service period, as well as failed changes and changes that caused incidents
- Key business events over the next service period that need particular attention from the supplier (e.g. quarter-end processing)
- Best practice and Service Improvement Programmes (SIPs).

Major service improvement initiatives and actions are controlled through SIPs with each supplier, including any actions for dealing with any failures or weaknesses. Progress of existing SIPs, or the need for a new initiative, is reviewed at service review meetings. Proactive or forward-thinking organizations not only use SIPs to deal with failures but also to improve a consistently achieved service. It is important that a contract provides suitable incentives to both parties to invest in service improvement. These aspects are covered in more detail in the Continual Service Improvement publication.

The governance mechanisms for suppliers and contracts are drawn from the needs of appropriate stakeholders at different levels within each organization, and are structured so that the organization's representatives face-off to their counterparts in the supplier's organization. Defining the responsibilities for each representative, meeting forums and processes ensure that each person is involved at the right time in influencing or directing the right activities.

The scale and importance of the service and/or supplier influence the governance arrangements needed. The more significant the dependency, the greater the commitment and effort involved in managing the relationship. The effort needed on the service provider side to govern an outsourcing contract should not be underestimated, especially in closely regulated industries, such as the finance and pharmaceutical sectors.

A key objective for Supplier Management is to ensure that the value of a supplier to the organization is fully realized. Value is realized through all aspects of the relationship, from operational performance assurance, responsiveness to change requests and demand fluctuations, through to contribution of knowledge and experience to the organization's capability. The service provider must also ensure that the supplier's priorities match the business's priorities. The supplier must understand which of its service levels are most significant to the business.

> **Example**
>
> A large multi-national company had software agreements in place with the same supplier in no less than 24 countries. By arranging a single global licensing deal with the supplier, the company made annual savings of £5,000,000.

To ensure that all activities and contacts for a supplier are consistent and coordinated, each supplier relationship should have a single nominated individual accountable for all aspects of the relationship.

> **Example**
>
> A nationwide retail organization had an overall individual owning the management of their major network services supplier. However, services, contracts and billing were managed by several individuals spread throughout the organization. The individual owner put forward a business case for single ownership of the supplier and all the various contracts, together with consolidation of all the individual invoices into a single quarterly bill. The estimated cost savings to the organization were in excess of £600,000 per annum.

Satisfaction surveys also play an important role in revealing how well supplier service levels are aligned to business needs. A survey may reveal instances where there is dissatisfaction with the service, yet the supplier is apparently performing well against its targets (and vice versa). This may happen where service levels are inappropriately defined and should result in a review of the contracts, agreements and targets. Some service providers publish supplier league tables based on their survey results, stimulating competition between suppliers.

For those significant supplier relationships in which the business has a direct interest, both the business (in conjunction with the procurement department) and IT will have established their objectives for the relationship, and defined the benefits they expect to realize. This forms a major part of the business case for entering into the relationship.

These benefits must be linked and complementary, and must be measured and managed. Where the business is seeking improvements in customer service, IT supplier relationships contributing to those customer services must be able to demonstrate improved service in their own domain, and how much this has contributed to improved customer service.

For benefits assessments to remain valid during the life of the contract, changes in circumstances that have occurred since the original benefits case was prepared must be taken into account. A supplier may have been selected on its ability to deliver a 5% saving of annual operational cost compared with other options, but after two years has delivered no savings. However, where this is due to changes to contract, or general industry costs that would have also affected the other options, it is likely that a relative cost saving is still being realized. A maintained benefits case shows that saving.

Benefits assessments often receive lower priority than cost-saving initiatives, and are given less priority in performance reports than issues and problem summaries, but it is important to the long-term relationship that achievements are recognized. A benefits report must make objective assessments against the original objectives, but may also include morale-boosting anecdotal evidence of achievements and added value.

> **Tip**
> It is important for both organizations, and for the longevity of the relationship, that the benefits being derived from the relationship are regularly reviewed and reported.

An assessment of the success of a supplier relationship, from a business perspective, is likely to be substantially based on financial performance. Even where a service is performing well, it may not be meeting one or both parties' financial targets. It is important that both parties continue to benefit financially from the relationship. A contract that squeezes the margins of a supplier too tightly may lead to under-investment by the supplier, resulting in a gradual degradation of service, or even threaten the viability of supplier. In either case this may result in adverse business impacts to the organization.

The key to the successful long-term Financial Management of the contract is a joint effort directed towards maintaining the financial equilibrium, rather than a confrontational relationship delivering short-term benefits to only one party.

Building relationships takes time and effort. As a result, the organization may only be able to build long-term relationships with a few key suppliers. The experience, culture and commitment of those involved in running a supplier relationship are at least as important as having a good contract and governance regime. The right people with the right attitudes in the relationship team can make a poor contract work, but a good contract does not ensure that a poor relationship team delivers.

A considerable amount of time and money is normally invested in negotiating major supplier deals, with more again at risk for both parties if the relationship is not successful. Both organizations must ensure that they invest suitably in the human resources allocated to managing the relationship. The personality, behaviours and culture of the relationship representatives all influence the relationship. For a partnering relationship, all those involved need to be able to respect and work closely and productively with their opposite numbers.

4.7.5.5 Contract renewal and/or termination

Contract reviews must be undertaken on a regular basis to ensure the contract is continuing to meet business needs. Contract reviews assess the contract operation holistically and at a more senior level than the service reviews that are undertaken at an operational level. These reviews should consider:

- How well the contract is working and its relevance for the future
- Whether changes are needed: services, products, contracts, agreements, targets
- What is the future outlook for the relationship – growth, shrinkage, change, termination, transfer, etc?
- Commercial performance of the contract, reviews against benchmarks or market assessments, suitability of the pricing structure and charging arrangements
- Guidance on future contract direction and ensuring best practice management processes are established
- Supplier and contract governance.

For high-value, lengthy or complex supply arrangements, the period of contract negotiation and agreement can be lengthy, costly and may involve a protracted period of negotiation. It can be a natural inclination to wish to avoid further changes to a contract for as long as possible. However, for the business to derive full value from the supplier relationship, the contract must be able to be regularly and quickly amended to allow the business to benefit from service developments.

Benchmarking provides an assessment against the marketplace. The supplier may be committed by the contract to maintaining charges against a market rate. To maintain the same margin, the supplier is obliged to improve its operational efficiency in line with its competitors. Collectively, these methods help provide an assessment of an improving or deteriorating efficiency.

The point of responsibility within the organization for deciding to change a supplier relationship is likely to depend on the type of relationship. The service provider may have identified a need to change supplier, based on the existing supplier's performance, but for a contractual relationship the decision needs to be taken in conjunction with the organization's procurement and legal departments.

The organization should take careful steps to:

■ Perform a thorough impact and Risk Analysis of a change of supplier on the organization and its business, especially during a period of transition. This could be particularly significant in the case of a strategic relationship.

■ Make a commercial assessment of the exit costs. This may include contractual termination costs if supplier liability is not clear, but the largest costs are likely to be associated with a transition project. For any significant-sized relationship, this typically includes a period of dual-supply as services are migrated. Any change associated with a change in supplier will increase costs, either immediately as fixed costs, or over time where borne by the supplier and reflected back in service charges.

■ Take legal advice on termination terms, applicable notice period and mechanisms, and any other consequences, particularly if the contract is to be terminated early.

■ Reassess the market to identify potential benefits in changing supplier.

A prudent organization undertakes most of these steps at the time the original contract is established, to ensure the right provisions and clauses are included, but this review activity needs to be reassessed when a change of supplier is being considered.

4.7.6 Triggers, inputs, outputs and interfaces

There are many events that could trigger Supplier Management activity. These include:

■ New or changed corporate governance guidelines

■ New or changed business and IT strategies, policies or plans

■ New or changed business needs or new or changed services

■ New or changed requirements within agreements, such as SLRs, SLAs, OLAs or contracts

■ Review and revision of designs and strategies

■ Periodic activities such as reviewing, revising or reporting, including review and revision of Supplier Management policies, reports and plans

■ Requests from other areas, particularly SLM and Security Management, for assistance with supplier issues

■ Requirements for new contracts, contract renewal or contract termination

■ Re-categorization of suppliers and/or contracts.

The key interfaces that Supplier Management has with other processes are:

■ ITSCM: with regard to the management of continuity service suppliers.

■ SLM: assistance with the determining of targets, requirements and responsibilities and their inclusion within underpinning agreements and contracts to ensure that they support all SLR and SLA targets. Also the investigation of SLA and SLR breaches caused by poor supplier performance.

■ ISM: in the management of suppliers and their access to services and systems, and their responsibilities with regard to conformance to ISM policies and requirements.

■ Financial Management: to provide adequate funds to finance Supplier Management requirements and contracts and to provide advice and guidance on purchase and procurement matters.

■ Service Portfolio Management: to ensure that all supporting services and their details and relationships are accurately reflected within the Service Portfolio.

4.7.6.1 Inputs

■ **Business information:** from the organization's business strategy, plans and financial plans, and information on their current and future requirements

■ **Supplier and contracts strategy:** this covers the sourcing policy of the service provider and the types of suppliers and contracts used. It is produced by the Service Strategy processes

■ **Supplier plans and strategies:** details of the business plans and strategies of suppliers, together with details of their technology developments and plans and statements and information on their current financial status and projected business viability

■ **Supplier contracts, agreements and targets:** of both existing and new contracts and agreements from suppliers

■ **Supplier and contract performance information:** of both existing and new contracts and suppliers

■ **IT information:** from the IT strategy and plans and current budgets

■ **Performance issues:** the Incident and Problem Management processes, with incidents and problems relating to poor contract or supplier performance

■ **Financial information:** from Financial Management, the cost of supplier service(s) and service provision, the cost of contracts and the resultant business benefit and the financial plans and budgets, together with the costs associated with service and supplier failure

■ **Service information:** from the SLM process, with details of the services from the Service Portfolio and the Service Catalogue, service level targets within SLAs and SLRs, and possibly from the monitoring of SLAs, service reviews and breaches of the SLAs. Also customer satisfaction data on service quality

■ **CMS:** containing information on the relationships between the business, the services, the supporting services and the technology.

4.7.6.2 Outputs

The outputs of Supplier Management are used within all other parts of the process, by many other processes and by other parts of the organization. Often this information is supplied as electronic reports or displays on shared areas or as pages on intranet servers to ensure the most up-to-date information is always used. The information provided is as follows:

■ **The Supplier and Contracts Database (SCD):** holds the information needed by all sub-processes within Supplier Management – for example, the data monitored and collected as part of Supplier Management. This is then invariably used as an input to all other parts of the Supplier Management process.

■ **Supplier and contract performance information and reports:** used as input to supplier and contract review meetings to manage the quality of service provided by suppliers and partners. This should include information on shared risk where appropriate.

■ **Supplier and contract review meeting minutes:** produced to record the minutes and actions of all review meetings with suppliers.

■ **Supplier Service Improvement Plans (SIPs):** used to record all improvement actions and plans agreed between service providers and their suppliers, wherever they are needed, and should be used to manage the progress of agreed improvement actions, including risk reduction measures.

■ **Supplier survey reports:** often many people within a service provider organization have dealings with suppliers. Feedback from these individuals should be collated to ensure that consistency in the quality of

service provided by suppliers is provided in all areas. These can be published as league tables to encourage competition between suppliers.

4.7.7 Key Performance Indicators

Many KPIs and metrics can be used to assess the effectiveness and efficiency of the Supplier Management process and activities. These metrics need to be developed from the service, customer and business perspective, such as:

■ Business protected from poor supplier performance or disruption:
  ● Increase in the number of suppliers meeting the targets within the contract
  ● Reduction in the number of breaches of contractual targets.

■ Supporting services and their targets align with business needs and targets:
  ● Increase in the number of service and contractual reviews held with suppliers
  ● Increase in the number of supplier and contractual targets aligned with SLA and SLR targets.

■ Availability of services is not compromised by supplier performance:
  ● Reduction in the number of service breaches caused by suppliers
  ● Reduction in the number of threatened service breaches caused by suppliers.

■ Clear ownership and awareness of supplier and contractual issues:
  ● Increase in the number of suppliers with nominated supplier managers
  ● Increase in the number of contracts with nominated contract managers.

4.7.8 Information Management

All the information required by Supplier Management should be contained within the SCD. This should include all information relating to suppliers and contracts, as well as all the information relating to the operation of the supporting services provided by suppliers. Information relating to these supporting services should also be contained within the Service Portfolio, together with the relationships to all other services and components. This information should be integrated and maintained in alignment with all other IT information management systems, particularly the Service Portfolio and the CMS.

4.7.9 Challenges, Critical Success Factors and risks

Supplier Management faces many challenges, which could include some of the following:

- Continually changing business and IT needs and managing significant change in parallel with delivering existing service
- Working with an imposed non-ideal contract, a contract that has poor targets or terms and conditions, or poor or non-existent definition of service or supplier performance targets
- Legacy issues, especially with services recently outsourced
- Insufficient expertise retained within the organization
- Being tied into long-term contracts, with no possibility of improvement, which have punitive penalty charges for early exit
- Situations where the supplier depends on the organization in fulfilling the service delivery (e.g. for a data feed) can lead to issues over accountability for poor service performance
- Disputes over charges
- Interference by either party in the running of the other's operation
- Being caught in a daily fire-fighting mode, losing the proactive approach
- Communication – not interacting often enough or quick enough or focusing on the right issues
- Personality conflicts
- One party using the contract to the detriment of the other party, resulting in win-lose changes rather than joint win-win changes
- Losing the strategic perspective, focusing on operational issues, causing a lack of focus on strategic relationship objectives and issues.

Key elements that can help to avoid the above issues are:

- Clearly written, well-defined and well-managed contract
- Mutually beneficial relationship
- Clearly defined (and communicated) roles and responsibilities on both sides
- Good interfaces and communications between the parties
- Well-defined Service Management processes on both sides
- Selecting suppliers who have achieved certification against internationally recognized certifications, such as ISO 9001, ISO/IEC 20000, etc.

The main CSFs for the Supplier Management process are:

- Business protected from poor supplier performance or disruption
- Supporting services and their targets align with business needs and targets
- Availability of services is not compromised by supplier performance
- Clear ownership and awareness of supplier and contractual issues.

The major areas of risk associated with Supplier Management include:

- Lack of commitment from the business and senior management to the Supplier Management process and procedures
- Lack of appropriate information on future business and IT policies, plans and strategies
- Lack of resources and/or budget for the ISM process
- Legacy of badly written and agreed contracts that don't underpin or support business needs or SLA and SLR targets
- Suppliers agree to targets and service levels within contracts that are impossible to meet, or suppliers fail or are incapable of meeting the terms and conditions of the contract
- Supplier personnel or organizational culture are not aligned to that of the service provider or the business
- Suppliers are not cooperative and are not willing to partake in and support the required Supplier Management process
- Suppliers are taken over and relationships, personnel and contracts are changed
- The demands of corporate supplier and contract procedures are excessive and bureaucratic
- Poor corporate financial processes, such as procurement and purchasing, do not support good Supplier Management.

Service Design
technology-related
activities

5

5 Service Design technology-related activities

This chapter considers the technology-related activities of requirement engineering and the development of technology architectures. The technology architectures cover aspects of Service Design in the following areas:

- Infrastructure Management
- Environmental Management
- Data and Information Management
- Application Management.

5.1 REQUIREMENTS ENGINEERING

Requirements engineering is the approach by which sufficient rigour is introduced into the process of understanding and documenting the business and user's requirements, and ensuring traceability of changes to each requirement. This process comprises the stages of elicitation, analysis (which feeds back into the elicitation) and validation. All these contribute to the production of a rigorous, complete requirements document. The core of this document is a repository of individual requirements that is developed and managed. Often these requirements are instigated by IT but ultimately they need to be documented and agreed with the business.

There are many guidelines on requirements engineering, including the Recommended Practice for Software Requirements Specifications (IEEE 830), The Software Engineering Body of Knowledge (SWEBOK), CMMI and the V-Model, which is described in detail in the Service Transition publication.

5.1.1 Different requirement types

A fundamental assumption here is that the analysis of the current and required business processes results in functional requirements met through IT services (comprising applications, data, infrastructure, environment and support skills).

It is important to note that there are commonly said to be three major types of requirements for any system – functional requirements, management and operational requirements, and usability requirements.

- Functional requirements are those specifically required to support a particular business function.

- Management and operational requirements (sometimes referred to as non-functional requirements) address the need for a responsive, available and secure service, and deal with such issues as ease of deployment, operability, management needs and security.

- Usability requirements are those that address the 'look and feel' needs of the user and result in features of the service that facilitate its ease of use. This requirement type is often seen as part of management and operational requirements, but for the purposes of this section it will be addressed separately.

5.1.1.1 Functional requirements

Functional requirements describe the things a service is intended to do, and can be expressed as tasks or functions that the component is required to perform. One approach for specifying functional requirements is through such methods as a system context diagram or a use case model. Other approaches show how the inputs are to be transformed into the outputs (data flow or object diagrams) and textual descriptions.

A system context diagram, for instance, captures all information exchanges between, on the one hand, the IT service and its environment and, on the other, sources or destinations of data used by the service. These information exchanges and data sources represent constraints on the service under development.

A use case model defines a goal-oriented set of interactions between external actors and the service under consideration. Actors are parties outside the service that interact with the service. An actor may reflect a class of user's roles that users can play, or other services and their requirements. The main purpose of use case modelling is to establish the boundary of the proposed system and fully state the functional capabilities to be delivered to the users. Use cases are also helpful for establishing communication between business and application developers. They provide a basis for sizing and feed the definition of usability requirements. Use cases define all scenarios that an application has to support and can therefore easily be expanded into test cases. Since use cases describe a service's functionality on a level that's understandable for both business and IT, they can serve as a vehicle to specify the functional elements of an SLA, such as the actual business deliverables from the service.

One level 'below' the use case and the context diagram, many other modelling techniques can be applied. These models depict the static and dynamic characteristics of the services under development. A conceptual data model (whether called object or data) describes the different 'objects' in the service, their mutual relationships and their internal structure. Dynamics of the service can be described using state models (e.g. state transition diagrams) that show the various states of the entities or objects, together with events that may cause state changes. Interactions between the different application components can be described using interaction diagrams (e.g. object interaction diagrams). Alongside a mature requirements modelling process, CASE tools can help in getting and keeping these models consistent, correct and complete.

5.1.1.2 Management and operational requirements

Management and operational requirements (or non-functional requirements) are used to define requirements and constraints on the IT service. The requirements serve as a basis for early systems and service sizing and estimates of cost, and can support the assessment of the viability of the proposed IT service. Management and operational requirements should also encourage developers to take a broader view of project goals.

Categories of management and operational requirements include:

- **Manageability**: Does it run? Does it fail? How does it fail?
- **Efficiency**: How many resources does it consume?
- **Availability and reliability**: How reliable does it need to be?
- **Capacity and performance**: What level of capacity do we need?
- **Security**: What classification of security is required?
- **Installation**: How much effort does it take to install the application? Is it using automated install procedures?
- **Continuity**: What level of resilience and recovery is required?
- **Controllability**: Can it be monitored, managed and adjusted?
- **Maintainability**: How well can the application be adjusted, corrected, maintained and changed for future requirements?
- **Operability**: Do the applications disturb other applications in their functionalities?
- **Measurability and reportability**: Can we measure and report on all of the required aspects of the application?

The management and operational requirements can be used to prescribe the quality attributes of the application being built. These quality attributes can be used to design test plans for testing the applications on the compliance to management and operational requirements.

5.1.1.3 Usability requirements

The primary purpose of usability requirements is to ensure that the service meets the expectations of its users with regard to its ease of use. To achieve this:

- Establish performance standards for usability evaluations
- Define test scenarios for usability test plans and usability testing.

Like the management and operational requirements, usability requirements can also be used as the quality attributes of design test plans for testing the applications on their compliance to usability requirements.

5.1.2 Requirements for support – the user view

Users have formally defined roles and activities as user representatives in requirements definition and acceptance testing. They should be actively involved in identifying all aspects of service requirements, including the three categories above, and also in:

- User training procedures and facilities
- Support activities and Service Desk procedures.

5.1.3 Requirements investigation techniques

There is a range of techniques that may be used to investigate business situations and elicit service requirements. Sometimes the customers and the business are not completely sure of what their requirements actually are and will need some assistance and prompting from the designer or requirements gatherer. This must be completed in a sensitive way to ensure that it is not seen as IT dictating business requirements again. The two most commonly used techniques are interviewing and workshops, but these are usually supplemented by other techniques, such as observation and scenarios.

5.1.3.1 Interviews

The interview is a key tool and can be vital in achieving a number of objectives, such as:

- Making initial contact with key stakeholders and establishing a basis for progress
- Building and developing rapport with different users and managers

- Acquiring information about the business situation, including issues and problems.

There are three areas that are considered during interviews:

- Current business processes that need to be fulfilled in any new business systems and services
- Problems with the current operations that need to be addressed
- New features required from the new business system or service and any supporting IT service.

The interviewing process is improved when the interviewer has prepared thoroughly as this saves time by avoiding unnecessary explanations and demonstrates interest and professionalism. The classic questioning structure of 'Why, What, Who, When, Where, How' provides an excellent framework for preparing for interviews.

It is equally important to formally close the interview by:

- Summarizing the points covered and the actions agreed
- Explaining what happens next, both following the interview and beyond
- Asking the interviewee how any further contact should be made.

It is always a good idea to write up the notes of the interview as soon as possible – ideally straight away and usually by the next day.

The advantages of interviewing are:

- Builds a relationship with the users
- Can yield important information
- Opportunity to understand different viewpoints and attitudes across the user group
- Opportunity to investigate new areas that arise
- Collection of examples of documents and reports
- Appreciation of political factors
- Study of the environment in which the new service will operate.

The disadvantages of interviewing are:

- Expensive in elapsed time
- No opportunity for conflict resolution.

5.1.3.2 Workshops

Workshops provide a forum in which issues can be discussed, conflicts resolved and requirements elicited. Workshops are especially valuable when time and budgets

are tightly constrained, several viewpoints need to be canvassed and an iterative and incremental view of service development is being taken.

The advantages of the workshop are:

- Gain a broad view of the area under investigation – having a group of stakeholders in one room will allow a more complete understanding of the issues and problems
- Increase speed and productivity – it is much quicker to have one meeting with a group of people than interviewing them one by one
- Obtain buy-in and acceptance for the IT service
- Gain a consensus view – if all the stakeholders are involved, the chance of them taking ownership of the results is improved.

There are some disadvantages, including:

- Can be time-consuming to organize – for example, it is not always easy to get all the necessary people together at the same time
- It can be difficult to get all of the participants with the required level of authority
- It can be difficult to get a mix of business and operational people to understand the different requirements.

The success or failure of a workshop session depends, in large part, on the preparatory work by the facilitator and the business sponsor for the workshop. They should spend time before the event planning the following areas:

- The objective of the workshop – this has to be an objective that can be achieved within the time constraints of the workshop.
- Who will be invited to participate in the workshop – it is important that all stakeholders interested in the objective should be invited to attend or be represented.
- The structure of the workshop and the techniques to be used. These need to be geared towards achieving the defined objective, e.g. requirements gathering or prioritization, and should take the needs of the participants into account.
- Arranging a suitable venue – this may be within the organization, but it is better to use a 'neutral' venue out of the office.

During the workshop, a facilitator needs to ensure that the issues are discussed, views are aired and progress is made towards achieving the stated objective. A record needs to be kept of the key points emerging from the discussion.

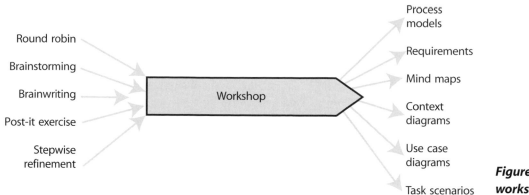

Figure 5.1 Requirements workshop techniques

At the end of the workshop, the facilitator needs to summarize the key points and actions. Each action should be assigned to an owner.

There are two main categories of technique required for a requirements workshop – techniques for discovery and techniques for documentation, as shown in Figure 5.1.

5.1.3.3 Observation

Observing the workplace is very useful in obtaining information about the business environment and the work practices. This has two advantages:

■ A much better understanding of the problems and difficulties faced by the business users
■ It will help devise workable solutions that are more likely to be acceptable to the business.

Conversely, being observed can be rather unnerving, and the old saying 'you change when being observed' needs to be factored into your approach and findings.

Formal observation involves watching a specific task being performed. There is a danger of being shown just the 'front-story' without any of the everyday variances, but it is still a useful tool.

5.1.3.4 Protocol Analysis

Protocol Analysis is simply getting the users to perform a task, and for them to describe each step as they perform it.

5.1.3.5 Shadowing

Shadowing involves following a user for a period such as a day to find out about a particular job. It is a powerful way to understand a particular user role. Asking for explanations of how the work is done, or the workflow, clarifies some of the already assumed aspects.

5.1.3.6 Scenario Analysis

Scenario Analysis is essentially telling the story of a task or transaction. Its value is that it helps a user who is uncertain what is needed from a new service to realize it more clearly. Scenarios are also useful when analysing or redesigning business processes. A scenario will trace the course of a transaction from an initial business trigger through each of the steps needed to achieve a successful outcome.

Scenarios provide a framework for discovering alternative paths that may be followed to complete the transaction. This is extremely useful in requirements elicitation and analysis because real-life situations, including the exceptional circumstances, are debated.

Scenarios offer significant advantages:

■ They force the user to include every step, so there are no taken-for-granted elements and the problem of tacit knowledge is addressed
■ By helping the user to visualize all contingencies, they help to cope with the uncertainty about future systems and services
■ A workshop group refining a scenario will identify those paths that do not suit the corporate culture
■ They provide a tool for preparing test scripts.

The disadvantages of scenarios are that they can be time-consuming to develop, and some scenarios can become very complex. Where this is the case, it is easier to analyse if each of the main alternative paths is considered as a separate scenario.

A popular approach to documenting scenario descriptions is to develop use case descriptions to support use case diagrams. However, there are also a number of graphical methods of documenting a scenario, such as storyboards, activity diagrams, task models and decision tree diagrams.

5.1.3.7 Prototyping

Prototyping is an important technique for eliciting, analysing, demonstrating and validating requirements. It is difficult for users to envisage the new service before it is actually built. Prototypes offer a way of showing the user how the new service might work and the ways in which it can be used. If a user is unclear what they need the service to do for them, utilizing a prototype often releases blocks to thinking and can produce a new wave of requirements. Incremental and iterative approaches to service development, such as the Dynamic Systems Development Method (DSDM), use evolutionary prototyping as an integral part of their development lifecycle.

There is a range of approaches to building prototypes. They may be built using an application development environment so that they mirror the service; images of the screens and navigations may be built using presentation software; or they may simply be 'mock-ups' on paper.

There are two basic methods of prototyping:

- The throw-away mock-up, which is only used to demonstrate the look and feel
- The incremental implementation, where the prototype is developed into the final system.

It is important to select consciously which is to be used, otherwise there is a danger that a poor-quality mock-up becomes the basis for the real system, causing problems later on.

There is a strong link between scenarios and prototyping because scenarios can be used as the basis for developing prototypes. In addition to confirming the users' requirements, prototyping can often help the users to identify new requirements.

Prototypes are successfully used to:

- Clarify any uncertainty on the part of the service developers and confirm to the user that what they have asked for has been understood
- Open the user up to new requirements as they understand what the service will be able to do to support them
- Show users the 'look and feel' of the proposed service and elicit usability requirements
- Validate the requirements and identify any errors.

Potential problems include:

- Endless iteration
- A view that if the prototype works, the full service can be ready tomorrow.

5.1.3.8 Other techniques

Other techniques that could be used, include:

- **Questionnaires**: can be useful to get a limited amount of information from a lot of people when interviewing them all would not be practical or cost-effective.
- **Special purpose records**: technique involves the users in keeping a record about a specific issue or task. For example, they could keep a simple five-bar gate record about how often they need to transfer telephone calls – this could provide information about the problems with this business process.
- **Activity sampling**: is a rather more quantitative form of observation and can be used when it is necessary to know how people spend their time – for example, how much time is spent on invoicing? How much time is spent on reconciling payments? How much time is spent on sorting out queries?

5.1.4 Problems with requirements engineering

Requirements, seen by users as the uncomplicated bit of a new service development, are actually the most problematic aspect, and yet the time allocated is far less than for the other phases.

Tight timescales and tight budgets – both the result of constraints on the business – place pressures on the development team to deliver a service. The trouble is that without the due time to understand and define the requirements properly, the service that is delivered on time may not be the service that the business thought it was asking for.

Studies carried out into IT project failures tell a common story. Many of the projects and unsatisfactory IT services suggest the following conclusions:

- A large proportion of errors (over 80%) are introduced at the requirements phase
- Very few faults (fewer than 10%) are introduced at design and development – developers are developing things right, but frequently not developing the right things
- Most of the project time is allocated to the development and testing phases of the project
- Less than 12% of the project time is allocated to requirements.

These findings are particularly significant because the cost of correcting errors in requirements increases dramatically the later into the development lifecycle they are found.

One of the main problems with requirements engineering is the lack of detailed skill and overall understanding of the area when people use it. If accurately performed, the work can integrate requirements from numerous areas in a few questions.

Other typical problems with requirements have been identified as:

- Lack of relevance to the objectives of the service
- Lack of clarity in the wording
- Ambiguity
- Duplication between requirements
- Conflicts between requirements
- Requirements expressed in such a way that it is difficult to assess whether or not they have been achieved
- Requirements that assume a solution rather than stating what is to be delivered by the service
- Uncertainty amongst users about what they need from the new service
- Users omitting to identify requirements
- Inconsistent levels of detail
- An assumption that user and IT staff have knowledge that they do not possess and therefore failing to ensure that there is a common understanding
- Requirements creep – the gradual addition of seemingly small requirements without taking the extra effort into account in the project plan.

Another problem is an apparent inability on the part of the users to articulate clearly what it is they wish the service to do for them. Very often they are deterred from doing so because the nature of the requirement is explained in a straightforward statement.

5.1.4.1 Resolving requirements engineering problems

Defining actors

There are some participants that must take part in the requirements process. They represent three broad stakeholder groups:

- The business
- The user community
- The service development team.

The user community should be represented by the domain expert (or subject-matter expert) and end-users.

Dealing with tacit knowledge

When developing a new service, the users will pass on to us their explicit knowledge, i.e. knowledge of procedures and data that is at the front of their minds and that they can easily articulate. A major problem when eliciting requirements is that of tacit knowledge, i.e. those other aspects of the work that a user is unable to articulate or explain.

Some common elements that cause problems and misunderstandings are:

- Skills – explaining how to carry out actions using words alone is extremely difficult.
- Taken-for-granted information – even experienced and expert business users may fail to mention information or clarify terminology, and the analyst may not realize that further questioning is required.
- Front-story/back-story – this issue concerns a tendency to frame a description of current working practices, or a workplace, in order to give a more positive view than is actually the case.
- Future systems knowledge – if the study is for a new service development, with no existing expertise or knowledge in the organization, how can the prospective users know what they want?
- The difficulty of an outsider assuming a common language for discourse, and common norms of communication. (If they do not have this, then the scope for misrepresentation of the situation can grow considerably.)
- Intuitive understanding, usually born of considerable experience. Decision makers are often thought to follow a logical, linear path of enquiry while making their decisions. In reality though, as improved decision-making skills and knowledge are acquired, the linear path is often abandoned in favour of intuitive pattern recognition.
- Organizational culture – without an understanding of the culture of an organization, the requirements exercise may be flawed.

Communities of practice are discrete groups of workers – maybe related by task, by department, by geographical location or some other factor – that have their own sets of norms and practices, distinct from other groups within the organization and the organization as a whole.

Table 5.1 Requirements engineering – tacit and explicit knowledge

	Tacit	Explicit
Individual	Skills, values, taken-for-granted, intuitiveness	Tasks, job descriptions, targets, volumes and frequencies
Corporate	Norms, back-story, culture, communities of practice	Procedures, style guides, processes, knowledge sharing

Example levels of tacit and explicit knowledge:

Table 5.2 Requirements engineering; examples of tacit and explicit knowledge (Maiden and Rugg, 1995)

Technique	Explicit knowledge	Tacit knowledge	Skills	Future requirements
Interviewing	√√	√	X	√
Shadowing	√√	√√	√√	X
Workshops	√√	√√	X	√√
Prototyping	√√	√√	√√	√√
Scenario analysis	√√	√√	X	√√
Protocol analysis	√√	√√	√√	X

5.1.5 Documenting requirements

The requirements document is at the heart of the process and can take a number of forms. Typically the document will include a catalogue of requirements, with each individual requirement documented using a standard template. One or more models showing specific aspects, such as the processing or data requirements, may supplement this catalogue.

Before they are formally entered into the catalogue, requirements are subject to careful scrutiny. This scrutiny may involve organizing the requirements into groupings and checking that each requirement is 'well-formed'.

Once the document is considered to be complete, it must be reviewed by business representatives and confirmed to be a true statement of the requirements, at this point in time. During this stage the reviewers examine the requirements and question whether they are well-defined, clear and complete.

As we uncover the requirements from our various users, we need to document them. This is best done in two distinct phases – building the requirements list and, later, developing an organized requirements catalogue. The list tends to be an informal document and can be presented as four columns, as shown in Table 5.3.

Table 5.3 Requirements list

Requirements	Source	Comments	Detail level

Each requirement in the list must be checked to see whether or not it is well formed and SMART (Specific, Measurable, Achievable, Realistic and Timely).

When checking the individual and totality of requirements, the following checklist can be used:

- Are the requirements, as captured, unambiguous?
- Is the meaning clear?
- Is the requirement aligned to the service development and business objectives, or is it irrelevant?
- Is the requirement reasonable, or would it be expensive and time-consuming to satisfy?
- Do any requirements conflict with one another such that only one may be implemented?
- Do they imply a solution rather than state a requirement?
- Are they atomic, or are they really several requirements grouped into one entry?
- Do several requirements overlap or duplicate each other?

There are several potential outcomes from the exercise:

- Accept the requirement as it stands
- Re-word the requirement to remove jargon and ambiguity
- Merge duplicated/overlapping requirements
- Take unclear and ambiguous requirements back to the users for clarification.

5.1.5.1 The requirements catalogue

The Requirements Catalogue is the central repository of the users' requirements, and all the requirements should be documented here, following the analysis of the list defined above. The Requirements Catalogue should form part of the overall Service Pipeline within the overall Service Portfolio. Each requirement that has been analysed is documented using a standard template, such as that shown in Table 5.4.

The key entries in the template are as follows:

- **Requirement ID** – this is a unique ID that never changes and is used for traceability – for example, to reference the requirement in design documents, test specifications or implemented code. This ensures that all requirements have been met and that all implemented functions are based on requirements.
- **Source** – the business area or users who requested the requirement or the document where the requirement was raised. Recording the source of a requirement helps ensure that questions can be answered or the need can be re-assessed in the future if necessary.

- **Owner** – the user who accepts ownership of the individual requirement will agree that it is worded and documented correctly, and will sign it off at acceptance testing when satisfied.
- **Priority** – the level of importance and need for a requirement. Normally approaches such as MoSCoW are used, where the following interpretation of the mnemonic applies:
  - **Must have** – a key requirement without which the service has no value.
  - **Should have** – an important requirement that must be delivered but, where time is short, could be delayed for a future delivery. This should be a short-term delay, but the service would still have value without them.
  - **Could have** – a requirement that would it be beneficial to include if it does not cost too much or take too long to deliver, but it is not central to the service.
  - **Won't have** (but want next time) – a requirement that will be needed in the future but is not required for this delivery. In a future service release, this requirement may be upgraded to a 'must have'.

The following should be clearly agreed during this prioritization activity:

- Requirement priorities can and do change over the life of a service development project.
- 'Should have' requirements need to be carefully considered because, if they are not delivered within the initial design stage, they may be impossible to implement later.

Table 5.4 Requirements template

IT service	Author		Date
Requirement ID	Requirement Name		
Source	Owner	Priority	Business Process
Functional Requirement Description			
Management and Operational and Usability Requirements	Description		
Justification			
Related Documents			
Related Requirements			
Comments			
Resolution			
Version No	Change History	Date	Change request

- Requirements are invariably more difficult and more expensive to meet later in the Service Lifecycle.
- It is not just the functional requirements that can be 'must haves' – some of the management and operational requirements should be 'must haves'.
- Requirement description – a succinct description of the requirement. A useful approach is to describe the requirement using the following structure:
  - Actor (or user role)
  - Verb phrase
  - Object (noun or noun phrase).
- Where the requirement incorporates complex business rules or data validation, decision table or decision tree may be more useful to define complex business rules, whilst data validation rules may be defined in a repository. If a supplementary technique is used to specify or model the requirement, there should be a cross-reference to the related document.
- Business process – a simple phrase to group together requirements that support a specific activity, such as sales, inventory, customer service, and so on.
- Justification – not all the requirements that are requested will be met. This may be due to time and budget constraints, or may be because the requirement is dropped in favour of a conflicting requirement. Often the requirement is not met because it adds little value to the business. The justification sets out the reasons for requesting the requirement.
- Related requirements – requirements may be related to each other for several reasons. Sometimes there is a link between the functionality required by the requirements or a high-level requirement is clarified by a series of more detailed requirements.
- Change history – the entries in this section provide a record of all the changes that have affected the requirement. This is required for Configuration Management and traceability purposes.

5.1.5.2 Full requirements documentation

An effective requirements document should comprise the following elements:

- A glossary of terms, to define each organizational term used within the requirements document. This will help manage the problem of local jargon and will clarify synonyms and homonyms for anyone using the document
- A scoping model, such as a system context diagram
- The Requirements Catalogue, ideally maintained as part of an overall Service Portfolio

- Supporting models, such as business process models, data flow diagrams or interaction diagrams.

Managing changes to the documentation

Changes may come about because:

- The scope of the new service has altered through budget constraints
- The service must comply with new regulation or legislation
- Changes in business priorities have been announced
- Stakeholders have understood a requirement better after some detailed analysis – for example, using scenarios or prototyping – and amended the original requirement accordingly.

There are a number of specialist support tools on the market to support requirements processes. These are sometimes called CARE (Computer Aided Requirements Engineering) or CASE (Computer Aided Software Engineering). Features include:

- Maintaining cross-references between requirements
- Storing requirements documentation
- Managing changes to the requirements documentation
- Managing versions of the requirements documentation
- Producing formatted requirements specification documents from the database
- Ensuring documents delivered by any solution project are suitable to enable support.

5.1.6 Requirements and outsourcing

The aim is to select standard packaged solutions wherever possible to meet service requirements. However, whether IT requirements are to be purchased off-the-shelf, developed in-house or outsourced, all the activities up to the production of a specification of business requirements are done in-house. Many IT service development contracts assume it is possible to know what the requirements are at the start, and that it is possible to produce a specification that unambiguously expresses the requirements. For all but the simplest services this is rarely true. Requirements analysis is an iterative process – the requirements will change during the period the application and service are being developed. It will require user involvement throughout the development process, as in the DSDM and other 'agile' approaches.

5.1.6.1 Typical requirements outsourcing scenarios

Typical approaches to contract for the development of IT systems to be delivered in support of an IT service are as follows:

■ Low-level requirements specification – the boundary between 'customer' and provider is drawn between the detailed requirements specification and any design activities. All the requirements that have an impact on the user have been specified in detail, giving the provider a very clear and precise implementation target. However, there is increased specification effort, and the added value of the provider is restricted to the less difficult aspects of development.

■ High-level requirements specification – the customer/provider boundary is between the high-level requirements and all other phases. The provider contract covers everything below the line. The customer is responsible for testing the delivered service against the business requirements. As it is easier to specify high-level requirements, there is reduced effort to develop contract inputs. However, there may be significant problems of increased cost and risk for both customer and provider, together with increased room for mistakes, instability of requirements and increased difficulty in knowing what information systems you want.

5.2 DATA AND INFORMATION MANAGEMENT

Data is one of the critical asset types that need to be managed in order to develop, deliver and support IT services effectively. Data/Information Management is how an organization plans, collects, creates, organizes, uses, controls, disseminates and disposes of its data/information, both structured records and unstructured data. It also ensures that the value of that data/information is identified and exploited, both in support of its internal operations and in adding value to its customer-facing business processes.

A number of terms are common in this area, including 'Data Management', 'Information Management' and 'Information Resource Management'. For the purposes of this publication, the term 'Data Management' is used as shorthand for all of the three above.

The role of Data Management described is not just about managing raw data: it's about managing all the contextual metadata – additional 'data about the data' – that goes with it, and when added to the raw data gives 'information' or 'data in context'.

Data, as the basis for the organization's information, has all the necessary attributes to be treated as an asset (or resource). For example, it is essential for 'the achievement of business objectives and the successful daily workings of an organization'. In addition, it can be 'obtained and preserved by an organization, but only at a financial cost'. Finally it can, along with other resources/assets, be used to 'further the achievement of the aims of an organization'.

Key factors for successful Data Management are as follows:

■ All users have ready access through a variety of channels to the information they need to do their jobs.

■ Data assets are fully exploited, through data sharing within the organization and with other bodies.

■ The quality of the organization's data is maintained at an acceptable level, and the information used in the business is accurate, reliable and consistent.

■ Legal requirements for maintaining the privacy, security, confidentiality and integrity of data are observed.

■ The organization achieves a high level of efficiency and effectiveness in its data and information-handling activities.

■ An enterprise data model to define the most important entities and their relationships – this helps to avoid redundancies and to avoid the deterioration of the architecture as it is changed over the years.

5.2.1 Managing data assets

If data isn't managed effectively:

■ People maintain and collect data that isn't needed

■ The organization may have historic information that is no longer used

■ The organization may hold a lot of data that is inaccessible to potential users

■ Information may be disseminated to more people than it should be, or not to those people to whom it should be

■ The organization may use inefficient and out-of-date methods to collect, analyse, store and retrieve the data

■ The organization may fail to collect data that it needs, reducing data quality and data integrity is lost, e.g. between related data sources.

In addition, whether or not information is derived from good-quality data is a difficult question to answer, because there are no measurements in place against which to compare it. For example, poor data quality often arises because of poor checks on input and/or updating procedures. Once inaccurate or incomplete data have been stored in the IT system, any reports produced using these data will reflect these inaccuracies or gaps. There may also be a lack of consistency between internally-generated management information from the operational systems, and from other internal, locally-used systems, created because the central data is not trusted.

One way of improving the quality of data is to use a Data Management process that establishes policy and standards, provides expertise and makes it easier to handle the data aspects of new services. This should then allow full Data/Information Asset Management to:

- Add value to the services delivered to customers
- Reduce risks in the business
- Reduce the costs of business processes
- Stimulate innovation in internal business processes.

5.2.2 Scope of Data Management

There are four areas of management included within the scope of Data/Information Management:

- **Management of data resources**: the governance of information in the organization must ensure that all these resources are known and that responsibilities have been assigned for their management, including ownership of data and metadata. This process is normally referred to as data administration and includes responsibility for:
  - Defining information needs
  - Constructing a data inventory and an enterprise data model
  - Identifying data duplication and deficiencies
  - Maintaining a catalogue/index of data/information content
  - Measuring the cost and value of the organization's data.
- **Management of data/information technology**: the management of the IT that underpins the organization's information systems; this includes processes such as database design and database administration. This aspect is normally handled by specialists within the IT function – see the Service Operation publication for more details.
- **Management of information processes**: business processes will lead to IT services involving one or other of the data resources of the organization. The processes of creating, collecting, accessing, modifying,

storing, deleting and archiving data – i.e. the data lifecycle – must be properly controlled, often jointly with the applications management process.
- **Management of data standards and policies**: the organization will need to define standards and policies for its Data Management as an element of an IT strategy. Policies will govern the procedures and responsibilities for Data Management in the organization; and technical policies, architectures and standards that will apply to the IT infrastructure that supports the organization's information systems.

The best practices scope of the Data Management process includes managing non-structured data that is not held in conventional database systems – for example, using formats such as text, image and audio. It is also responsible for ensuring process quality at all stages of the data lifecycle, from requirements to retirement. The main focus in this publication will be on its role in the requirements, design and development phases of the asset and Service Lifecycle.

The team supporting the Data Management process may also provide a business information support service. In this case they are able to answer questions about the meaning, format and availability of data internal to the organization, because they manage the metadata. They also are able to understand and explain what external data might be needed in order to carry out necessary business processes and will take the necessary action to source this.

Critically, when creating or redesigning processes and supporting IT services, it is good practice to consider re-using data and metadata across different areas of the organization. The ability to do this may be supported by a corporate data model – sometimes known as a common information model – to help support re-use, often a major objective for data management.

5.2.3 Data Management and the Service Lifecycle

It is recommended that a lifecycle approach be adopted in understanding the use of data in business processes. General issues include:

- What data is currently held and how can it be classified?
- What data needs to be collected or created by the business processes?
- How will the data be stored and maintained?
- How will the data be accessed, by whom and in what ways?

- How will the data be disposed of, and under whose authority?
- How will the quality of the data be maintained (accuracy, consistency, currency, etc.)?
- How can the data be made more accessible/available?

5.2.4 Supporting the Service Lifecycle

During requirements and initial design, Data Management can assist design and development teams with service-specific data modelling and give advice on the use of various techniques to model data.

During detailed ('physical') design and development, the Data Management function can provide technical expertise on database management systems and on how to convert initial 'logical' models of data into physical, product specific, implementations.

Many new services have failed because poor data quality has not been addressed during the development of the service, or because a particular development created its own data and metadata, without consultation with other service owners, or with Data Management.

5.2.5 Valuing data

Data is an asset and has value. Clearly in some organizations this is more obvious than in others. Organizations that are providers of data to other organizations – Yell, Dun and Bradstreet, and Reuters – can value data as an 'output' in terms of the price that they are charging external organizations to receive it. It's also possible to think of value in terms of what the internal data would be worth to another organization.

It's more common to value data in terms of what it's worth to the owner organization. There are a number of suggested ways of doing this:

- **Valuing data by availability**: one approach often used is to consider which business processes would not be possible if a particular piece of data were unavailable, and how much that non-availability of data would cost the business.
- **Valuing lost data**: another approach that's often used is to think about the costs of obtaining some data if it were to be destroyed.
- **Valuing data by considering the data lifecycle**: this involves thinking about how data is created or obtained in the first place, how it is made available to people to use, and how data is retired, either through archiving or physical destruction. It may be that some data is provided from an external source and then held internally, or it may be that data has to be

created by the organization's internal systems. In these two cases, the lifecycle is different and the processes that take place for data capture will be entirely separate. In both cases the costs of redoing these stages can be evaluated. The more highly valued the data, the more the effort that needs to be expended on ensuring its integrity, availability and confidentiality.

5.2.6 Classifying data

Data can be initially classified as operational, tactical or strategic:

- **Operational data**: necessary for the ongoing functioning of an organization and can be regarded as the lowest, most specific, level.
- **Tactical data**: usually needed by second-line management – or higher – and typically concerned with summarized data and historical data, typically year-to-year data or quarterly data. Often the data that's used here appears in management information systems that require summary data from a number of operational systems in order to deal with an accounting requirement, for example.
- **Strategic data**: often concerned with longer-term trends and with comparison with the outside world, so providing the necessary data for a strategic support system involves bringing together the operational and tactical data from many different areas with relevant external data. Much more data is required from external sources.

An alternative method is to use a security classification of data and documents. This is normally adopted as a corporate policy within an organization.

An orthogonal classification distinguishes between organization-wide data, functional-area data and service-specific data.

- Organization-wide data needs to be centrally managed.
- The next level of data is functional-area data that should be shared across a complete business function. This involves sharing data 'instances' – for example, individual customer records – and also ensuring that consistent metadata across that functional area, such as standard address formats, are being used.
- The final level is IT service-specific, where the data and metadata are valid for one IT service and do not need to be shared with other services.

5.2.7 Setting data standards

One of the critical aspects of data administration is to ensure that standards for metadata are in place – for example, what metadata is to be kept for different underlying 'data types'. Different details are kept about structured tabular data than for other areas. 'Ownership' is a critical item of this metadata, some sort of unique identifier is another, a description in business meaningful terms another, and a format might be another. The custodian or steward, someone in the IT department who takes responsibility for the day-to-day management of the data, is also recorded.

Another benefit of a Data Management process would be in the field of reference data. Certain types of data, such as postcodes or names of countries, may be needed across a variety of systems and need to be consistent. It is part of the responsibility of data administration to manage reference data on behalf of the whole business, and to make sure that the same reference data is used by all systems in the organization.

Standards for naming must be in place; so, for example, if a new type of data is requested in a new service, then there is a need to use names that meet these standards. An example standard might be 'all capitals, no underlining and no abbreviations'.

5.2.8 Data ownership

Data administration can assist the service developer by making sure responsibilities for data ownership are taken seriously by the business and by the IT department. One of the most successful ways of doing this is to get the business and the IT department to sign up to a data charter – a set of procedural standards and guidance for the careful management of data in the organization, by adherence to corporately defined standards. Responsibilities of a data owner are often defined here and may include:

- Agreeing a business description and a purpose for the data
- Defining who can create, amend, read and delete occurrences of the data
- Authorizing changes in the way data is captured or derived
- Approving any format, domain and value ranges
- Approving the relevant level of security, including making sure that legal requirements and internal policies about data security are adhered to.

5.2.9 Data migration

Data migration is an issue where a new service is replacing a number of (possibly just one) existing services, and it's necessary to carry across, into the new service, good-quality data from the existing systems and services. There are two types of data migration of interest to projects here: one is the data migration into data warehouses etc., for business intelligence/analytics purposes; the other is data migration to a new transactional, operational service. In both cases it will be beneficial if data migration standards, procedures and processes are laid down by Data Management. Data migration tools may have already been purchased on behalf of the organization by the Data Management team. Without this support, it's very easy to underestimate the amount of effort that's required, particularly if data consolidation and cleaning has to take place between multiple source systems, and the quality of the existing services' data is known to be questionable.

5.2.10 Data storage

One area where technology has moved on very rapidly is in the area of storage of data. There is a need to consider different storage media – for example, optical storage – and be aware of the size and cost implications associated with this. The main reason for understanding the developments in this area is that they make possible many types of data management areas that were considered too expensive before. For example, to store real-time video, which uses an enormous bandwidth, has, until the last two to three years, been regarded as too expensive. The same is true of the scanning of large numbers of paper documents, particularly where those documents are not text-based but contain detailed diagrams or pictures. Understanding technology developments with regard to electronic storage of data is critical to understanding the opportunities for the business to exploit the information resource effectively by making the best use of new technology.

5.2.11 Data capture

It is also very important to work with Data Management on effective measures for data capture. The aim here is to capture data as quickly and accurately as possible. There is a need to ensure that the data capture processes require the minimum amount of keying, and exploit the advantages that graphical user interfaces provide in terms of minimizing the number of keystrokes needed, also decreasing the opportunity for errors during data capture. It is reasonable to expect that the Data Management process has standards for, and can provide expertise on, effective methods of data capture in various environments, including 'non-structured' data capture using mechanisms such as scanning.

5.2.12 Data retrieval and usage

Once the data has been captured and stored, the next aspect to consider is the retrieval of information from the data. Services to allow easy access to structured data via query tools of various levels of sophistication are needed by all organizations, and generate their own specific architectural demands.

The whole area of searching within scanned text and other non-structured data such as video, still images or sound is a major area of expansion. Techniques such as automatic indexing, and the use of search engines to give efficient access via keywords to relevant parts of a document, are essential technologies that have been widely implemented, particularly on the internet. Expertise in the use of data or content within websites should exist within the Data Management as well as Content Management – standards and procedures that are vital for websites.

5.2.13 Data integrity and related issues

When defining requirements for IT services, it is vital that management and operational requirements related to data are considered. In particular, the following areas must be addressed:

- Recovery of lost or corrupted data
- Controlled access to data
- Implementation of policies on archiving of data, including compliance with regulatory retention periods
- Periodic data integrity checks.

Data integrity is concerned with ensuring that the data is of high quality and uncorrupted. It is also about preventing uncontrolled data duplication, and hence avoiding any confusion about what is the valid version of the data. There are several approaches that may assist with this. Various technology devices such as 'database locking' are used to prevent multiple, inconsistent, updating of data. In addition, prevention of illegal updating may be achieved through access control mechanisms.

5.3 APPLICATION MANAGEMENT

An application is defined here as the software program(s) that perform those specific functions that directly support the execution of business processes and/or procedures.

Applications, along with data and infrastructure components such as hardware, the operating system and middleware, make up the technology components that are part of an IT service. The application itself is only one component, albeit an important one of the service. Therefore it is important that the application delivered matches the agreed requirements of the business. However, too many organizations spend too much time focusing on the functional requirements of the new service and application, and insufficient time is spent designing the management and operational requirements (non-functional requirements) of the service. This means that when the service becomes operational, it meets all of the functionality required, but totally fails to meet the expectation of the business and the customers in terms of its quality and performance, and therefore becomes unusable.

Two alternative approaches are necessary to fully implement Application Management. One approach employs an extended Service Development Lifecycle (SDLC) to support the development of an IT service. SDLC is a systematic approach to problem solving and is composed of the following steps:

- Feasibility study
- Analysis
- Design
- Testing
- Implementation
- Evaluation
- Maintenance.

The other approach takes a global view of all services to ensure the ongoing maintainability and manageability of the applications:

- All applications are described in a consistent manner, via an Application Portfolio that is managed and maintained to enable alignment with dynamic business needs.
- Consistency of approach to development is enforced through a limited number of application frameworks and design patterns and through a 're-use' first philosophy.
- Common software components, usually to meet management and operational requirements, are created or acquired at an 'organizational' level and used by individual systems as they are designed and built.

Table 5.5 Application Portfolio attributes example

Application name	IT operations owner	New development cost
Application identifier	IT development owner	Annual operational costs
Application description	Support contacts	Annual support cost
Business process supported	Database technologies	Annual maintenance costs
IT services supported	Dependent applications	Outsourced components
Executive sponsor	IT systems supported	Outsource partners
Geographies supported	User interfaces	Production metrics
Business criticality	IT Architecture, including Network topology	OLA link
SLA link	Application technologies used	Support metrics
Business owner	Number of users	

5.3.1 The Application Portfolio

This is simply a full record of all applications within the organization and is dynamic in its content.

5.3.2 Linking Application and Service Portfolios

Some organizations maintain a separate Application Portfolio with separate attributes, while in other organizations the Application Portfolio is stored within the CMS, together with the appropriate relationships. Other organizations combine the Application Portfolio together with the Service Portfolio. It is for each organization to decide the most appropriate strategy for its own needs. What is clear is that there should be very close relationships and links between the applications and the services they support and the infrastructure components used.

5.3.3 Application frameworks

The concept of an application framework is a very powerful one. The application framework covers all management and operational aspects and actually provides solutions for all the management and operational requirements that surround an application.

Implied in the use of application frameworks is the concept of standardization. If an organization uses and has to maintain an application framework for every single application, there will not be many benefits of the use of an application framework.

An organization that wants to develop and maintain application frameworks, and to ensure the application frameworks comply with the needs of the application developers, must invest in doing so. It is essential that applications framework architectures are not developed in

isolation, but are closely related and integrated with all other framework and architectural activities. The Service, Infrastructure, Environment and Data Architectures must all be closely integrated with the **Application Architecture** and framework.

Architecture, application frameworks and standards

Architecture-related activities have to be planned and managed separately from individual system-based software projects. It is also important that architecture-related activities be performed for the benefit of more than just one application. Application developers should focus on a single application, while application framework developers should focus on more than one application, and on the common features of those applications in particular.

A common practice is to distinguish between various types of applications. For instance, not every application can be built on top of a Microsoft® Windows operating system platform, connected to a UNIX server, using HTML, Java applets, JavaBeans and a relational database. The various types of applications can be regarded as application families. All applications in the same family are based on the same application framework.

Utilizing the concept of an application framework, the first step of the application design phase is to identify the appropriate application framework. If the application framework is mature, a large number of the design decisions are given. If it is not mature, and all management and operational requirements cannot be met on top of an existing application framework, the preferred strategy is to collect and analyse the requirements that cannot be dealt with in the current version of the application framework. Based on the application requirements, new requirements can be defined for the application framework. Next, the application framework can be modified so that it can cope with the application requirements. In fact, the whole family of applications that corresponds to the application framework can then use the newly added or changed framework features.

Developing and maintaining an application framework is a demanding task and, like all other design activities, should be performed by competent and experienced people. Alternatively, application frameworks can be acquired from third parties.

5.3.4 The need for CASE tools and repositories

One important aspect of that overall alignment is the need to align applications with their underlying support structures. Application development environments traditionally have their own Computer Assisted/Aided Software Engineering (CASE) tools that offer the means to specify requirements, draw design diagrams (according to particular modelling standards), or even generate complete applications, or nearly complete application skeletons, almost ready to be deployed. These environments also provide a central location for storing and managing all the elements that are created during application development, generally called a repository. Repository functionality includes version control and consistency checking across various models. The current approach is to use metacase-tools to model domain-specific languages and use these to make the CASE-work more aligned to the needs of the business.

5.3.5 Design of specific applications

The requirements phase of the lifecycle was addressed earlier in the requirements engineering section. The design phase is one of the most important phases within the application lifecycle. It ensures that an application is conceived with operability and Application Management in mind. This phase takes the outputs from the requirements phase and turns them into the specification that will be used to develop the application.

The goal for designs should be satisfying the organization's requirements. Design includes the design of the application itself, and the design of the infrastructure and environment within which the application operates. Architectural considerations are the most important aspect of this phase, since they can impact on the structure and content of both application and operational model. Architectural considerations for the application (design of the Application Architecture) and architectural considerations for the environment (design of the IT Architecture) are strongly related and need to be aligned. Application Architecture and design should not be considered in isolation but should form an overall integrated component of service architecture and design.

Generally, in the design phase, the same models will be produced as have been delivered in the requirements phase, but during design many more details are added. New models include the architecture models, where the way in which the different functional components are mapped to the physical components (e.g. desktops, servers, databases and network) needs to be defined. The mapping, together with the estimated load of the system, should allow for the sizing of the infrastructure required.

Another important aspect of the architecture model is the embedding of the application in the existing environment. Which pieces of the existing infrastructure will be used to support the required new functions? Can existing servers or networks be used? With what impact? Are required functions available in existing applications that can be utilized? Do packages exist that offer the functionality needed or should the functions be built from scratch?

The design phase takes all requirements into consideration and starts assembling them into an initial design for the solution. Doing this not only gives developers a basis to begin working: it is also likely to bring up questions that need to be asked of the customers/users. If possible, application frameworks should be applied as a starting point.

It is not always possible to foresee every aspect of a solution's design ahead of time. As a solution is developed, new things will be learned about how to do things and also how not to.

The key is to create a flexible design, so that making a change does not send developers all the way back to the beginning of the design phase. There are a number of approaches that can minimize the chance of this happening, including:

- Designing for management and operational requirements
- Managing trade-offs
- Using application-independent design guidelines; using application frameworks
- Employing a structured design process/manageability checklist.

Design for management and operational requirements means giving management and operational requirements a level of importance similar to that for the functional requirements, and including them as a mandatory part of the design phase. This includes a number of management and operational requirements such as availability, capacity, maintainability, reliability and security. It is now inconceivable in modern application development projects that user interface design (usability requirements) would be omitted as a key design activity. However, many organizations ignore or forget manageability. Details of the necessary management and operational requirements are contained within the SDP and SAC in Appendices A and B.

5.3.6 Managing trade-offs

Managing trade-off decisions focuses on balancing the relationship among resources, the project schedule, and those features that need to be included in the application for the sake of quality.

When development teams try to complete this balancing, it is often at the expense of the management and operational requirements. One way to avoid that is to include management and operational requirements in the application-independent design guidelines – for example, in the form of an application framework. Operability and manageability effectively become standard components of all design processes – for example, in the form of an application framework – and get embedded into the working practices and culture of the development organization.

5.3.7 Typical design outputs

The following are examples of the outputs from an applications design forming part of the overall Service Design:

- Input and output design, including forms and reports
- A usable user interface (human computer interaction) design
- A suitable data/object model
- A process flow or workflow model
- Detailed specifications for update and read-only processes
- Mechanisms for achieving audit controls, security, confidentiality and privacy
- A technology specific 'physical' design
- Scripts for testing the systems design
- Interfaces and dependencies on other applications.

There are guidelines and frameworks that can be adopted to determine and define design outputs within Applications Management, such as Capability Maturity Model Integration (CMMI).

5.3.8 Design patterns

A design pattern is a general, repeatable solution to a commonly occurring problem in software design. Object-oriented design patterns typically show relationships and interactions between classes or objects, without specifying the final application classes or objects that are involved. Design patterns describe both a problem and a solution for common issues encountered during application development.

An important design principle used as the basis for a large number of the design patterns found in recent literature is that of separation of concern. Separation of concerns will lead to applications divided into components, with a strong cohesion and minimal coupling between components. The advantage of such an application is that modification can be made to individual components with little or no impact on other components.

In typical application development projects, more than 70% of the effort is spent on designing and developing generic functions and on satisfying the management and operational requirements. That is because each individual application needs to provide a solution for such generic features as printing, error handling and security.

Among others, the Object Management Group (OMG, www.omg.com) defined a large number of services that are needed in every application. OMG's Object Management Architecture (OMA) clearly distinguishes between functional and management and operational aspects of an application. It builds on the concept of providing a run-time environment that offers all sorts of facilities to an application.

In this concept, the application covers the functional aspects, and the environment covers all management and operational aspects. Application developers should, by definition, focus on the functional aspects of an application, while others can focus on the creation of the environment that provides the necessary management and operational services. This means that the application developers focus on the requirements of the business, while the architecture developers or application framework developers focus on the requirements of the application developers.

5.3.9 Developing individual applications

Once the design phase is completed, the application development team will take the designs that have been produced and move on to developing the application. Both the application and the related environment are made ready for deployment. Application components are coded or acquired, integrated and tested.

To ensure that the application is developed with management at the core, the development team needs to focus on ensuring that the developing phase continues to correctly address the management and operational aspects of the design (e.g. responsiveness, availability, security).

The development phase guidance covers the following topics:

- Consistent coding conventions
- Application-independent building guidelines
- Operability testing
- Management checklist for the building phase
- Organization of the build team roles.

5.3.10 Consistent coding conventions

The main reason for using a consistent set of design and coding conventions is to standardize the structure and coding style of an application so that everyone can easily read, understand and manage the application development process. Good design and coding conventions result in precise, readable and unambiguous source code that is consistent with the organizational coding and management standards and is as intuitive to follow as possible. Adding application operability into this convention ensures that all applications are built in a way that ensures that they can be fully managed all the way through their lifecycles.

A coding convention itself can be a significant aid to managing the application, as consistency allows the management tools to interact with the application in a known way. It is better to introduce a minimum set of conventions that everyone will follow rather than to create an overly complex set that encompasses every facet but is not followed or used consistently across the organization.

5.3.11 Templates and code generation

A number of development tools provide a variety of templates for creating common application components. Rather than creating all the pieces of an application from scratch, developers can customize an existing template. They can also re-use custom components in multiple applications by creating their own templates. Other development tools will generate large pieces of code (skeletons) based on the design models and coding conventions. The code could include hooks at the code

pieces that need to be added.

In this respect, templates and application frameworks should be considered IT assets. These assets not only guide the developing of applications, but also incorporate the lessons learned or intellectual capital from previous application development efforts. The more that standard components are designed into the solution, the faster applications can be developed, against lower costs in the long term (not ignoring the fact that development of templates, code generators and application frameworks requires significant investment).

5.3.12 Embedded application instrumentation

The development phase deals with incorporating instrumentation into the fabric of the application. Developers need a consistent way to provide instrumentation for application drivers/middleware components (e.g. database drivers) and applications that is efficient and easy to implement. To keep application developers from reinventing the wheel with every new application they develop, the computer industry provides methods and technologies to simplify and facilitate the instrumentation process.

These include:

- Application Response Measurement (ARMS)
- IBM Application Management Specification (AMS)
- Common Information Model (CIM) and Web-Based Enterprise Management (WBEM) from the Distributed Management Task Force (DMTF)
- Desktop Management Instrumentation (DMI)
- Microsoft Windows© Management Instrumentation (WMI)
- Java Management Extension (JMX).

Each of these technologies provides a consistent and richly descriptive model of the configuration, status and operational aspects of applications and services. These are provided through programming Application Program Interfaces (APIs) that the developer incorporates into an application, normally through the use of standard programming templates.

It is important to ensure that all applications are built to conform to some level of compliance for the application instrumentation. Ways to do this could include:

- Provide access to management data through the instrumentation API

- Publish management data to other management systems, again through the instrumentation API
- Provide applications event handling
- Provide a diagnostic hook.

5.3.13 Diagnostic hooks

Diagnostic hooks are of greatest value during testing and when an error has been discovered in the production service. Diagnostic hooks mainly provide the information necessary to solve problems and application errors rapidly and restore service. They can also be used to provide measurement and management information of applications.

The three main categories are:

- System-level information provided by the OS and hardware
- Software-level information provided by the application infrastructure components such as database, web server or messaging systems
- Custom information provided by the applications
- Information on component and service performance.

5.3.14 Major service outputs from development

The major outputs from the development phase are:

- Scripts to be run before or after deployment
- Scripts to start or stop the application
- Scripts to check hardware and software configurations of target environments before deployment or installation
- Specification of metrics and events that can be retrieved from the application and that indicate the performance status of the application
- Customized scripts initiated by Service Operation staff to manage the application (including the handling of application upgrades)
- Specification of access control information for the system resources used by an application
- Specification of the details required to track an application's major transactions
- SLA targets and requirements
- Operational requirements and documentation
- Support requirements
- Application recovery and backups
- Other IT SM requirements and targets.

Organizing for Service Design

6

6 Organizing for Service Design

For Service Design to be successful, it is essential to define the roles and responsibilities within the organization of the various activities.

When designing a service or a process, it is imperative that all the roles are clearly defined. A trademark of high-performing organizations is the ability to make the right decisions quickly and execute them effectively. Whether the decision involves a strategic choice or a critical operation, being clear on who has input, who decides and who takes action will enable the company to move forward rapidly.

The RACI model will be beneficial in enabling decisions to be made with pace and confidence. RACI is an acronym for the four main roles of:

- **Responsible** – the person or people responsible for getting the job done
- **Accountable** – only one person can be accountable for each task
- **Consulted** – the people who are consulted and whose opinions are sought
- **Informed** – the people who are kept up-to-date on progress.

Occasionally an expanded version of RACI is used called RACI-VS, with two further roles as follows:

- **Verifies** – the person or group that checks whether the acceptance criteria have been met
- **Signs off** – the person who approves the V decision and authorizes the product hand-off. This could be the A person.

A third variation of the RACI model is RASCI, where the S represents Supportive. This role provides additional resources to conduct the work, or plays a supportive role

in implementation, for example. This could be beneficial for IT service implementation.

The RACI chart in Table 6.1 shows the structure and power of RACI modelling with the activities down the left-hand side including the actions that need to be taken and decisions that must be made. Across the top, the chart lists the functional roles responsible for carrying out the initiative or playing a part in decision making.

Whether RACI or some other tool or model is used, the important thing is to not just leave the assignment of responsibilities to chance or leave it to the last minute to decide. Conflicts can be avoided and decisions can be made quickly if the roles are allocated in advance.

To build a RACI chart the following steps are required:

- Identify the activities/processes
- Identify/define the functional roles
- Conduct meetings and assign the RACI codes
- Identify any gaps or overlaps – for example, where there are two Rs or no Rs (see analysis below)
- Distribute the chart and incorporate feedback
- Ensure that the allocations are being followed.

6.1 FUNCTIONAL ROLES ANALYSIS

- Many As: Are duties segregated properly? Should someone else be accountable for some of these activities? Is this causing a bottleneck in some areas that will delay decisions?
- Many Rs: Is this too much for one function?
- No empty spaces: Does this role need to be involved in so many tasks?
- Also, does the type or degree of participation fit this role's qualifications?

Table 6.1 Example RACI matrix

	Director Service Management	Service Level Manager	Problem Manager	Security Manager	Procurement Manager
Activity 1	AR	C	I	I	C
Activity 2	A	R	C	C	C
Activity 3	I	A	R	I	C
Activity 4	I	A	R	I	
Activity 5	I	I	A	C	I

6.2 ACTIVITY ANALYSIS

- More than one A: only one role can be accountable.
- No As: at least one A must be assigned to each activity.
- More than one R: too many roles responsible often means that no one takes responsibility. Responsibility may be shared, but only if roles are clear.
- No Rs: at least one person must be responsible.
- Many Cs: Is there a requirement to consult with so many roles? What are the benefits and can the extra time be justified?
- No Cs and Is: Are the communication channels open to enable people and departments to talk to each other and keep each other up-to-date?

6.3 SKILLS AND ATTRIBUTES

The specific roles within ITIL Service Management all require specific skills, attributes and competences from the people involved to enable them to work effectively and efficiently. However, whatever the role, it is imperative that the person carrying out that role has the following attributes:

- Awareness of the business priorities, objectives and business drivers
- Awareness of the role IT plays in enabling the business objectives to be met
- Customer service skills
- Awareness of what IT can deliver to the business, including latest capabilities
- The competence, knowledge and information necessary to complete their role
- The ability to use, understand and interpret the best practice, policies and procedures to ensure adherence.

The following are examples of attributes required in many of the roles, dependent on the organization and the specific role:

- **Management skills** – both from a person management perspective and from the overall control of process
- **Meeting skills** – to organize, chair, document and ensure actions are followed up
- **Communications** – an important element of all roles is raising awareness of the processes in place to ensure buy-in and conformance. An ability to communicate at all levels within the organization will be imperative
- **Articulate** – both written, for reports etc., and verbal

- **Negotiation** – required for several aspects, such as procurement and contracts
- **Analytical** – to analyse metrics produced from the activity.

More information about the skills and competences of these roles can be found within the Skills Framework for the Information Age (SFIA – www.sfia.org.uk).

6.4 ROLES AND RESPONSIBILITIES

The following sections document the roles and responsibilities of the various roles within Service Design. In some organizations this could be a full-time individual and in others it could be several people, or it could be a part-time role. In smaller organizations many of these roles may be performed by a single person. This will depend on the size and volatility of the organization. The roles or job titles often vary between organizations. However, what is important is that the roles, responsibilities, processes, dependencies and interfaces are clearly defined and scoped for each individual organization. (See Appendix C for an example process document template.)

The following are illustrations of the main activities within each of the Service Design roles.

6.4.1 Process owner

A process owner is responsible for ensuring that their process is being performed according to the agreed and documented process and is meeting the aims of the process definition. This includes such tasks as:

- Documenting and publicizing the process
- Defining the Key Performance Indicators (KPIs) to evaluate the effectiveness and efficiency of the process
- Reviewing KPIs and taking action required following the analysis
- Assisting with and being ultimately responsible for the process design
- Improving the effectiveness and efficiency of the process
- Reviewing any proposed enhancements to the process
- Providing input to the ongoing Service Improvement Plan
- Addressing any issues with the running of the process
- Ensuring all relevant staff have the required training in the process and are aware of their role in the process
- Ensures that the process, roles, responsibilities and documentation are regularly reviewed and audited
- Interfaces with line management, ensuring that the process receives the necessary staff resources. (Line

management and process owners have complementary tasks – they need to work together to ensure efficient and effective processes. Often it is the task of line management to ensure the required training of staff.)

6.4.2 Service Design Manager

The key role and responsibilities of the Service Design Manager are covered throughout this publication and they are responsible for the overall coordination and deployment of quality solution designs for services and processes. Responsibilities of the role over and above those of line management of all people involved in Service Design roles include:

■ Taking the overall Service Strategies and ensuring they are reflected in the Service Design practice and the Service Designs that are produced to meet and fulfil the documented business requirements

■ Designing the functional aspects of the services as well as the infrastructure, environment applications and data management

■ Producing quality, secure and resilient designs for new or improved services, technology architecture, processes or measurement systems that meet all the agreed current and future IT requirements of the organization

■ Producing and maintaining all design documentation, including designs, plans, architectures and policies

■ Producing and maintaining all necessary SDPs

■ Measuring the effectiveness and efficiency of the Service Design process.

6.4.3 IT Planner

An IT Planner is responsible for the production and coordination of IT plans. The main objectives of the role are as follows:

■ Develop IT plans that meet and continue to meet the IT requirements of the business.

■ Coordinate, measure and review the implementation progress of all IT strategies and plans.

■ Produce and maintain the overall set of IT standards, policies, plans and strategies, encompassing all aspects of IT required to support an organization's business strategy. IT planning includes participation in the creation of SLAs and the planning of all aspects of infrastructure – internal and external, public or private, internet and intranet – necessary to ensure that the provision of IT services satisfies business.

■ Assume responsibility for all aspects of IT standards, policy and strategy implementation for IT as a whole

and for significant projects or major new strategic applications.

■ Recommend policy for the effective use of IT throughout the organization and work with IT Designers to ensure that overall plans and strategies are developed in conjunction with IT design for all areas of IT.

■ Review IT costs against budgets and new developments, initiating proposals to change IT plans and strategies where appropriate, in conjunction with Financial Management.

■ Assume full responsibility for the management, planning and coordination of IT systems and services, including investigation, analysis, specification, design, development, testing, maintenance, upgrade, transition and operation. It is essential that while performing these activities, the business, IT Management and all the Service Management processes are kept up-to-date with the progress of projects.

■ Obtain and evaluate proposals from suppliers of equipment, software, transmission services and other services, ensuring that all business and IT requirements are satisfied.

■ Identify internal and external influencing factors, forecast future needs and set plans for the effective use of IT within the organization.

■ Sponsor and monitor research, development and long-term planning for the provision and use of IT architectures, products and services

■ Review IT performance with all other areas and initiate any improvements in organization to ensure that service levels and targets continue to be met in all areas.

■ Take ultimate responsibility for prioritizing and scheduling the implementation of new or changed services within IT.

■ Work with senior management and other senior specialists and planners in formulating plans and making procurement decisions applicable to all areas of IT.

■ Recognize the key business drivers and those areas of business need that are not adequately supported by current and planned IT services, developing the plans and IT response to the business requirements.

■ Identify suitable applications, services and products, together with their environments, to meet business needs within the required planning timeframe.

■ Develop the initial plans for the implementation of authorized new IT services, applications and infrastructure support, identifying budgetary, technical and staffing constraints, and clearly listing costs and expected benefits.

■ Monitor the existing IT plans in relation to business needs and IT strategy to determine opportunities for improving business processes through the use of new technology, and to identify unforeseen risks to the achievement of forecast business benefit.

■ Investigate major options for providing IT services effectively and efficiently and recommend new innovative solutions, based on new approaches to processes, provision, recruitment and retention, and global supply contracts.

■ Produce feasibility studies, business models, IT models, business cases, SoRs and ITTs for recommended new IT systems, identifying the business impact, the probability of satisfying business needs, the anticipated business benefits and the risks and consequences of failure.

■ Oversee and coordinate the programme of planned IT project implementations and changes, taking appropriate action to identify and overcome problems and resolve conflict.

■ Conduct Post Implementation Reviews (PIRs) in conjunction with Change Management of those information systems introduced in pursuit of the plans, to assess the extent to which expected business benefits were realized.

■ Liaise with Strategy, Transition and Operations teams and processes to plan for their immediate and future needs.

■ Provide authoritative advice and guidance on relevant national and international standards, regulations, protocols and tariffs.

■ Document all work using required standards, methods and tools.

■ Ensure that all IT planning processes, roles, responsibilities and documentation are regularly reviewed and audited for efficiency, effectiveness and compliance.

■ Maintain a good overall knowledge of all IT product capabilities and the technical frameworks in which they operate.

■ Where required, assess changes for their conformance to the design strategies, including attendance at CAB meetings if appropriate.

6.4.4 IT Designer/Architect

An IT Designer/Architect is responsible for the overall coordination and design of the required technology. Often Designers and Architects within large organizations would specialize in one of the five aspects of design (see section 3). However, an integrated approach to design should always be adopted, therefore Designers and Architects need to work together within a formal method and framework to ensure consistent and compatible designs are produced. In smaller organizations, some or all of the roles are usually combined, and this is less of an issue, although a formal approach should still be used. Whenever designs are produced, they should always adopt an integrated approach, covering all areas, and should be accepted and signed off by all areas. All designers need to understand how architectures, strategies, designs and plans fit together and all the main aspects of design.

The Designer/Architect should produce a detailed process map that documents all the processes and their high-level interfaces. This ensures that the overall structure is not unnecessarily complex, that the process's central interfaces are part of the design, and provides an overview to everyone on how the customer and all other stakeholders interact with the processes.

To perform the role of Designer or Architect, it is necessary for staff to have good knowledge and practical experience of design philosophies and planning, including Programme, Project and Service Management, methods and principles. The main objectives of the IT Designer/Architect are as follows:

■ Produce and review the designs of all new or changed services, SLAs, OLAs and contracts.

■ Produce a process map of all of the processes and their high-level interfaces, to ensure integration, consistency and continuity across all processes.

■ Design secure and resilient technology architectures that meet all the current and anticipated future IT requirements of the organization.

■ Ensure that the design of all processes, roles, responsibilities and documentation is regularly reviewed and audited for efficiency, effectiveness and compliance.

■ Design an appropriate and suitable Service Portfolio, supporting all activities within the complete Service Lifecycle.

■ Design measurement systems and techniques to support the continual improvement of service provision and all supporting processes.

■ Produce and keep up-to-date all IT design, architectural, policy and specification documentation.

■ Produce and maintain all aspects of IT specification, including the overall designs, architectures, topologies and configurations of the infrastructure, environment, applications and data, and the design documentation of all IT systems. This should include not just the technology, but also the management systems, processes, information flows and external services.

■ Recommend proactive, innovative IT solutions for the improvement of IT design and operation whenever and wherever possible.

■ Translate logical designs into physical designs, taking account of business requirements, target environments, processes, performance requirements, existing systems and services, and any potential safety-related aspects.

■ Create and maintain IT design policies, philosophies and criteria, covering all areas including connectivity, capacity, interfaces, security, resilience, recovery, access and remote access, and ensuring that all new services meet their service levels and targets.

■ Work with Capacity Management and review IT traffic volumes and requirements, identifying trends in traffic flows and levels of service.

■ Propose design enhancements to IT infrastructure, capacity changes, continuity, backup and recovery arrangements, as required, and be aware of operational requirements, especially in terms of service levels, availability, response times, security and repair times. All these activities are performed in liaison with all of the Service Management processes.

■ Review IT costs against external service providers, new developments and new services, initiating proposals to change IT design where appropriate cost reductions and benefits can be achieved, in consultation with Financial Management.

■ Provide advice and guidance to management on the design and planning phases of IT systems, to ensure that requirements (particularly capacity, recovery, performance and security needs) are reflected in the overall specifications.

■ Provide advice and guidance to all areas of IT and Business Management, analysts, planners, designers and developers on all aspects of IT design and technology.

■ Interface with designers and planners from external suppliers and service providers, ensuring all external IT services are designed to meet their agreed service levels and targets.

■ Play a major role in the selection of any new IT infrastructure or technology solutions.

■ Assume technical responsibility for IT standards, policy and design for all significant projects or major application areas, assisting with the Impact Assessment and evaluation of major new IT design options.

■ Provide technical advice and guidance on relevant national and international standards, regulations, protocols and tariffs.

■ Take full responsibility for the design aspects of all stages of the lifecycle of IT systems, including investigation, analysis, specification, design, development, construction, testing, maintenance, upgrade, transition, operation and improvement.

■ Work with IT colleagues where appropriate, producing or updating IT and corporate design documentation and models.

■ Update or provide input to cost-benefit analyses, risk analyses, business cases, SoRs and ITTs and development plans, to take account of design decisions.

■ Obtain and assist with the evaluation and selection of proposals and solutions from suppliers of equipment, software and other IT service and product providers.

■ Construct, interpret and monitor test plans to verify correct operation of completed systems against their design objectives.

■ Document all work using required standards, methods and tools.

■ Maintain a good technical knowledge of all IT product capabilities and the technical frameworks in which they operate.

■ Where required, assess changes for their conformance to the design principles, including attendance at CAB meetings if appropriate.

Note: Often Designers and Architects within large organisations would specialise in one of the five aspects of design (see sections 3 and 4 for more detail). However, an integrated approach to design should always be adopted, therefore Designers and Architects need to work together within a formal method and framework to ensure consistent and compatible designs are produced. In smaller organisations, some or all of the roles are usually combined, and this is less of an issue, although a formal approach should still be used. Whenever designs are produced, they should always adopt a holistic approach, covering all areas, and should be accepted and signed off by all areas. All Designers need to understand how architectures, strategies, designs and plans fit together.

6.4.5 Service Catalogue Manager

The Service Catalogue Manager has responsibility for producing and maintaining the Service Catalogue. This includes responsibilities such as:

- Ensuring that all operational services and all services being prepared for operational running are recorded within the Service Catalogue
- Ensuring that all the information within the Service Catalogue is accurate and up-to-date
- Ensuring that all the information within the Service Catalogue is consistent with the information within the Service Portfolio
- Ensuring that the information within the Service Catalogue is adequately protected and backed up.

6.4.6 Service Level Manager

The Service Level Manager has responsibility for ensuring that the aims of Service Level Management are met. This includes responsibilities such as:

- Keeping aware of changing business needs
- Ensuring that the current and future service requirements of customers are identified, understood and documented in SLA and SLR documents
- Negotiating and agreeing levels of service to be delivered with the customer (either internal or external); formally documenting these levels of service in SLAs
- Negotiating and agreeing OLAs and, in some cases, other SLAs and agreements that underpin the SLAs with the customers of the service
- Assisting with the production and maintenance of an accurate Service Portfolio, Service Catalogue, Application Portfolio and the corresponding maintenance procedures
- Ensuring that targets agreed within underpinning contracts are aligned with SLA and SLR targets
- Ensuring that service reports are produced for each customer service and that breaches of SLA targets are highlighted, investigated and actions taken to prevent their recurrence
- Ensuring that service performance reviews are scheduled, carried out with customers regularly and are documented with agreed actions progressed
- Ensuring that improvement initiatives identified in service reviews are acted on and progress reports are provided to customers

- Reviewing service scope, SLAs, OLAs and other agreements on a regular basis, ideally at least annually
- Ensuring that all changes are assessed for their impact on service levels, including SLAs, OLAs and underpinning contracts, including attendance at CAB meetings if appropriate
- Identifying all key stakeholders and customers
- Developing relationships and communication with stakeholders, customers and key users
- Defining and agreeing complaints and their recording, management, escalation, where necessary, and resolution
- Definition recording and communication of all complaints
- Measuring, recording, analysing and improving customer satisfaction.

6.4.7 Availability Manager

An Availability Manager has responsibility for ensuring that the aims of Availability Management are met. This includes responsibilities such as:

- Ensuring that all existing services deliver the levels of availability agreed with the business in SLAs
- Ensuring that all new services are designed to deliver the levels of availability required by the business, and validation of the final design to meet the minimum levels of availability as agreed by the business for IT services
- Assisting with the investigation and diagnosis of all incidents and problems that cause availability issues or unavailability of services or components
- Participating in the IT infrastructure design, including specifying the availability requirements for hardware and software
- Specifying the requirements for new or enhanced event management systems for automatic monitoring of availability of IT components
- Specifying the reliability, maintainability and serviceability requirements for components supplied by internal and external suppliers
- Being responsible for monitoring actual IT availability achieved against SLA targets, and providing a range of IT availability reporting to ensure that agreed levels of availability, reliability and maintainability are measured and monitored on an ongoing basis
- Proactively improving service availability wherever possible, and optimizing the availability of the IT infrastructure to deliver cost-effective improvements that deliver tangible benefits to the business

- Creating, maintaining and regularly reviewing an AMIS and a forward-looking Availability Plan, aimed at improving the overall availability of IT services and infrastructure components, to ensure that existing and future business availability requirements can be met
- Ensuring that the Availability Management process, its associated techniques and methods are regularly reviewed and audited, and that all of these are subject to continual improvement and remain fit for purpose
- Creating availability and recovery design criteria to be applied to new or enhanced infrastructure design
- Working with Financial Management, ensuring the levels of IT availability required are cost-justified
- Maintaining and completing an availability testing schedule for all availability mechanisms
- Ensuring that all availability tests and plans are tested after every major business change
- Assisting Security and IT Service Continuity Management with the assessment and management of risk
- Assessing changes for their impact on all aspects of availability, including overall service availability and the Availability Plan
- Attending CAB meetings when appropriate.

6.4.8 IT Service **Continuity Manager**

The IT Service Continuity Manager is responsible for ensuring that the aims of IT Service Continuity Management are met. This includes such tasks and responsibilities as:

- Performing Business Impact Analyses for all existing and new services
- Implementing and maintaining the ITSCM process, in accordance with the overall requirements of the organization's Business Continuity Management process, and representing the IT services function within the Business Continuity Management process
- Ensuring that all ITSCM plans, risks and activities underpin and align with all BCM plans, risks and activities, and are capable of meeting the agreed and documented targets under any circumstances
- Performing risk assessment and risk management to prevent disasters where cost-justifiable and where practical
- Developing and maintaining the organization's continuity strategy
- Assessing potential service continuity issues and invoking the Service Continuity Plan if necessary

- Managing the Service Continuity Plan while it is in operation, including fail-over to a secondary location and restoration to the primary location
- Performing post mortem reviews of service continuity tests and invocations, and instigating corrective actions where required
- Developing and managing the ITSCM plans to ensure that, at all times, the recovery objectives of the business can be achieved
- Ensuring that all IT service areas are prepared and able to respond to an invocation of the continuity plans
- Maintaining a comprehensive IT testing schedule, including testing all continuity plans in line with business requirements and after every major business change
- Undertaking quality reviews of all procedures and ensuring that these are incorporated into the testing schedule
- Communicating and maintaining awareness of ITSCM objectives within the business areas supported and IT service areas
- Undertaking regular reviews, at least annually, of the Continuity Plans with the business areas to ensure that they accurately reflect the business needs
- Negotiating and managing contracts with providers of third-party recovery services
- Assessing changes for their impact on Service Continuity and Continuity Plans
- Attending CAB meetings when appropriate.

6.4.9 **Capacity Manager**

A Capacity Manager has responsibility for ensuring that the aims of Capacity Management are met. This includes such tasks as:

- Ensuring that there is adequate IT capacity to meet required levels of service, and that senior IT management is correctly advised on how to match capacity and demand and to ensure that use of existing capacity is optimized
- Identifying, with the Service Level Manager, capacity requirements through discussions with the business users
- Understanding the current usage of the infrastructure and IT services, and the maximum capacity of each component
- Performing sizing on all proposed new services and systems, possibly using modelling techniques, to ascertain capacity requirements
- Forecasting future capacity requirements based on business plans, usage trends, sizing of new services, etc.

- Production, regular review and revision of the Capacity Plan, in line with the organization's business planning cycle, identifying current usage and forecast requirements during the period covered by the plan
- Ensuring that appropriate levels of monitoring of resources and system performance are set
- Analysis of usage and performance data, and reporting on performance against targets contained in SLAs
- Raising incidents and problems when breaches of capacity or performance thresholds are detected, and assisting with the investigation and diagnosis of capacity-related incidents and problems
- Identifying and initiating any tuning to be carried out to optimize and improve capacity or performance
- Identifying and implementing initiatives to improve resource usage – for example, demand management techniques
- Assessing new technology and its relevance to the organization in terms of performance and cost
- Being familiar with potential future demand for IT services and assessing this on performance service levels
- Ensuring that all changes are assessed for their impact on capacity and performance and attending CAB meetings when appropriate
- Producing regular management reports that include current usage of resources, trends and forecasts
- Sizing all proposed new services and systems to determine the computer and network resources required, to determine hardware utilization, performance service levels and cost implications
- Assessing new techniques and hardware and software products for use by Capacity Management that might improve the efficiency and effectiveness of the process
- Performance testing of new services and systems
- Reports on service and component performance against targets contained in SLAs
- Maintaining a knowledge of future demand for IT services and predicting the effects of demand on performance service levels
- Determining performance service levels that are maintainable and cost-justified
- Recommending tuning of services and systems, and making recommendations to IT management on the design and use of systems to help ensure optimum use of all hardware and operating system software resources
- Acting as a focal point for all capacity and performance issues.

6.4.10 Security Manager

The Security Manager is responsible for ensuring that the aims of Information Security Management are met. This includes such tasks and responsibilities as:

- Developing and maintaining the Information Security Policy and a supporting set of specific policies, ensuring appropriate authorization, commitment and endorsement from senior IT and business management
- Communicating and publicizing the Information Security Policy to all appropriate parties
- Ensuring that the Information Security Policy is enforced and adhered to
- Identifying and classifying IT and information assets (Configuration Items) and the level of control and protection required
- Assisting with Business Impact Analyses
- Performing Security Risk Analysis and risk management in conjunction with Availability and IT Service Continuity Management
- Designing security controls and developing security plans
- Developing and documenting procedures for operating and maintaining security controls
- Monitoring and managing all security breaches and handling security incidents, taking remedial action to prevent recurrence wherever possible
- Reporting, analysing and reducing the impact and volumes of all security incidents in conjunction with Problem Management
- Promoting education and awareness of security
- Maintaining a set of security controls and documentation, and regularly reviewing and auditing all security controls and procedures
- Ensuring all changes are assessed for impact on all security aspects, including the Information Security Policy and security controls, and attending CAB meetings when appropriate
- Performing security tests
- Participating in any security reviews arising from security breaches and instigating remedial actions
- Ensuring that the confidentiality, integrity and availability of the services are maintained at the levels agreed in the SLAs and that they conform to all relevant statutory requirements
- Ensuring that all access to services by external partners and suppliers is subject to contractual agreements and responsibilities
- Acting as a focal point for all security issues.

6.4.11 Supplier Manager

The Supplier Manager has responsibility for ensuring that the aims of Supplier Management are met. This includes tasks such as:

■ Providing assistance in the development and review of SLAs, contracts, agreements or any other documents for third-party suppliers

■ Ensuring that value for money is obtained from all IT suppliers and contracts

■ Ensuring that all IT supplier processes are consistent and interface to all corporate supplier strategies, processes and standard terms and conditions

■ Maintaining and reviewing a Supplier and Contracts Database (SCD)

■ Review and Risk Analysis of all suppliers and contracts on a regular basis

■ Ensuring that any underpinning contracts, agreements or SLAs developed are aligned with those of the business

■ Ensuring that all supporting services are scoped and documented and that interfaces and dependencies between suppliers, supporting services and supplier processes are agreed and documented

■ Ensuring that all roles and relationships between lead and any sub-contracted suppliers are documented, maintained and subject to contractual agreement

■ Reviewing lead suppliers' processes to ensure that any sub-contracted suppliers are meeting their contractual obligations

■ Performing contract or SLA reviews at least annually, and ensuring that all contracts are consistent with organizational requirements and standard terms and conditions wherever possible

■ Updating contracts or SLAs when required, ensuring that the Change Management process is followed

■ Maintaining a process for dealing with contractual disputes, and ensuring that any disputes are dealt with in an efficient and effective manner

■ Maintaining a process for dealing with the expected end, early end or transfer of a service

■ Monitoring, reporting and regularly reviewing supplier performance against targets, identifying improvement actions as appropriate and ensuring these actions are implemented

■ Ensuring changes are assessed for their impact on suppliers, supporting services and contracts and attending CAB meetings when appropriate

■ Coordinating and supporting all individual IT supplier and contract managers, ensuring that each supplier/contract has a nominated owner within the service provider organization.

Technology
considerations

7

7 Technology considerations

It is generally recognized that the use of Service Management tools is essential for the success of all but the very smallest process implementations. However, it is important that the tool being used supports the processes – not the other way around. As a general rule, don't modify processes to fit the tool. However, with the use of tools to support processes, there is a need to be pragmatic and recognize that there may not be a tool that supports the designed process totally, so an element of process re-design may be necessary. Don't limit the requirements to functionality: consider the product's ability to perform, enlarge the size of the databases, recover from failure and maintain data integrity. Does the product conform to international standards? Is it efficient enough to enable you to meet your Service Management Requirements?

Often organizations believe that by purchasing or developing a tool all their problems will be solved, and it is easy to forget that we are still dependent on the process, the function and, most importantly, the people. Remember:

> 'a fool with a tool is still a fool'

7.1 SERVICE DESIGN TOOLS

There are many tools and techniques that can be used to assist with the design of services and their associated components. These tools and techniques enable:

- Hardware design
- Software design
- Environmental design
- Process design
- Data design.

The tools and techniques are many and varied, including both proprietary and non-proprietary, and are useful in:

- Speeding up the design process
- Ensuring that standards and conventions are followed
- Offering prototyping, modelling and simulation facilities
- Enabling 'What if?' scenarios to be examined
- Enabling interfaces and dependencies to checked and correlated
- Validating designs before they are developed and implemented to ensure that they satisfy and fulfil their intended requirements.

Developing Service Designs can be simplified by the use of tools that provide graphical views of the service and its constituent components, from the business processes, through the service and SLA to the infrastructure, environment, data and applications, processes, OLAs, teams, contracts and suppliers. Some Configuration Management tools provide such facilities, and are sometimes referred to as an element of Business Service Management (BSM) tools. They can contain or be linked to 'auto-discovery' tools and mechanisms and allow the relationships between all of these elements to be graphically represented, providing the ability to drill down within each component and obtain detailed information if needed.

If these types of tool also contain financial information, and are then linked to a 'Metrics Tree' providing KPIs and metrics of the various aspects of the service, then the service can be monitored and managed through all stages of its lifecycle. Sharing this single, centralized set of service information allows everybody in the service provider organization and the business to access a single, consistent, 'real-world' view of the service and its performance, and provides a solid base for the development of good relationships and partnerships between the service provider and its customers.

These types of tools not only facilitate the design processes, but also greatly support and assist all stages in the Service Lifecycle, including:

- Management of all stages of the Service Lifecycle
- All aspects of the service and its performance
- Service achievement, SLA, OLA, contractual and supplier measurement, reporting and management
- Consolidated metrics and Metrics Trees, with views from management dashboards down to detailed component information, performance and fault analysis and identification
- Consistent and consolidated views across all processes, systems, technologies and groups
- Relationships and integration of the business and its processes with IT services, systems and processes
- A comprehensive set of search and reporting facilities, enabling accurate information and analysis for informed decision-making
- Management of service costs
- Management of relationships, interfaces and inter-dependencies

- Management of the Service Portfolio and Service Catalogue
- A Configuration Management System (CMS)
- A Service Knowledge Management System (SKMS).

The following generic activities will be needed to implement such an approach:

- Establish the generic lifecycle for IT Assets (Requirements, Design and Develop, Build, Test, Deploy, Operate and Optimize, Dispose) and define the principal processes, policies, activities and technologies within each stage of the lifecycle for each type of asset
- Formalize the relationships between different types of IT asset, and the relationship between IT asset acquisition and management and other IT disciplines
- Define all roles and responsibilities involved in IT asset activities
- Establish measures for understanding the (Total) Cost of Ownership of an IT service
- Establish policies for the re-use of IT assets across services, e.g. at the corporate level
- Define a strategy for the acquisition and management of IT assets, including how it should be aligned with other IT and business strategies.

For the applications asset type, additionally:

- Define a strategy for the acquisition and management of IT assets, including how it should be aligned with other IT and business strategies
- Document the role played by applications in the delivery of IT services to the business
- Ensure the generic IT asset lifecycle model is adapted to an applications lifecycle, tailored to different application types
- Set standards for the use of different approaches to developing applications, and recognize the role of development methodologies, including those based on 're-use' (see the section on Design and Development for further discussion)
- Ensure that procedures are in place to consider all requirement types (such as operability, service performance, maintainability, security) in the early stages of application development
- Set standards for deciding on the optimal delivery of applications to the organization, such as the use of Application Service Providers, customized developments, COTS and package customization.

For the data/information asset type, additionally:

- Establish how the general principles of IT asset acquisition and management can help to manage the data/information resources of an organization.

Ensure that data designs are undertaken in the light of:

- The importance of standardized and re-usable metadata
- The need for data quality
- The value of data to an organization
- The need for data administration and database administration skills
- Understanding the 'corporate' (or common/cooperative) subject area and individual service ('system') views of data
- The need to manage data of non-traditional data types such as text, scanned images, video and audio
- Awareness of the major storage, security and legal issues for data
- Specify how the generic IT assets lifecycle model can be adapted to the data asset type.

For the IT infrastructure and environmental asset type, additionally:

- Establish standards for acquisition and management of the IT infrastructure and environmental equipment (including hardware, power, O/S software, dbms software, middleware and networks) and ensure they provide a stable yet adaptable foundation that underpins the provision of IT services to the business
- Establish how the generic IT assets lifecycle model should be adapted to a specific IT infrastructure lifecycle
- Establish activities to optimize the usage of IT infrastructure assets through their re-use
- Specify the need for tools and describe how their overall use and integration assists in the management of an effective IT infrastructure and related services.

For the skills (people, competencies), additionally:

- Formalize how the competencies of individuals responsible for the IT assets and related services can be regarded as an asset within the organization and are managed as such
- Specify how the IT asset lifecycle applies to people assets, particularly in terms of measurable competencies, such as skill, knowledge, understanding, qualifications, experience, attitude and behaviour

■ Ensure the documentation of the competencies currently in place and specify how these can be re-used or enhanced

■ Ensure organization standards are compatible with existing standard competency frameworks for the IT sector, such as SFIA+ (Skills For The Information Age) skills and competences are incorporated into roles and responsibilities.

In addition, in order to establish effective interfaces and dependencies:

■ Define the interfaces that IT asset acquisition and management has with IT-enabled Business Change, IT Project Management and IT Security

■ Formalize the interfaces that IT asset acquisition and management have with functions and processes outside IT

■ Finally formalize measurement and reporting in this area by:
  ● Identifying suitable metrics and the reports on IT assets for distribution throughout the organization as appropriate
  ● Formalizing quality control and measurement in the acquisition and management of IT assets.

7.2 SERVICE MANAGEMENT TOOLS

Tools will enable the Service Design processes to work more effectively. Tools will increase efficiency and effectiveness, and provide a wealth of management information, leading to the identification of weak areas. The longer-term benefits to be gained from the use of tools are cost savings and increased productivity, which in turn can lead to an increase in the quality of the IT service provision.

The use of tools will enable the centralization of key processes and the automation and integration of core Service Management processes. The raw data collected by the tools can be analysed, resulting in the identification of 'trends'. Preventative measures can then be implemented, again improving the quality of the IT service provision.

Some points that organizations should consider when evaluating Service Management tools include:

■ Data structure, data handling and integration

■ Integration of multi-vendor infrastructure components, and the need to absorb new components in the future – these will place particular demands on the data-handling and modelling capabilities of the tool

■ Conformity to international open standards

■ Flexibility in implementation, usage and data sharing

■ Usability – the ease of use permitted by the user interface

■ Support for monitoring service levels

■ Distributed clients with a centralized shared database (e.g. client server)

■ Conversion requirements for previously tracked data

■ Data backup, control and security

■ Support options provided by the tool vendor

■ Scalability at increasing of capacity (the number of users, volume of data and so on).

Consideration must be given to the exact requirements for the tool. What are the mandatory requirements and what are the desired requirements? Generally the tool should support the processes, not the other way round, so minimize modification of the processes to fit the tool. Where possible, it is better to purchase a fully integrated tool (although not at the expense of efficiency and effectiveness) to underpin many (if not all) Service Management processes. If this is not possible, consideration must be given to the interfaces between the various tools.

It is essential to have a Statement of Requirements (SoR) for use during the selection process – this statement can be used as a 'tick list'. The tool requirements should be categorized using the MoSCoW analysis:

■ M – MUST have this

■ S – SHOULD have this if at all possible

■ C – COULD have this if it does not affect anything else

■ W – WON'T have this time but WOULD like in the future.

The tool must be adequately flexible to support your required access rights. You must be able to determine who is permitted to access what data and for what purpose, e.g. read access to customers.

In the early stages, consideration must also be given to the platform on which the tool will be expected to operate – this may be on existing hardware and software or a new purchase. There may be restrictions laid down by IT strategy – for example, all new products may have to reside on specific servers. This might restrict which products could be included in the evaluation process. Make sure that the procurement fits within existing approved budgets.

There are many Service Management tools available. Details can be found on the internet, Service Management publications, from asking other organizations, from asking consultants or attending seminars and conferences to see what products are available.

During the early stages of the selection process, think about vendor and tool credibility. Are they still going to be supporting the purchase in a few months' or a year's time? Consider the past record of the supplier as well as that of the tool. Telephone the supplier's Service Desk to see how easy it is to get through, and ask some test questions to assess their technical competence. Ask the vendor to arrange a visit to a reference site to see what the experience is with the tool in practice – if possible without the vendor or supplier present. Make sure that the organization has similar requirements of the tool. See the tool in operation and speak to the users about their experiences, both initially and ongoing.

Assess the training needs of the organization and evaluate the capability of the supplier to provide the appropriate training. Also the ongoing training and tool update (upgrades and changes in user requirements) will need to be assessed to ascertain the support and training costs. In particular, consider training costs, training location, time required, how soon after training the tool will be in use, and during the implementation project ensure that sufficient training is provided – think about how the new tool will impact both IT and customer. Also ensure that interfaces with other tools and telephony are functioning correctly. It is wise to identify whether the planned combination has been used (or tried) elsewhere and with what results. Consider periods of parallel running alongside existing solutions before finally going live.

When evaluating tools, a 100% fit to requirements should not be expected and will almost certainly not be found. The '80/20 rule' should be brought into effect instead. A tool is deemed to be fit for its purpose if it meets 80% or more of the business's operational requirements. Those operational requirements should be categorized as discussed earlier.

Any product should be rejected as unsuitable if not all of the mandatory requirements ('must haves') are met. In some circumstances, it will be impossible to find an existing software product that will either meet all of the mandatory requirements or provide an 80% match. In this situation, the product offering the best functional design should be selected and the unsuitable elements re-written. This enhancement process should be done by the vendor if at all possible. In some cases, part of the enhancement costs may be met by the purchaser. Some products have been designed to include user hooks – this provides accessibility to site-written code at key procedural points, without the need for the package to be modified.

It doesn't end when the product has been selected. In many ways this could be considered as only the beginning. The tool now has to be implemented. Once the hardware platform has been prepared and the software loaded, data population needs to be considered. What, where from, how and when? Timing is important to the testing, implementation and the go-live processes. Resources must be available to ensure success. In other words, don't schedule implementation during a known busy period, such as year-end processing. Today 'software as a service' products are available where hardware and software are not required. These products give network-based access to and management of commercially available software. These types of products will still require planning and implementation, but this should simplify the process as no dedicated hardware is required.

Consideration should also be given to managed service providers and Application Service Providers who may be able to provide the same functionality.

Whatever tool or type of tool is chosen, the fulfilment of the requirements can be differentiated between:

- **Out-of-the box** – the requirement is fulfilled
- **Configuration** – the tool can be configured with x days of effort to fulfil the requirement and this will be preserved over product upgrades
- **Customization** – the tool must be reprogrammed with x days of effort to fulfil the requirement, and this may have to be repeated on every product upgrade.

Extensive customization of any product is always best avoided because of the high costs incurred at product upgrade. Vendors may be unwilling to support old releases, and purchasers may be unable to resource the necessary re-application of any bespoke customization. Customization may also release the vendor from much of their support obligations – this would be disastrous if, as a result, your Service Management system is unavailable for any length of time. Further costs would be incurred in providing the bespoke training that would be required. It would be impossible to take advantage of any cheap scheduled training courses being run by the software supplier.

The process of tool evaluation is shown in Figure 7.1.

Figure 7.1 shows the standard approach of identifying requirements before identifying products, but pragmatically there may be some element of overlap, where exploration of tools on the market opens one's eyes to new options that change the requirements. These stages are targeted primarily at the evaluation of packaged software products, but a similar approach could also be used when evaluating custom-built software. Produce a clear Statement of Requirements (SoR) that identifies the

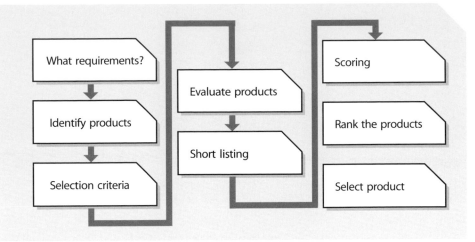

Figure 7.1 Service Management tool evaluation process

business requirements together with the mandatory facilities and those features that it would be 'nice to have'. Also identify the site policies and standards to which the product must conform. Such standards may include it running under particular system software, or on specific hardware.

Remember the considerations about the supplier's suitability, and carry out a formal evaluation of the products under consideration.

If well-developed and appropriate tools are used to support the processes, the results achieved will be far greater and often the overall costs of service provision will be less. Selecting the right tool means paying attention to a number of issues:

■ An 80% fit to all functional and technical requirements
■ A meeting of ALL mandatory requirements
■ Little (if any) product customization required
■ Adherence of tool and supplier to Service Management best practice
■ A sound data structure and handling
■ Integration with other Service Management and Operational Management tools
■ Support of open standards and interfaces
■ Business-driven not technology-driven
■ Administration and maintenance costs within budget
■ Acceptable levels of maintenance and release policies
■ Security and integrity
■ Availability of training and consultancy services
■ Good report generation
■ Scalability and growth.

Implementing
Service Design

8

8 Implementing Service Design

This section of the publication considers the task of implementing the Service Design processes and tackles issues such as:

- Where do we start?
- How do we improve?
- How do we know we are making progress?

The activities of implementing and improving Service Design need to be focused on the needs and desires of the customer and the business. Therefore these activities should be driven and prioritized by:

- Business needs and business impacts
- Risks to the services and processes.

The activities will be influenced significantly by the requirements outlined in the SLRs and by the agreements made in the SLAs.

8.1 BUSINESS IMPACT ANALYSIS

A valuable source of input when trying to ascertain the business needs, impacts and risks is the Business Impact Analysis (BIA). The BIA is an essential element of the overall business continuity process (see section 4.7) and will dictate the strategy for risk reduction and disaster recovery. Its normal purpose is to identify the effect a disaster would have on the business. It will show which parts of the organization will be most affected by a major incident and what effect it will have on the company as a whole. It therefore enables the recognition of the most critical business functions to the company's survival and where this criticality differs depending on the time of the day, week, month or year. Additionally experience has shown that the results from the BIA can be an extremely useful input for a number of other areas as well, and will give a far greater understanding of the service than would otherwise be the case.

The BIA could be divided into two areas:

- One by business management, which has to investigate the impact of the loss (or partial loss) of a business process or a business function. This includes the knowledge of manual workarounds and their costs.
- A second role located in Service Management is essential to break down the effects of service loss to the business. This element of the BIA shows the

impact of service disruption to the business. The services can be managed and influenced by Service Management. Other aspects also covered in 'Business BIA' cannot be influenced by Service Management.

As part of the design phase of a new or changed service, a BIA should be conducted to help define the business continuity strategy and to enable a greater understanding about the function and importance of the service. This will enable the organization to define:

- Which are the critical services, what constitutes a major incident on these services, and the subsequent impact and disruption caused to the business – important in deciding when and how to implement changes
- Acceptable levels and times of service outage levels – again important in the consideration of change and implementation schedules
- Critical business and service periods – important periods to avoid
- The cost of loss of service – important for Financial Management
- The potential security implications of a loss of service – important considerations in the management of risk.

8.2 SERVICE LEVEL REQUIREMENTS

As part of the Service Level Management process (see Chapter 4), the Service Level Requirements for all services will be ascertained and the ability to deliver against these requirements will be assessed and finally agreed in a formal SLA. For new services, the requirements must be ascertained at the start of the development process, not after completion. Building the service with Service Level Requirements uppermost in mind is essential from a Service Design perspective.

8.3 RISKS TO THE SERVICES AND PROCESSES

When implementing the Service Design and ITSM processes, business-as-usual practices must not be adversely affected. This aspect must be considered during the production and selection of the preferred solution to ensure that disruption to operational services is minimized.

This assessment of risk should then be considered in detail in the Service Transition activities as part of the implementation process.

8.4 IMPLEMENTING SERVICE DESIGN

The process, policy and architecture for the design of IT services outlined in this publication will need to be documented and utilized to ensure the appropriate innovative IT services can be designed and implemented to meet current and future agreed business requirements.

The IT Service Management processes outlined in Chapter 4 of this publication and in the other publications in this series will also need to be implemented to ensure service delivery that matches the requirements of the business.

The question often asked is 'Which process shall I implement first?' The real answer is all of them, as the true value of implementing all of the Service Management processes is far greater than the sum of the individual processes. All the processes are interrelated, and in some cases are totally dependent on others. What is ultimately required is a single, integrated set of processes, providing management and control of a set of IT services throughout their entire lifecycle.

While recognising that, to get the complete benefit of implementing IT service Management, all of the processes need to be addressed, it is also recognized that it is unlikely that organizations can do everything at once. It is therefore recommended that the areas of greatest need be addressed first. A detailed assessment needs to be undertaken to ascertain the strengths and weaknesses of IT service provision. This should be undertaken by performing customer satisfaction surveys, talking to customers, talking to IT staff and analysing the processes in action. From this assessment, short-, medium- and long-term strategies can be developed.

It may be that 'quick wins' need to be implemented in the short term to improve the current situation, but these improved processes may have to be discarded or amended as part of the medium- or long-term strategies. If 'quick wins' are implemented, it is important that they are not done at the expense of the long-term objectives, so these must be considered at all times. However, every organization will have to start somewhere, and the starting point will be wherever the organization is now in terms of IT Service Management maturity.

Implementation priorities should be set against the goals of a SIP. For example, if availability of IT services is a critical issue, focus on those processes aimed at maximizing availability (e.g. Incident Management,

Problem Management, Change Management and Availability Management). Throughout the implementation process, key players must be involved in the decision-making process. These will include receivers as well as providers of the service. There can be a tendency, when analysing the areas of greatest need, to go straight for tools to improve the situation. Workshops or focus groups will be beneficial in understanding the requirements and the most suitable process for implementation that will include people, processes, products and partners.

The first thing to do is to establish a formal process and method of implementation and improvement of Service Design, with the appropriate governance in place. This formal process should be based around the six-stage process illustrated in Figure 8.1. More information can also be found on this process in the Continual Service Improvement publication.

It is important that when implementing or improving processes a structured Project Management method is used. The improvement process can be summarized as, first, understanding the vision by ascertaining the high-level business objectives. The 'vision-setting' should set and align business and IT strategies. Second, assessing the current situation to identify strengths that can be built on and weaknesses that need to be addressed. So 'Where are we now?' is an analysis of the current position in terms of the business, organization, people and process. Third, 'Where do we want to be?' is a development of the principles defined in the vision-setting, agreeing the priorities for improvement, and fourth, detailing the SIP to achieve higher-quality service provision. Next, measurements and metrics need to be put in place to show that the milestones have been achieved and that the business objectives and business priorities have been met. Finally the process should ensure that the momentum for quality improvement is maintained.

The following are key elements for successful alignment of IT with business objectives:

■ Vision and leadership in setting and maintaining strategic direction, clear goals, and measurement of goal realization in terms of strategic direction
■ Acceptance of innovation and new ways of working
■ Thorough understanding of the business, its stakeholders and its environment
■ IT staff understanding the needs of the business
■ The business understanding the potential of IT
■ Information and communication available and accessible to everyone who needs it

- Separately allocated time to familiarize with the material
- Continuous tracking of technologies to identify opportunities for the business.

The implementation/improvement cycle is useful in checking the alignment between the business and IT, as shown in Figure 8.1.

8.4.1 What is the vision?

The starting point for all of these activities is the culture and environment of the service provider organization. The people and the culture have to be appropriate and acceptable to improvement and change. Therefore, before attempting anything else, the culture within the service provider needs to be reviewed to ensure that it will accept and facilitate the implementation of the required changes and improvements. The following key steps need to be completed to achieve this stage of the cycle:

- Establish a vision, aligned with the business vision and objectives
- Establish the scope of the project/programme
- Establish a set of high-level objectives
- Establish governance, sponsorship and budget
- Obtain senior management commitment
- Establish a culture focused on:
  - Quality
  - Customer and business focus
  - A learning environment
  - Continual improvement
  - Commitment to the 'improvement cycle'
  - Ownership and accountability.

8.4.2 Where are we now?

Once the vision and high-level objectives have been defined, the service provider then needs to review the current situation, in terms of what processes are in place and the maturity of the organization. The steps and activities that need to be completed here are:

- A review, assessment or a more formal audit of the current situation, using a preferred technique:
  - An internal review or audit
  - Maturity assessment
  - An external assessment or benchmark
  - An ISO/IEC 20000 audit
  - An audit against COBIT
  - A Strengths, Weaknesses, Opportunities and Threats (SWOT) analysis
  - A risk assessment and management methodology
- The review should include:
  - The culture and maturity of the service provider organization
  - The processes in place and their capability and maturity
  - The skills and competence of the people
  - The services and technology
  - The suppliers, contracts and their capability
  - The quality of service and the current measurements, metrics and KPIs
  - A report summarizing the findings and recommendations.

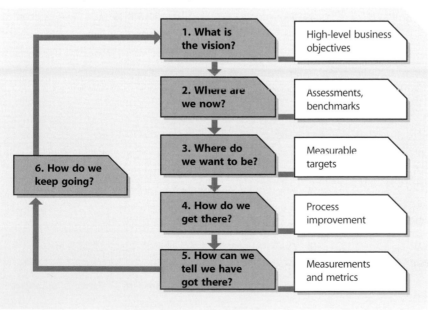

Figure 8.1   Implementation/improvement cycle

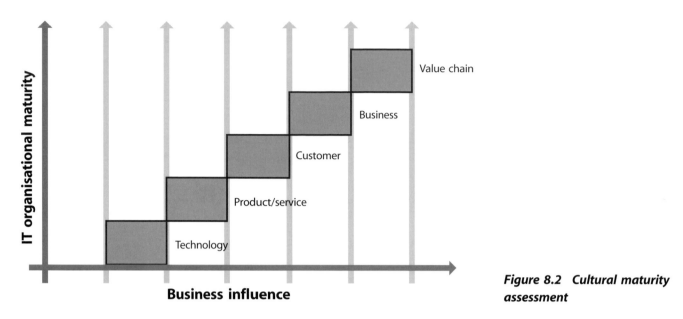

Figure 8.2 Cultural maturity assessment

The review of the culture should include assessing it in terms of the capability and maturity of the culture within the IT service provider organization, as shown in Figure 8.2.

This assessment should be based on the fact that each growth stage represents a transformation of IT organization and as such will require:

- Changes in people (skills and competences)
- Processes and ways of working
- Technology and tools (to support and enable the people and processes)
- Steering (the visions, goals and results)
- Attitude (the values and beliefs)
- The appropriate level and degree of interaction with the business, stakeholders, customers and users.

The assessment should also include a review of the capability and maturity of the Service Design processes, as shown in Figure 8.3.

This review and should include all aspects of the processes and their use including the:

- Vision: steering, objectives and plans
- Process maturity, functionality, usage, application, effectiveness and efficiency together with ownership, management and documentation
- People: the roles, responsibilities, skills and knowledge of the people
- Products, including the tools and technology used to automate the processes
- Culture: the focus, attitudes and beliefs.

The above framework can be used to provide consistency of process assessment. Assessing these two aspects will determine the current state of the organization and its Service Management capability and maturity. When starting out on the implementation or improvement of Service Design, or any set of processes, it is important to

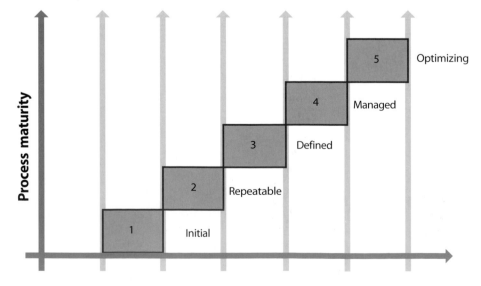

Figure 8.3 Process maturity framework

build on the strengths of the existing cultures and processes and rapidly identify and improve the weaknesses. A more detailed explanation of this framework is contained in Appendix H.

8.4.3 Where do we want to be?

Based on the current state assessment, and the vision and high-level objectives, a future desired state can be defined. This should be expressed in terms of planned outcomes, including some or all of:

■ Improved IT service provision alignment with total business requirements

■ Improved quality of Service Design

■ Improvements in service levels and quality

■ Increases in customer satisfaction

■ Improvements in process performance.

8.4.4 How do we get there?

A set of improvements should then be identified to move forward from the current state to the agreed future state. A plan to implement these improvements should then be developed, incorporating Service Transition and Service Operation, and should include:

■ The improvement actions

■ The approach to be taken and the methods to be used

■ Activities and timescales

■ Risk assessment and management

■ Resources and budgets

■ Roles and responsibilities

■ Monitoring, measurement and review.

8.4.5 How can we tell when we have got there?

Often organizations instigate improvement initiatives without considering or designing the measurement system from the outset. The success of the initiative cannot, therefore, be ascertained because we have no benchmark before, during or after the implementation. It is imperative that the measurements are designed before the implementation. A defined set of metrics needs to be utilized in order to ensure that the desired future state is achieved. This desired future state needs to be expressed in measurable terms such as:

■ X% reduction in Service Design non-conformances

■ X% increase in customer satisfaction

■ X% increase in the service availability of critical services.

Thus once the improvement actions and plans have been completed, checks and reviews should be completed in order to determine:

■ Did we achieve our desired new state and objectives?

■ Are there any lessons learnt and could we do it better next time?

■ Did we identify any other improvement actions?

8.4.6 How do we keep going?

Having improved, we now need to consolidate and move on. The organization and the culture must recognize that we can always get better, and therefore must establish an environment of continual improvement. So, once we have achieved the new desired state, we must review the vision and objectives, identify more improvement actions and repeat the six-stage process again. So this stage is all about:

■ Developing a learning environment

■ Establishing a desire to improve throughout the organization

■ Recognizing and reinforcing the message that quality and improvement are everybody's job

■ Maintaining the momentum on improvement and quality.

8.5   MEASUREMENT OF SERVICE DESIGN

The success of the Service Design and the success of the improvement to the processes around the Service Design must be measured, the data must be analysed and reported on. Where the design or process does not meet the requirements of the business as a whole, changes to the process may be required and the results of those changes must also be measured. Continuous measurement, analysis and reporting are mandatory requirements for both the Service Design process and the ITSM processes.

There are measurement methods available that enable the analysis of service improvement. The Balanced Scorecard is a method developed by Robert Kaplan and David Norton as a concept for measuring a company's activities in terms of its vision and strategies. It gives a comprehensive view of the performance of a business. The system forces managers to focus on the important performance metrics that drive success. It balances a financial perspective with customer, internal process and learning and growth perspectives. More information can be found on the Balanced Scorecard method in the Continual Service Improvement publication.

Six Sigma is a methodology developed by Bill Smith at Motorola Inc. in 1986, and was originally designed to manage process variations that cause defects, defined as unacceptable deviation from the mean or target, and to systematically work towards managing variation to eliminate those defects. Six Sigma has now grown beyond defect control and is often used to measure improvement in IT process execution. (Six Sigma is a registered service mark and trademark of Motorola Inc.)

Six Sigma (DMADV) is an improvement system used to develop new processes at Six Sigma quality levels and is defined as:

- **Define** – formally define the goals of the design activity that are consistent with customer demands and organization strategy
- **Measure** – identify Critical Success Factors, capabilities, process capability and risk assessment
- **Analyse** – develop and design alternatives, create high-level design and evaluate design capability to select the best design
- **Design** – develop detailed design, optimize design and plan for design verification
- **Verify** – set up pilot runs, implement production process and hand over to process owners.

The Six Sigma (DMAIC) process (define, measure, analyse, improve, control) is an improvement system for existing processes falling below specification and looking for incremental improvement.

8.5.1 Prerequisites for success

There are a number of prerequisites required for the Service Design and the successful introduction of new or revised processes. Often these prerequisites for success (PFSs) are elements of one process required by another. For example, fully completed and up-to-date Business Service Catalogue and Technical Service Catalogue are required before Service Level Management can design the SLA and supporting agreement structure, and before SLM can set up and agree the SLAs. Problem Management will depend on a mature Incident Management process. The PFSs can be much wider than just ITSM process interdependencies. For example, the design of availability and capacity for a new service cannot be achieved without details of the business plan for the utilization of the new service. The design of the service will be impossible without the Service Portfolio and Service Transition Pack. There are many more examples of these PFSs that need to be considered and planned before high process maturity levels can be achieved. Low maturity in one process will

mean that high levels of maturity will not be achievable in other processes.

8.5.2 Critical Success Factors and Key Performance Indicators

Critical Success Factor (CSF) is a term for an element that is necessary for an organization or project to achieve its mission. CSFs can be used as a means for identifying the important elements of success.

CSFs are the things that have to be got right in the Service Design and within each ITSM process. Key Performance Indicators (KPIs) are measures that quantify objectives and enable the measurement of performance. KPIs should be set and measured against the design and for each of the processes to ensure the CSFs are met. Together, CSFs and KPIs establish the baseline and mechanisms for tracking performance.

It is recommended that each IT organization focuses on a small sub-set of CSFs and KPIs at any one time. The required CSFs and KPIs should be set at the beginning of the Continual Service Improvement Plan (CSIP).

It is important that CSFs are agreed during the design phase of a service and of the processes, and that Key Performance Indicators (KPIs) are set, measured and reported on to indicate the quality of the Service Design and the Service Design processes. There is a requirement to be able to analyse how well the service infrastructure was designed. It is possible to arrive at a good design in a very resource-inefficient manner, and vice versa, so we need to look at the quality as well as resources required to achieve the required quality. KPIs around the success of delivery of the service indicate the effectiveness of the Service Design are applicable – for example, does the service meet the (defined) business requirements for availability, reliability, throughput, security, maintainability, serviceability, functionality etc.? KPIs around the resource estimates, however, will show us how efficient we were in the design.

These should be defined as part of QA planning and release acceptance. These KPIs could be supported by similar component metrics.

KPIs for the process of Service Design include:

- Percentage of Service Design requirement specifications produced on time (and to budget)
- Percentage of Service Design plans produced on time
- Percentage of Service Transition packs completed on time
- Percentage of QA and acceptance criteria plans produced on time

- Accuracy of Service Design – for example, was the correct infrastructure built to support the service?
- Percentage accuracy of the cost estimate of the whole Service Design phase
- Accuracy of SLA(s), OLA(s) and contract(s) – do they really support the required level of service?

To judge service provision and ITSM process performance, clearly defined objectives with measurable targets should be set. Confirmation needs to be sought that these objectives and the milestones set in the Continual Service Improvement (CSI) stage of the lifecycle have been reached and that the desired service quality or desired improvement in quality has been achieved. It is vital when designing services or processes that KPIs are designed from the outset and collected regularly and at important milestones. For example, when designing at the completion of each significant stage of the programme, a Post Implementation Review (PIR) should be conducted to ensure the objectives have been met. The PIR will include a review of supporting documentation and the general awareness amongst staff of the refined processes.

A comparison is required of what has been achieved against the original goals set in the project. Once this has been confirmed, new improvement targets should be defined. To confirm that the milestones have been reached, KPIs need to be constantly monitored. These KPIs include customer satisfaction targets, so there will be a need to survey customers planned at various stages to confirm that changes made are improving the customer perception of the service quality. It is possible that the services have higher availability, that there are fewer incidents and that response times have improved, but at the same time the customer's perception of service quality has not improved. Clearly this is as important, and will need to be addressed by talking to customers to ascertain their concerns. Confirmation will need to be sought that CSIs put in place are addressing the customer's primary needs.

For further information on service improvement practices, please refer to the Continual Service Improvement publication.

Challenges, Critical Success Factors and risks

9

9 Challenges, Critical Success Factors and risks

9.1 CHALLENGES

With every undertaking there will be challenges or difficulties to face and to overcome. This will be especially true when attempting to design new services and processes that meet the requirements of all stakeholders within the business. Experience has shown that the following will help to overcome the challenges:

- Understanding the business requirements and the business priorities and ensuring that these are uppermost in mind when designing the processes and the services.
- Communications will be vitally important both in explaining what is happening and how individuals will be affected and in listening to the requirements and needs of the individuals. It's vitally important to communicate with people about concerns that relate to their daily job.
- Involve as many people as possible in the design. Setting up focus groups or steering groups can be very effective in getting the right solution as well as gaining wider support.
- Gaining commitment from senior management as well as from all levels of staff.

Examples of challenges that may be faced include:

- The need to ensure alignment with current architectural directions, strategy and policies. An example of this may be that the procured infrastructure may have poor monitoring and control features.
- The use of diverse and disparate technologies and applications.
- Documentation and adherence to agreed practices and processes.
- Unclear or changing requirements from the business. This may be unavoidable in some cases because business needs are likely to change. The important thing is to ensure that there is a very close relationship between the IT service provider organization and the business customer of the service, so that any changing requirements can be identified as quickly as possible.
- A lack of awareness and knowledge of service and business targets and requirements.
- Linked to the above point, it may be that certain

facilities are not built into the design. Again, it is imperative that representatives of every user of the designed service or process are involved throughout the process to reduce the chance of this happening. Details of service testing (an important element here) are contained within the Service Transition publication.

- A resistance to planning, or a lack of planning leading to unplanned initiatives and unplanned purchases.
- Inefficient use of resources causing wasted spend and investment.
- As mentioned previously, a good knowledge and appreciation of the business impacts and priorities is imperative.
- Poor relationships, communication or lack of cooperation between the IT service provider and the business may result in the design not achieving the business requirements.
- Resistance to work within the agreed strategy.
- Use of, and therefore the constraints of, old technology and legacy systems.
- Required tools are too costly or too complex to implement or maintain with the current staff skills.
- Lack of information, monitoring and measurements.
- Unreasonable targets and timescales previously agreed in the SLAs and OLAs.
- Over-commitment of available resources with an associated inability to deliver (e.g. projects always late or over budget).
- Poor Supplier Management and/or poor supplier performance.
- Lack of focus on service availability.
- Lack of awareness and adherence to the operational aspects of security policies and procedures.
- Ensuring normal daily operation or business as usual is considered as part of the design.
- Cost and budgetary constraints.
- Ascertaining the ROI and the realization of business benefit.

9.2 RISKS

There are a number of risks directly associated with the Service Design phase of the Service Lifecycle. These risks need to be identified to ensure that they are not realized. They include the following:

- If any of the PFSs for Service Design are not met, then the Service Design or Service Management process will not be successful.

- If maturity levels of one process are low, it will be impossible to achieve full maturity in other processes.

- Business requirements are not clear to IT staff.

- Business timescales are such that insufficient time is given for proper Service Design.

- Insufficient testing, resulting in poor design and therefore poor implementation.

- An incorrect balance is struck between innovation, risk and cost while seeking a competitive edge, where desired by the business.

- The fit between infrastructures, customers and partners is not sufficient to meet the overall business requirements.

- A coordinated interface is not provided between IT planners and business planners.

- The policies and strategies, especially the Service Management strategy, are not available from Service Strategy, or its content is not clearly understood.

- There are insufficient resources and budget available for Service Design activities.

- The risk of services developed in isolation using their 'own' assets and infrastructure. This can appear to be cheaper in isolation, but can be much more costly in the long term because of the financial savings of corporate buying and the extra cost of supporting different architecture.

- Insufficient time given to the design phase, or insufficient training given to the staff tasked with the design.

- Insufficient engagement or commitment with the application's functional development, leading to insufficient attention to Service Design requirements.

Afterword

Afterword

Service Design, as described in this publication, covers the design of appropriate and innovative IT services to meet current and future agreed business requirements. Service Design develops a Service Design Package and looks at selecting the appropriate Service Design model. In this publication we have also examined the various sourcing models available and given some benefits and disadvantages to each.

The publication also discusses the fundamentals of the design processes and the five aspects of the design:

- The design of the service solutions, including all of the functional requirements, resources and capabilities needed and agreed
- The design of Service Management systems and tools, especially the Service Portfolio for the management and control of services through their lifecycle
- The design of the technology architectures and management architectures and tools required to provide the services
- The design or specification of the processes needed to design, transition, operate and improve the services, the architectures and the processes themselves
- The design of the measurement systems, methods and metrics for the services, the architectures and their constituent components and the processes.

The definition of Service Design is:

> 'The design of appropriate and innovative IT services, including their architectures, processes, policies and documentation, to meet current and future agreed business requirements'.

The publication has explained that the better and more careful the design, the better the solution taken into live operation. It is also highly likely that the better the design, the less re-work time that will need to be undertaken during the transition and live phases.

The scope of this publication includes the design of services, as well as the design of Service Management systems and processes. Service Design is not limited to new services, but includes change necessary to increase or maintain value to customers over the lifecycle of services.

This publication explains that pragmatism sometimes overrides the perfect solution where we know what it would be, but the amount of effort and cost does not justify the perfect solution. As always it will depend on the business needs and the business requirements. As always it is imperative that whatever is done within IT has a direct benefit to the overall business.

Appendix A: The Service Design Package

Appendix A: The Service Design Package

A 'Service Design Package' or SDP should be produced during the design stage, for each new service, major change to a service or removal of a service or changes to the 'Service Design Package' itself. This pack is then passed from Service Design to Service Transition and details all aspects of the service and its requirements through all of the subsequent stages of its lifecycle. The SDP should contain:

Table A.1 Contents of the Service Design Package

Category	Sub-category	Description of what is in the SDP
Requirements	Business requirements	The initial agreed and documented business requirements
	Service applicability	This defines how and where the service would be used. This could reference business, customer and user requirements for internal services
	Service contacts	The business contacts, customer contacts and stakeholders in the service
Service Design	Service functional requirements	The changed functionality of the new or changed service, including its planned outcomes and deliverables, in a formally agreed Statement of Requirements (SoR)
	Service Level Requirements	The SLR, revised or new SLA, including service and quality targets
	Service and operational management requirements	Management requirements to manage the new or changed service and its components, including all supporting services and agreements, control, operation, monitoring, measuring and reporting
	Service Design and topology	The design, transition and subsequent implementation and operation of the service solution and its supporting components, including: ■ The service definition and model, for transition and operation ■ All service components and infrastructure (including H/W, S/W, networks, environments, data, applications, technology, tools, documentation), including version numbers and relationships, preferably within the CMS ■ All user, business, service, component, transition, support and operational documentation ■ Processes, procedures, measurements, metrics and reports ■ Supporting products, services, agreements and suppliers
Organizational Readiness Assessment	Organizational Readiness Assessment	'Organizational Readiness Assessment' report and plan, including: business benefit, financial assessment, technical assessment, resource assessment and organizational assessment, together with details of all new skills, competences, capabilities required of the service provider organization, its suppliers, supporting services and contracts

Table A.1 Contents of the Service Design Package (continued)

Category	Sub-category	Description of what is in the SDP
Service Lifecycle Plan	Service Programme	An overall programme or plan covering all stages of the lifecycle of the service, including the timescales and phasing, for the transition, operation and subsequent improvement of the new service including:
		■ Management, coordination and integration with any other projects, or new or changed activities, services or processes
		■ Management of risks and issues
		■ Scope, objectives and components of the service
		■ Skills, competences, roles and responsibilities
		■ Processes required
		■ Interfaces and dependencies with other services
		■ Management of teams, resources, tools, technology, budgets, facilities required
		■ Management of suppliers and contracts
		■ Progress reports, reviews and revision of the programme and plans
		■ Communication plans and training plans
		■ Timescales, deliverables, targets and quality targets for each stage
	Service Transition Plan	Overall transition strategy, objectives, policy, risk assessment and plans including:
		■ Build policy, plans and requirements, including service and component build plans, specifications, control and environments, technology, tools, processes, methods and mechanisms, including all platforms
		■ Testing policy, plans and requirements, including test environments, technology, tools, processes, methods and mechanisms
		■ Testing must include:
		● Functional testing
		● Component testing, including all suppliers, contracts and externally provided supporting products and services
		● User acceptance and usability testing
		● System compatibility and integration testing
		● Service and component performance and capacity testing
		● Resilience and continuity testing
		● Failure, alarm and event categorization, processing and testing
		● Service and component, security and integrity testing
		● Logistics, release and distribution testing
		● Management testing, including control, monitoring, measuring and reporting, together with backup, recovery and all batch scheduling and processing

Table A.1 Contents of the Service Design Package (continued)

Category	Sub-category	Description of what is in the SDP
	Service Transition Plan	■ Deployment policy, release policy, plans and requirements, including logistics, deployment, roll-out, staging, deployment environments, cultural change, organisational change, technology, tools, processes, approach, methods and mechanisms, including all platforms, knowledge, skill and competence transfer and development, supplier and contract transition, data migration and conversion
	Service Operational Acceptance Plan	Overall operational strategy, objectives, policy, risk assessment and plans including: ■ Interface and dependency management and planning ■ Events, reports, service issues, including all changes, releases, resolved incidents, problems and known errors, included within the service and any errors, issues or non-conformances within the new service ■ Final service acceptance
	Service Acceptance Criteria	Development and use of Service Acceptance Criteria (SAC) for progression through each stage of the Service Lifecycle, including: ■ All environments ■ Guarantee and pilot criteria and periods

Appendix B: Service Acceptance Criteria (example)

B

Appendix B: Service Acceptance Criteria (example)

The Service Acceptance Criteria (SAC) is a set of criteria used to ensure that the service meets its expected functionality and quality and that the service provider is ready to deliver the new service once it has been deployed.

Table B.1 Service Acceptance Criteria

Criteria	Responsibility
Have the 'go-live' date and the guarantee period been agreed with all concerned parties, together with final acceptance criteria?	Change, Service Level
Have the deployment project and schedule been documented agreed and made public to all affected personnel?	Change, Incident
Has the SLA/SLR been reviewed, revised and agreed with all concerned parties?	Service Level
Has the service been entered/updated in the Service Catalogue/Service Portfolio within the CMS and appropriate relationships established for all supporting components?	Service Level, Configuration
Have all customers and stakeholders been identified and recorded in the CMS?	Service Level, Business Relationship
Have all operational risks associated with running the new service been assessed and mitigation actions completed where appropriate?	Business Continuity, Availability
Have contingency and fail-over measures been successfully tested and added to the overall resilience test schedule?	Business Continuity, Availability
Can all SLA/SLR targets be monitored, measured, reported and reviewed, including availability and performance?	Service Level, Availability
Have all users been identified/approved and their appropriate accounts created for them?	Account Management
Can all workload characteristics, performance and capacity targets be measured and incorporated into Capacity Plans?	Capacity
Have all operational processes, schedules and procedures been agreed, tested, documented and accepted (e.g. site documentation, backups, housekeeping, archiving, retention)?	Operations, Business Continuity
Have all batch jobs and printing requirements been agreed, tested, documented and accepted?	Operations
Have all test plans been completed successfully?	Test Manager
Have all security checks and tests been competed successfully?	Security Compliance
Are appropriate monitoring and measurement tools and procedures in place to monitor the new service, together with an out-of-hours support rota?	Systems Management
Have all ongoing operational workloads and costs been identified and approved?	Operations, IT Finance
Are all service and component operational costs understood and incorporated into financial processes and the cost model?	IT Finance
Have incident and problem categories and processes been reviewed and revised for the new service, together with any known errors and deficiencies?	Incident, Problem Reporting
Have all new suppliers been identified and their associated contracts drawn up accordingly?	Contract and Supplier Management

Table B.1 Service Acceptance Criteria (continued)

Criteria	Responsibility
Have all support arrangements been reviewed and revised – SLAs, SLRs, OLAs and contracts agreed, with documentation accepted by all teams (including suppliers, support teams, Supplier Management, development teams and application support)?	Project Manager
Has appropriate technical support documentation been provided and accepted by Incident, Problem and all IT support teams?	Incident, Problem
Have all RFCS and release records been authorized and updated?	Change
Have all service, SLA, SLR, OLA and contract details, together with all applications and infrastructure component details, been entered on the CMS?	Project Management Support Teams, Configuration
Have appropriate S/W licences been purchased or reallocated licences used?	Configuration
Have any new H/W components been stored in the DL with details recorded in the CMS?	Configuration
Have all new S/W components been lodged in the DL with details recorded in the CMS?	Configuration
Have all maintenance and upgrade plans been agreed, together with release policies, frequencies and mechanisms?	Release and Deployment
Have all users been trained, and has user documentation been accepted and supplied to all users?	Project Manager
Are all relationships, interfaces and dependencies with all other internal and external systems and services documented, agreed and supported?	Project Manager
Have appropriate business managers signed off acceptance of new service?	Project Manager

Appendix C: Process documentation templates (example)

C

Appendix C: Process documentation templates (example)

C1   PROCESS FRAMEWORK

When designing a new or revised process for any of the Service Management processes, it is recommended that a process specification or framework be produced. The specification should be kept at a fairly high level, but it needs to detail the scope and interfaces of the process. More detailed procedures and work instructions will also be needed to ensure consistency of the process and its application. The typical contents of a Process Framework or Specification are:

- Process name, description and administration (documentation administration: version, change control, author, etc.)
- Vision and mission statements
- Objectives
- Scope and terms of reference
- Process overview:
  - Description and overview
  - Inputs
  - Procedures
  - Activities
  - Outputs
  - Triggers
  - Tools and other deliverables
  - Communication
- Roles and responsibilities:
  - Operational responsibilities
  - Process owner
  - Process members
  - Process users
  - Other roles
- Associated documentation and references
- Interfaces and dependencies to:
  - Other SM processes
  - Other IT processes
  - Business processes
- Process measurements and metrics: reviews, assessments and audits
- Deliverables and reports produced by the process:
  - Frequency
  - Content
  - Distribution
- Glossary, acronyms and references.

Appendix D: Design and planning documents and their contents

Appendix D: Design and planning documents and their contents

This appendix contains suggested details of the types of design documents, plans and standards documents that should be produced and maintained by IT, and also outlines the minimum contents of IT technology architectures and plans. However, it should be stressed again that all these documents should be frequently and regularly reviewed and revised and should be actively used within everyday IT processes and procedures.

They must also be maintained in alignment with all similar documents in use within the business and the overall organization.

D1 DESIGN AND ARCHITECTURAL DOCUMENTS AND STANDARDS

The design documents and standards developed and maintained by IT should include:

- Design and planning standards, policies, processes and procedures
- Application architectures, design methods and standards
- Business requirements, business impact assessment and prioritization and business case methods and standards
- Functional requirements standards
- SoR and ITT standards and methods for their evaluation
- IT technology architectures, design standards and policies, covering all areas of technology, including mainframe, server, desktop, laptop, hand-held and mobile devices, telephony systems, storage, backup, network and network addressing
- Operating systems, systems software, utilities and firmware architectures, design policies and standards
- Data, information and database architectures, design policies and standards, including information flows, Knowledge Management, information security and access, Data Management, data storage, data warehousing, data analysis and data mining
- Management systems, platforms, tools and agents and their architectures and design polices and standards, including functionality, domains, interfaces, management protocols, event and alarm handling and categorization, automation and escalation
- Cabling architectures, designs and standards

- Development standards, methods and policies
- Testing methods, polices and standards
- Handover, acceptance and sign-off standards and methods
- Partners, supplier and contract standards and policies
- Communications policies and standards
- Document and document library standards and policies
- Internet and intranet architectures, design standards and policies, including e-commerce and e-business
- E-mail and groupware architectures, design standards and policies
- Environmental requirements, design policies and standards
- IT security design policies and standards, including fire walling, virus checking, service and system access levels, methods and policies, remote access, user account and password management
- Procurement standards and policies
- Programme standards and policies, project methods and project planning and review policies and standards
- Quality standards and policies
- User interfaces and standards.

D2 IT PLANS

IT should produce and maintain a number of plans in order to coordinate and manage the overall development and quality of IT services. These should include:

- **IT business plans**: the business plans for the development of IT services
- **Strategic plans**: providing plans for the achievement of the long-term vision, mission and objectives of IT
- **Tactical plans**: providing plans for the achievement of the short- and medium-term vision, mission and objectives of ICT
- **Functional plans**: providing plans for the achievement of the vision, mission and objectives of key IT functions
- **Operational plans**: providing plans for the development and improvement of operational processes, procedures and methods

- **Project plans and programmes**:
  - IT and business programmes
  - IT projects
- **Processes plans and programmes**:
  - Objectives and targets
  - Process improvement
  - Roles and responsibilities
- **Transition plans**:
  - Build plans and schedules
  - Testing and release schedules
  - Development and test environments
  - Transition schedules
- **Service Management plans**:
  - Service Quality Plan(s)
  - Service Improvement Plans and Programmes
  - Financial Plans and budgets
  - IT Service Continuity and Recovery Plans and Business Continuity Plans
  - Capacity Plan
  - Availability Plan
  - Service Support Plans
  - Release Plans and schedules
  - Configuration Management Plans
  - Change Management Plans and the Change Schedule
  - Service Desk, Incident Management and Problem Management Plans
  - Supplier and Contract Plans.

All IT plans should be developed, maintained and reviewed in line within the business and the overall organization. This should be achieved using the impact assessment process of a suitable Change Management system. Organizations should take the legal requirements for systems into consideration and also look into International and national standards and regulation and the need for corporate governance.

Appendix E:
Environmental architectures and standards

E

Appendix E: Environmental architectures and standards

This appendix contains details of environmental architectures and standards. Every organization should produce an environmental policy for equipment location, with minimum agreed standards for particular concentrations of equipment. Additionally, minimum standards should be agreed for the protection of buildings containing equipment and equipment room shells. The following tables cover the major aspects that need to be considered, with example characteristics.

Table E.1   Building/site

Access	Secure perimeters, secure entrances, audit trail
Building and site protection	Security fencing, video cameras, movement and intruder detectors, window and door alarms, lightning protectors, good working environment (standard)
Entry	Multiple controlled points of entry
External environment	Minimize external risks
Services	Where possible and justifiable, alternate routes and suppliers for all essential services, including network services

Table E.2   Major equipment room

Access	Secure controlled entry, combination lock, swipe card, video camera (if business critical and unattended)
Location	First floor wherever possible, with no water, gas, chemical or fire hazards within the vicinity, above, below or adjacent
Visibility	No signage, no external windows
Shell	External shell: waterproof, airtight, soundproofed, fire-resistant (0.5 hours to 4 hours depending on criticality)
Equipment delivery	Adequate provision should be made for the delivery and positioning of large delicate equipment
Internal floor	Sealed
Separate plant room	Uninterruptible Power Supply (UPS). Electrical supply and switching, air-handling units, dual units and rooms if business critical
External	Generator for major data centres and business-critical systems

Table E.3   Major data centres

Access	Secure controlled entry, combination lock, swipe card, video camera (if business critical and unattended)
Temperature	Strict control, 22° (± 3°). Provide for up to 550W/m2. 6° variation throughout the room and a maximum of 6° per hour
Humidity control	Strict control: 50% (± 10%)
Air quality	Positive pressure, filtered intake low gaseous pollution (e.g. sulphur dioxide ≤ 0.14 ppm), dust levels for particles > 1 micron, less than 5 x 106 particles/m3. Auto shut-down on smoke or fire detection
Power	Power Distribution Unit (PDU), with three-phase supply to non-switched boxes, one per piece of equipment, with appropriate rated circuit-breakers for each supply. Alternatively, approved power distribution strips can be used. Balanced three-phase loadings. UPS (online or line interactive with Simple Network Management Protocol (SNMP) Management) to ensure voltage supplied is within ± 5% of rating with minimal impulse, sags, surges and over/under voltage conditions
False floors	Antistatic, liftable floor tiles 600 x 600mm on pedestals, with alternate pedestals screwed to the solid floor. Minimum of 600mm clearance to solid floor. Floor loadings of up to 5kN/m2 with a recommended minimum of 3m between false floor and ceiling
Internal walls	From false floor to ceiling, fire-resistant, but with air flow above and below floor level
Fire detection/prevention	HSSD or VESDA multi-level alarm with auto FM200 (or alternative halon replacement) release on 'double-knock' detection
Environmental detectors	For smoke, temperature, power, humidity, water and intruder with automated alarm capability. Local alarm panels with repeater panels and also remote alarm capability
Lighting	Normal levels of ceiling lighting with emergency lighting on power failure
Power safety	Clean earth should be provided on the PDU and for all equipment. With clearly marked remote power-off buttons on each exit. Dirty power outlets, clearly marked, should also be supplied
Fire extinguishers	Sufficient electrical fire extinguishers with adequate signage and procedures
Vibration	Vibrations should be minimal within the complete area
Electromagnetic interference	Minimal interference should be present (1.5V/m ambient field strength)
Installations	All equipment should be provided and installed by qualified suppliers and installers to appropriate electrical and health and safety standards
Network connections	The equipment space should be flood-wired with adequate capacity for reasonable growth. All cables should be positioned and secured to appropriate cable trays
Disaster recovery	Fully tested recovery plans should be developed for all major data centres including the use of stand-by sites and equipment

Table E.4   Regional data centres and major equipment centres

Access	Secure controlled entry, combination lock, swipe card, video camera (if business critical and unattended)
Temperature	Temperature control, 22° (± 5°), preferable
Humidity control	Strict control: 50% (± 10%), preferable
Air quality	Positive pressure, filtered intake low gaseous pollution (e.g. sulphur dioxide ≤ 0.14 ppm), dust levels for particles > 1 micron, less than 5 x 106 particles/m3. Auto shut-down on smoke or fire detection
Power	PDU with three-phase supply to non-switched boxes, one per piece of equipment, with appropriate rated circuit-breakers for each supply. Alternatively, approved power distribution strips can be used. Balanced three-phase loadings. Room UPS to ensure voltage supplied is within ± 5% of rating with minimal impulse, sags, surges and over/under voltage conditions
False floors	Antistatic, liftable floor tiles 600 x 600mm on pedestals, with alternate pedestals screwed to the solid floor. Minimum of 600mm clearance to solid floor. Floor loadings of up to 5kN/m2 with a recommended minimum of 3m between false floor and ceiling
Internal walls	From false floor to ceiling, fire-resistant, but with air flow above and below floor level
Fire detection/prevention	Generally fire detection but not suppression, although HSSD or VESDA multi-level alarm with auto FM200 (or alternative halon replacement) release on 'double-knock' detection may be included if business-critical systems are contained
Environmental detectors	For smoke, temperature, power, humidity, water and intruder with automated alarm capability
Lighting	Normal levels of ceiling lighting with emergency lighting on power failure
Power safety	Clean earth should be provided on the PDU and for all equipment. With clearly marked remote power-off buttons on each exit. Dirty power outlets, clearly marked, should also be supplied
Fire extinguishers	Sufficient electrical fire extinguishers with adequate signage and procedures
Vibration	Vibrations should be minimal within the complete area
Electromagnetic interference	Minimal interference should be present (1.5V/m ambient field strength)
Installations	All equipment should be provided and installed by qualified suppliers and installers to appropriate electrical and health and safety standards
Network connections	The equipment space should be flood-wired with adequate capacity for reasonable growth. All cables should be positioned and secured to appropriate cable trays
Disaster recovery	Fully tested recovery plans should be developed for all regional data centres, including the use of stand-by sites and equipment where appropriate

Table E.5   Server or network equipment rooms

Access	Secure controlled entry, by combination lock, swipe card or lock and key. In some cases equipment may be contained in open offices in locked racks or cabinets
Temperature	Normal office environment, but if in closed/locked rooms adequate ventilation should be provided
Humidity control	Normal office environment
Air quality	Normal office environment
Power	Clean power supply with a UPS-supplied power to the complete rack
False floors	Recommended minimum of 3m between floor and ceiling with all cables secured in multi-compartment trunking
Internal walls	Wherever possible all walls should be fire-resistant
Fire detection/prevention	Normal office smoke/fire detection systems, unless major concentrations of equipment
Environmental detectors	For smoke, power, intruder with audible alarm capability
Lighting	Normal levels of ceiling lighting with emergency lighting on power failure
Power safety	Clean earth should be provided for all equipment. With clearly marked power-off buttons
Fire extinguishers	Sufficient electrical fire extinguishers with adequate signage and procedures
Vibration	Vibrations should be minimal within the complete area
Electromagnetic interference	Minimal interference should be present (1.5V/m ambient field strength)
Installations	All equipment should be provided and installed by qualified suppliers and installers to appropriate electrical and health and safety standards
Network connections	The equipment space should be flood-wired with adequate capacity for reasonable growth. All cables should be positioned and secured to appropriate cable trays
Disaster recovery	Fully tested recovery plans should be developed where appropriate

Table E.6   Office environments

Access	All offices should have the appropriate secure access depending on the business, the information and the equipment contained within them
Lighting, temperature, humidity and air quality	A normal clean, comfortable and tidy office environment, conforming to the organization's health, safety and environmental requirements
Power	Clean power supply for all computer equipment, with UPS facilities if appropriate
False floors	Preferred if possible, but all cables should be contained within appropriate trunking
Fire detection/prevention and extinguishers	Normal office smoke/fire detection systems and intruder alerting systems, unless there are major concentrations of equipment. Sufficient fire extinguishers of the appropriate type, with adequate signage and procedures
Network connections	The office space should preferably be flood-wired with adequate capacity for reasonable growth. All cables should be positioned and secured to appropriate cable trays. All network equipment should be secured in secure cupboards or cabinets
Disaster recovery	Fully tested recovery plans should be developed where appropriate

Appendix F: Sample SLA and OLA

Appendix F: Sample SLA and OLA

This appendix contains examples of SLAs and OLAs and their contents. It is not recommended that every SLA or OLA should necessarily contain all of the sections listed within the following sample documents. It is suggested that these areas are considered when preparing document templates, but that they are only incorporated into the actual documents themselves where they are appropriate and relevant. So the following outlines should only be considered as guidelines or checklists.

SERVICE LEVEL AGREEMENT (SLA – SAMPLE)

This agreement is made between...and

....

The agreement covers the provision and support of the ABC services which..... (brief service description).

This agreement remains valid for 12 months from the (date) until (date). The agreement will be reviewed annually. Minor changes may be recorded on the form at the end of the agreement, providing they are mutually endorsed by the two parties and managed through the Change Management process.

Signatories:

Name...Position......................................Date..............

Name...Position......................................Date..............

Service description:

The ABC Service consists of.... (a fuller description to include key business functions, deliverables and all relevant information to describe the service and its scale, impact and priority for the business).

Scope of the agreement:

What is covered within the agreement and what is excluded?

Service hours:

A description of the hours that the customers can expect the service to be available (e.g. 7 x 24 x 365, 08:00 to 18:00 – Monday to Friday).

Special conditions for exceptions (e.g. weekends, public holidays) and procedures for requesting service extensions (who to contact – normally the Service Desk –- and what notice periods are required).

This could include a service calendar or reference to a service calendar.

Details of any pre-agreed maintenance or housekeeping slots, if these impact on service hours, together with details of how any other potential outages must be negotiated and agreed – by whom and notice periods etc.

Procedures for requesting permanent changes to service hours.

Service availability:

The target availability levels that the IT service provider will seek to deliver within the agreed service hours. Availability targets within agreed service hours, normally expressed as percentages (e.g. 99.5%), measurement periods, method and calculations must be stipulated. This figure may be expressed for the overall service, underpinning services and critical components or all three. However, it is difficult to relate such simplistic percentage availability figures to service quality, or to customer business activities. It is therefore often better to try to measure service unavailability in terms of the customer's inability to conduct its business activities. For example, 'sales are immediately affected by a failure of IT to provide an adequate POS support service'. This strong link between the IT service and the customer's business processes is a sign of maturity in both the SLM and the Availability Management processes.

Agreed details of how and at what point this will be measured and reported, and over what agreed period should also be documented.

Reliability:

The maximum number of service breaks that can be tolerated within an agreed period (may be defined either as number of breaks e.g. four per annum, or as a Mean Time Between Failures (MTBF) or Mean Time Between Systems Incidents (MTBSI)).

Definition of what constitutes a 'break' and how these will be monitored and recorded.

Customer support:

Details of how to contact the Service Desk, the hours it will be available, the hours support is available and what to do outside these hours to obtain assistance (e.g. on-call support, third-party assistance etc.) must be documented. The SLA may also include reference to internet/Intranet Self Help and/or Incident logging. Metrics and measurements should be included such as telephone call answer targets (number of rings, missed calls etc.)

Targets for Incident response times (how long will it be before someone starts to assist the customer – may include travelling time etc.)

A definition is needed of 'response' – Is it a telephone call back to the customer or a site visit? – as appropriate.

Arrangements for requesting support extensions, including required notice periods (e.g. request must be made to the Service Desk by 12 noon for an evening extension, by 12 noon on Thursday for a week-end extension)

Note. Both Incident response and resolution times will be based on whatever Incident impact/priority codes are used – details of the classification of Incidents should also be included here.

Note. In some cases, it may be appropriate to reference out to third-party contacts and contracts and OLAs – but not as a way of diverting responsibility.

Contact points and escalation:

Details of the contacts within each of the parties involved in the agreement and the escalation processes and contact points. This should also include the definition of a complaint and procedure for managing complaints.

Service performance:

Details of the expected responsiveness of the IT service (e.g. target workstation response times for average, or maximum workstation response times, sometimes expressed as a percentile – e.g. 95% within two seconds), details of expected service throughput on which targets are based, and any thresholds that would invalidate the targets).

This should include indication of likely traffic volumes, throughput activity, constraints and dependencies (e.g. the number of transactions to be processed, number of concurrent users, and amount of data to be transmitted over the network). This is important so that performance issues that have been caused by excessive throughput outside the terms of the agreement may be identified.

Batch turnaround times:

If appropriate, details of any batch turnaround times, completion times and key deliverables, including times for delivery of input and the time and place for delivery of output where appropriate.

Functionality (if appropriate):

Details of the minimal functionality to be provided and the number of errors of particular types that can be tolerated before the SLA is breached. Should include severity levels and the reporting period.

Change Management:

Brief mention of and/or reference out to the organization's Change Management procedures that must be followed – just to reinforce compliance. Also targets for approving, handling and implementing RFCs, usually based on the category or urgency/priority of the change, should also be included and details of any known changes that will impact on the agreement, if any.

Service Continuity:

Brief mention of and/or reference out to the organization's Service Continuity Plans, together with details of how the SLA might be affected or reference to a separate Continuity SLA, containing details of any diminished or amended service targets should a disaster situation occur. Details of any specific responsibilities on both sides (e.g. data backup, off-site storage). Also details of the invocation of plans and coverage of any security issues, particularly any customer responsibilities (e.g. coordination of business activities, business documentation, backup of freestanding PCs, password changes).

Security:

Brief mention of and/or reference out to the organization's Security Policy (covering issues such as password controls, security violations, unauthorized software, viruses etc.). Details of any specific responsibilities on both sides (e.g. Virus Protection, Firewalls).

Printing:

Details of any special conditions relating to printing or printers (e.g. print distribution details, notification of large centralized print runs, or handling of any special high-value stationery).

Responsibilities:

Details of the responsibilities of the various parties involved within the service and their agreed responsibilities, including the service provider, the customer and the users.

Charging (if applicable):

Details of any charging formulas used, charging periods, or reference out to charging policy documents, together with invoicing procedures and payment conditions etc. must be included. This should also include details of any financial penalties or bonuses that will be paid if service targets do not meet expectations. What will the penalties/bonuses be and how will they be calculated, agreed and collected/paid (more appropriate for third-party situations). If the SLA covers an outsourcing relationship, charges should be detailed in an Appendix as they are often covered by commercial in-confidence provisions.

It should be noted that penalty clauses can create their own difficulties. They can prove a barrier to partnerships if unfairly invoked on a technicality and can also make service provider staff unwilling to admit to mistakes for fear of penalties being imposed. This can, unless used properly, be a barrier to developing effective relationships and problem solving.

Service reporting and reviewing:

The content, frequency, content, timing and distribution of service reports, and the frequency of associated service review meetings. Also details of how and when SLAs and the associated service targets will be reviewed and possibly revised, including who will be involved and in what capacity.

Glossary:

Explanation of any unavoidable abbreviations or terminology used, to assist customer understanding.

Amendment sheet:

To include a record of any agreed amendments, with details of amendments, dates and signatories. It should also contain details of a complete change history of the document and its revisions.

It should be noted that the SLA contents given above are examples only. They should not be regarded as exhaustive or mandatory, but they provide a good starting point.

OPERATIONAL LEVEL AGREEMENT (OLA – SAMPLE)

This agreement is made between..and

....

The agreement covers the provision of the support service providing..... (brief service description).

This agreement remains valid for 12 months from the (date) until (date).

The agreement will be reviewed annually. Minor changes may be recorded on the form at the end of the agreement, providing they are mutually endorsed by the two parties and managed through the Change Management process.

Signatories:

Name..Position..Date...............

Name..Position..Date...............

Details of previous amendments:

Support service description:

Comprehensive explanation and details of the support service being provided.

Scope of the agreement:

What is covered within the agreement and what is excluded?

Service hours:

A description of the hours for which the support service is provided.

Service targets:

The targets for the provision of the support service and the reporting and reviewing processes and frequency.

Contact points and escalation:

Details of the contacts within each of the parties involved within the agreement and the escalation processes and contact points.

Service Desk and incident response times and responsibilities:

The responsibilities and targets agreed for the progress and resolution of Incidents and support of the Service Desk.

Problem response times and responsibilities:

The responsibilities and targets agreed for the progress and resolution of Problems.

Change Management:

The responsibilities and targets agreed for the progress and implementation of changes.

Release Management:

The responsibilities and targets agreed for the progress and implementation of releases.

Configuration Management:

The responsibilities for the ownership, provision and maintenance of accurate Configuration Management information.

Information Security Management:

The responsibilities and targets agreed for the support of the Security Policy(s) and the Information Security Management process.

Availability Management:

Responsibility for ensuring that all components within their support domain are managed and supported to meet and continue to meet all of the service and component availability targets.

Service Continuity Management:

Responsibility for ensuring that all components within their support domain have up-to-date and tested recovery plans that support agreed and documented business requirements. This should include assistance with the technical assessment of risk and its subsequent management and mitigation.

Capacity Management:

Responsibility for supporting the needs of the Capacity Management process within the agreed scope of their technical domain.

Service Level Management:

Assistance with the definition and agreement of appropriate targets within SLAs, SLRs and OLAs, concerning components within the scope of their technical domain.

Supplier Management:

Assistance with the management of contracts and suppliers, again principally within the scope of their technical domain.

Provision of information:

The provision and maintenance of accurate information, including financial data for all components within the agreed scope of their technical domain.

Glossary:

Explanation of any unavoidable abbreviations or terminology used, to assist understanding of terms contained within the agreement.

Amendment sheet:

To include a record of any agreed amendments, with details of amendments, dates and signatories. It should also contain details of a complete change history of the document and its revisions.

Appendix G: Example Service Catalogue

Appendix G: Example Service Catalogue

The Service Catalogue is key document containing valuable information on the complete set of services offered. It should preferably be stored as a set of 'service' CIs within a CMS, maintained under change Management. As it is such a valuable set of information it should be available to anyone within the organization. Every new service should immediately be entered into the Service Catalogue once its initial definition of requirements has been documented and agreed. So as well as the information below, the Service Catalogue should record the status of every service, through the stages of its defined lifecycle.

Table G.1 Example Service Catalogue

Service Name	Service Description	Service type	Supporting services	Business Owner(s)	Business Unit(s)	Service Manager(s)	Business Impact	Business Priority	SLA	Service Hours	Business Contacts	Escalation Contacts	Service Reports	Service Reviews	Security Rating
Service 1															
Service 2															
Service 3															
Service 4															

Appendix H: The Service Management process maturity framework

H

Appendix H: The Service Management process maturity framework

The process maturity framework (PMF) can be used either as a framework to assess the maturity of each of the Service Management processes individually, or to measure the maturity of the Service Management process as a whole. This is an approach that has been widely used in the IT industry for a number of years, with many proprietary models being used by a number of organizations. This particular PMF has been developed to bring a common, best practice approach to the review and assessment of Service Management process maturity. This framework, which is shown in Figure H.1, can be used by organizations to internally review their own Service Management processes as well as third-party organizations brought in as external reviewers, assessors or auditors.

The use of the PMF in the assessment of Service Management processes relies on an appreciation of the IT Organization Growth Model. The maturity of the Service Management processes is heavily dependent on the stage of growth of the IT organization as a whole. It is difficult, if not impossible, to develop the maturity of the Service Management processes beyond the maturity and capability of the overall IT organization. The maturity of

the IT organization is not just dependent on the maturity of the Service Management processes. Each level requires a change of a combination of elements in order to be fully effective. Therefore a review of processes will require an assessment to be completed against the five areas of:

- Vision and steering
- Process
- People
- Technology
- Culture.

These are the five areas described within the PMF for assessing process maturity. The major characteristics of each level of the PMF are as follows.

Initial (Level 1)

The process has been recognized but there is little or no process management activity and it is allocated no importance, resources or focus within the organization. This level can also be described as 'ad hoc' or occasionally even 'chaotic'.

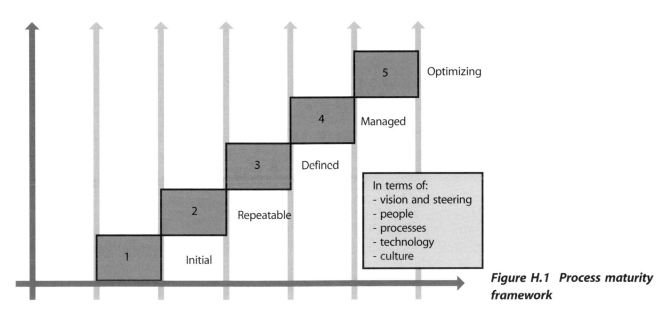

Figure H.1 Process maturity framework

Table H.1   PMF Level 1: initial

Vision and steering	Minimal funds and resources with little activity
	Results temporary, not retained
	Sporadic reports and reviews
Process	Loosely defined processes and procedures, used reactively when problems occur
	Totally reactive processes
	Irregular, unplanned activities
People	Loosely defined roles or responsibilities
Technology	Manual processes or a few specific, discrete tools (pockets/islands)
Culture	Tool and technology-based and driven with a strong activity focus

Repeatable (Level 2)

The process has been recognized and is allocated little importance, resource or focus within the operation. Generally activities related to the process are uncoordinated, irregular, without direction and are directed towards process effectiveness.

Table H.2   PMF Level 2: repeatable

Vision and steering	No clear objectives or formal targets
	Funds and resources available
	Irregular, unplanned activities, reporting and reviews
Process	Defined processes and procedures
	Largely reactive process
	Irregular, unplanned activities
People	Self-contained roles and responsibilities
Technology	Many discrete tools, but a lack of control
	Data stored in separate locations
Culture	Product and service-based and driven

Defined (Level 3)

The process has been recognized and is documented but there is no formal agreement, acceptance or recognition of its role within the IT operation as a whole. However, the process has a process owner, formal objectives and targets with allocated resources, and is focused on the efficiency as well as the effectiveness of the process. Reports and results are stored for future reference.

Table H.3 PMF Level 3: defined

Vision and steering	Documented and agreed formal objectives and targets
	Formally published, monitored and reviewed plans
	Well-funded and appropriately resourced
	Regular, planned reporting and reviews
Process	Clearly defined and well-publicized processes and procedures
	Regular, planned activities
	Good documentation
	Occasionally proactive process
People	Clearly defined and agreed roles and responsibilities
	Formal objectives and targets
	Formalized process training plans
Technology	Continuous data collection with alarm and threshold monitoring
	Consolidated data retained and used for formal planning, forecasting and trending
Culture	Service and Customer-oriented with a formalized approach

Managed (Level 4)

The process has now been fully recognized and accepted throughout IT. It is service focused and has objectives and targets that are based on business objectives and goals. The process is fully defined, managed and has become proactive, with documented, established interfaces and dependencies with other IT process.

Table H.4 PMF Level 4: managed

Vision and steering	Clear direction with business goals, objectives and formal targets, measured progress
	Effective management reports actively used
	Integrated process plans linked to business and IT plans
	Regular improvements, planned and reviewed
Process	Well-defined processes, procedures and standards, included in all IT staff job descriptions
	Clearly defined process interfaces and dependencies
	Integrated Service Management and systems development processes
	Mainly proactive process
People	Inter- and intra-process team working
	Responsibilities clearly defined in all IT job descriptions
Technology	Continuous monitoring measurement, reporting and threshold alerting to a centralized set of integrated toolsets, databases and processes
Culture	Business focused with an understanding of the wider issues

Optimizing (Level 5)

The process has now been fully recognized and has strategic objectives and goals aligned with overall strategic business and IT goals. These have now become 'institutionalized' as part of the everyday activity for everyone involved with the process. A self-contained continual process of improvement is established as part of the process, which is now developing a pre-emptive capability.

Table H.5   PMF Level 5: optimizing

Vision and steering	Integrated strategic plans inextricably linked with overall business plans, goals and objectives
	Continuous monitoring, measurement, reporting alerting and reviews linked to a continual process of improvement
	Regular reviews and/or audits for effectiveness, efficiency and compliance
Process	Well-defined processes and procedures part of corporate culture
	Proactive and pre-emptive process
People	Business aligned objectives and formal targets actively monitored as part of the everyday activity
	Roles and responsibilities part of an overall corporate culture
Technology	Well-documented overall tool architecture with complete integration in all areas of people, processes and technology
Culture	A continual improvement attitude, together with a strategic business focus. An understanding of the value of IT to the business and its role within the business value chain

This maturity framework is aligned with the Software Engineering Institute Capability Maturity Model® Integration (SEI CMMI) and their various maturity models including the evolving CMMI-SVC, which focuses on the delivery of services.

Appendix I: Example contents of a Statement of Requirement (SoR) and/or Invitation to Tender (ITT)

Appendix I: Example contents of a Statement of Requirement (SoR) and/or Invitation to Tender (ITT)

The following is an example of a minimum set of contents that should be included in an ITT or SOR:

- A description of the services, products and/or components required
- All relevant technical specifications, details and requirements
- An SLR where applicable
- Availability, reliability, maintainability and serviceability requirements
- Details of ownership of hardware, software, buildings, facilities, etc.
- Details of performance criteria to be met by the equipment and the supplier(s)
- Details of all standards to be complied with (internal, external, national and international)
- Legal and regulatory requirements (industry, national, EU and international)
- Details of quality criteria
- Contractual timescales, details and requirements, terms and conditions
- All commercial considerations: costs, charges, bonus and penalty payments and schedules
- Interfaces and contacts required
- Project management methods to be used
- Reporting, monitoring and reviewing procedures and criteria to be used during and after the implementation
- Supplier requirements and conditions
- Sub-contractor requirements
- Details of any relevant terms and conditions
- Description of the supplier response requirements:
  - Format
  - Criteria
  - Conditions
  - Timescales
  - Variances and omissions
  - Customer responsibilities and requirements
- Details of planned and possible growth
- Procedures for handling changes
- Details of the contents and structure of the responses required.

Appendix J: The typical contents of a Capacity Plan

J

Appendix J: The typical contents of a Capacity Plan

The typical contents of a Capacity Plan are as follows.

1   INTRODUCTION

This section briefly explains the background to this issue of the Capacity Plan, how it was produced and what it contains. For example:

- The current services, technology and resources
- The organization's current levels of capacity
- Problems being experienced or envisaged due to over- or under-capacity
- The degree to which service levels are being achieved
- What has changed since the last issue of the plan.

2   MANAGEMENT SUMMARY

Much of the Capacity Plan, by necessity, contains technical detail that is not of interest to all readers of the plan. The management summary should highlight the main issues, options, recommendations and costs. It may be necessary to produce a separate executive summary document that contains the main points from each of the sections of the main plan.

3   BUSINESS SCENARIOS

It is necessary to put the plan into the context of the current and envisaged business environment. For example, a British airline planned to move a large number of staff into its headquarters building. A ratio of 1.7 people per desktop terminal was forecast. Capacity Management was alerted and was able to calculate the extra network traffic that would result.

It is important to mention explicitly all known business forecasts so that readers can determine what is within and what is outside the scope of the plan. It should include the anticipated growth in existing services, the potential new services and existing services scheduled for closure.

4   SCOPE AND TERMS OF REFERENCE OF THE PLAN

Ideally, the Capacity Plan should encompass all IT resources. This section should explicitly name those elements of the IT infrastructure that are included and those that are excluded, if any.

5   METHODS USED

The Capacity Plan uses information gathered by the sub-processes. This sub-section, therefore, should contain details of how and when this information was obtained – for example, business forecasts obtained from business plans, workload forecasts obtained from customers, service level forecasts obtained by the use of modelling tools.

6   ASSUMPTIONS MADE

It is important that any assumptions made, particularly those concerning the business drivers for IT Capacity, are highlighted early on in the plan. If they are the cornerstones on which more detailed calculations are built, then it is vital that all concerned understand this.

7   SERVICE SUMMARY

The service summary section should include:

- **Current and recent service provision**: for each service that is delivered, provide a service profile. This should include throughput rates and the resulting resource utilization – for example, of memory, storage space, transfer rates, processor usage and network usage. Short-, medium- and long-term trends should be presented here.
- **Service forecasts**: the business plans should provide Capacity Management with details of the new services planned and the growth or contraction in the use of existing services. This sub-section should report on new services and the demise of legacy systems.

8   RESOURCE SUMMARY

The resource summary section should include:

- **Current and recent resource usage**: this sub-section concentrates on the resulting resource usage by the services. It reports, again, on the short-, medium- and long-term trends in resource usage, broken down by hardware platform. This information has been gathered and analysed by the sub-processes of Service Capacity Management and Component Capacity Management and so should be readily available.
- **Resource forecasts**: this sub-section forecasts the likely resource usage resulting from the service forecasts. Each business scenario mentioned above

should be addressed here. For example, a carpet wholesale business in the North of England could accurately predict what the peak and average processor usage would be before they decided to take over a rival business. It was proved that an upgrade would not be required. This was fed into the cost model, leading to a successful takeover.

9 OPTIONS FOR SERVICE IMPROVEMENT

Building on the results of the previous section, this section outlines the possible options for improving the effectiveness and efficiency of Service Delivery. It could contain options for merging different services on a single processor, upgrading the network to take advantage of technological advances, tuning the use of resource or service performance, rewriting legacy systems, purchasing new hardware or software etc.

10 COSTS FORECAST

The costs associated with these options should be documented here. In addition, the current and forecasted cost of providing IT services should be included. In practice, Capacity Management obtains much of this information from the Financial Management process and the IT Financial Plan.

11 RECOMMENDATIONS

The final section of the plan should contain a summary of the recommendations made in the previous plan and their status – for example, rejected, planned, implemented – and any variances from the plan. Any new recommendations should be made here, i.e. which of the options mentioned in the plan is preferred, and the implications if the plan and its recommendations are not implemented should also be included.

The recommendations should be quantified in terms of the:

- Business benefits to be expected
- Potential impact of carrying out the recommendations
- Risks involved
- Resources required
- Cost, both set-up and ongoing.

Appendix K: The typical contents of a recovery plan

K

Appendix K: The typical contents of a recovery plan

The typical contents of an ITSCM recovery plan are as follows.

GENERIC RECOVERY PLAN

1 DOCUMENT CONTROL

This document must be maintained to ensure that the systems, Infrastructure and facilities included, appropriately support business recovery requirements.

1.1 Document distribution

Copy	Issued to	Date	Position
1.			
2.			
3.			
4.			

1.2 Document revision

This document will be reviewed every X months.

Current Revision: *date*

Next Revision: *date*

Revision Date	Version No	Summary of Changes

1.3 Document approval

This document must be approved by the following personnel:

Name	Title	Signature

2 SUPPORTING INFORMATION

2.1 Introduction

This document details the instructions and procedures that are required to be followed to recover or continue the operation of systems, Infrastructure, services or facilities to maintain Service Continuity to the level defined or agreed with the business.

2.2 Recovery strategy

The *systems, Infrastructure, services* or *facilities* will be recovered to *alternative* systems, Infrastructure, services or facilities.

It will take approximately *X hours* to recover the *systems, Infrastructure, services* or *facilities*. The system will be recovered to the last known point of stability/data integrity, *which is point in day/timing*.

The required recovery time for this system, Infrastructure, service or facility is:

The recovery time and procedures for this system, *Infrastructure, services* or *facility* was last tested on:

2.3 Invocation

The following personnel are authorized to invoke this plan:

1

2

2.4 Interfaces and dependencies on other plans

Details of the inter-relationships and references with all other continuity and recovery plans and how the interfaces are activated.

2.5 General guidance

All requests for information from the media or other sources should be referred to the *Company procedure*.

When notifying personnel of a potential or actual disaster, follow the defined operational escalation procedures, and in particular:

- Be calm and avoid lengthy conversation
- Advise them of the need to refer information requests to escalation point
- Advise them of expectations and actions (avoid giving them details of the Incident unless absolutely necessary)
- If the call is answered by somebody else:
  - Ask if the contact is available elsewhere
  - If they cannot be contacted, leave a message to contact you on a given number
  - Do not provide details of the incident
  - Always document call time details, responses and actions.

All activities and contact/escalation should be clearly and accurately recorded. To facilitate this, actions should be in a checklist format and there should be space to record the date and time the activity was started and completed, and who carried out the activity.

2.6 Dependencies

System, Infrastructure, service, facility or *interface* dependencies should be documented (in priority order) so that related recovery plans or procedures that will need to be invoked in conjunction with this recovery plan can be identified and actioned. The person responsible for invocation should ensure recovery activities are coordinated with these other plans.

System	Document Reference	Contact

2.7 Contact lists

Lists of all contact names, organizations and contact details and mechanisms:

Name	Organization/Role	Title	Contact Details

2.8 Recovery team

The following staff/functions are responsible for actioning these procedures or ensuring the procedures are actioned and recording any issues or problems encountered. Contact will be made via the normal escalation procedures.

Name	Title	Contact Details

2.9 Recovery team checklist

To facilitate the execution of key activities in a timely manner, a checklist similar to the following should be used.

Task	Target completion	Actual completion
Confirm invocation		
Initiate call tree and escalation procedures		
Instigate and interface with any other recovery plans necessary (e.g. BCP, Crisis Management, Emergency Response Plan)		
Arrange for backup media and documentation to be shipped to recovery site(s)		
Establish recovery teams		
Initiate recovery actions		
Confirm progress reporting		
Inform recovery team of reporting requirements		
Confirm liaison requirements with all recovery teams		

Advise customers and management of estimated recovery completion		

3   RECOVERY PROCEDURE

Enter recovery instructions/procedures or references to all recovery procedures here.

Content/format should be in line with company standards for procedures. If there are none, guidance should be issued by the Manager or Team Leader for the area responsible for the system, Infrastructure, services or facility. The only guideline is that the instructions should be capable of being executed by an experienced professional without undue reliance on local knowledge.

Where necessary, references should be made to supporting documentation (and its location), diagrams and other information sources. This should include the document reference number (if it exists). It is the responsibility of the plan author to ensure that this information is maintained with this plan. If there is only a limited amount of supporting information, it may be easier for this to be included within the plan, providing this plan remains easy to read/follow and does not become too cumbersome.

Further information

REFERENCES

1. Service Strategy
2. Service Transition
3. Service Operation
4. Continual Service Improvement
5. Peter Drucker
6. COBIT – ISACA
7. CMMI – CMU
8. eSCM-Service Portfolio – CMU
9. PRINCE2 – OGC
10. ISO 9000
11. ISO/IEC 20000
12. ISO 27001
13. Enterprise Architecture – Gartner
14. Plan Do Check Act – W Edwards Deming
15. Balanced Scorecard – Kaplan/Norton
16. Service Oriented Architecture – OASIS
17. Management of Risk – OGC
18. Recommended Practice for Software Requirements Specification (IEEE 830)
19. The Software Engineering Body of Knowledge (SWEBOK)
20. Object management architecture – OMG
21. Common Information Model (CIM) – DMTF
22. Web-Based Enterprise Management (WEBM) – DMTF
23. Application Management Specification – IBM
24. Windows Management Instrumentation – Microsoft
25. Desktop Management Instrumentation – Windows
26. Six Sigma – Motorola Inc
27. Dynamics of Software Development – Jim McCarthy
28. Requirements engineering; examples of tacit and explicit knowledge (Maiden & Rugg, 1995)
29. Business Analysis – Deborah Paul and Donald Yeates
30. Principles of Data Management – Keith Gordon
31. Practical Data Migration – John Morris

Glossary

Acronyms list

ACD	Automatic Call Distribution	DIKW	Data–to–Information–to–Knowledge–to–Wisdom
AM	Availability Management	ELS	Early Life Support
AMIS	Availability Management Information System	eSCM–CL	eSourcing Capability Model for Client Organizations
ASP	Application Service Provider		
BCM	Business Capacity Management	eSCM–SP	eSourcing Capability Model for Service Providers
BCM	Business Continuity Management	FMEA	Failure Modes and Effects Analysis
BCP	Business Continuity Plan	FTA	Fault Tree Analysis
BIA	Business Impact Analysis	IRR	Internal Rate of Return
BRM	Business Relationship Manager	ISG	IT Steering Group
BSI	British Standards Institution	ISM	Information Security Management
BSM	Business Service Management	ISMS	Information Security Management System
CAB	Change Advisory Board	ISO	International Organization for Standardization
CAB/EC	Change Advisory Board/Emergency Committee		
		ISP	Internet Service Provider
CAPEX	Capital Expenditure	IT	Information Technology
CCM	Component Capacity Management	ITSCM	IT Service Continuity Management
CFIA	Component Failure Impact Analysis	ITSM	IT Service Management
CI	Configuration Item	itSMF	IT Service Management Forum
CMDB	Configuration Management Database	IVR	Interactive Voice Response
CMIS	Capacity Management Information System	KEDB	Known Error Database
CMM	Capability Maturity Model	KPI	Key Performance Indicator
CMMI	Capability Maturity Model Integration	LOS	Line of Service
CMS	Configuration Management System	M_o_R	Management of Risk
COTS	Commercial off the Shelf	MTBF	Mean Time Between Failures
CSF	Critical Success Factor	MTBSI	Mean Time Between Service Incidents
CSI	Continual Service Improvement	MTRS	Mean Time to Restore Service
CSIP	Continual Service Improvement Plan	MTTR	Mean Time To Repair
CSP	Core Service Package	NPV	Net Present Value
CTI	Computer Telephony Integration		

OGC	Office of Government Commerce
OLA	Operational Level Agreement
OPEX	Operational Expenditure
OPSI	Office of Public Sector Information
PBA	Pattern of Business Activity
PIR	Post-Implementation Review
PFS	Prerequisite for Success
PSO	Projected Service Outage
QA	Quality Assurance
QMS	Quality Management System
RCA	Root Cause Analysis
RFC	Request for Change
ROI	Return on Investment
RPO	Recovery Point Objective
RTO	Recovery Time Objective
SoC	Separation of Concerns
SAC	Service Acceptance Criteria
SACM	Service Asset and Configuration Management
SCD	Supplier and Contract Database
SCM	Service Capacity Management
SDP	Service Design Package
SFA	Service Failure Analysis
SIP	Service Improvement Plan
SKMS	Service Knowledge Management System
SLA	Service Level Agreement
SLM	Service Level Management
SLP	Service Level Package
SLR	Service Level Requirement
SMO	Service Maintenance Objective
SOP	Standard Operating Procedures
SOR	Statement of requirements
SPI	Service Provider Interface
SPM	Service Portfolio Management
SPO	Service Provisioning Optimization
SPOF	Single Point of Failure

TO	Technical Observation
TOR	Terms of Reference
TCO	Total Cost of Ownership
TCU	Total Cost of Utilization
TQM	Total Quality Management
UC	Underpinning Contract
UP	User Profile
VBF	Vital Business Function
VOI	Value on Investment
WIP	Work in Progress

Definitions list

The publication names included in parentheses after the name of a term identify where a reader can find more information about that term. This is either because the term is primarily used by that publication or because additional useful information about that term can be found there. Terms without a publication name associated with them may be used generally by several publications, or may not be defined in any greater detail than can be found in the glossary, i.e. we only point readers to somewhere they can expect to expand on their knowledge or to see a greater context. Terms with multiple publication names are expanded on in multiple publications.

Where the definition of a term includes another term, those related terms are highlighted in a second colour. This is designed to help the reader with their understanding by pointing them to additional definitions that are all part of the original term they were interested in. The form 'See also Term X, Term Y' is used at the end of a definition where an important related term is not used with the text of the definition itself.

Acceptance

Formal agreement that an IT Service, Process, Plan, or other Deliverable is complete, accurate, Reliable and meets its specified Requirements. Acceptance is usually preceded by Evaluation or Testing and is often required before proceeding to the next stage of a Project or Process. *See also* Service Acceptance Criteria.

Accounting

(Service Strategy) The Process responsible for identifying actual Costs of delivering IT Services, comparing these with budgeted costs, and managing variance from the Budget.

Activity

A set of actions designed to achieve a particular result. Activities are usually defined as part of Processes or Plans, and are documented in Procedures.

Agreed Service Time

(Service Design) A synonym for Service Hours, commonly used in formal calculations of Availability. *See also* Downtime.

Agreement

A Document that describes a formal understanding between two or more parties. An Agreement is not legally binding, unless it forms part of a Contract. *See also* Service Level Agreement, Operational Level Agreement.

Alert

(Service Operation) A warning that a threshold has been reached, something has changed, or a Failure has occurred. Alerts are often created and managed by System Management tools and are managed by the Event Management Process.

Analytical Modelling

(Service Strategy) (Service Design) (Continual Service Improvement) A technique that uses mathematical Models to predict the behaviour of a Configuration Item or IT Service. Analytical Models are commonly used in Capacity Management and Availability Management. *See also* Modelling.

Application

Software that provides Functions that are required by an IT Service. Each Application may be part of more than one IT Service. An Application runs on one or more Servers or Clients. *See also* Application Management, Application Portfolio.

Application Management

(Service Design) (Service Operation) The Function responsible for managing Applications throughout their Lifecycle.

Application Portfolio

(Service Design) A database or structured Document used to manage Applications throughout their Lifecycle. The Application Portfolio contains key Attributes of all Applications. The Application Portfolio is sometimes implemented as part of the Service Portfolio, or as part of the Configuration Management System.

Application Service Provider (ASP)

(Service Design) An External Service Provider that provides IT Services using Applications running at the Service Provider's premises. Users access the Applications by network connections to the Service Provider.

Application Sizing

(Service Design) The Activity responsible for understanding the Resource Requirements needed to support a new Application, or a major Change to an existing Application. Application Sizing helps to ensure that the IT Service can meet its agreed Service Level Targets for Capacity and Performance.

Architecture

(Service Design) The structure of a System or IT Service, including the Relationships of Components to each other and to the environment they are in. Architecture also includes the Standards and Guidelines that guide the design and evolution of the System.

Assessment

Inspection and analysis to check whether a Standard or set of Guidelines is being followed, that Records are accurate, or that Efficiency and Effectiveness targets are being met. *See also* Audit.

Asset

(Service Strategy) Any Resource or Capability. Assets of a Service Provider including anything that could contribute to the delivery of a Service. Assets can be one of the following types: Management, Organization, Process, Knowledge, People, Information, Applications, Infrastructure, and Financial Capital.

Asset Management

(Service Transition) Asset Management is the Process responsible for tracking and reporting the value and ownership of financial Assets throughout their Lifecycle. Asset Management is part of an overall Service Asset and Configuration Management Process.

Attribute

(Service Transition) A piece of information about a Configuration Item. Examples are: name, location, Version number, and Cost. Attributes of CIs are recorded in the Configuration Management Database (CMDB). *See also* Relationship.

Audit

Formal inspection and verification to check whether a Standard or set of Guidelines is being followed, that Records are accurate, or that Efficiency and Effectiveness targets are being met. An Audit may be carried out by internal or external groups. *See also* Certification, Assessment.

Automatic Call Distribution (ACD)

(Service Operation) Use of Information Technology to direct an incoming telephone call to the most appropriate person in the shortest possible time. ACD is sometimes called Automated Call Distribution.

Availability

(Service Design) Ability of a Configuration Item or IT Service to perform its agreed Function when required. Availability is determined by Reliability, Maintainability, Serviceability, Performance and Security. Availability is usually calculated as a percentage. This calculation is often based on Agreed Service Time and Downtime. It is Best Practice to calculate Availability using measurements of the Business output of the IT Service.

Availability Management

(Service Design) The Process responsible for defining, analysing, Planning, measuring and improving all aspects of the Availability of IT Services. Availability Management is responsible for ensuring that all IT Infrastructure, Processes, Tools, Roles, etc. are appropriate for the agreed Service Level Targets for Availability.

Availability Management Information System (AMIS)

(Service Design) A virtual repository of all Availability Management data, usually stored in multiple physical locations. *See also* Service Knowledge Management System.

Availability Plan

(Service Design) A Plan to ensure that existing and future Availability Requirements for IT Services can be provided Cost Effectively.

Back-out

See Remediation.

Backup

(Service Design) (Service Operation) Copying data to protect against loss of Integrity or Availability of the original.

Balanced Scorecard

(Continual Service Improvement) A management tool developed by Drs Robert Kaplan (Harvard Business School) and David Norton. A Balanced Scorecard enables a Strategy to be broken down into Key Performance Indicators. Performance against the KPIs is used to demonstrate how well the Strategy is being achieved. A Balanced Scorecard has four major areas, each of which has a small number of KPIs. The same four areas are considered at different levels of detail throughout the Organization.

Baseline

(Continual Service Improvement) A Benchmark used as a reference point. For example:

- An ITSM Baseline can be used as a starting point to measure the effect of a Service Improvement Plan
- A Performance Baseline can be used to measure changes in Performance over the lifetime of an IT Service
- A Configuration Management Baseline can be used to enable the IT Infrastructure to be restored to a known Configuration if a Change or Release fails.

Benchmark

(Continual Service Improvement) The recorded state of something at a specific point in time. A Benchmark can be created for a Configuration, a Process, or any other set of data. For example, a benchmark can be used in:

- Continual Service Improvement, to establish the current state for managing improvements
- Capacity Management, to document performance characteristics during normal operations.

See also Benchmarking, Baseline.

Benchmarking

(Continual Service Improvement) Comparing a Benchmark with a Baseline or with Best Practice. The term Benchmarking is also used to mean creating a series of Benchmarks over time, and comparing the results to measure progress or improvement.

Best Practice

Proven Activities or Processes that have been successfully used by multiple Organizations. ITIL is an example of Best Practice.

Brainstorming

(Service Operation) A technique that helps a team to generate ideas. Ideas are not reviewed during the Brainstorming session, but at a later stage. Brainstorming is often used by Problem Management to identify possible causes.

Budget

A list of all the money an Organization or Business Unit plans to receive, and plans to pay out, over a specified period of time. See also Budgeting, Planning.

Budgeting

The Activity of predicting and controlling the spending of money. Consists of a periodic negotiation cycle to set future Budgets (usually annual) and the day-to-day monitoring and adjusting of current Budgets.

Build

(Service Transition) The Activity of assembling a number of Configuration Items to create part of an IT Service. The term Build is also used to refer to a Release that is authorized for distribution. For example Server Build or laptop Build. See also Configuration Baseline.

Business

(Service Strategy) An overall corporate entity or Organization formed of a number of Business Units. In the context of ITSM, the term Business includes public sector and not-for-profit organizations, as well as companies. An IT Service Provider provides IT Services to a Customer within a Business. The IT Service Provider may be part of the same Business as its Customer (Internal Service Provider), or part of another Business (External Service Provider).

Business Capacity Management (BCM)

(Service Design) In the context of ITSM, Business Capacity Management is the Activity responsible for understanding future Business Requirements for use in the Capacity Plan. See also Service Capacity Management.

Business Case

(Service Strategy) Justification for a significant item of expenditure. Includes information about Costs, benefits, options, issues, Risks, and possible problems. See also Cost Benefit Analysis.

Business Continuity Management (BCM)

(Service Design) The Business Process responsible for managing Risks that could seriously affect the Business. BCM safeguards the interests of key stakeholders, reputation, brand and value-creating activities. The BCM Process involves reducing Risks to an acceptable level and planning for the recovery of Business Processes should a disruption to the Business occur. BCM sets the Objectives, Scope and Requirements for IT Service Continuity Management.

Business Continuity Plan (BCP)

(Service Design) A Plan defining the steps required to Restore Business Processes following a disruption. The Plan will also identify the triggers for Invocation, people to be involved, communications, etc. IT Service Continuity Plans form a significant part of Business Continuity Plans.

Business Customer

(Service Strategy) A recipient of a product or a Service from the Business. For example, if the Business is a car manufacturer then the Business Customer is someone who buys a car.

Business Impact Analysis (BIA)

(Service Strategy) BIA is the Activity in Business Continuity Management that identifies Vital Business Functions and their dependencies. These dependencies may include Suppliers, people, other Business Processes, IT Services, etc. BIA defines the recovery requirements for IT Services. These requirements include Recovery Time Objectives, Recovery Point Objectives and minimum Service Level Targets for each IT Service.

Business Objective

(Service Strategy) The Objective of a Business Process, or of the Business as a whole. Business Objectives support the Business Vision, provide guidance for the IT Strategy, and are often supported by IT Services.

Business Operations

(Service Strategy) The day-to-day execution, monitoring and management of Business Processes.

Business Perspective

(Continual Service Improvement) An understanding of the Service Provider and IT Services from the point of view of the Business, and an understanding of the Business from the point of view of the Service Provider.

Business Process

A Process that is owned and carried out by the Business. A Business Process contributes to the delivery of a product or Service to a Business Customer. For example, a retailer may have a purchasing Process that helps to deliver Services to its Business Customers. Many Business Processes rely on IT Services.

Business Relationship Management

(Service Strategy) The Process or Function responsible for maintaining a Relationship with the Business. Business Relationship Management usually includes:

- Managing personal Relationships with Business managers
- Providing input to Service Portfolio Management
- Ensuring that the IT Service Provider is satisfying the Business needs of the Customers

This Process has strong links with Service Level Management.

Business Service

An IT Service that directly supports a Business Process, as opposed to an Infrastructure Service, which is used internally by the IT Service Provider and is not usually visible to the Business.

The term Business Service is also used to mean a Service that is delivered to Business Customers by Business Units. For example, delivery of financial services to Customers of a bank, or goods to the Customers of a retail store. Successful delivery of Business Services often depends on one or more IT Services.

Business Service Management (BSM)

(Service Strategy) (Service Design) An approach to the management of IT Services that considers the Business Processes supported and the Business value provided.

This term also means the management of Business Services delivered to Business Customers.

Business Unit

(Service Strategy) A segment of the Business that has its own Plans, Metrics, income and Costs. Each Business Unit owns Assets and uses these to create value for Customers in the form of goods and Services.

Call

(Service Operation) A telephone call to the Service Desk from a User. A Call could result in an Incident or a Service Request being logged.

Call Centre

(Service Operation) An Organization or Business Unit that handles large numbers of incoming and outgoing telephone calls. *See also* Service Desk.

Capability

(Service Strategy) The ability of an Organization, person, Process, Application, Configuration Item or IT Service to carry out an Activity. Capabilities are intangible Assets of an Organization. *See also* Resource.

Capacity

(Service Design) The maximum Throughput that a Configuration Item or IT Service can deliver whilst meeting agreed Service Level Targets. For some types of CI, Capacity may be the size or volume, for example a disk drive.

Capacity Management

(Service Design) The Process responsible for ensuring that the Capacity of IT Services and the IT Infrastructure is able to deliver agreed Service Level Targets in a Cost Effective and timely manner. Capacity Management considers all Resources required to deliver the IT Service, and plans for short-, medium- and long-term Business Requirements.

Capacity Management Information System (CMIS)

(Service Design) A virtual repository of all Capacity Management data, usually stored in multiple physical locations. *See also* Service Knowledge Management System.

Capacity Plan

(Service Design) A Capacity Plan is used to manage the Resources required to deliver IT Services. The Plan contains scenarios for different predictions of Business demand, and costed options to deliver the agreed Service Level Targets.

Capacity Planning

(Service Design) The Activity within Capacity Management responsible for creating a Capacity Plan.

Category

A named group of things that have something in common. Categories are used to group similar things together. For example, Cost Types are used to group similar types of Cost. Incident Categories are used to group similar types of Incident, CI Types are used to group similar types of Configuration Item.

Certification

Issuing a certificate to confirm Compliance to a Standard. Certification includes a formal Audit by an independent and Accredited body. The term Certification is also used to mean awarding a certificate to verify that a person has achieved a qualification.

Change

(Service Transition) The addition, modification or removal of anything that could have an effect on IT Services. The Scope should include all IT Services, Configuration Items, Processes, Documentation, etc.

Change Advisory Board (CAB)

(Service Transition) A group of people that advises the Change Manager in the Assessment, prioritization and scheduling of Changes. This board is usually made up of representatives from all areas within the IT Service Provider, representatives from the Business and Third Parties such as Suppliers.

Change History

(Service Transition) Information about all changes made to a Configuration Item during its life. Change History consists of all those Change Records that apply to the CI.

Change Management

(Service Transition) The Process responsible for controlling the Lifecycle of all Changes. The primary objective of Change Management is to enable beneficial Changes to be made, with minimum disruption to IT Services.

Change Request

See Request for Change.

Change Schedule

(Service Transition) A Document that lists all approved Changes and their planned implementation dates. A Change Schedule is sometimes called a Forward Schedule of Change, even though it also contains information about Changes that have already been implemented.

Change Window

(Service Transition) A regular, agreed time when Changes or Releases may be implemented with minimal impact on Services. Change Windows are usually documented in SLAs.

Charging

(Service Strategy) Requiring payment for IT Services. Charging for IT Services is optional, and many Organizations choose to treat their IT Service Provider as a Cost Centre.

Classification

The act of assigning a Category to something. Classification is used to ensure consistent management and reporting. CIs, Incidents, Problems, Changes, etc. are usually classified.

Client

A generic term that means a Customer, the Business or a Business Customer. For example, Client Manager may be used as a synonym for Account Manager.

The term client is also used to mean:

- A computer that is used directly by a User, for example a PC, Handheld Computer, or Workstation
- The part of a Client-Server Application that the User directly interfaces with. For example an e-mail Client.

Closed

(Service Operation) The final Status in the Lifecycle of an Incident, Problem, Change, etc. When the Status is Closed, no further action is taken.

Closure

(Service Operation) The act of changing the Status of an Incident, Problem, Change, etc. to Closed.

COBIT

(Continual Service Improvement) Control Objectives for Information and related Technology (COBIT) provides guidance and Best Practice for the management of IT Processes. COBIT is published by the IT Governance Institute. See www.isaca.org for more information.

Cold Standby

See Gradual Recovery.

Commercial Off-The-Shelf (COTS)

(Service Design) Application software or Middleware that can be purchased from a Third Party.

Compliance

Ensuring that a Standard or set of Guidelines is followed, or that proper, consistent accounting or other practices are being employed.

Component

A general term that is used to mean one part of something more complex. For example, a computer System may be a component of an IT Service, an Application may be a Component of a Release Unit. Components that need to be managed should be Configuration Items.

Component Capacity Management

(Service Design) (Continual Service Improvement) The Process responsible for understanding the Capacity, Utilization and Performance of Configuration Items. Data is collected, recorded and analysed for use in the Capacity Plan. *See also* Service Capacity Management.

Component CI

(Service Transition) A Configuration Item that is part of an Assembly. For example, a CPU or Memory CI may be part of a Server CI.

Component Failure Impact Analysis (CFIA)

(Service Design) A technique that helps to identify the impact of CI failure on IT Services. A matrix is created with IT Services on one edge and CIs on the other. This enables the identification of critical CIs (that could cause the failure of multiple IT Services) and of fragile IT Services (that have multiple Single Points of Failure).

Concurrency

A measure of the number of Users engaged in the same Operation at the same time.

Confidentiality

(Service Design) A security principle that requires that data should only be accessed by authorized people.

Configuration

(Service Transition) A generic term, used to describe a group of Configuration Items that work together to deliver an IT Service, or a recognizable part of an IT Service. Configuration is also used to describe the parameter settings for one or more CIs.

Configuration Baseline

(Service Transition) A Baseline of a Configuration that has been formally agreed and is managed through the Change Management process. A Configuration Baseline is used as a basis for future Builds, Releases and Changes.

Configuration Control

(Service Transition) The Activity responsible for ensuring that adding, modifying or removing a CI is properly managed, for example by submitting a Request for Change or Service Request.

Configuration Identification

(Service Transition) The Activity responsible for collecting information about Configuration Items and their Relationships, and loading this information into the CMDB. Configuration Identification is also responsible for labelling the CIs themselves, so that the corresponding Configuration Records can be found.

Configuration Item (CI)

(Service Transition) Any Component that needs to be managed in order to deliver an IT Service. Information about each CI is recorded in a Configuration Record within the Configuration Management System and is maintained throughout its Lifecycle by Configuration Management. CIs are under the control of Change Management. CIs typically include IT Services, hardware, software, buildings, people, and formal documentation such as Process documentation and SLAs.

Configuration Management

(Service Transition) The Process responsible for maintaining information about Configuration Items required to deliver an IT Service, including their Relationships. This information is managed throughout the Lifecycle of the CI. Configuration Management is part of an overall Service Asset and Configuration Management Process.

Configuration Management System (CMS)

(Service Transition) A set of tools and databases that are used to manage an IT Service Provider's Configuration data. The CMS also includes information about Incidents, Problems, Known Errors, Changes and Releases; and may contain data about employees, Suppliers, locations, Business Units, Customers and Users. The CMS includes tools for collecting, storing, managing, updating, and presenting data about all Configuration Items and their Relationships. The CMS is maintained by Configuration Management and is used by all IT Service Management Processes. *See also* Service Knowledge Management System.

Continual Service Improvement (CSI)

(Continual Service Improvement) A stage in the Lifecycle of an IT Service and the title of one of the Core ITIL publications. Continual Service Improvement is responsible for managing improvements to IT Service Management Processes and IT Services. The Performance of the IT Service Provider is continually measured and improvements are made to Processes, IT Services and IT Infrastructure in order to increase Efficiency, Effectiveness, and Cost Effectiveness. *See also* Plan–Do–Check–Act.

Continuous Availability

(Service Design) An approach or design to achieve 100% Availability. A Continuously Available IT Service has no planned or unplanned Downtime.

Continuous Operation

(Service Design) An approach or design to eliminate planned Downtime of an IT Service. Note that individual Configuration Items may be down even though the IT Service is Available.

Contract

A legally binding Agreement between two or more parties.

Control

A means of managing a Risk, ensuring that a Business Objective is achieved, or ensuring that a Process is followed. Example Controls include Policies, Procedures, Roles, RAID, door locks, etc. A control is sometimes called a Countermeasure or safeguard. Control also means to manage the utilization or behaviour of a Configuration Item, System or IT Service.

Control perspective

(Service Strategy) An approach to the management of IT Services, Processes, Functions, Assets, etc. There can be several different Control Perspectives on the same IT Service, Process, etc., allowing different individuals or teams to focus on what is important and relevant to their specific Role. Example Control Perspectives include Reactive and Proactive management within IT Operations, or a Lifecycle view for an Application Project team.

Cost

The amount of money spent on a specific Activity, IT Service, or Business Unit. Costs consist of real cost (money), notional cost such as people's time, and Depreciation.

Cost Benefit Analysis

An Activity that analyses and compares the costs and the benefits involved in one or more alternative courses of action. See also Business Case, Return on Investment.

Cost Effectiveness

A measure of the balance between the Effectiveness and Cost of a Service, Process or activity. A Cost Effective Process is one that achieves its Objectives at minimum Cost. See also KPI, Return on Investment, Value for Money.

Countermeasure

Can be used to refer to any type of Control. The term Countermeasure is most often used when referring to measures that increase Resilience, Fault Tolerance or Reliability of an IT Service.

Crisis Management

(IT Service Continuity Management) Crisis Management is the Process responsible for managing the wider implications of Business Continuity. A Crisis Management team is responsible for Strategic issues such as managing media relations and shareholder confidence, and decides when to invoke Business Continuity Plans.

Critical Success Factor (CSF)

Something that must happen if a Process, Project, Plan, or IT Service is to succeed. KPIs are used to measure the achievement of each CSF. For example a CSF of 'protect IT Services when making Changes' could be measured by KPIs such as 'percentage reduction of unsuccessful Changes', 'percentage reduction in Changes causing Incidents', etc.

Culture

A set of values that is shared by a group of people, including expectations about how people should behave, their ideas, beliefs, and practices. See also Vision.

Customer

Someone who buys goods or Services. The Customer of an IT Service Provider is the person or group that defines and agrees the Service Level Targets. The term Customers is also sometimes informally used to mean Users, for example 'this is a Customer-focused Organization'.

Dashboard

(Service Operation) A graphical representation of overall IT Service Performance and Availability. Dashboard images may be updated in real-time, and can also be included in management reports and web pages. Dashboards can be used to support Service Level Management, Event Management or Incident Diagnosis.

Deliverable

Something that must be provided to meet a commitment in a Service Level Agreement or a Contract. Deliverable is also used in a more informal way to mean a planned output of any Process.

Demand Management

Activities that understand and influence Customer demand for Services and the provision of Capacity to meet these demands. At a Strategic level Demand Management can involve analysis of Patterns of Business Activity and User Profiles. At a tactical level it can involve use of Differential Charging to encourage Customers to use IT Services at less busy times. See also Capacity Management.

Dependency

The direct or indirect reliance of one Process or Activity on another.

Deployment

(Service Transition) The Activity responsible for movement of new or changed hardware, software, documentation, Process, etc. to the Live Environment. Deployment is part of the Release and Deployment Management Process.

Design

(Service Design) An Activity or Process that identifies Requirements and then defines a solution that is able to meet these Requirements. See also Service Design.

Detection

(Service Operation) A stage in the Incident Lifecycle. Detection results in the Incident becoming known to the Service Provider. Detection can be automatic, or can be the result of a user logging an Incident.

Development

(Service Design) The Process responsible for creating or modifying an IT Service or Application. Also used to mean the Role or group that carries out Development work.

Development Environment

(Service Design) An Environment used to create or modify IT Services or Applications. Development Environments are not typically subjected to the same degree of control as Test Environments or Live Environments. *See also* Development.

Diagnosis

(Service Operation) A stage in the Incident and Problem Lifecycles. The purpose of Diagnosis is to identify a Workaround for an Incident or the Root Cause of a Problem.

Differential Charging

A technique used to support Demand Management by charging different amounts for the same IT Service Function at different times.

Document

Information in readable form. A Document may be paper or electronic. For example, a Policy statement, Service Level Agreement, Incident Record, diagram of computer room layout. *See also* Record.

Downtime

(Service Design) (Service Operation) The time when a Configuration Item or IT Service is not Available during its Agreed Service Time. The Availability of an IT Service is often calculated from Agreed Service Time and Downtime.

Driver

Something that Influences Strategy, Objectives or Requirements. For example, new legislation or the actions of competitors.

Economies of scale

(Service Strategy) The reduction in average Cost that is possible from increasing the usage of an IT Service or Asset.

Effectiveness

(Continual Service Improvement) A measure of whether the Objectives of a Process, Service or Activity have been achieved. An Effective Process or activity is one that achieves its agreed Objectives. *See also* KPI.

Efficiency

(Continual Service Improvement) A measure of whether the right amount of resources has been used to deliver a Process, Service or Activity. An Efficient Process achieves its Objectives with the minimum amount of time, money, people or other resources. *See also* KPI.

Environment

(Service Transition) A subset of the IT Infrastructure that is used for a particular purpose. For example: Live Environment, Test Environment, Build Environment. It is possible for multiple Environments to share a Configuration Item, for example Test and Live Environments may use different partitions on a single mainframe computer. Also used in the term Physical Environment to mean the accommodation, air conditioning, power system, etc.

Environment is also used as a generic term to mean the external conditions that influence or affect something.

Error

(Service Operation) A design flaw or malfunction that causes a Failure of one or more Configuration Items or IT Services. A mistake made by a person or a faulty Process that affects a CI or IT Service is also an Error.

Escalation

(Service Operation) An Activity that obtains additional Resources when these are needed to meet Service Level Targets or Customer expectations. Escalation may be needed within any IT Service Management Process, but is most commonly associated with Incident Management, Problem Management and the management of Customer complaints. There are two types of Escalation, Functional Escalation and Hierarchic Escalation.

eSourcing Capability Model for Service Providers (eSCM-SP)

(Service Strategy) A framework to help IT Service Providers develop their IT Service Management Capabilities from a Service Sourcing perspective. eSCM-SP was developed by Carnegie Mellon University, US.

Estimation

The use of experience to provide an approximate value for a Metric or Cost. Estimation is also used in Capacity and Availability Management as the cheapest and least accurate Modelling method.

Evaluation

(Service Transition) The Process responsible for assessing a new or Changed IT Service to ensure that Risks have been managed and to help determine whether to proceed with the Change.

Evaluation is also used to mean comparing an actual Outcome with the intended Outcome, or comparing one alternative with another.

Event

(Service Operation) A change of state that has significance for the management of a Configuration Item or IT Service.

The term Event is also used to mean an Alert or notification created by any IT Service, Configuration Item or Monitoring tool. Events typically require IT Operations personnel to take actions, and often lead to Incidents being logged.

Event Management

(Service Operation) The Process responsible for managing Events throughout their Lifecycle. Event Management is one of the main Activities of IT Operations.

Exception Report

A Document containing details of one or more KPIs or other important targets that have exceeded defined Thresholds. Examples include SLA targets being missed or about to be missed, and a Performance Metric indicating a potential Capacity problem.

Expanded Incident Lifecycle

(Availability Management) Detailed stages in the Lifecycle of an Incident. The stages are Detection, Diagnosis, Repair, Recovery, Restoration. The Expanded Incident Lifecycle is used to help understand all contributions to the Impact of Incidents and to Plan how these could be controlled or reduced.

External Service Provider

(Service Strategy) An IT Service Provider that is part of a different Organization to its Customer. An IT Service Provider may have both Internal Customers and External Customers.

External Sourcing

See Outsourcing.

Facilities Management

(Service Operation) The Function responsible for managing the physical Environment where the IT Infrastructure is located. Facilities Management includes all aspects of managing the physical Environment, for example power and cooling, building Access Management, and environmental Monitoring.

Failure

(Service Operation) Loss of ability to Operate to Specification, or to deliver the required output. The term Failure may be used when referring to IT Services, Processes, Activities, Configuration Items, etc. A Failure often causes an Incident.

Fast Recovery

(Service Design) A Recovery Option that is also known as Hot Standby. Provision is made to Recover the IT Service in a short period of time: typically less than 24 hours. Fast Recovery typically uses a dedicated Fixed Facility with computer Systems, and software configured ready to run the IT Services. Fast Recovery may take up to 24 hours if there is a need to Restore data from Backups.

Fault

See Error.

Fault Tolerance

(Service Design) The ability of an IT Service or Configuration Item to continue to Operate correctly after Failure of a Component part. *See also* Resilience, Countermeasure.

Fault Tree Analysis (FTA)

(Service Design) (Continual Service Improvement) A technique that can be used to determine the chain of events that leads to a Problem. Fault Tree Analysis represents a chain of events using Boolean notation in a diagram.

Financial Management

(Service Strategy) The Function and Processes responsible for managing an IT Service Provider's Budgeting, Accounting and Charging Requirements.

Fit for Purpose

An informal term used to describe a Process, Configuration Item, IT Service, etc. that is capable of meeting its objectives or Service Levels. Being Fit for Purpose requires suitable design, implementation, control and maintenance.

Fulfilment

Performing Activities to meet a need or Requirement. For example, by providing a new IT Service, or meeting a Service Request.

Function

A team or group of people and the tools they use to carry out one or more Processes or Activities. For example the Service Desk.

The term Function also has two other meanings:

■ An intended purpose of a Configuration Item, Person, Team, Process, or IT Service. For example one Function of an e-mail Service may be to store and forward outgoing mails, one Function of a Business Process may be to dispatch goods to Customers.

■ To perform the intended purpose correctly, 'The computer is Functioning'.

Governance

Ensuring that Policies and Strategy are actually implemented, and that required Processes are correctly followed. Governance includes defining Roles and responsibilities, measuring and reporting, and taking actions to resolve any issues identified.

Gradual Recovery

(Service Design) A Recovery Option that is also known as Cold Standby. Provision is made to Recover the IT Service in a period of time greater than 72 hours. Gradual Recovery typically uses a Portable or Fixed Facility that has environmental support and network cabling, but no computer Systems. The hardware and software are installed as part of the IT Service Continuity Plan.

Guideline

A Document describing Best Practice, which recommends what should be done. Compliance with a guideline is not normally enforced. *See also* Standard.

High Availability

(Service Design) An approach or design that minimizes or hides the effects of Configuration Item Failure on the users of an IT Service. High Availability solutions are designed to achieve an agreed level of Availability and make use of techniques such as Fault Tolerance, Resilience and fast Recovery to reduce the number of Incidents, and the Impact of Incidents.

Hot Standby

See Fast Recovery or Immediate Recovery.

Immediate Recovery

(Service Design) A Recovery Option that is also known as Hot Standby. Provision is made to Recover the IT Service with no loss of Service. Immediate Recovery typically uses Mirroring, Load Balancing and Split Site technologies.

Impact

(Service Operation) (Service Transition) A measure of the effect of an Incident, Problem or Change on Business Processes. Impact is often based on how Service Levels will be affected. Impact and Urgency are used to assign Priority.

Incident

(Service Operation) An unplanned interruption to an IT Service or reduction in the Quality of an IT Service. Failure of a Configuration Item that has not yet affected Service is also an Incident. For example, Failure of one disk from a mirror set.

Incident Management

(Service Operation) The Process responsible for managing the Lifecycle of all Incidents. The primary Objective of Incident Management is to return the IT Service to Customers as quickly as possible.

Incident Record

(Service Operation) A Record containing the details of an Incident. Each Incident record documents the Lifecycle of a single Incident.

Indirect Cost

(Service Strategy) A Cost of providing an IT Service, which cannot be allocated in full to a specific customer. For example, the Cost of providing shared Servers or software licences. Also known as Overhead.

Information Security Management (ISM)

(Service Design) The Process that ensures the Confidentiality, Integrity and Availability of an Organization's Assets, information, data and IT Services. Information Security Management usually forms part of an Organizational approach to Security Management that has a wider scope than the IT Service Provider, and includes handling of paper, building access, phone calls, etc., for the entire Organization.

Information Security Management System (ISMS)

(Service Design) The framework of Policy, Processes, Standards, Guidelines and tools that ensures an Organization can achieve its Information Security Management Objectives.

Information Security Policy

(Service Design) The Policy that governs the Organization's approach to Information Security Management.

Information Technology (IT)

The use of technology for the storage, communication or processing of information. The technology typically includes computers, telecommunications, Applications and other software. The information may include Business data, voice, images, video, etc. Information Technology is often used to support Business Processes through IT Services.

Infrastructure Service

An IT Service that is not directly used by the Business, but is required by the IT Service Provider so they can provide other IT Services. For example directory services, naming services, or communication services.

Insourcing

See Internal Sourcing.

Integrity

(Service Design) A security principle that ensures data and Configuration Items are modified only by authorized personnel and Activities. Integrity considers all possible causes of modification, including software and hardware Failure, environmental Events, and human intervention.

Intermediate Recovery

(Service Design) A Recovery Option that is also known as Warm Standby. Provision is made to Recover the IT Service in a period of time between 24 and 72 hours. Intermediate Recovery typically uses a shared Portable or Fixed Facility that has Computer Systems and Network Components. The hardware and software will need to be configured, and data will need to be restored, as part of the IT Service Continuity Plan.

Internal Service Provider

(Service Strategy) An IT Service Provider that is part of the same Organization as its Customer. An IT Service Provider may have both Internal Customers and External Customers.

Internal Sourcing

(Service Strategy) Using an Internal Service Provider to manage IT Services.

International Organization for Standardization (ISO)

The International Organization for Standardization (ISO) is the world's largest developer of Standards. ISO is a non-governmental organization that is a network of the national standards institutes of 156 countries. See www.iso.org for further information about ISO.

ISO 9000

A generic term that refers to a number of international Standards and Guidelines for Quality Management Systems. See www.iso.org for more information. *See also* ISO.

ISO 9001

An international Standard for Quality Management Systems. *See also* ISO 9000, Standard.

ISO/IEC 20000

ISO Specification and Code of Practice for IT Service Management. ISO/IEC 20000 is aligned with ITIL Best Practice.

ISO/IEC 27001

(Service Design) (Continual Service Improvement) ISO Specification for Information Security Management. The corresponding Code of Practice is ISO/IEC 17799. *See also* Standard.

IT Infrastructure

All of the hardware, software, networks, facilities, etc. that are required to develop, Test, deliver, Monitor, Control or support IT Services. The term IT Infrastructure includes all of the Information Technology but not the associated people, Processes and documentation.

IT Operations

(Service Operation) Activities carried out by IT Operations Control, including Console Management, Job Scheduling, Backup and Restore, and Print and Output Management. IT Operations is also used as a synonym for Service Operation.

IT Service

A Service provided to one or more Customers by an IT Service Provider. An IT Service is based on the use of Information Technology and supports the Customer's Business Processes. An IT Service is made up from a combination of people, Processes and technology and should be defined in a Service Level Agreement.

IT Service Continuity Management (ITSCM)

(Service Design) The Process responsible for managing Risks that could seriously affect IT Services. ITSCM ensures that the IT Service Provider can always provide minimum agreed Service Levels, by reducing the Risk to an acceptable level and Planning for the Recovery of IT Services. ITSCM should be designed to support Business Continuity Management.

IT Service Continuity Plan

(Service Design) A Plan defining the steps required to Recover one or more IT Services. The Plan will also identify the triggers for Invocation, people to be involved, communications, etc. The IT Service Continuity Plan should be part of a Business Continuity Plan.

IT Service Management (ITSM)

The implementation and management of Quality IT Services that meet the needs of the Business. IT Service Management is performed by IT Service Providers through an appropriate mix of people, Process and Information Technology. *See also* Service Management.

IT Service Provider

(Service Strategy) A Service Provider that provides IT Services to Internal Customers or External Customers.

IT Steering Group (ISG)

A formal group that is responsible for ensuring that Business and IT Service Provider Strategies and Plans are closely aligned. An IT Steering Group includes senior representatives from the Business and the IT Service Provider.

ITIL

A set of Best Practice guidance for IT Service Management. ITIL is owned by the OGC and consists of a series of publications giving guidance on the provision of Quality IT Services, and on the Processes and facilities needed to support them. See www.itil.co.uk for more information.

Job Description

A Document that defines the Roles, responsibilities, skills and knowledge required by a particular person. One Job Description can include multiple Roles, for example the Roles of Configuration Manager and Change Manager may be carried out by one person.

Job Scheduling

(Service Operation) Planning and managing the execution of software tasks that are required as part of an IT Service. Job Scheduling is carried out by IT Operations Management, and is often automated using software tools that run batch or online tasks at specific times of the day, week, month or year.

Key Performance Indicator (KPI)

(Service Design) (Continual Service Improvement) A Metric that is used to help manage a Process, IT Service or Activity. Many Metrics may be measured, but only the most important of these are defined as KPIs and used to actively manage and report on the Process, IT Service or Activity. KPIs should be selected to ensure that Efficiency, Effectiveness, and Cost Effectiveness are all managed. *See also* Critical Success Factor.

Knowledge Base

(Service Transition) A logical database containing the data used by the Service Knowledge Management System.

Knowledge Management

(Service Transition) The Process responsible for gathering, analysing, storing and sharing knowledge and information within an Organization. The primary purpose of Knowledge Management is to improve Efficiency by reducing the need to rediscover knowledge. *See also* Service Knowledge Management System.

Known Error

(Service Operation) A Problem that has a documented Root Cause and a Workaround. Known Errors are created and managed throughout their Lifecycle by Problem Management. Known Errors may also be identified by Development or Suppliers.

Lifecycle

The various stages in the life of an IT Service, Configuration Item, Incident, Problem, Change, etc. The Lifecycle defines the Categories for Status and the Status transitions that are permitted. For example:

- The Lifecycle of an Application includes Requirements, Design, Build, Deploy, Operate, Optimize
- The Expanded Incident Lifecycle includes Detect, Respond, Diagnose, Repair, Recover, Restore
- The Lifecycle of a Server may include: Ordered, Received, In Test, Live, Disposed, etc.

Line of Service (LOS)

(Service Strategy) A Core Service or Supporting Service that has multiple Service Level Packages. A line of Service is managed by a Product Manager and each Service Level Package is designed to support a particular market segment.

Live

(Service Transition) Refers to an IT Service or Configuration Item that is being used to deliver Service to a Customer.

Live Environment

(Service Transition) A controlled Environment containing Live Configuration Items used to deliver IT Services to Customers.

Maintainability

(Service Design) A measure of how quickly and Effectively a Configuration Item or IT Service can be restored to normal working after a Failure. Maintainability is often measured and reported as MTRS.

Maintainability is also used in the context of Software or IT Service Development to mean ability to be Changed or Repaired easily.

Major Incident

(Service Operation) The highest Category of Impact for an Incident. A Major Incident results in significant disruption to the Business.

Managed Services

(Service Strategy) A perspective on IT Services that emphasizes the fact that they are managed. The term Managed Services is also used as a synonym for Outsourced IT Services.

Management Information

Information that is used to support decision making by managers. Management Information is often generated automatically by tools supporting the various IT Service Management Processes. Management Information often includes the values of KPIs such as 'Percentage of Changes leading to Incidents', or 'first-time fix rate'.

Management of Risk (M_o_R)

The OGC methodology for managing Risks. M_o_R includes all the Activities required to identify and Control the exposure to Risk, which may have an impact on the achievement of an Organization's Business Objectives. See www.m-o-r.org for more details.

Management System

The framework of Policy, Processes and Functions that ensures an Organization can achieve its Objectives.

Manual Workaround

A Workaround that requires manual intervention. Manual Workaround is also used as the name of a Recovery Option in which the Business Process Operates without the use of IT Services. This is a temporary measure and is usually combined with another Recovery Option.

Maturity

(Continual Service Improvement) A measure of the Reliability, Efficiency and Effectiveness of a Process, Function, Organization, etc. The most mature Processes and Functions are formally aligned to Business Objectives and Strategy, and are supported by a framework for continual improvement.

Mean Time Between Failures (MTBF)

(Service Design) A Metric for measuring and reporting Reliability. MTBF is the average time that a Configuration Item or IT Service can perform its agreed Function without interruption. This is measured from when the CI or IT Service starts working, until it next fails.

Mean Time Between Service Incidents (MTBSI)

(Service Design) A Metric used for measuring and reporting Reliability. MTBSI is the mean time from when a System or IT Service fails, until it next fails. MTBSI is equal to MTBF + MTRS.

Mean Time To Repair (MTTR)

The average time taken to repair a Configuration Item or IT Service after a Failure. MTTR is measured from when the CI or IT Service fails until it is repaired. MTTR does not include the time required to Recover or Restore. MTTR is sometimes incorrectly used to mean Mean Time to Restore Service.

Mean Time to Restore Service (MTRS)

The average time taken to restore a Configuration Item or IT Service after a Failure. MTRS is measured from when the CI or IT Service fails until it is fully restored and delivering its normal functionality. *See also* Maintainability, Mean Time to Repair.

Metric

(Continual Service Improvement) Something that is measured and reported to help manage a Process, IT Service or Activity. *See also* KPI.

Middleware

(Service Design) Software that connects two or more software Components or Applications. Middleware is usually purchased from a Supplier, rather than developed within the IT Service Provider. *See also* Off the Shelf.

Model

A representation of a System, Process, IT Service, Configuration Item, etc. that is used to help understand or predict future behaviour.

Modelling

A technique that is used to predict the future behaviour of a System, Process, IT Service, Configuration Item, etc. Modelling is commonly used in Financial Management, Capacity Management and Availability Management.

Monitoring

(Service Operation) Repeated observation of a Configuration Item, IT Service or Process to detect Events and to ensure that the current status is known.

Objective

The defined purpose or aim of a Process, an Activity or an Organization as a whole. Objectives are usually expressed as measurable targets. The term Objective is also informally used to mean a Requirement. *See also* Outcome.

Off-The-Shelf

See Commercial Off-The-Shelf.

Office of Government Commerce (OGC)

OGC owns the ITIL brand (copyright and trademark). OGC is a UK Government department that supports the delivery of the government's procurement agenda through its work in collaborative procurement and in raising levels of procurement skills and capability within departments. It also provides support for complex public sector projects.

Off-shore

(Service Strategy) Provision of Services from a location outside the country where the Customer is based, often in a different continent. This can be the provision of an IT Service, or of supporting Functions such as Service Desk. *See also* On-shore.

On-shore

(Service Strategy) Provision of Services from a location within the country where the Customer is based. *See also* Off-shore.

Operate

To perform as expected. A Process or Configuration Item is said to Operate if it is delivering the Required outputs. Operate also means to perform one or more Operations. For example, to Operate a computer is to do the day-to-day Operations needed for it to perform as expected.

Operation

(Service Operation) Day-to-day management of an IT Service, System, or other Configuration Item. Operation is also used to mean any pre-defined Activity or Transaction. For example loading a magnetic tape, accepting money at a point of sale, or reading data from a disk drive.

Operational

The lowest of three levels of Planning and delivery (Strategic, Tactical, Operational). Operational Activities include the day-to-day or short-term Planning or delivery of a Business Process or IT Service Management Process. The term Operational is also a synonym for Live.

Operational Cost

Cost resulting from running the IT Services. Often repeating payments. For example staff costs, hardware maintenance and electricity (also known as 'current expenditure' or 'revenue expenditure').

Operational Level Agreement (OLA)

(Service Design) (Continual Service Improvement) An Agreement between an IT Service Provider and another part of the same Organization. An OLA supports the IT Service Provider's delivery of IT Services to Customers. The OLA defines the goods or Services to be provided and the responsibilities of both parties. For example there could be an OLA:

- Between the IT Service Provider and a procurement department to obtain hardware in agreed times
- Between the Service Desk and a Support Group to provide Incident Resolution in agreed times.

See also Service Level Agreement.

Optimize

Review, Plan and request Changes, in order to obtain the maximum Efficiency and Effectiveness from a Process, Configuration Item, Application, etc.

Organization

A company, legal entity or other institution. Examples of Organizations that are not companies include International Standards Organization or itSMF. The term Organization is sometimes used to refer to any entity that has People, Resources and Budgets. For example a Project or Business Unit.

Outcome

The result of carrying out an Activity; following a Process; delivering an IT Service, etc. The term Outcome is used to refer to intended results, as well as to actual results. *See also* Objective.

Outsourcing

(Service Strategy) Using an External Service Provider to manage IT Services.

Overhead

See Indirect cost.

Partnership

A relationship between two Organizations that involves working closely together for common goals or mutual benefit. The IT Service Provider should have a Partnership with the Business, and with Third Parties who are critical to the delivery of IT Services. *See also* Value Network.

Passive Monitoring

(Service Operation) Monitoring of a Configuration Item, an IT Service or a Process that relies on an Alert or notification to discover the current status.

Pattern of Business Activity (PBA)

(Service Strategy) A Workload profile of one or more Business Activities. Patterns of Business Activity are used to help the IT Service Provider understand and plan for different levels of Business Activity.

Performance

A measure of what is achieved or delivered by a System, person, team, Process, or IT Service.

Performance Management

(Continual Service Improvement) The Process responsible for day-to-day Capacity Management Activities. These include monitoring, threshold detection, Performance analysis and Tuning, and implementing changes related to Performance and Capacity.

Pilot

(Service Transition) A limited Deployment of an IT Service, a Release or a Process to the Live Environment. A pilot is used to reduce Risk and to gain User feedback and Acceptance. *See also* Test, Evaluation.

Plan

A detailed proposal that describes the Activities and Resources needed to achieve an Objective. For example a Plan to implement a new IT Service or Process. ISO/IEC 20000 requires a Plan for the management of each IT Service Management Process.

Plan-Do-Check-Act

(Continual Service Improvement) A four-stage cycle for Process management, attributed to Edward Deming. Plan-Do-Check-Act is also called the Deming Cycle.

PLAN: Design or revise Processes that support the IT Services.

DO: Implement the Plan and manage the Processes.

CHECK: Measure the Processes and IT Services, compare with Objectives and produce reports.

ACT: Plan and implement Changes to improve the Processes.

Planned Downtime

(Service Design) Agreed time when an IT Service will not be available. Planned Downtime is often used for maintenance, upgrades and testing. *See also* Change Window, Downtime.

Planning

An Activity responsible for creating one or more Plans. For example, Capacity Planning.

PMBOK

A Project management Standard maintained and published by the Project Management Institute. PMBOK stands for Project Management Body of Knowledge. See www.pmi.org for more information. *See also* PRINCE2.

Policy

Formally documented management expectations and intentions. Policies are used to direct decisions, and to ensure consistent and appropriate development and implementation of Processes, Standards, Roles, Activities, IT Infrastructure, etc.

Portable Facility

(Service Design) A prefabricated building, or a large vehicle, provided by a Third Party and moved to a site when needed by an IT Service Continuity Plan. *See also* Recovery Option.

Post-Implementation Review (PIR)

A Review that takes place after a Change or a Project has been implemented. A PIR determines if the Change or Project was successful, and identifies opportunities for improvement.

Practice

A way of working, or a way in which work must be done. Practices can include Activities, Processes, Functions, Standards and Guidelines. *See also* Best Practice.

Prerequisite for Success (PFS)

An Activity that needs to be completed, or a condition that needs to be met, to enable successful implementation of a Plan or Process. A PFS is often an output from one Process that is a required input to another Process.

Pricing

(Service Strategy) The Activity for establishing how much Customers will be Charged.

PRINCE2

The standard UK government methodology for Project management. See www.ogc.gov.uk/prince2 for more information. *See also* PMBOK.

Priority

(Service Transition) (Service Operation) A Category used to identify the relative importance of an Incident, Problem or Change. Priority is based on Impact and Urgency, and is used to identify required times for actions to be taken. For example, the SLA may state that Priority 2 Incidents must be resolved within 12 hours.

Problem

(Service Operation) A cause of one or more Incidents. The cause is not usually known at the time a Problem Record is created, and the Problem Management Process is responsible for further investigation.

Problem Management

(Service Operation) The Process responsible for managing the Lifecycle of all Problems. The primary objectives of Problem Management are to prevent Incidents from happening, and to minimize the Impact of Incidents that cannot be prevented.

Procedure

A Document containing steps that specify how to achieve an Activity. Procedures are defined as part of Processes. *See also* Work Instruction.

Process

A structured set of Activities designed to accomplish a specific Objective. A Process takes one or more defined inputs and turns them into defined outputs. A Process may include any of the Roles, responsibilities, tools and management Controls required to reliably deliver the outputs. A Process may define Policies, Standards, Guidelines, Activities, and Work Instructions if they are needed.

Process Control

The Activity of planning and regulating a Process, with the Objective of performing the Process in an Effective, Efficient, and consistent manner.

Process Owner

A Role responsible for ensuring that a Process is Fit for Purpose. The Process Owner's responsibilities include sponsorship, Design, Change Management and continual improvement of the Process and its Metrics. This Role is often assigned to the same person who carries out the Process Manager Role, but the two Roles may be separate in larger Organizations.

Pro-forma

A template, or example Document containing example data that will be replaced with the real values when these are available.

Programme

A number of Projects and Activities that are planned and managed together to achieve an overall set of related Objectives and other Outcomes.

Project

A temporary Organization, with people and other Assets required to achieve an Objective or other Outcome. Each Project has a Lifecycle that typically includes initiation, Planning, execution, Closure, etc. Projects are usually managed using a formal methodology such as PRINCE2.

Quality

The ability of a product, Service, or Process to provide the intended value. For example, a hardware Component can be considered to be of high Quality if it performs as expected and delivers the required Reliability. Process Quality also requires an ability to monitor Effectiveness and Efficiency, and to improve them if necessary. *See also* Quality Management System.

Quality Management System (QMS)

(Continual Service Improvement) The set of Processes responsible for ensuring that all work carried out by an Organization is of a suitable Quality to reliably meet Business Objectives or Service Levels. *See also* ISO 9000.

RACI

(Service Design) (Continual Service Improvement) A Model used to help define Roles and Responsibilities. RACI stands for Responsible, Accountable, Consulted and Informed. *See also* Stakeholder.

Reciprocal Arrangement

(Service Design) A Recovery Option. An agreement between two Organizations to share resources in an emergency. For example, Computer Room space or use of a mainframe.

Record

A Document containing the results or other output from a Process or Activity. Records are evidence of the fact that an activity took place and may be paper or electronic. For example, an Audit report, an Incident Record, or the minutes of a meeting.

Recovery

(Service Design) (Service Operation) Returning a Configuration Item or an IT Service to a working state. Recovery of an IT Service often includes recovering data to a known consistent state. After Recovery, further steps may be needed before the IT Service can be made available to the Users (Restoration).

Recovery Option

(Service Design) A Strategy for responding to an interruption to Service. Commonly used Strategies are Do Nothing, Manual Workaround, Reciprocal Arrangement, Gradual Recovery, Intermediate Recovery, Fast Recovery, Immediate Recovery. Recovery Options may make use of dedicated facilities, or Third Party facilities shared by multiple Businesses.

Redundancy

See Fault Tolerance.

The term Redundant also has a generic meaning of obsolete, or no longer needed.

Relationship

A connection or interaction between two people or things. In Business Relationship Management it is the interaction between the IT Service Provider and the Business. In Configuration Management it is a link between two Configuration Items that identifies a dependency or connection between them. For example Applications may be linked to the Servers they run on. IT Services have many links to all the CIs that contribute to them.

Relationship Processes

The ISO/IEC 20000 Process group that includes Business Relationship Management and Supplier Management.

Release

(Service Transition) A collection of hardware, software, documentation, Processes or other Components required to implement one or more approved Changes to IT Services. The contents of each Release are managed, tested, and deployed as a single entity.

Release and Deployment Management

(Service Transition) The Process responsible for both Release Management and Deployment.

Release Management

(Service Transition) The Process responsible for Planning, scheduling and controlling the movement of Releases to Test and Live Environments. The primary Objective of Release Management is to ensure that the integrity of the Live Environment is protected and that the correct Components are released. Release Management is part of the Release and Deployment Management Process.

Release Record

(Service Transition) A Record in the CMDB that defines the content of a Release. A Release Record has Relationships with all Configuration Items that are affected by the Release.

Reliability

(Service Design) (Continual Service Improvement) A measure of how long a Configuration Item or IT Service can perform its agreed Function without interruption. Usually measured as MTBF or MTBSI. The term Reliability can also be used to state how likely it is that a Process, Function, etc. will deliver its required outputs. See also Availability.

Repair

(Service Operation) The replacement or correction of a failed Configuration Item.

Request for Change (RFC)

(Service Transition) A formal proposal for a Change to be made. An RFC includes details of the proposed Change, and may be recorded on paper or electronically. The term RFC is often misused to mean a Change Record, or the Change itself.

Request Fulfilment

(Service Operation) The Process responsible for managing the Lifecycle of all Service Requests.

Requirement

(Service Design) A formal statement of what is needed. For example, a Service Level Requirement, a Project Requirement or the required Deliverables for a Process. See also Statement of Requirements.

Resilience

(Service Design) The ability of a Configuration Item or IT Service to resist Failure or to Recover quickly following a Failure. For example an armoured cable will resist failure when put under stress. See also Fault Tolerance.

Resolution

(Service Operation) Action taken to repair the Root Cause of an Incident or Problem, or to implement a Workaround. In ISO/IEC 20000, Resolution Processes is the Process group that includes Incident and Problem Management.

Resource

(Service Strategy) A generic term that includes IT Infrastructure, people, money or anything else that might help to deliver an IT Service. Resources are considered to be Assets of an Organization. See also Capability, Service Asset.

Response Time

A measure of the time taken to complete an Operation or Transaction. Used in Capacity Management as a measure of IT Infrastructure Performance, and in Incident Management as a measure of the time taken to answer the phone, or to start Diagnosis.

Responsiveness

A measurement of the time taken to respond to something. This could be Response Time of a Transaction, or the speed with which an IT Service Provider responds to an Incident or Request for Change, etc.

Restoration of Service

See Restore.

Restore

(Service Operation) Taking action to return an IT Service to the Users after Repair and Recovery from an Incident. This is the primary Objective of Incident Management.

Retire

(Service Transition) Permanent removal of an IT Service, or other Configuration Item, from the Live Environment. Retired is a stage in the Lifecycle of many Configuration Items.

Return on Investment (ROI)

(Service Strategy) (Continual Service Improvement) A measurement of the expected benefit of an investment. In the simplest sense it is the net profit of an investment divided by the net worth of the assets invested.

Return to Normal

(Service Design) The phase of an IT Service Continuity Plan during which full normal operations are resumed. For example, if an alternate data centre has been in use, then this phase will bring the primary data centre back into operation, and restore the ability to invoke IT Service Continuity Plans again.

Review

An evaluation of a Change, Problem, Process, Project, etc. Reviews are typically carried out at predefined points in the Lifecycle, and especially after Closure. The purpose of a Review is to ensure that all Deliverables have been provided, and to identify opportunities for improvement. *See also* Post-Implementation Review.

Rights

(Service Operation) Entitlements, or permissions, granted to a User or Role. For example the Right to modify particular data, or to authorize a Change.

Risk

A possible event that could cause harm or loss, or affect the ability to achieve Objectives. A Risk is measured by the probability of a Threat, the Vulnerability of the Asset to that Threat, and the Impact it would have if it occurred.

Risk Assessment

The initial steps of Risk Management. Analysing the value of Assets to the business, identifying Threats to those Assets, and evaluating how Vulnerable each Asset is to those Threats. Risk Assessment can be quantitative (based on numerical data) or qualitative.

Risk Management

The Process responsible for identifying, assessing and controlling Risks. *See also* Risk Assessment.

Role

A set of responsibilities, Activities and authorities granted to a person or team. A Role is defined in a Process. One person or team may have multiple Roles, for example the Roles of Configuration Manager and Change Manager may be carried out by a single person.

Root Cause

(Service Operation) The underlying or original cause of an Incident or Problem.

Running Costs

See Operational Cost.

Scalability

The ability of an IT Service, Process, Configuration Item, etc. to perform its agreed Function when the Workload or Scope changes.

Scope

The boundary, or extent, to which a Process, Procedure, Certification, Contract, etc. applies. For example the Scope of Change Management may include all Live IT Services and related Configuration Items, the Scope of an ISO/IEC 20000 Certificate may include all IT Services delivered out of a named data centre.

Security

See Information Security Management.

Security Management

See Information Security Management.

Security Policy

See Information Security Policy.

Separation of Concerns (SoC)

(Service Strategy) An approach to Designing a solution or IT Service that divides the problem into pieces that can be solved independently. This approach separates 'what' is to be done from 'how' it is to be done.

Server

(Service Operation) A computer that is connected to a network and provides software Functions that are used by other Computers.

Service

A means of delivering value to Customers by facilitating Outcomes Customers want to achieve without the ownership of specific Costs and Risks.

Service Acceptance Criteria (SAC)

(Service Transition) A set of criteria used to ensure that an IT Service meets its functionality and Quality Requirements and that the IT Service Provider is ready to Operate the new IT Service when it has been Deployed. *See also* Acceptance.

Service Asset

Any Capability or Resource of a Service Provider. *See also* Asset.

Service Capacity Management (SCM)

(Service Design) (Continual Service Improvement) The Activity responsible for understanding the Performance and Capacity of IT Services. The Resources used by each IT Service and the pattern of usage over time are collected, recorded, and analysed for use in the Capacity Plan. *See also* Business Capacity Management, Component Capacity Management.

Service Catalogue

(Service Design) A database or structured Document with information about all Live IT Services, including those available for Deployment. The Service Catalogue is the only part of the Service Portfolio published to Customers, and is used to support the sale and delivery of IT Services. The Service Catalogue includes information about deliverables, prices, contact points, ordering and request Processes.

Service Continuity Management

See IT Service Continuity Management.

Service Culture

A Customer-oriented Culture. The major Objectives of a Service Culture are Customer satisfaction and helping Customers to achieve their Business Objectives.

Service Design

(Service Design) A stage in the Lifecycle of an IT Service. Service Design includes a number of Processes and Functions and is the title of one of the Core ITIL publications. *See also* Design.

Service Design Package

(Service Design) Document(s) defining all aspects of an IT Service and its Requirements through each stage of its Lifecycle. A Service Design Package is produced for each new IT Service, major Change, or IT Service Retirement.

Service Desk

(Service Operation) The Single Point of Contact between the Service Provider and the Users. A typical Service Desk manages Incidents and Service Requests, and also handles communication with the Users.

Service Failure Analysis (SFA)

(Service Design) An Activity that identifies underlying causes of one or more IT Service interruptions. SFA identifies opportunities to improve the IT Service Provider's Processes and tools, and not just the IT Infrastructure. SFA is a time-constrained, project-like activity, rather than an ongoing process of analysis.

Service Hours

(Service Design) (Continual Service Improvement) An agreed time period when a particular IT Service should be Available. For example, 'Monday-Friday 08:00 to 17:00 except public holidays'. Service Hours should be defined in a Service Level Agreement.

Service Improvement Plan (SIP)

(Continual Service Improvement) A formal Plan to implement improvements to a Process or IT Service.

Service Knowledge Management System (SKMS)

(Service Transition) A set of tools and databases that are used to manage knowledge and information. The SKMS includes the Configuration Management System, as well as other tools and databases. The SKMS stores, manages, updates, and presents all information that an IT Service Provider needs to manage the full Lifecycle of IT Services.

Service Level

Measured and reported achievement against one or more Service Level Targets. The term Service Level is sometimes used informally to mean Service Level Target.

Service Level Agreement (SLA)

(Service Design) (Continual Service Improvement) An Agreement between an IT Service Provider and a Customer. The SLA describes the IT Service, documents Service Level Targets, and specifies the responsibilities of the IT Service Provider and the Customer. A single SLA may cover multiple IT Services or multiple customers. *See also* Operational Level Agreement.

Service Level Management (SLM)

(Service Design) (Continual Service Improvement) The Process responsible for negotiating Service Level Agreements, and ensuring that these are met. SLM is responsible for ensuring that all IT Service Management Processes, Operational Level Agreements, and Underpinning Contracts, are appropriate for the agreed Service Level Targets. SLM monitors and reports on Service Levels, and holds regular Customer reviews.

Service Level Package (SLP)

(Service Strategy) A defined level of Utility and Warranty for a particular Service Package. Each SLP is designed to meet the needs of a particular Pattern of Business Activity. *See also* Line of Service.

Service Level Requirement (SLR)

(Service Design) (Continual Service Improvement) A Customer Requirement for an aspect of an IT Service. SLRs are based on Business Objectives and are used to negotiate agreed Service Level Targets.

Service Level Target

(Service Design) (Continual Service Improvement) A commitment that is documented in a Service Level Agreement. Service Level Targets are based on Service Level Requirements, and are needed to ensure that the IT Service design is Fit for Purpose. Service Level Targets should be SMART, and are usually based on KPIs.

Service Management

Service Management is a set of specialized organizational capabilities for providing value to Customers in the form of Services.

Service Management Lifecycle

An approach to IT Service Management that emphasizes the importance of coordination and Control across the various Functions, Processes, and Systems necessary to manage the full Lifecycle of IT Services. The Service Management Lifecycle approach considers the Strategy, Design, Transition, Operation and Continuous Improvement of IT Services.

Service Manager

A manager who is responsible for managing the end-to-end Lifecycle of one or more IT Services. The term Service Manager is also used to mean any manager within the IT Service Provider. Most commonly used to refer to a Business Relationship Manager, a Process Manager, an Account Manager or a senior manager with responsibility for IT Services overall.

Service Operation

(Service Operation) A stage in the Lifecycle of an IT Service. Service Operation includes a number of Processes and Functions and is the title of one of the Core ITIL publications. *See also* Operation.

Service Owner

(Continual Service Improvement) A Role that is accountable for the delivery of a specific IT Service.

Service Portfolio

(Service Strategy) The complete set of Services that are managed by a Service Provider. The Service Portfolio is used to manage the entire Lifecycle of all Services, and includes three Categories: Service Pipeline (proposed or in Development); Service Catalogue (Live or available for Deployment); and Retired Services. *See also* Service Portfolio Management.

Service Portfolio Management (SPM)

(Service Strategy) The Process responsible for managing the Service Portfolio. Service Portfolio Management considers Services in terms of the Business value that they provide.

Service Provider

(Service Strategy) An Organization supplying Services to one or more Internal Customers or External Customers. Service Provider is often used as an abbreviation for IT Service Provider.

Service Reporting

(Continual Service Improvement) The Process responsible for producing and delivering reports of achievement and trends against Service Levels. Service Reporting should agree the format, content and frequency of reports with Customers.

Service Request

(Service Operation) A request from a User for information or advice, or for a Standard Change or for Access to an IT Service. For example to reset a password, or to provide standard IT Services for a new User. Service Requests are usually handled by a Service Desk, and do not require an RFC to be submitted. *See also* Request Fulfilment.

Service Strategy

(Service Strategy) The title of one of the Core ITIL publications. Service Strategy establishes an overall Strategy for IT Services and for IT Service Management.

Service Transition

(Service Transition) A stage in the Lifecycle of an IT Service. Service Transition includes a number of Processes and Functions and is the title of one of the Core ITIL publications. *See also* Transition.

Service Warranty

(Service Strategy) Assurance that an IT Service will meet agreed Requirements. This may be a formal Agreement such as a Service Level Agreement or Contract, or may be a marketing message or brand image. The Business value of an IT Service is created by the combination of Service Utility (what the Service does) and Service Warranty (how well it does it). *See also* Warranty.

Serviceability

(Service Design) (Continual Service Improvement) The ability of a Third-Party Supplier to meet the terms of its Contract. This Contract will include agreed levels of Reliability, Maintainability or Availability for a Configuration Item.

Shift

(Service Operation) A group or team of people who carry out a specific Role for a fixed period of time. For example there could be four shifts of IT Operations Control personnel to support an IT Service that is used 24 hours a day.

Simulation modelling

(Service Design) (Continual Service Improvement) A technique that creates a detailed model to predict the behaviour of a Configuration Item or IT Service. Simulation Models can be very accurate but are expensive and time consuming to create. A Simulation Model is often created by using the actual Configuration Items that are being modelled, with artificial Workloads or Transactions. They are used in Capacity Management when accurate results are important. A simulation model is sometimes called a Performance Benchmark.

Single Point of Failure (SPOF)

(Service Design) Any Configuration Item that can cause an Incident when it fails, and for which a Countermeasure has not been implemented. A SPOF may be a person, or a step in a Process or Activity, as well as a Component of the IT Infrastructure. *See also* Failure.

SMART

(Service Design) (Continual Service Improvement) An acronym for helping to remember that targets in Service Level Agreements and Project Plans should be Specific, Measurable, Achievable, Relevant and Timely.

Specification

A formal definition of Requirements. A Specification may be used to define technical or Operational Requirements, and may be internal or external. Many public Standards consist of a Code of Practice and a Specification. The Specification defines the Standard against which an Organization can be Audited.

Stakeholder

All people who have an interest in an Organization, Project, IT Service, etc. Stakeholders may be interested in the Activities, targets, Resources, or Deliverables. Stakeholders may include Customers, Partners, employees, shareholders, owners, etc. *See also* RACI.

Standard

A mandatory Requirement. Examples include ISO/IEC 20000 (an international Standard), an internal security standard for Unix configuration, or a government standard for how financial Records should be maintained. The term Standard is also used to refer to a Code of Practice or Specification published by a Standards Organization such as ISO or BSI. *See also* Guideline.

Standby

(Service Design) Used to refer to Resources that are not required to deliver the Live IT Services, but are available to support IT Service Continuity Plans. For example a Standby data centre may be maintained to support Hot Standby, Warm Standby or Cold Standby arrangements.

Statement of requirements (SOR)

(Service Design) A Document containing all Requirements for a product purchase, or a new or changed IT Service. *See also* Terms of Reference.

Status

The name of a required field in many types of Record. It shows the current stage in the Lifecycle of the associated Configuration Item, Incident, Problem, etc.

Strategic

(Service Strategy) The highest of three levels of Planning and delivery (Strategic, Tactical, Operational). Strategic Activities include Objective setting and long-term Planning to achieve the overall Vision.

Strategy

(Service Strategy) A Strategic Plan designed to achieve defined Objectives.

Supplier

(Service Strategy) (Service Design) A Third Party responsible for supplying goods or Services that are required to deliver IT Services. Examples of suppliers include commodity hardware and software vendors, network and telecom providers, and outsourcing Organizations. *See also* Underpinning Contract, Supply Chain.

Supplier and Contract Database (SCD)

(Service Design) A database or structured Document used to manage Supplier Contracts throughout their Lifecycle. The SCD contains key Attributes of all Contracts with Suppliers, and should be part of the Service Knowledge Management System.

Supplier Management

(Service Design) The Process responsible for ensuring that all Contracts with Suppliers support the needs of the Business, and that all Suppliers meet their contractual commitments.

Supply Chain

(Service Strategy) The Activities in a Value Chain carried out by Suppliers. A Supply Chain typically involves multiple Suppliers, each adding value to the product or Service. *See also* Value Network.

Support Group

(Service Operation) A group of people with technical skills. Support Groups provide the Technical Support needed by all of the IT Service Management Processes. *See also* Technical Management.

Support Hours

(Service Design) (Service Operation) The times or hours when support is available to the Users. Typically these are the hours when the Service Desk is available. Support Hours should be defined in a Service Level Agreement, and may be different from Service Hours. For example, Service Hours may be 24 hours a day, but the Support Hours may be 07:00 to 19:00.

Supporting Service

(Service Strategy) A Service that enables or enhances a Core Service. For example, a Directory Service or a Backup Service.

SWOT Analysis

(Continual Service Improvement) A technique that reviews and analyses the internal strengths and weaknesses of an Organization and the external opportunities and threats that it faces SWOT stands for Strengths, Weaknesses, Opportunities and Threats.

System

A number of related things that work together to achieve an overall Objective. For example:

■ A computer System including hardware, software and Applications
■ A management System, including multiple Processes that are planned and managed together. For example, a Quality Management System
■ A Database Management System or Operating System that includes many software modules that are designed to perform a set of related Functions.

System Management

The part of IT Service Management that focuses on the management of IT Infrastructure rather than Process.

Tactical

The middle of three levels of Planning and delivery (Strategic, Tactical, Operational). Tactical Activities include the medium-term Plans required to achieve specific Objectives, typically over a period of weeks to months.

Technical Management

(Service Operation) The Function responsible for providing technical skills in support of IT Services and management of the IT Infrastructure. Technical Management defines the Roles of Support Groups, as well as the tools, Processes and Procedures required.

Technical Service

See Infrastructure Service.

Technical Support

See Technical Management.

Terms of Reference (TOR)

(Service Design) A Document specifying the Requirements, Scope, Deliverables, Resources and schedule for a Project or Activity.

Test

(Service Transition) An Activity that verifies that a Configuration Item, IT Service, Process, etc. meets its Specification or agreed Requirements. *See also* Acceptance.

Third Party

A person, group, or Business that is not part of the Service Level Agreement for an IT Service, but is required to ensure successful delivery of that IT Service. For example, a software Supplier, a hardware maintenance company, or a facilities department. Requirements for Third Parties are typically specified in Underpinning Contracts or Operational Level Agreements.

Third-line Support

(Service Operation) The third level in a hierarchy of Support Groups involved in the resolution of Incidents and investigation of Problems. Each level contains more specialist skills, or has more time or other resources.

Threat

Anything that might exploit a Vulnerability. Any potential cause of an Incident can be considered to be a Threat. For example a fire is a Threat that could exploit the Vulnerability of flammable floor coverings. This term is commonly used in Information Security Management and IT Service Continuity Management, but also applies to other areas such as Problem and Availability Management.

Threshold

The value of a Metric that should cause an Alert to be generated, or management action to be taken. For example 'Priority 1 Incident not solved within four hours', 'more than five soft disk errors in an hour', or 'more than 10 failed changes in a month'.

Throughput

(Service Design) A measure of the number of Transactions, or other Operations, performed in a fixed time. For example, 5,000 e-mails sent per hour, or 200 disk I/Os per second.

Total Cost of Ownership (TCO)

(Service Strategy) A methodology used to help make investment decisions. TCO assesses the full Lifecycle Cost of owning a Configuration Item, not just the initial Cost or purchase price.

Transaction

A discrete Function performed by an IT Service. For example transferring money from one bank account to another. A single Transaction may involve numerous additions, deletions and modifications of data. Either all of these complete successfully or none of them is carried out.

Transition

(Service Transition) A change in state, corresponding to a movement of an IT Service or other Configuration Item from one Lifecycle status to the next.

Trend Analysis

(Continual Service Improvement) Analysis of data to identify time related patterns. Trend Analysis is used in Problem Management to identify common Failures or fragile Configuration Items, and in Capacity Management as a Modelling tool to predict future behaviour. It is also used as a management tool for identifying deficiencies in IT Service Management Processes.

Tuning

The Activity responsible for Planning changes to make the most efficient use of Resources. Tuning is part of Performance Management, which also includes Performance monitoring and implementation of the required Changes.

Underpinning Contract (UC)

(Service Design) A Contract between an IT Service Provider and a Third Party. The Third Party provides goods or Services that support delivery of an IT Service to a Customer. The Underpinning Contract defines targets and responsibilities that are required to meet agreed Service Level Targets in an SLA.

Urgency

(Service Transition) (Service Design) A measure of how long it will be until an Incident, Problem or Change has a significant Impact on the Business. For example a high Impact Incident may have low Urgency, if the Impact will not affect the Business until the end of the financial year. Impact and Urgency are used to assign Priority.

Usability

(Service Design) The ease with which an Application, product, or IT Service can be used. Usability Requirements are often included in a Statement of Requirements.

Use Case

(Service Design) A technique used to define required functionality and Objectives, and to design Tests. Use Cases define realistic scenarios that describe interactions between Users and an IT Service or other System.

User

A person who uses the IT Service on a day-to-day basis. Users are distinct from Customers, as some Customers do not use the IT Service directly.

Utility

(Service Strategy) Functionality offered by a Product or Service to meet a particular need. Utility is often summarized as 'what it does'.

Validation

(Service Transition) An Activity that ensures a new or changed IT Service, Process, Plan, or other Deliverable meets the needs of the Business. Validation ensures that Business Requirements are met even though these may have changed since the original design. *See also* Verification, Acceptance.

Value Chain

(Service Strategy) A sequence of Processes that creates a product or Service that is of value to a Customer. Each step of the sequence builds on the previous steps and contributes to the overall product or Service. *See also* Value Network.

Value for Money

An informal measure of Cost Effectiveness. Value for Money is often based on a comparison with the Cost of alternatives. *See also* Cost Benefit Analysis.

Value Network

(Service Strategy) A complex set of relationships between two or more groups or organizations. Value is generated through exchange of knowledge, information, goods or Services. *See also* Value Chain, Partnership.

Variance

The difference between a planned value and the actual measured value. Commonly used in Financial Management, Capacity Management and Service Level Management, but could apply in any area where Plans are in place.

Verification

(Service Transition) An Activity that ensures a new or changed IT Service, Process, Plan, or other Deliverable is complete, accurate, Reliable and matches its design specification. *See also* Validation, Acceptance.

Version

(Service Transition) A Version is used to identify a specific Baseline of a Configuration Item. Versions typically use a naming convention that enables the sequence or date of each Baseline to be identified. For example Payroll Application Version 3 contains updated functionality from Version 2.

Vision

A description of what the Organization intends to become in the future. A Vision is created by senior management and is used to help influence Culture and Strategic Planning.

Vital Business Function (VBF)

(Service Design) A Function of a Business Process that is critical to the success of the Business. Vital Business Functions are an important consideration of Business Continuity Management, IT Service Continuity Management and Availability Management.

Vulnerability

A weakness that could be exploited by a Threat. For example an open firewall port, a password that is never changed, or a flammable carpet. A missing Control is also considered to be a Vulnerability.

Warm Standby

See Intermediate Recovery.

Warranty

(Service Strategy) A promise or guarantee that a product or Service will meet its agreed Requirements. *See also* Service Warranty.

Work Instruction

A Document containing detailed instructions that specify exactly what steps to follow to carry out an Activity. A Work Instruction contains much more detail than a Procedure and is only created if very detailed instructions are needed.

Workaround

(Service Operation) Reducing or eliminating the Impact of an Incident or Problem for which a full Resolution is not yet available. For example by restarting a failed Configuration Item. Workarounds for Problems are documented in Known Error Records. Workarounds for Incidents that do not have associated Problem Records are documented in the Incident Record.

Workload

The Resources required to deliver an identifiable part of an IT Service. Workloads may be Categorized by Users, groups of Users, or Functions within the IT Service. This is used to assist in analysing and managing the Capacity, Performance and Utilization of Configuration Items and IT Services. The term Workload is sometimes used as a synonym for Throughput.

Index

Index

Engineering Mathematics

Engineering Mathematics

A PROGRAMMED APPROACH

Second edition

C.W. Evans

School of Mathematical Studies
University of Portsmouth

CHAPMAN & HALL
University and Professional Division

London · Glasgow · New York · Tokyo · Melbourne · Madras

Published by Chapman & Hall, 2-6 Boundary Row, London SE1 8HN

Chapman & Hall, 2-6 Boundary Row, London SE1 8HN, UK

Blackie Academic & Professional, Wester Cleddens Road,
Bishopbriggs, Glasgow G64 2NZ, UK

Chapman & Hall, 29 West 35th Street, New York NY10001, USA

Chapman & Hall Japan, Thomson Publishing Japan, Hirakawacho
Nemoto Building, 6F, 1-7-11 Hirakawa-cho, Chiyoda-ku, Tokyo 102,
Japan

Chapman & Hall Australia, Thomas Nelson Australia, 102 Dodds
Street, South Melbourne, Victoria 3205, Australia

Chapman & Hall India, R. Seshadri, 32 Second Main Road, CIT East,
Madras 600 035, India

First edition 1989
Reprinted 1991
Second edition 1992
Reprinted 1993

© 1989, 1992 C.W. Evans

Typeset in 10/12pt Times by Best-set Typesetter Ltd., Hong Kong
Printed in Singapore by Fong & Sons Printers Pte Ltd

ISBN 0 412 45640 0

A catalogue record for this book is available from the British Library
Library of Congress Cataloging-in-Publication Data available

To my family, friends and students,
past, present and future.

Contents

Acknowledgements

Inevitably with a book of this size there are many people who have assisted in one way or another. Although it is invidious to mention just a few, some have been particularly helpful. T. Mayhew of Mayhew Telonics supplied an updated version of the company's SCIWAYS ROM; a scientific microchip. The bulk of the manuscript was prepared initially on a wordprocessor using this ROM. F. Smiley checked through the examples and produced solutions to all the exercises. Many anonymous readers commented on the initial draft of the manuscript and without exception their comments proved useful. Dr Dominic Recaldin commissioned the book and has always been most supportive. Indeed many staff, both past and present, of Van Nostrand Reinhold and Chapman and Hall have assisted enthusiastically in the production of this book. Lastly, the author's family must not go unmentioned for supplying a unique blend of patience, exasperation and forbearance. To these, and all others who have assisted in the preparation of this book, the author extends his warmest thanks.

Preface

The second edition differs from the first in three respects. First, the format is different. Wide margins are now provided so that readers can pencil in small individual notes and comments which may be of assistance to them later on. Second, each chapter has been provided with extra exercises. Generally these are of the more routine variety and have been incorporated before the assignment. All the exercises are supplied with answers which are located at the end of the book. Third, some marginal diagrams and references have been included to help illuminate the material and occasionally to indicate where a topic fits into the overall scheme.

It is hoped that students will find in the new edition plenty to sustain the development of their mathematical knowledge and skills. The author thanks all those who have contributed to the production of this book.

C W E

Preface to the first edition

Students reading for degrees and diplomas in Engineering and Applied Science arrive with a wide variety of mathematical backgrounds. Nevertheless by the end of the first year of study all of them must have achieved a minimum standard in mathematics and also have acquired sufficient skill to enable them to cope with the more advanced mathematical topics in the second year. Experience has shown that many students are unable to cope with the traditional mathematics textbooks because they find them remote and the concepts difficult to handle.

Today, more than ever before, pressure is on institutes of higher education to increase productivity. Inevitably this means that staff have less time to help students and the problem is particularly acute in mathematics because self-help groups usually lack the necessary competence. This book is written to help the student acquire the skill and confidence needed to succeed.

The work is divided up into **chapters** and each chapter is written broadly to the same general plan. The learning objectives are listed and the text follows in which ideas are illustrated by means of examples. **Workshop** sessions are provided in the form of steps where the student is invited to respond. Depending on the response offered it may be possible for the student to advance quickly through these steps. Otherwise further help is given to clear up difficulties. In this way the student who is able to cope can move ahead speedily whereas the student who is experiencing difficulty is given a helping hand. If problems persist the student is encouraged to return to the text and make sure that nothing has been overlooked.

After the mathematical material has been introduced and assimilated a **Practical** section is given where a physical problem which uses some of the mathematics is solved. The student who feels able to cope is encouraged to try it unaided straight away but all are invited to contribute to the solution at the earliest possible stage. Finally the chapter is summarized and an **Assignment** is provided. The student is expected to work through this; hints and solutions are provided at the end of the book. **Further exercises** are supplied at the end of each chapter for those who can spend time on them.

Each chapter has been carefully selected to reflect the present day demands. There are indications that with the rise of computer technology discrete mathematics is receiving more attention. In order to reflect this trend a chapter has been included on difference equations. Notation can be a problem particularly when students have differing mathematical back-grounds. Some may have studied traditional mathematics with plenty of practice at calculus, while others may have experienced more modern ap-proaches with emphasis on sets, functions and matrices. The approach adopted here is a unique blend of the two. Modern notation has been used only when it seems desirable for clarity but never for its own sake.

The approach adopted differs from some superficially similar texts because the development is analytical and open ended. The work is developed from initial statements and although proofs are seldom supplied the flavour of an evolving subject is preserved. Directions in which the subject can be taken are often indicated so that the student is not left with the false impression that mathematics is a fossilized relic of the classical age.

Another unusual feature of the book is that common mistakes are high-lighted. The author has had the pleasure of teaching mathematics to degree and diploma students for over twenty years and has been able to draw on this experience to show the pitfalls which usually take their toll. In this way an attentive student should be able to avoid making similar mistakes.

Most of the exercises which appear here have been specifically con-structed for the book. However some have been adapted from examples in common use which have their origins lost in time. If any problem has appeared elsewhere in essentially the same form as it appears here then the borrowing is unintentional and the author apologizes to those concerned. He also welcomes constructive criticism from those who use this book.

C.W.E.

To the student

There are essentially two different ways in which you can use this book. Each of them depends on your past experience of the topic; whether it is a new topic or one with which you are familiar.

NEW TOPICS

☐ Work your way through the chapter with the aid of a note pad, making sure that you follow the worked examples in the text.
☐ When you come to a workshop be resolute and do not read the solutions until you have tried to work them out.
☐ Attempt the assignment at the end of the chapter. If there are any difficulties return to the workshop.
☐ Spend as much time as possible on the further exercises.

FAMILIAR TOPICS

☐ Start with the assignment, which follows the text, and see how it goes.
☐ If all is well continue with the further exercises.
☐ If difficulties arise with the assignment backtrack to the workshop.
☐ If difficulties arise in the workshop backtrack to the text.
☐ Read through the chapter to ensure you are thoroughly familiar with the material.

SPECIAL SYMBOL

☐ The symbol ! is used in the margins and has a special meaning.
☐ It highlights an area where common mistakes and misunderstandings occur. Here it is important to concentrate with even more care than usual. The symbol does not imply that the material is necessarily more difficult but it does indicate that care should be taken.

Engineering Mathematics   A programmed approach
C.W. Evans

This bookmark is intended to be used as a page mask. It should stop
your eyes from glancing inadvertently down the page when you are
trying a worked example on your own. On the reverse side of the
bookmark is a table of standard integrals and derivatives together
with several formulas. These are frequently needed in applications to
engineering and science.

From time to time as you read through the text you will encounter a
think line like this:

Normally this represents a breathing space; it means that you can
stop at this point if you wish without interrupting the flow of the text
too much.
   All examples begin with the symbol □ and end with the symbol ■.
These should help you to judge whether the length and likely complexity of an example will fit into the time you have allocated for
study.

QUICK REFERENCE GUIDE

$f'(x)$	$f(x) = F'(x)$	$F(x)$
nx^{n-1}	x^n	$x^{n+1}/(n+1)\,(n \neq -1)$
$-\sin x$	$\cos x$	$\sin x$
$\sec^2 x$	$\tan x$	$\ln|\sec x|$
$\sec x \tan x$	$\sec x$	$\ln|\sec x + \tan x|$
$-\operatorname{cosec}^2 x$	$\cot x$	$\ln|\sin x|$
$-\operatorname{cosec} x \cot x$	$\operatorname{cosec} x$	$\ln|\operatorname{cosec} x - \cot x|$
$1/x$	$\ln x$	$x \ln x - x$
$a^x \ln a$	$a^x\,(a > 0)$	$a^x/\ln a$
$\cosh x$	$\sinh x$	$\cosh x$
$\operatorname{sech}^2 x$	$\tanh x$	$\ln \cosh x$
$-\operatorname{sech} x \tanh x$	$\operatorname{sech} x$	$2\tan^{-1}(e^x)$
$-\operatorname{cosech}^2 x$	$\coth x$	$\ln|\sinh x|$
$-\operatorname{cosech} x \coth x$	$\operatorname{cosech} x$	$\ln|\tanh(x/2)|$
$2x/(1-x^2)^2$	$1/(1-x^2)$	$\tfrac{1}{2}\ln|(1+x)/(1-x)|$
$-2x/(1+x^2)^2$	$1/(1+x^2)$	$\tan^{-1}x$
$x/(1-x^2)^{3/2}$	$1/\sqrt{(1-x^2)}$	$\sin^{-1}x$
$-x/(1+x^2)^{3/2}$	$1/\sqrt{(1+x^2)}$	$\ln[x + \sqrt{(1+x^2)}]$
$-x/(x^2-1)^{3/2}$	$1/\sqrt{(x^2-1)}$	$\ln|x + \sqrt{(x^2-1)}|$
$-x/(1-x^2)^{1/2}$	$\sqrt{(1-x^2)}$	$\{x\sqrt{(1-x^2)} + \sin^{-1}x\}/2$
$x/(1+x^2)^{1/2}$	$\sqrt{(1+x^2)}$	$\{x\sqrt{(1+x^2)} + \ln[x + \sqrt{(x^2+1)}]\}/2$
$x/(x^2-1)^{1/2}$	$\sqrt{(x^2-1)}$	$\{x\sqrt{(x^2-1)} - \ln|x + \sqrt{(x^2-1)}|\}/2$
$e^{ax}(a\cos bx - b\sin bx)$	$e^{ax}\cos bx$	$e^{ax}(a\cos bx + b\sin bx)/(a^2+b^2)$
$e^{ax}(a\sin bx + b\cos bx)$	$e^{ax}\sin bx$	$e^{ax}(a\sin bx - b\cos bx)/(a^2+b^2)$

1 Binomial expansion $\displaystyle (a+b)^n = \sum_{r=0}^{n} \binom{n}{r} a^r b^{n-r} \quad (n \in \mathbb{N})$

2 Taylor's expansion $\displaystyle f(a+h) = \sum_{r=0}^{n-1} \frac{h^r}{r!} f^{(r)}(a) + R_n$

where $\displaystyle R_n = \frac{h^n}{n!} f^{(n)}(a + \theta h) \quad \theta \in (0,1)$

3 Newton's formula $\displaystyle x_{n+1} = x_n - \frac{f(x_n)}{f'(x_n)}$

4 Triple vector product $\mathbf{a} \times (\mathbf{b} \times \mathbf{c}) = (\mathbf{a}\cdot\mathbf{c})\mathbf{b} - (\mathbf{a}\cdot\mathbf{b})\mathbf{c}$

5 Leibniz's theorem $\displaystyle (uv)_n = \sum_{r=0}^{n} \binom{n}{r} u_r v_{n-r} \quad (n \in \mathbb{N})$

6 Integration by parts $\displaystyle \int u\,dv = uv - \int v\,du$

Numbers and logarithms　　　　1

Mathematical language consists of words like 'number', 'function', 'set' and many others. We may have an intuitive idea of what some of these mean, but before we start to use them it would be a good idea if we agreed on the meanings.

After studying this chapter you should be able to
☐ Classify real numbers into natural numbers, integers, rational numbers and irrational numbers;
☐ Apply the rules of indices and logarithms correctly;
☐ Use the binomial expansion for $(1 + x)^n$, where n is a positive integer.
At the end of this chapter we shall solve a practical problem involving the force on a magnetic pole.

1.1 NUMBERS

When we learn to count we begin with the **natural numbers**. These are the positive whole numbers, and they are generated by repeatedly adding 1 to itself. Here are the first few natural numbers:

$$1, 2, 3, 4, 5, 6$$

We shall use the convention of showing three dots to indicate that we have not written down all the numbers in the set. The set of natural numbers can then be displayed informally as

$$1, 2, 3, 4, 5, 6, \ldots$$

The set of natural numbers is usually denoted by $\mathbb{N}$, and we can emphasize that it is a set by using curly brackets:

$$\mathbb{N} = \{1, 2, 3, 4, 5, \ldots\}$$

The expression on the right is the **set** of all natural numbers. (Sets are discussed in more detail in Chapter 2.)

If a number p is a natural number we write $p \in \mathbb{N}$, whereas if p is not a natural number we write $p \notin \mathbb{N}$. The symbol $\in$ can be replaced mentally by the words 'is a member of the set' and the symbol $\notin$ by the words 'is not a member of the set'.

Example □ Decide if $p \in \mathbb{N}$ or $p \notin \mathbb{N}$ in each of the following cases:
a $p = 3$
b $p^2 = 2$
c $p^2 - 3p + 2 = 0$
Have a go at this and check if you obtained the correct answers.

Here are the answers:
a 3 is a natural number, so $3 \in \mathbb{N}$.
b $p = \pm\sqrt{2} = \pm1.414$ (to three decimal places or 3DP), so $p \notin \mathbb{N}$.
c $(p - 1)(p - 2) = 0$, so $p = 1$ or $p = 2$ and therefore $p \in \mathbb{N}$. ■

All right so far?

The natural numbers are quite good enough for counting your possessions or even your money, but they are insufficient for anything slightly more sophisticated such as borrowing money.

The **integers** consist of the positive and negative whole numbers, including 0. The set of them is denoted by $\mathbb{Z}$. So

$$\mathbb{Z} = \{0, \pm1, \pm2, \pm3, \ldots\}$$

The integers are quite sufficient to represent profit and loss, for example, because the equation

$$a + x = b$$

can be solved to give an integer value for x whatever integer values are given to the constants a and b.

Example □ Decide in each case whether or not $p \in \mathbb{Z}$:
a $p^2 = 4$
b $p^3 = 2p$
c $p^2 - 2p - 1 = 0$
Try to solve this.

Here we go!

a $p = \pm 2$, and so in any event $p \in \mathbb{Z}$.

b Either $p = 0$ or $p^2 = 2$, so the solutions are 0, $\sqrt{2}$ and $-\sqrt{2}$. Only the first of these is an integer, so $p \notin \mathbb{Z}$.

c $p = 1 \pm \sqrt{2}$, and so $p \notin \mathbb{Z}$. ∎

We observe of course that every natural number is an integer. This is expressed by saying that $\mathbb{N}$ is a subset of $\mathbb{Z}$, and we write

$$\mathbb{N} \subset \mathbb{Z}$$

In general a set A is a **subset** of a set B if whenever x is a member of the set A then x is also a member of the set B. In symbols:

$$A \subset B \text{ if and only if whenever } x \in A \text{ then } x \in B$$

We can also write $B \supset A$ to denote the same property.

It follows that if both $A \subset B$ and $B \subset A$ then the two sets A and B have precisely the same elements and that we can write $A = B$.

Although the integers are sufficient for simple barter of discrete (individually distinct) objects, they are unable to cope with division. This concept can be represented mathematically by the equation

$$ax = b$$

For example:

$$3x = 15 \text{ implies } x = 5 \ (\in \mathbb{Z})$$
$$4x = 15 \text{ implies } x = 3.75 \ (\notin \mathbb{Z})$$

Any number which can be expressed in the form p/q, where p and q are integers, is known as a **rational number**. The set of rational numbers is represented by $\mathbb{Q}$.

Of course if p is an integer then $p = p/1$ and so can be expressed as the quotient of two integers. Consequently any integer is also a rational number. That is,

$$\mathbb{Z} \subset \mathbb{Q}$$

We therefore have

$$\mathbb{N} \subset \mathbb{Z} \subset \mathbb{Q}$$

There are numbers which are not rational numbers, for example $\sqrt{2}$. These are known as **irrational numbers**.

It is interesting to see why $\sqrt{2}$ is an irrational number. We give an indirect proof: we shall suppose that $\sqrt{2}$ is rational and deduce from this a contradiction. Suppose then that

$$\sqrt{2} = \frac{p}{q}$$

where p and q are integers. We can suppose further that there is no integer which divides both p and q, for if there were we could cancel it out and thereby reduce p and q to smaller numbers.

Squaring the equation gives

$$2 = \frac{p^2}{q^2}$$

so that

$$p^2 = 2q^2$$

Now this implies that p^2 is even, and so p must be even too. Therefore if we put $p = 2r$, r is an integer. We then obtain, substituting for p,

$$(2r)^2 = 2q^2$$
$$4r^2 = 2q^2$$
$$2r^2 = q^2$$

Now this implies that q^2 is even, and so q must be even too. However, this is the crunch! We have deduced that both p and q are even, and yet we know that p and q have no common factor. This contradiction shows that our initial assumption that $\sqrt{2}$ was a rational number must be false.

It is interesting to remark that when the irrationality of $\sqrt{2}$ was first discovered, in ancient times, it caused philosophical consternation.

1.2 REAL NUMBERS

So there it is: we have natural numbers, integers, rational numbers and now irrational numbers too. For our purposes we shall regard a **real number** as any number which can be represented by a decimal expansion. The set of all real numbers will be denoted by $\mathbb{R}$. Therefore

$$\mathbb{N} \subset \mathbb{Z} \subset \mathbb{Q} \subset \mathbb{R}$$

Any real number which is not a rational number is called an irrational number. The decimal expansion for an irrational number has the remarkable property that it never terminates and never recurs! For example π, the ratio of the circumference of a circle to its diameter, is an irrational number and can be approximated in various ways depending on the accuracy required:

$$\sqrt{10}, \ \frac{22}{7}, \ 3.14, \ 3.142, \ 3.141\,592\,654$$

Engineers and applied scientists are seldom interested in things irrational.

Luckily any irrational number can be approximated by a rational number to any required degree of accuracy.

___

Of more tangible value is the ability to solve equations which are likely to arise from practical considerations. We have already seen that the equation $ax = b$ can be solved, when $a \neq 0$, using real numbers. The equation

$$ax = b$$

is known as a **linear equation**. The equation

$$ax^2 + bx + c = 0$$

is a **quadratic equation**, and as you probably know its solution can be written using the formula

$$x = \frac{-b \pm \sqrt{(b^2 - 4ac)}}{2a} \qquad (a \neq 0)$$

The derivation of this formula will be given in section 10.1. Can you derive it yourself first?

If $b^2 - 4ac \geq 0$ then x is a real number. However, if $b^2 - 4ac < 0$ then there is no real number x which satisfies the equation. This unsatisfactory state of affairs is overcome by extending the number system to produce the **complex numbers** $\mathbb{C}$. We then have

$$\mathbb{N} \subset \mathbb{Z} \subset \mathbb{Q} \subset \mathbb{R} \subset \mathbb{C}$$

Complex numbers have particular applications in physics and electrical engineering. In mathematics they are needed, for example, in the study of linear difference equations and differential equations – equations which can arise in practical problems. In later chapters we shall be considering equations of this kind and so we shall also need to find out about complex numbers (Chapter 10).

___

1.3 Workshop

1

▷**Exercise**   Suppose A is one of the following numbered sets: (1) $\mathbb{N}$ (2) $\mathbb{Z}$ (3) $\mathbb{Q}$ (4) $\mathbb{R}$ (5) $\mathbb{C}$. From each of the following equations obtain the numbered set with the *least* number for which it is true that $p \in A$, for all p:

a $p^2 - 2p + 1 = 0$
b $p^2 + 5p + 6 = 0$
c $p^2 + p + 1 = 0$
d $2p^2 = 4$
e $(\sqrt{2})^p = 16$
f $4p^2 - 4p = 3$

For instance, if $p^2 + 2p + 1 = 0$ we obtain $(p + 1)^2 = 0$ and so $p = -1$. Therefore $p \in \mathbb{Z}$ but $p \notin \mathbb{N}$, so that the required answer is set 2.

Now you carry on. When you have sorted out equation **a**, move to step 2 and see if you've managed to get it right.

---

2   We can factorize **a** as $(p - 1)^2 = 0$. Therefore $p \in \mathbb{N}$ and so set 1.

If you managed that, try **c** and then move to step 4. If you made a mistake, try **b** and then move to step 3.

---

3   We can factorize **b** as $(p + 2)(p + 3) = 0$, and so $p = -2$ or $p = -3$. Therefore $p \in \mathbb{Z}$ but $p \notin \mathbb{N}$, so set 2.

Do we get the idea? Now try **c** and then move on to step 4.

---

4   We are not able to factorize quadratic **c**, and if we use the formula for its solution we obtain $p = [-1 \pm \sqrt{(1 - 4)}]/2$. This means that $p \in \mathbb{C}$ because $b^2 - 4ac < 0$. Therefore $p \in \mathbb{C}$ and the answer is set 5.

If you managed that, try **e** and then move ahead to step 6. If something went adrift, have a go at **d** and then move to step 5.

---

5   For **d** we have $2p^2 = 4$, so that $p^2 = 2$ and therefore $p = \pm \sqrt{2}$. Thus $p \in \mathbb{R}$ but $p \notin \mathbb{Q}$, and the answer is set 4.

There should be no trouble now. If there is a problem then you had better read through sections 1.1 and 1.2 again so that you see how numbers are classified.

Now try part **e** and then move forward to step 6.

---

6   For **e** we have $(\sqrt{2})^p = 16$, and so $p = 8$. Therefore $p \in \mathbb{N}$ and the answer is set 1.

Good! Now for part **f**. When you are ready, take the final step.

---

7   For **f** we have $4p^2 - 4p - 3 = 0$, and so $(2p - 3)(2p + 1) = 0$. It follows that $p = 3/2$ or $p = -1/2$. Therefore $p \in \mathbb{Q}$ but of course $p \notin \mathbb{Z}$, and so the answer is set 3.

Fine!

1.4 THE REAL NUMBER SYSTEM

Here is a list of the **algebraic rules** which are obeyed by the real numbers. Suppose that a, b and c are arbitrary real numbers.

Rules of addition
  1 closure rule $a + b \in \mathbb{R}$
  2 associative rule $(a + b) + c = a + (b + c)$
  3 identity rule $0 + a = a + 0 = a$
  4 inverse rule $a + (-a) = (-a) + a = 0$
  5 commutative rule $a + b = b + a$

Rules of multiplication
  6 closure rule $ab \in \mathbb{R}$
  7 associative rule $(ab)c = a(bc)$
  8 identity rule $a1 = 1a = a$
  9 inverse rule $aa^{-1} = a^{-1}a = 1 \quad (a \neq 0)$
  10 commutative rule $ab = ba$
  11 distributive rule $a(b + c) = ab + ac$

Rules of order
  12 trichotomy rule $a > 0$ or $a < 0$ or $a = 0$
  13 arithmetic rule $a > 0$ and $b > 0$ implies $a + b > 0$, $ab > 0$
  14 comparison rule $a > b$ if and only if $a + (-b) > 0$

It is possible to deduce from these rules all the algebraic properties of the real numbers that we need.

☐ Show that if $a > 0$ and $b > 0$ and $a^2 > b^2$ then $a > b$. In words, the **Example** inequality is preserved when we take the positive square root.

   We prove this by an indirect method: we show that only $a > b$ is possible, because if any of the alternatives were to hold then a contradiction would result. There are just three possibilities: **a** $a = b$ **b** $a < b$ **c** $a > b$.

a We can reject $a = b$ immediately, since then $a^2 - b^2 = (a + b)(a - b) = 0$ which contradicts $a^2 - b^2 > 0$.
b If $a < b$ then $b - a > 0$, and we know that $b + a > 0$. Therefore $(b + a)(b - a) > 0$ and so $b^2 - a^2 > 0$ which is a contradiction.

Only case **c** remains, and we deduce that $a > b$.   ∎

A similar method can be used to show that if $a \geqslant 0$ and $b \geqslant 0$ and $a^2 \geqslant b^2$ then $a \geqslant b$.

   It is essential to note that in order to apply this property both a and b must be positive. For example $(-3)^2 > 2^2$ but $-3 < 2$. Trouble soon occurs if you overlook considerations of this kind.

THE TRIANGLE INEQUALITY

One useful notation which we shall employ from time to time is the **modulus** symbol. We write $|a|$ for the absolute value of a. Thus if $a \in \mathbb{R}$,

$$|a| = a \qquad \text{when } a \geqslant 0$$
$$|a| = -a \qquad \text{when } a < 0$$

For example, $|-3| = 3$ and $|5| = 5$.

An inequality involving the modulus sign which we shall encounter occasionally is the **triangle inequality**. It can be interpreted physically as saying that the sum of the lengths of two sides of a triangle is always greater than or equal to the length of the third side. Geometrically this is obvious, but algebraically it is not quite so clear. Here it is:

$$|a + b| \leqslant |a| + |b| \quad \text{whenever } a, b \in \mathbb{R}$$

If you substitute a few numbers, you will soon convince yourself of the truth of this assertion.

To prove it we proceed as follows:

$$
\begin{aligned}
(|a| + |b|)^2 &= |a|^2 + 2|a||b| + |b|^2 \\
&= a^2 + 2|a||b| + b^2 \\
&\geqslant a^2 + 2ab + b^2 \\
&= (a + b)^2 \\
&= |a + b|^2
\end{aligned}
$$

So that, taking the positive square root,

$$|a| + |b| \geqslant |a + b|$$

or

$$|a + b| \leqslant |a| + |b|$$

There is a form of the triangle inequality for complex numbers (Chapter 10, Further exercises 6) and vectors (Chapter 14, Further exercises 7). We shall find inequalities useful when we come to limits in section 4.4.

THE AXIOM OF COMPLETENESS

One essential property of the real number system which we have not mentioned hitherto is the axiom of completeness.

A set S of real numbers is said to be **bounded** if and only if there exist numbers M and m such that $m \leqslant x \leqslant M$ whenever $x \in S$. M and m are then known as **upper bounds** and **lower bounds** respectively.

For example, three upper bounds for the set of negative real numbers are 0, 1 and 97. Of course any positive real number is an upper bound for this set. However, the least upper bound is 0 because any number less than 0 is not an upper bound.

In a similar way we see that the greatest lower bound of the set of numbers of the form $1/n$, where n is a natural number, is 0 because first it is a lower bound and secondly any number greater than 0 is not a lower bound.

We need this terminology to state the **axiom of completeness**: Every non-empty subset of real numbers which has an upper bound has a least upper bound.

MATHEMATICAL INDUCTION

Although we have described the axiom of completeness, it will not impinge directly on the work we do. It is important to the subject because it under-pins much of it. One consequence is a method of proof known as mathematical induction.

Suppose we have some statement $S(n)$ which we wish to prove true for all $n \in \mathbb{N}$. The **principle of mathematical induction** says that we need only prove two things:
1 $S(1)$ is true;
2 If $S(k)$ is true then $S(k + 1)$ is true.
There are many ways of thinking about induction. One analogy is that of a petrol engine. In order for the engine to fire it must first be turned over. This corresponds to condition 1. However, each time the engine turns over it generates enough electricity to fire the engine again. This corresponds to condition 2. Provided condition 2 continues to hold the engine will run even if the battery is flat. If you have had the experience of driving a car with a flat battery you will appreciate the need for both these conditions!

We are not going to make a song and dance out of mathematical induction. However, we shall look at two examples just to see how the method is applied.

□ Suppose $S(n)$ is the statement

Example

$$1 + 2 + 3 + \ldots + n = \tfrac{1}{2}n(n + 1)$$

We wish to show that $S(n)$ is true for all $n \in \mathbb{N}$. In words, we wish to prove that the sum of the first n natural numbers is one-half the product of n and $n + 1$.

By induction we must show two things:
1 $S(1)$ is true;
2 If $S(k)$ is true then $S(k + 1)$ is true.
We proceed as follows:
1 To show $S(1)$ is true is easy. We merely need to show that

$$1 = \tfrac{1}{2}1(1 + 1)$$

To see this we evaluate the right-hand side.
2 Suppose $S(k)$ is true for some $k \in \mathbb{N}$. Then

$$1 + 2 + 3 + \ldots + k = \tfrac{1}{2}k(k + 1)$$

(This is known as the **induction hypothesis**.)
We must show $S(k + 1)$ is true. Therefore we must show

$$1 + 2 + 3 + \ldots + (k + 1) = \tfrac{1}{2}(k + 1)\,[(k + 1) + 1]$$

We have simply replaced n by $k + 1$ in the statement $S(n)$. To show this we shall take the left-hand side and demonstrate that it reduces to the right-hand side. Remember we are entitled to use the induction hypothesis.

$$\begin{aligned}
\text{LHS} &= 1 + 2 + 3 + \ldots + k + (k + 1) \\
&= [1 + 2 + \ldots + k] + (k + 1) \\
&= \tfrac{1}{2}k(k + 1) + (k + 1) \quad \text{(using the induction hypothesis)} \\
&= \tfrac{1}{2}(k + 1)(k + 2) \\
&= \tfrac{1}{2}(k + 1)[(k + 1) + 1] \\
&= \text{RHS} \quad\blacksquare
\end{aligned}$$

That's all there is to it. Of course a proof by induction differs from a deductive proof because we need to have a shrewd idea that the formula which we wish to prove is true. However, it is a very useful technique because it is often possible to spot a pattern in mathematical work, infer a formula and then use induction to settle the matter. In fact there will be various occasions when we shall point out where a proof by induction would be appropriate.

Right, now here is one for you to try.

Example □ Show that if $n \in \mathbb{N}$ then

$$1^2 + 3^2 + 5^2 + \ldots + (2n - 1)^2 = n(4n^2 - 1)/3$$

In words, we have a formula for the sum of the squares of the first n odd numbers.

You have the statement $S(n)$, so you can write down the induction hypothesis $S(k)$ and also the statement which we must deduce $S(k + 1)$. Don't forget too that we must check that $S(1)$ holds.

Try it yourself and see how it goes.

$S(n)$ is the statement

$$1^2 + 3^2 + 5^2 + \ldots + (2n - 1)^2 = n(4n^2 - 1)/3$$

for all $n \in \mathbb{N}$.

1 To show $S(1)$ is true we check that when $n = 1$ the formula works. The left-hand side is $1^2 = 1$. The right-hand side is $1 \times (4 \times 1^2 - 1)/3 = 1$. Therefore $S(1)$ holds.

2 The induction hypothesis $S(k)$ is that, for some $k \in \mathbb{N}$,

$$1^2 + 3^2 + 5^2 + \ldots + (2k - 1)^2 = k(4k^2 - 1)/3$$

We must deduce $S(k + 1)$; that is, we must show

$$1^2 + 3^2 + 5^2 + \ldots + [2(k + 1) - 1]^2 = (k + 1)[4(k + 1)^2 - 1]/3$$

Remember we are entitled to use the induction hypothesis to establish this. We work on the left-hand side:

$$1^2 + 3^2 + 5^2 + \ldots + [2(k + 1) - 1]^2$$
$$= 1^2 + 3^2 + 5^2 + \ldots + (2k + 1)^2$$
$$= [1^2 + 3^2 + 5^2 + \ldots + (2k - 1)^2] + (2k + 1)^2$$
$$= k(4k^2 - 1)/3 + (2k + 1)^2$$

Here we have used the induction hypothesis. So the left-hand side simplifies to

$$= k(2k - 1)(2k + 1)/3 + (2k + 1)^2$$
$$= (2k + 1)[k(2k - 1) + 3(2k + 1)]/3$$
$$= (2k + 1)[2k^2 - k + 6k + 3]/3$$
$$= (2k + 1)[2k^2 + 5k + 3]/3$$

A glance at the expression we wish to obtain gives us the clue to factorizing:

$$= (2k + 1)(k + 1)(2k + 3)/3$$
$$= (k + 1)(4k^2 + 8k + 3)/3$$
$$= (k + 1)[4(k + 1)^2 - 1]/3$$

This is the right-hand side of $S(k + 1)$.

We have shown the two parts:

1 $S(1)$ holds;

2 If $S(k)$ holds then $S(k + 1)$ holds.

Therefore by induction we have shown that $S(n)$ holds for all $n \in \mathbb{N}$. ■

Finally we remark that although we used only $S(k)$, our induction hypothesis, we would have been entitled to use $S(r)$ for all $r \leq k$. When this is done it is usually known as using **strong induction**.

1.5 INDICES AND LOGARITHMS

Years ago all calculations of any difficulty had to be performed using tables of logarithms. It was therefore essential to become skilled in the use of these tables. With modern calculators this is no longer necessary, but it remains important to have a clear understanding of the rules which underlie them.

For example we shall use them in the Workshop 19.5 when we study differential equations.

INDICES

We shall first explain what is meant by a^r, where r is any real number and a is a strictly positive real number. You have probably done this before, but it is possible that you have only a very vague idea of what the raised symbol or **index** r means.

$r \in \mathbb{N}$

Suppose $r = n$, a *natural* number, and that a is any real number. We define

$$a^1 = a, \ a^2 = aa$$

and in general

$$a^n = aa^{n-1} \quad \text{where } n > 1$$

It follows that a^n is the product of a with itself n times.
If $a \neq 0$, we define $a^0 = 1$ and

$$a^{-n} = \frac{1}{a^n} \qquad (n \in \mathbb{N})$$

This extends the definition to a^r, where r is any integer.
When we consider this definition carefully, we obtain when $a \neq 0$:
1 $a^p a^q = a^{p+q}$
2 $(a^p)^q = a^{pq}$
where p and q are any integers. These two rules are often referred to as the
laws of indices, and as we extend the definition of a^n we shall have as a top
requirement that these rules remain true. One of the prices we have to pay
for this obsession is that we must restrict a so that $a > 0$. Therefore in what
follows we shall presuppose that a is a strictly positive real number.

$r \in \mathbb{Q}$

Suppose that r is a *rational* number. Remember that if r is a rational number it is of the form p/q, where p and q are integers. We define $a^{p/q}$ to be
the positive real solution of the equation $x^q = a^p$.
    That there is one and only one such real number follows from the inter-
mediate value theorem, which is outside the scope of our work.

Example □ $2^{1/2}$ is the positive real solution of the equation $x^2 = 2$, so that $2^{1/2} = \sqrt{2}$
$\simeq 1.414$. (The symbol $\simeq$ means 'approximately equal to'.)   ■

$r \in \mathbb{R}$

Lastly we need to extend the definition to a^r where r is any *real* number. If
r is rational then the definition has already been given. We may therefore
suppose that r is irrational. Suppose $r_1, r_2, r_3, \ldots$ are successive rational
approximations to r. We consider the numbers

$$a^{r_1}, \ a^{r_2}, \ a^{r_3}, \ \ldots$$

each one of which has been defined. The number, to which these are successive approximations, is the number we call a^r.

_____

It will be appreciated that this last idea is quite sophisticated, and it leaves
a number of questions unanswered. For instance, how do we know that the
numbers

$$a^{r_1}, \ a^{r_2}, \ a^{r_3}, \ \ldots$$

successively approximate to a number at all? Such questions are rather subtle and will not be discussed fully here.

It is sufficient for our purposes that we have an idea of what is meant by a^r when $a > 0$. It is particularly important to realize that the laws of indices

1 $a^r a^s = a^{r+s}$

2 $(a^r)^s = a^{rs}$

hold whenever $a > 0$.

Note that we do not define a^r when $a < 0$ unless r is an integer. This is to avoid violating the laws of indices.

☐ Using a calculator and employing six successive approximations to π, **Example** obtain six successive approximations to 2^π.

We have $\pi = 3.14159\ldots$, from which we obtain the successive approximations

$$2^3, \ 2^{3.1}, \ 2^{3.14}, \ 2^{3.141}, \ 2^{3.1415}, \ 2^{3.14159}$$

That is,

$$8, \ 8.574, \ 8.815, \ 8.821, \ 8.824, \ 8.825 \qquad ■$$

LOGARITHMS

From the laws of indices we obtain the laws of logarithms. Logarithms are important because they provide a transformation which enables the arithmetical processes of multiplication and division to be replaced by those of addition and subtraction.

Suppose $a = b^c$. Then c is said to be the power to which b has been raised to produce a. We can write then

$$c = \log_b a$$

which is called the logarithm of a to the base b. So $a = b^c$ is equivalent to $c = \log_b a$. In words, the **logarithm** of a number is the power to which the base must be raised to obtain the number.

Any positive number, except 1, is suitable as a base. In practice, two bases are used:

1 Base 10: this produces the **common logarithms**;

2 Base e: this produces the **natural logarithms** (also known as Naperian logarithms).

The number e ($\simeq 2.71828$) is an irrational number. The reason why it is chosen and called the natural base will become clearer when we deal with differentiation (Chapter 4).

It is usual to write $y = \log x$ instead of $y = \log_{10} x$, and $y = \ln x$ instead of $y = \log_e x$.

When we transform the laws of indices into logarithmic notation, the **laws of logarithms** result:

Formulas using logarithms are common in applications.

1 $\log_c (ab) = \log_c a + \log_c b$
2 $\log_c (a/b) = \log_c a - \log_c b$
3 $\log_c (a^r) = r \log_c a$
4 $\log_a b = \log_c b / \log_c a \quad (a \neq 1)$
The last rule is usually called the **formula for a change of base**.

Example □ Use the laws of indices to deduce

$$\log_c (ab) = \log_c a + \log_c b$$

Let $\log_c a = x$ and $\log_c b = y$. Then $a = c^x$ and $b = c^y$, and so $ab = c^x c^y = c^{x+y}$. Consequently $x + y = \log_c (ab)$.   ∎

Now one for you to try.

Example □ Deduce, using the laws of indices,

$$\log_c (a/b) = \log_c a - \log_c b$$

Have a go at this, it's very similar to the previous example.

This is what you should write. Let $\log_c a = x$ and $\log_c b = y$. Then $a = c^x$ and $b = c^y$, and so

$$\frac{a}{b} = \frac{c^x}{c^y} = c^x (c^y)^{-1} = c^x c^{-y} = c^{x-y}$$

Therefore

$$\log_c (a/b) = x - y = \log_c a - \log_c b$$ ∎

Was all well? If you would like some more practice then try this.

Example □ Deduce, using the laws of indices,
a $\log_c (a^r) = r \log_c a$
b $\log_a b = \log_c b / \log_c a$

Here is the working:
a Suppose $\log_c a = b$. Then $a = c^b$, and therefore $a^r = (c^b)^r = c^{rb}$. Consequently, $\log_c (a^r) = rb = r \log_c a$.
b Suppose $\log_c b = y$ and $\log_c a = x$. Then $b = c^y$ and $a = c^x$, and so

$$b^x = (c^y)^x = c^{xy} = (c^x)^y = a^y.$$

It follows that

$$b = (b^x)^{1/x} = (a^y)^{1/x} = a^{y/x}$$

from which

$$\log_a b = \frac{y}{x} = \frac{\log_c b}{\log_c a}$$

Note that $\log_c a \neq 0$, since if $\log_c a = 0$ then $a = 1$.   ■

Logarithms are quite important for solving algebraic equations in which indices are present. However, it is easy to make mistakes. One of the commonest errors is to assume that the logarithm of a sum is the sum of the logarithms. This kind of rule is known as a **linearity rule**. Unfortunately logarithms do not comply with it. Let us be specific and examine how the error is usually made.

☐ Solve the equation   **Example**

$$4^x + 2^x - 2 = 0$$

You try this first and then examine the correct working afterwards.

The following is the correct working. First,

$$4^x + 2^x - 2 = 0$$

So

$$2^{2x} + 2^x - 2 = 0$$
$$(2^x)^2 + 2^x - 2 = 0$$

Consequently

$$(2^x + 2)(2^x - 1) = 0$$

So either $2^x + 2 = 0$ or $2^x = 1$. Now $2^x > 0$ for all real numbers x. So the only possibility is $2^x = 1$, from which $x = 0$.   ■

Now let's examine some *incorrect* working of the type which is frequently seen by examiners. In order not to mislead the unwary still further we shall avoid the equality sign – it cuts against the grain to use it – and instead use the symbol ∥. See how many errors you can spot in the following incorrect working of the previous example.

Taking logarithms

$$x \ln 4 + x \ln 2 - \ln 2 \parallel 0$$

So

$$2x \ln 2 + x \ln 2 - \ln 2 \parallel 0$$
$$(3x - 1) \ln 2 \parallel 0$$

So $x \parallel 1/3$.

!

The trouble is that on rare occasions nonsense like this can even lead to the correct answer! There are two glaring errors:

1 You cannot 'take logarithms' of both sides in the way that has been shown. The temptation to saunter through the equation from left to right dispensing logarithmic transformations on every term encountered is so strong that some students find it irresistible. However, as we have said, taking logarithms is not a linear operation and so the procedure is not valid.

2 Without even bothering to mention it, the assumption has been made that $\ln 0 = 0$. However, since $e^0 = 1$, $e^0 \neq 0$. In fact $\ln 0$ has no meaning.

Here is an example for you to try. Do be careful!

Example ☐ Obtain all real solutions of the equation

$$2^{2x} - 2^{x+5} + 256 = 0$$

When you have solved the problem, look to see if you are right.

The easiest way to solve this is to put $u = 2^x$ and obtain a quadratic equation in u. For if $u = 2^x$,

$$2^{2x} = (2^x)^2 = u^2$$

and

$$2^{x+5} = 2^x 2^5 = 32u$$

If you prefer you could use 'the formula' (see p. 5).

So the equation becomes

$$u^2 - 32u + 256 = 0$$
$$u^2 - 2^5 u + 2^8 = 0$$
$$(u - 2^4)(u - 2^4) = 0$$

Therefore $u = 2^x = 2^4$, and so $x = 4$. ■

Right then. If you made an error, here is another chance to redeem yourself.

Example ☐ Solve the equation

$$6^x - 27 \times 2^x - 8 \times 3^x + 216 = 0$$

Try hard with this one and then we'll see how you have got on.

It's a bit tricky, isn't it? The key to the whole thing is to notice that $6^x = 2^x 3^x$, so the equation can be rewritten as

$$2^x 3^x - 27 \times 2^x - 8 \times 3^x + 216 = 0$$

This is of the form

$$uv - 27u - 8v + 216 = 0$$

and luckily we can factorize this as

$$(u - 8)(v - 27) = 0$$

So

$$(2^x - 8)(3^x - 27) = 0$$

Consequently $2^x = 8$ or $3^x = 27$, and in either event we deduce that $x = 3$.

■

If you managed that you did very well! For those who are still seeking to redeem themselves the next problem offers a chance.

□ Solve the equation   **Example**

$$10^x - 16 \times 5^x - 25 \times 2^x + 400 = 0$$

Off you go!

This is just like the previous one, isn't it? We have $10^x = 5^x 2^x$, and so

$$5^x 2^x - 16 \times 5^x - 25 \times 2^x + 400 = 0$$

Therefore

$$(2^x - 16)(5^x - 25) = 0$$

So either $2^x = 16$ in which case $x = 4$, or $5^x = 25$ in which case $x = 2$. There are therefore *two* solutions: $x = 2$ and $x = 4$.   ■

1.6 THE BINOMIAL THEOREM

It is easy to verify, by direct multiplication, that

$$(1 + x)^0 = 1$$
$$(1 + x)^1 = 1 + x$$
$$(1 + x)^2 = 1 + 2x + x^2$$
$$(1 + x)^3 = 1 + 3x + 3x^2 + x^3$$
$$(1 + x)^4 = 1 + 4x + 6x^2 + 4x^3 + x^4$$

Blaise Pascal (1623–1662), French mathematician and child prodigy who abandoned mathematics for religious work.

A pattern is emerging for these coefficients which is often referred to as **Pascal's triangle**. Let's look at it:

```
              1
           1     1
          ①     ②    1
          1     ③    3    1
          1     4    6    4    1
```

Each entry consists of the sum of the entry above and the entry above and to the left. The circled numbers illustrate this: 3 is the sum of 2 and 1.
   Using this idea, see if you can write down the next line.

Here it is:

$$1 \quad 5 \quad 10 \quad 10 \quad 5 \quad 1$$

So we may conjecture

$$(1 + x)^5 = 1 + 5x + 10x^2 + 10x^3 + 5x^4 + x^5$$

and indeed direct multiplication will verify this fact.

It is convenient to use the notation

$$\binom{n}{r} = \frac{n!}{(n - r)! \, r!}$$

where n and r are positive integers and $r \leqslant n$. Therefore

$$\binom{3}{2} = \frac{3!}{(3 - 2)! \, 2!} = \frac{3!}{1! \, 2!} = \frac{3 \times 2 \times 1}{1 \times 1 \times 2} = 3$$

$$\binom{5}{2} = \frac{5!}{(5 - 2)! \, 2!} = \frac{5!}{3! \, 2!} = \frac{5 \times 4 \times 3 \times 2 \times 1}{3 \times 2 \times 1 \times 2 \times 1} = 10$$

Here we have used the notation

$$n! = n \times (n - 1) \times \ldots \times 3 \times 2 \times 1$$

where n is a natural number. Another way of writing this is

$$n! = n \times (n - 1) \times \ldots \times 3 \times 2 \times 1 = \prod_{r=1}^{n} r$$

The **product** symbol Π has been used here with the convention that we allow r to take on all integer values from 1 to n (including 1 and n) and multiply them all together. For convenience it is useful to define $0! = 1$. The exclamation mark ! is known as the **factorial** symbol; in words, $n!$ is 'n factorial'. Computer people now call the exclamation mark 'pling'.

One way to think of $n!$ is that it is the number of ways in which we can arrange n books on a shelf. For example, if $n = 3$ and we have three books A, B and C, the six possible arrangements are

ABC, BCA, CAB, ACB, BAC, CBA

This definition is even consistent with the definition of $0!$, for if there are no books there is only one way to arrange them, and that is to leave the shelf empty!

If we calculate $\binom{n}{r}$ for $n \in \{0, 1, 2, 3, 4, 5\}$ and $r \in \{0, 1, 2, 3, 4, 5\}$, $r \leqslant n$, we see that Pascal's triangle can be written

$$\binom{0}{0}$$

$$\binom{1}{0}\ \binom{1}{1}$$

$$\binom{2}{0}\ \binom{2}{1}\ \binom{2}{2}$$

$$\binom{3}{0}\ \binom{3}{1}\ \binom{3}{2}\ \binom{3}{3}$$

$$\binom{4}{0}\ \binom{4}{1}\ \binom{4}{2}\ \binom{4}{3}\ \binom{4}{4}$$

This enables us to conjecture the general formula for $(1 + x)^n$. We have

$$(1 + x)^n = \binom{n}{0} + \binom{n}{1}x + \binom{n}{2}x^2 + \ldots + \binom{n}{n}x^n$$

$$= \sum_{r=0}^{n} \binom{n}{r} x^r$$

The **summation** symbol Σ has been used here. The convention is that we allow r to take on all integer values from 0 to n (including 0 and n) and add the results. The formula which we have obtained is known as the **binomial theorem**; it could be proved by induction. We shall extend it later to other values of n.

□ Obtain the coefficient of x^7 in the expansion of $(1 + x)^{12}$.   **Example**

The coefficient of x^7 in the expansion of $(1 + x)^n$ is $\binom{n}{7}$. So the coefficient of x^7 in the expansion of $(1 + x)^{12}$ is

$$\binom{12}{7} = \frac{12!}{5! \ 7!} = \frac{12 \times 11 \times 10 \times 9 \times 8}{5 \times 4 \times 3 \times 2 \times 1} = 792 \qquad \blacksquare$$

Example □ The pattern in Pascal's triangle suggests the following identities:

a $\binom{n}{r} = \binom{n}{n-r}$

b $\binom{n}{r} = \binom{n-1}{r} + \binom{n-1}{r-1}$

Before obtaining these identities algebraically we shall see why it is that they are suggested by Pascal's triangle. The first one arises because each row appears to be symmetrical about its midpoint. In other words, reading from left to right or reading from right to left gives an identical sequence of numbers.

The second one says the entry in row n column r is obtained by adding the entry in row $n-1$ column r to the entry in row $n-1$ column $r-1$. This is a feature which we had already observed.

Now deduce these identities algebraically.

---

a $\binom{n}{n-r} = \frac{n!}{[n-(n-r)]! \ (n-r)!} = \frac{n!}{r! \ (n-r)!} = \binom{n}{r}$

b $\binom{n-1}{r} + \binom{n-1}{r-1} = \frac{(n-1)!}{(n-1-r)! \ r!} + \frac{(n-1)!}{[n-1-(r-1)]! \ (r-1)!}$

$= \frac{(n-1)!}{(n-r-1)! \ r!} + \frac{(n-1)!}{(n-r)! \ (r-1)!}$

$= \frac{(n-1)!}{(n-r-1)! \ (r-1)!} \left(\frac{1}{r} + \frac{1}{n-r} \right)$

$= \frac{(n-1)!}{(n-r-1)! \ (r-1)!} \left(\frac{n}{r(n-r)} \right)$

$= \frac{n!}{(n-r)! \ r!} = \binom{n}{r} \qquad \blacksquare$

We shall meet these coefficients again in Chapter 24 when we study probability.

Just to make sure we can handle these **binomial coefficients** without too much difficulty we shall take a few steps.

1.7 Workshop

1

Exercise Show that if n is any natural number,

$$\binom{n}{0} + \binom{n}{1} + \dots + \binom{n}{n} = 2^n$$

that is,

$$\sum_{r=0}^{n} \binom{n}{r} = 2^n$$

Have a go at this and then see if you did the right thing.

2

We merely need to use the binomial theorem

$$(1 + x)^n = \sum_{r=0}^{n} \binom{n}{r} x^r$$

and put $x = 1$ to obtain the required identity.

   If you were right then move ahead to step 4. If you didn't manage that, then try this.

▷ **Exercise**   If we choose any row in Pascal's triangle and alternate the signs, the sum is 0. For example, if $n = 5$ then

$$1 - 5 + 10 - 10 + 5 - 1 = 0$$

Prove that this property holds for all natural numbers n.

   When you have done this, take the next step.

3

Again we must use the binomial theorem

$$(1 + x)^n = \sum_{r=0}^{n} \binom{n}{r} x^r$$

However, this time we put $x = -1$ to deduce

$$0 = \sum_{r=0}^{n} \binom{n}{r} (-1)^r$$

which is precisely what we wish to show.

4

▷ **Exercise**   Obtain a relationship between h and k if the constant terms in the binomial expansions of

$$\left(hx^2 - \frac{k}{x^2} \right)^8 \quad \text{and} \quad \left(hx + \frac{k}{x} \right)^4$$

are equal.

   Be careful about this. Remember that we have not stated the expansion of $(a + b)^n$, and unless you are familiar with this you will need to do some elementary algebra before you apply the binomial theorem. When you are ready, step forward!

The expansion of $(a + b)^n$ appears on the bookmark.

5 We have

$$\left(hx^2 - \frac{k}{x^2}\right)^8 = (hx^2)^8 \left[1 + \left(\frac{-k}{hx^4}\right)\right]^8$$

We select the term in

$$\frac{1}{x^{16}} = \left(\frac{1}{x^4}\right)^4$$

in the binomial expansion of the expression in square brackets, for this will produce a constant term:

$$(hx^2)^8 \binom{8}{4}\left(\frac{-k}{hx^4}\right)^4 = \frac{h^8 k^4}{h^4} \frac{8 \times 7 \times 6 \times 5}{1 \times 2 \times 3 \times 4} = 70h^4 k^4$$

Also

$$\left(hx + \frac{k}{x}\right)^4 = h^4 x^4 \left[1 + \frac{k}{hx^2}\right]^4$$

so that this time we select the term in

$$\frac{1}{x^4} = \left(\frac{1}{x^2}\right)^2$$

This gives

$$h^4 x^4 \binom{4}{2}\left(\frac{k}{hx^2}\right)^2 = \frac{h^4 k^2}{h^2} \frac{4 \times 3}{1 \times 2} = 6h^2 k^2$$

Therefore

$$70h^4 k^4 = 6h^2 k^2$$
$$35h^2 k^2 = 3$$

This is the relationship which we were required to obtain.

If you made a mistake or feel you would like some more practice then do the next exercise. Otherwise you may move through to the top of the steps, step 7.

▷**Exercise**   Obtain the approximate value of

$$y = \left(1 + x + \frac{x^2}{2}\right)^5$$

if x is so small that terms in x of degree higher than 3 may be neglected. Do your very best with this one. Then step ahead.

6 We have

$$y = \left[1 + \left(x + \frac{x^2}{2}\right)\right]^5$$

Since terms of degree higher than 3 in x may be neglected, we obtain

$$y \simeq 1 + \binom{5}{1}\left(x + \frac{x^2}{2}\right) + \binom{5}{2}\left(x + \frac{x^2}{2}\right)^2 + \binom{5}{3}\left(x + \frac{x^2}{2}\right)^3$$

$$\simeq 1 + 5\left(x + \frac{x^2}{2}\right) + \frac{5 \times 4}{1 \times 2}\left(x^2 + \frac{2xx^2}{2}\right) + \frac{5 \times 4 \times 3}{1 \times 2 \times 3}x^3$$

$$= 1 + 5x + \frac{5x^2}{2} + 10x^2 + 10x^3 + 10x^3$$

$$= 1 + 5x + \frac{25x^2}{2} + 20x^3$$

Finally we remark that

$$\binom{n}{r} = \frac{n \times (n-1) \times (n-2) \times \ldots \times (n-r+1)}{1 \times 2 \times 3 \times \ldots \times r}$$

We can use this to extend the definition of $\binom{n}{r}$ to the situation where n is not necessarily a natural number. In fact we shall see later that

$$(1 + x)^n = \sum_{r=0}^{\infty} \binom{n}{r} x^r$$

is valid when n is any *real* number provided $-1 < x < 1$. However, until we consider the concept of infinite series (Chapter 9), the expression on the right will have no meaning for us.

Here is an example which we shall solve together. It shows one practical application of some of the things we have been doing.

_____ 1.8 Practical _____

ELECTRICAL FORCE

A magnetic pole, distance x from the plane of a coil of radius a, and on the axis of the coil, is subject to a force

$$F = \frac{kx}{(a^2 + x^2)^{5/2}} \qquad (k \text{ constant})$$

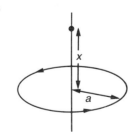

when a current flows in the coil. Show that:

a if x is small compared with a then

$$F \simeq \frac{kx}{a^5} - \frac{5kx^3}{2a^7}$$

b If x is large compared with a then

$$F \simeq \frac{k}{x^4} - \frac{5ka^2}{2x^6}$$

Try **a**, then move ahead for the solution.

---

a We have x/a is small, and so we rearrange the expression for F so that we can expand it by the binomial theorem:

$$F = \frac{kx}{(a^2 + x^2)^{5/2}}$$

$$= \frac{kx}{a^5[1 + (x/a)^2]^{5/2}}$$

$$= \frac{kx}{a^5}[1 + (x/a)^2]^{-5/2}$$

$$\simeq \frac{kx}{a^5}\left[1 - \frac{5}{2}\left(\frac{x}{a}\right)^2\right]$$

neglecting terms in x/a of degree higher than 2. So

$$F \simeq \frac{kx}{a^5} - \frac{5kx^3}{2a^7}$$

Now see if you can do the second part. Remember that here x is large compared with a.

---

b We rearrange the expression for F in terms of a/x, which is small, with a view to using the binomial expansion in a very similar way to that of **a**.

$$F = \frac{kx}{x^5\left[1 + \left(\dfrac{a}{x}\right)^2\right]^{5/2}}$$

$$= \frac{k}{x^4}\left[1 + \left(\frac{a}{x}\right)^2\right]^{-5/2}$$

$$\simeq \frac{k}{x^4}\left[1 - \frac{5}{2}\frac{a^2}{x^2}\right]$$

neglecting terms in a/x of degree higher than 2. So

$$F \simeq \frac{k}{x^4} - \frac{5ka^2}{2x^6}$$

SUMMARY

NUMBERS

We have seen that numbers can be classified into the following subsets:
- ☐ natural numbers $\mathbb{N}$
- ☐ integers $\mathbb{Z}$
- ☐ rational numbers $\mathbb{Q}$
- ☐ real numbers $\mathbb{R}$
- ☐ complex numbers $\mathbb{C}$

and that

$$\mathbb{N} \subset \mathbb{Z} \subset \mathbb{Q} \subset \mathbb{R} \subset \mathbb{C}$$

INDICES

We have defined what is meant by a^r and obtained the laws of indices:
- ☐ $a^r a^s = a^{r+s}$
- ☐ $(a^r)^s = a^{rs}$

LOGARITHMS

From the laws of indices we have deduced the laws of logarithms:
- ☐ $\log_c (ab) = \log_c a + \log_c b$
- ☐ $\log_c (a/b) = \log_c a - \log_c b$
- ☐ $\log_c (a^r) = r \log_c a$
- ☐ $\log_a b = \log_c b / \log_c a \quad (a \neq 1)$

THE BINOMIAL EXPANSION

If n is any natural number,

$$(1 + x)^n = \sum_{r=0}^{n} \binom{n}{r} x^r$$

EXERCISES (for answers see p. 738)

1 Find all real solutions of the following equations and classify them into real numbers, rational numbers, integers, natural numbers:

a $x^2 - x = 6$

b $3y^2 - 7y + 2 = 0$

c $u^2 + 1 = \dfrac{2}{u^2}$

d $v^2 + \dfrac{15}{v^2} = 8$

e $4x^2 - 4x + 1 = 0$

2 Simplify, using the laws of indices,

a $8^{5/3} \times 32^{1/5} \div 16^{3/4}$

b $12^{5/2} \times 27^{1/4} \div 6^{1/2}$,

c $\dfrac{(1 + x)^4(1 - x^4)}{(1 - x^2)^3}$

d $\dfrac{(a^2 - b^2)^5(a^4 - b^4)}{(a^2 + b^2)(a + b)^2}$

3 Solve the equations, where x is real,

a $e^{2x} = 4e^x + 5$

b $2^{2x} - 5.2^x + 4 = 0$

c $6^x - 9.2^x - 8.3^x + 72 = 0$

d $15^x + 15 = 3^{x+1} + 5^{x+1}$

4 Write down the first three terms in the binomial expansion, in ascending powers of x, of

a $(1 - 2x)^5$

b $(x + 3)^7$

c $(2x - 3)^8$

d $(4 - 5x)^{1/2}$

e $(3 + 5x)^{2/3}$

f $(x - 3)^{-2}$

5 Use mathematical induction to prove that for all $n \in \mathbb{N}$

a $1 + 3 + 5 + \ldots + (2n + 1) = n^2$

b $1^3 + 3^3 + 5^3 + \ldots + (2n - 1)^3 = n^2(2n^2 - 1)$

ASSIGNMENT (for answers see p. 738; see also Workshops on pp. 5 and 20)

1 For each of the following equations, classify the solutions in the hierarchy of natural numbers, integers, rational numbers, real numbers and complex numbers:

a $(2x - 1)(2x - 4) + 2 = 0$

b $x - \dfrac{1}{x} = 1 - \dfrac{5}{x}$

c $(x - 3)^2 + 6(x - 3) + 6 = 0$

d $\left(\sqrt{x} - \dfrac{1}{\sqrt{x}}\right)^2 = 1 - \dfrac{1}{x}$

2 Use the laws of indices to show that

$$\frac{(16)^{3/4}\,(25)^{1/2}}{(81)^{1/4}\,(125)^{1/3}} = \frac{8}{3}$$

3 Simplify

$$\frac{(1 - x^2)^3\,(1 - 3x + 2x^2)^4}{(1 - x - 2x^2)^6}\;\frac{(1 + x)^3}{(1 - x)^7}$$

4 Solve the equation $2^{3x} - 3 \times 2^{2x+1} + 2^{x+3} = 0$.

5 If $x = \log_a b$, $y = \log_b c$ and $z = \log_c a$, show that $xyz = 1$.

6 If $x = \log_a (bc)$, $y = \log_b (ca)$ and $z = \log_c (ab)$, show that $xyz = x + y + z + 2$.

7 If $x = \log_a (b/c)$, $y = \log_b (c/a)$ and $z = \log_c (a/b)$, prove that $xyz + x + y + z = 0$.

8 Determine the value of k if the coefficient of x^{12} in the binomial expansion of $(1 + kx^3)^{15}$ is known to be $455/27$.

9 Obtain the constant term in the binomial expansion of $[x - (1/x)]^8$.

10 The binomial expansions of $(1 + ax^3)^4$ and $(1 - bx^2)^6$ both have the same coefficient of x^6. Show that $3a^2 + 10b^3 = 0$.

11 Use mathematical induction to prove that, for all $n \in \mathbb{N}$,

    a $1^2 + 2^2 + 3^2 + \ldots + n^2 = n(n+1)(2n+1)/6$

    b $1^3 + 2^3 + 3^3 + \ldots + n^3 = [n(n+1)/2]^2$

FURTHER EXERCISES (for answers see p. 739)

1 Classify the roots of the following equations into complex numbers, real numbers, rational numbers, integers, natural numbers:

    a $u^2 + u - 2 = 0$
    b $u^2 + u + 2 = 0$
    c $u^2 + 2u - 2 = 0$
    d $u^2 - 3u + 2 = 0$
    e $u^2 + 3u + 2 = 0$
    f $2u^2 - 3u + 1 = 0$

2 Show that twice the coefficient of x^3 in $(3x + 2)^5$ is equal to three times the coefficient of x^3 in $(2x + 3)^5$.

3 Solve the equation $e^{2x} + e^x + e^{-2x} + e^{-x} = 3(e^{-2x} + e^x)$.

4 a Simplify

$$\frac{1 - x^4}{(1 - x)(1 + x^2)}$$

    b Use the laws of indices to show that

$$\frac{(25)^{1/2}\,(8)^{1/3}}{(27)^{1/3}\,(16)^{1/4}} = \frac{5}{3}$$

5 Establish that each of the following holds for all a, b and c:
 a $(a + b)(b + c)(c + a) = a(b^2 + c^2) + b(c^2 + a^2) + c(a^2 + b^2) + 2abc$
 b $a^2(b - c) + b^2(c - a) + c^2(a - b) + (a - b)(b - c)(c - a) = 0$

6 Use the fact that $(a - b)^2 \geqslant 0$ for all real numbers a and b to deduce

$$(a^2 + b^2)/2 \geqslant ab$$

so that if x and y are positive,

$$(x + y)/2 \geqslant \sqrt{(xy)}$$

(The arithmetic mean of two numbers is greater than or equal to the geometric mean.)

7 Write down the first four terms in the binomial expansion of
 a $(1 + x)^{10}$
 b $(1 + x)^{-1}$
 c $(1 - x)^{-1/2}$
 d $(1 - 3x)^{-5/3}$
 e $(4 - 7x)^{3/2}$

8 The field strength of a magnet at a point on the x-axis at distance x from the centre is given by

$$H = \frac{M}{2a}\left[\frac{1}{(x - a)^2} - \frac{1}{(x + a)^2}\right]$$

where M is the moment and $2a$ is the length of the magnet. Show that if x is large compared with a then $H \simeq 2M/x^3$.

9 The volume of a spherical raindrop of liquid decreases due to evaporation by one-half in 1 hour. The radius of the drop is given by $r = -kt + r_0$, where r_0 is the initial radius. If k is a constant and t denotes time, show that the time taken for the drop to evaporate completely is $(1 - 2^{-1/3})^{-1}$ hours.

10 The law governing radioactive decay is $p = p_0 e^{-kt}$, where p is the intensity at time t and p_0 is the initial intensity. Show that if $p = p_0/2$ when $t = h$ then the time taken for the initial radioactivity to decay 99% is $2h \log_2 10$.

11 A string is stretched between two points A and B distance l apart. A point P on the string distance d from A is pulled transversely through a small distance x. Show that the increase in the length of the string is approximately $lx^2/2d(1 - d)$.

12 Show that if two resistances are combined in series the total resistance is always greater than if they are combined in parallel.

13 The number n of terminals on a circuit board is known to satisfy the inequality $n^3 - 7n^2 + 5n - 35 < 0$. What is the maximum number?

14 The proportion p of purified oil which can be produced by an oil filter is known to satisfy $2(p^3 + 1) \leqslant (p - 2)^2$. Show that it can purify at most 50% of the oil.

15 The depth x to which a drill applied under constant pressure will sink into rock over time t is given by

$$x = \frac{1}{w} \ln \left(\frac{pvt}{w} + 1 \right)$$

where w, p and v are constants. Show that the time T taken to drill from a depth x to a depth $x + h$ is

$$T = \frac{w}{vp} e^{wx} (e^{wh} - 1)$$

Sets and functions 2

In Chapter 1 we examined algebraic rules which numbers obey. In this chapter we shall discuss some useful mathematical concepts: sets and functions.

After completing this chapter you should be able to
☐ Interpret and use simple set notation;
☐ Recognize open and closed intervals;
☐ Identify functions and use the convention of the maximal domain;
☐ Use standard notation for functions;
☐ Distinguish between an identity and an equation;
☐ Resolve a rational expression into partial fractions.
At the end of this chapter we shall solve a practical problem concerning a gas cylinder.

2.1 SET NOTATION

See sections 1.1 and 1.2 if you have forgotten what these symbols mean.

We have already described in Chapter 1 some standard sets $\mathbb{N}$, $\mathbb{Z}$, $\mathbb{Q}$, $\mathbb{R}$ and $\mathbb{C}$. In fact sets often arise in one form or another, so before we proceed any further we shall outline the set notation that is commonly employed.

A set can be described best by using the notation

$$\{x \mid P(x)\}$$

where $P(x)$ is some statement about x, for example $x \in \mathbb{Q}$. The notation means 'the set of all things x which satisfy the condition $P(x)$'.

Example ☐ $\{x \mid x \in \mathbb{Z}, x > 0\}$
This is the set of all elements x satisfying the two conditions
1 x is an integer;

2 x is strictly positive.

We already have a name for this set – the natural numbers. So

$$\mathbb{N} = \{x \mid x \in \mathbb{Z}, x > 0\} \qquad \blacksquare$$

If modulus signs are in use then to avoid any confusion the vertical line which appears in the notation $\{x \mid P(x)\}$ is usually replaced by a colon, so that we write

$$\{x : P(x)\}$$

Of course small finite sets can usually best be described by displaying their elements. For example $\{1, 2, 3, 4, 5\}$ is the set consisting of the first five natural numbers.

Whenever we are discussing sets there are two special sets which are always present. The first is the set consisting of all the elements we are considering: we call this the **universal set** and represent it by ε. The second is the set with no elements in it at all: we call this the **empty set** and represent it by $\varnothing$. Although these sets may appear trivial, they play an important role in the algebra of sets.

The symbols $\cup$, $\cap$ and $\sim$ are known respectively as the **union**, **intersection** and **complement** symbols. They are in common use and so we must become familiar with their meanings. Suppose A and B are two sets. Then, in notation and in words, the following are the meanings of the three symbols:

1 $A \cup B = \{x \mid x \in A \text{ or } x \in B, \text{ or both}\}$

A union B is the set of all elements which are either elements of A or elements of B or elements of both A and B.

2 $A \cap B = \{x \mid x \in A \text{ and } x \in B\}$

A intersection B is the set of all elements which are both elements of A and elements of B.

3 $\sim A = \{x \mid x \notin A\}$

The complement of A is the set of all elements which are not elements of A.

We shall sometimes write A' instead of $\sim A$ because it is often more convenient to do so. Of course if $x \notin A$, x remains an element of ε ($x \in \varepsilon$).

To get the feel to these definitions, and to infer some of the properties which follow from them, it helps to draw a diagram. Such a diagram is called a **Venn diagram** (Fig. 2.1).

If we consider sets with the operations of $\cup$, $\cap$ and $\sim$, we obtain an algebra known as a **Boolean algebra**. Boolean algebra has applications in the theory of switching circuits, logic and probability. For the moment we are going to confine our attention to the meanings of these symbols so that we are able to handle mathematical problems.

We shall use this notation when we consider probability (see Chapter 24).

Certain minimization techniques in electronic logic use Venn diagrams to simplify complicated logic equations.

George Boole (1815–1864), British mathematician who worked on logic and differential equations.

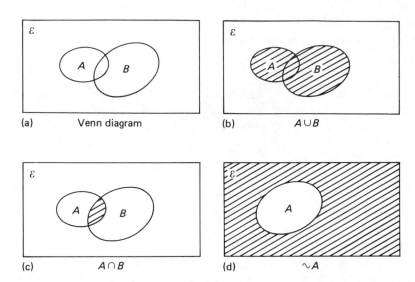

John Venn (1834–
1923), British logician
who used these
diagrams in his
writings.

(a) Venn diagram   **(b)** $A \cup B$

(c) $A \cap B$ **(d)** $\sim A$

Fig. 2.1 (a) Venn diagram (b) $A \cup B$ (c) $A \cap B$ (d) $\sim A$.

Example ☐ $\mathbb{Z} = \mathbb{N} \cup \{0\} \cup \{x \mid -x \in \mathbb{N}\}$
That is, the set of integers is the union of the natural numbers, zero, and
the numbers whose negatives are the natural numbers. ∎

There is one other piece of general set notation which we shall use. The
difference $A \setminus B$ of two sets is defined by

$$A \setminus B = \{x \mid x \in A \text{ and } x \notin B\}$$

The difference $A \setminus B$ is the set of all elements which are elements of A but
not elements of B.

Example ☐ $\mathbb{I} = \mathbb{R} \setminus \mathbb{Q}$ is the set of all real numbers which are not rational numbers;
that is, it is the set of irrational numbers. ∎

2.2 REAL INTERVALS

Suppose we consider

$$\{x \mid x \in \mathbb{R}, -1 \leqslant x \leqslant 1\}$$

This set consists of all those real numbers which lie between and include
-1 and 1. If we think of the real numbers as points on a straight line then
the set corresponds to a small section of that line. We call this set a closed
interval and represent it by $[-1, 1]$.

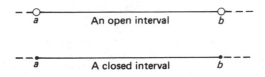

Fig. 2.2 Open and closed intervals.

In general, if a and b are real numbers, $a < b$, we define

$$[a, b] = \{x \mid x \in \mathbb{R}, a \leqslant x \leqslant b\}$$
$$(a, b) = \{x \mid x \in \mathbb{R}, a < x < b\}$$

These are called real intervals. The first one is called the **closed interval** between a and b, while the second is called the **open interval** between a and b (Fig. 2.2).

The important theoretical distinction between a closed interval and an open interval is that a closed interval includes the two end points a and b whereas an open interval does not include either a or b. Therefore

$$[a, b] = (a, b) \cup \{a, b\}$$
$$(a, b) = [a, b] \setminus \{a, b\}$$

Remember:

$$x \in [a, b] \text{ if and only if } x \in \mathbb{R} \text{ and } a \leqslant x \leqslant b$$
$$x \in (a, b) \text{ if and only if } x \in \mathbb{R} \text{ and } a < x < b$$

Note that in Chapter 3 we will introduce the symbol (a, b) as an ordered pair of numbers to represent a *point*, but here we are using it to represent an open *interval*. Surely this is unsatisfactory, what are we going to do about it?

Well, we shall adopt the view that the context should make clear whether (a, b) is an ordered pair of real numbers or an open interval. Some books have introduced the symbol $]a, b[$ to represent an open interval, but this is an ugly and unnecessary way of dealing with the problem. In fact in mathematical work it is quite common to use the same notation in different contexts for different things, and we should be sufficiently broad-minded to be flexible.

Now let's make sure we have the interval idea straight.

2.3 Workshop

Exercise   Represent the following sets as intervals:
a $[1, 2] \cup [2, 3]$

b $(0, 1) \cup \{1\} \cup (1, 3)$

c $[1, 2] \setminus \{1, 2\}$

Have a try at these and see how it goes. Then move to step 2.

2 For **a** we have $[1, 2] \cup [2, 3] = [1, 3]$, a closed interval.

The fact that 2 appears twice on the left but only once on the right need not concern us. Remember that, by definition, $A = B$ if and only if both $A \subset B$ and $B \subset A$.

Everything all right so far? If not then check carefully what you have done for **b** and **c** before you proceed.

3 For **b** we have $(0, 1) \cup \{1\} \cup (1, 3) = (0, 3)$, an open interval. Here, if we imagine the points on a line, we have glued together two open intervals with the missing point 1 to obtain another open interval.

Once more, if there were any problems at all then check again your answer to **c** before moving on.

4 Finally, for **c** we have $[1, 2] \setminus \{1, 2\} = (1, 2)$, an open interval.

Good.

5 Although we shall not always use interval notation, there are many occasions where it is desirable to do so.

2.4 FUNCTIONS

To handle practical problems analytically we need functions.

Mathematics is concerned with relationships between things, and it is through the generality of these relations that applications arise. For instance, there is a relationship between a force applied to the centre of a beam which is freely supported at each end and the deflection at that point. The force of course could arise from many different sources – a heavy weight suspended from it, or a man standing on it.

Equations often relate two or more variables. For example:

$$y = x^2 + 2$$

$$y = x + \frac{1}{x}$$

$$x^2 + y^2 = 1$$

When the relationship between two variables x and y is such that given any x there corresponds at most one y, we say that we have a **function** and write

$y = f(x)$. The set of numbers x for which $f(x)$ is defined is called the **domain** of the function, and each element in the domain is called an **argument** of the function.

A function therefore has two essential ingredients:
1 The domain, the set of arguments of the function, the possible values for x;
2 The rule f which assigns to each element in the domain a unique value $f(x)$.

Strictly there is another essential ingredient: the set consisting of all possible values of the function.

Although, when we specify the rule and the domain, we may not be able to say precisely what the values of the function will be, we are normally able to state some set which includes all the possible values. For example we may know all the values are real numbers. Therefore when we give a formal definition of a function we shall also specify a set which includes all the values of f. This set we shall call the **codomain**.

We write $f : A \rightarrow B$ to indicate that f is a function with domain A and codomain B. Then:
1 If $f : A \rightarrow B$ and $B \subset \mathbb{R}$ then f is said to be a **real-valued function**.
2 If $f : A \rightarrow B$ and both $A \subset \mathbb{R}$ and $B \subset \mathbb{R}$ then f is said to be a **real function**.

In this chapter we shall confine our attention to real functions.

□ $f : \mathbb{R} \rightarrow \mathbb{R}$ defined by $f(x) = x^2 + 2$ $(x \in \mathbb{R})$ **Example**
Here the rule is 'square the number and add 2'. This rule can be applied to all real numbers and there is no ambiguity about the result, so we have a function. ∎

□ $f : \mathbb{N} \rightarrow \mathbb{R}$ defined by $f(x) = x + x^{-1}$ $(x \in \mathbb{N})$ **Example**
Here the rule 'add the number to its reciprocal' can certainly be applied to every natural number, since 0 is not a natural number. The result in each case is a unique real number and consequently we have a function.

On the other hand if we attempted to extend this rule to $\mathbb{Z}$ we should no longer have a function because the number 0 in the domain has not been assigned a value. Indeed the rule could be applied to other sets of real numbers (in fact to any real number except 0), but we specified the domain as $\mathbb{N}$ and if we change the domain we change the function. ∎

THE MAXIMAL DOMAIN

In some cases an equation which defines a function is given but no indication is provided of either the domain or the codomain. Strictly speaking the definition is then deficient. One way round the difficulty is to take the co-domain as $\mathbb{R}$ and the domain to be all those real numbers for which the rule is valid. That is, $f : A \rightarrow \mathbb{R}$ and A is the maximal subset of $\mathbb{R}$ which satisfies the condition

This must not be confused with the argument of a complex number; see section 10.2.

Many people use the convention of the maximal domain without realizing it!

$$\text{if } x \in A \text{ then } f(x) \in \mathbb{R}$$

This convention is sometimes called the **convention of the maximal domain**.

Example □ Using the convention of the maximal domain, the equation $f(x) = x + x^{-1}$ defines a function $f : A \to \mathbb{R}$ where $A = \mathbb{R} \setminus \{0\}$.   ■

GRAPHS OF FUNCTIONS

Given a function $f : A \to B$ we may represent the elements of A as points on a horizontal axis and the elements of B as points on a vertical axis. The axes intersect at a point O called the origin. The case where $A \subset \mathbb{R}$ and $B \subset \mathbb{R}$ provides the usual rectangular cartesian coordinate system with the usual conventions (see Chapter 3). An example is shown in Fig. 2.3.

Graphs are used extensively in applications. We shall see how to draw them in Chapter 3 and section 5.3.

The definition of a function given earlier contains the undefined term 'rule', and one way to avoid this concept is to identify the function with the set of points which constitute its graph.

Before we take things any further we shall try a few steps just to ensure that everything has been understood clearly.

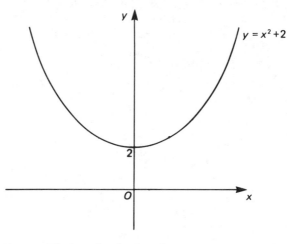

Fig. 2.3 The graph of a function.

2.5 Workshop

1 ▷ **Exercise**   Describe in words the following sets:
  a $\{x \mid x \in \mathbb{N} \text{ or } -x \in \mathbb{N} \text{ or } x = 0\}$
  b $\{x \mid x = p/q, p \in \mathbb{Z}, q \in \mathbb{Z}\}$
  c $\{x \mid \frac{1}{2}x \in \mathbb{N}\}$
  Try **a** and then take step 2.

Set **a** is the set of all things which are either natural numbers, have their 2 negatives equal to natural numbers, or are 0. We have a name for these: they are called the integers.

   If you were correct, try **c** and then move to step 4. If you were incorrect, try **b** and then move to step 3.

Set **b** consists of all things which can be expressed as the quotient of two 3 integers. We have already described this set as $\mathbb{Q}$, the set of rational numbers.

   If you didn't manage that then you should check that you understand the various categories of real number (Chapter 1) and also the use of set notation. You may need to spend some more time on it. If all was well, try **c** and then move ahead.

Set **c** consists of all those numbers which when divided by 2 are natura 4 numbers. We call these the strictly positive even integers.

   Now let's look at functions.

▷**Exercise**   Each of the following purports to be a function $f : A \to \mathbb{R}$ but has one or more deficiencies. Examine each definition carefully and state what is wrong.

a $A = \mathbb{Z}$ and $f(x) = x^{-1}$, $x \in A$
b $A = \{x \mid x \in \mathbb{R}, x > 0\}$ and $f(x) = y$ where $y^2 = 4x$
c $A = \mathbb{R}$ and $f(x) = \sqrt{(1 - x^2)}$

When you have examined all these carefully and made your decisions, move on to step 5 to see if you are correct.

a The difficulty here is 0. For all other integer values $f(x)$ is properly 5 defined and is a real number. However, the presence of 0 in the domain renders the definition faulty.

b From the equation we obtain $y = \pm 2\sqrt{x}$. Since $x > 0$ the values for y are always real numbers, but there is ambiguity: should we take $2\sqrt{x}$ or $-2\sqrt{x}$? This ambiguity is the defect.

c Unless the domain is restricted (and that means of course that it will be changed) we do not always obtain a value in the codomain. Although when $x^2 \leq 1$, $f(x) = \sqrt{(1 - x^2)}$ is uniquely defined, when $x^2 > 1$, $\sqrt{(1 - x^2)}$ is not a real number. The definition is therefore deficient.

In the context of **c**, however, note that $f : [-1, 1] \to \mathbb{R}$ defined by

$$f(x) = \sqrt{(1 - x^2)}, \ x \in [-1, 1]$$

is a well-defined function.

Did you manage all those? If you did, move on to step 7. Otherwise, try this exercise.

▷**Exercise**   Examine the following statements carefully, and say in each case why they do not define a function $f:[-1, 1] \to \mathbb{R}$.
a $f(x) = (x + 1)^{-1}, x \in [-1, 1]$
b $f(x) = y$ where $x^2 + y^2 = 1, x \in [-1, 1]$
c $f(x) = \ln x, x \in [-1, 1]$
Try them carefully before you step ahead.

6

a $f(x)$ is not defined when $x = -1$ and yet -1 is a point in the domain.
b From the equation it follows that $y = \pm \sqrt{(1 - x^2)}$ and, although this is defined for each $x \in [-1, 1]$, the value is not unique.
c $\ln x$ is a real number only when $x > 0$, and consequently $[-1, 1]$ cannot be the domain of this real function.
In the context of **c**, note that $f:[-1, 1] \to \mathbb{R}$ defined by

$$
\begin{aligned}
f(x) &= \ln x &&\text{if } x > 0 \\
f(x) &= \ln(-x) &&\text{if } x < 0 \\
f(x) &= 1 &&\text{if } x = 0
\end{aligned}
$$

is a well-defined function.
Now move on to step 7.

7

Exercise   In each of the following the codomain is $\mathbb{R}$. Use the convention of the maximal domain to determine the domain explicitly.
a $f(x) = [x (x - 1) (x - 2)]^{-1}$
b $f(x) = \sqrt{(x^2 - 1)}$
c $f(x) = \ln(1 + x)$
Furthermore, decide whether every real number is a value of the function. If there are some real numbers which are not values of the function, obtain at least one.
Try this exercise now. Then step ahead.

8

a $f(x)$ is defined for all real numbers except when $x(x - 1)(x - 2) = 0$. Therefore the domain of f is $\mathbb{R} \setminus \{0, 1, 2\}$. The question of possible values of the function is more tricky. However, it is not possible for $f(x)$ to be 0 and this is therefore a missing value.
b $\sqrt{(x^2 - 1)}$ is defined for all $x^2 - 1 \geq 0$, so we require $x^2 \geq 1$. This is true for either $x \geq 1$ or $x \leq -1$. Therefore the domain is $\mathbb{R} \setminus (-1, 1)$. Since $\sqrt{(x^2 - 1)} \geq 0$, it is impossible for the function to have any negative values. So for example $f(x)$ is never -1.
c $\ln(1 + x)$ is defined and real whenever $1 + x > 0$, that is $x > -1$.

Therefore the domain is $\{x \mid x \in \mathbb{R}, x > -1\}$. If $y = \ln(1 + x)$ then $1 + x = e^y$ and so $x = e^y - 1$. This formula assigns a value of x to every value of y. Consequently every number in the codomain is a possible value of the function.

The set of possible values of a function is called its **image set** or **range**. It is often denoted by $f(A)$. Therefore if $f : A \to B$ then

$$f(A) = \{y \mid y = f(x), x \in A\}$$

If you managed to get the exercise all right, proceed to step 10. Otherwise an extra exercise should help to make things clearer.

▷**Exercise** In each of these examples the codomain is $\mathbb{R}$. Using the convention of the maximal domain, obtain the domain of each function.
a $y = f(x) \geqslant 0$ and $x^2 + y^2 = 4$
b $f(x) = e^{-x}$
c $f(x) = (x^2 - 1)^{-1/2}$
In each case determine the image set of the function. When you are ready, move on to see if all is well.

a From the equation $x^2 + y^2 = 4$ we deduce that $y = \pm\sqrt{(4 - x^2)}$. However, we have been given the extra information that $y \geqslant 0$. Consequently $y = \sqrt{(4 - x^2)}$. This is a real number provided $x^2 \leqslant 4$, which means $-2 \leqslant x \leqslant 2$. Therefore the domain is $[-2, 2]$. Now $4 - x^2 \leqslant 4$ and so $y \leqslant 2$, and therefore $0 \leqslant f(x) \leqslant 2$. It follows that only real numbers which are in the closed interval $[0, 2]$ are values of the function: $f(A) = [0, 2]$.
b $f(x) = e^{-x}$ is defined for all $x \in \mathbb{R}$, so the domain of f is $\mathbb{R}$. Moreover $f(x) > 0$ for all $x \in \mathbb{R}$ and so if $y = e^{-x}$ then $x = -\ln y$. Therefore any strictly positive real number is a value of the function:
$$f(A) = \{r \mid r \in \mathbb{R}, r > 0\}.$$
c $f(x) = (x^2 - 1)^{-1/2}$ and this is only defined when $x^2 - 1 > 0$, so that either $x > 1$ or $x < 1$. The domain is therefore $\mathbb{R} \setminus [-1, 1]$. Now if $x^2 - 1$ is very small, $f(x)$ is very large, whereas if $x^2 - 1$ is very large, $f(x)$ is very small but positive. In fact we can easily see that all positive real numbers are values of the function. If $y = (x^2 - 1)^{-1/2}$ then $x^2 - 1 = y^{-2}$ and so $x = \pm\sqrt{(y^{-2} + 1)}$. We therefore obtain two suitable values for x for every positive real number y. However, no negative real number can be a value of the function because $f(x) > 0$, and so the image set is $f(A) = \{r \mid r \in \mathbb{R}, r > 0\}$.
If you managed that faultlessly then you may stride ahead to step 12. For those of us who are mortal there is another problem.

▷**Exercise** Each of the following purports to define a function $f : A \to \mathbb{R}$, where $A \subset \mathbb{R}$ and $y = f(x)$. Using the convention of the maximal domain,

The word 'range' is used in a different way in statistics: see section 23.15.

decide which are well-defined functions. For those that are, obtain the domain A and the image set $f(A)$.

a $x^2 + y^2 + 2xy = 1$

b $y = 1$ when $x \geq 2$

c $y = -1$ when $x < 0$
 $y = 0$ when $x = 0$
 $y = 1$ when $x > 0$

d $x^2 y = 1$

e $y = x^{1/2}$

Do each one in turn and check the result against the corresponding part of step 11.

11

a The equation gives $(x + y)^2 = 1$ and so $x + y = \pm 1$. This gives $y = -x \pm 1$. Given any real number x we see that, although y is meaningful, it is ambiguous and so we do not have a function.

b This is the constant function with domain $A = \{x \mid x \in \mathbb{R}, x \geq 2\}$. The set of values, the image set, is $f(A) = \{1\}$.

c Although no single formula gives y for all x, the condition for a function is satisfied and the domain is $\mathbb{R}$. The set of values is $f(A) = \{-1, 0, 1\}$.

d When $x \neq 0$ we deduce $y = x^{-2}$. Therefore $A = \mathbb{R} \setminus \{0\}$.
 Moreover every positive real number is a value, since if $y > 0$, $x = \pm y^{-1/2}$. Consequently $f(A) = \{r \mid r \in \mathbb{R}, r > 0\}$.

e $y = x^{1/2}$ is defined whenever $x > 0$, and therefore $A = \{r \mid r \in \mathbb{R}, r > 0\}$. The set of possible values is also $f(A) = \{r \mid r \in \mathbb{R}, r > 0\}$. This is a standard set and is sometimes represented by $\mathbb{R}^+$.

Strictly speaking $x = 0$ is excluded; see section 1.5.

---

12 There are one or two standard sets which we can introduce. We define

$$\mathbb{R}^+ = \{r \mid r \in \mathbb{R}, r > 0\}$$
$$\mathbb{R}_0^+ = \{r \mid r \in \mathbb{R}, r \geq 0\}$$
$$\mathbb{R}^- = \{r \mid r \in \mathbb{R}, r < 0\}$$
$$\mathbb{R}_0^- = \{r \mid r \in \mathbb{R}, r \leq 0\}$$

Finally, let us look again at the notation for a function. We have

$$f : A \to B$$

A is the domain, f is the rule, $f(A)$ is the image set and B is the codomain.

In practice it is often useful to write $y = f(x)$ and so to specify a variable y in terms of a variable x. The same function would be determined by using x and t, say, instead of y and x respectively. For this reason y and x are sometimes called **dummy variables**.

When the notation $y = f(x)$ is used it is customary to call x the **independent variable** and y the **dependent variable**. The reasoning behind this is that y is determined once x is known. Sometimes the fact that y is given in terms of x is indicated by writing $y = y(x)$ and saying that 'y is a function of x'. This notation has its uses and consequently its adherents. We shall try to use as much variety of notation as possible so that you will be able to increase your powers of communication.

2.6 IDENTITIES AND EQUATIONS

Often we come across equations of the form

$$f(x) = g(x)$$

There are two different types of such equations. If we look at two examples we shall see what the essential difference is:

1 $\sin x = \cos (\pi/2 - x)$
2 $\sin x = \cos (\pi/2 - 2x)$

Equation 1 is always true. It holds for all x and is known as an **identity**. If we wish to stress this fact we can write $\equiv$ instead of $=$.

On the other hand, equation 2 is not always true. In fact we can deduce from it some other conditions on x:

$$\sin x = \cos (\pi/2 - 2x) = \sin 2x = 2 \sin x \cos x$$

so that $\sin x = 0$ or $\cos x = 1/2$. Although in this case there are infinitely many solutions of the equation, it is not true for *all* x and so is not an identity.

> If you are unfamiliar with trigonometry then consider instead
> **1** $x^2 - x = x(x - 1)$
> **2** $x^2 - x = x(x + 1)$
> We consider trigonometry in detail in Chapter 3.

□ Obtain a and b if   **Example**

$$\frac{x}{x^2 - 4} \equiv \frac{a}{x - 2} + \frac{b}{x + 2}$$

By the convention of the maximal domain we see that the function on the left and the function on the right both have the same domain $\mathbb{R} \setminus \{-2, 2\}$. The expression on the right is

$$\frac{a(x + 2) + b(x - 2)}{(x - 2)(x + 2)} = \frac{a(x + 2) + b(x - 2)}{x^2 - 4}$$

We shall have an identity only if the corresponding numerators are identically equal

$$x \equiv a(x + 2) + b(x - 2)$$

In order to obtain a and b we are now entitled to put in any values of x, including $x = 2$ and $x = -2$. If we do this we deduce $2 = 4a$ and $-2 = -4b$. So $a = 1/2$ and $b = 1/2$. ∎

Identities are useful for putting mathematical expressions into different forms, and we shall often make use of them. Here are three useful algebraic identities involving two variables:

$$x^2 - y^2 = (x - y)(x + y)$$
$$x^3 - y^3 = (x - y)(x^2 + xy + y^2)$$
$$x^3 + y^3 = (x + y)(x^2 - xy + y^2)$$

Finally, we put all this into formal language. Suppose we have two functions $f : A \to \mathbb{R}$ and $g : B \to \mathbb{R}$. Then the equation $f(x) = g(x)$ is an identity if and only if

1 $A = B$;

2 $f(x) = g(x)$ for all $x \in A$.

We then write $f = g$ or $f(x) \equiv g(x)$.

2.7 POLYNOMIALS AND RATIONAL FUNCTIONS

Polynomials are relatively easy to handle. We shall see in Chapter 8 that many functions can be approximated by polynomials.

In general, a **polynomial** is a function f defined by

$$f(x) = a_n x^n + a_{n-1} x^{n-1} + \ldots + a_1 x + a_0$$

where the 'a's, which are known as the **coefficients**, are constants, and $n \in \mathbb{N}$. The expression $f(x)$ is then called a polynomial in x.

Example □ If f is defined by

$$f(x) = x^3 + 4x^2 + x + 1$$

then f is a polynomial and $x^3 + 4x^2 + x + 1$ is the corresponding polynomial in x.   ■

If the leading coefficient a_n is non-zero then the polynomial is said to have **degree** n.

Example □ $x^2 + 1 = 0$ and $2x^5 - x^3 + 1 = 0$ are polynomial equations of degree 2 and 5 respectively.   ■

A function which is the quotient of two polynomials is known as a **rational function**. If the degree of the numerator is n and the degree of the denominator is m then the degree of the rational function is defined to be $n - m$.

Example □ The functions

$$\frac{x^2 + 1}{2x + 3} \quad \text{and} \quad \frac{x^5 - 1}{x^7 + x - 2}$$

are examples of rational functions of degree $2 - 1 = 1$ and $5 - 7 = -2$ respectively.   ■

We may use the same techniques that we use for combining rational numbers to add together rational functions.

☐ Obtain

$$\frac{2x}{x^2 - 1} + \frac{x + 1}{(x - 1)(x - 2)}$$

We have

$$\frac{2x}{(x - 1)(x + 1)} + \frac{x + 1}{(x - 1)(x - 2)} = \frac{2x(x - 2) + (x + 1)^2}{(x - 1)(x + 1)(x - 2)}$$

$$= \frac{2x^2 - 4x + x^2 + 2x + 1}{(x^2 - 1)(x - 2)}$$

$$= \frac{3x^2 - 2x + 1}{x^3 - 2x^2 - x + 2}$$

This is a rational expression of degree −1.   ■

If we reverse this procedure we say we have put the rational expression into partial fractions. We shall now see how to do this.

2.8 PARTIAL FRACTIONS

To resolve a rational function into partial fractions we first ensure that the numerator is of degree less than the denominator. If this is not already the case we must *divide* the denominator into the numerator. For example, take the function

To integrate successfully you will need to be able to resolve partial fractions (see Chapter 15). They are also useful in other areas such as operational methods and the summation of series (Chapter 9).

$$R = \frac{2x^3 - 1}{x^3 + x^2 - x - 1}$$

Here the denominator needs to be divided into the numerator. We can use 'short' division by observing that

$$2x^3 - 1 = 2(x^3 + x^2 - x - 1) - 2x^2 + 2x + 1$$

so that

$$R = \frac{2x^3 - 1}{x^3 + x^2 - x - 1}$$

$$= 2 - \frac{2x^2 - 2x - 1}{x^3 + x^2 - x - 1}$$

Next we *factorize* the denominator as far as possible:

$$x^3 + x^2 - x - 1 = (x - 1)(x^2 + 2x + 1) = (x - 1)(x + 1)^2$$

To each factor of the denominator there corresponds a partial fraction. There are two cases:

1 If the factor is not repeated then the numerator of the partial fraction has degree less than its denominator.

For example, if the factor is $x - 1$ (that is, a polynomial of degree 1) then the corresponding numerator will be a constant, A say (that is, a polynomial of degree 0). Again, if the factor is $x^2 + 1$ (that is, a polynomial of degree 2) then the corresponding numerator will have the form $Ax + B$ (that is, a polynomial of degree 1).

2 If the factor is repeated r times then there correspond r partial fractions, one to each power of the factor.

For example, if the denominator was $(2x^2 + 1)^3$, we should obtain three corresponding partial fractions with denominators $2x^2 + 1$, $(2x^2 + 1)^2$ and $(2x^2 + 1)^3$ respectively. The form of each of the numerators is then identical and is determined by the factor itself; each numerator has degree less than that of the factor. So in this example we should obtain

$$\frac{Ax + B}{2x^2 + 1} + \frac{Cx + D}{(2x^2 + 1)^2} + \frac{Ex + F}{(2x^2 + 1)^3}$$

Finally, the unknown constants are obtained by using the fact that we require an identity.

Example □ Resolve into partial fractions

$$R = \frac{2x^3 - 1}{x^3 + x^2 - x - 1}$$

We have already shown that

$$R = 2 - \frac{2x^2 - 2x - 1}{x^3 + x^2 - x - 1}$$

$$= 2 - \frac{2x^2 - 2x - 1}{(x - 1)(x + 1)^2}$$

$$= 2 - \left[\frac{A}{x - 1} + \frac{B}{x + 1} + \frac{C}{(x + 1)^2} \right]$$

We therefore require

$$\frac{2x^2 - 2x - 1}{(x - 1)(x + 1)^2} \equiv \frac{A}{x - 1} + \frac{B}{x + 1} + \frac{C}{(x + 1)^2}$$

$$= \frac{A(x + 1)^2 + B(x - 1)(x + 1) + C(x - 1)}{(x - 1)(x + 1)^2}$$

So we require

$$2x^2 - 2x - 1 \equiv A(x + 1)^2 + B(x - 1)(x + 1) + C(x - 1)$$

We may either equate coefficients or put in values of x. In any case our aim is to determine A, B and C as easily as possible. Putting $x = 1$ gives $2 - 2 - 1 = 4A$, so $A = -1/4$. Putting $x = -1$ gives $2 + 2 - 1 = -2C$, so $C = -3/2$. Finally, putting $x = 0$ gives $-1 = A - B - C$, so $B = A - C + 1 = -1/4 + 3/2 + 1 = 9/4$.

Consequently

$$R = 2 - \left[\frac{(-1/4)}{x-1} + \frac{(9/4)}{x+1} + \frac{(-3/2)}{(x+1)^2} \right]$$

$$= 2 + \frac{1}{4(x-1)} - \frac{9}{4(x+1)} + \frac{3}{2(x+1)^2} \qquad \blacksquare$$

It is always possible to check your working by recombining the partial fractions. We shall write RHS to denote the right-hand side of an expression and LHS to denote the left-hand side. Then, for the previous example,

$$\text{RHS} = 2 + \frac{(x+1)^2 - 9(x-1)(x+1) + 6(x-1)}{4(x-1)(x+1)^2}$$

$$= 2 + \frac{(x^2 + 2x + 1) - 9(x^2 - 1) + 6(x-1)}{4(x-1)(x+1)^2}$$

$$= \frac{8(x-1)(x+1)^2 - 8x^2 + 8x + 4}{4(x-1)(x+1)^2}$$

$$= \frac{8(x^2-1)(x+1) - 8x^2 + 8x + 4}{4(x-1)(x+1)^2}$$

$$= \frac{8(x^3 - x + x^2 - 1) - 8x^2 + 8x + 4}{4(x-1)(x+1)^2}$$

$$= \frac{8x^3 - 4}{4(x-1)(x+1)^2}$$

$$= \frac{2x^3 - 1}{(x-1)(x+1)^2} = \text{LHS}$$

THE COVER-UP RULE

Although the technique always works, as you can see it can be rather long. A short cut is available for obtaining the partial fractions corresponding to factors which are *linear* (that is, polynomials of degree 1). This method is known as the **cover-up rule** and is simple to apply.

First we ensure, by dividing out if necessary, that the numerator of the rational expression has degree less than that of the denominator. Secondly we factorize the denominator and select the required factor. We cover up this factor and imagine that it has been put equal to zero. This will give a value for (say) x. Then we substitute this value for x in that part of the

We shall use this rule in a practical way in section 9.6.

rational expression which remains uncovered. This produces the required constant.

Example □ Take the rational function

$$R = \frac{2x^2 - 2x - 1}{(x - 1)(x + 1)^2}$$

The denominator is already factorized and is of greater degree than the numerator. Suppose we require the constant numerator corresponding to the factor $x - 1$. We cover up $x - 1$ and imagine it has been put equal to 0, and thus obtain $x = 1$. This is the value of x which we must substitute into the remnant to give the required constant:

$$\frac{2x^2 - 2x - 1}{\diagdown\!\!\!\!(x + 1)^2} \rightarrow \frac{2 \times 1 - 2 - 1}{\diagdown\!\!\!\!(1 + 1)^2} = -\frac{1}{4} \qquad ∎$$

It is interesting to notice that, in the case of a repeated linear factor, the cover-up technique produces the constant numerator corresponding to the denominator of highest degree. In the previous example,

$$\frac{2x^2 - 2x - 1}{(x - 1)\diagdown\!\!\!\!\diagdown} \rightarrow \frac{2(-1)^2 - 2(-1) - 1}{(-1 - 1)\diagdown\!\!\!\!\diagdown} = -\frac{3}{2}$$

The cover-up rule can be quite useful for cutting down the amount of algebra that would otherwise be necessary. Let's summarize the rule.

To obtain the constant numerator corresponding to a distinct linear factor $ax + b$, where a and b are constant:
1 Cover up the factor $ax + b$ in the denominator and imagine that it has been put equal to zero;
2 Substitute the value of x obtained in this way into the rest of the rational expression, and the result is the required constant.
Most students use a finger to cover up the linear factor but any other convenient part of the anatomy will do.

Now for some more steps.

_____ **2.9 Workshop** _____

Exercise Use the cover-up rule to resolve into partial fractions

$$\frac{3x + 1}{x(x - 2)}$$

First find the numerator corresponding to the fraction with denominator x, and then take step 2.

For the numerator corresponding to x we put $x = 0$ into $(3x + 1)/(x - 2)$, $\boxed{2}$ which gives $-1/2$.

Did you manage that all right? If you did then complete the resolution into partial fractions. If you made a mistake then take great care when obtaining the numerator corresponding to $x - 2$, and check algebraically by recombining your answer that it is correct.

As soon as you are ready, take another step.

For the numerator corresponding to $x - 2$ we put $x = 2$ into $(3x + 1)/x$, $\boxed{3}$ which gives $(6 + 1)/2 = 7/2$. Therefore

$$\frac{3x + 1}{x(x - 2)} = -\frac{1}{2x} + \frac{7}{2(x - 2)}$$

If you are still making mistakes, you must read again the section on the cover-up method to make sure you understand how to apply it correctly.

Now go on to this exercise.

▷**Exercise**   Resolve into partial fractions

$$\frac{x^4 + 2x - 3}{x^3 + 2x^2 + x}$$

First divide the denominator into the numerator and then move to step 4 to see if you have the right answer.

$$
\begin{aligned}
x^4 + 2x - 3 &= x(x^3 + 2x^2 + x) - 2x^3 - x^2 + 2x - 3 \qquad \boxed{4}\\
&= x(x^3 + 2x^2 + x) - 2(x^3 + 2x^2 + x) + 3x^2 + 4x - 3\\
&= (x - 2)(x^3 + 2x^2 + x) + 3x^2 + 4x - 3
\end{aligned}
$$

This method of short division is well worth practising.

So we have

$$\frac{x^4 + 2x - 3}{x^3 + 2x^2 + x} = x - 2 + \frac{3x^2 + 4x - 3}{x^3 + 2x^2 + x}$$

and

$$Q = \frac{3x^2 + 4x - 3}{x^3 + 2x^2 + x}$$

remains to be resolved.

Now factorize the denominator D of Q as far as possible and write down the form of the resolution. Then step ahead.

5

$$x^3 + 2x^2 + x = x(x^2 + 2x + 1) = x(x + 1)^2$$

Here the factors of the denominator are x and $x + 1$ (repeated). Therefore we shall obtain partial fractions with denominators x, $x + 1$ and $(x + 1)^2$, and the numerators will all be constant. So

$$Q = \frac{3x^2 + 4x - 3}{x^3 + 2x^2 + x} = \frac{A}{x} + \frac{B}{x + 1} + \frac{C}{(x + 1)^2}$$

Without using the cover-up method, obtain the constants A, B and C. Then go on to step 6.

6

If the partial fractions are recombined, the two numerators must be identically equal. Now

$$\frac{A}{x} + \frac{B}{x + 1} + \frac{C}{(x + 1)^2} = \frac{A(x + 1)^2 + Bx(x + 1) + Cx}{x(x + 1)^2}$$

Therefore we require

$$3x^2 + 4x - 3 \equiv A(x + 1)^2 + Bx(x + 1) + Cx$$

The constants A, B and C can be obtained either by substituting values of x into the identity, or by comparing the coefficients of powers of x on each side of it. In practice a mixture of the methods is usually the quickest.

Here if we put $x = 0$ we obtain $A = -3$. If we put $x = -1$ we obtain $3 - 4 - 3 = -C$, so $C = 4$. If we examine the coefficient of x^2 on each side of the identity we obtain $3 = A + B$, and so $B = 6$. Therefore

$$\frac{x^4 + 2x - 3}{x^3 + 2x^2 + x} = x - 2 - \frac{3}{x} + \frac{6}{x + 1} + \frac{4}{(x + 1)^2}$$

Here now is a problem which shows how the theory of partial fractions can be combined with the binomial theorem to produce an approximate formula.

_____2.10 Practical_____

LEAKING FUEL

The fuel reserve contained in a leaking gas cylinder is known to be given by the following formula:

$$R = 2P\left[\frac{(t + 1)^2 + t^2}{(2 + t)(1 + t^2)}\right]$$

where t represents time and P the initial reserve. Express R in partial fractions, and show that it can be approximated by

$$R \simeq \frac{P}{4}\,[(t + 3)^2 - 5]$$

provided t is small.

Try this first on your own. If you are successful you can then look to see if you have everything correct. If you are unsuccessful then read just enough to get going again and try once more. The full solution follows.

We have

$$R = 2P \left[\frac{2t^2 + 2t + 1}{(2 + t)\,(1 + t^2)} \right]$$

$$= 2P \left[\frac{A}{2 + t} + \frac{Bt + C}{1 + t^2} \right]$$

where A, B and C are constants. So

$$R = 2P \left[\frac{A(1 + t^2) + (2 + t)(Bt + C)}{(2 + t)(1 + t^2)} \right]$$

We obtain the identity

$$2t^2 + 2t + 1 \equiv A(1 + t^2) + (2 + t)(Bt + C)$$

It follows that

$$1 = A + 2C \qquad 2 = A + B \qquad 2 = 2B + C$$

from which $A = 1$, $B = 1$ and $C = 0$. Consequently,

$$R = 2P \left[\frac{1}{2 + t} + \frac{t}{1 + t^2} \right]$$

$$= 2P \left[\frac{1}{2}\left(1 + \frac{t}{2}\right)^{-1} + t(1 + t^2)^{-1} \right]$$

$$\simeq 2P \left[\frac{1}{2}\left(1 - \frac{t}{2} + \frac{t^2}{4}\right) + t \right]$$

Here we have neglected terms in t of degree higher than 2. So

$$R \simeq 2P \left[\frac{1}{2} + \frac{t}{4} + \frac{t^2}{8} + t \right]$$

$$= 2P \left[\frac{1}{2} + \frac{3t}{4} + \frac{t^2}{8} \right]$$

$$= \frac{P}{4} [4 + 6t + t^2]$$

$$= \frac{P}{4} [(t + 3)^2 - 5]$$

SUMMARY

These are the things you should be able to do after completing this chapter:

SETS

☐ Use standard set notation $\{x \mid P(x)\}$, and the notation $[a, b]$ for a closed interval and (a, b) for an open interval;
☐ Use the notation $\cap$, $\cup$ and $\sim$ for the intersection, the union and the complement respectively;
☐ Use other set notation such as $A \setminus B$ and $\mathbb{R}^+$.

FUNCTIONS

☐ Describe what is meant by a function f, its domain A, its codomain B and the image set $f(A)$;
☐ Use the notation $f : A \rightarrow B$ and the convention of the maximal domain;
☐ Recognize a polynomial and be able to state its degree;
☐ Recognize a rational function and be able to state its degree.

IDENTITIES

☐ Explain what is meant by an identity;
☐ Use algebraic methods to resolve rational functions into partial fractions.

EXERCISES (for answers see p. 739)

1 Resolve the following into partial fractions:

a $\dfrac{1}{(x - 1)(x - 3)}$

b $\dfrac{x}{x^2 + 7x + 12}$

c $\dfrac{2x + 1}{x^3 + 5x^2 + 6x}$

d $\dfrac{x - 7}{x^3 - 3x^2 - 9x - 5}$

2 Decide, in each case, which of the following are identities and which are equations. If they are equations then solve them.
 a $(2x + 3)^2 - 2(x + 3)(2x + 3) + (x + 3)^2 = x^2$
 b $\dfrac{x + 3}{x^2 + 3x + 2} - \dfrac{1}{x + 1} + \dfrac{1}{x + 2} = x$
 c $e^{2x} + 2 = 2(2e^x - 1)$
 d $\ln(x - 1) + \ln(x + 1) = \ln(2x)$

3 Express in set notation the domain of each of the following functions:
 a $\dfrac{x}{x - 3}$
 b e^{-x}
 c $(x^2 - 5x + 6)^{-1/2}$
 d $\ln(x - 1)$

4 Express x in terms of a, as simply as possible, in each of the following:
 a $\ln x = 2\ln(a + 1) - \ln(a^2 - 1)$
 b $e^x = \{e^{a+1} \cdot e^{a-1}\}^2$
 c $\ln(x^2 - 1) - \ln(x - 1) = \ln(a^2 - 1) - \ln(a + 1)$
 d $e^x \cdot (e^{-x})^2 = (e^{-a})^3(e^a)^4$

5 If $A = [1, 2]$, $B = [2, 4)$, $C = [3, 5]$ describe in terms of intervals
 a $A \cup B$
 b $A \setminus B$
 c $A \cap B'$
 d $B \cup C$
 e $(A \cup B) \cup C$
 f $(A \cup B) \cap C$

ASSIGNMENT (for answers see p. 739; see also Workshops on pp. 33, 36 and 46)

1 Identify each of the following sets:
 a $\sim\mathbb{R}_0{}^+$
 b $\mathbb{R}_0{}^+ \cap \mathbb{R}_0{}^-$
 c $\mathbb{R}_0{}^+ \cup \mathbb{R}_0{}^-$
 d $\mathbb{R}_0{}^+ \setminus \mathbb{R}_0{}^-$
 e $\mathbb{R}^+ \cap \mathbb{R}^-$
2 Represent each of the following sets using interval notation:
 a $\{x : x \in \mathbb{R}, |x| < 5\}$
 b $\{x : x \in \mathbb{R}, |x - 1| \leqslant 3\}$
 c $\{x : x \in \mathbb{R}, x^2 < 4\}$

d $\{x : x \in \mathbb{R}, x > 1\} \cap \{x : x \in \mathbb{R}, x < 4\}$
e $\{x : x \in \mathbb{R}, |x - 1| \leqslant 3\} \cup \{x : x \in \mathbb{R}, |x - 4| \leqslant 5\}$

3 Use the convention of the maximal domain to write down the domain of the real function f defined by
a $f(x) = (x^2 - 1)^{-1}$
b $f(x) = (x^2 - 1)^{-1/2}$
c $f(x) = (x^2 - 1)^{-1/2} + (1 - x^2)^{-1/2}$

4 Resolve into partial fractions:

a $\dfrac{x^2 + 2x - 1}{x^3 - x}$

b $\dfrac{3x^3 + 5x^2 - x - 1}{x^3 + x^2}$

c $\dfrac{4x^4 + x^3 - 11x^2 + x - 20}{x^4 - 3x^2 - 4}$

FURTHER EXERCISES (for answers see p. 740)

1 Express in partial fractions:

a $\dfrac{x^3 - 5}{(x - 1)^2 (x^2 - 3x + 2)}$

b $\dfrac{(x^2 + 1)^2}{(x^2 - 1)^3}$

2 By first expressing

$$\frac{1}{(n + 1)(n + 2)}$$

in partial fractions show that

$$\sum_{n=1}^{N} \frac{1}{(n + 1)(n + 2)} = \frac{N}{2(N + 2)}$$

3 Verify that

$$(x^2 + x\sqrt{2} + 1)(x^2 - x\sqrt{2} + 1) \equiv x^4 + 1$$

and thereby resolve $1/(x^4 + 1)$ into partial fractions.

4 Decide which of the following are identities and which equations. If they are equations then solve them.
a $(x - 1)^2 + (x - 4)^2 = (x - 2)^2 + (x - 3)^2 + 2^2$
b $\ln(x^4 - 1) = \ln(x - 1) + \ln(x + 1) + \ln(x^2 + 1)$
c $\ln(x + x^2) = \ln x + \ln x^2$

d $\ln (x^2 - 1)^3 = 3[\ln (x - 1) + \ln (x + 1)]$
e $e^{x^2}e^x = (e^x)^3$
f $e^x e^{2x} e^{3x} = (e^x)^6$

5 Show algebraically that the function defined by $y = [x(2 - x)]^{-1}$ when $x \in (0, 2)$ has a minimum value when $x = 1$.

6 If $x \in \mathbb{R}$ and $y = (3x^2 - 6x - 10)/(4x^2 + 8x + 5)$, obtain:
  a the least upper bound and the greatest lower bound;
  b the values of x for which the bounds are attained.

7 By putting $y = x - h$ or otherwise show that, if powers of $(x - y)/x$ higher than degree 2 may be neglected, then

$$\frac{x^2 - y^2}{2xy} \simeq \left(\frac{x - y}{x}\right) + \frac{1}{2}\left(\frac{x - y}{x}\right)^2$$

8 The flow of water through a pipe is given by $G = \sqrt{[(3d)^5 H/L]}$. If d decreases by 1% and H by 2%, use the binomial theorem to estimate the decrease in G.

9 The resonant frequency of a circuit of inductance L and capacitance C with negligible resistance is given by $f = 1/[2\pi\sqrt{(LC)}]$. If L and C increase respectively by 1% and 2%, estimate the percentage error in f.

10 The safe load W that can be carried by a beam of breadth b, depth d and length l is proportional to bd^3/l. Use the binomial theorem to estimate the percentage change in W if for a given beam the breadth is increased by 1%, the depth is decreased by 3% and the length is decreased by 3%.

11 The charge on a leaking capacitor is given by

$$Q = 2Q_0/[(1 + t)(2 + t)]$$

where t is time (seconds) and Q_0 is the initial charge (farads). Express Q in partial fractions, and show that it is approximately $(1 - 3t/2 + 7t^2/4)Q_0$ provided t is small.

12 The output of a system at time t is given by

$$A = 1 - [1 + t^4/(s + 1)]^{-1}$$

where s is the imposed signal and t is time in seconds. If $s = t(1 + t)^2$ at time t, resolve A into partial fractions and show that if terms in t of degree greater than 4 may be neglected then $A \simeq t^4$.

13 The Heaviside unit function H is defined by

$$H(t) = 1 \quad \text{when } t > 0$$
$$= 0 \quad \text{when } t < 0$$

  a Write down the domain and image set of H.
  b Show that if a constant voltage E is applied to a circuit, between time $t = 0$ and $t = 1$ only, then the voltage at time t is given by $E(t) = E[H(t) - H(t - 1)]$.

c Express by means of a single equation, using the Heaviside unit function, the current $i(t)$ in a circuit satisfying

$$
\begin{aligned}
i(t) &= t & \text{when } 0 < t < 1 \\
&= 2 - t & \text{when } 1 < t < 2 \\
&= 0 & \text{otherwise}
\end{aligned}
$$

Trigonometry and geometry 3

In the last two chapters we described some of the basic terminology which we need. We also picked up a few techniques which should prove useful later on. Soon we shall begin to develop the differential calculus, but before we do that we must make sure that we can handle any geometrical or trigonometrical problem that arises.

After working through this chapter you should be able to
☐ Use circular functions, recognize their graphs and be able to determine their domains;
☐ Solve equations involving circular functions;
☐ Recognize the equations of standard geometrical curves;
☐ Transform equations involving polar coordinates into those involving cartesian coordinates.
At the end of this chapter we shall solve practical problems in surveying and in circuits.

This chapter contains background work, and so it is possible that much of it will be familiar to you. If this is the case, then it is best to regard it as revision material. We shall be reviewing work on elementary trigonometry and coordinate geometry. If any section is very well known to you then simply read it through and devote your attention to that which is less familiar.

3.1 COORDINATE SYSTEMS

You are probably quite familiar with the **cartesian coordinate system**. In this system every point in the plane is determined uniquely by an ordered

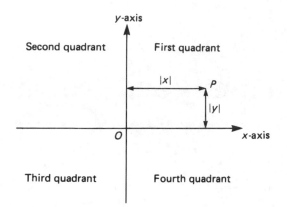

Fig. 3.1 The cartesian system.

pair of numbers (x, y). To do this, two fixed straight lines are laid at right angles to one another; these are called the x-axis and the y-axis. Their point of intersection is represented by O and is called the origin (Fig. 3.1). The quadrants so formed are labelled anticlockwise as the first quadrant, second quadrant, third quadrant and fourth quadrant respectively.

Given any point P, the absolute values of x and y are then obtained from the shortest distance of P to the y-axis and the x-axis respectively. The following conventions then hold:

First quadrant $x \geqslant 0, y \geqslant 0$
Second quadrant $x \leqslant 0, y \geqslant 0$
Third quadrant $x \leqslant 0, y \leqslant 0$
Fourth quadrant $x \geqslant 0, y \leqslant 0$

In this way, given any point in the plane we obtain a unique ordered pair (x, y) of real numbers. Conversely, given any ordered pair (x, y) of real numbers we obtain a unique point in the plane. We therefore identify the point P with the ordered pair (x, y) and refer to the point (x, y).

If P is the point (x, y), x and y are known as the cartesian coordinates of the point P; x is called the abscissa and y is called the ordinate.

This simple idea was initially due to the famous French philosopher Descartes and enabled algebra and geometry, two hitherto separate branches of mathematics, to be united. It is difficult to overestimate the benefits of this unification for science and technology, but Descartes threw it out almost as an afterthought to his philosophical treatise. The name 'cartesian system' comes from the latinized form of Descartes.

René Descartes (1596–1650), influential French philosopher and mathematician.

The cartesian system is not the only system which can be used to represent points in the plane. Another is the **polar coordinate system**.

In the polar coordinate system there is a fixed point O, called the origin,

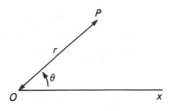

Fig. 3.2 The polar system.

and a fixed line emanating from O called the initial line OX (Fig. 3.2). It is convenient to identify the initial line with the positive x-axis, although this identification is by no means essential. A point P is then determined by r, its distance from O, and by θ, the angle XOP measured anticlockwise. In this way, given any point in the plane we obtain an ordered pair of real numbers (r, θ) where $r \geq 0$. Of course if we increase θ by 2π, a whole revolution, then we shall obtain the same point as before. In order to establish a unique representation we restrict θ so that $0 \leq \theta < 2\pi$.

There is a minor problem when $r = 0$, since we then lose our one-to-one correspondence between points in the plane and ordered pairs of real numbers of the form (r, θ). For example $(0, \pi)$ and $(0, \pi/2)$ both correspond to the origin. One way of avoiding this problem is to insist that if $r = 0$ then the origin will be the unique point $(0, 0)$: $r = 0, \theta = 0$. However, we shall not do this as the procedure creates more difficulties than it resolves. Instead we shall avoid representing the origin and insist that $r > 0$.

In fact the convention $0 \leq \theta < 2\pi$ is only used occasionally in coordinate geometry. Unfortunately we shall adopt a different convention, namely $-\pi < \theta \leq \pi$, when we deal with complex numbers (Chapter 10). The causes for this are historical and not mathematical, and this goes some way towards explaining why they are illogical.

The polar form of a complex number is discussed in section 10.2.

3.2 CIRCULAR FUNCTIONS

It is possible to define the circular functions $\cos \theta$ and $\sin \theta$ for any angle θ by using cartesian coordinate geometry and a circle centred at the origin with radius r. In Fig. 3.3, let X be the point where the circle crosses the positive x-axis, and let the point P on the circle be such that $\angle XOP = \theta$. If P is the point (x, y) then $OP = r > 0$ and

Trigonometrical functions are used in Surveying.

$$\cos \theta = \frac{x}{r} \qquad \sin \theta = \frac{y}{r}$$

It follows immediately that
1 If $0 < \theta < \pi/2$ then $\cos \theta > 0$ and $\sin \theta > 0$;
2 If $\pi/2 < \theta < \pi$ then $\cos \theta < 0$ and $\sin \theta > 0$;

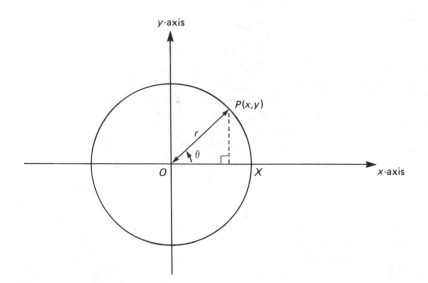

Fig. 3.3 The generating circle.

3 If $\pi < \theta < 3\pi/2$ then $\cos \theta < 0$ and $\sin \theta < 0$;
4 If $3\pi/2 < \theta < 2\pi$ then $\cos \theta > 0$ and $\sin \theta < 0$.

Example □ Use the definition to evaluate $\cos \theta$ and $\sin \theta$ when $\theta \in \{0, \pi/2, \pi, 2\pi\}$.
When

a $\theta = 0$ then $x = r$ and $y = 0$, so that

$$\cos \theta = r/r = 1 \text{ and } \sin \theta = 0/r = 0$$

b $\theta = \pi/2$ then $x = 0$ and $y = r$, so that

$$\cos \theta = 0/r = 0 \text{ and } \sin \theta = r/r = 1$$

c $\theta = \pi$ then $x = -r$ and $y = 0$, so that

$$\cos \theta = -r/r = -1 \text{ and } \sin \theta = 0/r = 0$$

d $\theta = 2\pi$ then P is in the same position as when $\theta = 0$, so that

$$\cos 2\pi = \cos 0 = 1 \text{ and } \sin 2\pi = \sin 0 = 0 \qquad \blacksquare$$

Now $\cos (\theta + 2\pi) = \cos \theta$ and $\sin (\theta + 2\pi) = \sin \theta$, so the circular functions are said to be **periodic functions**. In fact $T = 2\pi$ is the smallest positive
number such that both $\cos (\theta + T) \equiv \cos \theta$ and $\sin (\theta + T) \equiv \sin \theta$. Consequently $T = 2\pi$ is called the **period** of the circular functions. In other
words, if we increase the argument by 2π then the same value is obtained.

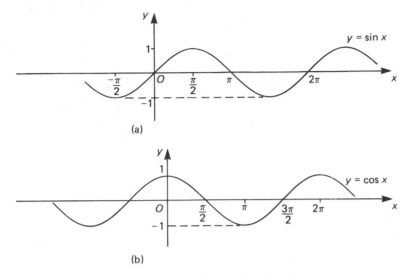

Those who study oscillators will become familiar with those curves. These occur in both electrical and mechanical systems.

Fig. 3.4 (a) The sine function (b) The cosine function.

We can use these general definitions to draw the graphs of the circular functions. In fact once their values are known for arguments in the interval $[0, \pi/2]$ the rest can be deduced by symmetry. You have probably seen the graphs of the sine and cosine functions before (Fig. 3.4).

The other circular functions, known as tangent, cotangent, secant and cosecant, can be defined in terms of cosine and sine. In fact

$$\tan \theta = \frac{\sin \theta}{\cos \theta} \qquad \cot \theta = \frac{\cos \theta}{\sin \theta}$$

$$\sec \theta = \frac{1}{\cos \theta} \qquad \operatorname{cosec} \theta = \frac{1}{\sin \theta}$$

However, whereas cosine and sine have the real numbers $\mathbb{R}$ as their domain, these subsidiary functions are not defined for all real numbers.

□ Obtain the domain of each of these subsidiary circular functions by **Example** using the convention of the maximal domain.

a $\tan \theta$ is defined whenever $\cos \theta \neq 0$. From Fig. 3.4 we see that this is when θ is not an odd multiple of $\pi/2$. Any odd number can be written in the form $2n + 1$ where $n \in \mathbb{Z}$. Therefore the domain of the tangent function is

$$A = \{x \,|\, x \in \mathbb{R}, \, x \neq (2n + 1)\, \pi/2, \, n \in \mathbb{Z}\}$$

b $\cot \theta$ is defined whenever $\sin \theta \neq 0$. So θ must not be a multiple of π. Therefore the domain of the cotangent function is

$$A = \{x \,|\, x \in \mathbb{R}, \, x \neq n\pi \,, \, n \in \mathbb{Z}\}$$

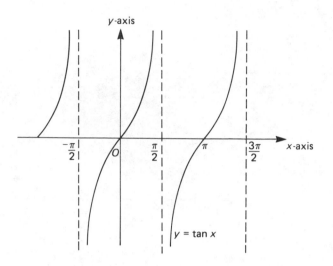

Fig. 3.5 The tangent function.

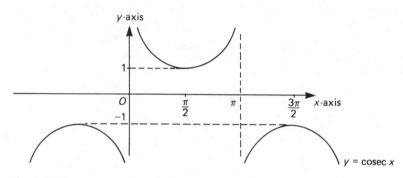

Fig. 3.6 The cosecant function.

The domains of the secant and cosecant are the same as those of the tangent and cotangent respectively. ∎

The graph of $y = \tan x$ shows that the tangent function has period π (Fig. 3.5).

The graph of the sine, cosine and tangent functions can be used to draw the graphs of the cosecant (Fig. 3.6), secant (Fig. 3.7) and cotangent functions. The graph of $y = \sec x$ has the same shape as the graph of $y = \operatorname{cosec} x$. To obtain the graph of $y = \operatorname{cosec} x$ from the graph of $y = \sec x$ we merely need to relocate the y-axis through $x = \pi/2$ and relabel.

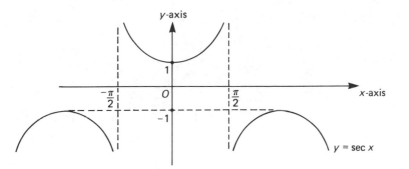

Fig. 3.7 The secant function.

You will remember that we write $\cos^n \theta$ instead of $(\cos \theta)^n$ when n is a natural number. This must not be confused with $\cos (n\theta)$, and you should be alert to the fact that this notation does not hold good when n is a negative integer. In particular,

$$\cos^{-1} \theta \neq (\cos \theta)^{-1}$$

We know that $(\cos \theta)^{-1}$ is $\sec \theta$, and in fact $\cos^{-1} \theta$ has a totally different meaning. Do watch out for this; it is a common mistake!

!

You may well have spent a long time in the past establishing identities between circular functions. We can deduce one well-known identity straight away:

$$\cos^2 \theta + \sin^2 \theta = 1$$

To show this we evaluate the expression on the left:

$$\cos^2 \theta + \sin^2 \theta = \frac{x^2}{r^2} + \frac{y^2}{r^2} = \frac{x^2 + y^2}{r^2} = 1$$

This is an identity; it holds for all θ.

All the remaining identities involving circular functions can be deduced from the expansion formula

$$\sin (A + B) = \sin A \cos B + \cos A \sin B$$

☐ Deduce from the expansion formula for $\sin (A + B)$ the expansion **Example** formulas for **a** $\sin (A - B)$ **b** $\cos (A + B)$.
a We have
$$\sin (A - B) = \sin (A + [-B])$$
$$= \sin A \cos [-B] + \cos A \sin [-B]$$

Now from the definitions (or from the graphs) we have

$$\cos [-B] = \cos B \quad \text{and} \quad \sin [-B] = -\sin B$$

from which we have

$$\sin (A - B) = \sin A \cos B - \cos A \sin B$$

b Putting $A = \pi/2$ enables us to deduce first

$$\sin (\pi/2 - B) = \sin \pi/2 \cos B - \cos \pi/2 \sin B = \cos B$$

Therefore

$$
\begin{aligned}
\cos (A + B) &= \sin (\pi/2 - [A + B]) \\
&= \sin ([\pi/2 - A] - B) \\
&= \sin (\pi/2 - A) \cos B - \cos (\pi/2 - A) \sin B \\
&= \cos A \cos B - \sin [\pi/2 - (\pi/2 - A)] \sin B \\
&= \cos A \cos B - \sin A \sin B
\end{aligned}
$$

Of course all this is rather algebraic and in some ways rather contrived, but the point is that starting with very little we can build up a host of identities. ∎

3.3 TRIGONOMETRICAL IDENTITIES

These identities are used frequently in applications. They can also be useful in mathematical processes such as integration (Chapter 16).

Here is a list of most of the trigonometrical identities that you will have met:

1 $\cos (A + B) = \cos A \cos B - \sin A \sin B$

2 $\cos (A - B) = \cos A \cos B + \sin A \sin B$

3 $\sin (A + B) = \sin A \cos B + \cos A \sin B$

4 $\sin (A - B) = \sin A \cos B - \cos A \sin B$

5 $\tan (A + B) = \dfrac{\tan A + \tan B}{1 - \tan A \tan B}$

6 $\tan (A - B) = \dfrac{\tan A - \tan B}{1 + \tan A \tan B}$

7 $\cos 2\theta = \cos^2 \theta - \sin^2 \theta = 1 - 2 \sin^2 \theta = 2 \cos^2 \theta - 1$

8 $\sin 2\theta = 2 \sin \theta \cos \theta$

9 $\tan 2\theta = \dfrac{2 \tan \theta}{1 - \tan^2 \theta}$

10 $\cos C + \cos D = 2 \cos \dfrac{C + D}{2} \cos \dfrac{C - D}{2}$

11 $\cos C - \cos D = -2 \sin \dfrac{C + D}{2} \sin \dfrac{C - D}{2}$

12 $\sin C + \sin D = 2 \sin \dfrac{C + D}{2} \cos \dfrac{C - D}{2}$

13 $\sin C - \sin D = 2 \cos \dfrac{C + D}{2} \sin \dfrac{C - D}{2}$

14 $1 + \tan^2 \theta = \sec^2 \theta$
15 $1 + \cot^2 \theta = \operatorname{cosec}^2 \theta$

You might like to have a go at deducing these from the identities we already have. If you need any hints then observe that identity 5 can be deduced by dividing 3 by 1. Similarly, 6 can be deduced by dividing 4 by 2. The identities 7, 8 and 9 are obtained from 1, 3 and 5 respectively by putting $A = B = \theta$. It is possible to deduce 10 by the addition of 1 and 3, whereas subtracting these identities results in 11. Similarly 12 and 13 can be deduced from 2 and 4. Lastly the identities 14 and 15 can be obtained by dividing $\cos^2 \theta + \sin^2 \theta = 1$ by $\cos^2 \theta$ and $\sin^2 \theta$ respectively.

3.4 THE FORM $a \cos \theta + b \sin \theta$

You probably already know that it is possible to express $a \cos \theta + b \sin \theta$ in the form $R \cos (\theta - \alpha)$. This is used quite frequently, and so we shall describe briefly how it is done (see Fig. 3.8).

We use this idea in complex numbers (Chapter 10) and differential equations (Chapter 20).

1 We put the point P (a,b) in the plane using cartesian coordinate geometry.
2 The angle α which can be read directly from the diagram is $\angle XOP$.
3 R is the distance OP.
It is easy to see why this works because we have

$$a \cos \theta + b \sin \theta = R[(a/R) \cos \theta + (b/R) \sin \theta]$$
$$= R(\cos \alpha \cos \theta + \sin \alpha \sin \theta]$$
$$= R \cos (\theta - \alpha)$$

☐ Express $\sin \theta - \cos \theta$ in the form $R \cos (\theta - \alpha)$.   **Example**
  We begin by expressing $\sin \theta - \cos \theta$ in the form $a \cos \theta + b \sin \theta$.
$\sin \theta - \cos \theta = -\cos \theta + \sin \theta$, and so $a = -1$ and $b = 1$. Putting the

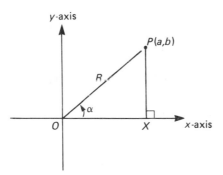

Fig. 3.8 Triangle relating a, b, R and α.

point $(-1, 1)$ on Fig. 3.8 shows that $R = \sqrt{2}$ and $\alpha = 3\pi/4$. Consequently

$$\sin \theta - \cos \theta = \sqrt{2} \cos (\theta - 3\pi/4) \qquad \blacksquare$$

3.5 SOLUTIONS OF EQUATIONS

We shall consider numerical methods of solving equations in Chapter 18.

To solve the equation $\sin \theta = \sin \alpha$, where α is constant, we need a formula which will express θ in terms of α. Of course $\theta = \alpha$ is one solution but in fact there are many others. The graph of $y = \sin x$ enables us to determine this formula (Fig. 3.9).

As we observed, $\theta = \alpha$ is one solution of the equation, and since the sine function has period 2π we can deduce that $\theta = 2\pi + \alpha$ is also a solution. Generalizing, we deduce that $\theta = 2k\pi + \alpha$ is a solution, where k is any integer. This provides a whole set of solutions.

However, we have not finished because the symmetry of the sine function gives another solution, $\theta = \pi - \alpha$. Moreover we can add any integer multiple of 2π to this and always obtain another solution. So $\theta = 3\pi - \alpha$ is a solution, and in general $\theta = (2k + 1)\pi - \alpha$ is a solution, where k is any integer. This provides a second set of solutions. If we glance at the graph we can see how all these solutions arise and also that there are no more.

We can write the general solution in the form

$$\theta = n\pi + (-1)^n \alpha$$

where n is any integer. We see that when n is even we obtain the first set of solutions, whereas if n is odd we obtain the second set.

Similar arguments can be used to show that:

1 If $\cos \theta = \cos \alpha$, where α is a constant, then $\theta = 2n\pi \pm \alpha$, where n is any integer.

2 If $\tan \theta = \tan \alpha$, where α is a constant, then $\theta = n\pi + \alpha$, where n is any integer.

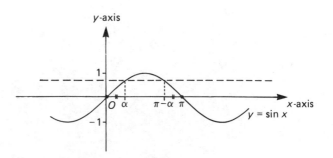

Fig. 3.9 Solutions of $\sin \theta = \sin \alpha$.

□ Obtain all the solutions of the equation sin $2x = \cos x$ in the interval **Example**
$[0, 2\pi]$.

We have $2 \sin x \cos x = \cos x$, so $\cos x = 0$ or $2 \sin x = 1$. Remember to
allow for the case $\cos x = 0$. If you don't you will lose some solutions and
this may be very important.

Now $\cos \pi/2 = 0$ and $\sin \pi/6 = 1/2$, so we have reduced the equation to
two cases: $\cos x = \cos \pi/2$, and $\sin x = \sin \pi/6$.

1 If $\cos x = \cos \pi/2$ then $x = 2n\pi \pm \pi/2$. Now we must pick out those
solutions in the required interval:

$$n = 0 \quad \Rightarrow x = \pm\pi/2, \ \pi/2 \text{ is in range}$$
$$n = 1 \quad \Rightarrow x = 2\pi \pm \pi/2, \ 3\pi/2 \text{ is in range}$$
$$n = -1 \Rightarrow x = -2\pi \pm \pi/2, \text{ out of range}$$

Clearly other integer values for n will be out of range.

2 If $\sin x = \sin \pi/6$ then $x = n\pi + (-1)^n (\pi/6)$. Again we pick out those
solutions which are in range:

$$n = 0 \quad \Rightarrow x = \pi/6, \text{ which is in range}$$
$$n = 1 \quad \Rightarrow x = \pi - \pi/6 = 5\pi/6, \text{ which is in range}$$
$$n = 2 \quad \Rightarrow x = 2\pi + \pi/6, \text{ out of range}$$
$$n = -1 \Rightarrow x = -\pi + \pi/6, \text{ out of range}$$

All other integer values for n will be out of range.
Finally we state the set of solutions in the interval $[0, 2\pi]$:

$$\{\pi/2, \ 3\pi/2, \ \pi/6, \ 5\pi/6\} \qquad \blacksquare$$

Have you met the symbol $\Rightarrow$ before? It is the one-way implication symbol;
it means 'implies'. It is quite useful; you sometimes see it on traffic signs!

Now it's time for you to solve some problems. If you are unsure of the
material, this is a good time to revise it. When you are ready, step ahead.

_____ 3.6 Workshop _____

▷**Exercise**   Solve the equation

$$\cos 2x = 3 \cos x - 2$$

to obtain all solutions in the interval $[-\pi, \pi]$.

You need to remember your trigonometrical identities. There is a lot to
be said for knowing them inside out.

If we use $\cos 2x = 2 \cos^2 x - 1$ we reduce the equations to a quadratic
equation in $\cos x$:

$$2 \cos^2 x - 1 = 3 \cos x - 2$$

so that

$$2 \cos^2 x - 3 \cos x + 1 = 0$$

Now this factorizes to give

$$(2 \cos x - 1)(\cos x - 1) = 0$$

from which either $\cos x = 1/2$ or $\cos x = 1$. However, $\cos \pi/3 = 1/2$ and $\cos 0 = 1$. So we can use the general solution of the equation $\cos \theta = \cos \alpha$, that is $\theta = 2n\pi \pm \alpha$, to obtain the general solution of this equation in the two cases:

1 $\cos x = \cos \pi/3 \Rightarrow x = 2n\pi \pm \pi/3$ where $n \in \mathbb{Z}$. We have to select those values of n which give solutions in the interval $[-\pi, \pi]$. We shall consider the positive and negative signs separately. If $x = 2n\pi + \pi/3$ then

$$\begin{aligned} n = -1 &\Rightarrow x = -5\pi/3, \text{ out of range} \\ n = 0 \ &\Rightarrow x = \pi/3, \text{ in range} \\ n = 1 \ &\Rightarrow x = 7\pi/3, \text{ out of range} \end{aligned}$$

If $x = 2n\pi - \pi/3$ then

$$\begin{aligned} n = -1 &\Rightarrow x = -7\pi/3, \text{ out of range} \\ n = 0 \ &\Rightarrow x = -\pi/3, \text{ in range} \\ n = 1 \ &\Rightarrow x = 5\pi/3, \text{ out of range} \end{aligned}$$

2 $\cos x = \cos 0 \Rightarrow x = 2n\pi$, and so $x = 0$ is the only solution in range. Therefore the solution set is $\{-\pi/3, 0, \pi/3\}$.

If you managed that, then go on to the next exercise.

▷**Exercise**   Obtain the general solution of the equation

$$\sin 2\theta = 2 \cos \theta + \sin \theta - 1$$

Try this one carefully. Don't forget those identities. Then step ahead.

We use $\sin 2\theta = 2 \sin \theta \cos \theta$ to obtain

$$\begin{aligned} 2 \sin \theta \cos \theta &= 2 \cos \theta + \sin \theta - 1 \\ 2 \sin \theta \cos \theta - 2 \cos \theta - \sin \theta + 1 &= 0 \end{aligned}$$

and this factorizes to give

$$(\sin \theta - 1)(2 \cos \theta - 1) = 0$$

from which $\sin \theta = 1$ or $\cos \theta = 1/2$. There are therefore two sets of solutions:

1 $\sin \theta = \sin \pi/2 \Rightarrow \theta = n\pi + (-1)^n \pi/2$, where $n \in \mathbb{Z}$;
2 $\cos \theta = \cos \pi/3 \Rightarrow \theta = 2n\pi \pm \pi/3$, where $n \in \mathbb{Z}$.

3.7 COORDINATE GEOMETRY

Coordinate geometry is an algebraic description of geometry. It is essential for us to be able to recognize certain geometrical objects when they are expressed in algebraic form. Straight lines, circles and other curves can be represented by equations and we shall study the simplest of these.

We begin by obtaining the coordinates of a point midway between two others.

☐ If P_1 and P_2 are the points (x_1, y_1) and (x_2, y_2) respectively, obtain the **Example** cartesian coordinates of the point M, the midpoint of P_1P_2 (Fig. 3.10).

Let M be the point (x, y). Then, using parallels,

$$x - x_1 = x_2 - x$$
$$y - y_1 = y_2 - y$$

So

$$x = \frac{x_1 + x_2}{2}, \qquad y = \frac{y_1 + y_2}{2}$$ ■

For example, the midpoints of the sides of the triangle with vertices $(2, 6)$, $(4, 0)$ and $(-6, 6)$ are given by

$$(\tfrac{1}{2}[2 + 4], \tfrac{1}{2}[6 + 0]) = (3, 3)$$
$$(\tfrac{1}{2}[2 - 6], \tfrac{1}{2}[6 + 6]) = (-2, 6)$$
$$(\tfrac{1}{2}[4 - 6], \tfrac{1}{2}[0 + 6]) = (-1, 3)$$

LOCUS PROBLEMS

We shall use the methods of coordinate geometry to obtain the equations of several curves. To do this we consider a general point $P(x, y)$ on the

Coordinate geometry is used extensively in applications.

Locus problems also arise in the theory of complex numbers, and we shall encounter them in section 10.3.

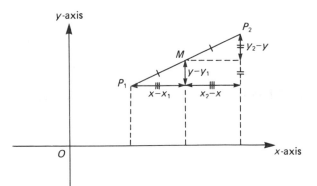

Fig. 3.10 The midpoint M of the line P_1P_2.

curve and obtain an equation relating x and y such that
1 If P is on the curve the equation holds;
2 If the equation holds then P is on the curve.
An equation which satisfies this condition is often called the **locus** of the point P; the Latin word *locus* means 'place'.

CHANGE OF AXES

When we identify a point P with an ordered pair of real numbers we must appreciate that this is relative to the cartesian coordinate system we have chosen. The same curve can have a very different equation if the axes are transformed in some way.

A **translation** is a change of axes in such a way that the new x-axis and the new y-axis are respectively parallel to the old ones. A **rotation** is a change of axes in which the origin remains fixed and axes rotate anti-clockwise through some angle θ.

Any movement of axes in the plane can be regarded as a translation followed by a rotation. We shall therefore consider the effects of these two transformations.

TRANSLATION

Suppose new axes X and Y are chosen which are parallel to the x and y axes. Suppose also the new origin O' is the point (h, k) relative to the system Oxy (see Fig. 3.11).

Then if P is a general point we may suppose that P is the point (x, y) relative to Oxy and (X, Y) relative to $O'XY$. We obtain

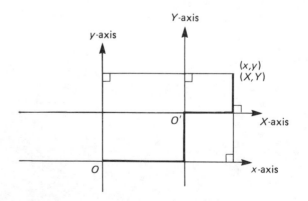

Fig. 3.11 A translation.

This is the change of coordinates corresponding to a translation of the origin to the point (h, k).

☐ If the origin is translated to the point $(1, 3)$, obtain the corresponding **Example** equation for the curve $x^2 + xy = y^2$.

Denoting the new axes by X and Y we have

$$x = X + 1, \qquad y = Y + 3$$

so that

$$(X + 1)^2 + (X + 1)(Y + 3) = (Y + 3)^2$$
$$X^2 + 2X + 1 + XY + Y + 3X + 3 = Y^2 + 6Y + 9$$
$$X^2 - Y^2 + XY + 5X - 5Y = 5$$

We may now drop the X and Y in favour of the usual x and y since we have done with the old coordinate system for good. Therefore the new equation is

$$x^2 - y^2 + xy + 5x - 5y = 5 \qquad\blacksquare$$

ROTATION

Suppose the axes Oxy are rotated anticlockwise through θ to produce OXY and that P is a general point. Let $OP = r$ and suppose that $\angle XOP = \alpha$ (Fig. 3.12).

Relative to OXY, P is the point $(r \cos \alpha, r \sin \alpha)$, whereas relative to Oxy, P is the point $(r \cos [\theta + \alpha], r \sin [\theta + \alpha])$. Therefore

$$X = r \cos \alpha, \qquad Y = r \sin \alpha$$
$$x = r \cos (\theta + \alpha), \qquad y = r \sin (\theta + \alpha)$$

So

$$x = r(\cos \theta \cos \alpha - \sin \theta \sin \alpha)$$
$$= X \cos \theta - Y \sin \theta$$

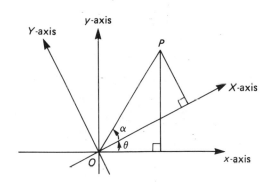

Fig. 3.12 A rotation.

$$y = r(\sin \theta \cos \alpha + \cos \theta \sin \alpha)$$
$$= X \sin \theta + Y \cos \theta$$

We therefore have the change of coordinates

$$x = X \cos \theta - Y \sin \theta$$
$$y = X \sin \theta + Y \cos \theta$$

for an anticlockwise rotation of the axes through an angle θ.

Example □ Obtain the equation of the curve $4x^2 + 6y^2 = 25$ if the axes are rotated anticlockwise through $\pi/4$.

Here $\theta = \pi/4$ and so the change of coordinates is

$$x = X(1/\sqrt{2}) - Y(1/\sqrt{2}) = (X - Y)/\sqrt{2}$$
$$y = X(1/\sqrt{2}) + Y(1/\sqrt{2}) = (X + Y)/\sqrt{2}$$

Substituting into the equation gives

$$2(X - Y)^2 + 3(X + Y)^2 = 25$$
$$2(X^2 - 2XY + Y^2) + 3(X^2 + 2XY + Y^2) = 25$$
$$5X^2 + 2XY + 5Y^2 = 25$$

So that reverting to x and y we have finally

$$5x^2 + 2xy + 5y^2 = 25 \qquad ∎$$

3.8 THE STRAIGHT LINE

A straight line can be fixed in the plane in several ways. First, we can specify a point $P_1 (x_1, y_1)$ on the straight line and also the slope m of the line. If $P (x, y)$ is a general point on the line, we have

$$m = \tan \theta = \text{slope } PP_1 = \frac{PM}{P_1M} = \frac{y - y_1}{x - x_1}$$

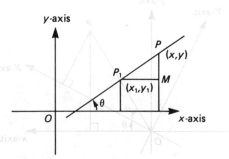

Fig. 3.13 Straight line; fixed slope through fixed point.

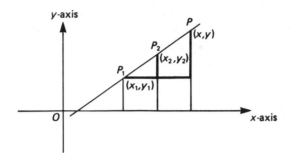

Fig. 3.14 Straight line; two fixed points.

Therefore

$$y - y_1 = m(x - x_1)$$

A second way of fixing a straight line is to specify two points $P_1 (x_1, y_1)$ and $P_2 (x_2, y_2)$ on the line (Fig. 3.14). Then if $P (x, y)$ is a general point on the line we have

$$\text{slope } PP_1 = \text{slope } P_2P_1$$

$$\frac{y - y_1}{x - x_1} = \frac{y_2 - y_1}{x_2 - x_1}$$

or

$$\frac{y - y_1}{y_2 - y_1} = \frac{x - x_1}{x_2 - x_1}$$

It is interesting to note that there are several other equivalent forms for this equation, and these can be obtained by equating the slopes of any two distinct pairs of points chosen from P_1, P_2 and P.

□ Putting slope PP_1 = slope PP_2 yields the equation **Example**

$$\frac{y - y_1}{y - y_2} = \frac{x - x_1}{x - x_2}$$

Show that this equation can be rewritten in the form

$$\frac{y - y_1}{y_2 - y_1} = \frac{x - x_1}{x_2 - x_1}$$

We have

$$(x - x_2)(y - y_1) = (x - x_1)(y - y_2)$$

So

$$xy - x_2 y - xy_1 + x_2 y_1 = xy - xy_2 - x_1 y + x_1 y_2$$

$$-x_2y - xy_1 + x_2y_1 = -xy_2 - x_1y + x_1y_2$$
$$x(y_2 - y_1) - x_1y_2 + x_1y_1 = y(x_2 - x_1) - y_1x_2 + y_1x_1$$
$$(x - x_1)(y_2 - y_1) = (y - y_1)(x_2 - x_1)$$

Therefore

$$\frac{y - y_1}{y_2 - y_1} = \frac{x - x_1}{x_2 - x_1}$$

as required. ∎

Example □ Obtain the equation of the straight line joining the points $(-3, 7)$ to $(5, 1)$.

We may use the formula

$$\frac{y - y_1}{y_2 - y_1} = \frac{x - x_1}{x_2 - x_1}$$

where $(x_1, y_1) = (-3, 7)$ and $(x_2, y_2) = (5, 1)$. So

$$\frac{y - 7}{1 - 7} = \frac{x - (-3)}{5 - (-3)}$$
$$\frac{y - 7}{-6} = \frac{x + 3}{8}$$
$$8(y - 7) = -6(x + 3)$$
$$8y + 6x = 56 - 18$$
$$4y + 3x = 19$$

This is the required equation. ∎

EQUATION OF A STRAIGHT LINE

Any equation of the form $ax + by = c$, where a, b and c are real constants, represents the equation of a straight line. Conversely, any straight line has an equation of the form $ax + by = c$ for some real constants a, b and c.

There are two other forms of the equation of a straight line which are often useful. One is for the straight line with slope m which has an intercept c on the y-axis. In other words, this is the line through $(0, c)$ with slope m:

$$y - c = m(x - 0)$$

Therefore

$$y = mx + c$$

This is the most commonly used equation of a straight line.

Another form is for the straight line which has intercepts a and b on the x-axis and y-axis respectively. In other words, we are looking for the straight line which passes through the points $(a, 0)$ and $(0, b)$ (Fig. 3.15). Therefore

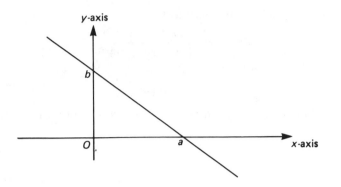

Fig. 3.15 Straight line; fixed intercepts.

$$\frac{y - b}{0 - b} = \frac{x - 0}{a - 0}$$

$$-\frac{y}{b} + 1 = \frac{x}{a}$$

So

$$\frac{x}{a} + \frac{y}{b} = 1$$

ANGLE BETWEEN TWO STRAIGHT LINES

Suppose we have two straight lines with slopes m_1 and m_2 respectively (Fig. 3.16). Then if $m_1 = \tan \theta_1$ and $m_2 = \tan \theta_2$ the angle θ between the lines is given by $\theta = \theta_1 - \theta_2$. So

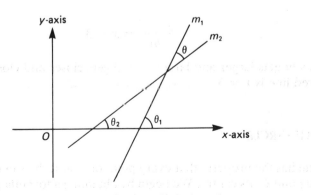

Fig. 3.16 Angle between two straight lines.

$$\tan \theta = \tan (\theta_1 - \theta_2)$$

$$= \frac{\tan \theta_1 - \tan \theta_2}{1 + \tan \theta_1 \tan \theta_2}$$

$$= \frac{m_1 - m_2}{1 + m_1 m_2}$$

This is valid provided $1 + m_1 m_2 \neq 0$. If $m_1 = m_2$ then $\tan \theta = 0$ as the straight lines are parallel.

Also

$$\cot \theta = \cot (\theta_1 - \theta_2)$$

$$= \frac{\cot \theta_1 \cot \theta_2 + 1}{\cot \theta_1 - \cot \theta_2}$$

$$= \frac{(1/m_1)(1/m_2) + 1}{(1/m_1) - (1/m_2)}$$

$$= \frac{1 + m_1 m_2}{m_2 - m_1}$$

If the lines are mutually perpendicular then $\theta = \pi/2$, so $\cot \theta = 0$ and therefore $m_1 m_2 = -1$.

One small point needs to be made. We have been considering straight lines with slope m. What happens if the line is parallel to the y-axis? We know that $\tan \theta$ is not defined when $\theta = \pi/2$, so what do we do? We divide through by m and note that, as θ approaches $\pi/2$, $1/m = \cot \theta$ approaches 0.

Example $\square$ Obtain the equation of the straight line parallel to the y-axis through the point (3, 7).

The equation of a straight line with slope m through the point (3, 7) is

$$x - 7 = m(x - 3)$$

So

$$\frac{y - 7}{m} = x - 3$$

Now as m gets larger and larger, $x - 3$ gets closer and closer to 0. So the required line is $x = 3$. $\blacksquare$

3.9 THE CIRCLE

A circle has the property that every point on it is at the same distance from a fixed point C, its centre. We begin by obtaining a formula for the distance between two points P and Q (Fig. 3.17).

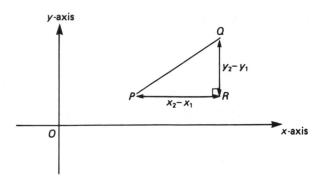

Fig. 3.17 Two points P and Q.

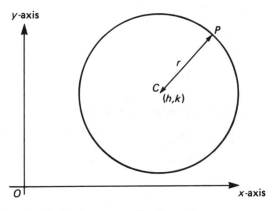

Fig. 3.18 Circle; centre (h, k), radius r.

Suppose P is (x_1, y_1) and Q is (x_2, y_2). Then

$$PQ^2 = PR^2 + RQ^2$$
$$= (x_2 - x_1)^2 + (y_2 - y_1)^2$$

So

$$PQ = \sqrt{[(x_2 - x_1)^2 + (y_2 - y_1)^2]}$$

Although we have shown this only in the case where P and Q are as on the diagram, the formula is valid wherever P and Q are positioned.

Suppose now we have a circle radius r with its centre at the point (h, k) (Fig. 3.18). Then if $P(x, y)$ is a general point on the circle, we have $PC^2 = r^2$. So

$$(x - h)^2 + (y - k)^2 = r^2$$

Conversely, any point (x, y) which satisfies this equation lies on the circle.

Here we are using
Pythagoras' theorem.
Pythagoras (c. 570–500 BC): Greek religious philosopher known principally for this theorem.

If we expand this equation we obtain

$$x^2 - 2hx + h^2 + y^2 - 2ky + k^2 = r^2$$

So

$$x^2 + y^2 - 2hx - 2ky + h^2 + k^2 - r^2 = 0$$

We can use this to obtain criteria for an equation to be the equation of a circle:

1 The equation must be of degree 2 in the two variables x and y;
2 The coefficient of x^2 must equal the coefficient of y^2;
3 There must be no xy term.

Such an equation is traditionally written in the form

$$x^2 + y^2 + 2gx + 2fy + c = 0$$

so that completing the square we obtain

$$(x + g)^2 + (y + f)^2 = g^2 + f^2 - c$$

Therefore provided $g^2 + f^2 - c > 0$ we have a circle. The circle has centre $(-g, -f)$ and radius $\sqrt{(g^2 + f^2 - c)}$.

The equation of the circle in general form is used in materials and structures and structural mechanics (Mohrs circle).

Example □ **a** Obtain the centre and radius of the circle

$$x^2 + y^2 - 4x + 6y + 8 = 0$$

b Obtain the equation of the circle with centre $(-1, 5)$ and radius 7 in the standard form

$$x^2 + y^2 + 2gx + 2fy + c = 0$$

The procedures are as follows:

a If we compare the given equation with the standard equation of the circle

$$x^2 + y^2 + 2gx + 2fy + c = 0$$

We have $g = -2$, $f = 3$ and $c = 8$. So the centre is the point $(2, -3)$ and the radius is

$$\sqrt{(g^2 + f^2 - c)} = \sqrt{(4 + 9 - 8)} = \sqrt{5}$$

b The equation of the circle is

$$(x - h)^2 + (y - k)^2 = r^2$$

where (h, k) is the centre and r is the radius. Here $h = -1$, $k = 5$ and $r = 7$, so that

$$(x + 1)^2 + (y - 5)^2 = 49$$
$$x^2 + 2x + 1 + y^2 - 10y + 25 = 49$$
$$x^2 + y^2 + 2x - 10y - 23 = 0 \quad \blacksquare$$

PARAMETRIC FORM

Another way of representing a curve is to express each of the two variables x and y in terms of some third variable θ which is known as a **parameter**. This is done in such a way that
1 Every value of θ corresponds to a unique point on the curve; and
2 Every point on the curve corresponds to a unique value of θ.
We can therefore talk about the point θ.

  If we were to eliminate θ we should obtain the cartesian equation of the curve.

☐ For the circle $x^2 + y^2 = a^2$ we have a parametric form $x = a\cos\theta$, **Example** $y = a\sin\theta$. ■

3.10 THE CONIC SECTIONS

If we take a right circular cone and cut it through in various positions we obtain standard curves known as the parabola, the ellipse and the hyperbola. Each of these curves can be defined as a locus in much the same way as we defined the circle as a locus.

  We consider a fixed straight line called the **directrix** and a fixed point S called the **focus** (Fig. 3.19). If P is a general point, suppose L is a point on the directrix such that the line PL and the directrix are perpendicular to one another. If the ratio PS/PL is a constant then the locus of P is one of the conic sections. The ratio $e = PS/PL$ is known as the **eccentricity**. We consider the three cases $e = 1$, $e < 1$ and $e > 1$.

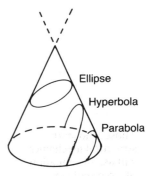

Ellipse

Hyperbola

Parabola

THE PARABOLA ($e = 1$)

Suppose we choose the x-axis to be the line through the focus S perpendicular to the directrix, and the origin to be the point on the x-axis midway between the focus and the directrix (Fig. 3.20). If S is the point $(a, 0)$ then

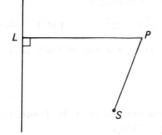

Fig. 3.19 Directrix and focus.

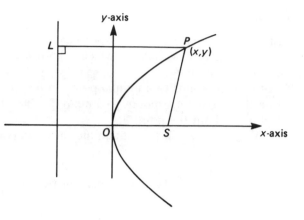

Fig. 3.20 The parabola.

the directrix has the equation $x = -a$. Now if P is a general point on the parabola we have

$$PS = \sqrt{[(x - a)^2 + y^2]}$$
$$PL = x + a$$

However, $PS = PL$ and so we have

$$(x - a)^2 + y^2 = (x + a)^2$$

Therefore we obtain the standard cartesian form for the parabola as

$$y^2 = (x + a)^2 - (x - a)^2 = 4ax$$

Those who study structural mechanics will use the equation of a parabola to represent suspension bridges. Surveyors also use the parabola for vertical curves. Mechanical engineers will learn that the velocity profile of a liquid flowing in a horizontal tube under certain conditions is parabolic.

Example ☐ Obtain the equation of the directrix and the position of the focus for the parabola $y^2 = 16x$.

We compare with the standard equation $y^2 = 4ax$ and obtain $a = 4$. Consequently the focus S is the point $(4, 0)$ and the equation of the directrix is $x + 4 = 0$.   ■

The usual parametric form of the parabola $y^2 = 4ax$ is $x = at^2$ and $y = 2at$. Clearly if we eliminate t we obtain

$$y^2 = 4a^2t^2 = 4a(at^2) = 4ax$$

So a general point t on the parabola is $(at^2, 2at)$.

THE ELLIPSE ($e < 1$)

It is convenient to choose our focus to be $(-ae, 0)$ and the directrix as the line $x = -a/e$ (Fig. 3.21). Then

$$PS^2 = (x + ae)^2 + y^2$$
$$PL^2 = (x + a/e)^2$$

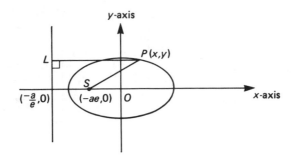

Fig. 3.21 The ellipse.

Now $PS/PL = e$, so that

$$(x + ae)^2 + y^2 = e^2(x + a/e)^2 = (ex + a)^2$$

Therefore

$$(x + ae)^2 - (ex + a)^2 + y^2 = 0$$
$$x^2(1 - e^2) - a^2(1 - e^2) + y^2 = 0$$
$$\frac{x^2}{a^2} + \frac{y^2}{a^2(1 - e^2)} = 1$$

Now $e < 1$, and so we may put $b^2 = a^2(1 - e^2)$ to obtain the standard cartesian form for the ellipse as

$$\frac{x^2}{a^2} + \frac{y^2}{b^2} = 1$$

The axes of symmetry are known as the major axis and the minor axis. The major axis has length $2a$ and the minor axis has length $2b$.

The symmetry of this curve suggests that it must be possible to define it in terms of another focus and another directrix. In fact the point $(ae, 0)$ provides a second focus, and the line $x = a/e$ the corresponding directrix. From Fig. 3.22

$$\frac{PS_1}{PL_1} = e = \frac{PS_2}{PL_2}$$

so that

$$PS_1 + PS_2 = ePL_1 + ePL_2$$
$$= e(PL_1 + PL_2) = eL_1L_2$$
$$= e(2a/e) = 2a$$

This says that at any point on the ellipse the sum of the distances to the foci is constant and equal to the length of the major axis. This property has practical uses. For example, gardeners sometimes use it to mark out the

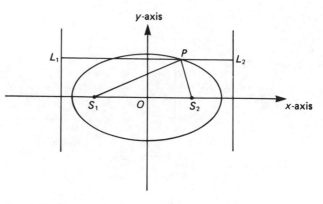

Fig. 3.22 The two foci of an ellipse.

boundary of an elliptical flower-bed. To do this two pegs are secured at the foci and a piece of rope equal in length to the major axis joins the two pegs. When the rope is held taut along the ground an ellipse can be traced out.

There are many possible parametric forms for the ellipse. The one which is usually employed is $x = a \cos \theta$ and $y = b \sin \theta$. Eliminating θ using $\cos^2 \theta + \sin^2 \theta = 1$ gives the ellipse in cartesian form.

THE HYPERBOLA ($e > 1$)

We choose the focus to be $(-ae, 0)$ and the directrix to be the line $x = -a/e$. However, since $e > 1$ the position of the focus is to the left of the directrix (Fig. 3.23). Then

$$PS^2 = (x + ae)^2 + y^2$$
$$PL^2 = (x + a/e)^2$$

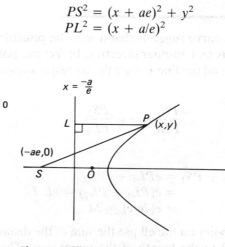

Fig. 3.23 The hyperbola.

Now $PS/PL = e$, so that

$$(x + ae)^2 + y^2 = e^2(x + a/e)^2 = (ex + a)^2$$

Therefore

$$(x + ae)^2 - (ex + a)^2 + y^2 = 0$$
$$x^2(1 - e^2) + y^2 = a^2(1 - e^2)$$
$$x^2(e^2 - 1) - y^2 = a^2(e^2 - 1)$$

Now $e > 1$, and so we may put $b^2 = a^2(e^2 - 1)$ to obtain the standard cartesian form for the hyperbola as

$$\frac{x^2}{a^2} - \frac{y^2}{b^2} = 1$$

There are several parametric forms for the hyperbola. The one which is usually chosen is $x = a \cosh u$, $y = a \sinh u$, which involves hyperbolic functions. Until we study these functions (Chapter 5) we shall have to be content with another parametric form, such as $x = a \sec \theta$, $y = b \tan \theta$. Note that

$$\frac{x^2}{a^2} - \frac{y^2}{b^2} = \sec^2 \theta - \tan^2 \theta = 1$$

The straight lines $y = \pm(b/a)x$ are the **asymptotes** of the hyperbola. The tangents approach these straight lines as $|x|$ increases in magnitude. Some books refer to them as 'tangents at infinity', but this does not really mean very much. If $b = a$ then the asymptotes are the straight lines $y = x$ and $y = -x$, which are mutually perpendicular, and the hyperbola is called a **rectangular hyperbola**. Moreover, if we rotate the curve anticlockwise through $\pi/4$ we can use the asymptotes as axes. This implies that the axes have been rotated clockwise through $\pi/4$.

Suppose $b = a$. Then we have $x^2 - y^2 = a^2$. For a rotation of $-\pi/4$ we have

$$x = X \cos (-\pi/4) - Y \sin (-\pi/4) = (X + Y)/\sqrt{2}$$
$$y = X \sin (-\pi/4) + Y \cos (-\pi/4) = (-X + Y)/\sqrt{2}$$

So

$$x^2 - y^2 = [(X + Y)^2 - (X - Y)^2]/2$$
$$= 2XY = a^2$$

So writing $c = a/\sqrt{2}$ and changing the notation X and Y to the more usual x and y, we have $xy = c^2$.

The usual parametric representation for the rectangular hyperbola $xy = c^2$ is $x = ct$ and $y = c/t$.

Now it's time to take a few more steps.

3.11 Workshop

1 **Exercise** Identify the polar equation

$$r^2 = 8 \operatorname{cosec} 2\theta$$

Here we are required to transform the equation into a form where the curve can be recognized.

by transforming it into cartesian coordinates, or otherwise.

The phrase 'or otherwise' is used quite often in examination questions. Theoretically it means that if you can think of a different method you are at liberty to use it. In practice it often means 'or otherwise try another question'!

2 We use $x = r \cos \theta$ and $y = r \sin \theta$, from which $r = \sqrt{(x^2 + y^2)}$ and $\tan \theta = y/x$. Given the equation $r^2 = 8 \operatorname{cosec} 2\theta$, if we multiply through by $\sin 2\theta$ we obtain

$$r^2 \sin 2\theta = 8$$

and since $\sin 2\theta = 2 \sin \theta \cos \theta$ we have

$$2r^2 \sin \theta \cos \theta = 8$$
$$r^2 \sin \theta \cos \theta = 4$$

That is, $xy = 4$.

We should now recognize this as the equation of a rectangular hyperbola in which the axes coincide with the asymptotes.

If that went well, then move ahead to step 4. Otherwise, try the next exercise. Remember that to transform from polar coordinates to cartesian coordinates we must use $x = r \cos \theta$ and $y = r \sin \theta$. Once r and θ have been eliminated it is then just a question of identifying the curve.

▷**Exercise** Identify the curve which has the equation in polar coordinates

$$r^2(\cos 2\theta - 3) + 10 = 0$$

When you have done this move forward.

3 If we remember the identity $\cos 2\theta = 2 \cos^2 \theta - 1$ it will help. In fact any of the three identities expressing $\cos 2\theta$ in terms of $\sin \theta$ and/or $\cos \theta$ will do. We obtain

$$r^2(2 \cos^2 \theta - 1 - 3) + 10 = 0$$
$$r^2(\cos^2 \theta - 2) + 5 = 0$$
$$r^2 \cos^2 \theta - 2r^2 + 5 = 0$$
$$x^2 - 2(x^2 + y^2) + 5 = 0$$
$$x^2 + 2y^2 = 5$$

We recognize this as the equation of an ellipse:

$$\frac{x^2}{5} + \frac{y^2}{(5/2)} = 1$$

The major axis has length $2a = 2\sqrt{5}$ and the minor axis has length $2b = 2\sqrt{(5/2)} = \sqrt{10}$.

If there are any problems remaining, then make sure you follow all the stages. You will have another chance to tackle one of these when you work through the problems at the end of the chapter. Now step ahead.

▷**Exercise**   Identify the curve which has the equation

$$(x + y)^2 = 4(xy + 1)$$

Be just a little careful here. Try it, then step forward.

This is one of those problems where you can be too clever! You may think that the equation has the form $Y^2 = 4X$, where $Y = x + y$ and $X = xy + 1$, and be led by this to conclude that the equation was that of a parabola. However, the change of coordinates does not correspond to a movement of axes and so does not preserve geometrical shapes. Instead we do something much more mundane. We multiply out and rearrange the equation:

$$(x + y)^2 = 4(xy + 1)$$
$$x^2 + 2xy + y^2 = 4xy + 4$$
$$x^2 - 2xy + y^2 = 4$$
$$(x - y)^2 - 4 = 0$$
$$[(x - y) - 2][(x - y) + 2] = 0$$

So $x - y - 2 = 0$ or $x - y + 2 = 0$, and we therefore have the equation of a pair of parallel straight lines $y = x - 2$ and $y = x + 2$.

If you were right, then on you stride to step 7. Otherwise try this exercise.

▷**Exercise**   Describe the geometrical curve which has the equation

$$(x + y)^2 = (x + 8)\,(x + 2y) + 8(x - 2y)$$

This should cause you no trouble.

6 We do the obvious thing and multiply out the equation with a view to simplifying it:

$$x^2 + 2xy + y^2 = x^2 + 8x + 2xy + 16y + 8x - 16y$$

Almost everything cancels out, and we are able to reduce the equation to

$$y^2 = 16x$$

We recognize this as the equation of a parabola in the standard form $y^2 = 4ax$, where $a = 4$. So the focus is the point $(4, 0)$ and the directrix is the line $x = -4$.

7 **Exercise** Obtain the condition that the line $y = mx + c$ intersects the parabola $y^2 = 4ax$ in two coincident points. Thereby obtain the equation of the tangent to the parabola $y^2 = 4ax$ with slope m.

We shall see in Chapter 6 how we can obtain the equation of the tangents to each of the conics at a general point by using calculus, but for the moment we shall restrict ourselves to algebraic methods.

8 The two 'curves' $y^2 = 4ax$ and $y = mx + c$ intersect when

$$(mx + c)^2 = 4ax$$
$$m^2x^2 + 2mcx + c^2 = 4ax$$
$$m^2x^2 + 2(mc - 2a)x + c^2 = 0$$

In general, if $(mc - 2a)^2 > m^2c^2$, there will be two real solutions for x and so two points where the straight line intersects the parabola. However, in the special case $(mc - 2a)^2 = m^2c^2$ the roots coincide and we have a tangent. This gives

$$m^2c^2 - 4amc + 4a^2 = m^2c^2 \text{ and so } mc = a$$

that is $c = a/m$. So the equation of the tangent is

$$y = mx + c = mx + \frac{a}{m}$$

If that went well, then finish with this exercise.

Exercise Obtain the equation of the tangent with slope m to the circle $x^2 + y^2 = r^2$.

This is just like the last one, and so there should be no problems. Try it, then take the final step.

9 We use the equation of the straight line in the form $y = mx + c$ and we wish to obtain c, given that this straight line is a tangent. Substituting into $x^2 + y^2 = r^2$ we have

$$x^2 + (mx + c)^2 = r^2$$
$$x^2 + m^2x^2 + 2mcx + c^2 = r^2$$
$$(m^2 + 1)x^2 + 2mcx + c^2 - r^2 = 0$$

If this quadratic equation is to have equal roots then

$$4m^2c^2 = 4(m^2 + 1)(c^2 - r^2)$$
$$m^2c^2 = m^2c^2 - m^2r^2 + c^2 - r^2$$
$$c^2 = (m^2 + 1)r^2$$

Therefore $c = \pm r\sqrt{(m^2 + 1)}$, and so there are two tangents:

$$y = mx \pm r\sqrt{(m^2 + 1)}$$

You didn't overlook the minus sign, did you?

Here now are a couple of problems which arise in applications.

3.12 Practical

TOWER HEIGHT

A surveyor finds that from the foot of a tower the elevation of a mast is 9θ but that from the top of the tower the elevation is only 8θ. The tower and the mast are both built on ground at the same horizontal level, and the height of the tower is h.

Show that the horizontal distance from the tower to the mast is

$$d = h \operatorname{cosec} \theta \cos 8\theta \cos 9\theta$$

Obtain an expression for l, the height of the mast, in terms of h and θ.

You should be able to try this on your own. When you have made an attempt, read on and examine the solution.

The arrangement is shown in Fig. 3.24. We have

$$l/d = \tan 9\theta$$

and

$$(l - h)/d = \tan 8\theta$$
$$l/d - h/d = \tan 8\theta$$

From these equations,

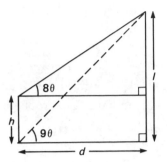

Fig. 3.24 Representation of tower and mast.

$$h/d = \tan 9\theta - \tan 8\theta$$

$$= \frac{\sin 9\theta}{\cos 9\theta} - \frac{\sin 8\theta}{\cos 8\theta}$$

$$= \frac{\sin 9\theta \cos 8\theta - \cos 9\theta \sin 8\theta}{\cos 9\theta \cos 8\theta}$$

$$= \frac{\sin (9\theta - 8\theta)}{\cos 9\theta \cos 8\theta}$$

$$= \frac{\sin \theta}{\cos 9\theta \cos 8\theta}$$

Therefore

$$d = h \operatorname{cosec} \theta \cos 8\theta \cos 9\theta$$

Also

$$l = d \tan 9\theta = h \operatorname{cosec} \theta \cos 8\theta \sin 9\theta$$

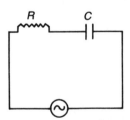

CIRCUIT ADMITTANCE

This problem uses some of the geometry we have developed.

The admittance of an RC series circuit may be represented by the point $P(x, y)$, where

$$x = R \bigg/ \left(R^2 + \frac{1}{\omega^2 C^2}\right)$$

$$y = \left(\frac{1}{\omega C}\right) \bigg/ \left(R^2 + \frac{1}{\omega^2 C^2}\right)$$

Eliminate ω to determine the admittance locus – the equation relating x and y. Show how P moves on this curve as ω increases from 0 without bound.

It is worth while seeing if you can sort this out for yourself before you move on.

We have

$$\frac{R}{x} = R^2 + \frac{1}{\omega^2 C^2} \tag{1}$$

$$\frac{1}{\omega Cy} = R^2 + \frac{1}{\omega^2 C^2} \tag{2}$$

So

$$\frac{R}{x} = \frac{1}{\omega Cy} \quad \text{or} \quad \frac{1}{\omega C} = \frac{Ry}{x}$$

Substituting back into (1) we have

$$\frac{R}{x} = R^2 + \frac{R^2 y^2}{x^2}$$
$$Rx = R^2 x^2 + R^2 y^2$$

Therefore

$$x^2 + y^2 - \frac{x}{R} = 0$$
$$\left(x - \frac{1}{2R}\right)^2 + y^2 = \frac{1}{4R^2}$$

So P is on a circle of centre $(1/2R, 0)$ and radius $1/2R$ (Fig. 3.25).
When $\omega \neq 0$ we have

$$x = \frac{R\omega^2 C^2}{R^2 \omega^2 C^2 + 1} \qquad y = \frac{\omega C}{R^2 \omega^2 C^2 + 1}$$

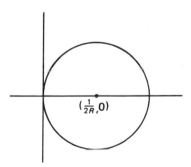

Fig. 3.25 The admittance locus.

As $\omega \to 0$ we have $(x, y) \to (0, 0)$, the origin. For $\omega > 0$ we have $y > 0$ and, as ω increases without bound, $(x, y) \to (1/R, 0)$. The movement of P is therefore confined to the upper semicircle (Fig. 3.26).

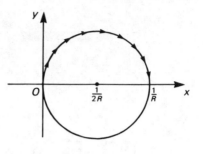

Fig. 3.26 The path of P.

SUMMARY

☐ We have defined the circular functions, drawn their graphs and deduced some of their properties. Two key identities are

$$\cos^2 \theta + \sin^2 \theta = 1$$
$$\sin (A + B) = \sin A \cos B + \cos A \sin B$$

☐ We have obtained the general solution of equations involving circular functions

$$\sin \theta = \sin \alpha \Rightarrow \theta = n\pi + (-1)^n \alpha$$
$$\cos \theta = \cos \alpha \Rightarrow \theta = 2n\pi \pm \alpha$$
$$\tan \theta = \tan \alpha \Rightarrow \theta = n\pi + \alpha$$

where n is any integer.

☐ We have obtained the standard equations of the straight line

a $y - y_1 = m(x - x_1)$ (slope m, through (x_1, y_1))

b $\dfrac{y - y_1}{y_2 - y_1} = \dfrac{x - x_1}{x_2 - x_1}$ (through (x_1, y_1) and (x_2, y_2))

c $y = mx + c$ (slope m, y-intercept c)

d $\dfrac{x}{a} + \dfrac{y}{b} = 1$ (x-intercept a, y-intercept b)

☐ We have shown that the angle between two straight lines with slopes m_1 and m_2 respectively is given by

$$\tan \theta = \frac{m_1 - m_2}{1 + m_1 m_2}$$

The lines are parallel if and only if $m_1 = m_2$.
The lines are mutually perpendicular if and only if $m_1 m_2 = -1$.

☐ We have obtained the equations in standard form of the conic sections

$$x^2 + y^2 + 2gx + 2fy + c = 0 \qquad \text{(the circle)}$$
$$y^2 = 4ax \qquad \text{(the parabola)}$$
$$\frac{x^2}{a^2} + \frac{y^2}{b^2} = 1 \qquad \text{(the ellipse)}$$
$$\frac{x^2}{a^2} - \frac{y^2}{b^2} = 1 \qquad \text{(the hyperbola)}$$

☐ We have transformed polar equations into cartesian equations using the relationships

$$x = r \cos \theta \qquad y = r \sin \theta$$

EXERCISES (for answers see p. 740)

1 Establish the following identities:
  a $\cos 3\theta = \cos\theta\,(\cos 2\theta - 2\sin^2\theta)$
  b $\sin 4\theta = 4(\sin\theta\cos^3\theta - \cos\theta\sin^3\theta)$
  c $\tan\theta + \cot\theta = \sec\theta\,\mathrm{cosec}\,\theta$
  d $\cos 2\theta + \sin 2\theta = (\cos\theta + \sin\theta)^2 - 2\sin^2\theta$
  e $\tan 3\theta = \dfrac{\tan\theta\,(3 - \tan^2\theta)}{(1 - \tan^2\theta)(1 - \tan\theta\tan 2\theta)}$

2 Solve the following equations in the interval $[0, 2\pi)$:
  a $\sin 3\theta = 1$
  b $\tan 4\theta = -1$
  c $\cos\theta + \sin\theta = 1$
  d $\cot^2\theta = 1$
  e $\cos\theta = 2\cos^2\theta - 1$
  f $\tan 3\theta = \dfrac{2\tan\theta}{1 - \tan^2\theta}$

3 Express in the form $R\cos(\theta - \alpha)$
  a $\cos\theta + 2\sqrt{2}\sin\theta$
  b $3\sin\theta - \sqrt{7}\cos\theta$
  c $4\cos\theta - 3\sin\theta$

4 Identify each of the following curves:
  a $(x + 4)^2 + (y + 3)^2 = 8x + 6y + 50$
  b $\dfrac{1}{x} + \dfrac{5}{y} + \dfrac{10}{xy} = 1$
  c $(y - 1)^2 - (x - 1)^2 = 2x - 1$
  d $x^2 + 4y = y^2 + 2x + 19$

5 Identify these polar equations by transforming them to cartesian form:
  a $\dfrac{\left(r + \dfrac{1}{r}\right)}{2} = \cos\theta - \sin\theta$
  b $r^2\cos 2\theta + 2r(\sin\theta - 2\cos\theta) = 1$
  c $r^2(1 + \cos^2\theta) = 4$
  d $r\sin 2\theta + 2\sin\theta - 2\cos\theta = \dfrac{10}{r}$

6 Determine the equation of each of the following:
  a the straight line through $(-1, 2)$ with slope 3
  b the straight line through $(1, -4)$ with slope -5
  c the straight line through $(2, 5)$ and $(-4, 6)$
  d the straight line through $(-1, 4)$ and $(3, 2)$
  e the straight line with x intercept -3 and y intercept 5
  f the straight line with x intercept 2 and y intercept -3
  g the straight line with slope 3 and y intercept -5
  h the straight line with slope -2 and y intercept 4

i the circle centre $(1, 2)$ with radius 4
j the circle centre $(2, -3)$ with radius 5

7 For each of the following straight lines determine the slope, the x intercept and the y intercept:

a $x + 4y = 12$
b $2x + 3y + 6 = 0$
c $2(x + 3) + 5(y - 2) = 7$
d $4(x - 2) + 3(y + 1) = 9$

8 For each of the following circles determine the centre and the radius:

a $x^2 + y^2 + 4x + 6y + 9 = 0$
b $x^2 + y^2 + 6x + 8y + 21 = 0$
c $x^2 + y^2 - 2x + 4y - 4 = 0$
d $(x - y)^2 + (x + y)^2 = 12x + 4y + 30$

ASSIGNMENT (for answers see p. 741; see also Workshops on pp. 65 and 82)

1 Show that

$$\frac{\cos \theta}{1 + \sin \theta} + \frac{1 + \sin \theta}{\cos \theta} = \frac{2}{\cos \theta}$$

2 Use the expansion formula for $\sin (A + B)$ to express $\sin 3\theta$ entirely in terms of $\sin \theta$. Hence, or otherwise, solve the equation

$$6 - 8 \sin^2 \theta = \operatorname{cosec} \theta$$

3 Obtain all solutions in the interval $[0, 2\pi]$ of the equation

$$2 \cos^3 \theta + \cos 2\theta = \cos \theta$$

4 Obtain the general solution of the equation

$$\sin 4\theta + 2 \sin 2\theta + 2 \sin^2 \theta = 2$$

5 Simplify and thereby identify each of the following equations as curves in the cartesian coordinate system:

a $(2x + y)^2 + (x - 2y)^2 = 16$
b $(x + y)(x + 5y) - 6x(y - 5) = 0$
c $(y + x)^2 = x(?y + 1) + 16$
d $(y + x)^2 = x(2y + x) + 16$
e $(3x - y)(x + y - 1)(x - y + 2) = 0$
In each case give a rough sketch.

6 Express in the form $R \cos (\theta - \alpha)$

a $\cos \theta + \sin \theta$
b $\sin \theta + \sqrt{3} \cos \theta$

7 By expressing the polar equation

$$r^2(1 - 7\cos 2\theta) = 10$$

in cartesian form, or otherwise, identify the curve.

FURTHER EXERCISES (for answers see p. 741)

1 Establish the following identities:
   a $\sin\theta/(1 + \cos\theta) = \tan(\theta/2)$
   b $(1 + \cos 2\theta)/(1 - \cos 2\theta) = \cot^2\theta$
   c $\cot\theta - \tan\theta = 2\cot 2\theta$
   d $\operatorname{cosec} 2\theta - \cot 2\theta = \tan\theta$
2 Solve each of the following equations to obtain $\theta \in \mathbb{R}$:
   a $\sec^2\theta = 1 + \tan\theta$
   b $\tan^4\theta = 9$
   c $1 + \sin\theta + \sin^2\theta = 0$
   d $2 - \cos\theta + 2\cos^2\theta - \cos^3\theta = 0$
   e $1 + \sin\theta + \cos\theta = 0$
3 Show that

$$\frac{\cos 2n\theta + \sin 2(n+1)\theta}{\cos(2n+1)\theta + \sin(2n+1)\theta} = \frac{\cos 2(n-1)\theta + \sin 2n\theta}{\cos(2n-1)\theta + \sin(2n-1)\theta}$$

Hence or otherwise show that

$$\frac{\cos 12\theta + \sin 14\theta}{\cos 13\theta + \sin 13\theta} = \frac{1 + \sin 2\theta}{\cos\theta + \sin\theta}$$

4 Show that the equation of the chord joining two points (a_1, b_1) and (a_2, b_2) on the rectangular hyperbola $xy = c^2$ is

$$\frac{x}{a_1 + a_2} + \frac{y}{b_1 + b_2} = 1$$

5 Show that

$$\frac{\sin\theta + \sin 3\theta + \sin 5\theta + \sin 7\theta}{\cos\theta + \cos 3\theta + \cos 5\theta + \cos 7\theta} = \tan 4\theta$$

6 A surveyor stands on the same horizontal level as a television mast at a distance d from its base. The angle of elevation of a point P on the mast is θ and the angle of elevation of the top of the mast is ϕ. Show that the distance from the point P to the top of the mast is $d \sin(\phi - \theta)/\cos\theta\cos\phi$.

7 A simple pendulum of length L swings so that it subtends an angle θ with the vertical. Show that the height of the pendulum bob above its lowest position is $2L\sin^2(\theta/2)$.

8 Obtain the axis of symmetry and the position of the focus of the conic $2y^2 = x + 4y$.

9 A symmetrical parabolic arch has a span of 24 metres and a height of 20 metres. Determine the height of the arch at a distance 3 metres from the axis of symmetry.

10 A symmetrical road bridge has the shape of half an ellipse. Its span is 30 metres and its height is 20 metres. Determine the height at a distance of 12 metres from the axis of symmetry.

11 A symmetrical parabolic bridge has a height of 4 metres and a span of 8 metres. A vehicle is 4 metres broad and has a height just over 3 metres. Can the vehicle pass under the bridge? Determine the maximum head height which a vehicle 3 metres wide can have to pass under the bridge without contact.

12 A beam of length l lies in a vertical plane and rests against a cylindrical drum of radius a which is lying on its side. The foot of the beam is a distance x from the point of contact of the cylinder and the ground. Calculate the height of the top of the beam above the ground.

13 In a plane representing an electric field, O and A denote the cross-sections of charged wires. The distance OA is 8 units. When the point P moves in this plane in such a way that $OP = 3AP$ then P moves on an equipotential surface. Show that the equipotential surface is a circle of radius 3 units.

14 Two rods AB and AC of length p and q ($p > q$) respectively are jointed together at one end A. The other ends, B and C, are secured to a wall with B vertically above C so that the distance BC is h. If C is moved a distance x down the wall away from B, show that A drops or rises by an amount $x/2 - (p^2 - q^2)x/2h(h + x)$.

Limits, continuity and differentiation

4

Now that we have acquired the basic algebraic and geometrical tools that we need, we can begin to develop the calculus.

After completing this chapter you should be able to
☐ Evaluate simple limits using the laws of limits;
☐ Decide, in simple cases, whether a function is continuous or not;
☐ Perform the processes of elementary differentiation;
☐ Obtain higher-order derivatives of a product using Leibniz's theorem;
☐ Apply differentiation to calculate rates of change.
At the end of this chapter we shall solve practical problems concerning cylinder pressure and the seepage of water into soil.

The calculus is one of the most widely applied mathematical processes.

4.1 LIMITS

One of the most important concepts in mathematics and therefore in its applications is that of a **limit**. We are often concerned with the long-term effects of things, or with what is likely to happen at a point of crisis – profitability, state of health, buoyancy, or stability of a structure. Such considerations often involve a limiting process.

We shall meet this idea in several ways. In the first instance we consider the limit of a function at a *point*. Suppose $y = f(x)$ has the property that $f(x)$ can be arbitrarily close to l just by choosing x ($\neq a$) sufficiently close to a. If so, we say that $f(x)$ tends to a limit l as x tends to a, and write

$$f(x) \to l \quad \text{as} \quad x \to a$$

Alternatively we say that f has a limit l at a, and write

$$l = \lim_{x \to a} f(x)$$

We do not insist that $f(a)$ is defined, or, if it is defined, that its value shall be equal to l. In other words, the point a need not be in the domain of the function and, even if it is, the value at the point a need not be l. Indeed we are not interested at all in what happens at $x = a$; we are interested only in what happens when x is *near a*.

!

□ Suppose

Example

$$y = f(x) = \frac{x^2 - 3x + 2}{x - 1}$$

then the domain of this function consists of all real numbers other than $x = 1$; so $f(x)$ is not defined when $x = 1$. On the other hand, when $x \neq 1$ we may simplify the expression for y to

$$y = \frac{(x - 2)(x - 1)}{x - 1} = x - 2$$

The function is shown in Fig. 4.1: we use a hollow circle to represent a missing point. Now $f(x)$ can be made arbitrarily close to -1 just by choosing x sufficiently near to 1. Therefore

$$\lim_{x \to 1} f(x) = \lim_{x \to 1} (x - 2) = -1$$

However, we cannot make $f(x)$ equal to -1 because $f(x)$ is not defined when x is equal to 1. ■

□ Obtain $\lim_{x \to a} f(x)$ in each of the following cases:

Example

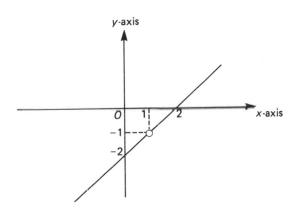

Fig. 4.1 The graph of f.

a $f(x) = \dfrac{x^2 - 4x + 3}{x^2 - 2x - 3}$ $a = 3$

b $f(x) = \dfrac{e^{2x} - 1}{e^x - e^{-x}}$ $a = 0$

a We have

$$f(x) = \frac{(x - 3)(x - 1)}{(x - 3)(x + 1)}$$

so that when $x \neq 3$

$$f(x) = \frac{x - 1}{x + 1}$$

Therefore as $x \to 3$,

$$f(x) \to \frac{3 - 1}{3 + 1} = \frac{2}{4} = \frac{1}{2}$$

b We have

$$f(x) = \frac{e^{2x} - 1}{e^x - e^{-x}}$$

If we try to put $x = 0$ straight away we get

$$f(x) \to \frac{0}{0}$$

which is undefined. Therefore we must be more subtle. If we multiply numerator and denominator by e^x (which is always non-zero) we obtain

$$f(x) = \frac{e^x(e^{2x} - 1)}{e^{2x} - 1} = e^x$$

provided $x \neq 0$. So that as $x \to 0$, $f(x) \to e^0 = 1$.   ■

4.2 THE LAWS OF LIMITS

Whenever we wish to determine the **initial** or the **final** value of a process the problem of determining a limit usually arises.

The following rules are often known as **the laws of limits**:

1 $\lim\limits_{x \to a} [f(x) + g(x)] = \lim\limits_{x \to a} f(x) + \lim\limits_{x \to a} g(x)$

2 $\lim\limits_{x \to a} [kf(x)] = k \lim\limits_{x \to a} f(x)$ $k \in \mathbb{R}$

3 $\lim\limits_{x \to a} [f(x)\, g(x)] = \lim\limits_{x \to a} f(x)\, \lim\limits_{x \to a} g(x)$

4 If $\lim\limits_{x \to a} g(x) \neq 0$, then $\lim\limits_{x \to a} [f(x)/g(x)] = \left[\lim\limits_{x \to a} f(x)\right] \Big/ \left[\lim\limits_{x \to a} g(x)\right]$

These rules are to be interpreted carefully in the following way. If the right-hand side exists then the left-hand side exists and the two are equal. If the right-hand side does not exist, then the rule cannot be applied.

!

☐ From the graphs of the circular functions (Figs 3.4, 3.5) it is clear that **Example**

$$\lim_{x\to 0} \sin x = 0$$

$$\lim_{x\to 0} \cos x = 1$$

$$\lim_{x\to 0} \tan x = 0$$

Obtain

a $\lim_{x\to 0} \dfrac{\sin x - 1}{2 \cos x}$

b $\lim_{x\to 0} \dfrac{\cos x - 1}{2 \sin x}$

a Using the laws of limits,

$$\lim_{x\to 0} \frac{\sin x - 1}{2 \cos x} = \frac{\lim_{x\to 0} (\sin x - 1)}{\lim_{x\to 0} (2 \cos x)}$$

$$= \frac{\lim_{x\to 0} (\sin x - 1)}{2 \lim_{x\to 0} (\cos x)} = \frac{0 - 1}{2 \times 1} = -\frac{1}{2}$$

Here the procedure is justified by the result; if you like, the end justifies the means! However, if the application of the rules produces at any stage an expression which is meaningless, we shall need to think again!

b If we go straight into the laws of limits we shall meet a problem:

$$\lim_{x\to 0} \frac{\cos x - 1}{2 \sin x} = \frac{\lim_{x\to 0} (\cos x - 1)}{\lim_{x\to 0} (2 \sin x)}$$

$$= \frac{\lim_{x\to 0} (\cos x) - 1}{2 \lim_{x\to 0} (\sin x)} = \frac{1 - 1}{2 \times 0} = \frac{0}{0}$$

At each stage we were able to carry out the simplification only on the understanding that the expression which resulted would be meaningful. However, 0/0 is indeterminate and so the procedure fails. The problem must be tackled differently. One way to sort things out is to try to express $f(x)$ in an alternative form when $x \neq 0$:

$$f(x) = \frac{\cos x - 1}{2 \sin x} = \frac{(\cos x - 1)(\cos x + 1)}{2 \sin x(\cos x + 1)}$$

We shall meet in section 8.4 L'Hospital's rule for dealing with indeterminate forms.

$$= \frac{\cos^2 x - 1}{2 \sin x(\cos x + 1)} = \frac{-\sin^2 x}{2 \sin x(\cos x + 1)}$$

$$= \frac{-\sin x}{2(\cos x + 1)} \qquad \text{provided } x \neq 0$$

Therefore

$$\lim_{x \to 0} f(x) = \lim_{x \to 0} \frac{-\sin x}{2(\cos x + 1)}$$

$$= \frac{-\lim_{x \to 0} \sin x}{2 \lim_{x \to 0} \cos x + 2} = \frac{0}{2 + 2} = 0 \qquad \blacksquare$$

4.3 Workshop

1

Exercise   Here are two limits for you to try; they are very similar to the ones we have just done.

a $\displaystyle \lim_{x \to 0} \frac{(\sin x - 1) \tan x}{2 \cos x}$

b $\displaystyle \lim_{x \to 0} \frac{(\cos x - 1) \cot x}{2 \sin x}$

When you have completed **a**, take the next step and see if you are right.

2   For **a** we have

$$\lim_{x \to 0} \frac{(\sin x - 1) \tan x}{2 \cos x} = \frac{\lim_{x \to 0} (\sin x - 1) \tan x}{\lim_{x \to 0} (2 \cos x)}$$

$$= \frac{\lim_{x \to 0} (\sin x - 1) \lim_{x \to 0} \tan x}{2 \lim_{x \to 0} \cos x}$$

$$= \frac{-1 \times 0}{2 \times 1} = 0$$

How did you get on with that? If you made a mistake, look carefully at the laws of limits and see how they are applied. Problem **b**, like the example we have just done, requires some work before we take limits. Try it and see how it goes; then step ahead.

3   In **b** we cannot apply the laws of limits directly because the result is meaningless. However,

$$\frac{(\cos x - 1) \cot x}{2 \sin x} = \frac{(\cos x - 1) \cos x}{2 \sin^2 x}$$

$$= \frac{(\cos x - 1) \cos x}{2(1 - \cos^2 x)}$$

$$= \frac{(\cos x - 1) \cos x}{2(1 - \cos x)(1 + \cos x)}$$

$$= \frac{-\cos x}{2(1 + \cos x)}$$

Therefore

$$\lim_{x \to 0} \frac{(\cos x - 1) \cot x}{2 \sin x} = \lim_{x \to 0} \frac{-\cos x}{2(1 + \cos x)}$$

$$= \frac{-1}{2(1 + 1)} = -\frac{1}{4}$$

Did you manage that?

The important fact that we need to remember about the limit of a function is that we are not at all concerned with the values of the function at the point. We are only interested in the values of the function *near* the point. In Fig. 4.2

$$\lim_{x \to a} f(x) = l \neq f(a)$$

Although the 'limit l of $f(x)$ as x tends to a' is only meaningful if l is a real number, we shall allow a slight extension of the notation. It is convenient but slightly absurd to write

$$\lim_{x \to a} f(x) = \infty$$

provided $f(x)$ can be made arbitrarily large just by choosing x sufficiently

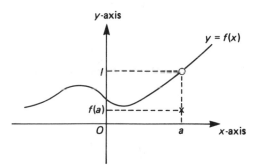

Fig. 4.2 The limit of a function.

close to a ($x \neq a$). That is, $f(x)$ can be made larger than any pre-assigned real number merely by choosing x close enough to the point a. Similarly,

$$\lim_{x \to a} f(x) = -\infty$$

means that $f(x)$ can be made less than any pre-assigned number merely by choosing x sufficiently close to a ($x \neq a$).

Example □ We have

$$\lim_{x \to 0} \operatorname{cosec}^2 x = \infty$$

The notation is slightly misleading because of course there is no limit! ■

Likewise we write

$$\lim_{x \to \infty} f(x) = l$$

if $f(x)$ can be made arbitrarily close to l merely by choosing x sufficiently large, and

$$\lim_{x \to -\infty} f(x) = l$$

if $f(x)$ can be made arbitrarily close to l merely by choosing the magnitude of x sufficiently large, where $x < 0$.

4.4 RIGHT AND LEFT LIMITS

We can extend the idea of a limit in a number of ways. One way, which is quite useful for applications, arises when $f(x)$ can be made arbitrarily close to r by choosing x ($>a$) sufficiently close to a. Here we are considering values of x greater than a, and so the limit is obtained as we approach the point a from the right-hand side. We call it a **right-hand limit** (Fig. 4.3). We write

A practical application of this will arise in section 8.8.

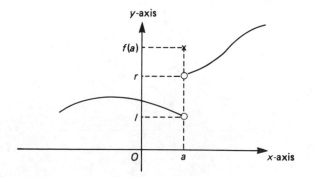

Fig. 4.3 Right-hand and left-hand limits.

$$\lim_{x \to a+} f(x) = r$$

Similarly, if $f(x)$ can be made arbitrarily close to l by choosing x ($<a$) sufficiently close to a, we have a **left-hand limit** (Fig. 4.3). We write

$$\lim_{x \to a-} f(x) = l$$

If

$$\lim_{x \to a+} f(x) = \lim_{x \to a-} f(x) = k$$

then

$$\lim_{x \to a} f(x) = k$$

INEQUALITIES

There is one further property of limits which we shall find particularly useful later and which we now describe briefly. It enables us to compare limits by comparing the functions which give rise to them.

Suppose
1 For all x in some open interval containing the point a, $0 \leqslant f(x) \leqslant g(x)$;
2 Both $\lim_{x \to a} f(x)$ and $\lim_{x \to a} g(x)$ exist.

Then

$$0 \leqslant \lim_{x \to a} f(x) \leqslant \lim_{x \to a} g(x)$$

In section 1.4 we considered some simple inequalities.

It must be stressed that both requirements must be met before we assert confidently that one limit is bounded above by another. Here are the conditions in words:
1 Each function must be positive, and one must be greater than the other;
2 Both limits must exist.
An analogous property holds for right-hand and left-hand limits.

4.5 CONTINUITY

Most of the functions which we have met in our mathematical work have the property

$$\lim_{x \to a} f(x) = f(a)$$

This in effect says that there are no breaks in the graph of the function. Specifically, if for some point a we have

$$\lim_{x \to a} f(x) = f(a)$$

then the function f is said to be **continuous** at a. Moreover, if the function f is continuous at all points of its domain we say it is a **continuous function**.

Intuitively, then, a continuous function has its graph all in one piece. However, this statement can be a little misleading.

Example □ $y = \tan x$ is defined whenever x is not an odd multiple of $\pi/2$. It is continuous at all points where it is defined, and so is a continuous function. However, the graph is certainly not in one piece (Fig. 4.4).   ■

The function in Fig. 4.5, although satisfying the requirements of a

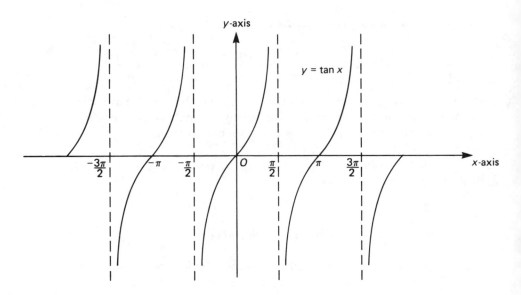

Fig. 4.4 The tangent function.

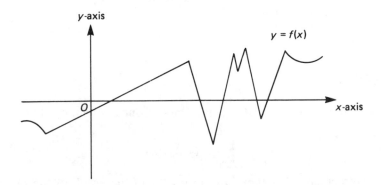

Fig. 4.5 A continuous function.

continuous function, is not the kind of function with which we are familiar. It isn't smooth, and there are several points at which it is impossible to draw a tangent.

4.6 DIFFERENTIABILITY

Suppose $y = f(x)$ is a smooth curve and that x determines a general point P on it (Fig. 4.6). Suppose also that h is small and Q corresponds to $x = a + h$. Using the notation shown in the diagram, the slope of the chord PQ is given by

$$\text{slope } PQ = \frac{QR}{PR} = \frac{f(a+h) - f(a)}{(a+h) - a} = \frac{f(a+h) - f(a)}{h}$$

Suppose now we consider what happens as h is made small $(h \neq 0)$. Q moves closer to P, and intuitively the slope of the chord PQ becomes arbitrarily close to the slope of the tangent at P. So

$$\text{slope of tangent at } P = \lim_{h \to 0} \frac{f(x+h) - f(x)}{h}$$

If this limit exists then the function f is said to be differentiable at the point a. If f is differentiable at all its points then f is said to be a **differentiable function**. We write

$$\frac{dy}{dx} = \lim_{h \to 0} \frac{f(x+h) - f(x)}{h}$$

We call this the **derivative** of f at x, and represent it by $f'(x)$. The process by which $f'(x)$ is calculated from $f(x)$ is called **differentiation** with respect to x.

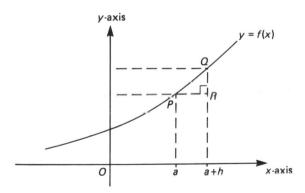

Fig. 4.6 Two neighbouring points on a smooth curve.

DIFFERENTIALS

Although we have used the notation dy/dx for the derivative of f at x, we have given no meaning to dy and dx which would enable them to be used separately. It is important to appreciate that the derivative is a *limit*; we may write $\delta x = h$ and $\delta y = f(x + h) - f(x)$ so that

$$\frac{dy}{dx} = \lim_{\delta x \to 0} \frac{\delta y}{\delta x}$$

but once the limit has been taken dy and dx become welded together and cannot be separated.

Nevertheless it is convenient to have an interpretation for dy and dx so that they can be used separately and are consistent with this definition of a derivative. Accordingly we define dx to be any change in x (not necessarily small) and define dy by the formula $dy = f'(x)\,dx$. This is consistent with the definition of a derivative because when $dx \neq 0$ we have $dy/dx = f'(x)$ as before. When dx and dy are used in this way they are called **differentials**. Note that if dx is a change in x, dy is not the corresponding change in y. However, if dx is numerically small then dy does *approximate* to the corresponding change in y.

RULES

The laws of limits enable us to deduce **rules for differentiation**. In what follows it will be supposed that $u = u(x)$ and $v = v(x)$ can be differentiated with respect to x and that k is a real constant.

1 $\dfrac{d}{dx}(u + v) = \dfrac{du}{dx} + \dfrac{dv}{dx}$ (the sum rule)

2 $\dfrac{d}{dx}(ku) = k\dfrac{du}{dx}$ (the factor rule)

3 $\dfrac{d}{dx}(uv) = u\dfrac{dv}{dx} + v\dfrac{du}{dx}$ (the product rule)

4 Suppose $y = y(u)$ and $u = u(x)$ are both differentiable. Then

$\dfrac{dy}{dx} = \dfrac{dy}{du}\dfrac{du}{dx}$ (the chain rule)

These are the basic rules for differentiation and, together with the derivatives of a few functions, they can be used to obtain the derivative of any function you are likely to need. Here is a short list of **derivatives**; if you were cast away on a desert island these would be sufficient for you to deduce all the standard forms:

1 $\dfrac{d}{dx}(x^n) = nx^{n-1}$ $(n \in \mathbb{R})$

2 $\dfrac{d}{dx}(e^x) = e^x$

3 $\dfrac{d}{dx}(\sin x) = \cos x$

Imagine for the moment that we are marooned on a desert island. There is a ship ready but the captain has gone mad and will not rescue us unless we can supply some simple derivatives. Let's try to build up some of the standard forms. See also Table 15.1, p. 407.

☐ Deduce the quotient rule   **Example**

$$\frac{d}{dx}\left(\frac{u}{v}\right) = \left(v\frac{du}{dx} - u\frac{dv}{dx}\right)\bigg/ v^2$$

We use the product rule and the chain rule to achieve the required form:

$$\text{LHS} = \frac{d}{dx}\left(\frac{u}{v}\right) = \frac{d}{dx}(uv^{-1})$$

$$= u\frac{d}{dx}(v^{-1}) + v^{-1}\frac{d}{dx}(u) \qquad \text{(product rule)}$$

$$= u\frac{d}{dv}(v^{-1})\frac{dv}{dx} + v^{-1}\frac{du}{dx} \qquad \text{(chain rule)}$$

$$= u(-v^{-2})\frac{dv}{dx} + v^{-1}\frac{du}{dx} \qquad \text{(derivative 1)}$$

$$= \left(v\frac{du}{dx} - u\frac{dv}{dx}\right)\bigg/ v^2 = \text{RHS} \qquad \text{(elementary algebra)}$$

■

☐ Use the rules and the standard forms to obtain   **Example**

a $\dfrac{d}{dx}(\cos x)$

b $\dfrac{d}{dx}(\tan x)$

c $\dfrac{d}{dx}(\sec x)$

d $\dfrac{d}{dx}(\ln x)$

e $\dfrac{d}{dx}(a^x) \qquad (a > 0)$

a We have $\cos x = \sin(\pi/2 - x)$. So

$$\frac{d}{dx}(\cos x) = \frac{d}{dx}[\sin (\pi/2 - x)]$$

Put $u = \pi/2 - x$; then

$$\frac{d}{dx}(\cos x) = \frac{d}{dx}(\sin u)$$

$$= \frac{d}{du}(\sin u)\,\frac{du}{dx} \qquad \text{(chain rule)}$$

$$= \cos u\,\frac{d}{dx}(\pi/2 - x) \qquad \text{(derivative 3)}$$

$$= \cos u\left[\frac{\pi}{2}\,\frac{d}{dx}(x^0) - \frac{d}{dx}(x)\right]$$

$$= \cos u\,(0 - 1) = -\cos (\pi/2 - x) = -\sin x$$

b We have

$$\frac{d}{dx}(\tan x) = \frac{d}{dx}\left(\frac{\sin x}{\cos x}\right)$$

$$= \left[\cos x\,\frac{d}{dx}(\sin x) - \sin x\,\frac{d}{dx}(\cos x)\right]\Big/\cos^2 x$$

$$= \frac{\cos^2 x + \sin^2 x}{\cos^2 x} = \frac{1}{\cos^2 x} = \sec^2 x$$

c We have

$$\frac{d}{dx}(\sec x) = \frac{d}{dx}[(\cos x)^{-1}]$$

Put $u = \cos x$. Then

$$\frac{d}{dx}(u^{-1}) = \frac{d}{du}(u^{-1})\,\frac{du}{dx}$$

$$= -u^{-2}\frac{d}{dx}(\cos x)$$

$$= \frac{-1}{\cos^2 x}(-\sin x) = \frac{\sin x}{\cos^2 x} = \sec x \tan x$$

d Let $y = \ln x$. Then $x = e^y$. So

$$\frac{d}{dx}(x) = \frac{d}{dx}(e^y) = \frac{d}{dy}(e^y)\,\frac{dy}{dx}$$

Therefore

$$1 = e^y\,\frac{dy}{dx} = x\,\frac{dy}{dx}$$

$$\frac{dy}{dx} = \frac{1}{x}$$

e Let $y = a^x$. Then $\ln y = \ln a^x = x \ln a$. So

$$\frac{d}{dx}(\ln y) = \frac{d}{dx}(x \ln a)$$

Therefore

$$\frac{d}{dy}(\ln y)\frac{dy}{dx} = \ln a$$

So

$$\frac{1}{y}\frac{dy}{dx} = \ln a$$

$$\frac{dy}{dx} = (\ln a)\, a^x \qquad\qquad \blacksquare$$

If $y = f(x)$ then $dy/dx = f'(x)$, and we say that $f(x)$ has been differentiated with respect to x. We may consider differentiating again with respect to x, and so we define the **higher-order derivatives**:

$$\frac{d^2y}{dx^2} = \frac{d}{dx}\left(\frac{dy}{dx}\right) = f''(x) = f^{(2)}(x)$$

$$\frac{d^3y}{dx^3} = \frac{d}{dx}\left(\frac{d^2y}{dx^2}\right) = f^{(3)}(x)$$

In general,

$$\frac{d^n y}{dx^n} = f^{(n)}(x)$$

is the result of differentiating n times with respect to x, and is known as the nth-order derivative of $f(x)$ with respect to x.

4.7 LEIBNIZ'S THEOREM

One rule which generalizes to higher-order derivatives is the product rule. The first few derivatives will establish the pattern. For the purposes of this section only we shall use a special subscript notation y_n to represent $d^n y/dx^n$.

The product rule is

$$\frac{d}{dx}(uv) = u\frac{dv}{dx} + \frac{du}{dx}v$$

so that

$$(uv)_1 = uv_1 + u_1 v$$

Now

$$\frac{d^2}{dx^2}(uv) = \frac{d}{dx}\left(u\frac{dv}{dx} + \frac{du}{dx}v\right)$$

$$= \left(u\frac{d^2v}{dx^2} + \frac{du}{dx}\frac{dv}{dx}\right) + \left(\frac{du}{dx}\frac{dv}{dx} + \frac{d^2u}{dx^2}v\right)$$

(using the product rule again)

$$= u\frac{d^2v}{dx^2} + 2\frac{du}{dx}\frac{dv}{dx} + \frac{d^2u}{dx^2}v$$

So

$$(uv)_2 = uv_2 + 2u_1v_1 + u_2v$$

Example □ Show by applying the product rule yet again that

$$(uv)_3 = uv_3 + 3u_1v_2 + 3u_2v_1 + u_3v$$

When you have managed this, read on.   ■

Here is the pattern which is emerging as we apply the product rule repeatedly. Look at it and see if it reminds you of anything:

$$(uv)_1 = uv_1 + u_1v$$
$$(uv)_2 = uv_2 + 2u_1v_1 + u_2v$$
$$(uv)_3 = uv_3 + 3u_1v_2 + 3u_2v_1 + u_3v$$

Refer back to section 1.6 if you need a refresher on binomial coefficients.

Look at the coefficients. Yes! They are the binomial coefficients. Remember

$$\binom{n}{r} = \frac{n!}{(n-r)!\,r!} \qquad (r \in \mathbb{N}_0, n \in \mathbb{N}_0; r \leqslant n)$$

So if we put them in we obtain

$$(uv)_1 = \binom{1}{0}uv_1 + \binom{1}{1}u_1v$$

$$(uv)_2 = \binom{2}{0}uv_2 + \binom{2}{1}u_1v_1 + \binom{2}{2}u_2v$$

$$(uv)_3 = \binom{3}{0}uv_3 + \binom{3}{1}u_1v_2 + \binom{3}{2}u_2v_1 + \binom{3}{3}u_3v$$

In general

$$(uv)_n = \binom{n}{0} u_0 v_n + \binom{n}{1} u_1 v_{n-1} + \binom{n}{2} u_2 v_{n-2}$$

$$+ \ldots + \binom{n}{r} u_r v_{n-r} + \ldots + \binom{n}{n} u_n v_0 \qquad (n \in \mathbb{N})$$

$$= \sum_{r=0}^{n} \binom{n}{r} u_r v_{n-r} \qquad \text{where } u_0 = u, \ v_0 = v$$

Remember that the summation sign simply tells us to let r take on all integer values between 0 and n and then add up the results.

This formula, which enables us to differentiate a product n times, is known as **Leibniz's theorem**. It can be proved by mathematical induction.

□ If $y = f(x) = x^3 e^{2x}$, obtain $f^{(n)}(x)$.

Example

Here we have a product, and so we use Leibniz's theorem. We must decide which factor to designate as u and which as v. The expansion will terminate after a few terms if we put $u = x^3$ because after differentiating u three times with respect to x the result is zero:

$$u = x^3, \qquad u_1 = 3x^2, \qquad u_2 = 6x, \qquad u_3 = 6$$

Now $v = e^{2x}$, so $v_1 = 2e^{2x}$, $v_2 = 2^2 e^{2x}$, and in general $v_n = 2^n e^{2x}$. Therefore

$$(uv)_n = u_0 v_n + \binom{n}{1} u_1 v_{n-1} + \binom{n}{2} u_2 v_{n-2} + \ldots$$

$$= x^3 2^n e^{2x} + \binom{n}{1} (3x^2)(2^{n-1} e^{2x})$$

$$+ \binom{n}{2} (6x)(2^{n-2} e^{2x}) + \binom{n}{3} (6)(2^{n-3} e^{2x})$$

$$= x^3 2^n e^{2x} + n(3x^2)(2^{n-1} e^{2x})$$

$$+ \frac{n(n-1)}{2} 6x \, 2^{n-2} e^{2x} + \frac{n(n-1)(n-2)}{1 \times 2 \times 3} 6 \, 2^{n-3} e^{2x}$$

$$= [x^3 2^n + 3nx^2 2^{n-1} + 3n(n-1)x \, 2^{n-2} + n(n-1)(n-2)2^{n-3}] \, e^{2x} \qquad \blacksquare$$

□ Obtain the nth derivative of $x^2 y$ with respect to x, where $y = y(x)$.   **Example**

Here we take $u = x^2$, so $u_1 = 2x$, $u_2 = 2$ and $v = y$. So

$$(x^2 y)_n = x^2 y_n + \binom{n}{1} 2x y_{n-1} + \binom{n}{2} 2 y_{n-2}$$

$$= x^2 y_n + 2nx y_{n-1} + n(n-1) y_{n-2} \qquad \blacksquare$$

□ If   **Example**

$$x \frac{dy}{dx} + y = x^2$$

Gottfried Wilhelm Leibniz (1646–1716); major German philosopher and mathematician; pioneer of the calculus.

show that

$$x \frac{d^{n+1}y}{dx^{n+1}} + (n + 1) \frac{d^n y}{dx^n} = 0 \qquad \text{for } n \geqslant 3$$

We differentiate each side of the equation with respect to x using Leibniz's theorem:

$$\left(x \frac{dy}{dx}\right)_n = (xy_1)_n$$

$$= xy_{n+1} + \binom{n}{1} 1y_n = xy_{n+1} + ny_n$$

Now

$$(x^2)_1 = 2x, \; (x^2)_2 = 2, \; (x^2)_n = 0 \qquad (n \geqslant 3)$$

Consequently for $n \geqslant 3$ we have

$$xy_{n+1} + ny_n + y_n = 0$$

So

$$x \frac{d^{n+1}y}{dx^{n+1}} + (n + 1) \frac{d^n y}{dx^n} = 0 \qquad \text{for } n \geqslant 3 \qquad \blacksquare$$

4.8 TECHNIQUES OF DIFFERENTIATION

Do not forget that very often if you pause and think for a few moments you can save yourself a lot of needless work. This is particularly true when it comes to differentiation, where a little algebraic simplification at the outset can make things very much easier.

Example □ Differentiate with respect to x

$$\left[\frac{1 - \sin x}{1 + \sin x}\right]^{1/2}$$

where $x \in (-\pi/2, \pi/2)$.

We could of course hit this head on and give it the full works, differentiating using the chain rule and the quotient rule. Instead we shall tame it first by multiplying numerator and denominator by $1 - \sin x$ inside the root. Algebraically this leaves everything the same, but from our point of view it will help greatly. So

$$\left[\frac{1 - \sin x}{1 + \sin x} \frac{(1 - \sin x)}{(1 - \sin x)}\right]^{1/2} = \left[\frac{(1 - \sin x)(1 - \sin x)}{(1 + \sin x)(1 - \sin x)}\right]^{1/2}$$

$$= \left[\frac{(1 - \sin x)^2}{(1 - \sin^2 x)}\right]^{1/2}$$

$$= \left[\frac{(1 - \sin x)^2}{\cos^2 x}\right]^{1/2}$$

$$= \left[\frac{(1 - \sin x)}{\cos x}\right]$$

$$= \sec x - \tan x$$

After all that excitement we mustn't forget to differentiate:

$$\frac{dy}{dx} = \sec x \tan x - \sec^2 x$$

Whenever we have a complicated expression to differentiate, it is worth looking to see if it can be simplified algebraically first. ∎

Before we consider any further techniques, here are a few steps to get you used to using the chain rule without making a formal substitution.

_____4.9 Workshop_____

▷**Exercise**   Differentiate with respect to t:
a $\ln (2t^2 + 1)$
b $\sin^3 t$
c $\sin 3t$
d $\sin t^3$
Try each one of these. Remember that the idea is to avoid having to write out all the details of a substitution. We differentiate with respect to 'the thing in brackets', then multiply by the derivative of 'the thing in brackets' with respect to t.

For **a** we have

$$\frac{d}{dt}[\ln (2t^2 + 1)] = \frac{d}{d(\ )}\ln (2t^2 + 1)\frac{d(\ )}{dt}$$

$$= \frac{1}{2t^2 + 1}\frac{d}{dt}(2t^2 + 1)$$

$$= \frac{4t}{2t^2 + 1}$$

If you made a mistake, check your working for **b**, **c** and **d** before you step ahead for the solutions.

For **b** we obtain

$$\frac{d}{dt}[\sin^3 t] = \frac{d}{dt}(\sin t)^3$$

$$= \frac{d}{d(\ )}(\sin t)^3 \frac{d(\ )}{dt}$$

$$= 3(\sin t)^2 \frac{d}{dt}(\sin t)$$

$$= 3\sin^2 t \cos t$$

If you made a mistake here, possibly you confused $\sin^3 t$ with either $\sin 3t$ or $\sin t^3$. It is important to realize that these are three different expressions.

---

4 Next, for **c** we have

$$\frac{d}{dt}[\sin 3t] = \frac{d}{d(\ )}\sin (3t)\frac{d}{dt}(3t)$$

$$= (\cos 3t)\,3 = 3\cos 3t$$

---

5 Finally, for **d** we obtain

$$\frac{d}{dt}[\sin t^3] = \frac{d}{d(\ )}\sin (t^3)\frac{d(\ )}{dt}$$

$$= \cos (t^3)\frac{d}{dt}(t^3) = 3t^2 \cos t^3$$

If you managed all those without difficulty you should be able to skip up the steps with ease. For further practice here is another problem.

▷**Exercise**   Differentiate with respect to u:
a exp (sin $2u$)
b ln [1 + sin^2 ($2u$ + 1)]
c exp $2u$ cos ($3u$ + 1)
Try them all and check your answers step by step.

---

6 For **a** we have

$$\frac{d}{du}[e^{\sin 2u}] = \frac{d}{d(\ )}[e^{(\sin 2u)}]\frac{d}{du}(\sin 2u)$$

$$= e^{\sin 2u}\frac{d}{du}(\sin 2u)$$

$$= e^{\sin 2u}\frac{d}{d(\ )}[\sin (2u)]\frac{d}{du}(2u)$$

$$= e^{\sin 2u} \cos 2u \, 2$$
$$= 2e^{\sin 2u} \cos 2u$$

Next, for **b** we obtain

$$\frac{d}{du} \ln [1 + \sin^2 (2u + 1)]$$

$$= \frac{d}{d[\ ]} \ln [1 + \sin^2 (2u + 1)] \frac{d}{du} [\ ]$$

$$= \frac{1}{1 + \sin^2 (2u + 1)} \frac{d}{du} [1 + \sin^2 (2u + 1)]$$

$$= \frac{1}{1 + \sin^2 (2u + 1)} \frac{d}{du} [\sin (2u + 1)]^2$$

$$= \frac{1}{1 + \sin^2 (2u + 1)} \frac{d}{d[\ ]} [\sin (2u + 1)]^2 \frac{d}{du} [\ ]$$

$$= \frac{1}{1 + \sin^2 (2u + 1)} 2 [\sin (2u + 1)] \frac{d}{du} \sin (2u + 1)$$

$$= \frac{1}{1 + \sin^2 (2u + 1)} 2 \sin (2u + 1) \cos (2u + 1) \, 2$$

$$= \frac{4 \sin (2u + 1) \cos (2u + 1)}{1 + \sin^2 (2u + 1)}$$

Finally, for **c** we have

$$\frac{d}{du} [e^{2u} \cos (3u + 1)]$$

$$= e^{2u} \frac{d}{du} [\cos (3u + 1)] + \cos (3u + 1) \frac{d}{du} [e^{2u}]$$

$$= e^{2u} [-\sin (3u + 1)] \, 3 + \cos (3u + 1) \, e^{2u} \, 2$$

$$= e^{2u} [-3 \sin (3u + 1) + 2 \cos (3u + 1)]$$

Now we are ready to continue.

4.10 LOGARITHMIC DIFFERENTIATION

It is not always possible to simplify an expression, but if it is a product or a quotient it may help to 'take logarithms' before differentiating. By this means we avoid the use of the product rule, but more importantly we avoid the very awkward quotient rule. Two examples will illustrate this technique.

Example □ Differentiate with respect to x

$$y = \frac{(1 + x) \sin^2 x}{(1 + 4x) (1 - x)^3}$$

Before taking logarithms we should be assured that both sides are positive. This is certainly true if $x \in (-1, 1)$, and so we shall suppose that we are within this interval. Using the laws of logarithms (see Chapter 1)

$$\ln y = \ln (1 + x) + \ln (\sin^2 x) - \ln (1 + 4x) - \ln (1 - x)^3$$
$$= \ln (1 + x) + 2 \ln (\sin x) - \ln (1 + 4x) - 3 \ln (1 - x)$$

Now differentiating throughout with respect to x gives

$$\frac{1}{y} \frac{dy}{dx} = \frac{1}{1 + x} + \frac{2 \cos x}{\sin x} - \frac{4}{1 + 4x} - \frac{3(-1)}{1 - x}$$

$$\frac{dy}{dx} = \left(\frac{1}{1 + x} + \frac{2 \cos x}{\sin x} - \frac{4}{1 + 4x} + \frac{3}{1 - x} \right) \frac{(1 + x) \sin^2 x}{(1 + 4x) (1 - x)^3} \quad ■$$

Example □ Differentiate x^x with respect to x (>0).
Let $y = x^x$. Then

$$\ln y = \ln (x^x) = x \ln x$$

So

$$\frac{d}{dx} (\ln y) = \frac{d}{dx} (x \ln x) = x \frac{d}{dx} (\ln x) + (\ln x) 1$$

Therefore

$$\frac{1}{y} \frac{dy}{dx} = x \frac{1}{x} + \ln x$$

So

$$\frac{dy}{dx} = y(1 + \ln x) = x^x(1 + \ln x) \quad ■$$

4.11 IMPLICIT DIFFERENTIATION

Occasionally when y is given in terms of x this is not expressed explicitly; instead, y and x are related by an equation. We sometimes say that y is given **implicitly** in terms of x. For example if x and y are related by the equation

$$x^2 + 3xy + y^3 = 5$$

then y is given implicitly in terms of x.

To differentiate y with respect to x it is not necessary first to express y explicitly in terms of x. Instead we can differentiate both sides of the equation with respect to x and use the chain rule. Here

$$\frac{d}{dx} f(y) = f'(y) \frac{dy}{dx}$$

☐ Obtain the first derivative of y with respect to x at the point $(1, 1)$ if   **Example**

$$x^2 + 3xy + y^3 = 5$$

We should check that the point $(1, 1)$ lies on the curve. It does because $x = 1$ and $y = 1$ satisfy the equation. Now we go through the equation, differentiating with respect to x and using the chain rule:

$$2x + 3x \frac{dy}{dx} + 3y + 3y^2 \frac{dy}{dx} = 0$$

$$3(x + y^2) \frac{dy}{dx} = -2x - 3y$$

$$\frac{dy}{dx} = \frac{-2x - 3y}{3(x + y^2)}$$

When $x = 1$ and $y = 1$ we obtain

$$\frac{dy}{dx} = \frac{-5}{6}$$ ■

4.12 PARAMETRIC DIFFERENTIATION

If a function is defined parametrically then it is better to use the chain rule to obtain its derivative in terms of the parameter. Of course theoretically we could eliminate the parameter and differentiate in the ordinary way. However, in practice this may not be possible.

Therefore if $y = y(t)$ and $x = x(t)$ we have

For example, the position of a point (x, y) can depend on temperature or time. This practical situation occurs frequently.

$$\frac{dy}{dx} = \frac{dy}{dt} \frac{dt}{dx}$$

and because

$$1 = \frac{dx}{dx} = \frac{dx}{dt} \frac{dt}{dx}$$

we obtain

$$\frac{dy}{dx} = \frac{dy}{dt} \Big/ \frac{dx}{dt}$$

There is one very important point to watch out for, and it is a frequent cause of error. Although

$$\frac{dy}{dx} = \frac{dy}{dt}\frac{dt}{dx}$$

a similar result does *not* hold for second-order derivatives. In symbols,

$$\frac{d^2y}{dx^2} \neq \frac{d^2y}{dt^2}\frac{d^2t}{dx^2}$$

!

In fact if you look carefully you will see that not even the notation leads you to believe this will work. Nevertheless many examination scripts contain attempts at solutions to differentiation problems which try to use this. It is a very popular mistake!

In order to obtain the second-order derivative it is necessary to use the chain rule again because the first derivative will be in terms of t:

$$\frac{d^2y}{dx^2} = \frac{d}{dx}\left(\frac{dy}{dx}\right) = \frac{d}{dt}\left(\frac{dy}{dx}\right)\frac{dt}{dx}$$

$$= \frac{d}{dt}\left(\frac{dy}{dt}\frac{dt}{dx}\right)\frac{dt}{dx}$$

Example □ If $y = \cos t + \sin t$ and $x = \tan t$, obtain the first-order and second-order derivatives of y with respect to x.

As you can see, it would not be easy to eliminate t. So we use the chain rule

$$\frac{dy}{dx} = \frac{dy}{dt}\frac{dt}{dx}$$

Now

$$\frac{dy}{dt} = \frac{d}{dt}(\cos t + \sin t)$$

$$= -\sin t + \cos t$$

Also

$$\frac{dx}{dt} = \frac{d}{dt}(\tan t) = \sec^2 t$$

Therefore the first-order derivative is

$$\frac{dy}{dx} = \frac{dy}{dt}\frac{dt}{dx} = \frac{-\sin t + \cos t}{\sec^2 t}$$

$$= -\sin t \cos^2 t + \cos^3 t$$

We use the chain rule again to obtain the second-order derivative:

$$\frac{d^2y}{dx^2} = \frac{d}{dt}(\cos^3 t - \sin t \cos^2 t)\frac{dt}{dx}$$

$$= \{3\cos^2 t\,(-\sin t) - [\sin t\, 2\cos t\,(-\sin t) + \cos^2 t\cos t]\}\cos^2 t$$

See how we use the chain rule here without the formal substitution. To differentiate $\cos^3 t$ with respect to t, we first differentiate $\cos^3 t$ with respect to $\cos t$ to obtain $3\cos^2 t$ and then multiply this by $-\sin t$, the derivative of $\cos t$ with respect to t.

Now we simplify:

$$\frac{d^2y}{dx^2} = (-3\cos^2 t\sin t + 2\sin^2 t\cos t - \cos^3 t)\cos^2 t$$

$$= (-3\cos t\sin t + 2\sin^2 t - \cos^2 t)\cos^3 t$$
$$= [-3\cos t\sin t + 2(1 - \cos^2 t) - \cos^2 t]\cos^3 t$$
$$= (-3\cos t\sin t + 2 - 3\cos^2 t)\cos^3 t$$
$$= 2\cos^3 t - 3\cos^4 t(\cos t + \sin t)$$

If you use the chain rule correctly and don't invent your own version, nothing should go wrong. ∎

4.13 RATES OF CHANGE

We can apply differentiation to obtain the rates at which variables change.

□ A spherical balloon is pumped up at a constant rate of 1 m³/s. Obtain **Example** the rate of change of the radius at the instant when it is 0.5 m.

We may denote the volume of the balloon by V and the radius by r. As time increases, r and V change. We have the following relationship between V and r:

$$V = \frac{4}{3}\pi r^3$$

We know that dV/dt is constant at 1 m³/s, and we wish to determine dr/dt. This is a simple application of the chain rule:

$$\frac{dV}{dt} = \frac{4}{3}3\pi r^2\frac{dr}{dt}$$

$$= 4\pi r^2\frac{dr}{dt}$$

Therefore substituting into this equation we obtain

$$\frac{dr}{dt} = \frac{1}{4\pi(0.5)^2} = \frac{1}{\pi}\ \text{m/s} \qquad\qquad ∎$$

Are you ready for some steps? If not then read through the chapter again to familiarize yourself with it.

_____4.14 Workshop_____

1

Exercise Evaluate the following limit:

$$\lim_{x \to \pi/2} \left(\frac{2 \tan x}{1 - \tan^2 x} \right)$$

As soon as you have had a crack at this, move on and see if you are right.

2 We cannot put $x = \pi/2$ since $\tan \pi/2$ is not defined. Therefore some other approach must be used. Here is one:

$$\tan 2x = \frac{2 \tan x}{1 - \tan^2 x}$$

So

$$\lim_{x \to \pi/2} \left(\frac{2 \tan x}{1 - \tan^2 x} \right) = \lim_{x \to \pi/2} (\tan 2x) = 0$$

If this has worked out well you may proceed directly to step 4. If you didn't get the limit correct then you will need to make sure you follow what has been done before you proceed. If you feel you would like some more practice then here is another problem.

▷**Exercise** Determine the following limit:

$$\lim_{x \to \pi/2} \left(\frac{1 - \sin x}{2 \cos^2 x} \right)$$

When you are ready, take the next step.

3 If we attempt to put $x = \pi/2$ we obtain the undefined expression $0/0$. Here is one way of proceeding:

$$\frac{1 - \sin x}{2 \cos^2 x} = \frac{1 - \sin x}{2(1 - \sin^2 x)} = \frac{1}{2(1 + \sin x)}$$

$$\to \frac{1}{2(1 + 1)} = \frac{1}{4} \text{ as } x \to \pi/2$$

Now step ahead.

▷**Exercise**   A function f is defined by

$$f(x) = \frac{2 \sin x}{\sec x \tan x} \qquad (x \neq 0)$$

$$f(x) = 2 \qquad\qquad (x = 0)$$

Use the convention of the maximal domain to describe the domain. Then decide whether or not the function is continuous at 0.

Make a good attempt at this one, then move to step 5 for the answer.

By the convention of the maximal domain (Chapter 2) the function is defined at all points where $\sec x \tan x$ is not zero. Now $\sec x$ is never zero, and $\tan x$ is only zero when x is a multiple of π. So the domain consists of all the real numbers except for a non-zero multiple of π. ($f(0)$ is defined separately.) Notationally the domain is

$$A = \{r \,|\, r \in \mathbb{R}, r \neq n\pi, \text{ where } n \in \mathbb{Z}, n \neq 0\}$$

If

$$\lim_{x \to 0} f(x) = f(0)$$

then the function is continuous at 0. We have

$$\lim_{x \to 0} f(x) = \lim_{x \to 0} \left(\frac{2 \sin x}{\sec x \tan x} \right)$$

$$= \lim_{x \to 0} \left(\frac{2 \sin x \cos^2 x}{\sin x} \right)$$

$$= \lim_{x \to 0} (2 \cos^2 x) = 2$$

Also by definition $f(0) = 2$, and so the function f is continuous at 0.

If you had trouble with the description of the domain it may repay you to concentrate some attention on Chapter 2.

Before we leave limits and continuity here is one more problem. It should cause no difficulty now.

▷**Exercise**   The real function f is defined by

$$f(x) = \frac{e^{2x} - 1}{e^x - 1} \qquad (x \neq 0)$$

$$f(x) = k \qquad\qquad (x = 0)$$

Calculate the value of k if it is known that f is continuous.

Best foot forward!

6 For continuity we require $f(x) \to f(0)$ as $x \to 0$, so that

$$k = \lim_{x \to 0} \frac{e^{2x} - 1}{e^x - 1}$$

$$= \lim_{x \to 0} \frac{(e^x - 1)(e^x + 1)}{e^x - 1}$$

$$= \lim_{x \to 0} (e^x + 1) = 1 + 1 = 2$$

Now move on to the next exercise.

▷ **Exercise**   Obtain the nth derivative with respect to x of

$$x^3 \frac{d^3 y}{dx^3}$$

where $y = y(x)$ and n is any natural number.

Leibniz was one of the great philosophers, but you shouldn't need to ponder too deeply about this.

7 We must calculate $(x^3 y_3)_n$, where we are using the subscript notation to denote differentiation with respect to x. Now

$$(uv)_n = uv_n + n u_1 v_{n-1} + \ldots + u_n v$$

Put $u = x^3$: then $u_1 = 3x^2$, $u_2 = 6x$, $u_3 = 6$. It follows that $u_r = 0$ for $r > 3$. Put $v = y_3$: then $v_1 = y_4$, $v_2 = y_5$, $\ldots$, $v_r = y_{r+3}$. Substituting into Leibniz's formula, we obtain

$$(x^3 y_3)_n = x^3 y_{n+3} + n\, 3x^2 y_{n+2} + \frac{n(n-1)}{1 \times 2} 6x y_{n+1} + \frac{n(n-1)(n-2)}{1 \times 2 \times 3} 6 y_n$$

$$= x^3 y_{n+3} + n\, 3x^2 y_{n+2} + 3n(n-1)x y_{n+1} + n(n-1)(n-2)y_n$$

$$= x^3 \frac{d^{n+3} y}{dx^{n+3}} + 3nx^2 \frac{d^{n+2} y}{dx^{n+2}} + 3n(n-1)x \frac{d^{n+1} y}{dx^{n+1}}$$

$$+ n(n-1)(n-2)\frac{d^n y}{dx^n}$$

Did that go well? If it didn't, here is another problem. If it did, you can miss this one out and step ahead to step 9.

▷ **Exercise**   Show that if

$$x \frac{dy}{dx} + y = e^{2x}$$

then

$$x \frac{d^{n+1}y}{dx^{n+1}} + (n+1) \frac{d^n y}{dx^n} = 2^n e^{2x} \qquad (n \in \mathbb{N}_0)$$

Step ahead for the answer.

Using the subscript notation, we have

$$xy_1 + y = e^{2x}$$

If throughout we differentiate n times with respect to x we obtain

$$(xy_1)_n + y_n = (e^{2x})_n$$

Now $(e^{2x})_1 = 2e^{2x}$, so $(e^{2x})_2 = 2^2 e^{2x}$ and in general $(e^{2x})_n = 2^n e^{2x}$. Using Leibniz's formula on the first term in the equation, we have

$$[xy_{n+1} + n(1)y_n] + y_n = 2^n e^{2x}$$

So

$$x \frac{d^{n+1}y}{dx^{n+1}} + (n+1) \frac{d^n y}{dx^n} = 2^n e^{2x} \qquad (n \in \mathbb{N}_0)$$

One last exercise will reinforce much that we have covered.

>**Exercise** Suppose that $y = e^{2x} + e^{3x}$ and $z = x^3 y$. Calculate $d^{12}z/dx^{12}$ when $x = 0$.

Think about this and then try it out for yourself before stepping on.

We could evaluate $x^3 y$ and differentiate the result twelve times, but that would be tedious. Instead we apply Leibniz's formula to differentiate z n times:

$$z_n = (x^3 y)_n$$

$$= x^3 y_n + n\, 3x^2 y_{n-1} + \frac{n(n-1)}{1 \times 2} 6xy_{n-2} + \frac{n(n-1)(n-2)}{6} 6y_{n-3}$$

Now $y = e^{2x} + e^{3x}$, so $y_1 = 2e^{2x} + 3e^{3x}$, and in general $y_r = 2^r e^{2x} + 3^r e^{3x}$. So putting $x = 0$ in the expression for z_n produces

$$z_n = 0 + 0 + 0 + n(n-1)(n-2)(2^{n-3}1 + 3^{n-3}1)$$
$$= n(n-1)(n-2)(2^{n-3} + 3^{n-3})$$

Finally when $n = 12$ we obtain

$$\frac{d^{12}z}{dx^{12}} = 12 \times 11 \times 10 \ (2^9 + 3^9) = 26\,657\,400$$

Now for two applications.

4.15 Practical

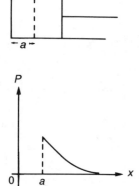

CYLINDER PRESSURE

The pressure inside a cylinder is given by

$$P = \frac{k}{\pi a^2 x}$$

where a and k are constants and x is allowed to change; initially $x = a$. Obtain the pressure gradient dP/dt, in terms of the initial pressure P_0, at the instant when x has doubled its initial value if x is moving at a constant rate of 1 m/s.

Try this; it is not at all difficult.

We require dP/dt, and so we differentiate through the equation using the chain rule. We obtain

$$\frac{dP}{dt} = \frac{-k}{\pi a^2 x^2} \frac{dx}{dt}$$

Now $dx/dt = 1$, and so when $x = 2a$

$$\frac{dP}{dt} = \frac{-k}{4\pi a^4}$$

The initial pressure is given by $P_0 = k/\pi a^3$, so $k = P_0 \pi a^3$. Therefore the pressure gradient when $x = 2a$ is given by

$$\frac{dP}{dt} = -\frac{P_0 \pi a^3}{4\pi a^4} = -\frac{P_0}{4a}$$

WATER SEEPAGE

Let's apply differentiation to solve another problem.

A crater, in the shape of part of a sphere of radius r, has been dug in porous soil by construction workers. The work has been interrupted by heavy rain. Water is falling at a constant rate w m³/s per unit horizontal surface area and is seeping into the surrounding soil at a constant rate of p m³/s per unit area of soil–water contact. When the water pool has depth h and surface diameter $2a$ it can be shown that the area of soil–water contact is $\pi(h^2 + a^2)$ and that the volume of water then present is $\pi h(h^2 + 3a^2)/6$.

Obtain the rate at which the depth h is increasing. Deduce that if $p = w/2$ then

$$\frac{dh}{dt} = \frac{w(a^2 - h^2)}{2a^2}$$

Deduce also that, in the steady state (when $dh/dt = 0$),

$$p = wa^2/(a^2 + h^2)$$

Try this problem, and then follow the solution through stage by stage when you are ready.

The water pool is shown in Fig. 4.7. We have

$$r^2 = (r - h)^2 + a^2$$
$$= r^2 - 2hr + h^2 + a^2$$

So $2hr - h^2 = a^2$.

Now the rate at which the volume is increasing can be obtained by considering the water which comes in and subtracting the water which seeps out. The amount which comes in each second is proportional to the air–surface area: the amount which seeps out is proportional to the soil–water area. Therefore

$$\frac{dV}{dt} = w\pi a^2 - p\pi(a^2 + h^2)$$

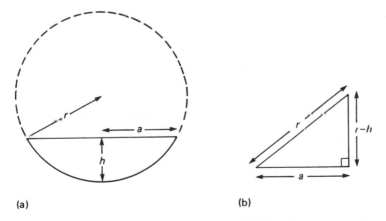

(a)   **(b)**

Fig. 4.7 (a) Representation of the crater (b) Triangle relating r, h and a.

If you didn't get to this stage, see if you can make the next move on your own before you check ahead.

We have

$$V = \frac{\pi h^3}{6} + \frac{\pi a^2 h}{2}$$

$$= \frac{\pi h^3}{6} + \frac{\pi h}{2}(2hr - h^2)$$

$$= \pi r h^2 - \frac{\pi h^3}{3}$$

So

$$\frac{dV}{dt} = 2\pi r h \frac{dh}{dt} - \pi h^2 \frac{dh}{dt}$$

$$= \pi(2rh - h^2)\frac{dh}{dt}$$

$$= \pi h(2r - h)\frac{dh}{dt}$$

If you have been unsuccessful to this stage, see if you can take over the problem now. It's simply a question of substitution to find the rate of increase of water depth.

Therefore

$$\pi h(2r - h)\frac{dh}{dt} = \pi(wa^2 - pa^2 - ph^2)$$

$$h(2r - h)\frac{dh}{dt} = (w - p)a^2 - ph^2$$

$$a^2 \frac{dh}{dt} = (w - p)a^2 - ph^2$$

$$\frac{dh}{dt} = w - p - p\left(\frac{h}{a}\right)^2$$

If $p = w/2$ then we deduce that

$$\frac{dh}{dt} = \frac{w}{2} - \frac{w}{2}\left(\frac{h}{a}\right)^2 = \frac{w(a^2 - h^2)}{2a^2}$$

Finally we require the formula for the steady-state seepage rate. We have

$\mathrm{d}h/\mathrm{d}t = 0$, and so

$$0 = w - p - p\left(\frac{h}{a}\right)^2$$

$$w = p + p\left(\frac{h}{a}\right)^2$$

$$p = \frac{wa^2}{a^2 + h^2}$$

SUMMARY

☐ To evaluate $\lim\limits_{x \to a} f(x)$ we examine the behaviour of $f(x)$ near the point a but not at the point a.

☐ We can use the laws of limits freely provided the result is meaningful: $0/0$, ∞/∞, and $0\,\infty$ are not meaningful.

☐ A function is continuous if $\lim\limits_{x \to a} f(x) = f(a)$ for all points a in its domain.

☐ We define

$$\frac{\mathrm{d}y}{\mathrm{d}x} = \lim_{h \to 0} \frac{f(x + h) - f(x)}{h}$$

and from this definition the rules of elementary differentiation follow. We considered some of the techniques of differentiation too.

☐ Leibniz's theorem

$$(uv)_n = uv_n + \binom{n}{1} u_1 v_{n-1} + \ldots + \binom{n}{n} u_n v$$

can be used to differentiate a product n times.

EXERCISES (for answers see p. 741)

1 Differentiate each of the following with respect to x:
  a $3x^2 + 5x + 1$
  b $x^3 - 2x^2$
  c $x^{1/2} + x^{-1/2}$
  d $(x + 2)^6$
  e $\sin(3x + 4)$
  f $\tan^2 3x$
  g $\ln(2x^2 + 1)$
  h $x^2 \sin x^2$

2 Differentiate each of the following with respect to t:

a $\dfrac{(t^2 + 1)(t + 2)}{(t^2 + 2)(t + 1)}$

b $\dfrac{(t + 1)^3(t + 2)^3}{(t + 3)^2}$

c $\dfrac{\sin t \cos 2t}{\sec t}$

d $\dfrac{e^t + 1}{e^t - 1}$

3 If x varies with t, obtain an expression for dy/dt in terms of x and the variable $\alpha = dx/dt$ in each of the following:

a $y = x^3$

b $y = \sin x^2$

c $y = \ln(\sin x)$

d $y^2 = e^x$

4 Obtain

a $\displaystyle\lim_{x \to 0} \left\{ \dfrac{e^x + 1}{e^x - 1} \right\}$

b $\displaystyle\lim_{x \to 0} \left\{ \dfrac{e^x - 1}{\ln(x + 1)^2} \right\}$

c $\displaystyle\lim_{x \to 0} \left\{ \dfrac{\tan 2x}{\sin 3x} \right\}$

d $\displaystyle\lim_{x \to \infty} \left\{ \dfrac{3 \ln x + 1}{2 \ln x - 5} \right\}$

ASSIGNMENT (for answers see p. 742; see also Workshops on pp. 98, 111 and 118)

1 Obtain

a $\displaystyle\lim_{x \to \pi/4} \dfrac{\sin x - \cos x}{\cos 2x}$

b $\displaystyle\lim_{x \to \pi/3} \dfrac{2\cos x - 1}{\sin 3x}$

c $\displaystyle\lim_{x \to \pi/2} \dfrac{\tan x}{\cos x - 1}$

d $\displaystyle\lim_{x \to \infty} \dfrac{2e^x + 1}{3e^x - 1}$

2 Obtain the value of $f(0)$ if the following functions are known to be continuous at 0:

a $f(x) = \dfrac{\cos x - 1}{2 \sin x}$

b $f(x) = \dfrac{\sin^2 x}{\cos^3 x - 1}$

3 Show that if $y = \sin^2 (2x)$ then

$$\frac{d^2y}{dx^2} = 8 - 16y$$

4 Differentiate each of the following with respect to x:

  a $x^{\ln x}$

  b $e^{3x} \tan 2x$

5 If $x^2 + 2xy - y^2 = 16$, show that

$$\frac{dy}{dx} = \frac{y + x}{y - x}$$

6 If $x = t + \sin t$ and $y = t + \cos t$, obtain dy/dx and show that

$$(1 + \cos t)^3 \frac{d^2y}{dx^2} = \sin t - \cos t - 1$$

FURTHER EXERCISES (for answers see p. 742)

1 Differentiate each of the following with respect to x:

  a $(2x + 1)(4x - 7)$

  b $(x - 1)(x - 2)(x - 3)$

  c $(x^2 - 1)^{1/2}$

  d $(x^2 + 3)/(x^2 - 3)$

  e $(a + bx^m)^n$, a, b, m and n constant.

  f $\tan (ax + b)$, a and b constant.

  g $\sqrt{(\operatorname{cosec} x^2)}$

2 Obtain the first four derivatives with respect to x of

  a x^9

  b $\sqrt{(x + 1)}$

  c $\cos^2 x$

  d $x^2 e^x$.

3 If $y^2 = \sec 2x$, show that $d^2y/dx^2 = 3y^5 - y$.

4 If $y = \sin 2t$ and $x = \cos t$, obtain d^2y/dx^2.

5 If $x = \cos^3 \theta$ and $y = \sin^3 \theta$, obtain dy/dx and show that

$$\frac{d^2y}{dx^2} = \frac{1}{3 \cos^4 \theta \sin \theta}$$

6 Use the chain rule to show that

$$\frac{d^2y}{dx^2}\left(\frac{dx}{dy}\right)^3 + \frac{d^2x}{dy^2} = 0$$

7 If y is real and satisfies the equation $y^3 + y = x$, show that $dy/dx = y/(3x - 2y)$.

8 Show that

a $\lim\limits_{x \to 3} [(x^2 - x - 6)/(x^2 + x - 12)] = 5/7$

b $\lim\limits_{x \to 0} \{[(1 + x)^2 - (1 - x)^2]/2x\} = 2$

c $\lim\limits_{x \to 0} \{[(a + x)^3 - (a - x)^3]/2x\} = 3a^2$

9 Evaluate

a $\lim\limits_{x \to 0} \{[1/(x - 1) - 1/x]/[1/(x - 2) + 1/x]\}$

b $\lim\limits_{x \to 1} \{[1/(x - 1) - 1/x] [1/(x - 2) + 1/x]\}$

10 Show that, for $x > 0$,

$$\sqrt{(x^2 + x + 1)} < x + 1/2 + 3/8x$$
$$\sqrt{(x^2 - x + 1)} < x - 1/2 + 1/2x$$

Deduce that

$$\lim\limits_{x \to \infty} [\sqrt{(x^2 + x + 1)} + \sqrt{(x^2 - x + 1)} - 2x] = 0$$

11 The rate at which the surface area of a bubble is increasing is kA, where A is its surface area and k is a constant. If the bubble is spherical, obtain the corresponding rate at which the volume is increasing.

12 Show that if a probe moves in a straight line in such a way that its speed is proportional to the square root of its distance from a fixed point on the line, then its acceleration is constant.

13 The retaining strut on a step ladder breaks, and as the ladder collapses the vertical angle increases at a constant rate. Show that the rate of increase of the distance between the feet is proportional to the height.

14 A uniform beam is clamped horizontally at one end and carries a variable load $w = w(x)$, where x is the distance from the fixed end. If the transverse deflection of the beam is $y(x) = -x^2 e^{-x}$, obtain an expression for w, given that $w = EI \, d^4y/dx^4$ and EI is the flexural rigidity of the beam.

15 A mooring buoy in the shape of a right circular cone, with the diameter of its base equal to its slant height, is submerged in the sea. Marine mud is deposited on it uniformly across the surface at a constant rate ϱ. Calculate the rate at which the surface area is increasing in terms of the height of the cone.

16 The content V cm^3 and the depth p cm of water in a vessel are connected by the relationship $V = 3p^2 - p^3$ ($p > 2$). Show that if water is poured in at a constant rate of Q cm^3/s then, at the moment when the depth is p, it is increasing at a rate $\sigma = Q[3p(2 - p)]^{-1}$.

17 A beam of length l m has one end resting on horizontal ground and the other leaning against a vertical wall at right angles to it. It begins to slip downwards. Show that when the foot of the beam is x m from the wall and moving at h m/s away from it, the top is descending at a rate $xh/(l^2 - x^2)^{1/2}$ m/s.

18 A rope l m long is attached to a heavy weight and passed over a pulley h m above the ground ($2h < l$). The other end of the rope is tied to a vehicle which moves at a constant rate u in a radial direction away from the vertical line of the weight and the pulley. Calculate (a) the rate at which the weight is rising when the vehicle is x m from the vertical line of the weight and the pulley, and (b) the rate at which the angle between the rope and the ground is changing.

19 Sand falls from a chute and forms a conical pile in such a way that the vertical angle remains constant. Suppose r is the base radius and h is the height at time t.

a Show that if r is increasing at a rate α cm/s then the volume is increasing at a rate $\pi r h \alpha$ cm^3/s.

b Show that if the height h is increasing at a rate β cm/s then the exposed surface area is increasing at a rate $2\pi r \beta \sqrt{(h^2 + r^2)}/h$ cm^2/s.

(The volume of the cone is $\pi r^2 h/3$ and the surface area is $\pi r l$, where l is the slant height.)

20 A body moves in a straight line in accordance with the equation $s = t^2/(1 + t^2)$, where t is time in seconds and s is the distance travelled in metres. Show that $0 \leqslant s < 1$. Show also that the speed u and acceleration f are given at time t by

$$u = \sin \theta \ (1 + \cos \theta)/2$$
$$f = (2 \cos \theta - 1) \ (1 + \cos \theta)^2/2$$

where $t = \tan (\theta/2)$.

21 A landmark on a distant hill is x metres from a water tower. The angle of elevation from the top of the tower is observed to be θ degrees, whereas the angle of elevation from the foot of the tower is observed to be $\theta + h$ degrees.

a How high is the water tower?

b Show that if h is small then the height of the water tower is approximately $\pi x h/180 \cos^2 \theta$.

5   Hyperbolic functions

Although we have now explored some of the basic terminology of mathematics and developed the techniques of the differential calculus, we need to pause to extend our algebraic knowledge. In this chapter we shall describe a class of functions known as the hyperbolic functions which are very similar in some ways to the circular functions. We shall use the opportunity to consider in detail what is meant by an inverse function.

After studying this chapter you should be able to
☐ Use the hyperbolic functions and their identities;
☐ Solve algebraic equations which involve hyperbolic functions;
☐ Differentiate hyperbolic functions;
☐ Decide when a function has an inverse function;
☐ Express inverse hyperbolic functions in logarithmic form.
We shall also consider a practical problem concerning the sag of a chain.

5.1 DEFINITIONS AND IDENTITIES

The hyperbolic functions are in some ways very similar to the circular functions. Indeed when we deal with complex numbers (Chapter 10) we shall see that there is an algebraic relationship between the two. Initially we shall discuss the hyperbolic functions algebraically, but later we shall see that one of them arises in a physical context.

The functions cosine and sine are called circular functions because $x = \cos \theta$ and $y = \sin \theta$ satisfy the equation $x^2 + y^2 = 1$, which is the equation of a circle. The functions known as the hyperbolic cosine (cosh) and the hyperbolic sine (sinh) are called **hyperbolic functions** because $x = \cosh u$ and $y = \sinh u$ satisfy the equation $x^2 - y^2 = 1$, which is the equation of a rectangular hyperbola.

We shall define the hyperbolic functions and use these definitions to sketch their graphs. Here then are the definitions:

$$\cosh u = \frac{e^u + e^{-u}}{2} \qquad \sinh u = \frac{e^u - e^{-u}}{2}$$

Now the exponential function has domain $\mathbb{R}$ and consequently both $\cosh u$ and $\sinh u$ are defined for all real numbers u.

To obtain a sketch of the graphs of $y = \cosh x$ and $y = \sinh x$ we can use the graphs of $y = e^x$.

$y = \cosh x$
If the graphs of $y = e^x$ and $y = e^{-x}$ are both drawn on the same diagram (Fig. 5.1) then chords can be drawn parallel to the y-axis between these two curves. The midpoints of these chords then lie on the curve $y = \cosh x$.

The hyperbolic cosine curve is one which arises in practice. It is often called the **catenary**. If a heavy rope or chain is freely suspended between two fixed points, the shape it assumes is that of the catenary. This has to be taken into account when, for example, suspension bridges are designed. At one time surveyors had to make a 'catenary correction' when using steel tape measures, but with modern electronic measuring devices this is not necessary.

We shall meet the catenary again when we discuss intrinsic coordinates in section 6.4.

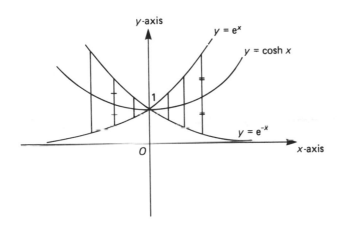

Fig. 5.1 The graph of $y = \cosh x$, by construction.

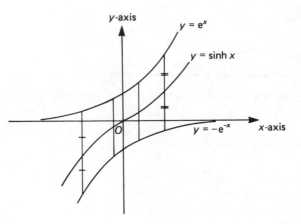

Fig. 5.2 The graph of $y = \sinh x$, by construction.

$y = \sinh x$

We draw the graphs of $y = e^x$ and $y = -e^{-x}$ on the same diagram (Fig. 5.2) and draw chords parallel to the y-axis between the two curves. The mid-points of the chords then lie on the curve $y = \sinh x$.

We define the hyperbolic tangent, cotangent, secant and cosecant by imitating the definitions for circular functions:

$$\tanh x = \frac{\sinh x}{\cosh x} \qquad \coth x = \frac{\cosh x}{\sinh x}$$

$$\operatorname{sech} x = \frac{1}{\cosh x} \qquad \operatorname{cosech} x = \frac{1}{\sinh x}$$

Strictly it is not necessary to know how to pronounce these new functions, but for completeness we shall indicate the standard practice. The hyperbolic functions cosh and coth are pronounced as they are written; sinh is pronounced 'shine'; tanh is pronounced 'than' but with a soft 'th' as in 'thank'; sech is pronounced 'sheck' and cosech as 'cosheck'.

From the definitions we obtain

$$\cosh x + \sinh x = \frac{e^x + e^{-x}}{2} + \frac{e^x - e^{-x}}{2} = e^x$$

$$\cosh x - \sinh x = \frac{e^x + e^{-x}}{2} - \frac{e^x - e^{-x}}{2} = e^{-x}$$

Therefore

$$\cosh^2 x - \sinh^2 x = (\cosh x + \sinh x)(\cosh x - \sinh x)$$
$$= e^x e^{-x} = 1$$

So we have the identity

$$\cosh^2 x - \sinh^2 x = 1$$

(this corresponds to the circular identity $\cos^2 x + \sin^2 x = 1$).

We can either appeal to the symmetry of the graphs or use the definitions to deduce that

$$\cosh(-x) = \cosh x$$
$$\sinh(-x) = -\sinh x$$

and therefore

$$\tanh(-x) = -\tanh x$$

We have already come across one identity involving hyperbolic functions:

$$\cosh^2 x - \sinh^2 x = 1$$

In fact corresponding to every identity involving circular functions there is an identity involving hyperbolic functions. There is a rule for converting identities involving circular functions into those involving hyperbolic functions. The rule is if there is a product of two sines or an *implied* product of two sines, the term changes sign. Although this can be applied in reverse it is easy to make mistakes, and so we shall avoid it altogether.

Here is a list of the main identities:

$$\cosh(x + y) = \cosh x \cosh y + \sinh x \sinh y$$
$$\cosh(x - y) = \cosh x \cosh y - \sinh x \sinh y$$
$$\sinh(x + y) = \sinh x \cosh y + \cosh x \sinh y$$
$$\sinh(x - y) = \sinh x \cosh y - \cosh x \sinh y$$

☐ Use the basic definitions to establish the identity   **Example**

$$\cosh(x + y) = \cosh x \cosh y + \sinh x \sinh y$$

We have

$$\text{LHS} = \frac{e^x + e^{-x}}{2} \frac{e^y + e^{-y}}{2} + \frac{e^x - e^{-x}}{2} \frac{e^y - e^{-y}}{2}$$

$$= \frac{1}{4}(e^x e^y + e^x e^{-y} + e^{-x} e^y + e^{-x} e^{-y}$$

$$+ e^x e^y - e^x e^{-y} - e^{-x} e^y + e^{-x} e^{-y})$$

$$= \frac{1}{4}(2e^{x+y} + 2e^{-(x+y)})$$

$$= \frac{e^{x+y} + e^{-(x+y)}}{2} = \text{RHS} \qquad \blacksquare$$

Now one for you to try!

Example □ Use the basic definitions to establish the identity

$$\sinh (x - y) = \sinh x \cosh y - \cosh x \sinh y$$

Make a good effort. Check carefully before you begin that you follow all the stages in the one we have just done – and then best foot forward!

We have

$$\sinh x \cosh y - \cosh x \sinh y$$

$$= \frac{e^x - e^{-x}}{2} \frac{e^y + e^{-y}}{2} - \frac{e^x + e^{-x}}{2} \frac{e^y - e^{-y}}{2}$$

$$= \frac{1}{4}[e^x e^y + e^x e^{-y} - e^{-x} e^y - e^{-x} e^{-y}$$

$$\quad - (e^x e^y - e^x e^{-y} + e^{-x} e^y - e^{-x} e^{-y})]$$

$$= \frac{1}{4}(e^x e^y + e^x e^{-y} - e^{-x} e^y - e^{-x} e^{-y}$$

$$\quad - e^x e^y + e^x e^{-y} - e^{-x} e^y + e^{-x} e^{-y})$$

$$= \frac{1}{4}(2e^{x-y} - 2e^{-x+y})$$

$$= \frac{e^{x-y} - e^{-(x-y)}}{2} = \sinh (x - y) \qquad \blacksquare$$

Good! If you need any more practice you can always try the other two identities.

We defined the hyperbolic functions in terms of exponential functions, and so it is perhaps not surprising that we need our work on logarithms (Chapter 1) when solving equations involving hyperbolic functions.

Example □ Obtain all the real solutions of the equation

$$\cosh x + \sinh x = 1$$

There are two approaches, each valid and so we shall solve the equation in two different ways.

1 We know $\cosh^2 x - \sinh^2 x = 1$, and so

$$(\cosh x - \sinh x)(\cosh x + \sinh x) = 1$$

Here $\cosh x + \sinh x = 1$, and therefore $\cosh x - \sinh x = 1$. So

$$(\cosh x + \sinh x) + (\cosh x - \sinh x) = 2$$

Therefore $2 \cosh x = 2$, so $\cosh x = 1$ and $x = 0$ is the only solution. Here we have used a hyperbolic identity to sort out the problem.

2 From the definitions,

$$\frac{e^x + e^{-x}}{2} + \frac{e^x - e^{-x}}{2} = 1$$

So $e^x = 1$ and therefore $x = 0$. ∎

In this example it was much easier and more direct to use the definitions at the outset. However, this is not always the case.

☐ Solve the equation

Example

$$8 \sinh x = 3 \operatorname{sech} x$$

We begin by writing the equation in terms of $\sinh x$ and $\cosh x$:

$$8 \sinh x = \frac{3}{\cosh x}$$

So $\sinh x \cosh x = 3/8$. Therefore $2 \sinh x \cosh x = 3/4$, and $\sinh 2x = 3/4$.

Now $(e^{2x} - e^{-2x})/2 = 3/4$. Therefore $2e^{2x} - 2e^{-2x} = 3$. Multiplying by e^{2x} gives

$$2(e^{2x})^2 - 2 = 3e^{2x}$$
$$2(e^{2x})^2 - 3e^{2x} - 2 = 0$$
$$(2e^{2x} + 1)(e^{2x} - 2) = 0$$

So either $2e^{2x} + 1 = 0$ or $e^{2x} - 2 = 0$. Since $e^{2x} > 0$, only $e^{2x} - 2 = 0$ is a possibility. So $2x = \ln 2$ and therefore $x = (\ln 2)/2 = \ln \sqrt{2}$. ∎

Why not try one yourself?

☐ Solve the equation

Example

$$3 \sinh 3x = 13 \sinh x$$

There are many approaches to this problem. If you obtain the correct answer it is probable that your working is basically correct.

Here is one solution:

$$3 \sinh 3x = 13 \sinh x$$
$$3(\sinh 3x - \sinh x) = 10 \sinh x$$

By identity,

$$3(2 \cosh 2x \sinh x) = 10 \sinh x$$

So either $\sinh x = 0$, from which $x = 0$; or $6 \cosh 2x = 10$, from which $3(e^{2x} + e^{-2x}) = 10$. For the latter case, multiply by e^{2x} to obtain

$$3(e^{2x})^2 + 3 = 10e^{2x}$$
$$(3e^{2x} - 1)(e^{2x} - 3) = 0$$

Therefore $e^{2x} = 1/3$ or $e^{2x} = 3$. So $2x = \ln(1/3) = -\ln 3$ or $2x = \ln 3$.
The three solutions are therefore $x = 0$ and $x = \pm\ln\sqrt{3}$. ∎

5.2 DIFFERENTIATION OF HYPERBOLIC FUNCTIONS

We may use the basic rules of differentiation to obtain the derivatives of the hyperbolic functions. All we need to do is use the basic definitions, remembering that

$$\cosh x = \frac{e^x + e^{-x}}{2} \quad \text{and} \quad \sinh x = \frac{e^x - e^{-x}}{2}$$

You might like to try these on your own. Afterwards you can look to see if you were correct.

_____

The derivative of $\cosh x$ is found as follows:

$$\frac{d}{dx}(\cosh x) = \frac{d}{dx}\frac{e^x + e^{-x}}{2}$$

$$= \frac{1}{2}\frac{d}{dx}e^x + \frac{1}{2}\frac{d}{dx}e^{-x}$$

$$= \frac{1}{2}e^x + \frac{1}{2}(-1)e^{-x}$$

$$= \frac{e^x - e^{-x}}{2} = \sinh x$$

The derivative of $\sinh x$ is found as follows:

$$\frac{d}{dx}(\sinh x) = \frac{d}{dx}\frac{e^x - e^{-x}}{2}$$

$$= \frac{1}{2}\frac{d}{dx}e^x - \frac{1}{2}\frac{d}{dx}e^{-x}$$

$$= \frac{1}{2} e^x - \frac{1}{2}(-1) e^{-x}$$

$$= \frac{e^x + e^{-x}}{2} = \cosh x$$

Therefore
1 When we differentiate the hyperbolic cosine we obtain the hyperbolic sine;
2 When we differentiate the hyperbolic sine we obtain the hyperbolic cosine.

Quite remarkable, isn't it?

The derivatives of the other hyperbolic functions can now be obtained from these by applying the rules for differentiation. Try some of these yourself. They are good exercise in differentiation and therefore well worth attempting.

Here is the working for each one.

$$\frac{d}{dx}(\tanh x) = \frac{d}{dx}\left(\frac{\sinh x}{\cosh x}\right)$$

$$= \frac{\cosh x \cosh x - \sinh x \sinh x}{\cosh^2 x}$$

$$= \frac{\cosh^2 x - \sinh^2 x}{\cosh^2 x}$$

$$= \frac{1}{\cosh^2 x} = \text{sech}^2 x$$

$$\frac{d}{dx}(\coth x) = \frac{d}{dx}\left(\frac{\cosh x}{\sinh x}\right)$$

$$= \frac{\sinh x \sinh x - \cosh x \cosh x}{\sinh^2 x}$$

$$= -\frac{\cosh^2 x - \sinh^2 x}{\sinh^2 x}$$

$$= \frac{-1}{\sinh^2 x} = -\text{cosech}^2 x$$

$$\frac{d}{dx}(\text{sech } x) = \frac{d}{dx}\left(\frac{1}{\cosh x}\right)$$

$$= \frac{d}{dx}(\cosh x)^{-1}$$

$$= -(\cosh x)^{-2} \sinh x$$

$$= -\frac{\sinh x}{\cosh^2 x} = -\text{sech } x \tanh x$$

$$\frac{d}{dx}(\operatorname{cosech} x) = \frac{d}{dx}\left(\frac{1}{\sinh x}\right)$$

$$= \frac{d}{dx}(\sinh x)^{-1}$$

$$= -(\sinh x)^{-2} \cosh x$$

$$= -\frac{\cosh x}{\sinh^2 x} = -\operatorname{cosech} x \coth x$$

Did you try those with success?

5.3 CURVE SKETCHING

The ability to give a rough sketch of a function is a valuable skill.

We are about to draw the graph of $y = \tanh x$, and so this is a good opportunity to refresh our memories about how to sketch curves which have equations expressed in cartesian form (Chapter 3). We have already used one method when we sketched the graphs of $y = \sinh x$ and $y = \cosh x$ (Figs 5.1, 5.2). There we were able to use a known graph $y = e^x$.

There are several things we can do to gain pieces of information which help us to sketch curves:

1 Obtain the points where the curve crosses the axes. This will certainly help to locate the curve.

2 Look to see if there are any values of x or y where the curve is not defined. For example, if there are any values of y which make $x^2 < 0$, the curve doesn't appear for these values of y.

3 Look to see if there are any values of x which make y large or any values of y which make x large.

4 Look to see if the graph is symmetrical about either or both of the axes. If when we replace x in the equation by $-x$ the same equation results, then the curve is symmetrical about the y-axis. Similarly if we replace y by $-y$ in the equation and the equation remains the same, then the curve is symmetrical about the x-axis.

Example □ $y^2 = 16x$ is symmetrical about the x-axis but not about the y-axis. This follows because $(-y)^2 = 16x$ but $y^2 \neq 16(-x)$. In the same way the curve $x^4 + 3x^2y = 4$ is symmetrical about the y-axis. ∎

5 Look to see if the graph is **skew symmetrical**, that is symmetrical with respect to the origin.

In other words, if we join a point on the curve to the origin and produce an equal length, do we always obtain another point on the curve? There is a simple test for this. If we replace x and y *simultaneously* in the equation of the curve by $-x$ and $-y$ respectively, the equation will remain the same if and only if the graph is symmetrical with respect to the origin.

☐ $x^2 + xy + y^4 = 16$ is symmetrical with respect to the origin because **Example**
$(-x)^2 + (-x)(-y) + (-y)^4 = 16$. Similarly $y = \sin x$ is symmetrical with
respect to the origin because $(-y) = \sin(-x)$. ∎

Another way of thinking about symmetry with respect to the origin is that
if we rotate the curve through π the graph will be unchanged.

6 Examine the behaviour of dy/dx, particularly near the origin and as
$|x| \to \infty$.

7 See if there are any points at which the curve attains a local maximum, a
local minimum or a point of inflexion. We shall see in Chapter 8 how to
obtain and classify these points.

THE GRAPH OF $y = \tanh x$

We now turn our attention to the problem of drawing the graph of $y = \tanh x$. We begin by finding out more about $\tanh x$:

1
$$\tanh x = \frac{\sinh x}{\cosh x} = \frac{e^x - e^{-x}}{e^x + e^{-x}}$$

$$= \frac{1 - e^{-2x}}{1 + e^{-2x}}$$

(dividing top and bottom by e^x). Now as $x \to \infty$ we have $e^{-x} \to 0$ and so
$e^{-2x} \to 0$. Consequently

$$\tanh x \to \frac{1 - 0}{1 + 0} = 1 \text{ as } x \to \infty$$

2
$$\tanh x = \frac{e^x - e^{-x}}{e^x + e^{-x}}$$

$$= \frac{e^{2x} - 1}{e^{2x} + 1}$$

(multiplying top and bottom by e^x)

$$= \frac{(e^{2x} + 1) - 2}{e^{2x} + 1} = 1 - \frac{2}{e^{2x} + 1}$$

Now e^{2x} is always positive, and so $\tanh x < 1$ for all x.

3
$$\tanh 0 = \frac{\sinh 0}{\cosh 0} = 0$$

4
$$\frac{d}{dx}(\tanh x) = \operatorname{sech}^2 x \leqslant 1$$

The maximum value of the slope is attained at the origin; it then decreases as x increases. In fact $dy/dx \to 0$ as $x \to \infty$.

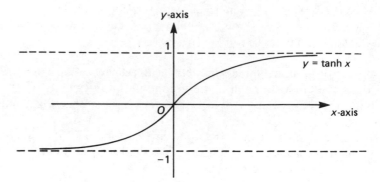

Fig. 5.3 The hyperbolic tangent function.

$$5 \qquad \tanh{(-x)} = \frac{\sinh{(-x)}}{\cosh{(-x)}} = \frac{e^{-x} - e^{x}}{e^{-x} + e^{x}} = -\tanh{x}$$

Consequently the curve is symmetrical with respect to the origin.
If we put all this information together we obtain a good idea of the shape
of the curve. This is shown in Fig. 5.3.

Now it's time for you to solve some problems. If you are unsure of the
material this is a good time to look back once more. If you are ready, then
here we go.

5.4 Workshop

1

Exercise   Using the definitions of the hyperbolic functions, show that

$$\cosh 2x = 1 + 2\sinh^2 x$$

Don't move on until you have attempted this!

2   Notice that we have been asked to use the definitions, so we must do so.
We must not assume the expansion formulas, for example. Now

$$\text{RHS} = 1 + 2\left(\frac{e^x - e^{-x}}{2}\right)^2$$

$$= 1 + 2\left(\frac{e^{2x} - 2 + e^{-2x}}{4}\right)$$

$$= \frac{e^{2x} + e^{-2x}}{2} = \text{LHS}$$

Did you get that right? If so, then move on to step 4. If not, possibly the trouble arose because you did not apply the definitions correctly. Let's see if we can sort things out in the next exercise.

▷**Exercise**   Use the definitions of the hyperbolic functions to show that

$$\tanh 2x = \frac{2 \tanh x}{1 + \tanh^2 x}$$

Remember: we must go back to the definitions.
    Try it, then step ahead.

3

We have

$$\tanh x = \frac{\sinh x}{\cosh x} = \frac{(e^x - e^{-x})/2}{(e^x + e^{-x})/2}$$

$$= \frac{e^x - e^{-x}}{e^x + e^{-x}} = \frac{e^{2x} - 1}{e^{2x} + 1}$$

So

$$1 + \tanh^2 x = 1 + \left(\frac{e^{2x} - 1}{e^{2x} + 1}\right)^2$$

$$= \frac{(e^{2x} + 1)^2 + (e^{2x} - 1)^2}{(e^{2x} + 1)^2}$$

$$= \frac{e^{4x} + 2e^{2x} + 1 + e^{4x} - 2e^{2x} + 1}{(e^{2x} + 1)^2}$$

$$= \frac{2(e^{4x} + 1)}{(e^{2x} + 1)^2}$$

Therefore

$$\frac{2 \tanh x}{1 + \tanh^2 x} = 2 \frac{e^{2x} - 1}{e^{2x} + 1} \frac{(e^{2x} + 1)^2}{2(e^{4x} + 1)}$$

$$= \frac{(e^{2x} - 1)\,(e^{2x} + 1)}{e^{4x} + 1}$$

$$= \frac{e^{4x} - 1}{e^{4x} + 1} = \tanh 2x$$

If you were unable to do this then look carefully at the working and go back to step 1. Otherwise step forward.

4

▷**Exercise**   Use the expansion formula for sinh $(x + y)$ and cosh $(x + y)$ to obtain the expansion formula

$$\tanh (x + y) = \frac{\tanh x + \tanh y}{1 + \tanh x \tanh y}$$

You can take this in your stride.

---

5 The expansion formulas we need are

$$\sinh (x + y) = \sinh x \cosh y + \cosh x \sinh y$$
$$\cosh (x + y) = \cosh x \cosh y + \sinh x \sinh y$$

Therefore

$$\tanh (x + y) = \frac{\sinh (x + y)}{\cosh (x + y)} = \frac{\sinh x \cosh y + \cosh x \sinh y}{\cosh x \cosh y + \sinh x \sinh y}$$

So that dividing numerator and denominator by $\cosh x \cosh y$ we obtain

$$\tanh (x + y) = \frac{\tanh x + \tanh y}{1 + \tanh x \tanh y}$$

If you succeeded in getting this right, then move on to step 7. Otherwise, check carefully so that you see what has been done and then tackle the next problem.

▷**Exercise**   Using the expansion formulas for $\sinh (x + y)$ and $\cosh (x + y)$, obtain the formula

$$\coth (x + y) = \frac{\coth x \coth y + 1}{\coth x + \coth y}$$

Try it, then move on.

---

6 As before we obtain

$$\coth (x + y) = \frac{\cosh x \cosh y + \sinh x \sinh y}{\sinh x \cosh y + \cosh x \sinh y}$$

So dividing numerator and denominator by $\sinh x \sinh y$ produces

$$\coth (x + y) = \frac{\coth x \coth y + 1}{\coth x + \coth y}$$

Now for another step!

7

Exercise   Obtain all real solutions of the equation

$$13 \tanh 3x = 12$$

Try this and move on only when you have made a good attempt.

Here is the working: **8**

$$\tanh 3x = \frac{e^{6x} - 1}{e^{6x} + 1} = \frac{12}{13}$$

So

$$13(e^{6x} - 1) = 12(e^{6x} + 1)$$

Consequently $e^{6x} = 25$ and therefore $6x = \ln 25 = 2 \ln 5$. So $x = (1/3) \ln 5$.

If you didn't get that right then you should check through each stage to make sure there are no misunderstandings. As soon as you are ready, try the next problem and take the final step.

▷**Exercise**   Obtain all the real solutions of the equation

$$4 \sinh 4x - 17 \sinh 3x + 4 \sinh 2x = 0$$

You may need to think about this a little.

At first sight this might seem rather tricky – until you realize that it is possible to combine two of these hyperbolic sines together, using an identity as follows:

$$4 \sinh 4x - 17 \sinh 3x + 4 \sinh 2x = 0$$
$$4(2 \sinh 3x \cosh x) - 17 \sinh 3x = 0$$

Therefore either $\sinh 3x = 0$ or $8 \cosh x = 17$. If $\sinh 3x = 0$ then $x = 0$. If $8 \cosh x = 17$ then

$$4(e^x + e^{-x}) = 17$$
$$4(e^x)^2 + 4 - 17e^x = 0$$
$$(4e^x - 1)(e^x - 4) = 0$$

Therefore either $e^x = 1/4$ or $e^x = 4$. From this we obtain $x = \ln(1/4) = -2 \ln 2$ or $x = 2 \ln 2$.

So the three solutions are $x = 0$ and $x = \pm 2 \ln 2$.

5.5 INJECTIVE FUNCTIONS

You will remember from Chapter 2 how we defined a function $f : A \rightarrow B$ to be a rule which assigned to each element x in the domain A a unique element y in the codomain B. We wrote $y = f(x)$.

Now there is nothing in the definition to suggest that two different

Although these next three sections are very mathematical they are essential for a complete understanding.

elements of A cannot be assigned to the same element of B. Indeed there are many functions which have this property.

Example □ Consider $y = x^2$. By the convention of the maximal domain we have domain $\mathbb{R}$: in other words, the domain consists of all the real numbers. Each real number x determines a unique value of y, but the same value of y is determined by two distinct arguments x. For instance

$$(-2)^2 = 4 = 2^2$$

so that when $x = 2$ or $x = -2$ we obtain the same value for y. ■

On the other hand there are some functions which do have the property that if $x_1 \neq x_2$ then $f(x_1) \neq f(x_2)$.

Example □ Consider $y = 1/x$. By the convention of the maximal domain this function has domain $\mathbb{R} \setminus \{0\}$: that is, the domain consists of all the real numbers except 0. In this instance if $x_1 \neq x_2$ then $f(x_1) \neq f(x_2)$.

To show this we simply show that if $f(x_1) = f(x_2)$ then it follows that $x_1 = x_2$. If $f(x_1) = f(x_2)$ then $1/x_1 = 1/x_2$, and so multiplying by $x_1 x_2$ we obtain $x_2 = x_1$. ■

A function $f: A \to B$ which has the property that, for all $x_1, x_2 \in A$, if $x_1 \neq x_2$ then $f(x_1) \neq f(x_2)$ is called an **injection** (or a **one-one function**).

In practice injections are easy to recognize from their graphs since any line parallel to the x-axis must cut the curve at most once. Algebraically we can deduce a function is an injection by considering the implications of the equation $f(x_1) = f(x_2)$. If we can deduce that $x_1 = x_2$ then we have an injection, whereas if we can find x_1 and x_2 which are unequal and have $f(x_1) = f(x_2)$ then we do not have an injection.

Example □ Decide which, if either, of the following functions is an injection: $y = \sinh x$; $y = \cosh x$.

Notice how the language has been misused here. The equation identifies an equation with a function, which is rather like identifying a person with his occupation. However, provided we know what is meant there is no difficulty. Mathematics is a language, and we must get used to various dialects – and even on occasion tolerate bad grammar!

First, suppose $\sinh x_1 = \sinh x_2$. Then

$$\frac{e^{x_1} - e^{-x_1}}{2} = \frac{e^{x_2} - e^{-x_2}}{2}$$

So

$$e^{x_1} - e^{x_2} = e^{-x_1} - e^{-x_2}$$

$$= \frac{1}{e^{x_1}} - \frac{1}{e^{x_2}}$$

$$= \frac{e^{x_2} - e^{x_1}}{e^{x_1}e^{x_2}}$$

$$e^{x_1} - e^{x_2} = (e^{x_2} - e^{x_1})\, e^{x_1 + x_2}$$

Now if $e^{x_1} - e^{x_2} \neq 0$ we have $e^{x_1 + x_2} = -1$, which is impossible. Therefore $e^{x_1} = e^{x_2}$ and consequently $x_1 = x_2$. So $y = \sinh x$ defines an injection.

Secondly, suppose $\cosh x_1 = \cosh x_2$. Then

$$\frac{e^{x_1} + e^{-x_1}}{2} = \frac{e^{x_2} + e^{-x_2}}{2}$$

So

$$e^{x_1} - e^{x_2} = e^{-x_2} - e^{-x_1}$$

$$= \frac{1}{e^{x_2}} - \frac{1}{e^{x_1}}$$

$$= \frac{e^{x_1} - e^{x_2}}{e^{x_1}e^{x_2}}$$

$$e^{x_1} - e^{x_2} = (e^{x_1} - e^{x_2})\, e^{x_1 + x_2}$$

Now if $e^{x_1} - e^{x_2} \neq 0$ we have $e^{x_1 + x_2} = 1$ and so $x_1 + x_2 = 0$, that is $x_1 = -x_2$. In other words, $y = \cosh x$ does not define an injection because $\cosh(-u) = \cosh u$ for all real numbers u.

We could if we wished deduce the same results by looking at the graphs. ∎

☐ Determine which, if any, of the following equations define functions **Example** which are injections: (a) $y = x^3$ (b) $y = 1/x^2$ (c) $y = \tanh x$.

When you have had a try at these, move on to check if you have them correct.

---

a Suppose $x_1^3 = x_2^3$. Then $x_1^3 - x_2^3 = 0$, and so

$$(x_1 - x_2)(x_1^2 + x_1 x_2 + x_2^2) = 0$$

If $x_1 \neq x_2$ then

$$x_1^2 + x_2^2 + x_1 x_2 = 0$$

But

$$x_1^2 + x_2^2 + x_1 x_2 = \tfrac{1}{2}(x_1 + x_2)^2 + \tfrac{1}{2}(x_1^2 + x_2^2)$$

is a sum of squares and is therefore only zero when both x_1 and x_2 are zero. Therefore we have an injection.

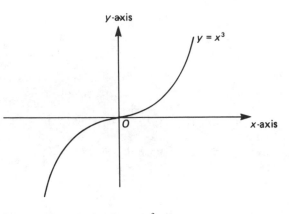

Fig. 5.4 The graph of $y = x^3$.

Alternatively a simple sketch of $y = x^3$ will establish the same result (Fig. 5.4).

b The domain of this function (by the convention of the maximal domain) is $\mathbb{R} \setminus \{0\}$. Moreover

$$\frac{1}{(-2)^2} = \frac{1}{4} = \frac{1}{(2)^2}$$

and so there are two points in the domain at which the value of the function is the same. Therefore the function is not an injection.

Again the graph $y = 1/x^2$ shows immediately that the function is not injective (Fig. 5.5).

c Suppose $\tanh x_1 = \tanh x_2$. Then

$$\frac{e^{2x_1} - 1}{e^{2x_1} + 1} = \frac{e^{2x_2} + 1}{e^{2x_2} + 1}$$

So

$$(e^{2x_1} - 1)(e^{2x_2} + 1) = (e^{2x_2} - 1)(e^{2x_1} + 1)$$
$$e^{2x_1} - e^{2x_2} = e^{2x_2} - e^{2x_1}$$
$$e^{2x_1} = e^{2x_2}$$

Therefore $e^{2(x_1 - x_2)} = 1$, so $x_1 - x_2 = 0$ and $x_1 = x_2$. So we have an injection. This property may be inferred directly from the graph of $y = \tanh x$ (Fig. 5.3). ∎

!

Although a graph enables us to see whether or not a function is an injection, the algebraic approach is necessary to establish the fact.

The special feature possessed by an injection can be represented diagrammatically as in Fig. 5.6.

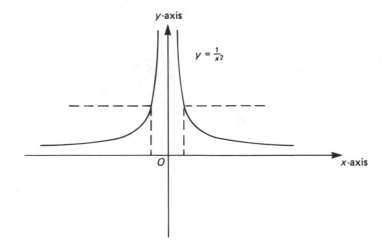

Fig. 5.5 The graph of $y = 1/x^2$.

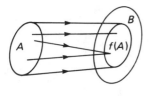

$f : A \rightarrow B$

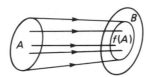

$f : A \rightarrow B$ (an injection)

Fig. 5.6

5.6 SURJECTIVE FUNCTIONS

When we introduced the notion of a function (Chapter 2) we observed that if $f : A \rightarrow B$ then it is possible to have members of the codomain B which are not in fact values of the function at all.

□ $f : \mathbb{R} \rightarrow \mathbb{R}$ defined by $f(x) = \tanh x$ whenever $x \in \mathbb{R}$. Here we know that **Example** $-1 < \tanh x < 1$ and so there is no $x \in \mathbb{R}$ such that $\tanh x = 2$. ■

In fact we gave a special name to the set of values of a function. Do you remember what it is called? It is the image set (or range) of the function and is denoted by $f(A)$.

However, for some functions the image set is indeed the codomain. Such functions are somewhat unusual and are given a special name: they are called **surjections** (or **onto functions**). The test of whether or not a function

$f : A \to B$ is a surjection is whether or not $f(A) = B$. That is, whether or not for each $y \in B$ there exists some $x \in A$ such that $f(x) = y$.

Example □ Consider the functions with codomain $\mathbb{R}$ defined by each of the following equations: (a) $y = \tan x$ (b) $y = \cosh x$.

A graph can often be useful in helping to decide whether or not a function is a surjection.

a From the graph of $y = \tan x$ (Fig. 5.7) it is clear that every real number is a value of the function. In fact given any $y \in \mathbb{R}$ there exists some $x \in (-\pi/2, \pi/2)$ such that $y = \tan x$. We conclude that the tangent function is a surjection.

b From the graph of $y = \cosh x$ (Fig. 5.8) it is clear that there are some

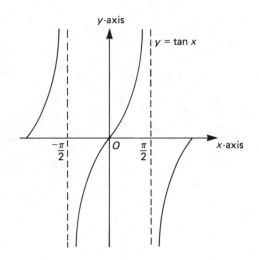

Fig. 5.7 The tangent function.

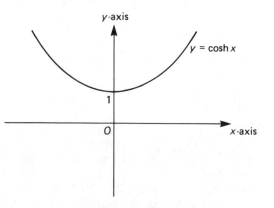

Fig. 5.8 The hyperbolic consine function.

real numbers y which are not values of the function. This is because $\cosh x \geq 1$ for all $x \in \mathbb{R}$, and therefore if $y < 1$ there is no real number x such that $y = \cosh x$. Consequently the hyperbolic cosine function is not a surjection. ∎

☐ For each of the following functions the convention of the maximal **Example** domain is to be used to obtain the domain and codomain. Decide in each case whether or not the function is a surjection.

a $y = \sinh x$
b $y = x^2$
c $y = x^3$.

Have a go at these. Don't be afraid to use the graphs to make your decisions.

---

a If we are given any real number y, it is possible to obtain a real number x such that $y = \sinh x$. This is clear from the graph (Fig. 5.9) and so we have a surjection.
b If x is any real number then $x^2 \geq 0$. Consequently if y is negative there is no real number x such that $y = x^2$ (Fig. 5.10). Therefore we do not have a surjection.
c From the graph (Fig. 5.11) it is clear that if y is any real number then there exists some real number x such that $y = x^3$. Therefore the function is indeed a surjection. ∎

Once more we can use a diagram to represent the special property a function has when it is a surjection: see Fig. 5.12.

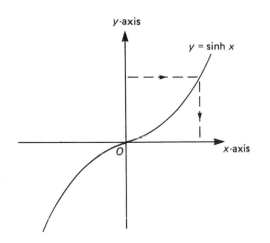

Fig. 5.9 The hyperbolic sinc function.

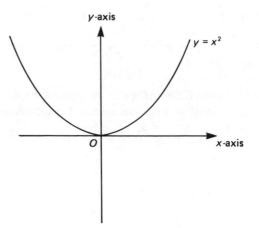

Fig. 5.10 The graph of $y = x^2$.

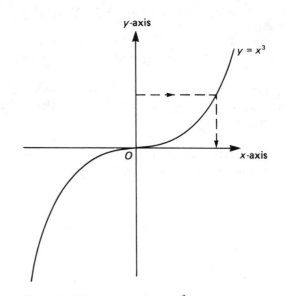

Fig. 5.11 The graph of $y = x^3$.

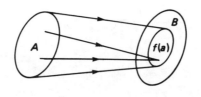

$f : A \to B$

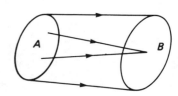

$f : A \to B$ (a surjection)

Fig. 5.12

5.7 BIJECTIVE FUNCTIONS

A function which is both an injection and a surjection is called a **bijection**. Such a function can be represented by Fig. 5.13.

Now if $f : A \rightarrow B$ is a bijection then to each $y \in B$ there corresponds a unique $x \in A$ such that $y = f(x)$. This means that the action of the function f can be reversed. Therefore there is a function $g : B \rightarrow A$ such that if $x \in A$ and $y = f(x)$ then $g(y) = x$.

The function g is called the **inverse function** of f and is usually represented by f^{-1}. Although there are good theoretical reasons for this notation, which we explore further in the context of linear operators (Chapter 22), it can cause problems to the unwary. You must remember that $f^{-1}(x)$ is not the same as $[f(x)]^{-1}$ and be vigilant about this, or nasty errors will be the result. You have been warned!

So if $f : A \rightarrow B$ is a bijection there exists an inverse function $f^{-1} : B \rightarrow A$ such that

1 If $x \in A$ then $f^{-1}[f(x)] = x$;
2 If $y \in B$ then $f[f^{-1}(y)] = y$.

We shall need this concept when we consider inverse operators in section 22.14.

!

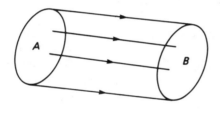

$f : A \rightarrow B$ (a bijection)

Fig. 5.13

□ Show that the function defined by $y = \sinh x$ is a bijection and give an **Example** explicit expression for its inverse function using logarithms.

By the convention of the maximal domain, the domain and codomain are both $\mathbb{R}$ and we have already shown that this function is both an injection and a surjection. Consequently it is a bijection and so has an inverse function.

Suppose $y = \sinh x$. We must reverse this formula to express x in terms of y:

$$y = \sinh x = \frac{e^x - e^{-x}}{2}$$

So $e^x - e^{-x} = 2y$. Therefore

$$(e^x)^2 - 2y(e^x) - 1 = 0$$

There are many areas where inverse functions are used: for instance, they arise in fluid mechanics and hydraulic engineering.

This is a quadratic equation in e^x and so we can solve it:

$$e^x = y \pm \sqrt{(y^2 + 1)}$$

At first sight this might appear to give two solutions. However, $\sqrt{(y^2 + 1)} > y$ for all real numbers y, and so, since e^x is always positive, the negative sign must be rejected. Consequently

$$e^x = y + \sqrt{(y^2 + 1)}$$

and so $x = \ln [y + \sqrt{(y^2 + 1)}]$.

Interchanging the symbols x and y (since it is usual to use x for points in the domain and y for points in the codomain) we deduce the inverse function is defined by

$$y = \ln [x + \sqrt{(x^2 + 1)}]$$

or

$$\sinh^{-1} x = \ln [x + \sqrt{(x^2 + 1)}] \qquad \blacksquare$$

5.8 PSEUDO-INVERSE FUNCTIONS

Bijections are comparatively rare, and so usually it is necessary to modify either the domain, the codomain or both in order to obtain a function which has an inverse. When this is done the inverse functions are not of course the inverses of the original functions, because the original functions are not bijections and so have no inverses. This fact is often obscured, but most people avoid the difficulty by giving these pseudo-inverse functions the name **principal inverse functions**.

An example will illustrate how this is done.

Example □ Obtain the principal inverse hyperbolic cosine function and express it in logarithmic form.

We already know that the function defined by $y = \cosh x$ is neither an injection nor a surjection (Fig. 5.14). We can obtain an injection by restricting the domain to $\mathbb{R}_0^+$, the positive real numbers including 0. The codomain must also be modified because, as we have observed, $\cosh x \geq 1$ for all real x.

Suppose now that $A = \mathbb{R}_0^+$, that $B = \{r \mid r \in \mathbb{R}, r \geq 1\}$ and that $f : A \to B$ is defined by $f(x) = \cosh x$ $(x \in A)$. Then f is a bijection and so has an inverse function $f^{-1} : B \to A$. To obtain $f^{-1}(y)$ explicitly we need to reverse the formula for $y = \cosh x$.

Suppose $y = \cosh x$. Then

$$y = \cosh x = \frac{e^x + e^{-x}}{2}$$

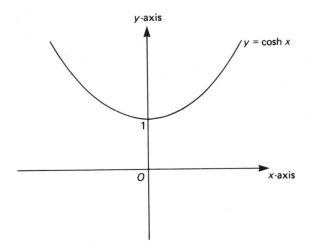

Fig. 5.14 The hyperbolic cosine function.

So $e^x + e^{-x} = 2y$. Therefore

$$(e^x)^2 - 2y(e^x) + 1 = 0$$

and so

$$e^x = y \pm V(y^2 - 1)$$

Now

$$y - V(y^2 - 1) = [y - V(y^2 - 1)] \frac{y + V(y^2 - 1)}{y + V(y^2 - 1)}$$

$$= \frac{[y - V(y^2 - 1)] \, [y + V(y^2 - 1)]}{y + V(y^2 - 1)}$$

$$= \frac{y^2 - (y^2 - 1)}{y + V(y^2 - 1)} = \frac{1}{y + V(y^2 - 1)}$$

So either

$$e^x = y + V(y^2 - 1)$$

or

$$e^x = [y + V(y^2 - 1)]^{-1}$$
$$e^{-x} = y + V(y^2 - 1)$$

Therefore

$$\pm x = \ln [y + V(y^2 - 1)]$$
$$x - \pm \ln [y + V(y^2 - 1)]$$

But $x \in A$ and so $x \geq 0$; therefore we must reject the negative value. So

$$x = \ln [y + \sqrt{(y^2 - 1)}]$$

The function defined in this way is called the principal inverse hyperbolic cosine function. Interchanging x and y we have

$$\cosh^{-1} x = \ln [x + \sqrt{(x^2 - 1)}]$$

Of course we could have chosen a different restriction such as $\mathbb{R}_0^-$ for the domain of the hyperbolic cosine. We have restricted the function so that continuity is not lost and selected positive numbers in preference to negative numbers. Until such a time as there is a campaign for equal rights for negative numbers, nobody is likely to object overmuch.   ∎

Example □ Show that $y = \ln x$ defines a bijection and obtain the inverse explicitly.
Try this. There is no need to modify the domain or codomain, but naturally you will need to use the convention of the maximal domain to obtain the domain and codomain.

The convention of the maximal domain gives the domain as $\mathbb{R}^+ = \{r \mid r \in \mathbb{R}, r > 0\}$ and the codomain as $\mathbb{R}$. The graph of $y = \ln x$ (Fig. 5.15) shows that we have a bijection. Now if $y = \ln x$ then $x = e^y$. Therefore the inverse function is the function $g : \mathbb{R} \to \mathbb{R}^+$ defined by $g(x) = e^x \ (x \in \mathbb{R})$.   ∎

Observe how we can obtain the graph of an inverse function from the graph of the function itself. Imagine that the graph $y = f(x)$ is drawn on a sheet of glass. Lift the sheet of glass away from the paper, turn it over and put it

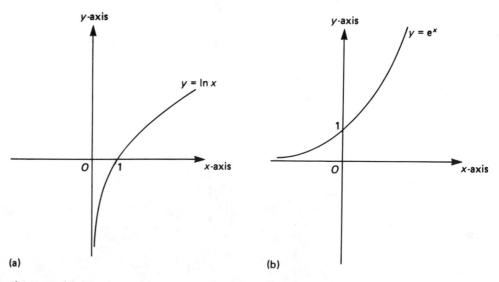

Fig. 5.15 (a) The logarithmic function (b) The exponential function.

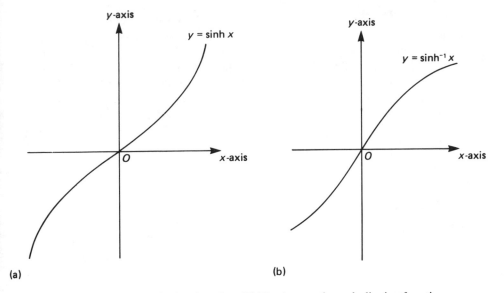

Fig. 5.16 (a) The hyperbolic sine function (b) The inverse hyperbolic sine function.

down with the x-axis where the y-axis was and the y-axis where the x-axis was. All that remains to be done is to relabel the x-axis and y-axis in the usual way.

☐ Fig. 5.16 shows the function $y = \sinh x$ and its inverse.　■ **Example**

5.9 DIFFERENTIATION OF INVERSE FUNCTIONS

In the case of the inverse hyperbolic functions we can differentiate them if we wish by using the logarithmic equivalent. However, this luxury is not generally available and when it isn't we must resort to the definition.

Suppose $y = f^{-1}(x)$. Then $f(y) = x$ and so, differentiating throughout with respect to x,

$$f'(y)\,\frac{dy}{dx} = 1$$

It is now simply a matter of eliminating y to obtain the derivative of the inverse function f^{-1}.

☐ The inverse sine function is defined as the inverse of the bijection **Example** obtained by restricting the domain of the sine function to the interval $[-\pi/2, \pi/2]$. Show that

$$\frac{dy}{dx} = \frac{1}{\sqrt{(1 - x^2)}}$$

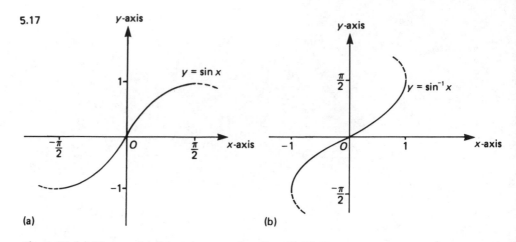

Fig. 5.17 (a) The graph of $y = \sin x$; $x \in [-\pi/2, \pi/2]$ (b) The graph of $y = \sin^{-1} x$.

and justify the choice of sign.

If $y = \sin^{-1} x$ then we know that $x = \sin y$. So differentiating throughout with respect to x we get

$$1 = \cos y \, \frac{dy}{dx}$$

Now $\cos^2 y + \sin^2 y = 1$, and so

$$\cos y = \pm \sqrt{(1 - \sin^2 y)} = \pm \sqrt{(1 - x^2)}$$

So we have

$$\frac{dy}{dx} = \frac{\pm 1}{\sqrt{(1 - x^2)}}$$

Now comes the crunch. If we had been sloppy about taking the square root and had ignored the negative sign, then we should be unaware that there was a crunch at all! A glance at the graph of $y = \sin^{-1} x$ (Fig. 5.17) tells us that the slope is always positive and so the negative can now be rejected with confidence. Naturally if we had taken a different restriction of the sine function to obtain our bijection, such as $[\pi/2, 3\pi/2]$, we could have obtained a negative slope instead! ∎

5.10 THE INVERSE CIRCULAR FUNCTIONS

Here is a complete list of the principal inverse circular functions. As you can see, the domains and codomains of the circular functions have had to be modified to produce bijections.

1 If $A = [-\pi/2, \pi/2]$ and $B = [-1, 1]$,

$$f : A \to B \text{ defined by } f(x) = \sin x \ (x \in A)$$

is a bijection and its inverse is the principal inverse sine function. Both the domain and the codomain needed modification.

2 If $A = [0, \pi]$ and $B = [-1, 1]$,

$$f : A \to B \text{ defined by } f(x) = \cos x \ (x \in A)$$

is a bijection and its inverse is the principal inverse cosine function. Both the domain and the codomain needed modification.

3 If $A = (-\pi/2, \pi/2)$ and $B = \mathbb{R}$,

$$f : A \to B \text{ defined by } f(x) = \tan x \ (x \in A)$$

is a bijection and its inverse is the principal inverse tangent function. The domain needed modification.

4 If $A = [0, \pi] \setminus \{\pi/2\}$ and $B = \{r : r \in \mathbb{R}, |r| \geqslant 1\}$,

$$f : A \to B \text{ defined by } f(x) = \sec x \ (x \in A)$$

is a bijection and its inverse is the principal inverse secant function. Both the domain and the codomain needed modification.

5 If $A = [-\pi/2, \pi/2] \setminus \{0\}$ and $B = \{r : r \in \mathbb{R}, |r| \geqslant 1\}$,

$$f : A \to B \text{ defined by } f(x) = \operatorname{cosec} x \ (x \in A)$$

is a bijection and its inverse is the principal inverse cosecant function. Both the domain and the codomain needed modification.

6 If $A = [0, \pi]$ and $B = \mathbb{R}$,

$$f : A \to B \text{ defined by } f(x) = \cot x \ (x \in A)$$

is a bijection and its inverse is the principal inverse cotangent function. The domain needed modification.

Now it's time to take a few steps. As soon as you are ready, press ahead.

5.11 Workshop

▷ **Exercise**   Show that the function defined by $y = \tanh x$ is not a bijection, but that by restricting the codomain to $(-1, 1)$ a bijection is obtained. The principal inverse hyperbolic tangent function $\tanh^{-1}$ is the inverse of this modified function. Deduce that

$$\tanh^{-1} x = \frac{1}{2} \ln \left(\frac{1 + x}{1 - x} \right)$$

and give a rough sketch of the graph.

Try this carefully before you proceed.

2 We saw when we drew the graph of $y = \tanh x$ (Fig. 5.3) that, for all real x, $-1 < \tanh x < 1$. Therefore it is necessary to restrict the codomain to $(-1, 1)$ to obtain a surjection. The function is an injection, and therefore if $A = \mathbb{R}$ and $B = (-1, 1)$ the function

$$f : A \rightarrow B \text{ defined by } f(x) = \tanh x \ (x \in A)$$

is a bijection and has an inverse function $\tanh^{-1}$.

We obtain the graph of $y = \tanh^{-1} x$ by interchanging the positions of the x-axis and the y-axis. We need a three-dimensional transformation to achieve this. Another way of looking at this transformation is as a two-stage operation. First we twist the graph of $y = \tanh x$ anticlockwise by $\pi/2$. Then we flip it over, that is we reflect it in the x-axis which is now vertical. Finally we relabel the axes (Fig. 5.18).

If $y = \tanh x$ then

$$y = \frac{e^{2x} - 1}{e^{2x} + 1}$$

$$y(e^{2x} + 1) = e^{2x} - 1$$

$$1 + y = e^{2x}(1 - y)$$

$$e^{2x} = \frac{1 + y}{1 - y}$$

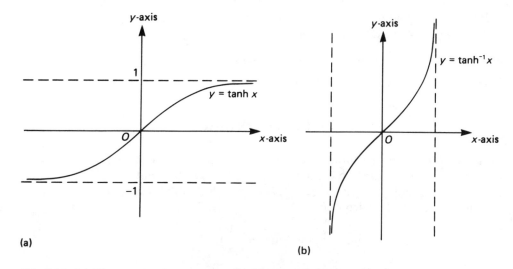

(a)

(b)

Fig. 5.18 (a) The graph of $y = \tanh x$ (b) The graph of $y = \tanh^{-1} x$.

Therefore

$$x = \frac{1}{2} \ln\left(\frac{1+y}{1-y}\right)$$

So

$$\tanh^{-1} x = \frac{1}{2} \ln\left(\frac{1+x}{1-x}\right)$$

If you managed to do all that correctly then you may move ahead to step 4. If there were unresolved problems then at this stage you should go through the theory of inverse functions once more. When you have smoothed out any difficulties, try the next exercise.

▷ **Exercise**   Explain why the function defined by $y = \operatorname{cosech} x$ is not a bijection. Show that by removing a single point from both the domain and the codomain a bijection can be obtained. The principal inverse hyperbolic cosecant is the inverse of this modified function. Draw its graph and show that

$$\operatorname{cosech}^{-1} x = \ln\left[\frac{1}{x} + \sqrt{\left(\frac{1}{x^2} + 1\right)}\right]$$

The graph of $y = \operatorname{cosech} x$ (Fig. 5.19) can be deduced easily from the graph of $y = \sinh x$ (Fig. 5.2). **3**

   There is no value of x for which $\operatorname{cosech} x = 0$, and so the function is not a surjection. Therefore there is no bijection, and consequently no inverse function. However, if we take

$$A = B = \{r \mid r \in \mathbb{R}, r \neq 0\}$$

then

$$f : A \to B \text{ defined by } f(x) = \operatorname{cosech} x \ (x \in A)$$

is a bijection. Its inverse can be drawn in the usual way (Fig. 5.20).
   Now if $y = \operatorname{cosech} x$ then $y = 1/\sinh x$. So $\sinh x = 1/y$, from which

$$x - \sinh^{-1}\left(\frac{1}{y}\right)$$

$$= \ln\left[\frac{1}{y} + \sqrt{\left(\frac{1}{y^2} + 1\right)}\right]$$

so that

$$\operatorname{cosech}^{-1} y = \ln\left[\frac{1}{y} + \sqrt{\left(\frac{1}{y^2} + 1\right)}\right] \ (y \neq 0)$$

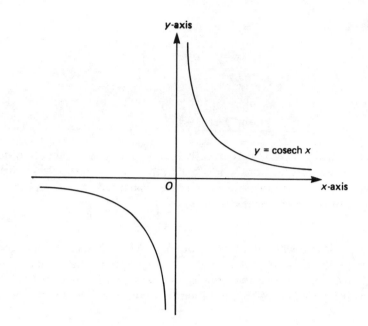

Fig. 5.19 The graph of $y = \operatorname{cosech} x$.

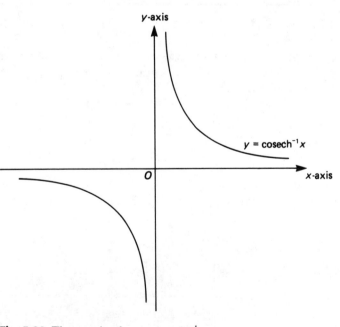

Fig. 5.20 The graph of $y = \operatorname{cosech}^{-1} x$.

or in terms of x

$$\text{cosech}^{-1} x = \ln\left[\frac{1}{x} + \sqrt{\left(\frac{1}{x^2} + 1\right)}\right]$$

Now we come to the problem of differentiation of inverse functions.

▷**Exercise** Differentiate $\text{cosec}^{-1} x$ with respect to x. $\boxed{4}$
  Try this, then step forward.

If $y = \text{cosec}^{-1} x$ then $x = \text{cosec } y$, so that differentiating with respect to x $\boxed{5}$

$$1 = -\text{cosec } y \cot y \frac{dy}{dx}$$

Now $1 + \cot^2 y = \text{cosec}^2 y$, so

$$\cot y = \pm\sqrt{(\text{cosec}^2 y - 1)} = \pm\sqrt{(x^2 - 1)}$$

Therefore

$$1 = \mp x\sqrt{(x^2 - 1)} \frac{dy}{dx}$$

$$\frac{dy}{dx} = \frac{\mp 1}{x\sqrt{(x^2 - 1)}}$$

It remains to decide which sign is the correct one. If we sketch the graph of $y = \text{cosec}^{-1} x$ (Fig. 5.21, overleaf) we see that the slope is negative, and so the negative sign must be chosen:

$$\frac{dy}{dx} = \frac{-1}{x\sqrt{(x^2 - 1)}}$$

If you discussed the choice of sign and succeeded in obtaining the correct derivative, then try one last problem. If you omitted to consider the sign or if you made an error, take care with this one.

▷**Exercise** Differentiate $\text{sech } x$ and $\text{sech}^{-1} x$ with respect to x.
  Have a go at both of these, then step ahead.

First, if $y = \text{sech } x$ then $y = (\cosh x)^{-1}$. Therefore, using the chain rule $\boxed{6}$
(Chapter 4),

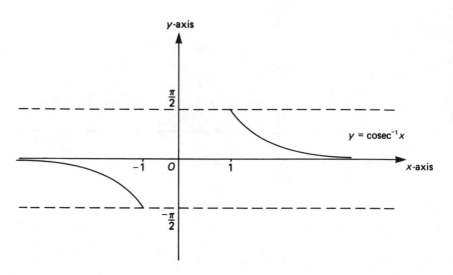

Fig. 5.21 The graph of $y = \operatorname{cosec}^{-1} x$.

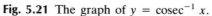

$$\frac{dy}{dx} = -(\cosh x)^{-2} \sinh x$$

$$= -\frac{\sinh x}{\cosh^2 x} = -\operatorname{sech} x \tanh x$$

Secondly, if $y = \operatorname{sech}^{-1} x$ then $x = \operatorname{sech} y$. So

$$1 = -\operatorname{sech} y \tanh y \frac{dy}{dx}$$

Now $1 - \tanh^2 y = \operatorname{sech}^2 y$, so

$$\tanh y = \pm \sqrt{(1 - \operatorname{sech}^2 y)} = \pm \sqrt{(1 - x^2)}$$

Therefore

$$1 = \mp x \sqrt{(1 - x^2)} \frac{dy}{dx}$$

$$\frac{dy}{dx} = \frac{\mp 1}{x \sqrt{(1 - x^2)}}$$

It remains to decide which sign is the correct one. If we sketch the graph of $y = \operatorname{sech}^{-1} x$ (Fig. 5.22) we see that the slope is negative, and so the negative sign must be chosen:

$$\frac{dy}{dx} = \frac{-1}{x \sqrt{(1 - x^2)}}$$

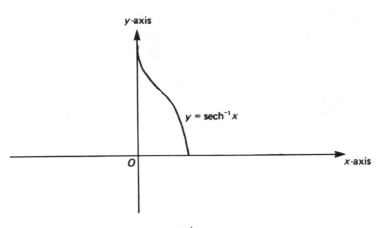

Fig. 5.22 The graph of $y = \text{sech}^{-1} x$.

5.12 THE INVERSE HYPERBOLIC FUNCTIONS

For the sake of completeness we state the bijections which have inverses known as the principal inverse hyperbolic functions:

1 If $A = B = \mathbb{R}$,

$$f : A \to B \text{ defined by } f(x) = \sinh x \ (x \in A)$$

is a bijection and its inverse is the inverse hyperbolic sine function. No modification to the domain or the codomain was needed.

2 If $A = \mathbb{R}_0^+$ and $B = \{r \,|\, r \in \mathbb{R}, r \geqslant 1\}$,

$$f : A \to B \text{ defined by } f(x) = \cosh x \ (x \in A)$$

is a bijection and its inverse is the principal inverse hyperbolic cosine function. Both the domain and the codomain needed to be modified.

3 If $A = \mathbb{R}$ and $B = (-1, 1)$,

$$f : A \to B \text{ defined by } f(x) = \tanh x \ (x \in A)$$

is a bijection and its inverse is the principal inverse hyperbolic tangent function. The codomain needed modification.

4 If $A = \mathbb{R}_0^+$ and $B = \{r \,|\, r \in \mathbb{R}, 0 < r \leqslant 1\} = (0, 1]$,

$$f : A \to B \text{ defined by } f(x) = \text{sech } x \ (x \in A)$$

is a bijection and its inverse is the principal inverse hyperbolic secant function. Both the domain and the codomain needed modification.

5 If $A = B = \mathbb{R} \setminus \{0\}$,

$$f : A \to B \text{ defined by } f(x) = \text{cosech } x \ (x \in A)$$

is a bijection and its inverse is the principal inverse hyperbolic cosecant function. Both the domain and the codomain needed modification.

6 If $A = \mathbb{R} \setminus \{0\}$ and $B = \{r : r \in \mathbb{R}, |r| > 1\}$,

$$f : A \to B \text{ defined by } f(x) = \coth x \; (x \in A)$$

is a bijection and its inverse is the principal inverse hyperbolic cotangent function. Both the domain and the codomain needed modification.

Now it remains only to work through an application.

5.13 Practical

SAGGING CHAIN

A chain hangs in the shape of the curve

$$y = c \cosh (x/c)$$

It is suspended from two points at the same horizontal level and at distance $2d$ apart. Obtain an expression for the sag at the midpoint, if the angle of slope at the ends is $\theta°$ to the horizontal.

It is worth while seeing if you can make progress on your own. We shall solve the problem stage by stage, so try it first and then see how it goes.

The sagging chain is shown in Fig. 5.23. Using the diagram, we have $dy/dx = \tan \theta$ when $x = d$. So $\tan \theta = \sinh (d/c)$. Therefore, using the result in section 5.7,

$$d/c = \sinh^{-1} (\tan \theta) = \ln [\tan \theta + \sqrt{(1 + \tan^2 \theta)}]$$
$$= \ln (\tan \theta + \sec \theta)$$

Consequently

$$c = d/\ln (\tan \theta + \sec \theta)$$

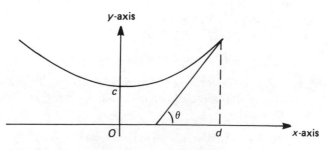

Fig. 5.23 The graph of $y = c \cosh (x/c)$.

Now that you know c, even if you weren't able to obtain it, you may be able to continue. Before doing so, make sure you follow all the stages.

The sag is the difference between the y value at $x = d$ and the y value at $x = 0$, namely c. Therefore

$$\text{sag} = c \cosh (d/c) - c = c \left[\cosh (d/c) - 1\right]$$

Now $\sinh (d/c) = \tan \theta$, and so

$$\cosh^2 (d/c) = 1 + \sinh^2 (d/c) = 1 + \tan^2 \theta = \sec^2 \theta$$

Therefore

$$\text{sag} = c (\sec \theta - 1) = d (\sec \theta - 1)/\ln (\tan \theta + \sec \theta)$$

Although in some ways this problem has been rather straightforward, it is not without practical significance. For instance, it would enable us to calculate the amount of clearance which a vehicle would have.

SUMMARY

☐ We defined the hyperbolic functions

$$\cosh x = \frac{e^x + e^{-x}}{2} \qquad \sinh x = \frac{e^x - e^{-x}}{2}$$

and drew their graphs.
☐ We obtained identities and solved equations involving hyperbolic functions.
☐ We differentiated the hyperbolic functions

$$\frac{d}{dx}(\cosh x) = \sinh x \qquad \frac{d}{dx}(\sinh x) = \cosh x$$

☐ We examined functions to see if they had inverses.
☐ We defined the principal inverse hyperbolic functions and obtained logarithmic equivalents

$$\cosh^{-1}x = \ln \left[x + \sqrt{(x^2 - 1)}\right]$$
$$\sinh^{-1}x = \ln \left[x + \sqrt{(x^2 + 1)}\right]$$

EXERCISES (for answers see p. 743)

1 Establish each of the following identities:
   a $2 \sinh^2 x = \cosh 2x - 1$

b $\coth(x + y) = \dfrac{\coth x \coth y + 1}{\coth y + \coth x}$

c $\tanh(x - y) = \dfrac{\tanh x - \tanh y}{1 - \tanh x \tanh y}$

d $8 \sinh^4 u + 4 \cosh 2u = 3 + \cosh 4u$

e $\cosh 4u = 8 \cosh^4 u - 4 \cosh 2u - 3$

2 Solve the following equations, where x is a real number:

a $1 + \sinh 2x = 10 \cosh x - \cosh 2x$

b $x \cosh x - \sinh x + 1 = \cosh x - x \sinh x + x$

c $\cosh 2x - 7(\cosh x - 1) - 1 = 7(\sinh x - 1) - \sinh 2x + 1$

d $12(\operatorname{sech} x - 1) = 1 - 13 \tanh^2 x$

3 Differentiate, with respect to t,

a $\operatorname{sech} 3t$

b $t^2 \sinh 2t$

c $\dfrac{\sinh t}{\cosh 2t}$

d $\operatorname{sech} t \operatorname{cosech} 2t$

e $\sqrt{(\operatorname{sech} t^2)}$

f $\operatorname{sech}^2 \sqrt{t}$

4 Differentiate, with respect to t,

a $\cosh^{-1}(2t^2 + 1)$

b $\tanh^{-1}(t^2 + 1)$

c $\sinh t \cosh^{-1} t$

d $\ln[\cosh^{-1} t]$

e $\cosh^{-1}[\ln t]$

f $\dfrac{1}{\sinh^{-1} t}$

ASSIGNMENT (for answers see p. 743; see also Workshop on pp. 140 and 157)

1 Solve for real x the equations

a $2 \sinh 2x = 1 + \cosh 2x$

b $2 \sinh 6x = 5 \sinh 3x$

2 Prove that if $a = \cosh x + \sinh x$ and $b = \cosh x - \sinh x$ then

a $ab = 1$

b $a^2 + b^2 = 2 \cosh 2x$

c $a^2 - b^2 = 2 \sinh 2x$

3 Solve the equation

$$1 + \sinh 2x \sinh 3x = (4/3) \sinh 3x + (3/4) \sinh 2x$$

4 Obtain all the real numbers x which satisfy the equation

$$2 \sinh 2x - 4 \sinh x - 3 \cosh x + 3 = 0$$

5 If $u = \cosh x + \sinh x$ and $v = \cosh x \sinh x$, show that $u^4 = 4u^2v + 1$.

6 If $y = \ln x$, show that

$$\cosh y = \frac{x^2 + 1}{2x} \quad \text{and} \quad \sinh y = \frac{x^2 - 1}{2x}$$

Hence, or otherwise, show that
  a If $\cosh y = a$ then $x = a \pm V(a^2 - 1)$; whereas
  b If $\sinh y = a$ then $x = a \pm V(a^2 + 1)$.

7 If

$$y = \frac{\sin^{-1} x}{V(1 + x^2)}$$

show that

$$(1 + x^2)\frac{dy}{dx} + xy = \left(\frac{1 + x^2}{1 - x^2}\right)^{1/2}$$

FURTHER EXERCISES (for answers see p. 743)

1 By first simplifying each expression, or otherwise, differentiate with respect to x
  a $\exp\left[\ln(x^{-1}) + 2\ln x\right]$
  b $\tan^{-1}\left[(1 - \cos x)/\sin x\right]$
  Simplify your answer as far as possible.

2 If $y = x\tan^{-1} x - \ln(1 + x^2)^{1/2}$, show that

$$(1 + x^2)\frac{d^2y}{dx^2} = 1$$

3 Differentiate with respect to x
  a $\cos^{-1}(3\cos x)$
  b $\tan^{-1}\left[(x^2 - 1)/2x\right]$
  c $\tan^{-1}\left[(1 + \sin x)/(1 - \sin x)\right]$

4 If $a = \sinh 2x$ and $b = \tanh x$, show that $2b + ab^2 = a$.

5 Show that
  a $\sinh(\sinh^{-1} a - \sinh^{-1} b) = aV(b^2 + 1) - bV(a^2 + 1)$
  b $\cosh(\sinh^{-1} a - \sinh^{-1} b) = V[(a^2 + 1)(b^2 + 1)] - ab$

6 Establish each of the following from the definitions:
  a $\operatorname{cosech}^2 u = \coth^2 u - 1$
  b $\cosh^2 u - \sinh^2 u = 1$
  c $\cosh 2u = \cosh^2 u + \sinh^2 u$
  d $\cosh(u + v) = \cosh u \cosh v + \sinh u \sinh v$
  e $\sinh(u + v) = \sinh u \cosh v + \cosh u \sinh v$

7 Solve
  a $\cosh 2x - 5\cosh x + 3 = 0$

b $2 \cosh x + \sinh x + \sinh 2x + 1 = 0$

c $\cosh x + \cosh 2x = 2$

8 A laser beam cuts a groove in a plate. The distance of the point of contact from a pivot is given at time t by $r = \alpha (t^2 - 2t + 2)$, where $0 \leqslant t \leqslant 10$ and α is positive.

   a What is the shortest distance from the groove to the pivot?

   b If the groove is in the shape of a straight line, determine the interval over which the beam etches the groove more than once.

   c Show that the cutting process consists of three phases: clean plate is cut; plate is cut a second time; clean plate is cut. Determine the lengths of the time intervals for each phase.

9 An automatic paint spraying machine sprays paint at a height h (metres) at time t (seconds) given by $h = \sin 2t + \cos 2t + 2$.

   a Determine the maximum and minimum heights at which the machine operates.

   b How long should the machine be applied if each point is to be painted twice?

   c At what time will the paint head be at its lowest height?

10 The input I and the output E of an experiment are related by $E = \cos 2I + \cos I + 2$. The experimenter wishes to be able to read the output and thereby determine the input uniquely. Practical considerations restrict possible inputs to $0 \leqslant I \leqslant 8$. What further restrictions should be imposed on the input given that the input must be an interval, and that small inputs are difficult to produce?

11 In a given volume of fluid an unknown number n of negatively charged particles of type A are present. It is proposed to count the particles by bombarding the fluid with positively charged particles of type B and type C. It is known that:

   a Each particle of type A bonds with 11 particles of other types.

   b Each particle of type B bonds with 7 particles of type A.

   c Each particle of type C bonds with 5 particles of type A.

   A mixture is made with 3 particles of type B to every 2 of type C. The mixture is introduced to the fluid until the overall mixture becomes stable and electrically neutral. This occurs when 605 particles have been introduced. Determine n.

   Suppose particles of type A can be further classified into either β particles (those which bond with particles of type B only) or γ particles (those which bond with particles of type C only). How many β particles and how many γ particles are present?

Further differentiation 6

In Chapter 4 we described how to differentiate simple functions. In this chapter we shall combine this knowledge with some of the geometrical ideas which we developed in Chapter 3 to obtain tangents and normals to plane curves.

After completing this chapter you should be able to
☐ Determine the equations of tangents and normals to plane curves;
☐ Use intrinsic coordinates and relate them to cartesian coordinates;
☐ Calculate the radius of curvature at a point on a curve and the position of the corresponding centre of curvature.
Finally in this chapter we shall solve a practical problem involving a moored dirigible.

6.1 TANGENTS AND NORMALS

We can apply differentiation directly to obtain the equations of the tangent and the normal at a general point (a, b) on a curve $f(x, y) = 0$. The normal is the straight line perpendicular to the tangent through the point of contact. Therefore if the slope of the tangent is m, the slope of the normal m' satisfies $mm' = -1$.

We know from our previous work (Chapter 4) that dy/dx is the slope of the curve at a general point. Therefore we have a general method for obtaining the equations of tangents and normals to plane curves:
1 Differentiate, with respect to x, throughout the equation $f(x, y) = 0$ to obtain the slope dy/dx at a general point (x, y).
2 Substitute $x = a$ and $y = b$ to obtain m, the slope of the curve at (a, b).
3 The equation of the **tangent** at (a, b) is then

$$y - b = m(x - a)$$

When practical problems are modelled mathematically it is often necessary to consider **trajectories**. Tangents and normals provide vital information.

4 The equation of the **normal** at (a, b) is

$$y - b = m'(x - a)$$

where $mm' = -1$.

! The only thing you have to be a little careful about is to make sure that the point (a, b) really is on the curve! You should check therefore that $x = a$, $y = b$ satisfy the equation $f(x, y) = 0$.

Example □ Determine the equations of the tangent and the normal at the point $(a, 2a)$ on the curve

$$xy^2 - x^3 = a^2y + ax^2$$

We follow the four stages of the general method:

1 Differentiating through the equation with respect to x gives

$$y^2 + x\,2y\,\mathrm{d}y/\mathrm{d}x - 3x^2 = a^2\,\mathrm{d}y/\mathrm{d}x + 2ax$$

So that

$$(2xy - a^2)\,\mathrm{d}y/\mathrm{d}x = 2ax - y^2 + 3x^2$$

Consequently

$$\mathrm{d}y/\mathrm{d}x = (2ax - y^2 + 3x^2)/(2xy - a^2)$$

2 At the point $(a, 2a)$ we therefore have

$$\mathrm{d}y/\mathrm{d}x = [2a^2 - (2a)^2 + 3a^2]/[2a(2a) - a^2]$$
$$= a^2/3a^2 = 1/3$$

3 We have $m = 1/3$, and so the equation of the tangent is

$$y - 2a = \tfrac{1}{3}(x - a)$$
$$3(y - 2a) = x - a$$
$$3y - 6a = x - a$$
$$3y = x + 5a$$

4 For the normal we have the slope $m' = -3$, since $mm' = -1$. Therefore the equation of the normal is

$$y - 2a = -3(x - a)$$
$$y - 2a = -3x + 3a$$
$$y + 3x = 5a$$ ■

If the curve is defined parametrically then the same principles apply. Naturally we shall obtain $\mathrm{d}y/\mathrm{d}x$ by using $\mathrm{d}y/\mathrm{d}x = (\mathrm{d}y/\mathrm{d}t)(\mathrm{d}t/\mathrm{d}x)$.

It is convenient to use a simplified notation, known as the **dot notation**. In this notation a derivative with respect to the parameter is indicated by the use of a dot over the variable: so $\dot{x} = \mathrm{d}x/\mathrm{d}t$. A second dot indicates a second-order derivative: so $\ddot{x} = \mathrm{d}^2x/\mathrm{d}t^2$. So we have shown $\mathrm{d}y/\mathrm{d}x = \dot{y}/\dot{x}$.

It is interesting to note that the dot is one of the few symbols to have survived from Newton's original work on the calculus. Much of the notation which we use today was introduced by the co-discoverer of the calculus, Leibniz.

Isaac Newton (1642–1727): major English mathematician who discovered and applied calculus to mechanics.

☐ Obtain the equations of the tangent and the normal at the general point **Example** p on the curve

$$x = p^2 + \sin 2p$$
$$y = 2p + 2 \cos 2p$$

We have

$$\dot{x} = 2p + 2 \cos 2p$$
$$\dot{y} = 2 - 4 \sin 2p$$

So

$$m = dy/dx = (2 - 4 \sin 2p)/(2p + 2 \cos 2p)$$
$$= (1 - 2 \sin 2p)/(p + \cos 2p)$$

For the tangent,

$$(y - 2p - 2 \cos 2p) = \frac{1 - 2 \sin 2p}{p + \cos 2p} (x - p^2 - \sin 2p)$$

from which

$$(y - 2p - 2 \cos 2p)(p + \cos 2p) = (1 - 2 \sin 2p)(x - p^2 - \sin 2p)$$

So

$$(p + \cos 2p)y - (1 - 2 \sin 2p)x$$
$$= 2(p + \cos 2p)^2 - (1 - 2 \sin 2p)(p^2 + \sin 2p)$$
$$= 2p^2 + 2 \cos^2 2p + 4p \cos 2p - p^2 + 2p^2 \sin 2p - \sin 2p + 2 \sin^2 2p$$
$$= p^2 + 2 + 4p \cos 2p + 2p^2 \sin 2p - \sin 2p$$

For the normal,

$$(y - 2p - 2 \cos 2p) = - \frac{p + \cos 2p}{1 - 2 \sin 2p} (x - p^2 - \sin 2p)$$

from which

$$(y - 2p - 2 \cos 2p)(1 - 2 \sin 2p) = -(p + \cos 2p)(x - p^2 - \sin 2p)$$

So

$$(1 - 2 \sin 2p)y + (p + \cos 2p)x$$
$$= 2(p + \cos 2p)(1 - 2 \sin 2p) + (p + \cos 2p)(p^2 + \sin 2p)$$
$$= (p + \cos 2p)(2 - 4 \sin 2p + p^2 + \sin 2p)$$
$$= (p + \cos 2p)(2 - 3 \sin 2p + p^2)$$ ■

Here now are a few steps to make sure we have the ideas straight.

6.2 Workshop

1

Exercise For the curve $y^2 = x^3 + x + 1$, obtain the equations of the tangent and the normal at the point $(0, 1)$.

As soon as you have done this, take a step and see if you are right.

2

We check that the point $(0, 1)$ does in fact lie on the curve, and then proceed to differentiate to obtain the slope at a general point.

$$2y \, dy/dx = 3x^2 + 1$$

so that

$$dy/dx = (3x^2 + 1)/2y$$

For the tangent at the point $(0, 1)$ we have

$$m = dy/dx = (0 + 1)/2 = 1/2$$

The equation is therefore

$$(y - 1) = \tfrac{1}{2}(x - 0) = x/2$$
$$y = x/2 + 1$$

For the normal at the point $(0, 1)$ the slope m' satisfies $mm' = -1$, and so $m' = -2$. The equation is therefore

$$(y - 1) = -2(x - 0)$$
$$y = -2x + 1$$

If there are any difficulties here it may be necessary for you to revise your work on the equations of the straight line in Chapter 3.

Another exercise follows. Are you ready?

▷**Exercise** The parametric equations of a curve are given as

$$x = t + 1/t, \qquad y = t - 1/t$$

Obtain the equations of the tangent and the normal at a general point t, and at the point where $t = 1$.

When you have done it, step forward.

3

We must obtain dy/dx at the point t. For this purpose we use the chain rule

$$dy/dx = (dy/dt)(dt/dx) = \dot{y}/\dot{x}$$

Now

$$\dot{x} = 1 - 1/t^2 = (t^2 - 1)/t^2$$
$$\dot{y} = 1 + 1/t^2 = (t^2 + 1)/t^2$$

So

$$m = dy/dx = (t^2 + 1)/(t^2 - 1)$$

at a general point t.

The equation of the tangent is therefore

$$[y - (t - 1/t)] = \frac{t^2 + 1}{t^2 - 1}[x - (t + 1/t)]$$

So

$$(t^2 - 1)[y - (t^2 - 1)/t] = (t^2 + 1)[x - (t^2 + 1)/t]$$
$$(t^2 - 1)y - (t^2 + 1)x = [(t^2 - 1)^2 - (t^2 + 1)^2]/t$$
$$= (-2)(2t^2)/t = -4t$$

using the algebraic identity $a^2 - b^2 \equiv (a - b)(a + b)$ for the difference of two squares. So the equation of the tangent at t is

$$(t^2 - 1)y - (t^2 + 1)x + 4t = 0$$

For the normal we use $mm' = -1$ and therefore

$$m' = -(t^2 - 1)/(t^2 + 1)$$

at a general point t. The equation is therefore

$$[y - (t - 1/t)] = -\frac{t^2 - 1}{t^2 + 1}[x - (t + 1/t)]$$

So

$$(t^2 + 1)[y - (t - 1/t)] + (t^2 - 1)[x - (t + 1/t)] = 0$$
$$(t^2 + 1)yt + (t^2 - 1)xt = [(t^4 - 1) + (t^4 - 1)]$$
$$= 2(t^4 - 1)$$

The equation of the normal at t is therefore

$$(t^2 + 1)yt + (t^2 - 1)xt = 2(t^4 - 1)$$

Now when $t = 1$ we hit a slight snag: m is not defined. However, we can argue by continuity that these equations will hold for all t. Therefore we take the limit as $t \to 1$ throughout the equation

$$(t^2 - 1)y - (t^2 + 1)x + 4t = 0$$

which we have shown to be the equation of the tangent at a general point $(t^2 \neq 1)$. We obtain straight away

$$0 - 2x + 4 = 0$$

and so the equation of the tangent is $x = 2$.

Similarly for the normal, from

$$(t^2 + 1)yt + (t^2 - 1)xt = 2(t^4 - 1)$$

by letting $t \rightarrow 1$ we obtain

$$2y + 0 = 0$$

and so the equation of the normal is $y = 0$ – which is, of course, the x-axis.

It is possible to give alternative arguments, but the conclusions should be the same.

Now try this final problem.

▷**Exercise**   Show that if a light source is positioned at the focus of a parabolic mirror it casts a beam parallel to the axis.

Before solving this we remark that the design of a car headlamp utilizes this property. Further, the reverse action will concentrate light at the focus. Therefore if the sun's rays strike a parabolic mirror, parallel to the axis, they are reflected to the focus. The first engineer to make use of this fact is reputed to have been Archimedes, when he set fire to the sails of the Roman fleet.

Archimedes (287 BC–212 BC): Greek geometer and applied mathematician without equal in his day. He anticipated by nearly 2000 years some of the ideas of the calculus.

4   We can use the equation of the parabola in standard form $y^2 = 4ax$ (Chapter 3), which we can regard as a cross-section through the mirror (Fig. 6.1). In parametric form this can be expressed by $x = at^2$, $y = 2at$. Therefore the slope of the tangent at a general point t is given by

$$m = \mathrm{d}y/\mathrm{d}x = \dot{y}/\dot{x} = 2a/2at = 1/t$$

So the slope of the normal at t is $-t$ (recall $mm' = -1$).

Now the basic property of light when it strikes a mirror is expressed by the equation

$$\text{angle of incidence} = \text{angle of reflection}$$

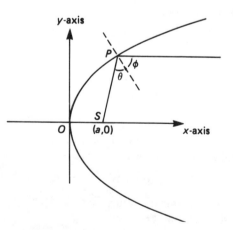

Fig. 6.1 The graph of $y^2 = 4ax$.

Let S be the focus $(a,0)$ and let P be a general point on the parabola. We must show that the angle ϕ, between the normal at P and the x-axis, is equal to the angle θ, between PS and the normal at P. Since both angles are acute, it suffices to show that $\tan \theta = \tan \phi$. Now

$$\tan \phi = [(-t) - 0]/[1 + (-t)0] = -t$$

The slope of PS is given by

$$(2at - 0)/(at^2 - a) = 2t/(t^2 - 1)$$

(recall that $m = (y_1 - y_2)/(x_1 - x_2)$). So

$$\tan \theta = \left[\frac{2t}{t^2 - 1} - (-t)\right] \Big/ \left[1 + (-t)\frac{2t}{t^2 - 1}\right]$$

$$= \frac{t^3 + t}{-t^2 - 1} = -t$$

6.3 INTRINSIC COORDINATES

We are familiar with the two coordinate systems which are used to describe plane curves and regions. These are the cartesian coordinate system and the polar coordinate system (see Chapter 3). In each of these systems we may represent a point in the plane by an ordered pair of numbers. For the cartesian system this is (x, y) and for the polar coordinate system (r, θ) (Fig. 6.2).

In these systems a curve is represented by an equation. For example $x^2 + y^2 = 1$ and $r = 1$ are, in these two systems respectively, the equations of a circle of unit radius centred at the origin.

In the cartesian system, points are described relative to two fixed mutually perpendicular straight lines known as the axes. In the polar coordinate system, points are described relative to a point called the origin and a straight line emanating from the origin called the initial line.

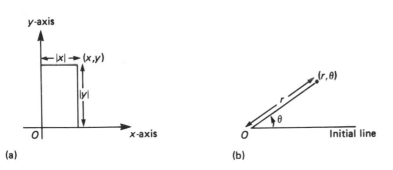

(a)   (b)

Fig. 6.2 (a) Cartesian coordinates (b) Polar coordinates.

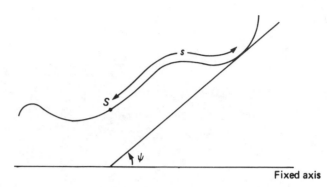

Fig. 6.3 Intrinsic coordinates.

We now describe another coordinate system, known as the **intrinsic coordinate system** (Fig. 6.3). Suppose we have a smooth curve, a fixed point S on the curve, and a fixed straight line. It will be convenient to think of the straight line as the x-axis. There are two possible ways in which we can move along the curve from S; we shall regard one as the positive direction, and the other as the negative direction. Given any real number s we therefore obtain a unique point on the curve by measuring a distance s (positive or negative) from S along the curve. The curve is smooth and so it has a tangent at all its points, and we shall suppose that there is an angle ψ at the point where the tangent meets the fixed axis.

A point on a curve in this system is then represented by an ordered pair (s, ψ), where s is the distance along the curve measured from S and ψ is the angle made by the tangent with the fixed axis.

This system, although useful, is not as versatile as the cartesian and polar coordinate systems, for it is not possible to represent a general point in the plane in terms of intrinsic coordinates. It is only possible to represent points on the curve.

6.4 THE CATENARY

The equation of the catenary in both intrinsic and cartesian form is used for suspended cables in structural mechanics.

Suppose a uniform chain or a heavy rope is freely suspended between two points; then the shape of the curve it assumes is known as the catenary (see section 5.1). Intrinsic coordinates enable us to determine the equation of the catenary quite easily. To do this we take the fixed line as the x-axis and S as the lowest point, and measure s positive to the right and negative to the left (Fig. 6.4). Suppose the mass per unit length is m. If P is a general point on the curve then P has coordinates (s, ψ).

We consider the forces on the portion of the rope SP (Fig. 6.5). There is a horizontal tension T_0 at S and a tension T in the direction of the tangent at P, and the rope is kept in equilibrium by its weight mgs which acts vertically downwards. We now resolve these forces vertically and horizontally to obtain

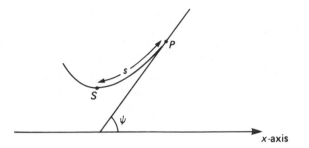

Fig. 6.4 The catenary.

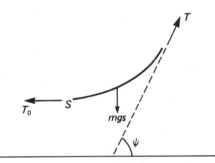

Fig. 6.5 Forces on the piece of rope.

$$mgs = T \sin \psi$$
$$T_0 = T \cos \psi$$

Eliminating T by dividing gives

$$mgs/T_0 = \tan \psi$$

which, on putting a constant $c = T_0/mg$, reduces to

$$s = c \tan \psi$$

This is the intrinsic equation of the catenary.

The catenary has many uses and needs to be considered whenever cables are strung between buildings. Although a light cable may not under normal circumstances be in the shape of a catenary, a severe winter's night with snow and ice on the cable can change the picture. When later we convert the equation of the catenary into cartesian coordinates, we shall find we are dealing with an old friend.

In order to link together the intrinsic coordinate system and the cartesian coordinate system, we shall need to locate the x and y axes. As we have said already, it is convenient to choose the x-axis as the fixed axis of the intrinsic coordinate system, and we shall choose the y-axis in such a way that S lies on it (Fig. 6.6).

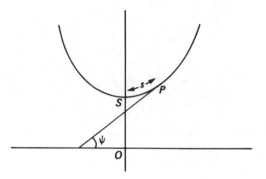

Fig. 6.6 Relating cartesian and intrinsic coordinates.

Then tan ψ is the slope of the curve at P, and so this is dy/dx. Therefore the *first linking equation* is

$$\tan \psi = dy/dx$$

Moreover, s is the length of the curve. So if δx and δy are small increases in x and y respectively, the corresponding increase in s is given by δs (Fig. 6.7). Therefore

$$(\delta x)^2 + (\delta y)^2 \simeq (\delta s)^2$$

It is reasonable to assume that as $\delta x \to 0$ the approximation will become good. Therefore dividing through by $(\delta x)^2$ and taking the limit as $\delta x \to 0$ we obtain

$$1 + (\delta y/\delta x)^2 \simeq (\delta s/\delta x)^2$$

So

$$1 + (dy/dx)^2 = (ds/dx)^2$$

If we choose s increasing with x we can take the positive square root to obtain the *second linking equation* as

$$ds/dx = [1 + (dy/dx)^2]^{1/2}$$

Example □ Transform the equation of the catenary $s = c \tan \psi$, in intrinsic coordinates, to an equation in cartesian coordinates.

It will be necessary to fix the catenary relative to the cartesian coordinate

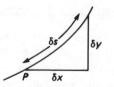

Fig. 6.7 Relating s, x and y.

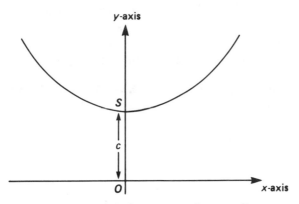

Fig. 6.8 Catenary relative to cartesian coordinates.

system, and so we shall choose S so that $OS = c$ (Fig. 6.8). The equation is
$s = c \tan \psi$, and we have the linking equations

$$\tan \psi = dy/dx$$
$$ds/dx = [1 + (dy/dx)^2]^{1/2}$$

Now

$$s = c \tan \psi = c\, dy/dx = cu$$

where $u = dy/dx$. Therefore differentiating this equation with respect to x
gives

$$ds/dx = c\, du/dx$$

from which

$$c^2(du/dx)^2 = (ds/dx)^2 = 1 + (dy/dx)^2$$
$$= 1 + u^2$$
$$dx/du = c/\sqrt{(1 + u^2)}$$

Now we already know that if $x = \sinh^{-1} u$ then $dx/du = 1/\sqrt{(1 + u^2)}$. So
$x = c \sinh^{-1} u + A$, where A is a constant. When $x = 0$ we have $dy/dx = 0$,
since this is the lowest point of the curve; consequently $A = 0$ and $x = c \sinh^{-1} u$.

However, $u = dy/dx$, and since we now have $u = \sinh x/c$ it follows that
$dy/dx = \sinh x/c$. Consequently $y = c \cosh x/c + B$, where B is a constant.
Finally when $x = 0$ we have $y = c$, and so $B = 0$. Therefore

$$y = c \cosh x/c$$

is the equation of the catenary in the cartesian coordinate system.   ■

Reversing the process
of differentiation is
known as integration.
We shall study this in
Chapter 15.

We first met the
catenary in section
5.1.

6.5 CURVATURE

The amount by which a curve bends determines the curvature of the curve.
If the curve bends sharply then the curvature is large, whereas if the curve

bends gently the curvature is small. In the intrinsic coordinate system we define the **curvature** $\varkappa$ by $\varkappa = d\psi/ds$. This is consistent with our intuitive idea because, for a small change in s, if ψ increases greatly then the curvature is high, whereas if ψ increases only gradually then the curvature is small.

The reciprocal of the curvature has the unit of length and is called the **radius of curvature** ϱ. So we have $\varrho = ds/d\psi$.

We now give a physical interpretation for the radius of curvature. Later we shall express it in terms of cartesian coordinates, and also determine a form suitable for calculating the radius of curvature if the curve is given parametrically.

Suppose that P is the point (s, ψ) and that Q is the point $(s + \delta s, \psi + \delta\psi)$ (Fig. 6.9). Suppose also that the normals to the curve at P and Q meet at C. Then since the angle between the tangents at P and Q is $\delta\psi$, the angle between the normals is also $\delta\psi$. Consequently $\angle PCQ = \delta\psi$, and because the length of the element of curve PQ is δs we conclude that

$$CP \, \delta\psi \simeq \delta s$$

The smaller that $\delta\psi$ becomes, the closer Q moves to P and the more CP comes to equalling CQ. Therefore as $\delta\psi \to 0$ the approximation $CP \simeq \delta s/\delta\psi$ becomes

$$CP = ds/d\psi = \varrho$$

that is, the radius of curvature.

The circle centred at C with radius ϱ is called the **circle of curvature**

The cartesian form for curvature is used in the theory of bending beams.

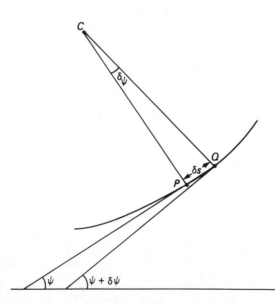

Fig. 6.9 Intersecting normals.

and the point C is called the **centre of curvature**. It is worth observing that if ϱ is negative this means that the curve is bending towards the x-axis (concave to the x-axis) and so in the opposite direction to the way shown in the diagram (convex to the x-axis).

THE CENTRE OF CURVATURE

To determine the coordinates of the centre of curvature it is best to use both cartesian coordinates and intrinsic coordinates at one and the same time.

Suppose that P is the point (x, y) in cartesian coordinates and also the point (s, ψ) relative to the curve in intrinsic coordinates. In Fig. 6.10 $\varrho > 0$, C has coordinates (X, Y) and T is the point (X, y). By similar triangles we have $\angle PCT = \psi$, and so

$$X = x - \varrho \sin \psi$$
$$Y = y + \varrho \cos \psi$$

Remarkably these formulas also work in the case $\varrho < 0$.

□ Show that if $\varrho < 0$ then the centre of curvature (X, Y) is given by   **Example**

$$X = x - \varrho \sin \psi$$
$$Y = y + \varrho \cos \psi$$

You will need a different diagram, but the working is very easy. It may help to put $p = |\varrho|$. Try it and see how you get on.

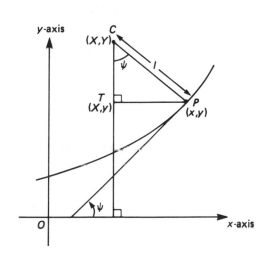

Fig. 6.10 The centre of curvature ($\varrho > 0$).

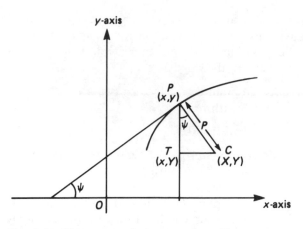

Fig. 6.11 The centre of curvature ($\varrho < 0$).

Put $p = |\varrho|$. Then $p > 0$ and we have a rather different figure, where now the curve bends towards the x-axis (Fig. 6.11). Now suppose T is the point (x, Y); then $\angle CPT = \psi$. So

$$X = x + p \sin \psi$$
$$Y = y - p \cos \psi$$

and therefore since $p = -\varrho$ we obtain

$$X = x - \varrho \sin \psi$$
$$Y = y + \varrho \cos \psi$$

as before. ■

We have seen how to determine the centre of curvature once the radius of curvature is known, and we have also seen how the sign of the radius of curvature can help us to decide which way the curve is bending. We now need a method of determining the radius of curvature without having to reduce a cartesian equation into one involving intrinsic coordinates.

THE RADIUS OF CURVATURE

Essentially there are two ways in which, using the cartesian coordinate system, a curve can be defined. It can be described directly by means of an equation involving x and y, or it can be described parametrically. In the parametric form x and y are each defined in terms of a third variable, for example t. Theoretically it could be argued that it is possible to eliminate t and thereby reduce the second case to the first one. However, in practice this may be very difficult to achieve. Therefore we shall deal with the two situations separately.

THE CARTESIAN FORM

We have $\varrho = ds/d\psi = (ds/dx)(dx/d\psi)$. Now

$$ds/dx = [1 + (dy/dx)^2]^{1/2}$$

and so it remains to obtain $dx/d\psi$ in cartesian form. Now $dy/dx = \tan \psi$, and so differentiating with respect to x

$$\begin{aligned}
d^2y/dx^2 &= \sec^2 \psi \ (d\psi/dx) \\
&= (1 + \tan^2 \psi)(d\psi/dx) \\
&= [1 + (dy/dx)^2](d\psi/dx)
\end{aligned}$$

Therefore the radius of curvature in cartesian form is

$$\varrho = \frac{[1 + (dy/dx)^2]^{1/2} \, [1 + (dy/dx)^2]}{d^2y/dx^2}$$

$$\varrho = \frac{[1 + (dy/dx)^2]^{3/2}}{d^2y/dx^2}$$

☐ For the curve $y = c \cosh (x/c)$ obtain (a) the radius of curvature at a **Example** general point (x, y) and (b) the position of the centre of curvature at the point where $x = c \ln 2$.

a We have $y = c \cosh (x/c)$, and so

$$dy/dx = c \ (1/c) \sinh (x/c) = \sinh (x/c)$$

Therefore

$$d^2y/dx^2 = (1/c) \cosh (x/c)$$

It follows that

$$1 + (dy/dx)^2 = 1 + \sinh^2 (x/c) = \cosh^2 (x/c)$$

and so

$$[1 + (dy/dx)^2]^{3/2} = \cosh^3 (x/c)$$

We now have

$$\begin{aligned}
\varrho &= \frac{[1 + (dy/dx)^2]^{3/2}}{d^2y/dx^2} \\
&= \frac{\cosh^3 (x/c)}{(1/c) \cosh (x/c)} = c \cosh^2 (x/c)
\end{aligned}$$

This is the radius of curvature at a general point. Observe that it is always positive; this is not surprising since the curve is always convex to the x-axis.

b When $x = c \ln 2$ we have $x/c = \ln 2$, and so

$$e^{x/c} = e^{\ln 2} = 2$$

So that, at $x = c \ln 2$,

$$\cosh (x/c) = \tfrac{1}{2}(e^{x/c} + e^{-x/c}) = \tfrac{1}{2}(2 + \tfrac{1}{2}) = 5/4$$
$$\sinh (x/c) = \tfrac{1}{2}(e^{x/c} - e^{-x/c}) = \tfrac{1}{2}(2 - \tfrac{1}{2}) = 3/4$$

The radius of curvature at $x = c \ln 2$ is therefore $25c/16$. Also, when $x = c \ln 2$ we have

$$y = c \cosh (x/c) = 5c/4$$

Furthermore

$$\tan \psi = dy/dx = \sinh (x/c) = 3/4$$

This gives $\sin \psi = 3/5$ and $\cos \psi = 4/5$.

Now C, the centre of curvature, is the point (X, Y), where

$$X = x - \varrho \sin \psi = c \ln 2 - (25c/16)\,(3/5)$$
$$= c \ln 2 - 15c/16$$
$$Y = y + \varrho \cos \psi = 5c/4 + (25c/16)\,(4/5)$$
$$= 5c/4 + 5c/4 = 5c/2$$

So when $x = c \ln 2$ the centre of curvature is

$$(c \ln 2 - 15c/16, 5c/2) \qquad\blacksquare$$

THE PARAMETRIC FORM

If x and y are each given in terms of a parameter t, then a small change δt in t will result in small changes δx and δy in x and y respectively. We have

$$(\delta s)^2 \simeq (\delta x)^2 + (\delta y)^2$$

As $\delta t \to 0$ both δx and δy tend to zero and this approximate formula becomes exact. Now

$$(\delta s/\delta t)^2 \simeq (\delta x/\delta t)^2 + (\delta y/\delta t)^2$$

so that as $\delta t \to 0$ we obtain

$$(ds/dt)^2 = (dx/dt)^2 + (dy/dt)^2$$

Therefore

$$\dot{s}^2 = \dot{x}^2 + \dot{y}^2$$

Now

$$\varrho = ds/d\psi = (ds/dt)\,(dt/d\psi)$$

We have seen how to find ds/dt; we need therefore to obtain $dt/d\psi$. The equation linking intrinsic coordinates with cartesian coordinates and which involves ψ is

$$\tan \psi = dy/dx = (dy/dt)\,(dt/dx) = \dot{y}/\dot{x}$$

We now differentiate throughout with respect to t and obtain

$$\sec^2 \psi \, \frac{d\psi}{dt} = \frac{\dot{x}\ddot{y} - \dot{y}\ddot{x}}{\dot{x}^2}$$

Now

$$\sec^2 \psi = 1 + \tan^2 \psi = 1 + (dy/dx)^2$$
$$= 1 + (\dot{y}/\dot{x})^2$$

so that

$$\dot{x}^2 \sec^2 \psi = \dot{x}^2 + \dot{y}^2 = \dot{s}^2$$

Substituting into the expression for ϱ we now have

$$\varrho = \frac{ds/dt}{d\psi/dt} = \frac{\dot{s}}{\dot{\psi}} = \frac{\dot{s}\dot{x}^2 \sec^2 \psi}{\dot{x}\ddot{y} - \dot{y}\ddot{x}}$$

$$= \frac{\dot{s}^3}{\dot{x}\ddot{y} - \dot{y}\ddot{x}} = \frac{(\dot{x}^2 + \dot{y}^2)^{3/2}}{\dot{x}\ddot{y} - \dot{y}\ddot{x}}$$

Therefore the radius of curvature in parametric form is

$$\varrho = \frac{(\dot{x}^2 + \dot{y}^2)^{3/2}}{\dot{x}\ddot{y} - \dot{y}\ddot{x}}$$

□ Obtain the radius of curvature at a general point, determined by the **Example** parameter θ, on the curve

$$x = \sin \theta + 2 \cos \theta$$
$$y = \cos \theta - 2 \sin \theta$$

We substitute into the formula

$$\varrho = \frac{(\dot{x}^2 + \dot{y}^2)^{3/2}}{\dot{x}\ddot{y} - \dot{y}\ddot{x}}$$

where the dot here indicates differentiation with respect to θ. We have

$$\dot{x} = \cos \theta - 2 \sin \theta$$
$$\dot{y} = -\sin \theta - 2 \cos \theta$$

So that squaring and adding,

$$\dot{x}^2 + \dot{y}^2 = (\cos \theta - 2 \sin \theta)^2 + (\sin \theta + 2 \cos \theta)^2$$
$$= \cos^2 \theta + 4 \sin^2 \theta - 4 \sin \theta \cos \theta + \sin^2 \theta + 4 \cos^2 \theta + 4 \sin \theta \cos \theta$$
$$= 5(\cos^2 \theta + \sin^2 \theta) = 5$$

Further,

$$\ddot{x} = -\sin \theta - 2 \cos \theta$$
$$\ddot{y} = -\cos \theta + 2 \sin \theta$$

so that

$$\dot{x}\ddot{y} - \dot{y}\ddot{x} = (\cos\theta - 2\sin\theta)(-\cos\theta + 2\sin\theta)$$
$$- (-\sin\theta - 2\cos\theta)(-\sin\theta - 2\cos\theta)$$
$$= -\cos^2\theta - 4\sin^2\theta + 4\sin\theta\cos\theta$$
$$- (\sin^2\theta + 4\cos^2\theta + 4\sin\theta\cos\theta)$$
$$= -5\cos^2\theta - 5\sin^2\theta = -5$$

Substituting into the formula for ϱ gives

$$\varrho = 5^{3/2}/(-5) = -\sqrt{5}$$

Now this means that there is a constant radius of curvature, and the only curve which has a constant radius of curvature is a circle. Therefore these parametric equations must define a circle. It is easy to confirm this by eliminating θ. We have

$$x = \sin\theta + 2\cos\theta$$
$$y = \cos\theta - 2\sin\theta$$

So

$$2x + y = 5\cos\theta$$
$$x - 2y = 5\sin\theta$$

If we square and add we obtain

$$(2x + y)^2 + (x - 2y)^2 = 25$$

which is $x^2 + y^2 = 5$.

The fact that ϱ is negative suggests that the circle is concave to the x-axis, and indeed since the circle in question is centred at the origin we can confirm this. ∎

Right! Are you ready for some steps?

6.6 Workshop

1

Exercise Express the equation of curve

$$s = \sec\psi\tan\psi + \ln(\sec\psi + \tan\psi)$$

in terms of cartesian coordinates, where the axes are to be chosen so that
1 when $x = 0$, $y = 0$;
2 when $x = 0$, $s = 0$.
As usual we suppose that the x-axis is parallel to the fixed axis of the intrinsic coordinate system.

Remember the linking equations, and see how you get on.

2

The linking equations are

$$\tan \psi = dy/dx$$
$$ds/dx = [1 + (dy/dx)^2]^{1/2}$$

So in general we have

$$ds/dx = [1 + (dy/dx)^2]^{1/2}$$
$$= (1 + \tan^2 \psi)^{1/2} = \sec \psi$$

since $1 + \tan^2 \psi = \sec^2 \psi$. Here

$$s = \sec \psi \tan \psi + \ln (\sec \psi + \tan \psi)$$

Therefore

$$ds/d\psi = \sec \psi \sec^2 \psi + \tan \psi \sec \psi \tan \psi$$
$$+ (\sec \psi + \tan \psi)^{-1} (\sec \psi \tan \psi + \sec^2 \psi)$$
$$= \sec \psi (\sec^2 \psi + \tan^2 \psi) + \sec \psi$$
$$= \sec \psi (\sec^2 \psi + \tan^2 \psi + 1)$$
$$= 2 \sec^3 \psi$$

since $1 + \tan^2 \psi = \sec^2 \psi$.

If you were stuck then try to get going from this point. Otherwise read on and see if you got everything right.

3

This means that

$$(ds/dx)(dx/d\psi) = 2 \sec^3 \psi$$

and we have already shown that

$$ds/dx = \sec \psi$$

Therefore

$$dx/d\psi = 2 \sec^2 \psi$$

It follows at once that

$$x = 2 \tan \psi + A$$

where A is a constant which we need to determine. We now have

$$dy/dx = \tan \psi = \tfrac{1}{2}(x - A)$$

and so

$$y = \tfrac{1}{4}x^2 - \tfrac{1}{2}Ax + B$$

where B is another constant which we need to determine.

See if you can determine these constants, and then take another step.

We have the initial conditions, and these will help us to fix A and B: **4**

1 When $x = 0$, $y = 0$ and so $B = 0$;
2 When $x = 0$, $s = 0$.

Now we have shown that when $x = 0$, $\tan \psi = -A/2 = C$ (say), and so $\sec \psi = \pm(1 + C^2)^{1/2}$. From the equation for s,

$$0 = C[\pm(1 + C^2)^{1/2}] + \ln [C \pm (1 + C^2)^{1/2}]$$

This has no meaning if the negative sign is chosen because the argument of the logarithm is then negative. Consequently the positive root for $\sec \psi$ must apply.

We have to solve the equation

$$\ln [C + (1 + C^2)^{1/2}] = -C(1 + C^2)^{1/2}$$

Now this is a tricky business. You should be able to spot that $C = 0$ is one solution, but it is quite a different matter to show that $C = 0$ is the only solution. You would not normally be expected to do this, but you might care to try out your algebraic skills!

There are several possible approaches. You could use the work we have not yet covered on maxima and minima (Chapter 8) and examine

$$y = x\sqrt{(1 + x^2)} + \ln [x + \sqrt{(1 + x^2)}]$$

You could then argue that if there are two values of x for which y is zero, then by continuity there must be a local maximum or a local minimum. It would then follow that dy/dx would be zero at some point. However, it is possible to show that $dy/dx = 2\sqrt{(x^2 + 1)}$ and so is never zero.

Nevertheless there is a purely algebraic approach. See if you can finish the problem off. If it's too much, just read through the solution and try to appreciate what is involved. Whatever your decision, take another step when you are ready.

---

5 We shall show that $C = 0$ is the only possible solution of

$$\ln [C + (1 + C^2)^{1/2}] = -C(1 + C^2)^{1/2}$$

Suppose $C > 0$. Then the right-hand side of the equation is negative, whereas the left-hand side is positive:

$$C + (1 + C^2)^{1/2} > 1$$

Suppose $C < 0$. Then

$$\exp [-C(1 + C^2)^{1/2}] = C + (1 + C^2)^{1/2}$$

We can rearrange the left-hand side of this by multiplying throughout by $-C + (1 + C^2)^{1/2}$. We then have

$$[-C + (1 + C^2)^{1/2}] \exp [-C(1 + C^2)^{1/2}] = -C^2 + (1 + C^2) = 1$$

However, the left-hand side is greater than 1 because

$$-C + (1 + C^2)^{1/2} > 1$$

and the exponential value of any positive number is always greater than 1.
  The only possibility which remains is $C = 0$.
  Finally, then, the equation of the curve in cartesian coordinates is

$$y = \tfrac{1}{4}x^2$$

If you managed that all on your own, you have handled an awkward problem successfully.
  Now for something rather different.

▷**Exercise**   For the curve

$$y = \tfrac{1}{2}x^2 - \tfrac{1}{4}\ln(x + 1) + x$$

obtain, at the origin, the radius of curvature and the centre of curvature.
  All you need to do is calculate the ingredients for the formulas and you are away! Work out the radius of curvature and take another step.

Here we go then. We need dy/dx and later d^2y/dx^2. So

$$y = \tfrac{1}{2}x^2 - \tfrac{1}{4}\ln(x + 1) + x$$
$$dy/dx = x - \tfrac{1}{4}(x + 1)^{-1} + 1$$
$$= \frac{4(x + 1)^2 - 1}{4(x + 1)}$$

Then

$$\left(\frac{ds}{dx}\right)^2 = 1 + \left(\frac{dy}{dx}\right)^2$$
$$= 1 + \frac{[4(x + 1)^2 - 1]^2}{16(x + 1)^2}$$
$$= \frac{16(x + 1)^2 + [4(x + 1)^2 - 1]^2}{16(x + 1)^2}$$
$$= \frac{[4(x + 1)^2 + 1]^2}{16(x + 1)^2}$$

Did you spot how to collect that together? If you multiply everything out you risk not being able to see the wood for the trees. It is always worth trying to stand back and see if there is a simple approach.
  So we have

$$\frac{ds}{dx} = \frac{4(x + 1)^2 + 1}{4(x + 1)}$$

Now

$$\frac{d^2y}{dx^2} = 1 + \frac{1}{4(x+1)^2}$$

$$= \frac{4(x+1)^2 + 1}{4(x+1)^2}$$

Then

$$\varrho = (ds/dx)^3/(d^2y/dx^2)$$

$$= \frac{[4(x+1)^2 + 1]^3}{[4(x+1)]^3} \frac{4(x+1)^2}{4(x+1)^2 + 1}$$

$$= \frac{[4(x+1)^2 + 1]^2}{16(x+1)}$$

$$= \frac{25}{16} \quad \text{when } x = 0$$

If you made a slip, check to find where you went wrong. Then see how you get on with the centre of curvature, and take another step.

---

7 We must obtain $\cos \psi$ and $\sin \psi$. Now $\tan \psi = dy/dx = 3/4$ when $x = 0$ so $\cos \psi = 4/5$ and $\sin \psi = 3/5$. We now have all the information we need to obtain the position of the centre of curvature:

$$X = x - \varrho \sin \psi = 0 - (25/16)(3/5) = -15/16$$
$$Y = y + \varrho \cos \psi = 0 + (25/16)(4/5) = 5/4$$

So the centre of curvature is $(-15/16, 5/4)$.

It is a good idea to practise the parametric formula, and so here is another exercise for you to try.

▷**Exercise** Determine the radius of curvature at the point where $t = 1$ on the curve defined parametrically by

$$x = t + t^2, \qquad y = 1 + t^4$$

When you have given this all you can, take the next step.

---

8 Don't forget the formula

$$\varrho = \frac{(\dot{x}^2 + \dot{y}^2)^{3/2}}{\dot{x}\ddot{y} - \dot{y}\ddot{x}}$$

Now $x = t + t^2$ and $y = 1 + t^4$. So $\dot{x} = 1 + 2t$ and $\dot{y} = 4t^3$. Therefore when $t = 1$ we have $\dot{x} = 3$ and $\dot{y} = 4$. Hence

$$(\dot{x}^2 + \dot{y}^2)^{3/2} = (9 + 16)^{3/2} = 125$$

Further, $\ddot{x} = 2$ and $\ddot{y} = 12t^2$. So when $t = 1$ we have $\ddot{x} = 2$ and $\ddot{y} = 12$. Hence

$$\dot{x}\ddot{y} - \dot{y}\ddot{x} = 3 \times 12 - 4 \times 2 = 36 - 8 = 28$$

Therefore $\varrho = 125/28$ when $t = 1$.

If you managed that then read through the next exercise and step. If there are still a few problems, then try the exercise yourself first.

▷**Exercise**   Obtain the position at the origin of the centre of curvature for the parametric curve

$$x = p + \sinh p, \qquad y = -1 + \cosh p$$

As soon as you have done this, move on to step 9.

When $p = 0$ we have $x = 0$ and $y = 0$, and so we begin by obtaining ϱ when $p = 0$. We have **9**

$$\dot{x} = 1 + \cosh p, \qquad \dot{y} = \sinh p$$
$$\ddot{x} = \sinh p, \qquad \ddot{y} = \cosh p$$

so that when $p = 0$,

$$\dot{x} = 2, \qquad \dot{y} = 0$$
$$\ddot{x} = 0, \qquad \ddot{y} = 1$$

The radius of curvature can now be found:

$$(\dot{x}^2 + \dot{y}^2)^{3/2} = (4 + 0)^{3/2} = 8$$
$$\dot{x}\ddot{y} - \dot{y}\ddot{x} = 2 \times 1 - 0 \times 0 = 2$$

Consequently $\varrho = 8/2 = 4$.

Is all well so far? If there are any problems, look through the work at this stage and then see if you can complete the problem by finding the position of the centre of curvature. Remember, you will need $\sin \psi$ and $\cos \psi$.

Here goes then. First, $\tan \psi = dy/dx = \dot{y}/\dot{x} = 0$ at the origin. We deduce **10**
that $\psi = 0$, and so $\sin \psi = 0$ and $\cos \psi = 1$. The centre of curvature is now the point $(x - \varrho \sin \psi, y + \varrho \cos \psi)$, and this is $(0 - 0, 0 + 4 \times 1) = (0, 4)$.

If any problems remain at this stage it is best to go back through the chapter again.

Now for a practical problem.

6.7 Practical

MOORED DIRIGIBLE

A dirigible is moored to a 200 m warp which is secured to a post. The tension at the post is equal to the weight of 50 m of warp and is inclined at

$\tan^{-1}(4/3)$ to the horizontal. Determine the tension and the direction of the warp at its upper end, and show that the dirigible is about 192 m above the post.

Make a real effort to solve this problem entirely on your own. As usual we shall give the solution stage by stage so that you can join in at whatever stage you can.

The warp is shown in Fig. 6.12. Let the tension at the top be T_1 inclined at an angle ϕ to the horizontal, and let the tension at the lower end be T_0 inclined at an angle θ to the horizontal.

Resolving the forces horizontally gives

$$T_1 \cos \phi = T_0 \cos \theta = 50w \,(3/5) = 30w$$

where w is the weight per metre. Resolving the forces vertically gives

$$200w + T_0 \sin \theta = T_1 \sin \phi$$

So

$$T_1 \sin \phi = 200w + 50w \,(4/5) = 240w$$

If you have not studied statics you may not have been able to obtain these equations. However, all should be well now we have obtained all the information we need.

Next we require ϕ, and we have shown

$$T_1 \cos \phi = 30w$$

$$T_1 \sin \phi = 240w$$

Therefore $\tan \phi = 240w/30w = 8$, and consequently $\phi = \tan^{-1} 8$ is the angle of inclination of the warp to the horizontal at the upper end.

We also require T_1. See if you can obtain this.

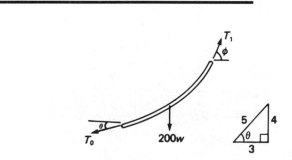

Fig. 6.12 Forces on the warp.

We have

$$T_1^2 \, (\sin^2 \phi + \cos^2 \phi) = (30w)^2 + (240w)^2$$

Therefore

$$T_1^2 = (30w)^2 (1 + 64)$$
$$T_1 = 30w\sqrt{65}$$

Lastly we must obtain the height of the dirigible above the post. For this we need to use the equation $y = c \cosh (x/c)$.

From $y = c \cosh (x/c)$ we obtain

$$dy/dx = \tan \psi = \sinh (x/c) = s/c$$

Now

$$\cosh^2 (x/c) - \sinh^2 (x/c) = 1$$

Therefore

$$(y/c)^2 - (s/c)^2 = 1$$
$$y^2 = s^2 + c^2$$

This formula is not in any way dependent on the details of this problem, and so can always be used when we have a catenary.

   The easiest way to proceed now is to consider the missing part of the catenary, length s_0, from the post to the lowest point (Fig. 6.13). Then

$$200 + s_0 = c \tan \phi$$
$$s_0 = c \tan \theta$$

See if you can complete things.

We have

$$200 = c (\tan \phi - \tan \theta) = c [8 - (4/3)] = 20c/3$$

Consequently $c = 30$ and $s_0 = c \tan \theta = 30(4/3) = 40$.
   Now

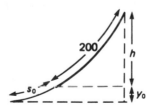

Fig. 6.13 Part of the catenary.

$$(h + y_0)^2 = (200 + s_0)^2 + c^2 = (240)^2 + (30)^2$$
$$h + y_0 = 30\sqrt{65}$$

Also

$$y_0^2 = s_0^2 + c^2 = (30)^2 + (40)^2 = (50)^2$$
$$y_0 = 50$$

Finally, $h = 30\sqrt{65} - 50 \approx 192$ m.

!

Notice how we leave any approximation to the last possible stage. We should always avoid premature approximation because it usually leads to greater inaccuracy.

SUMMARY

☐ We have shown how to find the equations of tangents and normals to plane curves.
☐ We have introduced intrinsic coordinates (s, ψ) and seen how to link them to the cartesian coordinate system:

$$\tan \psi = dy/dx$$
$$ds/dx = [1 + (dy/dx)^2]^{1/2}$$

☐ We have derived the equation of the catenary in intrinsic coordinates in the standard form $s = c \tan \psi$, and shown that this can be written in cartesian form as $y = c \cosh (x/c)$.
☐ We have introduced the ideas of
  a curvature $\varkappa = d\psi/ds$
  b radius of curvature $\varrho = ds/d\psi$
  c centre of curvature $(x - \varrho \sin \psi, y + \varrho \cos \psi)$.
☐ We have given cartesian and parametric forms for the radius of curvature:

$$\varrho = \frac{[1 + (dy/dx)^2]^{3/2}}{d^2y/dx^2}$$

$$\varrho = \frac{(\dot{x}^2 + \dot{y}^2)^{3/2}}{\dot{x}\ddot{y} - \dot{y}\ddot{x}}$$

EXERCISES (for answers see p. 743)

1 Obtain the equation of the tangent to each of the following curves at the point where $x = 0$:
a $y = x^2 + e^x$
b $y^2 = x^2 + \sqrt{(x^2 + 1)}$

c $y = \cos\left(\dfrac{\pi e^x}{2}\right)$

d $y = xy + x^2$

2 Obtain the equation of the normal to each of the following curves at the point where $y = 1$:

a $x^3 + y^3 = 2$

b $x^2y + y^2x = 6$

c $(x + y)^2 = x(x - y)$

d $x = \sin \pi y$

3 Obtain the radius of curvature of each of the following curves at the point $x = -1$:

a $(x + y)^2 = (x - y)^2 + 1$

b $y = xe^{1+x}$

c $x^2 + xy + y^2 = 1$

4 Obtain the radius of curvature at the point $t = 0$ on the curves

a $x = \sin t, \ y = \cosh t$

b $x = t + t^2, \ y = t - t^2$

c $x = t^3 + 1, \ y = t - 1$

d $x = \sin t, \ y = e^t$

ASSIGNMENT (for answers see p. 744; see also Workshops on pp. 173 and 186)

1 Obtain the radius of curvature and the position of the centre of curvature of the curve $y = x^2 + 1$ at $(0,1)$.

2 Show that for the curve described in intrinsic coordinates by $s = a\psi^2/2$ (where a is constant) the radius of curvature satisfies $\varrho^2 = 2as$.

3 Obtain the equations of the tangent and the normal at $x = 0$ for the curve $y = \exp x^2$.

4 Determine the radius of curvature of the curve $y = \exp x^2$ at $(0,1)$.

5 Prove that at any point on the rectangular hyperbola $xy = c^2$ the radius of curvature $\varrho = r^3/2c^2$, where r is the distance of the point to the origin.

6 Determine the equation of the tangent and the normal at a general point where $y = t$ on the curve $y^2 + 3xy + y^3 = 5$.

7 Obtain the equations of the tangent and the normal for the parametric curve $x = \frac{1}{2}t^2 - t, \ y = \frac{1}{2}t^2 + t$ at a general point t.

FURTHER EXERCISES (for answers see p. 744)

1 The parabola $y^2 = 4ax$ and the ellipse

$$\frac{x^2}{a^2} + \frac{y^2}{b^2} = 1$$

intersect at right angles. Show that $2a^2 = b^2$.

2 Show that the equation of the tangent at the point (x_1, y_1) on the curve

$$ax^2 + bxy + cy^2 + dx + ey + f = 0$$

where a, b, c, d, e and f are constants is given by

$$axx_1 + \tfrac{1}{2}b(xy_1 + x_1y) + cyy_1 + \tfrac{1}{2}d(x + x_1) + \tfrac{1}{2}e(y + y_1) + f = 0$$

(This equation is the general second-degree equation in x and y and includes the circle, parabola, ellipse and hyperbola. The transformations

$$uv \rightarrow \tfrac{1}{2}(uv_1 + u_1v)$$

$$u \rightarrow \tfrac{1}{2}(u + u_1)$$

where $u, v \in \{x, y\}$ enable the equation of the tangent at a point on any one of these curves to be written down straight away.)

3 Obtain the coordinates of the centre of curvature at the point $(1, 2)$ on the curve $(x - y)^2 = 2xy - x - y$.

4 Show that the perpendicular from the focus $(a, 0)$ on the parabola $y^2 = 4ax$ to any tangent intersects it on the y-axis.

5 P and Q are two points on the rectangular hyperbola $xy = 1$, constrained so that the line PQ is tangential to the parabola $y^2 = 8x$. Show that the locus of R, the midpoint of PQ, is also a parabola $y^2 + x = 0$.

6 Identify each of the following curves and give a rough sketch:
   a $xy - 2y - x + 1 = 0$
   b $xy + 12 = 3x + 4y$
   c $x^2 + 2y^2 + 4x + 12y + 18 = 0$
   d $2x^2 - y^2 - 4x + 6y = 15$
   e $(x + y)^2 = 2(x + 3)(y + 4) - 33$

7 For the equation defined parametrically by

$$x = \sin^3 \theta + 3 \sin \theta$$
$$y = \cos^3 \theta - 6 \cos \theta$$

obtain the coordinates (X, Y) of the centre of curvature at a general point. Eliminate θ and thereby obtain an equation relating X and Y; this is the locus of the centre of curvature, known as the **evolute** of the curve.

8 Show that for the parabola $y^2 = 4ax$ the locus of the centre of curvature (the evolute) is the curve $4(x - 2a)^3 = 27ay^2$.

9 Show that if $y = ax^2 + bx^3$ then at the origin $\varrho = 1/2a$ and $d\varrho/dx = -3b/2a^2$.

10 Determine the radius of curvature of the parametric curve

$$x = \cos^2 p \sin p$$
$$y = \sin^2 p \cos p$$

at a general point with parameter p.

11 The bending moment M at a point on a uniform strut subjected to loading is given by $M = EI/\rho$, where E and I are constants dependent on the material of the beam and ρ is the radius of curvature at the point. When suitable axes are chosen the profile of such a strut is defined parametrically by $x = a(t - \sin t)$, $y = a(1 - \cos t)$. Show that $M = (EI/4a) \operatorname{cosec} (t/2)$.

12 A curve is defined by the equations $x = 3 \tan^2 \theta$, $y = 1 + 2 \tan^3 \theta$. Prove that the radius of curvature at a general point with parameter θ is $6 \tan \theta \sec^3 \theta$.

13 A curve is defined parametrically by the equations

$$x = 2 \cos \theta - 2 \cos^2 \theta + 1$$
$$y = 2 \sin \theta + 2 \sin \theta \cos \theta$$

Show that the normal at a general point is

$$x \sin (\theta/2) + y \cos (\theta/2) = 3 \sin (3\theta/2)$$

14 A curve is defined parametrically by $x = a \sin 2\theta$, $y = a \sin \theta$. Show that

$$d^2y/dx^2 = \sin \theta \, (1 + 2 \cos^2 \theta)/4a \cos^3 2\theta$$

Obtain also the radius of curvature at the point $(0, a)$.

15 A uniform chain of length $2l$ and weight w per unit length is suspended between two points at the same level and has a maximum depth of sag d. Prove that the tension at the lowest point is $w(l^2 - d^2)/2d$, and that the distance between the points of suspension is

$$[(l^2 - d^2)/d] \ln [(l + d)/(l - d)]$$

16 When a body moves along a curve it experiences at any point an acceleration u^2/ρ along the normal, where u is its speed and ρ is the radius of curvature. Find this normal component of acceleration at the origin for the curve $y = x^2(x - 3)$ if the speed is a constant 12 m/s.

Partial differentiation 7

Now that we can apply some of the techniques of differentiation to functions of a single variable we shall see to what extent we can generalize these ideas to functions of several variables.

After completing this chapter you should be able to
☐ Use the language and standard notation for functions of several variables;
☐ Obtain first-order and second-order partial derivatives;
☐ Use the formulas for a change of variables correctly;
☐ Calculate an estimate of accuracy in using a formula where the variables have known errors.
At the end of this chapter we tackle practical problems of tank volume and oil flow.

7.1 FUNCTIONS

Refer back to section 2.4 if necessary for the meaning of a function.

We know that, given a real function f, we can draw a graph of it in the plane by writing $y = f(x)$. The set of arguments for which the function is defined is called the domain of f, and the set of values is called the range or image set of f (see Chapter 2).

What happens when we have a function of more than one variable? For example, suppose we consider the equation $z = (x + y) \sin x$. In this case, given any pair of real numbers x and y, we obtain a unique real number z. We have a function of *two* real variables, and we can write $f : \mathbb{R}^2 \to \mathbb{R}$ where

$$z = f(x, y) = (x + y) \sin x$$

This is just a generalization of the ideas we have already explored for a real function, which in this chapter we shall call a function of a single variable.

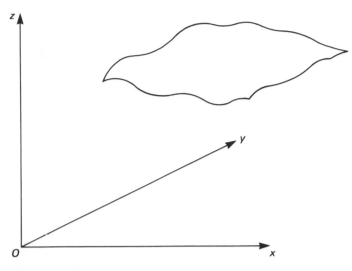

Fig. 7.1 A function of two variables.

It was a great asset when considering functions of a single variable to be able to draw the graph of the function. Here things are not quite so simple because in order to give a similar geometrical representation we shall need three axes Ox, Oy and Oz. Luckily we can represent situations like this by using a plane representation (Fig. 7.1). Instead of the 'curve' which we use to represent a function of a single variable, there corresponds a 'surface' for functions of two real variables.

However, once we extend the idea one stage further and consider functions of three real variables, we lose the picture altogether. Luckily we have the *algebraic* properties of the functions to enlighten us, and it is surprising how little we feel the loss of an adequate geometrical description. Nevertheless we can talk of 'hypersurfaces' for functions of more than two variables.

7.2 CONTINUITY

Intuitively a function of two variables is continuous at a point if the surface at the point has no 'cuts, holes or tears' in it. To put this a little more precisely, suppose (a, b) is a point in the domain of a function f; then f is continuous at the point (a, b) if $f(x, y)$ can be made arbitrarily close to $f(a, b)$ just by choosing (x, y) sufficiently close to (a, b) (Fig. 7.2).

Another way of thinking of this is that, whatever path of approach we use, as the point (x, y) approaches the point (a, b) the corresponding value $f(x, y)$ approaches the value $f(a, b)$.

In section 4.5 we considered this concept for real functions.

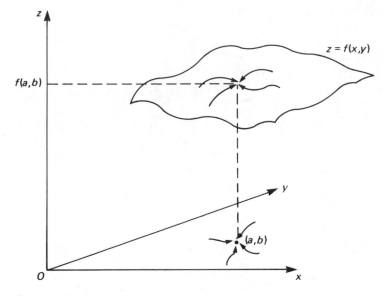

Fig. 7.2 Continuity at (a, b).

7.3 PARTIAL DERIVATIVES

When we considered functions of a single variable we saw that some functions which were continuous at a point were also differentiable there (Chapter 4). You probably recall the definition

$$\frac{\mathrm{d}f}{\mathrm{d}x} = f'(x) = \lim_{h \to 0} \frac{f(x + h) - f(x)}{h}$$

We make similar definitions for functions of several variables. For instance, suppose f is a function of two variables. Then we define

$$\frac{\partial f}{\partial x} = f_x(x, y) = \lim_{h \to 0} \frac{f(x + h, y) - f(x, y)}{h}$$

$$\frac{\partial f}{\partial y} = f_y(x, y) = \lim_{k \to 0} \frac{f(x, y + k) - f(x, y)}{k}$$

whenever these limits exist, and call these the **first-order partial derivatives** of f with respect to x and y respectively.

Notice the special symbol ∂ for partial differentiation. It must be carefully distinguished from the Greek delta δ and the d of ordinary differentiation.

At first sight these definitions seem rather formidable. However, when we examine them carefully we see that they tell us something very simple. If we look at the first one we notice that only the x part varies and that the

Partial differentiation is a basic tool used in many areas including hydraulic engineering, fluid mechanics, thermodynamics and elasticity.

!

y part is unchanged. This gives us the clue. We treat y as if it is constant, and differentiate in the ordinary way with respect to x.

Similarly, inspection of the second expression reveals that to obtain the first-order partial derivative with respect to y we simply differentiate in the ordinary way, treating x as if it is constant.

Geometrically we can think of the first-order partial derivative of f with respect to x as the slope of the curve where the plane parallel to the Oyz plane through the point (a, b) cuts the surface defined by f (Fig. 7.3). Similarly the first-order partial derivative of f with respect to y is represented as the slope of the curve where the Oxz plane through (a, b) cuts the surface defined by f.

Although we have defined partial derivatives for a function of two variables only, the definition can be extended in a similar way to functions of several variables.

To see how very easy it is to perform partial differentiation we shall do some examples.

□ Suppose   **Example**

$$z = f(x, y) = \sin 2x \cos y$$

Obtain $\partial z / \partial x$ and $\partial z / \partial y$.

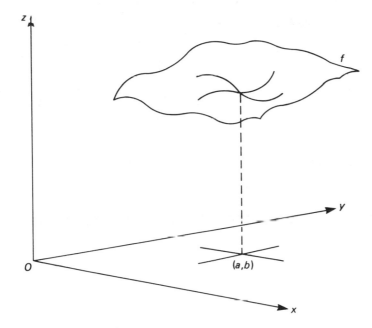

Fig. 7.3 Curves where planes cut f.

Remember that to differentiate partially with respect to a variable, all we need to do is to treat any other variables present as if they are constant. To begin with we wish to differentiate partially with respect to x, so we must treat y as if it is a constant. We obtain therefore

$$\frac{\partial z}{\partial x} = 2 \cos 2x \cos y$$

Likewise

$$\frac{\partial z}{\partial y} = -\sin y \sin 2x$$

It really is as simple as that! ∎

Now you try one.

Example ☐ If

$$u = f(s, t) = s^2 + 4st^2 - t^3$$

obtain $\partial u / \partial s$ and $\partial u / \partial t$.

Notice here we are using different letters for the variables. This should cause no problems. When you have done this problem, read on and see if it is correct.

Using our simple procedure we obtain

$$\frac{\partial u}{\partial s} = 2s + 4t^2$$

! Remember that we treat t as if it is constant. This does not mean that every term containing t automatically becomes zero when we differentiate. If you left out $4t^2$ you should think carefully about this point. Then check over your answer for $\partial u / \partial t$ before proceeding.

Differentiating with respect to t we obtain

$$\frac{\partial u}{\partial t} = 8st - 3t^2$$ ∎

7.4 HIGHER-ORDER DERIVATIVES

Suppose we have a function $f = f(x, y)$ of two real variables x and y for which the first-order partial derivatives exist. We can consider differentiating these first-order partial derivatives again with respect to x and y. There are four possibilities, and we call these the **second-order partial derivatives** of f:

Partial derivatives are used in many areas, such as hydrodynamics.

1 $\dfrac{\partial^2 f}{\partial x^2} = \dfrac{\partial}{\partial x}\left(\dfrac{\partial f}{\partial x}\right)$

2 $\dfrac{\partial^2 f}{\partial y\,\partial x} = \dfrac{\partial}{\partial y}\left(\dfrac{\partial f}{\partial x}\right)$

3 $\dfrac{\partial^2 f}{\partial x\,\partial y} = \dfrac{\partial}{\partial x}\left(\dfrac{\partial f}{\partial y}\right)$

4 $\dfrac{\partial^2 f}{\partial y^2} = \dfrac{\partial}{\partial y}\left(\dfrac{\partial f}{\partial y}\right)$

The definitions 1 and 4 are called the second-order partial derivatives of f with respect to x and y respectively. Definitions 2 and 3 are known as **mixed** second-order partial derivatives. It so happens that if these mixed derivatives are continuous at all points in a neighbourhood of the point (a, b), then they are equal at the point (a, b). It is very unusual to come across a function for which this condition does not hold, and so we shall assume that all the functions which we shall encounter have equal mixed second-order partial derivatives.

☐ Obtain all the first-order and second-order partial derivatives of the **Example** function f defined by

$$z = f(x, y) = x + \sin x^2 y + \ln y$$

We have

$$\frac{\partial z}{\partial x} = 1 + 2xy \cos x^2 y$$

$$\frac{\partial z}{\partial y} = x^2 \cos x^2 y + y^{-1}$$

So therefore:

$$\frac{\partial^2 z}{\partial x^2} = \frac{\partial}{\partial x}(1 + 2xy \cos x^2 y)$$
$$= 0 + 2xy(-2xy \sin x^2 y) + 2y \cos x^2 y$$
$$= -4x^2 y^2 \sin x^2 y + 2y \cos x^2 y$$

$$\frac{\partial^2 z}{\partial y\,\partial x} = \frac{\partial}{\partial y}(1 + 2xy \cos x^2 y)$$
$$= 2x \cos x^2 y - 2xy \sin x^2 y\,(x^2)$$
$$= 2x \cos x^2 y - 2x^3 y \sin x^2 y$$

$$\frac{\partial^2 z}{\partial x\, \partial y} = \frac{\partial}{\partial x}(x^2 \cos x^2 y + y^{-1})$$

$$= 2x \cos x^2 y - x^2 \sin x^2 y\, (2xy)$$
$$= 2x \cos x^2 y - 2x^3 y \sin x^2 y$$

$$\frac{\partial^2 z}{\partial y^2} = \frac{\partial}{\partial y}(x^2 \cos x^2 y + y^{-1})$$

$$= -x^2 \sin x^2 y\, (x^2) - y^{-2}$$
$$= -x^4 \sin x^2 y - y^{-2}$$

A partial check is provided by the fact that the two mixed derivatives are indeed equal. ∎

So that you will acquire plenty of practice, we shall take a few steps before proceeding any further.

7.5 Workshop

1

Exercise   Consider the following function of two real variables:

$$f(x, y) = \tan^{-1}\left(\frac{x}{y}\right)$$

Obtain the first-order partial derivatives f_x and f_y and thereby show that

$$x\frac{\partial f}{\partial x} + y\frac{\partial f}{\partial y} = 0$$

Try it first on your own and see how it goes. Then step ahead.

2

Differentiating partially with respect to x and with respect to y in turn gives

$$\frac{\partial f}{\partial x} = \frac{1}{[1 + (x/y)^2]}\frac{1}{y}$$

$$\frac{\partial f}{\partial y} = \frac{1}{[1 + (x/y)^2]}\frac{-x}{y^2}$$

Consequently

$$x\frac{\partial f}{\partial x} + y\frac{\partial f}{\partial y} = \frac{1}{[1 + (x/y)^2]}\frac{x - x}{y} = 0$$

If you managed that all right, you should move ahead to step 4. If something went wrong, then try this.

▷**Exercise**   Suppose

$$f(x, y) = \cos^3 (x^2 - y^2)$$

Derive the first-order partial derivatives and show that

$$y \frac{\partial f}{\partial x} + x \frac{\partial f}{\partial y} = 0$$

Try it carefully and take the next step.

3

Given that

$$f(x, y) = \cos^3 (x^2 - y^2)$$

we have

$$\frac{\partial f}{\partial x} = -3 \cos^2 (x^2 - y^2) \sin (x^2 - y^2) (2x)$$

$$\frac{\partial f}{\partial y} = -3 \cos^2 (x^2 - y^2) \sin (x^2 - y^2) (-2y)$$

It follows at once that

$$y \frac{\partial f}{\partial x} + x \frac{\partial f}{\partial y} = 0$$

If things are still going wrong there are only two possibilities. Either you are having difficulty with the ordinary differentiation, or you are forgetting when partially differentiating to treat the other variable as if it is a constant. Go back and review what you have done to make certain you can manage this correctly.

Assuming that all is now well, we can move ahead. Now we are going to test the work on second-order derivatives.

Familiarity with the material in Chapter 4 is essential here.

4

▷**Exercise**   Suppose $z = \ln \sqrt{(x^2 + y^2)}$. Show that **Laplace's equation** in two dimensions is satisfied, namely

$$\frac{\partial^2 z}{\partial x^2} + \frac{\partial^2 z}{\partial y^2} = 0$$

Laplace's equation has many applications and you will certainly come across it again from time to time. It is an example of a partial differential equation.

As soon as you have made a good attempt at this, move ahead to the next step.

Pierre Simon Laplace (1749–1827): French mathematician and astronomer who skilfully survived the revolution and its aftermath. He was ennobled in 1817.

5 It may help to simplify z before differentiating. Here we have

$$z = \tfrac{1}{2} \ln (x^2 + y^2)$$

using the laws of logarithms, and so

$$\frac{\partial z}{\partial x} = \frac{1}{2(x^2 + y^2)} (2x)$$

$$= \frac{x}{x^2 + y^2}$$

So

$$\frac{\partial^2 z}{\partial x^2} = \frac{(x^2 + y^2) - x(2x)}{(x^2 + y^2)^2}$$

$$= \frac{y^2 - x^2}{(x^2 + y^2)^2}$$

Now we don't need to do any more partial differentiation for this problem. Can you see why not? It is because of symmetry. Look back at the original expression for z; if we were to interchange x and y in it, it would not be altered. Therefore if we interchange x and y in this partial derivative we shall obtain a correct statement. So, by symmetry, we obtain

$$\frac{\partial^2 z}{\partial y^2} = \frac{x^2 - y^2}{(y^2 + x^2)^2}$$

Always keep an eye open for symmetry, it can save you a lot of time and effort!

Finally, adding these two second-order partial derivatives produces

We shall meet Laplace's equation in another form in section 7.8.

$$\frac{\partial^2 z}{\partial x^2} + \frac{\partial^2 z}{\partial y^2} = \frac{y^2 - x^2 + x^2 - y^2}{(x^2 + y^2)^2} = 0$$

If all's well then you can move ahead to step 7. However, if it went wrong then try this problem first.

▷**Exercise**   Given that

$$w = \sin (2x + y) - (x - 3y)^3$$

verify that the mixed partial derivatives are equal.

As soon as you have done it move on to the next step.

6 There is no symmetry here, so we have no alternative but to get our heads down and do the partial differentiation. Of course we only require the mixed second-order derivatives, and so we would be doing needless work if we obtained all four second-order derivatives. Did you? If you did, console yourself that you have at least practised some partial differentiation; your time was not completely wasted.

We have

$$\frac{\partial w}{\partial x} = 2 \cos (2x + y) - 3(x - 3y)^2$$

$$\frac{\partial w}{\partial y} = \cos (2x + y) - 3(x - 3y)^2 (-3)$$

$$= \cos (2x + y) + 9(x - 3y)^2$$

Differentiating again,

$$\frac{\partial^2 w}{\partial x \, \partial y} = -2 \sin (2x + y) + 18(x - 3y)$$

$$\frac{\partial^2 w}{\partial y \, \partial x} = -2 \sin (2x + y) - 6(x - 3y) (-3)$$

$$= -2 \sin (2x + y) + 18(x - 3y)$$

If trouble persists, make sure you can handle the chain rule for ordinary differentiation (Chapter 4).

▷ **Exercise**   Show that if f is a differentiable real function and if $z = f(x/y)$
then

7

$$x \frac{\partial z}{\partial x} + y \frac{\partial z}{\partial y} = 0$$

Try hard with this. Although it seems a little abstract we have already done all the necessary work before when we differentiated $\tan^{-1} (x/y)$ at the beginning of this workshop. As soon as you have made a good attempt read on.

We have straight away, using the chain rule for ordinary differentiation,

8

$$\frac{\partial z}{\partial x} = f'\left(\frac{x}{y}\right)\left(\frac{1}{y}\right)$$

Remember: first differentiate with respect to the bracketed terms, then multiply the result by the derivative of the bracketed terms with respect to x. Similarly,

$$\frac{\partial z}{\partial y} = f'\left(\frac{x}{y}\right)\left(\frac{-x}{y^2}\right)$$

Consequently,

$$x\frac{\partial z}{\partial x} + y\frac{\partial z}{\partial y} = f'\left(\frac{x}{y}\right)\left(\frac{x-x}{y}\right) = 0$$

You may have not managed that, but even if you did it is a good idea to try another exercise like that. Before tackling it, look very carefully at the previous exercise to make sure you have a good start.

▷**Exercise** Suppose f is a twice differentiable real function. Deduce that if $z = f(r)$, where $r = V(x^2 + y^2)$, then z satisfies the equation

$$\frac{\partial^2 z}{\partial x^2} + \frac{\partial^2 z}{\partial y^2} = \frac{1}{r}f'(r) + f''(r)$$

When you have tried it, take the next step.

9 Using exactly the same idea as before, we obtain

$$\frac{\partial z}{\partial x} = f'V(x^2 + y^2)\,\frac{1}{2}\,(x^2 + y^2)^{-1/2}\,2x$$

$$= f'V(x^2 + y^2)\,\frac{x}{V(x^2 + y^2)}$$

Now differentiating again we obtain

$$\frac{\partial^2 z}{\partial x^2} = f'V(x^2 + y^2)\,\frac{V(x^2 + y^2) - x\,(1/2)\,(x^2 + y^2)^{-1/2}\,2x}{(x^2 + y^2)}$$

$$+ f''V(x^2 + y^2)\,\frac{x^2}{x^2 + y^2}$$

$$= f'V(x^2 + y^2)\,\frac{(x^2 + y^2) - x^2}{(x^2 + y^2)^{3/2}} + f''V(x^2 + y^2)\,\frac{x^2}{x^2 + y^2}$$

$$= f'V(x^2 + y^2)\,\frac{y^2}{(x^2 + y^2)^{3/2}} + f''V(x^2 + y^2)\,\frac{x^2}{x^2 + y^2}$$

Similarly

$$\frac{\partial^2 z}{\partial y^2} = f'V(y^2 + x^2)\,\frac{x^2}{(y^2 + x^2)^{3/2}} + f''V(y^2 + x^2)\,\frac{y^2}{y^2 + x^2}$$

Adding we obtain

$$\frac{\partial^2 z}{\partial x^2} + \frac{\partial^2 z}{\partial y^2} = f'V(x^2 + y^2)\,\frac{x^2 + y^2}{(x^2 + y^2)^{3/2}} + f''V(x^2 + y^2)\,\frac{x^2 + y^2}{x^2 + y^2}$$

$$= f'V(x^2 + y^2)\,\frac{1}{(x^2 + y^2)^{1/2}} + f''V(x^2 + y^2)$$

Therefore

$$\frac{\partial^2 z}{\partial x^2} + \frac{\partial^2 z}{\partial y^2} = \frac{1}{r}f'(r) + f''(r)$$

We shall soon see that there is in fact a much easier way to do this.

A word about the notation for partial differentiation is not out of place at this point. Much has been written about the problems inherent with the notation, particularly when (as in the previous workshop) more than two symbols for independent variables are involved. It is necessary to be clear which are the independent variables.

!

For example, suppose that $z = x^2 + y^3$ and that $x = r\cos\theta$ and $y = r\sin\theta$. Here z is expressed in terms of two independent variables x and y. It is also possible to express z in terms of two other independent variables r and θ. It would be a mistake to express z in terms of mixtures such as r, x and y, or x and θ, and to attempt to form partial derivatives, because the variables would not be independent and so the partial derivatives we attempted to find would be incorrect. Major errors have followed from misunderstandings of this nature; many attempts have been made to improve the notation, but the result is generally unattractive and difficult to follow.

7.6 THE FORMULAS FOR A CHANGE OF VARIABLES: THE CHAIN RULE

In the final exercise in the previous workshop it would have been correct to use the abbreviated notation r instead of $\sqrt{(x^2 + y^2)}$, provided we obeyed the chain rule for ordinary differentation diligently. In fact we shall now state a version of the chain rule for functions of more than one variable.

If we write $f = f(x, y)$ where $x = x(u, v)$ and $y = y(u, v)$ we are using x and y in two ways: first as a dummy variable, and secondly as a function symbol. We have done this sort of thing before in the case of real functions, and shall find it particularly useful to avoid introducing many unwanted symbols. To express this in words: the function f is expressed in terms of the independent variables x and y, and the variables x and y are themselves expressed in terms of independent variables u and v.

Here now is the **chain rule**. Suppose that $f = f(x, y)$ and that $x = x(u, v)$ and $y = y(u, v)$. Then, if all the partial derivatives exist,

$$\frac{\partial f}{\partial u} = \frac{\partial f}{\partial x}\frac{\partial x}{\partial u} + \frac{\partial f}{\partial y}\frac{\partial y}{\partial u}$$

$$\frac{\partial f}{\partial v} = \frac{\partial f}{\partial x}\frac{\partial x}{\partial v} + \frac{\partial f}{\partial y}\frac{\partial y}{\partial v}$$

Notice how when we choose to differentiate with respect to one of the subsidiary variables we must be impartial. We differentiate with respect to each of the main variables in turn, multiplying the result in each case by the derivative of the main variable with respect to the subsidiary variable. This chain of products is then added together. The formula is reminiscent of the formula for differentiating a function of a single variable:

$$\frac{dy}{dx} = \frac{dy}{du}\frac{du}{dx}$$

Indeed, this is a special case of the more general rule.

However, there is one important point to watch. In the case of a single variable the formula looks right because we can imagine du as cancelling out. Indeed, if we extend the definitions to allow dy and dx to be used separately as differentials the procedure becomes justifiable. However, we must *never* cancel out symbols such as ∂x or ∂y. You can see why if you look at the formulas for a change of variables: it would give $1 = 2$!

To avoid unnecessary complications we shall justify the formula for a change of variables in a special case only. Suppose $f = f(x, y)$ and that $x = x(t)$, $y = y(t)$. You may like to think of t as time or temperature; then as t changes so too do x and y and consequently the value of f.

If δt is a small non-zero change in t and δx and δy are the corresponding changes in x and y respectively, these in turn produce a change δf in f. Now

$$\begin{aligned}
\delta f &= f(x+\delta x, y+\delta y) - f(x, y)\\
&= f(x+\delta x, y+\delta y) - f(x, y+\delta y) + f(x, y+\delta y) - f(x, y)\\
&= \frac{f(x+\delta x, y+\delta y) - f(x, y+\delta y)}{\delta x}\,\delta x + \frac{f(x, y+\delta y) - f(x, y)}{\delta y}\,\delta y
\end{aligned}$$

Dividing through by δt,

$$\frac{\delta f}{\delta t} = \frac{f(x+\delta x, y+\delta y) - f(x, y+\delta y)}{\delta x}\frac{\delta x}{\delta t} + \frac{f(x, y+\delta y) - f(x, y)}{\delta y}\frac{\delta y}{\delta t}$$

Now we consider that happens as δt tends to zero. We have $\delta x \to 0$, $\delta y \to 0$ and also

$$\frac{\delta x}{\delta t} \to \frac{dx}{dt}, \qquad \frac{\delta y}{\delta t} \to \frac{dy}{dt}, \qquad \frac{\delta f}{\delta t} \to \frac{df}{dt}$$

Moreover,

$$\frac{f(x, y + \delta y) - f(x, y)}{\delta y} \to \frac{\partial f}{\partial y}$$

$$\frac{f(x + \delta x, y + \delta y) - f(x, y + \delta y)}{\delta x} \rightarrow \frac{f(x + \delta x, y) - f(x, y)}{\delta x} \rightarrow \frac{\partial f}{\partial x}$$

Consequently,

$$\frac{df}{dt} = \frac{\partial f}{\partial x}\frac{dx}{dt} + \frac{\partial f}{\partial y}\frac{dy}{dt}$$

Here we have made a number of assumptions which we have not justified. Principal among these is that the limits exist and that we can select the order in which to take these limits. Nevertheless we have given a justification for the formula in the case where x and y are both functions of a single variable t, and it is a simple matter to extend this to the more general case.

It is important that we learn how to apply the chain rule correctly. Unfortunately it is sometimes possible to misapply the chain rule and still obtain a correct result. Diligent examiners are always on the lookout for errors of this kind, and so marks will be lost if you are sloppy!

□ If $z = (x + y)^2$ where $x = r \cos \theta$ and $y = r \sin \theta$, show that   **Example**

$$2r^2 \frac{\partial^2 z}{\partial r^2} + \frac{\partial^2 z}{\partial \theta^2} = 4r^2$$

We begin by finding the first-order partial derivatives:

$$\frac{\partial z}{\partial r} = \frac{\partial z}{\partial x}\frac{\partial x}{\partial r} + \frac{\partial z}{\partial y}\frac{\partial y}{\partial r}$$
$$= 2(x + y) \cos \theta + 2(x + y) \sin \theta$$
$$= 2(x + y) (\cos \theta + \sin \theta)$$

Do you follow it so far?
    See if you can obtain the other first-order partial derivative.

Here we are:

$$\frac{\partial z}{\partial \theta} = \frac{\partial z}{\partial x}\frac{\partial x}{\partial \theta} + \frac{\partial z}{\partial y}\frac{\partial y}{\partial \theta}$$
$$= 2(x + y)(-r \sin \theta) + 2(x + y)r \cos \theta$$
$$= 2r(x + y)(\cos \theta - \sin \theta)$$

There is not normally too much of a problem at this stage; it is when we differentiate again that some students, and unfortunately textbooks, overlook terms. It is important to remember that the chain rule must always be used when we differentiate with respect to a subsidiary variable.

So now

$$\frac{\partial^2 z}{\partial r^2} = \frac{\partial}{\partial r}\left(\frac{\partial z}{\partial r}\right)$$

$$= \frac{\partial}{\partial r}[2(x + y)](\cos\theta + \sin\theta) + 2(x + y)\frac{\partial}{\partial r}(\cos\theta + \sin\theta)$$

The second term is zero. Therefore, applying the chain rule to the first term,

$$\frac{\partial^2 z}{\partial r^2} = 2(\cos\theta + \sin\theta)\left[\frac{\partial}{\partial x}(x + y)\frac{\partial x}{\partial r} + \frac{\partial}{\partial y}(x + y)\frac{\partial y}{\partial r}\right]$$

$$= 2(\cos\theta + \sin\theta)(\cos\theta + \sin\theta)$$

$$= 2(\cos^2\theta + 2\sin\theta\cos\theta + \sin^2\theta)$$

$$= 2(1 + \sin 2\theta)$$

Also

$$\frac{\partial^2 z}{\partial\theta^2} = \frac{\partial}{\partial\theta}\left(\frac{\partial z}{\partial\theta}\right)$$

$$= 2(x + y)\frac{\partial}{\partial\theta}[r(\cos\theta - \sin\theta)] + 2r(\cos\theta - \sin\theta)\frac{\partial}{\partial\theta}(x + y)$$

$$= 2(x + y)[r(-\sin\theta - \cos\theta)] + 2r(\cos\theta - \sin\theta)(-r\sin\theta + r\cos\theta)$$

$$= 2r^2[-(\sin\theta + \cos\theta)^2 + (\cos\theta - \sin\theta)^2]$$

$$= 2r^2(-4\sin\theta\cos\theta)$$

$$= -4r^2\sin 2\theta$$

Therefore

$$2r^2\frac{\partial^2 z}{\partial r^2} + \frac{\partial^2 z}{\partial\theta^2} = 2r^2[2(1 + \sin 2\theta)] - 4r^2\sin 2\theta = 4r^2$$

As an exercise you may wish to check this by first eliminating x and y in the expression for z and then differentiating directly with respect to r and θ; it's much quicker!

7.7 THE TOTAL DIFFERENTIAL

This theory can be applied to the analysis of accumulation and propagation of errors in survey networks.

In the case of a differentiable function f of a single variable we originally defined dy/dx as a limit, so that the symbols dy and dx used on their own were meaningless. However, we found it useful to be able to use these symbols separately, and accordingly we extended the definition (Chapter 4). We call dx a differential, and we can think of it as a change in the value of x, not necessarily small. In fact it is any real number. The differential dy

is then defined by $dy = f'(x) \, dx$. Of course if dx happens to be small then dy is an approximation to the corresponding change in y.

In the case of a function of several variables we adopt a similar approach. Specifically, suppose that $z = f(x, y)$. Then the differentials dx and dy are defined to be any real numbers. You may choose to think of them as changes in x and y respectively which are not necessarily small. The differential dz is then defined by

$$dz = \frac{\partial z}{\partial x} \, dx + \frac{\partial z}{\partial y} \, dy$$

dz is usually called the **total differential**.

When we derived the special case of the chain rule (section 7.6), we showed that when dx and dy are small the total differential is approximately the corresponding change in z. We can therefore use this to obtain a rough estimate of the error caused by inaccuracies in measurement.

□ A surveyor estimates the area of a triangular plot of land using the **Example** formula

$$A = \tfrac{1}{2} \, ab \sin C$$

where a and b are the lengths of two sides and C is the included angle. If the sides are measured to an accuracy of 2% and the angle C, measured as 45°, is measured to within 1%, calculate approximately the percentage error in A.

You may have a go at this on your own if you wish.

Using the total differential,

$$dA = \frac{\partial A}{\partial a} \, da + \frac{\partial A}{\partial b} \, db + \frac{\partial A}{\partial C} \, dC$$

Now $da = \pm 0.02a$, $db = \pm 0.02b$ and $dC = \pm 0.01C$. Also

$$\frac{\partial A}{\partial a} = \frac{1}{2} b \sin C \qquad \frac{\partial A}{\partial b} = \frac{1}{2} a \sin C \qquad \frac{\partial A}{\partial C} = \frac{1}{2} ab \cos C$$

Substituting,

$$\begin{aligned} dA &= 1/2 \, b \sin C \, (\pm 0.02a) + 1/2 \, a \sin C \, (\pm 0.02b) \\ &\quad + 1/2 \, ab \cos C \, (\pm 0.01C) \\ &= 1/2 \, ab \sin C \, (\pm 0.02 \pm 0.02 \pm 0.01C \cot C) \end{aligned}$$

Now $C = 45° = \pi/4$, and so $\cot C = 1$. Therefore

$$dA = A \left[\pm 0.02 \pm 0.02 \pm 0.01 \, (\pi/4)\right]$$

The greatest error occurs when all have the same sign, so that

$$|dA| \leqslant 0.01A \left[2 + 2 + (\pi/4)\right] \simeq 0.048A$$

So the error is not more than 5% approximately. ∎

This theory, together with physical interpretations, is also used in fluid mechanics and hydraulic engineering.

Finally, we mention a few of the notations which are sometimes used for partial differentiation. Suppose that $z = f(x, y)$. Then

$$\frac{\partial z}{\partial x} \qquad \frac{\partial f}{\partial x} \qquad f_x \qquad f_1 \qquad D_1 f$$

are all equivalent and

$$\frac{\partial^2 z}{\partial x \, \partial y} \qquad \frac{\partial^2 f}{\partial x \, \partial y} \qquad f_{xy} \qquad f_{12} \qquad D_{12} f$$

are also equivalent to one another. There are many variations of these, and it is necessary to determine which notation is being used at any time. Our notation is the one which is most widely used.

So now we are ready to take steps. We are going to tackle a problem which is sometimes incorrectly solved in textbooks.

7.8 Workshop

1

Exercise   Transform the partial differential equation

$$\frac{\partial^2 z}{\partial x^2} + \frac{\partial^2 z}{\partial y^2} = 0$$

where z is expressed in terms of cartesian coordinates (x, y), into a partial differential equation in polar coordinates (r, θ), where $x = r \cos \theta$ and $y = r \sin \theta$.

Let us begin by writing down formulas which express the partial derivatives with respect to x and y in terms of the partial derivatives with respect to r and θ. When you have done this, take the next step.

We have

$$\frac{\partial z}{\partial x} = \frac{\partial z}{\partial r} \frac{\partial r}{\partial x} + \frac{\partial z}{\partial \theta} \frac{\partial \theta}{\partial x}$$

This is a straight application of the chain rule. Similarly,

$$\frac{\partial z}{\partial y} = \frac{\partial z}{\partial r}\frac{\partial r}{\partial y} + \frac{\partial z}{\partial \theta}\frac{\partial \theta}{\partial y}$$

If all is well, follow through the next step. If you made an error, write down formulas which express the partial derivatives with respect to r and θ in terms of those with respect to x and y. Don't move on until you have done this.

3

Here they are:

$$\frac{\partial z}{\partial r} = \frac{\partial z}{\partial x}\frac{\partial x}{\partial r} + \frac{\partial z}{\partial y}\frac{\partial y}{\partial r}$$

$$\frac{\partial z}{\partial \theta} = \frac{\partial z}{\partial x}\frac{\partial x}{\partial \theta} + \frac{\partial z}{\partial y}\frac{\partial y}{\partial \theta}$$

We now have a choice as to which pair to use. There are advantages and disadvantages either way. If we use the first pair we shall have to express r and θ explicitly in terms of x and y so that we can differentiate. If we use the second pair we can find the partial derivatives easily enough, but we shall then have to eliminate to obtain the differential equation and it might be difficult to find our way.

Let us be definite: we shall use the first pair. So we must obtain r and θ explicitly in terms of x and y, and then the partial derivatives. Do this and then take the next step.

4

We have $r^2 = x^2 + y^2$ and so $r = \sqrt{(x^2 + y^2)}$. Consequently,

$$\frac{\partial r}{\partial x} = \frac{x}{\sqrt{(x^2 + y^2)}}$$

$$\frac{\partial r}{\partial y} = \frac{y}{\sqrt{(x^2 + y^2)}}$$

Also $\tan \theta = y/x$ so that $\theta = \tan^{-1}(y/x)$. Therefore

$$\frac{\partial \theta}{\partial x} = \frac{-y}{(x^2 + y^2)}$$

$$\frac{\partial \theta}{\partial y} = \frac{x}{(x^2 + y^2)}$$

and so

$$\frac{\partial r}{\partial x} = \frac{x}{r} \qquad \frac{\partial r}{\partial y} = \frac{y}{r} \qquad \frac{\partial \theta}{\partial x} = \frac{-y}{r^2} \qquad \frac{\partial \theta}{\partial y} = \frac{x}{r^2}$$

Now substitute these expressions into the formulas for a change of variables, and take the next step.

5 We obtain

$$\frac{\partial z}{\partial x} = \frac{\partial z}{\partial r}\frac{\partial r}{\partial x} + \frac{\partial z}{\partial \theta}\frac{\partial \theta}{\partial x}$$

$$= \frac{\partial z}{\partial r}\frac{x}{r} + \frac{\partial z}{\partial \theta}\frac{(-y)}{r^2}$$

and

$$\frac{\partial z}{\partial y} = \frac{\partial z}{\partial r}\frac{\partial r}{\partial y} + \frac{\partial z}{\partial \theta}\frac{\partial \theta}{\partial y}$$

$$= \frac{\partial z}{\partial r}\frac{y}{r} + \frac{\partial z}{\partial \theta}\frac{x}{r^2}$$

Now we are ready for the second-order derivatives with respect to x and y respectively. You find the second-order partial derivative with respect to x – but be careful! This is the place at which we pass the bones of reputations bleached white by the sun.

6 Here we go! We must use the chain rule again and not overlook any terms:

$$\frac{\partial^2 z}{\partial x^2} = \frac{\partial}{\partial x}\left[\frac{\partial z}{\partial r}\frac{x}{r} + \frac{\partial z}{\partial \theta}\frac{(-y)}{r^2}\right]$$

$$= \frac{1}{r}\frac{\partial z}{\partial r}\frac{\partial x}{\partial x} + x\frac{\partial}{\partial x}\left(\frac{1}{r}\frac{\partial z}{\partial r}\right) - \frac{1}{r^2}\frac{\partial z}{\partial \theta}\frac{\partial y}{\partial x} - y\frac{\partial}{\partial x}\left(\frac{1}{r^2}\frac{\partial z}{\partial \theta}\right)$$

Here we have simply used the product rule but kept the two sets of variables apart. Since x and y are independent we can deduce that their partial derivatives with respect to each other are zero, and so the third term is zero. We must use the chain rule again to expand the remaining terms. So the second-order partial derivative of z with respect to x is

$$\frac{\partial^2 z}{\partial x^2} = \frac{1}{r}\frac{\partial z}{\partial r} + x\left[\frac{\partial}{\partial r}\left(\frac{1}{r}\frac{\partial z}{\partial r}\right)\frac{\partial r}{\partial x} + \frac{\partial}{\partial \theta}\left(\frac{1}{r}\frac{\partial z}{\partial r}\right)\frac{\partial \theta}{\partial x}\right]$$

$$- y\left[\frac{\partial}{\partial r}\left(\frac{1}{r^2}\frac{\partial z}{\partial \theta}\right)\frac{\partial r}{\partial x} + \frac{\partial}{\partial \theta}\left(\frac{1}{r^2}\frac{\partial z}{\partial \theta}\right)\frac{\partial \theta}{\partial x}\right]$$

This is where people make the error: they overlook the mixed derivative terms. As it happens they end up with the correct equation at the final stage, even though the second-order derivatives themselves are incorrect. To continue:

$$\frac{\partial^2 z}{\partial x^2} = \frac{1}{r}\frac{\partial z}{\partial r} + x\left[\left(\frac{1}{r}\frac{\partial^2 z}{\partial r^2} - \frac{1}{r^2}\frac{\partial z}{\partial r}\right)\frac{x}{r} + \left(\frac{1}{r}\frac{\partial^2 z}{\partial \theta \partial r}\right)\frac{(-y)}{r^2}\right]$$

$$- y \left[\left(\frac{-2}{r^3} \frac{\partial z}{\partial \theta} + \frac{1}{r^2} \frac{\partial^2 z}{\partial r \partial \theta} \right) \frac{x}{r} + \left(\frac{1}{r^2} \frac{\partial^2 z}{\partial \theta^2} \right) \frac{(-y)}{r^2} \right]$$

$$= \frac{1}{r} \frac{\partial z}{\partial r} + \frac{x^2}{r^2} \frac{\partial^2 z}{\partial r^2} - \frac{x^2}{r^3} \frac{\partial z}{\partial r} - \frac{xy}{r^3} \frac{\partial^2 z}{\partial \theta \partial r} + \frac{2xy}{r^4} \frac{\partial z}{\partial \theta} - \frac{xy}{r^3} \frac{\partial^2 z}{\partial r \partial \theta} + \frac{y^2}{r^4} \frac{\partial^2 z}{\partial \theta^2}$$

Well, there it is. Pretty tough going, isn't it? You have to keep a clear head and make sure you use the chain rule properly. If you didn't manage that then you are undoubtedly part of a huge majority, so you may take consolation in that. Also you may be relieved to know that the going seldom gets harder. Anyway, we still have the other second-order derivative to obtain: so off you go!

Hold on to your hats.   7

$$\frac{\partial^2 z}{\partial y^2} = \frac{\partial}{\partial y} \left(\frac{\partial z}{\partial r} \frac{y}{r} + \frac{\partial z}{\partial \theta} \frac{x}{r^2} \right)$$

$$= \frac{1}{r} \frac{\partial z}{\partial r} \frac{\partial y}{\partial y} + y \frac{\partial}{\partial y} \left(\frac{1}{r} \frac{\partial z}{\partial r} \right) + \frac{1}{r^2} \frac{\partial z}{\partial \theta} \frac{\partial x}{\partial y} + x \frac{\partial}{\partial y} \left(\frac{1}{r^2} \frac{\partial z}{\partial \theta} \right)$$

$$= \frac{1}{r} \frac{\partial z}{\partial r} + y \left[\frac{\partial}{\partial r} \left(\frac{1}{r} \frac{\partial z}{\partial r} \right) \frac{\partial r}{\partial y} + \frac{\partial}{\partial \theta} \left(\frac{1}{r} \frac{\partial z}{\partial r} \right) \frac{\partial \theta}{\partial y} \right]$$

$$+ x \left[\frac{\partial}{\partial r} \left(\frac{1}{r^2} \frac{\partial z}{\partial \theta} \right) \frac{\partial r}{\partial y} + \frac{\partial}{\partial \theta} \left(\frac{1}{r^2} \frac{\partial z}{\partial \theta} \right) \frac{\partial \theta}{\partial y} \right]$$

$$= \frac{1}{r} \frac{\partial z}{\partial r} + y \left[\left(\frac{1}{r} \frac{\partial^2 z}{\partial r^2} - \frac{1}{r^2} \frac{\partial z}{\partial r} \right) \frac{y}{r} + \left(\frac{1}{r} \frac{\partial^2 z}{\partial \theta \partial r} \right) \frac{x}{r^2} \right]$$

$$+ x \left[\left(\frac{-2}{r^3} \frac{\partial z}{\partial \theta} + \frac{1}{r^2} \frac{\partial^2 z}{\partial r \partial \theta} \right) \frac{y}{r} + \left(\frac{1}{r^2} \frac{\partial^2 z}{\partial \theta^2} \right) \frac{x}{r^2} \right]$$

$$= \frac{1}{r} \frac{\partial z}{\partial r} + \frac{y^2}{r^2} \frac{\partial^2 z}{\partial r^2} - \frac{y^2}{r^3} \frac{\partial z}{\partial r} + \frac{xy}{r^3} \frac{\partial^2 z}{\partial \theta \partial r} - \frac{2xy}{r^4} \frac{\partial z}{\partial \theta} + \frac{xy}{r^3} \frac{\partial^2 z}{\partial r \partial \theta} + \frac{x^2}{r^4} \frac{\partial^2 z}{\partial \theta^2}$$

Lastly we must add the two expressions for the second-order derivatives and equate to zero.

This is what you should get if you remember that $x^2 + y^2 = r^2$:   8

$$\frac{1}{r} \frac{\partial z}{\partial r} + \frac{\partial^2 z}{\partial r^2} + \frac{1}{r^2} \frac{\partial^2 z}{\partial \theta^2} = 0$$

so that

$$\frac{\partial^2 z}{\partial r^2} + \frac{1}{r^2} \frac{\partial^2 z}{\partial \theta^2} + \frac{1}{r} \frac{\partial z}{\partial r} = 0$$

This is **Laplace's equation** in two dimensions expressed in polar coordinates (see also section 7.5).

If you would like even more practice at this sort of work you can always try the other approach. The alternative method involves determining expressions for the second-order derivatives of z with respect to r and θ in terms of those with respect to x and y and then using Laplace's equation in cartesian coordinates to eliminate x and y. It helps to know the equation we are aiming to derive.

!
▪

You probably feel that those steps were quite steep, but if you persisted and completed the exercise you will have gained some useful experience. Remember to pay particular attention to brackets. They are not there for decorative purposes: they play a vital part. Students who pay scant attention to brackets rarely succeed in mathematics.

7.9 Practical

VOLUME ERROR

The volume of a hydraulic tank, in the shape of a ring, is calculated using the formula

$$V = \pi r^2 h - \pi s^2 h$$

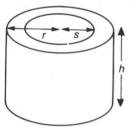

where h is the height and r and s are the external and internal radii respectively. If r and s were measured 3% too large, estimate the maximum error in V if h is correct to within 1%.

Try this. We need the formula for the total differential. Begin by writing this down for these symbols, obtain the partial derivatives and substitute into your equation.

This is correct:

$$dV = \frac{\partial V}{\partial r}\, dr + \frac{\partial V}{\partial s}\, ds + \frac{\partial V}{\partial h}\, dh$$

Now

$$\frac{\partial V}{\partial r} = 2\pi rh \qquad \frac{\partial V}{\partial s} = -2\pi sh \qquad \frac{\partial V}{\partial h} = \pi r^2 - \pi s^2$$

Also $dr = 0.03r$, $ds = 0.03s$, $dh = \pm 0.01h$. This gives

$$dV = 2\pi r^2 h(0.03) - 2\pi s^2 h(0.03) \pm (\pi r^2 - \pi s^2)\,(0.01h)$$
$$= V(0.06 \pm 0.01)$$

So the calculated value of V is between 5% and 7% too large.

It's all quite simple really. Remember the chain rule, and remember to put in brackets whenever necessary, and everything should be fine.

OIL FLOW

Here is a problem about oil – just to make sure everything is running smoothly!

The motion of a light oil flowing with speed u past a cylindrical bearing of radius a may be roughly described by the equation

$$\phi = u \cos \alpha \left(r + \frac{a^2}{r} \right) \cos \theta + zu \sin \alpha$$

where α is a constant and r, θ and z are independent variables. Show that ϕ satisfies the equation

$$\frac{\partial^2 \phi}{\partial r^2} + \frac{1}{r} \frac{\partial \phi}{\partial r} + \frac{1}{r^2} \frac{\partial^2 \phi}{\partial \theta^2} + \frac{\partial^2 \phi}{\partial z^2} = 0$$

Try it yourself first, and then we will look at it stage by stage.

Partial differential equations arise in many areas. For instance, those who study the theory of structures may meet them in the elastic theory of flat plates.

---

1 To solve this problem we merely need to show that ϕ satisfies the partial differential equation. Don't, whatever you do, take your starting-point as the partial differential equation and then try to deduce the expression for ϕ from it. We haven't been given enough information for that approach, even if we wished to attempt it that way.

We begin by finding the first-order partial derivatives:

$$\frac{\partial \phi}{\partial r} = u \cos \alpha \left(1 - \frac{a^2}{r^2} \right) \cos \theta$$

$$\frac{\partial \phi}{\partial \theta} = u \cos \alpha \left(r + \frac{a^2}{r^2} \right) (-\sin \theta)$$

$$\frac{\partial \phi}{\partial z} = u \sin \alpha$$

Check yours and see if they are right. The next step, of course, is to obtain the second-order derivatives we need.

---

2 Here we have

$$\frac{\partial^2 \phi}{\partial r^2} = u \cos \alpha \left(\frac{2a^2}{r^3} \right) \cos \theta$$

$$\frac{\partial^2 \phi}{\partial \theta^2} = -u \cos \alpha \left(r + \frac{a^2}{r} \right) \cos \theta$$

$$\frac{\partial^2 \phi}{\partial z^2} = 0$$

If you have these correct, it remains to substitute them into the left-hand side of the partial differential equation and confirm that the result is 0.

---

3 We obtain

$$\frac{\partial^2 \phi}{\partial r^2} + \frac{1}{r}\frac{\partial \phi}{\partial r} + \frac{1}{r^2}\frac{\partial^2 \phi}{\partial \theta^2} + \frac{\partial^2 \phi}{\partial z^2}$$

$$= u \cos \alpha \left(\frac{2a^2}{r^3}\right) \cos \theta + \frac{u \cos \alpha}{r}\left(1 - \frac{a^2}{r^2}\right) \cos \theta$$

$$- \frac{u \cos \alpha}{r^2}\left(r + \frac{a^2}{r}\right) \cos \theta$$

$$= 0$$

SUMMARY

We have
☐ Introduced the notion of partial differentiation and seen how to obtain partial derivatives of the first and second order.
☐ Derived the chain rule

$$\frac{\partial f}{\partial u} = \frac{\partial f}{\partial x}\frac{\partial x}{\partial u} + \frac{\partial f}{\partial y}\frac{\partial y}{\partial u}$$

$$\frac{\partial f}{\partial v} = \frac{\partial f}{\partial x}\frac{\partial x}{\partial v} + \frac{\partial f}{\partial y}\frac{\partial y}{\partial v}$$

and practised its use.
☐ Used the total differential

$$dz = \frac{\partial z}{\partial x}\,dx + \frac{\partial z}{\partial y}\,dy$$

to estimate errors in calculations which involve formulas with more than one independent variable.

EXERCISES (for answers see p. 744)

1 Obtain the first-order partial derivatives of the functions defined by the following formulas:
a $f(x,y) = x^3 + yx^2$
b $f(x,y) = \sin xy \cos (x + y)$
c $f(x,y) = (x + 2y)^3$

d $f(x, y) = \exp(x + y)\cos xy$
e $f(x, y) = \sqrt{\cosh(x + y)}$
f $f(x, y) = \cosh(x/y)$

2 Obtain the mixed second-order partial derivatives of each of the following functions defined by the formulas:
a $f(x, y) = \sqrt{(x^2 + y^2)} + \sin xy$
b $f(x, y) = \sqrt{(x + 2y)} + x^2 y$
c $f(x, y) = x^2 \sin(3x + 4y)$
d $f(x, y) = \sin(x^2/y^3)$

3 Obtain expressions in terms of u, v and partial derivatives with respect to u and v for $\partial z/\partial x$ and $\partial z/\partial y$ if
a $x = u^2 v^2$, $y = u + v$
b $x = u + 2v$, $y = 2u + v$
c $x = u + uv$, $y = v - uv$
d $x = \sqrt{(u^2 + v^2)}$, $y = u/v$

ASSIGNMENT (for answers see p. 745; see also Workshops on pp. 205 and 214)

1 Obtain the first-order partial derivatives of the functions defined by each of the following formulas:
a $f(x, y) = \sin x \cos y + xy^2$
b $f(x, y) = e^x \cos y + e^x \sin y$
c $z = \ln \sqrt{(x^2 + y^2)}$
d $z = (x + 2y)(x - 2y)^5$
e $z = \sin(u^2 - v^2)^2$

2 Verify the equality of the mixed second-order partial derivatives of the function f defined for all real x and y $(x^2 + y^2 \neq 0)$ by

$$f(x, y) = \ln(x^2 + y^2) + \cos(x + 2x^2 y)$$

3 Obtain an expression in terms of u and v and partial derivatives with respect to u and v for

$$\frac{\partial z}{\partial x} + \frac{\partial z}{\partial y}$$

if $x = c^u \cos v$ and $y = c^u \sin v$.

4 The force on a body is calculated using the formula

$$F = k\frac{m_1 m_2}{r^2}$$

where k is constant, m_1 and m_2 are masses and r is a distance. Calculate approximately the percentage error in F if the massses are measured to within 1% and the distance to within 5%.

FURTHER EXERCISES (for answers see p. 745)

1 If $x = r \cos \theta$ and $y = r \sin \theta$, and $z = f(x, y) = g(r, \theta)$, prove that
a $g_r = (xf_x + yf_y)/r$
b $g_\theta = xf_y - yf_x$
c $(g_r)^2 + \dfrac{1}{r^2} (g_\theta)^2 = (f_x)^2 + (f_y)^2$

2 Show that if $u = \ln x + \ln y$ and $v = xy$ then

$$\frac{\partial u}{\partial x} \frac{\partial v}{\partial y} = \frac{\partial v}{\partial x} \frac{\partial u}{\partial y}$$

3 If $z = f(x + y) + g(x - y)$, where f and g are both twice differentiable real functions, prove that

$$\frac{\partial^2 z}{\partial x^2} = \frac{\partial^2 z}{\partial y^2}$$

Hence or otherwise show that $z = \sin x \cos y$ and $z = e^x \sinh y$ each satisfy this partial differential equation.

4 If $z = x^m y^n$, where m and n are constants, show that

$$dz/z = m \, dx/x + n \, dy/y$$

5 If $z = \ln (x^2 + y^2)$, prove that $z_{xx} + z_{yy} = 0$. Show further that if $z = f(x^2 + y^2)$ then

$$z_{xx} + z_{yy} = 4tf''(t) + 4f'(t)$$

where $t = x^2 + y^2$.

6 If $z = f(y/x)$ show that $xz_x + yz_y = 0$. Hence or otherwise show that this partial differential equation is satisfied by each of the following:
a $z = \sin [(x^2 + y^2)/xy]$
b $z = \ln (y/x)$
c $z = \exp [(x - y)/(x + y)]$

7 A beam of very low weight, uniform cross-section and length l simply supported at both ends carries a concentrated load W at the centre. It is known that the deflection at the centre is given by $y = Wl^3/48EI$, where E is Young's modulus and I is a moment of inertia. E is constant but the following small percentage increases occur: 2ε in W, ε in l and 5ε in I. Show that the error in y is then negligible.

8 The second moment of area of a rectangle of breadth B and depth D about an axis through one horizontal edge is given by $I = BD^3/3$. If a small increase of $\delta\%$ in D takes place, estimate the change in B required if the calculated value of I is to remain constant.

9 In telecommunications, the transmission line equations may be written as

$$Ri + L \frac{\partial i}{\partial t} = -\frac{\partial v}{\partial x}$$

$$Gv + C \frac{\partial v}{\partial t} = -\frac{\partial i}{\partial x}$$

where R, L, G and C are constant. Show that both i and v satisfy the telegraphists' equation

$$\frac{\partial^2 y}{\partial x^2} = LC \frac{\partial^2 y}{\partial t^2} + (GL + RC) \frac{\partial y}{\partial t} + RGy$$

In the case of a distortionless line, $RC = LG$. If $w^2 = 1/LC$ and $a^2 = RG$, show that telegraphists' equation becomes

$$\frac{\partial^2 y}{\partial x^2} = \frac{1}{w^2} \frac{\partial^2 y}{\partial t^2} + \frac{2a}{w} \frac{\partial y}{\partial t} + a^2 y$$

10 The ratio r of the magnetic moments of two magnets was evaluated using the formula $r = (t_2^2 + t_1^2)/(t_2^2 - t_1^2)$, where t_1 and t_2 are the times of oscillation of the magnets when like poles are in the same direction and when like poles are in the opposite direction respectively. If e_1 is the percentage error in t_1 and e_2 is the percentage error in t_2, show that the percentage error in r is approximately $4t_1^2 t_2^2 (e_1 - e_2)/(t_2^4 - t_1^4)$.

11 The natural frequency of oscillation of an LRC series circuit is given by

$$f = \frac{1}{2\pi} \sqrt{\left(\frac{1}{LC} - \frac{R^2}{4L^2} \right)}$$

If L is increased by 1% and C is decreased by 1%, show that the percentage increase in f is approximately $R^2 C/(4L - R^2 C)$.

12 The heat generated in a resistance weld is given by $H = Ki^2 Rt$, where K is a constant, i is the current between the electrodes and t is the time for which current flows. H must not vary by more than 5% if the weld is to remain good. It is possible to control t to within 0.5% and R to within 2.5%. Estimate the maximum possible variation in current if the weld is to retain its quality.

Series expansions and their uses 8

In previous chapters we have described the processes of elementary differentiation for functions of a single variable. In Chapter 7 we extended some of these ideas to functions of several variables. There is much more to calculus than this, and our next task is to consider some other applications. We shall see in particular that series expansions play a vital role.

After studying this chapter you should be able to
- ☐ Obtain Taylor's expansion of a function about a point;
- ☐ Expand $f(x)$ as a power series in x using Maclaurin's theorem;
- ☐ Apply l'Hospital's rule correctly;
- ☐ Classify stationary points;
- ☐ Determine points of inflexion.

At the end of this chapter we shall solve a practical problem concerning a valve.

8.1 THE MEAN VALUE PROPERTY

The graph of a smooth function is shown in Fig. 8.1. By smooth we mean that the function is differentiable everywhere. Geometrically this implies that the curve has a tangent at all its points.

A and B are two points where this smooth curve crosses the x-axis. It can be shown that there is at least one point P on the curve between A and B with the property that the tangent at P is parallel to the x-axis. In symbols we can express this by saying that if $f(a) = 0$ and $f(b) = 0$ then there exists some point $c \in (a, b)$ such that $f'(c) = 0$.

Although this property is intuitively obvious, its proof requires quite advanced mathematical ideas and so we shall omit it. Surprisingly perhaps

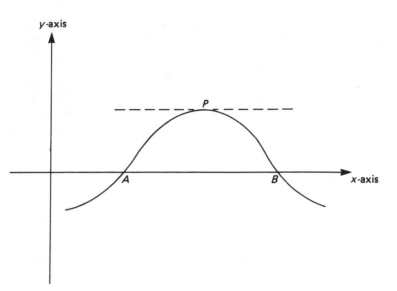

Fig. 8.1 A smooth function.

this simple theorem, known as **Rolle's theorem**, has quite profound consequences. In particular it leads to Taylor's expansion.

Michel Rolle (1652–
1719): French
mathematician who
wrote on geometry
and algebra.

We shall deduce one simple generalization straight away; this is known as
the mean value property.

Suppose we have a smooth curve and two points A and B on it (Fig.
8.2). The mean value property says that there is some point P on the curve

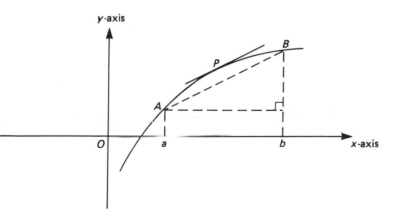

Fig. 8.2 The mean value property.

between A and B such that the tangent at P is parallel to the chord AB. Suppose A is the point $(a, f(a))$ and B is the point $(b, f(b))$. Then

$$\text{slope } AB = \frac{f(b) - f(a)}{b - a}$$

Consider $g = g(x)$ defined by

$$g(x) = f(x) - f(a) - \left[\frac{f(b) - f(a)}{b - a} \right](x - a)$$

Because g is a sum of differentiable functions, g is also differentiable. In fact

$$g'(x) = f'(x) - \frac{f(b) - f(a)}{b - a}$$

Now $g(a) = 0$ and $g(b) = 0$, and so by Rolle's theorem there exists $c \in (a, b)$ such that $g'(c) = 0$. That is,

$$f'(c) = \frac{f(b) - f(a)}{b - a}$$

for some c, $a < c < b$. This is precisely the **mean value property**.

8.2 TAYLOR'S THEOREM

Taylor's theorem is used extensively in numerical methods: see Chapter 18.

If we rearrange the formula which describes the mean value property we obtain

$$f(b) - f(a) = (b - a)f'(c) \qquad c \in (a, b)$$

So if we write $b = a + h$ then $c = a + \theta h$ for some $\theta \in (0, 1)$. Therefore

$$f(a + h) = f(a) + hf'(a + \theta h) \qquad \theta \in (0, 1)$$

It is possible to generalize this result so that, if we have a function which can be differentiated twice everywhere in an open interval containing the point a, then

$$f(a + h) = f(a) + hf'(a) + \frac{h^2}{2} f''(a + \theta h) \quad \text{for some } \theta \in (0, 1)$$

Therefore

$$f(a + h) = f(a) + hf'(a) + R_2$$

where

$$R_2 = \frac{h^2}{2} f''(a + \theta h) \quad \text{for some } \theta \in (0, 1)$$

Generalizing still further, if f is a real function which can be differentiated n times at all points in an open interval containing the point a, then

$$f(a + h) = f(a) + hf'(a) + \frac{h^2}{2!} f''(a) + \ldots + \frac{h^{n-1}}{(n-1)!} f^{(n-1)}(a) + R_n$$

where

$$R_n = \frac{h^n}{n!} f^{(n)}(a + \theta h) \quad \text{for some } \theta \in (0, 1)$$

This expansion is known as **Taylor's expansion** of f about the point a, and R_n is called the **remainder** after n terms.

So we have

$$f(a + h) = \sum_{r=0}^{n-1} \frac{h^r}{r!} f^{(r)}(a) + R_n$$

where

$$R_n = \frac{h^n}{n!} f^{(n)}(a + \theta h) \quad \text{for some } \theta \in (0, 1)$$

Brook Taylor (1685–1731): British mathematician known for contributions to the development of the calculus and the series named after him.

TAYLOR'S SERIES

If f is *infinitely* smooth, which means it can be differentiated an arbitrary number of times, and if $R_n \to 0$ as $n \to \infty$, then we obtain **Taylor's series**. This is an infinite series representation for $f(a + h)$:

$$f(a + h) = \sum_{r=0}^{\infty} \frac{h^r}{r!} f^{(r)}(a)$$

Questions of convergence of infinite series are discussed in Chapter 9.

If we use the variable x instead of h this becomes a power series in x:

$$f(a + x) = \sum_{r=0}^{\infty} \frac{x^r}{r!} f^{(r)}(a)$$

The special case where $a = 0$ is known as **Maclaurin's series**:

$$f(x) = \sum_{r=0}^{\infty} \frac{x^r}{r!} f^{(r)}(0)$$

Colin Maclaurin (1698–1746): Scottish mathematician and child prodigy. This special case of Taylor's series was named in his honour.

Although you may not have a clear understanding of what is meant by an infinite series until you study them in Chapter 9, be content for the time being to derive Taylor and Maclaurin expansions for known functions. However, one word of warning is in order.

It is not true that if we obtain a Taylor or Maclaurin series from a function that the series expansion is always *valid*. Nor is it true that if the series converges then the expansion is valid. In fact we are only entitled to write equality in the case where $R_n \to 0$ as $n \to \infty$. We shall therefore write

!

the equals sign on the understanding that we are restricting the domain of the function to those points for which $R_n \to 0$.

Here are two limits which can be quite useful in deciding whether or not $R_n \to 0$:

$$\lim_{n \to \infty} \frac{x^n}{n!} = 0 \qquad \text{for all } x \in \mathbb{R}$$

$$\lim_{n \to \infty} x^n = 0 \qquad \text{if } x \in (-1, 1)$$

Example □ Obtain the Maclaurin expansion for e^x.

Maclaurin's expansion is

$$f(x) = \sum_{n=0}^{\infty} \frac{x^n}{n!} f^{(r)}(0)$$

It is therefore necessary for us to calculate the values of successive derivatives of f at 0. If we put $f(x) = e^x$ we have $f(0) = e^0 = 1$. Moreover $f'(x) = e^x$, so that $f'(0) = e^0 = 1$. Clearly $f^{(n)}(x) = e^x$ for all $n \in \mathbb{N}$, and so $f^{(n)}(0) = 1$ for every n. Therefore

$$e^x = \sum_{n=0}^{\infty} \frac{x^n}{n!}$$

$$= 1 + x + \frac{x^2}{2!} + \frac{x^3}{3!} + \ldots + \frac{x^n}{n!} + \ldots$$

Here

$$R_n = \frac{c^n}{n!}$$

which tends to zero as n tends to infinity for all $c \in \mathbb{R}$. This shows in fact that this expansion is valid for all $x \in \mathbb{R}$. ■

THE EXPONENTIAL FUNCTION

We introduced the exponential function by stating that when e^x is differentiated with respect to x the result is e^x (Chapter 4). We have now used this to derive a representation of e^x as a power series in x. There are several ways of introducing the exponential function. Another way is to define $\exp x$ by means of the power series in x, and then to use deep theory of power series (Chapter 9) to show that $\exp x$ obeys the laws of indices and is unchanged when differentiated with respect to x. Yet another way to define the exponential function is by means of a limit:

$$\lim_{n \to \infty} \left(1 + \frac{x}{n} \right)^n$$

We shall give a very informal justification of this by showing how we can obtain the infinite series representation from it. First we expand $(1 + x/n)^n$ by means of the binomial theorem:

$$\left(1 + \frac{x}{n} \right)^n = 1 + n\left(\frac{x}{n} \right) + \frac{n(n-1)}{1 \times 2}\left(\frac{x}{n} \right)^2 + \frac{n(n-1)(n-2)}{1 \times 2 \times 3}\left(\frac{x}{n} \right)^3 + \ldots$$

$$= 1 + x + \frac{1(1 - 1/n)}{1 \times 2} x^2 + \frac{1(1 - 1/n)(1 - 2/n)}{1 \times 2 \times 3} x^3 + \ldots$$

Now as $n \to \infty$ we have for each fixed $r \in \mathbb{N}$

$$\left(1 - \frac{1}{n} \right)\left(1 - \frac{2}{n} \right)\left(1 - \frac{3}{n} \right) \ldots \left(1 - \frac{r}{n} \right) \to 1$$

In this way we see that

$$\lim_{n \to \infty} \left(1 + \frac{x}{n} \right)^n = 1 + x + \frac{x^2}{2!} + \frac{x^3}{3!} + \ldots, + \frac{x^n}{n!} + \ldots$$

$$= e^x$$

as foretold.

We must not disguise the fact that once again we have used properties of infinite series which, although plausible, require proof. Unfortunately there are many properties which appear plausible in the context of infinite series but which are *false*.

!

□ Use Maclaurin's expansion to obtain the binomial series for $(1 + x)^n$, **Example** where n is any real number.

Notice how Maclaurin's expansion and series are different names for the same thing. Some books distinguish between the expansion, which is the formula with remainder, and the series, which is an infinite series. However, there is no consensus on this terminology.

First we should remark that if r is any real number we have defined a^r only for $a > 0$. Therefore we must presuppose that $1 + x > 0$, so that $x > -1$. Now

$$f(x) = (1 + x)^n \qquad \text{so } f(0) - (1 + 0)^n = 1$$
$$f'(x) = n(1 + x)^{n-1} \qquad \text{so } f'(0) = n \times 1 = n$$
$$f''(x) = n(n - 1)(1 + x)^{n-2} \quad \text{so } f''(0) = n(n - 1)$$

In general,

$$f^{(r)}(x) = n(n - 1) \ldots (n - r + 1)(1 + x)^{n-r}$$

So

$$f^{(r)}(0) = n(n-1) \ldots (n-r+1)$$

Therefore in the Maclaurin expansion the coefficient of x^r is

$$\frac{n(n-1) \ldots (n-r+1)}{1 \times 2 \times 3 \times \ldots \times r}$$

But by definition this is the binomial coefficient $\binom{n}{r}$. Consequently we obtain

$$(1+x)^n = \binom{n}{0} + \binom{n}{1}x + \binom{n}{2}x^2 + \ldots + \binom{n}{r}x^r + \ldots$$

Again we stress that in order to be justified in using this infinite series as a representation for $(1+x)^n$ we should need to examine the remainder after r terms and show that it tends to 0 as $r \to \infty$. In fact this binomial expansion is only valid when $x \in (-1, 1)$, that is $-1 < x < 1$. ■

You may have come across some other power series. There are power series in x corresponding to the circular functions and the hyperbolic functions. Here are the main ones:

These series are often used in applications: for example, they arise in Surveying.

$$\cos x = \sum_{n=0}^{\infty} \frac{(-1)^n x^{2n}}{(2n)!} = 1 - \frac{x^2}{2!} + \frac{x^4}{4!} - \frac{x^6}{6!} + \ldots$$

$$\sin x = \sum_{n=0}^{\infty} \frac{(-1)^n x^{2n+1}}{(2n+1)!} = x - \frac{x^3}{3!} + \frac{x^5}{5!} - \frac{x^7}{7!} + \ldots$$

$$\cosh x = \sum_{n=0}^{\infty} \frac{x^{2n}}{(2n)!} = 1 + \frac{x^2}{2!} + \frac{x^4}{4!} + \frac{x^6}{6!} + \ldots$$

$$\sinh x = \sum_{n=0}^{\infty} \frac{x^{2n+1}}{(2n+1)!} = x + \frac{x^3}{3!} + \frac{x^5}{5!} + \frac{x^7}{7!} + \ldots$$

It can be shown that these are valid for all $x \in \mathbb{R}$. You will probably have observed the close similarity between the series expansions for the circular functions and their hyperbolic counterparts. We shall investigate this similarity when we consider complex numbers (Chapter 10).

Example □ Obtain the first four non-zero terms in the expansion of $\tan x$ as a power series in x.

Here we put

$$f(x) = \tan x$$

so $f(0) = \tan 0 = 0$.

$$f'(x) = \sec^2 x$$

so $f'(0) = \sec^2 0 = 1$.

$$f''(x) = 2 \sec x \sec x \tan x = 2 \sec^2 x \tan x$$

so $f''(0) = 0$.

$$\begin{aligned} f^{(3)}(x) &= 2 \sec^2 x \sec^2 x + 2 \tan x\, 2 \sec x \sec x \tan x \\ &= 2 \sec^4 x + 4 \sec^2 x \tan^2 x \\ &= 2 \sec^4 x + 4 \sec^2 x\, (\sec^2 x - 1) \\ &= 6 \sec^4 x - 4 \sec^2 x \end{aligned}$$

so $f^{(3)}(0) = 2$.

$$\begin{aligned} f^{(4)}(x) &= 24 \sec^3 x \sec x \tan x - 8 \sec x \sec x \tan x \\ &= 24 \sec^4 x \tan x - 8 \sec^2 x \tan x \end{aligned}$$

so $f^{(4)}(0) = 0$.

$$\begin{aligned} f^{(5)}(x) &= 24 \sec^4 x \sec^2 x + 24 \tan x\, 4 \sec^3 x \sec x \tan x \\ &\quad - 8 \sec^2 x \sec^2 x - 8 \tan x\, 2 \sec x \sec x \tan x \\ &= 24 \sec^6 x + 96 \sec^4 x\, (\sec^2 x - 1) - 8 \sec^4 x \\ &\quad - 16 \sec^2 x\, (\sec^2 x - 1) \\ &= 120 \sec^6 x - 120 \sec^4 x + 16 \sec^2 x \end{aligned}$$

so $f^{(5)}(0) = 16$.

$$\begin{aligned} f^{(6)}(x) &= 720 \sec^5 x \sec x \tan x - 480 \sec^3 x \sec x \tan x + 32 \sec x \sec x \tan x \\ &= 720 \sec^6 x \tan x - 480 \sec^4 x \tan x + 32 \sec^2 x \tan x \end{aligned}$$

so $f^{(6)}(0) = 0$.

$$\begin{aligned} f^{(7)}(x) &= 4320 \sec^5 x \sec x \tan x \tan x + 720 \sec^6 x \sec^2 x \\ &\quad - 1920 \sec^3 x \sec x \tan x \tan x - 480 \sec^4 x \sec^2 x \\ &\quad + 64 \sec x \sec x \tan x \tan x + 32 \sec^2 x \sec^2 x \\ &= 4320 \sec^6 x \tan^2 x + 720 \sec^8 x - 1920 \sec^4 x \tan^2 x \\ &\quad - 480 \sec^6 x + 64 \sec^2 x \tan^2 x + 32 \sec^4 x \end{aligned}$$

so $f^{(7)}(0) = 0 + 720 - 0 - 480 + 0 + 32 = 272$.

This is the fourth non-zero term, and so we can write down the expansion:

$$\tan x = 0 + x + 0 + 2\frac{x^3}{3!} + 0 + 16\frac{x^5}{5!} + 0 + 272\frac{x^7}{7!} + \dots$$

$$= x + \frac{x^3}{3} + \frac{2}{15}x^5 + \frac{17}{315}x^7 + \dots$$

This example shows that we should not always expect a discernible pattern to emerge. ■

Now for some steps – but make sure you have understood all the examples first.

8.3 Workshop

1

Exercise Differentiate $(\ln x)^x$ $(x > 1)$ with respect to x.

This is just a little differentiation to warm up on. Try it, then step forward.

2

Here we go then. It's easiest to put $y = (\ln x)^x$ and take logarithms:

$$\ln y = \ln [(\ln x)^x] = x \ln (\ln x)$$

so that

$$\frac{1}{y} \frac{dy}{dx} = \ln (\ln x) + x \frac{1}{\ln x} \frac{1}{x}$$

$$\frac{dy}{dx} = \ln (\ln x)(\ln x)^x + (\ln x)^{x-1}$$

If you were right then step ahead to step 4. If you were wrong, check carefully what you have done; then try the next problem.

▷**Exercise** Obtain dy/dx if $y = (\cosh x)^x$.

You know the method so there should be no serious problems.

3

We obtain $\ln y = x \ln (\cosh x)$. So, differentiating both sides with respect to x and using the product rule and chain rule, we have

$$\frac{1}{y} \frac{dy}{dx} = \ln (\cosh x) + x \frac{1}{\cosh x} \frac{d}{dx} (\cosh x)$$

$$= \ln (\cosh x) + x \frac{\sinh x}{\cosh x}$$

$$\frac{dy}{dx} = [\ln (\cosh x) + x \tanh x] (\cosh x)^x$$

Now move on to the next step.

4

Exercise Obtain the first four terms of Taylor's expansion for $y = \sin x$ about the point $x = \pi/4$ as a power series in x.

The difficulty with a question like this is sorting out what is really wanted. The trouble is that x has been used in three different ways here: first, as a dummy variable in the definition of sine; secondly, as a specific point; and thirdly, as the dummy variable in an algebraic description of the power series. Let's separate all these things so that we can proceed.

In general given $y = f(x)$ we obtain, using Taylor's expansion, $f(a + h)$ as a power series in h. Here $y = f(x) = \sin x$, $a = \pi/4$, and we can therefore obtain a power series in h for $\sin (\pi/4 + h)$. To satisfy the question we shall at the final stage replace h by x.

Right! You know what you have to do, so see how it goes.

We have

$$f(a + h) = f(a) + hf'(a) + \ldots$$

So we must evaluate successive derivatives at the point $\pi/4$:

$$f(x) = \sin x \quad \Rightarrow \quad f(a) = \sin \pi/4 = 1/\sqrt{2}$$
$$f'(x) = \cos x \quad \Rightarrow \quad f'(a) = \cos \pi/4 = 1/\sqrt{2}$$
$$f''(x) = -\sin x \quad \Rightarrow \quad f''(a) = -\sin \pi/4 = -1/\sqrt{2}$$
$$f^{(3)}(x) = -\cos x \Rightarrow f^{(3)}(a) = -\cos \pi/2 = -1/\sqrt{2}$$

This will give the first four non-zero terms, and so we have

$$f(a + h) = f(a) + hf'(a) + \tfrac{1}{2}h^2 f''(a) + \ldots$$
$$\sin (\pi/4 + h) = 1/\sqrt{2} + h/\sqrt{2} - h^2/2\sqrt{2} - h^3/6\sqrt{2} + \ldots$$

Finally, replacing h by x we have

$$\sin (\pi/4 + x) = 1/\sqrt{2} + x/\sqrt{2} - x^2/2\sqrt{2} - x^3/6\sqrt{2} + \ldots$$

Now try another problem.

▷ **Exercise** Obtain Maclaurin's expansion for $f(x) = \sin (x + \pi/4)$ as a power series in x as far as the term in x^3.

This shows how closely Taylor's expansion and Maclaurin's expansion are to one another. Superficially Taylor's expansion seems more general. However, not only can we deduce Maclaurin's expansion from Taylor's, but it is also possible to deduce Taylor's expansion from Maclaurin's. Try it, then step ahead.

We have

$$f(x) = f(0) + xf'(0) + \tfrac{1}{2}x^2 f''(0) + \ldots$$

We therefore need to obtain successive derivatives of f evaluated when $x = 0$. Now

$$f(x) = \sin (x + \pi/4) \quad \Rightarrow \quad f(0) = \sin \pi/4 = 1/\sqrt{2}$$
$$f'(x) = \cos (x + \pi/4) \quad \Rightarrow \quad f'(0) = \cos \pi/4 = 1/\sqrt{2}$$
$$f''(x) = \quad \sin (x + \pi/4) \quad \rightarrow \quad f''(0) = -1/\sqrt{2}$$

$$f^{(3)}(x) = -\cos (x + \pi/4) \Rightarrow f^{(3)}(0) = -\cos \pi/4 = -1/\sqrt{2}$$

Substituting into Maclaurin's expansion:

$$\sin (\pi/4 + x) = 1/\sqrt{2} + x/\sqrt{2} - x^2/2\sqrt{2} - x^3/6\sqrt{2} + \ldots$$

as before.

If you managed that successfully, then on you go to step 8. Otherwise, try a further exercise.

▷ **Exercise** Obtain an expansion of $\ln (1 + x)$ as a power series in x.

7 We use Maclaurin's expansion and so we put $f(x) = \ln (1 + x)$. We shall need to obtain successive derivatives of f at 0 to substitute into the expansion formula

$$f(x) = f(0) + xf'(0) + \tfrac{1}{2}x^2 f''(0) + \ldots$$

So:

$$f(x) = \ln (1 + x) \qquad\Rightarrow\qquad f(0) = \ln 1 = 0$$

$$f'(x) = \frac{1}{1 + x} \qquad\Rightarrow\qquad f'(0) = 1$$

$$f''(x) = \frac{-1}{(1 + x)^2} \qquad\Rightarrow\qquad f''(0) = -1$$

$$f^{(3)}(x) = \frac{(-1)(-2)}{(1 + x)^3} \qquad\Rightarrow f^{(3)}(0) = 2$$

$$f^{(4)}(x) = \frac{(-1)(-2)(-3)}{(1 + x)^4} \qquad\Rightarrow f^{(4)}(0) = -3!$$

$$f^{(5)}(x) = \frac{(-1)(-2)(-3)(-4)}{(1 + x)^5} \Rightarrow f^{(5)}(0) = 4!$$

We can see a pattern emerging:

$$f^{(n)}(0) = (-1)^{n+1}(n - 1)! \qquad \text{when } n \in \mathbb{N}$$

When we substitute into the Maclaurin expansion we obtain

$$f(0) + xf'(0) + \frac{x^2}{2!} f''(0) + \frac{x^3}{3!} f^{(3)}(0) + \ldots + \frac{x^n}{n!} f^{(n)}(0) + \ldots$$

$$= 0 + x(1) + \frac{x^2}{2!} (-1) + \frac{x^3}{3!} 2! + \frac{x^4}{4!} (-3!) + \ldots$$

$$+ \frac{x^n}{n!} (-1)^{n+1} (n - 1)! \ldots$$

$$= x - \frac{x^2}{2} + \frac{x^3}{3} - \frac{x^4}{4} + \ldots + (-1)^{n+1} \frac{x^n}{n} + \ldots$$

We have

$$\ln (1 + x) = \sum_{n=1}^{\infty} (-1)^{n+1} \frac{x^n}{n}$$

By examining the remainder after n terms it is possible to show that this series represents $\ln (1 + x)$ whenever $-1 < x \le 1$.

Now we go on to another problem.

▷**Exercise**   Given $y = \sin^{-1} x$, show that

8

$$(1 - x^2) \frac{d^2y}{dx^2} - x \frac{dy}{dx} = 0$$

Differentiate n times using Leibniz's theorem to deduce

$$(1 - x^2) \frac{d^{n+2}y}{dx^{n+2}} - (2n + 1) x \frac{d^{n+1}y}{dx^{n+1}} - n^2 \frac{d^n y}{dx^n} = 0$$

Hence or otherwise obtain a power series expansion for $\sin^{-1} x$.

This problem will help you to revise your work on Leibniz's theorem. Let's do it in three steps. First, obtain the equation for the second derivative.

If $y = \sin^{-1} x$ then $\sin y = x$. So differentiating throughout with respect to x we have

9

$$\cos y \frac{dy}{dx} = 1$$

Squaring we have

$$\cos^2 y \left(\frac{dy}{dx}\right)^2 = 1$$

and since $\cos^2 y = 1 - \sin^2 y = 1 - x^2$ we have

$$(1 - x^2)\left(\frac{dy}{dx}\right)^2 = 1$$

Now differentiating again throughout with respect to x,

$$(1 - x^2) 2 \frac{dy}{dx} \frac{d^2y}{dx^2} + (-2x)\left(\frac{dy}{dx}\right)^2 = 0$$

Since dy/dx is not zero we obtain

$$(1 - x^2) \frac{d^2y}{dx^2} - x \frac{dy}{dx} = 0$$

If you put a foot wrong then locate your error and take the next step, which is to use Leibniz's theorem.

10

We must consider the two terms in the last equation separately, since each is a product and will need to be differentiated n times by Leibniz's theorem.

For the first term, put $u = 1 - x^2$ and $v = y_2$, where the subscript n denotes the nth-order derivative with respect to x. We have $u_1 = -2x$, $u_2 = -2$ and $u_3 = 0$, so that $u_n = 0$ for $n \geqslant 3$. We also have $v_1 = y_3$, $v_2 = y_4$ and in general $v_n = y_{n+2}$. Now Leibniz's theorem gives

$$(uv)_n = uv_n + n u_1 v_{n-1} + \tfrac{1}{2}n(n-1) u_2 v_{n-2} + \ldots$$

Now since all the other terms are zero we have

$$(1 - x^2) \frac{d^{n+2}y}{dx^{n+2}} + n(-2x) \frac{d^{n+1}y}{dx^{n+1}} + \frac{n(n-1)}{2} (-2) \frac{d^n y}{dx^n}$$

$$= (1 - x^2) \frac{d^{n+2}y}{dx^{n+2}} - 2nx \frac{d^{n+1}y}{dx^{n+1}} - n(n-1) \frac{d^n y}{dx^n}$$

For the second term, if we put $u = x$ and $v = y_1$ then $u_1 = 1$ and $u_n = 0$ if $n > 1$. Also $v_1 = y_2$ and in general $v_n = y_{n+1}$. Therefore

$$(uv)_n = uv_n + n u_1 v_{n-1} + \ldots$$

and so we obtain

$$x \frac{d^{n+1}y}{dx^{n+1}} + n \frac{d^n y}{dx^n}$$

Finally we combine the two terms. So differentiating throughout the equation n times we obtain

$$(1 - x^2) \frac{d^{n+2}y}{dx^{n+2}} - 2nx \frac{d^{n+1}y}{dx^{n+1}} - n(n-1) \frac{d^n y}{dx^n} - x \frac{d^{n+1}y}{dx^{n+1}} - n \frac{d^n y}{dx^n} = 0$$

Therefore

$$(1 - x^2) \frac{d^{n+2}y}{dx^{n+2}} - (2n + 1) x \frac{d^{n+1}y}{dx^{n+1}} - n^2 \frac{d^n y}{dx^n} = 0$$

You did well if you managed to do that. Now you must think how you can use this to obtain Maclaurin's expansion.

11

If $y = f(x)$ then the equation is

$$(1 - x^2) f^{(n+2)}(x) - (2n + 1) x f^{(n+1)}(x) - n^2 f^{(n)}(x) = 0$$

but we require the values of the derivatives when $x = 0$. So the equation reduces to

$$f^{(n+2)}(0) - n^2 f^{(n)}(0) = 0$$
$$f^{(n+2)}(0) = n^2 f^{(n)}(0)$$

Now the equation was derived using Leibniz's theorem, and so is valid when $n \geqslant 1$. However, it also holds when $n = 0$ since it then reduces to the second-order equation. This means that the equation

$$f^{(n+2)}(0) = n^2 f^{(n)}(0)$$

can be used to generate all the coefficients in Maclaurin's expansion from $f(0)$ and $f'(0)$. Now $f(0) = \sin^{-1} 0 = 0$ and $f'(0) = 1$. So we deduce that $f^{(n)}(0) = 0$ if n is even, whereas

$$f^{(3)}(0) = 1^2 1$$
$$f^{(5)}(0) = 3^2 f^{(3)}(0) = 3^2 1^2$$
$$f^{(7)}(0) = 5^2 f^{(5)}(0) = 5^2 3^2 1^2$$

So we obtain the expansion

$$x + \frac{1^2}{3!}x^3 + \frac{3^2 1^2}{5!}x^5 + \ldots + \frac{(2r-1)^2 (2r-3)^2 \ldots 3^2 1^2}{(2r+1)!}x^{2r+1} + \ldots$$

Well, there it is. A bit of a monster, isn't it?

8.4 L'HOSPITAL'S RULE

L'Hospital's rule is extremely useful in the evaluation of a limit which might otherwise be difficult to obtain. Suppose we wish to evaluate

$$\lim_{x \to a} \frac{f(x)}{g(x)}$$

and either

$$\lim_{x \to a} f(x) = 0 \quad \text{and} \quad \lim_{x \to a} g(x) = 0$$

or

$$\lim_{x \to a} f(x) = \pm\infty \quad \text{and} \quad \lim_{x \to a} g(x) = \pm\infty$$

Then **l'Hospital's rule** says

$$\lim_{x \to a} \frac{f(x)}{g(x)} = \lim_{x \to a} \frac{f'(x)}{g'(x)}$$

provided the limit exists.

Guillame François Antoine de L'Hospital (1661– 1704): Maquis de St. Mesme; infant prodigy who wrote on geometry, algebra and mechanics.

Although we shall not prove it to be true generally, we can give an informal justification for this remarkable rule in the case where $f(a) = g(a) = 0$ and f' and g' are continuous at the point a:

$$\lim_{x \to a} \frac{f(x)}{g(x)} = \lim_{x \to a} \frac{f(x) - f(a)}{g(x) - g(a)}$$

$$= \lim_{x \to a} \left[\frac{f(x) - f(a)}{x - a} \quad \frac{x - a}{g(x) - g(a)} \right]$$

Now putting $x - a = h$ we obtain

$$\lim_{x \to a} \frac{f(x) - f(a)}{x - a} = \lim_{h \to 0} \frac{f(a + h) - f(a)}{h}$$

$$= f'(a) = \lim_{x \to a} f'(x)$$

Similarly

$$\lim_{x \to a} \frac{g(x) - g(a)}{x - a} = \lim_{x \to a} g'(x)$$

Therefore

$$\lim_{x \to a} \frac{f(x)}{g(x)} = \lim_{x \to a} \frac{f'(x)}{g'(x)}$$

Example □ Obtain

$$\lim_{x \to 0} \frac{\sin x - x}{x^3}$$

Here $f(x) = \sin x - x$ and $g(x) = x^3$. So

$$\lim_{x \to 0} f(x) = \lim_{x \to 0} [\sin x - x] = 0$$

$$\lim_{x \to 0} g(x) = \lim_{x \to 0} x^3 = 0$$

So we can use l'Hospital's rule:

$$f'(x) = \cos x - 1 \qquad g'(x) = 3x^2$$

but

$$\lim_{x \to 0} f'(x) = 1 - 1 = 0$$

$$\lim_{x \to 0} g'(x) = 3 \times 0 = 0$$

So we can use l'Hospital's rule again:

$$f''(x) = -\sin x \qquad g''(x) = 6x$$

As before,

$$\lim_{x \to 0} f''(x) = 0$$

$$\lim_{x \to 0} g''(x) = 0$$

So we use l'Hospital's rule once more:

$$f^{(3)}(x) = -\cos x \qquad g^{(3)}(x) = 6$$

So

$$\lim_{x \to 0} \frac{\sin x - x}{x^3} = \lim_{x \to 0} \frac{\cos x - 1}{3x^2}$$

$$= \lim_{x \to 0} \frac{-\sin x}{6x}$$

$$= \lim_{x \to 0} \frac{-\cos x}{6} = -\frac{1}{6}$$

The use of l'Hospital's rule at each stage is now justified because this final limit exists. ∎

☐ Obtain   **Example**

$$\lim_{x \to \pi/2} \frac{1 - \sin x}{\cot x}$$

When you have done this, see if you are correct.

First, $1 - \sin \pi/2 = 1 - 1 = 0$ and $\cot \pi/2 = 0$. So we may use l'Hospital's rule:

$$\lim_{x \to \pi/2} \frac{1 - \sin x}{\cot x} = \lim_{x \to \pi/2} \frac{-\cos x}{-\csc^2 x} = 0$$

Alternatively, if we wish we can avoid l'Hospital's rule and instead use algebraic simplification:

$$\lim_{x \to \pi/2} \frac{1 - \sin x}{\cot x} = \lim_{x \to \pi/2} \frac{(1 - \sin x) \sin x}{\cos x}$$

$$= \lim_{x \to \pi/2} \frac{(1 - \sin x) \sin x \cos x}{\cos^2 x}$$

$$= \lim_{x \to \pi/2} \frac{(1 - \sin x) \sin x \cos x}{1 - \sin^2 x}$$

$$= \lim_{x \to \pi/2} \frac{(1 - \sin x) \sin x \cos x}{(1 - \sin x)(1 + \sin x)}$$

$$= \lim_{x \to \pi/2} \frac{\sin x \cos x}{1 + \sin x}$$

$$= \frac{1.0}{1 + 1} = 0 \qquad \blacksquare$$

We first met an indeterminate form in section 4.2 but there we were able to tackle the problem algebraically.

One very important thing to remember about l'Hospital's rule is that you must not use it unless you have an **indeterminate form**. In other words, one of the following must hold:

$$\lim_{x \to a} f(x) = 0 \qquad \text{and} \qquad \lim_{x \to a} g(x) = 0$$

or

$$\lim_{x \to a} f(x) = \pm\infty \qquad \text{and} \qquad \lim_{x \to a} g(x) = \pm\infty$$

Indeterminate forms can be represented by 0/0 or ∞/∞: these expressions are meaningless and so indeterminate.

Why not check that you understand this by taking a few steps?

____8.5 Workshop____

Exercise   Evaluate the following limit:

$$\lim_{x \to 0} \frac{(e^x + 1)x}{e^{2x} - 1}$$

Move on only when you have done it – or when you think you can't do it.

▢2 If we put $x = 0$ straight away we obtain 0/0, which is indeterminate. However,

$$\frac{(e^x + 1)x}{e^{2x} - 1} = \frac{(e^x + 1)x}{(e^x + 1)(e^x - 1)}$$

$$= \frac{x}{e^x - 1}$$

Again this produces the indeterminate 0/0 if we try to substitute $x = 0$, but now we can easily use l'Hospital's rule:

$$\lim_{x \to 0} \frac{x}{e^x - 1} = \lim_{x \to 0} \frac{1}{e^x - 0}$$

$$= \lim_{x \to 0} \frac{1}{e^x} = 1$$

Did you get that right? If you did then you may go on to the next section. Otherwise, try this next exercise.

▷**Exercise** Evaluate the limit

$$\lim_{x \to 1} \frac{\sin \pi x}{\sin (\pi x + x - 1)}$$

Try very hard with this one. Then step forward.

If we attempt to put $x = 1$ we obtain the form 0/0, and so we shall use **3** l'Hospital's rule:

$$\lim_{x \to 1} \frac{\sin \pi x}{\sin (\pi x + x - 1)} = \lim_{x \to 1} \frac{\sin \pi x}{\sin [(\pi + 1)x - 1]}$$

$$= \lim_{x \to 1} \frac{\pi \cos \pi x}{(\pi + 1) \cos [(\pi + 1)x - 1]}$$

$$= \frac{\pi(-1)}{(\pi + 1)(-1)} = \frac{\pi}{\pi + 1}$$

REPEATED USE OF L'HOSPITAL'S RULE

We can use Taylor's theorem to justify the repeated use of l'Hospital's rule. Suppose that both the real functions f and g have a Taylor expansion about the point a, and that both

$$\lim_{x \to a} f^{(r)}(x) \quad \text{and} \quad \lim_{x \to a} g^{(r)}(x)$$

are zero for all integers r such that $0 \leqslant r < n$, but that

$$\lim_{x \to a} g^{(n)}(x) \neq 0$$

By Taylor's theorem we have

$$f(a + h) = f(a) + hf'(a) + \ldots + \frac{h^{n-1}}{(n-1)!} f^{(n-1)}(a) + \frac{h^n}{n!} f^{(n)}(a + \theta h)$$

$$g(a + h) = g(a) + hg'(a) + \ldots + \frac{h^{n-1}}{(n-1)!} g^{(n-1)}(a) + \frac{h^n}{n!} g^{(n)}(a + \phi h)$$

where $\theta, \phi \in (0, 1)$.

The continuity of the derivatives at the point a gives

$$f^{(r)}(a) = 0 = g^{(r)}(a)$$

for $0 \leqslant r < n$. Therefore these Taylor series reduce to

$$f(a + h) = \frac{h^n}{n!} f^{(n)}(a + \theta h)$$

$$g(a + h) = \frac{h^n}{n!} g^{(n)}(a + \phi h)$$

So that

$$\frac{f(a + h)}{g(a + h)} = \frac{f^{(n)}(a + \theta h)}{g^{(n)}(a + \phi h)}$$

Writing $x = a + h$ we have

$$\lim_{x \to a} \frac{f(x)}{g(x)} = \lim_{h \to 0} \frac{f(a + h)}{g(a + h)}$$

$$= \lim_{h \to 0} \frac{f^{(n)}(a + \theta h)}{g^{(n)}(a + \phi h)}$$

$$= \frac{f^{(n)}(a)}{g^{(n)}(a)}$$

$$= \lim_{x \to a} \frac{f^{(n)}(x)}{g^{(n)}(x)}$$

8.6 MAXIMA AND MINIMA

The theory of maxima and minima is used in structural mechanics when beam deflection is considered. Surveyors also need the theory for vertical curve calculations.

There are many situations in which we have an interest in those points where a function attains a maximum or a minimum value. For example:

1 A company may wish to maximize its profits, but increasing the price of its goods may decrease the demand. A reasonable question to ask is: 'What price will maximize profit?'

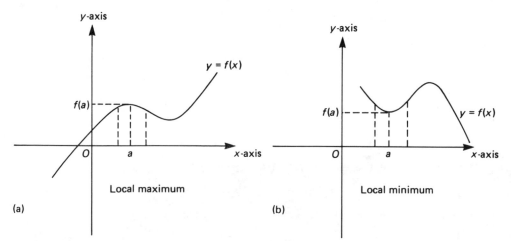

(a)   (b)

Fig. 8.3 (a) Local maximum (b) Local minimum.

2 An architect may be asked to design a library extension which, within a given budget, will maximize the available floor space.

3 An electrical engineer may wish to maximize the power in a circuit.

Suppose f is a real function which is defined at all points in some open interval containing the point a (Fig. 8.3). We say that f has a **local maximum** at the point a if and only if, for all h sufficiently small but non-zero,

$$f(a + h) - f(a) < 0$$

Similarly, f has a **local minimum** at the point a if and only if, for all h sufficiently small but non-zero,

$$f(a + h) - f(a) > 0$$

We shall confine our attention to functions which are infinitely smooth. As we have already remarked, this means that the function has derivatives of all orders.

It is intuitively obvious that if f is differentiable at either a local maximum or a local minimum then its derivative there is zero. Any point at which the derivative of f is zero is called a **stationary point** of f. The value of f at a stationary point is called a stationary value of f. (Stationary points are also sometimes known as turning points or critical points.)

A simple picture shows that not all stationary points are points at which f attains either a local maximum or a local minimum. Any point at which a curve crosses its tangent is called a **point of inflexion**. If we obtain the stationary points we shall obtain not only the points at which the function attains a local maximum or a local minimum but also some of the points of inflexion. In Fig. 8.4 A and I are local minima and E is a local maximum; A, C, E, G and I are stationary points, whereas B, C, D, F, G and H are points of inflexion.

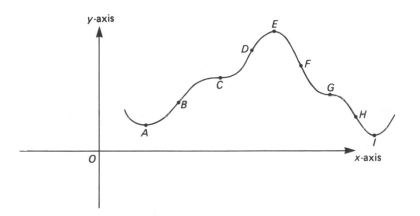

Fig. 8.4 Stationary points and points of inflexion.

As this makes clear, not every point of inflexion is a stationary point. We shall see later how to determine the points of inflexion of a function.

TESTING FOR MAXIMA AND MINIMA

There is an elementary method for determining local maxima and local minima which relies on the observation that at these points f' changes sign (Fig. 8.5):

1 As we pass through a local maximum, f' changes from positive to negative;

2 As we pass through a local minimum, f' changes from negative to positive.

It follows that if we examine the sign of f' on either side of the stationary point we should be able to classify it correctly. At a point of inflexion the sign is preserved.

However, it is possible to obtain a test for maxima and minima which does not involve examining the sign of f' on either side of the stationary point. Suppose that the function f has a stationary point at a, so that $f'(a) = 0$. By Taylor's theorem we know that

$$f(a + h) = f(a) + hf'(a) + \frac{h^2}{2!} f''(a) + \frac{h^3}{3!} f^{(3)}(a + \theta h)$$

where $0 < \theta < 1$. So in this case we have

$$f(a + h) - f(a) = \frac{h^2}{2!} f''(a) + \frac{h^3}{3!} f^{(3)}(a + \theta h)$$

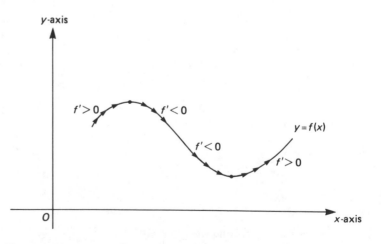

Fig. 8.5 The sign of f' near stationary points.

Now if $f''(a)$ is non-zero and $f^{(3)}(a + \theta h)$ is bounded, it is possible to choose h so small, $h \neq 0$, that the sign of the right-hand side of this equation is the same as the sign of the first term $(h^2/2!)f''(a)$, and the sign of this first term is of course the same as that of $f''(a)$. So if $f''(a) > 0$ we deduce that $f(a + h) - f(a) > 0$ for all h sufficiently small but non-zero, whereas if $f''(a) < 0$ then $f(a + h) - f(a) < 0$ for all h sufficiently small but non-zero. That is,

$$f''(a) > 0 \Rightarrow \text{local minimum}$$
$$f''(a) < 0 \Rightarrow \text{local maximum}$$

Therefore the following is the rule for obtaining the points at which $y = f(x)$ attains a local maximum or a local minimum:

1 Obtain all the stationary points, that is the points a at which $f'(a) = 0$.
2 For each stationary point a examine the sign of $f''(a)$:
  a if $f''(a) > 0$ then local minimum
  b if $f''(a) < 0$ then local maximum
  c if $f''(a) = 0$ then further testing is necessary.

□ Obtain and classify the stationary points of   **Example**

$$y = x^2 e^x$$

We first obtain dy/dx and then equate it to 0 for the stationary points:

$$\frac{dy}{dx} = x^2 e^x + 2xe^x = x(x + 2)e^x$$

Now $e^x \neq 0$: so $x(x + 2) = 0$, from which $x = 0$ and $x = -2$ are the stationary points.

Next we differentiate again and evaluate the second derivative at each stationary point to determine its sign there:

$$\frac{d^2y}{dx^2} = x^2 e^x + 2xe^x + 2xe^x + 2e^x = (x^2 + 4x + 2)e^x$$

The sign of this is the same as the sign of

$$x^2 + 4x + 2 = (x + 2)^2 - 2$$

So

$$x = 0 \quad \Rightarrow \quad \frac{d^2y}{dx^2} > 0 \Rightarrow \text{local minimum}$$

$$x = -2 \Rightarrow \frac{d^2y}{dx^2} < 0 \Rightarrow \text{local maximum} \qquad \blacksquare$$

TESTING FOR INFLEXION

We now turn our attention to the problem of what to do when $f''(a) = 0$ at the stationary point. As before we can use Taylor's theorem to obtain

$$f(a + h) = f(a) + hf'(a) + \frac{h^2}{2!} f''(a) + \frac{h^3}{3!} f^{(3)}(a) + \frac{h^4}{4!} f^{(4)}(a + \theta h)$$

for some $\theta \in (0, 1)$.

Now $f'(a) = 0$ and $f''(a) = 0$, so that this reduces to

$$f(a + h) - f(a) = \frac{h^3}{3!} f^{(3)}(a) + \frac{h^4}{4!} f^{(4)}(a + \theta h)$$

If $f^{(3)}(a) \neq 0$ and $f^{(4)}(a + \theta h)$ is bounded, the same argument as before shows that the sign of the right-hand side is the same as the sign of $(h^3/3!)f^{(3)}(a)$, which changes sign with h. So the sign of $f(a + h) - f(a)$ changes sign as h changes sign so we have therefore a point of inflexion.

Consequently if at a stationary point we have $f''(a) = 0$ and $f^{(3)}(a) \neq 0$ we obtain a point of inflexion. On the other hand if $f^{(3)}(a)$ is zero too, then we need to continue with our analysis. This leads to a complete test for maxima and minima.

MAXIMA AND MINIMA: COMPLETE TEST

To obtain and classify those points at which $y = f(x)$ attains a local maximum or a local minimum:

1 Determine the stationary points of f. That is, obtain those points at which $dy/dx = 0$.
2 Obtain for each stationary point the smallest value of n for which $d^n y/dx^n \neq 0$.
3 If n is odd then the function has a point of inflexion at the stationary point.
4 If n is even then the function attains either a local maximum or a local minimum at a:

$$d^n y/dx^n > 0 \text{ implies a local minimum}$$
$$d^n y/dx^n < 0 \text{ implies a local maximum}$$

AT POINTS OF INFLEXION

If we examine the slope of the curve as we pass through a point of inflexion we see that two situations can occur (Fig. 8.6):

1 dy/dx decreases as we approach the point of inflexion and increases thereafter;
2 dy/dx increases as we approach the point of inflexion and decreases thereafter.

If we were driving a car along a road which went up a hill with the shape of Fig. 8.6 we should be conscious of this change in slope at the point of inflexion.

When we interpret mathematically what this means we see that f' itself has either a local maximum or a local minimum at a point of inflexion. It

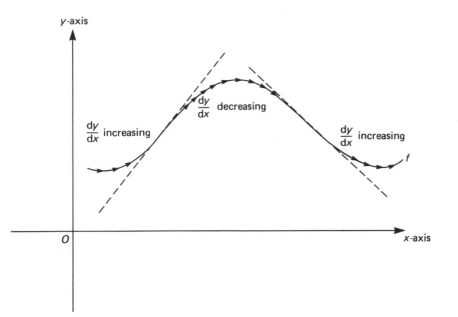

Fig. 8.6 The sign of dy/dx near points of inflexion.

follows that, at a point of inflexion, d^2y/dx^2 = 0. However, if the second order derivative is zero at a stationary point it does not necessarily follow that we have a point of inflexion. This is a very common misconception and it is possible that you too have fallen victim to it. In short:

$$\text{point of inflexion} \Rightarrow \frac{\mathrm{d}^2 y}{\mathrm{d}x^2} = 0$$

$$\frac{\mathrm{d}^2 y}{\mathrm{d}x^2} = 0 \nRightarrow \text{point of inflexion}$$

The next problem will help to reinforce this point.

□ Obtain and classify the stationary points of $y = x^4 \mathrm{e}^x$.   **Example**
    We begin by determining the stationary points:

$$\frac{\mathrm{d}y}{\mathrm{d}x} = x^4 \mathrm{e}^x + 4x^3 \mathrm{e}^x$$

Therefore we put $x^3(x + 4) = 0$ and deduce that the stationary points are $x = 0$ or $x = -4$. Now

$$\frac{\mathrm{d}^2 y}{\mathrm{d}x^2} = x^4 \mathrm{e}^x + 8x^3 \mathrm{e}^x + 12x^2 \mathrm{e}^x$$

$$= x^2(x^2 + 8x + 12)\mathrm{e}^x$$

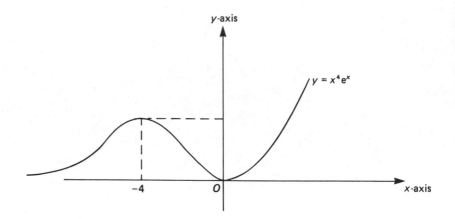

Fig. 8.7 The graph of $y = x^4 e^x$.

When $x = 0$ we obtain $d^2y/dx^2 = 0$, and so further testing is necessary. When $x = -4$ we obtain

$$\frac{d^2y}{dx^2} = 16(16 - 32 + 12)e^{-4} < 0$$

so there is a local maximum at $x = -4$. Now

$$\frac{d^3y}{dx^3} = x^4 e^x + 12x^3 e^x + 36x^2 e^x + 24x e^x$$

so that when $x = 0$, $d^3y/dx^3 = 0$ and still further testing is needed.

$$\frac{d^4y}{dx^4} = x^4 e^x + 16x^3 e^x + 72x^2 e^x + 96x e^x + 24 e^x$$

so that when $x = 0$ we obtain $d^4y/dx^4 = 24 > 0$, which corresponds to a local minimum. The stationary points are shown in Fig. 8.7.

Now you can be absolutely certain that if $d^2y/dx^2 = 0$ at a stationary point then there is no guarantee that it corresponds to a point of inflexion. In the words of the old song: 'It ain't necessarily so!' ∎

Now for some more steps.

8.7 Workshop

1 **Exercise** Obtain and classify all the stationary points of

$$y = x^2(x + 3)^2 e^x$$

This should cause very little difficulty provided you can determine the derivatives. Try it, then step ahead.

2

We have

$$y = (x^2 + 3x)^2 e^x$$

$$\frac{dy}{dx} = (x^2 + 3x)^2 e^x + 2(x^2 + 3x)(2x + 3)e^x$$

$$= (x^2 + 3x)(x^2 + 3x + 4x + 6)e^x$$

$$= x(x + 3)(x + 6)(x + 1)e^x$$

Equating to zero we obtain the stationary points $0, -3, -6, -1$.

Now we must differentiate again so that these can be classified as local maxima, local minima or points of inflexion. We could use the product rule, but there are five factors and algebraic simplification is tedious. We put

$$z = x(x + 3)(x + 6)(x + 1)e^x$$
$$\ln z = \ln x + \ln(x + 3) + \ln(x + 6) + \ln(x + 1) + x$$

So differentiating with respect to x,

$$\frac{1}{z}\frac{dz}{dx} = \frac{1}{x} + \frac{1}{x + 3} + \frac{1}{x + 6} + \frac{1}{x + 1} + 1$$

Multiplying through by z,

$$\frac{d^2y}{dx^2} = (x + 3)(x + 6)(x + 1)e^x + x(x + 6)(x + 1)e^x + x(x + 3)(x + 1)e^x$$

$$+ x(x + 3)(x + 6)e^x + x(x + 3)(x + 6)(x + 1)e^x$$

Now we examine each stationary point in turn:
1 $x = 0$: $d^2y/dx^2 = 18 > 0 \Rightarrow$ local minimum
2 $x = -3$: $d^2y/dx^2 = (-3)3(-2)e^{-3} > 0 \Rightarrow$ local minimum
3 $x = -6$: $d^2y/dx^2 = (-6)(-3)(-5)e^{-6} < 0 \Rightarrow$ local maximum
4 $x = -1$: $d^2y/dx^2 = (-1)2(5)e^{-1} < 0 \Rightarrow$ local maximum
If that was a personal success for you then skip through to step 4. Otherwise, try this exercise.

▷**Exercise**   Obtain and classify the stationary points of the function defined by

$$f(x) = x^3 e^{3x}$$

Have a go, then step forward.

3

We have

$$f'(x) = x^3 3e^{3x} + 3x^2 e^{3x}$$

so that, equating to 0 for stationary points,

$$3x^2(x + 1)e^{3x} = 0$$

from which $x = 0$ (repeated) and $x = -1$ are the stationary points.
    To classify these stationary points it is necessary to differentiate again:

$$\begin{aligned} f''(x) &= x^3 9e^{3x} + 9x^2 e^{3x} + 9x^2 e^{3x} + 6xe^{3x} \\ &= e^{3x}(9x^3 + 18x^2 + 6x) \\ &= 3xe^{3x}(3x^2 + 6x + 2) \end{aligned}$$

When $x = 0$ we obtain $f''(x) = 0$, and so further testing is necessary. When $x = -1$ we obtain

$$f''(x) = -3e^{-3}(3 - 6 + 2) > 0$$

so there is a local minimum. Differentiating again:

$$f^{(3)}(x) = e^{3x}(27x^2 + 36x + 6) + 3e^{3x}(9x^3 + 18x^2 + 6x)$$

When $x = 0$ we obtain $f^{(3)}(x) = 6 \neq 0$, and so when $x = 0$ there is a point of inflexion.
    Now step ahead.

Exercise   Obtain all the points of inflexion on the curve

$$y = x^6 - 5x^4 + 15x^2 + 1$$

Be careful: read the question. Try it, then step forward.

5

For a point of inflexion the slope has either a local maximum or a local minimum. Let s be the slope. Then

$$s = dy/dx = 6x^5 - 20x^3 + 30x$$

We must therefore examine this to see where s attains a local maximum or a local minimum.
    We first obtain the stationary points of s:

$$ds/dx = 30x^4 - 60x^2 + 30$$

So equating to 0 we have

$$\begin{aligned} 30x^4 - 60x^2 + 30 &= 0 \\ x^4 - 2x^2 + 1 &= 0 \\ (x^2 - 1)^2 &= 0 \end{aligned}$$

So $x = 1$ or $x = -1$. These are the stationary points of s, and so are candidates for points of inflexion of y.

We must continue the test to be certain:

$$d^2s/dx^2 = 120x^3 - 120x$$

When $x = 1$ we obtain 0, and when $x = -1$ we obtain 0 too. Therefore we differentiate again:

$$d^3s/dx^3 = 360x^2 - 120$$

So s has a point of inflexion at $x = 1$ and $x = -1$. This means that s does not attain either a local maximum or a local minimum, and so y has no points of inflexion.

Now we shall solve a practical problem in which l'Hospital's rule is used.

8.8 Practical

VALVE RESPONSE

The response x of a valve when subject to a certain input is given for $t > 0$ by

$$dx/dt = \sqrt{3} \, [1 - (x^2/\tan^2 t)]^{1/2}$$

where $x(t) \to 0$ as $t \to 0+$. Show that

$$dx/dt \to \sqrt{3}/2 \quad \text{as} \quad t \to 0+$$

Try this yourself first, and then move through the solution stage by stage.

The idea of a right-hand limit was discussed in section 4.4.

The physical situation enables us to assert that the limit exists. Suppose $dx/dt \to k$ as $t \to 0+$. We can see that the difficulty is centred on the term $x/\tan x$, for if we knew the limit of this as $t \to 0+$ we could calculate the limit of dx/dt using the laws of limits.

See if you can deal with the problem now.

We have, using l'Hospital's rule,

$$\lim_{t \to 0+} \frac{x}{\tan t} = \lim_{t \to 0+} \frac{dx/dt}{\sec^2 t}$$

Now $\sec^2 t \to 1$ as $t \to 0+$, and $dx/dt \to k$ as $t \to 0+$.
If you have been stuck, take over now.

Therefore we obtain

$$\lim_{t \to 0+} \frac{x}{\tan t} = \lim_{t \to 0+} \frac{dx/dt}{\sec^2 t} = \frac{\lim_{t \to 0+} (dx/dt)}{\lim_{t \to 0+} (\sec^2 t)} = \frac{k}{1} = k$$

So

$$k = \sqrt{3}(1 - k^2)^{1/2}$$
$$k^2 = 3(1 - k^2)$$
$$4k^2 = 3$$

It follows that $k = \pm\sqrt{3}/2$. However, $k \geq 0$ because $dx/dt > 0$. Consequently, as $t \to 0+$ we have shown that $dx/dt \to \sqrt{3}/2$.

We knew that the initial displacement was zero, and l'Hospital's rule has enabled us to determine the initial speed. Notice in particular that this is not an obvious result. Without l'Hospital's rule you might find it very difficult to confirm the limit.

SUMMARY

☐ We described the mean value theorem

$$\frac{f(b) - f(a)}{b - a} = f'(c)$$

for some $c \in (a, b)$.

☐ We generalized the mean value theorem to obtain Taylor's expansion about the point a

$$f(a + h) = \sum_{r=0}^{n-1} \frac{h^r}{r!} f^{(r)}(a) + R_n$$

where

$$R_n = \frac{h^n}{n!} f^{(n)}(a + \theta h) \quad \text{for some } \theta \in (0, 1)$$

☐ We obtained Maclaurin's expansion as the special case $a = 0$ of Taylor's expansion.

☐ We described l'Hospital's rule for determining a limit

$$\lim_{x \to a} \frac{f(x)}{g(x)} = \lim_{x \to a} \frac{f'(x)}{g'(x)}$$

provided $f(a)/g(a)$ is indeterminate.

☐ We used Taylor's expansion to deduce a complete test for maxima and minima.

EXERCISES (for answers see p. 745)

1 Obtain the first three non-zero terms of the Taylor expansion of each of the following:
   a $\exp(\sin x)$
   b $\text{sech } x$
   c $\dfrac{\ln(1 + x)}{1 + x}$

2 Obtain the stationary points of each of the following curves and classify them:
   a $y = x^4 - 10x^2 + 1$
   b $y = x(x - 1)\exp x$
   c $y = x^2 \exp(-x^2)$
   d $y = x^2 \ln(1 + x)$

3 Obtain the limit of x as t tends to 0, where
   a $x = \dfrac{2\sinh t - \sin 2t}{\cosh 2t - \cos 2t}$
   b $x = \dfrac{\exp(\sin t) - \cos t}{\cosh t - \exp(\sinh t)}$
   c $x = (\sin^2 t)^t$
   d $x = \dfrac{\ln t^3}{\ln(\sin t)}$

4 Obtain the limit of x as t tends to infinity, where
   a $x = \dfrac{\ln(t + 1)}{\ln(t^2 + 1)}$
   b $x = (\exp t + 1)^{1/t}$
   c $x = \dfrac{t}{\sqrt{(t^2 + 1)}}$
   d $x = \dfrac{\sinh t + t^2}{\cosh t + t}$

ASSIGNMENT (for answers see p. 746; see also Workshops on pp. 232, 240 and 248)

1 Differentiate with respect to x:
   a $\tanh^{-1}[\tan(x/2)]$
   b $(\sin x)^x \qquad x \in (0, \pi)$
   c $\tan^2 3x$
   d $x\cos^{-1}(1 - 2x^2)$
2 Obtain dy/dx if

$$\exp(xy) + x \ln y = \sin 2x$$

3 Show that the first four terms in the Maclaurin expansion of $\tan(x + \pi/4)$ and $\ln(1 + \sin x)$ are respectively
  a $1 + 2x + 2x^2 + 8x^3/3$
  b $0 + x - x^2/2 + x^3/6$
4 Express $e^x \cos x$ as a power series in x as far as, and including, the term in x^3.
5 Obtain and classify the stationary points, and any points of inflexion, of
  a $y = 3x^5 - 10x^3 + 15x + 1$
  b $y = x^4 - 4x^3 + 4x^2 + 7$
6 A dangerous chemical has to be stored in a cylindrical container of a given volume. The mass of metal used in the construction of the cylinder and the thickness of the material are constant. The cylinder is to stand on one flat end in an open space. If the surface area exposed to the atmosphere is to be a minimum, calculate the relationship between its diameter and its height.
7 Show that the minimum value of $1 + x \ln x$ is $(e - 1)/e$.
8 If $y = \exp(\sinh^{-1} x)$, deduce

$$(1 + x^2) \frac{d^2y}{dx^2} + x \frac{dy}{dx} - y = 0$$

and

$$(1 + x^2) \frac{d^{n+2}y}{dx^{n+2}} + (2n + 1)x \frac{d^{n+1}y}{dx^{n+1}} + (n^2 - 1) \frac{d^ny}{dx^n} = 0$$

Hence verify Maclaurin's expansion:

$$x + \sqrt{(1 + x^2)} = 1 + x + \frac{x^2}{2!} - \frac{8x^4}{4!} + \ldots$$

9 Obtain each of the following limits as $x \to 0$:
  a $\tan nx/\tan x$
  b $(e^x - 1 - x)/x^2$
  c $(1 - \cos \pi x)/x \tan \pi x$
  d $[\tan^{-1}(x - 1) + \pi/4]/x$
10 Obtain each of the following limits as $x \to \infty$:
  a $\sqrt{x} - \sqrt{(x - 1)}$
  b $xa^{1/x} - x$ where $a > 0$

FURTHER EXERCISES (for answers see p. 746)

1 Show that

$$\lim_{x \to 0} \frac{\sin(a \tan^{-1} bx)}{\tan(c \sin^{-1} dx)} = \frac{ab}{cd}$$

2 Prove that

a $(x + 1)e^x = 1 + 2x + \dfrac{3x^2}{2!} + \ldots + \dfrac{nx^{n-1}}{(n - 1)!} + \ldots$

b $(1 + 3x + x^2) \exp x = \displaystyle\sum_{n=0}^{\infty} \dfrac{(n + 1)^2 x^n}{n!}$

3 Prove that

a $\displaystyle\lim_{x \to 0} \dfrac{\exp ax - 1}{\exp bx - 1} = \dfrac{a}{b}$

b $\displaystyle\lim_{x \to 0} \dfrac{\exp (\sin x) - 1}{x} = 1$

c $\displaystyle\lim_{x \to 0} (\cos x)^{\operatorname{cosec}^2 x} = \dfrac{1}{\sqrt{e}}$

4 Prove that

a $\displaystyle\lim_{x \to 0+} x^x = 1$

b $\displaystyle\lim_{x \to 0+} [\ln (1 + x)]^x = 1$

c $\displaystyle\lim_{x \to 0+} (e^x - 1)^x = 1$

5 When a unit cube of rubber is deformed into a cube of length λ by the action of temperature T and external forces, the energy E is given by

$$E = cT(\lambda^2 + 2\lambda^{-1})$$

where c is a constant. Prove that if T is constant the energy is a minimum when $\lambda = 1$.

6 A steel girder 7 m long is moved on rollers along a passage 3 m wide into another passage at right angles to the first. What is the minimum width of the second passage for which this manoeuvre is possible?

7 A prospector has a fixed length of fencing available and has to enclose a rectangular plot on three sides. One side is adjacent to a river. Determine the ratio of the length to the breadth if the enclosed area is to be a maximum.

8 A dish is made in the shape of a right circular cone. Calculate the ratio of the height to the diameter of the surface which will give a maximum volume if (a) the slant height is specified (b) the area of the curved surface is specified.

9 A greenhouse is to be made in the shape of a cylinder with a hemispherical roof. The material for the roof is twice as expensive per unit area as the material for the sides. Show that if it is to enclose a given air space and the total cost of the materials is to be a minimum, then the height of the cylindrical part must equal the diameter of the hemisphere.

10 A resistor is made up of two resistors in parallel. The first branch consists of wire of resistance 1/3 ohms/metre and the second consists of wire of resistance 1/4 ohms/metre. If 2 m of wire are available altogether, obtain the maximum possible total resistance.

11 When an EMF of Ee^{-t} is applied to an LR series circuit, the current i satisfies the equation

$$\frac{di}{dt} + \frac{R}{L} i = \frac{E}{L} e^{-t}$$

If $E = 1$ volt, $R = 1$ ohm, $L = 1$ henry and $i(0) = 0$, calculate the first three non-zero terms in the Taylor expansion of $i(t)$ about 0.

12 The force F exerted by a current moving on a circle of radius r on a unit magnetic pole on the polar axis of a circle is

$$F = kx/(r^2 + x^2)^{5/2}$$

where k is a constant and x is the distance of the magnetic pole from the centre of the circle.

a Show that the maximum force occurs when $x = r/2$.

b Show that the maximum force is $k(4/5)^{5/2}/2r^4$.

13 A compound pendulum of length $2l$ metres is pivoted x metres from the centre of mass and has a period

$$T = 2\pi \left(\frac{l^2}{3gx} + \frac{x}{g} \right)^{1/2}$$

Show that for minimum period $x = l/\sqrt{3}$.

14 A beam of length l and weight w per unit length is clamped horizontally at both ends. Its deflection y at a distance x from one end is given by

$$y = \frac{wx^2}{24EI} (l - x)^2$$

where E and I are constants. Show that the maximum deflection of the beam is $wl^4/384EI$.

The bending moment M at x is given by $M = EI/\varrho$, where ϱ is the radius of curvature of y at x. For small deflections ϱ is approximately $1/|y''|$. Show that under these circumstances the bending moment at the point of maximum deflection is approximately $wl^2/24$.

15 When an alternating EMF E sin nt is applied to a quiescent LC circuit, the current i at time t is given by

$$i = \frac{nE}{L(n^2 - w^2)} (\cos wt - \cos nt)$$

where $w^2 = 1/LC$ and w is not equal to n.

Show that when n is tuned to the natural frequency w of the circuit

$$i = \frac{Et \sin wt}{2L}$$

9 Infinite series

In Chapter 8 we encountered several infinite series. In this chapter we shall clarify what we mean by infinite series and show that some of them behave rather unexpectedly.

After studying this chapter you should be able to
☐ Recognize an infinite series;
☐ Determine the sum to *n* terms of standard series;
☐ Examine for convergence directly by using the sum to *n* terms;
☐ Apply basic tests to examine a series for convergence or divergence;
☐ Determine the radius of convergence of a power series.
At the end of the chapter we shall solve practical problems concerning radioactive emission and a leaning tower.

9.1 SERIES

You have already come across infinite series. For example, the arithmetic series and the geometric series are quite well known. Here they are in standard notation.

The **arithmetic series** is of the form

$$a + (a + d) + (a + 2d) + (a + 3d) + \ldots$$

where *a* and *d* are real numbers. We can represent this, using the summation notation, by

$$\sum_{m=0}^{\infty} (a + md)$$

Here *a* is the first term and *d*, the difference between any two consecutive terms, is known as the **common difference**.

The **geometric series** is of the form

$$a + ar + ar^2 + ar^3 + \ldots$$

where a and r are real numbers. Again this can be represented in a more compact form by

$$\sum_{m=0}^{\infty} ar^m$$

Here r is known as the **common ratio**, since it is the ratio of any two consecutive terms.

Now we know how to add together any finite collection of numbers, but we do not as yet have a clear idea as to what can be meant by an infinite sum. Of course we could imagine the situation in which we never stop calculating, but such a dream (or maybe a nightmare) is not really helpful. To begin to make sense of the idea we shall first obtain the sums of some finite series. In fact we shall obtain the **sum to n terms** of the arithmetic series and the geometric series.

For the arithmetic series, suppose

$$S = a + (a + d) + (a + 2d) + \ldots + (a + [n - 1]d)$$

Then if we reverse the order of the terms,

$$S = (a + [n - 1]d) + (a + [n - 2]d) + (a + [n - 3]d) \ldots + a$$

The reason for doing this now becomes clear, for if we add together the two expressions for S we obtain

$$2S = (2a + [n - 1]d) + (2a + [n - 1]d) + \ldots + (2a + [n - 1]d)$$

which is a sum of n equal terms. Consequently

$$2S = n(2a + [n - 1]d)$$

So the sum to n terms of the arithmetic series is

$$S = \tfrac{1}{2}n(2a + [n - 1]d)$$

☐ Determine the sum of the first n natural numbers.   **Example**
We require $1 + 2 + 3 + \ldots + n$, which is the sum of the first n terms of an arithmetic series where $a = 1$ and $d = 1$. Therefore

$$S = \tfrac{1}{2}n(2 + [n - 1]) = \tfrac{1}{2}n(n + 1)$$

You may be able to use this to impress younger members of your family by declaring, after Christmas lunch, that you can add up the first 100 (say) whole numbers in an instant. This formula gives 5050, and by the time they have checked it you should have had a few moments' peace.   ■

For the geometric series, suppose

$$S = a + ar + ar^2 + \ldots + ar^{n-1}$$

Then multiplying through by r we obtain

$$Sr = ar + ar^2 + \ldots + ar^n$$

We have done this because, if we subtract Sr from S, terms cancel out in pairs and all that remains is the first term in S and the last term in Sr:

$$S - Sr = a - ar^n$$
$$S(1 - r) = a(1 - r^n)$$

So the sum to n terms of the geometric series is

$$S = a\frac{1 - r^n}{1 - r} \quad \text{provided } r \neq 1 \qquad \blacksquare$$

Example □ Determine the value of

$$1 + \tfrac{1}{2} + \tfrac{1}{4} + \ldots + (\tfrac{1}{2})^n$$

Here we require the sum of the first $n + 1$ terms of a geometric series in which the first term is 1 and the common ratio is 1/2. Using the formula we obtain

$$S = \frac{1 - (1/2)^{n+1}}{1 - (1/2)} = 2(1 - [\tfrac{1}{2}]^{n+1}) = 2 - (\tfrac{1}{2})^n \qquad \blacksquare$$

Each of these series is unusual in the sense that we have been able to determine formulas for S, the sum of the first n terms. Of course S depends upon n; therefore we shall in future denote the sum of the first n terms of an infinite series by s_n. In general we may write an **infinite series** in the form

$$\Sigma a_n = a_1 + a_2 + a_3 + \ldots + a_r + \ldots$$

Observe some of the general features. There are two sets of dots indicating missing terms. The first set of dots shows that terms occur between a_3 and the general term a_r. The second set of dots indicates that this is an infinite series and does not terminate.

We shall not normally adorn the summation sign Σ by writing $n = 1$ below and ∞ on top. However, if we wish to use a different dummy variable, or begin the sum at some other value of n, it is necessary to indicate this by an appropriate choice of labels.

9.2 CONVERGENCE AND DIVERGENCE

The two series which we have been considering display features which help us to describe the general situation.

We have seen that the sum of the first n natural numbers

$$1 + 2 + 3 + \ldots + n$$

is given by $s_n = \frac{1}{2}n(n + 1)$. We observe that in this instance $s_n \to \infty$ as $n \to \infty$. This means that the sum to n terms can be made arbitrarily large just by choosing n sufficiently large.

Again, the sum of the first n terms of the series

$$1 + \frac{1}{2} + \frac{1}{4} + \ldots + (\frac{1}{2})^n + \ldots$$

is given by $s_n = 2 - (1/2)^n$ and so $s_n \to 2$ as $n \to \infty$. This means that the sum to n terms can be made arbitrarily close to 2 just by choosing n sufficiently large.

In general, given an infinite series

$$\Sigma a_n = a_1 + a_2 + a_3 + \ldots + a_r + \ldots$$

suppose that s_n denotes the sum to n terms. Then:

1 If there exists a number s such that $s_n \to s$ as $n \to \infty$ then the series is said to **converge**. Moreover if s is known we can say that the series converges to s.

2 If there is no number s such that $s_n \to s$ as $n \to \infty$ then the series is said to **diverge**. If $s_n \to \infty$ as $n \to \infty$ then the series is said to diverge to ∞. If $s_n \to -\infty$ as $n \to \infty$ then the series is said to diverge to $-\infty$. A divergent series does not necessarily diverge either to ∞ or to $-\infty$; for example it might oscillate.

If it were always possible to obtain a straightforward formula for s_n it would be a relatively simple matter to examine a series to see if it converges or diverges. As it is, we can rarely obtain a simple formula for s_n and so tests have been devised to examine the behaviour of series which arise in practice.

In the examples the arithmetic series Σn diverges and the geometric series $\Sigma (1/2)^n$ converges (to 2). In fact *every* arithmetic series diverges; there really is a last straw which will break the camel's back!

For geometric series the situation is a little more subtle and we shall need to examine it closer. For the geometric series

$$\sum_{m=0}^{\infty} ar^m = a + ar + ar^2 + \ldots + ar^n + \ldots$$

we have

$$s_n = a\frac{1 - r^n}{1 - r} \quad \text{provided } r \neq 1$$

Then
1 If $|r| < 1$ we have $r^n \to 0$ as $n \to \infty$. So $s_n \to a/(1 - r)$ and the series converges.
2 If $r > 1$ then $r^n \to \infty$ as $n \to \infty$. So s_n does not tend to a limit as n tends to infinity and the series diverges.

3 If $r < -1$ then r^n increases in magnitude but alternates in sign as n tends to infinity. So once again s_n does not tend to a limit as n tends to infinity and the series consequently diverges.

4 It remains only to consider the cases $r = 1$ and $r = -1$. When $r = 1$ we obtain $s_n = na$; so the series diverges unless $a = 0$. When $r = -1$ we obtain $s_n = a$ if n is odd and $s_n = 0$ if n is even; again we conclude that the series diverges unless $a = 0$.

Consequently, if $a \neq 0$, the *geometric series*

$$\sum_{m=0}^{\infty} ar^m = a + ar + ar^2 + \ldots + ar^n + \ldots$$

converges when $|r| < 1$ and *diverges* when $|r| \geqslant 1$.

We have already discussed Taylor's series in section 8.2. The idea, from a different standpoint, arises again in section 22.9.

There are two types of series which arise in applications and which you are likely to encounter in theoretical work. These are power series and trigonometrical series.

A **power series** is a series of the form

$$a_0 + a_1 x + a_2 x^2 + a_3 x^3 + \ldots + a_r x^r + \ldots$$

where the 'a's are constants.

A **trigonometrical series** is a series of the form

$$(1/2)a_0 + (a_1 \cos x + b_1 \sin x) + (a_2 \cos 2x + b_2 \sin 2x)$$
$$+ \ldots + (a_r \cos rx + b_r \sin rx) + \ldots$$

where the 'a's and 'b's are constants. (The $(1/2)$ in the $(1/2)a_0$ term may seem strange, and strictly it is superfluous. However there are advantages in expressing the first term in this form and it is usual to do so.)

The discussion of trigonometrical series is an advanced topic and we shall not be considering it in this book. Power series will be discussed later in this chapter.

We have remarked that, although it is sometimes possible to examine the limit of s_n directly, in general this is not possible. To cope with the general situation we need some tests for convergence and divergence, and these we now describe.

9.3 TESTS FOR CONVERGENCE AND DIVERGENCE

There are very many tests which have been devised to examine infinite series to determine whether or not they converge or diverge. It is reasonable to ask whether there is one test which will settle the matter once and for all. Unfortunately there is no supertest; whatever test we have there is always a series which can be produced on which the test will fail.

Before we take things any further we should point out that this is a subtle area of mathematics where it is easy to make mistakes. Mathematical operations which we carry out on finite sums do not necessarily work when we attempt them on infinite series. Infinite series should therefore be treated with respect and, if in theoretical work you should come across one, it may be advisable to consult a competent mathematician rather than try to handle it yourself.

Nevertheless we are going to describe some basic tests which will enable us to examine most of the series which we are likely to meet at the moment.

TEST 1: THE DIVERGENCE TEST

The infinite series

$$\Sigma a_n = a_1 + a_2 + a_3 + \ldots + a_r + \ldots$$

diverges if

$$\lim_{n \to \infty} a_n \neq 0$$

To show this we examine the situation when Σa_n converges and show that then $\lim_{n \to \infty} a_n = 0$. Suppose that Σa_n converges to s. Now

$$a_1 + a_2 + \ldots + a_n = s_n$$
$$a_1 + a_2 + \ldots + a_{n-1} = s_{n-1}$$

Subtracting,

$$a_n = s_n - s_{n-1}$$

Therefore

$$\lim_{n \to \infty} a_n = \lim_{n \to \infty} (s_n - s_{n-1}) = s - s = 0$$

Consequently if Σa_n converges the nth term tends to 0 as n tends to ∞. However, we are told that the nth term does not tend to 0 as n tends to ∞. Therefore Σa_n cannot converge and so must diverge.

□ Examine for convergence $\Sigma(1 + 1/n)$.   **Example**
   Here $a_n = 1 + 1/n$ and so as $n \to \infty$ we have $a_n \to 1$, which is non-zero. So by the divergence test the series diverges. ∎

It is important to realize that this test is a divergence test; it can *never* be used to establish the convergence of a series. There are many divergent series which have their nth terms tending to zero.

TEST 2: THE COMPARISON TEST

Suppose Σa_n and Σb_n are real series such that $0 < a_n \leqslant b_n$. Then if Σb_n converges, so too does Σa_n.

We shall not justify this, but instead use it to examine the convergence of Σn^{-2}.

Example ☐ By considering s_n, the sum to n terms of the series $\Sigma[1/n(n + 1)]$, examine the series for convergence. Hence or otherwise establish the convergence of Σn^{-2}.

Now

$$\frac{1}{n(n + 1)} = \frac{1}{n} - \frac{1}{n + 1}$$

So

$$s_n = a_1 + a_2 + \ldots + a_n$$
$$= \left(1 - \frac{1}{2}\right) + \left(\frac{1}{2} - \frac{1}{3}\right) + \ldots + \left(\frac{1}{n} - \frac{1}{n + 1}\right)$$

These cancel out in pairs, leaving

$$s_n = 1 - \frac{1}{n + 1} \to 1 \quad \text{as } n \to \infty$$

Consequently $\Sigma[1/n(n + 1)]$ is convergent.

Now if n is any natural number, $n < n + 1$ and so $n(n + 1) < (n + 1)^2$. Therefore

$$0 < \frac{1}{(n + 1)^2} < \frac{1}{n(n + 1)}$$

Consequently by the comparison test $\Sigma(n + 1)^{-2}$ is convergent. Now in what way does this series differ from Σn^{-2}? It has the first term missing, and it is surely inconceivable that this single omission can affect the convergence. Therefore we conclude Σn^{-2} is convergent.

Although this line of reasoning may seem convincing, the statement requires proof. Luckily we can tighten things up without much difficulty. Let s_n be the sum to n terms of the first series and t_n the sum to n terms of the second series. Then $t_n = 1 + s_n - (n + 1)^{-2}$. Now s_n is known to converge to s (say), and consequently $t_n \to 1 + s - 0 = 1 + s$. ∎

The comparison test is particularly useful once a collection of series have been produced which are *known* to converge or to diverge. Here is the test again:

Suppose Σa_n and Σb_n are real series such that $0 < a_n \le b_n$. Then if Σb_n converges, so too does Σa_n.

It is worth remarking that if Σa_n diverges then so too does Σb_n. For if Σb_n were to converge then by the comparison test we could deduce the convergence of Σa_n.

Here is a series which at first sight looks very innocuous: $\Sigma\, 1/n$. Clearly the terms get smaller and smaller as n gets larger and larger, and it looks as if it is going to converge to a fairly small number. We might even be tempted to get a computer to estimate its value by, say, summing the first 1000 terms.

However, all is not as it seems. In fact the series *diverges* (very slowly), as we shall now show. We have

$$s_n = 1 + 1/2 + 1/3 + \ldots + 1/n$$

Now if $n = 2^m$ we have

$$s_n = 1 + \frac{1}{2} + \left(\frac{1}{3} + \frac{1}{4}\right) + \left(\frac{1}{5} + \frac{1}{6} + \frac{1}{7} + \frac{1}{8}\right) + \ldots + \left(\ldots + \frac{1}{2^m}\right)$$

Here we have grouped the terms together so that the last term in each bracket is a power of 2. Now in each bracket each term is greater than the last term in the bracket, and the number of terms in each bracket is a power of 2. Therefore

$$s_n > 1 + \frac{1}{2} + \left(\frac{1}{4} + \frac{1}{4}\right) + \left(\frac{1}{8} + \frac{1}{8} + \frac{1}{8} + \frac{1}{8}\right) + \ldots + \left(\ldots + \frac{1}{2^m}\right)$$

So

$$s_n > 1 + \tfrac{1}{2} + \tfrac{1}{2} + \tfrac{1}{2} + \ldots + \tfrac{1}{2} = 1 + \tfrac{1}{2}m$$

It follows that $s_n > 1 + m/2$ when $n = 2^m$. Now as m tends to ∞, n tends to ∞, and yet s_n is unbounded and so does not tend to a limit. Consequently $\Sigma\, 1/n$ is divergent.

This series is a member of the family $\Sigma\, 1/n^p$ where p is real. It can be shown that
1 When $p > 1$ the series converges;
2 When $p \leqslant 1$ the series diverges.

TEST 3: THE ALTERNATING TEST

Suppose $\Sigma\, a_n$ is an infinite series in which
1 The terms alternate in sign;
2 $|a_n| \geqslant |a_{n+1}|$ for all $n \in \mathbb{N}$;
3 $|a_n| \to 0$ as $n \to \infty$.
Then the series converges.

☐ Show that $\Sigma\,(-1)^n/n$ is convergent.   **Example**
    We observe that each of the conditions of the alternating test is satisfied:
1 The terms alternate in sign;
2 $|a_n| = 1/n > 1/(n + 1) = |a_{n+1}|$;
3 $1/n \to 0$ as $n \to \infty$.
So the conclusion is that the series is indeed convergent. ∎

Jean Le Rond
D'alembert (1717–
1783): French
mathematician and
encyclopaedist. The
ratio test is due to
him.

TEST 4: THE RATIO TEST

Suppose $\Sigma\, a_n$ is an infinite series and that

$$l = \lim_{n \to \infty} \left| \frac{a_{n+1}}{a_n} \right|$$

exists. Then
1 If $l < 1$, $\Sigma\, a_n$ converges;
2 If $l > 1$, $\Sigma\, a_n$ diverges;
3 If $l = 1$, no conclusion can be reached.

Example □ Discuss the behaviour of the series $\Sigma\, 1/n!$.
Here $a_n = 1/n!$ and so $a_{n+1} = 1/(n + 1)!$. Therefore

$$a_{n+1}/a_n = [1/(n + 1)!]/[1/n!] = n!/(n + 1)! = 1/(n + 1)$$

so that $|a_{n+1}/a_n| = 1/(n + 1) \to 0$ as $n \to \infty$. Of course $0 < 1$, and so we
deduce that the series is convergent. ■

TEST 5: THE ABSOLUTE CONVERGENCE TEST

Suppose $\Sigma\, a_n$ is an infinite series such that $\Sigma\, |a_n|$ converges. Then $\Sigma\, a_n$
converges.

Any series $\Sigma\, a_n$, real or complex, which has the property that $\Sigma\, |a_n|$ con-
verges is called an **absolutely convergent** series. This test tells us that if a
series is absolutely convergent then it is convergent. There are many series
which are convergent but which are not absolutely convergent. These series
are called **conditionally convergent**.

Example □ We have seen that $\Sigma\, [(-1)^n/n]$ is convergent but that $\Sigma\, (1/n)$ is divergent.
Since

$$\left| \frac{(-1)^n}{n} \right| = \frac{1}{n}$$

this implies that $\Sigma\, [(-1)^n/n]$ is conditionally convergent. ■

9.4 POWER SERIES

Taylor's series were
obtained in section
8.2.

Consider the power series $\Sigma\, a_n x^n$. We shall show that if $|a_n/a_{n+1}| \to R \neq 0$
as $n \to \infty$ then the power series
1 Converges whenever $|x| < R$;
2 Diverges whenever $|x| > R$.
R is known as the **radius of convergence** of the power series. Every power
series in x converges when $x = 0$, and if this is the only value of x for which

it converges we say it has zero radius of convergence and write $R = 0$. Some power series in x converge for all x, and we then say the power series has an infinite radius of convergence and write $R = \infty$.

If we were to extend these ideas to complex power series we should obtain a disc of convergence instead of an open interval (Chapter 10).

We apply the ratio test, but we have to be a little careful about the notation since a_n appears as the coefficient of x^n and not as the term itself. To avoid this confusion we shall call the nth term u_n. Now

$$u_{n+1}/u_n = a_{n+1}x^{n+1}/a_n x^n = x a_{n+1}/a_n$$

So

$$|u_{n+1}/u_n| = |x| |a_{n+1}/a_n|$$

Now $|a_n/a_{n+1}| \to R$ as $n \to \infty$, and since $R \neq 0$ we deduce that

$$|u_{n+1}/u_n| \to |x|/R \quad \text{as } n \to \infty$$

Consequently if $|x|/R < 1$ the series converges, whereas if $|x|/R > 1$ the series diverges. Finally, since $R > 0$ we have

$$|x| < R \Rightarrow \text{convergence}$$
$$|x| > R \Rightarrow \text{divergence}$$

In fact the radius of convergence of a power series is very useful because if $x \in (-R, R)$ it is possible to differentiate and integrate with respect to x term by term and obtain correct results.

It is important to realize that in general any operation on an infinite series may disturb its convergence. Such operations include rearranging terms, inserting or removing brackets, differentiating and integrating. Convergence of the series is *not* enough to ensure that we can perform these operations and obtain the expected results. We need special forms of convergence to ensure that. For algebraic operations we need *absolute* convergence and for calculus operations we need *uniform* convergence. We shall not describe uniform convergence in this book.

!

Well, now it's time to take a few steps.

9.5 Workshop

1

▷**Exercise** Discuss the behaviour of the series $\Sigma x^n/n!$ for all real x.
Try this and see how you get on.

2

This exercise is an application of the ratio test:

$$a_{n+1}/a_n = [x^{n+1}/(n + 1)!]/[x^n/n!] = x/(n + 1)$$

and so $|a_{n+1}/a_n| = |x|/(n + 1) \to 0$ as $n \to \infty$. Therefore the series is convergent for all real x. In fact you have seen this series before: it converges, if we start when $n = 0$, to e^x.

Did you manage that? Here is another exercise to try.

▷**Exercise** Discuss for all real x, $|x| \neq 1$, the convergence of the binomial series

$$\sum_{r=0}^{\infty} \binom{n}{r} x^r$$

where

$$\binom{n}{r} = \frac{n(n - 1)(n - 2) \ldots (n - r + 1)}{1 \times 2 \times 3 \times 4 \times \ldots \times r}$$

Here of course the dummy variable is r; n is constant. Make an effort and then take the next step.

---

3 We obtain

$$\frac{a_{r+1}}{a_r} = \frac{n(n - 1)(n - 2) \ldots (n - [r + 1] + 1)x^{r+1}}{1 \times 2 \times 3 \times 4 \times \ldots \times [r + 1]}$$

$$\times \frac{1 \times 2 \times 3 \times 4 \times \ldots \times r}{n(n - 1)(n - 2) \ldots (n - r + 1)x^r}$$

$$= \frac{(n - r)x}{r + 1}$$

Now

$$|a_{r+1}/a_r| = |(n - r)x/(r + 1)|$$
$$= |([n/r] - 1)x/(1 + [1/r])|$$
$$\to |-x/1| = |x| \quad \text{as } r \to \infty$$

Consequently if $|x| < 1$ the series converges, whereas if $|x| > 1$ the series diverges.

You may have found that one rather too algebraic. If you did then the next one may be more to your taste.

▷**Exercise** Discuss, for all real x, the convergence of the series $\sum x^n/n$.

As soon as you have tested the series, take the next step.

---

4 Here $a_n = x^n/n$ and so

$$a_{n+1}/a_n = [x^{n+1}/(n + 1)][n/x^n] = xn/(n + 1)$$

so that

$$|a_{n+1}/a_n| = |x| \{1/(1 + [1/n])\} \to |x| \quad \text{as } n \to \infty$$

So the ratio test shows that if $|x| < 1$ the series converges, whereas if $|x| > 1$ the series diverges.

There only remain the cases $x = 1$ and $x = -1$. When $x = 1$ the series reduces to $\Sigma 1/n$, which we have already shown to be divergent. When $x = -1$ the series reduces to $\Sigma (-1)^n/n$, which we have already shown to be convergent.

We conclude therefore that $\Sigma x^n/n$ is convergent when $-1 \leqslant x < 1$ and divergent when $x \geqslant 1$ or $x < -1$. In fact this is the series expansion corresponding to $\ln (1 - x)$.

Now let us look at a few series. Although the ratio test is very useful, we should not forget the other tests.

▷**Exercise** Determine whether $\Sigma 1/(n^2 + 1)$ is convergent or divergent. 5

Attempt this carefully and then move on to see if all is well.

The ratio test is of no use to us here. However, we do know that $\Sigma 1/n^2$ is 6 convergent, and this series is only slightly different.

Can we use the comparison test? Well, $n^2 < n^2 + 1$ for any natural number n, and so we have

$$0 < 1/(n^2 + 1) < 1/n^2$$

The convergence of $\Sigma 1/(n^2 + 1)$ now follows.

How about this one?

▷**Exercise** Examine for convergence $\Sigma (1 + 1/n)^n$.

At first sight this appears to be a pretty fearsome series to test. However, a 7 bell should sound. It may be a rather distant, muffled bell but it should sound nevertheless. Haven't we seen $(1 + 1/n)^n$ somewhere before? We have, you know. We have found the limit of it as $n \to \infty$ (Chapter 8). The limit is e, the natural base of logarithms.

This observation is all that we need to dispose of the problem once and for all. $(1 + 1/n)^n \to e$ as $n \to \infty$, and since $e \neq 0$ the divergence test shows that the series diverges.

Finally let us look at a limit.

▷**Exercise** Obtain the limit as $n \to \infty$ of $(1 + 2 + 3 + \ldots + n)/n^2$.

Try it, but be careful.

8 Perhaps you proceeded in the following manner:

$$(1 + 2 + 3 + \ldots + n)/n^2 = 1/n^2 + 2/n^2 + 3/n^2 + \ldots + 1/n$$

Then possibly you argued that there are n terms each of which is tending to 0 as $n \to \infty$, and concluded that the limit itself is zero.

Unfortunately this argument is flawed. Although it is true that the terms are getting smaller and smaller, there are more and more of them! If you got it wrong then have another try and take another step.

9 We know that

$$1 + 2 + 3 + \ldots + n = n(n + 1)/2$$

So

$$(1 + 2 + 3 + \ldots + n)/n^2 = n(n + 1)/2n^2$$
$$= (n + 1)/2n = (1 + 1/n)/2$$

As $n \to \infty$ we obtain the limit 1/2.

This is as far as we are going to take the topic of infinite series. There is much more that can be said, but it is important to realize that this is a sensitive area where even otherwise competent mathematicians are prone to error.

It is sometimes quite alarming to see what the uninformed will do with infinite series. It is always possible that the results could be catastrophic: bridges could fall down, aircraft disintegrate, dance floors cave in, buildings collapse, and power plants get out of control. Every infinite series should carry a government health warning!

Now here are some practical problems for you to try.

9.6 Practical

RADIOACTIVE EMISSION

Radioactive material is stored in a thick concrete drum. It is believed to ingress, by the end of each year, into the uncontaminated surrounding material a depth $d = Q/n$, where n is the number of years and the quantity Q is a constant. At the end of the first year, $d = 0.5$ cm.

First, if the surrounding concrete is 4 m thick, will this contain the material for all time? Secondly, if the material remains hazardous for 1000 years, what would be a safe thickness of concrete?

See if you can handle this problem. We will go through it stage by stage.

1 We have $d = Q/n$. When $n = 1$, $d = 0.5$, so that $Q = 0.5$. Now the depth of penetration after n years is given by

$$d = Q + \frac{Q}{2} + \frac{Q}{3} + \frac{Q}{4} + \ldots + \frac{Q}{n} = Q \sum_{r=1}^{n} \frac{1}{r}$$

Now you are at this stage, take over the solution.

---

2 We know that $\Sigma (1/n)$ is a divergent series, and so as $n \to \infty$ we infer that $d \to \infty$. The conclusion we draw is that whatever the value of Q (>0), penetration will eventually occur; so 4 m is certainly not enough.

Luckily the second part of the problem accords more with reality. See if you can finish it off.

---

3 As an exceedingly crude estimate we have

$$Q + \frac{Q}{2} + \frac{Q}{3} + \frac{Q}{4} + \ldots + \frac{Q}{1000} < 1000Q$$

Therefore provided $1000Q$ is less than the thickness T of the surrounding material, everything will certainly remain safe. So $T > 1000Q = 500$ cm $= 5$ m will do.

We could get away with considerably less concrete. In fact if you add the first 1000 terms you obtain $7.5Q$, and so in fact 0.0375 m is good enough!

Here is another problem.

LEANING TOWER

A tower is built in such a way that shortly after its construction it begins to lean. It is believed that the angle of tilt is increased at the end of each year by an amount $K/(1 + n^2)$, where K is constant and n is the age in years of the tower. At the end of the first year the angle of tilt was 3°.

a Assuming that the formula is correct, show that the tower will not fall flat.
b Show that eventually the angle of tilt will satisfy $4° \leqslant \theta \leqslant 5°$.
c Use a calculator to determine how many years it will take for the angle to become 4°.

Solve part **a**. It is not unlike the previous problem.

(by kind permission of Edwin Evans)

The leaning tower of Pisa was begun in 1174 and finished by 1356. Its height is 56.705 m and its maximum deviation from the perpendicular is 4.319 m. Galileo Galilei (1564–1642) performed experiments on the laws of gravity from the top of the leaning tower.

---

1 For **a** we have, when $n = 1$, $\theta = 3° = K + K/2$ and so $K = 2$. After n years the angle of tilt will be

$$\theta = K + \frac{K}{2} + \frac{K}{5} + \frac{K}{10} + \ldots + \frac{K}{1 + n^2}$$

We therefore need to examine $\Sigma\, 1/(1 + n^2)$ for convergence. The comparison test can be applied, for we know that $\Sigma\, 1/n^2$ is convergent. We have $1 + n^2 > n^2$, and so

$$0 < \frac{1}{1 + n^2} < \frac{1}{n^2}$$

The convergence of $\Sigma\, 1/n^2$ now implies the convergence of $\Sigma\, 1/(1 + n^2)$. So, provided $K\,\Sigma\, 1/(1 + n^2)$ converges to a number less than $90°$, the tower will not fall flat.

This matter will be settled provided we can sort out part **b**. Here is a hint:

$$n(n - 1) < n^2 + 1 < n(n + 1)$$

---

2 For **b**, using this inequality, we have for $n > 1$

$$\frac{1}{n(n + 1)} < \frac{1}{1 + n^2} < \frac{1}{n(n - 1)}$$

Refer back to section 2.8 for a refresher on the cover-up rule.

Add up the first N terms. Don't forget your work on partial fractions!

---

3 So

$$\sum_{n=2}^{N} \frac{1}{n(n + 1)} < \sum_{n=2}^{N} \frac{1}{1 + n^2} < \sum_{n=2}^{N} \frac{1}{n(n - 1)}$$

$$1 + \frac{1}{2} + \sum_{n=2}^{N} \frac{1}{n(n + 1)} < \sum_{n=0}^{N} \frac{1}{1 + n^2} < \frac{3}{2} + \sum_{n=2}^{N} \frac{1}{n(n - 1)}$$

$$\frac{3}{2} + \sum_{n=2}^{N} \left(\frac{1}{n} - \frac{1}{n + 1} \right) < \sum_{n=0}^{N} \frac{1}{1 + n^2} < \frac{3}{2} + \sum_{n=2}^{N} \left(\frac{1}{n - 1} - \frac{1}{n} \right)$$

$$2 - \frac{1}{N + 1} < \sum_{n=0}^{N} \frac{1}{1 + n^2} < \frac{5}{2} - \frac{1}{N}$$

Consequently

$$2K \leqslant \sum_{n=0}^{\infty} \frac{K}{1 + n^2} \leqslant \frac{5K}{2}$$

and so $4° \leqslant \theta \leqslant 5°$.

Lastly, start tapping the buttons on your calculator.

---

4 For **c** we must calculate

$$K \left(1 + \frac{1}{2} + \frac{1}{5} + \frac{1}{10} + \ldots + \frac{1}{1 + n^2} + \ldots \right)$$

until for some n the total exceeds 4°. In fact it takes 13 years for the tower to lean 4°.

SUMMARY

☐ We have seen how to represent an infinite series.
☐ We have explained what is meant by convergence and divergence.
☐ We have described some tests which can be applied to infinite series to see whether they converge or diverge. The tests we described were called
  a the divergence test
  b the comparison test
  c the alternating test
  d the ratio test
  e the absolute convergence test.
☐ We have defined the radius of convergence of a power series.

EXERCISES (for answers see p. 746)

1 Obtain the limit of the nth term of each of the following series and so show that each is divergent:

a $\sum \dfrac{n}{\sqrt{(n^2 + 1)}}$

b $\sum \dfrac{(\cosh n + n)}{(\sinh n + n)}$

c $\sum \dfrac{\ln (n^2 + 1)}{\ln (n^3 + 1)}$

d $\sum (2^n + 1)^{1/n}$

2 Obtain s_n, the sum to n terms of each of the following series, and thereby test for convergence:

a $\sum \dfrac{1}{4n^2 - 1}$

b $\sum \dfrac{2n + 1}{n^2(n + 1)^2}$

c $\sum \dfrac{1}{n\sqrt{(n + 1)} + (n + 1)\sqrt{n}}$

d $\sum \dfrac{1}{\sinh n \sinh (n - 1)}$

3 By using the comparison test show that each of the following series is divergent:

a $\sum \dfrac{1}{2n - 1}$

b $\sum \dfrac{1}{n - \sqrt{n}}$

c $\sum \dfrac{1}{n \sin n}$

d $\sum \dfrac{1}{n \tanh n}$

4 By using the comparison test show that each of the following series is convergent:

a $\sum \dfrac{1}{n^2 + 3}$

b $\sum \dfrac{1}{\sqrt{(n^4 + 1)}}$

c $\sum \dfrac{n}{\sqrt{(n^6 + 1)}}$

d $\sum \dfrac{2n + 1}{n^3 + 1}$

ASSIGNMENT (for answers see p. 746; see also Workshop on p. 267)

Examine each of the following series for convergence or divergence:
1 $\sum (n^2 - 1)/(n^2 + 1)$
2 $\sum 1/(n^2 + 2n)$
3 $\sum (-1)^n n^2/2^n$
4 $\sum n^{5/2}/(n^2 + 1)$
5 $\sum \sin n/n^2$
6 $\sum n!/3^n$
7 $\sum e^{nx}/n^2$
8 $\sum 1/\sqrt{n}$
9 $\sum n!/(2n)!$
10 $\sum 1/n(n^2 + 1)$
Determine the radius of convergence of each of the following power series:
11 $\sum x^n/2^n$
12 $\sum (n!)x^n/(2n)!$
13 $\sum x^{2n}/3^n$

14 $\Sigma x^n/n^3$
15 $\Sigma (x/n)^n$
16 $\Sigma (2x)^n/n$
17 $\Sigma (nx)^n$
18 $\Sigma (nx)^n/n!$
19 $\Sigma x^n/\sqrt{n}$
20 $\Sigma n^3 x^n$

FURTHER EXERCISES (for answers see p. 747)

1 Examine for convergence:

a $\displaystyle\sum_{n=0}^{\infty} \frac{n}{n+1}$

b $\displaystyle\sum_{n=1}^{\infty} \frac{2^{n-1}}{n^3}$

c $\displaystyle\sum_{n=0}^{\infty} \frac{n}{\sqrt{(n^2+1)}}$

d $\displaystyle\sum_{n=2}^{\infty} \frac{n}{\sqrt{(n^2-1)}}$

2 Classify each of the following series as absolutely convergent (AC) or conditionally convergent (CC):

a $\displaystyle\sum_{n=1}^{\infty} \frac{(-1)^n}{n^2}$

b $\displaystyle\sum_{n=0}^{\infty} \frac{(-1)^n n}{3^{n-1}}$

c $\displaystyle\sum_{n=0}^{\infty} \frac{(-1)^n n^2}{n^3+1}$

3 Show that if p and q are positive integers ($p < q$) then

$$1 + (p/q) + (p/q)^2 + \ldots + (p/q)^N < q/(q-p)$$

Deduce that

$$1 + (3/4) + (3/4)^2 + \ldots + (3/4)^n + \ldots \leqslant 4$$

4 Test for convergence or divergence:

a $\displaystyle\sum_{n=0}^{\infty} \frac{1}{1+nx}$

b $\displaystyle\sum_{n=0}^{\infty} \frac{1}{n+x}$

c $\displaystyle\sum_{n=0}^{\infty} \left(x^n + \frac{1}{x^n} \right)$

5 By first showing that $V(n^2 - 1) < n < (n + 1)$ and $V(n^2 + 1) < n + 1$, show that

$$\sum_{n=1}^{\infty} [V(n^2 + 1) + V(n^2 - 1)]^{-1}$$

is divergent.

6 Show that the radius of convergence of each of the following power series is 1. Investigate the convergence of each when $|x| = 1$.

a $\displaystyle\sum_{n=1}^{\infty} \frac{(-1)^n x^{2n}}{n}$

b $\displaystyle\sum_{n=1}^{\infty} \frac{x^n}{n(n + 1)}$

c $\displaystyle\sum_{n=1}^{\infty} \frac{n + 2}{n(n + 1)} x^n$

d $\displaystyle\sum_{n=1}^{\infty} \frac{(n + 1)}{n^2} x^n$

7 The quantity of liquid p_n which is extracted from pulp in the nth cycle of a pressure pump is given approximately by $p_n = p/(n^2 + 1)$, where p is the initial quantity extracted. Prove that the total quantity Q of liquid extracted is bounded and that $2p \leq Q \leq 5p/2$. Show that after 13 cycles at least $2p$ (80% of the upper bound) has been extracted. (In fact $Q = (\pi \coth \pi + 1)/2$, so that after 13 cycles 96% is extracted and after only 5 cycles 80% is extracted.)

8 The electromotive force $e(t)$ of period $2\pi/3$ supplied by a half-wave rectifier is believed to be represented by the series

$$e(t) = \frac{E}{\pi} + \frac{E}{2} \sin \omega t - \frac{2E}{\pi} \sum_{n=1}^{\infty} \frac{1}{4n^2 - 1} \cos 2n\omega t$$

By considering the first N terms and using the triangle inequality $|x + y| \leq |x| + |y|$ repeatedly, or otherwise, show that for all t

$$|e(t)| \leq 2E(1 + \pi/4)/\pi$$

9 When the power is shut down from a vertical power pounder the piston continues for a time to strike. After the nth stroke the time taken until the next stroke is $p^n u/f$ and the height of the recoil is $(p^n u)^2/f$. The dimensionless quantity p, the speed u and the acceleration f are constant, and $0 < p < 1$. If distances and times are measured in metres and seconds respectively, and if after the first stroke the time taken for the pounder to come to rest is less than t seconds, show that $p < (1 + u/ft)^{-1}$. Show also that if $u = 1$, $f = 1$ and $t = 1$ and $p = 1/4$ then the total distance travelled by the piston after the first stroke is about 13.3 cm.

10   Complex numbers

We have developed one-half of the calculus – differentiation. The other half is the reverse process, known as integration. However, before we consider that, we need to enlarge our algebraic knowledge. We have already mentioned, when we dealt with power series, that a familiarity with complex numbers would have enabled us to say more. Indeed this has not been the only occasion where the idea of a complex number has arisen. In this chapter we shall begin a short study of algebraic concepts that will lead via complex numbers, matrices and determinants to vectors. Only when we have done all this will we return to the calculus to gain the full stereophonic effect.

After working through this chapter you should be able to
☐ Solve equations involving complex numbers;
☐ Express a complex number in polar form;
☐ Represent sets of complex numbers as regions of the complex plane;
☐ Solve the equation $z^n = \alpha$ where $n \in \mathbb{N}$ and $\alpha \in \mathbb{C}$;
☐ Relate circular and hyperbolic functions using complex numbers.
At the end of this chapter we shall apply this work to the practical problem of an AC bridge.

10.1 GENESIS

If we consider the quadratic equation

$$ax^2 + bx + c = 0$$

where a, b and c are real numbers, $a \neq 0$, we obtain

$$x^2 + \frac{b}{a}x + \frac{c}{a} = 0$$

So, completing the square,

$$\left(x + \frac{b}{2a}\right)^2 - \frac{b^2}{4a^2} + \frac{c}{a} = 0$$

Notice how we add half the coefficient of x to complete the square. Then

$$\left(x + \frac{b}{2a}\right)^2 = \frac{b^2}{4a^2} - \frac{c}{a} = \frac{b^2 - 4ac}{4a^2}$$

If $b^2 - 4ac \geqslant 0$ then

$$x = \frac{-b \pm \sqrt{(b^2 - 4ac)}}{2a}$$

You will certainly have met this before (see Chapter 1). It is known as the formula for solving a quadratic equation, and we know that for real roots we require

$$b^2 - 4ac \geqslant 0$$

_____

What are we to do if $b^2 - 4ac < 0$? Clearly $\sqrt{(b^2 - 4ac)}$ is not a real number, because whenever we square a real number the result is positive.

Suppose nevertheless that there is a number, which we shall represent by i, which behaves with respect to addition and multiplication exactly as if it were a real number but which has the special property that $i^2 = -1$. If such a number exists then we can write

$$x = \frac{-b \pm i\sqrt{(4ac - b^2)}}{2a}$$

and obtain two roots.

So if we start with the real numbers, and augment them with this new number i, the operations of addition and multiplication will generate such numbers as

$$(2 + i)(1 - 3i) + (2 + 4i)^2 (i - 1)(2i + 1)$$

This is rather like adding an extra ingredient to a stew which is being cooked; the flavour permeates through.

Using the rules of elementary algebra, and the special property of i, namely $i^2 = -1$, any number which we generate can be reduced to the form

$$a + ib$$

where a and b are real numbers.

This problem was first encountered in section 1.2. Now we are able to resolve it.

We define the set of **complex numbers** $\mathbb{C}$ to be those numbers which can be expressed in the form $a + ib$, where a and b are real numbers:

$$\mathbb{C} = \{a + ib \,|\, a \in \mathbb{R}, b \in \mathbb{R}\}$$

a is called the **real** part of $a + ib$, and b is called the **imaginary** part of $a + ib$. These are rather unsatisfactory names because each of them is in fact a real number!

If $b = 0$ then $a + ib$ is a real number, whereas if $a = 0$ then $a + ib = ib$. A number of the form ib where b is real is often called a **pure imaginary** number.

> Electrical engineers find complex numbers very useful when describing circuit theory.

The complex numbers, with the usual operations of addition and multiplication, form a mathematical structure known as a **field**.

In the field of complex numbers, any quadratic equation

$$az^2 + bz + c = 0 \qquad a \neq 0$$

always has two roots. Of course if $b^2 = 4ac$ then the two roots are equal.

NOTATION

There are unwritten conventions about the use of letters to represent mathematical objects. These conventions are often broken, but here are some broad guidelines:
1 a, b, c and d are used for constants.
2 e is reserved for the natural base of logarithms.
3 f and g are used for functions.
4 i and j are reserved for complex numbers.
5 h, k, l, m, n, p, q, r, s and t are used for constants or variables.
6 u, v, w, x, y and z are used for functions or variables.

> In particular j is used extensively in electrical engineering to avoid confusion with i which is used for current.

It is often convenient to use a single letter to represent a complex number, and so that no confusion can arise it is customary to reserve z and w for this purpose. Other letters such as α and β can be used provided it is clear that the number is not real but complex.

So if $z = a + ib$ then
1 a is the real part of z; we write $a = \text{Re}(z)$.
2 b is the imaginary part of z; we write $b = \text{Im}(z)$.
Some books use $\mathscr{R}(z)$ and $\mathscr{I}(z)$ instead of $\text{Re}(z)$ and $\text{Im}(z)$ respectively.

EQUATING REAL AND IMAGINARY PARTS

Example □ Show that if $a + ib = c + id$, where a, b, c and d are real, then $a = c$ and $b = d$.

Suppose $a + ib = c + id$. Then $a - c = -i(b - d)$, so that squaring

$$(a - c)^2 = i^2(b - d)^2 = -(b - d)^2$$

Therefore

$$(a - c)^2 + (b - d)^2 = 0$$

Now $(a - c)^2$ is a positive real number and so too is $(b - d)^2$, and the sum of these two positive numbers is zero. It therefore follows that each of these real numbers must be zero. Therefore $a - c = 0$ and $b - d = 0$, so $a = c$ and $b = d$.

Of course we know that the converse is always true. That is, if $a = c$ and $b = d$ then $a + ib = c + id$. ■

This example has important consequences. It means that, given an equation involving complex numbers, we can equate the real parts and the imaginary parts and thereby obtain two real equations from one complex equation.

□ Obtain x and y in terms of a and b if   **Example**

$$\frac{1}{x + iy} + \frac{1}{a + ib} = 1$$

We obtain

$$\frac{1}{x + iy} = 1 - \frac{1}{a + ib} = \frac{a + ib - 1}{a + ib}$$

$$x + iy = \frac{a + ib}{a + ib - 1}$$

$$= \frac{a + ib}{(a - 1) + ib}$$

Now if we multiply numerator and denominator by $(a - 1) - ib$ the denominator will become a real number:

$$x + iy = \frac{a + ib}{(a - 1) + ib} \frac{(a - 1) - ib}{(a - 1) - ib}$$

$$= \frac{(a + ib)(a - 1 - ib)}{(a - 1)^2 + b^2}$$

$$= \frac{a(a - 1) + b^2 + i[b(a - 1) - ab]}{(a - 1)^2 + b^2}$$

$$= \frac{a(a - 1) + b^2 - ib}{(a - 1)^2 + b^2}$$

So that, equating real and imaginary parts,

$$x = \frac{a(a - 1) + b^2}{(a - 1)^2 + b^2} \quad \text{and} \quad y = \frac{-b}{(a - 1)^2 + b^2}$$ ■

This example shows that an equation involving complex numbers produces two equations involving real numbers, and that to obtain these equations we can *equate real and imaginary parts*.

10.2 THE COMPLEX PLANE: ARGAND DIAGRAM

We can obtain a geometrical representation for complex numbers by using the conventions of coordinate geometry (Chapter 3).

To each complex number $a + ib$ there is a unique point (a, b) in the plane Oxy. Conversely, given any point (a, b) in the plane Oxy, there is a unique complex number $a + ib$. There is therefore a one-to-one correspondence between the points in the plane Oxy and the complex numbers (Fig. 10.1).

When the plane is used in this way it is often called an **Argand diagram** or the **complex plane**. The x-axis is then called the **real axis** and the y-axis is called the **imaginary axis**.

Jean Robert Argand (1768–1822): French mathematician who wrote on the graphical representation of complex numbers.

POLAR FORM

Of course we know that a point in the plane can be expressed in polar coordinates rather than in cartesian coordinates (Fig. 10.2). We obtain from elementary trigonometry

$$a = r \cos \theta, \qquad b = r \sin \theta$$

so that

We first encountered polar coordinates in section 3.1.

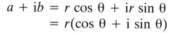
$$a + ib = r \cos \theta + ir \sin \theta$$
$$= r(\cos \theta + i \sin \theta)$$

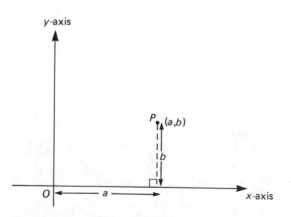

Fig. 10.1 Cartesian coordinates.

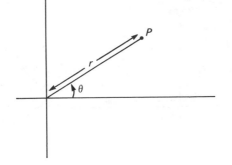

Fig. 10.2 Polar coordinates.

When a complex number is expressed in this way, we say it is expressed in **polar form**.

The easiest way to express a complex number in polar form is to put the complex number on the Argand diagram using the correspondence $a + ib \rightarrow (a, b)$, and then to read off the distance $r = \sqrt{(a^2 + b^2)}$ and the angle θ.

We use polar form when we solve difference equations in Chapter 21.

MODULUS AND ARGUMENT

The usual convention for polar coordinates is to take $r > 0$ and $0 \leqslant \theta < 2\pi$, so that a *unique* representation is obtained for every point other than the origin.

In the complex plane, the convention is slightly different. Here we take $r > 0$, as before, but $-\pi < \theta \leqslant \pi$. r is known as the **modulus** of the complex number: $r = \sqrt{(a^2 + b^2)}$. θ is known as the **argument** of the complex number: $\theta = \tan^{-1}(y/x)$ when $\theta \in (-\pi/2, \pi/2)$.

It follows that any non-zero complex number can be represented uniquely by the modulus r and the argument θ. The notation $r\angle\theta$ is often used to denote these essential ingredients. When a complex number is expressed in polar form where θ is the argument of the complex number, so that $-\pi < \theta \leqslant \pi$, it is said to be in **modulus-argument form**.

This should not be confused with the argument of a function (see section 2.4).

$\square$ Express the complex number $1 - 2i$ in the form $r\angle\theta$.

We begin by representing the complex number by a point on the Argand diagram (Fig. 10.3): $1 - 2i \rightarrow (1, -2)$. We calculate the modulus straight away using Pythagoras's theorem:

$$r^2 = a^2 + b^2 = 1^2 + (-2)^2 = 5$$

and therefore the modulus is $\sqrt{5}$. The argument can be read from the diagram using a little trigonometry. The acute angle α is given by $\tan^{-1} 2 \simeq 63°26'$ or $63.44°$, so that $r = \sqrt{5}$ and $\theta = -\tan^{-1} 2$.   ∎

Example

This representation is used in phasor analysis of a range of electrical networks operating under steady-state conditions, with sinusoidal excitations.

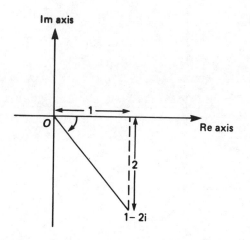

Fig. 10.3 Cartesian representation of $1 - 2i$.

Note that we can express the argument in degrees if we wish, but we must indicate clearly that we have done so. In many ways it is best to get used to the natural measure of angle, the so-called **radian** (π radians = 180 degrees). For instance, in the series expansion for the circular function

$$\cos x = 1 - \tfrac{1}{2}x^2 + \ldots$$

x is the natural measure of angle, and it would be incorrect to attempt to use degrees.

COMPLEX CONJUGATE

If $z = a + ib$, we denote the modulus of z by $|z|$ and the argument of z by $\arg z$.

Another useful concept, which we have already used implicitly, is known as the **complex conjugate** of z and is denoted by $\bar{z}$. If $z = a + ib$ then we define $\bar{z} = a - ib$. It follows that

$$z\bar{z} = (a + ib)(a - ib) = a^2 - (ib)^2$$
$$= a^2 + b^2 = |z|^2$$

which is a real number.

We can use this to reduce any rational expression involving complex numbers to the form $a + ib$, where a and b are real numbers. To achieve this we render the denominator real by multiplying numerator and denominator by the complex conjugate of the denominator. This is precisely what we did in a previous example. Here is another example to make the idea crystal clear.

☐ Express the following complex number in the standard cartesian form **Example**
$a + ib$, where a and b are real numbers:

$$\frac{(2 + i)^3}{(3 + 4i)^3}$$

We can simplify the numerator and denominator separately

$$\frac{(2 + i)(4 + 4i + i^2)}{(3 + 4i)(9 + 24i + 16i^2)} = \frac{(2 + i)(3 + 4i)}{(3 + 4i)(9 + 24i - 16)}$$

$$= \frac{2 + i}{(-7 + 24i)}$$

We now multiply numerator and denominator by the conjugate of the
denominator, since we know this will reduce the denominator to a real
number:

$$\frac{2 + i}{-7 + 24i} = \frac{(2 + i)(-7 - 24i)}{(-7)^2 + (24)^2}$$

$$= \frac{-14 + 24 - 55i}{49 + 576} = \frac{10 - 55i}{625}$$

$$= \frac{2 - 11i}{125} = \frac{2}{125} + i\frac{-11}{125}$$ ■

10.3 VECTORIAL REPRESENTATION

Another related geometrical method for representing complex numbers
is to regard them as directed line segments emanating from the origin.
More precisely, if $z = a + ib$ corresponds to P, the point (a, b) in the
complex plane, then we represent z by the line segment OP (Fig. 10.4).
It is easy to show that, with this representation, when two complex numbers are added together their sum is obtained by adding the corresponding
line segments according to the parallelogram law.

We shall encounter
the parallelogram law
again when we study
vectors in section
14.2.

To see this, suppose P and Q represent the complex numbers $a + ib$ and
$c + id$ respectively. Then the sum of the complex numbers is

$$(a + ib) + (c + id) = (a + c) + i(b + d)$$

We show that this is represented by the point R, where R is obtained from
P and Q by completing the parallelogram $POQR$.

If we complete the parallelogram $POQR$ as shown in Fig. 10.4 we have

$$OA = a, \qquad AP = b, \qquad OC = c, \qquad CQ = d$$

Moreover $OA - CD$, $AP - DB$ and $CQ = BR$ using parallels. So

$$OD = OC + CD = OC + OA = a + c$$
$$DR = DB + BR = AP + CQ = b + d$$

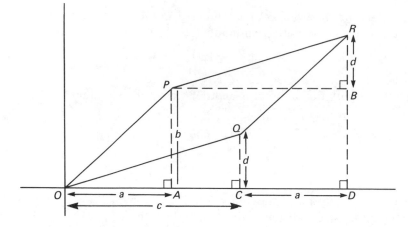

Fig. 10.4 Cartesian representation of $(a + ib) + (c + id)$.

This is the property we wished to show.

If the points P and Q represent the complex numbers z and α (Fig. 10.5) then since

$$z = (z - \alpha) + \alpha$$

the vector representing $z - \alpha$ is equal in length and parallel to PQ. This observation gives us a geometrical interpretation for $|z - \alpha|$ and arg $(z - \alpha)$ which we shall find useful when describing sets of points.

We shall refer to the 'point z' or the 'vector z' rather than the more correct but awkward 'point representing the complex number z' and 'vector representing the complex number z' respectively.

We can carry out operations involving multiplication geometrically in the Argand diagram if we observe the following properties:

1 $|zw| = |z| |w|$

2 $\left| \dfrac{z}{w} \right| = \dfrac{|z|}{|w|}$ provided $w \neq 0$

3 arg $(zw) = $ arg z + arg w

4 arg$\left(\dfrac{z}{w} \right) = $ arg z − arg w provided $w \neq 0$

To be strict, it may be necessary to add or subtract 2π to bring the argument in properties **3** and **4** within the range $-\pi < \theta \leqslant \pi$, that is the interval $(-\pi, \pi]$. However, if we add or subtract 2π from the polar angle of a complex number it has no geometrical effect in the complex plane. Therefore, if we are concerned solely with the geometrical effects of these operations, these algebraic details are irrelevant.

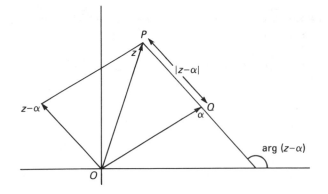

Fig. 10.5 Geometrical representation of $|z - \alpha|$.

To justify these properties, suppose $z = r(\cos \theta + i \sin \theta)$ and $w = s(\cos \phi + i \sin \phi)$. Then

$$zw = rs(\cos \theta + i \sin \theta)(\cos \phi + i \sin \phi)$$
$$= rs[\cos \theta \cos \phi - \sin \theta \sin \phi + i(\cos \theta \sin \phi + \cos \phi \sin \theta)]$$
$$= rs[\cos (\theta + \phi) + i \sin (\theta + \phi)]$$

so that properties **1** and **3** follow:

$$|zw| = rs = |z| |w|$$
$$\arg (zw) = \theta + \phi \qquad (\mathrm{mod}\ 2\pi)$$
$$= \arg z + \arg w \qquad (\mathrm{mod}\ 2\pi)$$

The expression mod 2π indicates that it may be necessary to add or subtract multiples of 2π to bring the argument within range.

We can readily deduce properties **2** and **4**. First, using property **1**,

$$|z| = \left| \frac{z}{w} w \right| = \left| \frac{z}{w} \right| |w|$$

Then dividing through by $|w|$ gives property **2**. Next, using property **3**,

$$\arg z = \arg \left(\frac{z}{w} w \right)$$
$$= \arg \left(\frac{z}{w} \right) + \arg w \qquad (\mathrm{mod}\ 2\pi)$$

Then subtracting $\arg w$ from each side gives property **4**.

We have shown that

1 When two complex numbers are multiplied the moduli are multiplied and the arguments are added;

2 When two complex numbers are divided the moduli are divided and the arguments are subtracted.

Example □ What is the effect in the complex plane of multiplying a complex number by i?

When we put i in polar form we obtain

$$i = 1(\cos \pi/2 + i \sin \pi/2)$$

so that the modulus is 1 and the argument is $\pi/2$. Suppose z is any complex number with modulus r and argument θ. Then iz is a complex number with modulus r and argument $\theta + \pi/2$. Therefore geometrically the effect is to **rotate** the vector representing z anticlockwise through $\pi/2$. ■

Example □ A complex number satisfies the equation

$$|z - i| = |z + i|$$

Determine the locus of the point which represents z in the Argand diagram.

We shall discuss two ways of solving this problem.

The idea of a locus was first introduced in section 3.7.

Geometrical method   In Fig. 10.6, $|z - i|$ is the distance between the point representing z and the point representing i. Likewise $|z + i|$ is the distance between the point representing z and the point representing $-i$. The equation tells us that these two distances are equal, and since this is the only constraint on z it follows that z lies on the perpendicular bisector of the line joining $-i$ to i. This is the real axis.

Algebraic method   Put $z = x + iy$ and examine what can be deduced from the equation $|z - i| = |z + i|$. We obtain

$$|(x + iy) - i| = |(x + iy) + i|$$
$$|(x + iy) - i|^2 = |(x + iy) + i|^2$$

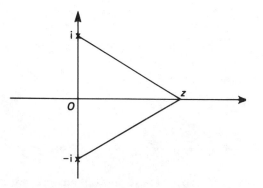

Fig. 10.6 Locus of z if $|z - i| = |z + i|$.

$$|x + i(y - 1)|^2 = |x + i(y + 1)|^2$$
$$x^2 + (y - 1)^2 = x^2 + (y + 1)^2$$
$$-2y = 2y$$
$$y = 0$$

Therefore z lies on the real axis, as we deduced before.   ■

In general there are two methods available for solving locus problems: the geometrical method and the algebraic method.

10.4 FURTHER PROPERTIES OF THE CONJUGATE

We have already seen that

$$z\bar{z} = |z|^2$$

and we have at once

$$z + \bar{z} = (a + ib) + (a - ib) = 2a = 2\,\mathrm{Re}(z)$$
$$z - \bar{z} = (a + ib) - (a - ib) = 2ib = 2i\,\mathrm{Im}(z)$$

☐ Show that the conjugate of a product is the product of the conjugates. **Example**
We have shown that if $z = r(\cos\theta + i\sin\theta)$ and $w = s(\cos\phi + i\sin\phi)$,
then

$$zw = rs[\cos(\theta + \phi) + i\sin(\theta + \phi)]$$

Therefore

$$\overline{zw} = rs[\cos(\theta + \phi) - i\sin(\theta + \phi)]$$

Now

$$\bar{z} = r(\cos\theta - i\sin\theta)$$
$$= r[\cos(-\theta) + i\sin(-\theta)]$$

and

$$\bar{w} = s(\cos\phi - i\sin\phi)$$
$$= s[\cos(-\phi) + i\sin(-\phi)]$$

So

$$\bar{z}\bar{w} = rs\,[\cos(-\theta - \phi) + i\sin(-\theta - \phi)]$$
$$= rs[\cos(\theta + \phi) - i\sin(\theta + \phi)] = \overline{zw}$$

as required.   ■

You will recall that, with one exception, we have defined a^n where n is any integer and a is any real number (Chapter 1). The exception is $a = 0$, for we do not define 0^0. The reason for this omission is that whatever definition we were to choose we should violate the laws of indices, and we wish to preserve these at all costs.

With the exception that we do not define 0^0 we now define, in the obvious way, z^n where n is any integer and z is any complex number. We define

$$z^0 = 1 \quad \text{provided } z \neq 0$$
$$z^{n+1} = zz^n \quad (n \in \mathbb{N})$$

Therefore z^n, when $n \in \mathbb{N}$, is a product of z with itself n times. Finally, we define

$$z^{-n} = 1/z^n \quad \text{when } n \in \mathbb{N}, z \neq 0$$

10.5 DE MOIVRE'S THEOREM

Abraham De Moivre (1667–1754): French Hugernot mathematician who fled to London. Worked as a tutor and insurance and gambling consultant. Pioneer of analytic trigonometry and theory of probability.

We have already seen how to express a complex number z in polar form. One of the advantages of doing so is that it is then possible to calculate z^n very easily. This is a consequence of **De Moivre's theorem**, which says that if n is any integer

$$(\cos \theta + i \sin \theta)^n = \cos n\theta + i \sin n\theta$$

We shall accept this without proof. The usual method of proof is to prove it first for natural numbers and then to extend the proof to all integers. If you are familiar with the method of proof known as mathematical induction (Chapter 1) you should have no difficulty in supplying the details.

We should be very wary of trying to use De Moivre's theorem for other values of n. For example, we have defined (section 1.5) $1^{1/2}$ to be the positive real root of the equation $x^2 = 1$, and so $1^{1/2} = 1$. However, if

$$(\cos \theta + i \sin \theta)^r = \cos r\theta + i \sin r\theta$$

were to hold for *all* real numbers r then

$$1 = 1^{1/2} = (\cos 2\pi + i \sin 2\pi)^{1/2} = \cos \pi + i \sin \pi = -1$$

You may find books that claim that for all real numbers r

$$(\cos \theta + i \sin \theta)^r = \cos r\theta + i \sin r\theta$$

and some which purport to prove it! The best that can be said of this is that the expression on the right is *one* of the values of the expression on the left, where the expression on the left may have been somewhat loosely defined.

If $z \in \mathbb{C}$, we shall not need to define z^n except when n is an integer.

There are several uses for De Moivre's theorem.

☐ Obtain $(1 + i)^{28}$.

We could expand by the binomial theorem, but this would be no easy task. Instead we begin by putting $z = 1 + i$ into polar form. If we put the point $(1, 1)$ on the Argand diagram we can read off the modulus and the argument straight away. We see that $r = \sqrt{2}$ and $\theta = \pi/4$. Therefore

$$z = \sqrt{2}(\cos \pi/4 + i \sin \pi/4)$$

So

$$z^{28} = (\sqrt{2})^{28}(\cos \pi/4 + i \sin \pi/4)^{28}$$
$$= 2^{14}(\cos 7\pi + i \sin 7\pi)$$

using De Moivre's theorem. Therefore

$$z^{28} = 2^{14}(\cos \pi + i \sin \pi) = -2^{14}$$ ■

Here we can see that De Moivre's theorem has helped us considerably. We can also use De Moivre's theorem to deduce trigonometrical identities.

☐ Use De Moivre's theorem to deduce identities for $\sin 3\theta$ and $\cos 3\theta$ in terms of $\sin \theta$ and $\cos \theta$ respectively.

It helps to use a shorthand notation. We write $c = \cos \theta$ and $s = \sin \theta$, so that

$$c + is = \cos \theta + i \sin \theta$$

Now by De Moivre's theorem

$$\cos 3\theta + i \sin 3\theta = (c + is)^3$$
$$= c^3 + 3c^2(is) + 3c(is)^2 + (is)^3$$
$$= c^3 + 3ic^2s - 3cs^2 - is^3$$

using $i^2 = -1$. So equating real and imaginary parts we have

$$\cos 3\theta = c^3 - 3cs^2$$
$$\sin 3\theta = 3c^2s - s^3$$

Now $c^2 + s^2 = 1$, and so

$$\cos 3\theta = c^3 - 3c(1 - c^2)$$
$$= 4c^3 - 3c$$
$$= 4 \cos^3 \theta - 3 \cos \theta$$
$$\sin 3\theta = 3(1 - s^2)s - s^3$$
$$= 3s - 4s^3$$
$$= 3 \sin \theta - 4 \sin^3 \theta$$ ■

☐ Simplify the expression

$$\frac{(\cos 3\theta + i \sin 3\theta)^6 (\cos 2\theta - i \sin 2\theta)^7}{(\sin 5\theta + i \cos 5\theta)^6 (\cos \theta - i \sin \theta)^8}$$

We begin by remarking that because

$$(\cos \theta + i \sin \theta)^n = \cos n\theta + i \sin n\theta$$

for any integer n, it follows that

$$(\cos \theta - i \sin \theta)^n = \cos n\theta - i \sin n\theta$$

There are many ways of seeing this. One way is to take the complex conjugate of each side of the equation using the property that the conjugate of a product is the product of the conjugates. Also

$$\sin \theta + i \cos \theta = -i^2 \sin \theta + i \cos \theta$$
$$= i(\cos \theta - i \sin \theta)$$

Using De Moivre's theorem we now have

$$\frac{(\cos 3\theta + i \sin 3\theta)^6 (\cos 2\theta - i \sin 2\theta)^7}{(\sin 5\theta + i \cos 5\theta)^6 (\cos \theta - i \sin \theta)^8}$$

$$= \frac{(\cos \theta + i \sin \theta)^{18} (\cos \theta - i \sin \theta)^{14}}{i^6(\cos 5\theta - i \sin 5\theta)^6 (\cos \theta - i \sin \theta)^8}$$

Now $i^2 = -1$ and so $i^6 = (-1)^3 = -1$. Therefore the expression becomes

$$= \frac{(\cos \theta + i \sin \theta)^{18} (\cos \theta - i \sin \theta)^{14}}{-(\cos \theta - i \sin \theta)^{30} (\cos \theta - i \sin \theta)^8}$$

$$= \frac{-(\cos \theta + i \sin \theta)^{18}}{(\cos \theta - i \sin \theta)^{24}}$$

$$= -(\cos \theta + i \sin \theta)^{42}$$

$$= -(\cos 42\theta + i \sin 42\theta) \qquad \blacksquare$$

It is now time for you to take some steps.

10.6 Workshop

1

Exercise Express the complex number

$$\frac{(\sqrt{3} + i)^2 (1 - i)^3}{(i - \sqrt{3})^3 (i + 1)^2}$$

in polar form.
   Try this carefully before you take the next step.

2 There are essentially two ways of proceeding. One method is to multiply everything out, simplify it down to obtain the cartesian form, and then produce the polar form. This is routine but long.

The better alternative is to put the complex numbers which appear in the expression into polar form and use De Moivre's theorem to simplify it. Thus

$$\sqrt{3} + i = 2(\cos \pi/6 + i \sin \pi/6)$$
$$1 - i = \sqrt{2}(\cos \pi/4 - i \sin \pi/4)$$

$$i - \sqrt{3} = -\sqrt{3} + i = 2\left(\cos \frac{5\pi}{6} + i \sin \frac{5\pi}{6} \right)$$

$$i + 1 = 1 + i = \sqrt{2}(\cos \pi/4 + i \sin \pi/4)$$

Then

$$\frac{(\sqrt{3} + i)^2 (1 - i)^3}{(i - \sqrt{3})^3 (i + 1)^2} = \frac{[2(\cos \pi/6 + i \sin \pi/6)]^2 [\sqrt{2}(\cos \pi/4 - i \sin \pi/4)]^3}{[2(\cos 5\pi/6 + i \sin 5\pi/6)]^3 [\sqrt{2}(\cos \pi/4 + i \sin \pi/4)]^2}$$

$$= \frac{[4(\cos \pi/3 + i \sin \pi/3)] [2\sqrt{2}(\cos 3\pi/4 - i \sin 3\pi/4)]}{[8(\cos 5\pi/2 + i \sin 5\pi/2)] [2(\cos \pi/2 + i \sin \pi/2)]}$$

$$= \frac{1}{\sqrt{2}} \left(\cos \left[\frac{1}{3} - \frac{3}{4} - \frac{5}{2} - \frac{1}{2} \right] \pi \right.$$

$$\left. + i \sin \left[\frac{1}{3} - \frac{3}{4} - \frac{5}{2} - \frac{1}{2} \right] \pi \right)$$

$$= \frac{1}{\sqrt{2}} \left(\cos \left[\frac{4 - 9 - 36}{12} \right] \pi + i \sin \left[\frac{4 - 9 - 36}{12} \right] \pi \right)$$

$$= \frac{1}{\sqrt{2}} \left(\cos \left[\frac{-41\pi}{12} \right] + i \sin \left[\frac{-41\pi}{12} \right] \right)$$

$$= \frac{1}{\sqrt{2}} \left(\cos \left[\frac{7\pi}{12} \right] + i \sin \left[\frac{7\pi}{12} \right] \right)$$

So $r = 1/\sqrt{2}$ and $\theta = 7\pi/12$, and the required polar form is

$$(1/\sqrt{2}) (\cos 7\pi/12 + i \sin 7\pi/12)$$

You can if you prefer express the complex number in the modulus-argument form as $(1/\sqrt{2}) \angle(7\pi/12)$.

If you managed that, except for possibly a numerical slip, then proceed at full speed to step 4. Otherwise, try this exercise.

▷ **Exercise**   Express the complex number

$$\frac{(1 + 4i) (2 - 3i)}{(i + 6)(1 + 3i)}$$

in the cartesian form $a + ib$.

There is no need for polar form here.

All we need to do is to rationalize the expression by multiplying numerator and denominator by the conjugate of the denominator. You can do this before you multiply out or afterwards; it's up to you to choose. So, multiplying out first, we have

$$\frac{(1 + 4i)(2 - 3i)}{(i + 6)(1 + 3i)} = \frac{2 + 8i - 3i - 12i^2}{i + 6 + 3i^2 + 18i}$$

$$= \frac{2 + 5i + 12}{19i + 6 - 3} = \frac{14 + 5i}{3 + 19i} \frac{3 - 19i}{3 - 19i}$$

$$= \frac{42 + 15i - 266i + 95}{9 + 361} = \frac{137 - 251i}{370}$$

So the number is

$$\frac{137}{370} - i\frac{251}{370}$$

Now step ahead.

4

Exercise   Describe the following set of points in the complex plane:

$$\{z : z \in \mathbb{C}, \arg(z - 1) < \pi/2\}$$

It is best to use a geometric method here because the algebraic method will involve you in work with inequalities which you may find too difficult.

5

Suppose we take a general point P in the set (Fig. 10.7). We know that if we join P to the point A, representing the complex number 1, and $\theta = \angle XAP$, then $\theta < \pi/2$. This follows because $\arg(z - 1) = \angle XAP$.

Any point in the lower half of the complex plane satisfies this condition,

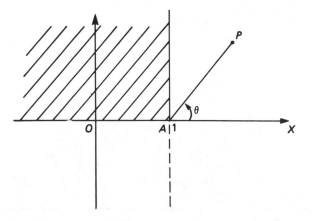

Fig. 10.7 $\{z : z \in \mathbb{C}, \arg(z - 1) < \pi/2\}$ (unshaded region).

and so too does any point in the upper plane to the right of the line defined by $\text{Re}(z) = 1$. We see therefore that we must exclude all points corresponding to complex numbers which have their real part less than or equal to 1 and their imaginary part greater than or equal to 0. This region is shown in the diagram.

If you managed to get that right then move on to the next section. Otherwise, try one more exercise.

▷**Exercise**   Describe the locus of the point z which moves in the complex plane in such a way that

$$|z - i| = 2|z - 1|$$

Only when you have tried this should you move on.

We can use either the geometrical method or the algebraic method. For the geometrical method you need to know that the locus of a point which moves so that the ratio of its distances from two fixed points is a constant is a circle. If you are not aware of this fact you might like to prove it. The only exception is when the ratio is 1, in which case the locus is a straight line. Once you know the locus is a circle, the centre and radius can be deduced from a diagram.

6

The algebraic method is more straightforward in this instance. Let $z = x + iy$. Then

$$|z - i| = 2|z - 1|$$

So

$$|(x + iy) - i| = 2|(x + iy) - 1|$$
$$|x + i(y - 1)| = 2|(x - 1) + iy|$$
$$|x + i(y - 1)|^2 = 4|(x - 1) + iy|^2$$
$$x^2 + (y - 1)^2 = 4[(x - 1)^2 + y^2]$$
$$x^2 + y^2 - 2y + 1 = 4(x^2 - 2x + 1 + y^2)$$
$$3x^2 + 3y^2 - 8x + 2y + 3 = 0$$
$$x^2 + y^2 - 8x/3 + 2y/3 + 1 = 0$$

This is the equation of a circle with centre $(4/3, -1/3)$ and radius $2\sqrt{2}/3$ (see Chapter 3).

10.7 THE *n*TH ROOTS OF A COMPLEX NUMBER

We are now in a position to solve the equation $z^n = \alpha$ where α is any complex number and $n \in \mathbb{N}$. The solutions of this equation are called the *n*th roots of α.

Suppose we have a polynomial in x

$$f(x) = c_n x^n + c_{n-1} x^{n-1} + \ldots + c_1 x + c_0 \qquad c_n \neq 0$$

If the coefficients

$$c_n, c_{n-1}, \ldots, c_1, c_0$$

are real numbers then we know there are at most n real roots of the equation $f(x) = 0$.

We began this chapter by looking at the quadratic equation and noticing that on occasion we did not have two real roots. This motivated the extension of the number system to complex numbers. We did this to ensure that every quadratic equation had two roots. It would not be surprising if when we turned our attention to polynomials of higher degree that further extensions of the number system would be required. However, it is a quite remarkable fact that when we allow complex numbers into the picture then the polynomial equation

$$f(z) = c_n z^n + c_{n-1} z^{n-1} + \ldots + c_1 z + c_0 = 0$$

always has n roots. Some of the roots may be repeated, but there are always n in total.

Unfortunately in general it is not possible to obtain formulas for solving polynomial equations of degree higher than 4. However, we can solve the equation $z^n = \alpha$ by using De Moivre's theorem, and this we now do.

We begin by expressing the number α in polar form:

$$\alpha = r(\cos \theta + i \sin \theta)$$

We observe first that if

$$z_0 = r^{1/n}[\cos (\theta/n) + i \sin (\theta/n)]$$

then

$$z_0^n = (r^{1/n})^n[\cos (\theta/n) + i \sin (\theta/n)]^n$$
$$= r[\cos n(\theta/n) + i \sin n(\theta/n)]$$

by De Moivre's theorem. So

$$z_0^n = r[\cos \theta + i \sin \theta] = \alpha$$

Therefore z_0 is one of the roots of the equation $z^n = \alpha$.

However, we can write α in the form

$$\alpha = r[\cos (\theta + 2k\pi) + i \sin (\theta + 2k\pi)]$$

where k is any integer. Therefore by the same token, if we put

$$z_k = r^{1/n}[\cos (\theta + 2k\pi)/n + i \sin (\theta + 2k\pi)/n]$$

it follows that z_k is one of the roots of the equation $z^n = \alpha$. Now this is true for *every* integer k, and so at first sight it might look as if we have an infinite number of solutions. However, if we allow k to take on $n + 1$ successive integer values the last one will be a repeat of the first. That is,

$$z_n = r^{1/n}[\cos{(\theta + 2n\pi)/n} + i \sin{(\theta + 2n\pi)/n}]$$
$$= r^{1/n}[\cos{(\theta/n + 2\pi)} + i \sin{(\theta/n + 2\pi)}]$$
$$= r^{1/n}[\cos{(\theta/n)} + i \sin{(\theta/n)}] = z_0$$

Therefore we obtain exactly n roots.

To sum up, the method for obtaining the nth roots of a complex number α is as follows:

1 Put the complex number α into polar form

$$\alpha = r(\cos{\theta} + i \sin{\theta})$$

2 Write α in the form

$$\alpha = r[\cos{(\theta + 2k\pi)} + i \sin{(\theta + 2k\pi)}]$$

where k is an arbitrary integer.

3 By De Moivre's theorem one of the roots of the equation $z^n = \alpha$ is

$$z_k = r^{1/n}[\cos{(\theta + 2k\pi)/n} + i \sin{(\theta + 2k\pi)/n}]$$

for every integer k.

4 Allow k to take on n successive integer values to determine the nth roots.

If we think in geometrical terms we see that each of the roots has the same modulus $r^{1/n}$ and the arguments increase by $2\pi/n$. This means that they are equally spaced around a circle centred at the origin (Fig. 10.8). This observation gives a geometrical method for obtaining the roots once the first one is known. Moreover, De Moivre's theorem, gives z_0 straight away:

$$z_0 = r^{1/n}[\cos{(\theta/n)} + i \sin{(\theta/n)}]$$

□ Obtain the fifth roots of i.   **Example**

We follow the method described. First, if we imagine i in the Argand diagram we see that $r = 1$ and $\theta = \pi/2$, so that

$$i = 1(\cos{\pi/2} + i \sin{\pi/2})$$

If k is any integer we can rewrite this as

$$i = 1[\cos{(\pi/2 + 2k\pi)} + i \sin{(\pi/2 + 2k\pi)}]$$

Using De Moivre's theorem we have that the fifth roots are

$$z_k = 1^{1/5}[\cos{(\pi/10 + 2k\pi/5)} + i \sin{(\pi/10 + 2k\pi/5)}]$$
$$= \cos{(\pi/10 + 2k\pi/5)} + i \sin{(\pi/10 + 2k\pi/5)}$$

Finally, we let k take five consecutive integer values, for example -2, -1, 0, 1, and 2, to obtain the five roots:

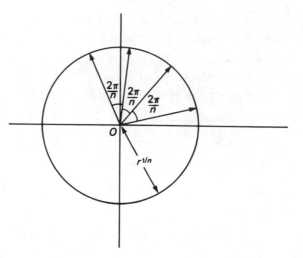

Fig. 10.8 The roots of $z^n = \alpha$.

$$z_{-2} = \cos{(\pi/10 - 4\pi/5)} + i\sin{(\pi/10 - 4\pi/5)}$$
$$= \cos{(7\pi/10)} - i\sin{(7\pi/10)}$$
$$z_{-1} = \cos{(\pi/10 - 2\pi/5)} + i\sin{(\pi/10 - 2\pi/5)}$$
$$= \cos{(3\pi/10)} + i\sin{(3\pi/10)}$$
$$z_0 = \cos{(\pi/10)} + i\sin{(\pi/10)}$$
$$z_1 = \cos{(\pi/10 + 2\pi/5)} + i\sin{(\pi/10 + 2\pi/5)}$$
$$= \cos{(\pi/2)} + i\sin{(\pi/2)} = i$$
$$z_2 = \cos{(\pi/10 + 4\pi/5)} + i\sin{(\pi/10 + 4\pi/5)}$$
$$= \cos{(9\pi/10)} + i\sin{(9\pi/10)}$$

We can easily check z_1:

$$i^5 = (i^2)^2 i = (-1)^2 i = i$$

You can if you prefer use the geometric method to write down z_0 and obtain the other roots using the fact that they are equally spaced around a circle centred at the origin. ∎

10.8 POWER SERIES

These Maclaurin expansions were given in section 8.2 and power series were further discussed in section 9.4.

You will have met the power series expansions for the exponential function and the circular functions (Chapter 8):

$$e^x = 1 + x + \frac{x^2}{2!} + \frac{x^3}{3!} + \ldots$$

$$\cos x = 1 - \frac{x^2}{2!} + \frac{x^4}{4!} - \frac{x^6}{6!} + \ldots$$

$$\sin x = x - \frac{x^3}{3!} + \frac{x^5}{5!} - \frac{x^7}{7!} + \ldots$$

In fact it is possible to take these series representations as the *definitions* of the functions themselves, since the series converge for all $x \in \mathbb{R}$. We should then of course have to derive all the usual properties of the functions.

CONVERGENCE

Suppose s_n is the sum to n terms of a complex series. Then we can extend the concept of convergence to infinite complex series. We say s_n converges to s if and only if $|s_n - s| \to 0$ as $n \to \infty$.

Since $|s_n - s|$ is the distance in the complex plane between the point s_n and the point s we see that, as in the real case, the series is convergent if and only if the distance between s_n and s can be made arbitrarily small merely by choosing n sufficiently large.

We discussed convergence of real series in Chapter 9.

We shall use the real series for e^x, $\cos x$ and $\sin x$ to extend the definitions of these functions to complex arguments by defining

$$e^z = 1 + z + \frac{z^2}{2!} + \frac{z^3}{3!} + \ldots$$

$$\cos z = 1 - \frac{z^2}{2!} + \frac{z^4}{4!} - \frac{z^6}{6!} + \ldots$$

$$\sin z = z - \frac{z^3}{3!} + \frac{z^5}{5!} - \frac{z^7}{7!} + \ldots$$

It can be shown that each of these series converges for all complex numbers z and in such a way that the algebraic identities which we have stated for these functions remain valid.

The series for $\exp z = e^z$ can be used to extend the definition of a^r, where a is a positive real number and $r \in \mathbb{R}$, to a^z where $z \in \mathbb{C}$. We define

$$a^z = e^{z \ln a}$$

Clearly a^z is defined *uniquely* by this formula, and is consistent with our previous definition in the special case when $z = r$, a real number.

We shall avoid attempting a general definition of z^w where z and w are *both* complex numbers. The reason for this is that we must either make a rather arbitrary choice for the definition or extend the definition of a function to allow more than one value to each argument. Each course of action has its own problems, and since the concept of z^w is without practical applications we shall do well to avoid it altogether.

EULER'S FORMULA

We have then

$$e^z = \sum_{r=0}^{\infty} \frac{z^r}{r!}$$

$$\cos z = \sum_{r=0}^{\infty} \frac{(-1)^r z^{2r}}{(2r)!}$$

$$\sin z = \sum_{r=0}^{\infty} \frac{(-1)^r z^{2r+1}}{(2r + 1)!}$$

If we replace z by iz in the series for e^z we obtain

$$e^{iz} = \sum_{k=0}^{\infty} \frac{(iz)^k}{k!}$$

$$= \sum_{r=0}^{\infty} \frac{(iz)^{2r+1}}{(2r + 1)!} + \sum_{r=0}^{\infty} \frac{(iz)^{2r}}{(2r)!}$$

Here we have assumed it is permissible, without affecting the convergence, to rearrange the terms in this series to sum the odd terms first and then the even terms. In fact the exponential series is a particularly tame one, and in this case the procedure can be justified. In general, however, (1) rearranging terms (2) removing or inserting brackets and (3) differentiating or integrating the terms can disturb the convergence of a series. The message as always is clear: infinite series can behave in unexpected ways and so they must be handled with care.

Luckily here we can throw caution to the wind and proceed!

$$e^{iz} = \sum_{k=0}^{\infty} \frac{(iz)^k}{k!}$$

$$= \sum_{r=0}^{\infty} \frac{(iz)^{2r}}{(2r)!} + \sum_{r=0}^{\infty} \frac{(iz)^{2r+1}}{(2r + 1)!}$$

Now

$$(iz)^{2r} = (i)^{2r} z^{2r} = (i^2)^r z^{2r} = (-1)^r z^{2r}$$
$$(iz)^{2r+1} = (i)^{2r+1} z^{2r+1} = (-1)^r i z^{2r+1}$$

So that

$$e^{iz} = \sum_{r=0}^{\infty} \frac{(-1)^r z^{2r}}{(2r)!} + i \sum_{r=0}^{\infty} \frac{(-1)^r z^{2r+1}}{(2r + 1)!}$$

$$= \cos z + i \sin z$$

We use this formula in Chapter 20 when solving differential equations.

That is

$$e^{iz} = \cos z + i \sin z$$

where z is any complex number. This is an important relationship known as **Euler's formula**, and it has many consequences.

Leonhard Euler (1707–1783): prolific Swiss mathematician who made major contributions to algebra, analysis and topology.

For instance if θ is real we obtain

$$e^{i\theta} = \cos \theta + i \sin \theta$$

In particular, if $\theta = \pi$ we have

$$e^{i\pi} = \cos \pi + i \sin \pi = -1$$

This quite remarkable formula relates two transcendental numbers e and π. **Transcendental numbers** are numbers which do not satisfy any polynomial equation with integer coefficients.

CIRCULAR AND HYPERBOLIC FUNCTIONS

Replacing z by $-z$ in Euler's formula gives

$$e^{-iz} = \cos (-z) + i \sin (-z)$$
$$= \cos z - i \sin z$$

So that

$$e^{iz} + e^{-iz} = 2 \cos z$$
$$e^{iz} - e^{-iz} = 2i \sin z$$

Equivalently

$$\cos z = \frac{e^{iz} + e^{-iz}}{2}$$

$$\sin z = \frac{e^{iz} - e^{-iz}}{2i}$$

Now if you remember the definitions of the hyperbolic functions you will notice the striking similarity between these relationships and the definitions

$$\cosh z = \frac{e^{z} + e^{-z}}{2}$$

$$\sinh z = \frac{e^{z} - e^{-z}}{2}$$

Here of course we have extended the domain and codomain of the hyperbolic functions to include all the complex numbers.

In fact there are some simple algebraic relationships between the hyperbolic and the circular functions:

1 $\cosh (iz) = \cos z$

2 $\cos (iz) = \cosh z$

3 $\sinh (iz) = i \sin z$
4 $\sin (iz) = i \sinh z$

These relationships are easy to derive. For instance to establish **4**:

$$\sin (iz) = \frac{e^{i(iz)} - e^{-i(iz)}}{2i}$$

$$= \frac{e^{-z} - e^{z}}{2i}$$

$$= \frac{i^2(e^{z} - e^{-z})}{2i} \qquad (\text{using } i^2 = -1)$$

$$= \frac{i(e^{z} - e^{-z})}{2} = i \sinh z$$

Why not have a go at the others? They are all very similar.

Here is the working. You can check and see if you have chosen the best way.

$$\cos (iz) = \frac{e^{i(iz)} + e^{-i(iz)}}{2}$$

$$= \frac{e^{-z} + e^{z}}{2}$$

$$= \frac{(e^{z} + e^{-z})}{2} = \cosh z$$

$$\cosh (iz) = \cos (i[iz]) = \cos (-z) = \cos z$$
$$\sinh (iz) = -i \sin (i[iz]) = -i \sin (-z) = i \sin z$$

As a result of the relationships between hyperbolic and circular functions it is possible to translate identities between them. For example,

$$\cos 2\theta = 1 - 2 \sin^2 \theta$$

is a well-known identity involving circular functions. So

$$\cos (2iz) = 1 - 2 \sin^2 (iz)$$
$$\cosh 2z = 1 - 2[i \sinh z]^2$$
$$= 1 + 2 \sinh^2 z$$

That is, we have deduced the hyperbolic identity

$$\cosh 2u = 1 + 2 \sinh^2 u$$

Now for some more steps.

_____ 10.9 Workshop_____

▷**Exercise**   Obtain the sixth roots of $32\sqrt{2}\,(1 - i)$.
    Don't forget the easiest way to put a complex number into polar form is to draw a diagram and read off r and θ directly.

We put the complex number $16(1 - i)$ into polar form to obtain

$$32\sqrt{2}\,(1 - i) = 64[\cos(-\pi/4) + i\sin(-\pi/4)]$$

By De Moivre's theorem one of the sixth roots is

$$z_0 = (64)^{1/6}[\cos(-\pi/24) + i\sin(-\pi/24)]$$
$$= 2\,\angle(-\pi/24)$$

The equal spacing property now enables us to write down all the roots:

$$z_0 = 2\,\angle(-\pi/24)$$
$$z_1 = 2\,\angle(-\pi/24 + 2\pi/6) = 2\,\angle(7\pi/24)$$
$$z_2 = 2\,\angle(7\pi/24 + 2\pi/6) = 2\,\angle(15\pi/24)$$
$$z_3 = 2\,\angle(15\pi/24 + 2\pi/6) = 2\,\angle(23\pi/24)$$
$$z_4 = 2\,\angle(23\pi/24 + 2\pi/6) = 2\,\angle(31\pi/24) = 2\,\angle(-17\pi/24)$$
$$z_5 = 2\,\angle(-17\pi/24 + 2\pi/6) = 2\,\angle(-9\pi/24)$$

We can check this by

$$z_6 = 2\,\angle(-9\pi/24 + 2\pi/6)$$
$$= 2\,\angle(-\pi/24) = z_0$$

If that went well then leap ahead to step 4. Otherwise, try this exercise.

▷**Exercise**   Obtain the seventh roots of -1.
    There is nothing new about this problem. You can use the geometrical method or the algebraic method.

For a change we shall use the algebraic method. We begin by putting -1 in polar form:

$$-1 = 1(\cos \pi + i\sin \pi)$$

So that for any integer k

$$-1 = \cos(\pi + 2k\pi) + i\sin(\pi + 2k\pi)$$
$$= \cos(2k + 1)\pi + i\sin(2k + 1)\pi$$

Using De Moivre's theorem we deduce that for every integer k

$$z_k = \cos(2k + 1)\pi/7 + i\sin(2k + 1)\pi/7$$
$$= \exp(2k + 1)i\pi/7$$

is a solution of the equation $z^7 = -1$.

Finally, allowing k to take on seven successive integer values provides us with all the roots:

$$z_{-3} = \exp(-5i\pi/7)$$
$$z_{-2} = \exp(-3i\pi/7)$$
$$z_{-1} = \exp(-i\pi/7)$$
$$z_0 = \exp(i\pi/7)$$
$$z_1 = \exp(3i\pi/7)$$
$$z_2 = \exp(5i\pi/7)$$
$$z_3 = \exp(7i\pi/7) = \exp i\pi = -1$$

It's worth looking out for situations in which we can use this theory. For example, suppose we were required to solve the equation

$$(w - 1)^7 + (w + i)^7 = 0$$

We can rearrange this to give

$$\left(\frac{w - 1}{w + i}\right)^7 = -1$$

Then if we put

$$z = \frac{w - 1}{w + i}$$

we merely need to solve $z^7 = -1$ and then express w in terms of z:

$$z(w + i) = w - 1$$
$$w(z - 1) = -iz - 1$$
$$w = \frac{-iz - 1}{z - 1}$$

Now, if you can manage it, here is a further problem.

4

Exercise   Obtain the general solution of the equation $\sinh z = -2$.
We need to remember that we are in the field of *complex* numbers.

5

Putting $z = x + iy$ we have

$$\sinh z = \sinh(x + iy)$$
$$= \sinh x \cosh iy + \cosh x \sinh iy$$
$$= \sinh x \cos y + \cosh x (i \sin y)$$
$$= \sinh x \cos y + i \cosh x \sin y$$

So that we have

$$-2 = \sinh x \cos y + i \cosh x \sin y$$

and equating real and imaginary parts

$$-2 = \sinh x \cos y$$
$$0 = \cosh x \sin y$$

Now $\cosh x$ is never zero and so we conclude that $\sin y = 0$. So $y = n\pi$, where n is any integer. We then have $\cos y = \cos n\pi = (-1)^n$, and so

$$-2 = (-1)^n \sinh x$$

from which

$$\sinh x = 2(-1)^{n+1}$$

Now

$$x = \sinh^{-1}[2(-1)^{n+1}] = \ln [2(-1)^{n+1} + \sqrt{(4 + 1)}]$$

so that

$$z = \ln [2(-1)^{n+1} + \sqrt{5}] + in\pi \qquad \text{where } n \in \mathbb{N}$$

If you succeeded in solving that problem then you can read through the next one and gloat over your achievement. For those who fell short of the target there is one more hurdle.

▷**Exercise**   Solve the equation $\tan z = i$.
   Don't attempt this until you feel confident that you understand the previous problem.

If we put $z = x + iy$ then we have

$$\tan z = \tan (x + iy)$$
$$= \frac{\tan x + \tan iy}{1 - \tan x \tan iy} = \frac{\tan x + i \tanh y}{1 - i \tan x \tanh y}$$

Therefore

$$(1 - i \tan x \tanh y)i = \tan x + i \tanh y$$
$$i + \tan x \tanh y = \tan x + i \tanh y$$

Equating real and imaginary parts we obtain

$$\tan x \tanh y = \tan x$$
$$1 = \tanh y$$

We conclude that $\tanh y = 1$, which is impossible for $y \in \mathbb{R}$. Consequently there is no $z \in \mathbb{C}$ satisfying the equation $\tan z = i$.

It is now time for us to apply some of this work. Check that you have understood all the material in this chapter. If there are any weak points then concentrate on them before you begin.

10.10 Practical

BALANCED BRIDGE

When the AC bridge shown in Fig. 10.9 is balanced, the complex impedances Z_1, Z_2, Z_3, Z_4 of the arms satisfy

$$Z_1 Z_3 = Z_2 Z_4$$

If the bridge is balanced, determine C and L in terms of R_1, R_2, R_3, C_1 and C_2.

Many electrical and electronic engineers prefer to reserve the symbol i to denote current, and consequently another symbol j is then used instead of the complex number i. We shall employ this notation in this example. We must be flexible about notation so that we can change it whenever the need arises.

If you are familiar with circuit theory you may be able to reach the first stage. If you are not then read it through to obtain the necessary equations.

1 We have the complex impedances

$$Z_1 = R_1 + \frac{1}{j\omega C_1}$$

$$Z_2 = R_2 + \frac{1}{j\omega C_2}$$

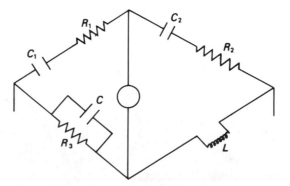

Fig. 10.9 An AC bridge.

$$Z_3 = \frac{1}{(1/R_3) + j\omega C}$$

$$Z_4 = j\omega L$$

Now that you have the necessary ingredients it should be possible for you to complete the solution.

---

2 We have

$$\left(R_1 + \frac{1}{j\omega C_1}\right) \frac{1}{(1/R_3) + j\omega C} = \left(R^2 + \frac{1}{j\omega C_2}\right) j\omega L$$

so that

$$R_1 + \frac{1}{j\omega C_1} = \left(R_2 + \frac{1}{j\omega C_2}\right)\left(\frac{1}{R_3} + j\omega C\right) j\omega L$$

Rationalizing terms:

$$R_1 - j\frac{1}{\omega C_1} = \left(R_2 - \frac{j}{\omega C_2}\right)\left(\frac{j\omega L}{R_3} - \omega^2 L C\right)$$

$$= -R_2\omega^2 L C + \frac{L}{R_3 C_2} + j\left(\frac{R_2\omega L}{R_3} + \frac{\omega L C}{C_2}\right)$$

Now, if you were stuck, take over the working at this stage.

---

3 Equating real and imaginary parts we obtain two equations:

$$R_1 = -R_2\omega^2 L C + \frac{L}{R_3 C_2} \tag{1}$$

$$-\frac{1}{\omega C_1} = \frac{R_2\omega L}{R_3} + \frac{\omega L C}{C_2} \tag{2}$$

From (1) we obtain

$$\frac{R_1}{C_2} = -R_2\omega\left(\frac{\omega L C}{C_2}\right) + \frac{L}{R_3 C_2^2}$$

So using (2) to eliminate C:

$$\frac{R_1}{C_2} = -R_2\omega\left(-\frac{1}{\omega C_1} - \frac{R_2\omega L}{R_3}\right) + \frac{L}{R_3 C_2^2}$$

$$-\frac{R_2}{C_1} + \frac{R_2^2\omega^2 L}{R_3} + \frac{L}{R_3 C_2^2}$$

Therefore to obtain L we have

$$\left(\frac{R_2^2\omega^2}{R_3} + \frac{1}{R_3 C_2^2}\right) L = \frac{R_1}{C_2} - \frac{R_2}{C_1}$$

That is,

$$L = \frac{[(R_1/C_2) - (R_2/C_1)]R_3 C_2^2}{1 + R_2^2 C_2^2 \omega^2}$$

Now see if you can determine C.

---

4 Using (1) we have

$$R_2 \omega^2 LC = \frac{L}{R_3 C_2} - R_1$$

So

$$
\begin{aligned}
C &= \frac{1}{\omega^2 R_2 R_3 C_2} - \frac{R_1}{R_2 \omega^2 L} \\
&= \frac{1}{\omega^2 R_2 R_3 C_2} - \frac{R_1(1 + R_2^2 C_2^2 \omega^2)}{R_2 \omega^2[(R_1/C_2) - (R_2/C_1)]R_3 C_2^2} \\
&= \frac{1}{\omega^2 R_2 R_3 C_2}\left[1 - \frac{R_1(1 + R_2^2 C_2^2 \omega^2)}{R_1 - (R_2/C_1)C_2}\right] \\
&= \frac{1}{\omega^2 R_2 R_3 C_2} \frac{R_1 C_1 - R_2 C_2 - R_1 C_1(1 + R_2^2 C_2^2 \omega^2)}{R_1 C_1 - R_2 C_2} \\
&= \frac{1}{\omega^2 R_2 R_3 C_2} \frac{R_2 C_2 + R_1 R_2^2 C_1 C_2^2 \omega^2}{R_2 C_2 - R_1 C_1} \\
&= \frac{1}{\omega^2 R_3} \frac{1 + R_1 R_2 C_1 C_2 \omega^2}{R_2 C_2 - R_1 C_1}
\end{aligned}
$$

SUMMARY

☐ We defined the complex numbers and showed how to arrange them in the cartesian form $a + ib$.

☐ We expressed complex numbers in polar form $r(\cos \theta + i \sin \theta)$.

☐ We gave two geometrical interpretations of complex numbers: as points in the Argand diagram, and as vectors in the complex plane.

☐ We described and applied De Moivre's theorem

$$(\cos \theta + i \sin \theta)^n = \cos n\theta + i \sin n\theta \quad (n \in \mathbb{Z})$$

☐ We saw how to obtain the nth roots of a complex number. If $z^n = \alpha = r(\cos \theta + i \sin \theta)$ then

$$z = r^{1/n}[\cos(\theta + 2k\pi)/n + i \sin (\theta + 2k\pi)/n]$$

for some integer k.

☐ We obtained the relationships between the circular functions and the hyperbolic functions

a $\cosh (iz) = \cos z$
b $\cos (iz) = \cosh z$
c $\sinh (iz) = i \sin z$
d $\sin (iz) = i \sinh z$

EXERCISES (for answers see p. 747)

1 Express in cartesian form $a + ib$, where a and b are real:
 a $(2 + 3i)(i - 4)^2$
 b $\dfrac{3 + i}{(2 + i)^2}$
 c $\dfrac{1}{2 + i} + \dfrac{i}{1 + 3i}$
 d $\exp (2 + 4i) + i$

2 Express in polar form $r(\cos \theta + i \sin \theta)$ where r and θ are real numbers $(r > 0, 0 \leqslant \theta < 2\pi)$:
 a $2/(\cos \pi/4 + i \sin \pi/4)$
 b $i(1 + i)^2$
 c $(\cos \pi/4 + i \sin \pi/4)^2 + (\cos \pi/2 + i \sin \pi/2)^5$
 d $\exp i$

3 Obtain all complex numbers z which satisfy the equation
 a $z^2 + 4z + 5 = 0$
 b $z^3 + i = (z - i)^3$
 c $z^4 + 2z^2 + 9 = 0$
 d $\dfrac{1}{z + i} + \dfrac{1}{z - i} = i$

4 Describe the set of points in the complex plane for which z satisfies

a $|z - 3i| = 5$

b $|z - i| + |z + i| = 4$

c $\left| \dfrac{z - 2i}{2z - i} \right| = 1$

ASSIGNMENT (for answers see p. 748; see also Workshops on pp. 292 and 303)

1 Express in the form $a + ib$

$$\frac{(1 + i)(2 - 3i)(1 + 4i)}{(3 + 2i)(3 + 5i)}$$

2 Express in polar form

$$\frac{(1 + i)\, i\, (\sqrt{3} - i)}{(1 + i\sqrt{3})(2 - 2i)}$$

3 Solve the equation

$$(z + i)^3 = i(z - i)^3$$

4 Simplify the expression

$$\frac{(\cos\theta - i\sin\theta)^9 (\cos 2\theta + i\sin 2\theta)^4}{(\cos 3\theta + i\sin 3\theta)^6 (\cos 4\theta - i\sin 4\theta)^2}$$

5 Use De Moivre's theorem to express $\cos 4\theta$ and $\sin 4\theta$ in terms of $\cos\theta$ and $\sin\theta$ only.

6 Express the complex expression $\tan(x + iy)$, where x and y are real numbers, in the form $a + ib$.

7 Solve the equation $\sin z = i$.

8 Describe the set of points in the complex plane which satisfy

$$\mathrm{Re}\left(\frac{z + i}{z - i}\right) = 0$$

FURTHER EXERCISES (for answers see p. 748)

1 If P is a point in the Argand diagram representing the complex number z, interpret the following as loci:

a $\arg[(z - 4)/(z + 4)] = \pi/2$

b $|z - i\sqrt{7}| + |z + i\sqrt{7}| = 8$

Determine z if z satisfies both **a** and **b**.

2 a Show that if $|3z - 2| = |z - 6|$ then $|z| = 2$.

b Determine z if $\arg(z + 2) = \pi/3$ and $\arg(z - 2) = 5\pi/6$.

c The centre of a square in the Argand diagram is represented by the complex number $1 + 3i$. Suppose one of the vertices is represented by $3 + 6i$: determine the complex numbers which represent the remaining vertices.

3 a Determine all the solutions of the equation $z^4 + 16 = 0$.
  b Obtain the roots of the equation $z^4 - 9z^2 + 400 = 0$.

4 a By expressing $1 + i\sqrt{3}$ in polar form, or otherwise, calculate $(1 + i\sqrt{3})^{12}$.
  b Obtain all the solutions of the equation $z^4 = 1$ and hence, or otherwise, solve the equation $(w + 1)^4 = (w - 1)^4$.

5 a Solve the equation $z^4 - 11z^2 + 49 = 0$.
  b Show that if $|2z - 5| = |z - 10|$ then $|z| = 5$.

6 Show that if $z = a + ib$ is any complex number,
  a $\mathrm{Re}\,(z) \leqslant |z|$
  b $|z| = |\bar{z}|$
  c $\mathrm{Re}\,(z) = \frac{1}{2}\{z + \bar{z}\}$
  Deduce that, whenever $z_1, z_2 \in \mathbb{C}$,

$$z_1\bar{z}_2 + z_2\bar{z}_1 = 2\,\mathrm{Re}\,(z_1\bar{z}_2) \leqslant 2|z_1 z_2|$$

By considering $(z_1 + z_2)(\bar{z}_1 + \bar{z}_2)$, or otherwise, deduce the triangle inequality

$$|z_1 + z_2| \leqslant |z_1| + |z_2|$$

We first met the triangle inequality in section 1.4. The triangle inequality for vectors is given in Chapter 14, Further exercises 7.

7 The admittance Y of an RC series circuit is given by $1/Y = R + 1/j\omega C$. Show that as ω varies from 0 to ∞ the admittance locus is a circle of radius $1/2R$ which passes through the origin.

8 In a transmission line the voltage reflection equation is

$$(Z - Z_0)/(Z + Z_0) = K \exp j\theta$$

where K is real, $Z = R + jX$ and $Z_0 = R_0 + jX_0$. Show that if $X_0 = 0$ then

$$\tan \theta = 2XR_0/(X^2 + R^2 - R_0^2)$$

9 For a certain network the input impedance is w and the output impedance is z, where $w = (z + j)/(z + 1)$.
  a Express z explicitly in terms of w.
  b Put $z = x + jy$ and $w = u + jv$ and thereby express x and y in terms of u and v.
  c Show that for z pure imaginary ($x = 0$) the input impedance w must lie on a circle.
  d Show that for z real ($y = 0$) the input impedance must lie on a straight line.

10 The impedance Z of an RC parallel circuit is given by $1/Z = 1/R + j\omega C$. Show that as ω varies from 0 to ∞ the impedance locus is a semicircle below the real axis.

11   Matrices

In Chapter 10 we extended our algebraic knowledge by examining some of the properties of complex numbers. In this chapter we continue our algebraic studies by describing a widely used algebraic concept known as a matrix.

After studying this chapter you should be able to
☐ Use matrix notation;
☐ Perform the basic operations of matrix algebra;
☐ Apply the rules of matrix algebra correctly and use the zero matrices O and the identity matrices I;
☐ Write equations in matrix form and solve matrix equations.
At the end of this chapter we shall apply matrix methods to some practical problems in electrical theory.

11.1 NOTATION

Matrices are very useful, for example they are used extensively in the finite element method (structural engineering) and in network analysis (electrical engineering). The general availability of high-speed computers has generated considerable interest in numerical methods and many of these methods use matrices. Wherever large amounts of data need to be handled in a logical and easily accessible manner, matrices prove useful.

What are matrices and where do they come from? You will remember, in elementary algebra, solving sets of simultaneous linear equations. If we were to examine the underlying structure of systems of equations of this kind, we should discover matrix algebra.

Luckily for us we do not have to consider the origins of matrices. We need only learn what they are and how to handle them.

A matrix is a rectangular array of elements arranged in rows and columns. For example,

$$\begin{bmatrix} 2 & 3 & 1 \\ 4 & -2 & 6 \end{bmatrix}$$

is an example of a matrix with two **rows**, three **columns** and six **elements**.

Matrices will be denoted by capital letters, and in general a matrix can be written as

$$A = \begin{bmatrix} a_{11} & a_{12} & a_{13} & \cdots & a_{1n} \\ a_{21} & a_{22} & a_{23} & \cdots & a_{2n} \\ \vdots & \vdots & \vdots & & \vdots \\ a_{m1} & a_{m2} & a_{m3} & \cdots & a_{mn} \end{bmatrix}$$

where the dots indicate elements which have not been displayed.

You will observe that each element in the matrix has been given two subscripts. These subscripts indicate the **address** of the element: the first subscript gives the number of the row, and the second subscript gives the number of the column. We say that the matrix has **order** m by n, which we write as $m \times n$ (in much the same way as carpenters describe the sizes of pieces of wood). We do not evaluate the product $m \times n$, for this would merely give the total number of elements in the matrix and no indication of its shape. For example a carpenter might talk about pieces of 4 by 2, but he would not talk about pieces of 8; that's a different story altogether!

If $m = n$ we say we have a **square matrix** of order n.

The notation

$$A = [a_{i,j}]$$

is a useful shorthand notation when the order of the matrix is known. The element shown is a typical element, for as i and j take on all possible values, each element of the matrix is obtained.

The type of bracket used for matrices is largely a matter of personal choice; some books use parentheses.

A matrix which has just one row or column is called an **algebraic vector**; so a matrix which has just one row is called a **row vector**, and a matrix with just one column is called a **column vector**. Vector notation is sometimes employed, so that algebraic vectors are denoted by **x** or **y**.

☐   **Example**

$$\begin{bmatrix} 2 \\ 3 \\ 4 \end{bmatrix} \qquad [1,5,7,1] \qquad [0,0,0]$$

These are respectively a column vector with three elements, a row vector with four elements and a row vector with three elements. ■

There is a convention which you may come across, known as the printer's convention (because it preserves text line spacing), in which a column vector is written horizontally as if it were a row vector! The fact that it is really a column vector is indicated by reserving curly brackets for the purpose. Thus {4, 2, 6, 1} may be used to represent the column vector

This convention should be used with caution, particularly if there is a possibility of confusion with a *set* of elements. We shall avoid its use altogether.

11.2 MATRIX ALGEBRA

EQUALITY

Two matrices A and B are **equal** and we write $A = B$ if and only if
1 A and B have the same order (i.e. the same size and shape);
2 Corresponding elements are equal.
We may write this more formally if we wish in the following way. Suppose that A and B are two matrices of order $m \times n$ and $r \times s$ respectively, and that $A = [a_{i,j}]$ and $B = [b_{i,j}]$. Then $A = B$ if and only if
1 $r = m$ and $s = n$;
2 $a_{i,j} = b_{i,j}$ for all i and j.
Don't be worried if you find this algebraic definition a little difficult at first. Compare it carefully with our informal definition and try to understand it.
   The definition of equality of matrices enables us to write a set of several algebraic equations by means of a single matrix equation.

Example □ Deduce the values of x, y and z if

$$\begin{bmatrix} x + y \\ y + z \\ x + z \end{bmatrix} = \begin{bmatrix} 4 \\ 6 \\ 8 \end{bmatrix}$$

See if you can do this. The working is given below.

_____

We obtain the three equations

$$x + y = 4$$
$$y + z = 6$$
$$x + z = 8$$

If we add all three equations and divide by 2 we obtain

$$x + y + z = 9$$

so that $x = 3$, $y = 1$ and $z = 5$. ■

Did you manage that? Let's continue! Now that we have decided when two matrices are equal, we consider how to add two matrices.

ADDITION

Two matrices are compatible for addition if and only if they have the *same order*. Addition is then performed by adding corresponding elements.

In symbols, suppose $A = [a_{i,j}]$ and $B = [b_{i,j}]$ are of order $m \times n$ and $r \times s$ respectively. Then $A + B$ exists if and only if $r = m$ and $s = n$, and

$$A + B = [c_{i,j}]$$

where

$$c_{i,j} = a_{i,j} + b_{i,j}$$

Once more try to follow this algebraic definition by comparing it with the working definition which is given above it.

Clearly if $A + B$ exists then $B + A$ also exists and the two are equal. We emphasize this because later when we introduce the operation of multiplication of matrices we shall see that generally AB and BA are *not* equal.

□ Obtain x, y, z and w if **Example**

$$\begin{bmatrix} 2x & -y - 1 \\ y & x \end{bmatrix} + \begin{bmatrix} -4x & 2y \\ x & y - 1 \end{bmatrix} = \begin{bmatrix} y & -z \\ -w & 0 \end{bmatrix}$$

Give this example a try. It gives a test of equality and addition. The correct working is given below.

We obtain

$$\begin{bmatrix} -2x & -y - 1 + 2y \\ y + x & x + y - 1 \end{bmatrix} = \begin{bmatrix} y & -z \\ -w & 0 \end{bmatrix}$$

From which $-2x = y$, $y - 1 = -z$, $y + x = -w$ and $x + y - 1 = 0$. It follows that $x = -1$, $y = 2$, $z = -1$ and $w = -1$. ■

So far so good!

TRANSPOSITION

The transpose A^T (or A') of a matrix A is obtained from A by interchanging each of its rows with each of its corresponding columns. So if A is of order $m \times n$ then the **transpose** of A is of order $n \times m$.

Example ☐ If

$$A = \begin{bmatrix} 2 & 1 & 3 \\ 4 & 6 & 5 \end{bmatrix} \quad \text{then} \quad A^\mathrm{T} = \begin{bmatrix} 2 & 4 \\ 1 & 6 \\ 3 & 5 \end{bmatrix}$$ ∎

In general we have $(A^\mathrm{T})^\mathrm{T} = A$. Note also that if $\mathbf{x}$ is a column vector then $\mathbf{x}^\mathrm{T}$ is a row vector. So the use of this concept obviates the need for the printer's convention.

More formally, if $A = [a_{i,j}]$ then $A^\mathrm{T} = [b_{i,j}]$, where $b_{i,j} = a_{j,i}$ for $i \in \{1, \ldots, n\}$ and $j \in \{1, \ldots, m\}$. If this algebraic form of the definition causes difficulties, try to understand it but don't be over-concerned.

SCALAR MULTIPLICATION

Any matrix A can be multiplied by any number. The multiplication is performed by multiplying every element in the matrix by the number. The numbers are often called scalars.

In symbols, if $A = [a_{i,j}]$ is a matrix of order $n \times m$ and k is a scalar then

$$kA = k[a_{i,j}] = [ka_{i,j}]$$

Example ☐ If

$$A = \begin{bmatrix} 2 & 1 \\ 3 & 4 \end{bmatrix} \quad B = \begin{bmatrix} 1 & 5 \\ 2 & 3 \end{bmatrix}$$

then

$$3A = \begin{bmatrix} 6 & 3 \\ 9 & 12 \end{bmatrix} \quad 4B = \begin{bmatrix} 4 & 20 \\ 8 & 12 \end{bmatrix}$$ ∎

MATRIX MULTIPLICATION

The rule for matrix multiplication is more complicated, and so we introduce it in two stages.

Stage 1
Suppose $\mathbf{x}$ and $\mathbf{y}$ are a row vector and a column vector respectively, each with the same number of elements. Specifically, let us suppose

$$\mathbf{x} = [x_1, \ldots, x_n] \qquad \mathbf{y} = \begin{bmatrix} y_1 \\ y_2 \\ \vdots \\ y_n \end{bmatrix}$$

Then we define

$$\mathbf{xy} = [x_1, \ldots, x_n] \begin{bmatrix} y_1 \\ y_2 \\ \vdots \\ y_n \end{bmatrix} = x_1 y_1 + x_2 y_2 + \ldots + x_n y_n$$

□   **Example**

$$[4, 3, 2] \begin{bmatrix} 6 \\ 7 \\ 5 \end{bmatrix} = 4 \times 6 + 3 \times 7 + 2 \times 5 = 24 + 21 + 10 = 55 \quad ∎$$

The order in which we write down these vectors is important. We have defined the product **xy** but we have not yet defined the product **yx**. When we do so, we shall see that the two are *not* equal.

Stage 2
We are now in a position to consider the general rule for multiplying two matrices A and B together to form a product AB. As a precondition we require that the number of columns of A equals the number of rows of B. If this precondition is not satisfied then the product AB will not be defined.

Suppose then that A has order $r \times s$ and that B has order $s \times t$. We regard the matrix A as made up of row vectors and the matrix B as made up of column vectors. We shall initially use dashed lines to help us to visualize this.

□ Let   **Example**

$$A = \begin{bmatrix} 1 & 4 & 7 \\ 2 & 3 & 5 \end{bmatrix} \qquad B = \begin{bmatrix} 1 & -1 & 2 \\ 2 & 1 & 0 \\ 3 & 0 & 4 \end{bmatrix}$$

We have

$$AB = \begin{bmatrix} 1 & 4 & 7 \\ \hline 2 & 3 & 5 \end{bmatrix} \begin{bmatrix} 1 & \vdots & -1 & \vdots & 2 \\ 2 & \vdots & 1 & \vdots & 0 \\ 3 & \vdots & 0 & \vdots & 4 \end{bmatrix}$$

Now the product AB has, in its ith row and jth column position, the product of the ith row of A with the jth column of B viewed as vectors.

For example, using the first row of A and the first column of B,

$$[1 \ 4 \ 7] \begin{bmatrix} 1 \\ 2 \\ 3 \end{bmatrix} = 1 \times 1 + 4 \times 2 + 7 \times 3 = 1 + 8 + 21 = 30$$

It follows that AB has 30 as the element in the first row and first column, that is the position $(1, 1)$.

Consequently,

$$AB = \begin{bmatrix} 1 & 4 & 7 \\ \hline 2 & 3 & 5 \end{bmatrix} \begin{bmatrix} 1 & -1 & 2 \\ 2 & 1 & 0 \\ 3 & 0 & 4 \end{bmatrix}$$

$$= \begin{bmatrix} 1 + 8 + 21 & -1 + 4 + 0 & 2 + 0 + 28 \\ 2 + 6 + 15 & -2 + 3 + 0 & 4 + 0 + 20 \end{bmatrix}$$

$$= \begin{bmatrix} 30 & 3 & 30 \\ 23 & 1 & 24 \end{bmatrix} \qquad \blacksquare$$

So that in general, if A has order $r \times s$ and B has order $s \times t$, then AB has order $r \times t$.

We shall sometimes write A^2 for AA, and in general $A^{n+1} = A^n A$ when $n \in \mathbb{N}$, $n > 1$.

We can write the matrix multiplication rule in symbols if we wish. Suppose $A = [a_{ij}]$ and $B = [b_{ij}]$. Then

$$AB = [c_{ij}]$$

where

$$c_{ij} = \sum_{k=1}^{s} a_{ik} b_{kj}$$

$$= a_{i1} b_{1j} + a_{i2} b_{2j} + \ldots + a_{is} b_{sj}$$

The summation sign Σ should cause no problems. Remember, it means we let k take on every possible integer value from 1 to s, and then add up all the terms.

As we can see, the rule is more involved and less intuitive than the other rules. However, it is quite simple to apply and you will be surprised how quickly you can get used to it.

One small point: you remember that when we multiplied a row vector by a column vector we obtained a number. However, if we use this definition we obtain a 1×1 matrix. One way round this slight contradiction is to say that we shall regard 1×1 matrices as numbers.

It can be shown that the **associative law**

$$A(BC) = (AB)C$$

holds whenever these products are defined. You should not assume that this rule is self-evident, however. It is the notation and the use of the word 'product' which may lead you to this erroneous conclusion. You have already met several examples of non-associative operations. For example, ordinary division for real numbers is non-associative: (3/2)/5 is not equal to 3/(2/5).

To reinforce the fact that we need to exercise caution when carrying out algebraic operations using objects with which we are unfamiliar, we remark that for matrices A and B the products AB and BA are not in general equal. In fact, we have a precondition that may not be satisfied in both cases, so that only one of the products may exist. If, however, A is of order $r \times s$ and B is of order $s \times r$ then AB is a square matrix of order r and BA is a square matrix of order s. Now matrices cannot be equal unless they have the same order, so that before we can even begin to consider equality we must have $r = s$. Even this is not enough to ensure equality! If A and B are both square matrices of order r then in general

$$AB \neq BA$$

Matrices for which $AB = BA$ are said to **commute**. This is a comparatively rare event!

You will come across another situation where the associative law does not hold when you meet the vector product in section 14.12.

!

Now we shall make sure we have our ideas straight.

11.3 Workshop

We shall use the following matrices to step through some exercises:

$$A = \begin{bmatrix} 1 & 3 \\ 6 & 1 \end{bmatrix} \qquad B = \begin{bmatrix} 1 & 3 & 1 \\ 2 & 1 & 5 \end{bmatrix} \qquad C = \begin{bmatrix} 1 & 3 \\ -1 & 1 \\ 2 & 4 \end{bmatrix}$$

$$D = \begin{bmatrix} 2 & 1 \\ 5 & 4 \end{bmatrix} \qquad E = \begin{bmatrix} 1 & 1 \\ 2 & 1 \end{bmatrix}$$

▷**Exercise**   Without evaluating them, write down all possible products of pairs of distinct matrices from the list which include the matrix A. (For instance, if you think AC exists include AC in your list, but if you believe that CA does not exist exclude CA from your list.) In each case write the order of the product alongside.

When you have completed this, look at the next step to see if you have the right answers!

2 Here are the correct answers:

$$AB \ (2 \times 3)$$
$$AD \ (2 \times 2)$$
$$AE \ (2 \times 2)$$
$$CA \ (3 \times 2)$$
$$DA \ (2 \times 2)$$
$$EA \ (2 \times 2)$$

Did you manage to get them all right? If you did then move on to step 5. If you made some mistakes, check back carefully to see the precondition for matrix multiplication and the rule for calculating the order of a product. Then solve this next problem.

▷ **Exercise** Write down a list of all the products of two matrices which have B as one of them. As before, write alongside the order of each product.

As soon as you have finished, take the next step to see if you are right.

3 Here are the answers:

$$BC \ (2 \times 2)$$
$$CB \ (3 \times 3)$$
$$DB \ (2 \times 3)$$
$$EB \ (2 \times 3)$$

If they are all right then move on to step 5. If there are still a few difficulties you should go back carefully over what we have done and then try this problem.

▷ **Exercise** If we consider pairs of distinct matrices from our original list, there are still four which we have not listed. Say which these are and give the orders of these products.

When you have completed this, look at the list in the next step.

4 Here are the answers:

$$CD \ (3 \times 2)$$
$$CE \ (3 \times 2)$$

$$DE \; (2 \times 2)$$
$$ED \; (2 \times 2)$$

Now let's move on to matrix multiplication.

5

▷**Exercise**   Obtain AB, AD, BC, AE, CD and DE.
   Try these, then look at the next step to see if you have all the answers right.

6

Here are the correct results:

$$AB = \begin{bmatrix} 1 & 3 \\ \hline 6 & 1 \end{bmatrix} \begin{bmatrix} 1 & 3 & 1 \\ 2 & 1 & 5 \end{bmatrix} = \begin{bmatrix} 7 & 6 & 16 \\ 8 & 19 & 11 \end{bmatrix}$$

$$AD = \begin{bmatrix} 1 & 3 \\ \hline 6 & 1 \end{bmatrix} \begin{bmatrix} 2 & 1 \\ 5 & 4 \end{bmatrix} = \begin{bmatrix} 17 & 13 \\ 17 & 10 \end{bmatrix}$$

$$BC = \begin{bmatrix} 1 & 3 & 1 \\ \hline 2 & 1 & 5 \end{bmatrix} \begin{bmatrix} 1 & 3 \\ -1 & 1 \\ 2 & 4 \end{bmatrix} = \begin{bmatrix} 0 & 10 \\ 11 & 27 \end{bmatrix}$$

$$AE = \begin{bmatrix} 1 & 3 \\ \hline 6 & 1 \end{bmatrix} \begin{bmatrix} 1 & 1 \\ 2 & 1 \end{bmatrix} = \begin{bmatrix} 7 & 4 \\ 8 & 7 \end{bmatrix}$$

$$CD = \begin{bmatrix} 1 & 3 \\ -1 & 1 \\ 2 & 4 \end{bmatrix} \begin{bmatrix} 2 & 1 \\ 5 & 4 \end{bmatrix} = \begin{bmatrix} 17 & 13 \\ 3 & 3 \\ 24 & 18 \end{bmatrix}$$

$$DE = \begin{bmatrix} 2 & 1 \\ \hline 5 & 4 \end{bmatrix} \begin{bmatrix} 1 & 1 \\ 2 & 1 \end{bmatrix} = \begin{bmatrix} 4 & 3 \\ 13 & 9 \end{bmatrix}$$

If you have these all correct then you can proceed to step 8. If some of the products didn't work out, try this next exercise.

▷**Exercise**   Calculate the products CA, CB, DA, DB, ED.
   When you have finished, check in step 7 to see if you have them right.

7

Here are the answers:

$$CA = \begin{bmatrix} 1 & 3 \\ -1 & 1 \\ 2 & 4 \end{bmatrix} \begin{bmatrix} 1 & 3 \\ 6 & 1 \end{bmatrix} = \begin{bmatrix} 1{\times}1{+}3{\times}6 & 1{\times}3{+}3{\times}1 \\ -1{\times}1{+}1{\times}6 & -1{\times}3{+}1{\times}1 \\ 2{\times}1{+}4{\times}6 & 2{\times}3{+}4{\times}1 \end{bmatrix} = \begin{bmatrix} 19 & 6 \\ 5 & -2 \\ 26 & 10 \end{bmatrix}$$

$$CB = \begin{bmatrix} 1 & 3 \\ \hline -1 & 1 \\ \hline 2 & 4 \end{bmatrix} \begin{bmatrix} 1 & 3 & 1 \\ 2 & 1 & 5 \end{bmatrix} = \begin{bmatrix} 7 & 6 & 16 \\ 1 & -2 & 4 \\ 10 & 10 & 22 \end{bmatrix}$$

$$DA = \begin{bmatrix} 2 & 1 \\ \hline 5 & 4 \end{bmatrix} \begin{bmatrix} 1 & 3 \\ 6 & 1 \end{bmatrix} = \begin{bmatrix} 8 & 7 \\ 29 & 19 \end{bmatrix}$$

$$DB = \begin{bmatrix} 2 & 1 \\ \hline 5 & 4 \end{bmatrix} \begin{bmatrix} 1 & 3 & 1 \\ 2 & 1 & 5 \end{bmatrix} = \begin{bmatrix} 4 & 7 & 7 \\ 13 & 19 & 25 \end{bmatrix}$$

$$ED = \begin{bmatrix} 1 & 1 \\ \hline 2 & 1 \end{bmatrix} \begin{bmatrix} 2 & 1 \\ 5 & 4 \end{bmatrix} = \begin{bmatrix} 7 & 5 \\ 9 & 6 \end{bmatrix}$$

There we are! Now step ahead.

8

Exercise Among the matrices we have been considering, there are two that commute. Find out which they are!

When you have done this, read on and see if you are right. It shouldn't take too long!

9

Here is the solution. We have seen that for two matrices to commute, they must both be square and have the same order. Therefore the only ones we need to consider are A, D and E. The products AD, AE, DA, ED and DE have already been found, and so there remains only EA to find:

$$EA = \begin{bmatrix} 1 & 1 \\ \hline 2 & 1 \end{bmatrix} \begin{bmatrix} 1 & 3 \\ 6 & 1 \end{bmatrix} = \begin{bmatrix} 7 & 4 \\ 8 & 7 \end{bmatrix} = AE$$

Consequently A and E commute.

11.4 MATRIX EQUATIONS

The simplest way to deal with this subject is by example.

Suppose we want to write the following equations in matrix form and thereby obtain u and v in terms of x, y and z:

$$\begin{aligned} u &= 3p + 4q & p &= 2x + 3y - z \\ v &= p - 3q & q &= x - y + 2z \end{aligned}$$

We have

$$\begin{bmatrix} u \\ v \end{bmatrix} = \begin{bmatrix} 3 & 4 \\ 1 & -3 \end{bmatrix} \begin{bmatrix} p \\ q \end{bmatrix}$$

and

$$\begin{bmatrix} p \\ q \end{bmatrix} = \begin{bmatrix} 2 & 3 & -1 \\ 1 & -1 & 2 \end{bmatrix} \begin{bmatrix} x \\ y \\ z \end{bmatrix}$$

These matrix equations may be verified easily by multiplying out and using the rule for equality. Observe that in each case the matrix consists of the coefficients and that it is multiplied by a column vector of the unknowns. So, writing

$$\mathbf{u} = \begin{bmatrix} u \\ v \end{bmatrix} \qquad \mathbf{p} = \begin{bmatrix} p \\ q \end{bmatrix} \qquad \mathbf{x} = \begin{bmatrix} x \\ y \\ z \end{bmatrix}$$

with

$$A = \begin{bmatrix} 3 & 4 \\ 1 & -3 \end{bmatrix} \qquad B = \begin{bmatrix} 2 & 3 & -1 \\ 1 & -1 & 2 \end{bmatrix}$$

we have

$$\mathbf{u} = A\mathbf{p} \quad \text{and} \quad \mathbf{p} = B\mathbf{x}$$

So substituting for **p** we have

$$\mathbf{u} = A(B\mathbf{x}) = (AB)\mathbf{x}$$

using the associative law. Now

$$AB = \begin{bmatrix} 3 & 4 \\ 1 & -3 \end{bmatrix} \begin{bmatrix} 2 & 3 & -1 \\ 1 & -1 & 2 \end{bmatrix} = \begin{bmatrix} 10 & 5 & 5 \\ -1 & 6 & -7 \end{bmatrix}$$

So that

$$\begin{bmatrix} u \\ v \end{bmatrix} = \begin{bmatrix} 10 & 5 & 5 \\ -1 & 6 & -7 \end{bmatrix} \begin{bmatrix} x \\ y \\ z \end{bmatrix}$$

Therefore

$$u = 10x + 5y + 5z$$
$$v = -x + 6y - 7z$$

Matrix methods for solving equations are used in the theory of structures.

Of course, we know we could have solved this problem by using elementary algebra. The point is that we have now developed matrix algebra to such an extent that we have an alternative method. This is just the beginning of the story.

11.5 ZERO, IDENTITY AND INVERSE MATRICES

Any matrix that has all its elements zero is called a **zero matrix** or a **null matrix** and is denoted by O. Once we decide on the order of the zero matrix, for example 3×2, then the zero matrix is uniquely determined.

Example □ The 3×2 zero matrix is

$$\begin{bmatrix} 0 & 0 \\ 0 & 0 \\ 0 & 0 \end{bmatrix}$$

■

If A is any matrix and O is the zero matrix of the same order as A then $A + O = A$.

We do not usually need to emphasize the order of O since its context clarifies the position. However, when we do need to show the order we write it underneath, as in the next example.

Example □

$$\begin{array}{ccc} A & O & = & O \\ 3 \times 2 & 2 \times 5 & & 3 \times 5 \end{array}$$

■

Observe how the rule for matrix multiplication determines the order of the zero matrix on the right once the order of the zero matrix on the left is given.

If we have a square matrix, the set of elements on the diagonal from the top left-hand corner to the bottom right-hand corner is known as the **leading diagonal**. Any square matrix which has its only non-zero elements on the leading diagonal is known as a **diagonal matrix**. Such a matrix is uniquely determined by the leading diagonal, so that

$$A = \text{diag } \{a, b, c, d\}$$

is a 4×4 matrix in which the elements on the leading diagonal are a, b, c and d respectively. That is,

$$A = \begin{bmatrix} a & 0 & 0 & 0 \\ 0 & b & 0 & 0 \\ 0 & 0 & c & 0 \\ 0 & 0 & 0 & d \end{bmatrix}$$

Any square matrix which has all the elements on the leading diagonal equal to 1 and all other elements 0 is known as an **identity matrix** and is represented by I.

☐ The 3 × 3 identity matrix is   **Example**

$$\begin{bmatrix} 1 & 0 & 0 \\ 0 & 1 & 0 \\ 0 & 0 & 1 \end{bmatrix} = \text{diag}\{1, 1, 1\}$$ ■

Suppose that A is an $n \times m$ matrix. Then we can easily show that

$$\begin{array}{ccccc} A & I & = & I & A & = & A \\ n \times m & m \times m & & n \times n & n \times m & & n \times m \end{array}$$

☐ Check this relation with the matrix   **Example**

$$A = \begin{bmatrix} 2 & 5 & 6 \\ 4 & 3 & 1 \end{bmatrix}$$ ■

Another name for the identity matrix is the **unit matrix**. The equation $AI = A = IA$ shows that in matrix algebra I plays much the same role as the number 1 does in elementary algebra.

The consideration of algebraic equations leads to a further important type of matrix. Take, for example,

$$ax + by = h$$
$$cx + dy = k$$

We have seen how to write these in matrix form:

$$\begin{bmatrix} a & b \\ c & d \end{bmatrix} \begin{bmatrix} x \\ y \end{bmatrix} = \begin{bmatrix} h \\ k \end{bmatrix}$$

or alternatively by the single matrix equation $A\mathbf{x} = \mathbf{h}$.

Suppose now that we can find another matrix B such that $BA = I$. Then if we pre-multiply both sides by B we obtain

$$B(A\mathbf{x}) = B\mathbf{h}$$
$$(BA)\mathbf{x} = B\mathbf{h}$$

That is,

$$I\mathbf{x} = B\mathbf{h}$$
$$\mathbf{x} = B\mathbf{h}$$

Consequently, this set of simultaneous equations can be solved, using matrices, if we can obtain the matrix B. The matrix B, for which $BA = I = AB$, is known as the **inverse** of the matrix A (see Chapter 13). Although we shall see later that not every square matrix has an inverse, the quest for inverses leads us to the study of determinants in the next chapter.

We examine the question of inverse matrices, in detail, in section 13.1.

As you know, any point in the plane can be expressed uniquely using rectangular cartesian coordinates as an ordered pair of numbers (x, y). If we write this as a column vector and pre-multiply it by a 2×2 real matrix we obtain another point. So any 2×2 real matrix can be regarded as a transformation of the plane to itself. Similarly any 3×3 real matrix can be regarded as a transformation of three-dimensional space to itself.

11.6 ALGEBRAIC RULES

These rules will have added significance for us when we study linear operators in Chapter 22.

Finally we state without further ado the algebraic rules which matrices obey. In each case we shall suppose that the matrices which appear in the equations are of the correct order so that the equations are meaningful.

1 $(A + B) + C = A + (B + C)$: addition is associative.
2 $A + B = B + A$: addition is commutative.
3 $A + O = O + A = A$: zero matrices exist.
4 $A(BC) = (AB)C$: multiplication is associative.
5 $AI = IA = A$: unit matrices exist. (Unless A is square the two matrices denoted by I will have different orders.)
6 $A(B + C) = (AB) + (AC)$: multiplication is distributive over addition.
7 $k(AB) = (kA)B = A(kB)$ where k is a scalar.

Perhaps the most important rules to remember are the following:

8 In general $AB \neq BA$.
9 If $AB = O$ it does *not* necessarily follow that either $A = O$ or $B = O$.

Example □

$$\begin{bmatrix} 1 & 1 \\ 2 & 2 \end{bmatrix} \begin{bmatrix} -1 & 1 \\ 1 & -1 \end{bmatrix} = \begin{bmatrix} 0 & 0 \\ 0 & 0 \end{bmatrix}$$ ∎

This means that we must be extra careful when multiplying by matrices to keep the order in which we are to perform the operations clear. We either **pre-multiply** or **post-multiply** by a matrix.

We cannot 'cancel out' matrix equations in the same way as we cancel out equations involving real or complex numbers.

Example □

$$\begin{bmatrix} -1 & 1 \\ 1 & -1 \end{bmatrix} \begin{bmatrix} 0 & 2 \\ 2 & 4 \end{bmatrix} = \begin{bmatrix} 2 & 2 \\ -2 & -2 \end{bmatrix}$$

Also

$$\begin{bmatrix} -1 & 1 \\ 1 & -1 \end{bmatrix}\begin{bmatrix} -2 & -1 \\ 0 & 1 \end{bmatrix} = \begin{bmatrix} 2 & 2 \\ -2 & -2 \end{bmatrix}$$

so that

$$\begin{bmatrix} -1 & 1 \\ 1 & -1 \end{bmatrix}\begin{bmatrix} 0 & 2 \\ 2 & 4 \end{bmatrix} = \begin{bmatrix} -1 & 1 \\ 1 & -1 \end{bmatrix}\begin{bmatrix} -2 & -1 \\ 0 & 1 \end{bmatrix}$$

but

$$\begin{bmatrix} 0 & 2 \\ 2 & 4 \end{bmatrix} \neq \begin{bmatrix} -2 & -1 \\ 0 & 1 \end{bmatrix} \qquad \blacksquare$$

Now let's apply some of the work we have done to a practical problem.

_____ **11.7 Practical** _____

ELECTRICAL NETWORKS

Obtain the transmission matrices for the circuits shown in Fig. 11.1(a) and (b). Use these to obtain the transmission matrix for the network in Fig. 11.1(c).

We shall solve this problem stage by stage. If you are not an electrical engineering student you may not be concerned with the underlying theory. If this is the case you may skip over the derivations of the series and shunt transmission matrices.

The transmission matrix is determined by the circuit configuration and is used to relate the output conditions to the input conditions.

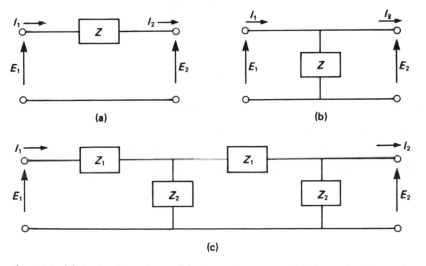

Fig. 11.1 (a) Series impedance (b) Shunt impedance (c) Cascade of impedances.

For the series impedance (Fig. 11.1(a)) we have

$$E_1 = E_2 + ZI_2$$
$$I_1 = I_2$$

When we write these equations in matrix form we obtain the transmission matrix:

$$\begin{bmatrix} E_1 \\ I_1 \end{bmatrix} = \begin{bmatrix} 1 & Z \\ 0 & 1 \end{bmatrix} \begin{bmatrix} E_2 \\ I_2 \end{bmatrix}$$

where

$$\begin{bmatrix} 1 & Z \\ 0 & 1 \end{bmatrix}$$

is the transmission matrix.

See if you can write down the transmission matrix for the shunt impedance before moving on.

For the shunt impedance (Fig. 11.1(b)) we have

$$E_1 = E_2$$
$$I_1 = (1/Z)E_2 + I_2$$

So in matrix form we have

$$\begin{bmatrix} E_1 \\ I_1 \end{bmatrix} = \begin{bmatrix} 1 & 0 \\ 1/Z & 1 \end{bmatrix} \begin{bmatrix} E_2 \\ I_2 \end{bmatrix}$$

where the transmission matrix is

$$\begin{bmatrix} 1 & 0 \\ 1/Z & 1 \end{bmatrix}$$

The network shown in Fig. 11.1(c) can be regarded as a cascade of series and shunt impedances as in Fig. 11.2. For each impedance we use the matrix equations

$$\begin{bmatrix} E_1 \\ I_1 \end{bmatrix} = \begin{bmatrix} a & b \\ c & d \end{bmatrix} \begin{bmatrix} E_2 \\ I_2 \end{bmatrix}$$

where

$$\begin{bmatrix} a & b \\ c & d \end{bmatrix}$$

is one of the two types of transmission matrix obtained.

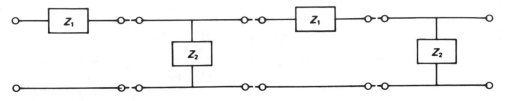

Fig. 11.2 Cascade of series and shunt impedances.

To obtain the transmission matrix of the whole network we put all the individual matrices together:

$$
\begin{bmatrix} E_1 \\ I_1 \end{bmatrix} = \begin{bmatrix} 1 & Z_1 \\ 0 & 1 \end{bmatrix} \begin{bmatrix} 1 & 0 \\ 1/Z_2 & 1 \end{bmatrix} \begin{bmatrix} 1 & Z_1 \\ 0 & 1 \end{bmatrix} \begin{bmatrix} 1 & 0 \\ 1/Z_2 & 1 \end{bmatrix} \begin{bmatrix} E_2 \\ I_2 \end{bmatrix}
$$

$$
= \begin{bmatrix} 1 + Z_1/Z_2 & Z_1 \\ 1/Z_2 & 1 \end{bmatrix} \begin{bmatrix} 1 + Z_1/Z_2 & Z_1 \\ 1/Z_2 & 1 \end{bmatrix} \begin{bmatrix} E_2 \\ I_2 \end{bmatrix}
$$

$$
= \begin{bmatrix} (1 + Z_1/Z_2)^2 + Z_1/Z_2 & Z_1(1 + Z_1/Z_2) + Z_1 \\ (1/Z_2)(1 + Z_1/Z_2) + 1/Z_2 & (Z_1/Z_2) + 1 \end{bmatrix} \begin{bmatrix} E_2 \\ I_2 \end{bmatrix}
$$

Therefore the transmission matrix is

$$
\begin{bmatrix} (1 + Z_1/Z_2)^2 + Z_1/Z_2 & Z_1(2 + Z_1/Z_2) \\ (1/Z_2)(2 + Z_1/Z_2) & 1 + Z_1/Z_2 \end{bmatrix}
$$

SUMMARY

☐ We have introduced matrices and explained the concepts of
   a equality of matrices
   b matrix addition
   c transposition of matrices
   d scalar multiplication
   e matrix multiplication
   f the matrices O and I.
☐ We have seen how to write a set of simultaneous linear equations in matrix form.
☐ We have listed the rules which matrices obey.
☐ We have seen that if a set of algebraic equations is expressed in the form $A\mathbf{x} = \mathbf{h}$ in which A is a square matrix, and if we can find a matrix B such that $BA = I$, then $\mathbf{x} = B\mathbf{h}$ and the equations are solved.

EXERCISES (for answers see p. 748)

The following exercises use the matrices

$$A = \begin{bmatrix} 1 & 2 \\ -1 & 3 \end{bmatrix} \qquad B = \begin{bmatrix} 1 & 3 \\ -2 & 4 \end{bmatrix}$$

$$C = \begin{bmatrix} -3 & 2 \\ 1 & -4 \end{bmatrix} \qquad D = \begin{bmatrix} 1 & -2 \\ -1 & 2 \end{bmatrix}$$

1 Calculate

a $A + B$　　　　　　　**b** $(A + B)C$　　　　　　**c** $(A^T + B^T)^T$

d $AD + BD$　　　　　　**e** $D^T D$　　　　　　　　**f** DD^T

2 If U, V and W are square matrices, obtain the expansion of $(U + V + W)^2$ and check your expansion in the case $U = A$, $V = B$, $W = C$.

3 Obtain the matrix X in each of the following:

a $A + X = B - X$

b $A + X = I$

c $(A + X)^T = B$

d $(A + X)C = I$

e $(A - X)B = C^T$

f $AX = BX + C$

4 Obtain the diagonal matrix X which satisfies

$$(AX)(BX)^T = D$$

ASSIGNMENT (for answers see p. 749; see also Workshop on p. 319)

1 Obtain the values of x and y if the matrix

$$A = \begin{bmatrix} \cos w & x \\ \sin w & y \end{bmatrix}$$

satisfies the equation $AA^T = I$, where A^T is the transpose of A.

2 By considering the matrices

$$A = \begin{bmatrix} 1 & 1 & 2 \\ 3 & 2 & -1 \\ 4 & 1 & 2 \end{bmatrix} \qquad B = \begin{bmatrix} 2 & -1 \\ 4 & 2 \\ 3 & -1 \end{bmatrix}$$

verify the identity $(AB)^T = B^T A^T$.

3 a Identify the matrices diag $\{1, 1\}$ and diag $\{0, 0, 0\}$.

b Show that if A = diag $\{a, b, c, d\}$ and B = diag $\{h, k, l, m\}$ then

$$AB = BA = \text{diag } \{ah, bk, cl, dm\}$$

Obtain also A^n.

4 Expand (a) $(A + B)^2$ (b) $(A + 2B)^2$ and check the expansions obtained with

$$A = \begin{bmatrix} 1 & 3 \\ 2 & 6 \end{bmatrix} \qquad B = \begin{bmatrix} 1 & 4 \\ 3 & 2 \end{bmatrix}$$

5 A square matrix M is **symmetric** if and only if it is equal to its transpose. Obtain a, b and c if

$$A = \begin{bmatrix} 3 & a & -1 \\ 2 & 5 & c \\ b & 8 & 2 \end{bmatrix}$$

is symmetric.

6 A square matrix M is **skew symmetric** if and only if $M^T = -M$. Obtain a, b, c, d, e and f if

$$A = \begin{bmatrix} a & 3 & e \\ d & b & f \\ -2 & 6 & c \end{bmatrix}$$

is skew symmetric.

7 Given the matrices

$$A = \begin{bmatrix} 1 & x & 1 \\ x & 2 & y \\ 1 & y & 3 \end{bmatrix} \qquad B = \begin{bmatrix} 3 & -3 & z \\ -3 & 2 & -3 \\ z & -3 & 1 \end{bmatrix}$$

obtain x, y and z if AB is symmetric. Show that A and B commute.

FURTHER EXERCISES (for answers see p. 749)

1 If

$$A = \begin{bmatrix} 1 & 2 & 1 \\ 2 & 4 & 2 \\ 3 & 6 & 3 \end{bmatrix} \qquad B = \begin{bmatrix} 1 & -3 & -2 \\ -1 & 2 & 1 \\ 1 & -1 & 0 \end{bmatrix}$$

verify that $AB = O$.

2 If $AB = O$ and $BC = I$ prove that

$$(A + B)^2(A + C)^2 = I$$

3 Show that if

$$A = \begin{bmatrix} 1 & 2 & 3 \\ 3 & 7 & 9 \\ 4 & 8 & 13 \end{bmatrix} \qquad B = \begin{bmatrix} 19 & -2 & -3 \\ -3 & 1 & 0 \\ -4 & 0 & 1 \end{bmatrix}$$

then $AB = BA = I$. Hence, or otherwise, solve each of the following systems of equations:

a $x + 2y + 3z = 1$
$3x + 7y + 9z = 4$
$4x + 8y + 13z = 3$

b $x + 3y + 4z = 2$
$2x + 7y + 8z = 6$
$3x + 9y + 13z = 4$

4 In atomic physics the Pauli spin matrices are

$$S_1 = \begin{bmatrix} 0 & 1 \\ 1 & 0 \end{bmatrix} \qquad S_2 = \begin{bmatrix} 0 & -i \\ i & 0 \end{bmatrix} \qquad S_3 = \begin{bmatrix} 1 & 0 \\ 0 & -1 \end{bmatrix}$$

where $i^2 = -1$. Verify

a $S_1 S_2 = i S_3$
b $S_2 S_1 = -i S_3$
c $S_1^2 = S_2^2 = S_3^2 = I$

5 Obtain the transmission matrices of the three cascade circuits shown in Fig. 11.3.

6 If there exists a positive integer n such that $A^n = 0$ then the square matrix A is said to be **nilpotent**. Verify that

$$A = \begin{bmatrix} 0 & 1 & a \\ 0 & 0 & 1 \\ 0 & 0 & 0 \end{bmatrix}$$

is nilpotent.

7 Show that if A is any square matrix then
a AA^T is symmetric;
b $A + A^T$ is symmetric;
c $A - A^T$ is skew symmetric.
Verify this general property by considering the matrix

$$A = \begin{bmatrix} 1 & 2 & 3 \\ 4 & 5 & 6 \\ 7 & 8 & 9 \end{bmatrix}$$

8 Suppose

$$A = \begin{bmatrix} 5 & 11 & 4 \\ 2 & 9 & 5 \\ 3 & 6 & 2 \end{bmatrix} \qquad B = \begin{bmatrix} -12 & 2 & 19 \\ 11 & -2 & -17 \\ -15 & 3 & 23 \end{bmatrix}$$

a Verify that $AB = I = BA$.
b Use **a** and the rules of matrices to write down $A^T B^T$.
c Use **a** and **b** to write each of the following systems in matrix form and thereby solve them:

i $-12x + 2y + 19z = 1$
$11x - 2y - 17z = 2$

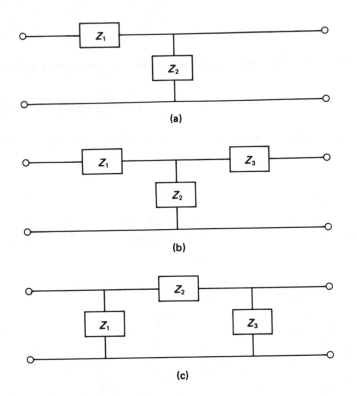

Fig. 11.3 Cascades of impedances.

$$-15x + 3y + 23z = 3$$

ii $\quad -12u + 11v - 15w = 1$
$$2u - 2v + 3w = 2$$
$$19u - 17v + 23w = 3$$

9 If $1 + \alpha + \alpha^2 = 0$, show that $\alpha^3 = 1$. Hence or otherwise show that if

$$A = \begin{bmatrix} 1 & 1 & 1 \\ 1 & \alpha^2 & \alpha \\ 1 & \alpha & \alpha^2 \end{bmatrix} \qquad B = \frac{1}{3}\begin{bmatrix} 1 & 1 & 1 \\ 1 & \alpha & \alpha^2 \\ 1 & \alpha^2 & \alpha \end{bmatrix}$$

then $AB = I$.

Three inputs e_1, e_2 and e_3 are expressed in terms of three outputs E_1, E_2 and E_3 by

$$e_1 = E_1 + E_2 + E_3$$
$$e_2 = E_1 + \alpha^2 E_2 + \alpha E_3$$
$$e_3 = E_1 + \alpha E_2 + \alpha^2 E_3$$

Express E_1, E_2 and E_3 explicitly in terms of e_1, e_2 and e_3.

12 Determinants

In Chapter 11 we explained what is meant by a matrix and examined the elementary properties of matrices. To take the story any further we shall need the concept of a determinant; the subject of this next chapter.

After you have completed this chapter you should be able to
☐ Distinguish between matrices and determinants;
☐ Evaluate determinants;
☐ Use Cramer's rule;
☐ Calculate minors and cofactors;
☐ Simplify determinants.
At the end of this chapter we shall apply determinants to the practical problem of a Wheatstone bridge.

12.1 NOTATION

A determinant is a number which is calculated from the elements in a square matrix. If we have a square matrix, we may represent its determinant using the row and column notation of matrices. To distinguish the two concepts we enclose the elements of a determinant between vertical parallel lines. We can write the determinant of the square matrix A as either $|A|$ or det A.

Example ☐

$$A = \begin{bmatrix} 1 & 3 \\ 2 & 4 \end{bmatrix} \qquad \det A = \begin{vmatrix} 1 & 3 \\ 2 & 4 \end{vmatrix}$$

∎

The rule for evaluating a determinant is best introduced by considering the simplest cases. If A is a 1×1 matrix, then the determinant of A is merely the element itself.

☐ If $A = [-3]$ then $\det A = -3$.   ■ **Example**

In this instance the notation $|A|$ is unfortunate because it could become confused with the modulus sign. Luckily 1×1 determinants are so trivial they seldom arise.

Things are slightly more straightforward when we consider determinants of order two. We define

$$\begin{vmatrix} a_{11} & a_{12} \\ a_{21} & a_{22} \end{vmatrix} = a_{11}a_{22} - a_{21}a_{12}$$

☐   **Example**

$$\begin{vmatrix} \cosh u & \sinh u \\ \sinh u & \cosh u \end{vmatrix} = \cosh^2 u - \sinh^2 u = 1 \qquad ■$$

The rule is: top left times bottom right minus bottom left times top right.

The rule itself may seem rather strange and arbitrary. To see why it is like this, consider the following pair of simultaneous equations:

$$ax + by = h$$
$$cx + dy = k$$

If we perform elementary algebraic operations on these equations to express x and y explicitly in terms of h and k, we obtain

$$x = \frac{hd - kb}{ad - cb} \qquad y = \frac{ak - ch}{ad - cb}$$

We can write these equations in terms of second-order determinants as follows:

$$x = \frac{\begin{vmatrix} h & b \\ k & d \end{vmatrix}}{\begin{vmatrix} a & b \\ c & d \end{vmatrix}} \qquad y = \frac{\begin{vmatrix} a & h \\ c & k \end{vmatrix}}{\begin{vmatrix} a & b \\ c & d \end{vmatrix}}$$

12.2 CRAMER'S RULE

Gabriel Cramer (1704–1752): Swiss mathematician who revived the subject of determinants.

In fact these equations provide us with an algebraic method for solving equations, known as **Cramer's rule**:

1 Write down the equations with the constants on the right-hand side:

$$a_{11}x_1 + a_{12}x_2 = h_1$$
$$a_{21}x_1 + a_{22}x_2 = h_2$$

2 Calculate Δ, the determinant of the coefficients of the unknowns:

$$\Delta = \begin{vmatrix} a_{11} & a_{12} \\ a_{21} & a_{22} \end{vmatrix} = a_{11}a_{22} - a_{21}a_{12}$$

3 To obtain one of the unknowns, cover up its coefficients in the equations and imagine them to have been replaced by the corresponding constants from the right-hand side. Evaluate the determinant of the fictitious coefficients and equate it to the product of the unknown with Δ.

If you look carefully at the rule you will be able to see how to apply it easily. Try this example; the working is given below.

Example □ Obtain x and y explicitly in terms of u and v when

$$x \cos w + y \sin w = u$$
$$-x \sin w + y \cos w = v$$

Using Cramer's rule, we obtain

$$\Delta = \begin{vmatrix} \cos w & \sin w \\ -\sin w & \cos w \end{vmatrix} = \cos^2 w + \sin^2 w = 1$$

Therefore

$$\Delta x = x = \begin{vmatrix} u & \sin w \\ v & \cos w \end{vmatrix} = u \cos w - v \sin w$$

$$\Delta y = y = \begin{vmatrix} \cos w & u \\ -\sin w & v \end{vmatrix} = v \cos w + u \sin w$$

So

$$x = u \cos w - v \sin w$$
$$y = v \cos w + u \sin w$$

■

Cramer's rule extends to n equations in n unknowns and can be useful for dealing with purely algebraic systems. However, there are much more efficient ways of solving such systems of equations when the coefficients are numerical.

12.3 HIGHER-ORDER DETERMINANTS

We now turn our attention to determinants of order three:

$$\begin{vmatrix} a_{11} & a_{12} & a_{13} \\ a_{21} & a_{22} & a_{23} \\ a_{31} & a_{32} & a_{33} \end{vmatrix}$$

Before seeing how to evaluate this determinant, we shall consider an operation which can be performed either on a square matrix or on a determinant.

If the row and column in which an element is situated are deleted and the resulting determinant is evaluated, the result is known as the **minor** of the element. The minor of a_{ij} is represented by M_{ij}.

□   **Example**

$$A = \begin{bmatrix} 3 & 2 & 1 \\ 4 & 6 & -1 \\ 2 & 1 & 3 \end{bmatrix}$$

Then

$$M_{22} = \begin{vmatrix} 3 & 1 \\ 2 & 3 \end{vmatrix} = 9 - 2 = 7$$

$$M_{31} = \begin{vmatrix} 2 & 1 \\ 6 & -1 \end{vmatrix} = -2 - 6 = -8$$

When every element is replaced by its minor we obtain the **matrix of minors** M. In this example,

$$M = \begin{bmatrix} 19 & 14 & -8 \\ 5 & 7 & -1 \\ -8 & -7 & 10 \end{bmatrix}$$

Check these calculations carefully and see if you agree!   ■

An idea closely associated with that of a minor is that of a **cofactor**. This is sometimes known as the **signed minor** because it has the same absolute value as the minor. We define

$$A_{ij} = (-1)^{i+j} M_{ij}$$

This rule is by no means as complicated as it looks. We see that
1 If $i + j$ is odd then $(-1)^{i+j} = -1$;
2 If $i + j$ is even then $(-1)^{i+j} = 1$.

So that to obtain the cofactor we take the minor, and if $i + j$ is odd we change its sign, whereas if $i + j$ is even we leave it as it is. That is,

$$A_{ij} = M_{ij} \quad \text{if } i + j \text{ is even}$$
$$A_{ij} = -M_{ij} \quad \text{if } i + j \text{ is odd}$$

An easy way to see whether or not to change the sign of a minor when calculating the cofactor is to note that the rule provides us with a sign convention:

$$\begin{bmatrix} + & - & + & - & + & . & . & . \\ - & + & - & + & . & . & . & . \\ + & . & . & . & . & . & . & . \\ . & . & & & & & & \\ . & . & & & & & & \end{bmatrix}$$

where $+$ indicates that the sign is unchanged, and $-$ indicates that the sign must be changed.

We now return to the evaluation of the third-order determinant:

$$\begin{vmatrix} a_{11} & a_{12} & a_{13} \\ a_{21} & a_{22} & a_{23} \\ a_{31} & a_{32} & a_{33} \end{vmatrix} = a_{11}M_{11} - a_{12}M_{12} + a_{13}M_{13} = a_{11}A_{11} + a_{12}A_{12} + a_{13}A_{13}$$

In fact we can evaluate this determinant in terms of the elements in any row or any column provided we multiply each element by its appropriate cofactor and add the results. So, for instance,

$$|A| = a_{12}A_{12} + a_{22}A_{22} + a_{32}A_{32}$$
$$= a_{31}A_{31} + a_{32}A_{32} + a_{33}A_{33}$$

Check this carefully from the previous example.

It will help to fix the ideas of minor and cofactor in your mind so that you can be sure you know the difference. Here is an example for you to try.

Example □ Evaluate the determinant given below by using **a** the elements of the second row **b** the elements of the third column:

$$\begin{vmatrix} 8 & 7 & 6 \\ 3 & 9 & 1 \\ 2 & 2 & 4 \end{vmatrix}$$

Here is the working:

a $|A| = a_{21}A_{21} + a_{22}A_{22} + a_{23}A_{23}$

$$= -3 \times \begin{vmatrix} 7 & 6 \\ 2 & 4 \end{vmatrix} + 9 \times \begin{vmatrix} 8 & 6 \\ 2 & 4 \end{vmatrix} - \begin{vmatrix} 8 & 7 \\ 2 & 2 \end{vmatrix}$$

$$= -3(7 \times 4 - 6 \times 2) + 9(8 \times 4 - 2 \times 6) + (-1)(8 \times 2 - 2 \times 7)$$

$$= (-3) \times 16 + 9 \times 20 - 2 = -48 + 180 - 2 = 130$$

b $|A| = a_{13}A_{13} + a_{23}A_{23} + a_{33}A_{33}$

$$= 6 \times \begin{vmatrix} 3 & 9 \\ 2 & 2 \end{vmatrix} - \begin{vmatrix} 8 & 7 \\ 2 & 2 \end{vmatrix} + 4 \times \begin{vmatrix} 8 & 7 \\ 3 & 9 \end{vmatrix}$$

$$= 6(6 - 18) - (16 - 14) + 4(72 - 21)$$

$$= -72 - 2 + 204 = 130 \qquad\blacksquare$$

Although we shall have little need to evaluate determinants of order higher than three, we remark that the same rule applies:
1 Select any row or any column;
2 Multiply each element in it by its cofactor;
3 Obtain the total.
As we can see, to evaluate a fourth-order determinant we shall have to evaluate four determinants of order three. This is equivalent to evaluating twelve determinants of order two. Similarly, to evaluate a fifth-order determinant requires the evaluation of sixty determinants of order two. The evaluation of determinants of high order is therefore a very inefficient way of using a computer, and should be avoided.

MIXED COFACTORS

One curious property of determinants is that if we multiply each element in a row by the corresponding cofactor in another row, the sum is always zero. We shall need this property a little later, and so it is worth illustrating it.

☐ In the previous example the cofactors of the second row were $-16, 20$ **Example** and -2 respectively. Therefore using these with the elements in the first row gives

$$8 \times (-16) + 7 \times 20 + 6 \times (-2) = 0$$

Likewise with the elements in the third row we obtain

$$2 \times (-16) + 2 \times 20 + 4 \times (-2) = 0$$

as claimed.   ■

☐ Check this property for the columns by using the cofactors of the third **Example** column with the elements in columns 1 and 2 in turn.   ■

12.4 RULES FOR DETERMINANTS

From time to time we shall need to evaluate third-order determinants. A number of rules have been devised which enable us to simplify determinants before we evaluate them. Of course, we know that if we change the elements in a matrix, we obtain a different matrix. However, we should remember that a determinant can be *evaluated*; it is a number, and it is possible for several ostensibly different determinants to have the same value. It is this property which is used to both theoretical and practical advantage when determinants are simplified before being evaluated.

Rule 1 The value of a determinant is the same as the value of its transpose.

In other words if we interchange each of the rows with each of the corresponding columns, the value of the determinant does not change.

Example □ Check that the determinants of these two matrices are the same:

$$\begin{bmatrix} 2 & 3 & 4 \\ 5 & 11 & 6 \\ 7 & -4 & 8 \end{bmatrix} \qquad \begin{bmatrix} 2 & 5 & 7 \\ 3 & 11 & -4 \\ 4 & 6 & 8 \end{bmatrix}$$ ∎

Of course, this rule by itself is not going to simplify the numbers inside the determinant. However, it does tell us the mathematical equivalent of 'What's sauce for the goose is sauce for the gander', or in this case 'What's true for rows is true for columns'! So for any statement we make about the rows of a determinant there is a corresponding statement about the columns of a determinant.

Rule 2 If two rows of a determinant are interchanged then the determinant changes sign.

For example, if a determinant had the value 54 then, were we to interchange two of its rows, the new determinant would have the value −54.
  For instance, if we evaluate the determinant

$$\begin{vmatrix} 1 & 3 & 7 \\ 2 & 9 & 6 \\ 5 & 4 & 9 \end{vmatrix}$$

we obtain the number −166. Again, if we interchange the second and third rows we obtain

$$\begin{vmatrix} 1 & 3 & 7 \\ 5 & 4 & 9 \\ 2 & 9 & 6 \end{vmatrix}$$

which you should be able easily to verify has the value 166.

One useful consequence of this rule is that if a determinant has two rows the same, then it must be zero. This is easy to see if we consider the effect of interchanging the equal rows. On the one hand the determinant has not been changed at all, and yet on the other hand, by rule 2, the determinant has changed signs. Consequently $D = -D$ and so $2D = 0$; therefore $D = 0$. This is a very useful rule, so let us repeat it:

If a determinant has two identical rows or two identical columns, it is zero.

Rule 3 A determinant may be multiplied by a number by selecting any single row (or column) and multiplying all its elements by the number. So

$$3 \times \begin{vmatrix} 2 & 1 & 2 \\ 1 & 2 & 3 \\ 4 & -1 & 6 \end{vmatrix} = \begin{vmatrix} 6 & 1 & 2 \\ 3 & 2 & 3 \\ 12 & -1 & 6 \end{vmatrix}$$

Here we have multiplied all the elements in the first column by 3.

There are two important points to note here:

1 The rule is in marked contrast to the rule for multiplying a matrix by a number (where every element in the matrix must be multiplied by the number).
2 The principal application of the rule is its reverse. That is, we simplify the arithmetic by taking out a common factor from a row or a column.

!

□   **Example**

$$\begin{vmatrix} 18 & 9 & 4 \\ 6 & 15 & 12 \\ 12 & 3 & 16 \end{vmatrix} = 6 \times \begin{vmatrix} 3 & 9 & 4 \\ 1 & 15 & 12 \\ 2 & 3 & 16 \end{vmatrix}$$

$$= 6 \times 3 \times \begin{vmatrix} 3 & 3 & 4 \\ 1 & 5 & 12 \\ 2 & 1 & 16 \end{vmatrix}$$

$$= 6 \times 3 \times 4 \times \begin{vmatrix} 3 & 3 & 1 \\ 1 & 5 & 3 \\ 2 & 1 & 4 \end{vmatrix}$$

Here we have taken out factors from the first column, second column and third column in turn. ■

Rule 4 The value of a determinant is unchanged if a constant multiple of the elements of a chosen row is added to the corresponding elements of another row.

Of course, the constant multiple can be negative, so it is possible to subtract a multiple of one row from another row. This is illustrated by the following example: the new notation is explained after the example.

Example □

$$
\begin{vmatrix} 1 & 2 & 3 \\ 2 & 3 & 4 \\ 4 & 5 & 6 \end{vmatrix} = \begin{vmatrix} 1 & 2 & 3 \\ 0 & -1 & -2 \\ 4 & 5 & 6 \end{vmatrix} \qquad (r2 = r2 - 2r1)
$$

$$
= \begin{vmatrix} 1 & 2 & 3 \\ 0 & -1 & -2 \\ 0 & -3 & -6 \end{vmatrix} \qquad (r3 = r3 - 4r1)
$$

$$
= 3 \times \begin{vmatrix} 1 & 2 & 3 \\ 0 & -1 & -2 \\ 0 & -1 & -2 \end{vmatrix} = 0 \qquad \text{(two equal rows)} \qquad ■
$$

With practice it is often possible to perform several of these operations at the same time. In order to check back it is important to record, alongside the determinant, the operations which have been performed. In this way can easily check for errors. Notice also the use of this strange notation. For example, $r2 = r2 - 2r1$ means the new row 2 is equal to the old row 2 minus twice the old row 1. The equality sign is used here in the same way as it is used in computer programming. Columns are referred to by the letter c.

One word of warning: when using this rule you must keep the row you are subtracting fixed. This can easily be overlooked if you attempt several operations of this kind together. The best way to check that your operations are valid is to see if they could all take place in a logical sequence, one at a time.

Here is an example for you to try. There are many ways of doing the problem; one way is shown below.

Example □ Simplify and thereby evaluate the determinant

$$
\begin{vmatrix} 13 & 15 & 18 \\ 15 & 17 & 21 \\ 14 & 16 & 27 \end{vmatrix}
$$

Here is a solution:

$$
\begin{vmatrix} 13 & 15 & 18 \\ 15 & 17 & 21 \\ 14 & 16 & 27 \end{vmatrix} = \begin{vmatrix} 13 & 15 & 18 \\ 2 & 2 & 3 \\ 1 & 1 & 9 \end{vmatrix} \qquad \begin{array}{l} (r2 = r2 - r1) \\ (r3 = r3 - r1) \end{array}
$$

$$
= 3 \times \begin{vmatrix} 13 & 15 & 6 \\ 2 & 2 & 1 \\ 1 & 1 & 3 \end{vmatrix} \qquad (c3 = c3/3)
$$

$$
= 3 \times \begin{vmatrix} 13 & 15 & 6 \\ 0 & 0 & -5 \\ 1 & 1 & 3 \end{vmatrix} \qquad (r2 = r2 - 2r3)
$$

$$
= 3 \times [-(-5)] \times \begin{vmatrix} 13 & 15 \\ 1 & 1 \end{vmatrix} = -30 \qquad \blacksquare
$$

☐ Solve the equation   **Example**

$$
\begin{vmatrix} w^2 - 1 & w + 1 & w - 1 \\ w + 1 & w - 1 & w + 1 \\ w - 1 & 2w & 0 \end{vmatrix} = 0
$$

We are looking for all values of w which satisfy this equation. We should be very unwise to multiply out the determinant straight away because this would result in an equation of the fourth degree and solutions might be difficult to spot. Instead we use the rules for simplifying determinants:

$$
\begin{vmatrix} w^2 - 1 & 2w & w - 1 \\ w + 1 & 2w & w + 1 \\ w - 1 & 2w & 0 \end{vmatrix} = 0 \qquad (c2 = c2 + c3)
$$

$$
2w \begin{vmatrix} w^2 - 1 & 1 & w - 1 \\ w + 1 & 1 & w + 1 \\ w - 1 & 1 & 0 \end{vmatrix} = 0 \qquad (c2 = c2/2w)
$$

$$
2w \begin{vmatrix} w^2 - w & 0 & w - 1 \\ w + 1 & 1 & w + 1 \\ w - 1 & 1 & 0 \end{vmatrix} = 0 \qquad (r1 = r1 - r3)
$$

$$
2w(w - 1) \begin{vmatrix} w & 0 & 1 \\ w + 1 & 1 & w + 1 \\ w - 1 & 1 & 0 \end{vmatrix} = 0 \qquad (c1 = c1/(w - 1))
$$

$$
2w(w - 1) \begin{vmatrix} w - 1 & 0 & 1 \\ 0 & 1 & w + 1 \\ w - 1 & 1 & 0 \end{vmatrix} = 0 \qquad (c1 = c1 - c3)
$$

$$2w(w - 1)^2 \begin{vmatrix} 1 & 0 & 1 \\ 0 & 1 & w + 1 \\ 1 & 1 & 0 \end{vmatrix} = 0 \qquad (c1 = c1/(w - 1))$$

Expanding the determinant in terms of the first column gives

$$2w(w - 1)^2[-(w + 1) + (-1)] = 2w(w - 1)^2(-w - 2) = 0$$

So that $w = 0$, $w = 1$ (repeated root) or $w = -2$.   ∎

Before we leave this section we remark that if A and B are square matrices of order n then the product AB is also square of order n. The following rule holds:

$$\det AB = \det A \det B$$

Therefore the same rule that we used for multiplying matrices together can be used for multiplying determinants.

Example □ Check this property with the matrices

$$\begin{bmatrix} 2 & 3 & -5 \\ 1 & -1 & 6 \\ 4 & 2 & 3 \end{bmatrix} \qquad \begin{bmatrix} 1 & 3 & 9 \\ 4 & -2 & 6 \\ -1 & 5 & 7 \end{bmatrix}$$ ∎

Here are some steps for you to take to check that everything is all right.

12.5 Workshop

1

Exercise Using Cramer's rule, express u and v explicitly in terms of $t(t \neq -1)$ from the following:

$$\begin{aligned} tu \quad + (2t + 1)v &= (t + 1)^2 \\ (t - 1)u + \quad 2tv &= t(t + 1) \end{aligned}$$

Try it, then move to step 2 for the solution.

2 We obtain

$$\begin{aligned} \Delta &= \begin{vmatrix} t & 2t + 1 \\ t - 1 & 2t \end{vmatrix} \\ &= 2t^2 - (t - 1)(2t + 1) \\ &= 2t^2 - (2t^2 - t - 1) \\ &= t + 1 \end{aligned}$$

Now

$$\Delta u = (t + 1)u = \begin{vmatrix} (t + 1)^2 & 2t + 1 \\ t(t + 1) & 2t \end{vmatrix}$$

$$= (t + 1)^2 2t - t(t + 1)(2t + 1)$$

$$= (t^2 + 2t + 1)2t - t(2t^2 + 3t + 1)$$

$$= 2t^3 + 4t^2 + 2t - 2t^3 - 3t^2 - t$$

$$= t^2 + t = t(t + 1)$$

Consequently $u = t$. To obtain v, either substitute u into one of the equations or use Cramer's rule again. You should obtain $v = 1$.

If you were successful then move straight on to step 3. Otherwise, here is a similar problem to try.

▷**Exercise**   Solve, using Cramer's rule,

$$3x + 2y = 1$$
$$4x - y = 5$$

You should obtain $\Delta = -11$ and thereby the correct result $x = 1$ and $y = -1$.

If you came unstuck with the first exercise, go back and give it another go before going on to step 3.

▷**Exercise**   Evaluate the determinant

◰ **3**

$$\begin{vmatrix} 2 & 1 & -1 \\ 3 & 0 & 1 \\ 1 & 2 & 2 \end{vmatrix}$$

in terms of the second row and the second column.

Try it, then step ahead.

First, expanding in terms of the second row the determinant is

◰ **4**

$$-3 \begin{vmatrix} 1 & -1 \\ 2 & 2 \end{vmatrix} + 0 \begin{vmatrix} 2 & -1 \\ 1 & 2 \end{vmatrix} - 1 \begin{vmatrix} 2 & 1 \\ 1 & 2 \end{vmatrix}$$

$$= -3[2 - (-2)] + 0 - (2 \times 2 - 1 \times 1)$$

$$= -3 \times 4 - 4 + 1 = -12 - 4 + 1 = -15$$

Next, expanding in terms of the second column the determinant is

$$(-1) \begin{vmatrix} 3 & 1 \\ 1 & 2 \end{vmatrix} + 0 \begin{vmatrix} 2 & -1 \\ 1 & 2 \end{vmatrix} - 2 \begin{vmatrix} 2 & -1 \\ 3 & 1 \end{vmatrix}$$

$$= (-1)(3 \times 2 - 1 \times 1) + 0 - 2[2 \times 1 - 3 \times (-1)]$$

$$= (-1)(6 - 1) - 2(2 + 3)$$
$$= (-1) \times 5 - 2 \times 5 = -5 - 10 = -15$$

Don't forget the sign convention. Of course, if there are zero elements in the row or column we do not normally bother to write down the minors which correspond to them, because their contribution to the value of the determinant is zero.

If you got this one right, move ahead to step 5. If not, try this similar problem.

▷**Exercise** Evaluate the following determinant in terms of the third row and the second column:

$$\begin{vmatrix} 3 & 5 & 1 \\ 2 & 1 & 0 \\ 1 & 4 & -1 \end{vmatrix}$$

The answer is 14.
Now step forward.

5 **Exercise** Simplify, and thereby evaluate, the determinant

$$\begin{vmatrix} 15 & 20 & 28 \\ 28 & 42 & 59 \\ 21 & 32 & 45 \end{vmatrix}$$

Have a go, then step ahead.

6 There are many ways of proceeding. Here is one of them.
Fix the first row and subtract multiples of it from the others:

$$\begin{vmatrix} 15 & 20 & 28 \\ -2 & 2 & 3 \\ 6 & 12 & 17 \end{vmatrix} \quad \begin{array}{l} (r2 = r2 - 2r1) \\ (r3 = r3 - r1) \end{array}$$

Now fix the second column and subtract multiples from the others. We are trying to produce zeros and reduce the large numbers:

$$\begin{vmatrix} 35 & 20 & 8 \\ 0 & 2 & 1 \\ 18 & 12 & 5 \end{vmatrix} \quad \begin{array}{l} (c1 = c1 + c2) \\ (c3 = c3 - c2) \end{array}$$

We can produce a second zero in the second row:

$$\begin{vmatrix} 35 & 4 & 8 \\ 0 & 0 & 1 \\ 18 & 2 & 5 \end{vmatrix} \quad (c2 = c2 - 2c3)$$

$$= (-1)\begin{vmatrix} 35 & 4 \\ 18 & 2 \end{vmatrix}$$

$$= (-1)(70 - 72) = 2$$

If all is well you may move on to step 7. If not, check back carefully. Are you remembering to keep a note of the operations you have been using?

Now try this exercise.

▷**Exercise** Simplify the following determinant and then evaluate it:

$$\begin{vmatrix} 18 & 23 & 32 \\ 32 & 41 & 59 \\ 25 & 32 & 47 \end{vmatrix}$$

The correct answer is 3.

Now let's check that we can use these operations algebraically.

▷**Exercise** Solve the equation

7

$$\begin{vmatrix} 2x - 3 & 3x - 5 & 4x - 8 \\ 3x - 5 & 5x - 9 & 6x - 12 \\ 4x - 6 & 6x - 10 & 9x - 19 \end{vmatrix} = 0$$

Try it, then step forward for the solution.

Here is one way of solving this problem. There are alternative approaches, but it would be unwise to evaluate the determinant straight away because this would result in a cubic equation which on occasions might be difficult to solve.

8

There are no obvious factors, and so we look to see whether or not subtracting rows or columns will produce any. Alternatively we should like to produce some zeros.

We have, using r2 = r2 − r1 and r3 = r3 − 2r1,

$$\begin{vmatrix} 2x - 3 & 3x - 5 & 4x - 8 \\ x - 2 & 2x - 4 & 2x - 4 \\ 0 & 0 & x - 3 \end{vmatrix} = 0$$

This enables us to take out the factor $x - 3$ from the third row and the factor $x - 2$ from the second row. We obtain

$$(x-2)(x-3)\begin{vmatrix} 2x-3 & 3x-5 & 4x-8 \\ 1 & 2 & 2 \\ 0 & 0 & 1 \end{vmatrix} = 0$$

Therefore

$$(x-2)(x-3)[2(2x-3)-(3x-5)] = 0$$
$$(x-2)(x-3)(x-1) = 0$$

so that $x = 1$, $x = 2$ or $x = 3$.

If you got it right, move on to the next section. If not, have a go at another one of these exercises.

▷**Exercise** Solve the equation

$$\begin{vmatrix} 6u+1 & 3u+1 & 2u+1 \\ 9u+1 & 5u+1 & 3u+1 \\ 14u+4 & 7u+3 & 5u+3 \end{vmatrix} = 0$$

The correct answer is $u = 1$, $u = 0$ or $u = -1$.

Here now is a problem which can be solved by using determinants.

12.6 Practical

ELECTRICAL BRIDGE

Charles Wheatstone (1802–1878): British physicist. Coinventor of the electric telegraph and inventor of the electric clock.

A Wheatstone bridge (Fig. 12.1) has the following set of equations for the loop currents i_1, i_2 and i_3:

$$i_1 r_1 + (i_1 - i_2)R_4 + (i_1 - i_3)R_3 = E$$
$$(i_1 - i_3)R_3 - i_3 R_1 - (i_3 - i_2)r_2 = 0$$
$$(i_1 - i_2)R_4 + (i_3 - i_2)r_2 - i_2 R_2 = 0$$

When the bridge is balanced, no current flows through r_2. Show that $R_1 R_4 = R_2 R_3$ when the bridge is balanced.

See if you can sort this out using Cramer's rule. We shall tackle the problem stage by stage.

The first thing to realize is that we are interested in i_1, i_2 and i_3, so that these are the 'unknowns' in our equations. Therefore we rewrite the equations in this form:

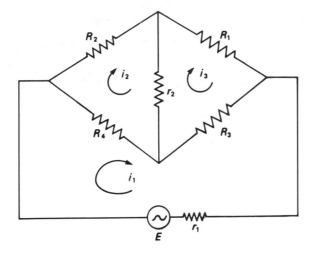

Fig. 12.1 A Wheatstone bridge.

$$(r_1 + R_4 + R_3)i_1 - R_4 i_2 - R_3 i_3 = E$$
$$R_3 i_1 + r_2 i_2 - (R_1 + R_3 + r_2)i_3 = 0$$
$$R_4 i_1 - (R_2 + R_4 + r_2)i_2 + r_2 i_3 = 0$$

Now use Cramer's rule delicately. We don't need it with all its weight.

We can argue in the following way. When the bridge is balanced there is no current through r_2 and so $i_2 = i_3$. Therefore $\Delta i_2 = \Delta i_3$. We do not need to calculate Δ itself, only Δi_2 and Δi_3. Write down the determinants Δi_2 and Δi_3 and see if you can complete the solution.

By Cramer's rule

$$\Delta i_2 = \begin{vmatrix} r_1 + R_4 + R_3 & E & -R_3 \\ R_3 & 0 & -(R_1 + R_3 + r_2) \\ R_4 & 0 & r_2 \end{vmatrix}$$

$$\Delta i_3 = \begin{vmatrix} r_1 + R_4 + R_3 & -R_4 & E \\ R_3 & r_2 & 0 \\ R_4 & -(R_2 + R_4 + r_2) & 0 \end{vmatrix}$$

When the bridge is balanced we can equate these two determinants. Do this and then check the final stage.

We expand the determinant Δi_2 in terms of the second column and the determinant Δi_3 in terms of the third column:

$$-E \begin{vmatrix} R_3 & -(R_1 + R_2 + r_2) \\ R_4 & r_2 \end{vmatrix} = E \begin{vmatrix} R_3 & r_2 \\ R_4 & -(R_2 + R_4 + r_2) \end{vmatrix}$$

That is,

$$-[R_3 r_2 + R_4(R_1 + R_3 + r_2)] = -R_3(R_2 + R_4 + r_2) - R_4 r_2$$

From which

$$R_1 R_4 = R_2 R_3$$

Determinants have their uses, independent of matrix work. Cramer's rule is one example of this, and we shall come across another occasion where a knowledge of determinants can be valuable. This will be when we derive a formula for the vector product of two vectors in terms of components (Chapter 14). We shall see then that this can be expressed using a determinant.

There are several other examples too. For instance, suppose we have a triangle in the plane with vertices (x_1, y_1), (x_2, y_2) and (x_3, y_3). The area of this triangle can be expressed neatly in terms of a determinant:

$$\pm \tfrac{1}{2} \begin{vmatrix} x_1 & y_1 & 1 \\ x_2 & y_2 & 1 \\ x_3 & y_3 & 1 \end{vmatrix}$$

Why not check this for yourself?

SUMMARY

In this chapter we have examined
□ The definition of a minor and a cofactor and the relationship between them

$$A_{ij} = (-1)^{i+j}M_{ij}$$

□ The procedure for evaluating determinants
  a Select any row or any column;
  b Multiply each element in it by its cofactor;
  c Obtain the total.
□ Cramer's rule for solving simultaneous equations.
□ Rules for simplifying determinants
  a The value of a determinant is the same as the value of its transpose.
  b If two rows of a determinant are interchanged, then the determinant changes sign.
  c A determinant may be multiplied by a number. Select any row (or column) and multiply all its elements by the number.
  d The value of a determinant is unchanged if a constant multiple of the elements of a chosen row are added to the corresponding elements of another row.

EXERCISES (for answers see p. 748)

1 Solve the following equations:

a $\begin{vmatrix} x+1 & 2 \\ 6 & x-3 \end{vmatrix} = 0$
    b $\begin{vmatrix} x-1 & 3 \\ 6 & x-4 \end{vmatrix} = 0$

c $\begin{vmatrix} x-2 & x \\ x & x-6 \end{vmatrix} = 0$
    d $\begin{vmatrix} x+1 & x+2 \\ x+2 & x+4 \end{vmatrix} = 0$

2 Evaluate the following determinants:

a $\begin{vmatrix} 2 & 0 & 1 \\ -1 & 1 & 2 \\ 3 & 0 & 4 \end{vmatrix}$
    b $\begin{vmatrix} 1 & 2 & 1 \\ -5 & 1 & -1 \\ 4 & 3 & 0 \end{vmatrix}$

c $\begin{vmatrix} 2 & 1 & 1 \\ 1 & 3 & 5 \\ 4 & 1 & 2 \end{vmatrix}$
    d $\begin{vmatrix} x+1 & x+2 & x+3 \\ x+2 & x+3 & x+1 \\ x+3 & x+1 & x+2 \end{vmatrix}$

3 Evaluate, by simplifying first,

a $\begin{vmatrix} 21 & 15 & 14 \\ 18 & 45 & 7 \\ 24 & 40 & 21 \end{vmatrix}$
    b $\begin{vmatrix} 75 & 48 & 90 \\ 125 & 64 & 75 \\ 50 & 32 & 45 \end{vmatrix}$

4 Use Cramer's rule to solve the simultaneous equations where a, u, v and w are known:

a $x\sqrt{(1 + a^2)} + ya = (1 + a^2)^{-1/2}$
 $xa + y\sqrt{(1 + a^2)} = 1/a$

b $x - y\exp(u + v) + z\exp(u - w) = \exp u$
 $x\exp(v - u) + y\exp 2v - z\exp(v - w) = \exp v$
 $x\exp(w - u) - y\exp(w + v) - z = -\exp w$

ASSIGNMENT (for answers see p. 749; see also Workshop on p. 344)

1 Solve the equation

$$\begin{vmatrix} x - 2 & 3 \\ 4 & x + 2 \end{vmatrix} = 0$$

2 Simplify and thereby evaluate

$$\begin{vmatrix} 19 & 18 & 25 \\ 22 & 21 & 29 \\ 20 & 28 & 32 \end{vmatrix}$$

3 Solve the equation

$$\begin{vmatrix} x + 1 & x & x - 4 \\ 2 & 1 & -4 \\ 3 & 5 & 1 \end{vmatrix} = 0$$

4 Obtain x if

$$\begin{vmatrix} x - 4 & x - 2 & x \\ x - 3 & x - 1 & x + 2 \\ x - 2 & x + 4 & 3x \end{vmatrix} = 0$$

5 Obtain M, the matrix of minors of the matrix

$$A = \begin{bmatrix} 7 & 6 & 9 \\ 4 & 5 & 6 \\ 7 & 8 & 10 \end{bmatrix}$$

6 Obtain C, the matrix of cofactors of the matrix

$$A = \begin{bmatrix} 5 & 2 & 4 \\ 4 & 3 & 5 \\ 2 & 2 & 3 \end{bmatrix}$$

FURTHER EXERCISES (for answers see p. 750)

1 Obtain w if

$$\begin{vmatrix} w-6 & w-4 & w-2 \\ w-5 & w-2 & w+2 \\ w-4 & w & w+6 \end{vmatrix} = 0$$

2 Show that

$$\begin{vmatrix} x^2 & 2x & -2 \\ 2x & 2-x^2 & 2x \\ 2 & -2x & -x^2 \end{vmatrix} = (x^2+2)^3$$

Hence or otherwise obtain the possible values of x if the determinant is known to have the value 27.

3 Obtain an expression for k in terms of a, b, c and d if

$$\begin{vmatrix} 1+a & 1 & 1 & 1 \\ 1 & 1+b & 1 & 1 \\ 1 & 1 & 1+c & 1 \\ 1 & 1 & 1 & 1+d \end{vmatrix} = abcd(k+1)$$

4 It is given that the arithmetic mean of the three numbers a, b and c is zero and that the root mean square (RMS) value is the square root of 8. Solve the equation

$$\begin{vmatrix} x+a & c & b \\ c & x+b & a \\ b & a & x+c \end{vmatrix} = 0$$

Note: the RMS value is the square root of the arithmetic mean of the squares of the numbers.

5 Show that if A is the matrix

$$\begin{bmatrix} 0 & \cos u & \sin u \\ \cos v & -\sin u \sin v & \cos u \sin v \\ \sin v & \sin u \cos v & -\cos u \cos v \end{bmatrix}$$

then det $A = 1$.

6 Solve the equation

$$\begin{vmatrix} x+1 & 2x+3 & 3x+5 \\ 3x+3 & 5x+7 & 7x+11 \\ 5x+6 & 8x+12 & 14x+24 \end{vmatrix} = 0$$

7 Simplify and then evaluate

$$\begin{vmatrix} 27 & 37 & 42 \\ 11 & 15 & 16 \\ 23 & 31 & 34 \end{vmatrix}$$

8 Without evaluating them, show that the following determinants are zero:

a
$$\begin{vmatrix} 1 & yz & yz(y + z) \\ 1 & zx & zx(z + x) \\ 1 & xy & xy(x + y) \end{vmatrix}$$

b
$$\begin{vmatrix} a + x & x + y & a - y \\ x + w & x - a & a + w \\ y + w & w - x & x + y \end{vmatrix}$$

9 Use Cramer's rule to express u and v explicitly in terms of w where

$$u + v \sin w = \sec w$$
$$u \tan w + v \cos w = 2 \sin w$$

10 The loop currents in a circuit satisfy

$$R_1 i_1 + R_2(i_1 - i_3) = 0$$
$$R_3 i_2 + R_4(i_2 - i_3) = 0$$
$$R_1 i_1 + R_3 i_2 = 0$$

where R_1, R_2, R_3 and R_4 are resistances. Show that if not all the currents are zero then

$$\frac{1}{R_1} + \frac{1}{R_2} + \frac{1}{R_3} + \frac{1}{R_4} = 0$$

13   Inverse matrices

We have seen what determinants are and how to expand and simplify them. Our next task is to see what part they play in matrix algebra.

When you have completed this chapter you should be able to
☐ Decide when a matrix is non-singular;
☐ Calculate the inverse of a non-singular matrix by the formula;
☐ List the elementary row transformations;
☐ Calculate the inverse of a non-singular matrix using row transformations;
☐ Apply the method of systematic elimination to solve simultaneous equations.
At the end of this chapter we shall solve a practical problem involving a binary code.

13.1 THE INVERSE OF A SQUARE MATRIX

We now turn our attention to the problem of finding the inverse of a square matrix A. This is the nearest we get to an operation of division for matrices. We are looking for a matrix B such that

$$AB = BA = I$$

where I is the identity matrix.

The fact that there is at most one such matrix can be deduced as follows. Suppose there is a square matrix A for which there are two matrices B and C such that

$$AB = BA = I$$
$$AC = CA = I$$

We first discussed this idea in section 11.5.

We have

$$C = CI = C(AB) = (CA)B = IB = B$$

So we have deduced $C = B$. That is, we have shown that if the square matrix A has an inverse then the inverse is *unique*. We denote the inverse of A, if it has one, by A^{-1}.

Suppose A is a square matrix. Then we have seen how to form from A a matrix C of cofactors (Chapter 12). That is, if

$$A = \begin{bmatrix} a_{11} & a_{12} & a_{13} \\ a_{21} & a_{22} & a_{23} \\ a_{31} & a_{32} & a_{33} \end{bmatrix}$$

then

$$C = \begin{bmatrix} A_{11} & A_{12} & A_{13} \\ A_{21} & A_{22} & A_{23} \\ A_{31} & A_{32} & A_{33} \end{bmatrix}$$

The transpose of C is known as the **adjoint** (or **adjugate**) matrix of A and is denoted by adj A. So

$$\text{adj } A = \begin{bmatrix} A_{11} & A_{21} & A_{31} \\ A_{12} & A_{22} & A_{32} \\ A_{13} & A_{23} & A_{33} \end{bmatrix}$$

From what we have done before, we deduce that

$$A(\text{adj } A) = (\text{adj } A)A = (\det A)I$$

We illustrate this property in the case of a 3×3 matrix:

$$\begin{bmatrix} a_{11} & a_{12} & a_{13} \\ a_{21} & a_{22} & a_{23} \\ a_{31} & a_{32} & a_{33} \end{bmatrix} \begin{bmatrix} A_{11} & A_{21} & A_{31} \\ A_{12} & A_{22} & A_{32} \\ A_{13} & A_{23} & A_{33} \end{bmatrix}$$

$$= \begin{bmatrix} a_{11}A_{11}+a_{12}A_{12}+a_{13}A_{13} & a_{11}A_{21}+a_{12}A_{22}+a_{13}A_{23} & a_{11}A_{31}+a_{12}A_{32}+a_{13}A_{33} \\ a_{21}A_{11}+a_{22}A_{12}+a_{23}A_{13} & a_{21}A_{21}+a_{22}A_{22}+a_{23}A_{23} & a_{21}A_{31}+a_{22}A_{32}+a_{23}A_{33} \\ a_{31}A_{11}+a_{32}A_{12}+a_{33}A_{13} & a_{31}A_{21}+a_{32}A_{22}+a_{33}A_{23} & a_{31}A_{31}+a_{32}A_{32}+a_{33}A_{33} \end{bmatrix}$$

$$= \begin{bmatrix} |A| & 0 & 0 \\ 0 & |A| & 0 \\ 0 & 0 & |A| \end{bmatrix} = |A|I$$

Consequently, if $|A|$ is non-zero then the inverse of A exists and is given by

$$A^{-1} = \frac{1}{|A|} \text{adj } A$$

Any square matrix with a zero determinant is called a **singular matrix**. (Singular is used here in the sense of 'unusual', as when Sherlock Holmes remarks to Dr Watson on a singular occurrence.) Consequently when a square matrix has a non-zero determinant, it is called a **non-singular matrix**. From what we have done we can now assert that every non-singular square matrix has a unique inverse given by the formula

$$A^{-1} = \frac{1}{|A|} \text{adj } A$$

It follows therefore that for such matrices if $AB = I$ then $BA = I$. However, this is a consequence of the algebraic structure satisfied by the elements of the matrices. Real and complex numbers are examples of what mathematicians call **fields**. If the elements in the matrices did not belong to fields then many of the conclusions we have reached would no longer hold.

Arthur Conan Doyle (1859–1930): Scottish novelist and doctor best known as the creator of the detective Sherlock Holmes and his assistant Dr Watson. He practised in Southsea.

13.2 ROW TRANSFORMATIONS

Although the formula for the inverse of a square matrix is very useful, there is a procedure which can often be used to obtain the inverse more quickly. This procedure is known as the method of row operations.

An operation on a matrix is called an **elementary row transformation** if and only if it is one of the following:
1 An interchange of two rows;
2 Multiplication of the elements in a row by a non-zero number;
3 Subtraction of the elements of one row from the corresponding elements of another row.

A sequence of elementary row transformations results in a **row transformation**. Of course the matrix will be changed as a result of a row transformation, but the matrix which results is said to be **row equivalent** to the original matrix.

An **elementary matrix** is a matrix obtained by performing an elementary row transformation on the identity matrix I. In fact, it is easy to see that an elementary row transformation can be effected by pre-multiplying the matrix by an elementary matrix.

Example □

$$E_1 A = \begin{bmatrix} 0 & 0 & 1 \\ 0 & 1 & 0 \\ 1 & 0 & 0 \end{bmatrix} \begin{bmatrix} a & b & c \\ d & e & f \\ g & h & i \end{bmatrix}$$

$$= \begin{bmatrix} g & h & i \\ d & e & f \\ a & b & c \end{bmatrix}$$

E_1 has been obtained from the identity matrix by interchanging row 1 and row 3. ∎

Example □

$$E_2 A = \begin{bmatrix} 1 & 0 & 0 \\ 0 & k & 0 \\ 0 & 0 & 1 \end{bmatrix} \begin{bmatrix} a & b & c \\ d & e & f \\ g & h & i \end{bmatrix}$$

$$= \begin{bmatrix} a & b & c \\ kd & ke & kf \\ g & h & i \end{bmatrix}$$

E_2 has been obtained from the identity matrix by multiplying row 2 by k. ∎

Example □

$$E_3 A = \begin{bmatrix} 1 & 0 & 0 \\ 0 & 1 & -1 \\ 0 & 0 & 1 \end{bmatrix} \begin{bmatrix} a & b & c \\ d & e & f \\ g & h & i \end{bmatrix}$$

$$= \begin{bmatrix} a & b & c \\ d-g & e-h & f-i \\ g & h & i \end{bmatrix}$$

E_3 has been obtained from the identity matrix by subtracting row 3 from row 2. ∎

Suppose now it is possible, using a sequence of elementary row transformations, to reduce a matrix A to the identity matrix I. Then

$$(E_s \ \dots \ E_2 E_1)A = I$$

It follows that

$$E_s \ \dots \ E_2 E_1 = A^{-1}$$

Moreover,

$$A^{-1} = E_s \, \ldots \, E_2 E_1 = E_s \, \ldots \, E_2 E_1 I$$

This provides a method for obtaining the inverse of a matrix A.

13.3 OBTAINING INVERSES

To obtain the inverse of a non-singular matrix using row transformations:
1 Write down an array consisting of the matrix A on the left-hand side and an identity matrix of the same order on the right-hand side.
2 Perform a sequence of elementary row transformations on the *entire array* with the object of converting the matrix A into an identity matrix.
3 As the matrix A on the left is transformed into the identity matrix I, so the identity matrix I on the right becomes transformed into the inverse of A.

As we carry out this procedure we shall observe at each stage that the matrix on the left gets to look more and more like an identity matrix, whereas the matrix on the right gets to look more and more like the inverse of A. It's rather like watching Dr Jekyll turn into Mr Hyde!

The best way of carrying out the procedure is to work systematically column by column, starting on the left. As a first step, we arrange things so that we obtain 1 in the (1, 1) position. We then subtract multiples of the first row from the other rows so that the first column becomes the first column of an identity matrix. When an element is fixed and its row is used in this way the element is called a **pivot**; it may help to encircle the pivot at each stage.

Robert Louis Stevenson (1850–1894): Scottish author best known for *Treasure Island*, *Kidnapped* and *Dr Jekyll and Mr Hyde*.

□ Use the method of elementary row operations to obtain the inverse of the matrix   **Example**

$$\begin{bmatrix} 6 & 13 & 9 \\ 3 & 7 & 5 \\ 2 & 3 & 2 \end{bmatrix}$$

We begin with the array

$$\left[\begin{array}{ccc|ccc} 6 & 13 & 9 & 1 & 0 & 0 \\ 3 & 7 & 5 & 0 & 1 & 0 \\ 2 & 3 & 2 & 0 & 0 & 1 \end{array}\right]$$

Subtract row 3 from row 2 to obtain a leading element 1 in row 2:

$$\left[\begin{array}{ccc|ccc} 6 & 13 & 9 & 1 & 0 & 0 \\ 1 & 4 & 3 & 0 & 1 & -1 \\ 2 & 3 & 2 & 0 & 0 & 1 \end{array}\right]$$

Interchange row 1 and row 2 to obtain 1 in the correct position:

$$\begin{bmatrix} ① & 4 & 3 & \vdots & 0 & 1 & -1 \\ 6 & 13 & 9 & \vdots & 1 & 0 & 0 \\ 2 & 3 & 2 & \vdots & 0 & 0 & 1 \end{bmatrix}$$

Subtract multiples of row 1 from row 2 and row 3 to produce the zeros in the first column:

$$\begin{bmatrix} 1 & 4 & 3 & \vdots & 0 & 1 & -1 \\ 0 & -11 & -9 & \vdots & 1 & -6 & 6 \\ 0 & -5 & -4 & \vdots & 0 & -2 & 3 \end{bmatrix}$$

Subtract twice row 3 from row 2 to obtain -1 in the (2, 2) position:

$$\begin{bmatrix} 1 & 4 & 3 & \vdots & 0 & 1 & -1 \\ 0 & -1 & -1 & \vdots & 1 & -2 & 0 \\ 0 & -5 & -4 & \vdots & 0 & -2 & 3 \end{bmatrix}$$

Change the sign of row 2:

$$\begin{bmatrix} 1 & 4 & 3 & \vdots & 0 & 1 & -1 \\ 0 & ① & 1 & \vdots & -1 & 2 & 0 \\ 0 & -5 & -4 & \vdots & 0 & -2 & 3 \end{bmatrix}$$

Subtract four times row 2 from row 1 and add five times row 2 to row 3:

$$\begin{bmatrix} 1 & 0 & -1 & \vdots & 4 & -7 & -1 \\ 0 & 1 & 1 & \vdots & -1 & 2 & 0 \\ 0 & 0 & 1 & \vdots & -5 & 8 & 3 \end{bmatrix}$$

Finally, add row 3 to row 1 and subtract row 3 from row 2:

$$\begin{bmatrix} 1 & 0 & 0 & \vdots & -1 & 1 & 2 \\ 0 & 1 & 0 & \vdots & 4 & -6 & -3 \\ 0 & 0 & 1 & \vdots & -5 & 8 & 3 \end{bmatrix}$$

Check:

$$\begin{bmatrix} 6 & 13 & 9 \\ 3 & 7 & 5 \\ 2 & 3 & 2 \end{bmatrix} \begin{bmatrix} -1 & 1 & 2 \\ 4 & -6 & -3 \\ -5 & 8 & 3 \end{bmatrix} = \begin{bmatrix} 1 & 0 & 0 \\ 0 & 1 & 0 \\ 0 & 0 & 1 \end{bmatrix}$$

Notice how we move column by column through the matrix, working from the left. Only when the column has been reduced to the appropriate column of an identity matrix do we proceed to the next column. ■

Here is an example for you to try. Remember to make a note of the row operations at each stage so that, if you make a mistake, it can be corrected later. By the way, it is always worth checking by multiplication that you have the correct result. In practice it is only necessary to check the product one way round; so we check either $AB = I$ or $BA = I$ but not both.

□ Obtain the inverse of the matrix   **Example**

$$\begin{bmatrix} 6 & 11 & 5 \\ 18 & 34 & 15 \\ 13 & 25 & 11 \end{bmatrix}$$

When you have completed this example, check below to see if you have the correct answer.

There are many ways of proceeding to reduce the array using row transformations. Here is one of the ways:

$$\begin{bmatrix} 6 & 11 & 5 & | & 1 & 0 & 0 \\ 18 & 34 & 15 & | & 0 & 1 & 0 \\ 13 & 25 & 11 & | & 0 & 0 & 1 \end{bmatrix}$$

To obtain 1 in row 3 we transform r3 = r3 − 2r1, and to reduce the numbers we put r2 = r2 − 3r1:

$$\begin{bmatrix} 6 & 11 & 5 & | & 1 & 0 & 0 \\ 0 & 1 & 0 & | & -3 & 1 & 0 \\ 1 & 3 & 1 & | & -2 & 0 & 1 \end{bmatrix}$$

Interchanging row 1 and row 3 produces 1 in the first row:

$$\begin{bmatrix} ① & 3 & 1 & | & -2 & 0 & 1 \\ 0 & 1 & 0 & | & -3 & 1 & 0 \\ 6 & 11 & 5 & | & 1 & 0 & 0 \end{bmatrix}$$

To complete the first column, r3 = r3 − 6r1:

$$\begin{bmatrix} 1 & 3 & 1 & | & -2 & 0 & 1 \\ 0 & ① & 0 & | & -3 & 1 & 0 \\ 0 & -7 & -1 & | & 13 & 0 & -6 \end{bmatrix}$$

The second column is completed by r1 = r1 − 3r2 and r3 = r3 + 7r2:

$$\begin{bmatrix} 1 & 0 & 1 & | & 7 & -3 & 1 \\ 0 & 1 & 0 & | & -3 & 1 & 0 \\ 0 & 0 & -1 & | & -8 & 7 & -6 \end{bmatrix}$$

Add row 3 to row 1 and then change the sign of row 3 to produce

$$\begin{bmatrix} 1 & 0 & 0 & \vdots & -1 & 4 & -5 \\ 0 & 1 & 0 & \vdots & -3 & 1 & 0 \\ 0 & 0 & 1 & \vdots & 8 & -7 & 6 \end{bmatrix}$$

Check:

$$\begin{bmatrix} 6 & 11 & 5 \\ 18 & 34 & 15 \\ 13 & 25 & 11 \end{bmatrix} \begin{bmatrix} -1 & 4 & -5 \\ -3 & 1 & 0 \\ 8 & -7 & 6 \end{bmatrix} = \begin{bmatrix} 1 & 0 & 0 \\ 0 & 1 & 0 \\ 0 & 0 & 1 \end{bmatrix}$$ ∎

!

The rules for simplifying determinants and the use of row operations have features in common. However, you must *never* use column operations when obtaining the inverse of a matrix by row operations. (As a matter of interest there is a parallel theory using column operations instead of row operations, but the two must be kept distinct.)

13.4 SYSTEMATIC ELIMINATION

Elementary row transformations can be used to solve a system of simultaneous equations directly. To do so we use a matrix known as the **augmented matrix**. This is a matrix consisting of the matrix of coefficients with an extra column for the constants on the right-hand side. Such a matrix can be written down once we are given a system of equations; conversely, given any matrix we can write down a system of equations for which it is the augmented matrix.

Example □

$$\begin{array}{cc} ax + by = h \\ cx + dy = k \end{array} \qquad \begin{bmatrix} a & b & \vdots & h \\ c & d & \vdots & k \end{bmatrix}$$

equations   augmented matrix   ∎

Karl Frederick Gauss (1777–1855): German mathematician of the first rank who made substantial contributions to every major field of mathematics, and also to astronomy, geodesics and electricity.

If we now perform row transformations on the augmented matrix we shall produce an equivalent system of equations. The method of **systematic elimination**, otherwise known as the **Gauss elimination method**, makes use of this fact.

We perform row operations on the augmented matrix with the object of reducing it to a state in which each row has at least as many leading zeros as the previous row. In other words, if the first three elements in a row are zero then at least the first three elements of each subsequent row will be zero.

When this procedure has been completed the equations can be reconstituted. There will then be one of three possibilities:

1 The equations have a unique solution;

2 The equations are inconsistent;
3 The equations have more than one solution.
It will be clear which of these possibilities holds. If it is either 1 or 3 then
the solution can be determined by back substitution. In case 3, some of
the unknowns can be chosen arbitrarily.
   We shall illustrate all three cases.

□ Decide whether or not the following system of simultaneous equations **Example**
is consistent and, if it is, obtain the solution:

$$x + 2y - 3z = 1$$
$$x - y + 4z = 5$$
$$2x + y - 3z = 2$$
$$4x - 2y - 2z = 4$$
$$x + y + 3z = 6$$

Here we have five equations in three unknowns. The augmented matrix is

$$\begin{bmatrix} ① & 2 & -3 & | & 1 \\ 1 & -1 & 4 & | & 5 \\ 2 & 1 & -3 & | & 2 \\ 4 & -2 & -2 & | & 4 \\ 1 & 1 & 3 & | & 6 \end{bmatrix}$$

To produce zeros in the first column we use r2 = r2 - r1, r3 = r3 - 2r1,
r4 = r4 - 4r1 and r5 = r5 - r1:

$$\begin{bmatrix} 1 & 2 & -3 & | & 1 \\ 0 & -3 & 7 & | & 4 \\ 0 & -3 & 3 & | & 0 \\ 0 & -10 & 10 & | & 0 \\ 0 & -1 & 6 & | & 5 \end{bmatrix}$$

Divide row 3 by -3 and interchange with row 2:

$$\begin{bmatrix} 1 & 2 & -3 & | & 1 \\ 0 & ① & -1 & | & 0 \\ 0 & -3 & 7 & | & 4 \\ 0 & -10 & 10 & | & 0 \\ 0 & -1 & 6 & | & 5 \end{bmatrix}$$

Now r3 = r3 + 3r2, r4 = r4 + 10r2 and r5 = r5 + r2:

$$\begin{bmatrix} 1 & 2 & -3 & | & 1 \\ 0 & 1 & -1 & | & 0 \\ 0 & 0 & 4 & | & 4 \\ 0 & 0 & 0 & | & 0 \\ 0 & 0 & 5 & | & 5 \end{bmatrix}$$

Lastly, r3 = r3/4 and r5 = r5 − 5r3:

$$\begin{bmatrix} 1 & 2 & -3 & | & 1 \\ 0 & 1 & -1 & | & 0 \\ 0 & 0 & 1 & | & 1 \\ 0 & 0 & 0 & | & 0 \\ 0 & 0 & 0 & | & 0 \end{bmatrix}$$

So two of the equations are redundant, and the new equations are

$$\begin{aligned} x + 2y - 3z &= 1 \\ y - z &= 0 \\ z &= 1 \end{aligned}$$

From these, by back substitution, $z = 1$, $y = z = 1$ and

$$x = -2y + 3z + 1 = 2. \qquad \blacksquare$$

You should always check the solution by substituting it directly into the *original* equations. It is only the work of a moment, and if a mistake has occurred you then have an opportunity to locate and correct it. It is not unknown for examiners to reserve a mark or two for evidence that the solution has been checked. It is usually easy to check it mentally, but always indicate at the end of your solution that it has been checked; 'solution checks' is often enough.

Example □ Given the equations

$$\begin{aligned} 2x - y + z &= 3 \\ x + 2y + z &= 5 \\ 3x - 4y + z &= 1 \\ 5x + 5y + 4z &= 18 \end{aligned}$$

decide whether or not they are consistent. If they are consistent, solve them.

The augmented matrix is

$$\begin{bmatrix} 2 & -1 & 1 & | & 3 \\ 1 & 2 & 1 & | & 5 \\ 3 & -4 & 1 & | & 1 \\ 5 & 5 & 4 & | & 18 \end{bmatrix}$$

Interchanging rows 1 and 2 gives

$$\begin{bmatrix} ① & 2 & 1 & | & 5 \\ 2 & -1 & 1 & | & 3 \\ 3 & -4 & 1 & | & 1 \\ 5 & 5 & 4 & | & 18 \end{bmatrix}$$

Then r2 = r2 − 2r1, r3 = r3 − 3r1 and r4 = r4 − 5r1 give

$$\begin{bmatrix} 1 & 2 & 1 & | & 5 \\ 0 & -5 & -1 & | & -7 \\ 0 & -10 & -2 & | & -14 \\ 0 & -5 & -1 & | & -7 \end{bmatrix}$$

Since row 3 and row 4 are multiples of row 2, the system reduces to just two equations:

$$\begin{aligned} x + 2y + z &= 5 \\ -5y - z &= -7 \end{aligned}$$

This shows that the equations are consistent, and in fact it is possible to choose one of the variables arbitrarily. So if we put $z = t$, we can express the remaining variables in terms of t. Therefore if $z = t$ then $y = -(t - 7)/5$ and

$$\begin{aligned} x &= -2y - z + 5 \\ &= [2(t - 7)/5] - t + 5 \\ &= (-3t + 11)/5 \end{aligned}$$ ∎

□ Solve, if possible, the system of equations   **Example**

$$\begin{aligned} w + 3x - y + z &= 4 \\ 2w - x + y - z &= 7 \\ 5w + x + y - z &= 20 \end{aligned}$$

The augmented matrix is

$$\begin{bmatrix} ① & 3 & -1 & 1 & | & 4 \\ 2 & -1 & 1 & -1 & | & 7 \\ 5 & 1 & 1 & -1 & | & 20 \end{bmatrix}$$

First, r2 = r2 − 2r1 and r3 = r3 − 5r1 give

$$\begin{bmatrix} 1 & 3 & -1 & 1 & \vdots & 4 \\ 0 & -7 & 3 & -3 & \vdots & -1 \\ 0 & -14 & 6 & -6 & \vdots & 0 \end{bmatrix}$$

Next, r3 = r3 − 2r2 produces

$$\begin{bmatrix} 1 & 3 & -1 & 1 & \vdots & 4 \\ 0 & -7 & 3 & -3 & \vdots & -1 \\ 0 & 0 & 0 & 0 & \vdots & 2 \end{bmatrix}$$

The system is clearly inconsistent since the final 'equation' has become now $0 = 2$. ∎

Here now are a few steps which will enable you to see how you are progressing.

13.5 Workshop

▷**Exercise**   Use the formula to obtain the inverse of the matrix

$$\begin{bmatrix} 3 & 5 & 9 \\ 1 & 2 & 3 \\ 4 & 7 & 15 \end{bmatrix}$$

Check your answer by multiplication.

If everything works out right, proceed to step 4. Otherwise, go on to step 2.

2   If the product does not produce an identity matrix, check carefully all the stages:
1 the matrix of minors
2 the matrix of cofactors
3 the adjoint matrix
4 the determinant
5 the final multiplication.
Now see if you can get it right. If all is well move on to step 4. If not, go to step 3.

3   So we still have problems. If you have gone through all the stages in step 2 and checked for errors, there can be only one explanation. You must have 'simplified' the matrix in some way. Did you use row transformations, or the rules for simplifying determinants? If you did then you have made a *fatal* error. Remember, whenever we use row transformations we change the matrix. So you have found the inverse of a row equivalent matrix and not the one in which we are interested.

Award yourself a wooden spoon, solve the problem correctly and move on to step 4.

▷**Exercise**   Use the method of row transformations to obtain the inverse of **4** the matrix

$$\begin{bmatrix} 3 & 1 & 2 \\ 7 & 3 & 4 \\ 9 & 3 & 8 \end{bmatrix}$$

You can check your answer by multiplication. If it is right, move on to step 7. If not, go to step 5.

If you have managed to convert the matrix on the left into an identity **5** matrix but the matrix on the right didn't turn out to be the inverse, move on to step 6.

If you have been unable to convert the matrix on the left into an identity matrix you have not been approaching the problem systematically. Remember to move across the matrix column by column:
1 Get the non-zero element into the correct position; then
2 Convert this element into a 1; then
3 Subtract multiples of this row from the others to produce the zeros.
Only when all this has been done do we move to the next column.

Try again, and if all is well now move on to step 7. If there are still problems, move to step 6.

There are a number of possible sources of error: **6**
1 You may have simply made an arithmetical slip. Errors have a habit of hiding away in the parts where you least expect to find them. Have a good look and see if you can spot one or two.
2 You may have carried out some illegal operation. For instance it is usually advisable to make sure that at each stage the row in which the pivot lies remains unaltered. Are you sure that you have performed each row operation on the entire row of six elements?
3 You may have used column transformations as well as row transformations. You must stick to row transformations; mixing transformations is strictly against the law!
Once you have located your error, make the necessary amendments and obtain the correct inverse.

7 **Exercise** Discuss the solution of the following system of equations:

$$x + 2y - z = 2$$
$$x - y + z = 5$$
$$3x + 3y + az = b + 8$$

in the three cases **a** $a = -1, b = 1$ **b** $a = -1, b = 2$ **c** $a = 1, b = 7$.

You may consider the cases separately if you wish, or you may choose to operate on the augmented matrix algebraically. Whichever method you decide on, complete the problem and take the final step to see if all is well.

8 The augmented matrix is

$$\begin{bmatrix} 1 & 2 & -1 & \vdots & 2 \\ 1 & -1 & 1 & \vdots & 5 \\ 3 & 3 & a & \vdots & b+8 \end{bmatrix}$$

This reduces to

$$\begin{bmatrix} 1 & 2 & -1 & \vdots & 2 \\ 0 & -3 & 2 & \vdots & 3 \\ 0 & 0 & a+1 & \vdots & b-1 \end{bmatrix}$$

So

a $a = -1, b = 1$ gives a redundant row, and the solution in terms of z is $y = (2z - 3)/3$ and $x = 3 - z/3$.

b $a = -1, b = 2$ produces a final equation $0 = 1$, and so the equations are inconsistent.

c $a = 1, b = 7$ gives a unique solution $z = 3$, $y = 1$ and $x = 3$.

13.6 PIVOTING

When we used the method of systematic elimination we avoided arithmetical complications by choosing the pivot with care. In particular we tried to perform our arithmetic with integers. On occasions we interchanged rows rather than divide through a row by a number which would have resulted in decimal representations. This is one way of keeping the arithmetic exact and so avoiding errors.

If we were programming a computer to perform this elimination method we should in each case reduce the non-zero element on the leading diagonal to 1 by dividing throughout the row. It would require some sophisticated programming to detect the presence of suitable rows which could be manipulated by the rules to produce, without division, a pivot 1.

The approach which the computer would take is shown in the following scheme:

$$
\begin{bmatrix} * & * & * & * \\ * & * & * & * \\ * & * & * & * \end{bmatrix} \rightarrow
\begin{bmatrix} 1 & * & * & * \\ * & * & * & * \\ * & * & * & * \end{bmatrix} \rightarrow
$$

$$
\begin{bmatrix} 1 & * & * & * \\ 0 & * & * & * \\ 0 & * & * & * \end{bmatrix} \rightarrow
\begin{bmatrix} 1 & * & * & * \\ 0 & 1 & * & * \\ 0 & * & * & * \end{bmatrix} \rightarrow
$$

$$
\begin{bmatrix} 1 & * & * & * \\ 0 & 1 & * & * \\ 0 & 0 & * & * \end{bmatrix} \rightarrow
\begin{bmatrix} 1 & * & * & * \\ 0 & 1 & * & * \\ 0 & 0 & 1 & * \end{bmatrix}
$$

In the first transformation, row 1 is divided by the element in the (1, 1) position.

In the second transformation, multiples of row 1 are subtracted from the other rows to produce the zeros in column 1. Attention then turns to column 2.

In the third transformation, we divide row 2 by the element now in the (2, 2) position to produce 1 in the (2, 2) position. Then multiples of row 2 are subtracted from the other rows to produce the required zeros in column 2.

If a zero were to appear on the leading diagonal, a complication would arise. In such circumstances it would be necessary to locate a non-zero element in the same column below the leading diagonal and by means of a row interchange to bring it to the leading diagonal.

One of the problems which arises in practice with this method is due to round-off error in the numerical approximation.

One method of minimizing the effects of round-off error is to use **partial pivoting**. Partial pivoting consists of rearranging the equations in such a way that the numerically largest non-zero elements occur on the leading diagonal.

The solution of equations using matrices of error distribution problems is required in Surveying.

□ Here is a set of equations before partial pivoting: **Example**

$$
\begin{aligned}
x + 5y - z &= 8 \\
4x - y + 2z &= 5 \\
2x + 3y - 6z &= 1
\end{aligned}
$$

In the first equation the largest coefficient is 5, in the second it is 4 and in the third it is -6. Therefore the system of equations after partial pivoting becomes

$$4x - y + 2z = 5$$
$$x + 5y - z = 8$$
$$2x + 3y - 6z = 1$$

■

Partial pivoting ensures that when the rows are divided by the elements on the leading diagonal the numbers are reduced and errors are therefore controlled.

We shall now solve a practical problem involving binary arithmetic. In binary arithmetic there are just two numbers, 0 and 1. The following algebraic rules are satisfied:

$$0 \times 0 = 0 \qquad 0 + 0 = 0$$
$$0 \times 1 = 0 \qquad 1 + 0 = 1$$
$$1 \times 0 = 0 \qquad 0 + 1 = 1$$
$$1 \times 1 = 1 \qquad 1 + 1 = 0$$

Most people have come across binary arithmetic; computers use it.

13.7 Practical

CODEWORDS

A seven-bit binary code consists of codewords $x_1 x_2 \ldots x_7$ which satisfy the condition $H\mathbf{x}^T = O$, where $\mathbf{x} = [x_1, x_2, \ldots, x_7]$, O is the 7×1 zero vector and

$$H = \begin{bmatrix} 0 & 0 & 0 & 1 & 1 & 1 & 1 \\ 0 & 1 & 1 & 0 & 0 & 1 & 1 \\ 1 & 0 & 1 & 0 & 1 & 0 & 1 \end{bmatrix}$$

Obtain all the codewords.
 See how this goes. We shall attack the problem one stage at a time.

We have the set of equations

$$x_4 + x_5 + x_6 + x_7 = 0$$
$$x_2 + x_3 + x_6 + x_7 = 0$$
$$x_1 + x_3 + x_5 + x_7 = 0$$

If we remember that in binary arithmetic $1 + 1 = 0$ we see that these are equivalent to

$$x_4 = x_5 + x_6 + x_7$$

$$x_2 = x_3 + x_6 + x_7$$
$$x_1 = x_3 + x_5 + x_7$$

Can you see how many codewords there will be? When you have decided, move to the next stage and see if you are right.

We have expressed three of the unknowns x_4, x_2 and x_1 in terms of the other four. Each of these four has two possible values, 0 or 1. Consequently the total number of codewords is $2 \times 2 \times 2 \times 2 = 2^4 = 16$. Once we enumerate these 16 possibilities for x_3, x_5, x_6 and x_7 the equations will determine the other bits and so the codewords will be obtained.

We shall do this in two stages. First determine all the codewords which have $x_3 = 0$.

We enumerate (x_3, x_5, x_6, x_7) and use the equations to obtain x_4, x_2 and x_1 and thereby the codeword $x_1 x_2 \ldots x_7$:

1 $(0, 0, 0, 0) \Rightarrow x_4 = 0, x_2 = 0, x_1 = 0 \Rightarrow 0000000$
2 $(0, 0, 0, 1) \Rightarrow x_4 = 1, x_2 = 1, x_1 = 1 \Rightarrow 1101001$
3 $(0, 0, 1, 0) \Rightarrow x_4 = 1, x_2 = 1, x_1 = 0 \Rightarrow 0101010$
4 $(0, 0, 1, 1) \Rightarrow x_4 = 0, x_2 = 0, x_1 = 1 \Rightarrow 1000011$
5 $(0, 1, 0, 0) \Rightarrow x_4 = 1, x_2 = 0, x_1 = 1 \Rightarrow 1001100$
6 $(0, 1, 0, 1) \Rightarrow x_4 = 0, x_2 = 1, x_1 = 0 \Rightarrow 0100101$
7 $(0, 1, 1, 0) \Rightarrow x_4 = 0, x_2 = 1, x_1 = 1 \Rightarrow 1100110$
8 $(0, 1, 1, 1) \Rightarrow x_4 = 1, x_2 = 0, x_1 = 0 \Rightarrow 0001111$

If something went wrong, check through things carefully and then obtain the remaining eight codewords.

We now put $x_3 = 1$:

9 $(1, 0, 0, 0) \Rightarrow x_4 = 0, x_2 = 1, x_1 = 1 \Rightarrow 1110000$
10 $(1, 0, 0, 1) \Rightarrow x_4 = 1, x_2 = 0, x_1 = 0 \Rightarrow 0011001$
11 $(1, 0, 1, 0) \Rightarrow x_4 = 1, x_2 = 0, x_1 = 1 \Rightarrow 1011010$
12 $(1, 0, 1, 1) \Rightarrow x_4 = 0, x_2 = 1, x_1 = 0 \Rightarrow 0110011$
13 $(1, 1, 0, 0) \Rightarrow x_4 = 1, x_2 = 1, x_1 = 0 \Rightarrow 0111100$
14 $(1, 1, 0, 1) \Rightarrow x_4 = 0, x_2 = 0, x_1 = 1 \Rightarrow 1010101$
15 $(1, 1, 1, 0) \Rightarrow x_4 = 0, x_2 = 0, x_1 = 0 \Rightarrow 0010110$
16 $(1, 1, 1, 1) \Rightarrow x_4 = 1, x_2 = 1, x_1 = 1 \Rightarrow 1111111$

It is interesting to note that each pair of codewords differs by at least three bits. This is an example of an error-correcting linear code.

13.8 CONCLUDING REMARKS

The important concept of linear independence which arises in sections 20.2 and 21.2 is discussed more fully in section 22.7.

Before we end this chapter there are two points which should be made:

1 We have only touched on the theory of matrices. There is much more to them than this. For example we have solved systems of equations by using an elimination method, but we have not examined the theory behind the technique we have used. The key idea is that of the **rank** of a matrix, which is the number of linearly independent rows. It can be shown that

   a The rank of a matrix is unaltered when a row transformation is performed on it;

   b A set of equations is consistent if and only if the rank of the matrix of coefficients is the same as the rank of the augmented matrix.

2 When matrices are used in conjunction with differential equations some very powerful techniques become available. One of the most fruitful ideas arises from considering the equation

$$A\mathbf{x} = \lambda\mathbf{x}$$

See question 7 in the Further exercises.

where A is a square matrix and λ is a scalar. The non-zero vectors $\mathbf{x}$ which satisfy this equation are known as **eigenvectors** and the corresponding values of λ are then called the **eigenvalues**. One of the further exercises gives you an opportunity to examine the consequences of this equation. It is possible to express many differential and difference equations as eigenvalue problems.

SUMMARY

We now summarize what we have learnt in this chapter:
□ The formula for calculating the inverse of a matrix:

$$A^{-1} = \frac{1}{|A|} \text{adj } A$$

□ The meanings of the terms singular matrix and non-singular matrix

$$A \text{ is singular} \Leftrightarrow |A| = 0$$

□ The operations on a matrix known as elementary row transformations
a an interchange of two rows;
b multiplication of the elements in a row by a non-zero number;
c subtraction of the elements of one row from the corresponding elements of another row.
□ The method of obtaining the inverse of a matrix by using row transformations

$$A|I \rightarrow I|A^{-1}$$

□ The use of row transformations to solve systems of simultaneous algebraic equations

$$\begin{bmatrix} * & * & * & | & * \\ * & * & * & | & * \\ * & * & * & | & * \end{bmatrix} \rightarrow \begin{bmatrix} 1 & * & * & | & * \\ 0 & 1 & * & | & * \\ 0 & 0 & 1 & | & * \end{bmatrix}$$

EXERCISES (for answers see p. 750)

1 Use the formula to obtain the inverses of each of the following matrices:

a $\begin{bmatrix} 3 & 8 & 2 \\ 4 & 10 & 3 \\ 2 & 5 & 1 \end{bmatrix}$
  b $\begin{bmatrix} 5 & 3 & 8 \\ 7 & 5 & 11 \\ 3 & 2 & 5 \end{bmatrix}$

c $\begin{bmatrix} 11 & 7 & 18 \\ 4 & 3 & 6 \\ 14 & 9 & 23 \end{bmatrix}$
  d $\begin{bmatrix} 8 & 5 & 13 \\ 10 & 7 & 16 \\ 13 & 9 & 21 \end{bmatrix}$

2 Obtain x for each of the following matrices if each one is singular:

a $\begin{bmatrix} x+1 & x+2 & x+5 \\ 5 & 9 & 4 \\ x+3 & x+7 & x+2 \end{bmatrix}$

b $\begin{bmatrix} x+2 & x+3 & 7 \\ 2 & 5 & -3 \\ x+4 & 9 & x+3 \end{bmatrix}$

c $\begin{bmatrix} x-1 & x+1 & x+4 \\ x-4 & x+2 & -3 \\ x-2 & 3x & x+1 \end{bmatrix}$

d $\begin{bmatrix} -x & x+1 & x+2 \\ x-3 & x-1 & -x+2 \\ -x+2 & 2x & x-1 \end{bmatrix}$

3 Use the method of row transformations to obtain the inverses of the matrices in question 1.

4 Use the method of row transformations to solve the following sets of simultaneous equations:

a $3x + 5y + 8z = 3$
$4x + 6y + 11z = 5$
$2x + 3y + 5z = 7$

b $4x + 2y + 3z = 5$
$6x + 3y + 5z = 8$
$11x + 5y + 8z = 7$

c $18x + 6y + 5z = -1$
$11x + 4y + 3z = 7$
$7x + 3y + 2z = 9$

d $7x + 3y + 8z = 4$
$5x + 2y + 5z = 5$
$11x + 5y + 13z = 6$

ASSIGNMENT (for answers see p. 751; see also Workshop on p. 367)

1 Obtain the inverse of the matrix

$$\begin{bmatrix} 2 & 4 & 7 \\ 3 & 7 & 9 \\ 1 & 2 & 3 \end{bmatrix}$$

2 An **orthogonal matrix** is a matrix which has its inverse equal to its transpose. Verify that

$$A = \frac{1}{3}\begin{bmatrix} 1 & -2 & 2 \\ 2 & -1 & -2 \\ -2 & -2 & -1 \end{bmatrix}$$

is an orthogonal matrix.

3 If

$$A = \begin{bmatrix} 3 & 2 & 4 \\ 2 & -2 & -6 \\ 4 & -6 & -1 \end{bmatrix} \qquad X = \begin{bmatrix} -2 & -2 & 1 \\ -2 & 1 & -2 \\ 1 & -2 & -2 \end{bmatrix}$$

show that $X^{\mathrm{T}}AX$ is a diagonal matrix.

4 Prove that if A and B are non-singular square matrices of the same order then AB is also non-singular and $(AB)^{-1} = B^{-1}A^{-1}$.

FURTHER EXERCISES (for answers see p. 751)

1 If A is a non-singular matrix, show in general that adj A is also non-singular and give an explicit formula for the inverse of adj A.

2 Obtain the relationship between the determinant of a square matrix A and the determinant of adj A, its adjoint matrix.

3 A company employs 45 people and there are three different grades of employee. The pay and profits are as follows:

Grade	Pay/hour (£)	Profit/hour (£)
1	2	4
2	4	-3
3	6	4

Obtain the numbers of employees in the various grades if the total wage bill is £200 per hour and the total profit is £75 per hour.

4 Show that if $AB = O$ and if either A or B is a non-singular square matrix then either $A = O$ or $B = O$.

5 Prove that, if A is a non-singular matrix, $(A^{\mathrm{T}})^{-1} = (A^{-1})^{\mathrm{T}}$.

6 Show that if the simultaneous equations

$$ax + by + h = 0$$
$$cx + dy + k = 0$$
$$ex + fy + l = 0$$

are consistent, then

$$\begin{vmatrix} a & b & h \\ c & d & k \\ e & f & l \end{vmatrix} = 0$$

By means of an example, show that this condition is no guarantee of consistency.

7 If

$$A = \begin{bmatrix} 7 & 8 & 9 \\ 0 & 3 & 3 \\ -2 & -4 & -4 \end{bmatrix}$$

k is known as an eigen value and *X* as the corresponding eigen vector. You may use these in stability work and vibrations. See also section 13.8.

and the equation $AX = kX$ is satisfied for some non-zero matrix X, prove that det $(A - kI) = 0$. Hence or otherwise obtain the three possible values of k.

8

$$A = \begin{bmatrix} 1 & -1 & 2 \\ 3 & 4 & 0 \\ -2 & 2 & -4 \end{bmatrix}$$

show that **a** A is singular and **b** A satisfies the equation $A^3 - A^2 - 9A = 0$.

9 If the input and output of a system are denoted by **y** and **x** respectively and are related by an equation of the form $\mathbf{y} = M\mathbf{x}$ where M is a matrix, then M is called a transmission matrix. If the transmission matrix M for a waveguide below cutoff is

$$\begin{bmatrix} \cosh a & Z \sinh a \\ (1/Z) \sinh a & \cosh a \end{bmatrix}$$

then

Transmission matrices arose in section 11.7.

a Show that M is non-singular and obtain its inverse;

b Show that for a cascade of n such waveguides the transmission matrix is

$$\begin{bmatrix} \cosh na & Z \sinh na \\ (1/Z) \sinh na & \cosh na \end{bmatrix}$$

10 If I is the 3×3 identity matrix and

$$S = \begin{bmatrix} 0 & 1 & 0 \\ -1 & 0 & 2 \\ 0 & -2 & 0 \end{bmatrix}$$

show that the matrix A given by $A = (I + S)(I - S)^{-1}$ is orthogonal. Hence, or otherwise, solve the matrix equation $AX = K$ where

$$X = \begin{bmatrix} x \\ y \\ z \end{bmatrix} \qquad K = \begin{bmatrix} 2 \\ 1 \\ 3 \end{bmatrix}$$

Vectors 14

In Chapter 13 we used the term vector to mean an algebraic vector. The vectors which we describe in this chapter have rather more structure and are widely used in applications.

After completing this chapter you should be able to
☐ Apply the rules of vector addition and scalar multiplication;
☐ Obtain the scalar product of two vectors;
☐ Obtain the vector product of two vectors;
☐ Use triple scalar products and triple vector products;
☐ Use vector methods to solve simple problems;
☐ Differentiate vectors.
At the end of the chapter we look at a simple practical problem in particle dynamics.

14.1 DESCRIPTIONS

You probably have an intuitive idea of what is meant by magnitude and direction. **Magnitude** gives a measure of how large something is, and **direction** an indication of where it applies. For example, meteorologists talk of a north-easterly wind of force 6. There the magnitude is 6 on the Beaufort scale and the direction is from the north-east.

Some concepts which arise in practice are adequately described purely in terms of a magnitude. Mass, volume, height, speed and time are all examples of quantities of this kind, and we call them **scalar quantities**.

Other concepts need not only a magnitude to describe them but also a direction. Velocity and displacement are examples in which both a magnitude and a direction are involved; we call these **vector quantities**.

Vectors are used in many areas of opplication. Fluid mechanics, hydraulic cngincering and structural mechanics are three areas where some engineering students apply them first.

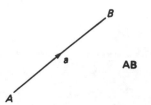

Fig. 14.1 Representation of a vector quantity.

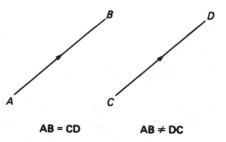

AB = CD   **AB ≠ DC**

Fig. 14.2 Equivalent and non-equivalent vector quantities.

In brief, two scalar quantities of the same type can be compared by their magnitudes, whereas two vector quantities of the same type cannot be compared adequately in this way. We shall use real numbers to represent scalar quantities and directed line segments to represent vector quantities.

So to represent a vector quantity we choose an initial point A and construct a directed line segment **AB** with the same direction as the vector quantity and with length AB proportional to its magnitude (Fig. 14.1). It is sometimes convenient to represent the vector quantity **AB** by means of the notation **a**, but then we usually need to refer to a diagram showing AB with an arrowhead somewhere on it so that the direction of the vector quantity is unambiguous.

Two parallel directed line segments with the same direction will be regarded as equivalent vector quantities (Fig. 14.2).

Although anything with both magnitude and direction can be thought of as a vector quantity, it would be wrong to think that all such things are vectors. A set of **vectors** is a set of vector quantities with operations known as **vector addition** and **scalar multiplication**. We must describe how each of these operations is performed.

14.2 VECTOR ADDITION

Vector addition is performed by the **parallelogram law**. Suppose we take two vector quantities **OP** and **OQ** and construct the parallelogram $OPRQ$

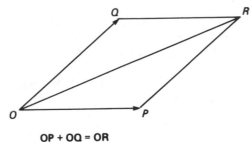

OP + OQ = OR

Fig. 14.3 The parallelogram law.

We first met the parallelogram law when we considered complex numbers in section 10.3.

Mechanical and Civil Engineers will use vector addition in many applications, such as resolving forces acting on structures.

(Fig. 14.3). Then a necessary condition for **OP** and **OQ** to be vectors is

$$\mathbf{OP} + \mathbf{OQ} = \mathbf{OR}$$

Many vector quantities are in fact examples of vectors because they combine according to the parallelogram law. However, others do not satisfy this condition and so are not vectors.

☐ A light aircraft travels the shortest route from London to Oxford and **Example** then from Oxford to York. The pilot keeps records of fuel consumed, travelling time and distance travelled.

For each leg, represent the journeys as vector quantities; the magnitude is the quantity recorded by the pilot, the direction is the direction of travel. Decide, in each case, which are vectors. You may neglect the curvature of the earth.

In Fig. 14.4 we may represent the journey from London to Oxford by **OP** and the journey from Oxford to York by **PR**. For these to constitute a set of vectors we require the journey from London to York to be represented by **OR**, where $OPRQ$ is a parallelogram.

If the magnitudes are proportional to the fuel consumption, then in general

$$\mathbf{OP} + \mathbf{PR} \neq \mathbf{OR}$$

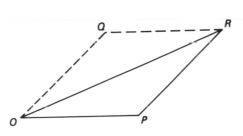

Fig. 14.4 The parallelogram.

To see why this is, we merely consider the situation in which there is a strong wind blowing in the direction from York to London. This would affect fuel consumption disproportionately. Therefore we do not have a set of vectors.

If the magnitudes are proportional to travelling time, then again we do not have a set of vectors for reasons similar to those given for fuel consumption.

If the magnitudes are proportional to the distances travelled then

$$\mathbf{OP} + \mathbf{PR} = \mathbf{OR}$$

These are a set of vectors, for if he had travelled from London, in the direction of **OR** and with distance OR, he would have arrived at York. ■

When no confusion is likely to occur we shall represent a vector by the notation **a** and its magnitude by $|\mathbf{a}|$.

When we employ this notation then it is often necessary to refer to a diagram.

! Note that we shall avoid the temptation to write the magnitude of **a** simply as a. This is because when we consider differentiation of vectors a conflict of notation can lead to error.

Example □ In Fig. 14.5 the parallelogram law is $\mathbf{a} + \mathbf{b} = \mathbf{c}$. The word resultant is often used for the vector obtained by adding two vectors. The resultant is usually shown on the diagram by means of a double arrow. ■

We have said that parallel vectors with the same magnitude and direction are equivalent to one another. Therefore every vector has a representative in the form of a vector emanating from a single point O. The terminology **free vector** for a vector which can start anywhere, and **localized vector** for a vector which must start from a fixed point, is in common usage.

It is convenient for us to be able to represent vectors in terms of coordinates. Suppose $Oxyz$ is a rectangular three-dimensional coordinate system (Fig. 14.6). We introduce three **unit vectors** **i**, **j** and **k** emanating from the origin O in the direction Ox, Oy and Oz respectively, each having a unit magnitude.

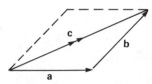

Fig. 14.5 The resultant.

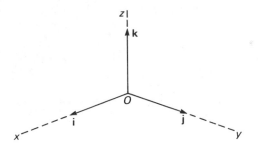

Fig. 14.6 The unit vectors **i**, **j** and **k**.

0 is a special vector called the **zero vector**; it has zero magnitude and arbitrary direction. Any vector which has magnitude 1 is called a **unit vector**.

BINARY OPERATIONS

We know how to add and multiply scalars, since these rules are the usual rules for dealing with real numbers.

We have also described the rule for adding two vectors **a** and **b** together to produce **a** + **b**. This is known as a **binary operation**:

$$(\mathbf{a}, \mathbf{b}) \rightarrow \mathbf{a} + \mathbf{b}$$

We think of this as the parallelogram law. Later we shall describe two further binary operations on vectors which produce a scalar known as the **scalar product**, and a vector known as the **vector product**.

Before this we need to describe how to multiply a scalar by a vector. We shall call this operation **scalar multiplication**. However, it must not be confused with the scalar product, which is an operation we shall describe later.

14.3 SCALAR MULTIPLICATION

If **a** is a vector and p is a real number then we define $p\mathbf{a}$ to be a vector with the following properties (Fig. 14.7):

1 If $p > 0$ then $p\mathbf{a}$ has the same direction as **a** and magnitude p times that of **a**.

2 If $p < 0$ then $p\mathbf{a}$ has the opposite direction to **a** and magnitude $(-p)$ times that of **a**.

3 If $p - 0$ then $p\mathbf{a}$ has arbitrary direction and magnitude 0.

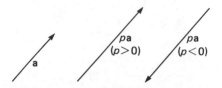

Fig. 14.7 Scalar multiplication.

Having dealt with vector addition and scalar multiplication, we can summarize the position so far in a set of rules. Suppose p and q are any real numbers (scalars) and $\mathbf{a}$, $\mathbf{b}$ and $\mathbf{c}$ are arbitrary vectors. Then the following rules hold:

$$\mathbf{a} + \mathbf{b} = \mathbf{b} + \mathbf{a}$$
$$(\mathbf{a} + \mathbf{b}) + \mathbf{c} = \mathbf{a} + (\mathbf{b} + \mathbf{c})$$
$$\mathbf{a} + \mathbf{0} = \mathbf{0} + \mathbf{a} = \mathbf{a}$$
$$\mathbf{a} + (-\mathbf{a}) = (-\mathbf{a}) + \mathbf{a} = \mathbf{0}$$

$$p(\mathbf{a} + \mathbf{b}) = p\mathbf{a} + p\mathbf{b}$$
$$p(q\mathbf{a}) = (pq)\mathbf{a}$$
$$(p + q)\mathbf{a} = p\mathbf{a} + q\mathbf{a}$$

Example ☐ Show that there is only one zero vector $\mathbf{0}$.

Suppose that there are two zero vectors $\mathbf{0}_1$ and $\mathbf{0}_2$. Then with $\mathbf{a} = \mathbf{0}_1$ and $\mathbf{0} = \mathbf{0}_2$ we can use ·

$$\mathbf{a} + \mathbf{0} = \mathbf{0} + \mathbf{a} = \mathbf{a}$$

to obtain

$$\mathbf{0}_1 + \mathbf{0}_2 = \mathbf{0}_2 + \mathbf{0}_1 = \mathbf{0}_1$$

Whereas with $\mathbf{a} = \mathbf{0}_2$ and $\mathbf{0} = \mathbf{0}_1$ we obtain

$$\mathbf{0}_2 + \mathbf{0}_1 = \mathbf{0}_1 + \mathbf{0}_2 = \mathbf{0}_2$$

Therefore $\mathbf{0}_1 = \mathbf{0}_2$. ∎

This is quite an interesting result because originally we defined $\mathbf{0}$ to be a vector with zero magnitude and arbitrary direction. It might be thought therefore that there are an *infinity* of zero vectors. This example has shown that this is not the case. If you have nothing, it doesn't matter what you do with it!

14.4 COMPONENTS

Suppose we have a rectangular cartesian coordinate system $Oxyz$ and that, relative to this system, P is the point (a_1, a_2, a_3) (Fig. 14.8). We have

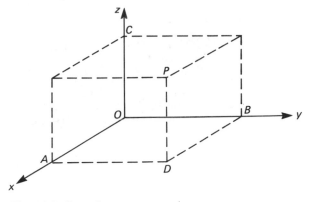

Fig. 14.8 Cartesian representation.

defined **i**, **j** and **k** to be unit vectors in the directions Ox, Oy and Oz respectively. Using the diagram,

$$\begin{aligned}
\mathbf{r} = \mathbf{OP} &= \mathbf{OD} + \mathbf{DP} \\
&= \mathbf{OA} + \mathbf{AD} + \mathbf{DP} \\
&= \mathbf{OA} + \mathbf{OB} + \mathbf{OC} \\
&= a_1\mathbf{i} + a_2\mathbf{j} + a_3\mathbf{k}
\end{aligned}$$

Also

$$\begin{aligned}
|\mathbf{r}| = OP &= \sqrt{(OD^2 + DP^2)} \\
&= \sqrt{(OA^2 + AD^2 + DP^2)} \\
&= \sqrt{(a_1^2 + a_2^2 + a_3^2)}
\end{aligned}$$

When a vector is expressed in this way we say it has been expressed in terms of **components**. (These are also known as resolutes or projections.)

If **r** is a vector it is customary to represent a unit vector in the same direction by $\hat{\mathbf{r}}$. We then have

$$\mathbf{r} = |\mathbf{r}|\, \hat{\mathbf{r}}$$

or equivalently

$$\hat{\mathbf{r}} = \frac{1}{|\mathbf{r}|}\, \mathbf{r}$$

☐ If $\mathbf{a} = 3\mathbf{i} - 4\mathbf{j} + 5\mathbf{k}$ and $\mathbf{b} = \mathbf{i} - 5\mathbf{j} + 7\mathbf{k}$, obtain (a) $\mathbf{a} + \mathbf{b}$ (b) a unit **Example** vector in the direction of $\mathbf{a} - \mathbf{b}$ (c) a unit vector in the opposite direction to $\mathbf{a} - \mathbf{b}$.
a We have

$$\begin{aligned}
\mathbf{a} + \mathbf{b} &= (3\mathbf{i} - 4\mathbf{j} + 5\mathbf{k}) + (\mathbf{i} - 5\mathbf{j} + 7\mathbf{k}) \\
&= 4\mathbf{i} - 9\mathbf{j} + 12\mathbf{k}
\end{aligned}$$

b First,

$$\mathbf{a} - \mathbf{b} = (3\mathbf{i} - 4\mathbf{j} + 5\mathbf{k}) - (\mathbf{i} - 5\mathbf{j} + 7\mathbf{k})$$
$$= 2\mathbf{i} + \mathbf{j} - 2\mathbf{k}$$

Therefore

$$|\mathbf{a} - \mathbf{b}| = \sqrt{[(2)^2 + (1)^2 + (-2)^2]} = \sqrt{9} = 3$$

So the required vector is

$$\frac{1}{3}(\mathbf{a} - \mathbf{b}) = \frac{2}{3}\mathbf{i} + \frac{1}{3}\mathbf{j} - \frac{2}{3}\mathbf{k}$$

c The required vector is

$$-\frac{1}{3}(\mathbf{a} - \mathbf{b}) = -\frac{2}{3}\mathbf{i} - \frac{1}{3}\mathbf{j} + \frac{2}{3}\mathbf{k} \qquad \blacksquare$$

14.5 THE SCALAR PRODUCT

Given any two vectors **a** and **b**, we define the **scalar product a · b** by the formula

$$\mathbf{a} \cdot \mathbf{b} = |\mathbf{a}||\mathbf{b}| \cos \theta$$

where θ is the angle between the two vectors (Fig. 14.9).

We observe that **a · b** is always a scalar, and this is why it is called the scalar product. Sometimes it is known as the **dot product** because of this notation, and to avoid confusion with scalar multiplication.

Note that since $\cos \theta = \cos (2\pi - \theta)$ it does not matter whether the included angle or the excluded angle between the two vectors is chosen. Moreover,

$$\mathbf{b} \cdot \mathbf{a} = |\mathbf{b}||\mathbf{a}| \cos \theta = \mathbf{a} \cdot \mathbf{b}$$

That is, **a · b = b · a** for all vectors **a** and **b**. This is known as the **commutative rule**, and we have shown that it holds for the scalar product. Later we shall see that for the other type of product, the vector product, the commutative law does *not* hold.

Example □ Show that if **a** and **b** are non-zero vectors then

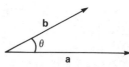

Fig. 14.9 The angle between two vectors.

$$\mathbf{a} \cdot \mathbf{b} = 0$$

if and only if **a** and **b** are mutually perpendicular.

Suppose first that $\mathbf{a} \cdot \mathbf{b} = 0$. Then

$$|\mathbf{a}||\mathbf{b}| \cos \theta = 0$$

and since neither **a** nor **b** is the zero vector we conclude that $|\mathbf{a}| \neq 0$ and $|\mathbf{b}| \neq 0$. Consequently $\cos \theta = 0$ and so $\theta = \pi/2$ (or $3\pi/2$); therefore **a** and **b** are mutually perpendicular.

Conversely, if **a** and **b** are mutually perpendicular then $\theta = \pi/2$ (or $3\pi/2$) and it follows that $\mathbf{a} \cdot \mathbf{b} = 0$. ∎

We have also

$$\mathbf{a} \cdot \mathbf{a} = |\mathbf{a}||\mathbf{a}| \cos \theta = |\mathbf{a}|^2$$

so that

$$\mathbf{i} \cdot \mathbf{i} = \mathbf{j} \cdot \mathbf{j} = \mathbf{k} \cdot \mathbf{k} = 1$$
$$\mathbf{i} \cdot \mathbf{j} = \mathbf{j} \cdot \mathbf{k} = \mathbf{k} \cdot \mathbf{i} = 0$$

14.6 DIRECTION RATIOS AND DIRECTION COSINES

If we multiply a vector by a positive number we preserve the direction of the vector. Likewise if we multiply it by a negative number the direction is reversed. It follows that if

$$\mathbf{r} = l\mathbf{i} + m\mathbf{j} + n\mathbf{k}$$

where the components l, m and n are non-zero, then the ratio $l : m : n$ determines the direction (but not the sense) of the vector. Any three numbers which are in these proportions are known as **direction ratios**.

Another way of fixing the direction of a vector is by means of a unit vector in the same direction. Suppose that

$$\mathbf{u} = u_1\mathbf{i} + u_2\mathbf{j} + u_3\mathbf{k}$$

is a unit vector in the direction of the vector **r**. Then if α, β and γ are the angles between this vector and the axes Ox, Oy and Oz respectively (Fig. 14.10) we have

$$u_1 = \mathbf{u} \cdot \mathbf{i} = (1)(1) \cos \alpha = \cos \alpha$$
$$u_2 = \mathbf{u} \cdot \mathbf{j} = (1)(1) \cos \beta = \cos \beta$$
$$u_3 = \mathbf{u} \cdot \mathbf{k} = (1)(1) \cos \gamma = \cos \gamma$$

Therefore

$$\mathbf{u} = \cos \alpha\mathbf{i} + \cos \beta\mathbf{j} + \cos \gamma\mathbf{k}$$

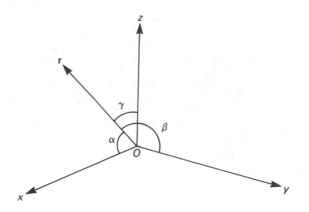

Fig. 14.10 Direction cosines.

These cosines are called the **direction cosines**.

Note that

$$|\mathbf{u}|^2 = 1 = \cos^2 \alpha + \cos^2 \beta + \cos^2 \gamma$$

Therefore the direction cosines are not independent of one another and cannot all be chosen arbitrarily.

14.7 APPLICATIONS

We can use the scalar product to obtain the component of one vector in the direction of another. For example, suppose we have two vectors **a** and **b** and we require the component of **a** in the direction of **b**. We first obtain a unit vector $\mathbf{u} = \hat{\mathbf{b}}$, and then $\mathbf{a} \cdot \mathbf{u} = |\mathbf{a}|\,(1)\cos\theta$ is the required component.

Extending this idea, suppose we have a particle which is subject to a constant force **F**. The work done by the force is defined to be the magnitude of the force multiplied by the distance moved in the direction of the force. Equivalently the work done by the force is the displacement multiplied by the component of the force in the direction of the displacement. It follows that if the particle is displaced by **s** then the work done by **F** is simply $\mathbf{F} \cdot \mathbf{s}$ (Fig. 14.11).

Example □ A force of 3 newtons is applied from the origin to a particle placed at the point $P\,(1, 2, 2)$ and subject to a system of forces. The particle is displaced to $Q\,(3, 4, 5)$. If all distances are in metres, calculate the work W done by the force.

We have

$$\mathbf{F} = \mathbf{i} + 2\mathbf{j} + 2\mathbf{k}$$

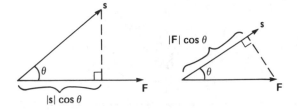

Fig. 14.11 The work done by a force.

and

$$\mathbf{PQ} = \mathbf{PO} + \mathbf{OQ} = \mathbf{OQ} - \mathbf{OP}$$
$$= (3\mathbf{i} + 4\mathbf{j} + 5\mathbf{k}) - (\mathbf{i} + 2\mathbf{j} + 2\mathbf{k}) = 2\mathbf{i} + 2\mathbf{j} + 3\mathbf{k}$$

So

$$W = \mathbf{F} \cdot \mathbf{s} = (\mathbf{i} + 2\mathbf{j} + 2\mathbf{k}) \cdot (2\mathbf{i} + 2\mathbf{j} + 3\mathbf{k})$$
$$= 2 + 4 + 6 = 12 \text{ Nm}$$

14.8 ALGEBRAIC PROPERTIES

There are a number of algebraic properties which follow from the definition of the scalar product.

Suppose $\mathbf{a}$, $\mathbf{b}$ and $\mathbf{c}$ are vectors and p is a scalar. Then

$$p(\mathbf{a} \cdot \mathbf{b}) = (p\mathbf{a}) \cdot \mathbf{b}$$
$$(\mathbf{a} + \mathbf{b}) \cdot \mathbf{c} = \mathbf{a} \cdot \mathbf{c} + \mathbf{b} \cdot \mathbf{c}$$

This is the **distributive rule** for the dot product. Note that we are using the convention of elementary algebra that multiplication takes precedence over addition. Without this convention we should need to include more brackets:

$$(\mathbf{a} + \mathbf{b}) \cdot \mathbf{c} = (\mathbf{a} \cdot \mathbf{c}) + (\mathbf{b} \cdot \mathbf{c})$$

□ Prove that if p is any scalar and $\mathbf{a}$ and $\mathbf{b}$ are arbitrary vectors then **Example**

$$p(\mathbf{a} \cdot \mathbf{b}) = (p\mathbf{a}) \cdot \mathbf{b}$$

We have

$$p(\mathbf{a} \cdot \mathbf{b}) = p|\mathbf{a}||\mathbf{b}| \cos \theta$$

First, if $p \geqslant 0$ then $|p\mathbf{a}| = p|\mathbf{a}|$. So

$$p(\mathbf{a} \cdot \mathbf{b}) = p|\mathbf{a}||\mathbf{b}| \cos \theta$$
$$= |p\mathbf{a}||\mathbf{b}| \cos \theta$$
$$= (p\mathbf{a}) \cdot \mathbf{b}$$

Next, if $p < 0$ then $|p\mathbf{a}| = (-p)|\mathbf{a}|$. So

$$
\begin{aligned}
p(\mathbf{a} \cdot \mathbf{b}) &= -[(-p)|\mathbf{a}|\,|\mathbf{b}|\cos\theta] \\
&= -|p\mathbf{a}|\,|\mathbf{b}|\cos\theta \\
&= |p\mathbf{a}|\,|\mathbf{b}|\cos(\pi - \theta) \\
&= (p\mathbf{a}) \cdot \mathbf{b}
\end{aligned}
$$

■

Here is a very simple formula which enables us to determine the scalar product when the vectors are given in terms of coordinates. Suppose $\mathbf{a} = a_1\mathbf{i} + a_2\mathbf{j} + a_3\mathbf{k}$ and $\mathbf{b} = b_1\mathbf{i} + b_2\mathbf{j} + b_3\mathbf{k}$. Then

$$\mathbf{a} \cdot \mathbf{b} = a_1 b_1 + a_2 b_2 + a_3 b_3$$

This is easy to establish, as you will see later in this chapter.

Example □ Obtain the acute angle between two diagonals which each pass through the centre of a cube. We remark that without the use of vectors this would be quite a difficult problem.

Judicious use of vectors can enable awkward distances and angles to be calculated in Surveying.

Consider a unit cube and position it in such a way that one corner is at the origin O and the axes Ox, Oy and Oz lie along the edges incident at O (Fig. 14.12). It does not matter which pair of the four principal diagonals we choose, as any pair is equivalent to any other. At first sight the diagonals EB and AD may appear to give a different angle from the pair EB and CF, but a few moments' consideration will show that this is not really so.

Using the diagram we require the angle between OP and AD:

$$
\begin{aligned}
\mathbf{OP} &= \mathbf{OA} + \mathbf{AF} + \mathbf{FP} = \mathbf{OA} + \mathbf{OB} + \mathbf{OC} = \mathbf{i} + \mathbf{j} + \mathbf{k} \\
\mathbf{AD} &= \mathbf{AF} + \mathbf{FP} + \mathbf{PD} = \mathbf{OB} + \mathbf{OC} - \mathbf{OA} = \mathbf{j} + \mathbf{k} - \mathbf{i}
\end{aligned}
$$

Now $\mathbf{OP} \cdot \mathbf{AD} = |\mathbf{OP}||\mathbf{AD}|\cos\theta$, where θ is the angle between OP and AD. Therefore

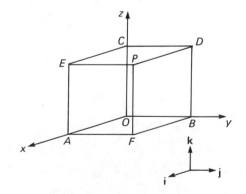

Fig. 14.12 A cube relative to $Oxyz$.

$$(\mathbf{i} + \mathbf{j} + \mathbf{k}) \cdot (-\mathbf{i} + \mathbf{j} + \mathbf{k}) = |\mathbf{i} + \mathbf{j} + \mathbf{k}||-\mathbf{i} + \mathbf{j} + \mathbf{k}| \cos \theta$$
$$-1 + 1 + 1 = \sqrt{3} \sqrt{3} \cos \theta$$

and therefore $\theta = \cos^{-1} (1/3)$.   ■

14.9 THE VECTOR PRODUCT

We now introduce another binary operation known as the vector product. Remember that in general a binary operation takes two things and produces from it a third. We use binary operations all the time. For example, whenever we add two numbers together we are performing a binary operation.

Let us review the binary operations involving vectors which we have encountered so far:

1 scalar multiplication $(p, \mathbf{a}) \rightarrow p\mathbf{a}$
2 vector addition $(\mathbf{a}, \mathbf{b}) \rightarrow \mathbf{a} + \mathbf{b}$
3 scalar product $(\mathbf{a}, \mathbf{b}) \rightarrow \mathbf{a} \cdot \mathbf{b}$

We have seen that given two vectors $\mathbf{a}$ and $\mathbf{b}$ the scalar product results in a scalar $\mathbf{a} \cdot \mathbf{b}$. The new operation which we shall now consider produces from two vectors $\mathbf{a}$ and $\mathbf{b}$ another vector $\mathbf{a} \times \mathbf{b}$. The vector product is sometimes known as the **cross product** because of this notation. An alternative notation is $\mathbf{a} \wedge \mathbf{b}$.

Those studying structural mechanics are certain to use both the dot product and the cross product.

Suppose $\mathbf{a}$ and $\mathbf{b}$ are any two non-zero vectors. Then we can choose representatives emanating from O (Fig. 14.13). Moreover, unless they are parallel to one another, they determine a plane in which each of them lies. There are two unit vectors perpendicular to this plane passing through O. It will be convenient to use the special symbols $\odot$ and $\oplus$; the first indicates a vector coming out of the plane towards you, and the second indicates a vector going into the plane away from you. The symbols are inspired by an arrow. The point shows it coming towards you, the tail feathers show it going away.

We shall use $\mathbf{n}$ for a unit vector normal to the plane. We define the **vector product** as

$$\mathbf{a} \times \mathbf{b} = |\mathbf{a}||\mathbf{b}| \sin \theta \, \mathbf{n}$$

where the direction of $\mathbf{n}$ is obtained by the right hand rule.

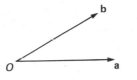

Fig. 14.13 Two vectors emanating from O.

The right-hand rule has many applications in engineering, and particularly in electromagnetism, where it can be used as a simple method of determining relationships between currents and magnetic fields.

The **right-hand rule** is sometimes known as the corkscrew rule. Ordinary wood screws, jar tops etc. have a right-hand thread. Imagine rotating a screw which is in a piece of wood from the direction **a** to the direction **b** (Fig. 14.14). Then the screw would tend to come out of the wood, and so the direction of **n** is out of the plane towards you. Conversely, if **a** and **b** are reversed then as we rotate the screw from **a** to **b** the screw goes into the wood (Fig. 14.15), and the direction of **n** is into the plane away from you.

For the sake of completeness, if either **a** or **b** is **0** then we define **a** × **b** = **0** too.

We have in all cases

$$|\mathbf{a} \times \mathbf{b}| = |\mathbf{a}|\,|\mathbf{b}|\,|\sin\,\theta|$$

but of course **a** × **b** = −**b** × **a** because the unit vectors concerned have opposite directions.

We can show that

$$\mathbf{a} \times \mathbf{b} = -\mathbf{b} \times \mathbf{a}$$

algebraically by using the definition (see also Fig. 14.16). We have

$$\mathbf{a} \times \mathbf{b} = |\mathbf{a}|\,|\mathbf{b}|\,\sin\,\theta\,\mathbf{n}$$

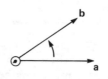

Fig. 14.14 a × **b** (out of the plane).

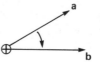

Fig. 14.15 a × **b** (into the plane).

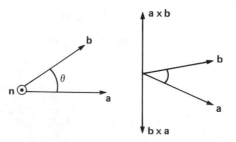

Fig. 14.16 The vector product.

So

$$\mathbf{b} \times \mathbf{a} = |\mathbf{b}||\mathbf{a}| \sin (2\pi - \theta) \mathbf{n}$$
$$= -|\mathbf{a}||\mathbf{b}| \sin \theta \mathbf{n} = -\mathbf{a} \times \mathbf{b}$$

☐ Show that if $\mathbf{a}$ and $\mathbf{b}$ are non-zero vectors then $\mathbf{a} \times \mathbf{b} = \mathbf{0}$ if and only if $\mathbf{a}$ **Example**
and $\mathbf{b}$ are parallel.

Suppose $\mathbf{a} \times \mathbf{b} = \mathbf{0}$. Then $|\mathbf{a} \times \mathbf{b}| = 0$. So $|\mathbf{a}||\mathbf{b}||\sin \theta| = 0$, and since $\mathbf{a}$
and $\mathbf{b}$ are non-zero it follows that $\sin \theta = 0$. So $\theta = 0$ or $\theta = \pi$ and the
vectors are parallel.

Conversely, suppose the vectors $\mathbf{a}$ and $\mathbf{b}$ are parallel. Then either $\theta = 0$
or $\theta = \pi$, and it follows that

$$\mathbf{a} \times \mathbf{b} = |\mathbf{a}||\mathbf{b}| \sin \theta \mathbf{n} = 0\mathbf{n} = \mathbf{0} \qquad \blacksquare$$

It follows of course that $\mathbf{a} \times \mathbf{a} = \mathbf{0}$, and in fact we can easily obtain the
vector products of the vectors $\mathbf{i}$, $\mathbf{j}$ and $\mathbf{k}$ (Fig. 14.17):

$$\mathbf{i} \times \mathbf{j} = \mathbf{k} \qquad \mathbf{j} \times \mathbf{i} = -\mathbf{k}$$
$$\mathbf{j} \times \mathbf{k} = \mathbf{i} \qquad \mathbf{k} \times \mathbf{j} = -\mathbf{i}$$
$$\mathbf{k} \times \mathbf{i} = \mathbf{j} \qquad \mathbf{i} \times \mathbf{k} = -\mathbf{j}$$

Corresponding to the algebraic properties we derived for the scalar product,
there are similar properties for the vector product. Suppose $\mathbf{a}$ and $\mathbf{b}$ are
arbitrary vectors and that p is a scalar. Then

$$p(\mathbf{a} \times \mathbf{b}) = (p\mathbf{a}) \times \mathbf{b}$$
$$(\mathbf{a} + \mathbf{b}) \times \mathbf{c} = \mathbf{a} \times \mathbf{c} + \mathbf{b} \times \mathbf{c}$$

☐ Prove that if p is a scalar and $\mathbf{a}$ and $\mathbf{b}$ are arbitrary vectors then   **Example**

$$p(\mathbf{a} \times \mathbf{b}) = (p\mathbf{a}) \times \mathbf{b}$$

Fig. 14.18 illustrates the alternatives.

If $p > 0$ then

$$(p\mathbf{a}) \times \mathbf{b} = |p\mathbf{a}||\mathbf{b}| \sin \theta \mathbf{n}$$
$$= p|\mathbf{a}||\mathbf{b}| \sin \theta \mathbf{n}$$
$$= p(\mathbf{a} \times \mathbf{b})$$

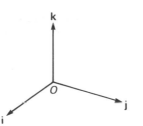

Fig. 14.17 The standard unit vectors.

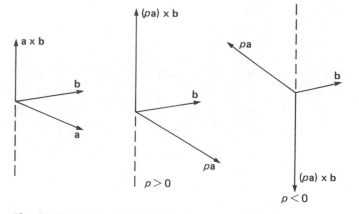

Fig. 14.18 Verification that $(p\mathbf{a}) \times \mathbf{b} = p(\mathbf{a} \times \mathbf{b})$.

If $p < 0$ then

$$
\begin{aligned}
(p\mathbf{a}) \times \mathbf{b} &= |p\mathbf{a}| |\mathbf{b}| \sin \theta \, (-\mathbf{n}) \\
&= (-p) |\mathbf{a}| |\mathbf{b}| \sin \theta \, (-\mathbf{n}) \\
&= p|\mathbf{a}| |\mathbf{b}| \sin \theta \, \mathbf{n} \\
&= p(\mathbf{a} \times \mathbf{b})
\end{aligned}
$$

If $p = 0$ the conclusion is immediate. ∎

Here is a formula which enables us to determine the vector product when the vectors are given in terms of coordinates. Suppose $\mathbf{a} = a_1\mathbf{i} + a_2\mathbf{j} + a_3\mathbf{k}$ and $\mathbf{b} = b_1\mathbf{i} + b_2\mathbf{j} + b_3\mathbf{k}$. Then

$$
\begin{aligned}
\mathbf{a} \times \mathbf{b} &= (a_2b_3 - a_3b_2)\mathbf{i} - (a_1b_3 - a_3b_1)\mathbf{j} + (a_1b_2 - a_2b_1)\mathbf{k} \\
&= \begin{vmatrix} \mathbf{i} & \mathbf{j} & \mathbf{k} \\ a_1 & a_2 & a_3 \\ b_1 & b_2 & b_3 \end{vmatrix}
\end{aligned}
$$

Notice how useful the determinant notation is here, and how easy it is to remember this formula provided we know how to expand determinants (Chapter 12). The first row consists of the unit vectors $\mathbf{i}$, $\mathbf{j}$ and $\mathbf{k}$. The next two rows consist of the components of the vectors $\mathbf{a}$ and $\mathbf{b}$ respectively. It is interesting also to notice that, by the rules of determinants, if we interchange two rows the determinant changes sign. This gives another proof that $\mathbf{a} \times \mathbf{b} = -\mathbf{b} \times \mathbf{a}$. The formula is quite easy to obtain, as you will see later in the chapter.

Let's summarize what we have learnt so far:
☐ We began with scalar quantities and vector quantities.

□ We added vectors together using the parallelogram law.
□ We multiplied vectors by scalars.
□ We expressed vectors in terms of components.
□ We defined the scalar product of two vectors.
□ We defined the vector product of two vectors.
Right! Are you ready for some steps? If necessary you can read through all
we have covered once more.

_____ 14.10 Workshop _____

1

▷**Exercise** A man travels over the surface of the earth, first from Moscow
to Paris and then from Paris to Cairo. Representing these journeys as
vector quantities, where the magnitude of each is the shortest distance over
the earth's surface, decide whether or not they are a set of vectors.
    Think carefully about this before you decide.

2

They do *not* constitute a set of vectors because the parallelogram law does
not in general apply where distances are measured over the curved surface
of the earth.
    If you were wrong, don't worry: we are only just getting warmed up! Try
this exercise.

▷**Exercise** If $a = a_1 i + a_2 j + a_3 k$, show that

$$a \cdot i = a_1 \qquad a \cdot j = a_2 \qquad a \cdot k = a_3$$

Try this using the rules carefully. Then step ahead.

3

First,

$$\begin{aligned} a \cdot i &= (a_1 i + a_2 j + a_3 k) \cdot i \\ &= a_1(i \cdot i) + a_2(j \cdot i) + a_3(k \cdot i) \\ &= a_1 1 + a_2 0 + a_3 0 = a_1 \end{aligned}$$

If you didn't manage that you should now be able to obtain $a \cdot j$ and $a \cdot k$.
    Then go on to the next exercise.

▷**Exercise** If $a = a_1 i + a_2 j + a_3 k$ and $b = b_1 i + b_2 j + b_3 k$, show that

$$a \cdot b = a_1 b_1 + a_2 b_2 + a_3 b_3$$

Try this using the results of the previous exercise.

4

The working is

$$\begin{aligned}
\mathbf{a} \cdot \mathbf{b} &= \mathbf{a} \cdot (b_1\mathbf{i} + b_2\mathbf{j} + b_3\mathbf{k}) \\
&= (\mathbf{a} \cdot \mathbf{i})b_1 + (\mathbf{a} \cdot \mathbf{j})b_2 + (\mathbf{a} \cdot \mathbf{k})b_3 \\
&= a_1b_1 + a_2b_2 + a_3b_3
\end{aligned}$$

This should have caused no difficulty. If it did then repeat the exercise, taking the vector **a** in components instead of **b**.

Then go on to the next exercise.

▷**Exercise** Without expressing the vectors in terms of components, show that

$$\mathbf{a} \cdot (\mathbf{b} + \mathbf{c}) = \mathbf{a} \cdot \mathbf{b} + \mathbf{a} \cdot \mathbf{c}$$

Don't assume any algebraic properties that we have not already discussed. Try it, then step forward.

---

5 We have

$$\mathbf{a} \cdot (\mathbf{b} + \mathbf{c}) = (\mathbf{b} + \mathbf{c}) \cdot \mathbf{a}$$

because the scalar product is commutative. Then

$$= \mathbf{b} \cdot \mathbf{a} + \mathbf{c} \cdot \mathbf{a}$$

using the distributive rule. Finally

$$= \mathbf{a} \cdot \mathbf{b} + \mathbf{a} \cdot \mathbf{c}$$

again using the commutative property of the dot product.

That was a little algebraic perhaps, so let's solve a more practical problem.

▷**Exercise** A rectangular building has a square cross-section and is twice as long as it is wide. Two thin wires are to be inserted joining the corners at the top of one end of the building to the diagonally opposite corners at the bottom of the far end. Calculate the cosine of the angle between these two wires (Fig. 14.19).

This is very similar to the problem in the text involving the cube. If you can do that, you can do this.

---

6 We set up the building in a coordinate system (Fig. 14.20) just as we did for the cube (Fig. 14.12). Then in Fig. 14.20 we have

$$|\mathbf{OB}| = 2|\mathbf{OA}| = 2|\mathbf{OC}|$$

So, taking $|\mathbf{OA}| = 1$, we have

$$\begin{aligned}
\mathbf{OP} &= \mathbf{OA} + \mathbf{AF} + \mathbf{FP} \\
&= \mathbf{OA} + \mathbf{OB} + \mathbf{OC} = \mathbf{i} + 2\mathbf{j} + \mathbf{k}
\end{aligned}$$

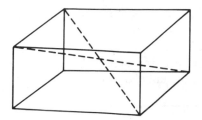

Fig. 14.19 Building with diagonals.

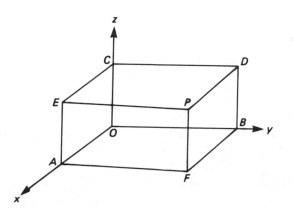

Fig. 14.20 Building relative to *Oxyz*.

$$\mathbf{AD} = \mathbf{AF} + \mathbf{FP} + \mathbf{PD}$$
$$= \mathbf{OB} + \mathbf{OC} - \mathbf{OA} = -\mathbf{i} + 2\mathbf{j} + \mathbf{k}$$

Now

$$\mathbf{OP} \cdot \mathbf{AD} = |\mathbf{OP}||\mathbf{AD}| \cos \theta$$

So

$$(\mathbf{i} + 2\mathbf{j} + \mathbf{k}) \cdot (-\mathbf{i} + 2\mathbf{j} + \mathbf{k}) = |\mathbf{i} + 2\mathbf{j} + \mathbf{k}||-\mathbf{i} + 2\mathbf{j} + \mathbf{k}| \cos \theta$$

Therefore

$$-1 + 4 + 1 = \sqrt{(1 + 4 + 1)}\sqrt{(1 + 4 + 1)} \cos \theta$$
$$4 = 6 \cos \theta$$

so that $\cos \theta = 2/3$.

If you didn't get that right, try the cube again without looking at the solution. Then repeat the building exercise.

Now let's see if we can handle the vector product.

▷**Exercise** Expand

a $\mathbf{a} \times (\mathbf{b} + \mathbf{c})$

b $(\mathbf{a} + \mathbf{b}) \times (\mathbf{c} + \mathbf{d})$

To do this you need to use the same techniques as at step 5 for the scalar product, although the formulas differ a little. Try it and see how it goes.

7

a We have

$$\begin{aligned}
\mathbf{a} \times (\mathbf{b} + \mathbf{c}) &= -(\mathbf{b} + \mathbf{c}) \times \mathbf{a} \\
&= -(\mathbf{b} \times \mathbf{a} + \mathbf{c} \times \mathbf{a}) \\
&= -\mathbf{b} \times \mathbf{a} - \mathbf{c} \times \mathbf{a} \\
&= \mathbf{a} \times \mathbf{b} + \mathbf{a} \times \mathbf{c}
\end{aligned}$$

b First write $\mathbf{e} = \mathbf{c} + \mathbf{d}$. Then

$$\begin{aligned}
(\mathbf{a} + \mathbf{b}) \times (\mathbf{c} + \mathbf{d}) &= (\mathbf{a} + \mathbf{b}) \times \mathbf{e} \\
&= \mathbf{a} \times \mathbf{e} + \mathbf{b} \times \mathbf{e} \\
&= \mathbf{a} \times (\mathbf{c} + \mathbf{d}) + \mathbf{b} \times (\mathbf{c} + \mathbf{d}) \\
&= \mathbf{a} \times \mathbf{c} + \mathbf{a} \times \mathbf{d} + \mathbf{b} \times \mathbf{c} + \mathbf{b} \times \mathbf{d}
\end{aligned}$$

Did you manage that all right? If you didn't then you must be extra specially careful about the next problem.

▷**Exercise** Simplify $(\mathbf{a} + \mathbf{b}) \times (\mathbf{a} - \mathbf{b})$

Do be careful!

8

We have

$$\begin{aligned}
(\mathbf{a} + \mathbf{b}) \times (\mathbf{a} - \mathbf{b}) &= \mathbf{a} \times \mathbf{a} + \mathbf{b} \times \mathbf{a} - \mathbf{a} \times \mathbf{b} - \mathbf{b} \times \mathbf{b} \\
&= 0 + \mathbf{b} \times \mathbf{a} - \mathbf{a} \times \mathbf{b} - 0 \\
&= 2(\mathbf{b} \times \mathbf{a})
\end{aligned}$$

Did you fall into the trap of cancelling out $\mathbf{a} \times \mathbf{b}$ and deducing the incorrect answer $\mathbf{0}$? You must remember that for the vector product the commutative law does *not* hold.

Now try one last exercise.

▷**Exercise** Obtain the formula for the vector product of $\mathbf{a} = a_1\mathbf{i} + a_2\mathbf{j} + a_3\mathbf{k}$ and $\mathbf{b} = b_1\mathbf{i} + b_2\mathbf{j} + b_3\mathbf{k}$.

This is not too hard now that we know how to multiply out. Do this carefully, and remember to write down the vector products in the right order.

9

We have

$$\begin{aligned}
\mathbf{a} \times \mathbf{b} &= (a_1\mathbf{i} + a_2\mathbf{j} + a_3\mathbf{k}) \times \mathbf{b} \\
&= a_1(\mathbf{i} \times \mathbf{b}) + a_2(\mathbf{j} \times \mathbf{b}) + a_3(\mathbf{k} \times \mathbf{b})
\end{aligned}$$

$$= a_1\mathbf{i} \times (b_1\mathbf{i} + b_2\mathbf{j} + b_3\mathbf{k})$$
$$+ a_2\mathbf{j} \times (b_1\mathbf{i} + b_2\mathbf{j} + b_3\mathbf{k})$$
$$+ a_3\mathbf{k} \times (b_1\mathbf{i} + b_2\mathbf{j} + b_3\mathbf{k})$$
$$= a_1b_2(\mathbf{i} \times \mathbf{j}) + a_1b_3(\mathbf{i} \times \mathbf{k}) + a_2b_1(\mathbf{j} \times \mathbf{i})$$
$$+ a_2b_3(\mathbf{j} \times \mathbf{k}) + a_3b_1(\mathbf{k} \times \mathbf{i}) + a_3b_2(\mathbf{k} \times \mathbf{j})$$
$$= a_1b_2\mathbf{k} - a_1b_3\mathbf{j} - a_2b_1\mathbf{k}$$
$$+ a_2b_3\mathbf{i} + a_3b_1\mathbf{j} - a_3b_2\mathbf{i}$$

Therefore we have

$$\mathbf{a} \times \mathbf{b} = (a_2b_3 - a_3b_2)\mathbf{i} - (a_1b_3 - a_3b_1)\mathbf{j} + (a_1b_2 - a_2b_1)\mathbf{k}$$
$$= \begin{vmatrix} \mathbf{i} & \mathbf{j} & \mathbf{k} \\ a_1 & a_2 & a_3 \\ b_1 & b_2 & b_3 \end{vmatrix}.$$

Well, now it's time to move on.

We have seen that if $\mathbf{a}$ and $\mathbf{b}$ are vectors then $\mathbf{a} \times \mathbf{b}$ is also a vector. We can therefore consider the effect of combining this vector with a third vector $\mathbf{c}$. There are two operations that we need to examine: the triple scalar product and the triple vector product.

14.11 THE TRIPLE SCALAR PRODUCT

We now describe what is meant by the symbol

$$\mathbf{a} \cdot \mathbf{b} \times \mathbf{c}$$

What *can* it mean? There are only two possible ways of inserting brackets so that the operations can be performed consecutively, and these are

$$\mathbf{a} \cdot (\mathbf{b} \times \mathbf{c}) \quad \text{and} \quad (\mathbf{a} \cdot \mathbf{b}) \times \mathbf{c}$$

However, a few moments' thought shows that the expression $(\mathbf{a} \cdot \mathbf{b}) \times \mathbf{c}$ has no meaning. This is because it purports to calculate the vector product of a scalar $\mathbf{a} \cdot \mathbf{b}$ with a vector $\mathbf{c}$. Now we defined the vector product as a binary operation in which two *vectors* were combined. Consequently the expression $(\mathbf{u} \cdot \mathbf{b}) \times \mathbf{c}$ is meaningless.

On the other hand the expression $\mathbf{a} \cdot (\mathbf{b} \times \mathbf{c})$ does have a meaning, and so it is this which we take as the definition of the symbol $\mathbf{a} \cdot \mathbf{b} \times \mathbf{c}$ when brackets are not inserted. Therefore

$$\mathbf{a} \cdot \mathbf{b} \times \mathbf{c} = \mathbf{a} \cdot (\mathbf{b} \times \mathbf{c})$$

Now $\mathbf{a}$ is a vector and $\mathbf{b} \times \mathbf{c}$ is also a vector; consequently $\mathbf{a} \cdot (\mathbf{b} \times \mathbf{c})$ is a scalar. For this reason this product of the three vectors is called a **triple scalar product**.

Example □ Obtain the triple scalar product $\mathbf{a} \cdot \mathbf{b} \times \mathbf{c}$ of three vectors in terms of components.

If you wish you can try this yourself. It is not difficult now that we know how to obtain the scalar product and the vector product in terms of components. Suppose

$$\mathbf{a} = a_1\mathbf{i} + a_2\mathbf{j} + a_3\mathbf{k}$$
$$\mathbf{b} = b_1\mathbf{i} + b_2\mathbf{j} + b_3\mathbf{k}$$
$$\mathbf{c} = c_1\mathbf{i} + c_2\mathbf{j} + c_3\mathbf{k}$$

Here is a *neat* way of deducing the result. Remember that

$$\mathbf{a} \cdot \mathbf{b} = (a_1\mathbf{i} + a_2\mathbf{j} + a_3\mathbf{k}) \cdot (b_1\mathbf{i} + b_2\mathbf{j} + b_3\mathbf{k})$$
$$= a_1b_1 + a_2b_2 + a_3b_3$$

and this can be thought of as having been obtained in the following way. The unit vectors $\mathbf{i}$, $\mathbf{j}$ and $\mathbf{k}$ in the second vector have each been replaced by the components a_1, a_2 and a_3 of the first vector. Using this idea we have

$$\mathbf{a} \cdot \mathbf{b} \times \mathbf{c} = \mathbf{a} \cdot (\mathbf{b} \times \mathbf{c})$$

$$= (a_1\mathbf{i} + a_2\mathbf{j} + a_3\mathbf{k}) \cdot \begin{vmatrix} \mathbf{i} & \mathbf{j} & \mathbf{k} \\ b_1 & b_2 & b_3 \\ c_1 & c_2 & c_3 \end{vmatrix}$$

$$= \begin{vmatrix} a_1 & a_2 & a_3 \\ b_1 & b_2 & b_3 \\ c_1 & c_2 & c_3 \end{vmatrix} \qquad \blacksquare$$

One immediate consequence of this is that if two of the vectors have the same direction then the triple scalar product is *zero*. This is a consequence of the rule for determinants that if two rows are equal then the determinant is zero.

Using the work we did on determinants (Chapter 12) you will now be able to write down several equivalent expressions for $\mathbf{a} \cdot \mathbf{b} \times \mathbf{c}$. Remember, if we interchange the corresponding elements in two rows of a determinant then the determinant changes sign. So

$$\mathbf{a} \cdot \mathbf{b} \times \mathbf{c} = -\begin{vmatrix} b_1 & b_2 & b_3 \\ a_1 & a_2 & a_3 \\ c_1 & c_2 & c_3 \end{vmatrix} = -\mathbf{b} \cdot \mathbf{a} \times \mathbf{c}$$

$$= \begin{vmatrix} b_1 & b_2 & b_3 \\ c_1 & c_2 & c_3 \\ a_1 & a_2 & a_3 \end{vmatrix} = \mathbf{b} \cdot \mathbf{c} \times \mathbf{a}$$

In fact the rules for determinants enable us to deduce that the important ingredient in a triple scalar product is not the relative positions of the signs $\times$ and $\cdot$, or the precise order of the vectors **a**, **b** and **c**, but the **cyclic order** of the vectors **a**, **b** and **c**.

If we preserve the cyclic order so that **b** follows **a**, **c** follows **b**, and **a** follows **c**, it does not matter where we put the dot and cross; we will obtain the same result. However, if we reverse the cyclic order so that **b** follows **c**, **c** follows **a**, and **a** follows **b**, then wherever we put the dot and cross the result will have the *opposite* sign. So

$$\mathbf{a} \cdot \mathbf{b} \times \mathbf{c} = \mathbf{c} \times \mathbf{a} \cdot \mathbf{b}$$
$$\mathbf{b} \times \mathbf{c} \cdot \mathbf{a} = -\mathbf{a} \cdot \mathbf{c} \times \mathbf{b}$$

For this reason a triple scalar product is sometimes written as $[\mathbf{a}, \mathbf{b}, \mathbf{c}]$; this defines the cyclic order, and is all that is needed. So

$$[\mathbf{a}, \mathbf{b}, \mathbf{c}] = [\mathbf{b}, \mathbf{c}, \mathbf{a}] = [\mathbf{c}, \mathbf{a}, \mathbf{b}]$$
$$= -[\mathbf{a}, \mathbf{c}, \mathbf{b}] = -[\mathbf{c}, \mathbf{b}, \mathbf{a}] = -[\mathbf{b}, \mathbf{a}, \mathbf{c}]$$

PHYSICAL INTERPRETATIONS

If we consider the magnitude of $\mathbf{a} \times \mathbf{b}$, the vector product of two vectors **a** and **b**, we see that

$$|\mathbf{a} \times \mathbf{b}| = |\mathbf{a}| |\mathbf{b}| |\sin \theta|$$

This is equal to the area of the parallelogram formed by the two vectors (Fig. 14.21).

If now we consider $\mathbf{a} \cdot (\mathbf{b} \times \mathbf{c})$ we have

$$\mathbf{a} \cdot (\mathbf{b} \times \mathbf{c}) = |\mathbf{a}| |\mathbf{b} \times \mathbf{c}| \cos \phi$$

where ϕ is the angle between **a** and $\mathbf{b} \times \mathbf{c}$ (Fig. 14.22). Now $\mathbf{b} \times \mathbf{c}$ is perpendicular to the plane of **b** and **c**, and so it follows that $|\mathbf{a}| \cos \phi$ is the height of the parallelepiped Π formed by the vectors **a**, **b** and **c**. Therefore

$$\mathbf{a} \cdot (\mathbf{b} \times \mathbf{c}) = \text{height of } \Pi \times \text{area of base of } \Pi$$
$$= \text{volume of } \Pi$$

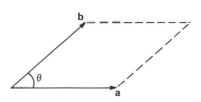

Fig. 14.21 The magnitude of $\mathbf{a} \times \mathbf{b}$.

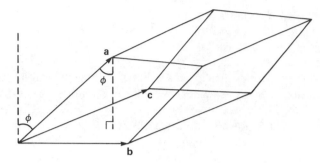

Fig. 14.22 The triple scalar product.

Strictly speaking we have relied a little too much on the diagram for, were **b** and **c** interchanged, cos θ would be negative. Nevertheless we have shown that the *magnitude* of **a** · **b** × **c** can be interpreted as the volume of the parallelepiped Π formed from the three vectors **a**, **b** and **c**.

Observe that this accords with several of the properties we have already discovered. In particular it shows that the triple scalar product depends only on the cyclic order of the three vectors concerned.

14.12 THE TRIPLE VECTOR PRODUCT

We have considered the scalar product of the vector **a** and the vector **b** × **c**. We now turn our attention to the vector product of these vectors. The result **a** × (**b** × **c**) will be a vector and so we call it a triple vector product.

At the outset it is important to realize that

$$\mathbf{a} \times (\mathbf{b} \times \mathbf{c}) \neq (\mathbf{a} \times \mathbf{b}) \times \mathbf{c}$$

Indeed there is no reason at all why these two triple vector products should be equal. However, the use of the product notation and the fact that the associative law usually holds for products leads the unwary to expect that it will hold. It certainly does not hold, and this means of course that we must be scrupulously careful to insert brackets correctly in any mathematical expression we write down. More marks are lost in examinations as a result of missing brackets than are lost through numerical inaccuracy.

The failure of the associative law makes theoretical development very difficult. In section 11.2 we observed that matrix multiplication is associative. Matrix algebra is therefore relatively straight-forward.

What then is **a** × (**b** × **c**)? We know it is a vector because it is the result of taking the vector product of two vectors **a** and **b** × **c**. Moreover it is perpendicular to both **a** and **b** × **c**. Now **b** × **c** itself is perpendicular to the plane containing the vectors **b** and **c**, and since we have only three dimensions at our disposal we can make a deduction. Can you see what it is?

The implication is that $\mathbf{a} \times (\mathbf{b} \times \mathbf{c})$ must be in the *same plane* as $\mathbf{b}$ and $\mathbf{c}$. Now any vector in the plane of $\mathbf{b}$ and $\mathbf{c}$ can be written in the form $p\mathbf{b} + q\mathbf{c}$ where p and q are scalars. So we have deduced that

$$\mathbf{a} \times (\mathbf{b} \times \mathbf{c}) = p\mathbf{b} + q\mathbf{c}$$

It remains only to determine the scalars p and q.

If we take the dot product with $\mathbf{a}$ of each side of the last relation we obtain

$$0 = p(\mathbf{a} \cdot \mathbf{b}) + q(\mathbf{a} \cdot \mathbf{c})$$

So defining a new scalar t by

$$p = t(\mathbf{a} \cdot \mathbf{c})$$

we have

$$q = -t(\mathbf{a} \cdot \mathbf{b})$$

and therefore

$$\mathbf{a} \times (\mathbf{b} \times \mathbf{c}) = t[(\mathbf{a} \cdot \mathbf{c})\mathbf{b} - (\mathbf{a} \cdot \mathbf{b})\mathbf{c}]$$

It remains only to obtain the scalar t.

No loss of generality is obtained if we choose our coordinate system so that $\mathbf{a} = \lambda\mathbf{i}$, and since the expansion must hold for all $\mathbf{b}$ and $\mathbf{c}$ we can examine the component in the direction of $\mathbf{k}$. The right-hand side gives

$$t[\lambda c_1 b_3 - \lambda b_1 c_3]$$

The left-hand side gives, since $\mathbf{i} \times \mathbf{j} = \mathbf{k}$, the product of λ with the coefficient of $\mathbf{j}$ in $\mathbf{b} \times \mathbf{c}$. This is

$$-\lambda[b_1 c_3 - b_3 c_1] = \lambda[c_1 b_3 - b_1 c_3]$$

It follows that $t = 1$, and therefore the **triple vector product** is given by

$$\mathbf{a} \times (\mathbf{b} \times \mathbf{c}) = (\mathbf{a} \cdot \mathbf{c})\mathbf{b} - (\mathbf{a} \cdot \mathbf{b})\mathbf{c}$$

We are now in a position to calculate the other triple vector product $(\mathbf{a} \times \mathbf{b}) \times \mathbf{c}$. We have

$$\begin{aligned}
(\mathbf{a} \times \mathbf{b}) \times \mathbf{c} &= -\mathbf{c} \times (\mathbf{a} \times \mathbf{b}) \\
&= -[(\mathbf{c} \cdot \mathbf{b})\mathbf{a} - (\mathbf{c} \cdot \mathbf{a})\mathbf{b}] \\
&= (\mathbf{c} \cdot \mathbf{a})\mathbf{b} - (\mathbf{c} \cdot \mathbf{b})\mathbf{a} \\
&= (\mathbf{a} \cdot \mathbf{c})\mathbf{b} - (\mathbf{b} \cdot \mathbf{c})\mathbf{a}
\end{aligned}$$

So we have the two triple vector products

$$\mathbf{a} \times (\mathbf{b} \times \mathbf{c}) = (\mathbf{a} \cdot \mathbf{c})\mathbf{b} - (\mathbf{a} \cdot \mathbf{b})\mathbf{c}$$
$$(\mathbf{a} \times \mathbf{b}) \times \mathbf{c} = (\mathbf{a} \cdot \mathbf{c})\mathbf{b} - (\mathbf{b} \cdot \mathbf{c})\mathbf{a}$$

These have a similar structure, which makes the expansion easy to remember if you are prepared to learn a little chant. To expand a triple vector product write down the middle vector and multiply it by the dot product of the others; then subtract the other *bracketed* vector multiplied by the dot product of the remaining two.

Example □ Write down the triple vector product $\mathbf{a} \times (\mathbf{b} \times \mathbf{c})$ of the vectors $\mathbf{a} = 2\mathbf{i} + \mathbf{j} - \mathbf{k}$, $\mathbf{b} = \mathbf{i} + \mathbf{j} - \mathbf{k}$ and $\mathbf{c} = \mathbf{i} + 2\mathbf{j} - \mathbf{k}$.
We have

$$\mathbf{a} \times (\mathbf{b} \times \mathbf{c}) = (\mathbf{a} \cdot \mathbf{c})\mathbf{b} - (\mathbf{a} \cdot \mathbf{b})\mathbf{c}$$

and

$$\mathbf{a} \cdot \mathbf{c} = 2 \times 1 + 1 \times 2 + (-1) \times (-1) = 5$$
$$\mathbf{a} \cdot \mathbf{b} = 2 \times 1 + 1 \times 1 + (-1) \times (-1) = 4$$

So

$$\mathbf{a} \times (\mathbf{b} \times \mathbf{c}) = 5(\mathbf{i} + \mathbf{j} - \mathbf{k}) - 4(\mathbf{i} + 2\mathbf{j} - \mathbf{k})$$
$$= \mathbf{i} - 3\mathbf{j} - \mathbf{k}$$

Alternatively, we could determine $\mathbf{b} \times \mathbf{c}$ first and then $\mathbf{a} \times (\mathbf{b} \times \mathbf{c})$. Do this and check the answer. ■

14.13 DIFFERENTIATION OF VECTORS

All the vectors we have considered in the examples have been constant vectors. However, there is no reason why this should be so. Suppose O is a fixed point and P is a general point on a curve. As P moves along the curve the vector **OP** changes in both magnitude and direction (Fig. 14.23).

OP is called the **position vector** of the point P. We may write $\mathbf{OP} = \mathbf{r}(t)$ to represent this vector, where t is a parameter. It may be helpful to think

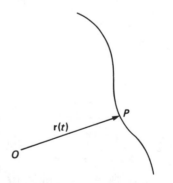

Fig. 14.23 A variable position vector.

_____14.14 Workshop_____

▷**Exercise** Obtain the equation satisfied by a point (x, y, z) which is in the ⌐1⌐
same plane as the points $(1, -1, 2)$, $(3, 1, -1)$ and $(1, 1, -2)$.

Think carefully about this. Remember that the triple scalar product can be interpreted as the volume of the parallelepiped formed from the three vectors.

Suppose we let the three fixed points be A, B and C. Then the vectors **OA**, ⌐2⌐
OB and **OC** are the position vectors of the points. If P is in the same plane as A, B and C then the vectors **AP**, **AB** and **AC** are coplanar. It therefore follows that their triple scalar product is zero.

If you didn't manage to argue this through then don't be concerned. Store the idea away in your mind for future use and see if you can complete the problem.

We have ⌐3⌐

$$\mathbf{AP} = \mathbf{AO} + \mathbf{OP} = -\mathbf{OA} + \mathbf{OP} = -(\mathbf{i} - \mathbf{j} + 2\mathbf{k}) + (x\mathbf{i} + y\mathbf{j} + z\mathbf{k})$$
$$= (x - 1)\mathbf{i} + (y + 1)\mathbf{j} + (z - 2)\mathbf{k}$$
$$\mathbf{AB} = \mathbf{AO} + \mathbf{OB} = -\mathbf{OA} + \mathbf{OB} = -(\mathbf{i} - \mathbf{j} + 2\mathbf{k}) + (3\mathbf{i} + \mathbf{j} - \mathbf{k})$$
$$= 2\mathbf{i} + 2\mathbf{j} - 3\mathbf{k}$$
$$\mathbf{AC} = \mathbf{AO} + \mathbf{OC} = -\mathbf{OA} + \mathbf{OC} = -(\mathbf{i} - \mathbf{j} + 2\mathbf{k}) + (\mathbf{i} + \mathbf{j} - 2\mathbf{k})$$
$$= 2\mathbf{j} - 4\mathbf{k}$$

The triple scalar product is zero, and so

$$\begin{vmatrix} x - 1 & y + 1 & z - 2 \\ 2 & 2 & -3 \\ 0 & 2 & -4 \end{vmatrix} = 0$$

This gives

$$(x - 1)(-8 + 6) - 2[-4(y + 1) - 2(z - 2)] = 0$$
$$-2(x - 1) + 8(y + 1) + 4(z - 2) = 0$$
$$x - 1 - 4y - 4 - 2z + 4 = 0$$
$$x - 4y - 2z = 1$$

Did you get there? Don't forget to check that A, B and C each satisfy this equation.

If all was well you can move on to step 5. If there were difficulties then try the next problem carefully. It is always better to spend a few seconds *planning* what you intend to do.

▷**Exercise** Obtain the volume of the tetrahedron formed by the points O,

A, B and C, where O is the origin and A, B, C are the points $(1, -1, 2)$, $(3, 1, -1)$ and $(1, 1, -2)$.

You need to know that a tetrahedron has

$$\text{volume} = \frac{1}{3} \text{ area of base} \times \text{height}$$

4 The area of the triangle formed by two vectors is half the area of the parallelogram which they form. Therefore the required volume will be one-sixth of the volume of the parallelepiped formed by the three vectors **OA**, **OB** and **OC**.

The triple scalar product gives the volume of the parallelepiped.

$$\mathbf{OA} = \mathbf{i} - \mathbf{j} + 2\mathbf{k}$$
$$\mathbf{OB} = 3\mathbf{i} + \mathbf{j} - \mathbf{k}$$
$$\mathbf{OC} = \mathbf{i} + \mathbf{j} - 2\mathbf{k}$$

So we obtain

$$\begin{vmatrix} 1 & -1 & 2 \\ 3 & 1 & -1 \\ 1 & 1 & -2 \end{vmatrix} = (-2 + 1) + (-6 + 1) + 2(3 - 1)$$

$$= -1 - 5 + 4 = -2$$

expanding in terms of the first row. The magnitude of this is therefore 2 and the required volume is $\frac{2}{6} = \frac{1}{3}$.

5 **Exercise** Show that if $\mathbf{u} \cdot \mathbf{v} \neq -1$ then $\mathbf{x} = \mathbf{u}$ is the only solution of the equation

$$\mathbf{x} + (\mathbf{u} \wedge \mathbf{x}) \wedge \mathbf{v} = \mathbf{u}$$

Notice that this question uses the wedge notation for the vector product.

It is clear that $\mathbf{x} = \mathbf{u}$ is certainly a solution of the equation, but we must show it is the *only* solution.

6 Expanding the triple vector product we obtain

$$\mathbf{x} + (\mathbf{u} \cdot \mathbf{v})\mathbf{x} - (\mathbf{v} \cdot \mathbf{x})\mathbf{u} = \mathbf{u}$$

However, if we take the dot product with $\mathbf{v}$ of both sides of the equation

$$\mathbf{x} + (\mathbf{u} \wedge \mathbf{x}) \wedge \mathbf{v} = \mathbf{u}$$

we obtain a triple scalar product in which two of the vectors are the same:

$$(\mathbf{u} \wedge \mathbf{x}) \wedge \mathbf{v} \cdot \mathbf{v}$$

Consequently this product is zero and therefore

$$\mathbf{x} \cdot \mathbf{v} = \mathbf{u} \cdot \mathbf{v}$$

So

$$\mathbf{v} \cdot \mathbf{x} = \mathbf{u} \cdot \mathbf{v}$$

We now have

$$\mathbf{x} + (\mathbf{u} \cdot \mathbf{v})\mathbf{x} - (\mathbf{u} \cdot \mathbf{v})\mathbf{u} = \mathbf{u}$$
$$[1 + (\mathbf{u} \cdot \mathbf{v})]\mathbf{x} = [1 + (\mathbf{u} \cdot \mathbf{v})]\mathbf{u}$$

Since $1 + (\mathbf{u} \cdot \mathbf{v}) \neq 0$ we conclude that $\mathbf{x} = \mathbf{u}$.

If you managed that all right then move on to the practical. Otherwise, try a final exercise.

▷**Exercise** Obtain the general solution of the equation

$$\mathbf{u} \wedge \mathbf{x} + \mathbf{v} \wedge \mathbf{x} = \mathbf{u} \wedge \mathbf{v}$$

where $\mathbf{u}$ and $\mathbf{v}$ are non-parallel vectors.

Remember some of the tricks we have used before and see if you can sort this out. The argument is similar, in some ways, to the one we used to expand a triple vector product.

We have

$$[\mathbf{u} + \mathbf{v}] \wedge \mathbf{x} = \mathbf{u} \wedge \mathbf{v}$$

The right-hand side is a vector perpendicular to the plane of $\mathbf{u}$ and $\mathbf{v}$, whereas the left-hand side is a vector perpendicular to the plane of $\mathbf{u} + \mathbf{v}$ and $\mathbf{x}$. It follows that $\mathbf{x}$ is in the plane of $\mathbf{u}$ and $\mathbf{v}$, so $\mathbf{x} = h\mathbf{u} + k\mathbf{v}$ where h and k are scalars. Substituting this expression for $\mathbf{x}$ into the vector equation gives

$$[\mathbf{u} + \mathbf{v}] \wedge [h\mathbf{u} + k\mathbf{v}] = \mathbf{u} \wedge \mathbf{v}$$
$$h(\mathbf{u} \wedge \mathbf{u}) + h(\mathbf{v} \wedge \mathbf{u}) + k(\mathbf{u} \wedge \mathbf{v}) + k(\mathbf{v} \wedge \mathbf{v}) = \mathbf{u} \wedge \mathbf{v}$$

Now $\mathbf{u} \wedge \mathbf{u} = 0 = \mathbf{v} \wedge \mathbf{v}$ and $\mathbf{v} \wedge \mathbf{u} = -\mathbf{u} \wedge \mathbf{v}$. Therefore

$$(-h + k)\mathbf{u} \wedge \mathbf{v} = \mathbf{u} \wedge \mathbf{v}$$

Now $\mathbf{u} \wedge \mathbf{v} \neq 0$, and so $-h + k = 1$. Therefore

$$\mathbf{x} = h\mathbf{u} + (h + 1)\mathbf{v} = h(\mathbf{u} + \mathbf{v}) + \mathbf{v}$$

where h is an arbitrary scalar.

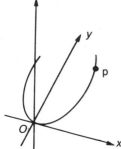

_____ 14.15 Practical _____

PARTICLE DYNAMICS

A particle has position $P\ (t, t^2, t^3)$ at time t, relative to a rectangular cartesian coordinate system $Oxyz$. Obtain, for the particle at time t, the velocity, the speed and the magnitude of the acceleration. Distances are measured in metres, and time is measured in seconds.

All you have to do is put this in vector form; the rest is easy.

Let **OP** be the position vector of the particle. Then, in the usual notation, we have

$$\mathbf{OP} = \mathbf{r}(t) = t\mathbf{i} + t^2\mathbf{j} + t^3\mathbf{k}$$

The velocity is obtained by differentiating:

$$\dot{\mathbf{r}}(t) = \mathbf{i} + 2t\mathbf{j} + 3t^2\mathbf{k}$$

The magnitude of this gives the speed:

$$\text{speed} = \sqrt{(1 + 4t^2 + 9t^4)} \text{ m/s}$$

For the acceleration we must differentiate again:

$$\ddot{\mathbf{r}}(t) = 2\mathbf{j} + 6t\mathbf{k}$$

and the magnitude of this is $\sqrt{(4 + 36t^2)}$ m/s^2.

James Clerk Maxwell (1831–1879): Scottish mathematician who applied mathematics to the study of electricity.

Vectors are very useful indeed; they enable us to solve problems in three dimensions without having to try to visualize them. When they are used in conjunction with matrices and operators they become a very powerful mathematical instrument. For example Maxwell's equations can be expressed by this method, and these form the cornerstone of electromagnetics. We shall gain some insight into how each of these mathematical ingredients functions separately, but the powerful combination is outside the scope of our present studies.

SUMMARY

In this chapter we have covered the following topics:
☐ Vector algebra; addition and scalar multiplication of vectors

$$(\mathbf{a}, \mathbf{b}) \rightarrow \mathbf{a} + \mathbf{b}$$
$$(p, \mathbf{a}) \rightarrow p\mathbf{a}$$

☐ The scalar product and the vector product

$$\mathbf{a} \cdot \mathbf{b} = |\mathbf{a}|\,|\mathbf{b}|\cos\theta$$
$$\mathbf{a} \times \mathbf{b} = |\mathbf{a}|\,|\mathbf{b}|\sin\theta\,\mathbf{n}$$

where θ is the angle between the vectors and $\mathbf{n}$ is a unit vector.
☐ The use of position vectors.
☐ Triple scalar products

$$[\mathbf{a}, \mathbf{b}, \mathbf{c}] = \begin{vmatrix} a_1 & a_2 & a_3 \\ b_1 & b_2 & b_3 \\ c_1 & c_2 & c_3 \end{vmatrix}$$

☐ Triple vector products

$$\mathbf{a} \times (\mathbf{b} \times \mathbf{c}) = (\mathbf{a} \cdot \mathbf{c})\mathbf{b} - (\mathbf{a} \cdot \mathbf{b})\mathbf{c}$$
$$(\mathbf{a} \times \mathbf{b}) \times \mathbf{c} = (\mathbf{a} \cdot \mathbf{c})\mathbf{b} - (\mathbf{b} \cdot \mathbf{c})\mathbf{a}$$

☐ Differentiation of vectors.

EXERCISES (for answers see p. 751)

1 Determine $\mathbf{a} + \mathbf{b}$, $\mathbf{a} \cdot \mathbf{b}$, $\mathbf{a} \times \mathbf{b}$ for each of the following:
  a $\mathbf{a} = 2\mathbf{i} + \mathbf{j} + 3\mathbf{k}$, $\mathbf{b} = \mathbf{i} - 3\mathbf{j} + \mathbf{k}$
  b $\mathbf{a} = \mathbf{i} + 4\mathbf{j} - 5\mathbf{k}$, $\mathbf{b} = 2\mathbf{i} + 2\mathbf{j} + 3\mathbf{k}$
  c $\mathbf{a} = -\mathbf{i} + 2\mathbf{j} - 3\mathbf{k}$, $\mathbf{b} = \mathbf{i} + 3\mathbf{j} - 2\mathbf{k}$
  d $\mathbf{a} = \mathbf{i} + \mathbf{j} + 2\mathbf{k}$, $\mathbf{b} = -3\mathbf{i} + 4\mathbf{j} - \mathbf{k}$
2 Obtain two unit vectors perpendicular to each of the following:
  a $\mathbf{a} = \mathbf{i} + 3\mathbf{j} - 5\mathbf{k}$, $\mathbf{b} = \mathbf{i} + \mathbf{j}$
  b $\mathbf{a} = \mathbf{i} + 2\mathbf{j} + 3\mathbf{k}$, $\mathbf{b} = 3\mathbf{i} + 2\mathbf{j} - \mathbf{k}$
  c $\mathbf{a} = -\mathbf{i} + \mathbf{j} - \mathbf{k}$, $\mathbf{b} = \mathbf{i} - \mathbf{j} - \mathbf{k}$
  d $\mathbf{a} = (\mathbf{i} + \mathbf{j}) \times (\mathbf{j} + \mathbf{k})$, $\mathbf{b} = (\mathbf{i} - \mathbf{j}) \times (\mathbf{j} - \mathbf{k})$
3 Obtain the triple scalar product $[\mathbf{a}, \mathbf{b}, \mathbf{c}]$ for each of the following
  a $\mathbf{a} = \mathbf{i} + \mathbf{j}$, $\mathbf{b} = \mathbf{j} + \mathbf{k}$, $\mathbf{c} = \mathbf{k} + \mathbf{i}$
  b $\mathbf{a} = 2\mathbf{i} + \mathbf{j} + \mathbf{k}$, $\mathbf{b} = \mathbf{i} + 2\mathbf{j} + \mathbf{k}$, $\mathbf{c} = \mathbf{i} + \mathbf{j} + 2\mathbf{k}$
  c $\mathbf{a} = 3\mathbf{i} - 2\mathbf{j} - \mathbf{k}$, $\mathbf{b} = \mathbf{i} + 3\mathbf{j} - 2\mathbf{k}$, $\mathbf{c} = 2\mathbf{i} + \mathbf{j} - 3\mathbf{k}$
  d $\mathbf{a} = (\mathbf{i} + \mathbf{j}) \times \mathbf{k}$, $\mathbf{b} = (\mathbf{j} + \mathbf{k}) \times \mathbf{i}$, $\mathbf{c} = (\mathbf{k} + \mathbf{i}) \times \mathbf{j}$
4 Obtain the triple vector products $\mathbf{a} \times (\mathbf{b} \times \mathbf{c})$ and $(\mathbf{a} \times \mathbf{b}) \times \mathbf{c}$ for each of the sets of vectors given in exercise 3.

5 Obtain d$\mathbf{r}$/dt for each of the vectors given below:

a $\mathbf{r} = \cos t\mathbf{i} - \sin t\mathbf{j} + t\mathbf{k}$

b $\mathbf{r} = \cos 3t\mathbf{i} + \sin 5t\mathbf{j} + t^2\mathbf{k}$

c $\mathbf{r} = (1 + t^2)^2\mathbf{i} + (1 + t^3)^3\mathbf{j} + (1 + t^4)^4\mathbf{k}$

d $\mathbf{r} = (t\mathbf{i} - t^2\mathbf{j} + t^3\mathbf{k}) \wedge (t^3\mathbf{i} + t^2\mathbf{j} + t\mathbf{k})$

ASSIGNMENT (for answers see p. 752; see also Workshops on pp. 393 and 405)

1 For the vectors $\mathbf{a} = 2\mathbf{i} + \mathbf{j} - \mathbf{k}$ and $\mathbf{b} = \mathbf{i} + \mathbf{j} + 2\mathbf{k}$ obtain
   (a) the scalar product $\mathbf{a} \cdot \mathbf{b}$
   (b) the cosine of the angle between the vectors $\mathbf{a}$ and $\mathbf{b}$
   (c) the vector product $\mathbf{a} \times \mathbf{b}$
   (d) the area of the parallelogram formed by the two vectors $\mathbf{a}$ and $\mathbf{b}$.
2 Obtain a unit vector parallel to the Oyz plane and perpendicular to $\mathbf{i} + 4\mathbf{j} - 3\mathbf{k}$.
3 By putting $\mathbf{d} = \mathbf{b} \times \mathbf{c}$ initially or otherwise show that

$$(\mathbf{a} \times \mathbf{b}) \times (\mathbf{b} \times \mathbf{c}) = [\mathbf{a}, \mathbf{b}, \mathbf{c}]\mathbf{b}$$

4 Show that
   (a) $[\mathbf{a} + \mathbf{b}, \mathbf{b} + \mathbf{c}, \mathbf{c} + \mathbf{a}] = 2[\mathbf{a}, \mathbf{b}, \mathbf{c}]$
   (b) $[\mathbf{a} \times \mathbf{b}, \mathbf{b} \times \mathbf{c}, \mathbf{c} \times \mathbf{a}] = [\mathbf{a}, \mathbf{b}, \mathbf{c}]^2$
5 Solve the equation $\mathbf{a} \wedge \mathbf{x} + (\mathbf{b} \cdot \mathbf{x})\mathbf{a} = \mathbf{b}$, if $\mathbf{a} \cdot \mathbf{b} \neq 0$.
6 Obtain the constant t if the vectors $\mathbf{i} - \mathbf{j} + 2\mathbf{k}$, $5\mathbf{i} + t\mathbf{j} + 3\mathbf{k}$ and $-3\mathbf{i} + 2\mathbf{j} + \mathbf{k}$ are coplanar.
7 Show that if $\mathbf{u}$, $\mathbf{v}$ and $\mathbf{w}$ are dependent on the parameter t and differentiable with respect to t then

$$\frac{d}{dt}[\mathbf{u}, \mathbf{v}, \mathbf{w}] = \left[\frac{d\mathbf{u}}{dt}, \mathbf{v}, \mathbf{w}\right] + \left[\mathbf{u}, \frac{d\mathbf{v}}{dt}, \mathbf{w}\right] + \left[\mathbf{u}, \mathbf{v}, \frac{d\mathbf{w}}{dt}\right]$$

FURTHER EXERCISES (for answers see p. 752)

1 ABC is a triangle; D is the midpoint of BC, and E is the midpoint of AC. Prove that $\mathbf{AB} = 2\ \mathbf{ED}$.
2 For the vector $\mathbf{a} = (\mathbf{i} - 2\mathbf{j} + 2\mathbf{k})/3$ and $\mathbf{b} = (-3\mathbf{i} - 5\mathbf{j} + 4\mathbf{k})/5$ determine
   (a) the angle between $\mathbf{a}$ and $\mathbf{b}$
   (b) two unit vectors perpendicular to the plane of $\mathbf{a}$ and $\mathbf{b}$.
3 By eliminating z and using differentiation, or otherwise, determine the vector

$$\mathbf{a} = x\mathbf{i} + y\mathbf{j} + z\mathbf{k}$$

which has all of the following properties:

(a) **a** is perpendicular to $\mathbf{i} + \mathbf{j} + \mathbf{k}$;

(b) **a** has twice the magnitude of $\mathbf{i} + \mathbf{j} + \mathbf{k}$;

(c) y is a minimum.

4 Suppose **a**, **b**, **c** and **d** are position vectors from the origin to the points A, B, C and D respectively.

(a) By expanding $(\mathbf{a} \wedge \mathbf{b}) \wedge (\mathbf{c} \wedge \mathbf{d})$ in two different ways, or otherwise, show that

$$[\mathbf{a}, \mathbf{b}, \mathbf{c}]\mathbf{d} + [\mathbf{a}, \mathbf{c}, \mathbf{d}]\mathbf{b} = [\mathbf{b}, \mathbf{c}, \mathbf{d}]\mathbf{a} + [\mathbf{a}, \mathbf{b}, \mathbf{d}]\mathbf{c}$$

(b) Show that

$$(\mathbf{b} \wedge \mathbf{c}) \cdot (\mathbf{a} \wedge \mathbf{d}) + (\mathbf{c} \wedge \mathbf{a}) \cdot (\mathbf{b} \wedge \mathbf{d}) + (\mathbf{a} \wedge \mathbf{b}) \cdot (\mathbf{c} \wedge \mathbf{d}) = 0$$

5 The path of a point is given vectorially by the equation

$$\mathbf{r} = (\cos^2 \theta)\mathbf{i} + (\cos \theta \sin \theta)\mathbf{j} + (\cos \theta)\mathbf{k}$$

Determine expressions for $\mathbf{r} \cdot \mathbf{r}$ and $\mathbf{r} \wedge \mathbf{r}$. Obtain the vector $\mathbf{r}$ which has (a) minimum magnitude (b) maximum magnitude.

6 The position vector of a moving point P is given by

$$\mathbf{r} = (\cos \omega t)\mathbf{i} + (\sin \omega t)\mathbf{j} + t\mathbf{k}$$

where t is time. Show that the direction of motion makes a constant angle α with the Oz axis, where $\omega = \tan \alpha$.

7 Show that $\mathbf{a} \cdot \mathbf{b} \le |\mathbf{a}| \, |\mathbf{b}|$ for any two vectors **a** and **b**. By using

$$|\mathbf{a} + \mathbf{b}|^2 = (\mathbf{a} + \mathbf{b}) \cdot (\mathbf{a} + \mathbf{b})$$

or otherwise, deduce the triangle inequality $|\mathbf{a} + \mathbf{b}| \le |\mathbf{a}| + |\mathbf{b}|$.

8 Show that W, the work done by a constant force $\mathbf{F} = \alpha\mathbf{i} + \beta\mathbf{j} + \gamma\mathbf{k}$ in moving a mass from the point (a_1, b_1, c_1) to the point (a_2, b_2, c_2), is given by

$$W = \alpha(a_2 - a_1) + \beta(b_2 - b_1) + \gamma(c_2 - c_1)$$

We first met the triangle inequality in section 1.4. The triangle inequality for complex numbers is given in Chapter 10, Further exercises 6.

9 An electron is constrained to move on a curve. Its position vector at time t is given by

$$\mathbf{r} = (2 \cos t)\mathbf{i} + (2 \sin t)\mathbf{j} + t\mathbf{k}$$

Show that its velocity and acceleration each have constant magnitude.

10 Suppose

$$\mathbf{u} = (\cos t)\mathbf{i} + (\sin t)\mathbf{j} + e^{-t}\mathbf{k}$$
$$\mathbf{v} = (-\sin t)\mathbf{i} + (\cos t)\mathbf{j} + e^{t}\mathbf{k}$$
$$\mathbf{r} = \mathbf{u} \times \mathbf{v}$$

Show that $\dot{\mathbf{r}}$ is always in the **i**, **j** plane and that $\dot{\mathbf{r}}$ has magnitude $2\sqrt{(2)} \cosh t$.

11 The position vector of a point mass at time t is

$$\mathbf{r} = (\cos^2 t)\mathbf{i} + (\sin t \cos t)\mathbf{j} + (\sin t)\mathbf{k}$$

Determine the velocity $\dot{\mathbf{r}}$ and the acceleration $\ddot{\mathbf{r}}$. Show also that $|\mathbf{r}| = 1$ and that, at time t, $|\dot{\mathbf{r}}| = \sqrt{(1 + \cos^2 t)}$.

(a) The curvature $\varkappa$ is given by the formula

$$\varkappa = |\dot{\mathbf{r}} \times \ddot{\mathbf{r}}|/|\dot{\mathbf{r}}|^3$$

Show that the curvature at time t is $(3 \cos^2 t + 5)^{1/2}/(1 + \cos^2 t)^{3/2}$.

(b) The torsion τ is given by the formula

$$1/\tau = (\dot{\mathbf{r}} \times \ddot{\mathbf{r}} \cdot \dddot{\mathbf{r}})/|\dot{\mathbf{r}} \times \ddot{\mathbf{r}}|^2$$

Show that the torsion at time t is $(3 + 5 \sec^2 t)/6 \sec t$.

12 An electron moves with constant angular velocity on a circle of radius 1. Show that when suitable axes are chosen its position vector can be expressed in the form

$$\mathbf{r} = (\cos \omega t)\mathbf{i} + (\sin \omega t)\mathbf{j}$$

Confirm, using vectors, that
(a) The velocity of the electron is perpendicular to the vector $\mathbf{r}$;
(b) The acceleration $\ddot{\mathbf{r}}$ is directed towards the centre of the circle.

13 A particle is constrained to move on the curve defined by $x = 2 \cos t$, $y = 2 \sin t$, $z = t\sqrt{5}$ relative to a rectangular cartesian coordinate system $Oxyz$. If distances are measured in metres and time t in seconds, show that the magnitude of the velocity is 3 m/s and the magnitude of the acceleration is 2 m/s².

15   Integration 1

Now that our algebraic knowledge has been increased by studying complex numbers, matrices, determinants and vectors we return to the calculus to begin our work on integration.

After studying this chapter you should be able to
- ☐ Write down indefinite integrals of simple functions;
- ☐ Apply the four basic rules of integration correctly;
- ☐ Perform simple substitutions to determine integrals;
- ☐ Obtain integrals by putting simple rational functions into partial fractions.

At the end of the chapter we look at practical problems in gas compression and structural stress.

15.1 THE CONCEPT OF INTEGRATION

Integration is sometimes thought of as falling into two parts: indefinite integration and definite integration. We shall deal with integration in this way, and the link between the two will then become clear.

It is best to think of indefinite integration as the reverse procedure to that of differentiation. We know that given a differentiable real function F there is a unique real function f such that $F' = f$. We call f the derivative of F (Chapter 4).

Suppose we try to reverse this procedure. For any real function f:

1 Under what circumstances does there exist a real function F such that $F' = f$?

2 If there is a function F with this property, is it unique?

We shall not answer question 1 since it is beyond the scope of our work, but question 2 can be answered straight away: *no*! If *F* exists it is not the only function with this property.

Example □ We know that both *f* and *g* defined by

$$f(x) = x + 1 \quad \text{and} \quad g(x) = x \quad \text{when } x \in \mathbb{R}$$

have a derivative *h* defined by

$$h(x) = 1 \quad \text{when } x \in \mathbb{R}$$

In other symbols, if $y = x + 1$ and $z = x$ then

$$\frac{dy}{dx} = \frac{dz}{dx}$$

■

Suppose we have two real functions *F* and *G* which have the same derivative. What can we say about them? Suppose $F' = G'$: then $F' - G' = 0$ and therefore $(F - G)' = 0$. Consequently the function $F - G$ has the zero function as its derivative. Now it so happens that the only differentiable function, defined for all real *x*, which has zero derivative is a constant function.

In other symbols, if

$$\frac{dy}{dx} = \frac{dz}{dx}$$

'then

$$\frac{dy}{dx} - \frac{dz}{dx} = 0$$

$$\frac{d}{dx}(y - z) = 0$$

Therefore

$$y - z = \text{constant}$$

Consequently to integrate a real function *f* we must
1 Determine any function *F* with derivative *f*;
2 Add an arbitrary constant.
This will then represent all those functions which have derivative *f*.

It is convenient to use a dummy variable such as *x* or *t* when describing functions, and the same is true when it comes to representing an indefinite integral.

We shall meet this again when we consider differential equations in section 19.1.

Of course it is the presence of an arbitrary constant which gives rise to the name 'indefinite' integral. Suppose

$$\frac{\mathrm{d}}{\mathrm{d}x} F(x) = f(x)$$

Then we write

$$\int f(x)\ \mathrm{d}x = F(x) + C$$

where C is an arbitrary constant. We call this the **indefinite integral** of $f(x)$ with respect to x, and refer to $f(x)$ as the **integrand**. We shall also say that $f(x)$ is integrable, and we mean by this that the indefinite integral with respect to x exists.

Our work on differentiation will stand us in good stead, since we can write down a number of indefinite integrals. For example:

$$\int e^x\ \mathrm{d}x = e^x + C$$

$$\int \cos x\ \mathrm{d}x = \sin x + C$$

$$\int \sec^2 x\ \mathrm{d}x = \tan x + C$$

These are examples of **standard forms**. When we wish to perform an integration we shall attempt to reduce the integrand to a sum of standard forms. The techniques of integration may not at first seem quite as straightforward as the techniques of differentiation. However, practice will soon overcome this problem.

A list of standard forms is given in Table 15.2, page 418.

15.2 RULES FOR INTEGRATION

The rules for integration follow from the rules for differentiation. We shall suppose that $u = u(x)$ and $v = v(x)$ are real functions which are integrable and that c is a constant.

Sum rule

$$\int (u + v)\ \mathrm{d}x = \int u\ \mathrm{d}x + \int v\ \mathrm{d}x$$

This means that if we express the integrand as the sum of two parts we can then integrate each separately and add the results. You should not presume that this rule is self-evident, however reasonable it may appear; the corresponding property does not hold for products!

Factor rule

$$\int cu \, dx = c \int u \, dx$$

This means that we can divide the integrand by a constant and take this outside the integral sign. This rule only holds for constants, so that

$$\int 3 \tan x \, dx = 3 \int \tan x \, dx$$

but

$$\int x \tan x \, dx \neq x \int \tan x \, dx$$

Product rule

$$\int u \frac{dv}{dx} \, dx = uv - \int v \frac{du}{dx} \, dx$$

We shall use this rule in section 15.6.

This is usually called the formula for **integration by parts** and it is useful for integrating certain products. It is an awkward rule to remember, and some students prefer to learn it in words. So here is the chant: 'The integral of a product of two functions is the first times the integral of the second, minus the integral of, the integral of the second times the derivative of the first.' You may well prefer to remember the formula!

Substitution rule

$$\int f(x) \, dx = \int f[g(u)]g'(u) \, du$$

where $x = g(u)$.

This is easy to apply because we make the substitution $x = g(u)$ and then

$$\frac{dx}{du} = g'(u)$$

which leads quite naturally to the substitution $dx = g'(u) \, du$.

There is one additional requirement. To every x there must correspond a value of u such that $x = g(u)$ and $g'(u)$ must remain bounded on any finite interval.

We shall use this rule in section 16.1.

The substitution rule is perhaps the most useful rule for integration.

One little remark about arbitrary constants is in order. We do not allow arbitrary constants to proliferate each time we split an integral into two. This is because they can all be collected together in a sum which is itself an arbitrary constant. To avoid these constants appearing left, right and centre we shall suppose that the last integral to be determined is the guardian of the arbitrary constant. It's rather like a waiter watching customers at a table in a café. He doesn't mind if some of them leave, provided somebody is still sitting there to pay the bill. If the last customer gets up and walks out he says 'Oi! What about the bill?' or words to that effect. We must do the same; the last integral sign remaining owes a debt of the arbitrary constant.

☐ Using the rules for differentiation and the definition of the indefinite **Example** integral deduce **a** the sum, **b** the factor, **c** the product and **d** the substitution rules.

We shall suppose that

$$\int u(x) \, dx = U(x) + A$$

$$\int v(x) \, dx = V(x) + B$$

where A and B are arbitrary constants. As usual we shall write $U = U(x)$ and $V = V(x)$.

a By definition, $U'(x) = u(x)$ and $V'(x) = v(x)$. Now

$$(U + V)' = U' + V' = u + v$$

Consequently

$$\int (u + v) \, dx = U + V + C$$

$$= \int u \, dx + \int v \, dx$$

b By definition, $(cU)' = cU' = cu$. Therefore

$$\int cu \, dx = cU(x) + K$$

where K is an arbitrary constant. So

$$\int cu \, dx = c \int u \, dx$$

c The product rule for differentiation gives

$$\frac{d}{dx} (uv) = u \frac{dv}{dx} + v \frac{du}{dx}$$

Therefore by the sum rule

$$\int \frac{d}{dx}(uv)\, dx = \int u \frac{dv}{dx}\, dx + \int v \frac{du}{dx}\, dx$$

So

$$uv = \int v \frac{du}{dx} + \int u \frac{dv}{dx}$$

Rearranging,

$$\int u \frac{dv}{dx} = uv - \int v \frac{du}{dx}$$

d We have

$$\frac{d}{dx}\left[\int f(x)\, dx\right] = f(x) = f[g(u)]$$

So

$$\frac{d}{dx}\left[\int f(x)\, dx\right] \frac{dx}{du} = f[g(u)] \frac{dx}{du}$$

Therefore by the chain rule for differentiation

$$\frac{d}{du}\left[\int f(x)\, dx\right] = f[g(u)]g'(u)$$

and so

$$\int f(x)\, dx = \int f[g(u)]g'(u)\, du \qquad \blacksquare$$

Table 15.1 Standard derivatives

$f(x)$	$f'(x)$
x^n (n constant)	nx^{n-1}
e^x	e^x
$\ln x$ ($x > 0$)	x^{-1}
$\sin x$	$\cos x$
$\cos x$	$-\sin x$
$\tan x$	$\sec^2 x$
$\sec x$	$\sec x \tan x$
$\cot x$	$-\operatorname{cosec}^2 x$
$\operatorname{cosec} x$	$-\operatorname{cosec} x \cot x$
$\sinh x$	$\cosh x$
$\cosh x$	$\sinh x$
$\sin^{-1} x$	$1/\sqrt{(1 - x^2)}$
$\tan^{-1} x$	$1/(1 + x^2)$
$\sinh^{-1} x$	$1/\sqrt{(1 + x^2)}$
$\cosh^{-1} x$	$1/\sqrt{(x^2 - 1)}$

STANDARD FORMS

We shall now build up a table of standard forms which we shall use to integrate more complicated functions. To begin with we list some well-known derivatives in Table 15.1, as these will form the basis of the integrals table which we shall devise.

On the basis of these, and remembering that we can take any constant factor outside the integral sign, but not expressions which depend on x, it is possible to list the standard integrals in Table 15.2. We use the notation

$$\int f(x) \, dx = F(x) + C$$

in the table.

Table 15.2 Standard integrals

$f(x)$	$F(x)$
x^n ($n \neq -1$, constant)	$x^{n+1}/(n+1)$
e^x	e^x
x^{-1} ($x > 0$)	$\ln x$
$\cos x$	$\sin x$
$\sin x$	$-\cos x$
$\sinh x$	$\cosh x$
$\cosh x$	$\sinh x$
$1/(1 + x^2)$	$\tan^{-1} x$
$1/\sqrt{(1 - x^2)}$	$\sin^{-1} x$
$1/\sqrt{(1 + x^2)}$	$\sinh^{-1} x$
$1/\sqrt{(x^2 - 1)}$	$\cosh^{-1} x$
$\sec^2 x$	$\tan x$
$\sec x \tan x$	$\sec x$
$\operatorname{cosec}^2 x$	$-\cot x$
$\operatorname{cosec} x \cot x$	$-\operatorname{cosec} x$

A further list of standard forms is given in section 16.4. Others are derived in sections 15.5 and 15.6. They all appear on the bookmark.

☐ We shall extend Table 15.2, using the rules of integration, to obtain **Example**

$$\int x^{-1} \, dx \quad \text{when } x < 0$$

We use the substitution rule and put $x = -t$. Then $t > 0$ since $x < 0$. Also $dx/dt = -1$, and so we obtain

$$\int x^{-1} \, dx = \int \frac{1}{x} \frac{dx}{dt} \, dt$$

$$= \int \frac{1}{(-t)} (-1) \, dt$$

$$= \int \frac{1}{t} \, dt$$

It is necessary to be able to obtain integrals using elementary algebraic substitutions, in work on the theory of structures.

But since $t > 0$ we know this integral is $\ln t + C$. So substituting back we have

$$\int x^{-1}\, dx = \ln(-x) + C \quad \text{when } x < 0$$

Of course we can combine both cases, $x > 0$ and $x < 0$, in one formula:

$$\int x^{-1}\, dx = \ln|x| + C \quad \text{when } x \neq 0$$

It is important to remember this, as occasionally it is possible to produce incorrect working by overlooking the possibility that $x < 0$. On the other hand, if x is clearly positive the modulus signs are entirely superfluous and should be omitted. ∎

A word or two about the arbitrary constant is not out of place here. We know that given any real number y there exists a positive number x such that $y = \ln x$. This number x is equal to e^y, in fact. Therefore any arbitrary constant C can be written in the form $\ln k$ where $k > 0$.

One advantage of doing this is that we can then use the laws of logarithms to put the integral in a tidier form. One disadvantage is that it may take some algebraic work on your part to confirm that the answer you have obtained to an integration is equivalent to the one which it is stated you should obtain! For instance,

$$\ln(x^2 - 1) - \ln(x + 1) + C$$

is equivalent to

$$\ln k(x - 1)$$

where C and k (>0) are arbitrary constants.

Now let's do some integrations. In these we rearrange the integrand and then use standard forms together with the sum and factor rule.

15.3 Workshop

1

Exercise Obtain

$$I = \int e^x \cosh x\, dx$$

See if you can rearrange the integrand so that it becomes a sum of standard forms. When you have done so, take the next step.

If we use the definition of cosh x we see that we can split the integral into
two. We have

$$I = \int e^x \frac{e^x + e^{-x}}{2} dx$$

$$= \frac{1}{2} \int (e^{2x} + 1)dx$$

$$= \frac{1}{2} \int e^{2x} dx + \frac{1}{2} \int dx$$

It is customary to use dx algebraically in this way and not to insist that it
appears on the far right as in the standard notation

$$I = \frac{1}{2} \int e^{2x} dx + \frac{1}{2} \int 1 dx$$

We obtain

$$I = \frac{1}{2} \frac{e^{2x}}{2} + \frac{1}{2} x + C$$

$$= \frac{e^{2x}}{4} + \frac{x}{2} + C$$

Now try this one. You have to think carefully.

▷**Exercise**   Obtain

$$\int \frac{dx}{1 + \sin x}$$

When you are ready, take the next step.

If you have split the integral into two by writing

$$\int dx + \int \frac{dx}{\sin x}$$

then you have made an algebraic blunder because

$$\frac{1}{A + B} \neq \frac{1}{A} + \frac{1}{B}$$

You can readily confirm this by putting $A = 1$ and $B = 1$. Instead, we
multiply the numerator and denominator by $1 - \sin x$. On the one hand the
integrand is unaltered, but on the other hand we can use the rules of
elementary trigonometry to simplify it. So

$$\int \frac{dx}{1 + \sin x} = \int \frac{(1 - \sin x)}{(1 - \sin x)} \frac{dx}{(1 + \sin x)}$$

$$= \int \frac{1 - \sin x}{1 - \sin^2 x} \, dx$$

$$= \int \frac{1 - \sin x}{\cos^2 x} \, dx = \int (\sec^2 x - \sec x \tan x) \, dx$$

$$= \int \sec^2 x \, dx - \int \sec x \tan x \, dx$$

using the sum and factor rules.

Now each of these is a standard form which we included in Table 15.2. See then if you can write the answer down straight away. If not, you had better look back at the table and then write down the answer. Whichever way you proceed, as soon as you have finished move on to the final step.

4 This is what you should have written down:

$$\int \frac{dx}{1 + \sin x} = \int \sec^2 x \, dx - \int \sec x \tan x \, dx$$

$$= \tan x - \sec x + C$$

Refer back to Chapter 3 to refresh your knowledge of trigonometrical identities.

You may not have managed to tackle these steps, but do not worry at this stage. If we look at what we have done there are one or two features which we can remember for future use. First, we need to know our trigonometrical formulas forwards, backwards and inside out! Also, simple algebraic identities will often assist us.

We have said that we are content if we can resolve the integrand into a sum of standard forms, but in general two guidelines can be of help. They are

1 Remove denominators;
2 Resolve roots.

In the workshop we had a denominator which we wished to remove. How did we do it? We had to remember almost simultaneously that

$$1 - \sin^2 x = \cos^2 x$$
$$(1 - \sin x) (1 + \sin x) = 1 - \sin^2 x$$

This realization showed us that we needed to multiply numerator and denominator by $1 - \sin x$ to proceed effectively.

So we must train ourselves to inspect the integrand and to plan ahead. It's all a matter of practice.

15.4 INTEGRATION BY INSPECTION

Sometimes when we inspect an integrand it is possible to see straight away how to integrate it. One very common situation, where this is the case, is when the integral is of the form

$$\int \frac{f'(x)}{f(x)}\, dx$$

If we use the substitution rule and put $u = f(x)$ then we obtain, differentiating with respect to x, $u' = f'(x)$, and so

$$\int \frac{f'(x)}{f(x)}\, dx = \int \frac{1}{u}\, du = \ln |u| + C$$
$$= \ln |f(x)| + C$$

☐ Render the following integrals: **Example**

$$\int \frac{2x}{x^2 + 4}\, dx \qquad \int \frac{4x + 3}{x^2 + 1}\, dx$$

The first integral has the desired form: the numerator is the derivative of the denominator. So, without making a formal substitution, we can write down straight away

$$\int \frac{2x}{x^2 + 4}\, dx = \ln (x^2 + 4) + C$$
$$= \ln k(x^2 + 4)$$

where k is constant. Note that we do not need to include modulus signs here since the argument is clearly *positive*.

The second integral needs to be manipulated slightly but is essentially the same. See if you can do it. When you have finished, read on and see if you are right.

You're not looking, are you? You really have tried your best? Well then, here it is:

$$\int \frac{4x + 3}{x^2 + 1}\, dx = 2 \int \frac{2x}{x^2 + 1}\, dx + 3 \int \frac{dx}{x^2 + 1}$$

Here we have used the sum rule and the factor rule to split things up. Notice particularly that only constants can appear to the left of each integral sign. The first integral is the logarithmic type which we have been discussing, and the second integral is a standard form. So we can write straight away

$$I = 2 \ln (x^2 + 1) + 3 \tan^{-1} x + C \qquad \blacksquare$$

The logarithmic type is a special case of a more general type, and we should be on the lookout for this too. This is an integral of the form

$$\int g(u) \, du$$

where $u = f(x)$ and g is a function which has a known integral.

Example □ Obtain each of the following integrals:

$$\int \frac{x^2}{\sqrt{(x^3 + 1)}} \, dx \qquad \int x \sqrt{(1 + x^2)} \, dx$$

Why not see if you can do something with these by yourself?

For the first integral, if we put $u = x^3 + 1$ then $du/dx = 3x^2$ and we can use the factor rule to adjust the numerator to include the 3. Moreover, we know

$$\int \frac{du}{\sqrt{u}} = \int u^{-1/2} \, du = 2u^{1/2} + C$$

In words: raise the index by 1 and divide by the number so obtained. Therefore we have

$$\int \frac{x^2}{\sqrt{(x^3 + 1)}} \, dx = \frac{1}{3} \int \frac{3x^3}{\sqrt{(x^3 + 1)}} \, dx$$

$$= \frac{2}{3} \sqrt{(x^3 + 1)} + C$$

! It is a common error to get this wrong by half recognizing the general form and ignoring the root sign by writing down a logarithm. Don't be one of those who makes that particular mistake! Now you have a go at the second integral.

Here we are then. It's a simple example of the general type, although an adjustment of the constant is necessary:

$$\int x \sqrt{(1 + x^2)} \, dx = \frac{1}{2} \int 2x \sqrt{(1 + x^2)} \, dx$$

$$= \frac{1}{2} \frac{2}{3} (1 + x^2)^{3/2} + C = \frac{1}{3} (1 + x^2)^{3/2} + C \qquad \blacksquare$$

15.5 INTEGRATION BY PARTIAL FRACTIONS

One type of integrand can be dealt with routinely. This is when the integrand is a quotient of two polynomials, for example

$$\frac{x^4 + 2x - 3}{x^3 + 2x^2 + x}$$

It is then possible to split the integrand into a sum of a number of partial fractions.

We shall use the example to illustrate the method. We first divide the denominator into the numerator so that, for the quotient which results, the degree of the numerator is less than the degree of the denominator. The rest of the integrand is then a polynomial, which we can integrate without difficulty.

We have

$$\frac{x^4 + 2x - 3}{x^3 + 2x^2 + x} = x - 2 + \frac{3x^2 + 4x - 3}{x^3 + 2x^2 + x}$$

We dealt with partial fractions in Chapter 2. You may need to refer back in order to refresh your memory.

The rational expression

$$Q = \frac{3x^2 + 4x - 3}{x^3 + 2x^2 + x}$$

remains to be resolved. We factorize the denominator of Q:

$$x^3 + 2x^2 + x = x(x^2 + 2x + 1) = x(x + 1)^2$$

Here the factors of the denominator are x and $x + 1$ (repeated). Therefore we obtain partial fractions with denominators x, $x + 1$ and $(x + 1)^2$ and *constant* numerators. So

$$Q = \frac{3x^2 + 4x - 3}{x^3 + 2x^2 + x} = \frac{A}{x} + \frac{B}{x + 1} + \frac{C}{(x + 1)^2}$$

If the partial fractions are recombined the two numerators must be identically equal. Now

$$\frac{A}{x} + \frac{B}{x + 1} + \frac{C}{(x + 1)^2} = \frac{A(x + 1)^2 + Bx(x + 1) + Cx}{x(x + 1)^2}$$

Therefore we require

$$3x^2 + 4x - 3 \equiv A(x + 1)^2 + Bx(x + 1) + Cx$$

The constants A, B and C can be obtained either by substituting values of x into the identity or by comparing the coefficients of powers of x on each side of it. In practice a mixture of the methods is usually the quickest.

Here if we put $x = 0$ we obtain $A = -3$. If we put $x = -1$ we obtain $3 - 4 - 3 = -C$, so $C = 4$. If we examine the coefficient of x^2 on each side of the identity we obtain $3 = A + B$ and so $B = 6$. Therefore

$$\frac{x^4 + 2x - 3}{x^3 + 2x^2 + x} = x - 2 - \frac{3}{x} + \frac{6}{x + 1} + \frac{4}{(x + 1)^2}$$

Each of these can be integrated without trouble. Try it and see how you get on.

We integrate term by term to obtain

$$\frac{x^2}{2} - 2x - 3 \ln |x| + 6 \ln |x + 1| - \frac{4}{x + 1} + C$$

Did you manage that? All we have done is to apply the ideas which we developed earlier and to integrate by sight. If you are having a few difficulties, then to begin with you can make the substitutions algebraically. However, as soon as possible you should train yourself to carry out these substitutions mentally. Otherwise you may lose time in examinations going through tedious algebraic routines that can be avoided.

STANDARD FORMS

Our table of standard integrals (Table 15.2) had two important omissions which we can now make good. They are the integrals of the tangent function and the secant function.

For the *tangent* function we have

$$\int \tan x \, dx = \int \frac{\sin x}{\cos x} \, dx$$

Now if we differentiate $\cos x$ with respect to x we obtain $-\sin x$. Therefore by the factor and substitution rules we have

$$\int \tan x \, dx = - \int \frac{-\sin x}{\cos x} \, dx = -\ln |\cos x| + C$$
$$= \ln |\sec x| + C$$

For the *secant* function we rearrange the integrand in a cunning way:

$$\int \sec x \, dx = \int \frac{\sec x \, (\sec x + \tan x)}{\sec x + \tan x} \, dx$$

The reason is that if we differentiate $\sec x + \tan x$ with respect to x we obtain

$$\sec x \tan x + \sec^2 x = \sec x \, (\sec x + \tan x)$$

So in fact the numerator is now the derivative of the denominator. (Of course you would not be expected to pluck that technique out of thin air on your own, but just savour for a moment the elegance of the move and remember it for future use.) Consequently

$$\int \sec x \, dx = \ln |\sec x + \tan x| + C$$

Now you try to integrate the cotangent function and the cosecant function. When you have done them, check the answers below. The methods are very similar.

For the *cotangent* function we have

$$\int \cot x \, dx = \ln |\sin x| + C$$

For the *cosecant* function we have

$$\int \text{cosec} \, x \, dx = \ln |\text{cosec} \, x - \cot x| + C$$

These integrals augment Table 15.2.

Did you manage to sort out the sign in the second one?

There are some other obvious omissions in our table of integrals, for instance $\int \ln x \, dx$. This can be rectified provided we use the product rule known as the formula for integration by parts. We now consider this rule in some detail.

15.6 INTEGRATION BY PARTS

If we have an integrand which is the product of two *different* types of function, for example
1 exponential × circular
2 polynomial × exponential
3 polynomial × circular
the formula for integration by parts can often resolve it. Here is the formula again:

We first stated this rule in section 15.2.

$$\int u \frac{dv}{dx} \, dx = uv - \int v \frac{du}{dx} \, dx$$

or equivalently

$$\int u \, dv = uv - \int v \, du$$

Given a product, we shall need to decide which part to call u and which part dv. There are four broad principles to adopt:

1 We must be able to write down v easily.

2 If there is a polynomial then the polynomial is usually u.

3 If having made a choice a more complicated integral results, then start again with the opposite choice.

4 If having decided on the correct choice for u and dv a further integration by parts is necessary, maintain the same type of functions for u and dv.

Example □ Obtain

$$\int x e^{5x}\, dx$$

Here using principle 2 we have $u = x$ and $dv = e^{5x}\, dx$, so that $v = e^{5x}/5$. We do not need to include an arbitrary constant; if we include it, it will only cancel out later. Also $du = 1\, dx = dx$, so therefore

$$\int x e^{5x}\, dx = \frac{x}{5} e^{5x} - \frac{1}{5} \int e^{5x}\, dx$$

$$= \frac{x}{5} e^{5x} - \frac{1}{25} e^{5x} + C \qquad \blacksquare$$

Sometimes it doesn't matter which way we choose u and dv.

Example □ Obtain the following integral:

$$I = \int e^x \cos x\, dx$$

Here whichever choice we make we are bound to succeed. For instance $u = \cos x$, $dv = e^x\, dx$ gives $du = -\sin x\, dx$ and $v = e^x$. So

$$I = \int e^x \cos x\, dx = e^x \cos x - \int e^x(-\sin x)\,dx$$

Now the integral on the right is no *worse* than the one we started with, so we continue integrating by parts. Maintaining our choice of types of function for u and v gives $u = \sin x$ and $dv = e^x$. If we were to choose them the other way round we should get back where we started!

So we have $du = \cos x$ and $v = e^x$, and so

$$I = e^x \cos x + \int e^x \sin x\, dx$$

$$= e^x \cos x + \left[e^x \sin x - \int e^x \cos x\, dx \right]$$

$$= e^x \cos x + e^x \sin x - I$$

So

$$2I = e^x \cos x + e^x \sin x$$

We discussed this aspect of arbitrary constants in section 15.2.

'Oi! What about the constant?' Oh yes, we forgot the waiter in the café, didn't we? We have removed the last integral sign, and we overlooked the fact that it is the guardian of some arbitrary constants. Therefore

$$2I = e^x \cos x + e^x \sin x + \text{constant}$$

That is,

$$I = \frac{1}{2}(e^x \cos x + e^x \sin x) + C$$

Now you try the same problem but with the opposite choice for u and dv. That is, you choose $u = e^x$ and $dv = \cos x$. It will still work out; keep calm, and keep a clear head!   ∎

Sometimes an integrand does not look like a product at all, but nevertheless can be determined using integration by parts. One such integral is $\int \ln x \, dx$. Suppose we put $u = \ln x$ and $dv = dx$; then we obtain $v = x$ and $du = x^{-1} \, dx$. So the integral of the *logarithm* function is

$$\int \ln x \, dx = x \ln x - \int x \frac{1}{x} \, dx$$

$$= x \ln x - x + C$$

Integration by parts is always worth considering.

_____ 15.7 Workshop _____

It's time now to look at some integrals. We shall do this bearing in mind that all of them can be solved by the methods we have used in this chapter. It is important that you get used to looking at the integral and deciding *before* you start which approach you are going to adopt. Sometimes an integral looks quite fierce but on closer inspection we see that in reality it is very easy. The opposite is also true, unfortunately.

The integrals we are going to inspect also form the problems for this chapter. If you feel confident you can tackle them on your own and omit these steps altogether. However, you may prefer to take things a little more slowly and in that way build up confidence. These steps give ideas for the methods, but not the full solutions.

▷**Exercise**   Inspect these integrals:

1 $\int \dfrac{x + 1}{x} \, dx$ **2** $\int \dfrac{x}{x + 1} \, dx$ **3** $\int \tan^2 x \, dx$

When you have decided which approach to adopt, take the next step. Don't be afraid to try a few moves on paper.

2

1 We can split the integral into two, each a standard form.

2 It's best to put $u = x + 1$, or equivalently to rewrite the numerator as $(x + 1) - 1$.

3 We cannot integrate $\tan^2 x$ as it stands, but we can integrate $\sec^2 x$. Remember: $1 + \tan^2 x = \sec^2 x$.

If you have all those right, then move on to step 4. Otherwise, consider the next three integrals.

▷**Exercise** Inspect these integrals:

4 $\int \dfrac{x + 1}{x - 1}\,dx$ **5** $\int \dfrac{x + 1}{x^2 - 1}\,dx$ **6** $\int x\,e^{-x^2}\,dx$

When you have decided what to do, take another step.

3

4 This is like problem 2. We can substitute $u = x - 1$.

5 There is a common factor which can be cancelled.

6 This is a case for a substitution: $u = x^2$ will get rid of the floating x. Now move ahead to step 4.

4

Exercise Inspect these integrals:

7 $\int \dfrac{2x}{x^2 + x}\,dx$ **8** $\int \dfrac{e^x}{e^x + 1}\,dx$ **9** $\int \sin^2 x \cos x\,dx$

Move on when you are ready.

5

7 Cancel out the x.

8 Put $u = e^x + 1$.

9 Note that when we differentiate $\sin x$ with respect to x we obtain $\cos x$. Therefore substitute $u = \sin x$.

Now take a look at the next three.

▷**Exercise** Inspect these integrals:

10 $\int \dfrac{\sin x}{\cos^2 x + 1}\,dx$ **11** $\int \dfrac{e^x}{e^{2x} + 1}\,dx$ **12** $\int \sin^{-1} x\,dx$

When you have made your decisions, take the next step.

6

Things are not quite so straightforward now.

10 We can reduce this to a standard form by putting $u = \cos x$.

11 A standard form is obtained by putting $u = e^x$.

12 A substitution isn't really going to help much here. This is one of those

cases where integration by parts is the best method; we can differentiate $\sin^{-1} x$.
If you managed all those then move ahead to step 8. Otherwise, try these
before you step ahead.

▷**Exercise**   Inspect these integrals:

13 $\displaystyle\int x\,\sqrt{(x^2 + 4)}\,dx$ **14** $\displaystyle\int \frac{\sin 2x}{\sqrt{(\cos^2 x + 9)}}\,dx$ **15** $\displaystyle\int x\,\ln x\,dx$

Only move on when you have made a clear decision in each case.

---

13 At first sight this might seem difficult, but note that if $u = x^2 + 4$ then $\boxed{7}$
    $du = 2x\,dx$ and so the floating x can be removed.
14 If we differentiate $\cos^2 x$ with respect to x we obtain $-2\cos x \sin x = -\sin 2x$. This is conveniently present in the numerator to make the
    substitution work smoothly.
15 This is a product of two different types of function and so is a clear
    candidate for integration by parts.
Now take the next step.

▷**Exercise**   Inspect these integrals: $\boxed{8}$

16 $\displaystyle\int x\,\tan^{-1} x\,dx$ **17** $\displaystyle\int \frac{x + 2}{x^2 - 5x + 6}\,dx$ **18** $\displaystyle\int \tan^3 x\,dx$

As soon as you have decided for all three, take another step.

---

16 This is a clear candidate for integration by parts. $\boxed{9}$
17 The denominator factorizes and so we can use partial fractions.
18 This is certainly different from problem 3, although we get the hint
    from that one. We take $\tan^2 x$ and rewrite it as $\sec^2 x - 1$, so that
    $\tan^3 x = \tan x \sec^2 x - \tan x$. We can handle each of these.
Try the final three.

▷**Exercise**   Inspect these integrals:

19 $\displaystyle\int \frac{dx}{x^4 - 1}$ **20** $\displaystyle\int \frac{x^3\,dx}{x^4 - 1}$ **21** $\displaystyle\int \frac{x^3\,dx}{\sqrt{(x^4 + 1)}}$

Then take the final step.

---

19 We can factorize $x^4 - 1$ and this will enable us to use partial fractions.
20 Substitute $u = x^4 - 1$ rather than use partial fractions.
21 The square root presents the difficulty. However, if you remember the

guidelines there should be no serious problem. Put $u = x^4 + 1$; then $du = 4x^3\,dx$ and the substitution can be carried through successfully.

15.8 Practical

GAS COMPRESSION

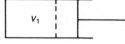

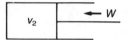

The work done in compressing a gas from one volume to another can be expressed by

$$W = \int p\,dv$$

If the volume v_1 is compressed to the volume v_2 and if $pv^n = c$, where c is a constant and $n \neq 1$, show that

$$W = \frac{c}{1 - n}\,(v_2^{1-n} - v_1^{1-n})$$

Obtain W in the case $n = 1$.

See how you get on with this. We will offer the solution stage by stage.

---

1 There is one small point to note. W has been used in two different ways. First, it is the general symbol for the work done. Secondly, it is the amount of work done in compressing the gas from v_1 to v_2. To avoid confusion we shall refer to the second as W^*.

We have, if $n \neq 1$,

$$W = \int \frac{c}{v^n}\,dv = c \int v^{-n}\,dv$$

$$= \frac{cv^{1-n}}{1 - n} + A$$

where A is a constant.

If you did not get this, try now to calculate A.

---

2 When $v = v_1$ no work has been done, and so we have

$$0 = W_1 = \frac{cv_1^{1-n}}{1 - n} + A$$

So

$$A = -\frac{cv_1^{1-n}}{1 - n}$$

Therefore

$$W = \frac{cv^{1-n}}{1-n} - \frac{cv_1^{1-n}}{1-n}$$

when $v = v_2$ we have $W = W^*$, which is

$$W^* = \frac{cv_2^{1-n}}{1-n} - \frac{cv_1^{1-n}}{1-n} = \frac{c}{1-n}(v_2^{1-n} - v_1^{1-n})$$

Now you deal with the case $n = 1$.

---

3 If $n = 1$ then

$$W = \int \frac{c}{v}\, dv = c\ln v + A$$

As before, when $v = v_1$, $W = 0$. Therefore

$$0 = c\ln v_1 + A$$

and so, replacing A,

$$W = c\ln v - c\ln v_1$$

So when $v = v_2$,

$$W^* = c\ln v_2 - c\ln v_1 = c\ln(v_2/v_1)$$

STRESS

In a thick cylinder, subject to internal pressure, the radial stress P at a distance r from the axis of the cylinder is given by

$$\int \frac{dP}{a-P} = 2\int \frac{dr}{r}$$

where a is a constant. If the stress has magnitude P_0 at the inner wall ($r = r_0$) and if it may be neglected at the outer wall ($r = r_1$), show that

$$P = \frac{P_0 r_0^2}{r_1^2 - r_0^2}\left(\frac{r_1^2}{r^2} - 1\right)$$

Again we present the solution stage by stage.

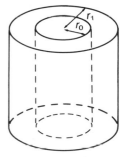

---

1 Rearranging the integral we have

$$-\int \frac{(-1)}{a-P}\, dP = 2\int \frac{dr}{r}$$

So

$$-\ln |a - P| = 2 \ln |r| + A$$

That is,

$$-\ln |a - P| = 2 \ln |r| + \ln k = \ln kr^2$$

$$\frac{1}{|a - P|} = kr^2$$

where $k > 0$ is the arbitrary constant.

There are two cases to consider: $a > P$ and $a < P$.

---

2 If $a > P$ then

$$\frac{1}{a - P} = kr^2$$

$$a - P = \frac{1}{kr^2}$$

When $P = P_0$, $r = r_0$ and so $a - P_0 = 1/kr_0^2$. When $P = 0$, $r = r_1$ and therefore $a = 1/kr_1^2$. Now $r_1 > r_0$ and $P_0 > 0$, so that

$$P_0 = a - \frac{1}{kr_0^2} = \frac{1}{kr_1^2} - \frac{1}{kr_0^2} < 0$$

which is a contradiction. Therefore the case $a > P$ cannot arise and there remains only $a < P$.

---

3 When $a < P$ we have

$$\frac{1}{a - P} = -kr^2$$

$$a - P = -\frac{1}{kr^2}$$

When $r = r_0$, $P = P_0$ and so $a - P_0 = -1/kr_0^2$. When $r = r_1$, $P = 0$ and so $a = -1/kr_1^2$. Consequently

$$P_0 = \frac{1}{kr_0^2} - \frac{1}{kr_1^2} = \frac{1}{k}\left(\frac{1}{r_0^2} - \frac{1}{r_1^2}\right)$$

from which

$$\frac{1}{k} = \frac{P_0 r_0^2 r_1^2}{r_1^2 - r_0^2}$$

and

$$a = -\frac{1}{kr_1^2} = \frac{-P_0 r_0^2}{r_1^2 - r_0^2}$$

Further,

$$P = a + \frac{1}{kr^2} = -\frac{1}{kr_1^2} + \frac{1}{kr^2}$$

$$= \frac{1}{kr_1^2}\left(-1 + \frac{r_1^2}{r^2}\right)$$

$$= \frac{P_0 r_0^2}{r_1^2 - r_0^2}\left(\frac{r_1^2}{r^2} - 1\right)$$

SUMMARY

To obtain an integral we first inspect the integrand. The following checklist can then help us to proceed:
☐ Is this an integral which can be done by sight?
☐ Is there a simple substitution which will reduce it to a standard form? (Don't forget to substitute for dx too!)
☐ Is it possible to rearrange the integrand so that it becomes a sum of standard forms?
☐ Can the integrand be rearranged using the theory of partial fractions?
☐ Can the integral be obtained by integration by parts?
Remember also that if you make a substitution you must always carry it through. Never allow two variables to appear together under the integral sign.

EXERCISES (for answers see p. 752)

1 Obtain each of the following integrals:

a $\displaystyle\int (1 + 2x + 3x^3)\,dx$

b $\displaystyle\int \{\exp x + 2\exp(-x)\}\,dx$

c $\displaystyle\int \left\{1 + \frac{1}{\sqrt{(1 + x^2)}}\right\}\,dx$

d $\displaystyle\int \sec x\,(\sec x + \tan x)\,dx$

2 Use a simple substitution to obtain each of the following integrals:

a $\displaystyle\int (1 + 2x)^7 \, dx$

b $\displaystyle\int \cos 3x \, dx$

c $\displaystyle\int x^2 \sin x^3 \, dx$

d $\displaystyle\int \frac{1}{4 + x^2} \, dx$

3 Resolve into partial fractions to obtain each of the following:

a $\displaystyle\int \frac{dx}{(2 + x)(1 - 3x)}$

b $\displaystyle\int \frac{dx}{x^3 + 3x}$

c $\displaystyle\int \frac{dx}{x^3 - 4x}$

d $\displaystyle\int \frac{dx}{(x^2 + 1)(x^2 + 4)}$

4 Use the method of integration by parts to obtain each of the following:

a $\displaystyle\int 2x \cos 3x \, dx$

b $\displaystyle\int x \exp 3x \, dx$

c $\displaystyle\int x^3 \exp x^2 \, dx$

d $\displaystyle\int x^2 \ln (x^2 + 1) \, dx$

5 Obtain the following integrals:

a $\displaystyle\int \left(\frac{x}{2} + \frac{2}{x} \right) dx$

b $\displaystyle\int \frac{dx}{1 + \cos x}$

c $\displaystyle\int x^2 \exp x^3 \, dx$

d $\displaystyle\int x \sec^2 x^2 \, dx$

ASSIGNMENT (for answers see p. 753; see also Workshops on pp. 420 and 429)

Obtain each of the following integrals. If you are stuck at any stage, hints are given in section 15.7.

1 $\int \dfrac{x + 1}{x} \, dx$ 　　　　**2** $\int \dfrac{x}{x + 1} \, dx$ 　　　　**3** $\int \tan^2 x \, dx$

4 $\int \dfrac{x + 1}{x - 1} \, dx$ 　　　**5** $\int \dfrac{x + 1}{x^2 - 1} \, dx$ 　　　**6** $\int x \, e^{-x^2} \, dx$

7 $\int \dfrac{2x}{x^2 + x} \, dx$ 　　　**8** $\int \dfrac{e^x}{e^x + 1} \, dx$ 　　　**9** $\int \sin^2 x \cos x \, dx$

10 $\int \dfrac{\sin x}{\cos^2 x + 1} \, dx$ 　**11** $\int \dfrac{e^x}{e^{2x} + 1} \, dx$ 　**12** $\int \sin^{-1} x \, dx$

13 $\int x \sqrt{(x^2 + 4)} \, dx$ 　**14** $\int \dfrac{\sin 2x}{\sqrt{(\cos^2 x + 9)}} \, dx$ 　**15** $\int x \ln x \, dx$

16 $\int x \tan^{-1} x \, dx$ 　**17** $\int \dfrac{x + 2}{x^2 - 5x + 6} \, dx$ 　**18** $\int \tan^3 x \, dx$

19 $\int \dfrac{dx}{x^4 - 1}$ 　　**20** $\int \dfrac{x^3 \, dx}{x^4 - 1}$ 　　**21** $\int \dfrac{x^3 \, dx}{\sqrt{(x^4 + 1)}}$

FURTHER EXERCISES (for answers see p. 753)

1 Obtain each of the following integrals:

a $\int x \cos x^2 \, dx$ 　　　**b** $\int \dfrac{1}{\sqrt{(x + 3)}} \, dx$

c $\int \dfrac{e^t - 1}{e^t + 1} \, dt$ 　　　**d** $\int \dfrac{x^3}{1 + x^4} \, dx$

2 Resolve each integral:

a $\int \dfrac{du}{u \ln u}$ 　　　**b** $\int (\sin^3 \theta + \cos^3 \theta) \, d\theta$

c $\int \sec^{-1} t \, dt$ 　　　**d** $\int \dfrac{\ln x}{x} \, dx$

3 Render each of the following:

a $\int \tan^{-1} u \, du$ 　　　**b** $\int \dfrac{dx}{1 - \cos x}$

c $\int \dfrac{dx}{(x - 1)^2 (x + 1)}$ 　**d** $\int \dfrac{\cos 2\theta \, d\theta}{(1 - \sin \theta)(1 - \cos \theta)}$

4 When a constant EMF E is applied to a coil with inductance L and resistance R the current i is given by the equation

$$\int \frac{L \, di}{E - Ri} = \int dt$$

Determine the current i at time t if $i = 0$ when $t = 0$.

5 By Newton's law of cooling the surface temperature θ at time t of a sphere in isothermal surroundings of temperature θ_0 is given by the equation

$$\int \frac{d\theta}{\theta - \theta_0} = -kt$$

When $t = 0$, $\theta = \theta_1$. Show that at time t

$$\theta = (\theta_1 - \theta_0)e^{-kt} + \theta_0$$

6 When a uniform beam of length L is clamped horizontally at each end and carries a load of w per unit length, the deflection y at distance x from one end satisfies

$$\frac{d^4y}{dx^4} = \frac{w}{EI}$$

where EI is constant and is the flexural rigidity of the beam. Use the information that $y = 0 = dy/dx$ at both $x = 0$ and $x = L$ to obtain an expression for the deflection y at a general point.

7 A spherical drop of liquid evaporates at a rate proportional to its surface area. Show that if r is the radius then dr/dt is constant. Given that the volume halves in 30 minutes, determine how long it will take for the drop to evaporate completely.

8 If $c_p \equiv \cos p\theta$ and $s_p \equiv \sin p\theta$, verify that if m and n are real constants

$$\frac{d}{d\theta} \frac{c_n + s_n}{c_m + s_m} = \frac{(n - m)c_{n+m} - (n + m)s_{n-m}}{(c_m + s_m)^2}$$

Hence, or otherwise, obtain

$$\int \frac{\cos 3\theta - 3\sin \theta}{1 + \sin 2\theta} \, d\theta$$

9 The acceleration of a missile is given by $f = \alpha \, e^{-t} \cosh u$ where α is constant, t is time in seconds and u is its speed in kilometres per second. Show that this leads to the integral equation

$$\int \text{sech} \, u \, du = \alpha \int e^{-t} \, dt$$

Obtain the speed at time t if initially it is zero, and show that as $t \to \infty$, $u \to \ln [\tan (\pi/4 + \alpha/2)]$.

Integration 2 16

In this chapter we shall extend our table of standard forms still further and learn how to deal with more difficult integrands.

After studying this chapter you should be able to
- ☐ Use trigonometrical substitutions to resolve algebraic integrands;
- ☐ Apply the standard algebraic substitutions to resolve trigonometrical integrands;
- ☐ Manipulate integrands and use tables of standard forms to resolve them;
- ☐ Assess an integrand to plan a suitable method of integration.

At the end of the chapter we consider practical problems in particle dynamics and ballistics.

16.1 INTEGRATION BY SUBSTITUTION

Although we have extended our table of standard forms slightly, there are still a few gaps. Three of these are the integrals

$$\int \sqrt{(1 + x^2)}\, dx \qquad \int \sqrt{(1 - x^2)}\, dx \qquad \int \sqrt{(x^2 - 1)}\, dx$$

We shall now consider how to determine these. To do so we deal further with integration by substitution.

Sometimes it is not possible to reduce an integrand to standard forms either by inspection or by the use of partial fractions. In such circumstances a substitution is worth considering. Remember the broad guidelines:

1 Remove denominators;
2 Resolve roots.

We need the substitution rule. This was stated in section 15.2.

It is a good idea to review sections 3.1 to 3.4 in order to brush up on your trigonometry.

A good facility with trigonometry and elementary algebra is essential for this. Before going any further it is vital that you are aware of the essential difference in kind between the two integrals $\int \sqrt{(1 + x)}\,dx$ and $\int \sqrt{(1 + x^2)}\,dx$. The first integral can be obtained by inspection. See if you can write the answer down.

If we differentiate $(1 + x)^{3/2}$ with respect to x we obtain

$$\frac{3}{2}(1 + x)^{1/2} = \frac{3}{2}\sqrt{(1 + x)}$$

so that

$$\int \sqrt{(1 + x)}\,dx = \frac{2}{3}(1 + x)^{3/2} + C$$

It is unfortunately a common error for students to write

$$\int \sqrt{(1 + x^2)}\,dx \text{ as } \frac{1}{3x}(1 + x^2)^{3/2} + C$$

using broadly the same style of argument. This is incorrect because $2x$ is not constant, so the factor rule cannot be used in this way. Indeed, were we to differentiate this result correctly we should not obtain the integrand.

So then we have a problem. How are we to determine $\int \sqrt{(1 + x^2)}\,dx$? The answer is that we must make a substitution.

It is no good putting $u^2 = 1 + x^2$ because, although at first this may appear to resolve the root, when we substitute for dx in terms of du another one appears. We must make a *trigonometrical* substitution, and for this purpose it helps to recall one of the following two identities:

$$1 + \tan^2 t = \sec^2 t$$
$$1 + \sinh^2 t = \cosh^2 t$$

For example, using the first we put $x = \tan t$. Then $dx = \sec^2 t\,dt$ and so

$$\sqrt{(1 + x^2)} = \sqrt{(1 + \tan^2 t)} = \sqrt{\sec^2 t} = \sec t$$

provided we choose t in the interval $(-\pi/2, \pi/2)$. This is certainly possible since for all real x there exists t in this interval such that $x = \tan t$. Now

$$\int \sqrt{(1 + x^2)}\,dx = \int \sec t \sec^2 t\,dt = \int \sec^3 t\,dt$$

How are we to determine $\int \sec^3 t\,dt$? If you think the answer is simply $(1/4)$ $\sec^4 t + C$ you had better think again! For, if we differentiate $(1/4)\,\sec^4 t$ with respect to t we obtain $\sec^3 t \sec t \tan t$, which is not the integrand.

At first sight, then, this integral may seem difficult. However, suppose we rewrite $\sec^3 t$ as a product $\sec^2 t \sec t$. We can then integrate by parts. If $dv = \sec^2 t \, dt$ then $v = \tan t$, whereas if $u = \sec t$ then $du = \sec t \tan t \, dt$. Consequently

$$\int \sec t \sec^2 t \, dt = \sec t \tan t - \int \tan t \sec t \tan t \, dt$$

$$= \sec t \tan t - \int \sec t \tan^2 t \, dt$$

Now $\sec^2 t = 1 + \tan^2 t$, and so this becomes

$$\int \sec^3 t \, dt = \sec t \tan t - \int \sec t \, (\sec^2 t - 1) \, dt$$

$$= \sec t \tan t - \int (\sec^3 t - \sec t) \, dt$$

Consequently

$$2 \int \sec^3 t \, dt = \sec t \tan t + \int \sec t \, dt$$

$$= \sec t \tan t + \ln |\sec t + \tan t| + \text{constant}$$

and so

$$\int \sec^3 t \, dt = \frac{1}{2} \sec t \tan t + \frac{1}{2} \ln |\sec t + \tan t| + C$$

It is worth remarking that for $t \in (-\pi/2, \pi/2)$, $\sec t + \tan t$ which equals $(1 + \sin t)/\cos t$ is positive, and so the modulus signs are superfluous.

It remains only to substitute back in terms of x. We had $x = \tan t$, so $\sec t = \sqrt{(1 + x^2)}$. Therefore finally

$$\int \sqrt{(1 + x^2)} \, dx = \frac{1}{2} x \sqrt{(1 + x^2)} + \frac{1}{2} \ln [x + \sqrt{(1 + x^2)}] + C$$

We will now use some steps to look at the other two integrals in the trio introduced at the start of the chapter.

_____ 16.2 Workshop _____

▷**Exercise**   Determine the integrals

$$\int \sqrt{(1 - x^2)} \, dx \qquad \int \sqrt{(x^2 - 1)} \, dx$$

For $\int \sqrt{(1 - x^2)} \, dx$, decide what you should do and then take the next step.

2 We shall need to make a substitution, and to resolve the square root we shall wish to make $1 - x^2$ a perfect square. Appropriate identities which suggest the substitution to use are

$$1 - \sin^2 t = \cos^2 t$$
$$1 - \tanh^2 t = \text{sech}^2 t$$

Accordingly we should choose $x = \sin t$ (or $x = \cos t$) or $x = \tanh t$ (or $x = \text{sech}\, t$). Which one we choose depends on mood and temperament! Let us be definite and select $x = \sin t$ so that we all do the same thing.

One small observation should be made before proceeding. If $x = \sin t$ then $|x| \leqslant 1$, but this is no problem since the integrand is not defined when $x^2 > 1$.

If you managed to sort out the integrand along these lines, then make the substitution and move ahead to step 4.

If you couldn't do it then look carefully at the identities and try your skill with the other integral. In other words, decide which substitution you would choose to obtain $\int \sqrt{(x^2 - 1)}\, dx$. As soon as you are ready take the next step.

3 The identities which are of use to us for $\int \sqrt{(x^2 - 1)}\, dx$ are

$$\sec^2 t - 1 = \tan^2 t$$
$$\cosh^2 t - 1 = \sinh^2 t$$

So you should substitute either $x = \sec t$ or $x = \cosh t$. The substitution $x = \cosh t$ presumes that $x \geqslant 1$. For the integral to exist we require $x^2 \geqslant 1$ so that either $x \geqslant 1$ or $x \leqslant -1$. The case $x \leqslant -1$ needs to be considered separately. The substitution $u = -x$ shows that when $x \leqslant -1$

$$\int \sqrt{(x^2 - 1)}\, dx = -\int \sqrt{(u^2 - 1)}\, du$$

where $u \geqslant 1$.

We shall return to this point once we have determined the integral in the case $x \geqslant 1$.

Of course it is always possible that you will think of a totally different approach which is nevertheless correct. The test will be whether or not you come up with the correct answer eventually.

Now return to $\int \sqrt{(1 - x^2)}\, dx$, substitute $x = \sin t$, simplify and take another step.

4 When $x = \sin t$ we have $dx = \cos t\, dt$ and $\sqrt{(1 - x^2)} = \cos t$. Once more we note that if we take $t \in (-\pi/2, \pi/2)$ then every $x \in (-1, 1)$ is attained. Also then $\cos t$ is positive, and so no modulus sign is needed when the value of the square root is calculated. We obtain

$$\int \sqrt{(1 - x^2)}\,dx = \int \cos^2 t \, dt$$

If you managed that then think how you are going to resolve this integral. When you have decided, try it, then move to step 6 and see if all is well.

If this did not work out correctly, look carefully to see where you made a mistake. Then try putting $x = \cosh t$ in the integral $\int \sqrt{(x^2 - 1)}\,dx$. When you are satisfied with your answer, take a further step.

If we put $x = \cosh t$ then $dx = \sinh t \, dt$ and $\sqrt{(x^2 - 1)} = \sinh t$. So   **5**

$$\int \sqrt{(x^2 - 1)}\,dx = \int \sinh^2 t \, dt$$

All's well now!

Now return to the determination of $\int \sqrt{(1 - x^2)}\,dx$, and consider what to do about obtaining $\int \cos^2 t \, dt$. As soon as you have decided, move to step 6 to see if you are correct. It helps to remember a simple trigonometrical identity!

We have   **6**

$$\int \cos^2 t \, dt = \frac{1}{2} \int (1 + \cos 2t)\,dt$$

$$= \frac{t}{2} + \frac{\sin 2t}{4} + C$$

$$= \tfrac{1}{2} t + \tfrac{1}{2} \sin t \cos t + C$$

Did you get that? If so, substitute back in terms of x and then move on to step 8.

If something went wrong, try again this time with $\int \sinh^2 t \, dt$ in the determination of $\int \sqrt{(x^2 - 1)}\,dx$. When you have sorted things out, move to step 7.

We have   **7**

$$\int \sinh^2 t \, dt = \frac{1}{2} \int (\cosh 2t - 1)\,dt$$

$$= \frac{\sinh 2t}{4} - \frac{t}{2} + C$$

$$= \tfrac{1}{2} \sinh t \cosh t - \tfrac{1}{2} t + C$$

It's just a few trigonometrical identities and simple use of the substitution rule.

Now let's go back to the solution of $\int \sqrt{(1 - x^2)}\,dx$. We had $x = \sin t$, and we found that

$$\int \sqrt{(1 - x^2)}\,dx = \int \cos^2 t \, dt$$
$$= \tfrac{1}{2}t + \tfrac{1}{2}\sin t \cos t + C$$

Substitute back in terms of x, and when you are ready take a step.

---

8 We have $x = \sin t$ where $t \in (-\pi/2, \pi/2)$, and so $t = \sin^{-1} x$ and

$$\cos t = \sqrt{(1 - \sin^2 t)} = \sqrt{(1 - x^2)}$$

Consequently

$$\int \sqrt{(1 - x^2)}\,dx = \tfrac{1}{2}\sin^{-1} x + \tfrac{1}{2}x\sqrt{(1 - x^2)} + C$$

If you managed that, then all well and good. You may move on to the next section.

If things went wrong, then try the twin brother of the one we have just looked at. Given that, when $x = \cosh t$,

$$\int \sqrt{(x^2 - 1)}\,dx = \int \sinh^2 t \, dt$$
$$= \tfrac{1}{2}\sinh t \cosh t - \tfrac{1}{2}t + C$$

substitute back to express the integral in terms of x. When you have done that, take the last step.

---

9 If $x = \cosh t$ then

$$t = \cosh^{-1} x = \ln\,[x + \sqrt{(x^2 - 1)}]$$

Also $\sinh t = \sqrt{(x^2 - 1)}$, so that

$$\int \sqrt{(x^2 - 1)}\,dx = \frac{1}{2}x\sqrt{(x^2 - 1)} - \frac{1}{2}\cosh^{-1} x + C$$

Alternatively

$$\int \sqrt{(x^2 - 1)}\,dx = \frac{1}{2}x\sqrt{(x^2 - 1)} - \frac{1}{2}\ln\,[x + \sqrt{(x^2 - 1)}] + C$$

---

10 Remember that we have considered the case $x \geq 1$ only. You should use the substitution rule to confirm that when $x \leq -1$

$$\int \sqrt{(x^2 - 1)}dx = \frac{1}{2}x\sqrt{(x^2 - 1)} - \frac{1}{2}\ln\,[-x - \sqrt{(x^2 - 1)}] + C$$

So that in general, when $x^2 \geqslant 1$

$$\int \sqrt{(x^2 - 1)}\,dx = \frac{1}{2}x\,\sqrt{(x^2 - 1)} - \frac{1}{2}\ln|x + \sqrt{(x^2 - 1)}| + C$$

Let's list the three standard forms discussed so far in this chapter:

$$\int \sqrt{(1 + x^2)}\,dx = \frac{1}{2}x\,\sqrt{(1 + x^2)} + \frac{1}{2}\ln[x + \sqrt{(1 + x^2)}] + C$$

$$\int \sqrt{(1 - x^2)}\,dx = \frac{1}{2}x\,\sqrt{(1 - x^2)} + \frac{1}{2}\sin^{-1} x + C$$

$$\int \sqrt{(x^2 - 1)}\,dx = \frac{1}{2}x\,\sqrt{(x^2 - 1)} - \frac{1}{2}\ln|x + \sqrt{(x^2 - 1)}| + C$$

Notice the common pattern.

16.3 SPECIAL SUBSTITUTIONS

There are a number of integrals which are best dealt with by the use of special substitutions.

THE t SUBSTITUTION

Consider the two integrals

$$\int \frac{dx}{4 + 3\cos x} \qquad \int \frac{\sin x\,dx}{10 + \cos x}$$

Trigonometrical and standard integrals arise in the theory of structures and in many other areas.

These can be resolved by making the substitution $t = \tan(x/2)$, known universally as the t **substitution**. We shall need to remember the special formulas which are a consequence of this substitution. Here they are:

$$\sin x = \frac{2t}{1 + t^2} \qquad \cos x = \frac{1 - t^2}{1 + t^2}$$

$$\tan x = \frac{2t}{1 - t^2} \qquad \frac{dx}{dt} = \frac{2}{1 + t^2}$$

We must also remember of course that $t = \tan(x/2)$, and to express the result of the integration in terms of x. Surprisingly, some students remember the substitutions but forget what t is!

The derivation of these special formulas involves the use of the half-angle formulas of elementary trigonometry. See if you can derive the one for $\cos x$ yourself. Afterwards we shall see how to use these formulas to obtain integrals.

Here we go then!

$$\cos x = 2 \cos^2 (x/2) - 1$$

$$= \frac{2}{\sec^2 (x/2)} - 1$$

$$= \frac{2}{1 + \tan^2 (x/2)} - 1$$

$$= \frac{2}{1 + t^2} - 1$$

$$= \frac{2 - (1 + t^2)}{1 + t^2}$$

$$= \frac{1 - t^2}{1 + t^2}$$

If you didn't manage that, then look at the working carefully. Observe the chain of thought: we express $\cos x$ in terms of $\cos^2 (x/2)$, which itself can be expressed in terms of $\sec^2 (x/2)$, which itself can be expressed in terms of $\tan^2 (x/2)$.

Now you try $\sin x$ and $\tan x$.

Now

$$\sin x = 2 \sin (x/2) \cos (x/2)$$

$$= 2 \tan (x/2) \cos^2 (x/2)$$

$$= \frac{2 \tan (x/2)}{\sec^2 (x/2)}$$

$$= \frac{2 \tan (x/2)}{1 + \tan^2 (x/2)}$$

$$= \frac{2t}{1 + t^2}$$

Also

$$\tan x = \frac{2 \tan (x/2)}{1 - \tan^2 (x/2)}$$

$$= \frac{2t}{1 - t^2}$$

Alternatively we can obtain $\tan x$ by dividing $\sin x$ by $\cos x$; at any rate we have a useful check that all is well.

Lastly obtain the substitution which enables us to put dx in terms of dt. Don't move on until you have made an attempt!

Here is the correct working. $t = \tan(x/2)$, and so differentiating with respect to x using the chain rule:

$$\frac{dt}{dx} = \frac{1}{2}\sec^2(x/2)$$

$$= \frac{1}{2}[1 + \tan^2(x/2)]$$

$$= \frac{1 + t^2}{2}$$

$$\frac{dx}{dt} = \frac{2}{1 + t^2}$$

That wasn't too bad, was it? Let's hope you didn't forget the 1/2 when you applied the chain rule.

We shall now concern ourselves with the mechanics of the t substitution. When do we use it, and how does it work?
If the integrand
1 contains circular functions only
2 is free of powers or roots
3 is difficult to resolve by other means
then the t substitution *may* be of use.

The t substitution converts a trigonometrical integrand into an algebraic integrand consisting of a rational function. Unfortunately the process can be tedious because it is often necessary to use partial fractions to complete the integration. However, the good thing about integrals of this kind is that they are not inherently difficult. One thing, of course: we must remember to substitute back to eliminate t finally.

Well now, let's have a go at one. Let us look at the first of the two integrals introduced at the beginning of this section, namely

$$\int \frac{dx}{4 + 3\cos x}$$

You make the substitutions and see what you get.

We have

$$4 + 3\cos x = 4 + \frac{3(1 - t^2)}{1 + t^2}$$

$$= \frac{4(1 + t^2) + 3(1 - t^2)}{1 + t^2}$$

$$= \frac{7 + t^2}{1 + t^2}$$

So we have

$$\int \frac{dx}{4 + 3 \cos x} = \int \frac{(1 + t^2)}{(7 + t^2)} \frac{2\,dt}{(1 + t^2)}$$

$$= \int \frac{2\,dt}{7 + t^2} = \frac{2}{7} \int \frac{dt}{1 + (t/\sqrt{7})^2}$$

$$= \frac{2}{\sqrt{7}} \tan^{-1}(t/\sqrt{7}) + C$$

So that

$$\int \frac{dx}{4 + 3 \cos x} = \frac{2}{\sqrt{7}} \tan^{-1} \left[\frac{\tan(x/2)}{\sqrt{7}} \right] + C$$

Not very pretty, is it? However, we were lucky! We didn't need to use partial fractions.

Now you try the second integral, namely

$$\int \frac{\sin x \, dx}{10 + \cos x}$$

and don't forget your work on partial fractions. Only when you have completed it should you move on and see if you are correct.

─────────────

Here we go then:

$$10 + \cos x = 10 + \frac{1 - t^2}{1 + t^2}$$

$$= \frac{10(1 + t^2) + 1 - t^2}{1 + t^2}$$

$$= \frac{11 + 9t^2}{1 + t^2}$$

So

$$\int \frac{\sin x \, dx}{10 + \cos x} = \int \frac{(1 + t^2)}{(11 + 9t^2)} \frac{2t}{(1 + t^2)} \frac{2\,dt}{(1 + t^2)}$$

$$= \int \frac{4t \, dt}{(11 + 9t^2)(1 + t^2)}$$

Now

$$\frac{4t}{(11 + 9t^2)(1 + t^2)} = \frac{A + Bt}{11 + 9t^2} + \frac{C + Dt}{1 + t^2}$$

So

$$4t \equiv (A + Bt)(1 + t^2) + (C + Dt)(11 + 9t^2)$$

First, $t = 0$ gives $0 = A + 11C$. The coefficient of t^2 gives $0 = A + 9C$. Therefore $A = 0$ and $C = 0$. The coefficient of t gives $4 = B + 11D$. The coefficient of t^3 gives $0 = B + 9D$. Consequently $D = 2$ and $B = -18$. You should check that this works by recombining the partial fractions into a rational expression.

So we have

$$\frac{4t}{(11 + 9t^2)(1 + t^2)} = \frac{-18t}{11 + 9t^2} + \frac{2t}{1 + t^2}$$

You could actually have done this by the cover-up method by replacing t^2 by u and ignoring the numerator initially. So we now have

$$\int \frac{\sin x \, dx}{10 + \cos x} = \int \frac{4t \, dt}{(11 + 9t^2)(1 + t^2)}$$

$$= \int \frac{-18t \, dt}{11 + 9t^2} + \int \frac{2t \, dt}{1 + t^2}$$

$$= -\ln (11 + 9t^2) + \ln (1 + t^2) + \ln k$$

$$= \ln k \left[\frac{1 + t^2}{11 + 9t^2} \right]$$

$$= \ln k \left[\frac{1 + \tan^2(x/2)}{11 + 9 \tan^2(x/2)} \right]$$

This simplifies even more. Can you sort it out?

Here is the working:

$$\int \frac{\sin x \, dx}{10 + \cos x} = \ln k \left[\frac{\sec^2(x/2)}{11 + 9 \tan^2(x/2)} \right]$$

$$= \ln k \left[\frac{1}{11 \cos^2(x/2) + 9 \sin^2(x/2)} \right]$$

$$= \ln k \left[\frac{1}{2 \cos^2(x/2) + 9} \right]$$

$$= \ln k \left[\frac{1}{\cos x + 10} \right]$$

$$= -\ln (\cos x + 10) + C$$

Now this is rather strange, isn't it? All that work: surely we could have done this quicker!

Could we? Yes, of course we could. We should have integrated by sight! Apart from a constant factor, the numerator of the integrand is the derivative of the denominator. The lesson to be learnt is quite plain: always look before you leap!

!

If you managed to spot this on your own, award yourself a special bonus. You can feel proud of yourself. If you didn't spot it, don't be alarmed; you were led into the longer method deliberately in order to make a point.

THE s SUBSTITUTION

If the integrand contains squares of circular functions then another substitution, which we shall call the s substitution, can be of use. As an example we shall consider the integral

$$\int \frac{dx}{9 \sin^2 x + 4 \cos^2 x}$$

The substitution is $s = \tan x$. Do not confuse this with the t substitution; here we do not have the half-angle.

We obtain at once the corresponding special formulas. First,

$$\frac{ds}{dx} = \sec^2 x = 1 + \tan^2 x = 1 + s^2$$

so that

$$\frac{dx}{ds} = \frac{1}{1 + s^2}$$

Also

$$\cos^2 x = \frac{1}{\sec^2 x} = \frac{1}{1 + s^2}$$
$$\sin^2 x = 1 - \cos^2 x$$
$$= 1 - \frac{1}{\sec^2 x} = 1 - \frac{1}{1 + s^2} = \frac{s^2}{1 + s^2}$$

You do not need to remember these formulas because you can, if you wish, obtain them directly using a right-angled triangle (Fig. 16.1).

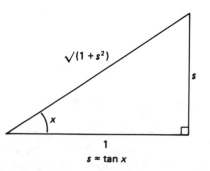

$s = \tan x$

Fig. 16.1

Now you try the substitutions on the integral which we have taken as an example.

Here goes then. When $s = \tan x$,

$$9 \sin^2 x + 4 \cos^2 x = 9 - 5 \cos^2 x = 9 - \frac{5}{1 + s^2} = \frac{4 + 9s^2}{1 + s^2}$$

So

$$\int \frac{dx}{9 \sin^2 x + 4 \cos^2 x} = \int \frac{(1 + s^2)}{(4 + 9s^2)} \frac{ds}{(1 + s^2)}$$

$$= \int \frac{ds}{(4 + 9s^2)} = \frac{1}{4} \int \frac{ds}{1 + (3s/2)^2}$$

$$= \frac{1}{4} \frac{2}{3} \tan^{-1} \left(\frac{3s}{2} \right) + C$$

$$= \frac{1}{6} \tan^{-1} \left(\frac{3 \tan x}{2} \right) + C$$

We could have done this more quickly by dividing numerator and denominator by $\cos^2 x$ at the outset.

If you didn't get it right, then here is another integral to determine:

$$\int \frac{\tan x \, dx}{5 \sin^2 x - 3 \cos^2 x}$$

If you were all right, then read through the working just to check there are no surprises.

When $s = \tan x$ it follows that

$$5 \sin^2 x - 3 \cos^2 x = \frac{5s^2}{1 + s^2} - \frac{3}{1 + s^2} = \frac{5s^2 - 3}{1 + s^2}$$

So

$$\int \frac{\tan x \, dx}{5 \sin^2 x - 3 \cos^2 x} = \int \frac{(1 + s^2)}{(5s^2 - 3)} \frac{s \, ds}{(1 + s^2)}$$

$$= \int \frac{s \, ds}{(5s^2 - 3)} = \frac{1}{10} \ln |5s^2 - 3| + C$$

$$= \frac{1}{10} \ln |5 \tan^2 x - 3| + C$$

As in the previous example, we can reduce the integral a little more quickly if we divide numerator and denominator by $\cos^2 x$ first.

GUIDELINES FOR THE *t* AND *s* SUBSTITUTIONS

We have the following guidelines for these special substitutions. However, they should only be used if it is not possible to perform the integration by more direct means.

1 If the integrand contains circular functions without powers, consider putting $t = \tan(x/2)$.

2 If the integrand contains squares of circular functions, consider putting $s = \tan x$.

16.4 INTEGRATION USING STANDARD FORMS

Another technique of indefinite integration which we shall discuss briefly is the use of standard forms. We should always bear in mind that we already know the following standard forms:

These augment the list of standard forms given in Table 15.2 and those derived in sections 15.5 and 15.6. They are all given on the bookmark.

1 $\displaystyle\int \frac{dx}{1 + x^2} = \tan^{-1} x + C$

2 $\displaystyle\int \frac{dx}{1 - x^2} = \frac{1}{2} \ln \left| \frac{1 + x}{1 - x} \right| + C$

3 $\displaystyle\int \frac{dx}{\sqrt{(1 - x^2)}} = \sin^{-1} x + C$

4 $\displaystyle\int \frac{dx}{\sqrt{(1 + x^2)}} = \sinh^{-1} x + C$
$$= \ln [x + \sqrt{(1 + x^2)}] + C$$

5 $\displaystyle\int \frac{dx}{\sqrt{(x^2 - 1)}} = \cosh^{-1} |x| + C$
$$= \ln |x + \sqrt{(x^2 - 1)}| + C$$

6 $\displaystyle\int \sqrt{(x^2 - 1)}\, dx = \{x\sqrt{(x^2 - 1)} - \ln |x + \sqrt{(x^2 - 1)}|\}/2 + C$

7 $\displaystyle\int \sqrt{(x^2 + 1)}\, dx = \{x\sqrt{(x^2 + 1)} + \ln [x + \sqrt{(x^2 + 1)}]\}/2 + C$

8 $\displaystyle\int \sqrt{(1 - x^2)}\, dx = [x\sqrt{(1 - x^2)} + \sin^{-1} x]/2 + C$

We have derived most of these in the course of our work, but there remain two which we have not. Before going any further, and by way of revision, you should tackle them. Do you know which ones they are? They are numbers 2 and 5.

Consequently if the integrand is of the form $1/Q$, $1/\sqrt{Q}$ or $\sqrt{Q}$, where Q is a quadratic, then we can always determine the integral by a routine procedure. All we need do is remember the procedure for 'completing the square'. That is, given a quadratic of the form $x^2 + ax + b$ we must express it in the form $(x + h)^2 \pm k^2$.

Do you remember how to do this? It is simplicity itself! We take h as half the coefficient of x, calculate $(x + h)^2$ and then add or subtract a positive number k^2 so that the constant agrees with b. In algebraic terms we obtain

$$(x + \tfrac{1}{2}a)^2 + b - \tfrac{1}{4}a^2$$

which looks much more complicated than it is.

Here is a numerical example.

☐ Express $x^2 - 4x + 9$ in the form $(x + h)^2 \pm k^2$.   **Example**
The coefficient of x is -4, so h is -2. Now $(x - 2)^2 = x^2 - 4x + 4$, so that

$$x^2 - 4x + 9 = (x - 2)^2 + 5$$

So here $k^2 = 5$.   ■

How does this help with integration? Well, when we see an integrand which is of the form $1/Q$, $1/\sqrt{Q}$ or $\sqrt{Q}$, where Q is a quadratic, we complete the square and substitute $X = x + h$. The integral will thereby be reduced to one of the standard forms. Be careful, however. Any stray x terms or other functions in the integrand change its nature completely and the method cannot be used.

So here is an example:

$$\int \frac{dx}{\sqrt{(x^2 + 6x + 18)}}$$

Completing the square:

$$x^2 + 6x + 18 = (x + 3)^2 + 9$$

So the integral becomes

$$\int \frac{dx}{\sqrt{[(x + 3)^2 + 3^2]}}$$

and the substitution $X = x + 3$ reduces it to a standard form. Now you complete this part of the calculation, and you will get the idea.

We have

$$\int \frac{dX}{\sqrt{(X^2 + 3^2)}} = \frac{1}{3} \int \frac{dX}{\sqrt{[(X/3)^2 + 1]}}$$

$$= \int \frac{d(X/3)}{\sqrt{[1 + (X/3)^2]}}$$

$$= \ln \{(X/3) + \sqrt{[1 + (X/3)^2]}\} + C$$

$$= \ln \{(x + 3)/3 + \sqrt{[1 + [(x + 3)/3]^2]}\} + C$$
$$= \ln k \, [x + 3 + \sqrt{(x^2 + 6x + 18)}]$$

Here we have absorbed some stray constants.

Now you try this one completely on your own:

$$\int \frac{\mathrm{d}x}{\sqrt{(15 - 2x - x^2)}}$$

Don't worry if things get in a mess. Help is at hand!

We complete the square but have to change the sign. So

$$x^2 + 2x - 15 = (x + 1)^2 - 16$$
$$15 - 2x - x^2 = 16 - (x + 1)^2$$

The integral is therefore

$$\int \frac{\mathrm{d}x}{\sqrt{[16 - (x + 1)^2]}}$$

Putting $X = x + 1$ we obtain

$$\int \frac{\mathrm{d}X}{\sqrt{(16 - X^2)}} = \frac{1}{4} \int \frac{\mathrm{d}X}{\sqrt{[1 - (X/4)^2]}}$$
$$= \int \frac{\mathrm{d}(X/4)}{\sqrt{[1 - (X/4)^2]}}$$
$$= \sin^{-1}(X/4) + C = \sin^{-1}[(x + 1)/4] + C$$

So there it is.

16.5 REDUCTION FORMULAS

Sometimes it is possible to avoid unnecessary work when obtaining an integral by using a reduction formula. This is best illustrated using an example.

Example □ Obtain

$$\int \tan^7 x \, \mathrm{d}x$$

The idea is to deal with a whole family of integrals at once. Suppose

$$I_n = \int \tan^n x \, \mathrm{d}x$$

so that $I_7 = \int \tan^7 x \, dx$ is the required integral. We try to obtain an equation which expresses I_n in terms of the same integral for smaller values of n. We have here

$$I_n = \int \tan^n x \, dx = \int \tan^{n-2}x \tan^2 x \, dx$$

$$= \int \tan^{n-2} x(\sec^2 x - 1)\,dx$$

$$= \int \tan^{n-2} x \sec^2 x \, dx - \int \tan^{n-2} x \, dx$$

$$= \int \tan^{n-2} x \sec^2 x \, dx - I_{n-2}$$

Now we can write down the integral immediately – can't we? You do it and then move on!

We have

$$I_n = \frac{\tan^{n-1} x}{n - 1} - I_{n-2} \qquad \text{when } n > 1$$

So that

$$I_7 = \frac{\tan^6 x}{6} - I_5 \qquad \text{putting } n = 7$$

$$I_5 = \frac{\tan^4 x}{4} - I_3 \qquad \text{putting } n = 5$$

$$I_3 = \frac{\tan^2 x}{2} - I_1 \qquad \text{putting } n = 3$$

Furthermore, we know that

$$I_1 = \int \tan x \, dx = \ln |\sec x| + \text{constant}$$

So substituting we obtain

$$I_7 = \frac{1}{6} \tan^6 x - \frac{1}{4} \tan^4 x + \frac{1}{2} \tan^2 x - \ln |\sec x| + C \qquad \blacksquare$$

By producing a reduction formula we have avoided repeating the same stage three times. Usually integration by parts is used in forming a reduction formula. However, do not rush into a reduction formula unnecessarily; it is often possible to make a simple substitution to resolve a difficult integral. Now here is one for you to try.

Example □ Obtain, by first deducing a reduction formula,

$$\int x^4 \, e^x \, dx$$

As soon as you have obtained the reduction formula, read on and see if you have it correct.

We put

$$I_n = \int x^n \, e^x \, dx$$

and integrate by parts:

$$I_n = x^n \, e^x - \int n \, x^{n-1} \, e^x \, dx$$

So

$$I_n = x^n \, e^x - nI_{n-1} \qquad n \text{ any integer}$$

Good! Now put in values of n so that we reduce things down to a very simple integral, and finish it off.

Putting $n = 4, 3, 2, 1, 0$ in turn we obtain:

$$I_4 = x^4 \, e^x - 4I_3$$
$$I_3 = x^3 \, e^x - 3I_2$$
$$I_2 = x^2 \, e^x - 2I_1$$
$$I_1 = x^1 \, e^x - 1I_0$$

Now

$$I_0 = \int e^x \, dx = e^x + \text{constant}$$

Finally we have

$$I_4 = x^4 \, e^x - 4x^3 \, e^x + 12x^2 \, e^x - 24x \, e^x + 24 \, e^x + C$$
$$= (x^4 - 4x^3 + 12x^2 - 24x + 24)e^x + C \qquad ∎$$

If you have followed everything so far in these integration chapters you should be able to make progress with all the usual integrals. However, it is important to know that not every integral can be obtained *analytically*. Sometimes two integrals may look superficially similar but are in fact totally different. To illustrate the point, $\int \sqrt{(\tan x)} \, dx$ and $\int \sqrt{(\sin x)} \, dx$ *look* alike, but the second cannot be obtained analytically using elementary functions whereas the first can. However, the integral of $\sqrt{\tan x}$, with respect to x, is a very hard nut to crack, and you would be best advised to leave it well alone! You have been warned.

_____ 16.6 Workshop _____

Now it's time to take steps. We are going to approach things in the same way as we did in the previous chapter. We are going to look at some integrals and decide the best approach. The integrals also form the assignment for this chapter. We are not at this stage going to obtain the integrals. Experience shows that the key to integration is not the ability to deal with technical detail but the ability to stand back and *plan ahead*. So out with the magnifying glass and on with the deerstalker:

   We are going to inspect some more integrals. Examine each carefully and decide how you would proceed. You may like to make a few jottings to explore your ideas, but you should not at this stage complete the integration.

▷**Exercise**   Inspect these integrals:

$$1 \int \frac{\cos x + 1}{\sin x - 1}\, dx \qquad 2 \int e^{\sin x} \cos x\, dx \qquad 3 \int \frac{x\, dx}{x^3 - 1}$$

When you have decided, take the next step.

1 At first sight you may think of going for the t substitution, but this may not be best. The integrand simplifies into a sum of standard forms if we multiply numerator and denominator by $\sin x + 1$.
2 Do not go for integration by parts; things will only get worse. In fact the integral can be obtained by sight, can it not $(u - \sin x)$?
3 This is a clear case for using partial fractions. The derivative of the denominator is not the numerator, and there is no obvious substitution to employ.

If all your answers agree with these, then move on to step 4. If some of your answers look as if they will not resolve the integral, then try these next three.

▷**Exercise**   Inspect these integrals:

$$4 \int \frac{\cos x}{\sin^2 x - 1}\, dx \qquad 5 \int e^{\sin^2 x} \sin 2x\, dx \qquad 6 \int \frac{x\, dx}{x^2 - 1}$$

When you are ready, read on!

3

4 If we simplify the integrand we obtain a standard form straight away. Alternatively we can put $u = \sin x$ and use a standard form. We could even use partial fractions following this substitution, but this is then rather long.

5 This is the sort of situation where it helps if we know our trigonometrical identities and can use them smoothly. When $u = \sin^2 x$ we obtain $du = 2 \sin x \cos x \, dx = \sin 2x \, dx$. Therefore this substitution resolves the integral.

6 There is obviously a method using partial fractions available to us. However, it is quite unnecessary to go to these lengths since, apart from a constant factor, the numerator is the derivative of the denominator.

Good! Now let's look at some more.

4

Exercise Inspect these integrals:

$$7 \int \sin^5 x \, dx \qquad 8 \int \cos^4 x \, dx \qquad 9 \int \cos 2x \sin x \, dx$$

As soon as you have decided on a suitable method, look in the next step to see if you are right.

5

7 Odd powers of sine or cosine should cause us no difficulty. Here we keep one sine and convert the even power into cosines using $\cos^2 x + \sin^2 x = 1$. Finally we use the substitution rule, putting $u = \cos x$.

8 Even powers of sine or cosine must be converted into multiple angles. The key formulas to use here are $\cos^2 x = (1 + \cos 2x)/2$ and $\sin^2 x = (1 - \cos 2x)/2$. In this example we can convert the integrand into one containing a quadratic term in $\cos 2x$, which in turn, using the double-angle formulas again, can be converted into terms of $\cos 4x$. All terms are then integrable by sight.

9 There are several approaches here which work. For example, we could write $\cos 2x = 2 \cos^2 x - 1$ and then integrate term by term. Alternatively we could use the formula

$$2 \sin A \cos B = \sin (A + B) + \sin (A - B)$$

If you are all right with these, then move ahead to step 8. If not, look carefully at the integrands we have been considering and by making rough notes convince yourself that the approaches which have been suggested do in fact work. Then examine the next three integrals.

6

Exercise Inspect these integrals:

10 $\int \sec^6 x \, dx$ **11** $\int \sec^5 x \, dx$ **12** $\int \sec^5 x \tan x \, dx$

When you have decided what to do with these, take another step.

7

10 If we were to put $u = \tan x$ we should obtain $du = \sec^2 x \, dx$. So if we split $\sec^6 x$ into a product of $\sec^4 x$ with $\sec^2 x$, it remains only to express $\sec^4 x$ in terms of $\tan x$. The identity $\sec^2 x = 1 + \tan^2 x$ is all we need.

11 Although superficially this may seem the same as the previous integral, in fact the odd power makes all the difference. Here we need to think in terms of integration by parts, writing the integrand as $\sec^3 x \sec^2 x$.

12 This may look more involved than the others, but in reality it is much simpler. If $u = \sec x$ then $du = \sec x \tan x \, dx$, and the necessary $\tan x$ term is obligingly part of the integrand. A simple application of the substitution rule enables us to complete it.

Now try the last two exotic creatures.

8

▷**Exercise**   Inspect these integrals:

13 $\int \frac{1}{x} \left(x + \frac{1}{x} \right)^{11} \left(x - \frac{1}{x} \right) dx$ **14** $\int (1 + \sin x)^7 \cos x \, dx$

How will you proceed? Make an attempt at **13** and take another of the steps.

9

13 You could multiply out and integrate term by term – all 24 terms! You may wonder if there is a better method. Yes, there is: the integral can be found by sight ($u = x + x^{-1}$).

If you are right then move on to the text following. Otherwise, try **14** and take the last step.

10

14 This is much the same as the previous integral. Of course it is possible to expand out the bracket so that the integrand snakes away all over the page, but we should never overlook a very simple substitution. Think carefully about which substitution to make!

That's it then. With judicious use of the rules of integration you should now be able to tackle any integral you are given. The key to success is experience, and this can only be obtained through practice. Therefore tackle as many integrals as possible; then it will have to be a very exceptional integral which catches you out!

We now consider two practical problems. One of the tasks of the next chapter will be to show how useful integration is when it comes to solving problems which arise in engineering and science.

16.7 Practical

PARTICLE ATTRACTION

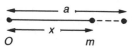

A particle is attracted towards a fixed point O by a force inversely proportional to the square of its distance from O and directly proportional to its mass m. If it starts from rest at a distance a from O, its distance x from O at time t satisfies the equation

$$\frac{dx}{dt} = \pm \sqrt{(2k)} \left(\frac{1}{x} - \frac{1}{a} \right)^{1/2}$$

where k is a positive constant. Show that the time taken to reach O is

$$a^{3/2} \pi / 2 \sqrt{(2k)}$$

As a first stage, integrate the differential equation with respect to t by writing it as two integrals.

---

1 We have

$$\pm \sqrt{(2k)} \int dt = \int \frac{dx}{\sqrt{[(1/x) - (1/a)]}}$$

Now we have a difficulty. How are we to resolve the integral on the right? Remember the guidelines: remove denominators, resolve roots. Remember also $\sec^2 \theta - 1 = \tan^2 \theta$. Try something, then move on.

---

2 We shall put $1/x = (1/a) \sec^2 \theta$, so that $x = a \cos^2 \theta$. Initially $\theta = 0$ and $x = a$, and as θ increases, x decreases. We have

$$dx/d\theta = -2a \cos \theta \sin \theta$$

so that

$$\pm \sqrt{(2k)} \, t = \int \frac{-2a \cos \theta \sin \theta}{\sqrt{(1/a)} \tan \theta} d\theta$$

Now see if you can resolve this integral.

---

3 We have, using elementary trigonometry,

$$\pm\sqrt{(2k)}\ t = -2a\sqrt{a}\int\cos^2\theta\ d\theta$$

$$= -a\sqrt{a}\int 2\cos^2\theta\ d\theta$$

$$= -a\sqrt{a}\int(\cos 2\theta + 1)\ d\theta$$

$$= -a\sqrt{a}\left(\frac{1}{2}\sin 2\theta + \theta\right) + C$$

where C is the arbitrary constant.

Now determine C and complete the solution.

---

4 When $t = 0$, $x = a$ and so $\theta = 0$. Consequently $C = 0$.

As $x \to 0$, $\cos\theta \to 0$, and $\theta \to \pi/2$. Therefore if T is the time required to reach O we have

$$\pm\sqrt{(2k)}\ T = -a\sqrt{a}\left(0 + \frac{\pi}{2}\right)$$

Now $T > 0$, so

$$T = \frac{a\sqrt{(a)}\,\pi}{\sqrt{(2k)}} = \frac{\pi a^{3/2}}{2\sqrt{(2k)}}$$

BALL BEARING MOTION

A ball bearing of mass m is projected vertically upwards with speed u in a liquid which offers resistance of magnitude mkv, where v is the speed of the bearing and k is a constant. Given that

$$-m\frac{d^2x}{dt^2} = mg + mk\frac{dx}{dt}$$

where x is the height, t is the time and g is the acceleration due to gravity, show that the greatest height attained is

$$\frac{u}{k} - \frac{g}{k^2}\ln\left(1 + \frac{ku}{g}\right)$$

Determine also the maximum speed the ball bearing will attain when falling through the liquid.

The equation may be integrated with respect to t to express dx/dt in terms of x and t. At the maximum height, $dx/dt = 0$; it will therefore be useful if we can obtain the time T to reach the maximum height. If we substitute $v = dx/dt$ we can calculate the time t in terms of v. Make this substitution, then look ahead for confirmation.

1 If we put $v = dx/dt$ the equation becomes

$$-dv/dt = g + kv$$

Therefore

$$\int \frac{dv}{g + kv} = -\int dt$$

So

$$\frac{1}{k} \ln (g + kv) = -t + C$$

where C is the arbitrary constant.

Next determine C and the time T taken for the ball bearing to reach its greatest height.

---

2 When $t = 0$, $v = u$ and so

$$\frac{1}{k} \ln (g + ku) = C$$

Therefore

$$\frac{1}{k} \ln (g + kv) = -t + \frac{1}{k} \ln (g + ku)$$

$$kt = \ln \left(\frac{g + ku}{g + kv} \right)$$

The maximum height is when $v = 0$, so we have

$$kT = \ln \left(\frac{g + ku}{g} \right)$$

$$= \ln \left(1 + \frac{k}{g} u \right)$$

So

$$T = \frac{1}{k} \ln \left(1 + \frac{k}{g} u \right)$$

Now that we know how long it takes to reach its maximum height, we can return to the differential equation to obtain the greatest height. See if you can do it; you must integrate term by term. Do this and then move on.

3 Dividing out m we have

$$-\frac{d^2x}{dt^2} = g + k\frac{dx}{dt}$$

So that, integrating with respect to t,

$$-\frac{dx}{dt} = gt + kx + A$$

where A is the arbitrary constant. Now when $t = 0$, $x = 0$ and $dx/dt = u$ so that $A = -u$. So

$$-\frac{dx}{dt} = gt + ku - u$$

At the maximum height $dx/dt = 0$ and we know T. Try to finish the solution.

---

4 We obtain

$$gT - u + kX = 0$$

where X is the greatest height. Therefore

$$X = \frac{1}{k}(u - gT)$$

$$= \frac{1}{k}\left[u - \frac{g}{k}\ln\left(1 + \frac{ku}{g}\right)\right]$$

$$= \frac{u}{k} - \frac{g}{k^2}\ln\left(1 + \frac{ku}{g}\right)$$

Lastly we must obtain the terminal velocity: that is, the maximum speed which the ball bearing will attain when falling freely through the liquid.

The key thing to realize is that at the maximum speed there is no acceleration and so $d^2x/dt^2 = 0$. Therefore

$$g + k\frac{dx}{dt} = 0$$

So

$$\frac{dx}{dt} = -\frac{g}{k}$$

The negative sign indicates that the ball bearing is falling.

SUMMARY

We have seen how to tackle integrals using a number of techniques.
☐ Trigonometrical and algebraic substitutions. Remember:
   a remove denominators
   b resolve roots.
☐ Reduction of the integral to a sum of standard forms.
☐ Use of the special substitutions

$$t = \tan x/2$$

and

$$s = \tan x$$

☐ Resolution of a quadratic Q where the integral is one of three types:

$$1/Q, \ 1/\sqrt{Q}, \ \sqrt{Q}$$

☐ Use of reduction formulas.

EXERCISES (for answers see p. 753)

1 Simplify, and thereby resolve, each of the following:

   a $\displaystyle\int \frac{\exp 2x + 1}{\exp x + 1} \, dx$

   b $\displaystyle\int \frac{\sin 2x + 2\cos x}{1 + \sin x} \, dx$

   c $\displaystyle\int \ln(x \exp x) \, dx$

   d $\displaystyle\int \frac{\sqrt{(1 + x^2)}}{(1 + x)^2 - 2x} \, dx$

2 Use appropriate substitutions, where necessary, to obtain

   a $\displaystyle\int x \tan(1 + x^2) \, dx$

   b $\displaystyle\int \frac{x \sin \sqrt{(1 + x^2)}}{\sqrt{(1 + x^2)}} \, dx$

   c $\displaystyle\int \frac{\sin 2x}{(1 + \sin^2 x)} \, dx$

   d $\displaystyle\int \sin 3x \cos 4x \, dx$

3 Obtain each of the following integrals by reducing it to a sum of standard forms:

a $\displaystyle\int \frac{\sin 2x}{2(1 + \sin x)}\,dx$

b $\displaystyle\int \frac{2 - x^2}{\sqrt{(1 - x^2)}}\,dx$

c $\displaystyle\int \frac{dx}{\{\sqrt{(x^2 + 1)} + \sqrt{(x^2 - 1)}\}}$

d $\displaystyle\int \frac{2x^2\,dx}{\sqrt{(1 + x^2)} - \sqrt{(1 - x^2)}}$

4 Use the t substitution to obtain the following integrals:

a $\displaystyle\int \frac{dx}{(4 - 3\tan x)}$

b $\displaystyle\int \frac{dx}{5\cos x - 12\sin x}$

5 Use a reduction formula to obtain each of the following integrals:

a $\displaystyle\int \cosh^7 x\,dx$

b $\displaystyle\int x^5 \cos x\,dx$

ASSIGNMENT (for answers see p. 754; see also Workshops on pp. 441 and 457)

Obtain each of the following integrals. If you are stuck at any stage, hints are given in section 16.6.

1 $\displaystyle\int \frac{\cos x + 1}{\sin x - 1}\,dx$ 2 $\displaystyle\int e^{\sin x} \cos x\,dx$ 3 $\displaystyle\int \frac{x\,dx}{x^3 - 1}$

4 $\displaystyle\int \frac{\cos x}{\sin^2 x - 1}\,dx$ 5 $\displaystyle\int e^{\sin^2 x} \sin 2x\,dx$ 6 $\displaystyle\int \frac{x\,dx}{x^2 - 1}$

7 $\displaystyle\int \sin^5 x\,dx$ 8 $\displaystyle\int \cos^4 x\,dx$ 9 $\displaystyle\int \cos 2x \sin x\,dx$

10 $\displaystyle\int \sec^6 x\,dx$ 11 $\displaystyle\int \sec^5 x\,dx$ 12 $\displaystyle\int \sec^5 x \tan x\,dx$

13 $\displaystyle\int \frac{1}{x}\left(x + \frac{1}{x}\right)^{11}\left(x - \frac{1}{x}\right)\,dx$ 14 $\displaystyle\int (1 + \sin x)^7 \cos x\,dx$

FURTHER EXERCISES (for answers see p. 754)

1 Obtain each of the following integrals:

(a) $\displaystyle\int \operatorname{cosec}^3 x \, dx$

(b) $\displaystyle\int \tanh^3 x \, dx$

(c) $\displaystyle\int \frac{d\theta}{3 \cos \theta + 4 \sin \theta}$

2 Obtain each of the following integrals:

(a) $\displaystyle\int \frac{1}{x^2} \sqrt{\left(1 - \frac{1}{x}\right)} \, dx$

(b) $\displaystyle\int \tan^2 (\theta/2) \tan \theta \, d\theta$

(c) $\displaystyle\int \frac{1 + \sin \theta}{1 + \cos \theta} \exp \theta \, d\theta$

3 Determine:

(a) $\displaystyle\int \frac{1 - \tan^2 x}{1 + \tan x + \tan^2 x} \, dx$

(b) $\displaystyle\int \frac{d\theta}{5 + 12 \tan \theta}$

(c) $\displaystyle\int \frac{x + 2}{(x^2 + 2x + 2)^2} \, dx$

4 Obtain each of the following:

(a) $\displaystyle\int \frac{dx}{\cos x - \sin x}$

(b) $\displaystyle\int \frac{dx}{\sin^3 x + 3 \sin x}$

(c) $\displaystyle\int \cos 3x \cos 5x \, dx$

5 If $I_n = \int \sec^n x \, dx$, show that for $n \geqslant 2$

$$(n - 1)I_n = \sec^{n-2} x \tan x + (n - 2)I_{n-2}$$

6 If $I_n = \int \tan^n x \, dx$, show that for $n \geqslant 2$

$$I_n = \frac{1}{n - 1} \tan^{n-1} x - I_{n-2}$$

7 If $I_n = \int x^m (\ln x)^n \, dx$, show that if $n \in \mathbb{N}$

$$(m + 1)I_n = x^{m+1} (\ln x)^n - nI_{n-1}$$

8 A particle moves on a curve defined parametrically in the polar co-ordinate system by $r = \sec u$ and $\theta = \tan u - u$. Show that if the intrinsic coordinates s and ψ are each measured from the line $\theta = 0$ then

(a) $\left(\dfrac{ds}{d\theta}\right)^2 = \left(\dfrac{dr}{d\theta}\right)^2 + r^2$

(b) $\dfrac{dr}{d\theta} = r \cot (\psi - \theta)$

Hence or otherwise show that the particle moves on the spiral $s = \psi^2/2$.

Integration 3   17

In Chapters 15 and 16, we were learning the techniques of integration. This chapter will be concerned with applications.

After studying this chapter you should be able to
☐ Evaluate definite integrals;
☐ Examine simple improper integrals for convergence;
☐ Apply methods of integration to determine volumes of revolution, centres of mass, moments of inertia and other quantities.
At the end of this chapter we look at a practical problem concerning the radius of gyration of a body.

17.1 DEFINITE INTEGRATION

Suppose that $f(x)$ is integrable with respect to x for all $x \in [a, b]$ where a and b are real numbers, $a < b$. In other words this means that we can find

$$\int f(x) \, dx = F(x) + C$$

whenever $a \leqslant x \leqslant b$. In such circumstances we define the **definite integral** of $f(x)$ with respect to x, with upper limit of integration b and lower limit of integration a, by

$$\int_a^b f(x) \, dx = [F(x)]_a^b = F(b) - F(a)$$

So the procedure for finding a definite integral is to first find the indefinite integral, ignoring the arbitrary constant, and then subtract its value at the lower limit of integration from its value at the upper limit of integration.

The only point to watch is that if we use a substitution when we are performing the indefinite integral we must take care either to change the limits of integration or to substitute back in terms of the original variable before evaluating the definite integral.

☐ Evaluate

$$\int_0^1 (1 + x)^2 \, dx$$

We have

$$\int_0^1 (1 + x)^2 \, dx = [\tfrac{1}{3}(1 + x)^3]_0^1$$

$$= \tfrac{1}{3}[(1 + 1)^3 - (1 + 0)^3] = \tfrac{1}{3}(8 - 1) = 7/3$$

Alternatively, if we make a substitution $u = 1 + x$ then we have $u = 2$ when $x = 1$ and $u = 1$ when $x = 0$. So

$$\int_0^1 (1 + x)^2 \, dx = \int_1^2 u^2 \, dt = [\tfrac{1}{3}u^3]_1^2 = 7/3 \qquad ■$$

We shall see later that a physical interpretation can be given for the definite integral.

17.2 IMPROPER INTEGRALS

Suppose that $f(x)$ is integrable with respect to x for all $x \in (a, b)$, where a and b are real numbers, $a < b$. In other words, this means that we can find

$$\int f(x) \, dx = F(x) + C$$

whenever $a < x < b$.

It may be that $f(x)$ is not defined when $x = a$ or $x = b$. We extend the definition of the definite integral under such circumstances by

$$\int_a^b f(x) \, dx = \lim_{x \to b-} F(x) - \lim_{x \to a+} F(x)$$

provided the limits exist.

Remember that $x \to b-$ means that x approaches b through numbers less than b, whereas $x \to a+$ means that x approaches a through numbers greater than a. You might like to imagine yourself imprisoned by the interval (a, b); then the left boundary is a and the right boundary is b, and all values in the interval are between these two extremes.

Right and left limits were considered in section 4.4.

Of course if the integral exists throughout a *closed* interval $[a, b]$ it is not necessary to take limits. Equally if the integral of $f(x)$ with respect to x exists for $a \le x < b$ then there is no need to take limits at a. We should then have

$$\int_a^b f(x)\, dx = \lim_{x \to b-} F(x) - F(a)$$

It is possible to use these ideas to extend the definition further so that infinite integrals may be considered. An **infinite integral** occurs when either the upper limit of integration is ∞ or the lower limit of integration is $-\infty$, or both. For example, if the integral of $f(x)$ with respect to x exists throughout the interval $[0, \infty)$ then

We first considered limits in section 4.1.

$$\int_0^\infty f(x)\, dx = \lim_{x \to \infty} F(x) - F(0)$$

provided the limit exists. If the limit exists the integral is said to **converge**; if it does not then it is said to **diverge**.

Example □ Evaluate each of the following integrals, if the integrals exist:

$$\int_0^\infty e^{-t}\, dt \qquad \int_0^1 x^{-1}\, dx$$

For the first integral we have

$$\int e^{-t}\, dt = -e^{-t} + C$$

So that

$$\int_0^\infty e^{-t}\, dt = [-e^{-t}]_0^\infty$$
$$= \lim_{t \to \infty} (-e^{-t}) - (-e^0)$$
$$= 0 - (-1) = 1$$

In the second integral the integrand is not defined when $x = 0$, and since $x > 0$ throughout the interval we have

$$\int x^{-1}\, dx = \ln x + C$$

So that

$$\int_0^1 x^{-1}\, dx = \ln 1 - \lim_{x \to 0+} (\ln x)$$

However, a graph of the logarithmic function shows that $\ln x \to -\infty$ as $x \to 0+$, so that the limit does not *exist*. Consequently the improper integral does not exist. ■

17.3 AREA UNDER THE CURVE

At this stage an important question has to be considered. How can we tell when $f(x)$ is integrable with respect to x? We used the phrase '$f(x)$ is integrable with respect to x' in connection with the indefinite integral to mean that we could obtain a function F such that $F'(x) = f(x)$. However, this idea is too narrow when we come to the definite integral and we shall need to modify it. In particular we shall show that if a function $f:[a, b] \to \mathbb{R}$ is continuous then it has a definite integral over the interval.

To do this we show that we can physically identify the definite integral of a positive continuous function between the limits a and b with the area A of the region enclosed by the x-axis, the curve $y = f(x)$ and the lines $x = a$ and $x = b$.

Suppose that the function $f:[a, b] \to \mathbb{R}$ is continuous, and suppose $A(t)$ is the area enclosed by the x-axis, the curve $y = f(x)$ and the lines $x = a$ and $x = t$, so that $A(a) = 0$ and $A(b) = A$ (Fig. 17.1). If t changes by a small amount δt then the corresponding change in the area of the shaded region is $A(t + \delta t) - A(t)$. Furthermore, suppose that $f^*(t)$ is the *maximum* value of $f(x)$ when $x \in [t, t + \delta t]$, and that $f_*(t)$ is the *minimum* value of $f(x)$ when $x \in [t, t + \delta t]$. Then

$$f_*(t)\,\delta t \leq A(t + \delta t) - A(t) \leq f^*(t)\,\delta t$$

since $f_*(t)\,\delta t$ underestimates the value of $A(t + \delta t) - A(t)$ whereas $f^*(t)\,\delta t$ overestimates the value of $A(t + \delta t) - A(t)$. Now if $\delta t \neq 0$ we have

$$f_*(t) \leq \frac{A(t + \delta t) - A(t)}{\delta t} \leq f^*(t)$$

As $\delta t \to 0$ we notice that both $f^*(t) \to f(t)$ and $f_*(t) \to f(t)$. Also

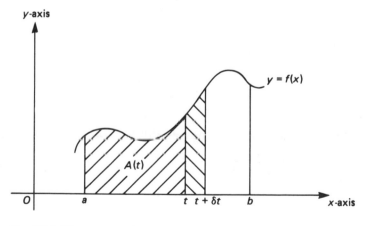

Fig. 17.1 The area under a curve.

$$\frac{A(t + \delta t) - A(t)}{\delta t} \rightarrow \frac{\mathrm{d}A}{\mathrm{d}t}$$

Therefore

$$f(t) \leqslant \frac{\mathrm{d}A}{\mathrm{d}t} \leqslant f(t)$$

so that $\mathrm{d}A/\mathrm{d}t = f(t)$. Consequently

$$\int f(t) \, \mathrm{d}t = A(t) + C$$

Now $A(a) = 0$ and $A(b) = A$, so that

$$A = A(b) - A(a) = \int_a^b f(x) \, \mathrm{d}x$$

This was what we wanted to show.

    It should be stressed that in this argument we have tacitly used a number of properties of continuous functions without justification.

> The concept of an integral as the area under a curve is widely used: for example, it is used in structural mechanics and hydraulic engineering.

We can use the idea of a definite integral of a continuous function having a physical representation as the area 'under a curve' as a springboard to apply the calculus to a wide variety of different situations.

    Suppose we look again at the area under the curve. We can imagine the interval $[a, b]$ divided up into n subintervals each of equal length δx. A typical subinterval can be represented as $[x, x + \delta x]$ (Fig. 17.2). Each sub-interval corresponds to a strip of area δA which we can approximate by $f(x) \, \delta x$. This is the area of a rectangular region, and may be either an overestimate or an underestimate for the true area. However, $f(x) \, \delta x$ will

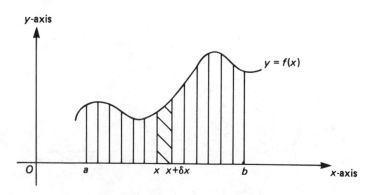

Fig. 17.2 Subdivision into strips.

approximate the true area when δx is very small. We may represent the total area in an informal way by

$$A = \sum \delta A \simeq \sum_{x=a}^{x=b} f(x)\,\delta x$$

where the summation sign $\sum$ indicates that we are adding up the corresponding elements. In the second sum, a and b show that we are summing these elements from $x = a$ until $x = b$; in other words, over the interval $[a, b]$.

Now we already know what happens as $\delta x \to 0$ because we have already shown that

$$A = \int_a^b f(x)\,dx$$

So a remarkable transformation occurs. As $\delta x \to 0$, the approximation becomes equality, the δ becomes d and the ugly duckling of a sigma sign becomes a beautiful swan of an integral sign!

We use this single example to infer a general method which we shall use to apply the calculus to a variety of problems. To fix the language for future use we shall refer to the idea of **partitioning** the interval $[a, b]$ into subintervals, and the corresponding portion of area δA which results will be termed an **element** of area. There are two conditions which are satisfied in this example and which must be satisfied in general:

1 The element which we choose and on which we base our approximation must be *typical*. That is, each element must be of this form and the approximation must be valid for each one.

2 By decreasing δx and so increasing the number of elements we must be certain that we could make the approximation arbitrarily close to the *true* result.

If and only if these two conditions are satisfied can we pronounce the magic words 'as δx tends to zero the approximation becomes good' and then carry out the following replacements:

$$\delta \to d \qquad \simeq \to = \qquad \sum \to \int$$

Let's try to visualize this in a more practical way.

17.4 VOLUME OF REVOLUTION

There are many ways of obtaining the volume of an egg, but one of them is closely related to the idea of integration and so we shall discuss it briefly. We can boil it, shell it and slice it up with an egg slicer. The egg will then have been converted into several small disc-like portions (Fig. 17.3). Then

A slice of egg   Egg slicer with sliced egg

Fig. 17.3

we can measure the radius and thickness of each portion and calculate approximately its volume. We can then add up all the volumes corresponding to each of the slices and in that way obtain an approximation to the volume of the egg.

Some observations are worth making:

1 The smaller the gaps between the wires of the egg slicer, the closer the slices will be to discs and so the better the approximation.

2 If we choose a slice at random it is typical of the others; they can each be approximated by a disc.

3 We could obtain an approximation as close as we desired to the true volume of the egg just by making the subdivisions smaller and smaller.

Let us now look at this problem more systematically. The egg can be regarded as a solid of revolution. That is, we may suppose the region surrounded by the curve $y = f(x) \geq 0$, the x-axis and the lines $x = a$ and $x = b$ has been rotated through 2π degrees about the x-axis. In this way the egg is obtained (Fig. 17.4).

Now suppose we partition the interval $[a, b]$ into equal parts each of width δx. A typical element of volume will be a disc-like shape with its

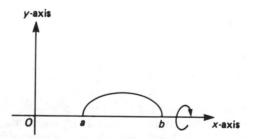

Fig. 17.4 Generating a solid of revolution.

Fig. 17.5 A typical element.

centre a distance x from the origin. The radius will be the height $y = f(x)$ of the curve at x. So the volume of a typical element is approximately $\pi y^2 \, \delta x$ (Fig. 17.5). We may represent the sum of all the elements by writing

$$V = \sum \delta V \simeq \sum_{x=a}^{x=b} \pi y^2 \, \delta x$$

Now the two basic requirements are certainly satisfied and so we can pronounce the magic spell: 'as δx tends to zero the approximation becomes good'. Hey presto! We obtain

$$V = \int_{x=a}^{x=b} \pi y^2 \, dx$$

$$V = \int_{a}^{b} \pi y^2 \, dx$$

We should realize just how powerful this method is. Unfortunately it is easy to misuse it and thereby to obtain an incorrect result. For example, if we were to attempt to obtain the surface area of an egg by the same procedure we should still obtain discs as elements. It might be tempting to approximate the curved surface area of each disc by $2\pi y \, \delta x$, since $2\pi y$ is the perimeter and δx is the width of a typical disc. However,

$$A \neq \int_{x=a}^{x=b} 2\pi y \, dx$$

What has gone wrong? Can you see?

The error here is that the element we have chosen does not typify the *extreme* case. For example, if $y = f(x)$ is particularly steep then the width of each element does not relate to the surface area (Fig. 17.6). Instead it is the length δs of the corresponding element of curve which is important. So, for a typical element, the curved surface area is approximately $2\pi y \, \delta s$. Hence the surface area required is

Fig. 17.6 An element.

$$A = \sum \delta A \simeq \sum_{x=a}^{x=b} 2\pi y \, \delta s$$

$$A = \int_{x=a}^{x=b} 2\pi y \, ds$$

We have a powerful method which can be used not only to calculate quantities which we already know about, but also to calculate quantities which may become of importance in the future and which have not even been considered at present.

————————————————Workshop————————————————

This chapter differs from the others in the book because there is no formal workshop; the workshop is dispersed among the text which follows. The reason for this is that we are about to derive a wide variety of formulas using, over and over again, the same basic principles of integral calculus. Therefore you can select for detailed study those which are particularly relevant to your branch of engineering. You will of course wish to use the others for practice and examples. In some ways it is like going on a 'field trip'!

17.5 LENGTH OF A CURVE

We begin by developing the formula for the length s of a curve $y = f(x)$ between the points where $x = a$ and $x = b$ (Fig. 17.7):

$$s = \int_a^b \left[1 + \left(\frac{dy}{dx} \right)^2 \right]^{1/2} dx$$

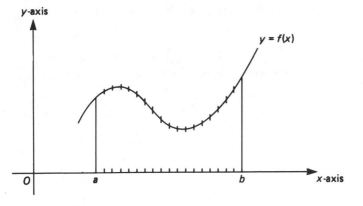

Fig. 17.7 Subdivision of a curve.

Suppose $y = f(x)$ is defined for $x \in [a, b]$. We wish to obtain the length of the curve over this interval. Dividing $[a, b]$ into subintervals each of length δx corresponds to a subdivision of the curve into portions of length δs. However, not all the subdivisions of the curve will necessarily have the same length even if δx becomes small (Fig. 17.8). We shall suppose that the curve is sufficiently smooth that when δx is small δs is given by the formula

$$(\delta s)^2 \simeq (\delta x)^2 + (\delta y)^2$$

and that this approximation becomes good as $\delta x \to 0$. So

$$\left(\frac{\delta s}{\delta x}\right)^2 \simeq 1 + \left(\frac{\delta y}{\delta x}\right)^2$$

and as $\delta x \to 0$

$$\left(\frac{ds}{dx}\right)^2 = 1 + \left(\frac{dy}{dx}\right)^2$$

so that

$$\frac{ds}{dx} = \left[1 + \left(\frac{dy}{dx}\right)^2\right]^{1/2}$$

Fig. 17.8 Relating x, y and s.

assuming that s increases with x, so that $ds/dx \geq 0$. Now we have

$$s \simeq \sum_{x=a}^{x=b} \delta s$$

As $\delta x \to 0$ the approximation becomes good, and so

$$s = \int_{x=a}^{x=b} ds$$

$$= \int_{x=a}^{x=b} \frac{ds}{dx} \, dx$$

Consequently we achieve the required formula for the length of a curve:

$$s = \int_a^b \left[1 + \left(\frac{dy}{dx} \right)^2 \right]^{1/2} dx$$

We remark that we are now in a position to give a formula for the surface area A produced by revolution of the curve around the x-axis:

$$A = 2\pi \int_a^b y \left[1 + \left(\frac{dy}{dx} \right)^2 \right]^{1/2} dx$$

Now for an example.

Example □ Obtain the length of the curve

$$y = \frac{x^2}{2} - \frac{1}{4} \ln x$$

between $x = 1$ and $x = 2$.
    Try it yourself first.

We have

$$\frac{dy}{dx} = x - \frac{1}{4x}$$

Therefore

$$\left(\frac{ds}{dx} \right)^2 = 1 + \left(x - \frac{1}{4x} \right)^2$$

$$= \left(x + \frac{1}{4x} \right)^2$$

$$\frac{ds}{dx} = x + \frac{1}{4x}$$

Consequently

$$s = \int_1^2 \left(x + \frac{1}{4x} \right) dx$$

$$= \left[\frac{x^2}{2} + \frac{1}{4} \ln x \right]_1^2$$

$$= \frac{3}{2} + \frac{1}{4} \ln 2 \qquad \blacksquare$$

Sometimes a curve is described parametrically in the form $x = x(t)$, $y = y(t)$. We shall show that the length of the curve between the points $t = t_1$ and $t = t_2$ is given by

$$s = \int_{t_1}^{t_2} \sqrt{(\dot{x}^2 + \dot{y}^2)} \, dt$$

where $\dot{x} = x'(t)$ and $\dot{y} = y'(t)$.

Why not try this? It is not difficult.

If we partition the interval $[t_1, t_2]$ into equal parts each of length δt, this will produce corresponding elements δx and δy. We have

$$(\delta s)^2 \simeq (\delta x)^2 + (\delta y)^2$$

and as $\delta t \to 0$ the approximation becomes good. Now

$$\left(\frac{\delta s}{\delta t} \right)^2 \simeq \left(\frac{\delta x}{\delta t} \right)^2 + \left(\frac{\delta y}{\delta t} \right)^2$$

So as $\delta t \to 0$

$$\left(\frac{ds}{dt} \right)^2 = \left(\frac{dx}{dt} \right)^2 + \left(\frac{dy}{dt} \right)^2$$

Now assuming that s increases with t we have

$$s = \int_{t=t_1}^{t=t_2} ds$$

$$= \int_{t=t_1}^{t=t_2} \frac{ds}{dt} \, dt$$

$$= \int_{t_1}^{t_2} \left[\left(\frac{dx}{dt} \right)^2 + \left(\frac{dy}{dt} \right)^2 \right]^{1/2} dt$$

Therefore the parametric formula for the length of a curve is

$$s = \int_{t_1}^{t_2} \sqrt{(\dot{x}^2 + \dot{y}^2)} \, dt$$

Here now is a problem using this formula.

Example ☐ Obtain the length of the curve $x = \theta + \sin \theta$, $y = 1 + \cos \theta$ between $\theta = 0$ and $\theta = \pi$.

When you have done this, move forward for the solution.

We need to convince ourselves that the curve doesn't do anything totally unexpected such as producing a figure of eight! One of the assumptions which we made was that, as the parameter increased, so too did the length of the curve. When $\theta = 0$ we have $x = 0$ and $y = 2$. Then as θ increases from 0 to π we see that x increases from 0 to π and y decreases from 2 to 0 (Fig. 17.9). As a matter of fact this is an interesting curve known as a cycloid. It is the curve described by a point on the rim of a car tyre as it moves along the road.

Now

$$x'(\theta) = 1 + \cos \theta$$
$$y'(\theta) = -\sin \theta$$

so that

$$\dot{x}^2 + \dot{y}^2 = (1 + \cos \theta)^2 + (-\sin \theta)^2$$
$$= 1 + 2 \cos \theta + \cos^2 \theta + \sin^2 \theta$$
$$= 1 + 2 \cos \theta + 1 = 2(1 + \cos \theta)$$

Now $1 + \cos \theta = 2 \cos^2 (\theta/2)$, so that

$$\dot{x}^2 + \dot{y}^2 = 4 \cos^2 (\theta/2)$$

Finally

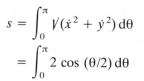

$$s = \int_0^\pi \sqrt{(\dot{x}^2 + \dot{y}^2)} \, d\theta$$

$$= \int_0^\pi 2 \cos (\theta/2) \, d\theta$$

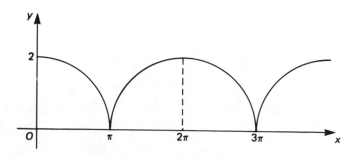

Fig. 17.9 A cycloid.

Note that cos $(\theta/2)$ is positive over the interval:

$$s = [4 \sin (\theta/2)]_0^\pi = 4 - 0 = 4 \qquad ■$$

17.6 CENTRES OF MASS

Suppose we have n particles of mass $m_1, m_2, \ldots, m_n$ positioned at points $(x_1, y_1, z_1), \ldots, (x_n, y_n, z_n)$ respectively relative to a rectangular cartesian coordinate system $Oxyz$. The centre of mass is the point $(\bar{x}, \bar{y}, \bar{z})$ where

The centre of mass of a body is an important property used by mechanical and civil engineers in mechanics and structures.

$$M\bar{x} = \sum_{r=1}^{n} m_r x_r$$

$$M\bar{y} = \sum_{r=1}^{n} m_r y_r$$

$$M\bar{z} = \sum_{r=1}^{n} m_r z_r$$

and

$$M = \sum_{r=1}^{n} m_r$$

In many situations the system of particles behaves as if the mass M is concentrated at the centre of mass. If all the particles have equal mass then we have

$$\bar{x} = \frac{1}{n} \sum_{r=1}^{n} x_r$$

$$\bar{y} = \frac{1}{n} \sum_{r=1}^{n} y_r$$

$$\bar{z} = \frac{1}{n} \sum_{r=1}^{n} z_r$$

which is a purely geometrical property and is often called the **centroid** of the n points. We shall now use these concepts to obtain the position of centre of mass of a solid body and the position of a centroid of a uniform lamina.

☐ Determine the position of the centre of mass of a uniform solid hemi- **Example** sphere of radius a.
   Try this if you like.

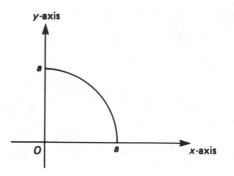

Fig. 17.10 Generating a hemisphere.

We first need to know the positions of the centroids of some simple objects. By symmetry, the centre of mass of a uniform rod is at the centre and the centre of mass of a uniform disc is also at the centre.

The hemisphere may be regarded as a solid of revolution obtained by rotating the portion of the circle $x^2 + y^2 = a^2$, $x \geq 0$ about the x-axis (Fig. 17.10). If we divide the interval $[0, a]$ into elements of length δx we divide up the hemisphere into discs each of radius y and width δx (Fig. 17.11).

Suppose the density of the hemisphere is ϱ. Then the mass of the elemental disc is $\varrho \pi y^2 \, \delta x$ approximately. So

$$M\bar{x} \simeq \sum_{x=0}^{x=a} \varrho \pi y^2 \, \delta x \, x$$

and

$$M \simeq \sum_{x=0}^{x=a} \varrho \pi y^2 \, \delta x$$

As $\delta x \to 0$ these approximations become good and so consequently

$$M\bar{x} = \int_0^a \varrho \pi x y^2 \, \mathrm{d}x$$

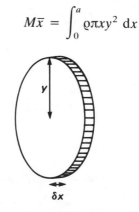

Fig. 17.11 A typical element.

$$M = \int_0^a \varrho \pi y^2 \, dx$$

Therefore

$$M = \int_0^a \varrho \pi \, (a^2 - x^2) \, dx$$

$$= \varrho \pi \left[a^2 x - \frac{x^3}{3} \right]_0^a$$

$$= 2\varrho \pi a^3/3$$

$$M\bar{x} = \int_0^a \varrho \pi \, (a^2 x - x^3) \, dx$$

$$= \varrho \pi \left[\frac{a^2 x^2}{2} - \frac{x^4}{4} \right]_0^a$$

$$= \varrho \pi a^4/4$$

Hence

$$\bar{x} = \varrho \pi \frac{a^4}{4} \frac{3}{2 \, \varrho \pi a^3} = \frac{3a}{8}$$

By symmetry, $\bar{y} = 0$ and $\bar{z} = 0$. ■

☐ Obtain the position of the centroid of an arc of a circle, radius r, sub- **Example** tending an angle 2α at the centre.

Why not see if you can manage this on your own?

Using polar coordinates we can partition the arc into equal lengths each subtending an angle $\delta\theta$ at the centre (Fig. 17.12). So for each element of arc $\delta s = r \, \delta\theta$. Furthermore, referring to the diagram we can use symmetry to deduce that $\bar{y} = 0$, and it remains only to calculate $\bar{x}$. In order to determine the position of the centroid it may help to consider the circle as having a unit linear density. You may if you wish introduce a constant linear density ϱ, but this is unnecessary.

We have $r \, \delta\theta$ is the mass of a typical element and $r \cos \theta$ is the distance of the element from the y-axis. So

$$M\bar{x} \simeq \sum_{\theta=-\alpha}^{\theta=\alpha} r \, \delta\theta \, r \cos \theta$$

As $\delta\theta$ tends to zero the approximation becomes good and so

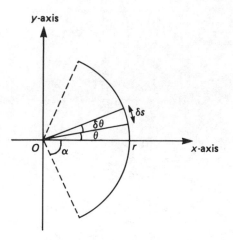

Fig. 17.12 Arc partitioned into equal lengths.

$$M\bar{x} = \int_{-\alpha}^{\alpha} r \, d\theta \, r \cos \theta$$

Moreover, M = length of arc × density = $2\alpha r$. So

$$\bar{x} = \frac{1}{2\alpha r} \int_{-\alpha}^{\alpha} r^2 \cos \theta \, d\theta$$

$$= \frac{r}{2\alpha} [\sin \theta]_{-\alpha}^{\alpha} = \frac{r \sin \alpha}{\alpha}$$

Of course α is expressed in terms of radians and not degrees.   ∎

Example □ Obtain the position of the centroid of a sector of a circle, radius a, subtending an angle 2α at the centre.

We divide the sector into elements each consisting of an arc subtending an angle 2α at the centre O (Fig. 17.13). The width of a typical arc with all its points distance r from O is δr. Now here we take the density per unit area as 1. We may consider each arc as having its mass concentrated at its centroid. In each case the centroid is at

$$\left(\frac{r \sin \alpha}{\alpha}, 0 \right)$$

and the mass of an element is $2\alpha r \, \delta r$. Consequently

$$M\bar{x} \simeq \sum_{r=0}^{r=a} 2\alpha r \, \delta r \, \frac{r \sin \alpha}{\alpha}$$

As δr tends to zero the approximation becomes good and therefore

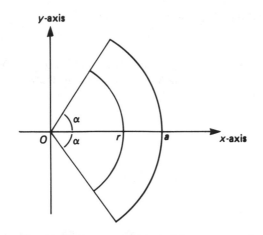

Fig. 17.13 Sector partitioned into concentric arcs.

$$M\bar{x} = \int_0^a 2\alpha r \, dr \, \frac{r \sin \alpha}{\alpha}$$

$$= 2 \sin \alpha \int_0^a r^2 \, dr$$

Now M is the area of the sector, so $M = \alpha a^2$. So

$$\bar{x} = \frac{2 \sin \alpha}{\alpha a^2} \int_0^a r^2 \, dr$$

$$= \frac{2 \sin \alpha}{\alpha a^2} \left[\frac{r^3}{3} \right]_0^a$$

$$= \frac{2a \sin \alpha}{3\alpha}$$

Once again we can appeal to symmetry to deduce that $\bar{y} = 0$.   ∎

17.7 THE THEOREMS OF PAPPUS

In the days before calculus, many techniques were employed to calculate volumes and surface areas. Two such techniques are attributed to Pappus, but their rediscovery 1300 years later by Guldin led to his name being linked with them also. These are the theorems.

Pappus of Alexandria (c. AD 320): the last great Greek geometer whose 'Synagoge' incorporates many Greek writings.

Theorem 1   Suppose an arc rotates about an axis in its plane, which it does not cross. Then the curved surface area of the region which it describes is

Paul Guldin (1577–1643): Jesuit mathematician and physicist. Thought by some to have been a plagiarist but this is largely discounted now.

equal to the product of the length of arc and the distance travelled by the centroid of the arc.

To justify this we shall take the x-axis as the axis about which the curve is rotated and take $y = f(x)$, positive, as the curve itself (Fig. 17.14). If the arc is rotated through an angle θ then the surface area S swept out is easily obtained using calculus as

$$S = \int_{x=a}^{x=b} \theta y \, \mathrm{d}s$$

and of course the length of arc is given by

$$\int_{x=a}^{x=b} \mathrm{d}s$$

Now we need to obtain the position of the centroid. It will be sufficient for our purposes to obtain $\bar{y}$. As usual we partition the interval $[a, b]$ so that we obtain subintervals each of width δx. We have

$$\bar{y} \int_{x=a}^{x=b} \mathrm{d}s = \int_{x=a}^{x=b} y \, \mathrm{d}s$$

and the distance travelled by the centroid of the arc is $\theta\bar{y}$. Then

$$S = \int_{x=a}^{x=b} \theta y \, \mathrm{d}s$$
$$= \theta \int_{x=a}^{x=b} y \, \mathrm{d}s$$
$$= \theta\bar{y} \int_{x=a}^{x=b} \mathrm{d}s$$

that is, the distance travelled by the centroid times the length of the arc.

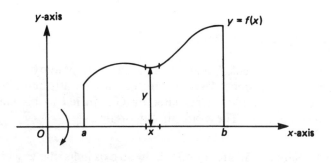

Fig. 17.14 Rotation of a curve.

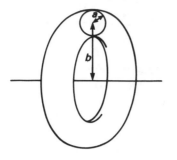

Fig. 17.15 Rotation of a circle.

☐ Obtain the surface area of a torus with inner radius $b - a$ and outer **Example**
radius $b + a$.

A torus is sometimes known as an anchor ring, a tyre shape or a quoit.
Try this example first, then look ahead. Calculus is not needed!

We can consider the torus as a circle of radius a rotated through 2π about
an axis distance b ($>a$) from its centre (Fig. 17.15). The length of arc is the
circumference of the circle $= 2\pi a$. The distance travelled by the centroid
is $2\pi b$, since the centroid of a circle is at its centre. Therefore the surface
area is

$$(2\pi a)\,(2\pi b) \;=\; 4\pi^2 ab \qquad\qquad ■$$

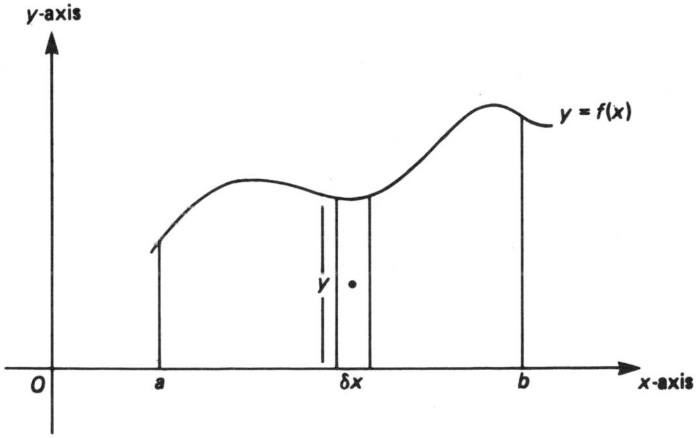

Fig. 17.16 Rotation of a region.

The second theorem of Pappus is very similar to the first. However, instead of rotating an arc we rotate a plane region.

Theorem 2   Suppose a region rotates about an axis in its plane, which it does not cross. Then the volume of the shape which it describes is equal to the product of the area of the region and the distance travelled by the centroid of the region.

See if you can justify this in the special case of the area enclosed by the curve $y = f(x)$, positive, the x-axis and the lines $x = a$ and $x = b$ rotating about the x-axis. The argument is very similar to the one we used for the first theorem.

If the region is rotated through an angle θ (Fig. 17.16) then the volume V swept out is given by

$$V = \int_{x=a}^{x=b} \frac{1}{2}y^2\theta \, \mathrm{d}x$$

and the area of the region is given by

$$\int_{x=a}^{x=b} y \, \mathrm{d}x$$

Now we need to obtain $\bar{y}$, the distance of the centroid of the region from the x-axis. We partition the interval $[a, b]$ so that we obtain subintervals each of width δx. Then, using the fact that the centroid of each strip is at its midpoint, we have

$$\bar{y} \int_{x=a}^{x=b} y \, \mathrm{d}x = \int_{x=a}^{x=b} \frac{1}{2}y^2 \, \mathrm{d}x$$

and the distance travelled by the centroid of the region is $\theta\bar{y}$. Then

$$V = \int_{x=a}^{x=b} \frac{1}{2}y^2\theta \, \mathrm{d}x$$

$$= \theta \int_{x=a}^{x=b} \frac{1}{2}y^2 \, \mathrm{d}x$$

$$= \theta\bar{y} \int_{x=a}^{x=b} y \, \mathrm{d}x$$

that is, the distance travelled by the centroid times the area of the region. It is easy to adapt this argument to the more general case.

Pappus's theorems can be used the other way round to obtain the positions of centroids. See if you can do that with this example.

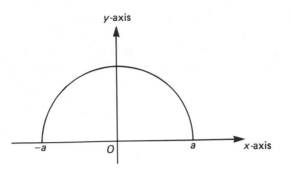

Fig. 17.17 Rotation of a semicircular region.

☐ Determine the position of the centroid of a semicircular region.   **Example**
   Move on when you have tried this. You do not need calculus.

We can arrange the semicircle in a symmetric way as shown in Fig. 17.17.
Then $\bar{x} = 0$ since the centroid must lie on the axis of symmetry. It remains
only to determine $\bar{y}$.

   Now if we rotate this region through 2π about the diameter, which is on
the x-axis, we obtain a sphere as the solid of revolution. Using Pappus's
second theorem we now have

$$\frac{4}{3}\,\pi a^3 = \frac{\pi a^2}{2}\,2\pi\bar{y}$$

So

$$\bar{y} = \frac{4a}{3\pi} \qquad\qquad ■$$

17.8 MOMENTS OF INERTIA

The product of the mass of a particle and its distance from some fixed axis
is called the **first moment** of the particle about the axis. The product of the
mass of a particle with the square of its distance from some fixed axis is
called the **second moment** of the particle about the axis.

   We have already used first moments implicitly when calculating the
positions of centres of mass. Another name for the second moment is the
moment of inertia of the particle about the axis. Moments of inertia are
important in dynamics and so we shall consider the concept briefly.

Moments of inertia
are considered in
structural mechanics,
fluid dynamics and
hydraulic
engineering, and also
in many other areas of
application.

Suppose we have a system of particles with masses $m_1, m_2, m_3, \ldots, m_n$ situated at the points $(x_1, y_1, z_1), (x_2, y_2, z_2), \ldots, (x_n, y_n, z_n)$ respectively relative to a rectangular cartesian coordinate system $Oxyz$ (Fig. 17.18). We denote by I_{Ox}, I_{Oy} and I_{Oz} the moments of inertia of the system about the axes Ox, Oy and Oz respectively. So

$$I_{Ox} = \sum_{i=1}^{n} m_i(y_i^2 + z_i^2)$$

$$I_{Oy} = \sum_{i=1}^{n} m_i(z_i^2 + x_i^2)$$

$$I_{Oz} = \sum_{i=1}^{n} m_i(x_i^2 + y_i^2)$$

If we sum these moments of inertia we obtain

$$I_{Ox} + I_{Oy} + I_{Oz} = 2 \Sigma m_i r_i^2$$

where r_i is the distance of the particle (x_i, y_i, z_i) from O. Note that the summation Σ is taken over all possible values of $i \in \{1, 2, \ldots, n\}$ and so we can simplify the notation by leaving out the limits.

Example □ Obtain the moment of inertia of a hollow spherical shell about a diameter.

We can partition the surface of the spherical shell into elements of area δA. So if the shell has uniform density ϱ each element has a mass $\varrho\,\delta A$. Then taking the origin at the centre of the shell we deduce by symmetry $I_{Ox} = I_{Oy} = I_{Oz}$. We also have

$$I_{Ox} + I_{Oy} + I_{Oz} = 3 \Sigma \varrho\,\delta A\, r^2 = 2Mr^2$$

where r is the radius of the shell and M is its mass. Therefore

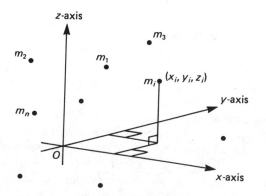

Fig. 17.18 System of particles.

$$3I_{Ox} = 2Mr^2$$

$$I_{Ox} = \frac{2}{3} Mr^2$$ ∎

17.9 THE PERPENDICULAR AXIS THEOREM

An interesting relationship holds when all the particles in a system are in the same plane:

If a system of particles is coplanar then the moment of inertia of the system, about an axis perpendicular to its plane, is equal to the sum of the moments of inertia of the system about two mutually perpendicular axes, in the plane of the system, provided that all three axes are concurrent.

We may take the axis as Oz and the particles in the plane Oxy (Fig. 17.19). Then

$$I_{Ox} = \Sigma \, m_i y_i^2$$
$$I_{Oy} = \Sigma \, m_i x_i^2$$

So

$$I_{Ox} + I_{Oy} = \Sigma \, m_i(x_i^2 + y_i^2) = \Sigma \, m_i r_i^2 = I_{Oz}$$

This is a useful theorem, but it can only be used when the particles are coplanar. Naturally this extends to a plane lamina when we apply calculus, but it must *never* be misapplied to a solid body.

☐ Obtain the moments of inertia of a uniform solid disc of mass m and **Example** radius a about an axis through the centre perpendicular to its plane, and about a diameter.

Try this and see how it goes.

_____

We begin by considering a uniform ring of radius r and uniform linear density ϱ (Fig. 17.20). Using polar coordinates, the perimeter can be split into elements each of length $r \, \delta\theta$. We therefore obtain an approximation for the moment of inertia about an axis Oz through the centre perpendicular to its plane:

$$I_{Oz} \simeq \sum_{\theta=0}^{2\pi} \varrho r \, \delta\theta \, r^2$$

The approximation becomes good as $\delta\theta$ tends to 0. Therefore

$$I_{Oz} = \int_0^{2\pi} \varrho r^3 \, d\theta = \varrho r^3 2\pi$$

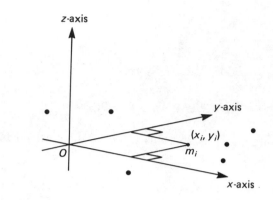

Fig. 17.19 System of coplanar particles.

But $M = 2\pi r\varrho$, so $I_{Oz} = Mr^2$.

Turning now to the disc, we split it into concentric rings as elements. A typical element has radius r and width δr. Using ϱ now for the area density, we have that the mass of an element is approximately $\varrho 2\pi r\, \delta r$; so it will contribute $\varrho 2\pi r\, \delta r\, r^2$ to the moment of inertia of the disc about Oz. Consequently

$$I_{Oz} \simeq \sum_{r=0}^{a} \varrho 2\pi r^3\, \delta r$$

and the approximation becomes good as δr tends to 0. Therefore

$$I_{Oz} = \int_0^a 2\pi\varrho r^3\, dr$$

$$= 2\pi\varrho \left[\frac{r^4}{4}\right]_0^a$$

$$= \pi\varrho a^4/2$$

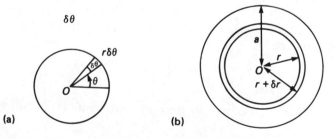

Fig. 17.20 (a) A uniform ring (b) Disc partitioned into concentric rings.

Now $m = \varrho\pi a^2$, and so the moment of inertia about an axis through the centre is $I_{Oz} = \frac{1}{2}ma^2$.

Lastly by symmetry $I_{Ox} = I_{Oy}$ and by the perpendicular axis theorem $I_{Ox} + I_{Oy} = I_{Oz}$. So the moment of inertia about a diameter is $I_{Ox} = I_{Oy} = \frac{1}{4}ma^2$. ■

Remember these results, because we often need them when calculating moments of inertia of other solids.

17.10 THE PARALLEL AXIS THEOREM

Another useful theorem which can be applied to solid bodies is known as the parallel axis theorem:

The moment of inertia of a system of particles about an axis is equal to the sum of the moment of inertia of the system about a parallel axis through the centre of mass and the product of the mass of the system with the square of the distance between the two axes.

Before we justify this we should note the reason for its importance. When calculating moments of inertia it is an error to assume that the mass of an element can be regarded as concentrated at the centre of mass. The parallel axis theorem must be used to obtain moments of inertia of elements about a given axis.

Suppose we are given a system of particles and a fixed axis (Fig. 17.21). We choose rectangular cartesian axes in such a way that

1 O is the centre of mass;
2 The fixed axis AB is parallel to the axis Oz;
3 The negative x-axis meets the fixed axis at A.

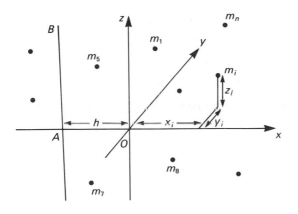

Fig. 17.21 System of particles and parallel axes.

We shall denote the fixed axis by AB and suppose that the distance between the two axes AB and Oz is h. Now

$$I_{AB} = \Sigma\, m_i[(x_i + h)^2 + y_i^2]$$
$$= \Sigma\, m_i(x_i^2 + y_i^2 + 2hx_i + h^2)$$

But $\Sigma\, m_i x_i = 0$ because O is the centre of mass of the system. Consequently

$$I_{AB} = \Sigma\, m_i(x_i^2 + y_i^2) + h^2\,\Sigma\, m_i$$
$$= I_{Oz} + Mh^2$$

where M is the mass of the system.

Example □ Obtain the moment of inertia of a solid right circular cone about an axis through its vertex parallel to its base.

If you wish you can try this first on your own.

We take the height as h, the base radius as a and the mass as M. It will be convenient to take the axes as shown in Fig. 17.22 and the density as ϱ. So $M = \pi a^2 h \varrho / 3$. We begin by slicing the cone into elements; a typical element is a disc with its centre at distance x from O, and with radius y and thickness δx. Regarding the cone as a solid of revolution we have

$$y = \frac{a}{h}x$$

Now the mass of an elemental disc is $\varrho\pi y^2\,\delta x$, and so the moment of inertia of the element about its diameter is $(1/4)\,(\varrho\pi y^2\,\delta x)\,y^2$. By the parallel axis theorem this element contributes

$$\tfrac{1}{4}(\varrho\pi y^2\,\delta x)\,y^2 + (\varrho\pi y^2\,\delta x)\,x^2$$

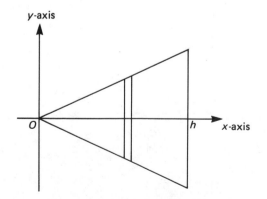

Fig. 17.22 Cross-section of solid right circular cone.

towards I_{Oy}. Therefore summing for all elements we have

$$I_{Oy} \simeq \sum_{x=0}^{h} \left(\frac{1}{4}y^2 + x^2\right) \varrho\pi y^2 \; \delta x$$

The approximation becomes good as δx tends to 0, and so

$$I_{Oy} = \int_{0}^{h} \varrho\pi \left(\frac{1}{4}y^2 + x^2\right) y^2 \; dx$$

Now

$$\left(\frac{y^2}{4} + x^2\right) y^2 = \left(\frac{a^2 x^2}{4h^2} + x^2\right) \left(\frac{a^2 x^2}{h^2}\right)$$

$$= Kx^4$$

where

$$K = \frac{(a^2 + 4h^2)\, a^2}{4h^4}$$

So

$$I_{Oy} = \varrho\pi K \int_{0}^{h} x^4 \; dx$$

$$= \varrho\pi K \left[\frac{x^5}{5}\right]_{0}^{h}$$

$$= \frac{\pi}{5} \varrho K h^5$$

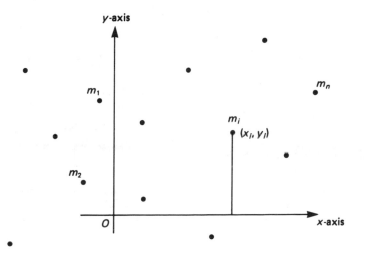

Fig. 17.23 System of particles with axes.

Now

$$\varrho = \frac{3M}{ha^2\pi}$$

so that

$$I_{Oy} = \frac{3M}{ha^2\pi} \frac{\pi h^5}{5} \frac{a^2 + 4h^2}{4h^4} a^2$$

$$= \frac{3M}{20}(a^2 + 4h^2) \qquad \blacksquare$$

It is possible to define the product of inertia of a particle relative to two axes. For example, given the axes Ox and Oy and a system of particles (Fig. 17.23) then, in our usual notation, the **product of inertia** H_{xy} relative to these axes is given by

$$H_{xy} = \Sigma\, m_i x_i y_i$$

In order to generalize this to laminae and solid bodies we should need to extend the ideas of integration further to define double integrals and triple integrals. This is a simple matter but is beyond the scope of our present studies.

17.11 AVERAGE VALUES

We now look at two other quantities which are often calculated using integration. They are the mean value of a function over an interval, and the root mean square value of a function over an interval.

The **mean value** (MV) of f over the interval $[a, b]$ is given by

$$MV = \frac{1}{b - a}\int_a^b f(x)\ dx$$

We have already shown, if $f(x) \geqslant 0$ when $x \in [a, b]$, that the integral is the area enclosed by the curve, the x-axis and the lines $x = a$ and $x = b$ (Fig. 17.24). Therefore dividing by $b - a$ gives the average height of the curve.

If $f(x) \leqslant 0$, when $x \in [a, b]$, then a negative integral will be calculated. Consequently the mean value of the sine function, for instance, over the interval $[-\pi, \pi]$ is zero because $\sin(-x) = \sin x$ for all $x \in [-\pi, \pi]$. Therefore in this example as much of the area lies below the x-axis as lies above it.

In many applications this is an inadequate representation of the effect of the function over the interval. For instance, the effects of receiving

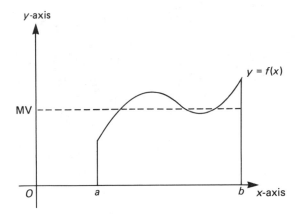

Fig. 17.24 The mean value of a function.

alternating current are certainly not zero! To obtain a more meaningful statistic, the RMS value is introduced.

The **root mean square value**, known as the RMS value, of a function f over the interval $[a, b]$ is the square root of the mean of the squares of the function:

$$\text{RMS} = \sqrt{\left\{ \frac{1}{b-a} \int_a^b [f(x)]^2 \, dx \right\}}$$

RMS values arise in electrical applications when alternating currents are considered.

□ Obtain the mean value and the RMS value of $y = x^3 + 1$ over the **Example** interval $[-1, 1]$.

You can try this yourself if you wish. It is just a matter of substituting into the integrals and evaluating them. Why not have a go? We shall see who gets there first!

For the mean value we begin with

$$\int_{-1}^{1} (x^3 + 1) \, dx = \left[\frac{1}{4} x^4 + x \right]_{-1}^{1}$$

$$= \left(\frac{1}{4} + 1 \right) - \left(\frac{1}{4} - 1 \right) = 2$$

The length of the interval is $1 - (-1) = 2$ and so MV $= 2/2 = 1$.

For the RMS value we must first obtain

$$\int_{-1}^{1} (x^3 + 1)^2 \, dx = \int_{-1}^{1} (x^6 + 2x^3 + 1) \, dx$$

$$= \left[\frac{1}{7}x^7 + \frac{2}{4}x^4 + x \right]_{-1}^{1}$$

$$= \left(\frac{1}{7} + \frac{1}{2} + 1 \right) - \left(-\frac{1}{7} + \frac{1}{2} - 1 \right)$$

$$= \frac{2}{7} + 2 = \frac{16}{7}$$

We divide by the length of the interval and take the positive square root to obtain RMS = $\sqrt{[(16/7)/2]} = \sqrt{(8/7)}$. ∎

17.12 RADIUS OF GYRATION

The moment of inertia I of a body of mass m about a given axis has dimensions ML^2; that is, it is the product of a mass with the square of a length. You possibly know that mass M, length L and time T are the basic building blocks in terms of which we can express many physical concepts. For example, acceleration has the dimensions LT^{-2}.

Indeed it is possible, by considering algebraic relationships between the ingredients in a physical problem, to derive the actual relationship by using dimensional analysis. In the case of a moment of inertia we see that $\sqrt{(I/m)}$ has the dimension of length ($\sqrt{(ML^2M^{-1})} = L$) and is called the **radius of gyration**.

The following practical problem involves the radius of gyration and uses polar coordinates.

————————— 17.13 Practical —————————

METAL SPRING

Example □ A plane wire has the shape of the curve $r = f(\theta)$ where $\theta \in [\theta_1, \theta_2]$ in the polar coordinate system. Show that the radius of gyration k about an axis through the origin perpendicular to the plane of the curve satisfies

$$k^2 \int_{\theta_1}^{\theta_2} \sqrt{\left[\left(\frac{dr}{d\theta} \right)^2 + r^2 \right]} \, d\theta = \int_{\theta_1}^{\theta_2} r^2 \sqrt{\left[\left(\frac{dr}{d\theta} \right)^2 + r^2 \right]} \, d\theta$$

Hence or otherwise show that if $r = a \exp \theta$ and $\theta \in [0, \ln 10]$ then $k = a\sqrt{37}$.

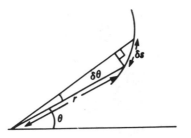

Fig. 17.25 Neighbouring points on $r = f(\theta)$.

It's a good idea to try this on your own first without looking at the solution. This is a problem in which you have to produce your own formula. We shall solve it stage by stage. Join in the solution when you feel you can.

---

1 We partition the spring into elements each of length δs (Fig. 17.25). Then if ϱ is linear density, we have that the mass of a typical element is $\varrho \, \delta s$. So the moment of inertia of this element about the required axis is given by

$$I_{\delta s} \simeq r^2 \varrho \, \delta s$$

The approximation becomes good as $\delta s \to 0$.

Use this to write down the mass m of the spring and the moment of inertia about the given axis.

---

2 We obtain immediately

$$m = \int_{\theta = \theta_1}^{\theta = \theta_2} \varrho \, ds$$

$$I = \int_{\theta = \theta_1}^{\theta = \theta_2} r^2 \varrho \, ds$$

Now use the definition of the radius of gyration to obtain an expression for k.

---

3 We have $k^2 m = I$, and so

$$k^2 \int_{\theta = \theta_1}^{\theta = \theta_2} \varrho \, ds = \int_{\theta = \theta_1}^{\theta = \theta_2} r^2 \varrho \, ds$$

Since ϱ is constant this becomes

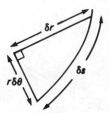

Fig. 17.26 Relating r, θ and s.

$$k^2 \int_{\theta=\theta_1}^{\theta=\theta_2} \mathrm{d}s = \int_{\theta=\theta_1}^{\theta=\theta_2} r^2 \, \mathrm{d}s$$

The next thing to do is to express $\mathrm{d}s/\mathrm{d}\theta$ in terms of $\mathrm{d}r/\mathrm{d}\theta$. See if you can do it.

---

4 We have, using Pythagoras's theorem (Fig. 17.26),

$$(\delta r)^2 + (r \, \delta\theta)^2 \simeq (\delta s)^2$$

So

$$\left(\frac{\delta r}{\delta\theta}\right)^2 + r^2 \simeq \left(\frac{\delta s}{\delta\theta}\right)^2$$

where the approximation becomes good as $\delta\theta \to 0$. Therefore

$$\left(\frac{\mathrm{d}r}{\mathrm{d}\theta}\right)^2 + r^2 = \left(\frac{\mathrm{d}s}{\mathrm{d}\theta}\right)^2$$

Consequently

$$k^2 \int_{\theta_1}^{\theta_2} \sqrt{\left[\left(\frac{\mathrm{d}r}{\mathrm{d}\theta}\right)^2 + r^2\right]} \, \mathrm{d}\theta = \int_{\theta_1}^{\theta_2} r^2 \sqrt{\left[\left(\frac{\mathrm{d}r}{\mathrm{d}\theta}\right)^2 + r^2\right]} \, \mathrm{d}\theta$$

Right! Now see if you can determine k for the portion of the spiral $r = a \exp \theta$ which has been specified.

---

5 We have $r = a \exp \theta$, $\theta_1 = 0$ and $\theta_2 = \ln 10$. So therefore $\mathrm{d}r/\mathrm{d}\theta = a \exp \theta$, and consequently

$$\left(\frac{\mathrm{d}r}{\mathrm{d}\theta}\right)^2 + r^2 = a^2 \, e^{2\theta} + a^2 \, e^{2\theta} = 2a^2 \, e^{2\theta}$$

Now from the previous relation we have

$$k^2 \int_0^{\ln 10} (\sqrt{2})a\ e^\theta\ d\theta = \int_0^{\ln 10} (a\ e^\theta)^2\ (\sqrt{2})\,(a\ e^\theta)\,d\theta$$

$$k^2 a(\sqrt{2}) \int_0^{\ln 10} e^\theta\ d\theta = a^3(\sqrt{2}) \int_0^{\ln 10} e^{3\theta}\ d\theta$$

So

$$k^2[e^\theta]_0^{\ln 10} = a^2 \left[\frac{1}{3}e^{3\theta}\right]_0^{\ln 10}$$

$$k^2(10 - 1) = \frac{a^2}{3}(1000 - 1)$$

from which $k^2 = 37a^2$, that is $k = a\sqrt{37}$.

SUMMARY

We have seen how to
☐ Evaluate definite integrals.

$$\int_a^b f(x)\,\mathrm{d}x = F(b) - F(a)$$

if $F(x) = \int f(x)\,\mathrm{d}x$ exists for $x \in [a, b]$.
☐ Examine improper integrals for convergence.

$$\int_a^b f(x)\,\mathrm{d}x = \lim_{x \to b-} F(x) - \lim_{x \to a+} F(x)$$

if $F(x) = \int f(x)\,\mathrm{d}x$ exists for $x \in (a, b)$.
☐ Apply integral calculus to obtain formulas.

(a) Area under a curve $= \displaystyle\int_a^b y\,\mathrm{d}x$

(b) Volume of revolution $= \displaystyle\int_a^b \pi y^2\,\mathrm{d}x$

(c) Curved surface area of revolution $= \displaystyle\int_{x=a}^{x=b} 2\pi y\,\mathrm{d}s$

(d) Length of a curve $= \displaystyle\int_{x=a}^{x=b} \mathrm{d}s$

(e) Mean value $= \dfrac{1}{(b-a)} \displaystyle\int_a^b y\,\mathrm{d}x$

(f) Root mean square value $= \sqrt{\left\{\dfrac{1}{(b-a)} \displaystyle\int_a^b y^2\,\mathrm{d}x\right\}}$

if $y = f(x)$ is continuous for $x \in [a, b]$.
☐ Apply integral calculus to obtain centres of mass and moments of inertia of solid bodies.
☐ Use the theorems of Pappus to determine positions of centroids, lengths of curves, volumes and surface areas of revolution.

EXERCISES (for answers see p. 755)

1 Obtain the area enclosed by the curve $y = f(x)$, the x-axis and the ordinates at $x = a$ and $x = b$ for

a $y = \dfrac{1}{1 + x^2}$, $a = 0$, $b = 1$

b $y = x^2 + x$, $a = 0$, $b = 1$

c $y = \dfrac{x}{1 + x^2}$, $a = 0$, $b = 1$

d $y = \sin x + \sin 2x$, $a = 0$, $b = \pi$

2 Obtain the area enclosed by the curves

a $y = x^4$, $y = x$

b $y = 2x^2 + x$, $y = x^3 + 2x$

c $y = \dfrac{(x^3 + x^2 - 1)}{(x + 1)}$, $y = \dfrac{(x^2 + x - 1)}{(x + 1)}$

d $y = x \exp x^2$, $y = x \exp x$

3 Find the volume of revolution when $y = f(x) > 0$ is rotated through 2π about the x-axis

a $y = 1 - x^2$

b $y = x(1 - x) \exp x$

c $y = 2 - \cosh x$

d $y = (2 - x) \ln x$

4 Obtain the mean value of each of the following over the interval $[a, b]$:

a $y = \sin^2 x$, $a = 0$, $b = \pi$

b $y = \cosh x$, $a = 0$, $b = 1$

c $y = \ln x$, $a = 1$, $b = 2$

d $y = \tan x$, $a = 0$, $b = \pi/4$

5 Obtain the RMS values of each of the following over the interval $[a, b]$:

a $y = \cosh x$, $a = 0$, $b = 1$

b $y = \tan x$, $a = 0$, $b = \pi/4$

c $y = \sin x$, $a = 0$, $b = \pi$

d $y = \dfrac{x^2 + 1}{x^2}$, $a = 1$, $b = 2$

ASSIGNMENT (for answers see p. 755; see also Workshop on p. 476)

1 Obtain the length of the curve $e^y = \sec x$ between the points where $x = 0$ and $x = \pi/4$.

2 Determine the length of the curve $y = c \cosh(x/c)$ from $x = 0$ to $x = c \ln 2$.

3 Obtain the area enclosed by the curve $x = \cos^3 \theta$, $y = \sin^3 \theta$ where $\theta \in [0, 2\pi]$.

4 Sketch the polar curve $r = 2 \sin \theta$ and obtain the area of the region it encloses.

5 The portion of the curve

$$y = \tfrac{1}{2}x^2 - \tfrac{1}{4} \ln(1 + x) + x$$

between $x = 0$ and $x = 1$ is rotated about the x-axis through 2π radians. Obtain the area of the curved surface generated.

6 Obtain the position of the centre of mass of a uniform solid right circular cone of mass M, height h and base radius a.

7 Determine the moment of inertia of a uniform semicircular lamina of mass m and radius a about (a) its axis of symmetry (b) the bounding diameter. (Watch out for bounding diameters!)

8 Obtain the moment of inertia of a solid hemisphere of mass M and radius a about a tangent parallel to its plane face.

FURTHER EXERCISES (for answers see p. 755)

1 By putting $x = \tan \theta$ and then $\theta = \pi/4 - \phi$, or otherwise, show that

$$\int_0^1 \frac{\ln(1 + x)}{1 + x^2}\, dx = \frac{\pi}{8} \ln 2$$

2 Obtain the area of the region enclosed by the curves $y^2 = ax$ and $y^3 = ax^2$ and the position of its centroid.

3 Determine the length of the curve $4y = x^2 - \ln(x^2)$ between $x = 1$ and $x = 4$.

4 If

$$y = \tfrac{1}{4}x^2 + \tfrac{1}{4}x - \tfrac{1}{2}\ln(2x + 1)$$

obtain the radius of curvature at the origin and the length of the curve between $x = -1/4$ and $x = 1/4$.

5 If

$$y = \tfrac{1}{2}\ln(1 - x) - \tfrac{1}{2}\ln(1 + x) + \tan^{-1}x$$

where $-1 < x < 1$, show that if the length of arc s is measured from the point where the curve crosses the x-axis then

$$s = -x - \tfrac{1}{2}\ln(1 - x) + \tfrac{1}{2}\ln(1 + x) + \tan^{-1}x$$

Hence, or otherwise, deduce that

$$y - s - x = \ln(1 - x) - \ln(1 + x)$$
$$y + s + x = 2\tan^{-1}x$$

6 Determine the moment of inertia of a solid right circular cone mass M, height h and base radius a about its axis of symmetry.

7 Evaluate where possible each of the following integrals:

(a) $\displaystyle\int_0^\infty x \ln x\, dx$

(b) $\displaystyle\int_0^\infty x\, e^{-x}\, dx$

(c) $\displaystyle\int_0^1 (1 - x^2)^{-1/2}\, dx$

8 Prove that the area of the cardioid $r = a(1 + \cos \theta)$ is $3\pi a^2/2$ and that its perimeter is $8a$.

9 Show that the area of the ellipse

$$\frac{x^2}{a^2} + \frac{y^2}{b^2} = 1$$

is πab.

   A solid circular ring of overall diameter 1.2 m is made from metal of elliptical cross-section. Each such ellipse has a major axis of length 0.4 m and a minor axis of length 0.2 m, and is such that its major axis is parallel to the axis of symmetry of the ring. Show that the volume of metal is $0.02\pi^2$ m^3.

10 A flat uniform metal plate PQR is in the shape of a triangle. Show that the moment of inertia of the plate about an axis through P parallel to QR is $Mh^2/2$, where M is the mass and h is the length of the perpendicular from P to QR. Without further integration prove that the moment of inertia about QR is $Mh^2/6$.

11 Show that when $3ay^2 = x(a - x)^2$ between $x = 0$ and $x = a$ is rotated about the x-axis through a complete revolution, the volume of the solid swept out is $\pi a^3/36$ and the surface area is $\pi a^2/3$.

12 If

$$I_n = \int_0^1 x^n \cos \pi x \, dx$$

and if n is a natural number, show that

$$\pi^2 I_n + n + n(n - 1) I_{n-2} = 0 \qquad (n > 1)$$

Hence, or otherwise, evaluate

$$\int_0^1 x^4 \cos \pi x \, dx$$

18 Numerical techniques

In Chapters 14, 15 and 16 we investigated the technique of integration and saw how to apply it to a variety of situations. We noted that some integrals cannot be determined analytically using elementary functions. In the case of definite integrals a numerical method can often be employed. In this chapter we discuss some numerical techniques and include in this some methods for determining definite integrals.

After working through this chapter you should be able to
☐ Solve an equation of the form $f(x) = 0$ using one of four numerical techniques;
☐ Approximate derivatives of the first and second order and estimate the error involved;
☐ Apply the trapezoidal rule and Simpson's rule to evaluate definite integrals.
We shall then solve a practical problem concerning the approximation of the temperature in a heat-conducting fin.

18.1 THE SOLUTION OF THE EQUATION $f(x) = 0$

Numerical methods for solving equations arise in materials and structures, fluid dynamics and hydraulic engineering.

We know how to solve quadratic equations; there is a simple formula for doing this. It is even possible to write a complicated set of procedures and formulas which will enable us to solve cubic equations and quartic equations explicitly. However, in general it is impossible to do this for polynomial equations of degree greater than four, and it is impossible to solve many other types of algebraic equation explicitly.

In order to obtain solutions of algebraic equations of the form $f(x) = 0$ a number of numerical techniques have been developed, and we shall look at some of them. We shall not, however, submerge ourselves in a quagmire of detail but shall be content to see the overall method. With digital computers and programmable calculators readily available, much of the laborious and painful process of dealing with numerical techniques has been removed.

18.2 GRAPHICAL METHODS

If we cannot solve an equation of the form $f(x) = 0$ analytically, we can often obtain a solution by giving a rough sketch of the graph $y = f(x)$ and locating approximately those values of x at which the curve crosses the x-axis. Sometimes it is easier to rewrite the equation $f(x) = 0$ in the form $g(x) = h(x)$ and to determine the points at which the curves $y = g(x)$ and $y = h(x)$ intersect. In order to increase the accuracy of the approximation it may be necessary to draw the graphs in greater detail over a smaller interval, but provided we can calculate the values and have enough patience we should be able to obtain any degree of accuracy required.

However, there are obvious drawbacks with using a graphical method. Sketching graphs can be time consuming and liable to error even with a computer program, but perhaps more seriously it is difficult to estimate the accuracy of the solution which is obtained. A much more satisfactory method from many points of view is a numerical method, and we shall consider several of these in this chapter.

18.3 ITERATIVE METHODS

Many numerical methods use a recurrence relation of the form

$$x_{n+1} = F(x_n)$$

and we require $x_n \to a$ as $n \to \infty$, where a satisfies the equation $f(x) = 0$. We call x_n the nth **iterate** and x_0 the initial approximation or **starting value**. Therefore if h_n is the error in the nth iterate we have

$$x_n = a + h_n$$

Moreover, if the process is to converge then as $n \to \infty$ we have $x_n \to a$, so that

$$a = F(a) \quad \text{and} \quad f(a) = 0$$

Now $x_{n+1} = F(x_n)$, so

$$
\begin{aligned}
a + h_{n+1} &= F(a + h_n) \\
&= F(a) + h_n F'(a) + \tfrac{1}{2} h_n^2 F''(a + \theta h_n)
\end{aligned}
$$

where $\theta \in (0, 1)$. Here we are assuming that F has a Taylor expansion about the point a, and we are using the form of Taylor's theorem with the remainder after two terms (see Chapter 8).

For convergence we require $a = F(a)$, and so we obtain

$$h_{n+1} = h_n[F'(a) + \tfrac{1}{2}h_n F''(a + \theta h_n)]$$

Moreover, if the process is to converge we require for large n

$$|h_{n+1}| < |h_n|$$

That is, the error in the $(n + 1)$th iterate must eventually become less than the error in the nth iterate.

It can be shown that if the process is to converge and if F'' is bounded then

$$|F'(a)| < 1$$

Example □ Consider the equation

$$x^2 - 5x + 6 = 0$$

which we know to have roots at $x = 2$ and $x = 3$.

First, suppose we rewrite the equation as

$$x = 5 - \frac{6}{x} = F(x)$$

Then

$$F'(x) = \frac{6}{x^2}$$

So when $x = 2$, $F'(x) = 3/2 > 1$, and when $x = 3$, $F'(x) = 6/9 = 2/3 < 1$. This means that we expect the iteration

$$x_{n+1} = 5 - \frac{6}{x_n}$$

to converge near $x = 3$ but diverge near $x = 2$.

Secondly, suppose we rewrite the equation as

$$x = \frac{6}{5 - x} = G(x)$$

Then

$$G'(x) = -\frac{6}{(5 - x)^2}$$

So when $x = 2$, $G'(x) = -6/9$ and therefore $|G'(x)| < 1$; and when $x = 3$, $G'(x) = -6/4$ and therefore $|G'(x)| > 1$. This means that we expect the iteration

$$x_{n+1} = \frac{6}{5 - x_n}$$

to converge near $x = 2$ but diverge near $x = 3$.   ■

The principal iterative method we shall consider is Newton's method. We begin, however, by considering some other numerical methods.

18.4 THE BISECTION METHOD

Suppose f is continuous and that we wish to solve the equation $f(x) = 0$. We first obtain two numbers a and b such that $f(a) < 0$ and $f(b) > 0$. We can then argue that somewhere in between a and b there is a solution of the equation (Fig. 18.1). This is a consequence of the intermediate value theorem, which is outside the scope of our work but is intuitively 'obvious'.

Let $c = (a + b)/2$. We then have one of three possibilities:
1 If $f(c) = 0$ we have found the required root.
2 If $f(c) < 0$ we can repeat the procedure with c replacing a.
3 If $f(c) > 0$ we can repeat the procedure with c replacing b.
After a bisection of the interval we either obtain the solution or we halve the length of the interval. So, if we repeat the process indefinitely, we must eventually arrive at the solution. The procedure stops when a and b agree to the required number of decimal places. In practice we rarely find that $f(c)$ is exactly 0 at any stage. However, we should always check that the root does satisfy the equation $f(x) = 0$ approximately.

We can make this more systematic by writing down the nth step:
1 Let a_n and b_n 'bracket' the root so that $f(a_n) < 0$ and $f(b_n) > 0$.
2 Put $c_n = (a_n + b_n)/2$.
3 If $f(c_n) = 0$ then the root is c_n.

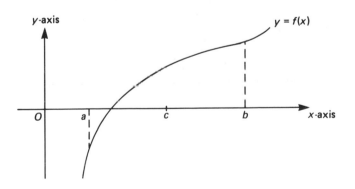

Fig. 18.1 The bisection method.

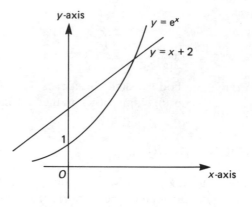

Fig. 18.2 The graphs of $y = e^x$ and $y = x + 2$.

4 If $f(c_n) < 0$ then $a_{n+1} = c_n$, $b_{n+1} = b_n$.
5 If $f(c_n) > 0$ then $a_{n+1} = a_n$, $b_{n+1} = c_n$.
We know that starting with $n = 0$ and $a_0 = a$, $b_0 = b$ we shall eventually obtain the root.

We now solve an equation using this method.

Example □ Obtain correct to three decimal places the positive root of $e^x = x + 2$.
A rough sketch of the equations $y = e^x$ and $y = x + 2$ reveals that there is indeed a positive root (Fig. 18.2).

Table 18.1

n	a_n	b_n	c_n	$f(c_n)$
0	1.000 00	2.000 00	1.500 00	0.981 69
1	1.000 00	1.500 00	1.250 00	0.240 34
2	1.000 00	1.250 00	1.125 00	−0.044 78
3	1.125 00	1.250 00	1.187 50	0.091 37
4	1.125 00	1.187 50	1.156 25	0.021 74
5	1.125 00	1.156 25	1.140 62	−0.011 91
6	1.140 63	1.156 25	1.148 44	0.004 83
7	1.140 63	1.148 44	1.144 54	−0.003 54
8	1.144 54	1.148 44	1.146 49	0.000 64
9	1.144 54	1.146 49	1.145 52	−0.001 44
10	1.145 52	1.146 49	1.146 01	−0.000 39

Put $f(x) = e^x - x - 2$. We begin by looking for two numbers which bracket the root: $f(1) = e - 3 < 0$ and $f(2) = e^2 - 5 > 0$. A table of values is the usual way to present the working (Table 18.1). As a general rule we must always work to two more places of decimals than that of the required accuracy, and so in this case we work to five. We can stop at $n = 10$ since no change to the third decimal place can now occur. So the required root is 1.146.   ■

The main problem with the bisection method is that if the root is close to a or b the process will still take a long time to converge.

18.5 THE *REGULA FALSI* METHOD

One way of trying to compensate a little for the shortcomings of the bisection method is to attempt to use the curve itself in helping to locate the root.

In the *regula falsi* method we join the points $(a, f(a))$ and $(b, f(b))$ by a straight line and determine the point where it crosses the axis (Fig. 18.3). We know from our work on coordinate geometry (Chapter 3) that the equation of the straight line joining $(a, f(a))$ to $(b, f(b))$ is

$$\frac{y - f(a)}{f(b) - f(a)} = \frac{x - a}{b - a}$$

So when $y = 0$ we obtain

$$x = a - \frac{(b - a)f(a)}{f(b) - f(a)}$$

$$= \frac{a[f(b) - f(a)] - (b - a)f(a)}{f(b) - f(a)}$$

$$= \frac{af(b) - bf(a)}{f(b) - f(a)}$$

This formula gives an improved approximation:

Regula falsi is Latin for 'the rule of false'; it is more generally called the **rule of false position**. It was very well known from ancient times and widely used until the 19th century.

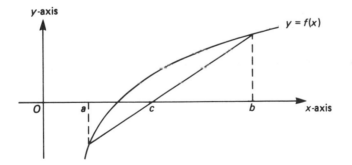

Fig. 18.3 The *regula falsi* method.

$$c_n = \frac{a_n f(b_n) - b_n f(a_n)}{f(b_n) - f(a_n)}$$

Example □ For the equation

$$f(x) = x^3 + 2x - 1$$

use the *regula falsi* method with $a = 0$ and $b = 1$ to obtain the first approximation c to the root.

We have $f(0) = -1$ and $f(1) = 1 + 2 - 1 = 2$, and so the interval $[0, 1]$ brackets the root. All we need to do now is to substitute $a = 0$ and $b = 1$ in

$$c_n = \frac{a_n f(b_n) - b_n f(a_n)}{f(b_n) - f(a_n)}$$

We obtain

$$c = \frac{0 \times 2 - 1 \times (-1)}{2 - (-1)} = \frac{1}{3}$$

The bisection method would have given $c = 1/2$. Furthermore $f(1/3) < 0$, and so if we were required to continue we should take $a_1 = 1/3$ and $b_1 = 1$. ∎

18.6 THE SECANT METHOD

In the bisection method and the *regula falsi* method, *both* ends of the interval are liable to become modified as the method progresses. A technique similar in some ways to the *regula falsi* method, but which does not have this feature, is the secant method.

Unlike the bisection and *regula falsi* methods we do not require two initial approximations which bracket the root; nor is it necessary to check the sign of the value of the function at each stage. However, we do require two starting values x_0 and x_1. Suppose x_n is the nth approximation. Then we can join the points $(x_{n-1}, f(x_{n-1}))$, $(x_n, f(x_n))$ by a straight line and determine the point where this cuts the x-axis (Fig. 18.4).

In fact we have already determined this point for this line! We had

$$c_n = \frac{a_n f(b_n) - b_n f(a_n)}{f(b_n) - f(a_n)}$$

and so putting $a_n = x_{n-1}$, $b_n = x_n$ we obtain

$$x_{n+1} = \frac{x_{n-1} f(x_n) - x_n f(x_{n-1})}{f(x_n) - f(x_{n-1})}$$

Example □ If $f(x) = x^2 - 5$, obtain the formula corresponding to the secant method which gives x_{n+1} in terms of x_n and x_{n-1}.

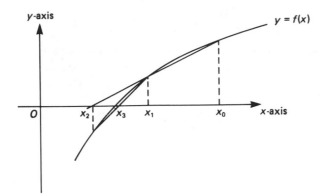

Fig. 18.4 The secant method.

We have

$$x_{n-1}f(x_n) - x_nf(x_{n-1}) = x_{n-1}(x_n^2 - 5) - x_n(x_{n-1}^2 - 5)$$
$$= x_nx_{n-1}(x_n - x_{n-1}) + 5(x_n - x_{n-1})$$
$$= (x_nx_{n-1} + 5)(x_n - x_{n-1})$$

and

$$f(x_n) - f(x_{n-1}) = x_n^2 - 5 - (x_{n-1}^2 - 5)$$
$$= x_n^2 - x_{n-1}^2$$
$$= (x_n - x_{n-1})(x_n + x_{n-1})$$

So

$$x_{n+1} = \frac{(x_nx_{n-1} + 5)(x_n - x_{n-1})}{(x_n - x_{n-1})(x_n + x_{n-1})}$$
$$= \frac{x_nx_{n-1} + 5}{x_n + x_{n-1}} \qquad \blacksquare$$

Two advantages of the secant method are that it is not necessary to choose starting values which bracket the root, and that we do not have to stop at each stage and check whether the function is positive or negative at the point.

The main disadvantage of this method is that convergence is no longer guaranteed. Although we shall not discuss the detailed circumstances in which convergence occurs, if

1 The starting values are chosen sensibly
2 The value of f' is non-zero at the root
3 The second-order derivative f'' is bounded then the method will work.

18.7 NEWTON'S METHOD

We mentioned in Chapter 6 that Newton was the mathematician who discovered and applied the calculus to a wide variety of problems.

Yet another method, due originally to Newton, involves using the tangent to the curve (Fig. 18.5). Suppose x_n is an approximate root; then for many curves the tangent will cut the x-axis at a point which is closer to the true root. From the diagram

$$\text{slope of curve at } P = \frac{PR}{QR}$$

Therefore

$$f'(x_n) = \frac{f(x_n)}{x_n - x_{n+1}}$$

so that

$$x_{n+1} = x_n - \frac{f(x_n)}{f'(x_n)}$$

This is Newton's formula. It is an iterative formula because we obtain a new approximation each time n increases. We need just one starting value x_0.

Example □ Given the equation $f(x) = x^2 - 5$, obtain the iterative formula corresponding to Newton's method. Perform three iterations starting with $x = 2$ and $x = 3$. In each case work to three decimal places.

We have $f'(x) = 2x$, and so the formula gives

$$x_{n+1} = x_n - \frac{f(x_n)}{f'(x_n)}$$

$$x_{n+1} = x_n - \frac{x_n^2 - 5}{2x_n}$$

$$= \frac{2x_n^2 - (x_n^2 - 5)}{2x_n}$$

$$= \frac{x_n^2 + 5}{2x_n}$$

First we have $x_0 = 2$, and so

$$x_1 = \frac{x_0^2 + 5}{2x_0} = \frac{4 + 5}{4} = 2.25$$

$$x_2 = \frac{x_1^2 + 5}{2x_1} = \frac{(2.25)^2 + 5}{2(2.25)} = 2.236$$

$$x_3 = \frac{x_2^2 + 5}{2x_2} = \frac{(2.236)^2 + 5}{2(2.236)} = 2.236$$

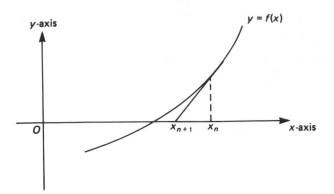

Fig. 18.5 Newton's method.

Secondly we have $x_0 = 3$, so

$$x_1 = \frac{x_0^2 + 5}{2x_0} = \frac{9 + 5}{6} = 2.333$$

$$x_2 = \frac{x_1^2 + 5}{2x_1} = \frac{(2.333)^2 + 5}{4.666} = 2.238$$

$$x_3 = \frac{x_2^2 + 5}{2x_2} = \frac{(2.238)^2 + 5}{2(2.238)} = 2.236 \qquad \blacksquare$$

Newton's method is usually very good and can be applied to many problems. The number of correct decimal places is approximately doubled with each iteration.

The disadvantages with Newton's method are similar to those of the secant method. Principally we are not assured of convergence (Fig. 18.6), and certainly if f' is zero at a root then problems will occur. If f' is numerically small at any of the iterates then arithmetical difficulties such as rounding errors and arithmetic overflow will result.

There are two ways round this problem. One is to try it and see. That is, assume everything will be all right until shown otherwise. If a computer has been given the burden of calculation then either it will return an error message or it will calculate and calculate *ad nauseam*. A better method, but

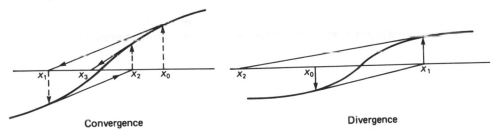

Fig. 18.6 Convergence and divergence of Newton's method.

one which requires some effort, is to try to anticipate any problems by making a rough sketch of $y = f(x)$.

Now we shall take a few steps.

18.8 Workshop

1

Exercise   The bisection method is used to solve an equation $f(x) = 0$ and it is found that $f(0) = -1$ and $f(1) = 2$. If arithmetic is performed to seven decimal places, how many times will the method have to be applied to obtain a solution correct to five decimal places?

Give this some careful thought: it's not too difficult. Then step forward.

2

We need a_n and b_n to agree to five decimal places, and this will only be guaranteed if the difference between the two numbers is less than $0.000\,000\,1$. For example, consider the numbers $0.435\,674\,9$ and $0.435\,675\,0$. The first rounds to $0.435\,67$ and the second to $0.435\,68$.

So we have in general

$$|a_n - b_n| < 0.000\,000\,1$$

Now

$$|a_0 - b_0| = 1$$
$$|a_1 - b_1| = 1/2$$
$$|a_2 - b_2| = 1/4$$
$$|a_3 - b_3| = 1/8$$

In general, $|a_n - b_n| = 2^{-n}$. Therefore we must have $2^{-n} < 0.000\,000\,1$, which means we require $2^n > 10\,000\,000$. It follows at once that 24 applications are necessary to be certain.

If you got that right, move ahead to step 4.

If you went wrong then try this one.

▷**Exercise**   Arithmetic is performed to five decimal places, and after 12 applications of the bisection method a solution is stable to three decimal places. What was the maximum length of the interval initially?

Try this and then take a step. It may help to write down some numbers.

3

We need to ask the question: how different can the two numbers be if they agree to three decimal places? For example, $1.462\,50$ and $1.463\,49$ both agree to three decimal places. So we see that the difference between the two numbers is no more than $0.000\,99$.

Suppose $|a_0 - b_0| = r$. Then $|a_n - b_n| = 2^{-n}r$, and so we require $2^{-n}r <$ 0.000 99 when $n = 12$. Consequently $r < (0.000\,99)\,(4096) = 4.055\,04$, and this is the maximum length of the interval between a_0 and b_0.

Now for a rather different type of question.

▷**Exercise** A computer programmer wishes to apply Newton's method to solve an equation of the form $f(x) = 0$. He intends the computer to handle the derivative, and uses the approximation

$$f'(x_n) = \frac{f(x_n) - f(x_{n-1})}{x_n - x_{n-1}}$$

where x_n is the nth iterate. What is the iterative formula corresponding to this adaptation? How many starting values are needed?

Work your way through this and on to the next step.

4

We begin with the formula which Newton's method provides:

$$x_{n+1} = x_n - \frac{f(x_n)}{f'(x_n)}$$

So approximating the derivative in the prescribed fashion gives

$$
\begin{aligned}
x_{n+1} &= x_n - \frac{f(x_n)(x_n - x_{n-1})}{f(x_n) - f(x_{n-1})} \\
&= \frac{x_n[f(x_n) - f(x_{n-1})] - f(x_n)[x_n - x_{n-1}]}{f(x_n) - f(x_{n-1})} \\
&= \frac{f(x_n)x_{n-1} - f(x_{n-1})x_n}{f(x_n) - f(x_{n-1})}
\end{aligned}
$$

5

Clearly we shall need *two* starting values to set things going.

The computer programmer may *think* he is using Newton's method, but in fact he is using the secant method, isn't he?

If you made a mistake or would like some more practice, try the exercise below and take the following step; otherwise simply read it through.

▷**Exercise** Work out the iterative formula corresponding to Newton's method if it is intended to solve the equation $\sin x - x = 0$ by this method.

The key formula involves calculating

$$x - \frac{f(x)}{f'(x)}$$

6

Now $f(x) = \sin x - x$ and so $f'(x) = \cos x - 1$. Therefore

$$x - \frac{f(x)}{f'(x)} = x - \frac{\sin x - x}{\cos x - 1}$$

$$= \frac{x\,(\cos x - 1) - (\sin x - x)}{\cos x - 1}$$

$$= \frac{x\cos x - \sin x}{\cos x - 1}$$

So

$$x_{n+1} = \frac{x_n \cos x_n - \sin x_n}{\cos x_n - 1}$$

is the iterative formula which we require.

18.9 APPROXIMATIONS TO DERIVATIVES

We have seen that Newton's method uses the *derivative* of the function to produce an iterative formula. Unless we are going to tell the computer the derivative of the function when we supply it with the data (the function and the starting value), it will be necessary to produce some approximate formulas for derivatives. In fact you will need these formulas if ever you consider the numerical solutions of ordinary or partial differential equations.

Let us begin by recalling Taylor's expansion

$$f(x + h) = f(x) + hf'(x) + \frac{h^2}{2!} f''(c)$$

for some $c \in (x, x + h)$ (Chapter 8). This is the form of Taylor's expansion where the remainder is given after two terms. So therefore

$$\frac{f(x + h) - f(x)}{h} = f'(x) + \tfrac{1}{2} h f''(c)$$

This gives at once an approximate formula for the derivative together with an estimate of the error involved:

$$f'(x) \simeq \frac{f(x + h) - f(x)}{h}$$

If M is an upper bound for the modulus of f'' on the interval $(x, x + h)$ we can assert confidently that the error is at most $hM/2$. The fact that the error is no more than a constant multiple of h is expressed by saying that the error is of order h, which is written as $O(h)$. Of course as $h \to 0$ we have the error tends to 0 and the approximation becomes good.

A similar argument can be used to show that

$$f'(x) \simeq \frac{f(x) - f(x - h)}{h}$$

again with an error of $O(h)$.

We can obtain a better approximation if we take another term in Taylor's expansion:

$$f(x + h) = f(x) + hf'(x) + \frac{h^2}{2!} f''(x) + \frac{h^3}{3!} f^{(3)}(c_1)$$

for some $c_1 \in (x, x + h)$. Replacing h by $-h$ in this expansion gives

$$f(x - h) = f(x) - hf'(x) + \frac{h^2}{2!} f''(x) + \frac{h^3}{3!} f^{(3)}(c_2)$$

for some $c_2 \in (x - h, x)$. We shall use these to obtain an approximate formula of order h^2.

Subtracting the two expansions gives

$$f(x + h) - f(x - h) = 2hf'(x) + \frac{h^3}{3!} [f^{(3)}(c_1) + f^{(3)}(c_2)]$$

so that we obtain

$$\frac{f(x + h) - f(x - h)}{2h} = f'(x) + \frac{h^2}{12} [f^{(3)}(c_1) + f^{(3)}(c^2)]$$

Therefore if K is an upper bound for the modulus of $f^{(3)}$ on the interval $(x - h, x + h)$, we have

$$f'(x) \simeq \frac{f(x + h) - f(x - h)}{2h}$$

with an error no more than $h^2 K/6$. So the error is of order h^2.

Yet one more term in the Taylor expansion provides an approximation for a second-order derivative which is also of order h^2. You might like to see if you can work it out for yourself.

We have

$$f(x + h) = f(x) + hf'(x) + \frac{h^2}{2!} f''(x) + \frac{h^3}{3!} f^{(3)}(x) + \frac{h^4}{4!} f^{(4)}(c_1)$$

for some $c_1 \in (x, x + h)$. Replacing h by $-h$ in this expansion gives

$$f(x - h) = f(x) - hf'(x) + \frac{h^2}{2!} f''(x) - \frac{h^3}{3!} f^{(3)}(x) + \frac{h^4}{4!} f^{(4)}(c_2)$$

for some $c_2 \in (x - h, x)$. (The c_1 and c_2 are not necessarily the same as the c_1 and c_2 when we considered the remainder after three terms.)

Adding the two expansions gives

$$f(x + h) + f(x - h) = 2f(x) + h^2 f''(x) + \frac{h^4}{4!} [f^{(4)}(c_1) + f^{(4)}(c_2)]$$

Therefore if K is an upper bound for the modulus of $f^{(4)}$ on the interval $(x - h, x + h)$ we obtain

$$f''(x) \simeq \frac{f(x + h) - 2f(x) + f(x - h)}{h^2}$$

with an error of no more than $h^2 K / 12$. So the error is of order h^2.

Example □ The deflection of a beam is believed to satisfy the equation

$$\frac{d^2 y}{dx^2} = e^{x^2}$$

The deflection is 0 at both $x = 0$ and $x = 1$. Estimate, using a second-order approximation for the derivative, the approximate deflections at 0.2, 0.4, 0.6 and 0.8.

We have approximately

$$\frac{f(x + h) - 2f(x) + f(x - h)}{h^2} = e^{x^2}$$

Therefore taking $h = 0.2$ we have

$$\frac{f(x + 0.2) - 2f(x) + f(x - 0.2)}{0.04} = e^{x^2}$$

Consequently,

$$f(x + 0.2) - 2f(x) + f(x - 0.2) = 0.04 \, e^{x^2}$$

Putting $x = 0.2, 0.4, 0.6$ and 0.8 in turn gives

$$
\begin{aligned}
f(0.4) - 2f(0.2) + f(0) &= 0.041\,63 \\
f(0.6) - 2f(0.4) + f(0.2) &= 0.046\,94 \\
f(0.8) - 2f(0.6) + f(0.4) &= 0.057\,33 \\
f(1) - 2f(0.8) + f(0.6) &= 0.075\,86
\end{aligned}
$$

Therefore writing $f(0.2r) = f_r$ and using the information that $f_0 = f(0) = 0$ and $f_5 = f(1) = 0$, these equations become

$$
\begin{aligned}
f_2 - 2f_1 + 0 &= 0.041\,63 & (1) \\
f_3 - 2f_2 + f_1 &= 0.046\,94 & (2) \\
f_4 - 2f_3 + f_2 &= 0.057\,33 & (3) \\
0 - 2f_4 + f_3 &= 0.075\,86 & (4)
\end{aligned}
$$

Eliminating f_1 between (1) and (2) produces

$$2f_3 - 4f_2 + f_2 = 0.135\,51$$
$$2f_3 - 3f_2 = 0.135\,51 \qquad\qquad (5)$$

Eliminating f_4 between (3) and (4) produces

$$f_3 - 4f_3 + 2f_2 = 0.190\,52$$
$$-3f_3 + 2f_2 = 0.190\,52 \qquad\qquad (6)$$

Using (5) and (6) we can eliminate f_2:

$$4f_3 - 9f_3 = 0.842\,58$$

Therefore $-5f_3 = 0.842\,58$ and so $f_3 = -0.168\,52$. From (6),

$$2f_2 = 0.190\,52 + 3f_3 = -0.315\,04$$

Therefore $f_2 = -0.157\,52$. Equation (1) gives

$$2f_1 = f_2 - 0.041\,63 = -0.199\,15$$

So $f_1 = -0.099\,58$. Equation (4) gives

$$2f_4 = f_3 - 0.075\,86 = -0.244\,38$$

So $f_4 = -0.122\,19$.

We conclude that the deflections at 0.2, 0.4, 0.6 and 0.8 are approximately $-0.099\,58$, $-0.157\,52$, $-0.168\,52$ and $-0.122\,19$ respectively. If we were to analyse the approximation we should see that each of these could have an error not exceeding 0.0022. ■

Now for a few more steps.

―――――――――――― **18.10 Workshop** ――――――――――――

▷**Exercise**   Obtain a finite difference approximation of order h^2 for the differential equation

$$\frac{d^2y}{dx^2} + \frac{dy}{dx} + y = \tan x$$

When you have tried this, step ahead.

―――――――――――――――――――――――――――――――――――――――

We must use two approximations of order h^2, and we have just the right ones at our disposal. If we put $y = f(x)$ the equation becomes

$$f''(x) + f'(x) + f(x) = \tan x$$

If you got stuck then perhaps you would like to take over here. When you are ready, move on.

3 We have

$$f'(x) \simeq \frac{f(x + h) - f(x - h)}{2h}$$

$$f''(x) \simeq \frac{f(x + h) - 2f(x) + f(x - h)}{h^2}$$

So substituting into the equation:

$$\frac{f(x + h) - 2f(x) + f(x - h)}{h^2} + \frac{f(x + h) - f(x - h)}{2h} + f(x) \simeq \tan x$$

If we multiply up by $2h^2$ we obtain

$$2[f(x + h) - 2f(x) + f(x - h)]$$
$$+ h[f(x + h) - f(x - h)] + 2h^2 f(x) \simeq 2h^2 \tan x$$
$$(2 + h)f(x + h) - 2(2 - h^2)f(x) + (2 - h)f(x - h) \simeq 2h^2 \tan x$$

If you managed that all right, then step out of the workshop and on to the next section. If there was a problem, then try this for size.

▷**Exercise**   Derive the approximate formula for $f'(x)$ of order h

$$f'(x) \simeq \frac{f(x) - f(x - h)}{h}$$

and use it to obtain an approximate formula for

$$x^2 \frac{dy}{dx} + xy = \sin x$$

4 We use Taylor's expansion with the remainder after two terms:

$$f(x + h) = f(x) + hf'(x) + \frac{h^2}{2} f''(c)$$

where $c \in (x, x + h)$. Replacing h by $-h$ gives

$$f(x - h) = f(x) - hf'(x) + \frac{h^2}{2} f''(c)$$

where $c \in (x - h, x)$. Rearranging we obtain

$$f'(x) = \frac{f(x) - f(x - h)}{h} + \frac{h}{2} f''(c)$$

So

$$f'(x) \simeq \frac{f(x) - f(x - h)}{h}$$

where the approximation is of order h.

If you couldn't manage that, see now if you can do the last part and substitute into the differential equation.

5

We have

$$x^2 \frac{dy}{dx} + xy = \sin x$$

which becomes, on putting $y = f(x)$,

$$x^2 f'(x) + x f(x) = \sin x$$

Now

$$f'(x) \simeq \frac{f(x) - f(x - h)}{h}$$

and therefore

$$x^2 \frac{f(x) - f(x - h)}{h} + x f(x) \simeq \sin x$$

So

$$x^2 [f(x) - f(x - h)] + hx f(x) \simeq h \sin x$$

that is,

$$x(x + h) f(x) - x^2 f(x - h) \simeq h \sin x$$

It is worth remarking that the effect of multiplying through by h, as we have, is to change the order of the error; so now the error is of order h^2.

18.11 NUMERICAL INTEGRATION

Although we can differentiate almost any function that is likely to arise, the situation is very different when it comes to integration. Unfortunately not only is a certain amount of skill needed to perform integration, but also there are some functions for which no indefinite integral exists using elementary functions. For example,

Numerical integration is useful for fluid mechanics and hydraulic engineering.

$$\int e^{x^2} dx$$

cannot be determined.

Consequently the problem we solved numerically, giving the deflection of a beam, cannot be solved analytically. Of course it is very unusual to have an indefinite integral like this. In practical situations we usually need to determine a *definite* integral, and so a numerical method is appropriate.

You will remember that we were able to show that any definite integral could be given a physical interpretation in terms of an area (Chapter 17). In the next two sections we use this fact to derive some formulas which can be used to determine integrals approximately.

18.12 THE TRAPEZOIDAL RULE

Consider the curve $y = f(x) \geqslant 0$ on the interval $[a, b]$ where $a < b$ (Fig. 18.7). Suppose we wish to determine the definite integral

$$\int_a^b f(x)\,dx$$

We know that this is the area of the region enclosed by the curve, the x-axis and the lines $x = a$ and $x = b$.

In order to approximate this area we divide it up into n strips each parallel to the y-axis and each of equal width h. By doing this we partition the interval $[a, b]$ into n equal subintervals each of length $h = (b - a)/n$ formed by the points $x_k = a + kh$, where k increases from its initial value 0 by unit steps until the value $k = n$ is attained. There is a useful notation to represent this: $k = 0(1)n$.

Suppose that $y_k = f(x_k)$ for $k = 0(1)n$. Then (x_k, y_k) are the points where the edges of the strips cut the curve $y = f(x)$. If we join these points up we obtain a polygonal curve, and if h is small the area under the polygon will approximate the area under the curve.

The trapezoidal rule uses this approximation, and so each strip is approximated by a trapezium. You will recall that a trapezium is a quadrilateral with just one pair of parallel sides. If we look at a typical trapezium (Fig. 18.8) we have an area

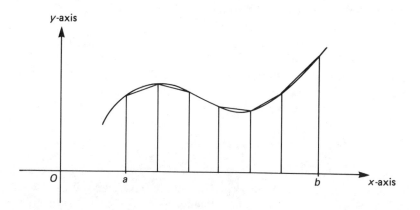

Fig. 18.7 The trapezoidal rule.

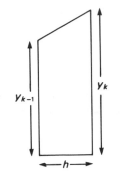

Fig. 18.8 A typical trapezium.

$$A_k = \tfrac{1}{2}h(y_{k-1} + y_k)$$

To obtain the total area A under the polygon we must add the values of A_k for $k = 1(1)n$:

$$
\begin{aligned}
A &= \sum_{1}^{n} A_k \\
&= \tfrac{1}{2}h[(y_0 + y_1) + (y_1 + y_2) + \ldots + (y_{n-1} + y_n)] \\
&= \tfrac{1}{2}h[y_0 + 2y_1 + 2y_2 + \ldots + 2y_{n-1} + y_n]
\end{aligned}
$$

Now $y_k = f(x_k) = f(a + kh)$ for $k = 0(1)n$ and $a + nh = b$, so

$$
\begin{aligned}
A &= \tfrac{1}{2}h[f(a) + 2f(a + h) + 2f(a + 2h) + \ldots \\
&\quad + 2f(a + \{n-1\}h) + f(b)] \\
&= \frac{h}{2}\left[f(a) + f(b) + 2\sum_{k=1}^{n-1} f(a + kh)\right]
\end{aligned}
$$

where $h = (b - a)/n$.

The formula written in this way looks rather complicated, but it is in fact very easy to apply. The trapezoidal method is as follows:

1 Partition the interval $[a, b]$ so that the area is divided up into equal strips of width h.
2 Calculate the corresponding y values.
3 Add the first value to the last value: call this P.
4 Add up all the other values: call this Q.
5 Calculate $P + 2Q$.
6 Multiply by h and divide by 2.

We have derived the **trapezoidal rule**:

$$\int_a^b f(x)\,\mathrm{d}x \simeq \frac{h}{2}\left[f(a) + f(b) + 2\sum_{k=1}^{n-1} f(a + kh)\right]$$

If the maximum value of the modulus of f'' on the interval (a, b) is M then it can be shown that the error is no more than

$$\frac{h^2}{12} M(b - a)$$

For functions which have graphs of high curvature this error can be quite sizeable, and so the trapezoidal rule is quite limited. Theoretically one could argue that it is always possible to increase accuracy by taking more and more strips. Unfortunately this often results in error due to rounding off, and in problems arising from dealing with large numbers of very small numbers.

18.13 SIMPSON'S RULE

A better rule is known as Simpson's rule. This is named after the colourful seventeenth-century charlatan, rogue, plagiarist, astrologer and writer of mathematical textbooks, Thomas Simpson. How much he had to do with this rule will probably never be known, but he certainly published it.

In the trapezoidal rule we approximate the curve by a polygonal curve. Simpson's rule uses, instead of segments of straight lines $y = mx + c$, segments of parabolas $y = ax^2 + bx + c$. In order to do this it is necessary to divide up the area under the curve into an even number of strips. This means that there will be an odd number of points in the partition of the interval $[a, b]$.

To simplify matters we shall consider the area under two strips which we place symmetrically about the origin (Fig. 18.9). The x values are there-

Thomas Simpson (1710–1761): British mathematician known to have exploited contemporary ignorance by associating mathematical symbols with fortune-telling.

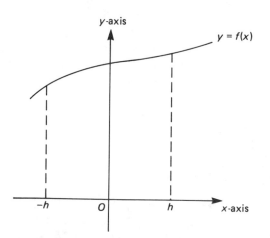

Fig. 18.9 A pair of strips.

fore $x = -h$, $x = 0$ and $x = h$, and the corresponding y values are $y = f(-h)$, $y = f(0)$ and $y = f(h)$ respectively. We are going to approximate the curve $y = f(x)$ by a parabola $y = ax^2 + bx + c$ passing through these three points.

The corresponding area is

$$\int_{-h}^{h} (ax^2 + bx + c)\, dx = [\tfrac{1}{3}ax^3 + \tfrac{1}{2}bx^2 + cx]_{-h}^{h}$$
$$= (\tfrac{1}{3}ah^3 + \tfrac{1}{2}bh^2 + ch)$$
$$\quad - [\tfrac{1}{3}a(-h)^3 + \tfrac{1}{2}b(-h)^2 + c(-h)]$$
$$= \tfrac{2}{3}ah^3 + 2ch$$

We must determine a and c.

The three points are to be on the parabola, and so they must satisfy its equation. Consequently

$$f(-h) = a(-h)^2 + b(-h) + c$$
$$f(0) = a0 + b0 + c$$
$$f(h) = ah^2 + bh + c$$

From the second $c = f(0)$, and then from the first and the third $f(-h) + f(h) = 2ah^2 + 2f(0)$. Using these, we have that the area under the parabola is

$$\tfrac{2}{3}ah^3 + 2ch = \tfrac{1}{3}h[f(-h) + f(h) - 2f(0)] + 2hf(0)$$
$$= \tfrac{1}{3}h[f(-h) + 4f(0) + f(h)]$$

We can now return to the general situation. You will remember that we divided the area under the curve into an even number of strips. To emphasize this we shall let $2n$ be the number of strips, so that $2nh = (b - a)$ (Fig. 18.10). The x values corresponding to this partition are therefore $x_k = a + kh$, where $k = 0(1)2n$. To apply what we have just discovered we shall need to take the strips in pairs. A typical pair of strips is defined by the partition $\{x_{k-1}, x_k, x_{k+1}\}$.

We have seen that the corresponding area under a parabola is

$$\tfrac{1}{3}h[f(x_{k-1}) + 4f(x_k) + f(x_{k+1})]$$

If we approximate the area under the whole curve by parabolic segments in this way we must total them all to obtain the corresponding area A:

$$A = \tfrac{1}{3}h\{[f(x_0) + 4f(x_1) + f(x_2)] + [f(x_2) + 4f(x_3) + f(x_4)] + \ldots$$
$$+ [f(x_{2n-2}) + 4f(x_{2n-1}) + f(x_{2n})]\}$$
$$= \tfrac{1}{3}h\{f(x_0) + f(x_{2n}) + 2[f(x_2) + f(x_4) + \ldots + f(x_{2n-2})]$$
$$+ 4[f(x_1) + f(x_3) + \ldots + f(x_{2n-1})]\}$$
$$= \frac{h}{3}\left[f(a) + f(b) + 2\sum_{r=1}^{n-1} f(a + 2rh) + 4\sum_{r=1}^{n} f(a + \{2r - 1\}h) \right]$$

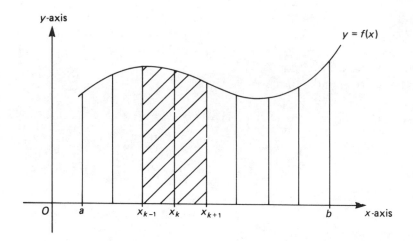

Fig. 18.10 Simpson's rule.

where $h = (b - a)/2n$.

Again we have quite a complicated formula, but it looks worse than it is. Here is Simpson's method:

1 Partition the interval $[a, b]$ into an even number of subintervals of equal length using points $x_0, x_1, \ldots, x_{2n}$.

2 Calculate the corresponding values of y.

3 Add the first value to the last value: call this P.

4 Add up all the values at the other even points: call this Q.

5 Add up all the values at the odd points: call this R.

6 Calculate $P + 2Q + 4R$.

7 Multiply by h and divide by 3.

We have derived **Simpson's rule**:

$$\int_a^b f(x) \, dx \simeq \frac{h}{3}\left[f(a) + f(b) + 2 \sum_{r=1}^{n-1} f(a + 2rh) \right.$$
$$\left. + 4 \sum_{r=1}^{n} f(a + \{2r - 1\}h) \right]$$

If the maximum value of the modulus of $f^{(4)}$ on the interval (a, b) is M, then it can be shown that the error is no more than

$$\frac{h^4}{180} M(b - a)$$

Of course if the curve happens to be a parabola then Simpson's rule will give an exact result. It may surprise you to learn that there are other integrals for which an exact result is obtained using Simpson's rule. For

Surveyors use Simpson's rule for cut and fill and mass haul problems.

example, the integral of a polynomial of degree three is exactly determined using Simpson's rule.

Now it's time for some more steps.

18.14 Workshop

1

▷**Exercise** Use Simpson's rule to obtain

$$\int_0^{\pi/2} \sqrt{\sin x}\; \mathrm{d}x$$

using six strips and performing arithmetic to five decimal places.

You will need to tabulate your work. Make sure you get the coefficients right. A table with the form shown below is probably the best way of proceeding. The totals can then be found and the appropriate factors used:

$$f(x_0)$$
$$f(x_1) \qquad f(x_2)$$
$$f(x_3) \qquad f(x_4)$$
$$f(x_5) \qquad f(x_6)$$
$$\vdots \qquad \vdots$$
$$f(x_{2n-1}) \qquad f(x_{2n-2})$$
$$f(x_{2n})$$

2

We have six strips, so $2nh = 6h = (b - a) = \pi/2$. Therefore $h = \pi/12$. There are seven points in the partition, and these are $x_k = k\pi/12$ where $k = 0(1)6$. The corresponding values of y_k are now calculated and arranged in the array:

0.000 00	0.508 74	0.707 11
	0.840 90	0.930 60
	0.982 82	
1.000 00		
1.000 00	2.332 46	1.637 71

The totals are given at the foot of each column.

Using 'four times the odd plus twice the even' we obtain

$$1.000\,00$$
$$9.329\,84$$
$$3.275\,42$$
$$\overline{13.605\,26}$$

from which

$$I \simeq \tfrac{1}{3}(\pi/12) \ (13.605\,26) \ = \ 1.187\,28$$

So the estimated value is 1.187.

This is an example where the estimate of error is very difficult to apply. To differentiate $\sqrt{\sin x}$ four times is bad enough, but that is not the least of our worries. It is not just that it is difficult to handle the trigonometry to examine the upper bound (which it is); more alarming, as $x \to 0+$ the fourth derivative increases without bound!

A good rule of thumb when dealing with numerical processes of this kind is to double the number of strips and recalculate the approximation. This should give an indication of how accurate the answer is.

If you made a mistake in the exercise, try the next one. If all was well, except possibly for a minor numerical slip, move on to the text following.

▷**Exercise**   Use Simpson's rule to obtain

$$\int_0^{\pi/2} \sqrt{\sin x} \ \mathrm{d}x$$

using twelve strips and performing arithmetic to five decimal places.

This would be no problem to a computer with a suitable program, but without one you will have to press a few buttons. After all, you have to pay a penalty for getting the last problem wrong, and you may as well make sure your calculator earns its keep. Don't duck out of this.

---

3   We have twelve strips, so $2nh = 12h = (b - a) = \pi/2$. Therefore $h = \pi/24$. There are thirteen points in the partition, and these are $x_k = k\pi/24$ where $k = 0(1)12$. The corresponding values of y_k are now calculated and arranged in the array:

0.000 00			
		0.361 28	0.508 74
		0.618 61	0.707 11
		0.780 23	0.840 90
		0.890 70	0.930 60
		0.961 19	0.982 82
	1.000 00	0.995 71	
	1.000 00	4.607 72	3.970 17

Using 'four times the odd plus twice the even' we obtain

$$\begin{array}{r} 1.000\,00 \\ 18.430\,88 \\ 7.940\,34 \\ \hline 27.371\,22 \end{array}$$

from which

$$I \simeq \tfrac{1}{3}(\pi/24)\ (27.371\,22) = 1.194\,29$$

So we estimate the value as 1.194.

Comparing this result with the one obtained previously, we see that they agree to two decimal places that the integral is 1.19. We might feel there is a possibility that still more strips could change the last decimal place, and so we will opt for 1.2 as an approximate value.

Well, that's almost all there is for this chapter. We have examined a number of numerical techniques, and some of these you may be able to employ when solving equations which cannot be handled analytically. Numerical analysis is a vast subject, and there are many different techniques which have been developed to deal with almost any problem which can arise. High-speed computers have revolutionized the approach to many of them, but you must remember that a computer does not always give the whole picture. The program has been written by a human being and things might have been overlooked. An answer given by a computer is not always right, any more than something printed in a book is always right. Forewarned is forearmed.

!

Now it's time to take your forearms off the desk and tackle a practical problem.

18.15 Practical

CONDUCTION

If $\theta = \theta(x)$ is the temperature at any point distance x from one end of a heat-conducting fin (Fig. 18.11), then θ satisfies the equation

$$\frac{d^2\theta}{dx^2} + \frac{1}{x}\frac{d\theta}{dx} - \frac{r^2}{x}\theta = 0$$

where

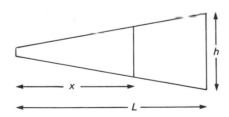

Fig. 18.11 Section of fin.

$$r^2 = \frac{2\sigma L}{kh} \left[1 + \left(\frac{h}{2L} \right)^2 \right]^{1/2}$$

Here h is the width of the fin, L is the length, σ is the coefficient of heat transfer and k is the thermal conductivity. It is given that $\theta(L) = \theta_1$ and $\theta(0) = \theta_0$, and the units are standardized so that $L = 1$, $\theta_0 = 20$, $\theta_1 = 100$ and $r = 2$. Approximate the equation by means of approximations of order h^2 where $h = 0.25$, and thereby estimate θ at $x = 0.25, 0.5$ and 0.75.

It is a good idea to see if you can do this by yourself. We have already solved a very similar problem, and so you have a blueprint with which to work. As usual we shall solve it stage by stage so that you can join in with the solution as soon as possible.

The first thing to do is to use the approximations in the equation.

---

1 We have

$$x \frac{d^2\theta}{dx^2} + \frac{d\theta}{dx} - r^2\theta = 0$$

So

$$x \frac{\theta(x + h) - 2\theta(x) + \theta(x - h)}{h^2}$$

$$+ \frac{\theta(x + h) - \theta(x - h)}{2h} - r^2\theta(x) = 0$$

$$2x[\theta(x + h) - 2\theta(x) + \theta(x - h)]$$
$$+ h[\theta(x + h) - \theta(x - h)] - 2h^2r^2\theta(x) = 0$$
$$2x[\theta(x + 0.25) - 2\theta(x) + \theta(x - 0.25)]$$
$$+ 0.25[\theta(x + 0.25) - \theta(x - 0.25)] - 0.5\theta(x) = 0$$
$$[2x + 0.25]\theta(x + 0.25) - [4x + 0.5]\theta(x) + [2x - 0.25]\theta(x - 0.25) = 0$$

Now we have the basic equation we need to estimate the required temperatures. To ease the notation we shall put $a = \theta(0.25)$, $b = \theta(0.5)$ and $c = \theta(0.75)$. Try it and see how it goes.

---

2 We use the boundary conditions and put $x = 0.25$, $x = 0.5$ and $x = 0.75$ in turn to obtain

$$0.75b - 1.5a + 0.25(20) = 0$$
$$1.25c - 2.5b + 0.75a = 0$$
$$1.75(100) - 3.5c + 1.25b = 0$$

Finally, solve these to obtain estimates of the temperatures that we require.

3 The equations become

$$3b - 6a + 20 = 0 \tag{1}$$
$$5c - 10b + 3a = 0 \tag{2}$$
$$700 - 14c + 5b = 0 \tag{3}$$

Equation (1) gives $a = (3b + 20)/6$, and equation (3) gives $c = (700 + 5b)/14$. Substituting these into (2) gives

$$3500 + 25b - 140b + 21b + 140 = 0$$

Therefore $94b = 3640$ and so $b = 38.723$. Lastly, substituting back we obtain

$$a = (3 \times 38.72 + 20)/6 = 22.695$$
$$c = (700 + 5 \times 38.72)/14 = 63.830$$

Therefore the temperatures where $x = 0.25$, $x = 0.5$ and $x = 0.75$ are 22.7, 38.7 and 63.8 approximately.

SUMMARY

Here is a list of the topics we have studied in this chapter:
☐ Solutions of the equation $f(x) = 0$ by
  a bisection method
  b *regula falsi*
  c secant method
  d Newton's method.
☐ Approximations for derivatives
  a approximations of order h

$$f'(x) \simeq \frac{f(x + h) - f(x)}{h}$$

$$f'(x) \simeq \frac{f(x) - f(x - h)}{h}$$

  b approximations of order h^2

$$f'(x) \simeq \frac{f(x + h) - f(x - h)}{2h}$$

$$f''(x) \simeq \frac{f(x + h) - 2f(x) + f(x - h)}{h^2}$$

☐ Numerical integration
  a trapezoidal rule
  b Simpson's rule.

EXERCISES (for answers see p. 756)

1 Solve the following equations by the bisection method giving your answers correct to four significant figures:

a $x = 2\sin^2 x$

b $\exp x = 1 + \cos x^2$

2 Using the *regula falsi* method and the equation

$$f(x) = x^3 \exp x - 1 = 0$$

obtain a formula to give a better approximation c in terms of a and b where $f(a) < 0$ and $f(b) > 0$. Obtain integer values of a and b.

3 Using the secant method and the equation

$$f(x) = x^3 + x - 5 = 0$$

obtain an iterative formula which gives x_{n+1} in terms of x_n and x_{n-1}. Calculate suitable integer starting values x_0 and x_1.

4 Use Newton's method to solve each of the following equations correct to five decimal places:

a $x^3 + x^2 = 4x - 1$

b $x - 2 = \ln x$

5 Use the trapezoidal method with six strips and working to five decimal places to estimate

a $\displaystyle\int_0^{\pi/2} \sin\sqrt{(x^2 + 1)}\,dx$

b $\displaystyle\int_0^{\pi/2} \ln(1 + \sin x)\,dx$

6 Use Simpson's rule, with six strips, working to five decimal places, to estimate

a $\displaystyle\int_0^1 \exp(1 - x^2)\,dx$

b $\displaystyle\int_0^{\pi/2} \cos\sqrt{x}\,dx$

ASSIGNMENT (for answers see p. 756; see also Workshops on pp. 516, 521 and 529)

1 The bisection method is used to solve the equation $e^x = 3x$ using $[0, 1]$ as the initial interval and working to five decimal places. How many steps are needed to guarantee accuracy to three decimal places? Solve the equation using this method to achieve this accuracy.

2 Calculate the iterative formula corresponding to Newton's method for solving the equation $f(x) = e^x - 3x = 0$. Solve this equation using 0 as a starting value to obtain a solution accurate to three decimal places.

3 Determine the iterative formula corresponding to the secant method for solving $f(x) = e^x - 3x = 0$. Work through three iterations with starting values $x_0 = 0$ and $x_1 = 1$.

4 By writing $y = f(x)$, and using approximations of order h^2 for the derivatives, obtain a finite difference approximation for the differential equation

$$\frac{d^2y}{dx^2} + 2\frac{dy}{dx} + y = \sec x$$

5 Using six strips and working to seven decimal places, estimate the value of

$$\int_0^1 x e^{x^2} dx$$

by Simpson's rule. Check the accuracy of your solution by (a) doubling the number of strips (b) obtaining the exact integral.

FURTHER EXERCISES (for answers see p. 756)

1 Use Simpson's rule to evaluate

$$\int_0^\pi \frac{dt}{\cos t + 2}$$

using five ordinates. Determine the integral directly and thereby show that Simpson's rule underestimates the integral by less than 0.28%.

2 Show graphically that the curves $y = e^x - 1$ and $y = \ln(x + 2)$ intersect at two points. Use Newton's method to obtain the larger of the roots of the equation $e^x = 1 + \ln(x + 2)$. Give your answer correct to two decimal places.

3 Use a graph to show that the equation $x^2 - 4 = \ln x$ has just two real roots. Obtain, using Newton's method, the larger of the roots correct to three decimal places.

4 Use any numerical method to obtain the roots of the equation $x = 2 - e^x$ correct to three decimal places.

5 Starting with the approximation $x = 0.6$, obtain the real root of the equation $x = e^{-x}$ correct to four decimal places.

6 Show that if α is an approximate root of the equation $x \ln x - x = a$ (where a is real) and if $p = \ln \alpha - \alpha$, then a better approximation is given by β where $\beta = (a + \alpha)/(p + \alpha)$.

7 Evaluate approximately

$$\int_0^1 \frac{dx}{1 + x^2}$$

using eight strips (seven ordinates) by (a) the trapezoidal rule (b) Simpson's rule. Work to five decimal places and show that the error in the result obtained by the trapezoidal rule is less than 0.0026. Determine the integral exactly and thereby show that Simpson's rule is accurate in this instance.

8 Simpson's rule gives the exact result if the function to be integrated is a polynomial of degree three or less. Use this fact and two strips to derive the formula $V = \pi h(3a^2 + 3b^2 + h^2)/6$ for the volume of a segment of a sphere of height h and base radii a and b.

9 The response u of a system is given at time t by the equation $du/dt = -u$ where the units have been standardized. Put $u = u(t)$ and approximate the derivative with an approximation of order h.

a Use the initial value $u(0) = 1$ with the step length $h = 0.2$ and five iterations to estimate $u(1)$.

b Use integration to obtain the exact solution and thereby calculate the percentage error in **a**.

(The numerical method outlined in this problem is usually known as Euler's method for solving a first-order differential equation.)

10 Write down Maclaurin's expansion (Taylor's expansion about the point 0) for the function $y = y(x)$ which has derivatives of all orders, and show that if $y' = 1 - xy$ and $y(0) = 0$ then

$$y(h) = h - h^3/3 + h^5/15 - h^7/105 + \ldots$$

Estimate the value of $y(0.5)$ to four decimal places.

19 First-order differential equations

Although we have studied integration as the reverse process of differentiation, integrals do not always present themselves explicitly in applications. Instead an equation involving derivatives is obtained and some method of eliminating these derivatives is needed. This is the subject of our next section of work, differential equations.

After studying this chapter you should be able
- ☐ Identify a differential equation and be able to state its order and degree;
- ☐ Recognize the standard form of three basic types of first-order differential equation;
- ☐ Solve variables separable, linear and homogeneous equations;
- ☐ Apply simple substitutions to convert equations into one of these three types.

At the end of this chapter we shall solve practical problems in circuits and vehicle braking.

19.1 TERMINOLOGY

You have already solved some first order differential equations, although you may not be aware of the fact! The process of integration is equivalent to the solution of a very simple first-order differential equation. If you don't forget to put in the arbitrary constant you will obtain the general solution.

What then is a differential equation, and what do we mean by saying that we have solved it? An ordinary **differential equation** is an equation involving two variables (say x and y) and ordinary derivatives. The highest-order derivative which is present determines the **order** of the differential equation. So for instance

$$\left(\frac{d^2y}{dx^2}\right)^3 + \left(\frac{dy}{dx}\right)^4 + y = 0$$

is a differential equation of the second order. Notice here that the second-order derivative occurs raised to the power of 3, and so this is a differential equation of the third **degree**. The first-order derivative occurs raised to the power of 4 but, since this is not the derivative which determines the order of the differential equation, this does not affect the degree of the equation. To avoid complications, and because differential equations of high degree do not arise often in applications, we shall confine our attention to equations of the first degree.

Example □ Identify the degrees and orders of the following differential equations:

a $\left(\frac{d^3y}{dx^3}\right)^2 - x\left(\frac{d^2y}{dx^2}\right)^4 + y = 0$

b $y\left(\frac{d^2y}{dx^2} + x\right) + \left(\frac{dy}{dx}\right)^3 + x = 0$

c $\left(\frac{d^2y}{dx^2}\right)^3 + \left(\frac{dy}{dx} + y\right)^2 = 0$

when you have made your decision, read on and check you are right.

Here are the results:
a This is a third-order equation of degree 2.
b This is a second-order equation of degree 1.
c This is a second-order equation of degree 3. ∎

Now that we have described what a differential equation is, we need to say what we mean by saying we have solved the equation. Usually we are given not only the differential equation itself but also some initial or boundary conditions which have to be satisfied too. For the moment, though, let us confine our attention to the differential equation itself.

A solution of the differential equation is an equation between the two variables concerned, x and y, which is
1 Free of derivatives;
2 Consistent with the differential equation.
Differential equations have many solutions, but we shall be interested in the **general solution**. Consider for example the equation

$$\frac{dy}{dx} = 1$$

By inspection we see that $y = x$ is a solution of this equation, and that so too is $y = x - 5$ or indeed $y = x + C$ where C is any constant. Moreover, any solution of this differential equation can be expressed in the form $y = x + C$ where C is some arbitrary constant.

We considered this in detail in section 15.1.

This should come as no surprise to us, of course. We began with a first-order differential equation and have obtained a solution which is necessarily free of the derivative. Therefore a process equivalent to a single integration must have occurred, and this is bound to result in the presence of an arbitrary constant.

Continuing this line of thought, we shall expect the general solution of a differential equation of order n and degree 1 to contain n independent arbitrary constants.

So we already know how to solve one very important type of first-order differential equation:

$$\frac{dy}{dx} = f(x)$$

To solve this equation we merely integrate both sides with respect to x; remembering not to omit the arbitrary constant.

In fact we can generalize this very slightly to deal with a whole class of differential equations. These are equations which can be expressed in the form

$$\frac{dy}{dx} = \frac{f(x)}{g(y)}$$

where f and g are real functions.

19.2 VARIABLES SEPARABLE EQUATIONS

Any differential equation which can be expressed in the form

$$\frac{dy}{dx} = \frac{f(x)}{g(y)}$$

where f and g are real functions, is known as a **variables separable** differential equation. It can be solved easily by writing it in the form

$$g(y)\frac{dy}{dx} = f(x)$$

and integrating both sides with respect to x. We obtain then

$$\int g(y)\, dy = \int f(x)\, dx$$

Naturally we do not obtain two independent arbitrary constants because the equation

$$G(y) + A = F(x) + B$$

where A and B are arbitrary constants can be replaced by

$$G(y) = F(x) + C$$

where $C = B - A$.

The problem of solving variables separable differential equations therefore is twofold:

1 Identifying which equations are variables separable;
2 Performing the necessary integrations.

Example □ Solve, for $y > 0$, the equation

$$\frac{dy}{dx} - xy = y$$

We may rewrite this equation in the form

$$\frac{dy}{dx} = y + xy = y(1 + x)$$

So that, since $y \neq 0$,

$$\frac{1}{y}\frac{dy}{dx} = 1 + x$$

Consequently

$$\int \frac{1}{y}\,dy = \int (1 + x)\,dx$$

And so

$$\ln y = x + \tfrac{1}{2}x^2 + C$$

Note that, strictly speaking, without the information that $y > 0$ we should have to represent the solution as

$$\ln |y| = x + \tfrac{1}{2}x^2 + C \qquad (y \neq 0)$$

and also include the solution $y = 0$. In fact we shall limit discussions of this kind in this chapter because to do so could obscure the methods. ■

Example □ Solve the differential equation

$$\frac{dy}{dx} = e^{x-y}$$

At first sight this may not look like a variables separable equation, but we need to remember from the laws of indices that

$$e^{x-y} = e^x/e^y$$

Now it is clear that we can put all the terms in x on the right and all the terms in y on the left and proceed to integrate throughout with respect to x. This produces

$$\int e^y \, dy = \int e^x \, dx$$

From which

$$e^y = e^x + C$$

where C as usual is the arbitrary constant. If we wish, we can make y the subject of the equation. Then

$$y = \ln (e^x + C)$$

By the way, don't make the mistake of delaying to put in the arbitrary constant. It must go in at the moment of integration; it cannot be added on as an afterthought. For instance, here we would obtain (ignoring the arbitrary constant)

$$e^y = e^x$$

From which

$$y = x$$

Whoops, forgot the arbitrary constant. So

$$y = x + C$$

No! This will not do. Watch out for this and similar errors.   ∎

Now let's take some steps to make sure we know how to separate the variables.

_____ **19.3 Workshop** _____

▷ **Exercise**   Obtain the general solution of the following differential equation:

$$\frac{dy}{dx} = \sin (x + y) + \sin (x - y)$$

If after you have given the matter some thought you can't see how the variables separate, then take another step for a clue. Otherwise try to solve the equation and move ahead to step 3.

2 The expansion formulas for sin $(x + y)$ and sin $(x - y)$ when added together reduce the left to the product of a sine and a cosine. Alternatively you can combine them using the addition formulas. The result is the same either way:

$$\frac{dy}{dx} = 2 \sin x \cos y$$

Now solve the equation, and when you have finished take the next step.

3 We have

$$\frac{dy}{dx} = 2 \sin x \cos y$$

from which, since $y \neq 0$,

$$\int \sec y \, dy = \int 2 \sin x \, dx$$

so that

$$\ln |\sec y + \tan y| = -2 \cos x + C$$

In order to cope with the trigonometry you will need to be familiar with the identities from section 3.3.

Here you would not be expected to rearrange the equation in order to make y the subject, as this is not particularly easy to do. Nevertheless, as a slight diversion and to help brush up our algebraic and trigonometrical skill, we shall have a go. Why not have a go at it yourself first? If you don't feel you could manage it, at least follow through the working carefully. You should be able to pick up a few useful tips.

4 We must take great care when dealing with exponentials and logarithms. It may be very tempting to expand out a logarithm, but if we replace the left-hand side by

$$\ln |\sec y| + \ln |\tan y|$$

we shall have made a bad mistake. Instead we remove the logarithm by using the definition to obtain

$$|\sec y + \tan y| = e^{-2 \cos x + C}$$

From which

$$|\sec y + \tan y| = A \, e^{-2 \cos x}$$

where A is another arbitrary constant (in fact positive since $C = \ln A$).
    Let us write

$$k = A\,e^{-2\cos x}$$

so that we now have

$$\sec y + \tan y = \pm k \tag{1}$$

Multiplying through by $\cos y$ gives

$$1 + \sin y = \pm k \cos y$$

Squaring produces

$$(1 + \sin y)^2 = k^2 \cos^2 y = k^2 (1 - \sin^2 y)$$
$$\sin^2 y + 2 \sin y + 1 = k^2 - k^2 \sin^2 y$$
$$(1 + k^2) \sin^2 y + 2 \sin y + (1 - k^2) = 0$$

This factorizes to give

$$(\sin y + 1)[(1 + k^2) \sin y + (1 - k^2)] = 0$$

Now $\sin y \neq -1$, as can be seen by considering the original equation (1), and consequently

$$\sin y = -\frac{1 - k^2}{1 + k^2}$$

Now

$$k^2 = A^2\,e^{-4\cos x}$$

Therefore finally we obtain

$$\sin y = \frac{A^2\,e^{-4\cos x} - 1}{A^2\,e^{-4\cos x} + 1}$$

Here now is another equation which, although not variables separable as it stands, can be transformed into a variables separable equation easily by means of a substitution.

▷ **Exercise** Solve

$$\frac{dy}{dx} = \sin(x + y)$$

Have a look at this and see if you can choose the substitution. Then step ahead.

Suppose we put $z = x + y$. Then we obtain, differentiating with respect to x,

5

$$\frac{dz}{dx} = 1 + \frac{dy}{dx}$$

So the equation becomes, on substituting,

$$\frac{dz}{dx} = 1 + \sin z$$

When we separate the variables we are left with two integrals to find – one easy, the other not so easy:

$$\int \frac{dz}{1 + \sin z} = \int dx$$

We shall concentrate on the integral on the left for the moment:

$$\int \frac{dz}{1 + \sin z} = \int \frac{1 - \sin z}{\cos^2 z} \, dz$$

$$= \int (\sec^2 z - \sec z \tan z) \, dz$$

$$= \tan z - \sec z + C$$

The solution is therefore

$$x = \tan z - \sec z + C$$

So that substituting back we obtain

$$x = \tan (x + y) - \sec (x + y) + C$$

19.4 LINEAR EQUATIONS

We are now ready to look at the next type of first-order differential equation. Any equation which can be written in the form

$$\frac{dy}{dx} + Py = Q$$

where P and Q depend on x only, is known as a **linear** first-order differential equation.

Here is an example:

$$x \frac{dy}{dx} = x^3 y + 1 + x^4$$

In order to arrange this in standard form we must divide by x and take the term in y to the left. When this is done we have

$$\frac{dy}{dx} - x^2 y = \frac{1}{x} + x^3$$

From which

$$P = -x^2 \qquad Q = \frac{1}{x} + x^3$$

Sometimes an equation is both variables separable and linear! See if you can construct an example which is both. It's not too difficult if you bear in mind the special features which each one has to have. Here is one example:

$$\frac{dy}{dx} = xy + x$$

Now let us see how to go about solving a linear differential equation. We shall first describe the process by which we obtain the solution and pick out the crucial steps later to obtain a direct method. Don't be too concerned if things seem a little complicated at first; we won't have to go through all this work whenever we want to solve an equation! To have a good understanding, however, it is best to have a peep behind the scenes.

The linear equation is an example of a general class of differential equations which can be solved by means of a device known as an integrating factor. An **integrating factor** is an expression which when multiplied through the equation makes it easy to integrate. Suppose in the case which we are considering $((dy/dx) + Py = Q)$ it is possible to multiply throughout by some expression I and thereby express the equation in the form

$$\frac{d}{dx}(Iy) = IQ$$

Of course you may object to this on the grounds that I may not exist. However, suspend disbelief for a little longer to discover the properties which I would have to possess.

Using the product rule we obtain

$$I\frac{dy}{dx} + y\frac{dI}{dx} = IQ$$

So that comparing with

$$I\frac{dy}{dx} + IPy = IQ$$

we deduce that

$$y\frac{dI}{dx} = IPy$$

$$\frac{\mathrm{d}I}{\mathrm{d}x} = IP$$

So there it is: we are looking for I satisfying the equation

$$\frac{\mathrm{d}I}{\mathrm{d}x} = IP$$

Any I which satisfies this will do, so that here (unusually) we can forget about an arbitrary constant!

Now this is a variables separable differential equation for I, since P depends solely on x. So separating the variables we obtain

$$\int \frac{\mathrm{d}I}{I} = \int P \, \mathrm{d}x$$

from which

$$\ln I = \int P \, \mathrm{d}x$$

The expression on the right can be obtained easily by direct integration, and so we have

$$I = \mathrm{e}^{\int P \, \mathrm{d}x}$$

Remarkably, then, it is possible to solve the linear type of differential equation by means of an integrating factor, and the equation then becomes

$$\frac{\mathrm{d}}{\mathrm{d}x}(Iy) = IQ$$

From this it follows immediately that

$$Iy = \int IQ \, \mathrm{d}x$$

Before we do an example we shall summarize this method for solving a linear differential equation:

1 Express the equation in the form

$$\frac{\mathrm{d}y}{\mathrm{d}x} + Py = Q \tag{1}$$

where P and Q depend solely on x.

2 Identify P and Q and calculate the integrating factor

$$I = \mathrm{e}^{\int P \, \mathrm{d}x}$$

3 Multiply equation (1) by I to reduce it to the form

$$\frac{\mathrm{d}}{\mathrm{d}x}(Iy) = IQ$$

4 Integrate throughout to obtain the solution

$$Iy = \int IQ \, \mathrm{d}x$$

There are just three other points to remember. First, we can ignore any arbitrary constant when calculating I. Secondly, we do not need to worry about how the integrating factor works. When we multiply through by I the left-hand side of the equation automatically becomes

$$\frac{\mathrm{d}}{\mathrm{d}x}(\text{integrating factor} \times y)$$

Thirdly, in the final integration we must include an arbitrary constant as usual.

Well now! It's time to work through an example.

□ Solve the differential equation   **Example**

$$\cos x \, \frac{\mathrm{d}y}{\mathrm{d}x} + y \sin x = \sin 2x$$

We arrange it in standard form by dividing throughout by $\cos x$. It helps if we remember the trigonometrical identity $\sin 2x = 2 \sin x \cos x$. So we now have

$$\frac{\mathrm{d}y}{\mathrm{d}x} + y \tan x = 2 \sin x$$

Of course we have now also assumed that $\cos x$ is non-zero, and we should ensure that we represent that fact in the solution.

The equation is now in standard form, and so we can identify P and Q:

$$P = \tan x \qquad Q = 2 \sin x$$

Now we calculate the integrating factor I. We have

$$\int P \, \mathrm{d}x = \int \tan x \, \mathrm{d}x = -\ln(\cos x) = \ln(\sec x)$$

So

$$I = e^{\ln(\sec x)} = \sec x$$

Strictly speaking we have assumed $\cos x > 0$, but this is also an integrating factor if $\cos x < 0$.

Multiplying through the equation by I produces

$$\frac{d}{dx}[(\sec x)y] = 2 \sin x \sec x = 2 \tan x$$

Integrating throughout with respect to x gives

$$(\sec x)y = \int 2 \tan x \, dx = -2 \ln (\cos x) + C$$

$$= \ln (\sec^2 x) + C = \ln (A \sec^2 x)$$

where C and A are arbitrary constants. Finally,

$$y = \cos x \ln (A \sec^2 x)$$

where A is a positive arbitrary constant. Note that the solution is not defined when $\cos x = 0$, and this is consistent with the remark we made earlier. ∎

Now it is time for you to try to solve one of these equations. Remember the four stages in the solution and you should have no difficulty.

19.5 Workshop

1

Exercise Solve the differential equation

$$x \frac{dy}{dx} = y + x^3$$

First put the equation into standard form and identify P and Q. As soon as you have done this, check ahead that you have got things right.

2

You must divide through by x to put the equation into the standard form. Observe that if $x = 0$ then $y = 0$; therefore our solution must include this possibility. If you did the rearrangement correctly you should obtain

$$\frac{dy}{dx} - \frac{y}{x} = x^2$$

from which $P = -x^{-1}$ and $Q = x^2$.

Did you include the minus sign? It is a common error to overlook it! If you made a slip then notice where things went wrong to avoid the mistake next time.

Now calculate the integrating factor. Only when you have done this should you read on!

3

You should have written down

$$\int P \, dx = \int -x^{-1} \, dx = -\ln x$$

If the integral caused problems, perhaps you differentiated instead of integrated. Remember: differentiation is not integration, and integration is not differentiation!

Next the integrating factor I is obtained from

$$I = \exp\left(-\ln x\right) = \exp\left(\ln x^{-1}\right) = x^{-1}$$

Maybe a slip or two has occurred here. If you wrote down $-x$ then you have misused the laws of logarithms. You should not include the arbitrary constant as it is superfluous at this stage.

Once you have corrected any errors, use the integrating factor to solve the equation. As soon as you have done this, take the next step to see the result.

Multiplying the equation by I produces straight away

$$\frac{d}{dx}\left(\frac{y}{x}\right) = \frac{x^2}{x} = x$$

There is no need to go back and wrestle with the equation. The chances are that if you have done so you will have made some sort of mistake.

Lastly, integrating with respect to x gives the solution

$$\frac{y}{x} = \frac{x^2}{2} + C$$

so that on multiplying up by x we obtain

$$y = \frac{x^3}{2} + Cx$$

Note that in this form we include the solution at $x = 0$.

That was quite straightforward, wasn't it? Notice the four stages to the solution, and how we followed each one through to the end.

Of course not all problems are quite as easy as this one. Often a rather unpleasant integral is produced and has to be sorted out. In the worst situations it is not possible to complete the second stage. In such circumstances we must either find another method or resort to some numerical technique to obtain the solution. However, the numerical option is only available if we have a boundary condition and therefore do not require the general solution.

Here is an exercise which is not quite as straightforward as the previous one but nevertheless can be solved by proceeding through all the stages.

▷**Exercise**   Solve the equation

$$\exp x \frac{dy}{dx} + y \exp 2x = \exp 3x$$

If you managed the previous one without mistakes you might like to have a go at this completely on your own. Make a real effort and see if you can manage it. When you have finished, look ahead at the answer and see if you are right. Even if your answer looks wrong it may nevertheless be correct because it is often possible to write solutions to differential equations in different forms. Therefore, if you are in doubt, differentiate your answer and see if it satisfies the differential equation; remember the chain rule!

If you made mistakes with the previous example then a few more steps are necessary. First, put the equation into standard form so that it is recognizable as a linear type and identify P and Q. Then step ahead.

---

5 To put it into standard form so that it is recognizable as a linear type it is necessary to divide throughout by $\exp x$. This gives

$$\frac{dy}{dx} + y \exp x = \exp 2x$$

from which it follows that

$$P = \exp x \qquad Q = \exp 2x$$

The laws of indices are given in section 1.5.

If you didn't manage that then you have forgotten the laws of indices and you would be well advised to brush up on them (Chapter 1).

Now obtain the integrating factor. When you have done so, take the next step.

---

6 Now $\int \exp x \, dx = \exp x$, so that

$$I = \exp e^x$$

You didn't make an incorrect simplification, did you? The answer is certainly not x.

Lastly, complete the solution and take the final steps.

---

7 Multiplying through the equation by I gives

$$\frac{d}{dx}[(\exp e^x)y] = \exp e^x \exp 2x$$

so that

$$(\exp e^x)y = \int \exp e^x \exp 2x \, dx$$

If you've made it to here, all that remains is to determine the rather nasty looking integral on the right. A substitution is called for; can you see what it is?

It's best to put $u = \exp x$. Then $du/dx = \exp x = u$, so the integral reduces to

$$\int u \exp u \, du$$

and this can be obtained by integration by parts:

$$\int u \exp u \, du = u \exp u - \int \exp u \, du = u \exp u - \exp u + C$$

So we have

$$(\exp e^x)y = \exp x \exp e^x - \exp e^x + C$$

and therefore

$$y = \exp x - 1 + C \exp -e^x$$

where C is an arbitrary constant.

19.6 BERNOULLI'S EQUATION

You will remember that when we were considering variables separable equations there were some equations which, although not variables separable as they stood, could be made so by means of a substitution. In a similar way it is sometimes possible to reduce an equation to a linear type by making a substitution. Although there are many different situations where this is true, one type of equation – known as Bernoulli's equation – is worthy of special note.

Bernoulli's equation is any equation which can be expressed in the form

$$\frac{dy}{dx} + Py = Qy^n$$

where P and Q depend solely on x, and n is constant ($n \neq 1$).

You will notice how similar this equation is to the standard form of the linear equation. In fact the only difference is the term in y on the right. To reduce the equation to a linear equation we make the substitution

$$z = \frac{1}{y^{n-1}}$$

The Bernoullis were a family of Belgian Swiss mathematicians who flourished in the 17th and 18th centuries. Nine members of the family attained fame. This equation is due to Jacques Bernoulli (1654–1705). However, most of the methods developed in this chapter are due to his brother Jean Bernoulli (1667–1748). The fame of the Bernoullis was matched only by their reputation for quarrelling with one another.

It then follows that

$$\frac{dz}{dx} = \frac{-(n-1)}{y^n}\frac{dy}{dx}$$

Now dividing through Bernoulli's equation by y^n gives

$$\frac{1}{y_n}\frac{dy}{dx} + \frac{P}{y^{n-1}} = Q$$

so that when the substitutions are made,

$$\frac{1}{-(n-1)}\frac{dz}{dx} + Pz = Q$$

This is now a linear type where the variables are z and x, so it can be solved by the standard technique. Finally, the solution of the original equation can be obtained by substituting back for z.

Let us do an example.

Example □ Obtain the general solution to the equation

$$\frac{dy}{dx} + \frac{y}{x} = xy^2$$

This is Bernoulli's equation in the case $n = 2$, so we make the substitution $z = y^{-1}$. Then

$$\frac{dz}{dx} = \frac{-1}{y^2}\frac{dy}{dx}$$

so that dividing the equation through by y^2 yields

$$\frac{1}{y^2}\frac{dy}{dx} + \frac{1}{xy} = x$$

from which

$$-\frac{dz}{dx} + \frac{z}{x} = x$$

$$\frac{dz}{dx} - \frac{z}{x} = -x$$

This is a linear type in standard form and so we solve it in the usual way. Why not have a go on your own?

$P = -x^{-1}$ and $Q = -x$, so that

$$\int P\,dx = \int -x^{-1}\,dx = -\ln x$$

Consequently

$$I = e^{-\ln x} = x^{-1}$$

Therefore

$$\frac{d}{dx}(x^{-1}z) = -xx^{-1} = -1$$

From which

$$\frac{z}{x} = -x + C$$

so that $z = -x^2 + Cx$. Now $z = y^{-1}$; therefore substituting gives

$$y = (-x^2 + Cx)^{-1}$$

where C is an arbitrary constant.   ∎

19.7 HOMOGENEOUS EQUATIONS

Finally we shall consider a type of differential equation known as homogeneous. Before describing how to recognize an equation of this kind we need to say what is meant by a homogeneous function.

Consider the two expressions

$$f(x,y) = x^2 + 2xy - y^2$$
$$g(x,y) = x^3 + 3xy - y^3$$

Suppose we replace x and y by tx and ty respectively. Then we obtain

$$f(tx,ty) = (tx)^2 + 2(tx)(ty) - (ty)^2$$
$$= t^2(x^2 + 2xy - y^2) = t^2 f(x,y)$$

We say that f is homogeneous of degree 2.

On the other hand,

$$g(tx,ty) = (tx)^3 + 3(tx)(ty) - (ty)^3$$

and it is not possible to extract all the 't's as factors.

In general, if f is a function of two variables x and y, we say that f is a **homogeneous function** of degree n if and only if

$$f(tx,ty) = t^n f(x,y)$$

Let us see how this applies to differential equations.

A first-order differential equation is said to be a **homogeneous equation** if and only if it can be expressed in the form

$$\frac{dy}{dx} = \frac{f(x,y)}{g(x,y)}$$

where f and g are both homogeneous functions of the same degree.

If the expression on the right is a quotient of two homogeneous functions of the same degree, then if we substitute $y = vx$ into it, all the 'x's cancel out and it reduces to terms in v. It follows that the substitution $y = vx$ reduces any homogeneous equation to a variables separable type.

Let us illustrate the method by means of an example.

Example ☐ Solve the equation

$$\frac{dy}{dx} = \frac{xy - y^2}{x^2 + xy}$$

We apply our simple test. We put $y = vx$ into the right of the equation and see what results. This gives

$$\frac{xvx - (vx)^2}{x^2 + xvx} = \frac{v - v^2}{1 + v}$$

which is an expression depending solely on v.

Now we use the same substitution $y = vx$ to reduce the equation to a variables separable type. Let us see how this works. If $y = vx$ then, differentiating with respect to x,

$$\frac{dy}{dx} = v + x\frac{dv}{dx}$$

so the equation becomes

$$v + x\frac{dv}{dx} = \frac{v - v^2}{1 + v}$$

Therefore

$$x\frac{dv}{dx} = \frac{v - v^2}{1 + v} - v$$

$$= \frac{v - v^2 - v(1 + v)}{1 + v}$$

$$= \frac{-2v^2}{1 + v}$$

This is now variables separable, and consequently

$$\int \frac{1 + v}{-2v^2}\,dv = \int \frac{1}{x}\,dx$$

Thus

$$\frac{1}{2v} - \frac{1}{2} \ln |v| = \ln |x| + C$$

where C is an arbitrary constant.

Finally, we substitute back to remove v from the equation since v was a term which we introduced ourselves:

$$\frac{x}{2y} - \frac{1}{2} \ln \left|\frac{y}{x}\right| = \ln |x| + C$$

which is

$$\frac{x}{2y} = \frac{1}{2} \ln \left|\frac{y}{x}\right| + \ln |x| + C$$

$$= \frac{1}{2} \ln |xy| + C \qquad \blacksquare$$

Ready to take a few steps?

_____ **19.8 Workshop** _____

⌐1

▷**Exercise** Consider the differential equation

$$\frac{dy}{dx} = \frac{y^2 - xy}{xy + x^2}$$

Make a substitution to reduce the right-hand side to terms in v. When you have done so, take the next step.

⌐2

Putting $y = vx$ into the right-hand side of the equation gives

$$\frac{(vx)^2 - x(vx)}{x(vx) + x^2}$$

Cancelling x^2 top and bottom results in

$$\frac{v^2 - v}{v + 1}$$

which depends solely on v.

All right so far? If not then make sure you know where you went wrong. Now complete the reduction to variables separable type and take another step.

⌐3

Substituting into the equation produces

$$x \frac{dv}{dx} + v = \frac{v^2 - v}{v + 1}$$

from which

$$x \frac{dv}{dx} = \frac{-2v}{v + 1}$$

That should have caused no problems. Now solve the equation in terms of v and x and take another step.

Separating the variables and integrating gives

$$\int \frac{1}{x} \, dx = \int \frac{v + 1}{-2v} \, dv$$

So

$$\ln |x| = -\frac{v}{2} - \frac{1}{2} \ln |v| + \ln k$$

where k is an arbitrary constant.

Check carefully if you have a different answer. Of course the constant may be expressed differently. Lastly, substitute back to eliminate v and take the final step.

4 You should obtain

$$\ln |x| = -\frac{y}{2x} - \frac{1}{2} \ln \left| \frac{y}{x} \right| + \ln k$$

Multiplying through by 2 and rearranging gives

$$2 \ln |x| + \ln \left| \frac{y}{x} \right| - 2 \ln k + \frac{y}{x} = 0$$

Using the laws of logarithms, in particular $2 \ln a = \ln a^2$ and $\ln (ab) = \ln a + \ln b$, produces the solution

$$x \ln (A |xy|) + y = 0$$

where A is an arbitrary constant ($A = k^{-2}$).

5

19.9 REDUCIBLE EQUATIONS

As with the other types of first-order equation we have discussed, there are some equations which although not homogeneous can be made so by means of a change of variable. For instance, consider an equation of the form

$$\frac{dy}{dx} = \frac{a_1x + b_1y + c_1}{a_2x + b_2y + c_2}$$

We wish to transform the variables x and y to obtain new variables X and Y. We take $X = x - A$ and $Y = y - B$. So the equation becomes

$$\frac{dY}{dX} = \frac{a_1X + b_1Y}{a_2X + b_2Y}$$

In order to achieve this objective we require

$$a_1A + b_1B + c_1 = 0$$
$$a_2A + b_2B + c_2 = 0$$

This means that we can think of (A, B) as the point at which the pair of straight lines

$$a_1x + b_1y + c_1 = 0$$
$$a_2x + b_2y + c_2 = 0$$

intersects. (We shall consider later the case of parallel lines, where there is no point of intersection.)

So now we have a simple method. Let us state precisely what we have to do. To solve the **reducible equation**

$$\frac{dy}{dx} = \frac{a_1x + b_1y + c_1}{a_2x + b_2y + c_2}$$

1 Obtain the point (A, B) where the straight lines

$$a_1x + b_1y + c_1 = 0$$
$$a_2x + b_2y + c_2 = 0$$

intersect.

2 Change variables by writing $X = x - A$ and $Y = y - B$ so that

$$\frac{dy}{dx} = \frac{dY}{dx} = \frac{dY}{dX}\frac{dX}{dx} = \frac{dY}{dX}1 = \frac{dY}{dX}$$

3 The equation then becomes

$$\frac{dY}{dX} = \frac{a_1X + b_1Y}{a_2X + b_2Y}$$

which is homogeneous and can be solved in the usual way.

4 Replace X and Y by $x - A$ and $y - B$ respectively to obtain the solution to the original equation.

Time now for an example. We shall see that sometimes a nasty integral results. However, if we remember our work on integration (Chapters 15–17) and a few basic standard forms this task should present no great difficulty.

Example ☐ Solve the equation

$$\frac{dy}{dx} = \frac{x + y - 3}{2x - y - 3}$$

First solve the pair of simultaneous equations

$$x + y - 3 = 0$$
$$2x - y - 3 = 0$$

Subtracting gives at once

$$-x + 2y = 0$$

So $x = 2y$. Substituting for x in the first equation we obtain $3y - 3 = 0$, and therefore $y = 1$ and $x = 2$.

Now make the substitutions $X = x - A$ and $Y = y - B$; in this case, $X = x - 2$ and $Y = y - 1$. This produces

$$\frac{dY}{dX} = \frac{X + Y}{2X - Y}$$

Notice that we do not have to think very hard at this stage. First, the coefficients of X and Y are the same as the coefficients of x and y respectively in the original equation. Secondly, we can replace the derivative dy/dx by dY/dX since we have already considered the change of variable in detail.

Now solve the homogeneous equation

$$\frac{dY}{dX} = \frac{X + Y}{2X - Y}$$

As usual we make the substitution $Y = VX$ (it is neater to use capital letters throughout). This gives

$$X\frac{dV}{dX} + V = \frac{X + VX}{2X - VX} = \frac{1 + V}{2 - V}$$

Consequently

$$X\frac{dV}{dX} = \frac{1 + V}{2 - V} - V = \frac{1 - V + V^2}{2 - V}$$

As a result we obtain

$$\int \frac{dX}{X} = \int \frac{2 - V}{1 - V + V^2}\, dV$$

$$= \int \frac{2 - V}{(V - 1/2)^2 + 3/4} \, dV$$

$$= -\frac{1}{2} \int \frac{(2V - 1) - 3}{(V - 1/2)^2 + 3/4} \, dV$$

The numerator has been split up so that one part is the derivative of the denominator and the other is constant. In this way the integral can be seen to be the sum of two, one a logarithm and the other an inverse tangent:

$$-\tfrac{1}{2} \ln \left[(V - 1/2)^2 + 3/4\right] + (3/2)(2/\sqrt{3}) \tan^{-1}[(V - 1/2)/(\sqrt{3}/2)] + \text{constant}$$

So the solution is

$$\ln X = -\tfrac{1}{2} \ln (V^2 - V + 1) + (\sqrt{3}) \tan^{-1} [(2V - 1)/\sqrt{3}] + \text{constant}$$

Now $Y = VX$, where $X = x - 2$ and $Y = y - 1$. So multiplying by 2 we obtain

$$2 \ln X + \ln (V^2 - V + 1) = 2(\sqrt{3}) \tan^{-1} [(2V - 1)/\sqrt{3}] + \text{constant}$$

Eliminating V,

$$\ln (Y^2 - YX + X^2) = 2(\sqrt{3}) \tan^{-1} [(2Y - X)/(\sqrt{3})X] + \text{constant}$$

Lastly, substituting in terms of x and y,

$$\ln \left[(y - 1)^2 - (y - 1)(x - 2) + (x - 2)^2\right]$$
$$= 2(\sqrt{3}) \tan^{-1} \{[2(y - 1) - (x - 2)]/(\sqrt{3})(x - 2)\} + C$$

Therefore

$$\ln[y^2 - 2y + 1 - (xy - x - 2y + 2) + x^2 - 4x + 4]$$
$$= 2(\sqrt{3}) \tan^{-1} [(2y - x)/(\sqrt{3})(x - 2)] + C$$

Finally,

$$\ln(x^2 + y^2 - xy - 3x + 3) = 2(\sqrt{3}) \tan^{-1} [(2y - x)/(\sqrt{3})(x - 2)] + C$$

where C is an arbitrary constant.   ∎

Whew!

We now dispose of the problem of **parallel lines** which we mentioned earlier. If the simultaneous equations

$$a_1 x + b_1 y + c_1 = 0$$
$$a_2 x + b_2 y + c_2 = 0$$

have no point of intersection, then the differential equation can be converted into a variables separable equation quite easily by substituting

$$z = a_2 x + b_2 y + c_2$$

In fact there are many substitutions which will have the same effect. For instance,

$$z = a_2x + b_2y$$
$$z = a_1x + b_1y$$
$$z = a_1x + b_1y + c_1$$

Here is an example of this kind.

Example □ Solve the differential equation

$$\frac{dy}{dx} = \frac{2x - 4y - 3}{x - 2y + 1}$$

We observe that the equations

$$2x - 4y - 3 = 0$$
$$x - 2y + 1 = 0$$

have no common solution, and so we put

$$z = x - 2y + 1$$

Then

$$\frac{dz}{dx} = 1 - 2\frac{dy}{dx} = 1 - 2\frac{2z - 5}{z}$$

Therefore

$$\frac{dz}{dx} = \frac{z - 4z + 10}{z} = \frac{-3z + 10}{z}$$

Consequently,

$$x = \int \frac{z}{-3z + 10}\, dz$$

$$= -\frac{1}{3}\int \frac{(-3z + 10) - 10}{-3z + 10}\, dz$$

Observe how we can rearrange the numerator so that the denominator divides into it, leaving a simple integral. So

$$x = -\frac{1}{3}\int dz - \frac{10}{9}\int \frac{-3}{-3z + 10}\, dz$$

Here we have arranged things so that the numerator in the second integral is the derivative of the denominator. Then

$$x = -\frac{z}{3} - \frac{10}{9}\ln(-3z + 10) + C$$

To be strict we should take the modulus of $-3z + 10$ when finding the logarithm. One way to avoid any problems (which are unlikely to occur) is to use the laws of logarithms and rewrite the solution as

$$x = -\frac{z}{3} - \frac{5}{9} \ln (-3z + 10)^2 + C$$

Eliminating z produces

$$x = -\frac{x - 2y + 1}{3} - \frac{5}{9} \ln (-3x + 6y + 7)^2 + C \qquad \blacksquare$$

That wasn't too bad, was it? Now you do one – and be careful with the integral.

☐ Obtain the general solution to the differential equation   **Example**

$$\frac{dy}{dx} = \frac{x - 2y + 3}{-2x + 4y + 7}$$

When you have completed your working, follow through the solution and see how things differ.

First we examine the two equations

$$x - 2y + 3 = 0$$
$$-2x + 4y + 7 = 0$$

and see at once that they have no common solution.

Next make a substitution. $z = -2x + 4y + 7$ is suitable, but you may prefer $z = x - 2y$. Even if you have solved this problem successfully it is a good idea to follow through the substitution $z = x - 2y$ to see how it all comes eventually to the same thing. When $z = -2x + 4y + 7$ we have

$$\frac{dz}{dx} = -2 + 4\frac{dy}{dx} = -2 + 4\frac{-(z - 7)/2 + 3}{z}$$

So

$$\frac{dz}{dx} = \frac{-2z - 2(z - 7) + 12}{z} = \frac{-4z + 26}{z}$$

Therefore

$$\int \frac{z\,dz}{-4z + 26} = \int dx$$

It follows that

$$x = -\frac{1}{4}\int \frac{z - (13/2) + (13/2)}{z - (13/2)}\,dz$$

$$= -\frac{z}{4} - \frac{13}{8} \int \frac{dz}{z - (13/2)}$$

$$= -\frac{z}{4} - \frac{13}{8} \ln |z - (13/2)| + C$$

So that, substituting back, the solution is

$$x = -\frac{-2x + 4y + 7}{4} - \frac{13}{8} \ln |-2x + 4y + (1/2)| + C$$

So

$$2x + 4y - 7 = -\frac{13}{2} \ln |-2x + 4y + (1/2)| + 4C$$

$$4x + 8y - 14 + 13 \ln |-2x + 4y + (1/2)| = A$$

where A is the arbitrary constant.

Although your answer may not look like this, it may be equivalent. Check to see if it is. For example, using the laws of logarithms, it is possible to express this answer in the form

$$4x + 8y - 14 + 13 \ln |-4x + 8y + 1| = B$$

where B is an arbitrary constant. One way to check if two answers are equivalent is in each case to put the constant on the right and the rest of the solution on the left. Then subtract the two left-hand sides; if they differ by a constant, all is well. ■

19.10 BOUNDARY CONDITIONS

We have not mentioned the situation where we are given some boundary condition which the differential equation and therefore its solution must satisfy. In these circumstances we are not greatly interested in the general solution.

There are many methods for solving differential equations, and some of these make use of the boundary condition at the outset. However, for first-order differential equations we shall continue to solve them analytically by first obtaining the general solution and then determining the arbitrary constant. A single example will suffice to show how this is done; it really is very easy indeed!

Example □ Solve the equation

$$\frac{dy}{dx} = \tan (2x + y) - 2$$

given that $y = 3\pi/2$ when $x = 0$. This initial condition is sometimes written as $y(0) = 3\pi/2$, a useful shorthand notation.

Before reading any further, see if you can solve the equation on your own. You never know your own strength until you test it!

If we attempt to expand out the tangent we shall soon find things difficult. It is clear also that the equation does not obviously fall into any one of the categories which we have discussed. So we shall need to adapt it. We note that if $z = 2x + y$ then

$$\frac{dz}{dx} = 2 + \frac{dy}{dx} = 2 + \tan z - 2 = \tan z$$

so that the equation becomes variables separable. We have therefore

$$\int dx = \int \cot z \, dz = \int \frac{\cos z}{\sin z} \, dz$$

so that

$$x = \ln |\sin z| + C = \ln |\sin (2x + y)| + C$$

Now we use the initial condition and substitute into the equation the pair of values for x and y to determine C. We obtain

$$0 = \ln |\sin [0 + (3\pi/2)]| + C$$
$$= \ln |-1| + C = \ln 1 + C = 0 + C$$

So $C = 0$, and consequently

$$x = \ln |\sin (2x + y)|$$

or

$$\sin^2 (2x + y) = e^{2x} \qquad \blacksquare$$

Now it's time to consider some applications. We shall solve two problems, one electrical and one mechanical. You can either take your pick or solve them both. We shall tackle them stage by stage so that you can participate in the solution whenever you wish.

19.11 Practical

CIRCUIT CURRENT

An RL series circuit has an EMF $E \sin \omega t$ where E is constant. The current i satisfies, at time t,

$$L \frac{di}{dt} + Ri = E \sin \omega t$$

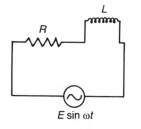

$E \sin \omega t$

Obtain the current at time t if initially it is zero.
   Try it and see how it goes.

This is clearly a first-order linear equation:

$$\frac{di}{dt} + \frac{R}{L} i = \frac{E}{L} \sin \omega t$$

We have $P = R/L$, so

$$\int P \, dt = \int \frac{R}{L} \, dt = \frac{Rt}{L}$$

Therefore the integrating factor is $e^{Rt/L}$.
   Now solve the equation.

We have

$$\frac{d}{dt} (e^{Rt/L} \, i) = \frac{E}{L} \sin \omega t \, e^{Rt/L}$$

Consequently

$$e^{Rt/L} \, i = \frac{E}{L} \int e^{Rt/L} \sin \omega t \, dt$$

Now

$$\int e^{ax} \sin bx \, dx = \frac{e^{ax}}{a^2 + b^2} (a \sin bx - b \cos bx) + C$$

Write down the solution and move on to the next stage.

We have

$$e^{Rt/L} \, i = \frac{(E/L) e^{Rt/L}}{(R^2/L^2) + \omega^2} \left(\frac{R}{L} \sin \omega t - \omega \cos \omega t \right) + C$$

where C is the arbitrary constant. Determine C and complete the solution.

We have

$$i = \frac{E}{R^2 + \omega^2 L^2} (R \sin \omega t - \omega L \cos \omega t) + C \, e^{-Rt/L}$$

When $t = 0$, $i = 0$, and therefore

$$C = \frac{E\omega L}{R^2 + \omega^2 L^2}$$

Consequently

$$i = \frac{E}{R^2 + \omega^2 L^2}(R \sin \omega t - \omega L \cos \omega t + \omega L \, e^{-Rt/L})$$

VEHICLE BRAKING

The brakes of a vehicle are applied when the speed is u. Subsequently its speed v satisfies the equation

$$v \frac{dv}{dx} = \left(-2 - \frac{v}{3u}\right) a$$

where a is a constant and x is the distance travelled after braking. Obtain the distance the vehicle travels after the brakes are applied before it comes to rest.

Move on when you have sorted out the equation.

The equation is variables separable:

$$v \frac{dv}{dx} = \frac{-6u - v}{3u} a$$

So

$$\int \frac{3uv \, dv}{-6u - v} = a \int dx$$

Obtain these integrals and thereby the general solution.

We have

$$ax = -3u \int \frac{v \, dv}{v + 6u}$$

$$= -3u \int \frac{v + 6u - 6u}{v + 6u} dv$$

$$= -3u \int dv + 18u^2 \int \frac{dv}{v + 6u}$$

$$= -3uv + 18u^2 \ln(v + 6u) + C$$

where C is an arbitrary constant.

Determine C and complete the solution.

When $x = 0$, $v = u$, and so

$$0 = -3u^2 + 18u^2 \ln 7u + C$$

Therefore

$$C = 3u^2 - 18u^2 \ln 7u$$

Consequently

$$ax = -3uv + 18u^2 \ln (v + 6u) + 3u^2 - 18u^2 \ln 7u$$

When $v = 0$, $x = d$ the stopping distance, so

$$ad = 0 + 18u^2 \ln 6u + 3u^2 - 18u^2 \ln 7u$$
$$= 18u^2 \ln (6/7) + 3u^2$$

Therefore

$$d = (1/a)[18u^2 \ln (6/7) + 3u^2]$$

SUMMARY

We have solved first-order ordinary differential equations which are of the following types:

☐ Variables separable

$$\frac{dy}{dx} = \frac{f(x)}{g(y)}$$

☐ Linear

$$\frac{dy}{dx} + Py = Q$$

☐ Homogeneous

$$\frac{dy}{dx} = \frac{f(x, y)}{g(x, y)}$$

We have seen that other equations can be reduced to these by means of substitutions. In particular we considered:

☐ Bernoulli's equation

$$\frac{dy}{dx} + Py = Qy^n$$

☐ Reducible

$$\frac{dy}{dx} = \frac{a_1 x + b_1 y + c_1}{a_2 x + b_2 y + c_2}$$

EXERCISES (for answers see p. 756)

1 Solve, by separating the variables,

a $x\dfrac{dy}{dx} = xy + y$

b $x^2(y + 1)\dfrac{dy}{dx} = y(x + 1)$

c $\exp(x + y)\dfrac{dy}{dx} = \dfrac{x}{y}$

2 Solve the linear equations

a $\dfrac{y}{x} + \dfrac{dy}{dx} = \exp x$

b $\dfrac{y}{x} - \dfrac{dy}{dx} + x^2 \exp x = 0$

c $\dfrac{dy}{dx} + y \cot x = \cos x$

3 Solve the homogeneous equations

a $\dfrac{dy}{dx} = \dfrac{2x + y}{x - y}$

b $(x + 4y)\dfrac{dy}{dx} = x - 2y$

c $(x^2 + xy)\dfrac{dy}{dx} = y^2 - xy$

4 Solve each of the following equations:

a $\dfrac{dy}{dx} + 2xy = y^2 \exp x^2$

b $x\dfrac{dy}{dx} - y = x^2y^2$

c $(x + y - 3)\dfrac{dy}{dx} = 2x - y$

ASSIGNMENT (for answers see p. 757; see also Workshops on pp. 541, 548 and 555)

Solve each of the following differential equations:

1 $e^y \dfrac{dy}{dx} = \dfrac{2x}{x^2 + 1}$

2 $\dfrac{dx}{dt} = x \sec^2 t$

3 $2 \sec 2u \dfrac{dv}{du} = \left(y + \dfrac{1}{y}\right)$

4 $\dfrac{dy}{dx} = \dfrac{y^2 - x + xy^2 - 1}{2xy}$

5 $\dfrac{dy}{d\theta} + y \cot \theta + 1 = 0$

6 $x \ln x \dfrac{dy}{dx} + y = \dfrac{x^2}{\sqrt{(x^2 + 1)}}$

7 $x + \dfrac{dx}{dt} = 2e^t$

8 $x \dfrac{dy}{dx} + y = 2x$

9 $\dfrac{dy}{dx} = \dfrac{x + y}{x}$

10 $\dfrac{ds}{dt} = \dfrac{2s^2 + t^2}{2st}$

11 $\dfrac{dy}{dx} = \dfrac{2y^2 - xy + x^2}{2xy - x^2}$

12 $\dfrac{dy}{dx} = \dfrac{y}{x} + \cos\left(\dfrac{y}{x}\right)$

FURTHER EXERCISES (for answers see p. 757)

Solve each of the differential equations 1 to 10:

1 $\dfrac{dy}{dx} = \dfrac{x^2}{y^2 - x^2} + \dfrac{y}{x}$

2 $\dfrac{x}{x + y}\dfrac{dy}{dx} = \dfrac{y}{x}$

3 $\sin 2t \dfrac{dx}{dt} = 2(\sin t - x)$

4 $x + y \dfrac{dy}{dx} = (x^2 + y^2) \cot x$

5 $\dfrac{du}{dv} = \dfrac{2u - 5}{v - 3}$

6 $(6x + y) \dfrac{dy}{dx} = x - 6y$

7 $\dfrac{dp}{dq} = \dfrac{q + 3p - 9}{3q - p - 7}$

8 $x \dfrac{dy}{dx} = y + x \tan\left(\dfrac{y}{x}\right)$

9 $x^2 \dfrac{dy}{dx} = (x - y)^2 + xy$ where $y(1) = 0$

10 $\cos^2 \theta \dfrac{dr}{d\theta} + r \cos \theta = 1 + \sin \theta$ given $r = 1$ when $\theta = 0$

11 A circuit consists of two branches in parallel. One branch consists of a resistance R ohms and a capacitance C farads. The other branch consists of another resistance R ohms and an inductance L henries. When an EMF $E \sin \omega t$ is applied, the branch currents i_1 and i_2 satisfy the two relations

$$L \frac{di_1}{dt} + Ri_1 = E \sin \omega t$$

$$R \frac{di_2}{dt} + \frac{1}{C} i_2 = \omega E \cos \omega t$$

Show that if the circuit is initially quiescent and is tuned so that $CR^2 = L$ then the total current $i_1 + i_2$ will be $(E/R) \sin \omega t$.

12 An EMF $E \sin \omega t$ is applied to an RC series circuit. Show that the current i is given by

$$RC \frac{di}{dt} + i = \omega EC \cos \omega t$$

Initially the circuit was quiescent. Obtain an expression for the charge on the capacitor at time t.

13 The rate of decay of a radioactive substance is proportional to the quantity Q which remains. Initially $Q = Q_0$. Show that if it takes T hours for the quantity to reduce by 50% it will take $T(\log_2 Q_0 - \log_2 Q_1)$ hours for the quantity to reduce from Q_0 to Q_1.

14 Newton's law of cooling states that the rate of fall of temperature of a body is approximately proportional to the excess temperature over that of its surroundings. If θ_1 is the temperature initially and θ_0 is the surrounding temperature ($\theta_1 > \theta_0$) and if it takes T minutes to cool to $(\theta_1 + \theta_0)/2$, show that the time taken to cool to $(\theta_1 + n\theta_0)/(n + 1)$, where n is a positive integer, is $T \log_2 (n + 1)$.

Second-order differential equations

20

In Chapter 19 we solved some of the first-order differential equations which tend to arise in applications. We now turn our attention to second-order differential equations.

After studying this chapter you should be able to
☐ Recognize a second-order linear differential equation;
☐ Write down the general solution in the homogeneous case;
☐ Use the method of trial solutions to obtain a particular solution in the non-homogeneous case;
☐ Anticipate the breakdown case and remedy the situation;
☐ Solve a general linear second-order differential equation with constant coefficients.
At the end of the chapter we solve practical problems in filtering, circuits and mechanical oscillations.

20.1 LINEAR DIFFERENTIAL EQUATIONS

There are many types of second-order differential equation, but one in particular arises frequently in applications. This is known as a **linear** differential equation with **constant coefficients**. It can be expressed in the form

$$a \frac{d^2 y}{dx^2} + b \frac{dy}{dx} + cy = f(x)$$

where a, b and c are real constants ($a \neq 0$) and $f(x)$ depends solely on x.

The special case where $f(x)$ is identically zero is known as the homogeneous case. Since this equation is not only easy to solve but also of relevance in the solution of the general equation, the non-homogeneous case, we shall consider it first.

20.2 THE HOMOGENEOUS CASE

We are concerned with the differential equation

$$a \frac{d^2y}{dx^2} + b \frac{dy}{dx} + cy = 0$$

where a, b and c are real constants and a is non-zero.

This is a second-order differential equation and so its general solution will contain two independent arbitrary constants. Later we shall be able to reduce the solution of this equation to a simple routine, but first we see how the routine arises.

We show firstly that if $y = u$ and $y = v$ are solutions of the equation then so also is $y = Au + Bv$, where A and B are arbitrary constants. This is important because it implies that in order to obtain the general solution it is sufficient to obtain any two linearly independent solutions.

Note that if the identity $Au + Bv \equiv 0$, where A and B are constants, is satisfied only when both $A = 0$ and $B = 0$, then u and v are said to be **linearly independent**.

Suppose then

See also section 22.7 for a discussion of linear independence. The concept also arises in sections 13.8 and 21.2.

$$a \frac{d^2u}{dx^2} + b \frac{du}{dx} + cu = 0$$

and

$$a \frac{d^2v}{dx^2} + b \frac{dv}{dx} + cv = 0$$

To show that $y = Au + Bv$ is also a solution we shall substitute this value for y into the left-hand side of the differential equation and deduce the result is zero. Now from $y = Au + Bv$ we deduce, by differentiating, that

$$\frac{dy}{dx} = A \frac{du}{dx} + B \frac{dv}{dx}$$

$$\frac{d^2y}{dx^2} = A \frac{d^2u}{dx^2} + B \frac{d^2v}{dx^2}$$

So

$$a \frac{d^2y}{dx^2} + b \frac{dy}{dx} + cy$$

$$= a \left(A \frac{d^2u}{dx^2} + B \frac{d^2v}{dx^2} \right) + b \left(A \frac{du}{dx} + B \frac{dv}{dx} \right) + c(Au + Bv)$$

$$= A \left(a \frac{d^2u}{dx^2} + b \frac{du}{dx} + cu \right) + B \left(a \frac{d^2v}{dx^2} + b \frac{dv}{dx} + cv \right)$$

$$= 0 + 0 = 0$$

So we have shown that if $y = u$ and $y = v$ are any two solutions of the differential equation

$$a \frac{d^2y}{dx^2} + b \frac{dy}{dx} + cy = 0$$

then $y = Au + Bv$ is also a solution, where A and B are constants which may be arbitrarily chosen.

The outcome of all this is that if we can find two linearly independent solutions of this differential equation we can find the general solution. How are we to find these solutions? Well it so happens that it is fairly easy to spot one. Remember that when we differentiate e^x with respect to x the answer remains e^x. We adapt this observation very slightly and look for a solution of the form e^{mx}, where m is a constant; we shall wish to determine m.

Now if $y = e^{mx}$ is a solution it follows that

$$\frac{dy}{dx} = m\, e^{mx} \qquad \frac{d^2y}{dx^2} = m^2\, e^{mx}$$

Consequently, substituting these expressions into the differential equation,

$$am^2\, e^{mx} + bm\, e^{mx} + c\, e^{mx} = 0$$

and since e^{mx} is never zero we can divide through by it to obtain

$$am^2 + bm + c = 0$$

This is a very familiar equation, which you probably recognize straight away: it is a quadratic equation. Because of its importance in the solution of this differential equation it is given a special name: the **auxiliary equation**.

Notice the pattern, and see how easy it is to write down the auxiliary equation straight away from the differential equation. The second-order derivative is replaced by m^2, the first-order derivative is replaced by m, and y is replaced by 1. There is no need to think!

Given the auxiliary equation

$$am^2 + bm + c = 0$$

there are three situations which can occur:
1 The equation has two distinct real roots m_1 and m_2;
2 The equation has two equal roots m;
3 The equation has complex roots $m = \alpha \pm i\beta$.
We shall deal with each of these cases in turn.

The formula for solving a quadratic equation was obtained at the beginning of Chapter 10.

Case 1

The auxiliary equation $am^2 + bm + c = 0$ has distinct real roots m_1 and m_2.

Here we have now two distinct linearly independent solutions of the differential equation, namely $u = e^{m_1x}$ and $v = e^{m_2x}$. So the general solution is

$$y = A\,e^{m_1x} + B\,e^{m_2x}$$

where A and B are arbitrary constants.

Case 2

The auxiliary equation $am^2 + bm + c = 0$ has two equal roots m, necessarily real since $b^2 = 4ac$.

At first sight we may seem to be in difficulties since we have only one solution. However, in these circumstances it is easy to verify that $y = x\,e^{mx}$ is another solution. To see this we simply differentiate, substitute the results into the left-hand side of the differential equation and check that the outcome is zero. You may like to try this for yourself, but in either event here is the working in full.

If $y = x\,e^{mx}$ then

$$\frac{dy}{dx} = e^{mx} + mx\,e^{mx}$$

$$\frac{d^2y}{dx^2} = m\,e^{mx} + m\,e^{mx} + m^2x\,e^{mx} = 2m\,e^{mx} + m^2x\,e^{mx}$$

So substituting into the left-hand side of the auxiliary equation gives

$$a(2m\,e^{mx} + m^2x\,e^{mx}) + b(e^{mx} + mx\,e^{mx}) + cx\,e^{mx}$$
$$= (am^2 + bm + c)\,x\,e^{mx} + (2am + b)\,e^{mx}$$

Now $am^2 + bm + c = 0$ because the auxiliary equation is satisfied by m, and $2am + b = 0$ because the auxiliary equation has equal roots $m = -b/(2a)$. So we now have two linearly independent solutions of the differential equation, $u = e^{mx}$ and $v = x\,e^{mx}$. The general solution is consequently

$$y = A\,e^{mx} + Bx\,e^{mx} = (A + Bx)\,e^{mx}$$

where A and B are arbitrary constants.

Case 3

The auxiliary equation $am^2 + bm + c = 0$ has complex roots $m = \alpha \pm i\beta$.

This is similar to case 1. In fact if we were content to have a solution containing complex numbers we need go no further. However, the differential equation itself did not have any complex numbers in it and there is no reason why the solution should contain any; such equations often arise from practical situations where complex numbers would seem very out of place. Luckily we can express the solution in a form which is entirely free of complex numbers, and this we now do.

Following case 1 we have the general solution

$$y = P e^{(\alpha + i\beta)x} + Q e^{(\alpha - i\beta)x}$$

where P and Q are arbitrary constants. So

$$
\begin{aligned}
y &= e^{\alpha x}(P e^{i\beta x} + Q e^{-i\beta x}) \\
&= e^{\alpha x}[P(\cos \beta x + i \sin \beta x) + Q(\cos \beta x - i \sin \beta x)] \\
&= e^{\alpha x}[(P + Q) \cos \beta x + (Pi - Qi) \sin \beta x] \\
y &= e^{\alpha x}(A \cos \beta x + B \sin \beta x)
\end{aligned}
$$

Here we use Enler's formula derived in section 10.8.

where A and B are arbitrary constants.

The solution is now free of complex numbers. However, there are several different ways of expressing this. For example, another is

$$y = e^{\alpha x} R \cos (\beta x - \theta)$$

This was done in section 3.4.

where R and θ are arbitrary constants. This follows immediately from elementary trigonometry, since we can always express $a \cos \theta + b \sin \theta$ as $r \cos (\theta - \alpha)$.

In summary, to obtain the general solution of the equation

$$a \frac{d^2 y}{dx^2} + b \frac{dy}{dx} + cy = 0$$

where a, b and c are real constants ($a \neq 0$):
1 Write down the auxiliary equation $am^2 + bm + c = 0$.
2 Solve this quadratic equation to obtain the roots m_1 and m_2.
3 Select from three cases:

We shall meet the auxiliary equation in a different context when we study difference equations in section 21.3.

    a If the roots m_1 and m_2 are both real and distinct,

$$y = A e^{m_1 x} + B e^{m_2 x}$$

    b If the roots m_1 and m_2 are equal, so $m_1 = m_2 = m$,

$$y = (A + Bx) e^{mx}$$

    c If the roots m_1 and m_2 are complex, so $m = \alpha \pm i\beta$,

$$y = e^{\alpha x}(A \cos \beta x + B \sin \beta x)$$

where A and B are arbitrary constants.
It really is very easy. We shall see how simple it all is by taking some steps.

_____ 20.3 Workshop _____

1

Exercise   Obtain the general solutions of the following differential equations:

a $\dfrac{d^2y}{dx^2} - 6\dfrac{dy}{dx} + 5y = 0$

b $4\dfrac{d^2y}{dx^2} + 25y = 20\dfrac{dy}{dx}$

c $\dfrac{d^2y}{dx^2} + 25y = 0$

d $\dfrac{d^2y}{dx^2} + 25\dfrac{dy}{dx} = 0$

Four examples and only three cases; at least one case must occur more than once!

First write down the auxiliary equations for **a** and **b**. Remember that there is no need to do any mathematics at this stage: no differentiating, and no substituting into the differential equation. We have dealt with all that once and for all. We simply write down the auxiliary equation.

Done it? Step ahead.

Well then, here are the results you should obtain:
a $m^2 - 6m + 5 = 0$
b $4m^2 - 20m + 25 = 0$
If all is well, write down the auxiliary equations for **c** and **d** and move ahead to step 3.

If you have made an error, look back carefully through what we have done and see where you went wrong. When you are satisfied that you can write down an auxiliary equation correctly, taking care about signs, try doing so for **c** and **d**. If you are confident that you have done it correctly, then read on to check that all is well. If there are still problems you had better go back to the main text and read things through slowly and carefully so that you understand it properly.

Here then are the other two auxiliary equations:
c $m^2 + 25 = 0$
d $m^2 + 25m = 0$

Now the time has come to solve each of the four quadratic equations. Of course this is very elementary work, but it is surprising how many mistakes creep in at this stage. See if you can solve them correctly.

Here are the roots:
a $m = 1$ or $m = 5$
b $m = 5/2$ (repeated)
c $m = \pm 5i$
d $m = 0$ or $m = -25$

Is all well? We must decide for each one which case it is, and then write down the corresponding solution. To begin with, try **a** and **b**. When you have finished, move to the next step to check they are correct.

---

5 Here are the answers:
a $y = A e^x + B e^{5x}$
b $y = (A + Bx) e^{5x/2}$

where A and B are arbitrary constants. Of course it does not matter if you have A and B the other way round or have used some other letters.

If all is well you can now see if you can deal properly with **c** and **d**, and then move ahead to step 7.

If not, check carefully to see what went wrong. Look back at the summary of the method; possibly you identified the cases incorrectly. When you are confident that you know what went wrong, try these equations and see how it goes.

▷ **Exercise**   Obtain the general solutions of the following differential equations:

e $\dfrac{d^2y}{dx^2} - 14\dfrac{dy}{dx} + 49y = 0$

f $\dfrac{d^2y}{dx^2} + 6y = 5\dfrac{dy}{dx}$

First obtain the auxiliary equation, then the values for m and finally the correct form of the solution. Then step ahead.

---

6 The auxiliary equations are:
e $m^2 - 14m + 49 = 0$
f $m^2 - 5m + 6 = 0$
The roots are:
e $m = 7$ (repeated)
f $m = 2$ and $m = 3$
The solutions are:
e $y = (A + Bx) e^{7x}$
f $y = A e^{2x} + B e^{3x}$
where A and B are arbitrary constants.

If things are still going wrong it is best to read through the chapter again and see if you can get things straight. Otherwise, see if you can now deal properly with **c** and **d** and then take a further step to see how things worked out.

---

7 These are the solutions. For **c**, $m = \pm 5i$ so that $\alpha = 0$ and $\beta = 5$. Consequently,

c $y = e^0(A \cos 5x + B \sin 5x)$
    $= A \cos 5x + B \sin 5x$
d $y = A e^0 + B e^{-25x} = A + B e^{-25x}$

where A and B are arbitrary constants.

Here then are the general solutions **a–d** again:

a $y = A e^x + B e^{5x}$
b $y = (A + Bx) e^{5x/2}$
c $y = A \cos 5x + B \sin 5x$
d $y = A + B e^{-25x}$

where A and B are arbitrary constants.

All should be well with **d**, but **c** may have caused some difficulty. If you have a clean bill of health, you may move on to the next section of work.

Otherwise, here are two more equations where the roots of the auxiliary equation turn out to be complex numbers. Try these so that you can become confident that you can solve such equations.

▷**Exercise** Obtain the general solutions of the following differential equations:

g $\dfrac{d^2y}{dx^2} - 2\dfrac{dy}{dx} + 2y = 0$

h $\dfrac{d^2y}{dx^2} + 36y = 0$

When you have finished, move ahead to step 8 to see the results.

The auxiliary equations are:
g $m^2 - 2m + 2 = 0$
h $m^2 + 36 = 0$

| 8 |

The roots are:
g $m = 1 \pm i$, so $\alpha = 1$ and $\beta = 1$
h $m = \pm 6i$, so $\alpha = 0$ and $\beta = 6$
The solutions are:
g $y = e^x(A \cos x + B \sin x)$
h $y = e^0(A \cos 6x + B \sin 6x)$
    $= A \cos 6x + B \sin 6x$
where A and B are arbitrary constants.

If there are still problems then it is best to look back through the material of this chapter to sort things out.

20.4 THE NON-HOMOGENEOUS CASE

We now turn our attention once more to the solution of second-order linear differential equations with constant coefficients. As we said before, such an equation can be expressed in the form

$$a \frac{d^2y}{dx^2} + b \frac{dy}{dx} + cy = f(x) \tag{1}$$

where a, b and c are real constants ($a \neq 0$) and $f(x)$ depends solely on x.

We have disposed completely of the homogeneous case $f(x) \equiv 0$. However it turns out, as we shall see in a moment, that the solution of the homogeneous case is part and parcel of the solution of the non-homogeneous case.

Suppose for the moment that we know how to obtain a solution $y = v$ to the differential equation. This solution is a particular solution and is not likely to contain any arbitrary constants. Then substituting into (1) gives

$$a \frac{d^2v}{dx^2} + b \frac{dv}{dx} + cv = f(x) \tag{2}$$

Subtracting (2) from (1) and simplifying gives

$$a \frac{d^2}{dx^2}(y - v) + b \frac{d}{dx}(y - v) + c(y - v) = f(x) - f(x) = 0$$

so that putting $u = y - v$ we have

$$a \frac{d^2u}{dx^2} + b \frac{du}{dx} + cu = 0 \tag{3}$$

Now this is very significant, although its importance may not occur to you straight away. Just think. We know how to solve (3), so we can obtain u containing two arbitrary constants. Moreover, $y = u + v$ and so we can obtain the general solution to (1) provided we can obtain *any* solution at all to it.

We call u the **complementary function** (or complementary part) and v a **particular integral** (or particular solution). The problem of solving the **non-homogeneous** case has therefore essentially become reduced to that of obtaining a particular solution of the differential equation:

general solution (y) = complementary part (u) + particular solution (v)

20.5 THE PARTICULAR SOLUTION

We have already seen how to find the complementary part, so we now concentrate our attention on finding a particular solution. There are two principal methods which can be used to do this, and each has something to be said for it. The methods are known as
1 the method of the operator D
2 the method of trial solution.
The method of the operator D is a formal method using the linear operator D (differentiation) in an algebraic way to derive a particular solution.

We shall be discussing this method in the more general context of linear operators (Chapter 22) and so we shall not consider it here.

Instead we shall consider the method of **trial solution**. Basically what we do is we examine $f(x)$ and attempt to find a solution of the same form.

□ Consider the equation   **Example**

$$\frac{d^2y}{dx^2} + 5\frac{dy}{dx} + 6y = 24$$

Here $f(x) = 24$, and so we might wonder if there is a solution of the form $y = k$ where k is a constant.

To see if this is possible, we tentatively suppose that $y = k$ is a particular solution and substitute into the equation to see if we can find k. We have, if $y = k$,

$$\frac{dy}{dx} = 0 \qquad \frac{d^2y}{dx^2} = 0$$

So substituting,

$$0 + 0 + 6k = 24$$

So $k = 4$ and consequently $y = 4$ is a particular solution.

You can easily check that the complementary part is

$$u = A\,e^{-2x} + B\,e^{-3x}$$

So substituting,

$$y = A\,e^{-2x} + B\,e^{-3x} + 4 \qquad\qquad ■$$

There are two points to be careful about here:
1 Do *not* call the complementary part y. It is only part of the solution; by itself it does not even satisfy the equation. It is better to call it u or CP.
2 If there are initial conditions such as $y(0) = 1$ and $y'(0) = 2$ then we must obtain the general solution to the equation before we make any attempt to use them. We must *never* substitute these values into the complementary part in an attempt to determine the constants A and B.

How, then, are we to decide which trial solutions to use? Well, it is important to realize that it is not always possible to obtain an analytic solution to the differential equation by this method. In fact there are relatively few functions f for which particular solutions exist. However, we can construct a table and the recommended trial solution in some simple cases. There is a set of circumstances in which the trial solution will not work; we shall consider this later.

Suitable trial solutions for selected functions are shown in Table 20.1. In this table k is supposed constant, and the constants a, b, c and d are to be determined by trial solution.

Table 20.1

$f(x)$	Trial solution
Constant	Constant $y = k$
Polynomial, e.g. $x^2 + 1$	Polynomial of same degree $y = ax^2 + bx + c$
e^{kx}	$y = a\,e^{kx}$
$\sin kx$ or $\cos kx$	$y = a\cos kx + b\sin kx$
$\sinh kx$ or $\cosh kx$	$y = a\,e^{kx} + b\,e^{-kx}$ or $y = c\cosh kx + d\sinh kx$

Note that if $f(x)$ is a sum of several functions then the corresponding trial solution can be obtained by using an appropriate sum of trial solutions. A similar rule holds for products, provided we interpret the product of trial solutions in the widest sense. We shall later consider an example which illustrates this point.

Example □ Consider the equation

$$\frac{d^2y}{dx^2} - 7\frac{dy}{dx} + 10y = 2\,e^{-x}$$

From Table 20.1 we see that a suitable trial solution is $y = a\,e^{-x}$, where a is a constant which we shall need to obtain. (The presence of the factor 2 has no influence on the choice of trial solution.) Now differentiating we obtain

$$\frac{dy}{dx} = -a\,e^{-x} \qquad \frac{d^2y}{dx^2} = a\,e^{-x}$$

Therefore substituting,

$$a\,e^{-x} - 7(-a\,e^{-x}) + 10a\,e^{-x} = 2e^{-x}$$

Since e^{-x} is never zero we can divide out to obtain

$$a + 7a + 10a = 2$$

from which $a = 1/9$. So a particular solution (PS) is $y = e^{-x}/9$.

By way of revision, write down the complementary part (CP) and thereby the general solution (GS). It shouldn't take more than three minutes. When you have done it, move ahead to check the result.

Here it is then:

$$CP = A\,e^{2x} + B\,e^{5x}$$
$$PS = e^{-x}/9$$
$$GS = CP + PS$$

so that

$$y = A\,e^{2x} + B\,e^{5x} + e^{-x}/9$$

is the general solution.   ■

Now it's time for you to take a few steps on your own.

_____ 20.6 Workshop_____

▷**Exercise**   Solve the differential equations

a $\dfrac{d^2y}{dx^2} - 6\dfrac{dy}{dx} + 8y = 2x^2$

b $\dfrac{d^2y}{dx^2} + 2\dfrac{dy}{dx} + 5y = \cos 2x$

Write down in each case a suitable trial solution. Only when you have done this should you read on.

The trial solution for equation **a** is

$$y = ax^2 + bx + c$$

Don't forget to include $bx + c$. We must allow for the possibility of a *general* polynomial of degree 2, and this would include a term in x and a constant.
   If you didn't get that right then check your trial solution for equation **b** before taking the next step.

The trial solution for equation **b** is

$$y = a\cos 2x + b\sin 2x$$

It is worth remarking that we should use the same trial solution in the case $f(x) = \cos 2x + \sin 2x$.
   Good, now we can proceed to obtain particular solutions. Let's concentrate on equation **a** for the moment. Have a go!

From $y = ax^2 + bx + c$ it follows that

$$\frac{dy}{dx} = 2ax + b \qquad \frac{d^2y}{dx^2} = 2a$$

So on substituting into equation **a** we require the following equation to hold for all x:

$$2a - 6(2ax + b) + 8(ax^2 + bx + c) = 2x^2$$

Therefore

$$(8a - 2)x^2 + (8b - 12a)x + (8c - 6b + 2a) \equiv 0$$

Consequently $8a = 2$, from which $a = 1/4$. Next $8b - 12a = 0$, from which $b = 3/8$. Finally $8c - 6b + 2a = 0$, from which $4c = 3b - a = 9/8 - 1/4 = 7/8$ and $c = 7/32$.

Therefore a particular solution for **a** is

$$y = \frac{x^2}{4} + \frac{3x}{8} + \frac{7}{32}$$

If that didn't quite work out in the way it should, see where you went wrong and try extra carefully to find a particular solution for equation **b**. When it has been done, move to the next step.

---

5 Using $y = a \cos 2x + b \sin 2x$, we have

$$\frac{dy}{dx} = -2a \sin 2x + 2b \cos 2x$$

$$\frac{d^2y}{dx^2} = -4a \cos 2x - 4b \sin 2x$$

So substituting these into the differential equation, we are seeking to satisfy the identity

$$(-4a \cos 2x - 4b \sin 2x) + 2(-2a \sin 2x + 2b \cos 2x) \\ + 5(a \cos 2x + b \sin 2x) \equiv \cos 2x$$

So we require

$$(-4a + 4b + 5a) \cos 2x + (-4b - 4a + 5b) \sin 2x \equiv \cos 2x$$

It follows that $a + 4b = 1$ and $b - 4a = 0$. So $17a = 1$, and consequently $a = 1/17$ and $b = 4/17$.

A particular solution for **b** is therefore

$$y = \frac{\cos 2x + 4 \sin 2x}{17}$$

Lastly, write down the general solutions and take the final step.

---

6 Here are the answers. You should not have had any difficulty here.

a $y = A e^{2x} + B e^{4x} + \frac{x^2}{4} + \frac{3x}{8} + \frac{7}{32}$

b $y = e^{-x}(A \cos 2x + B \sin 2x) + \dfrac{\cos 2x + 4 \sin 2x}{17}$

where A and B are arbitrary constants.

20.7 THE BREAKDOWN CASE

As we mentioned earlier, there is one situation in which it is possible to anticipate that the trial solution will not work. This is known as the breakdown case – not because of its effect on a hard-working student, but because the standard trial solution does not produce a particular solution. To anticipate when this is going to arise it is essential that we find the complementary part of the solution first. There is much to be said in favour of doing this anyhow, since it is a routine procedure and in an examination represents easy marks.

Suppose the trial solution y which is suggested by Table 20.1 is already present, with some suitable choice of A and B, in the complementary part. This means that y satisfies the homogeneous equation; that is, the equation when $f(x) \equiv 0$. Consequently it cannot possibly satisfy the non-homogeneous equation: that is, the equation when $f(x) \neq 0$. So then it's a dead duck!

What are we to do about it? Luckily there is a simple remedy:

1 Locate the part of the trial solution which corresponds to the complementary part;
2 Multiply it by x and construct a new trial solution;
3 Check again with the complementary part;
4 Repeat this procedure, if necessary, to ensure that the trial solution contains no terms in the complementary part.

An example will illustrate the procedure adequately.

□ Solve the equation   **Example**

$$\frac{d^2y}{dx^2} - 6\frac{dy}{dx} + 9y = e^{3x}$$

First we find the complementary part. The auxiliary equation is

$$m^2 - 6m + 9 = 0$$

from which $(m - 3)^2 = 0$ and so $m = 3$ (repeated). Consequently

$$CP = (A + Bx)e^{3x}$$

Now we seek a particular solution. Here $f(x) = e^{3x}$, and so the standard trial solution is $y = a\,e^{3x}$. However, this is already part of the complementary part ($A = a$ and $B = 0$). So we try instead $y = ax\,e^{3x}$ and check if this is all right. Is it?

No it isn't, is it? If we choose $A = 0$ and $B = a$ then we see it is still part of the complementary part. We therefore repeat the prescription, and this time all is well: $y = ax^2 e^{3x}$ is suitable.

The main advantage in anticipating the breakdown case is that we avoid waste of time and effort, for the standard trial solution will fail anyway and we will find ourselves back at square one. ∎

We shall encounter the breakdown case in a different context in section 21.7.

A few steps will convince you how easy it is to anticipate the breakdown case and take appropriate action.

20.8 Workshop

1 **Exercise**   Suppose

$$CP = A e^{4x} + B e^{-2x}$$

and

$$f(x) = e^{-2x}$$

What would be an appropriate trial solution?

When you have completed your answer, take the next step and see if you were correct.

2 Our initial trial solution would be

$$y = a e^{-2x}$$

However, this is already present in the complementary part when $A = 0$ and $B = a$, and so we have the breakdown case. Consequently we select

$$y = ax e^{-2x}$$

and this is fine.

Did you manage that? If you did, then move to step 4. If you made an error, follow through the argument carefully and then do this one.

▷**Exercise**   Find an appropriate trial solution for

$$CP = (A + Bx) e^{-2x}$$
$$f(x) = e^{-2x}$$

Try it, then step ahead.

3 Our initial trial solution would be

$$y = a e^{-2x}$$

However, this is already present in the complementary part when $A = a$ and $B = 0$ and so we have the breakdown case. Consequently

$$y = ax\,e^{-2x}$$

but this too is the breakdown case. We see this by putting $A = 0$ and $B = a$. Therefore

$$y = ax^2\,e^{-2x}$$

and this will certainly do.
   Got it now? Step forward.

▷**Exercise**   Find an appropriate trial solution for

|4|

$$CP = (A\,e^{4x} + B\,e^{-2x})$$
$$f(x) = \cosh 2x + 1$$

Try it, then step ahead.

We can easily make a mistake here. If we use the standard trial solution in the form

|5|

$$y = a\cosh 2x + b\sinh 2x + c$$

we shall have failed to appreciate the difficulty. However, if we first express $f(x)$ in exponential form then the light will begin to dawn:

$$f(x) = \tfrac{1}{2}(e^{2x} + e^{-2x}) + 1$$

The e^{2x} term and the constant term are no problem, but the term in e^{-2x} is another matter altogether. If it had appeared on its own we should have the standard trial solution

$$y = a\,e^{-2x}$$

which is the breakdown case ($A = 0$ and $B = a$). So we should modify our trial solution and try instead

$$y = ax\,e^{-2x}$$

Consequently our trial solution should be, in the problem we are considering,

$$y = ax\,e^{-2x} + b\,e^{2x} + c$$

If you couldn't get that, try the next exercise. If you were successful, move to step 7.

▷**Exercise**   Find an appropriate trial solution for

$$CP = (A + Bx)\,e^{-2x}$$
$$f(x) = \cosh 2x + 1$$

Then take another step.

6

This is a very similar problem to the one we were considering in steps 4 and 5. However, here it is necessary to modify the trial solution twice. That is, $y = a\,e^{-2x}$ appears in the complementary part ($A = a$ and $B = 0$) and so too does $y = ax\,e^{-2x}$ ($A = 0$ and $B = a$), so that the component of the trial solution corresponding to e^{-2x} must be $ax^2\,e^{-2x}$.

Therefore our trial solution is

$$y = ax^2\,e^{-2x} + b\,e^{2x} + c$$

If there are still problems, read through the text carefully and try the exercises again. Then move on.

7

Exercise   Find an appropriate trial solution for

$$CP = e^{-2x}(A \cos x + B \sin x)$$
$$f(x) = e^{-2x} \cos x$$

Then take the final step.

8

If we had $f(x) = \cos x$ we should try

$$y = a \cos x + b \sin x$$

On the other hand, if we had $f(x) = e^{-2x}$ we should try

$$y = c\,e^{-2x}$$

For the product we can generalize and try

$$y = e^{-2x}(a \cos x + b \sin x)$$

where the constant c has been absorbed by a and b. However, this appears in the complementary part ($A = a$ and $B = b$), and so finally we try instead

$$y = x\,e^{-2x}(a \cos x + b \sin x)$$

!

There is a subtle point which is worth a remark. Suppose $f(x) = x \cos x$. Then corresponding to x we should normally try $ax + b$, and corresponding to $\cos x$ we should normally try $c \cos x + d \sin x$. We might therefore think that we should try

$$y = (ax + b)(c \cos x + d \sin x)$$

or, absorbing one of the constants,

$$y = (x + c)(a \cos x + b \sin x)$$

(a, b and c are different here, of course.) However, this presumes relationships between the coefficients which may not hold. Instead we must consider the generalized product and try

$$y = ax \cos x + bx \sin x + c \cos x + d \sin x$$

In summary, to obtain the general solution of a non-homogeneous second-order linear differential equation:

$$a\frac{d^2y}{dx^2} + b\frac{dy}{dx} + cy = f(x)$$

where a, b and c are real constants ($a \neq 0$):

1 Obtain u, the complementary part. This is the general solution to the equation

$$a\frac{d^2y}{dx^2} + b\frac{dy}{dx} + cy = 0$$

2 Obtain v, a particular solution of the equation

$$a\frac{d^2y}{dx^2} + b\frac{dy}{dx} + cy = f(x)$$

3 Then the general solution is given by $y = u + v$. That is, general solution = complementary part + particular solution.
4 If initial conditions are given then A and B, the two arbitrary constants generated by the complementary part, can now be determined.

20.9 HIGHER-ORDER EQUATIONS

The methods which we have developed can be generalized to higher-order linear differential equations with real constant coefficients. The generalization holds no surprises.

We begin by writing down the auxiliary equation and obtaining its roots. For example,

$$am^3 + bm^2 + cm + d = 0$$

where a, b, c and d are real constants.
The complementary part is constituted in the following way:
1 A distinct root m contributes

$$A\,e^{mx}$$

to the complementary part.

2 Equal roots $m_1 = m_2 = m_3\ (=m)$ contribute

$$(A + Bx + Cx^2)\, e^{mx}$$

to the complementary part.

3 Complex roots always occur in conjugate pairs $\alpha \pm i\beta$, and so these contribute

$$\exp(\alpha x)\{A \cos \beta x + B \sin \beta x\}$$

to the complementary part.

In this description A, B and C are of course arbitrary constants.

20.10 DAMPING

Suppose we consider the equation

$$a\,\frac{d^2 x}{dt^2} + b\,\frac{dx}{dt} + cx = f(t)$$

Then

1 If $b^2 - 4ac < 0$ and if the roots of the auxiliary equation are $\alpha \pm i\beta$ we have

$$\alpha = -\frac{b}{2a} \qquad \beta = \frac{\sqrt{(4ac - b^2)}}{2a}$$

The complementary part is then

Damped systems arise frequently in applications.

$$\exp(\alpha t)(A \cos \beta t + B \sin \beta t)$$

α is called the **damping factor**. If $\alpha < 0$ then as $t \to \infty$ the complementary part will decay. This means that the complementary part will tend to 0 as t tends to ∞. The angular frequency β is known as the **natural frequency** of the equation.

2 If $b^2 - 4ac = 0$ the system (the physical system which gives rise to the equation) is said to be **critically damped**, for then $\alpha = -b/(2a)$ and $\beta = 0$.

3 If $b^2 - 4ac > 0$ the system is said to be **overdamped**.

Example ☐ The equation of simple harmonic motion is

$$\frac{d^2 x}{dt^2} + \omega^2 x = 0$$

Simple harmonic motion (SHM) occurs in mechanical and electrical systems.

Here $\alpha = 0$ and $\beta = \omega$, so that $x = A \cos \omega t + B \sin \omega t$. The natural frequency is ω and there is no damping. ∎

20.11 RESONANCE

As an example, consider an LC series circuit to which an EMF $E \sin pt$ is applied; L, C, E and p are positive real constants. The charge q on the capacitor is given by

$$\frac{d^2q}{dt^2} + \frac{q}{LC} = \frac{E}{L} \sin pt$$

The auxiliary equation is

$$m^2 + \frac{1}{LC} = 0$$

and so $m = \pm i\omega$ where $\omega = 1/\sqrt{(LC)}$ is the natural frequency.

If p is set equal to ω then we have the breakdown case and consequently

$$q = A \cos \omega t + B \sin \omega t - \frac{Et}{2\omega L} \cos \omega t$$

The significance of this is that q is unbounded, so in practice the charge will increase until the capacitor fails. This contrasts sharply with the case where $p \neq \omega$:

$$q = A \cos \omega t + B \sin \omega t + \frac{E}{L(\omega^2 - p^2)} \sin pt$$

Here q remains bounded.

The frequency ω is called the **resonant frequency**. Resonance occurs when the frequency of f, the forcing function, is tuned to that of the natural frequency. Resonance occurs in a wide variety of situations. For instance, platoons of soldiers break step when marching over a bridge so that there is no danger of resonance undermining the structure.

20.12 TRANSIENT AND STEADY STATE

Any part of the solution x of a differential equation which tends to zero as the independent variable t tends to infinity is known as a **transient**. When t is large enough for the transients to be neglected, that which remains is known as the **steady state**. In this way we obtain the equation

Those studying structural mechanics or circuit theory will need to be able to give a physical interpretation of the arbitrary constants which arise in the solution of the differential equation.

$$\text{general solution} = \text{transient} + \text{steady state}$$

It is a mistake, however, to assume that the complementary part is necessarily the transient and that the particular solution is the steady state, although in some cases this is true.

☐ Solve the differential equation   **Example**

$$\frac{d^2x}{dt^2} + \frac{dx}{dt} - 6x = e^{-t}$$

Identify the transient and steady state.

The auxiliary equation is $m^2 + m - 6 = 0$, from which $m = -3$ or $m = 2$. The complementary part is therefore $A \, e^{-3t} + B \, e^{2t}$.

For a particular solution we try $x = a \, e^{-t}$, from which $x' = -a \, e^{-t}$ and $x'' = a \, e^{-t}$. Therefore $a \, e^{-t} - a \, e^{-t} - 6a \, e^{-t} = e^{-t}$. Consequently $a = -1/6$ and a particular solution is $x = -e^{-t}/6$.

The general solution is now

$$x = A \, e^{-3t} + B \, e^{2t} - e^{-t}/6$$

Here the transient is $A \, e^{-3t} - e^{-t}/6$ and the steady state is $B \, e^{2t}$. ■

Example □ Obtain the transient and steady state for the equation

$$4 \, \frac{d^2x}{dt^2} + 9x = e^{-2t}$$

Do this before you read any more.

You will have obtained the complementary part $A \cos (3t/2) + B \sin (3t/2)$ and a particular solution $e^{-2t}/25$. So the general solution is

$$x = A \cos (3t/2) + B \sin (3t/2) + e^{-2t}/25$$

Here the transient is the particular solution $e^{-2t}/25$, and the steady state is the complementary part $A \cos (3t/2) + B \sin (3t/2)$. ■

We now work through examples which include some initial conditions.

_____ 20.13 Practical _____

PRESSURE FILTER

The transpose displacement x of a circular pressure filter at time t is known to satisfy the equation

$$\frac{d^2x}{dt^2} + 2p \frac{dx}{dt} + p^2 = 0$$

where p is a constant. If initially there was no displacement and the speed of displacement x' was a constant q, obtain the displacement x at time t.

There is one nasty trap into which the unwary are likely to step. The equation is not a homogeneous linear equation, for there is no term in x. Let's rearrange it in standard form

$$\frac{d^2x}{dt^2} + 2p \frac{dx}{dt} = -p^2$$

Now we can proceed.

First we seek the complementary part. The auxiliary equation is

$$m^2 + 2mp = 0$$

from which $m(m + 2p) = 0$, so $m = 0$ or $m = -2p$. Therefore

$$CP = A\,e^0 + B\,e^{-2pt} = A + B\,e^{-2pt}$$

Note that the variables are x and t and not y and x respectively.

Now we want a particular solution. Here $f(t) = -p^2$, a constant, so we try $x = a$, a constant. This is the breakdown case; $A = a$ and $B = 0$.

Therefore we modify the trial solution and try $x = at$. With this choice of x we have $x' = a$ and $x'' = 0$, so that substituting we require $0 + 2ap = -p^2$ from which $a = -p/2$. So

$$PS = -\tfrac{1}{2}pt$$

Therefore the general solution is given by

$$x = A + B\,e^{-2pt} - \tfrac{1}{2}pt \tag{1}$$

Now we use the initial conditions to determine A and B. Differentiating throughout with respect to t we obtain

$$x' = -2Bp\,e^{-2pt} - \tfrac{1}{2}p \tag{2}$$

When $t = 0$ we obtain from (1) and (2)

$$0 = A + B$$
$$q = -2Bp - \tfrac{1}{2}p$$

So $B = -(p + 2q)/4p$, and $A = (p + 2q)/4p$.

Finally the solution is

$$x = \frac{p + 2q}{4p}\left(1 - e^{-2pt}\right) - \frac{pt}{2}$$

Here are two problems for *you* to try. The first is an electrical problem, the second a mechanical problem. You may choose which you wish to do.

LC CIRCUIT

An alternating EMF $E \sin nt$ is applied to a quiescent circuit consisting of an inductance L and a capacitance C in series. Obtain the current at time $t > 0$, if $\omega^2 = 1/(LC) \neq n^2$.

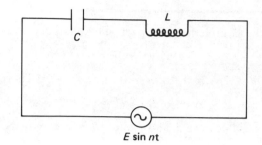

Fig. 20.1 An LC series circuit.

If you cannot cope with the electrical side of this problem, read through the first stage and take over the solution then.

The circuit is illustrated in Fig. 20.1. We have

$$L\frac{di}{dt} + \frac{q}{C} = E \sin nt$$

where i is the current and q is the charge on the capacitor. Now $i = dq/dt$, and so

$$\frac{di}{dt} = \frac{d^2q}{dt^2}$$

Therefore

$$\frac{d^2q}{dt^2} + \frac{1}{LC} q = \frac{E}{L} \sin nt$$

$$\frac{d^2q}{dt^2} + \omega^2 q = \frac{E}{L} \sin nt$$

so that ω is the natural frequency of the circuit. Next we must solve this differential equation.

We begin with the complementary part – a standard routine procedure. The auxiliary equation is

$$m^2 + \omega^2 = 0$$

so that $m = \pm j\omega$. (Notice that here because i denotes current we are adopting the usual practice of writing j instead of the complex number i.)
  With m in the form $\alpha \pm j\beta$ we see that $\alpha = 0$ and $\beta = \omega$. Consequently

$$CP = e^0(A \cos \omega t + B \sin \omega t)$$
$$= A \cos \omega t + B \sin \omega t$$

where A and B are arbitrary constants.

The next step is to find a particular solution.

A glance at the right-hand side of the equation enables us to infer the form of a particular solution. We try $q = a \sin nt + b \cos nt$ and differentiate twice with respect to t to obtain

$$\dot{q} = an \cos nt - bn \sin nt$$
$$\ddot{q} = -an^2 \sin nt - bn^2 \cos nt - n^2(a \sin nt + b \cos nt)$$

So substituting,

$$-n^2(a \sin nt + b \cos nt) + \omega^2(a \sin nt + b \cos nt) = (E/L) \sin nt$$

from which $a(\omega^2 - n^2) = E/L$ and $b(\omega^2 - n^2) = 0$. Since $\omega \neq n$ we can deduce

$$a = \frac{E}{L(\omega^2 - n^2)} \qquad b = 0$$

Therefore a particular solution is

$$q = \frac{E \sin nt}{L(\omega^2 - n^2)}$$

The general solution is then

$$q = A \cos \omega t + B \sin \omega t + \frac{E \sin nt}{L(\omega^2 - n^2)}$$

Initially the circuit is quiescent. This means there is no charge on the capacitor and there is no current. Use this information to obtain the arbitrary constants A and B.

When $t = 0$, $q = 0$ and so $A = 0$. Therefore

$$q = B \sin \omega t + \frac{E \sin nt}{L(\omega^2 - n^2)}$$

So

$$i = \frac{dq}{dt} = B\omega \cos \omega t + \frac{En \cos nt}{L(\omega^2 - n^2)}$$

When $t = 0$, $i = 0$ and so

$$B\omega + \frac{En}{L(\omega^2 - n^2)} = 0$$

$$B\omega = -\frac{En}{L(\omega^2 - n^2)}$$

Finally

$$i = -\frac{En \cos \omega t}{L(\omega^2 - n^2)} + \frac{En \cos nt}{L(\omega^2 - n^2)}$$

$$= \frac{En}{L(\omega^2 - n^2)} (\cos nt - \cos \omega t)$$

See Chapter 8,
Further exercise 15.
You may remember in the further exercises of Chapter 8 using l'Hospital's rule to obtain i when $\omega = n$. This of course corresponds to the breakdown case.

OSCILLATING BODY

A small body of mass m performs oscillations controlled by a spring of stiffness λ and subject to a frictional force of constant magnitude F (Fig. 20.2). The equation which describes the motion is

$$m\ddot{x} = -\lambda x + F$$

where x is the displacement from the position in which the spring has zero tension. The body is released from rest with a displacement a. Obtain the displacement when it next comes to rest.

Try this and see how it goes. We have one slight difficulty: some of the notation which we usually employ has been used here in a different way. We must be nimble in mind and prepared to use other symbols.

We begin as usual by obtaining the complementary part. Let us use u for the variable in the auxiliary equation. We then have

$$mu^2 + \lambda = 0$$

so that putting $\omega^2 = \lambda/m$ (positive) we obtain

$$u^2 + \omega^2 = 0$$

from which $u = \pm i\omega$. Consequently

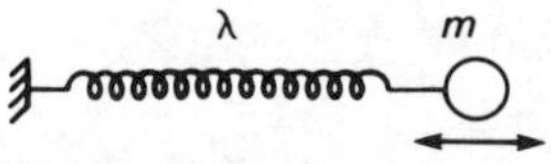

Fig. 20.2 Spring and mass.

$$CP = A \cos \omega t + B \sin \omega t$$

where A and B are arbitrary constants.

Now find a particular solution.

Here the forcing function is F, a constant. Therefore we look for a constant solution. Suppose $x = c$, a constant (we cannot use a). Then substituting, $\lambda c = F$ and so $c = F/\lambda$. A particular solution is therefore obtained:

$$PS = F/\lambda$$

The general solution is then

$$x = A \cos \omega t + B \sin \omega t + F/\lambda$$

Now complete the solution by first determining A and B.

When $t = 0$, $x = a$, so

$$a = A + F/\lambda$$
$$A = a - F/\lambda$$

Also when $t = 0$, $\dot{x} = 0$. Now

$$\dot{x} = -A\omega \sin \omega t + B\omega \cos \omega t$$

so that $0 = B$.

We have

$$x = (a - F/\lambda) \cos \omega t + F/\lambda$$

and also

$$\dot{x} = -(a - F/\lambda) \omega \sin \omega t$$

When the body is next at rest, $\dot{x} = 0$ and so we have $\sin \omega t = 0$. This first occurs when $\omega t = \pi$, and at this time $\cos \omega t = -1$. At this moment the displacement is

$$d = (a - F/\lambda)(-1) + F/\lambda = 2F/\lambda - a$$

SUMMARY

To obtain the general solution of a non-homogeneous second-order linear differential equation:

$$a\frac{d^2y}{dx^2} + b\frac{dy}{dx} + cy = f(x)$$

where a, b and c are real constants ($a \neq 0$):
□ The complementary part u is the general solution of the equation

$$a\frac{d^2y}{dx^2} + b\frac{dy}{dx} + cy = 0$$

To obtain this, write down and solve the auxiliary equation

$$am^2 + bm + c = 0$$

and obtain the roots m_1 and m_2. There are three cases:

a If the roots m_1 and m_2 are both real and distinct,

$$u = A\,e^{m_1 x} + B\,e^{m_2 x}$$

b If the roots m_1 and m_2 are equal, so $m_1 = m_2 = m$,

$$u = (A + Bx)\,e^{mx}$$

c If the roots m_1 and m_2 are complex, so $m = \alpha \pm i\beta$,

$$u = e^{\alpha x}(A \cos \beta x + B \sin \beta x)$$

A and B are arbitrary constants.
□ Examine u carefully to see whether $f(x)$ corresponds to the breakdown case. Then obtain v, a particular solution of the equation

$$a\frac{d^2y}{dx^2} + b\frac{dy}{dx} + cy = f(x)$$

using a trial solution.
□ Then

$$y = u + v$$

general solution = complementary part + particular solution

□ If boundary conditions are given then the constants A and B can be determined.

EXERCISES (for answers see p. 757)

1 Obtain the general solution of

  a $2\dfrac{d^2x}{dt^2} - 7\dfrac{dx}{dt} + 3x = 0$

  b $\dfrac{d^2x}{dt^2} - 2\dfrac{dx}{dt} + 10x = 0$

  c $9\dfrac{d^2y}{dx^2} - 24\dfrac{dy}{dx} + 16y = 0$

2 Obtain the general solution of

  a $2\dfrac{d^2x}{dt^2} - 9\dfrac{dx}{dt} - 5x = t$

  b $3\dfrac{d^2y}{dx^2} - 8\dfrac{dy}{dx} + 4y = e^{2x}$

  c $9\dfrac{d^2u}{dx^2} - 9\dfrac{du}{dx} + 2u = e^{x}$

  d $5\dfrac{d^2y}{dx^2} - 4\dfrac{dy}{dx} + y = \cos x$

3 Obtain the solution which satisfies the conditions that when $t = 0$, $x = 0$ and $dx/dt = 0$ for

  a $\dfrac{d^2x}{dt^2} - 6\dfrac{dx}{dt} + 10x = \sin t$

  b $3\dfrac{d^2x}{dt^2} - 16\dfrac{dx}{dt} + 5x = e^{5t}$

  c $25\dfrac{d^2x}{dt^2} - 30\dfrac{dx}{dt} + 9x = t\,e^{3t/5}$

ASSIGNMENT (for answers see p. 758; see also Workshops on pp. 574, 581 and 584)

Obtain the general solutions of each of the following differential equations:

1 $4\dfrac{d^2y}{dx^2} - 4\dfrac{dy}{dx} + y = e^{x}$

2 $\dfrac{d^2y}{dt^2} + 4\dfrac{dy}{dt} + 8y = \cos 2t$

3 $\dfrac{d^2x}{dt^2} + 2\dfrac{dx}{dt} - 3x = e^{2t}$

4 $\dfrac{d^2u}{dv^2} - 8\dfrac{du}{dv} + 16u = v^2$

5 $\dfrac{d^2s}{dt^2} + 6\dfrac{ds}{dt} + 10s = \cos t$

6 $\dfrac{d^2u}{dt^2} - 7\dfrac{du}{dt} + 10u = 1 + e^{5t}$

7 $\dfrac{d^2y}{dx^2} + 6\dfrac{dy}{dx} + 9y = e^{-3x} + e^x$

8 $\dfrac{d^2y}{du^2} - 3\dfrac{dy}{du} - 10y = \cosh 2u$

9 $\dfrac{d^2y}{dx^2} + 2\dfrac{dy}{dx} + 10y = e^{-x}\cos 3x$

10 $\dfrac{d^2y}{dw^2} + \dfrac{dy}{dw} - 2y = w\cos w$

FURTHER EXERCISES (for answers see p. 758)

1 A constant EMF E is applied to a series circuit with resistance R, capacitance C and inductance L. Given that

$$L\frac{di}{dt} + Ri + \frac{q}{C} = E$$

where, at time t, q is the charge on the capacitor and i is the current. Show that the system will oscillate if $4L > CR^2$.

2 The differential equation representing the simple harmonic motion (SHM) of a particle of unit mass is

$$\ddot{x} = -\lambda^2 x$$

where λ is a constant and the dots denote differentiation with respect to time. Solve this equation and express x in terms of t, given that x is zero when $t = 0$ and that the speed is u at $x = a$.

3 A capacitor of capacitance C discharges through a circuit of resistance R and inductance L. Show that if $CR^2 = 4L$ the discharge is just non-oscillatory. The initial voltage is E and $CR^2 = 4L$. Show that the charge q on the capacitor and the current i are given by

$$q = \frac{2E}{R}\left(\frac{2L}{R} + t\right)\exp(-Rt/2L)$$

$$i = -\frac{Et}{L}\exp(-Rt/2L)$$

4 The differential equation for the deflection y of a light cantilever of length c clamped horizontally at one end and with a concentrated load W at the other satisfies the equation

$$EI \frac{d^2y}{dx^2} = W(c - x)$$

where EI is the flexural rigidity and is constant. Show that the deflection at the free end is $Wc^3/3EI$.

5 The displacement x in metres at time t in seconds of a vibrating governor is given by the differential equation

$$\ddot{x} + x = \sin 2t$$

where dots denote differentiation. Initially the displacement and the speed are zero. Show that the next time the speed is instantaneously zero is when $t = 2\pi/3$ seconds.

6 An EMF $E \sin \omega t$ (where E and ω are constant) is applied to an RLC series circuit. The charge q on the capacitor and the current i are both initially zero. Show that if $CR^2 = 4L$ and $\omega^2 = 1/LC$ then at time t

$$i = (E/R) [\sin \omega t - \omega t \exp (-\omega t)]$$

7 The components of acceleration for a model which simulates the movement of a particle in a plane are

$$\ddot{x} = \omega \dot{y}$$
$$\ddot{y} = a\omega^2 - \omega \dot{x}$$

where a and ω are constant. When $t = 0$ the particle is stationary at the origin. Show that subsequently it describes the curve defined parametrically by

$$x = a(\theta - \sin \theta)$$
$$y = a(1 - \cos \theta)$$

where $\theta = \omega t$.

8 A light horizontal strut of length L and flexural rigidity EI carries a concentrated load W at its midpoint. It is supported at each end and subjected to a compressive force P. The deflection y at a point distance x from one end is given by

$$\frac{d^2y}{dx^2} + n^2y = -\frac{Wn^2x}{2P} \quad \left(0 \le x \le \frac{L}{2}\right)$$

where $n^2 = P/EI$. Solve this equation to show that the greatest deflection of the strut which occurs at its midpoint is

$$\frac{WL}{4P} \left[\frac{\tan (nL/2)}{nL/2} - 1\right]$$

9 The current i in an LRC series circuit satisfies

$$L \frac{d^2i}{dt^2} + R \frac{di}{dt} + \frac{1}{C}i = E \cos nt$$

where L, R, C, E and n are constant and t denotes time. Given that R is positive, show that the exponential terms in the solution of this equation are transient. Show further that when the transient terms are ignored,

$$i = E\,\frac{nR \sin nt + (1/C - Ln^2) \cos nt}{R^2 n^2 + (1/C - Ln^2)^2}$$

10 A beam of length L and of weight w per unit length is clamped horizontally at both ends. The beam is subject to an axial compressive load P. The deflection y is related to the distance x from one end by the equation

$$EIy'' + Py = G - \tfrac{1}{2}wLx + \tfrac{1}{2}wx^2 \qquad \left(0 \leqslant x \leqslant \frac{L}{2}\right)$$

Thomas Young (1773–1829): English physicist who worked on the theory of light, molecular measurements and elasticity.

where G is the clamping couple, E is Young's modulus and I is the moment of inertia, and the dashes indicate differentiation with respect to x. Show that

$$y = \frac{1}{P}\left[\left(\frac{w}{n^2} - G\right)\cos nx + \frac{wL}{2n}\sin nx + G - \frac{w}{n^2}\right.$$
$$\left. - \frac{1}{2}wLx + \frac{1}{2}wx^2\right]$$

where $n^2 = P/EI$.

21 Difference equations

In Chapters 19 and 20 we looked at the problems involved in solving differential equations. The purpose of this chapter is to do the same for difference equations.

Long before calculus was discovered, difference equations were used extensively. More recently they have gained a new importance, partly because of computer simulations of dynamical systems and the finite element method of analysing continuous structures.

After we have considered the solution of difference equations we shall draw together some common themes and introduce operational methods for solving both types of equation.

After completing this chapter you should be able to
☐ Identify a linear difference equation and put it in standard form;
☐ Solve homogeneous linear difference equations of the first and second order with constant coefficients;
☐ Use the method of trial solutions to obtain a particular solution for certain difference equations;
☐ Obtain the general solutions for many difference equations;
☐ Obtain solutions of difference equations satisfying prescribed boundary values.
At the end of this chapter we solve a practical problem in beam deflection.

21.1 VARIABLES

When a digital computer performs calculations it uses either input data or numbers which it has previously calculated. Similarly when a dynamical system is simulated numerically the appropriate responses at any given point are usually expressed in terms of known responses at other points. In these situations the mathematical functions which describe them are known as functions of **discrete** variables to distinguish them from functions of **continuous** variables.

To see the difference more clearly we can consider the graphs of the functions involved (Fig. 21.1). For a continuous variable the domain will consist of intervals, whereas for a discrete variable the domain will consist of isolated points.

When we come to algebraic descriptions, the distinction is highlighted even more clearly. We shall consider real-valued functions which are defined on real numbers.

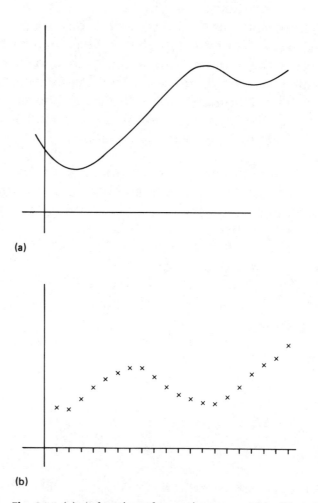

(a)

(b)

Fig. 21.1 (a) A function of a continuous variable (b) A function of a discrete variable.

1 For a function of a continuous variable the domain of the function is an interval, a collection of intervals or possibly even an infinite interval such as $\mathbb{R}$.

2 For a function of a discrete variable the domain of the function consists of isolated points, for example the set of integers $\mathbb{Z}$. Other examples are the set of natural numbers $\mathbb{N}$ or any finite set.

This distinction is often highlighted by the notation we employ. Continuous variables are usually denoted by x, y or t, whereas discrete variables are usually denoted by r, n or m. However, this agreement is very informal and often broken, so that it is always best to make it clear if the variable is continuous or discrete by indicating the domain of the function clearly.

☐ Classify the domains of the following functions as either continuous or **Example** discrete:

a $f : \mathbb{R} \to \mathbb{R}$ defined by $f(x) = \sin x$ when $x \in \mathbb{R}$.
b $f : (-1, 1) \to \mathbb{R}$ defined by $f(t) = \sin^{-1} t$ when $t \in (-1, 1)$.
c $f : \mathbb{Z} \to \mathbb{N}$ defined by $f(x) = x^2$ when $x \in \mathbb{Z}$.
d $f : A \to \mathbb{R}$ where $A = (-1, 1) \cup \{2, 3, 4\}$ defined by $f(t) = t^3$.

You may like to see if you can do these on your own.

Let us carefully analyse each case:

1 The domain consists of all the real numbers, and this is certainly a continuous set.
2 The domain is an open interval, and so this too is a continuous set.
3 The domain consists of the integers, and this is a discrete set.
4 The domain consists of a real interval together with some isolated points, and this is neither a discrete nor a continuous set.   ∎

The advent of computer technology has highlighted the need for mathematics involving discrete variables. In this chapter we are concerned with functions of discrete variables which are defined recursively: that is, the value at each stage is defined in terms of the values at previous stages. We shall wish to obtain explicit expressions for these functions. An example will illustrate the general idea.

☐ Suppose $u(n)$ is defined for all natural numbers n by the formula   **Example**

$$u(n + 2) = u(n + 1) + u(n)$$

where $u(1) = 1$ and $u(2) = 1$. The requirement then would be to obtain $u(n)$ explicitly in terms of n.   ∎

This equation first arose as a model discussed by Leonardo of Pisa, Fibonacci, in the twelfth century to describe a population of rabbits, where n denotes the number of months. Clearly there is an assumption that the first two rabbits have opposite gender!

Leonardo of Pisa (1170–1250): Italian who wrote on arithmetic, geometry and algebra. He was the most productive mathematician of the Middle Ages.

The formula $u(n + 2) = u(n + 1) + u(n)$ is often known as a **recursion**, but we shall use the other name in common use and call it a **difference equation**. We shall concern ourselves in particular with the solution of one type, known as a linear difference equation with constant coefficients.

To be specific, we shall be concerned with the equation

$$as(n + 2) + bs(n + 1) + cs(n) = f(n)$$

where a, b and c are constants and $f(n)$ depends only on n. We wish to determine $s(n)$ in terms of n. If a is non-zero we have a second-order difference equation, whereas if a is zero but b is non-zero we have a first-order difference equation. So Fibonacci's equation is a second-order difference equation.

It is important to realize that we are using function notation here, so that $s(n + 2) \neq sn + 2s$ just as $f(x + h) \neq fx + fh$. This may seem a trivial point to make, but it is surprising how often this notation can give rise to problems.

If you have already studied second-order differential equations (Chapter 20) you will soon find echoes of it in the work we are about to do.

As already stated, the equation which we shall be studying is

$$as(n + 2) + bs(n + 1) + cs(n) = f(n)$$

where a, b and c are constants and $f(n)$ depends only on n. We are seeking an explicit formula for $s(n)$ in terms of n, consistent with the difference equation and which satisfies any starting values which we may have, such as $s(1)$ or $s(2)$.

We shall consider the equation in two stages. In the first instance we shall confine our attention to the case where $f(n) \equiv 0$. This is known as the homogeneous case. Later we shall extend our discussion to the non-homogeneous case, where $f(n) \not\equiv 0$.

21.2 THE HOMOGENEOUS CASE

FIRST-ORDER EQUATIONS

This is a very straightforward situation. We must consider the equation

$$as(n + 1) + bs(n) = 0$$

where a and b are constant and $a \neq 0$. It will be convenient for us to assume that this difference equation holds for all natural numbers and also $n = 0$.

If we divide through by a and rearrange the equation we obtain

$$s(n + 1) = \frac{-b}{a} s(n) = ms(n)$$

where $m = -b/a$. Now this gives

$$s(1) = ms(0)$$
$$s(2) = ms(1) = m^2 s(0)$$
$$s(3) = ms(2) = m^3 s(0)$$

Now you don't need the insight of Einstein to spot the general formula for $s(n)$, do you? We have

$$s(n) = m^n s(0)$$

A formal proof of this formula can be given using mathematical induction. However, it would be an exceedingly sceptical student who would doubt this formula holds.

So then we have a general expression

$$s(n) = Am^n$$

where A is an arbitrary constant and m satisfies the equation $am + b = 0$. Clearly, since $A = s(0)$, A is fixed not by the difference equation but by the starting value. A different starting value will change the value of A.

So given a first-order difference equation

$$as(n + 1) + bs(n) = 0$$

the general solution is

$$s(n) = Am^n$$

where A is an arbitrary constant and m satisfies the equation $am + b = 0$.

☐ Obtain an explicit formula for $u(n)$ if

Example

$$u(n) - u(n + 1) = 2[u(n + 1) + u(n)]$$

and $u(1) = 2$.
   We begin by rearranging the equation in standard form:

$$3u(n + 1) + u(n) = 0$$

The equation for m is $3m + 1 = 0$, and so $m = -1/3$. Therefore $u(n) = A(-1/3)^n$ is the general solution. Finally, we use the starting value $u(1) = 2$ to give $2 = A(-1/3)$, and so $A = -6$. Therefore

$$u(n) = -6(-1/3)^n$$ ■

Now you try one.

☐ Solve the equation

Example

$$P(n + 1) - P(n) = 5P(n) + 3P(n + 1)$$

where n is a natural number and $P(3) = 9$.
   Try it on your own first, then look ahead.

Albert Einstein (1879–1955): German Swiss physicist who originated the theory of relativity. Settled in USA 1933.

We discussed mathematical induction in section 1.4.

Rearranging the equation into standard form gives

$$2P(n + 1) + 6P(n) = 0$$
$$P(n + 1) + 3P(n) = 0$$

The equation for m is $m + 3 = 0$, and so $m = -3$. Consequently, the general solution is $P(n) = A(-3)^n$ where A is an arbitrary constant. Lastly, using the starting value for n, $P(3) = 9 = A(-3)^3 = -27A$, so $A = (-1/3)$. Consequently

$$P(n) = (-1/3)(-3)^n = (-3)^{n-1}$$ ∎

SECOND-ORDER EQUATIONS

We have seen that to determine $s(n)$ completely, a first-order difference equation requires one boundary value. Similarly a second-order difference equation will require two boundary values if we are to determine $s(n)$ without any arbitrary constants. To put it another way, the general solution of a second-order difference equation must contain two independent arbitrary constants.

Example □ Show that if $p(n)$ and $q(n)$ are any two solutions of the difference equation

$$as(n + 2) + bs(n + 1) + cs(n) = 0$$

then $Ap(n) + Bq(n)$ is also a solution, where A and B are arbitrary constants.

We have

$$ap(n + 2) + bp(n + 1) + cp(n) = 0 \tag{1}$$
$$aq(n + 2) + bq(n + 1) + cq(n) = 0 \tag{2}$$

and must show that $s(n) = Ap(n) + Bq(n)$ also satisfies the difference equation. Now

$$s(n + 1) = Ap(n + 1) + Bq(n + 1)$$
$$s(n + 2) = Ap(n + 2) + Bq(n + 2)$$

so that

$$\begin{aligned} as(n + 2) + bs(n + 1) + cs(n) &= a[Ap(n + 2) + Bq(n + 2)] \\ &\quad + b[Ap(n + 1) + Bq(n + 1)] \\ &\quad + c[Ap(n) + Bq(n)] \\ &= A[ap(n + 2) + bp(n + 1) + cp(n)] \\ &\quad + B[aq(n + 2) + bq(n + 1) + cq(n)] \\ &= A0 + B0 = 0 \end{aligned}$$

using (1) and (2). So $s(n)$ satisfies the difference equation.   ∎

Now this example was not just an algebraic exercise. It gives us some important information which we shall now use.

We have the equation

$$as(n + 2) + bs(n + 1) + cs(n) = 0$$

where a, b and c are real constants and $a \neq 0$. We have shown that if we can obtain two solutions $p(n)$ and $q(n)$ then

$$s(n) = Ap(n) + Bq(n)$$

is also a solution.

Consequently the problem of solving the difference equation is reduced to that of finding two linearly independent solutions $p(n)$ and $q(n)$. We say that $p(n)$ and $q(n)$ are **linearly independent** if the equation $Ap(n) + Bq(n) = 0$ is satisfied only when the constants A and B are zero.

How are we to obtain two linearly independent solutions? At the moment we don't know any at all!

See section 22.7 for a discussion of linear independence. The concept also arises in sections 13.8 and 20.2.

21.3 THE AUXILIARY EQUATION

The clue comes from the work we did solving the first-order equation. There we found a solution of the form $s(n) = m^n$ where m was a constant.

Let's look and see if there is a solution of this form for the second-order equation. If $s(n) = m^n$ then $s(n + 1) = m^{n+1}$ and $s(n + 2) = m^{n+2}$, so that substituting we require

$$am^{n+2} + bm^{n+1} + cm^n = 0$$

which on dividing by m^n produces

$$am^2 + bm + c = 0$$

This quadratic equation, which can be written down directly from the difference equation, is given a special name to emphasize its importance. It is called the **auxiliary equation**.

This is the same equation that we met in a different context in section 20.2.

So we have shown that $s(n) = m^n$, where m is constant, is a solution of the difference equation

$$as(n + 2) + bs(n + 1) + cs(n) = 0$$

if

$$am^2 + bm + c = 0$$

Now the auxiliary equation has two roots m_1 and m_2, and depending on their nature there are three different situations which can arise:
1 distinct real roots
2 equal roots
3 complex roots.
We shall deal with them in turn.

Distinct real roots

If the auxiliary equation has distinct real roots m_1 and m_2 then the difference equation has two linearly independent solutions $p(n) = m_1^n$ and $q(n) = m_2^n$. So the general solution is

$$s(n) = Am_1^n + Bm_1^n$$

where A and B are arbitrary constants.

To see how straightforward this is, let's look at an example.

Example ☐ Obtain the solution to the equation $y(n + 2) = y(n + 1) + 6y(n)$ which satisfies the conditions $y(1) = 8$ and $y(2) = 14$.

You can try this first if you like.

The equation must first be written in standard form:

$$y(n + 2) - y(n + 1) - 6y(n) = 0$$

From this the auxiliary equation is

$$m^2 - m - 6 = 0$$

This factorizes to give

$$(m - 3)(m + 2) = 0$$

and so $m = 3$ or $m = -2$. The roots of the auxiliary equation are real and distinct, and consequently

$$y(n) = A3^n + B(-2)^n$$

is the general solution, where A and B are arbitrary constants.

To obtain A and B we substitute the values $n = 1$ and $n = 2$ into this solution:

$$y(1) = 3A - 2B = 8$$
$$y(2) = 9A + 4B = 14$$

Doubling the first and adding to the second gives $15A = 30$, so $A = 2$. Substituting into the first equation gives $B = -1$. So the solution is

$$y(n) = (2)3^n - (-2)^n \qquad \blacksquare$$

Equal roots

If the auxiliary equation has equal roots then $m_1 = m_2 = m$ and we have only one solution to our difference equation. We need another linearly independent solution.

Example ☐ Consider the difference equation

$$as(n + 2) + bs(n + 1) + cs(n) = 0$$

where a, b and c are real constants, $a \neq 0$. Show that if the auxiliary equation

$$am^2 + bm + c = 0$$

has equal roots then $s(n) = nm^n$ is a solution of the difference equation.

To show this it suffices to show that the left-hand side of the difference equation reduces to zero. We have if $s(n) = nm^n$ then $s(n + 1) = (n + 1)m^{n+1}$ and $s(n + 2) = (n + 2)m^{n+2}$. So

$$
\begin{aligned}
as(n + 2) + bs(n + 1) + cs(n) &= a(n + 2)m^{n+2} + b(n + 1)m^{n+1} + cnm^n \\
&= [a(n + 2)m^2 + b(n + 1)m + cn]m^n \\
&= [(am^2 + bm + c)n + (2am + b)m]m^n \\
&= 0
\end{aligned}
$$

This follows because
1 m is a root of the auxiliary equation and so $am^2 + bm + c = 0$;
2 The auxiliary equation has equal roots $m = (-b/2a)$ and so $2am + b = 0$.
This is most fortuitous, as we now have *two* linearly independent solutions $p(n) = m^n$ and $q(n) = nm^n$. Consequently we have all we need, and can write down the general solution

$$s(n) = Am^n + Bnm^n = (A + Bn)m^n \qquad \blacksquare$$

□ Solve the difference equation   **Example**

$$3v(n + 2) = 2[2v(n + 1) + v(n + 2) - 2v(n)]$$

given that n is any integer and that $v(0) = 7$ and $v(1) = 16$.
Try this on your own!

First we must rearrange the equation so that it is in standard form. We obtain

$$
\begin{aligned}
3v(n + 2) &= 4v(n + 1) + 2v(n + 2) - 4v(n) \\
v(n + 2) &- 4v(n + 1) + 4v(n) = 0
\end{aligned}
$$

The auxiliary equation is therefore

$$m^2 - 4m + 4 = 0$$

so that $(m - 2)^2 = 0$ and so $m = 2$ is a repeated root. Consequently,

$$v(n) = (A + Bn)2^n$$

where A and B are arbitrary constants.
Finally we obtain A and B by using the boundary conditions:

$$
\begin{aligned}
v(0) &= (A + 0)2^0 = A = 7 \\
v(1) &= (A + B)2^1 = 2A + 2B = 16
\end{aligned}
$$

so that $A = 7$ and $B = 1$. Therefore

$$v(n) = (7 + n)2^n$$ ∎

Complex roots

The auxiliary equation has real coefficients, and so if there are complex roots they form a conjugate pair (see Chapter 10). Using polar form we can write them as

$$m_1 = r(\cos \theta + i \sin \theta)$$
$$m_2 = r(\cos \theta - i \sin \theta)$$

The reasoning which we used for distinct real roots also holds for complex roots. However, the disadvantage is that the solution then appears to involve complex numbers. We shall show shortly that this is in fact an illusion.

We have

$$s(n) = Pm_1^n + Qm_2^n$$

where P and Q are arbitrary constants. So

$$s(n) = P[r(\cos \theta + i \sin \theta)]^n + Q[r(\cos \theta - i \sin \theta)]^n$$
$$= Pr^n(\cos n\theta + i \sin n\theta) + Qr^n(\cos n\theta - i \sin n\theta)$$

We first met De Moivre's theorem in section 10.5.

using De Moivre's theorem. So

$$s(n) = r^n[(P + Q) \cos n\theta + (iP - iQ) \sin n\theta]$$
$$= r^n(A \cos n\theta + B \sin n\theta)$$

where A and B are arbitrary constants.

Notice how we began by using P and Q as arbitrary constants. We reserved the symbols A and B for the arbitrary constants in the final form. At first sight it might appear that B is complex. However, it is P and Q which are complex; A and B are real.

Example □ Obtain the general solution of the difference equation

$$a(n + 1) + 4a(n - 1) = 0$$

which is known to hold for all integers n.

Why not try this on your own?

The first thing to note is that the difference equation is known to hold for all integers n. Therefore it holds if we replace n by $n + 1$. We shall refer to this procedure as 'increasing n by 1'. We obtain

$$a(n + 2) + 4a(n) = 0$$

which is now in standard form. The auxiliary equation is $m^2 + 4 = 0$, and so $m = \pm 2i$.

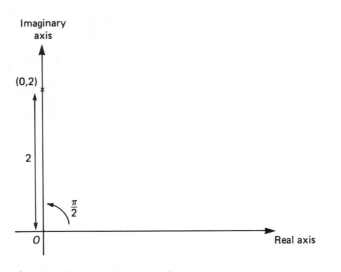

Fig. 21.2 Putting 2i in polar form.

The easiest way to put a complex number into polar form is to draw a diagram of the complex plane and read off the modulus and argument. Here, for $m = 2i$, we obtain $r = 2$ and $\theta = \pi/2$ (Fig. 21.2). Consequently the general solution is given by

$$a(n) = 2^n(A \cos n\pi/2 + B \sin n\pi/2) \qquad \blacksquare$$

We now summarize what we have discovered.

To solve the homogeneous linear difference equation

$$as(n + 2) + bs(n + 1) + cs(n) = 0$$

where a, b and c are real constants and $a \neq 0$:

1 Write down the auxiliary equation

$$am^2 + bm + c = 0$$

and solve it.

2 There are three cases in the selection of the general solution $s(n)$:

a distinct real roots m_1 and m_2:

$$s(n) = Am_1^n + Bm_2^n$$

b equal roots $m_1 = m_2 = m$:

$$s(n) = (A + Bn)m^n$$

c complex roots $m = r(\cos \theta \pm i \sin \theta)$:

$$s(n) = r^n(A \cos n\theta + B \sin n\theta)$$

where A and B are arbitrary constants.

Before we move on to the non-homogeneous case we shall take some very easy steps. This is all very straightforward and you should have no difficulty.

21.4 Workshop

1

Exercise   Obtain the general solution of the difference equation

$$t(n + 2) = t(n + 1) - t(n + 2)$$

As soon as you are ready, take the next step.

2

We have $2t(n + 2) - t(n + 1) = 0$, so the auxiliary equation is $2m^2 - m = 0$. That is, $m(2m - 1) = 0$, so $m = 0$ or $m = 1/2$; these are distinct real roots. Consequently

$$t(n) = A(0) + B(1/2)^n = B/2^n$$

where B is an arbitrary constant.

Alternatively we can decrease n by 1 throughout the difference equation and reduce it to a first-order equation.

If you are correct, move on to step 4. Perhaps some slip occurred in solving the quadratic; just to clear things up, try this next exercise.

▷**Exercise** $P(n)$ denotes the number of binary operations which take place in part of a computer program when n data points are supplied. If $P(n)$ satisfies the equation

$$P(n + 2) - P(n + 1) = 2[P(n + 1) - P(n)]$$

and the conditions $P(0) = 10$ and $P(3) = 24$, obtain an expression for $P(n)$ in terms of n.

Make a good attempt and then move on.

3

The equation becomes, when rearranged,

$$P(n + 2) - 3P(n + 1) + 2P(n) = 0$$

and so the auxiliary equation is

$$m^2 - 3m + 2 = 0$$
$$(m - 1)(m - 2) = 0$$

Therefore $m = 1$ or $m = 2$, distinct real roots, and we obtain

$$P(n) = A(1^n) + B(2^n) = A + B(2^n)$$

where A and B are arbitrary constants.

Now to obtain A and B we use the boundary conditions:

$$P(0) = 10 = A + B(2^0) = A + B$$
$$P(3) = 24 = A + B(2^3) = A + 8B$$

Subtracting, $14 = 7B$ so that $B = 2$ and $A = 8$. Finally, therefore,

$$P(n) = 8 + 2(2^n) = 8 + 2^{n+1}$$

Did you manage to get that correct? If not, and the error is a simple algebraic one, move ahead anyway. There's more practice to come.

▷**Exercise** Obtain the general solutions of the following difference equations:
a $U(n + 2) = 2[U(n + 1) - U(n)]$
b $y(n + 3) = 4[y(n + 2) - y(n + 1)]$
c $u(n + 2) = u(n + 1) + u(n)$
Do the lot before you check!

Here are the solutions.
  For **a** the equation is

$$U(n + 2) - 2U(n + 1) + 2U(n) = 0$$

So the auxiliary equation is

$$m^2 - 2m + 2 = 0$$
$$(m - 1)^2 + 1 = 0$$

So $m = 1 \pm i$. Expressing $1 + i$ in polar form we deduce that $r = \sqrt{2}$ and $\theta = \pi/4$. Consequently the solution for **a** is

$$U(n) = 2^{n/2}(A \cos n\pi/4 + B \sin n\pi/4)$$

In section 10.2 we showed how to put a complex number into polar form.

For **b** we have

$$y(n + 3) - 4y(n + 2) + 4y(n + 1) = 0$$

Decreasing n by 1 produces

$$y(n + 2) - 4y(n + 1) + 4y(n) = 0$$

which is now in standard form. The auxiliary equation is

$$m^2 - 4m + 4 = 0$$
$$(m - 2)^2 = 0$$

So $m = 2$, a repeated root. Therefore the solution for **b** is

$$y(n) = (A + Bn)2^n$$

The difference equation **c** defines the Fibonacci sequence when $u(1) = 1 = u(0)$. We have

$$u(n + 2) - u(n + 1) - u(n) = 0$$

which has auxiliary equation

$$m^2 - m - 1 = 0$$

So $m = (1 \pm \sqrt{5})/2$. These are distinct real roots, and consequently the solution for **c** is

$$u(n) = A[\tfrac{1}{2}(1 + \sqrt{5})]^n + B[\tfrac{1}{2}(1 - \sqrt{5})]^n$$

Did you get them all right? If you did then the next exercise is optional, although you should read through it. If things went wrong then it's time to sort them out. Go back and clear up your misunderstandings, then attempt the next exercise. You should not avoid it!

▷**Exercise**   Obtain the general solution of the recursion

$$6t(n) = t(n + 1) + 25t(n - 1)$$

Only when you are ready should you move on.

---

6 We need to increase n by 1 to put the equation in standard form:

$$6t(n + 1) = t(n + 2) + 25t(n)$$
$$t(n + 2) - 6t(n + 1) + 25t(n) = 0$$

The auxiliary equation is therefore

$$m^2 - 6m + 25 = 0$$
$$(m - 3)^2 + 16 = 0$$

So $m = 3 \pm 4i$.

Are we all right so far? If you have made an error, go back and correct it and then try again.

Now we must put the complex number $3 + 4i$ into polar form. Drawing a diagram is the easiest method, for we see at once that $r = 5$ and $\theta = \tan^{-1}(4/3)$. Consequently

$$t(n) = 5^n\{A \cos [n \tan^{-1}(4/3)] + B \sin [n \tan^{-1}(4/3)]\}$$

Do remember, by the way, that $\tan^{-1}(4/3)$ must be expressed in radians and not degrees!

We are now ready to consider the situation where there is a non-zero forcing function $f(n)$ appearing in the difference equation.

21.5 THE NON-HOMOGENEOUS CASE

We are concerned now with the difference equation

$$as(n + 2) + bs(n + 1) + cs(n) = f(n) \tag{1}$$

where a, b and c are real constants and $f(n)$ depends on n.

Suppose for the moment that we can devise some method of obtaining a particular solution $v(n)$ of this equation. Then

$$av(n + 2) + bv(n + 1) + cv(n) = f(n) \tag{2}$$

Subtracting (2) from (1) gives

$$a[s(n + 2) - v(n + 2)] + b[s(n + 1) - v(n + 1)] + c[s(n) - v(n)] = 0$$

Moreover, if we put $u(n) = s(n) - v(n)$ we have

$$au(n + 2) + bu(n + 1) + cu(n) = 0 \tag{3}$$

Now we have already seen how to solve equation (3); this is the homogeneous case. We call $u(n)$, the solution of this equation, the complementary part. Since $u(n) = s(n) - v(n)$ we have

$$s(n) = u(n) + v(n)$$

What does this show? Simply this: that if we can find any solution of equation (1) we need only add the solution of the corresponding homogeneous equation to obtain the general solution.

In summary, to solve the non-homogeneous equation

$$as(n + 2) + bs(n + 1) + cs(n) = f(n)$$

where a, b and c are real constants:

1 Write down the complementary part $u(n)$, that is the general solution of the homogeneous equation

$$as(n + 2) + bs(n + 1) + cs(n) = 0$$

2 Obtain a particular solution $v(n)$; this is any solution of the difference equation

$$as(n + 2) + bs(n + 1) + cs(n) = f(n)$$

3 The general solution is then the sum of the complementary part and a particular solution:

$$s(n) = u(n) + v(n)$$

4 Determine the arbitrary constants if starting values are given.

So then the general solution of a linear non-homogeneous difference equation with constant coefficients is the sum of two parts: the complementary part and a particular solution. We have already seen how to find the complementary part, and it remains therefore to describe a method for determining a particular solution.

21.6 THE PARTICULAR SOLUTION

If you have already studied second-order differential equations (Chapter 20) you will have seen several similarities between the two types of linear equation. The similarities continue in the method used to obtain a particular solution.

We are looking for any solution of the difference equation

$$as(n + 2) + bs(n + 1) + cs(n) = f(n)$$

where a, b and c are real constants and $f(n)$ depends on n. We use a method, known as the method of **trial solution**, to obtain a particular solution. To apply this method we inspect the **forcing function** $f(n)$ and look for a solution of the same form.

Example □ Obtain a particular solution for the difference equation

$$s(n + 2) - 4s(n + 1) + 4s(n) = n + 5$$

Here we examine $f(n)$ and observe that it is a polynomial in n of degree 1. Therefore we look for a solution which is also a polynomial in n of degree 1. So we look for a solution $s(n) = an + b$ where a and b are constants, which we must determine. Of course we shall want our solution to hold for all n, and so when we substitute into the difference equation we are looking for an identity.

See section 2.6 for the meaning of an identity.

Now if

$$s(n) = an + b$$

then

$$s(n + 1) = a(n + 1) + b$$
$$s(n + 2) = a(n + 2) + b$$

Therefore, substituting, we require

$$a(n + 2) + b - 4[a(n + 1) + b] + 4(an + b) \equiv n + 5$$
$$an + 2a + b - 4an - 4a - 4b + 4an + 4b \equiv n + 5$$
$$an - 2a + b \equiv n + 5$$

We can satisfy this by choosing $a = 1$ and $-2a + b = 5$. So $a = 1$ and $b = 7$. A particular solution is therefore

$$s(n) = n + 7$$

■

Table 21.1

$f(n)$	Trial solution
Polynomial in n, e.g. $2n^2 + 4$	Polynomial of the same degree $an^2 + bn + c$
k^n	ak^n
$\cos kn$ or $\sin kn$	$a \cos kn + b \sin kn$
$\cosh kn$ or $\sinh kn$	$a \cosh kn + b \sinh kn$ or $a\, e^{kn} + b\, e^{-kn}$

Since the method of trial solution involves inspecting $f(n)$, we give a short table (Table 21.1) showing possible values for $f(n)$ and the corresponding trial solutions which will normally work. The constants a, b and c have to be determined by substituting; k is a constant. If $f(n)$ is a sum of those shown in the table, then a suitable trial solution can be obtained using a sum of the corresponding trial solutions.

Table 21.1 is very short, and so the types of non-homogeneous equations that we shall be able to solve is very restricted. Nevertheless many linear difference equations which arise in practice do have $f(n)$ as one of these. To show how simple things are, we shall solve an example. Note the four stages in the solution: complementary part, particular solution, general solution and constants.

☐ Obtain the solution of the difference equation   **Example**

$$u(n + 2) - 4u(n) = 3^n$$

given that $u(0) = 1$ and $u(1) = 9$.

We begin by finding the complementary part. The auxiliary equation is

$$m^2 - 4 = 0$$
$$(m - 2)(m + 2) = 0$$

So $m = 2$ or $m = -2$. Therefore

$$CP = A2^n + B(-2)^n$$

where A and B are arbitrary constants.

Do not make the mistake of calling this $u(n)$ or substituting in to try to obtain A and B; this is only part of the solution.

Next we look for a particular solution. Here $f(n) = 3^n$, and so using Table 21.1 we see we must look for a solution of the form $u(n) = a3^n$. We substitute this tentatively into the equation, looking for an identity:

$$a3^{n+2} - 4(a3^n) \equiv 3^n$$

which, dividing through by 3^n, non-zero, gives

$$a3^2 - 4a \equiv 1$$

This is satisfied when $a = 1/5$, so a particular solution is

$$PS = 3^n/5$$

Therefore the general solution is given by

$$u(n) = CP + PS = A2^n + B(-2)^n + 3^n/5$$

Lastly we obtain A and B from the starting conditions. We have

$$u(0) = A(2^0) + B(-2)^0 + 3^0/5 = 1$$
$$A + B + 1/5 = 1$$
$$A + B = 4/5$$

Also

$$u(1) = A(2^1) + B(-2)^1 + 3/5 = 9$$
$$2A - 2B + 3/5 = 9$$
$$2A - 2B = 42/5$$

We have $A + B = 4/5$ and $A - B = 21/5$. Therefore adding, $2A = 5$ and $A = 5/2$; whereas subtracting, $2B = -17/5$ so $B = -17/10$. Hence

$$u(n) = 5(2^n)/2 - 17(-2)^n/10 + 3^n/5$$

21.7 THE BREAKDOWN CASE

You may remember the breakdown case for differential equations which we met in section 20.7.

There is one situation where the trial solution is bound to fail; this is known as the breakdown case. Suppose we are attempting to use a trial solution which is already present in the complementary part; a moment's reflection will show that this cannot possibly work. Can you see why not?

The answer is that the complementary part satisfies the equation when $f(n) \equiv 0$, so it cannot possibly satisfy the equation when $f(n) \neq 0$. What are we to do about it?

Luckily there is a simple remedy: if, with an appropriate choice of constants A and B, some of the trial solution is already present in the complementary part, 'multiply by n and try again.'

We now solve a problem which should make everything crystal clear.

Example □ Obtain the general solution of the difference equation

$$s(n + 2) - 6s(n + 1) + 9s(n) = 3^n + 1$$

In order to be in a position to anticipate the breakdown case, we always obtain the complementary part first. The auxiliary equation is

$$m^2 - 6m + 9 = 0$$
$$(m - 3)^2 = 0$$

So $m = 3$, a repeated root. Consequently,

$$CP = (A + Bn)3^n$$

We notice that $f(n)$ is here the sum of two types. The first part is 3^n, which normally has a corresponding trial solution $a3^n$. The second is 1, a constant, a polynomial of degree 0, which would normally have a trial solution b, where b is constant.

Now the first part of the trial solution will not do! The term $a3^n$ is already in the complementary part; $A = a$ and $B = 0$. We must remedy the situation: 'multiply by n and try again.' This now gives $an3^n$; is this all right?

No! We remain in difficulties. The term $an3^n$ is still present in the complementary part; $A = 0$ and $B = a$. Therefore 'multiply by n and try again.' This gives an^23^n. Are we all right now?

Yes! We have pulled clear of troubled waters. We only need to note in passing that the trial solution b corresponding to 1 gives no problems whatever.

So the trial solution which we shall use is

$$s(n) = an^23^n + b$$

So

$$s(n + 1) = a(n + 1)^2\, 3^{n+1} + b$$
$$s(n + 2) = a(n + 2)^2\, 3^{n+2} + b$$

Therefore, together,

$$s(n) = an^23^n + b$$
$$s(n + 1) = 3a(n^2 + 2n + 1)3^n + b$$
$$s(n + 2) = 9a(n^2 + 4n + 4)3^n + b$$

We substitute back into the equation to obtain a and b:

$$[9a(n^2 + 4n + 4) - 18a(n^2 + 2n + 1) + 9an^2]3^n + b - 6b + 9b \equiv 3^n + 1$$

This is satisfied if

$$9a(n^2 + 4n + 4) - 18a(n^2 + 2n + 1) + 9an^2 = 1$$
$$b - 6b + 9b - 1$$

This gives $18a = 1$ and $4b = 1$, so

$$PS = n^23^n/18 + 1/4$$

Finally, the general solution is the sum of CP and PS:

$$s(n) = (A + Bn)3^n + n^23^n/18 + 1/4$$

That's all there is to it.   ■

In summary, to solve the non-homogeneous difference equation

$$as(n + 2) + bs(n + 1) + cs(n) = f(n)$$

where a, b and c are constants and $f(n)$ depends only on n:

1 Obtain the complementary part: the solution of the equation in the special case $f(n) \equiv 0$, the homogeneous equation.

2 Obtain a particular solution by the method of trial solutions, using the complementary part to anticipate the breakdown case. If the breakdown case occurs, locate the part which corresponds to it, multiply by n and try again.

3 The general solution is the sum of the complementary part and a particular solution.

4 Determine the constants A and B from the general solution using the starting values of the difference equation.

Very well; now we are ready to attempt some steps.

_____ 21.8 Workshop _____

12

Exercise

a Obtain $u(n)$ if

$$u(n + 2) - 5u(n + 1) + 6u(n) = 2^n$$

given that $u(0) = 5$ and $u(1) = 8$.

b Solve the difference equation

$$t(n + 2) - 3t(n + 1) + 2t(n) = n + 1$$

if $t(0) = 2$ and $t(1) = 0$.

c Determine $p(n)$ in terms of n if $p(n)$ satisfies $p(0) = 1$, $p(1) = 2$ and the recurrence

$$p(n + 1) - p(n) = p(n) - p(n - 1) + \sin n\pi$$

Try them. If you manage them all, then read through to check everything is well. If you cannot do the first one then take the next step before attempting the others. Do *yourself* a favour and make a real effort. We solve each using the standard four stages:

1 complementary part
2 particular solution
3 general solution
4 constants.

2

In this step we solve **a**.

The auxiliary equation is

$$m^2 - 5m + 6 = 0$$
$$(m - 2)(m - 3) = 0$$

So $m = 2$ or $m = 3$. Therefore

$$CP = A2^n + B3^n$$

Next, $f(n) = 2^n$, so the usual trial solution is $a2^n$. However, this is already present in the complementary part; $A = a$ and $B = 0$. Therefore we try instead $an2^n$, and there is no problem with this. If $u(n) = an2^n$ then, substituting, we have

$$4a(n + 2)2^n - 10a(n + 1)2^n + 6an2^n \equiv 2^n$$
$$4an + 8a - 10an - 10a + 6an \equiv 1$$

We require $a = -1/2$, so

$$PS = -n2^{n-1}$$

The general solution is given by

$$u(n) = A2^n + B3^n - n2^{n-1}$$

Using the starting values

$$u(0) = A + B = 5$$
$$u(1) = 2A + 3B - 1 = 8$$
$$2A + 3B = 9$$

Solving, $A = 6$ and $B = -1$. So the required solution is

$$u(n) = 6(2^n) - 3^n - n2^{n-1}$$
$$= 3(2^{n+1}) - 3^n - n2^{n-1}$$

If you didn't manage that then look carefully at all the stages and check through each one. You are ready to move on when you have tried **b**.

In this step we solve **b**.

 The auxiliary equation is

$$m^2 - 3m + 2 = 0$$
$$(m - 2)(m - 1) = 0$$

So $m = 1$ or $m = 2$. Therefore

$$CP = A1^n + B2^n = A + B2^n$$

Here $f(n) = n + 1$, a polynomial of degree 1; so we try $t(n) = an + b$. We may not realize this is the breakdown case, so we can try to substitute as things stand. We require

$$a(n + 2) + b - 3[a(n + 1) + b] + 2(an + b) \equiv n + 1$$

Thus $a \equiv n + 1$, and this is impossible! The problem is b, which appears in the complementary part when $A = b$ and $B = 0$. Here we are unable to isolate the difficulty, since even if $f(n)$ had been n the trial solution would have been $an + b$ and the problem would have arisen. We must therefore apply the remedy to the *whole* of the trial solution, and try instead $an^2 + bn$. We then require

$$a(n + 2)^2 + b(n + 2) - 3[a(n + 1)^2 + b(n + 1)] + 2(an^2 + bn) \equiv n + 1$$
$$a(n^2 + 4n + 4) + bn + 2b - 3a(n^2 + 2n + 1)$$
$$- 3bn - 3b + 2an^2 + 2bn \equiv n + 1$$
$$4an + 4a + bn + 2b - 6an - 3a - 3bn - 3b + 2bn \equiv n + 1$$
$$-2an + a - b \equiv n + 1$$

This is satisfied when $a = -1/2$ and $a - b = 1$, so $b = -3/2$. Hence a particular solution is

$$\text{PS} = -n^2/2 - 3n/2$$

The general solution is given by

$$t(n) = A + B2^n - n^2/2 - 3n/2$$

To obtain the solution satisfying the starting values $t(0) = 2$ and $t(1) = 0$ we substitute:

$$t(0) = A + B = 2$$
$$t(1) = A + 2B - 1/2 - 3/2 = A + 2B - 2 = 0$$

Consequently $A = 2$ and $B = 0$. Therefore the required solution is

$$t(n) = 2 - n^2/2 - 3n/2$$

If that went wrong, make sure you understand why. Then tackle **c**.

---

4 Rearranging the equation into standard form we have

$$p(n + 1) - 2p(n) + p(n - 1) = \sin n\pi$$

So increasing n by 1,

$$p(n + 2) - 2p(n + 1) + p(n) = \sin (n + 1)\pi$$

The auxiliary equation is

$$m^2 - 2m + 1 = 0$$
$$(m - 1)^2 = 0$$

So $m = 1$ repeated. Therefore

$$\text{CP} = (A + Bn)1^n = A + Bn$$

Next, we have

$$f(n) = \sin (n + 1)\pi = \sin n\pi \cos \pi + \cos n\pi \sin \pi = -\sin n\pi$$

So we try $a \cos n\pi + b \sin n\pi$:

$$p(n) = a \cos n\pi + b \sin n\pi$$
$$p(n + 1) = a \cos (n + 1)\pi + b \sin (n + 1)\pi$$
$$p(n + 2) = a \cos (n + 2)\pi + b \sin (n + 2)\pi$$

Then we require

$$[a \cos (n + 2)\pi + b \sin (n + 2)\pi] - 2[a \cos (n + 1)\pi + b \sin (n + 1)\pi]$$
$$+ a \cos n\pi + b \sin n\pi \equiv \sin (n + 1)\pi$$

$$a(\cos n\pi \cos 2\pi - \sin n\pi \sin 2\pi) + b(\sin n\pi \cos 2\pi + \cos n\pi \sin 2\pi)$$
$$- 2a(\cos n\pi \cos \pi - \sin n\pi \sin \pi)$$
$$- 2b(\sin n\pi \cos \pi + \cos n\pi \sin \pi)$$
$$+ a \cos n\pi + b \sin n\pi \equiv -\sin n\pi$$

$$a \cos n\pi + b \sin n\pi + 2a \cos n\pi + 2b \sin n\pi$$
$$+ a \cos n\pi + b \sin n\pi \equiv -\sin n\pi$$

$$4a \cos n\pi + 4b \sin n\pi \equiv -\sin n\pi$$

Comparing coefficients of $\cos n\pi$ and $\sin n\pi$ we obtain $a = 0$ and $b = -1/4$. Therefore a particular solution is

$$\text{PS} = -\tfrac{1}{4} \sin n\pi$$

The general solution is now

$$p(n) = A + Bn - \tfrac{1}{4} \sin n\pi$$

Finally, $p(0) = 1$ and $p(1) = 2$, so that

$$p(0) = A - \tfrac{1}{4} \sin n\pi = A = 1$$
$$p(1) = A + B - \tfrac{1}{4} \sin \pi = A + B = 2$$

and so $B = 1$. Therefore

$$p(n) = 1 + n - \tfrac{1}{4} \sin n\pi$$

Now there is nothing wrong with this, but most of it is *unnecessary*. If n is an integer then $\sin n\pi = 0$, so that the difference equation is in fact homogeneous! The required solution is

$$p(n) = 1 + n$$

If you spotted that then award yourself three bonus points.

Now we apply some of this theory to a practical problem. There are links here with the work we did on numerical techniques and differential equations (Chapters 18–20). The problem concerns the approximation of a differential equation by a difference equation.

21.9 Practical

BENDING BEAM

The deflection y of a beam satisfies the differential equation

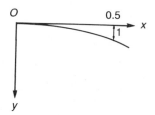

$$\frac{d^2y}{dx^2} - 9\frac{dy}{dx} + 8y = 0$$

The boundary conditions are $y(0) = 0$ and $y(0.5) = 1$.

Replace the derivatives by approximations of order h^2 where $h = 0.5$, and thereby approximate the differential equation by a difference equation. Solve both the original differential equation and also the difference equation, and thereby compare the two solutions.

You should be able to tackle this confidently now. We shall solve it stage by stage so that you may join in whenever you can. As a first move we solve the differential equation to obtain the true deflection.

This uses the work we did in Chapter 20.

The auxiliary equation is

$$m^2 - 9m + 8 = 0$$
$$(m - 1)(m - 8) = 0$$

Therefore $m = 1$ or $m = 8$.

There is no forcing function (the equation is homogeneous). Therefore

$$y = Ae^x + Be^{8x}$$

When $x = 0$, $y = 0$ and so $A + B = 0$. Therefore

$$y = A(e^x - e^{8x})$$

When $x = 0.5$, $y = 1$ and so $1 = A(e^{0.5} - e^4)$, from which $A \simeq -0.019$. Consequently

$$y = 0.019(e^{8x} - e^x)$$

Now replace the derivatives by the finite difference approximations. When you have sorted things out, move on to the next stage.

Refer to section 18.9 for these approximations.

The equation becomes

$$\frac{y(x + h) - 2y(x) + y(x - h)}{h^2} - 9\frac{y(x + h) - y(x - h)}{2h} + 8y(x) = 0$$

$$\frac{y(x + h) - 2y(x) + y(x - h)}{0.25} - 9\frac{y(x + h) - y(x - h)}{1} + 8y(x) = 0$$

$$4[y(x + h) - 2y(x) + y(x - h)] - 9[y(x + h) - y(x - h)] + 8y(x) = 0$$

$$-5y(x + h) + 13y(x + h) = 0$$

$$5y(x + h) - 13y(x - h) = 0$$

$$5y(x + 2h) - 13y(x) = 0$$

Solve this and move on to the next stage.

The auxiliary equation is

$$5m^2 - 13 = 0$$

from which $m = \pm\sqrt{(13/5)}$. So

$$y(x + nh) = A(13/5)^{n/2} + B(-1)^n (13/5)^{n/2}$$
$$= [A + B(-1)^n] (13/5)^{n/2}$$

where A and B are arbitrary constants. Taking $x = 0$ and $h = 0.5$ we have

$$y(n/2) = [A + B(-1)^n] (13/5)^{n/2}$$

Now $y(0) = 0$, so that $A + B = 0$. Therefore

$$y(n/2) = A[1 - (-1)^n] (13/5)^{n/2}$$

When $n = 1$, $y = 1$ we have $1 = A2\sqrt{(13/5)}$, so $A = 0.310$. Consequently,

$$y(n/2) = 0.310[1 - (-1)^n] (13/5)^{n/2}$$

Give some thought to what we have done, and then read carefully through the next stage.

We have a solved a finite difference equation which purports to approximate the differential equation from which it arose. However, if we compare the approximate solution with the true solution we have

True solution: $y(x) = 0.019 (e^{8x} - e^x)$
Approximation: $y(n/2) = 0.310[1 - (-1)^n] (13/5)^{n/2}$

Of course the approximation only makes claims to represent the solution when n is a positive integer, and the boundary conditions ensure that when $n = 0$ and $n = 1$ the solution is exact. However, all is not well. Indeed, we see that whenever n is an even integer the approximation gives a zero deflection, and this is certainly not the true deflection. The approximation is not only bad, it is useless! What has gone wrong?

The trouble is that we have used two approximations for the derivatives, each of order h^2. Although the error involved is bounded, the bound is dependent on higher-order derivatives. The true solution contains a term in e^{8x}, and so the third-order and fourth-order derivatives are very large even for small values of x.

The problem shows that we must be very careful indeed when replacing derivatives by finite difference approximations, and without careful analysis we should remain sceptical of the results.

Before ending this chapter we remark that there is nothing in the method we have used to solve difference equations which relies on n being an integer. In fact we could emphasize this by writing $s(x)$ instead of $s(n)$. The only adjustment that it would be wise to make is to the arbitrary constants A and B. If we have a difference equation in which there is a continuous variable x, then A and B can be 'periodic constants'. This means that if A and B depend on x then

$$A = A(x) \equiv A(x + 1) \qquad B = B(x) \equiv B(x + 1)$$

There it is then: we have dealt with first-order and second-order linear difference equations with constant coefficients. It is a simple matter to generalize this work to deal with higher-order equations of this type.

SUMMARY

To solve the homogeneous linear difference equation

$$as(n + 2) + bs(n + 1) + cs(n) = 0$$

where a, b and c are real constants and $a \neq 0$:
□ Write down the auxiliary equation

$$am^2 + bm + c = 0$$

and solve it.
□ There are three cases in the selection of the general solution $s(n)$:
  a distinct real roots m_1 and m_2:

$$s(n) = Am_1^n + Bm_2^n$$

  b equal roots $m_1 = m_2 = m$:

$$s(n) = (A + Bn)m^n$$

  c complex roots $m = r(\cos \theta \pm i \sin \theta)$:

$$s(n) = r^n(A \cos n\theta + B \sin n\theta)$$

where A and B are arbitrary constants.
To solve the non-homogeneous linear difference equation

$$as(n + 2) + bs(n + 1) + cs(n) = f(n)$$

where a, b and c are constants and $f(n)$ depends only on n:
□ Write down the complementary part $u(n)$: the general solution of the homogeneous equation

$$as(n + 2) + bs(n + 1) + cs(n) = 0$$

□ Anticipate the breakdown case and obtain a particular solution $v(n)$: any solution of the difference equation

$$as(n + 2) + bs(n + 1) + cs(n) = f(n)$$

□ The general solution is the sum of the complementary part and a particular solution:

$$s(n) = u(n) + v(n)$$

□ Determine the arbitrary constants if boundary values are available.

EXERCISES (for answers see p. 758)

1 Solve each of these first-order difference equations:

  a $\dfrac{1}{p_n} - \dfrac{3}{p_{n+1}} = 0$

b $\ln u_{n+1} - \ln u_n = \ln 2$

c $\dfrac{1}{t_n} = 4\left(\dfrac{1}{t_{n+1}} - \dfrac{1}{t_n}\right)$

d $6u(n + 1) = 7[u(n + 1) - u(n)]$

e $6(p_n - p_{n-1}) + 5p_{n-1} = 0$

f $7(q_{n+2} - q_{n+1}) = 4q_{n+1}$

g $9u_{n+1}{}^2 = 4u_n{}^2$

h $\dfrac{1}{s_n} - \dfrac{1}{s_{n+1}} = \dfrac{5}{s_{n+1}}$

2 Solve each of the following equations:

a $3(s_{n+1} - s_n) + s_{n-1} = (s_{n+1} - s_{n-1}) - 2(s_n - s_{n-1})$

b $s_{n+1} - s_n = (s_n - s_{n-1}) + s_n + s_{n+1}$

c $1 = (P_{n+1}/P_{n+2})(5 - 6P_n/P_{n+1})$

d $S_{n+2}/2S_{n+1} + 2S_n/S_{n+1} = 2$

3 Solve each of the following equations:

a $2(S_{n+2} - 2S_n) = 7(S_{n+1} - S_n)$

b $9(U_{n+2} - U_{n+1}) + 3(U_{n+1} - U_n) + 4U_n = 0$

c $4(S_{n+2} - S_{n+1}) + 4(S_{n+1} - S_n) + 5S_n = 0$

4 Obtain the general solution of each of the following difference equations:

a $2S(n + 2) - 5S(n + 1) + 2S(n) = 1$

b $2t(n + 2) - 3t(n + 1) - 2t(n) = 2^n$

c $16r(n + 2) - 8r(n + 1) + r(n) = 2^{-2n}$

ASSIGNMENT (for answers see p. 759; see also Workshops on pp. 612 and 620)

1 Write down the general solutions of each of the following linear difference equations, which are defined for all integers n:

a $Y(n + 2) - 7Y(n + 1) + 10Y(n) = 0$

b $u(n) = u(n - 1) + 6u(n - 2)$

c $25T(n) = -T(n - 2)$

d $p(n + 2) - 5p(n + 1) = 5[p(n + 1) - 5p(n)]$

e $2E(n + 2) = E(n + 1) + E(n)$

2 Obtain the solutions of each of the following difference equations:

a $S(n + 2) - S(n + 1) = S(n + 1) - S(n)$, where $S(1) = 1$ and $S(2) = 3$

b $S(n + 2) = 3S(n + 1)$, where $S(0) = 1$

c $T(n + 1) = T(n - 1) + n(n - 1)$, where $T(0) = 1$ and $T(1) = 0$

d $v(n + 2) = v(n) + n + 1$, where $v(0) = 5$ and $v(1) = 3$.

3 Solve the difference equation

$$s(n + 1) - s(n) = s(n) - s(n - 1)$$

where $s(1) = a$ and $s(2) - s(1) = d$ and a and d are constants. Explain the significance of this result.

4 Solve the difference equations
  a $p(n) - p(n - 1) = n^2$, given that $p(1) = 1$
  b $q(n) - q(n - 1) = n^3$, given that $q(1) = 1$.
5 By eliminating $p(n)$ or $q(n)$, or otherwise, solve the simultaneous equations

$$p(n + 1) - p(n) = q(n)$$
$$q(n + 1) - q(n) = -p(n)$$

FURTHER EXERCISES (for answers see p. 759)

1 Obtain the general solution of the recurrence relation

$$s(n) - s(n - 1) - s(n - 2) = n^2$$

2 Solve, in terms of $T(1)$ and n, the difference equation

$$2T(n) - T(n - 1) = nc$$

where c is a constant.
3 Show that the solution of the difference equation

$$u(n) + u(n - 1) = \sin n\alpha$$

which satisfies the condition $u(1) = 0$ is

$$u(n) = \frac{\sin \alpha \, (1 + 2 \cos \alpha) \, (-1)^n}{2(1 + \cos \alpha)} + \frac{\sin (n + 1) \, \alpha + \sin n\alpha}{2(1 + \cos \alpha)}$$

4 The response $r(n)$ of a system in the nth phase is given in terms of previous responses by

$$r(n) = n[r(n - 1) + r(n - 2)]$$

By putting $s(n) = r(n) - (n + 1) r(n - 1)$, show that $s(n) + s(n - 1) = 0$ and thereby obtain $s(n)$. Put $t(n) = r(n)/(n + 1)!$ to obtain a linear difference equation for $t(n)$. Hence, or otherwise, show that

$$r(n) = (n + 1)! \left\{ r(0) + [r(1) - 2r(0)] \left[\frac{1}{2!} - \frac{1}{3!} + \ldots + \frac{(-1)^{n+1}}{(n + 1)!} \right] \right\}$$

Show further that as $n \to \infty$

$$\frac{r(n)}{(n + 1)!} \to r(0) + \frac{r(1) - 2r(0)}{e}$$

5 The amount $e(n)$ extracted in successive cycles of a filtering process satisfies the equation

$$e(n) \, e(n - 1) = k/n$$

where k is a constant. By expressing $e(n)$ in terms of $e(n - 2)$, or otherwise, determine the amount extracted in terms of $e(1)$ when the cycle number is (a) odd (b) even.

6 The signal-to-noise ratio $\varrho(n)$ after an input has been smoothed n times through a filter satisfies

$$e\varrho(n + 1) - \varrho(n) = e - 1$$

where e is the natural base of logarithms. Obtain $\varrho(n)$ in terms of n if initially the ratio was 50%.

7 The height $h(t)$ in metres at time t in seconds of a prototype aircraft above ground under test conditions satisfies the equation

$$h(t + 2) - 2 \cos \alpha h(t + 1) + h(t) = 200 (1 - \cos \alpha)$$

The flutter angle α is constant and satisfies the strict inequality $0 < \alpha < \pi/2$. When $t = 0$ the height is 100 m, and when $t = 1$ the height is $100 + \sin \alpha$ m. By obtaining an explicit expression for $h(t)$, decide if the aircraft will remain airborne. If the aircraft does not crash, determine its maximum and minimum heights during the test.

8 The probabilities of faults developing in three different components in a microcomputer after n periods of operation are denoted by $p(n)$, $q(n)$ and $r(n)$ respectively. Theoretical considerations show that

$$p(n) = p(n - 1) + \tfrac{1}{4} q(n - 1)$$
$$q(n) = \tfrac{1}{2} q(n - 1)$$
$$r(n) = \tfrac{1}{4} q(n - 1) + r(n - 1)$$

Obtain $p(n)$, $q(n)$ and $r(n)$ in terms of $p(0)$, $q(0)$ and $r(0)$. Hence, or otherwise, show that as $n \to \infty$

$$p(n) \to p(0) + \tfrac{1}{2} q(0)$$
$$q(n) \to 0$$
$$r(n) \to r(0) + \tfrac{1}{2} q(0)$$

Linear operators 22

In Chapters 20 and 21 we obtained particular solutions to differential and difference equations using the method of trial solutions. In this chapter we shall discuss another method which uses linear operators.

After studying this chapter you should be able to
☐ Test a function for linearity;
☐ Decide when a set of vectors is linearly independent;
☐ Use the algebraic properties of linear operators;
☐ Use the operator D to obtain particular solutions to differential equations;
☐ Use the operator Δ to obtain particular solutions to difference equations.
Finally we shall consider a practical problem involving the resonant frequency of a baffle plate.

22.1 LINEAR FUNCTIONS

The word 'linear' occurs many times in mathematical work, for example in terms such as linear algebra and linear mathematics. What do we mean by linear, and why is the term so important?

Certain mathematical things which we do have features in common. If you have studied differential equations and difference equations (Chapters 19–21) you will already have observed a common theme. The methods used to solve second-order linear differential equations and those used to solve second-order linear difference equations had so much in common that it is reasonable to suspect they are both special cases of something more general. The key to the whole thing lies in the word 'linearity'.

We shall start by explaining what is meant by **linearity** when applied to a function:

Suppose $f: \mathbb{R} \to \mathbb{R}$. Then f is linear if and only if, given any $a, b \in \mathbb{R}$,

$$f(ax + by) = af(x) + bf(y)$$

whenever $x, y \in \mathbb{R}$.

Example □ Decide which of the following are linear functions:
    a $f(x) = 3x$
    b $f(x) = x + 1$
    c $f(x) = x^2$
In each case we must examine the condition $f(ax + by) = af(x) + bf(y)$ and see if it is satisfied or not.
    a $\begin{aligned} f(ax + by) &= 3(ax + by) \\ &= a(3x) + b(3y) \\ &= af(x) + bf(y) \end{aligned}$
    So f is linear.
    b $\begin{aligned} f(ax + by) &= (ax + by) + 1 \\ &= a(x + 1) + b(x + 1) + 1 - a - b \\ &\neq af(x) + bg(x) \end{aligned}$
    So f is not linear.
You try the next one.

    c $\begin{aligned} f(ax + by) &= (ax + by)^2 \\ &= ax^2 + by^2 + 2abxy \\ &= af(x) + bg(y) + 2abxy \end{aligned}$
    So again f is not linear.   ■

! One thing needs to be stressed: a linear function has very little to do with straight lines. Even more importantly, the absence of quadratic terms and those of higher degree does not decide linearity.

    In order to extend the idea of linearity further we shall first need to describe some algebraic structures.

22.2 VECTOR SPACES

These algebraic concepts were the subjects of Chapters 10 to 14.

We have already discussed some mathematical objects – matrices, vectors and complex numbers – which satisfy algebraic rules that are slightly different from the rules familiar in elementary algebra. Sometimes several distinct kinds of mathematical object possess a common structure, and when they do it helps to give that structure a special name. One mathematical structure in particular frequently arises, and this is called a **real vector space**. It may help to think of the elements of a real vector space as the vectors which we have already encountered (Chapter 14), but we shall be talking about an abstract idea and so there are several other objects which also have the same structure. For this reason we use bold symbols only for variables that have previously been introduced as vectors.

In what follows we shall suppose that a and b are real numbers and that u, v and w are arbitrary objects in the real vector space V which we are going to describe.

22.3 THE ADDITION RULES

Here are the addition rules which are satisfied by a real vector space.

The closure rule

$$u + v \in V$$

This means that if we take any two vectors and add them together, the result is itself a vector.

The associative rule

$$u + (v + w) = (u + v) + w$$

This means that if we add v and w together and add the result to u we obtain the same as adding u and v together and adding w to the result.

Identity element
There exists a vector **O** such that

$$u + \mathbf{O} = \mathbf{O} + u = u$$

This means that there must be a zero vector in V.

Additive inverses
To any u there exists v such that

$$u + v = v + u = \mathbf{O}$$

This means that given any vector u there is another one v which when added to it gives the zero vector. It can be shown that v is unique and we represent it as $-u$.

You may be interested to know that the four conditions which we have just stated are the conditions that V, with the operation $+$, forms a **group**.

Commutative rule

$$u + v = v + u$$

This means that the sum of two vectors is independent of the order in which we add them together.

Although groups have interesting structure, we need more for a real vector space. We shall need to be able to multiply the elements in V by real numbers.

22.4 THE SCALAR MULTIPLICATION RULES

The closure rule

$$au \in V$$

If we multiply a vector by a real number the result is always a vector.

The identity element

$$1u = u$$

If we multiply a vector by 1 the result is the same vector.

Associativity condition

$$a(bu) = (ab)u$$

The result of multiplying a vector by one number after another is the same as multiplying the vector by the product of the two numbers.

Distributive conditions

$$a(u + v) = au + av$$

If we add two vectors together and multiply the result by a number, the result is the same as if we had multiplied each vector by the number and added the vectors obtained.

$$(a + b)v = av + bv$$

If we multiply a vector by the sum of two numbers, the result is the same as multiplying it by each of the numbers and adding the vectors obtained.

These then are the conditions which must be satisfied before we have a real vector space V. We shall call the elements in V vectors.

Although we have probably had in mind a set of two- or three-dimensional vectors, in fact there are many mathematical objects which have the structure of a real vector space. Here is a list of just a few:

1 complex numbers
2 the set of all polynomials in x with real coefficients
3 the set of differentiable real functions
4 the set of convergent power series
5 geometrical vectors.

22.5 LINEAR COMBINATIONS

If we are given a set of vectors

$$v_1, v_2, v_3, \ldots, v_n$$

and a set of real numbers

$$a_1, a_2, a_3, \ldots, a_n$$

then the vector

$$v = (a_1 v_1 + a_2 v_2 + \ldots + a_n v_n)$$
$$= \sum_{r=1}^{n} a_r v_r$$

is called a **linear combination** of the vectors $v_1, v_2, \ldots, v_n$. The real numbers $a_1, a_2, \ldots, a_n$ are called the **coefficients** of the linear combination.

☐ Suppose we consider the vectors $v_1 = \mathbf{i} + \mathbf{j}$ and $v_2 = 2\mathbf{i} - \mathbf{j}$ in the plane. **Example**
Then if $a_1 = 5$ and $a_2 = -4$ we obtain a linear combination

$$v = 5(\mathbf{i} + \mathbf{j}) - 4(2\mathbf{i} - \mathbf{j}) = -3\mathbf{i} + 9\mathbf{j} \qquad ∎$$

You may need to refer back to Chapter 14 if you have forgotten your work on vectors.

22.6 LINEAR DEPENDENCE

If there is a linear combination of a set of vectors

$$v_1, v_2, \ldots, v_n$$

other than

$$a_1 = a_2 = \ldots = a_n = 0$$

such that

$$\mathbf{O} = \sum_{r=1}^{n} a_r v_r$$

then the vectors $v_1, v_2, \ldots, v_n$ are **linearly dependent**.

In other words, if we can find a linear combination of the set of vectors which produces the zero vector and in which not *all* the coefficients are zero, then we have a linearly dependent set of vectors.

Example □ The vectors $\mathbf{i} + \mathbf{j} - \mathbf{k}$, $\mathbf{i} - \mathbf{j} + \mathbf{k}$ and $\mathbf{i} + 2\mathbf{j} - 2\mathbf{k}$ are linearly dependent. To see this, we only need observe that

$$3(\mathbf{i} + \mathbf{j} - \mathbf{k}) - (\mathbf{i} - \mathbf{j} + \mathbf{k}) - 2(\mathbf{i} + 2\mathbf{j} - 2\mathbf{k}) = \mathbf{0}$$

22.7 LINEAR INDEPENDENCE

Given a set of vectors

The concept of linear independence has already arisen in sections 13.8, 20.2 and 21.2.

$$v_1, v_2, \ldots, v_n$$

if the equation

$$\mathbf{O} = \sum_{r=1}^{n} a_r v_r$$

necessarily implies

$$a_1 = a_2 = \ldots = a_n = 0$$

then the vectors are said to be **linearly independent**.

In other words, if the *only* linear combination of the vectors which produces the zero vector is the one in which all the coefficients are zero, then the vectors are linearly independent.

Example □ Show that

$$\mathbf{i} + \mathbf{j} \qquad \mathbf{j} + \mathbf{k} \qquad \mathbf{k} + \mathbf{i}$$

is a linearly independent set of vectors in three dimensions.

Consider the equation

$$a(\mathbf{i} + \mathbf{j}) + b(\mathbf{j} + \mathbf{k}) + c(\mathbf{k} + \mathbf{i}) = \mathbf{O}$$

where a, b and c are real numbers. We have

$$(a + c)\mathbf{i} + (a + b)\mathbf{j} + (b + c)\mathbf{k} = \mathbf{O}$$

Now this implies

$$a + c = 0$$
$$a + b = 0$$
$$b + c = 0$$

from which it follows that $a = 0$, $b = 0$ and $c = 0$. So the vectors are linearly independent. ∎

22.8 BASES

A set of vectors is said to **span** the vector space if every vector in the space can be expressed as a linear combination of them.

A set of vectors is said to form a **basis** of the vector space if
1 It is a linearly independent set;
2 It spans the space.

☐ In the set of vectors in three dimensions, **i**, **j** and **k** form the usual basis. **Example** However, this is not the only basis; another example is provided by the vectors **i** + **j**, **j** + **k**, **k** + **i**.

We have already shown that these vectors are linearly independent. It remains only to show that they span the space. We must show that an arbitrary vector $a\mathbf{i} + b\mathbf{j} + c\mathbf{k}$ in the vector space can be expressed as a linear combination of **i** + **j**, **j** + **k**, **k** + **i**. Why not see if you can do this?

We are looking for numbers r, s and t such that

$$a\mathbf{i} + b\mathbf{j} + c\mathbf{k} = r(\mathbf{i} + \mathbf{j}) + s(\mathbf{j} + \mathbf{k}) + t(\mathbf{k} + \mathbf{i})$$
$$= (r + t)\mathbf{i} + (r + s)\mathbf{j} + (s + t)\mathbf{k}$$

from which we obtain the equations

$$a = r + t$$
$$b = r + s$$
$$c = s + t$$

We now solve these to obtain

$$r = \tfrac{1}{2}(a + b - c)$$
$$s = \tfrac{1}{2}(-a + b + c)$$
$$t = \tfrac{1}{2}(a - b + c)$$
■

22.9 THE BASIS THEOREM

If a vector space has a basis with a finite number n of vectors in it, then every basis for it has n vectors.

A vector space with a finite basis is called a **finite dimensional** vector space. The number of elements in its basis determines its dimension.

We shall not prove the basis theorem, but we observe that in the previous example there were three vectors in each of the bases. Some vector spaces do not have a finite basis and so are not finite dimensional.

We can turn the problem around by taking a set of vectors and considering all possible linear combinations of them. This is known as the **span** of the vectors. We have already done this with complex numbers when we introduced the new symbol i to the real numbers and so generated, among other things, a two-dimensional real vector space spanned by the set of vectors {1, i}.

This is a particularly fruitful idea. For example, suppose we consider real functions and the set of vectors

$$1, x, x^2, x^3, \ldots, x^n, \ldots$$

Taylor expansions were obtained in section 8.2.

The set of linear combinations consists of all those functions which can be represented by Taylor expansions about the origin. Unfortunately, this is a fairly restricted class of functions.

However, if instead we take the set of vectors

$$1, \cos x, \sin x, \cos 2x, \sin 2x, \ldots, \cos nx, \sin nx, \ldots$$

Joseph Fourier (1768–1830): French mathematician. Influential in mathematical physics and on the theory of real functions.

and consider the span of these, then we obtain all those functions which can be represented by trigonometrical series about the origin. This is a much wider class of functions and even includes discontinuous ones. Considerations of this kind would lead us to the theory of Fourier series.

22.10 TRANSFORMATIONS

A **transformation** is a function from one vector space to another. In other words, if you give a vector to a transformation it will give you back another vector – not necessarily in the same space.

We shall reserve the word **operator** for a transformation from a vector space to itself. So that if you give a vector to an operator, it will give you another vector in the same space.

Let $\mathscr{F}$ consist of all real functions which can be differentiated and integrated an arbitrary number of times and which each have the real numbers $\mathbb{R}$ as their domain. Then $\mathscr{F}$ has the algebraic structure of a real vector space. We shall reserve the symbol $\mathscr{F}$ in this chapter to denote this space.

We have already met many operators on $\mathscr{F}$, so let's list a few:
1 differentiation
2 integration
3 taking a finite difference.

22.11 THE ZERO AND IDENTITY OPERATORS

There are two special operators, known as the **zero operator** O and the **identity operator** I, which behave in the algebraic structure of operators rather like 0 and 1 do in real numbers. Here they are:

O: $V \to V$ is defined by O[v] = **0** for all $v \in V$.

In other words, every vector is transformed into the zero vector.

I: $V \to V$ is defined by I[v] = v for all $v \in V$.

In other words, every vector is transformed into itself.

22.12 LINEAR OPERATORS

Suppose that a and b are any two real numbers and suppose also that T is an operator on the real vector space V. Then T is linear if and only if

$$T[au + bv] = aT[u] + bT[v]$$

whenever u and v are vectors in V. In other words, T is an operator which is also linear.

☐ For each of the following values of T, decide if T is a linear operator on the vector space $\mathscr{F}$:

Example

a T = I, the identity operator.
b T = O, the zero operator.
c T = exp, the exponential operator.
d T defined by $T[f(x)] = [f(x)]^2$.
e T = D defined by $D[f(x)] = f'(x)$; D is known as the **differential opera-tor**.
f T = ∫ defined by

We shall use the operator D in section 22.15 to solve differential equations.

$$\int [f(x)] = \int f(x)\, \mathrm{d}x$$

g T = Δ defined by

$$\Delta[f(x)] = f(x + 1) - f(x)$$

Δ is known as the **forward difference operator**.

We shall use the operator Δ in section 22.15 to solve difference equations.

In each case we have to decide whether or not

$$T[af + bg] = aT[f] + bT[g]$$

We consider each side separately.
a T = I
   LHS = I[$af + bg$] = $af + bg$
   RHS = aI[f] + bI[g] = $af + bg$
   Therefore LHS = RHS and we have linearity.
b T = O
   LHS = O[$af + bg$] = 0
   RHS = aO[f] + bO[g] = 0 + 0 = 0
   Therefore LHS = RHS and we have linearity.
c T = exp
   LHS = exp [$af + bg$] = exp [af] exp [bg]
   RHS = a exp f + b exp g
   But a exp f + b exp g ≠ exp [$af + bg$], and so we do not have a linear operator.

d $Tf = f^2$
  LHS $= [af + bg]^2$
  RHS $= af^2 + bg^2$
  But $[af + bg]^2 \neq af^2 + bg^2$, and so we do not have a linear operator.
e $T = D$
  LHS $= [af + bg]' = af' + bg'$
  RHS $= af' + bg'$
  Therefore LHS $=$ RHS and we have a linear operator.
f $T = \int$

$$\text{LHS} = \int [af + bg] = \int [af(x) + bg(x)] \, dx$$

$$= a \int f(x) \, dx + b \int g(x) \, dx$$

$$= a \int [f] + b \int [g] = \text{RHS}$$

So we have a linear operator.
Perhaps you would like to try to sort out the last one on your own.

---

g $T = \Delta$
  LHS $= \Delta[af + bg]$
     $= [af(x + 1) + bg(x + 1)] - [af(x) + bg(x)]$
     $= a[f(x + 1) - f(x)] + b[g(x + 1) - g(x)]$
     $= a\Delta[f] + b\Delta[g] = \text{RHS}$
So once more we have a linear operator.   ■

If you didn't manage that then try the same exercise with ∇, known as the **backward difference operator**. It is defined by $\nabla[f(x)] = f(x) - f(x - 1)$. The working is very similar and the conclusion is the same.

  We have seen how to test if an operator is linear, and in doing so we have met some operators which we shall be using later. We shall also use the **translation operator** E, defined by

$$E[f(x)] = f(x + 1)$$

You might like to check that E is linear.

Let's list the main operators again:
D   the differential operator
Δ   the forward difference operator
E   the translation operator
I   the identity operator
O   the zero operator

This is the cast of our play. We shall see later how these operators can be used to obtain particular solutions to differential and difference equations.

22.13 ALGEBRAIC RULES FOR OPERATORS

Suppose we have two operators S and T defined on the same vector space V. Then if a is a real number we define S + T and aT by

$$(S + T)[v] = S[v] + T[v]$$
$$(a\text{T})[v] = a\text{T}[v]$$

where $v \in V$.

For example, $2\Delta + \nabla$ has the following action on $\mathscr{F}$:

$$(2\Delta + \nabla)[f] = (2\Delta)[f] + \nabla[f]$$
$$= 2\Delta[f] + \nabla[f]$$

So

$$(2\Delta + \nabla)[f(x)] = 2\{f(x + 1) - f(x)\} + \{f(x) - f(x - 1)\}$$
$$= 2f(x + 1) - f(x) - f(x - 1)$$

Equality of operators

If we have two operators S and T, then we shall say that S and T are equal and write S = T if and only if they operate in identical ways. Therefore S = T if and only if $S[v] = T[v]$ whenever $v \in V$.

☐ In the vector space $\mathscr{F}$ **Example**

$$\Delta[f(x)] = f(x + 1) - f(x)$$
$$= E[f(x)] - I[f(x)]$$
$$= (E - I)[f(x)]$$

so that $\Delta = E - I$.   ∎

Composition of operators

If S and T are operators on the same vector space V, we define ST by

$$(ST)[v] = S(T[v])$$

whenever $v \in V$. Note that in general $ST \neq TS$.

☐ Suppose S and T and defined on $\mathscr{F}$ by   **Example**

$$S[f(x)] = [f(x)]^2$$
$$T[f(x)] = 2f(x)$$

Show that $ST \neq TS$.

We consider the action of each side on $f(x)$:

$$(ST)[f(x)] = S(T[f(x)]$$
$$= S[2f(x)] = [2f(x)]^2 = 4[f(x)]^2$$
$$(TS)[f(x)] = T(S[f(x)])$$
$$= T([f(x)]^2) = 2[f(x)]^2$$

So ST ≠ TS.   ∎

However, equality does occur *sometimes*.

Example □ Show that on the vector space $\mathscr{F}$, EΔ = ΔE.
   We consider the action of each operator:

$$(EΔ)[f(x)] = E(Δ[f(x)])$$
$$= E[f(x + 1) - f(x)]$$
$$= f(x + 2) - f(x + 1)$$

$$(ΔE)[f(x)] = Δ(E[f(x)])$$
$$= Δ[f(x + 1)]$$
$$= f(x + 2) - f(x + 1)$$

as before.   ∎

If R, S and T are operators, it follows from the definitions that

$$(R + S)T = RT + ST$$
$$R(S + T) = RS + RT$$

Powers of operators
If T is an operator we define T^2 by

$$T^2 = TT$$

In general we define T^n by

$$T^n = TT^{n-1}$$

whenever $n \in N$, $n > 1$.

Example □ Show that

$$(Δ - ∇ + 2I)E = E^2 + I$$

We consider the action of each side on an arbitrary element of $\mathscr{F}$:

$$\{(Δ - ∇ + 2I)E\}[f(x)] = (Δ - ∇ + 2I)[f(x + 1)]$$
$$= Δ[f(x + 1)] - ∇[f(x + 1)] + 2f(x + 1)$$
$$= \{f(x + 2) - f(x + 1)\} - \{f(x + 1) - f(x)\}$$
$$+ 2f(x + 1)$$
$$= f(x + 2) + f(x)$$

Whereas

$$(E^2 + I)[f(x)] = E^2[f(x)] + I[f(x)]$$
$$= E(E[f(x)]) + I[f(x)]$$

$$= E[f(x + 1)] + I[f(x)]$$
$$= f(x + 2) + f(x) \qquad \blacksquare$$

Since the operators have the same action, they are equal.

☐ Show that   **Example**

$$(\Delta + I)^2 = \Delta^2 + 2\Delta + I$$

Again we can show that the action of the two operators is equal. We have already shown that $E = \Delta + I$, and therefore

$$(\Delta + I)^2 [f(x)] = E^2[f(x)] = f(x + 2)$$

On the other hand,

$$
\begin{aligned}
(\Delta^2 + 2\Delta + I)[f(x)] &= \Delta^2[f(x)] + 2\Delta[f(x)] + I[f(x)] \\
&= \Delta(\Delta[f(x)]) + 2\Delta[f(x)] + f(x) \\
&= \Delta[\{f(x + 1) - f(x)\}] + 2\Delta[f(x)] + f(x) \\
&= \Delta[f(x + 1)] + \Delta[f(x)] + f(x) \\
&= f(x + 2) - f(x + 1) + f(x + 1) - f(x) + f(x) \\
&= f(x + 2)
\end{aligned}
$$

as before.

However, we have developed enough algebra of operators to be able to show this directly:

$$
\begin{aligned}
(\Delta + I)^2 &= (\Delta + I)(\Delta + I) \\
&= \Delta(\Delta + I) + I(\Delta + I) \\
&= \Delta\Delta + \Delta I + I\Delta + II \\
&= \Delta^2 + \Delta + \Delta + I = \Delta^2 + 2\Delta + I \qquad \blacksquare
\end{aligned}
$$

From now on we shall assume without further justification that we can multiply out expressions with operators using the usual algebraic rules but being careful not to assume commutativity. In general, remember,

$$ST \neq TS$$

You may have detected something familiar about the rules for operators. If you are exceptionally perspicacious (this has nothing to do with the temperature in the room) you may have realized that the algebra involved is the same as *matrix* algebra. Indeed if we consider real vector spaces consisting of algebraic vectors then the linear transformations turn out to be nothing more or less than our old friends the matrices. If we confine our attention to vectors with n elements then the transformations become operators and we have square $n \times n$ matrices.

Although we are not going to pursue this line any further, it is interesting to notice how the fabric of mathematics interlinks and interweaves.

The algebraic rules for matrices were given in section 11.6.

Now that we know how to combine operators together, we can rewrite equations that we have already encountered in terms of them.

Example ☐ Express the difference equation

$$u(x + 2) - 3u(x + 1) + 2u(x) = x$$

in terms of **a** the translation operator E and **b** the forward difference operator Δ.

a We have

$$E[u(x)] = u(x + 1)$$

and

$$E^2[u(x)] = E\{E[u(x)]\}$$
$$= E[u(x + 1)] = u(x + 2)$$

So the equation is

$$(E^2 - 3E + 2I)[u(x)] = x$$

b We have already shown that Δ = E − I and so E = Δ + I. Then

$$E^2 = (\Delta + I)^2 = \Delta^2 + 2\Delta + I$$

So that

$$E^2 - 3E + 2I = \Delta^2 + 2\Delta + I - 3(\Delta + I) + 2I$$
$$= \Delta^2 - \Delta$$

Therefore the equation is

$$(\Delta^2 - \Delta)[u(x)] = x$$ ■

22.14 INVERSE OPERATORS

If we have a pair of operators S and T such that

$$ST = TS = I$$

we say that S is the **inverse** of T and write $S = T^{-1}$. It then follows by symmetry that T is the inverse of S and $T = S^{-1}$. (It is a simple matter to prove that an operator has at most one inverse.)

Example ☐ Show that if T satisfies

$$T[f(x)] = f(x - 1)$$

then $T = E^{-1}$.

We must show two things:

$$T[E[f(x)]] = f(x)$$
$$E[T[f(x)]] = f(x)$$

This is straightforward:

$$T[E[f(x)]] = T[f(x + 1)] = f(x)$$
$$E[T[f(x)]] = E[f(x - 1)] = f(x) \qquad \blacksquare$$

Why are inverses important to us? Well, let's think back to our difference equation at the end of section 22.13. We had

$$(E^2 - 3E + 2I) [u(x)] = x$$

Suppose we can find an inverse T for the operator

$$S = E^2 - 3E + 2I$$

From the equation,

$$(E^2 - 3E + 2I)[u(x)] = x$$
$$S[u(x)] = x$$

and so

$$T(S[u(x)]) = T[x]$$

taking the value of T at each side. However, this gives

$$u(x) = T[x]$$

and so we obtain $u(x)$.

Unfortunately there is a slight snag: given an operator S, we don't always have an inverse operator T. In such circumstances we must make the best of a bad job and see what we can do with what we have available. We illustrate the difficulty with D, the differential operator.

We have $D[f] = f'$ for every differentiable function f. For example, $D[\sin x] = \cos x$. If an inverse operator D^{-1} exists it must therefore have the property that $D^{-1}[\cos x] = \sin x$. However, $D[\sin x + 1] = \cos x$ and so by the same argument we must have $D^{-1}[\cos x] = \sin x + 1$.

This ambiguity shows that in fact D has no inverse. The trouble is, D does not define a bijection (Chapter 5), so there is no hope of finding an inverse operator D^{-1}. To get round this we define D^{-1} rather loosely, so that if $D[f] = g$ then $f = D^{-1}[g]$ means any solution of the equation $D[f(x)] = g$. In other words, $D^{-1}[g]$ will be a **particular solution** of the equation $D[f] = g$.

If you have forgotten what a bijection is then refer back to section 5.7.

Now if you remember the work we did on differential and difference equations (Chapters 19–21) you will remember that the general solution of the equations we considered turned out to be the sum of two parts. One was the complementary part and the other was a particular solution. The arguments which we used can be generalized to similar equations involving linear operators. However, we have a different method for obtaining particular solutions.

22.15 THE OPERATIONAL METHOD

We treat T as an algebraic symbol and from the equation $T[f] = g$ obtain a particular solution. We shall not justify the seemingly outrageous algebraic practices which will be used to obtain these solutions, but suffice it to say that they can be justified for the types of function we shall be considering.

   Traditionally these operator methods have been used to obtain particular solutions to differential equations, but in fact they can be used in the same way to obtain particular solutions to difference equations.

DIFFERENTIAL EQUATIONS: OPERATOR D

The operator D was introduced in section 22.12.

Suppose $P(D)$ is a polynomial in D of degree n. Then the equation

$$P(D) [y] = f(x)$$

is an nth-order differential equation.

Example □ If $P(D) = D^3 + D - I$, a polynomial of degree 3, then

$$P(D) [y] = x^2$$

is the equation

$$(D^3 + D - I) [y] = x^2$$

$$\frac{d^3y}{dx^3} + \frac{dy}{dx} - y = x^2$$

a third-order differential equation. ■

We shall want some techniques for obtaining particular solutions, and these solutions will depend on the form of $f = f(x)$.

   We choose $f(x) = e^{ax}$ as an example for detailed discussion. We have $D[e^{ax}] = a\,e^{ax}$ and $D^2[e^{ax}] = a^2\,e^{ax}$. So in general

$$P(D)[e^{ax}] = P(a)\,e^{ax}$$

In other words, if an operator consists of a polynomial in D then its action on e^{ax} is to replace D by a in the polynomial and multiply the result by e^{ax}. Consider the differential equation

$$P(D)[y] = e^{ax}$$

a particular solution may be represented formally by

$$y = \frac{1}{P(D)} [e^{ax}]$$

We now show that if $P(a) \neq 0$

$$y = \frac{1}{P(a)} (e^{ax})$$

To do this we must show that the equation $P(D)[y] = e^{ax}$ is satisfied. Now

$$P(D)[y] = P(D) \left[\frac{1}{P(a)} e^{ax} \right]$$

$$= \frac{1}{P(a)} P(D)[e^{ax}] \quad \text{(since D is linear)}$$

$$= \frac{1}{P(a)} P(a)e^{ax} = e^{ax}$$

So y is a particular solution.

We can represent this operational rule symbolically in the following way:

$$\frac{I}{P(D)} [e^{ax}] = \frac{1}{P(a)} (e^{ax}) \quad \text{provided } P(a) \neq 0$$

Here is a list of this and similar operational rules which can be used for the operator D. We shall not justify them all, but instead we see how they can be applied to obtain particular solutions to differential equations.

1     $\dfrac{I}{P(D)} [e^{ax}] = \dfrac{1}{P(a)} (e^{ax})$ provided $P(a) \neq 0$

2     $\dfrac{I}{P(D^2)} [\sin ax] = \dfrac{1}{P(-a^2)} (\sin ax)$ provided $P(-a^2) \neq 0$

3     $\dfrac{I}{P(D^2)} [\cos ax] = \dfrac{1}{P(-a^2)} (\cos ax)$ provided $P(-a^2) \neq 0$

4     $\dfrac{I}{P(D)} [e^{ax} f(x)] = e^{ax} \dfrac{I}{P(D + aI)} [f(x)]$

Rules 2 and 3 can be used to handle sines and cosines in much the same way as rule 1 does for exponentials. Rule 4 enables us to handle the situation when $P(a) = 0$.

However, we must not disguise the fact that when we use the operational procedure we will perform operations which we have not justified.

□ Obtain a particular solution of the equation   **Example**

$$(D^2 + 2D + I)[y] = \cos x$$

We write

$$y = \frac{I}{D^2 + 2D + I}[\cos x]$$

$$= \frac{I}{-I + 2D + I}[\cos x]$$

$$= \frac{I}{2D}[\cos x]$$

$$= \frac{D}{2D^2}[\cos x]$$

$$= \frac{D}{-2I}[\cos x]$$

$$= -\frac{1}{2}D[\cos x] = \frac{1}{2}\sin x \qquad \blacksquare$$

Notice how we have shamelessly misused rule 3 to make only partial substitutions in P(D) and then have carried out dextrous algebraic operations with D to wrestle a particular solution out of it. Never mind, it works! Feel free to do the same; it is good to let your hair down once in a while!

Now we shall solve the same problem again, this time using complex numbers.

$$y = \frac{I}{D^2 + 2D + I}[\cos x]$$

$$= \frac{I}{D^2 + 2D + I}[\text{Re}\,(e^{ix})]$$

$$= \text{Re}\left\{\frac{I}{D^2 + 2D + I}[(e^{ix})]\right\}$$

$$= \text{Re}\left\{e^{ix}\frac{I}{[D + iI]^2 + 2[D + iI] + I}[1]\right\}$$

$$= \text{Re}\left\{e^{ix}\frac{I}{D^2 + 2iD - I + 2D + 2iI + I}[1]\right\}$$

$$= \text{Re}\left\{e^{ix}\frac{I}{D^2 + 2iD + 2D + 2iI}[1]\right\}$$

$$= \text{Re}\left\{\frac{1}{2i}e^{ix}\left(I + \frac{D^2 + 2iD + 2D}{2i}\right)^{-1}[1]\right\}$$

We now argue that, if we expand by the binomial theorem, since D[1] = 0 we need only consider the first term. Consequently

$$y = \text{Re}\left\{\frac{1}{2i}e^{ix}I[1]\right\}$$

$$= \text{Re} \left\{ \frac{1}{2i} e^{ix} 1 \right\}$$

$$= \text{Re} \left\{ \frac{\cos x + i \sin x}{2i} \right\}$$

$$= \text{Re} \left\{ \frac{i \cos x - \sin x}{-2} \right\}$$

$$= \frac{1}{2} \sin x$$

as before.

Although we have used complex numbers freely, you should realize that we have not justified their use here. The use too of the binomial theorem in this cavalier way is another instance of where the theory we have developed has been left behind. We shall have to regard all this as a situation in which the ends justify the means.

Notice how much quicker the first method was. This is often the situation; one method is quick and relatively straightforward while another is long and heavy going.

DIFFERENCE EQUATIONS: OPERATOR Δ

The operator Δ was introduced in section 22.12.

In much the same way as we have obtained particular solutions to differential equations, we can also obtain particular solutions to difference equations. We shall find that the binomial theorem is a useful standby here too.

There are rules for Δ too. Here is an example of one of them:

For another rule refer to Further exercise 10 at the end of this chapter.

$$\frac{I}{P(\Delta)} [(a + 1)^n] = \frac{1}{P(a)} (a + 1)^n \quad \text{provided } P(a) \neq 0$$

However, before we solve a problem we shall show there is an interesting link between D and Δ. Here is the connection:

$$\Delta = \exp D - I$$

We shall give a justification for this extraordinary operator equation. Suppose f is an element of $\mathscr{F}$. Then

$$E[f(x)] = f(x + 1)$$

$$= f(x) + f'(x) + \frac{1}{2!} f''(x) + \ldots + \frac{1}{n!} f^{(n)}(x) + \ldots$$

Taylor's expansion is given in section 8.2.

using Taylor's expansion with $h = 1$. Now we know that questions of convergence may arise, but if we accept only functions which can be represented by a Taylor expansion then we have

$$E[f(x)] = f(x) + D[f(x)] + \frac{1}{2!} D^2[f(x)] + \ldots + \frac{1}{n!} D^n[f(x)] + \ldots$$

$$= \left(I + D + \frac{D^2}{2!} + \ldots + \frac{D^n}{n!} + \ldots \right)[f(x)]$$
$$= \exp D[f(x)]$$

So $E = \exp D$. Since we have previously shown that $E = \Delta + I$, we obtain

$$\Delta = \exp D - I$$

Example □ Obtain a particular solution to the difference equation

$$u(x + 1) - 2u(x) = x^2$$

We begin by writing the equation in terms of the translation operator E, where $u = u(x)$:

$$(E - 2I)[u] = x^2$$
$$([\Delta + I] - 2I)[u] = x^2$$
$$(\Delta - I)[u] = x^2$$

Then

$$u = \frac{I}{\Delta - I}[x^2]$$
$$= -(I - \Delta)^{-1}[x^2]$$

Now

$$\Delta[x^2] = (x + 1)^2 - x^2 = 2x + 1$$

So

$$\Delta^2[x^2] = \Delta[2x + 1] = [2(x + 1) + 1] - [2x + 1] = 2$$

and therefore $\Delta^n[x^2] = 0$ if $n > 2$. This means that we only need to consider the first three terms in the binomial expansion:

$$u = -(I + \Delta + \Delta^2)[x^2]$$
$$= -x^2 - (2x + 1) - 2$$
$$= -x^2 - 2x - 3$$

If you have already studied difference equations (Chapter 21) you might like to obtain the particular solution again using the method of trial solutions. ■

_____22.16 Workshop_____

Exercise Decide whether or not, in the vector space $\mathcal{F}$, the following set of vectors is linearly dependent or linearly independent:

$$\{1, x^2, x^2 + x, x + 1, x^4\}$$

Remember the key question is whether or not there is a linear combination of the vectors which is the zero vector and in which not *all* the coefficients are zero.

As soon as you have made an attempt, read on and see how things went.

We must consider the equation   **2**

$$a + bx^2 + c(x^2 + x) + d(x + 1) + ex^4 = 0$$

where a, b, c, d and e are real numbers. Can we find a set of coefficients, not all zero, which satisfy this? We deduce

$$a + d + (c + d)x + (b + c)x^2 + ex^4 = 0$$

This must be satisfied for all x; it must be an identity, and so

$$a + d = 0$$
$$c + d = 0$$
$$b + c = 0$$
$$e = 0$$

It follows therefore that $a = c = -b = -d$ and $e = 0$.

So there are coefficients which are not all zero. For instance, taking $a = 1$ we have

$$1 + (-1)x^2 + (1)(x^2 + x) + (-1)(x + 1) + (0)x^4 = 0$$

Consequently the vectors are linearly dependent.

If you managed that you can move ahead to step 4. Otherwise try this exercise.

▷ **Exercise**   Decide, in the vector space consisting of geometrical vectors in three-dimensional space, whether the set of vectors

$$\{\mathbf{i} + 2\mathbf{j} + \mathbf{k}, \mathbf{i} + \mathbf{j} + 2\mathbf{k}, 2\mathbf{i} + \mathbf{j} + \mathbf{k}\}$$

is a linearly independent set or not.

When you have made the effort, move on.

We look for coefficients which are not all zero which satisfy the equation   **3**

$$a(\mathbf{i} + 2\mathbf{j} + \mathbf{k}) + b(\mathbf{i} + \mathbf{j} + 2\mathbf{k}) + c(2\mathbf{i} + \mathbf{j} + \mathbf{k}) = \mathbf{O}$$

If this equation is to hold then

$$(a + b + 2c)\mathbf{i} + (2a + b + c)\mathbf{j} + (a + 2b + c)\mathbf{k} = \mathbf{O}$$

Consequently

$$a + b + 2c = 0$$
$$2a + b + c = 0$$
$$a + 2b + c = 0$$

Adding these together and dividing by 4 gives $a + b + c = 0$ and we therefore deduce that $a = 0$, $b = 0$ and $c = 0$. Since all the coefficients must necessarily be zero, we deduce that the vectors are linearly independent.

If there are any persistent difficulties here, you had better return to the text to see if you can sort them out. Then step ahead.

4 **Exercise**   Show that the operator δ defined on $\mathscr{F}$ by

$$\delta[f(x)] = f(x + \tfrac{1}{2}) - f(x - \tfrac{1}{2})$$

is a linear operator. (δ is known as the **central difference operator**.) Remember the test for linearity and see how things work out.

5   We must show that if a and b are arbitrary real numbers then

$$\delta[af(x) + bg(x)] = a\delta[f(x)] + b\delta[g(x)]$$

$$\begin{aligned}
\text{LHS} &= \{af(x + \tfrac{1}{2}) + bg(x + \tfrac{1}{2})\} - \{af(x - \tfrac{1}{2}) + bg(x - \tfrac{1}{2})\} \\
&= a\{f(x + \tfrac{1}{2}) - f(x - \tfrac{1}{2})\} + b\{g(x + \tfrac{1}{2}) - g(x - \tfrac{1}{2})\} \\
&= a\delta[f(x)] + b\delta[g(x)] = \text{RHS}
\end{aligned}$$

! Make sure you didn't try to sort out each term individually first. If you wrote

$$\text{LHS} = af(x + \tfrac{1}{2}) - af(x - \tfrac{1}{2}) + bg(x + \tfrac{1}{2}) - bg(x - \tfrac{1}{2})$$

then you *assumed* linearity at the outset and your argument is wrong! If you are certain that you did not make any error, move ahead to step 7. Otherwise try this exercise.

▷**Exercise**   Consider $\mathbb{C}$, the real vector space of complex numbers, and suppose that T is defined by

$$T(z) = z + iz$$

Is T a linear operator?

6   T is certainly an operator since every vector z becomes transformed into another vector. We must investigate whether T is linear. For linearity we must show

$$T[az + bw] = aT[z] + bT[w]$$

where z and w are any two complex numbers and a and b are real numbers.

$$T[az + bw] = \{az + bw\} + i\{az + bw\}$$
$$= a(z + iz) + b(w + iw)$$
$$= aT[z] + bT[w]$$

So T is linear.

▷**Exercise**   Verify the following operator identities for the vector space $\mathscr{F}$: ⌐7⌐

$$\Delta = \nabla E$$
$$(\Delta + \nabla)E = E^2 - I$$

Make a good effort and then move on.

We can verify equality by showing that each operator has the same action ⌐8⌐ on the vectors in $\mathscr{F}$. First,

$$\nabla E[f(x)] = \nabla[f(x + 1)] = f(x + 1) - f(x) = \Delta[f(x)]$$

Secondly,

$$(\Delta + \nabla)E[f(x)] = (\Delta + \nabla)[f(x + 1)]$$
$$= \Delta[f(x + 1)] + \nabla[f(x + 1)]$$
$$= \{f(x + 2) - f(x + 1)\} + \{f(x + 1) - f(x)\}$$
$$= f(x + 2) - f(x)$$
$$= E^2[f(x)] - I[f(x)]$$
$$= (E^2 - I)[f(x)]$$

If all is well you can go ahead to step 10. If things didn't go right, make sure you follow what we have done and then try the next exercise.

▷**Exercise**   Show that

$$(\Delta - \nabla)E = (E - 1)^2$$

Step forward when you are ready!

Once more we can consider the action of each operator on $f(x)$: ⌐9⌐

$$\text{LHS} = (\Delta - \nabla)E[f(x)]$$
$$= (\Delta - \nabla)[f(x + 1)]$$
$$= \Delta[f(x + 1)] - \nabla[f(x + 1)]$$
$$= f(x + 2) - f(x + 1) - \{f(x + 1) - f(x)\}$$
$$= f(x + 2) - 2f(x + 1) + f(x)$$
$$\text{RHS} = (E - 1)^2[f(x)]$$

$$= (E - I)[(E - I)[f(x)]]$$
$$= (E - I)[E[f(x)] - I[f(x)]]$$
$$= (E - I)[f(x + 1) - f(x)]$$
$$= E[f(x + 1) - f(x)] - I[f(x + 1) - f(x)]$$
$$= f(x + 2) - f(x + 1) - f(x + 1) + f(x)$$
$$= f(x + 2) - 2f(x + 1) + f(x)$$

10 We can establish these operator identities *directly* once we know how E, Δ and ∇ interrelate. It is easy to show that

$$\Delta = E - I \qquad \nabla = I - E^{-1}$$

▷**Exercise**   Show by using operator identities that

$$(\Delta + \nabla)E = E^2 - I$$

See how you get on.

11 We notice that the right-hand side only has E and I, so we start with the left and eliminate Δ and ∇:

$$(\Delta + \nabla)E = (E - I + I - E^{-1})E$$
$$= (E - E^{-1})E = EE - E^{-1}E$$
$$= E^2 - I$$

If you managed that then on you go to step 13. If not, make sure you follow things before moving ahead to the next problem.

▷**Exercise**   Show by using operator identities that

$$(\Delta - \nabla)E = (E - I)^2$$

12 Once again we eliminate Δ and ∇ from the left-hand side:

$$(\Delta - \nabla)E = (E - I - \{I - E^{-1}\})E$$
$$= (E - 2I + E^{-1})E$$
$$= EE - 2IE + E^{-1}E$$
$$= E^2 - 2E + I$$
$$= E^2 - E - E + I$$
$$= E(E - I) - (E - I)$$
$$= E(E - I) - I(E - I)$$
$$= (E - I)^2$$

You may have shortened this a little by using the fact that E and I commute and therefore $E^2 - 2E + I = (E - I)^2$.

Now let's find some particular solutions to differential and difference equations.

───

▷**Exercise**   Obtain, by the use of operator methods, a particular solution to the differential equation

13

$$\frac{d^2y}{dx^2} - 2\frac{dy}{dx} + y = e^x$$

If we had found the complementary part first we should have recognized this as the breakdown case. One good characteristic which the operator method has is that it is easy to handle the breakdown case.

Have a go at this and see how you get on.

───

We begin by writing the equation in terms of the operator D:

14

$$(D^2 - 2D + I)[y] = e^x$$
$$(D - I)^2[y] = e^x$$

So a particular solution is

$$y = \frac{I}{(D - I)^2}[e^x]$$

Now this is an occasion where $P(a) = 0$, and so we need to use the rule which enables us to pull the exponential function past the domain of the operator:

$$y = e^x \frac{I}{(\{D + I\} - I)^2}[1]$$

$$= e^x \frac{I}{D^2}[1]$$

$$= e^x D^{-2}[1]$$

This means we must integrate 1 twice with respect to x. We can ignore any arbitrary constants because we are looking for any solution.

$$y = e^x D^{-1}[x]$$
$$= e^x\{\tfrac{1}{2}x^2\}$$
$$= \tfrac{1}{2}x^2 e^x$$

Did you manage that? It's quicker than the trial solution method.

If you would like another one of these then try the next exercise. Otherwise you can move forward to step 16.

▷**Exercise**   Obtain a solution to the differential equation

$$\frac{d^2x}{dt^2} - 3\frac{dx}{dt} + 2x = \sin 2t$$

using the operator D.

Notice that we are using different variables here. This should cause no difficulties, but don't give the answer in terms of y and x, will you?

---

15 Expressing the equation in terms of the operator D we have

$$(D^2 - 3D + 2I)[x] = \sin 2t$$

Therefore

$$x = \frac{I}{D^2 - 3D + 2I}[\sin 2t]$$

$$= \frac{I}{-4I - 3D + 2I}[\sin 2t]$$

$$= \frac{I}{-2I - 3D}[\sin 2t]$$

$$= \frac{-2I + 3D}{(-2I)^2 - (3D)^2}[\sin 2t]$$

$$= \frac{-2I + 3D}{(-2I)^2 - 9(-4I)}[\sin 2t]$$

$$= \frac{-2I + 3D}{40}[\sin 2t]$$

$$= \frac{1}{20}(-\sin 2t + 3\cos 2t)$$

---

16 We have only stated one rule for Δ, but if we regard $\Delta^{-1}[f]$ as *any* solution of the equation $\Delta y = f$ then we can easily obtain some results. For example, $\Delta[x] = 1$, so $\Delta^{-1}[1] = x$. Again, $\Delta[x^2] = 2x + 1$, so $x^2 = 2\Delta^{-1}[x] + \Delta^{-1}[1]$. Therefore

$$\Delta^{-1}[x] = \tfrac{1}{2}[x^2 - x] = \tfrac{1}{2}x(x - 1)$$

Δ^{-1} is often called **indefinite summation**.

▷**Exercise**   Obtain, using an operator method, a solution of the difference equation

$$y(x + 2) - y(x) = x$$

Remember: first express the equation in operator form and then proceed.

17

$$(E^2 - I)[y] = x$$
$$([\Delta + I]^2 - I)[y] = x$$
$$(\Delta^2 + 2\Delta)[y] = x$$
$$(\Delta + 2I)\Delta[y] = x$$

From which a particular solution is

$$y = \frac{I}{(\Delta + 2I)\Delta}[x]$$

$$= \frac{I}{(\Delta + 2I)}\Delta^{-1}[x]$$

$$= \frac{I}{(\Delta + 2I)}[\tfrac{1}{2}(x^2 - x)]$$

$$= \tfrac{1}{2}(I + \tfrac{1}{2}\Delta)^{-1}[\tfrac{1}{2}(x^2 - x)]$$

$$= \tfrac{1}{4}(I + \tfrac{1}{2}\Delta)^{-1}[x^2 - x]$$

Since $\Delta^3[x^2] = 0$ we may stop the binomial expansion at the second degree term. Therefore

$$y = \tfrac{1}{4}(I - \tfrac{1}{2}\Delta + \tfrac{1}{4}\Delta^2)[x^2 - x]$$

$$= \tfrac{1}{4}([x^2 - x] - \tfrac{1}{2}[2x + 1 - 1] + \tfrac{1}{4}[2])$$

$$= \tfrac{1}{4}(x^2 - x - x + \tfrac{1}{2})$$

$$= \tfrac{1}{4}x^2 - \tfrac{1}{2}x + \tfrac{1}{8}$$

Did you manage that? If you did then you have learned the technique. Now for another problem.

▷**Exercise**   Show that if r is any natural number and $x^{(r)}$ is defined by

$$x^{(r)} = x(x - 1)(x - 2) \ldots (x - r + 1)$$

then $\Delta x^{(r)} = r x^{(r-1)}$. Obtain a particular solution of the difference equation

$$y(x + 2) - 6y(x + 1) + 9y(x) = x(x - 1)$$

Do this before you take the next step.

18

We have

$$\Delta[x^{(r)}] = [x + 1]^{(r)} - x^{(r)}$$

$$= (x + 1)x(x - 1) \ldots (x - r + 2) - x(x - 1)(x - 2) \ldots (x - r + 1)$$

$$= x(x - 1)(x - 2) \ldots (x - r + 2)\{(x + 1) - (x - r + 1)\}$$

$$= rx(x - 1)(x - 2) \ldots (x - \{r - 1\} + 1)$$

$$= rx^{(r-1)}$$

The equation in terms of the operator E is

$$(E^2 - 6E + 9I)[y(x)] = x(x - 1)$$

Using $E = \Delta + I$ this becomes

$$(\{\Delta + I\}^2 - 6\{\Delta + I\} + 9I)[y(x)] = x(x - 1)$$
$$(\Delta^2 + 2\Delta + I - 6\{\Delta + I\} + 9I)[y(x)] = x(x - 1)$$
$$(\Delta^2 - 4\Delta + 4I)[y(x)] = x(x - 1)$$
$$(\Delta - 2I)^2[y(x)] = x(x - 1)$$

A particular solution is therefore

$$y(x) = \frac{I}{(\Delta - 2I)^2}[x(x - 1)]$$
$$= \tfrac{1}{4}(I - \tfrac{1}{2}\Delta)^{-2}[x(x - 1)]$$

Now $\Delta[x(x - 1)] = 2x$ and $\Delta^2[x(x - 1)] = 2$. So we need only terms in Δ of degree 2 or less when we take the binomial expansion:

$$y(x) = \frac{1}{4}\Big\{I + (-2)\Big(-\frac{1}{2}\Delta\Big)$$
$$+ \frac{(-2)(-3)}{1 \times 2}\Big(-\frac{1}{2}\Delta\Big)^2\Big\}[x(x - 1)]$$
$$= \frac{1}{4}\Big\{I + \Delta + \frac{3}{4}\Delta^2\Big\}[x(x - 1)]$$
$$= \frac{1}{4}\Big\{x(x - 1) + 2x + \frac{3}{4}(2)\Big\}$$
$$= \frac{1}{8}\{2x(x - 1) + 4x + 3\}$$
$$= \frac{1}{8}\{2x^2 + 2x + 3\}$$

Fine! Now for one last problem.

The binomial theorem was discussed in section 1.6.

▷**Exercise** Obtain a particular solution to the difference equation

$$u(x + 2) - u(x + 1) + u(x) = 2^x$$

You will need the one rule we had for the operator Δ.

---

19 As usual we begin by writing the equation in terms of the operator E:

$$(E^2 - E + I)[u(x)] = 2^x$$

Then we use $E = \Delta + I$ to obtain

$$([\Delta + I]^2 - [\Delta + I] + I)[u(x)] = 2^x$$
$$(\Delta^2 + 2\Delta + I - \Delta - I + I)[u(x)] = 2^x$$
$$(\Delta^2 + \Delta + I)[u(x)] = 2^x$$

A particular solution is

$$u(x) = \frac{I}{\Delta^2 + \Delta + I}[(1 + 1)^x]$$

$$u(x) = \frac{1}{1 + 1 + 1}(1 + 1)^x$$

$$u(x) = \tfrac{1}{3}2^x$$

Before we leave this topic, we stress that there is much more that could be said. The practices which we have adopted have overtaken the theory in several places. For example, $\mathscr{F}$ contained only functions defined for all real numbers and which could be integrated and differentiated repeatedly, and yet we have been using the operators on functions which are not defined everywhere. You do not need to lose any sleep over this; it is a *mathematical* dilemma.

Now it's time for an application.

22.17 Practical

RESONATING BAFFLE PLATE

A light spring is suspended vertically and supports a mass m in the form of a baffle plate. It is kept in sinusoidal motion with amplitude X and angular frequency ω. Assuming that the resistance to motion is proportional to the velocity of the mass and that the extension of the spring is proportional to the restoring force, it can be shown that

$$m \frac{d^2y}{dt^2} + k \frac{dy}{dt} + ny = X \sin \omega t$$

where k is the resisting force per unit velocity, n is the restoring force per unit displacement and y is the vertical displacement.

If $k = 0$, determine the resonant frequency p of the system and the displacement at time t when ω is set to this resonant frequency. Initially the baffle plate is at rest and there is no displacement.

Although there is some algebra to be handled, you should be able to complete the first stage – which is to obtain the complementary part (CP).

1 The equation becomes, on dividing by m,

$$\frac{d^2y}{dt^2} + \frac{k}{m}\frac{dy}{dt} + \frac{n}{m}y = \frac{X}{m}\sin \omega t$$

We cannot use m as the variable in the auxiliary equation, so we shall use λ instead:

$$\lambda^2 + (k/m)\lambda + (n/m) = 0$$

When $k = 0$ we have $\lambda^2 = -n/m$, so that putting $p^2 = n/m$ we obtain $\lambda = \pm ip$. Consequently

$$CP = A \cos pt + B \sin pt$$

where $p = \sqrt{(n/m)}$ is the resonant frequency.

The next stage is to obtain a particular solution using operational methods. The method of trial solutions is available to us, but we shall use the operator D.

---

2 If $\omega = p$ the equation becomes

$$\frac{d^2y}{dt^2} + p^2y = \frac{X}{m}\sin \omega t$$

$$(D^2 + p^2I)[y] = (X/m)\sin pt$$

So a particular solution is

$$
\begin{aligned}
y &= \frac{I}{D^2 + p^2I}\left[\frac{X}{m}\sin pt\right]\\
&= \frac{X}{m}\frac{I}{D^2 + p^2I}[\sin pt]\\
&= \frac{X}{m}\frac{I}{D^2 + p^2I}[\operatorname{Im}(e^{ipt})]\\
&= \frac{X}{m}\operatorname{Im}\left\{\frac{I}{D^2 + p^2I}[e^{ipt}]\right\}\\
&= \frac{X}{m}\operatorname{Im}\left\{\frac{e^{ipt}}{[D + ipI]^2 + p^2I}[1]\right\}\\
&= \frac{X}{m}\operatorname{Im}\left\{\frac{e^{ipt}}{D^2 + 2ipD}[1]\right\}\\
&= \frac{X}{m}\operatorname{Im}\left\{\frac{e^{ipt}}{D + 2ipI}[t]\right\}\\
&= \frac{X}{m}\operatorname{Im}\left\{\frac{1}{2ip}e^{ipt}\left(I + \frac{D}{2ip}\right)^{-1}[t]\right\}
\end{aligned}
$$

$$= \frac{X}{m} \operatorname{Im} \left\{ \frac{1}{2ip} e^{ipt} \left(I - \frac{D}{2ip} \right) [t] \right\}$$

$$= \frac{X}{m} \operatorname{Im} \left\{ \frac{1}{2ip} e^{ipt} \left(t - \frac{1}{2ip} \right) \right\}$$

$$= \frac{X}{m} \operatorname{Im} \left\{ -\frac{1}{4p^2} [\cos pt + i \sin pt] [2ipt - 1] \right\}$$

$$= \frac{X}{m} \left\{ -\frac{2pt}{4p^2} \cos pt + \frac{\sin pt}{4p^2} \right\}$$

$$= \frac{X}{4mp^2} (\sin pt - 2pt \cos pt)$$

We therefore have the general solution

$$y = A \cos pt + B \sin pt + \frac{X}{4mp^2} (\sin pt - 2pt \cos pt)$$

It is interesting to note that the operational method has thrown up an unwanted term. The term

$$\frac{X}{4mp^2} \sin pt$$

is already present in the complementary part and is therefore superfluous to the particular solution. We can make things a little easier for ourselves if we absorb this term into the complementary part by redefining the arbitrary constant B. We obtain then the general solution

$$y = A \cos pt + B \sin pt - \frac{X}{2mp} t \cos pt$$

Now all you have to do is to use the boundary conditions to complete the solution.

---

3 When $t = 0$, $y = 0$, so $A = 0$. Then

$$y = B \sin pt - \frac{X}{2mp} t \cos pt$$

When $t = 0$, $dy/dt = 0$. We have

$$\frac{dy}{dt} = Bp \cos pt - \frac{X}{2mp} \cos pt + \frac{Xt}{2m} \sin pt$$

Therefore

$$0 = Bp - \frac{X}{2mp}$$

and so $B = X/2mp^2$.

Finally,

$$y = \frac{X}{2mp^2} \sin pt - \frac{X}{2mp} t \cos pt$$

$$= \frac{X}{2mp^2} (\sin pt - pt \cos pt)$$

If we look back through the chapters we shall see that we first developed the differential calculus and then later the integral calculus. This led on to the solutions of differential equations. We studied difference equations too because of their present-day usage and the similar techniques which could be applied to them. In this chapter we built a bridge between linear difference and differential equations and saw that they were closely linked.

This is as far as we are going to take our discussions on the solution of differential equations and difference equations. Other analytic methods exist for solving more complicated equations. For instance power series can be used to solve ordinary differential equations; the principal technique there is known as the method of Frobenius.

Although we have not discussed the solution of partial differential equations, one of the main analytic methods makes use of trigonometrical series and the theory of Fourier series. Other analytic methods for solving ordinary and partial differential equations use integral transforms. Broadly speaking, Laplace transforms are used for ordinary differential equations and Fourier transforms are used for partial differential equations.

Power series can also be used in the solution of difference equations, but there the techniques involve producing generating functions and examining coefficients.

Alternative methods for dealing with all these equations involve numerical techniques. In recent years, because high-speed computers have become common, extensive use of these methods has been made. In the chapter on numerical techniques we noted *en passant* a crude elementary method for solving first-order ordinary differential equations: Euler's method. Here, as in so much mathematical work, it is Taylor's series which underlies it. Improvements in this technique result in the highly accurate Runge-Kutta methods, which have been used extensively in the USA and (it is said) contributed to the successful moon landing. Other techniques, for example predictor-corrector methods, have been employed successfully too.

It is possible to express differential and difference equations in terms of matrix theory, and when this is done another arsenal of powerful methods becomes available. When operators are used in conjunction with vectors they produce a mathematical implement of much power and diversity which can be widely applied; for example to fluid dynamics, the theory of

Ferdinand Frobenius (1849–1917): German mathematician who made major contributions to group theory and worked on differential equations.

Fourier and Laplace transforms are used extensively in advanced engineering mathematics.

Carl Runge (1856–1927), Wilhelm Kutta (1867–1944): German mathematicians. Runge did his work in 1895 and Kutta in 1901.

elasticity, electrical field theory and many other areas. As we may observe, it is when two of three of the topics we have studied singly are put together that we obtain exceedingly powerful mathematical techniques. It will be in the second year of your course that you will consider some of the ideas which we have outlined here.

SUMMARY

Here is a list of some of the things we have learnt about in this chapter.
- ☐ **Vector spaces**
  - **a** Linear combination.
  - **b** Linear dependence and independence.
  - **c** Basis and dimension.
- ☐ **Transformations**
  - **a** Linear operators.
  - **b** Algebraic rules for operators.
- ☐ **Operator methods**
  - **a** The operators I and O.
  - **b** The translation operator E.
  - **c** The forward difference operator Δ.
  - **d** The differential operator D.

We have also seen how operator methods can be used to obtain particular solutions to both differential equations and difference equations.

EXERCISES (for answers see p. 759)

1 Decide whether or not in $\mathscr{F}$ the following sets of vectors are linearly dependent or linearly independent:
 a $\{\sinh x, e^x, e^{-x}\}$
 b $\{x + 1, x^2 + 1, x^2 + x\}$
 c $\{\operatorname{cosec} 2x, \cot 2x, \tan x\}$
 d $\{\coth x, \tanh x, \coth 2x\}$
 e $\{x^2 - x, x^2 + x, x\}$

2 Decide whether or not the following three-dimensional vectors are linearly dependent or linearly independent:
 a $\{\mathbf{i} - \mathbf{j} + 2\mathbf{k}, -\mathbf{i} + 2\mathbf{j} + \mathbf{k}, 2\mathbf{i} + \mathbf{j} - \mathbf{k}\}$
 b $\{\mathbf{i} + 2\mathbf{j}, \mathbf{j} + 2\mathbf{k}, \mathbf{k} + 2\mathbf{i}\}$
 c $\{\mathbf{i} + 2\mathbf{j} + 3\mathbf{k}, 3\mathbf{i} + \mathbf{j} + 2\mathbf{k}, 2\mathbf{i} + 3\mathbf{j} + \mathbf{k}\}$
 d $\{\mathbf{i} + 2\mathbf{j} + \mathbf{k}, 2\mathbf{i} + \mathbf{j} - \mathbf{k}, \mathbf{i} - \mathbf{j} - 2\mathbf{k}\}$

3 Express entirely in terms of the operator Δ
 a $E(\nabla + I)(E + I)$

b $E(\nabla + E + I)^2 E$

c $(\nabla - E)(\nabla + I)E^2$

4 Express entirely in terms of the operator D

  a $\ln E . \ln (\Delta + I)$

  b $(-\nabla + I)(I + \Delta)E$

  c $(E^2 + I)(\Delta - I)$

5 Use operator methods to obtain particular solutions to the following equations:

  a $\dfrac{d^2y}{dx^2} - 5\dfrac{dy}{dx} + 6y = e^{2x}$

  b $U(n + 2) - U(n + 1) + U(n) = 2^n$

  c $\dfrac{d^2y}{dx^2} + y = \sin x$

ASSIGNMENT (for answers see p. 760; see also Workshop on p. 650)

1 Show that in $\mathscr{F}$ the following sets of vectors are linearly independent:

  a $\{1, x + 1, x^2 - x\}$

  b $\{1, \sin x, \cos x, \sin 2x\}$

2 Show that in $\mathscr{F}$ the following sets of vectors are linearly dependent:

  a $\{x, x^2 + x + 1, x^2 - x + 1\}$

  b $\{1, \cos^2 x, \sin^2 x\}$

3 Establish the following operator identities:

  a $\nabla E = \Delta = E\nabla$

  b $\nabla = I - E^{-1}$

4 Establish each of the following:

  a $\Delta[a^x] = a^x(a - 1)$

  b $\Delta[\sin ax] = 2 \sin \tfrac{1}{2}a \cos a(x + \tfrac{1}{2})$

5 Using operator methods, obtain a particular solution for each of the following equations:

  a $y(x + 3) - 4y(x + 2) + y(x + 1) + 6y(x) = x$

  b $u(x + 2) - 2u(x + 1) + 4u(x) = 2^x$

  c $y''(x) + 4y(x) = \cos 2x$

FURTHER EXERCISES (for answers see p. 760)

1 Decide which of the following sets of vectors in $\mathscr{F}$ are linearly dependent and which are linearly independent. If they are linearly dependent, obtain a linear combination which is 0.

  a $\{1, \cos 2x, \cos^2 x\}$

  b $\{1, x^2 + 1, (x + 1)^3, (x - 1)^3\}$

2 Obtain the operator identities

  a $\nabla\Delta = \Delta\nabla = E - 2I + E^{-1}$

  b $\nabla(\Delta + E) = 2\Delta - \nabla$

  c $D = \ln(I + \Delta)$

3 Deduce

  a $\Delta[\log_a x] = \log_a(1 + x^{-1})$

  b $\Delta[\cos ax] = -2\sin\tfrac{1}{2}a\sin a(x + \tfrac{1}{2})$

4 Obtain a particular solution for each of the following equations:

  a $u(x + 2) - 4u(x + 1) + 4u(x) = x(x - 1)$

  b $y''(x) + 4y(x) = \cos x$

  c $y''(x) + 4y(x) = x\cos 2x$

  d $y''(x) + y'(x) - 2y(x) = e^x$

5 The operators D_1 and D_2 are defined as follows:

$$D_1[uv] = vD[u]$$
$$D_2[uv] = uD[v]$$

where u and v are differentiable functions.

  a Show that $D[uv] = (D_1 + D_2)[uv]$.

  b By considering $D''[uv]$ and using the binomial theorem, deduce Leibniz's theorem.

6 Give formal verifications of the following operational formulas:

  a $\Delta = E - I$

  b $E = \exp D$

  c $\Delta[\log_a n!] = \log_a(n + 1)$

Show that if $a \in (0, 1)$, the general solution of the equation

$$y(x + 1) - ay(x) = x$$

where a is constant, is

$$y(x) = Aa^x + \frac{x}{(1 - a)} - \frac{1}{(1 - a)^2}$$

Identify the transient and the steady state and obtain the solution which satisfies $y(1) = 0$.

7 The terminals of a generator producing a constant voltage E are connected across a capacitor of C farads, a cable of resistance R ohms and a coil of self-inductance L henries in series. At time t the charge on the capacitor satisfies

$$L\frac{d^2q}{dt^2} + R\frac{dq}{dt} + \frac{q}{C} = E$$

At time $t = 0$ there is no charge on the capacitor and no current in the circuit. Show that if $LC = 1/2n^2$ and $RC = 1/n$ then

$$q = EC\{1 - \exp(-nt)(\cos nt + \sin nt)\}$$

8 The depth $d(n)$ in metres to which a beam can be driven by a pile-driver into soft mud is given in terms of the number n of impacts by

$$\Delta[d(n + 1)] = \Delta[d(n)] - 0.002$$

provided n is less than 50. Initially the depth was 0.1 metres, and after a single blow the depth increased to 0.199 metres. Obtain an expression for $d(n)$ in terms of n, and thereby show that after 30 blows the depth will be 2.2 metres.

9 A computer program contains a loop which uses at each step numbers which have been calculated in the previous step. If $t(n)$ is the time taken to execute the nth step, it is found that

$$\tfrac{1}{2}\{\Delta[t(n + 2)] + \Delta[t(n)]\} = \Delta[t(n + 1)] + 3$$

Obtain $t(n)$ given that the times taken to execute the first three loops are 5, 15 and 37 microseconds respectively. Use induction, or otherwise, to show that

$$\Sigma r^3 = \{\tfrac{1}{2}n(n + 1)\}^2$$

and hence or otherwise show that, if the program takes N steps to complete, the total time taken is

$$N(10 + 7N + 2N^2 + N^3)/4 \quad \text{microseconds}$$

10 Verify that $\Delta^{-2}[1] = \dfrac{x^2}{2}$. Use the operator rule

$$\frac{1}{P(\Delta)}[(a + 1)^n f(n)] = (a + 1)^n \frac{1}{P(\Delta + a\mathrm{E})}[f(n)]$$

where $P(\Delta)$ is a polynomial in Δ to obtain particular solutions of

a $4U(n + 2) - 4U(n + 1) + U(n) = 2^{-n}$
b $S(n + 2) - 3S(n + 1) + 2S(n) = 2^n$

23 Descriptive statistics

This chapter represents a complete change of mood. We leave the crystal world of mathematics, where there is order and clarity, to visit the opaque world of statistics, where there is randomness and uncertainty.

After working through this chapter you should be able to
- [ ] Use the basic terminology of statistics;
- [ ] Distinguish between population statistics and sample statistics;
- [ ] Present data in a pictorial form to highlight its features;
- [ ] Calculate the basic measures of location – mean, mode and median;
- [ ] Calculate the basic measures of spread – range, mean absolute deviation and variance.

At the end of the chapter we look at a practical problem in production testing.

23.1 TERMINOLOGY

The subject of statistics arises in everyday conversation, in newspapers and on television. Whenever statistics are mentioned they are usually accompanied by the word 'data'. Strictly speaking 'data' is a plural word, the singular being 'datum', but nowadays it is common practice to use it as if it is singular.

Data is the information with which we start, the outcome of the activity or experiment. For example, data could consist of heights, weights, colours, temperature, lifetimes or examination scores. Very often data is in a numerical form; you will be able to think of many other examples. Data, when it has been obtained and not modified in any way, is usually called **raw data**.

The moment we calculate something from the data we have produced a **statistic**.

Once more, just to get the terminology clear:

1 The information which has been collected is called data;

2 Anything which we calculate from the data is known as a statistic.

The measurement in which we are interested – height, temperature or whatever – is often called the **variate**. The set of all the values which the variate takes is known as the **population**. For example, the population could consist of

1 The tensile strengths of hawsers produced by a certain process;

2 The times taken for gauges on fuel tanks to register correctly after they are first switched on;

3 The numbers of faulty bricks in each production batch from a brickworks.

In industrial applications it is not usually feasible to collect data from the whole population. For instance, to obtain the data an item may have to be tested to destruction. No manufacturer would allow his entire output to be destroyed! Even if destruction is not involved it may be too expensive to collect the data corresponding to the population.

23.2 RANDOM SAMPLES

Of course, to say anything with certainty we should need the data from the entire population. However, the theory of statistics enables us to say something with a specified probability by analysing **samples** selected at random from the population.

The procedure by which a **random sample** is selected is fraught with danger, and so a few words are required to clarify things. To choose a random sample from the population we have to select a sample of, say, 100 items at random. How do we select at random? We must ensure that

1 The entire population is available to us;

2 The selection process is in no way likely to bias the results.

For example, suppose a newspaper wishes to predict the result of an election the next day. The editor may ask his reporters to dial numbers at random and ask the people who reply how they intend to vote.

This would not be a random sample of the electorate. First, he will have restricted the population to those people who are telephone subscribers. Secondly, by telephoning at a set time he has restricted that population to those who may be at home then: self-employed, mothers with children, retired people, unemployed etc. The editor will therefore have made a number of fundamental statistical errors. However, this will not deter him from publishing his results and maybe getting a correct prediction!

So then in engineering and science we shall be concerned with **sample statistics**. The data which we have will usually be a random sample taken from the population, and we shall wish to calculate statistics from this data which will enable us to make statements about the underlying population. Our interest is not in the sample but in the population.

In section 23.17 we highlight one of the differences between sample statistics and population statistics.

23.3 POPULATION STATISTICS

There are fundamental differences between the theory of population statistics and the theory of sample statistics, and to reinforce this difference we shall consider an example. Remember that the purpose for which we are examining the data is the thing of overriding importance. We must ask ourselves at each stage: 'What are we trying to find out, and why?'

In the simplest of all situations we have all the data available and we wish merely to obtain information concerning it. For example, suppose a class of students sits an examination. Then there are several statistics which may be of interest: the class average, the range of marks or the top mark. As far as the examiner is concerned his interest in the marks may begin and end with the class of students. The population is in this instance the marks obtained by these students in the examination, and the statistics obtained are population statistics.

Suppose now we consider a public examination, such as 'A' level, where candidates sit the examination at a number of examination centres. In this situation if an examiner were given random samples of scripts it may be possible, using the data obtained, to estimate various statistics for the population. The resulting statistics are sample statistics. The population here, of course, consists of the complete set of marks from all the candidates.

23.4 DATA

Numerical data falls broadly into two categories: discrete data and continuous data.

Discrete data is data which can only take *isolated* values. Usually, but not always, discrete data consists of natural numbers. Examples include
1 The number of cars parked on consecutive days at a certain time in a car park;
2 The number of defective microchips produced by a machine process each week.

Continuous data is data which could take any value in some specified *interval* or set of intervals. Examples are:

1 The weight of ball bearings produced by a machine under normal working conditions;

2 The heights of a group of students in a class.

In the second of these examples of continuous data, if the shortest student has height 1.43 m and the tallest has height 2.04 m then there is no reason in theory why a student in the class could not have height 1.76 m. Of course practical considerations limit the accuracy to which we can measure any height, and so in practice there is often little distinction between discrete and continuous data. However, there are some important theoretical distinctions to be made and so we should decide at the outset whether the data is discrete or continuous.

We shall not consider situations in which the data is a mixture of discrete and continuous because to do so would involve very advanced mathematical ideas.

23.5 PICTORIAL REPRESENTATIONS

Faced with a collection of data, the statistician usually wishes to display the information in a clear easily understood and unbiased way. A table of data is often very difficult to assess and so pictorial methods have been devised. By carefully selecting the pictorial representation it is often possible to present data in a way which highlights certain characteristics and suppresses others.

To begin with we confine our attention to discrete data; it is a simple matter to modify things for continuous data. A single item of data is called a **data point**; the **frequency** of a data point is the number of times it occurs in the data.

23.6 PIE CHARTS

A pie chart represents the data as a 'pie'. To each distinct data point is assigned a slice of pie with an area proportional to the point's frequency. Although a pie chart is a satisfactory representation if there are only a few distinct data points, it loses much of its visual impact when there are many.

Example □ A selection of motorists were asked the question: 'Should traffic lights, wherever possible, be replaced by roundabouts?' The results were 63% 'yes', 21% 'no' and 16% 'don't know'. These are displayed in the pie chart to good visual effect (Fig. 23.1). ∎

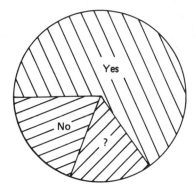

Fig. 23.1 A good pie chart.

☐ Twelve television programmes were each assigned a number, and **Example**
members of the public were asked to select the one they liked most. Those
who could not decide were excluded from the sample. The results are
shown in the pie chart (Fig. 23.2), but this does not give a very good visual
effect because there are too many slices.   ■

23.7 BAR CHARTS

A better way of presenting discrete data visually, when there are many
distinct data points, is to construct a bar chart.

To do this we use rectangular cartesian axes and assign an x value to each
distinct data point. Vertical bars are constructed joining each point (x, f) to
the x-axis, where f is the frequency of the data point corresponding to x.

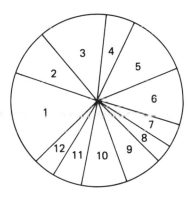

Fig. 23.2 A poor pie chart.

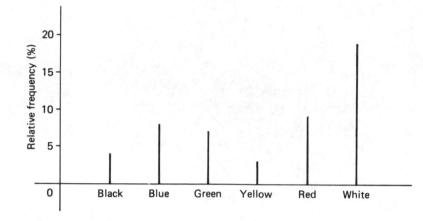

Fig. 23.3 A bar chart.

Example □ Fifty potential customers were asked to say which colour car they preferred from those in current production. The results were as follows:

Colour	black	white	red	blue	green	yellow
Frequency	4	19	9	8	7	3

In this case there are many ways we can order the colours. For instance we could arrange them according to popularity, in the order of the spectrum, or alphabetically. The choice of order will depend very much on what we want to show.

With a suitable choice of scales we can produce a bar chart for each of these orders, for example Fig. 23.3. ■

23.8 HISTOGRAMS

If we have continuous data then a bar chart may no longer be appropriate, as most of the data points will be distinct. We therefore need to group the data.

To do this we begin by examining the range of the data – the difference between the highest value which appears and the lowest. Depending on the quantity which we have, we partition the data into a number of **class intervals**, not necessarily of equal length. In practice the number chosen should be not less than four and not more than twenty. The square root of the number of data points gives a good guide to the maximum number of class intervals we should use.

□ Suppose continuous data consists of 100 points, the smallest of which is **Example**
2.13 m and the largest 9.87 m. The range of the data is then 9.87 − 2.13 =
7.74. So, if the data is fairly evenly distributed, it seems sensible to choose
eight intervals: 2.00–2.99, 3.00–3.99, . . . , 7.00–7.99. Each of these is
called a class interval.

The midpoint of each interval is called its **class mark**. So the class marks
in this case are 2.495, 3.495, . . . , 7.495. The end points of each interval
are called **class limits**. Notice that the interval 3.00–3.99 will contain any
data point x such that $2.995 \leqslant x < 3.995$, so the length of the class interval
is 1. These critical numbers 2.995, 3.995, . . . , 6.995 are usually called **class
boundaries**. In this way we group the data into class intervals and calculate
the frequency – the number of data points in each one.

If we wish to calculate statistics from this grouped data we must regard
all the data points in the class interval as concentrated at the class mark.
Although it could be misleading to do so, it would be possible to construct
a bar chart corresponding to this data.

To construct a histogram we use the rectangular cartesian coordinate
system and draw rectangles with intervals between the class boundaries as
their bases and each having an area proportional to the frequency. If the
class intervals are all of equal length then the heights of these rectangles
will also be proportional to the frequencies (Fig. 23.4).   ■

A smooth curve drawn through the midpoints of the tops of the rectangles
is known as a **frequency curve**. If the midpoints are joined instead by
straight lines we obtain a **frequency polygon**. One advantage of having
equal class intervals is that the area under a frequency polygon is then the
area of the histogram.

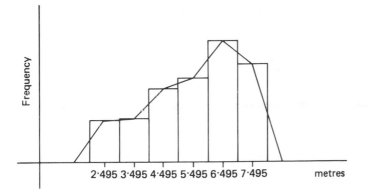

Fig. 23.4 A histogram and frequency polygon.

Table 23.1 Number of cars at 10.00 a.m. on 120 days

51,	53,	55,	56,	57,	58,	61,	62,	62,	65,	67,	69,	70,	70,	72,
73,	73,	74,	74,	75,	75,	76,	76,	76,	77,	77,	77,	78,	78,	78,
79,	79,	79,	80,	80,	80,	80,	81,	81,	81,	82,	82,	83,	83,	83,
83,	83,	83,	84,	84,	85,	85,	85,	85,	85,	85,	86,	86,	87,	87,
87,	88,	88,	89,	89,	89,	90,	90,	90,	90,	90,	90,	91,	91,	91,
92,	92,	92,	93,	93,	93,	93,	93,	94,	95,	95,	95,	95,	95,	96,
96,	97,	97,	98,	98,	98,	99,	99,	100,	101,	104,	105,	106,	107,	107,
107,	108,	108,	109,	110,	110,	111,	111,	112,	114,	116,	117,	119,	119,	120

Grouped data for bar chart production

Interval	Class mark	Frequency
51–60	55.5	6
61–70	65.5	8
71–80	75.5	23
81–90	85.5	35
91–100	95.5	27
101–110	105.5	12
111–120	115.5	9

23.9 GROUPED DATA

Sometimes in the case of discrete data there are too many observations for a useful bar chart to be constructed without first **grouping** the data.

Example □ The number of cars parked in a factory car park at 10.00 a.m. was counted on 120 consecutive working days. The results are shown in Table 23.1.

Some graphical indication of how much the car park is used is required. In order to obtain a bar chart we can consider the intervals 51–60, 61–70, . . . , 111–120. The class marks are 55.5, 65.5, . . . , 115.5. The groups are shown in Table 23.1, and the resulting bar chart in Fig. 23.5.

Unfortunately with this choice of interval each of the class marks cannot possibly be a data point. For instance, the car park never has 65.5 cars in it. Although from one point of view this is a disadvantage, it has one advantage: it emphasizes that the data has been grouped.

23.10 CUMULATIVE FREQUENCY DIAGRAMS

If the data is numerical, it is possible to arrange it in ascending order of magnitude. We can then calculate the **cumulative frequency** at each data point. The cumulative frequency is the total number of data points which

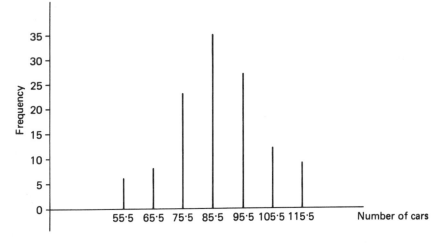

Fig. 23.5 Bar chart.

are less than, or equal to, the chosen point. If we divide the cumulative frequency by the total number of data points we obtain the **relative cumulative frequency**. The relative cumulative frequency will therefore increase from 0 to 1 as we go through the data. An example will show how this works.

☐ Consider again the data of the cars in the car park (Table 23.1). The **Example** data increases from 50 to 120, and so we have the cumulative and relative frequencies shown in Table 23.2. From this table it is an easy matter to construct a relative cumulative frequency diagram (Fig. 23.6).

Cumulative frequencies are particularly important if we are setting a standard or a **quota**. In the previous example the company may decide to build on the car park and may wish to leave enough space so that 85% utilization of the present car park will be preserved. Table 23.2 could suggest that 105 car-parking spaces will have to be provided. ■

We have seen how data may be presented in a pictorial way, but we have not yet calculated any statistics. This we now do. Let's just go through some of the terminology again to make sure we have it clear in our minds:
1 The variate is the name given to the quantity in which we are interested;
2 Data consists of the results which are available to us;
3 An individual value of the data is called a data point;
4 Numerical data consists of data in numerical form;
5 The frequency of a data point is the number of times the data point appears in the data;
6 Anything which is calculated from the data is called a statistic.
Right! Now that we have that straight we can move ahead.

Table 23.2 Cumulative frequency for cars in car park

Numbers of cars	Cumulative frequency	Relative frequency
50	0	0.000
55	3	0.025
60	6	0.050
65	10	0.083
70	14	0.117
75	21	0.175
80	37	0.308
85	56	0.467
90	72	0.600
95	89	0.742
100	99	0.825
105	102	0.850
110	111	0.925
115	115	0.958
120	120	1.000

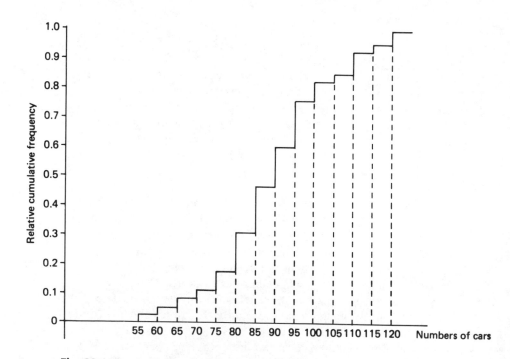

Fig. 23.6 A cumulative frequency diagram.

23.11 MEASURES OF LOCATION AND MEASURES OF SPREAD

Most useful statistics can be classified into either measures of location or measures of spread. We shall now explain what these terms mean.

A measure of **location**, also known as a measure of **central tendency**, attempts to indicate roughly the position around which the data is clustered. The usefulness of this statistic in any instance must be judged by the extent to which it typifies the data. There are three principal measures of location in common use: these are the mean, the mode and the median. Each has the same units as the data points themselves.

A measure of **spread**, also known as a measure of **dispersion**, gives an indication of how widely the data is distributed. Broadly speaking, if the measure of spread is large then the data is widely dispersed, whereas if it is small then it is closely bunched together. There are three principal measures of spread: the range, the mean absolute deviation and the standard deviation.

We shall consider each of these types of statistic in some detail.

23.12 THE MEAN

Suppose we have n distinct data points $x_1, x_2, \ldots, x_n$ and that these appear with frequencies $f_1, f_2, \ldots, f_n$ respectively in the data. Then the (arithmetic) **mean** $\bar{x}$ is obtained by totalling the data and dividing by the total number N of data points:

$$\bar{x} = \frac{1}{N}(f_1 x_1 + f_2 x_2 + \ldots + f_n x_n)$$

$$= \frac{1}{N} \sum_{r=1}^{n} f_r x_r$$

where

$$N = \sum_{r=1}^{n} f_r$$

Although the mean is not the only measure of location, it is by far the most widely used.

□ Ten students took an examination, and the results were **Example**

$$72, 81, 43, 39, 47, 21, 35, 51, 63, 52$$

We can easily calculate the mean mark $\bar{x}$:

$$\bar{x} = \frac{1}{10}(72 + 81 + 43 + \ldots + 52) = 50.4 \qquad \blacksquare$$

Two disadvantages of the mean are immediately apparent:
1 The mean may not be a possible value of the data. This is certainly the

case in this example where examination scripts are assigned integer values.

2 If the data is non-numerical, for example colours, then the mean does not exist.

Another disadvantage of relying on the mean as the only statistic is provided by the following cautionary tale.

Example □ An entertainer is engaged to provide recreation for a mixed party of people and, discovering that the mean age is 14, arranges a disco. However, the party consists of a playgroup and some adult helpers and the ages are

$$5, 3, 4, 4, 3, 5, 2, 38, 25, 51$$

This example illustrates how a measure of location as the sole statistic can sometimes give a misleading impression. ■

23.13 THE MODE

Suppose we have n distinct data points $x_1, x_2, x_3, \ldots, x_n$ and that these occur with frequencies $f_1, f_2, f_3, \ldots, f_n$ respectively.

The point x_r corresponding to the largest frequency f_r is called the **mode**. If there is only one mode then the distribution of data is called **unimodal**, whereas if there are two modes it is called **bimodal**. The terminology may be extended as appropriate. This statistic is particularly valuable if one of the data points occurs with a frequency much greater than any of the others.

Example □ A total of 100 welders were asked to try four different types of eye shield to say which one they preferred. The results were as follows:

Type	1	2	3	4
Number	19	14	13	54

The mode here is type 4. ■

Although the mode has its uses as a measure of location, it can give a misleading impression. For example if there are several data points each with almost the same frequency, an undue emphasis could be placed on one of them.

23.14 THE MEDIAN

If we have numerical data, it is possible to arrange it in ascending order of magnitude. The data point which appears in the middle is then known as the **median**.

One immediate problem arises: what are we to do if there is an even number of data points? Let's consider some of the options:

1 We could take the mean of the two central points. This compromise, although attractive in some ways, destroys one of the advantages of the median: that it is a data point itself.

2 We could allow two medians, as we do with the mode. This non-uniqueness is the principal disadvantage because, unlike the situation with the mode, the only information it gives is that there is an even number of data points.

3 We could choose a data point at random and discard it. In this way an odd number of data points is obtained together with a unique statistic. The disadvantage is that the original data could produce two different values of this statistic.

4 We could adopt the view that the median is an inappropriate statistic if there is an even number of data points. Which option do you think we choose?

In fact we choose option 1 for the following reason. If there is a significant difference between the two central points then the median is an inappropriate statistic to use as a measure of location. Nevertheless, since the median should represent the middle of the distribution the mean of the two may be taken. If there is no significant difference then it doesn't matter which one is selected. Unless it is important that the median be a typical data point we can take the mean of the two.

!

Remember when we are calculating statistics we are not simply performing a numerical exercise. We are attempting to represent significant features of the data.

If we draw a frequency curve (Fig. 23.7) we can see that for a unimodal symmetrical distribution the mean, mode and median all coincide, whereas for a skewed distribution they are often quite distinct.

☐ Obtain measures of location for the following sample data: **Example**
a Numbers of rivets which fail under test conditions:

$$2, 5, 5, 12, 14, 16$$

b Number of errors received in a set of test codewords:

$$2, 2, 2, 2, 3, 3, 3, 3, 3$$

c Voltage measurements:

$$1.1, 1.2, 1.3, 1.3, 1.4, 1.7, 1.8, 1.8$$

We calculate each of the three principal measures of location:

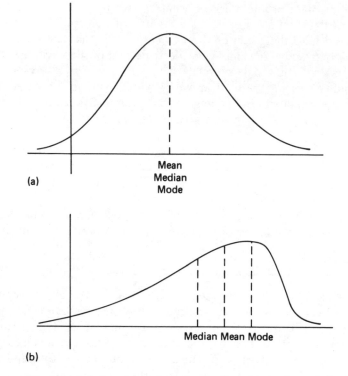

Fig. 23.7 (a) A symmetrical distribution (b) A skewed distribution.

a mean = (2 + 5 + 5 + 12 + 14 + 16)/6 = 9 rivets
mode = 5 rivets
median = $\frac{1}{2}$(5 + 12) = 8.5 rivets
b mean = (4 × 2 + 5 × 3)/9 = 23/9 ≃ 2.556 errors
mode = 3 errors
median = 3 errors
c mean = (1/8) (Σ) = 11.6/8 = 1.45 volts
modes = 1.3 and 1.8 volts
median = $\frac{1}{2}$(1.3 + 1.4) = 1.35 volts

Note that very few data points are involved, so if the data had been the entire population it is doubtful if the statistics would have been worth calculating at all. ■

Now let's consider some measures of spread.

23.15 THE RANGE

This should not be confused with the word 'range' as used in section 2.5.

One of the simplest measures of spread is known as the **range**. This is simply the difference between the largest data point and the smallest. Although in many circumstances this is a perfectly adequate measure of spread, it has one serious drawback. It is unduly affected by freak values of the data.

For example, suppose a manufacturing process resulted in components which usually had a lifetime between 36 and 50 hours, satisfying the retailer's specification. A single faulty component (lifetime 0 hours) would change the range from 14 hours to 50 hours. This could be a very misleading statistic because it might lead to the belief that the process was generally unsatisfactory.

23.16 THE MEAN ABSOLUTE DEVIATION

At first sight it seems a good idea to calculate the average deviation from the mean.

Suppose we have n distinct data points $x_1, x_2, x_3, \ldots, x_n$ and these appear with frequencies $f_1, f_2, f_3, \ldots, f_n$ respectively. The number of data points is N and the mean is $\bar{x}$:

$$N = \sum_{r=1}^{n} f_r$$

$$\bar{x} = \frac{1}{N} \sum_{r=1}^{n} f_r x_r$$

We should then obtain, for the average deviation,

$$\frac{1}{N}[f_1(x_1 - \bar{x}) + f_2(x_2 - \bar{x}) + \ldots + f_n(x_n - \bar{x})]$$

$$= \frac{1}{N}(f_1 x_1 + f_2 x_2 + \ldots + f_n x_n) - \frac{\bar{x}}{N}(f_1 + f_2 + \ldots + f_n)$$

$$= \bar{x} - \frac{\bar{x}}{N}N = 0$$

So the mean deviation is zero whatever the data! Back to the drawing board!

One way round this problem is to consider the absolute value of the deviations and take the mean of these. This is then known as the **mean absolute deviation** (MAD):

$$\text{MAD} = \frac{1}{N}(f_1 |x_1 - \bar{x}| + f_2 |x_2 - \bar{x}| + \ldots + f_n |x_n - \bar{x}|)$$

Although it is easy enough to calculate this statistic, the problems with the modulus signs inhibit theoretical work and so this measure of spread does not play a large part in statistical theory.

23.17 THE STANDARD DEVIATION

Without doubt the most important measure of spread is the standard deviation.

Suppose we have n distinct data points $x_1, x_2, x_3, \ldots, x_n$ and these appear with frequencies $f_1, f_2, f_3, \ldots, f_n$ respectively. As before, the total number N of data points is therefore given by

$$N = \sum_{r=1}^{n} f_r$$

We can calculate the mean $\bar{x}$ of the data, and we wish to obtain a measure of how widely the data is dispersed about the mean. The **standard deviation** s of the data is defined by

$$s = \sqrt{\left[\frac{1}{N-1} \sum_{r=1}^{n} f_r(x_r - \bar{x})^2\right]}$$

This is (almost) the root mean square: the only change is that we are dividing by $N - 1$ instead of N. Since this strange definition can cause some confusion, we shall explain why it is the way it is.

You will remember that we stressed that there was a fundamental difference between population statistics and sample statistics. The statistics we calculate from samples chosen at random from some population are intended to estimate as closely as possible the corresponding statistics for the population. To reinforce this we use different symbols for the statistics corresponding to the population from those corresponding to the sample.

The **population mean** is denoted by μ and the **population standard deviation** is denoted by σ. If we are given a random sample, the mean $\bar{x}$ of the sample is an unbiased estimate for μ. If the data consists of the entire population we have

$$\sigma = \sqrt{\left[\frac{1}{N} \sum_{r=1}^{n} f_r(x_r - \mu)^2\right]}$$

Indeed in general, if the data consists of a random sample from the population and if the population mean μ is known, then the formula

$$s = \sqrt{\left[\frac{1}{N} \sum_{r=1}^{n} f_r(x_r - \mu)^2\right]}$$

would give an **unbiased estimate** for σ.

However, it is relatively rare that μ is known, and so we have to estimate μ by calculating the mean $\bar{x}$ of the sample. When we do this, it can be shown that an unbiased estimate for the population standard deviation is given by

$$s = \sqrt{\left[\frac{1}{N-1} \sum_{r=1}^{n} f_r(x_r - \bar{x})^2\right]}$$

!

The distinction was emphasized in section 23.3.

Observe that, unless N is small, the difference between the results obtained by dividing by N and those obtained by dividing by $N - 1$ are negligible.

Most calculators now enable calculations to be made routinely for both the standard deviation of a population and the standard deviation of a sample.

The square of the standard deviation is called the **variance** and is somewhat easier to work with algebraically than the standard deviation. However, the standard deviation has the advantage that it has the same dimension as the data. If we divide the standard deviation by the mean we obtain a dimensionless quantity known as the **coefficient of variation**.

We shall use variance in sections 24.15 and 24.19.

_____ **23.18 Workshop** _____

⏎ 1

▷**Exercise**   The number of working days lost by each of twenty employees in a small firm during the past twelve months was

$$5, 6, 8, 12, 4, 5, 15, 7, 12, 11,$$
$$6, 0, 2, 4, 5, 5, 8, 10, 12, 11$$

Represent the data using a pie chart and a bar chart.

Have a go at this. It may be necessary to group the data in order to sharpen its impact.

⏎ 2

We begin by constructing a frequency table so that we can assess the situation:

Days lost	Frequency
0	1
2	1
4	2
5	4
6	2
7	1
8	2
10	1
11	2
12	3
15	1

There are not many data points, and if this had been continuous data we should have had to draw a histogram with not more than four or five class intervals. It therefore seems sensible to group the data into four (or five) intervals here:

Class interval	Frequency
0–3	2
4–7	9
8–11	5
12–15	4

Using these we obtain diagrams which reflect the main features of the information (Fig. 23.8).

If all was well, move ahead to step 4. If not, here is a little more practice.

▷**Exercise**   Repeat the previous exercise using six class intervals 0–2, 3–5, . . . , 15–17.

3

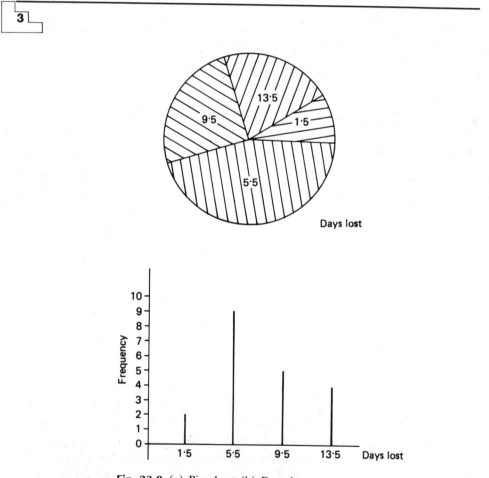

Fig. 23.8 (a) Pie chart (b) Bar chart.

We obtain the following frequency table:

Class interval	Frequency
0–2	2
3–5	6
6–8	5
9–11	3
12–14	3
15–17	1

Diagrams can then be produced as before.
  Now for a histogram.

▷**Exercise**   The following gives the time taken in hours for 30 samples of soil ⌐**4**
to dry out at room temperature:

> 5.43, 4.98, 5.24, 5.59, 4.89, 5.01, 4.97, 4.99, 5.11, 5.23,
> 5.52, 5.61, 5.31, 5.67, 5.51, 5.23, 5.47, 5.55, 4.87, 4.91,
> 4.84, 5.34, 5.16, 4.86, 5.12, 5.45, 5.48, 5.15, 5.23, 5.42

Group the data into class intervals 4.8–4.9, 5.0–5.1, ... , 5.6–5.7. Then
draw a histogram, construct a frequency polygon, and produce a cumulative frequency diagram.
  It's very simple to do all this. Keep an eye on the class boundaries.

⌐**5**

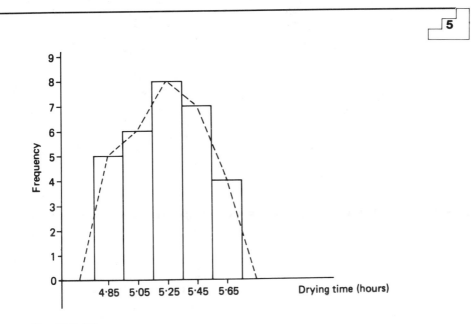

Fig. 23.9 Histogram.

We put the data points into the appropriate class intervals in preparation for drawing the histogram:

Class interval	Class mark	Frequency
4.8–4.9	4.85	5
5.0–5.1	5.05	6
5.2–5.3	5.25	8
5.4–5.5	5.45	7
5.6–5.7	5.65	4

It's best to make a tally to avoid overlooking data points.

The histogram and frequency polygon are then shown in Fig. 23.9. Notice particularly how by extending the class intervals on either side and giving them frequencies of zero we obtain an area under the frequency polygon which is equal to the area of the histogram. Indeed, had we drawn a histogram using relative frequencies the area enclosed would have been unity. We shall see later that this would imply that the frequency polygon would then be the graph of a probability density function.

We need to note that when we come to the cumulative frequencies we must use the class boundaries 4.95, 5.15, 5.35, 5.55, 5.75. The cumulative frequencies are as follows:

Class boundary	Cumulative frequency
4.95	5
5.15	11
5.35	19
5.55	26
5.75	30

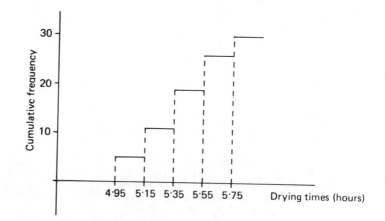

Fig. 23.10 Cumulative frequency diagram.

The cumulative frequency diagram is shown in Fig. 23.10.
  Make sure that you had
1 no gaps between your rectangles in your histogram
2 each class mark in the centre of the class interval
3 class boundaries as the boundary markers.
If everything was correct then proceed at full speed to the next section. If
not, here is more practice.

▷**Exercise**   Draw another histogram using the same data and the following
class intervals: 4.80–5.04, 5.05–5.14, 5.15–5.24, 5.25–5.34, 5.35–5.44,
5.45–5.96. Draw a frequency polygon. Is the area under the frequency
polygon the same as that of the histogram?

Class interval	Class mark	Frequency
4.80–5.04	4.920	9
5.05–5.14	5.095	2
5.15–5.24	5.195	6
5.25–5.34	5.295	2
5.35–5.44	5.395	2
5.45–5.96	5.705	9

The histogram required is shown in Fig. 23.11, together with the frequency
polygon. In this case the area under the frequency polygon is *not* the same
as that of the histogram.

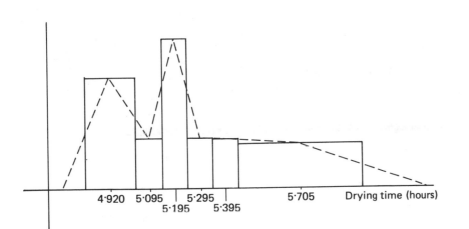

Fig. 23.11 Histogram and frequency polygon.

_____**23.19 Practical**_____

LOAD BEARING

Ten 4-metre girders were taken from a production line and each one was tested for central load bearing when freely supported at each end. The results in kilonewtons were as follows:

4.562, 4.673, 4.985, 4.657, 4.642,
4.784, 4.782, 4.832, 4.637, 4.596

Calculate the mean, mode, median, range, mean absolute deviation and standard deviation for this data.

It's just a question of pressing the buttons really! Work them out and take the next step to see if they are all right.

_____

There are ten observations and the total is 47.150. So the mean is 4.715 kilonewtons.

_____

It is necessary to put the data into class intervals to obtain a meaningful mode. The obvious intervals to choose are 4.55–4.64, 4.65–4.74, 4.75–4.84, 4.85–4.94, 4.95–5.04. Taking the class marks as the representatives, we then have:

Class mark	Number
4.595	4
4.695	2
4.795	3
4.895	0
4.995	1

In this way we obtain a mode of 4.595. However, we should indicate the fact that this has been obtained from continuous data by giving fewer decimal places than in the data: so the mode is 4.60. We remark further that this is a poor statistic to use here in view of the almost bimodal nature of the sample.

_____

When we arrange the data in ascending order we obtain

4.562, 4.596, 4.637, 4.642, 4.657,
4.673, 4.782, 4.784, 4.832, 4.985

There are an even number of data points, so we average the middle two: the median is (4.657 + 4.673)/2 = 4.665 kilonewtons.

To find the range we must subtract the smallest value which appears in the data from the largest. The range is $4.985 - 4.562 = 0.423$ kilonewtons.

To find the mean absolute deviation we begin by subtracting the mean, 4.715, from each of the data points to give the deviations from the mean and the absolute deviations. These are shown in columns 2 and 3 of Table 23.3. The total absolute deviation is 1.046, and so dividing by the total number we obtain MAD = 0.1046 kilonewtons.

Finally we require standard deviation. The squared deviations from the mean are shown in column 4 of Table 23.3. The sum of these is 0.149 950 and the total number is 10. It remains to divide by 9 and take the square root: the standard deviation s is then 0.129 08 kilonewtons.

Did you manage all those?

In the old days we used to insist that students present the numerical work clearly in a tabulated form as shown here. Although there is a lot to be said in favour of this practice, now that calculators and computers are generally available it is usually quicker to tap in the numbers. It's a good idea to do the calculation twice, though, just to check you haven't pressed the wrong buttons!

!

Table 23.3

Data	Deviations from mean	Absolute deviations	Squared deviations
1	2	3	4
4.562	−0.153	0.153	0.023 409
4.596	−0.119	0.119	0.014 161
4.637	−0.078	0.078	0.006 084
4.642	−0.073	0.073	0.005 329
4.657	−0.058	0.058	0.003 364
4.673	−0.042	0.042	0.001 764
4.782	0.067	0.067	0.004 489
4.784	0.069	0.069	0.004 761
4.832	0.117	0.117	0.013 689
4.985	0.270	0.270	0.072 900
47.149		1.046	0.149 950

SUMMARY

We have seen how to display data pictorially using
☐ pie charts
☐ bar charts
☐ histograms.
We have examined the principal examples of statistics:
☐ Measures of location
  a mean
  b mode
  c median.
☐ Measures of spread
  a range
  b mean absolute deviation
  c standard deviation.

EXERCISES (for answers see p. 760)

1 Decide whether the following data is discrete or continuous:
  a Defective batteries in batches
  b Quantity of impurities in water supply
  c Faulty tyres in spot testing
  d Over-stressed components after wind tunnel exposure
  e Anti-cyclones each day in the Northern hemisphere
  f Percentage of pollutants in engine exhaust
  g Percentage of faulty components in production
2 The amount of time devoted to a new piece of research was initially one sixth of the time available. Two other pieces of development were under way, production and testing, and these took equal times. It was decided to increase the amount of time devoted to the new work to 25% and to devote twice as much of the remaining time to production as to testing. Represent this change by means of pie charts.
3 Calculate for each of the following lists of data (i) the mean, (ii) the mode, (iii) the median, (iv) the range:
  a Resistances (ohms)

$$3, 2, 1.5, 1.5, 2, 1.5, 3, 2, 2, 1.5, 2, 2$$

  b Percentage of water in soil samples

$$30.0, 29.6, 21.5, 22.0, 23.5, 18.1, 19.5, 23.0, 24.2, 21.9, 18.7,$$
$$14.1, 17.9, 18.3, 19.7$$

  c Deflections of a beam (metres)

0.113, 0.121, 0.119, 0.110, 0.118, 0.123, 0.121, 0.171, 0.153, 0.161, 0.169, 0.173

In each case give a suitable visual display of the data and comment on the suitability of the statistics you have calculated in reflecting its true nature.

4 Data consists of the digits 0, 1, 2, 3, ..., 9 used in the decimal representation of the first 100 natural numbers. Obtain the mean, mode, median and range.

5 Data consists of the number of days in each month over a four year period. Obtain the mean, mode, median and range.

ASSIGNMENT (for answers see p. 760; see also Workshop on p. 683)

A machine collects measured quantities of soil and deposits them in boxes for analysis in the laboratory. Fifty boxes were taken at random and inspected. It was found that the following numbers of stones were in the boxes:

45, 47, 43, 46, 42, 47, 44, 48, 41, 47,
46, 44, 45, 43, 43, 42, 45, 44, 43, 42,
43, 49, 42, 40, 44, 48, 44, 46, 42, 46,
42, 44, 45, 44, 44, 42, 42, 41, 44, 43,
45, 43, 44, 41, 43, 48, 47, 40, 46, 46

1 State whether the data is discrete or continuous.
2 Without grouping the data, display it as a bar chart.
3 Grouping the data as 40–41, 42–43, 44–45, 46–47, 48–49, present it as a pie chart. Then present it as a histogram, and draw a corresponding frequency polygon.
4 Calculate the mean, mode and median from the raw data.
5 Calculate the range and variance.

FURTHER EXERCISES (for answers see p. 760)

1 Two consignments of carbon brushes were examined for defects. Each consignment consisted of 100 boxes each containing 50 brushes. Five boxes from each assignment were selected at random and the number of defective brushes in each one was counted. The results were
a 8, 3, 5, 2, 3
b 20, 5, 2, 3, 5
Calculate for each sample (i) the mean (ii) the mode (iii) the median (iv) the range (v) the standard deviation.
2 Samples of lubricant were chosen and the specific gravity (SG) was measured. The frequencies of samples in SG classes were as follows:

SG	1.11–1.12	1.12–1.13	1.13–1.14	1.14–1.15	1.15–1.16	1.16–1.17	1.17–1.18
Frequency	1	3	8	16	20	11	5

Draw a histogram showing percentage frequency against specific gravity interval.

3 A construction site uses five different grades of sand. On a typical day the number of bags of each type drawn from the store is as follows:

Grade	1	2	3	4	5
Number	12	28	10	16	8

Represent this information using (a) a pie chart (b) a bar chart.

4 The lengths of a sample of 30 steel drive belts produced by a machine were measured in metres to the nearest millimetre. The results were as follows:

2.975, 3.245, 3.254, 3.156, 2.997, 2.995, 3.005, 3.057, 3.046, 3.142, 3.116, 3.052, 3.017, 3.084, 3.119, 3.143, 3.063, 3.158, 3.196, 3.203, 3.225, 3.183, 3.193, 3.174, 3.148, 3.053, 3.202, 3.153, 3.037, 3.048

a Display the data on a histogram by grouping the data into class intervals 2.95–3.00, 3.05–3.10, ..., 3.25–3.30.
b Write down the class boundaries.
c Using the same class intervals, draw a relative frequency diagram.
d Calculate the mean and standard deviation of (i) the raw data (ii) the grouped data.

5 Suppose data consists of n distinct data points $x_1, x_2, \ldots, x_n$ with frequencies $f_1, f_2, \ldots, f_n$ respectively. Suppose also that N is the total number of data points. Show that, if s is the standard deviation,

$$(N - 1)s^2 = \sum_{r=1}^{n} f_r x_r^2 - N\bar{x}^2$$

(In the days before electronic calculators this formula could be used to ease the arithmetical burden.)

Probability 24

To take our story any further requires some probability theory, and that is the subject of this chapter.

After completing this chapter you should be able to
☐ Use the terminology of statistics correctly – experiment, sample space, event, random variable etc.;
☐ Use the rules of probability correctly;
☐ Obtain the mean and variance of a probability distribution;
☐ Use the binomial, Poisson and normal distributions;
☐ Approximate the binomial and Poisson distributions by the normal distribution;
☐ Use normal probability paper to estimate the mean and variance of a distribution.
At the end of this chapter we look at a practical problem of statistics in engineering.

24.1 CONCEPTS

In order to use sample statistics effectively we need to employ some of the theory of probability. It is necessary first to fix some of the terminology:
1 The word **experiment** is used to denote any activity which has an outcome.
2 The set of all possible outcomes of an experiment is called the **sample space** S.
3 Each of the possible outcomes is called a **sample point**.
4 An **event** E is any collection of sample points.

☐ The outcomes of the activity of throwing two dice can be represented as **Example** ordered pairs of numbers. So the sample space may be represented as follows:

$$(1,1), (1,2), (1,3), (1,4), (1,5), (1,6)$$
$$(2,1), (2,2), (2,3), (2,4), (2,5), (2,6)$$
$$(3,1), (3,2), (3,3), (3,4), (3,5), (3,6)$$
$$(4,1), (4,2), (4,3), (4,4), (4,5), (4,6)$$
$$(5,1), (5,2), (5,3), (5,4), (5,5), (5,6)$$
$$(6,1), (6,2), (6,3), (6,4), (6,5), (6,6)$$

There are 36 sample points in the sample space.

If E is the event 'the total sum is greater than 7', then

$$E = \{(x,y) \mid x + y > 7\}$$
$$= \{(2,6), (3,5), (3,6), (4,4), (4,5), (4,6), (5,3),$$
$$(5,4), (5,5), (5,6), (6,2), (6,3), (6,4), (6,5), (6,6)\}$$

So E consists of 15 sample points. ■

If there are no sample points in an event E then $E = \emptyset$, the empty set. If every sample point is in the event E then $E = S$, the sample space.

We shall define **probability** in such a way that every event will have a probability in the interval $[0, 1]$. If an event is certain to occur we say it has probability 1, whereas if an event cannot occur we say it has probability 0. So:

1 The event S has probability 1 because one of the points in the sample space must be the result of the experiment.

2 The event $\emptyset$ has probability 0 since by definition the experiment must have an outcome.

It often helps to picture things by using a Venn diagram (see Chapter 2). In this it is usual to represent the sample space S by means of a large rectangle. The sample points are then shown inside the rectangle, and an event is represented by means of a loop; the interior of the loop represents the points in the event (Fig. 24.1).

If x is a sample point in S, the sample space, we denote by $P(x)$ the probability that x will occur. If E is an event we then define $P(E)$ by

There are three approaches to probability which we discuss in sections 24.10, 24.11 and 24.12.

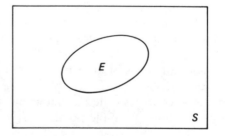

Fig. 24.1 A Venn diagram.

$$P(E) = \sum_{x \in E} P(x)$$

The probability of an event E is the sum of the probabilities of the sample points in E.

In the Venn diagram the probability of an event E is the proportion of the sample space covered by E. We see at once that $P(S) = 1$ and $P(\emptyset) = 0$, which is consistent with the definition. Now we have already seen that

$$P(S) = \sum_{x \in S} P(x) = 1$$

and so we may write

$$P(E) = \frac{\displaystyle\sum_{x \in E} P(x)}{\displaystyle\sum_{x \in S} P(x)}$$

Although Venn diagrams are very useful there is one snag: they may lead us to draw conclusions which are false. For example, not every sample space is bounded.

24.2 THE RULES OF PROBABILITY

We can use Venn diagrams, together with the interpretation we have put on probability, to deduce the basic rules of probability. In the sections that follow we shall suppose that E and F are any two events in the sample space S (see Fig. 24.2).

To begin with we must bring to mind the basic terminology of set theory (see Chapter 2):

1 Union: $E \cup F = \{x \mid x \in E \text{ or } x \in F, \text{ or both}\}$
2 Intersection: $E \cap F = \{x \mid x \in E \text{ and } x \in F\}$
3 Complement: $E' = \{x \mid x \in S \text{ but } x \notin E\}$

There are rules of set theory which can be deduced formally from these definitions. However, for our purposes they can be inferred easily from Venn diagrams. Here are the rules:

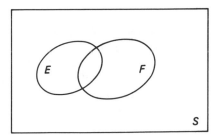

Fig. 24.2 Two events E and F.

$$E \cup F = F \cup E$$
$$E \cap F = F \cap E$$
$$(E \cup F)' = E' \cap F'$$
$$(E \cap F)' = E' \cup F'$$
$$E \cap (F \cup G) = (E \cap F) \cup (E \cap G)$$
$$E \cup (F \cap G) = (E \cup F) \cap (E \cup G)$$

You might like to draw a few Venn diagrams to convince yourself of the truth of these.

Now for the first rule of probability.

24.3 THE SUM RULE

The probability that either the event E or the event F (or both) will occur is the sum of the probability that E will occur with the probability that F will occur less the probability that both E and F will occur:

$$P(E \cup F) = P(E) + P(F) - P(E \cap F)$$

To see this we merely need to note that the area enclosed by both E and F is the area enclosed by E, together with the area enclosed by F, but less the area of the overlap $E \cap F$, which we would otherwise have counted twice.

Example ☐ The probability that a drilling machine will break down is 0.35. The probability that the lights will fail is 0.28. It is known that the probability that one or the other (or possibly both) will occur is 0.42. Obtain the probability that both the machine will break down and the lights will fail.

Let E be 'the drilling machine will break down' and F be 'the lights will fail'. Then $P(E) = 0.35$, $P(F) = 0.28$ and $P(E \cup F) = 0.42$. Now

$$P(E \cup F) = P(E) + P(F) - P(E \cap F)$$

Therefore

$$P(E \cap F) = P(E) + P(F) - P(E \cup F)$$
$$= 0.35 + 0.28 - 0.42 = 0.21 \quad\blacksquare$$

24.4 MUTUALLY EXCLUSIVE EVENTS

Sometimes two events E and F in a sample space S have no sample points in common, so that $E \cap F = \emptyset$. In such circumstances the events E and F are said to be **mutually exclusive** events. For mutually exclusive events the addition law of probability becomes simplified:

$$P(E \cup F) = P(E) + P(F)$$

24.5 CONDITIONAL PROBABILITY

We write $P(E \mid F)$ for the probability that the event E will occur, given that the event F does occur.

If we think about this for a few seconds, we see that the precondition that the event F does occur effectively reduces the sample space that we are considering to the points in the event F. We require the proportion of those which are in the event E. Consequently

$$P(E \mid F) = \frac{\sum\limits_{x \in E \cap F} P(x)}{\sum\limits_{x \in F} P(x)}$$

$$= \frac{P(E \cap F)}{P(F)}$$

☐ A car mechanic knows that the probability of a vehicle having a flat **Example** battery is 0.24. He also knows that if the vehicle has a flat battery then the probability that the starter motor needs replacing is 0.47. A vehicle is brought in for his attention. What is the probability that it both has a flat battery and needs a new starter motor?

Suppose E is 'the starter motor needs replacing' and F is 'the vehicle has a flat battery'. We know $P(E \mid F) = 0.47$ and $P(F) = 0.24$ and require $P(E \cap F)$. Using

$$P(E \mid F) = \frac{P(E \cap F)}{P(F)}$$

we deduce that $P(E \cap F) = 0.47 \times 0.24 = 0.1128$.   ■

24.6 THE PRODUCT RULE

From the equation

$$P(E \mid F) = \frac{P(E \cap F)}{P(F)}$$

we obtain, on multiplying through by $P(F)$,

$$P(E \cap F) = P(E \mid F)P(F)$$

By symmetry therefore we also have

$$P(E \cap F) = P(E)P(F \mid E)$$

The probability that both the event E and the event F will occur is the product of the probability that E will occur with the probability that F will occur, given that E does occur.

24.7 INDEPENDENT EVENTS

Two events E and F are said to be **independent** if $P(E) = P(E \mid F)$, because the event F has no effect whatever on E as far as probability is concerned. Whenever two events E and F are independent the product rule becomes simplified to

$$P(E \cap F) = P(E)P(F)$$

At first sight the condition that two events E and F are independent looks asymmetrical. However, it is a simple algebraic matter to deduce that this is equivalent to

$$P(F) = P(F \mid E)$$

Can you see why? Give it a whirl and then see if you are right.

Suppose that E and F are independent, so that $P(E) = P(E \mid F)$. We have $P(E \cap F) = P(E)P(F)$ but $P(E \cap F) = P(E)P(F \mid E)$. Equating these two expressions and dividing by $P(E)$ gives

$$P(F) = P(F \mid E)$$

The argument fails if $P(E) = 0$, but this would imply $E = \varnothing$. So $P(F) = P(F \mid E)$ since there is no condition to satisfy.

24.8 COMPLEMENTATION RULE

The events E and E' satisfy $E \cup E' = S$ and $E \cap E' = \varnothing$. Therefore $P(E) + P(E') = P(S) = 1$, from which

$$P(E') = 1 - P(E)$$

Example □ The probability that a telephone switchboard is jammed is 0.25. The probability that a customer will attempt to telephone is 0.15. These events are known to be independent. However, if a customer telephones but fails to get connected the probability that an order will be lost is 0.75. Calculate
a The probability that a customer will telephone while the switchboard is jammed, resulting in a lost order;
b The probability that the order will not be lost even though the telephone switchboard is jammed and the customer tried to telephone.
You might like to try this on your own.

We begin by identifying the events. Let E be 'the telephone switchboard is jammed', F be 'a customer will attempt to telephone' and G be 'an order will be lost'.

We know $P(E) = 0.25$, $P(F) = 0.15$. Now $E \cap F$ is the event 'a customer will attempt to telephone and the switchboard is jammed'. Since E and F are independent,

$$P(E \cap F) = P(E)P(F) = 0.25 \times 0.15 = 0.0375$$

For **a** we require $P[(E \cap F) \cap G]$. We know that $P[G \mid (E \cap F)] = 0.75$, so

$$\frac{P[G \cap (E \cap F)]}{P(E \cap F)} = 0.75$$

Now

$$\begin{aligned} P[(E \cap F) \cap G] &= P[G \cap (E \cap F)] \\ &= P(E \cap F) \times 0.75 \\ &= 0.0375 \times 0.75 = 0.028\,125 \end{aligned}$$

For **b**, G' is the event 'the order will not be lost'. We require $P[G' \mid (E \cap F)]$. We have

$$\begin{aligned} P[G' \mid (E \cap F)] &= 1 - P[G \mid (E \cap F)] \\ &= 1 - 0.75 = 0.25 \end{aligned}$$ ■

Although we have seen how to use the rules of probability, we have yet to define fully what is meant by probability.

24.9 A RANDOM VARIABLE

A random variable X is a numerically valued function defined on the sample space S; so $X:S \to \mathbb{R}$. For example, if we consider the experiment of tossing a coin then we could define X by

$$\text{heads} \to 1$$
$$\text{tails} \to 0$$

However, there is no restriction on the way we define X. We could, if we wished to be perverse, define X instead by

$$\text{heads} \to \pi$$
$$\text{tails} \to e$$

The important thing is that X assigns numerical values to the outcome of an experiment. In this way outcomes which we regard as equivalent to one another can be assigned the same numerical value, whereas those which are regarded as distinct can be assigned different values.

In a slight misuse of the function notation, we write $X = r$ if the random variable X has value r at the sample point. We also write $P(X = r)$ for the probability that X has the value r at the sample point.

There are three basic approaches to probability; these are described in the next three sections.

24.10 THE ANALYTICAL METHOD

We begin by looking at an example.

Example ☐ Suppose that a box contains 100 microcomputer discs and that 15 of them are defective in some way. If one of the discs is selected at random from the box, what is the probability that it is defective?

Of course we know that it will be either good or defective, so the question we are really asking is: what proportion of the discs is defective? The answer to this is clear; there are 15 defectives and 100 discs altogether, and so the proportion of defectives is $15/100 = 3/20 = 0.15$.

This then is what we define as the probability p of selecting a defective:

$$p = \frac{\text{number of defectives}}{\text{total number}}$$

We observe that if every disc in the box is defective we shall obtain $p = 1$, whereas if none of the discs is defective we shall obtain $p = 0$; this is consistent with our earlier definition.

Looked at in this way, we see we can define a random variable X on the sample space S consisting of each of the discs:

$$\text{bad disc} \rightarrow 0$$
$$\text{good disc} \rightarrow 1$$

Then $P(X = 0) = 0.15$ and $P(X = 1) = 0.85$, so that $P(X = 0) + P(X = 1) = 1$; a disc is either defective or satisfactory. ∎

Now let's analyse what we have done. Suppose the discs were numbered $1, 2, 3, \ldots, 100$. Then we can represent the discs as $D_1, D_2, D_3, \ldots, D_{100}$ of which we know there are 15 defective.

Now if we consider these labelled discs, there are 100 sample points in S because each of the labelled discs is a possible outcome of the experiment. Moreover, the selection procedure is random so each disc has the same probability of being chosen.

If E is the event that 'the disc is defective' then there are 15 sample points in this event because there are 15 defective discs. So we obtain

$$P\,(\text{disc defective}) = \frac{|E|}{|S|} = \frac{15}{100}$$

where $|A|$ denotes the number of elements in the finite set A.

In general, if each point in a finite sample space is equally likely the probability of an event E is

$$P(E) = \frac{\text{number of points in } E}{\text{number of points in } S} = \frac{|E|}{|S|}$$

There are two problems which arise with this approach:
1 We may not know the number of sample points in the event E.
2 The number of sample points in S may not be finite.

24.11 THE RELATIVE FREQUENCY METHOD

We may not know how many defective discs are in the box. For example, a machine could be making and packaging the discs and it may not be known how many are defective.

One way of proceeding is to select each disc in turn and test it. We then obtain

$$P(n) = \frac{\text{number of defective discs}}{\text{number of discs tested}}$$

where n is the number of discs tested. This would give an estimate of the probability p, and we could argue that as $n \to N$ (the total number) we should have $p(n) \to p$, the probability of a defective. Indeed, we could extend this idea to an infinite population and then obtain $p(n) \to p$ as $n \to \infty$.

☐ A coin is thrown to test the probability that it will show heads. Given **Example** the following results, taken in order, show how an estimate of the probability varies:

H H T H T H H H T H T T T H H T

where H denotes heads and T denotes tails.

We can construct a table of the relative frequency $p(n)$, that is the number of heads which have shown in n throws:

n	$p(n)$	n	$p(n)$
1	1/1	9	6/9
2	2/2	10	7/10
3	2/3	11	7/11
4	3/4	12	7/12
5	3/5	13	7/13
6	4/6	14	8/14
7	5/7	15	9/15
8	6/8	16	9/16

What are we to make of this? We can argue that if the coin is fair then, if we throw it $2m$ times, we should expect for large m that there would be m heads. However, we don't know anything about the coin in question here.

We could perhaps turn the argument round and use this as a method of testing whether or not the coin is fair. However, this leaves a number of open questions, such as 'How many times do we need to throw the coin to establish the probability?'   ■

The major problem with the relative frequency method is that $p(n)$ changes as n changes, and consequently a fluke situation could give misleading results.

24.12 THE MATHEMATICAL METHOD

We must remember that a sample space S consists of all possible outcomes of an experiment and that a random variable assigns a number to each sample point. Therefore if we assign probabilities to the set of values $X(S)$ of the random variable, we automatically assign probabilities to the sample points:

$$S \to X(S) \to \mathbb{R}$$

It is convenient on some occasions to think of probabilities as assigned to the sample space, and on others to think of them as assigned to the values of the random variable.

Suppose S is a sample space and X is a random variable. A **probability density function** (PDF) is a real-valued function with domain $X(S)$ such that

1 If $r \in X(S)$ then $P(r) \geq 0$;

2 $\Sigma P(r) = 1$.

Here we suppose that the random variable is discrete. Continuous random variables are discussed in section 24.18.

where the sum is taken over every element of $X(S)$. So a probability density function is a function which assigns weights to the values of the random variable in such a way that they are all non-negative and total to 1.

Whenever we have a probability density function we say that P defines a **probability distribution**.

Example □ Obtain h if P defines a probability distribution on $\{1,2,3\}$ as follows:

r	1	2	3
$P(X = r)$	1/4	h	h^2

Obtain also
a the probability that X is greater than 1
b the probability that X is not equal to 2.
We have $\Sigma P(X = r) = 1$ for all values of the random variable X, and so

$$\tfrac{1}{4} + h + h^2 = 1$$
$$(h + \tfrac{1}{2})^2 = 1$$
$$h + \tfrac{1}{2} = \pm 1$$
$$h = -\tfrac{1}{2} \pm 1$$

However, we can reject the negative sign because all probabilities must be positive. We conclude therefore that $h = 1/2$.

a $P(X > 1) = P(X = 2) + P(X = 3) = 1/2 + (1/2)^2 = 1/2 + 1/4 = 3/4$
b $P(X \neq 2) = 1 - P(X = 2) = 1 - 1/2 = 1/2$ ∎

In the case of a discrete random variable X which can take values $x_1, x_2, \ldots, x_n, \ldots$ with probabilities, $p_1, p_2, \ldots, p_n, \ldots$ respectively we obtain

$$p_r \geqslant 0 \quad \text{for all } r \in \mathbb{N}$$
$$\Sigma p_r = 1$$

where the sum is taken over all $r \in \mathbb{N}$.

There are many discrete probability distributions. However there are two, the binomial distribution and the Poisson distribution, which have many applications. We shall discuss them briefly.

We need one extra piece of terminology first. A single occurrence of an experiment is called a **trial**.

24.13 THE BINOMIAL DISTRIBUTION

Before describing the binomial distribution we shall state the circumstances in which it can be used. It is most important to be sure that these conditions hold before attempting to apply the binomial distribution.

The binomial distribution may be applied whenever an experiment occurs with the following characteristics:

1 There are only two possible outcomes of each trial. For reference purposes we shall call these 'success' and 'failure'.
2 The probability p of success in a single trial is constant. Note that this implies that the probability q of failure is constant too, because $p + q = 1$.
3 The outcomes of successive trials are independent of one another.

We can think of many examples where these conditions hold, such as tossing a coin with outcome heads or tails, or rolling dice to obtain a six. A third example is selecting, one by one at random, electrical components from a box and then testing and replacing them. In this case, if we do not replace a component then the probability of choosing a defective next time will change. However, for a large quantity of components in the box the binomial conditions will be satisfied approximately.

In general, suppose there are n trials and that we define the random variable X as the number of successes. We shall examine the possibilities.

If there is just one trial, we then have only two possibilities: F (failure) or S (success). We know that $P(F) = q$ and $P(S) = p$ where $p + q = 1$, so

$$P(X = 0) = q \qquad P(X = 1) = p$$

If there are two trials then the possibilities are FF, SF, FS, SS. So

$$P(X = 0) = q^2$$
$$P(X = 1) = pq + qp = 2pq$$
$$P(X = 2) = p^2$$

Now you list the possible outcomes for three trials and thereby calculate $P(X = 0)$, $P(X = 1)$, $P(X = 2)$ and $P(X = 3)$.

Here are the possible outcomes:

FFF, FFS, FSF, SFF, FSS, SFS, SSF, SSS

From these,

$$P(X = 0) = q^3$$
$$P(X = 1) = 3pq^2$$
$$P(X = 2) = 3p^2q$$
$$P(X = 3) = p^3$$

In the general situation where there are n trials we have

$$P(X = r) = \binom{n}{r} p^r q^{n-r}$$

You will observe that this is the general term in the expansion of $(p + q)^n$ using the binomial theorem (see Chapter 1). Indeed this observation confirms straight away that we have a probability distribution. Each term is positive and the sum of them all is $(p + q)^n$, which is 1 since $p + q = 1$.

Example □ A company has eight faulty machines. It is stated by the servicing engineer that if a machine is serviced there is a 75% probability that it will last a further three years. The company has all eight machines serviced. If the servicing engineer is correct, estimate
a The probability that none of the machines will last a further three years;
b The probability that at least six of the machines will last a further three years;
c The probability that at least one of the machines will last a further three years.

The probability that if a machine is serviced it will last a further three years is $p = 0.75$, and we may suppose that the lifetimes of the machines are independent of one another.

The conditions for a binomial distribution are satisfied with $n = 8$. So if the random variable X is defined as the number of machines which will last a further three years, we have

$$P(X = r) = \binom{8}{r} (0.75)^r (0.25)^{8-r}$$

a We must calculate

$$P(X = 0) = (0.75)^0(0.25)^8$$
$$= (0.25)^8 = 0.000\,015\,26$$

This is negligible.

b We must obtain

$$P(X \geqslant 6) = P(X = 6) + P(X = 7) + P(X = 8)$$

$$= \binom{8}{6} (0.75)^6 (0.25)^2 + \binom{8}{7} (0.75)^7 (0.25) + (0.75)^8$$

$$= 0.311\,462\,4 + 0.266\,967\,8 + 0.100\,112\,9 = 0.678\,543\,1$$
$$= 0.6785 \text{ to four decimal places}$$

c We require

$$P(X > 0) = 1 - P(X = 0) = 1 - 0.000\,015\,26 = 0.999\,984\,74$$

So it is almost certain that at least one of the machines will last a further three years. ∎

24.14 THE MEAN OF A PROBABILITY DISTRIBUTION

In much the same way as we defined the mean of a population, we define the mean of a discrete probability distribution by

$$\mu = \Sigma P(X = r)r$$

where the sum is taken over all possible values of the random variable X. Here we can think of $P(X = r)$ as the relative frequency with which the random variable X attains the value r in a long sequence of trials.

The mean μ of the probability distribution is also known as the **expectation** of random variable.

☐ A businessman knows that if he sends a letter to a householder there is **Example** a 0.5% probability that he will receive an order for new windows which will give him a profit of £600. If he doesn't receive an order the cost to him in postage and administration is 30p. What is his expected gain?

Writing S for success and F for failure we have $S \to 600$, $F \to -0.3$. So defining the random variable X as his expected win, we have $P(X - 600) = 0.005$ and $P(X - 0.3) = 0.995$. Therefore

$$\mu = 600 \times 0.005 + (-0.3) \times 0.995 = 2.7015$$

So if he sends out a lot of letters, on average he will expect to gain £2.70 for each one. ∎

☐ Obtain the mean μ corresponding to the binomial distribution.   **Example**
We have

$$P(X = r) = \binom{n}{r} p^r q^{n-r}$$

for $r \in \{0, 1, 2, \ldots, n\}$. Then

$$\mu = \sum_{r=0}^{n} \binom{n}{r} p^r q^{n-r} r$$

$$= \sum_{r=1}^{n} \frac{n(n-1) \ldots (n-r+1)}{1 \times 2 \times 3 \times \ldots \times r} p^r q^{n-r} r$$

$$= np \sum_{r=1}^{n} \frac{(n-1) \ldots (n-r+1)}{1 \times 2 \times 3 \times \ldots \times r} p^{r-1} q^{n-r} r$$

If we put $s = r - 1$ we obtain

$$\mu = np \sum_{s=0}^{n-1} \frac{(n-1) \ldots ([n-1]-s+1)}{1 \times 2 \times 3 \times \ldots \times (s+1)} p^s q^{n-s-1}(s+1)$$

$$= np \sum_{s=0}^{n-1} \frac{(n-1) \ldots ([n-1]-s+1)}{1 \times 2 \times 3 \times \ldots \times s} p^s q^{n-s-1}$$

Now s is a dummy variable, and so we can call it what we like. Therefore we shall revert to using r; the old r is dead and gone! If you object to this practice, give it some thought and you will realize you are simply being sentimental about good old r. Then

$$\mu = np \sum_{r=0}^{n-1} \frac{(n-1) \ldots ([n-1]-r+1)}{1 \times 2 \times 3 \times \ldots \times r} p^r q^{n-r-1}$$

$$= np \sum_{r=0}^{n-1} \binom{n-1}{r} p^r q^{n-1-r}$$

$$= np(p+q)^{n-1} = np$$

We knew this anyway, didn't we? We knew that if a single trial has constant probability p of success, then if we perform n trials the mean will be np. ∎

24.15 THE VARIANCE OF A PROBABILITY DISTRIBUTION

The variance for a continuous distribution is given in section 24.19.

The variance of a probability distribution is defined as the expected value of $(X - \mu)^2$. As with the mean, this is consistent with the definition of a population variance.

Recall that

$$\sigma^2 = \frac{\Sigma f_r(x_r - \mu)^2}{\Sigma f_r}$$

where there are n distinct data points, the sums are taken for $r \in \{1, 2,$

$\dots, n\}$ and $\Sigma f_r = N$, the total number of data points. If we divide through each term in the numerator by Σf_r we obtain instead of each frequency f_r a relative frequency p_r, so that

$$\sigma^2 = \Sigma p_r(x_r - \mu)^2$$

So for the variance we have

$$\begin{aligned}
V(X) = \sigma^2 = E(X - \mu)^2 &= \Sigma P(X = r)(r - \mu)^2 \\
&= \Sigma P(X = r)(r^2 - 2\mu r + \mu^2) \\
&= \Sigma P(X = r)r^2 - 2\mu \Sigma P(X = r)r + \mu^2 \Sigma P(X = r)
\end{aligned}$$

where, of course, the sums are taken over all possible values of the random variable.

Now we have a probability distribution, and consequently

$$\Sigma P(X = r) = 1$$
$$\Sigma P(X = r)r = \mu$$

So that substituting these into the expression for V we obtain

$$\begin{aligned}
V(X) = \sigma^2 &= \Sigma P(X = r)r^2 - 2\mu\mu + \mu^2 \\
&= \Sigma P(X = r)r^2 - \mu^2
\end{aligned}$$

Therefore we have shown that

$$V(X) = \sigma^2 = E(X - \mu)^2 = E(X^2) - [E(X)]^2$$

This formula can be useful when calculating the variance of a probability distribution. It can be shown using elementary algebra that for the binomial distribution the variance is npq. The standard deviation is therefore $\sqrt{(npq)}$.

In summary, for the binomial distribution, mean $= np$ and variance $= npq$, where n is the number of experiments and p is the probability of success in a single trial.

24.16 THE POISSON DISTRIBUTION

Suppose we have a situation in which incidents occur randomly. Then we have a Poisson distribution if the following conditions are satisfied:

1 On average there are λ incidents in a unit time interval, where λ is a constant.
2 In a small time interval δT, the probability of two or more incidents occurring is zero.
3 If two time intervals have no points in common, the number of incidents occurring in each one is independent of the other.

If the random variable X is defined as the number of incidents which occur in a time interval of length T, then we obtain the following probability distribution:

Siméon-Denis Poisson (1781–1840): French mathematician known for his work on integrals, Fourier series, electromagnetic theory and probability.

$$P(X = r) = e^{-\mu} \frac{\mu^r}{r!} \quad \text{for } r \in \mathbb{N}_0$$

where $\mu = \lambda T$. (You will recall that $\mathbb{N}_0 = \{0, 1, 2, 3, \ldots\}$ is the set of non-negative integers.) To see that this is a probability density function, we note first that all its values are positive and secondly that their sum is

$$\sum_{r=0}^{\infty} e^{-\mu} \frac{\mu^r}{r!} = e^{-\mu} e^{\mu} = 1$$

Example $\square$ A company has three telephone lines and receives on average six calls every five minutes. Assuming a Poisson distribution, what is the probability that more than three calls will be received during a given two-minute period.

We have six calls every five minutes on average, and so $\lambda = 1.2$ per minute. The time interval T in which we are interested is of length 2, and so $\mu = \lambda T = 2.4$. If X is the number of calls which are being received in the two-minute interval, we have

$$P(X = r) = e^{-1.2} \frac{(1.2)^r}{r!} \quad \text{for } r \in \mathbb{N}_0$$

So we require

$$
\begin{aligned}
P(X > 3) &= 1 - P(X \leq 3) \\
&= 1 - \{P(X = 0) + P(X = 1) + P(X = 2) + P(X = 3)\} \\
&= 1 - e^{-1.2} \left[1 + 1.2 + \frac{(1.2)^2}{2} + \frac{(1.2)^3}{6} \right] \\
&= 1 - 0.966 = 0.034
\end{aligned}
$$
$\blacksquare$

It is a simple algebraic exercise to show that the expectation of the Poisson random variable is μ. We do not therefore have a conflict of notation, as would otherwise be the case. Why not try and deduce this for yourself?

We have

$$P(X = r) = e^{-\mu} \frac{\mu^r}{r!} \quad \text{for } r \in \mathbb{N}_0$$

So

$$
\begin{aligned}
E(X) &= \sum_{r=0}^{\infty} P(X = r) r = \sum_{r=0}^{\infty} e^{-\mu} \frac{\mu^r}{r!} r \\
&= \sum_{r=1}^{\infty} e^{-\mu} \frac{\mu^r}{(r-1)!}
\end{aligned}
$$

Putting $s = r - 1$,

$$E(X) = \mu \sum_{s=0}^{\infty} e^{-\mu} \frac{\mu^s}{s!}$$

$$= \mu$$

Note that the sum of all the probabilities of the random variable is 1. A similar but more involved algebraic exercise can be used to show that the variance is also μ.

In summary, for the Poisson distribution, mean $= \mu$, variance $= \mu$ and $\mu = \lambda T$, where λ is the number of incidents per unit time interval and T is the length of the time interval.

24.17 APPROXIMATION FOR THE BINOMIAL DISTRIBUTION

If n is large there is a problem in calculating the coefficients of the binomial expansion. However, if p is also small then for the binomial distribution

$$\sigma^2 = npq = np(1 - p) \simeq np = \mu$$

so that the mean and variance are approximately equal.

It is not difficult to show that if $n \to \infty$ and $p \to 0$ in such a way that np remains constant, then the Poisson distribution is a good approximation for the binomial distribution. Clearly we shall require $np^2 \simeq 0$, and this will hold provided μ^2 is much smaller than n. If $n > 20$ and $\mu = np < 5$ then the approximation will be good enough for most purposes.

□ It is known that 5% of all bricks manufactured at a brick works are sub- **Example** standard. A customer buys 30 which are selected randomly. What is the probability that at least four are substandard?

Here $n = 30$ and $p = 0.05$, so that $np = 0.6$ and the Poisson distribution is certainly appropriate. Let the random variable X denote the number of defective bricks in the sample. Then

$$P(X = r) = e^{-0.6} \frac{(0.6)^r}{r!}$$

We are dealing with an approximation, and so we must ignore the fact that these probabilities are defined for r greater than 30. Then

$$P(X \geqslant 4) = 1 - P(X \leqslant 3)$$

$$= 1 - e^{-0.6} \left[1 + 0.6 + \frac{(0.6)^2}{2!} + \frac{(0.6)^3}{3!} \right] = 0.003\,36 \quad ■$$

24.18 CONTINUOUS DISTRIBUTIONS

Given a discrete probability distribution, we can represent it pictorially by means of a histogram with unit area. The probability of each value of the

Discrete distributions were discussed in section 24.12.

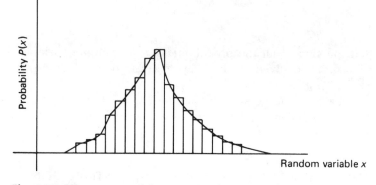

Fig. 24.3 Histogram and frequency polygon.

random variable is then shown as the corresponding area of the histogram. If the random variable has a large number of values within each closed interval, the frequency polygon will approach that of a smooth curve (Fig. 24.3). We can use this to picture probability density functions corresponding to continuous random variables.

In order to extend the idea of a probability density function to *continuous* random variables, we shall need to employ calculus. Suppose $f : \mathbb{R} \to \mathbb{R}$ is a probability density function corresponding to a continuous random variable X. Then f satisfies the condition

$$f(x) \geq 0 \quad \text{for all } x \in \mathbb{R}$$

Given any $a, b \in \mathbb{R}$, $a < b$, we require $P(a < X < b)$. Suppose we partition the interval $[a, b]$ into an equal number of subintervals each of length δx (Fig. 24.4). Then, selecting an arbitrary point x,

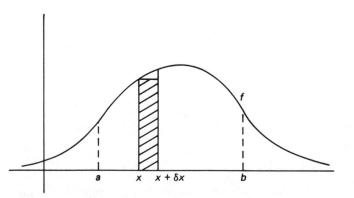

Fig. 24.4 Graph of a probability density function.

$$P(x < X < x + \delta x) \simeq f(x)\,\delta x$$

using a discrete approximation. So

$$P(a < X < b) \simeq \sum_{x=a}^{x=b} f(x)\,\delta x$$

Moreover, the approximation becomes good as $\delta x \to 0$, so that

$$P(a < X < b) = \int_a^b f(x)\,dx$$

We know also that, taken over all possible values of the random variable X, the total probability must be 1. Consequently

$$P(-\infty < X < \infty) = \int_{-\infty}^{\infty} f(x)\,dx = 1$$

It's best to think of the probability that X takes on a value between $X = a$ and $X = b$ as the *area* under the probability curve $y = f(x)$ between $x = a$ and $x = b$. Notice in particular that the area under a point is zero, and so for a continuous distribution $P(X = a) = 0$ for every $a \in \mathbb{R}$. Consequently

$$P(a < X < b) = P(a \leqslant X \leqslant b)$$

You should note that this is certainly not so for discrete distributions. Later we shall be using a continuous distribution as an approximation to a discrete distribution, and we shall have to take account of this difference then.

Remember the two conditions which need to be satisfied if $f: \mathbb{R} \to \mathbb{R}$ is to be a probability density function:

1 $f(x) \geqslant 0$ for all $x \in \mathbb{R}$

2 $\displaystyle\int_{-\infty}^{\infty} f(x)\,dx = 1$

□ The function $f: [0, 1] \to \mathbb{R}$ defined by $f(x) = 3kx^2$ is known to be a prob- **Example** ability density function. Obtain the value of k. Obtain also the probability that if an observation were chosen at random it would be (a) less than 1/2 (b) between 1/4 and 1/2.

We note that because the domain of f is an interval $[0, 1]$, we have a continuous random variable. We require

$$f(x) \geqslant 0 \quad \text{for all } x \in [0, 1]$$

and this implies that $3kx^2 \geqslant 0$ and so $k \geqslant 0$. Next we have

$$\int f(x)\,dx = 1$$

where the integral must be taken over the domain of f. In this case this is the interval $[0, 1]$. So

$$1 = \int_0^1 3kx^2 \, \mathrm{d}x = [kx^3]_0^1 = k$$

Therefore $k = 1$.

Consequently

a $P\left(X < \frac{1}{2}\right) = \int_0^{1/2} 3x^2 \, \mathrm{d}x = [x^3]_0^{1/2} = \frac{1}{8}$

b $P\left(\frac{1}{4} < X < \frac{1}{2}\right) = \int_{1/4}^{1/2} 3x^2 \, \mathrm{d}x = [x^3]_{1/4}^{1/2} = \frac{1}{8} - \frac{1}{64} = \frac{7}{64}$ ∎

24.19 MEAN AND VARIANCE

The variance for a discrete distribution was obtained in section 24.15.

The formula for the mean of a continuous distribution involves an integral instead of a sum. The form of this can be deduced, using the calculus, from the formula for a discrete distribution. We obtain

$$\mu = E(X)$$
$$= \int_{-\infty}^{\infty} f(x) \, x \, \mathrm{d}x$$

We defined the variance of a discrete distribution in terms of expectation, and this formula will hold good for continuous distributions too:

$$V(X) = \sigma^2 = E(X - \mu)^2$$
$$= \int_{-\infty}^{\infty} (x - \mu)^2 \, f(x) \, \mathrm{d}x$$
$$= \int_{-\infty}^{\infty} x^2 f(x) \, \mathrm{d}x - 2\mu \int_{-\infty}^{\infty} xf(x) \, \mathrm{d}x + \mu^2 \int_{-\infty}^{\infty} f(x) \, \mathrm{d}x$$
$$= E(X^2) - 2\mu\mu + \mu^2$$
$$= E(X^2) - \mu^2$$
$$= E(X^2) - [E(X)]^2$$

Example □ Obtain the mean and variance of the probability density function $f : [0, 1] \to \mathbb{R}$ defined by $f(x) = 3x^2$.

We have already shown that we have a PDF, and so we need only calculate what is required:

$$\mu = E(X) = \int_0^1 3x^2 x \, \mathrm{d}x$$
$$= 3 \int_0^1 x^3 \, \mathrm{d}x$$
$$= \frac{3}{4} [x^4]_0^1 = \frac{3}{4}$$

Also

$$E(X^2) = \int_0^1 3x^2 x^2 \, dx$$

$$= 3 \int_0^1 x^4 \, dx$$

$$= \frac{3}{5} [x^5]_0^1 = \frac{3}{5}$$

So

$$V(X) = E(X^2) - \mu^2$$

$$= \frac{3}{5} - \frac{9}{16} = \frac{3}{80}$$ ∎

Although there are many continuous distributions, one in particular – the normal distribution – is of great importance and application. We shall discuss this distribution now.

24.20 THE NORMAL DISTRIBUTION

The probability density function for the normal distribution is an ugly-looking beast. Luckily we shall not need to handle it at all because the indefinite integral cannot be obtained explicitly in terms of elementary functions. Therefore tables have had to be constructed so that the probabilities can be calculated. Part of our task will be acquiring the skill necessary to use the tables. For the sake of completeness, and for your general edification, here is the probability density function itself:

$$f(x) = \frac{1}{\sigma\sqrt{(2\pi)}} \exp\left[-\frac{(x-\mu)^2}{2\sigma^2}\right] \qquad x \in \mathbb{R}$$

where $\sigma > 0$ is the standard deviation and μ is the mean.

Although the graph is symmetrical about $x = \mu$ and its height is $1/\sigma\sqrt{(2\pi)}$, its shape depends on σ. For instance, if we take $\mu = 0$ then for $\sigma = 3$ we have a low-humped curve, whereas for $\sigma = 1$ we obtain the more familiar bell-shaped curve (Fig. 24.5).

The **standard normal distribution** has $\mu = 0$ and $\sigma = 1$, and it is areas under the standard normal curve which are tabulated. If the continuous random variable X is normally distributed with mean μ and variance σ^2, and if

$$Z = \frac{X - \mu}{\sigma}$$

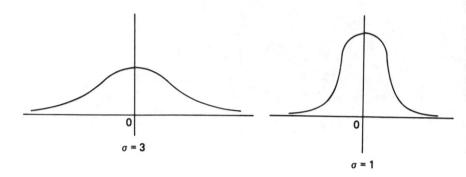

Fig. 24.5 Normal distributions with mean 0.

then Z is normally distributed with mean 0 and variance 1.

There are several ways in which the area under the standard normal curve can be tabulated. However, we confine our attention to just one of them. The curve is symmetrical and so the area under the upper half of the curve will be sufficient. In Table 24.1 we give the area under the upper tail; this is the shaded area shown in Fig. 24.6. When $Z = 0$ the area under the upper tail is 0.5, because the total area is 1 and the curve is symmetrical. Also as Z tends to ∞ the area under the upper tail tends to 0.

Suppose now $a \le b$ and that we require $P(a < Z < b)$. We observe from Fig. 24.6 that

$$P(a < Z < b) = P(Z > a) - P(Z > b)$$

So if $a \ge 0$ we can use the table straight away to obtain the required probability. If $a < 0$ then we must use the symmetry of the standard normal curve.

Example □ A random variable X is normally distributed with mean 0 and variance 1. Obtain the probability that a sample chosen at random will be **a** greater

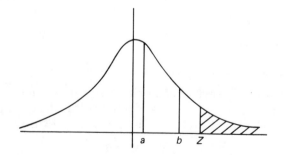

Fig. 24.6 Standard normal distribution.

than 2.12 **b** between 0.55 and 2.15 **c** greater than -1.34 but less than 2.43.

In each case we reduce the probabilities to those corresponding to areas under the upper tail:

a We require $P(X > 2.12) = 0.0170$, directly from the table. Notice how we use the left-hand column to obtain the row corresponding to 2.1 and then move across the columns to find the area corresponding to 2.12.

b To obtain $P(0.55 < X < 2.15)$, we use

$$P(0.55 < X < 2.15) = P(X > 0.55) - P(X > 2.15)$$
$$= 0.2912 - 0.0158 = 0.2754$$

c For $P(-1.34 < X < 2.43)$ we must use the symmetry and the fact that the total area under the curve is 1:

$$P(-1.34 < X < 2.43) = 1 - P(X > 1.34) - P(X > 2.43)$$
$$= 1 - 0.0901 - 0.0075 = 0.9024 \qquad ■$$

The normal distribution applies in many situations, and this can be shown whenever large quantities of data are collected. It is comparatively rare for a non-normal distribution to arise in practice. Here is another example to show how we use standard normal tables when we are solving a problem where the mean and variance are not 0 and 1 respectively.

☐ A manufacturing process produces dry cell batteries which have a mean **Example** shelf life of 2.25 years and a standard deviation of 3.5 months. Assuming the distribution is normal:

a Obtain the probability that an item selected at random will have a shelf life of at least 2.5 years.

b If three items are selected at random, obtain the probability that at least two will have a shelf life of more than 2.5 years.

We have $\mu = 2.25$ and $\sigma = 0.2917$, so that using the standard normal distribution we put

$$Z = \frac{X - \mu}{\sigma} = \frac{X - 2.25}{0.2917}$$

a When $X = 2.5$ we have $Z = 0.857$, so that

$$P(X \geqslant 2.5) = P(Z \geqslant 0.857) = 0.1957$$

Notice that we have interpolated the value corresponding to 0.857 from those given in Table 24.1:

$$0.85 \rightarrow 0.1977 \qquad 0.86 \rightarrow 0.1949$$

so the difference is 0.0028. Multiplying by 0.7 gives approximately 0.0020 as the corresponding difference between 0.85 and 0.857.

b If we select three items at random we have a binomial distribution where

Table 24.1 Standard normal distribution: area under upper tail

Z	0.00	0.01	0.02	0.03	0.04	0.05	0.06	0.07	0.08	0.09	
0.0	0.5000	0.4960	0.4920	0.4880	0.4840	0.4801	0.4761	0.4721	0.4681	0.4641	0.0
0.1	0.4602	0.4562	0.4522	0.4483	0.4443	0.4404	0.4364	0.4325	0.4286	0.4247	0.1
0.2	0.4207	0.4168	0.4129	0.4090	0.4052	0.4013	0.3974	0.3936	0.3897	0.3859	0.2
0.3	0.3821	0.3783	0.3745	0.3707	0.3369	0.3632	0.3594	0.3557	0.3520	0.3483	0.3
0.4	0.3446	0.3409	0.3372	0.3336	0.3300	0.3264	0.3228	0.3192	0.3156	0.3121	0.4
0.5	0.3085	0.3050	0.3015	0.2981	0.2946	0.2912	0.2877	0.2843	0.2810	0.2776	0.5
0.6	0.2743	0.2709	0.2676	0.2643	0.2611	0.2578	0.2546	0.2514	0.2483	0.2451	0.6
0.7	0.2420	0.2389	0.2358	0.2327	0.2296	0.2266	0.2236	0.2206	0.2177	0.2148	0.7
0.8	0.2119	0.2090	0.2061	0.2033	0.2005	0.1977	0.1949	0.1922	0.1894	0.1867	0.8
0.9	0.1841	0.1814	0.1788	0.1762	0.1736	0.1711	0.1685	0.1660	0.1635	0.1611	0.9
1.0	0.1587	0.1562	0.1539	0.1515	0.1492	0.1469	0.1446	0.1423	0.1401	0.1379	1.0
1.1	0.1357	0.1335	0.1314	0.1292	0.1271	0.1251	0.1230	0.1210	0.1190	0.1170	1.1
1.2	0.1151	0.1131	0.1112	0.1093	0.1075	0.1056	0.1038	0.1020	0.1003	0.0985	1.2
1.3	0.0968	0.0951	0.0934	0.0918	0.0901	0.0885	0.0869	0.0853	0.0838	0.0823	1.3
1.4	0.0808	0.0793	0.0778	0.0764	0.0749	0.0735	0.0721	0.0708	0.0694	0.0681	1.4
1.5	0.0668	0.0655	0.0643	0.0630	0.0618	0.0606	0.0594	0.0582	0.0571	0.0559	1.5
1.6	0.0548	0.0537	0.0526	0.0516	0.0505	0.0495	0.0485	0.0475	0.0465	0.0455	1.6
1.7	0.0446	0.0436	0.0427	0.0418	0.0409	0.0401	0.0392	0.0384	0.0375	0.0367	1.7
1.8	0.0359	0.0351	0.0344	0.0336	0.0329	0.0322	0.0314	0.0307	0.0301	0.0294	1.8
1.9	0.0287	0.0281	0.0274	0.0268	0.0262	0.0256	0.0250	0.0244	0.0239	0.0233	1.9

	0.00	0.01	0.02	0.03	0.04	0.05	0.06	0.07	0.08	0.09
2.0	0.0228	0.0222	0.0217	0.0212	0.0207	0.0202	0.0197	0.0192	0.0188	0.0183
2.1	0.0179	0.0174	0.0170	0.0166	0.0162	0.0158	0.0154	0.0150	0.0146	0.0143
2.2	0.0139	0.0136	0.0132	0.0129	0.0125	0.0122	0.0119	0.0116	0.0113	0.0110
2.3	0.0107	0.0104	0.0102	0.0099	0.0096	0.0094	0.0091	0.0089	0.0087	0.0084
2.4	0.0082	0.0080	0.0078	0.0075	0.0073	0.0071	0.0069	0.0068	0.0066	0.0064
2.5	0.0062	0.0060	0.0059	0.0057	0.0055	0.0054	0.0052	0.0051	0.0049	0.0048
2.6	0.0047	0.0045	0.0044	0.0043	0.0041	0.0040	0.0039	0.0038	0.0037	0.0036
2.7	0.0035	0.0034	0.0033	0.0032	0.0031	0.0030	0.0029	0.0028	0.0027	0.0026
2.8	0.0026	0.0025	0.0024	0.0023	0.0023	0.0022	0.0021	0.0021	0.0020	0.0019
2.9	0.0019	0.0018	0.0018	0.0017	0.0016	0.0016	0.0015	0.0015	0.0014	0.0014
3.0	0.0014	0.0013	0.0013	0.0012	0.0012	0.0011	0.0011	0.0010	0.0010	0.0010
3.1	0.0010	0.0009	0.0009	0.0009	0.0008	0.0008	0.0008	0.0008	0.0007	0.0007
3.2	0.0007	0.0007	0.0006	0.0006	0.0006	0.0006	0.0006	0.0005	0.0005	0.0005
3.3	0.0005	0.0005	0.0005	0.0004	0.0004	0.0004	0.0004	0.0004	0.0004	0.0003
3.4	0.0003	0.0003	0.0003	0.0003	0.0003	0.0003	0.0003	0.0003	0.0003	0.0002
3.5	0.00023	0.00022	0.00022	0.00021	0.00020	0.00019	0.00019	0.00018	0.00017	0.00017
3.6	0.00016	0.00015	0.00015	0.00014	0.00014	0.00013	0.00013	0.00012	0.00012	0.00011
3.7	0.00011	0.00010	0.00010	0.00010	0.00009	0.00009	0.00008	0.00008	0.00008	0.00008
3.8	0.00007	0.00007	0.00007	0.00006	0.00006	0.00006	0.00006	0.00005	0.00005	0.00005
3.9	0.00005	0.00005	0.00004	0.00004	0.00004	0.00004	0.00004	0.00004	0.00003	0.00003

$p = 0.1957$. Using Y as the random variable, suppose Y is the number selected with a shelf life of at least 2.5 years. Then

$$P(Y = r) = \binom{3}{r}(0.1957)^r(0.8043)^{3-r}$$

We require

$$
\begin{aligned}
P(Y \geqslant 2) &= P(Y = 2) + P(Y = 3) \\
&= 3 \times (0.1957)^2 \times (0.8043) + (0.1957)^3 \\
&= 0.0924 + 0.0075 = 0.0999
\end{aligned}
$$

24.21 DISCRETE APPROXIMATIONS

We have seen that when p is small and n is large the binomial distribution can be approximated by the Poisson distribution. Of course if p is close to 1 then the approximation can still be used since then $q = 1 - p$ is small.

Problems arise when n is large and neither p nor q is small. In such circumstances the normal distribution becomes a good approximation to the binomial distribution where

$$
\begin{aligned}
\mu \text{ (normal)} &= \mu \text{ (binomial)} = np \\
\sigma^2 \text{ (normal)} &= \sigma^2 \text{ (binomial)} = npq
\end{aligned}
$$

In a similar way, when $\mu > 10$, the Poisson distribution can be approximated by the normal distribution. Once again it is the mean and variance of the distributions which enable the approximation to be effected:

$$
\begin{aligned}
\mu \text{ (normal)} &= \mu \text{ (Poisson)} = \mu \\
\sigma^2 \text{ (normal)} &= \sigma^2 \text{ (Poisson)} = \mu
\end{aligned}
$$

24.22 CONTINUITY CORRECTION

We noticed earlier that one of the differences between discrete and continuous distributions is that, if X is a random variable, the probability that X takes a particular value is always zero for a continuous distribution. For example, if X is a Poisson random variable we have

$$P(X < 9) = P(X \leqslant 8)$$

whereas if X is a normal random variable we have

$$P(X < 8) = P(X \leqslant 8)$$

To compensate for this difference when we use these approximations, we apply a continuity correction and find $P(X < 8.5)$ instead of $P(X \leqslant 8)$ or $P(X < 9)$.

☐ Of the fire extinguishers produced by a factory, 25% are known to be **Example**
faulty. If 30 extinguishers are selected at random, what is the probability
that at least 17 will be satisfactory?

We have a binomial distribution with $n = 30$ and $p = 0.25$, so that $q =$
0.75. Let the random variable X be the number of faulty fire extinguishers
selected. Then we require $P(X < 14)$. There are too many terms to handle,
and so we approximate using the normal distribution. X is approximately
normally distributed with mean $\mu = 30 \times 0.25 = 7.5$ and $\sigma = \sqrt{(7.5 \times 0.75)}$
$= 2.372$.

We require $P(X < 13.5)$, using the continuity correction, and when $X =$
13.5 we have

$$Z = \frac{X - \mu}{\sigma} = \frac{13.5 - 7.5}{2.372} = 2.53$$

$$P(X < 13.5) = P(Z < 2.53) = 1 - P(Z > 2.53)$$
$$= 1 - 0.0057 = 0.9943 \qquad \blacksquare$$

24.23 NORMAL PROBABILITY PAPER

One way of checking whether or not data is normally distributed is to use
special graph paper known as normal probability paper. If we draw the
cumulative frequency curve for the normal distribution we shall obtain an
S-shaped curve (Fig. 24.7). You can do this yourself if you like because the
values which you require are simply the areas under the probability curve,
which we already know from our table of the standard normal distribution
(Table 24.1).

Normal probability paper distorts the y-axis in such a way that the

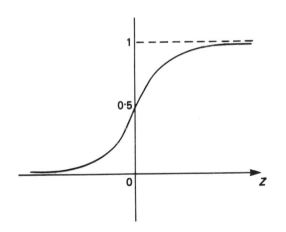

Fig. 24.7 Cumulative frequency curve for the normal distribution.

cumulative frequency curve becomes a straight line. Therefore by calculating the relative cumulative frequencies we can see if our data is approximately normally distributed. We shall illustrate this using some data which we displayed in Chapter 23.

Example □ The number of cars parked in a factory car park at 10.00 a.m. was counted on 120 consecutive working days. The results were given in Table 23.1.

We constructed Table 23.2 to give the relative cumulative frequencies. If we multiply these by 100 they become percentages. From this data we can draw Fig. 24.8.

If the data is normally distributed, the mean can be obtained from this graph. It is the median of the distribution – the value of the random variable X corresponding to a relative cumulative frequency on the axis of symmetry. This is marked as 50% on the graph paper. Here $\mu = 87$.

The table of the standard normal distribution (Table 24.1) shows that when $Z = 1$ the area under the upper tail is 0.1587, and so the cumulative frequency is about 0.84. We can therefore estimate the standard deviation by obtaining the differences between the two values of the random variable X with relative cumulative frequencies of 50% and 84% respectively:

$$\sigma = 102 - 87 = 15$$

■

24.24 Workshop

1

Exercise Two brothers work for a large multinational company. It is announced that 25% of the workforce are to be made redundant. A message is received to say that one of the brothers (it is not known which one) will not be losing his job. Assuming that each employee has an equal probability of being made redundant and that these events are independent of one another, what is the probability that both brothers will remain in employment?

Watch out! In this problem you have to be extra careful. When you have decided on your answer, move on to step 2.

2

!

At first sight you might think this is ridiculously easy and argue as follows: each employee has 0.75 probability of remaining in employment; one brother is already secure; so for both to be safe the probability must be 0.75.

However, this argument is faulty; the error is quite subtle. The point is that we do not know which brother rang home. If the problem had named the brothers as Jim and Tom and had said that Jim rang home then indeed the probability of both holding their jobs would have been 0.75.

If you made that error try again.

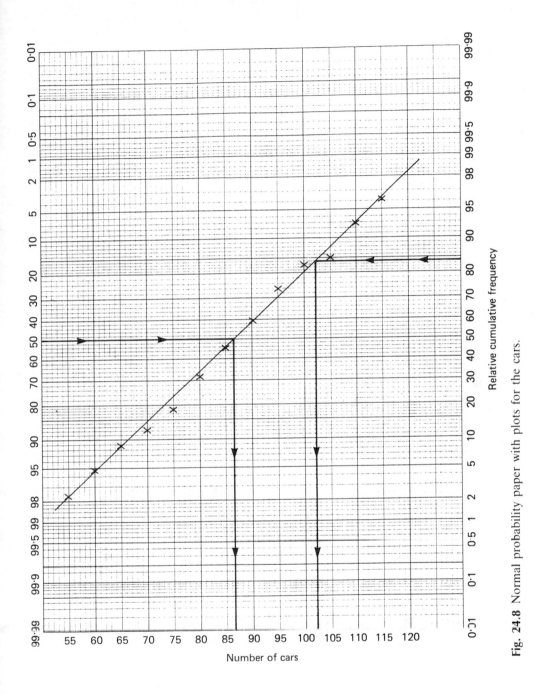

Fig. 24.8 Normal probability paper with plots for the cars.

3 Let's call the brothers Jim and Tom. Let E be 'Jim retains his job' and F be 'Tom retains his job'. We want $P(E \cap F \mid E \cup F)$. Now

$$P(E \cup F) = P(E) + P(F) - P(E \cap F)$$

and since E and F are independent events,

$$P(E \cap F) = P(E)\,P(F)$$

However, $P(E) = P(F) = 0.75$, so that

$$P(E \cup F) = 0.75 + 0.75 - 0.75 \times 0.75$$

Now

$$P(E \cap F \mid E \cup F) = \frac{P[(E \cap F) \cap (E \cup F)]}{P(E \cup F)}$$

$$= \frac{P(E \cap F)}{P(E \cup F)} = \frac{(0.75)^2}{0.75 + 0.75 - (0.75)^2} = 0.6$$

Here is another problem.

▷**Exercise**   In a builders' yard there are two boxes: one contains rods and the other contains clamps. The rods should fit into the clamps. However, 10% of the rods are slightly bent and unusable, and 25% of the clamps are twisted and also unusable. A workman rushes into the yard and selects a rod and a clamp at random from the boxes. Obtain the probability that **a** they are both usable **b** at least one is usable.
Try this and then move on.

4 Let E be 'the rod is usable' and F be 'the clamp is usable'. Then $P(E) = 0.9$ and $P(F) = 0.75$.

a We require $P(E \cap F)$, and since by the nature of the problem E and F are independent we have

$$P(E \cap F) = P(E)\,P(F) = 0.9 \times 0.75 = 0.675$$

b We require $P(E \cup F)$, and so we use

$$P(E \cup F) = P(E) + P(F) - P(E \cap F)$$
$$= 0.9 + 0.75 - 0.675 = 0.975$$

If you managed that then move ahead to step 6. If you didn't make it, then try this.

▷**Exercise**   In the previous exercise, obtain the probability that neither rod nor clamp is usable.

We require $P(E' \cap F')$. As before, E' and F' are independent events, and so

[5]

$$P(E' \cap F') = P(E') P(F') = 0.1 \times 0.25 = 0.025$$

Now we move on to probability density functions.

[6]

▷**Exercise**   The following gives the probability distribution for the random variable X. Obtain h and k if the mean is known to be 3.4.

X	1	3	5	7
$P(X)$	$h + k$	h	$2h - k$	k

When you have done this, step forward.

[7]

For a probability distribution we have that total probability must be 1. Therefore

$$P(1) + P(3) + P(5) + P(7) = 1$$

So

$$(h + k) + h + (2h - k) + k = 1$$
$$4h + k = 1$$

We are also told that the mean is 3.4. Now $\mu = E(X)$, so

$$1P(1) + 3P(3) + 5P(5) + 7P(7) = 3.4$$
$$(h + k) + 3h + 5(2h - k) + 7k = 3.4$$
$$14h + 3k = 3.4$$

From this pair of simultaneous equations we have $h = 0.2$ and $k = 0.2$. Finally, we need to check that all the probabilities are positive; they are.
   If you could not do that exercise, don't worry. The next one is similar for continuous distributions.

▷**Exercise**   The function $f : [0, 2] \to \mathbb{R}$ defined by

$$f(x) = k(x + a) \qquad 0 \leqslant x \leqslant 2$$

is known to be a probability density function. The mean of the distribution is 7/6. Obtain the constants a and k.
   When you have made an attempt, move on to the next step.

[8]

We must obtain the definite integral of f over the interval $[0, 2]$ and equate it to 1 if we are to have a PDF:

$$\int_0^2 k(x + a) \, dx = \frac{k}{2} [(x + a)^2]_0^2$$

Equating to 1 we obtain

$$2 = k[(2 + a)^2 - a^2]$$
$$= k(4a + 4)$$
$$1 = 2k(a + 1)$$

The expectation determines the mean, and so we have

$$\mu = \frac{7}{6} = \int_0^2 xf(x) \, dx = \int_0^2 k(x^2 + ax) \, dx$$
$$\frac{7}{6} = k \left[\frac{x^3}{3} + \frac{ax^2}{2} \right]_0^2$$

from which

$$7 = k(16 + 12a)$$

We have the two equations

$$1 = 2k(a + 1)$$
$$7 = 4k(3a + 4)$$

Eliminating k we have

$$4(3a + 4) = 14(a + 1)$$

It follows that $a = 1$. Substituting back into either of the equations for k gives $k = 1/4$.

▷ **Exercise**   There is a fixed probability that every time a record-making machine operates it will produce a record which is warped. The records are packaged in boxes of five, and 1000 boxes were chosen at random and tested. The numbers warped $(0, 1, 2, 3, 4$ or $5)$ were obtained, and the results are as follows:

Number faulty	0	1	2	3	4	5
Number of boxes	41	143	284	343	169	20

Fit a binomial distribution to this data and calculate the corresponding theoretical frequencies.

When you have done this problem, take another step.

9

Let the random variable X be the number of warped discs in a package of five. We know that the total number of observations N is 1000, and we can determine $\bar{x}$ from the data which estimates μ, the mean of the binomial distribution. So

$$\frac{1}{1000}(41 \times 0 + 143 \times 1 + 284 \times 2 + 343 \times 3 + 169 \times 4 + 20 \times 5) = 2.516$$

Now $\mu = np$ and $n = 5$, so we can obtain an estimate for $p = 0.5032$, the probability that the machine will produce a warped disc each time it operates. Therefore

$$P(X = r) = \binom{5}{r}(0.5032)^r(0.4968)^{5-r}$$

for $r \in \{0, 1, 2, 3, 4, 5\}$.

If we calculate these and multiply them by 1000 we shall obtain the theoretical frequencies:

X	0	1	2	3	4	5
$P(X)$	0.030	0.153	0.311	0.315	0.159	0.032

You will notice that we have had to 'fiddle' the arithmetic so that the probabilities add up to 1 as they must. This is because we have chosen to display the probabilities to only three decimal places. Strictly speaking we should leave the probabilities exact, working out the arithmetic to as many places as necessary, and adjust the theoretical frequencies to bring them into line with reality.

If something went wrong with this, press ahead nevertheless – provided you are sure that you understand it.

▷**Exercise** A company finds that on average there is a claim for damages which it must pay seven times in every ten years. It has expensive insurance to cover this situation. The premium has just been increased, and the firm is considering letting the insurance lapse for 12 months as it can afford to meet a single claim. Assuming a Poisson distribution, what is the probability that there will be at least two claims during the year?

See how you get on with this.

10

Assuming a Poisson distribution, we use a time interval of one year to obtain $\lambda = 0.7$, $T = 1$ and so $\mu = \lambda T = 0.7$. We have

$$P(X = r) = e^{-0.7}\frac{(0.7)^r}{r!}$$

for $r \in \mathbb{N}_0$.

Writing $P(r)$ for $P(X = r)$ we require

$$P(X \geqslant 2) = 1 - P(0) - P(1)$$
$$= 1 - e^{-0.7}(1 + 0.7) = 0.1558$$

▷**Exercise** A company manufactures carpet tacks which it sells in boxes. The number of tacks in each box is a random variable which is normally distributed with mean 35.5 and standard deviation 2.35. The company prints on each box a figure indicating the average minimum contents, and wants this figure to be such that 95% of the boxes have at least this number of tacks in them. What figure should be printed on the boxes?

Try this one before you take the next step.

---

11 Suppose the random variable X is the number of tacks in each box. Then X is normally distributed with mean 35.5 and standard deviation 2.35. We use the standard transformation

$$Z = \frac{X - 35.5}{2.35}$$

so that then Z is normally distributed with mean 0 and standard deviation 1.

We are looking for a number A such that $P(Z > A) = 0.95$. To find this number we must look at the areas under the normal curve. We observe that

$$P(Z > 1.645) = 0.05$$

and so by symmetry

$$P(Z > -1.645) = 0.95$$

Now if

$$Z = \frac{X - 35.5}{2.35} > -1.645$$

we have

$$X - 35.5 > -1.645 \times 2.35$$
$$X > 35.5 - 1.645 \times 2.35 = 31.63$$

Consequently if the company prints the figure of 31 on the packet at least 95% of the packets will have at least the contents stated.

Did you manage that? If you did you can do a hop, skip and a jump to step 13. For those who made an error, here is a supplementary question.

▷**Exercise**   The company goes ahead and prints the figure 31 on the box. What percentage contains fewer than 31 matches?

Tally ho!

---

12 We are looking for $P(X > 31)$, and we already have the transformation we require to the standard normal distribution:

$$Z = \frac{X - 35.5}{2.35}$$

When $X = 31$ this gives

$$Z = \frac{31 - 35.5}{2.35} = -1.915$$

$$P(Z > -1.915) = P(Z < 1.915)$$
$$= 1 - P(Z > 1.915) = 1 - 0.0278 = 0.9722$$

So that less than 3% contain fewer than 31 matches.

13

▷**Exercise**   A company finds that occasionally an export order has been lost
through poor communications. It keeps a record of events of this kind and
discovers that on average 15 orders each year are lost in this way.
Assuming a Poisson distribution, what is the probability that at least 20
orders will be lost during the current year due to poor communications?

   You will need to use the normal approximation here unless you have
itchy fingers. Don't forget the continuity correction.

14

Suppose the random variable X is the number of orders lost due to poor
communications. Then with $\lambda = 15$ and $T = 1$ we have $\mu = 15$ lost per year.

   Since $\mu > 10$ we can use the normal approximation and assert that X is
approximately normally distributed with mean 15 and variance 15. We
require $P(X \geq 20) = P(X > 19)$, and so using the continuity correction
we shall determine $P(X > 19.5)$. Transforming to the standard normal
distribution:

$$Z = \frac{X - 15}{3.873}$$

So when $X = 19.5$ we have $Z = 1.162$, and consequently

$$P(X > 19.5) = P(Z > 1.162) = 0.1226$$

We conclude that there is about a 12¼% probability that at least 20 orders
will be lost in the current year.

   If you managed that then you can leap ahead to step 16. Those who are
left can try this.

▷**Exercise**   A company repairs second-hand television sets which it then
guarantees. The probability that any one set will have to be returned to it
within twelve months for repair is 0.35. A retailer orders 40 sets which he
then sells. Determine the probability that at least half of these sets will
have to be returned for repair within twelve months.

   You may assume we have a binomial distribution. Try hard before
looking at the solution.

15 We have $p = 0.35$ and $n = 40$, so we use the normal approximation: $\mu = np = 14$ and $\sigma^2 = npq = 9.1$. The random variable X is the number of faulty sets in the sample, and we require $p(X \geqslant 20) = P(X > 19)$. So we determine using the continuity correction $P(X > 19.5)$. Transforming to standard normal,

$$Z = \frac{X - 14}{3.017}$$

we see that when $X = 19.5$, $Z = 1.823$. So

$$P(X > 19.5) = P(Z > 1.823) = 0.0342$$

So the probability that at least half will have to be returned is rather less than 3.5%.

There it is then.

16 Now for some practice at drawing. You will need a sheet of normal probability paper. Make sure you know what it looks like. It is not unknown for students in the panic of examinations to use a sheet of logarithmic graph paper by mistake!

▷**Exercise**   The following data represents the lifetimes in hours of 60 dry cell batteries which were tested to destruction:

28.2, 23.4, 21.1, 26.3, 22.7, 25.2, 25.3, 22.7, 24.3, 25.3,
26.3, 24.5, 24.3, 24.8, 26.7, 27.4, 25.6, 22.6, 21.3, 22.6,
20.6, 25.1, 27.4, 25.9, 27.9, 22.1, 25.0, 24.3, 23.6, 24.8,
23.5, 21.8, 27.7, 24.3, 26.4, 20.6, 24.8, 25.1, 23.5, 24.6,
23.7, 25.4, 25.3, 24.7, 23.5, 26.5, 24.6, 24.9, 24.3, 25.4,
25.1, 22.5, 23.6, 25.1, 24.7, 24.9, 25.1, 23.2, 24.7, 23.1

Using class boundaries of

20, 21, 22, 23, 24, 25, 26, 27, 28, 29

show, using normal probability paper, that the data is approximately normally distributed. From your graph estimate the mean and standard deviation.

17 We must begin by calculating the relative cumulative frequencies:

Class boundary	Cumulative frequency	Relative frequency
21	2	0.033
22	5	0.083
23	11	0.183
24	20	0.333
25	36	0.600
26	50	0.833
27	55	0.917
28	59	0.983
29	60	1.000

Using this we are able to plot the necessary points on a sheet of normal probability paper (Fig. 24.9). The line of central symmetry marked 50% gives the estimate for the mean as 24.5. The difference between the 84% percentile and the 50% percentile gives an estimate for the standard deviation as $26.2 - 24.5 = 1.7$.

It is interesting to compare these with the values which we obtain from the raw data using a calculator; $\bar{x} = 24.498$ and $s = 1.7198$.

_____ **24.25 Practical** _____

FAULTY SCAFFOLDING

A box contains a large number of clamps, 40% of which are defective. It is impossible for a construction worker to distinguish visually between the good ones and the bad ones. He selects ten clamps at random and constructs a piece of scaffolding using two clamps for each section. The scaffolding will be dangerous if
1 Either both the clamps on any one section are defective;
2 Or four or more clamps are defective.
Otherwise the scaffolding will be safe. Obtain the probability that the scaffolding will be dangerous.

We shall solve this problem stage by stage so that you may join in the solution at whichever stage you can. First try to analyse the problem to see what is needed.

_____

We shall define events E as 'both the clamps on a section are defective' and F as 'at least four clamps are defective'. We require $P(E \cup F)$. Now

$$P(E \cup F) = 1 - P[(E \cup F)']$$
$$= 1 - P[E' \cap F']$$

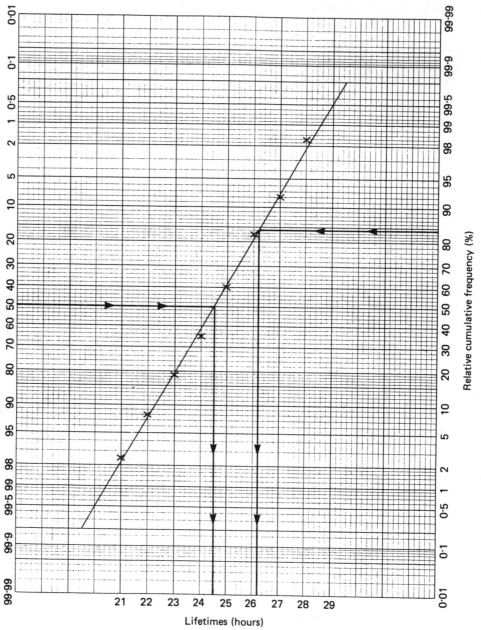

Fig. 24.9 Normal probability paper with plots for lifetimes.

where E' is 'at least one clamp on each section is good' and F' is 'at most three clamps are defective'.

Now let X be 'the number of defective clamps'. Can you carry on?

We require

$$P(E' \cap F')_{*} = P(E' \cap [X = 0]) + P(E' \cap [X = 1])$$
$$+ P(E' \cap [X = 2]) + P(E' \cap [X = 3])$$

To continue with the solution you will need to remember that if A and B are any two events,

$$P(A \cap B) = P(A)P(B|A)$$

Given that there is at most one defective clamp chosen, at least one clamp on every section will be good. Therefore only the binomial probabilities come into the first two terms:

$$P(E' \cap [X = 0]) = P(X = 0)P(E'|X = 0)$$
$$= (0.6)^{10} \times 1 = (0.6)^{10} = 0.006\,047$$
$$P(E' \cap [X = 1]) = P(X = 1)P(E'|X = 1)$$
$$= [10 \times (0.4) \times (0.6)^9] \times 1 = 0.040\,311$$

Things get a little more complicated when two or more clamps are defective.

We consider first $P(E'|X = 2)$. There are five sections and two defective clamps. There are ten ways of placing the first clamp, which leaves nine ways of placing the second. Therefore the probability that a given section contains two defective clamps is

$$\frac{2}{10} \times \frac{1}{9}$$

Now there are five sections, and so the total probability that any one of the sections has two defective clamps (given that there are exactly two defective clamps in the pile) is

$$5 \times \frac{2}{10} \times \frac{1}{9} = \frac{1}{9}$$

Therefore

$$P(E'|X = 2) = 1 - \frac{1}{9} = \frac{8}{9}$$

Try now to complete the calculation of $P(E' \cap [X = 2])$.

We have

$$P(E' \cap [X = 2]) = P(X = 2)P(E'|X = 2)$$

$$= \binom{10}{2}(0.4)^2(0.6)^8\left(\frac{8}{9}\right) = 0.107\,495$$

In order to calculate $P(E'|X = 3)$ you need to use an argument similar to that just used. See if you can do it yourself.

We have

$$P(E'|X = 3) = 1 - 5 \times \frac{3}{10} \times \frac{2}{9} = \frac{2}{3}$$

$$P(E' \cap [X = 3]) = P(X = 3)P(E'|X = 3)$$

$$= \binom{10}{3}(0.4)^3(0.6)^7\left(\frac{2}{3}\right) = 0.143\,327$$

You can certainly finish it off now.

If we add up the probabilities which we have calculated we obtain

$$P(E' \cap F') = 0.297\,18$$

Therefore the required probability is

$$P(E \cup F) = 0.702\,82$$

This is the last of our chapters and if you have completed your studies of the material contained in this book you may soon face your sessional examination. You should be able to do this confidently and calmly certain in the knowledge that you have at your fingertips a variety of experience and technique. In the second and subsequent years of your course you will be able to build on this and develop into an engineer who is able to use mathematics to his or her advantage and does not need to fight shy of mathematical methods.

SUMMARY

There has been quite a lot to learn in this chapter, and so we will just summarize the main points.

PROBABILITY RULES

E and F are events in the sample space S:

$$P(E \cup F) = P(E) + P(F) - P(E \cap F)$$
$$P(E \cap F) = P(E)P(F|E)$$

If $E \cap F = \varnothing$ then E and F are mutually exclusive events. For mutually exclusive events,

$$P(E \cup F) = P(E) + P(F)$$

If $P(E|F) = P(E)$ then E and F are independent events. For independent events,

$$P(E \cap F) = P(E)P(F)$$

BINOMIAL DISTRIBUTION

$$P(X = r) = \binom{n}{r} p^r q^{n-r}$$

where there are n trials and p is the constant probability of success in each one; $p + q = 1$.

POISSON DISTRIBUTION

$$P(X = r) = e^{-\mu} \frac{\mu^r}{r!}$$

where λ is the average number of incidents in unit time, T is the length of the time interval and $\mu = \lambda T$.

NORMAL DISTRIBUTION

If the random variable X is normally distributed with mean μ and variance σ^2 and if

$$Z = \frac{X - \mu}{\sigma}$$

then Z is normally distributed with mean 0 and variance 1.

continued overleaf

continued from previous page

APPROXIMATIONS

If $n > 20$ and $p < 0.3$,

$$\text{binomial} \rightarrow \text{Poisson } (\mu = np)$$

If $n > 20$ and $0.3 \leqslant p \leqslant 0.7$,

$$\text{binomial} \rightarrow \text{normal } (\mu = np, \sigma^2 = npq)$$

If $\mu > 10$,

$$\text{Poisson} \rightarrow \text{normal } (\sigma^2 = \mu)$$

EXERCISES (for answers see p. 761)

1 The probability that an electrical component will function properly after n hours of operation is $10/(10 + n)$. Obtain the probability that the component will still function properly after 200 hours given that it was functioning properly after 150 hours.

2 A lifting apparatus has five cables which can be put under strain. In a single lift at least one cable is under strain. Suppose that the probability that n cables are put under strain is a/n^2, where a is a constant. Determine (a) the value of a (b) the probability that there are at least three cables under strain (c) the probability that there are four cables under strain, given that there are three cables under strain.

3 A machine produces square sheets of chipboard with mean side length 4 metres and standard deviation 0.05 m. Obtain the mean area of each sheet.

4 A probability density function is $f(x) = \log_k x(1 \leqslant x \leqslant 2)$. Obtain (a) the value of k (b) the mean of the distribution.

5 The probability that a glass fibre will shatter during an experiment is believed to follow a Poisson distribution. In an apparatus containing 100 glass fibres it was found that on average seven shattered. Obtain the probability that during a single demonstration of the experiment (a) two glass fibres will shatter (b) at least one glass fibre will shatter. How would your answers differ if the distribution was thought to be binomial?

6 The probability that the nth stage of a production process will be completed on time is $p(n) = 1/(n + 1)$. A certain production process has five stages. Obtain the probability that (a) it will be completed on time (b) it will be completed on time given that the first three stages were completed on time (c) none of the stages will be completed on time. Obtain the corresponding results if $p(n) = n/(n + 1)$.

ASSIGNMENT (for answers see p. 761; see also Workshop on p. 720)

1 The number of collisions requiring garage services on site on a busy stretch of motorway in any one week is known to be a Poisson random variable with mean 9.43. If there are more than two collisions in a day an auxiliary truck needs to be hired. Determine the probability that an extra truck will need to be hired.

2 A factory assembly is responsible for putting together three indepen-dent parts of a microcomputer: the case, the keyboard and the circuit board. The probabilities that these components are substandard are 0.1, 0.15 and 0.07 respectively. Determine the probability that, if a computer is examined, two or more of these components will be substandard.

3 The probability that a factory medical officer will be away is 0.4. The probability that medical assistance will be required is 0.2. The prob-ability that both the medical officer will be away and medical assistance will be required is 0.1.

   a If medical assistance is required, what is the probability that the medical officer is away?

   b If the medical officer is away, what is the probability that medical assistance will be required?

4 There is a probability 0.005 that a welding machine will produce a faulty joint when it is operated. The machine welds 1000 rivets. Determine the probability that at least three of these are faulty.

5 The function defined by $p(x) = kx$ when $x \in [0, 2]$ is known to be a probability density function. Determine (a) k (b) the mean of the distribution (c) the variance of the distribution.

FURTHER EXERCISES (for answers see p. 761)

1 Illustrate by means of diagrams the following laws of probability:

$$P(E \cup F) = P(E) + P(F) - P(E \cap F)$$
$$P(\sim E) = 1 - P(E)$$
$$P[\sim(E \cup F)] = P[(\sim E) \cap (\sim F)]$$

   where E and F are two events.

2 a Calculate the mean and variance of the first n natural numbers.

   b A fair die is thrown twice and the scores shown are r and s. Represent the sample space of this experiment and show the subspaces corresponding to the following events:

$$E = \{(r, s) : |r - s| = 1\}$$
$$F = \{(r, s) : r + s > 6\}$$
$$G = \{(r, s) : rs \leqslant 6\}$$

Calculate $P(E \cap F)$, $P(F \mid E)$, $P(E \cup F \cup G)$, and $P[(E \cup F) \cap G]$.

3 The probability that a cement mixer will break down during a shift is 0.04. If there are six cement mixers working on site at the start of the shift, obtain the probability that by the end of the shift
a none will have broken down
b at least two will have broken down.

4 Consignments of bricks are subjected to the following inspection procedure. N bricks are selected at random from the consignment and tested. If the number of defective bricks is less than four the consignment is accepted. Otherwise it is rejected. Determine the smallest value of N if the probability of acceptance of a large consignment in which 50% are defective is to be no more than 0.1.

5 The average number of lorries per hour delivering cement to a building site during an 8-hour shift is 0.5. The workforce can handle up to three loads per shift. Further loads must be redirected to another site. Obtain, assuming a Poisson distribution,
a the probability that a lorry arriving during the shift will be redirected to another site
b the tonnage of cement which the workers on the site expect to handle during the shift if each lorry carries 6 tonnes of cement.

6 The numbers of people telephoning a certain number for advice on 40 consecutive working days was recorded as follows:

$$
\begin{array}{cccccccccccc}
3 & 0 & 0 & 1 & 0 & 2 & 1 & 0 & 1 & 1 \\
0 & 3 & 4 & 1 & 2 & 0 & 2 & 1 & 3 & 1 \\
1 & 0 & 1 & 2 & 0 & 2 & 1 & 0 & 1 & 2 \\
3 & 1 & 1 & 0 & 2 & 1 & 0 & 3 & 1 & 2
\end{array}
$$

Calculate the median and mode for this data and represent it by a bar chart. Fit a Poisson distribution to this data and compare the theoretical frequencies with those actually obtained.

7 The weights of ball bearings are normally distributed with a mean of 0.845 newtons and a standard deviation of 0.025 newtons. Determine the percentage of ball bearings with weights
a between 0.800 N and 0.900 N
b greater than 0.810 N.

8 The probability that a loom will break down and require attention during a shift is 0.04. If ten looms are in working order at the start of the shift, determine the probability that during the shift
a none will break down
b not more than two will break down.

9 The number of employees in a firm required to appear before magistrates on driving summonses is a Poisson random variable with mean 4.5 per month. Determine the probability that in any one week at least one employee will receive a summons.

10 The number of telephone calls received by a receptionist between

9.00 a.m. and 9.30 a.m. follows a Poisson distribution with mean 12. Determine the probability

a that on any given day at that time there will be fewer than 8 calls

b that the total number of calls on three consecutive days at that time will be less than 30.

11 Over a ten-week period the number of weeks $f(r)$ in which r employees forgot to clock off was recorded. Fit a Poisson distribution to the data and compare the observed frequencies with the actual ones. The data is as follows:

r	0	1	2	3	4	5
$f(r)$	4	4	1	0	1	0

Hints and solutions

CHAPTER 1

EXERCISES

1 a $x = -2$ or $x = 3$; integers
 b $y = 1/3$ or $y = 2$; rational numbers
 c $u = \pm 1$; integers
 d $v = \pm\sqrt{5}$, $v = \pm\sqrt{3}$; real numbers
 e $x = 1/2$ repeated; rational numbers
2 a 8
 b $2^{9/2} \times 3^{11/4}$
 c $(1 + x)^2(1 + x^2)/(1 - x)^2$
 d $(a - b)^6(a + b)^4$
3 a $x = \ln 5$
 b $x = 0$ or $x = 2$
 c $x = 2$ or $x = 3$
 d $x = \ln 5/\ln 3$ or $x = \ln 3/\ln 5$
4 a $1 - 10x + 40x^2$
 b $3^7 + 7.3^6 x + 21.3^5 x^2$
 c $3^8 - 16.3^7 x + 112.3^6 x^2$
 d $2 - 5x/4 - 25x^2/64$
 e $3^{2/3} + 10.3^{-4/3} x - 25.3^{-10/3} x^2$
 f $1/9 + 2x/27 + x^2/27$

ASSIGNMENT

1 a Rational numbers; 1, 3/2 **b** complex numbers
 c real numbers; $\pm\sqrt{3}$ **d** natural numbers; 1, 2
3 $(1 - 2x)^{-2}$
4 $x = 1$ or $x = 2$
6 Hint: express x, y and z to base e and expand xyz
8 $k = \pm 1/3$
9 70

FURTHER EXERCISES

1 a Integers; $u = 1, u = -2$ **b** complex; $u = (-1 \pm \sqrt{-7})/2$
  c real; $u = -1 \pm \sqrt{3}$ **d** natural numbers; $u = 1, u = 2$
  e integers; $u = -1, u = -2$ **f** rationals; $u = 1$ and $u = 1/2$
3 $x = \ln 2$
4 a $1 + x$
7 a $1 + 10x + 45x^2 + 120x^3$ **b** $1 - x + x^2 - x^3$
  c $1 + x/2 + 3x^2/8 + 5x^3/16$ **d** $1 + 5x + 20x^2 + 220x^3/3$
  e $8 - 21x + 147x^2/16 + 343x^3/128$
12 Hint: if R_1 and R_2 are in series, $R = R_1 + R_2$; if in parallel,
  $1/R = 1/R_1 + 1/R_2$
13 $n = 6$

CHAPTER 2

EXERCISES

1 a $-1/2(x - 1) + 1/2(x - 3)$
  b $-3/(x + 3) + 4/(x + 4)$
  c $1/6x + 3/2(x + 2) - 5/3(x + 3)$
  d $-1/18(x - 5) + 4/3(x + 1)^2 + 1/18(x + 1)$
2 a Identity
  b $x = (-1 \pm \sqrt{5})/2$; equation
  c $x = \ln 2$; equation
  d $x = 1 \pm \sqrt{2}$; equation
3 a $\mathbb{R} \setminus \{3\}$
  b $\mathbb{R}$
  c $\mathbb{R} \setminus \{2, 3\}$
  d $\mathbb{R}_0^+ \setminus [0, 1]$
4 a $x = (a + 1)/(a - 1)$
  b $x = 4a$
  c $x = a - 2$
  d $x = -a$
5 a $[1, 4)$
  b $[1, 2)$
  c $[1, 2)$
  d $[2, 5]$
  e $[1, 5]$
  f $[3, 4)$

ASSIGNMENT

1 a $\mathbb{R}^-$ **b** $\{0\}$ **c** $\mathbb{R}$ **d** $\mathbb{R}^+$ **e** $\varnothing$
2 a $(-5, 5)$ **b** $[-2, 4]$ **c** $(-2, 2)$ **d** $(1, 4)$ **e** $[-2, 9]$

3 a $\mathbb{R} \setminus \{-1, 1\}$ **b** $\{x : x \in \mathbb{R}, |x| > 1\}$ **c** $\emptyset$
4 a $1/x + 1/(x - 1) - 1/(x + 1)$ **b** $3 - 1/x^2 + 2/(x + 1)$
   c $4 + 1/(x^2 + 1) + 1/2(x - 2) + 1/2(x + 2)$

FURTHER EXERCISES

1 a $3/(x - 2) - 2/(x - 1) + 1/(x - 1)^2 + 4/(x - 1)^3$ **b** $1/4(x - 1) -$
   $1/4(x + 1) + 1/4(x - 1)^2 + 1/4(x + 1)^2 + 1/2(x - 1)^3 - 1/2(x + 1)^3$
3 $[(x + \sqrt{2})/(x^2 + x\sqrt{2} + 1) - (x - \sqrt{2})/(x^2 - x\sqrt{2} + 1)]/2\sqrt{2}$
4 Identities: **a, b, d, f.** Equations: **c** $x = (1 + \sqrt{5})/2$
   e $x = 0$ or $x = 2$
6 Hint: rearrange as a quadratic in x and use the fact that it has real roots.
   Answers: **a** 3 and $-3\frac{1}{4}$ **b** $-5/3$ and $-5/8$
8 3.5%
9 1.5% decrease
10 5% decrease
12 $A = 1 - 1/(1 + t + t^2) - t/(1 + t^2)$
13 a $\mathbb{R} \setminus \{0\}, \{0, 1\}$ **c** $i(t) = tH(t) + 2(1 - t)H(t - 1) - (2 - t)H(t - 2)$

CHAPTER 3

EXERCISES

2 a $\{\pi/6, 5\pi/6, 3\pi/2\}$
  b $\{3\pi/16, 7\pi/16, 11\pi/16, 15\pi/16, 19\pi/16, 23\pi/16, 27\pi/16, 31\pi/16\}$
  c $\{0, \pi/2\}$
  d $\{\pi/4, 3\pi/4, 5\pi/4, 7\pi/4\}$
  e $\{0, 2\pi/3, 4\pi/3\}$
  f $\{0, \pi\}$
3 a $3\cos(\theta - \alpha)$ where $\alpha = \cos^{-1}(1/3)$
  b $4\cos(\theta - \alpha)$ where $\alpha = \pi - \sin^{-1}(3/4)$
  c $5\cos(\theta - \alpha)$ where $\alpha = -\cos^{-1}(4/5)$
4 a Circle, centre $(0, 0)$, radius 5
  b rectangular hyperbola, centre $(1, 5)$
  c pair of straight lines; $y = x + 1$, $y = -x + 1$
  d rectangular hyperbola, centre $(1, 2)$
5 a Circle, centre $(1, -1)$, radius 1
  b rectangular hyperbola, centre $(2, 1)$
  c ellipse, centre $(0, 0)$, lengths of axes $2\sqrt{2}$ and 4 (minor axis on x-axis)
  d rectangular hyperbola, centre $(-1, 1)$
6 a $y - 3x = 5$
  b $y + 5x = 1$
  c $6y + x = 32$
  d $2y + x = 7$
  e $3y - 5x = 15$

f $2y = 3x - 6$
g $y = 3x - 5$
h $2x + y = 4$
i $x^2 + y^2 - 2x - 4y - 11 = 0$
j $x^2 + y^2 - 4x + 6y - 12 = 0$

7 a Slope $= -1/4$, x intercept $= 12$, y intercept $= 3$
b slope $= -2/3$, x intercept $= -3$, y intercept $= -2$
c slope $= -2/5$, x intercept $= 11/2$, y intercept $= 11/5$
d slope $= -4/3$, x intercept $= 7/2$, y intercept $= 14/3$

8 a Centre $= (-2, -3)$, radius $= 2$
b centre $= (-3, -4)$, radius $= 2$
c centre $= (1, -2)$, radius $= 3$
d centre $= (3, 1)$, radius $= 5$

ASSIGNMENT

2 $\{n\pi/3 + (-1)^n \pi/18 : n \in \mathbb{Z}\}$
3 $\{\pi/4, 3\pi/4, \pi, 5\pi/4, 7\pi/4\}$
4 Hint: put in terms of 2θ. Answers:
$\{n\pi \pm \pi/2 : n \in \mathbb{Z}\} \cup \{(n\pi/2) + (-1)^n(\pi/12) : n \in \mathbb{Z}\}$
5 a Circle centre 0, radius $4/\sqrt{5}$ **b** ellipse $(x + 15)^2 + 5y^2 = 225$
c circle centre $(1/2, 0)$, radius $(1/2)\sqrt{65}$
d pair of straight lines $y = \pm 4$
e three straight lines $y = 3x$, $x + y = 1$, $y = x + 2$
6 a $\sqrt{(2)} \cos(\theta - \pi/4)$ **b** $2\cos(\theta - \pi/6)$
7 Hyperbola $4y^2 - 3x^2 = 5$

FURTHER EXERCISES

2 a $\theta = n\pi$ or $\theta = n\pi + \pi/4$ **b** $\theta = n\pi \pm \pi/3$ **c** no roots
d no roots   **e** $n\pi - \pi/4 - (-1)^n \pi/4$
8 $y = 1; (-15/8, 1)$
9 18.75 metres
10 12 metres
11 No: 55/16 metres
12 $2axl/(x^2 + a^2)$

CHAPTER 4

EXERCISES

1 a $6x + 5$
b $3x^2 - 4x$
c $x^{-1/2}/2 - x^{-3/2}/2$
d $6(x + 2)^5$

    e $3\cos(3x+4)$

    f $6\tan 3x \sec^2 3x$

    g $4x/(2x^2+1)$

    h $2x^3\cos x^2 + 2x\sin x^2$

2 a $(t^2+1)(t+2)\{2t/(t^2+1)+1/(t+2)-2t/(t^2+2)-1/(t+1)\}/$
    $(t^2+2)(t+1)$

    b $(t+1)^3(t+2)^3\{3/(t+1)+3/(t+2)-2/(t+3)\}/(t+3)^2$

    c $\cos 4t$

    d $-2e^t/(e^t-1)^2$

3 a $3x^2\alpha$

    b $2\alpha x\cos x^2$

    c $\alpha\cot x$

    d $\pm\alpha e^{x/2}/2$

4 a 1

    b $1/2$

    c $2/3$

    d $3/2$

ASSIGNMENT

1 a $-1/\sqrt{2}$ **b** hint: $\sin 3x = \sin x\,(4\cos^2 x - 1)$; answer $1/\sqrt{3}$

    c $-\infty$ **d** $2/3$

2 a Hint: use half-angle formula; answer 0

    b hint: $\cos^3 x - 1 = (\cos x - 1)(\cos^2 x + \cos x + 1)$; answer $-2/3$

4 a $2\ln x\; x^{\ln x - 1}$ **b** $(2\sec^2 2x + 3\tan 2x)\,e^{3x}$

6 $dy/dx = (1 - \sin t)/(1 + \cos t)$

FURTHER EXERCISES

1 a $16x - 10$ **b** $3x^2 - 12x + 11$ **c** $x(x^2 - 1)^{-1/2}$

    d $-12x(x^2 - 3)^{-2}$ **e** $bmnx^{m-1}\,(a + bx^m)^{n-1}$ **f** $a\sec^2(ax + b)$

    g $-x\cot x^2\sqrt{\operatorname{cosec} x^2}$

2 a $9x^8, 72x^7, 504x^6, 3024x^5$

    b $(x + 1)^{-1/2}/2, -(x + 1)^{-3/2}/4, 3(x + 1)^{5/2}/8, -15(x + 1)^{-7/2}/16$

    c $-2\sin x\cos x = -\sin 2x, -2\cos 2x, 4\sin 2x, -8\cos 2x$

    d $x^2e^x + 2xe^x, x^2e^x + 4xe^x + 2e^x, x^2e^x + 6xe^x + 6e^x,$
    $x^2e^x + 8xe^x + 12e^x$

4 $-6\cot t - 2\cot^3 t$

6 Hint: $(dy/dx)(dx/dy) = 1$, differentiate this

9 a -1 **b** -2

11 $kA^{3/2}/4\sqrt{\pi}$

14 $w = -EI\,e^{-x}\,(x - 6)(x - 2)$

15 $6\varrho/h$

18 a $xu(x^2 + h^2)^{-1/2}$ **b** decreasing at $hu/(x^2 + h^2)$

21 $x[\tan(\theta + h) - \tan\theta]$

CHAPTER 5

EXERCISES

2 a $x = \ln 5$
  b $x = 0$ or $x = 1$
  c $x = \ln 3$ or $x = \ln 4$
  d $x = \pm\ln(2/3)$
3 a $-3\operatorname{sech} 3t \tanh 3t$
  b $2t^2 \cosh 2t + 2t \sinh 2t$
  c $\operatorname{sech} 2t \cosh t (1 - 2\tanh t \tanh 2t)$
  d $-\operatorname{sech} t \operatorname{cosech} 2t (2\coth 2t + \tanh t)$
  e $-t \tanh t^2 \sqrt{\operatorname{sech} t^2}$
  f $-(\operatorname{sech}^2 \sqrt{t} \tanh \sqrt{t})/\sqrt{t}$
4 a $2/\sqrt{(t^2 + 1)}$
  b $-2/t(t^2 + 2)$
  c $(\sinh t)/\sqrt{(t^2 - 1)} + \cosh t \cosh^{-1} t$
  d $(t^2 - 1)^{-1/2}/\cosh^{-1} t$
  e $1/t\sqrt{[(\ln t)^2 - 1]}$
  f $-\{(\sinh^{-1} t)^2 \sqrt{(t^2 + 1)}\}^{-1}$

ASSIGNMENT

1 a $x = (1/2)\ln 3$ **b** $x = 0$ or $x = \pm(1/3)\ln 2$
3 $x = \frac{1}{2}\ln 3$, $x = \frac{1}{3}\ln 2$
4 $x = \ln 2$ or $x = 0$

FURTHER EXERCISES

1 a 1 **b** 1/2
3 a $3\sin x (1 - 9\cos^2 x)^{-1/2}$ **b** $2(x^2 + 1)^{-1}$ **c** $\cos x (1 + \sin^2 x)^{-1}$
7 a $x = \ln(2 \pm \sqrt{3})$ **b** $x = \ln(\sqrt{2} - 1)$ **c** $x = 0$
8 Hint: $r = \alpha[(t - 1)^2 + 1]$ **a** min. $r = \alpha$ **b** $[1,2]$ **c** $1, 1, 8$
9 Hint: $h = \sqrt{(2)} \cos(2t - \pi/4) + 2$ **a** $2 \pm \sqrt{2}$ **b** π seconds
   c $5\pi/8$
10 $I \in [\pi + \cos^{-1}(1/4), 2\pi]$
11 $n = 341$, 'β' $= 231$, 'γ' $= 110$

CHAPTER 6

EXERCISES

1 a $y = x + 1$
  b $y + 1 = 0$, $y - 1 = 0$

   c $y = -\pi x/2$
   d $y = 0$
2 a $y = x$
   b $5y - 8x + 11 = 0, 5y + 3x + 4 = 0$
   c $9y - 3x = 10$
   d $y - 1 = \pi x$
3 a $-17^{3/2}/32$
   b 1
   c $5\sqrt{5}/6, -\sqrt{2}/3$
4 a 1
   b $-1/\sqrt{2}$
   c infinite
   d $2\sqrt{2}$

ASSIGNMENT

1 $\varrho = 1/2$, centre $(0, 3/2)$
3 Tangent $y = 1$; normal $x = 0$
4 $\varrho = 1/2$
6 Tangent $y(t^2 + 2t^3 + 5) + 3t^2 x = t^4 + 10t$; normal
   $9t^3(y - t) - 3t(2t^3 + t^2 + 5)x = (t^3 + t^2 - 5)(2t^3 + t^2 + 5)$
7 Tangent $y(t - 1) - x(t + 1) = t^2$; normal $y(t + 1) + x(t - 1) = t(t^2 + 2)$

FURTHER EXERCISES

3 $(71/6, -1/6)$
6 a Rectangular hyperbola centre $(2, 1)$
   b pair of straight lines $x = 4, y = 3$
   c ellipse centre $(-2, -3)$, major axis 4, minor axis $2\sqrt{(2)}$
   d hyperbola centre $(1, 3)$ **e** circle centre $(4, 3)$ radius 4
7 $X = -2\sin^3\theta, Y = -2\cos^3\theta; X^{2/3} + Y^{2/3} = 2^{2/3}$
10 $(\cos^6 p + \sin^6 p)^{3/2}/(\cos^6 p + \sin^6 p + 1)$
14 $4a$
16 864 m/s^2

CHAPTER 7

EXERCISES

1 a $f_x = 3x^2 + 2xy, f_y = x^2$
   b $f_x = -\sin xy \sin(x + y) + y \cos(x + y) \cos xy$
     $f_y = -\sin xy \sin(x + y) + x \cos(x + y) \cos xy$
   c $f_x = 3(x + 2y)^2, f_y = 6(x + 2y)^2$
   d $f_x = (-y \sin xy + \cos xy) \exp(x + y)$

$f_y = (-x \sin xy + \cos xy) \exp(x + y)$

e $f_x = \sinh(x + y)/2\sqrt{\cosh(x + y)} = f_y$

f $f_x = (1/y) \sinh(x/y), f_y = -(x/y^2) \sinh(x/y)$

2 a $f_{xy} = -xy/(x^2 + y^2)^{3/2} + \cos xy - xy \sin xy$

b $f_{xy} = 2x - (x + 2y)^{-3/2}/2$

c $f_{xy} = -12x^2 \sin(3x + 4y) + 8x \cos(3x + 4y)$

d $f_{xy} = (6x^3/y^7) \sin(x^2/y^3) - (6x/y^4) \cos(x^2/y^3)$

3 a $z_x = (z_u - z_v)/2uv(v - u), z_y = (uz_u - vz_v)/(u - v)$

b $z_x = -z_u/3 + 2z_v/3, z_y = 2z_u/3 - z_v/3$

c $z_x = [(u - 1)z_u - vz_v]/[u - v - 1], z_y = [uz_u - (1 + v)z_v]/[u - v - 1]$

d $z_x = (uz_u + vz_v)/(u^2 + v^2)^{1/2}, z_y = (v^3 z_u - uv^2 z_v)/(u^2 + v^2)$

ASSIGNMENT

1 a $f_x = \cos x \cos y + y^2; f_y = -\sin x \sin y + 2xy$

b $f_x = e^x \cos y + e^x \sin y; f_y = -e^x \sin y + e^x \cos y$

c $\partial z/\partial x = x/(x^2 + y^2); \partial z/\partial y = y/(x^2 + y^2)$

d $\partial z/\partial x = 2(x - 2y)^4(3x + 4y); \partial z/\partial y = -8(x - 2y)^4(x + 3y)$

e $\partial z/\partial u = 4u(u^2 - v^2) \cos(u^2 - v^2)^2;$

$\partial z/\partial v = -4v(u^2 - v^2) \cos(u^2 - v^2)^2$

3 $e^{-u} \cos v (\partial z/\partial u + \partial z/\partial v) + e^{-u} \sin v (\partial z/\partial u - \partial z/\partial v)$

4 Approximately 12%

FURTHER EXERCISES

8 Decrease of 3δ%

12 1%

CHAPTER 8

EXERCISES

1 a $1 + x + x^2/2$

b $1 - x^2/2 + 5x^4/24$

c $x - 3x^2/2 + 11x^3/6$

2 a $x = 0$, max; $x = \pm\sqrt{5}$, min

b $x = (-1 + \sqrt{5})/2$, min; $x = (-1 - \sqrt{5})/2$, max

c $x = 0$, min; $x = 1$, max; $x = -1$, max

d $x = 0$, point of inflexion

3 a 0

b -1

c 1 (take logarithms)

d 3

4 a 1/2
  b e (take logarithms)
  c 1
  d 1

ASSIGNMENT

1 a $(1/2) \sec x$ **b** $(\sin x)^x [x \cot x + \ln (\sin x)]$ **c** $6 \tan 3x \sec^2 3x$
  d Hint: put $x = \sin t$, then $dy/dx = 2 [\sin^{-1} x + x(1 - x^2)^{-1/2}]$
2 $dy/dx = [2y \cos 2x - y \ln y - y^2 \exp (xy)]/[xy \exp (xy) + x]$
4 $1 + x - \frac{1}{3}x^3$
5 a Stationary points at ± 1, points of inflexion at $0, \pm 1$
  b stationary points at $0, 1, 2; 0$ (min.), 1 (max.), 2 (min.)
6 Diameter = twice height
9 a n **b** 1/2 **c** $\pi/2$ **d** 1/2
10 a 0   **b** Hint: put $u = 1/x$; $\ln a$

FURTHER EXERCISES

6 $3[(7/3)^{2/3} - 1]^{3/2}$ metres; approximately 2 metres.
7 Length $= 2 \times$ breadth
8 a $\sqrt{2}/4$ **b** $\sqrt{2}/2$
10 $14 - 8\sqrt{3}$ ohms
11 $i(t) = t - t^2/2 + t^3/3 + \ldots$
15 Hint: use L'Hospital's rule

CHAPTER 9

EXERCISES

1 a 1
  b 1
  c 2/3
  d 2 (take logarithms)
2 a $n/(2n + 1)$
  b $1 - 1/(n + 1)^2$
  c $1 - 1/\sqrt{(n + 1)}$
  d $-\operatorname{cosech} 1 (\coth n - \coth 1)$

ASSIGNMENT

1 Divergent: divergence test
2 Convergent: comparison test
3 Convergent: ratio test

   4 Divergent: divergence test
   5 Convergent: comparison test
   6 Divergent: ratio test
   7 $x \leqslant 0$ convergent, $x > 0$ divergent: ratio and comparison tests
   8 Divergent: comparison test
   9 Convergent: ratio test
  10 Convergent: s_n explicitly
  11 $R = 2$
  12 $R = \infty$
  13 $R = \sqrt{3}$
  14 $R = 1$
  15 $R = \infty$
  16 $R = 1/2$
  17 $R = 0$
  18 $R = 1/e$
  19 $R = 1$
  20 $R = 1$

FURTHER EXERCISES

1 a Divergent   **b** divergent   **c** divergent   **d** divergent
2 a Absolutely convergent   **b** absolutely convergent
  c conditionally convergent
4 a Hint: $n + nx > 1 + nx$; divergent   **b** divergent
  c divergent (if $|x| > 1$ then $|x|^n \to \infty$, if $|x| < 1$ then $|x|^{-n} \to \infty$)
6 a Convergent   **b** convergent
  c convergent when $x = -1$, divergent when $x = 1$
  d convergent when $x = -1$, divergent when $x = 1$

CHAPTER 10

EXERCISES

1 a $54 + 29i$
  b $(13 - 9i)/25$
  c $(7 - i)/10$
  d $c^2 \cos 4 + i[e^2 \sin 4 + 1]$
2 a $2[\cos(7\pi/4) + i \sin(7\pi/4)]$
  b $2[\cos \pi + i \sin \pi]$
  c $2[\cos \pi/2 + i \sin \pi/2]$
  d $1[\cos 1 + i \sin 1]$
3 a $-2 \pm i$
  b $0, i$
  c $+1 + \sqrt{2}, \pm 1 - \sqrt{2}$

    d $i(-1 \pm \sqrt{2})$
4 a Circle, centre $(0, 3)$, radius 5
  b ellipse, foci $(0, \pm 1)$, semi-axes 2, $\sqrt{3}$
  c circle, centre $(0, 0)$, radius 1

ASSIGNMENT

1 $(195 - 104i)/221$
2 $(1/2)(\cos \pi/2 + i \sin \pi/2)$
3 $z = i(w + 1)/(w - 1)$ where $w = \exp i\,(\pi/6 + 2k\pi/3)$, $k \in \{-1, 0, 1\}$
4 $\cos 11\theta - i \sin 11\theta$
5 $\cos 4\theta = \cos^4 \theta - 6 \cos^2 \theta \sin^2 \theta + \sin^4 \theta$,
  $\sin 4\theta = 4 \cos^3 \theta \sin \theta - 4 \cos \theta \sin^3 \theta$
6 $(\tan x \operatorname{sech}^2 y + i \tanh y \sec^2 x)/(1 + \tan^2 x \tanh^2 y)$
7 $z = n\pi + \ln\left[(-1)^n + \sqrt{2}\right]$
8 $z = x + iy$ lies on the circle $x^2 + y^2 = 1$

FURTHER EXERCISES

1 a Semicircle $x^2 + y^2 = 16$ $(y \geqslant 0)$
  b $x^2/9 + y^2/16 = 1$ (ellipse); $z = 4i$
2 a $-1 + i\sqrt{3}$ **c** $-2 + 5i$, -1, $4 + i$
3 a $2 \exp (\pi i/4)$, $2 \exp (3\pi i/4)$, $2 \exp (-\pi i/4)$, $2 \exp (-3\pi i/4)$
  b $(\pm 7 \pm i\sqrt{31})/2$
4 a 2^{12} **b** $z = \pm 1$, $\pm i$; 0, $\pm i$
5 a $(\pm 5 \pm i\sqrt{3})/2$ **b** Hint: square and use $|z|^2 = z\bar{z}$

CHAPTER 11

EXERCISES

1 a $\begin{bmatrix} 2 & 5 \\ -3 & 7 \end{bmatrix}$ **b** $\begin{bmatrix} -1 & -16 \\ 16 & -34 \end{bmatrix}$ **c** $\begin{bmatrix} 2 & 5 \\ -3 & 7 \end{bmatrix}$

  d $\begin{bmatrix} -3 & 6 \\ -10 & 20 \end{bmatrix}$ **e** $\begin{bmatrix} 2 & -4 \\ -4 & 8 \end{bmatrix}$ **f** $\begin{bmatrix} 5 & -5 \\ -5 & 5 \end{bmatrix}$

2 $(U + V + W)^2 = U^2 + V^2 + W^2 + UV + UW + VU + VW + WU + WV$

3 a $\begin{bmatrix} 0 & 1/2 \\ -1/2 & 1/2 \end{bmatrix}$ **b** $\begin{bmatrix} 0 & -2 \\ 1 & -2 \end{bmatrix}$ **c** $\begin{bmatrix} 0 & -4 \\ 4 & 1 \end{bmatrix}$

  d $\begin{bmatrix} -1.4 & -2.2 \\ 0.9 & -3.3 \end{bmatrix}$ **e** $\begin{bmatrix} 2 & 1 \\ -1 & 4 \end{bmatrix}$ **f** $\begin{bmatrix} 4 & -6 \\ 3 & -2 \end{bmatrix}$

4 diag $\{\pm 1, 0\}$

ASSIGNMENT

1 $x = \sin w, y = -\cos w$ or $x = -\sin w, y = \cos w$

3 a $I(2 \times 2)\, O(3 \times 3)$ **b** $A^n = \text{diag}\{a^n, b^n, c^n, d^n\}$

4 a $(A + B)^2 = A^2 + AB + BA + B^2$

 b $(A + 2B)^2 = A^2 + 4AB + 4BA + 4B^2$

5 $a = 2, b = -1, c = 8$

6 $a = 0, b = 0, c = 0, d = -3, e = 2, f = -6$

7 $x = 3, y = 3, z = -1$ or $x = \mp 4\sqrt{2/3}, y = 2/3, z = \pm 2\sqrt{2}$

FURTHER EXERCISES

2 Hint: use $A(BC) = (AB)C$ to deduce $A = O$

3 a $x = 2, y = 1, z = -1$ **b** $x = 4, y = 2, z = -2$

5 a $\begin{bmatrix} 1 + Z_1/Z_2 & Z_1 \\ 1/Z_2 & 1 \end{bmatrix}$

 b $\begin{bmatrix} 1 + Z_1/Z_2 & Z_1 + Z_3 + Z_1 Z_3/Z_2 \\ 1/Z_2 & Z_3/Z_2 + 1 \end{bmatrix}$

 c $\begin{bmatrix} 1 + Z_2/Z_3 & Z_2 \\ 1/Z_1 + 1/Z_3 + Z_2/Z_1 Z_3 & Z_2/Z_1 + 1 \end{bmatrix}$

6 $n = 3$

8 c i $x = 39, y = 35, z = 21$ **ii** $u = 18, v = 47, w = 20$

9 $E_1 = (1/3)(e_1 + e_2 + e_3), E_2 = (1/3)(e_1 + \alpha e_2 + \alpha^2 e_3),$

 $E_3 = (1/3)(e_1 + \alpha^2 e_2 + \alpha e_3)$

CHAPTER 12

EXERCISES

1 a $x = -3$ or $x = 5$

 b $x = -2$ or $x = 7$

 c $x = 3/2$

 d $x = 0$

2 a 5   **b** -24 **c** 9   **d** $-9x - 18$

3 a 5775   **b** 18,000

4 a $x = 0, y = 1/a\sqrt{(1 + a^2)}$

 b $x = \exp u, y = \exp(-v), z = \exp w$

ASSIGNMENT

1 $x = \pm 4$

2 8

3 $x = 1/2$

4 $x = 5$

5 $M = \begin{bmatrix} 2 & -2 & -3 \\ -12 & 7 & 14 \\ -9 & 6 & 11 \end{bmatrix}$

6 $C = \begin{bmatrix} -1 & -2 & 2 \\ 2 & 7 & -6 \\ -2 & -9 & 7 \end{bmatrix}$

FURTHER EXERCISES

1 An identity; true for all w
2 $x = \pm 1$
3 $k = 1/a + 1/b + 1/c + 1/d$
4 $x = 0$ or $x = \pm 6$
6 $x = -1, x = -2, x = -2$
7 -12
8 a Hint:

$$D = \frac{1}{xyz} \begin{vmatrix} x & 1 & y + z \\ y & 1 & z + x \\ z & 1 & x + y \end{vmatrix}$$

b Hint: $C_1 - C_2$
9 $u = \cos w, v = \tan w$
10 Hint: $\Delta = 0$

CHAPTER 13

EXERCISES

1 a $\begin{bmatrix} -5 & 2 & 4 \\ 2 & -1 & -1 \\ 0 & 1 & -2 \end{bmatrix}$
b $\begin{bmatrix} 3 & 1 & -7 \\ -2 & 1 & 1 \\ -1 & -1 & 4 \end{bmatrix}$

c $\begin{bmatrix} 15 & 1 & -12 \\ -8 & 1 & 6 \\ -6 & -1 & 5 \end{bmatrix}$
d $\begin{bmatrix} 3 & 12 & -11 \\ -2 & -1 & 2 \\ -1 & -7 & 6 \end{bmatrix}$

2 a $x = 2$ **b** $x = 1$ **c** $x = 3$ or $x = -3 \pm \sqrt{13}$
d $x = 1/3$ or $x = 5$
4 a $x = 35, y = -6, z = -9$
b $x = -6, y = 13, z = 1$
c $x = 4, y = 17, z = -35$
d $x = 3, y = 5, z = -4$

ASSIGNMENT

$$
1 \quad \begin{bmatrix} -3 & -2 & 13 \\ 0 & 1 & -3 \\ 1 & 0 & -2 \end{bmatrix}
$$

3 diag $\{27, 54, -81\}$
4 Hint: pre-multiply and post-multiply AB by the expression suggested

FURTHER EXERCISES

1 $(\operatorname{adj} A)^{-1} = (1/|A|)A$
2 $|\operatorname{adj} A| = |A|^{n-1}$ where n is the order
3 Grade, number: $1, 10; 2, 15; 3, 20$
4 Hint: if a matrix is non-singular it has an inverse
5 Hint: verify that $A^{\mathrm{T}}(A^{-1})^{\mathrm{T}} = (A^{-1})^{\mathrm{T}}A^{\mathrm{T}} = I$
6 Example: $x + y + 1 = 0, 2x + 2y + 2 = 0, 2x + 2y + 3 = 0$
7 $k = 1, k = 2, k = 3$

9 a $M^{-1} = \begin{bmatrix} \cosh a & -Z \sinh a \\ -(1/Z) \sinh a & \cosh a \end{bmatrix}$

   b Use induction
10 $x = 3, y = -2, z = 1$

CHAPTER 14

EXERCISES

1 a $\mathbf{a} + \mathbf{b} = 3\mathbf{i} - 2\mathbf{j} + 4\mathbf{k}, \mathbf{a} \cdot \mathbf{b} = 2, \mathbf{a} \times \mathbf{b} = 10\mathbf{i} + \mathbf{j} - 7\mathbf{k}$
  b $\mathbf{a} + \mathbf{b} = 3\mathbf{i} + 6\mathbf{j} - 2\mathbf{k}, \mathbf{a} \cdot \mathbf{b} = -5, \mathbf{a} \times \mathbf{b} = 22\mathbf{i} - 13\mathbf{j} - 6\mathbf{k}$
  c $\mathbf{a} + \mathbf{b} = 5\mathbf{j} - 5\mathbf{k}, \mathbf{a} \cdot \mathbf{b} = 11, \mathbf{a} \times \mathbf{b} = 5\mathbf{i} - 5\mathbf{j} - 5\mathbf{k}$
  d $\mathbf{a} + \mathbf{b} = -2\mathbf{i} + 5\mathbf{j} + \mathbf{k}, \mathbf{a} \cdot \mathbf{b} = -1, \mathbf{a} \times \mathbf{b} = -9\mathbf{i} - 5\mathbf{j} + 7\mathbf{k}$
2 a $\pm(1/3\sqrt{6})\{5\mathbf{i} - 5\mathbf{j} - 2\mathbf{k}\}$
  b $\pm(1/3\sqrt{5})\{4\mathbf{i} - 5\mathbf{j} + 2\mathbf{k}\}$
  c $\pm(1/\sqrt{2})\{\mathbf{i} + \mathbf{j}\}$
  d $\pm(1/\sqrt{2})\{\mathbf{i} - \mathbf{k}\}$
3 a 2 **b** 4 **c** -14 **d** 0
4 a $\mathbf{a} \times (\mathbf{b} \times \mathbf{c}) - \mathbf{j} - \mathbf{i}, (\mathbf{a} \times \mathbf{b}) \times \mathbf{c} = \mathbf{k} - \mathbf{i}$
  b $\mathbf{a} \times (\mathbf{b} \times \mathbf{c}) = 5\mathbf{j} - 5\mathbf{k}, (\mathbf{a} \times \mathbf{b}) \times \mathbf{c} = -5\mathbf{i} + 5\mathbf{j}$
  c $\mathbf{a} \times (\mathbf{b} \times \mathbf{c}) = 9\mathbf{i} + 22\mathbf{j} - 17\mathbf{k}, (\mathbf{a} \times \mathbf{b}) \times \mathbf{c} = -26\mathbf{i} + 43\mathbf{j} - 3\mathbf{k}$
  d $\mathbf{a} \times (\mathbf{b} \times \mathbf{c}) = -\mathbf{i} - \mathbf{j} + 2\mathbf{k}, (\mathbf{a} \times \mathbf{b}) \times \mathbf{c} = \mathbf{i} - 2\mathbf{j} + \mathbf{k}$
5 a $\dot{\mathbf{r}} = -\sin t \mathbf{i} - \cos t \mathbf{j} + \mathbf{k}$
  b $\dot{\mathbf{r}} = -3\sin 3t \mathbf{i} + 5\cos 5t \mathbf{j} + 2t\mathbf{k}$
  c $\dot{\mathbf{r}} = 4t(1 + t^2)\mathbf{i} + 9t^2(1 + t^3)^2\mathbf{j} + 16t^3(1 + t^4)^3\mathbf{k}$
  d $\dot{\mathbf{r}} = -t^2(3 + 5t^2)\mathbf{i} - 2t(1 - 3t^4)\mathbf{j} + t^2(3 + 5t^2)\mathbf{k}$

ASSIGNMENT

1 (a) 1 (b) 1/6 (c) $3\mathbf{i} - 5\mathbf{j} + \mathbf{k}$ (d) $\sqrt{35}$
2 $\pm(1/5)(3\mathbf{j} + 4\mathbf{k})$
5 $\mathbf{x} = (1/|\mathbf{a}|^2)[\mathbf{a} - \mathbf{a} \wedge \mathbf{b}]$
6 $t = -4$

FURTHER EXERCISES

2 (a) $\pi/4$ (b) $\pm(2\mathbf{i} - 10\mathbf{j} - 11\mathbf{k})/15$
3 $\sqrt{2}(\mathbf{i} - 2\mathbf{j} + \mathbf{k})$
4 (a) Hint: put $\mathbf{e} = \mathbf{c} \wedge \mathbf{d}$
  (b) Hint: $(\mathbf{x} \wedge \mathbf{y}) \cdot (\mathbf{z} \wedge \mathbf{w}) = (\mathbf{x} \cdot \mathbf{z})(\mathbf{y} \cdot \mathbf{w}) - (\mathbf{y} \cdot \mathbf{z})(\mathbf{x} \cdot \mathbf{w})$
5 $\mathbf{r} \cdot \mathbf{r} = 2\cos^2\theta; \mathbf{r} \wedge \mathbf{r} = 0$
  (a) $\cos\theta = 0 \Rightarrow \theta = \pi/2 \Rightarrow \mathbf{r} = \mathbf{0}$
  (b) $\cos^2\theta = 1 \Rightarrow \mathbf{r} = \mathbf{i} \pm \mathbf{k}$ (no calculus needed)
9 $\sqrt{5}$ and 2

CHAPTER 15

EXERCISES

1 a $x + x^2 + 3x^4/4 + C$
  b $e^x - 2e^{-x} + C$
  c $x + \sinh^{-1}x + C$
  d $\tan x + \sec x + C$
2 a $(1 + 2x)^8/16 + C$
  b $(1/3)\sin 3x + C$
  c $-(1/3)\cos x^3 + C$
  d $(1/2)\tan^{-1}(x/2) + C$
3 a $(1/7)\ln|x + 2| - (1/7)\ln|3x - 1| + C$
  b $(1/3)\ln|x| - (1/6)\ln(x^2 + 3) + C$
  c $-(1/4)\ln|x| + (1/8)\ln|x^2 - 4| + C$
  d $(1/3)\tan^{-1}x - (1/6)\tan^{-1}(x/2) + C$
4 a $(2x/3)\sin 3x + (2/9)\cos 3x + C$
  b $(x/3)\exp 3x - (1/9)\exp 3x + C$
  c $\{(x^2 - 1)/2\}\exp x^2 + C$
  d $(x^3/3)\ln(x^2 + 1) - 2x^3/9 + 2x/3 - (2/3)\tan^{-1}x + C$
5 a $x^2/4 + \ln x^2 + C$
  b $-\cot x + \operatorname{cosec} x + C$
  c $(1/3)\exp x^3 + C$
  d $(1/2)\tan x^2 + C$

ASSIGNMENT

1 $x + \ln|x| + C$
2 $x - \ln|x + 1| + C$
3 $\tan x - x + C$
4 $x + \ln(x - 1)^2 + C$
5 $\ln|x - 1| + C$
6 $-(1/2)\exp(-x^2) + C$
7 $\ln(x + 1)^2 + C$
8 $\ln(e^x + 1) + C$
9 $(1/3)\sin^3 x + C$
10 $-\tan^{-1}(\cos x) + C$
11 $\tan^{-1}(e^x) + C$
12 $x\sin^{-1} x + \sqrt{(1 - x^2)} + C$
13 $(1/3)(x^2 + 4)^{3/2} + C$
14 $-2\sqrt{(\cos^2 x + 9)} + C$
15 $(x^2/2)\ln x - x^2/4 + C$
16 $[(x^2 + 1)/2]\tan^{-1} x - x/2 + C$
17 $5\ln|x - 3| - 4\ln|x - 2| + C$
18 $(1/2)\tan^2 x + \ln(\cos x) + C$
19 $(1/4)\ln|(x - 1)/(x + 1)| - (1/2)\tan^{-1} x + C$
20 $(1/4)\ln|x^4 - 1| + C$
21 $(1/2)(x^4 + 1)^{1/2} + C$

FURTHER EXERCISES

1 a $(1/2)\sin x^2 + C$ **b** $2\sqrt{(x + 3)} + C$ **c** $2\ln(1 + e^t) - t + C$
   d $(1/4)\ln(1 + x^4) + C$
2 a $\ln(\ln u) + C$ **b** $-(\cos\theta - \sin\theta) + (1/3)(\cos^3\theta - \sin^3\theta) + C$
   c $t\sec^{-1} t - \cosh^{-1} t + C$ **d** $(1/2)(\ln x)^2 + C$
3 a $u\tan^{-1} u - (1/2)\ln(1 + u^2) + C$ **b** $\sin x/(\cos x - 1) + C$
   c $(1/4)\ln[(x + 1)/(x - 1)] - 1/2(x - 1) + C$
   d $\ln\{(1 - \sin\theta)(1 - \cos\theta)\} + 2/(1 - \sin\theta - \cos\theta) + C$
4 $i = (E/R)[1 - \exp(-Rt/L)]$
6 $wx^2(x - L)^2/24EI$
7 $30/(1 - 2^{-1/3})$ minutes; 2 hours 25 minutes (approx.)
8 $(\cos 2\theta + \sin 2\theta)/(\cos\theta + \sin\theta) + C$
9 $u = \ln\{\tan[\pi/4 + (\alpha/2)(1 - e^t)]\}$

CHAPTER 16

EXERCISES

1 a $e^x + x - 2\ln(e^x + 1) + C$
   b $2\sin x + C$

    c $x \ln x - x + x^2/2 + C$
    d $\sinh^{-1} x + C$
 2 a $\ln \sqrt{\sec(1 + x^2)} + C$
    b $-\cos \sqrt{(1 + x^2)} + C$
    c $\ln(1 + \sin^2 x) + C$
    d $-(1/14) \cos 7x + (1/2) \cos x + C$
 3 a $\sin x - \ln(1 + \sin x) + C$
    b $(3/2) \sin^{-1} x + (x/2)\sqrt{(1 - x^2)} + C$
    c $(x/4)\{\sqrt{(x^2 + 1)} - \sqrt{(x^2 - 1)}\}$
       $+ (1/4) \ln |[x + \sqrt{(x^2 + 1)}] \cdot [x + \sqrt{(x^2 - 1)}]| + C$
    d $(x/2)\{\sqrt{(1 + x^2)} + \sqrt{(1 - x^2)}\} + \ln \sqrt{[x + \sqrt{(1 + x^2)}]}$
       $+ (1/2) \sin^{-1} x + C$
 4 a $(1/25)\{3 \ln[(1 + t^2)/(2t^2 + 3t - 2)] + 8 \tan^{-1} t\} + C$
    where $t = \tan(x/2)$
    b $(1/13) \ln |[5 + \tan(x/2)]/[1 - 5 \tan(x/2)]| + C$
    c $(1/7) \cosh^6 x \sinh x + (6/35) \cosh^4 x \sinh x + (8/35) \cosh^2 x \sinh x$
       $+ (16/35) \sinh x + C$
    d $x^5 \sin x + 5x^4 \cos x - 20x^3 \sin x - 60x^2 \cos x + 120x \sin x$
       $+ 120 \cos x + C$

ASSIGNMENT

 1 $\ln(1 - \sin x) - \cos x/(1 - \sin x) + C$
 2 $\exp \sin x + C$
 3 $(1/3) \ln(x - 1) - (1/6) \ln(x^2 + x + 1) + (1/\sqrt{3}) \tan^{-1}[(2x + 1)/\sqrt{3}] + C$
 4 $-\ln(\sec x + \tan x) + C$
 5 $\exp \sin^2 x + C$
 6 $(1/2) \ln(x^2 - 1) + C$
 7 $-\cos x + (2/3) \cos^3 x - (1/5) \cos^5 x + C$
 8 $3x/8 + (1/4) \sin 2x + (1/32) \sin 4x + C$
 9 $-(2/3) \cos^3 x + \cos x + C$
10 $\tan x + (2/3) \tan^3 x + (1/5) \tan^5 x + C$
11 Hint: obtain the integral of $\sec^3 x$ first. Answer:
    $(1/4) \sec^3 x \tan x + (3/8) \sec x \tan x + (3/8) \ln(\sec x + \tan x) + C$
12 $(1/5) \sec^5 x + C$
13 $(1/12)(x + 1/x)^{12} + C$
14 $(1/8)(1 + \sin x)^8 + C$

FURTHER EXERCISES

 1 (a) Hint: put $\operatorname{cosec}^2 x = 1 + \cot^2 x$; answer
       $-(1/2) \operatorname{cosec} x \cot x + (1/2) \ln |\operatorname{cosec} x - \omega t x| + C$
    (b) hint: put $\tanh^2 x = 1 - \operatorname{sech}^2 x$; answer $\ln(\cosh x) + (1/2) \operatorname{sech}^2 x + C$
    (c) hint: standard t substitution; answer
       $(1/5) \ln \{[1 + 3 \tan(\theta/2)]/[3 - \tan(\theta/2)]\} + C$

2 (a) Hint: put $u = 1 - 1/x$; answer $(2/3)(1 - 1/x)^{3/2} + C$
  (b) hint: put $u = \cos\theta$; answer $\ln[(1 + \cos\theta)^2/\cos\theta] + C$
  (c) hint: express $(1 + \sin\theta)/(1 + \cos\theta)$ in terms of $\theta/2$; answer
      $\exp\theta\tan\theta/2 + C$
3 (a) $\ln(1 + \sin x \cos x) + C$ (b) hint: put $u = \tan\theta$; answer
      $(12/169)\ln(5\cos\theta + 12\sin\theta) + (5\theta/169) + C$
  (c) $x/2(x^2 + 2x + 2) + (1/2)\tan^{-1}(x + 1) + C$
4 (a) $(1/\sqrt{2})\ln\{[(\sqrt{2} + 1) + \tan x/2]/[(\sqrt{2} - 1) - \tan x/2]\} + C$
  (b) Hint: put $u = \cos x$; answer $(1/12)\ln[(1 - \cos x)^2(2 + \cos x)] -$
      $(1/12)\ln(1 + \cos x)^2(2 - \cos x) + C$
  (c) $(1/16)(\sin 8x + 4\sin 2x) + C$
5 Hint: $\sec^n x = \sec^{n-2} x \sec^2 x$
6 Hint: $\tan^n x = \tan^{n-2} x \tan^2 x$
7 Hint: integrate by parts
8 Hint: show that $d^2s/d\psi^2 = 1$

CHAPTER 17

EXERCISES

1 a $\pi/4$ b $5/6$ c $\ln\sqrt{2}$ d 2
2 a $3/10$ b $1/12$ c $1/6$ d $(3 - e)/2$
3 a $16\pi/15$ b $\pi e^2/4 - 7\pi/4$ c $\pi[9\ln(2 + \sqrt{3}) - 6\sqrt{3}]$
  d $[72(\ln 2)^2 - 264\ln 2 + 149]\pi/27$
4 a $1/2$ b $(e^2 - 1)/(2e)$ c $2\ln 2 - 1$ d $(2/\pi)\ln 2$
5 a $(2 + \sinh 2)^{1/2}/2$ b $(4/\pi - 1)^{1/2}$ c $1/\sqrt{2}$ d $(1019/120)^{1/2}$

ASSIGNMENT

1 $\ln(\sqrt{2} + 1)$
2 $3c/4$
3 $3\pi/8$
4 π
5 $\pi[3 - (5/4)\ln 2 - (1/16)(\ln 2)^2]$
6 On the axis of symmetry, $h/4$ from the centre of the base
7 (a) $ma^2/4$ (b) $ma^2/4$
8 $13Ma^2/20$

FURTHER EXERCISES

2 $a^2/15$; $(\bar{x}, \bar{y}) = (3a/8, 15a/28)$
3 $15/4 + \ln 2$
4 $25/32$; $l = \frac{1}{8} + \frac{1}{2}\ln 3$
6 $3Ma^2/10$
7 (a) Does not exist: $x^2(\ln x^2 - 1) \to \infty$ as $x \to \infty$

(b) $1: xe^{-x} + e^{-x} \to 0$ as $x \to \infty$, $xe^{-x} + e^{-x} \to 1$ as $x \to 0$
(c) $\pi/2$
9 Hint: use Pappus's theorem
12 $-4/\pi^2 + 24/\pi^4$

CHAPTER 18

EXERCISES

1 a $x = 1.849$ **b** $x = 0.6486$
2 $c = \{ab(b^2 e^b - a^2 e^a) + b - a\}/\{b^3 e^b - a^3 e^a\}$, $a = 0$, $b = 1$
3 $x_{n+1} = \{x_n x_{n-1}(x_n + x_{n-1}) + 5\}/\{x_n^2 + x_n x_{n-1} + x_{n-1}^2 + 1\}$
    $x_0 = 1, x_1 = 2$
4 a $x = 0.273\,89$ **b** $x = 3.146\,19$
5 a $1.468\,14$ **b** $0.737\,43$
6 a $2.030\,10$ **b** $1.005\,71$

ASSIGNMENT

1 At most 17 steps (in fact 11 will do); 0.619
2 $x_{n+1} = (x_n - 1)/(1 - 3 \exp[-x_n])$; 0.619 (4 steps)
3 $x_{n+1} = (x_{n-1} \exp x_n - x_n \exp x_{n-1})/[\exp x_n - \exp x_{n-1} - 3(x_n - x_{n-1})]$:
    $x_2 = 0.780\,202\,717$, $x_3 = 0.496\,678\,604$, $x_4 = 0.635\,952\,246$
4 $(1 + h)f(x + h) - (2 - h^2)f(x) + (1 - h)f(x - h) \simeq h^2 \sec x$
5 $0.859\,533\,8$ (a) $0.859\,166\,6$ (b) $0.859\,140\,9$

FURTHER EXERCISES

2 0.69
3 2.187
4 0.443
5 0.5671
7 (a) $T = 0.784\,75$ (b) $S = 0.785\,40$
8 Hint: consider volume of rotation using $x^2 + y^2 = r^2$ between ordinates
    a and b
9 $u(t + h) = (1 - h)u(t)$; $u(0.2r) \simeq (0.8)^r$, so
    a $u(1) \simeq 0.327\,68$ **b** 10.93% underestimate
10 0.4603

CHAPTER 19

EXERCISES

1 a $y = Axe^x$
    b $y + \ln(y/x) + 1/x = C$

c $(y - 1)e^{x+y} + x + 1 = Ce^x$

2 a $xy = (x - 1)e^x + C$

  b $y = x(x - 1)e^x + Cx$

  c $y = (1/2)\sin x + C\operatorname{cosec} x$

3 a $\ln \sqrt{(2x^2 + y^2)} = (1/\sqrt{2})\tan^{-1}(y/x\sqrt{2}) + C$

  b $(x + y)^3(x - 4y)^2 = A$

  c $\ln(xy) + y/x = A$

4 a $y = (\exp{-x^2})/(C - x)$

  b $x/y = C - x^3/3$

  c $y^2 + 2xy - 2x^2 - 6y = C$

ASSIGNMENT

1 $e^y = \ln(x^2 + 1) + C$

2 $\ln x = \tan t + C$

3 $\ln(y^2 + 1) = \frac{1}{2}\sin 2u + C$

4 $y^2 - 1 = Axe^x$

5 $y = \cot\theta + C\operatorname{cosec}\theta$

6 $y\ln x = (x^2 + 1)^{1/2} + C$

7 $x = e^t + Ce^{-t}$

8 $xy = x^2 + C$

9 $Ax = \exp(y/x)$

10 $s^2 = t^2(\ln t + C)$

11 $x^2\ln x = y^2 - xy + Cx^2$

12 $\sec(y/x) + \tan(y/x) = Ax$

FURTHER EXERCISES

1 $\ln x = y^3/3x^3 - y/x + C$

2 $\ln x = -x/y + C$

3 $x\sin t = C\cos t + 1$

4 $x^2 + y^2 = A\sin^2 x$

5 $u = 5/2 + A(v - 3)^2$

6 $x^2 - 12xy - y^2 = C$

7 $\ln[(q - 3)^2 + (p - 2)^2] = 6\tan^{-1}[(p - 2)/(q - 3)] + C$

8 $x = k\sin(y/x)$

9 $y = x\ln x/(1 + \ln x)$

10 $r = \sec\theta$

12 Hint: obtain a differential equation for q first; answer
$EC[\sin\omega t + \omega RC\{\exp(-t/RC) - \cos\omega t\}]/[1 + (RC\omega)^2]$

CHAPTER 20

EXERCISES

1 a $x = Ae^{t/2} + Be^{3t}$

  b $x = e^t\{A\cos 3t + B\sin 3t\}$

    c $y = (A + Bx)e^{4x/3}$

2 a $x = Ae^{-t/2} + Be^{5t} - t/5 + 9/25$

  b $y = Ae^{2x/3} + Be^{2x} + xe^{2x}/4$

  c $u = Ae^{2x/3} + Be^{x/3} + e^x/2$

  d $y = e^{2x/5}[A\cos(x/5) + B\sin(x/5)] - [\cos x + \sin x]/8$

3 a $x = (2/39)[1 - e^{3t}]\cos t + (1/13)[1 + e^{3t}]\sin t$

  b $x = (3/196)[e^{t/3} - e^{5t}] + (t/14)e^{5t}$

  c $x = (t^3/150)e^{3t/5}$

ASSIGNMENT

1 $y = (A + Bx)e^{x/2} + e^x$

2 $y = e^{-2t}(A\cos 2t + B\sin 2t) + (1/20)\cos 2t + (1/10)\sin 2t$

3 $x = Ae^t + Be^{-3t} + (1/5)e^{2t}$

4 $u = (A + Bv)e^{4v} + v^2/16 + v/16 + 3/128$

5 $s = e^{-3t}(A\cos t + B\sin t) + (1/13)\cos t + (2/39)\sin t$

6 $u = Ae^{2t} + Be^{5t} + (1/10) + (1/3)te^{5t}$

7 $y = (A + Bx)e^{-3x} + (1/2)x^2e^{-3x} + (1/16)e^x$

8 $y = Ae^{5u} + Be^{-2u} - (1/24)e^{2u} - (1/14)ue^{-2u}$

9 $y = e^{-x}(A\cos 3x + B\sin 3x) + (x/6)e^{-x}\sin 3x$

10 $y = Ae^w + Be^{-2w} - (3w/10)\cos w + (w/10)\sin w + (1/25)\cos w + (11/50)\sin w$

FURTHER EXERCISES

1 Hint: complex roots of auxiliary equation $\Rightarrow$ oscillations

2 Hint: obtain $x = x(t)$, differentiate and eliminate t to obtain the second constant; answer $x = \sqrt{[(u/\lambda)^2 + a^2]}\sin\lambda t$

7 Hint: express as a differential equation involving x and θ only and solve

CHAPTER 21

EXERCISES

1 a $p_n = A3^n$ **b** $u_n = A2^n$ **c** $t_n = A(4/5)^n$ **d** $u_n = A7^n$

  e $p_n = A/6^n$ **f** $q_n = A(11/7)^n$ **g** $u_n = A(2/3)^n(\pm 1)^n$ **h** $s_n = A6^n$

2 a $s_n = A/2^n$ **b** $s_n = A(1/3)^n$ **c** $p_n = A2^n + B3^n$ **d** $s_n = (A + Bn)2^n$

3 a $s_n = A/2^n + B3^n$ **b** $u_n = (A + Bn)/3^n$

  c $s_n = \{A\cos(n\pi/2) + B\sin(n\pi/2)\}/2^n$

4 a $S(n) = A/2^n + B2^n - 1$

  b $t(n) = A2^n + B(-1/2)^n + n2^n/10$

  c $r(n) = (A + Bn)/2^{2n} + n^2/2^{2n+1}$

ASSIGNMENT

1 a $Y(n) = A2^n + B5^n$ **b** $u(n) = A3^n + B(-2)^n$
  c $T(n) = (A \cos n\pi/2 + B \sin n\pi/2)/5^n$ **d** $p(n) = (A + Bn)5^n$
  e $E(n) = A + B(-1/2)^n$
2 a $S(n) = 2n - 1$ **b** $S(n) = 3^n$
  c $T(n) = 5/8 + (3/8)(-1)^n + n^3/6 - n^2/4 - n/6$
  d $V(n) = 31/8 + (9/8)(-1)^n + n^2/4$
3 $s(n) = [a + (n - 1)d]$, the nth term of an arithmetic series in standard notation
4 a $p(n) = n(n + 1)(2n + 1)/6$, the sum of the first n squares
  b $q(n) = [n(n + 1)/2]^2$, the sum of the first n cubes
5 $p(n) = 2^{n/2} (A \cos n\pi/4 + B \sin n\pi/4)$
  $q(n) = 2^{n/2} (-A \sin n\pi/4 + B \cos n\pi/4)$

FURTHER EXERCISES

1 $s(n) = A[(1 + \sqrt{5})/2]^n + B[(1 - \sqrt{5})/2]^n - (n^2 + 6n + 13)$
2 $T(n) = T(1)/2^{n-1} + (n - 1)c$
5 a $e(2n + 1) = [2n(2n - 2) \ldots 2e(1)]/[(2n + 1)(2n - 1) \ldots 3]$
  b $e(2n) = [(2n - 1)(2n - 3) \ldots 3 \times 1]/[(2n)(2n - 2) \ldots 2e(1)]$
6 $\varrho(n) = 1 - (1/2)e^{-n}$
7 Airborne, $h(t) = 100 + \sin \alpha t$; maximum height 101 metres, minimum height 99 metres
8 $p(n) = p(0) + (1/2)q(0) - q(0)(1/2)^{n+1}, q(n) = q(0)(1/2)^n,$
  $r(n) = r(0) + (1/2)q(0) - q(0)(1/2)^{n+1}$

CHAPTER 22

EXERCISES

1 a Dependent, $\sinh x - e^x/2 + e^{-x}/2 = 0$
  b independent
  c dependent, $\operatorname{cosec} 2x - \cot 2x - \tan x = 0$
  d dependent, $2 \coth 2x = \coth x + \tanh x$
  e dependent, $(x^2 - x) - (x^2 + x) + 2x = 0$
2 a Independent
  b independent
  c independent
  d dependent, $\mathbf{i} + 2\mathbf{j} + \mathbf{k} - (2\mathbf{i} + \mathbf{j} - \mathbf{k}) + (\mathbf{i} - \mathbf{j} - 2\mathbf{k}) = \mathbf{O}$
3 a $2\Delta^2 + 5\Delta + 2I$
  b $\Delta^4 + 8\Delta^3 + 20\Delta^2 + 16\Delta + 4I$
  c $-2\Delta^3 - 3\Delta^2 - 3\Delta - I$
4 a D^2 **b** e^D **c** $e^{3D} - 2e^{2D} + e^D - 2I$
5 a $y = -xe^{2x}$ **b** $u(n) = 2^n/3$ **c** $y = -[2x \cos x - \sin x]/4$

ASSIGNMENT

2 a $-2x + (x^2 + x + 1) - (x^2 - x + 1) \equiv 0$ **b** $1 - \cos^2 x - \sin^2 x \equiv 0$
5 a $(x + 1)/4$ **b** 2^{x-2} **c** $(\cos 2x + 4x \sin 2x)/16$

FURTHER EXERCISES

1 a Linearly dependent; $\cos 2x - 2\cos^2 x + 1 \equiv 0$
   b linearly dependent; $4 - 6(x^2 + 1) + (x + 1)^3 - (x - 1)^3 \equiv 0$
4 a $x^2 + 3x + 6$ **b** $(1/3) \cos x$
   c $(x/16) \cos 2x - (1/64) \sin 2x + (x^2/8) \sin 2x$ **d** $x \, \mathrm{e}^x/3$
6 Transient Aa^x; steady state $x/(1 - a) - 1/(1 - a)^2$,
   $y(x) = [a^x + x - (ax + 1)]/(1 - a)^2$
8 $d(n) = (1/10) + (n/10) - (n^2/1000)$
9 $t(n) = 1 + 3n + n^3$
10 a $U(n) = n^2/2^{n+1}$ **b** $S(n) = n \, 2^{n-1}$

CHAPTER 23

EXERCISES

1 a Discrete   **b** continuous   **c** discrete   **d** discrete   **e** discrete
   f continuous   **g** discrete
3 a Mean = 2 ohms, mode = 2 ohms, median = 2 ohms, range = 1.5 ohms
   b mean = 21.47%, equimodal but for grouped data approximately 19%,
      median = 19.7%, range = 15.9%
   c mean = 0.1377 m, mode (ungrouped) = 0.121 m but grouped data is
      bimodal, median = 0.122 m, range = 0.063 m
4 Mean = 4.69, mode = 1, median = 5, range = 9
5 Mean = 30.4375, mode = 31, median = 31, range = 3

ASSIGNMENT

1 Discrete   **4** 44.1, 44, 44   **5** 9, 4.8265

FURTHER EXERCISES

1 a(i) 4.2   (ii) 8   (iii) 3   (iv) 6   (v) 2.39
   b(i) 7   (ii) 20   (iii) 5   (iv) 18   (v) 7.38
4 b 2.925, 3.025, 3.125, 3.225, 3.325   **d**(i) $\bar{x} = 3.115$,
   $s = 0.0813$ (raw data)   (ii) $\bar{x} = 3.118$, $s = 0.0898$ (grouped data)
5 Hint: expand $\Sigma f_r(x_r - \bar{x})^2$

CHAPTER 24

EXERCISES

1 16/21

2 a $a = 3600/5269$
   b 769/5269
   c 9/16

3 $16.0025\,\text{m}^2$ $E(x^2) = V(x) + [E(x)]^2$

4 a 4/e   **b** $1 + 1/[4\ln 4 - 4]$

5 a 2.28×10^{-3} **b** 0.0676 (answers respectively 2.26×10^{-3} and 0.0676)

6 a 1/6!   **b** 1/30   **c** 1/6 ($a = 1/6$, $b = 2/3$, $c = 1/6!$)

ASSIGNMENT

1 0.154 (note $\mu = 1.347$)

2 0.0304

3 a 0.5   **b** 0.25

4 0.875

5 (a) $k = 1/2$ (b) $\mu = 4/3$ (c) $\sigma^2 = 2/9$

FURTHER EXERCISES

2 a $\mu = (n + 1)/2$, $\sigma^2 = (n^2 - 1)/12$ (population statistics)
   b $P(E \cap F) = 1/6$, $P(F \mid E) = 3/5$, $P(E \cup F \cup G) = 11/12$,
   $P[(E \cup F) \cap G] = 1/6$

3 a 0.7828   **b** 0.0216

4 Hint: we require $(0.1)2^N > 1 + N + N(N - 1)/2 + N(N - 1)(N - 2)/6$,
   and so $N = 12$

5 a 0.001 75   **b** 2.96 tonnes

6 Median = mode = 1; actual frequencies $(10, 15, 9, 5, 1)$; theoretical
   frequencies $(11, 14, 9, 4, 1)$

7 a 95%   **b** 92%

8 a 0.6648   **b** 0.9938

9 0.6753

10 a 0.0968   **b** 0.14

11 $\mu = 1$; $\{4, 4, 2, 1, 0, 0\}$

Subject index

Symbols index